Caldera OpenLinux

QUE®

Installing OpenLinux from LIZARD (Linux Wizard)

Caldera OpenLinux offers unparalleled ease of installation. Follow these steps to install OpenLinux for Linux:

1. Select the desired language. Your options are English, German, French, and Italian.
2. Slowly move your mouse; it will be auto-detected.
3. Choose one of the following installation targets:
   - Entire disk
   - Prepared partitions (use this option if you have chosen the Windows options)
   - Custom (experts only)

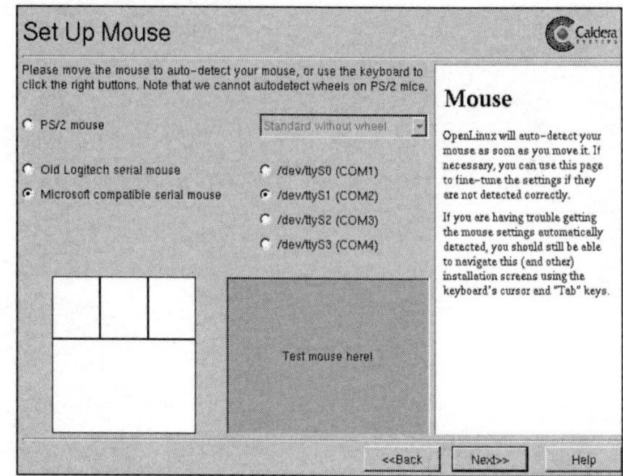

Figure 1

4. Select the package set that you want to install (remember your partition size when making selections).
5. Select the keyboard (model and layout). The defaults are Generic 101 and U.S.
6. The video adapter is auto-detected. It defaults to 256K video RAM. Select Probe to determine the exact video RAM.

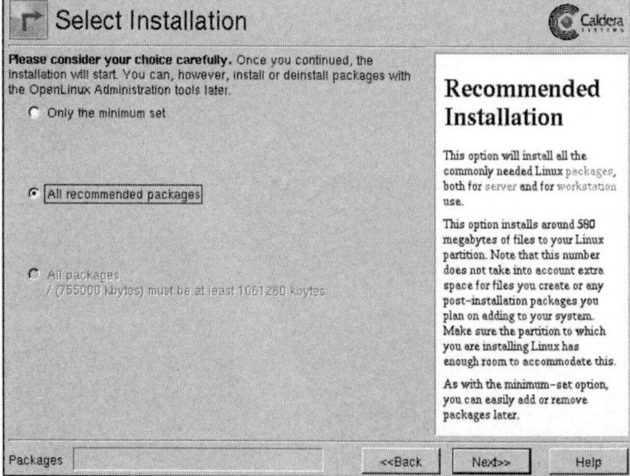

Figure 2

7. Select monitor settings from a large prebuilt listing of monitor makes and models.
8. Select the desired video mode, color depth, and resolution.
9. Set the password for the root account.

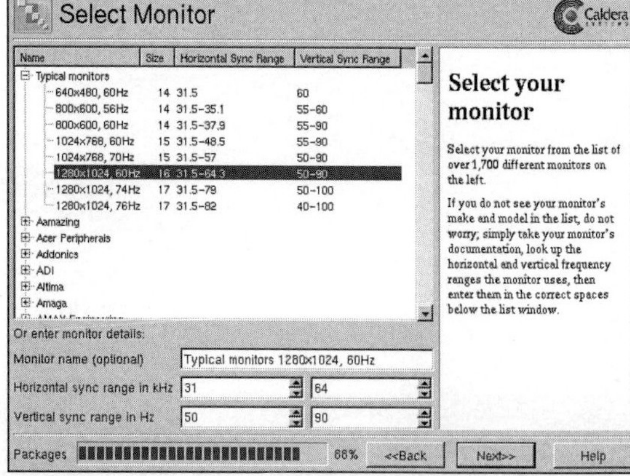

Figure 3

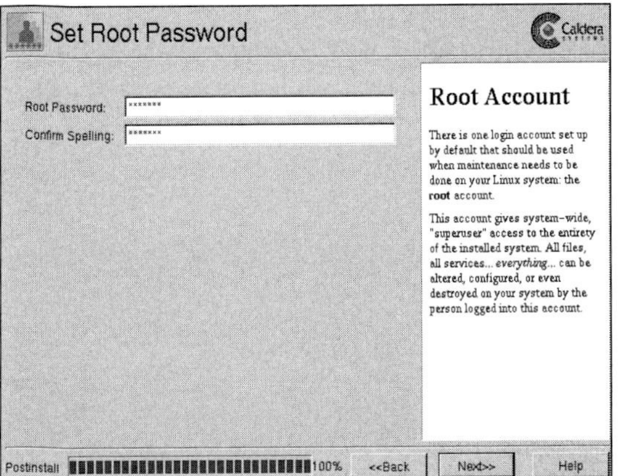

Figure 4

10. You can add additional users and passwords. Add as many users as you want. Passwords are set for each user.
11. Set one of the following as your networking option:
    - No networking
    - Use DHCP (IP address set at boot time)
    - Statically assigned (if you are connected to a network during installation, the appropriate network numbers will be auto-detected; you must supply the IP address)
12. Set the time zone by finding the correct area on the map or by manually selecting the correct zone in the combo box.

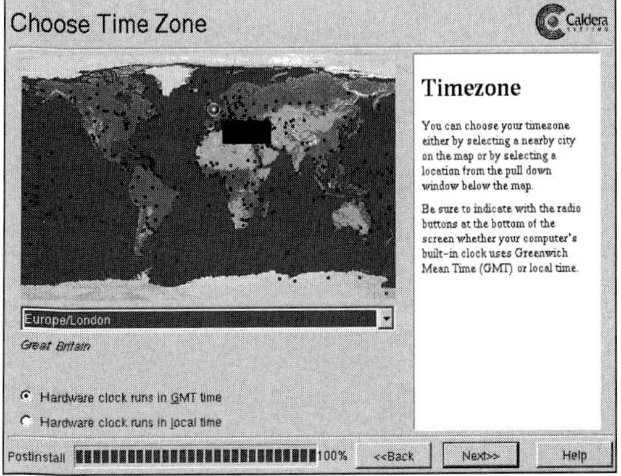

Figure 5

13. The installation entertainment appears. Play onscreen games 'til the cows come home.

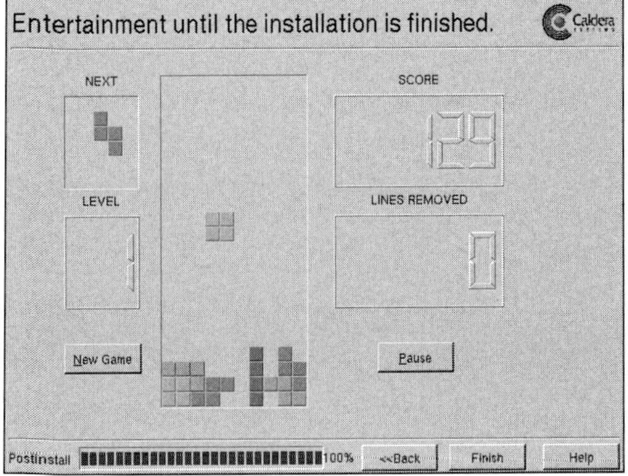

Figure 6

The LIZARD installation is automatic. After the installation is complete, the Caldera Systems logo appears, followed by a series of screens on which user input is required.

Installing OpenLinux for Microsoft Windows

The following Windows instructions simply prepare your system for OpenLinux. If you have no other OS installed, see the preceding section, "Installing OpenLinux from LIZARD (Linux Wizard)." Follow these steps:

1. Insert the CD-ROM in the CD-ROM drive; the installation program automatically runs. If it doesn't, click the CD-ROM icon in the My Computer folder and run `\winsetup\setup`. The main menu appears.

2. Click Install Products to begin the installation process. There are two installation methods. The first installs icons and start menu options within your Windows system. The second installs most items directly from the CD.

Figure 7

3. Click Full Install Preparation—English (or other language). This option installs the utilities that are necessary to perform the other options that are listed. These utilities can be accessed at any time from within the Windows program group in which they are installed.

   The OpenLinux Install Preparation screen appears.

4. It is strongly recommended that you exit other applications before proceeding with this step. Select Next when you are ready.

5. Read the Software License Agreement. Then click the Yes button to continue.

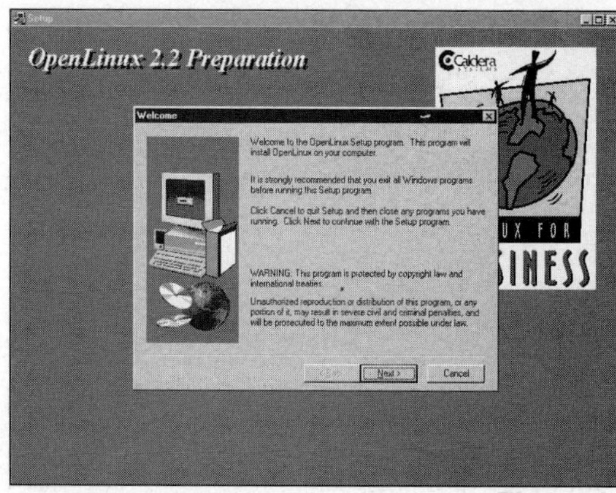

Figure 8

6. Select a destination directory in which to install the OpenLinux program group. The default directory is C:\Program Files\OpenLinux. Click the Next button to continue.

7. Change the name of the Program Folder in which you want to install these components. The default folder is OpenLinux. Then click the Next button.

8. OpenLinux creates a program group for you. Now you are ready to do the following:

   - Read the README file
   - Browse the CD for documents
   - View special offers from Caldera Systems' Web site
   - Create an installation disk (only if your CD-ROM doesn't support power on boot)
   - Create a module disk (only if your CD-ROM doesn't support power on boot)

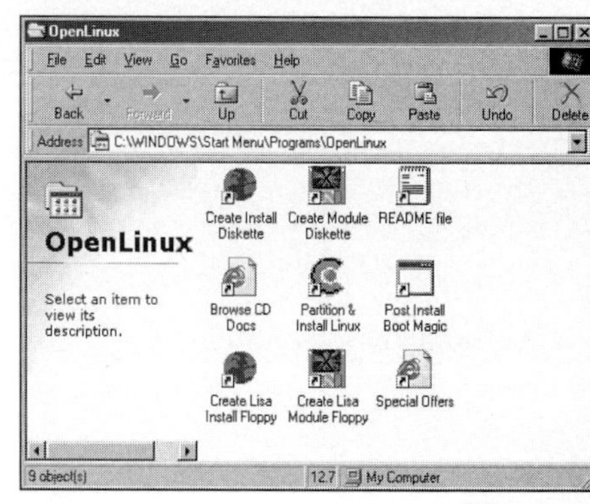

Figure 9

Linux and KDE Keystrokes

From the K menu, go to Setting, Keys, and then to Global Keys.

Table 1 Keyboard Shortcuts (Standard)

Action	Shortcut	Action	Shortcut
Close	Ctrl+W	Next	Ctrl+PageDown
Copy	Ctrl+C	Open	Ctrl+O
Cut	Ctrl+X	Paste	Ctrl+V
End	Ctrl+End	Print	Ctrl+P
Find	Ctrl+F	Prior	PageUp
Help	F1	Quit	Ctrl+Q
Home	Ctrl+Home	Replace	Ctrl+R
Insert	Ctrl+Insert	Save	Ctrl+5
New	Ctrl+N	Undo	Ctrl+2

Table 2 Keyboard Shortcuts (Global)

Action	Shortcut	Action	Shortcut
Execute command	Alt+F2	Switch to desktop 5	Ctrl+F5
Kill Window Mode	Ctrl+Alt+Esc	Switch to desktop 6	Ctrl+F6
Pop up menu	Alt+F1	Switch to desktop 7	Ctrl+F7
Switch to desktop 1	Ctrl+F1	Switch to desktop 8	Ctrl+8
Switch to desktop 2	Ctrl+F2	Task manager	Ctrl+Escape
Switch to desktop 3	Ctrl+F3	Window close	Alt+F4
Switch to desktop 4	Ctrl+F4	Window operations menu	Alt+F3

Administration and Networking Hints

Even though MS-DOS and Linux have several commands that are similar, Linux offers additional parameters that enrich most of these commands.

Table 3 Linux Versus DOS Commands

Linux Command	MS-DOS Equivalent	Linux Command	MS-DOS Equivalent
`.`	`.`	`mkdir`	`mkdir` or `md`
`..`	`..`	`mv`	`move` and/or `rename`
`>`	`>`	none	`find x y`
`cat x`	`type`	`passwd`	none
`cat x y`	`copy x,y`	`path`	`path`
`cd`	`cd`	`pr x`	none
`chmod`	`chmod` or `attrib`	`ps`	`mem /c`
`chown`	none	`rm x`	`del x` or `erase x`
`cp`	`copy`	`rmdir`	`rmdir` or `rd`
`echo`	`echo`	`spell x`	none
`find x`	none	`su`	none
`head x`	none	`tail x`	none
`lpr x`	`dir>prn`	`touch`	none
`ls`	`dir`	`vi`	`edit`
`man x`	none	`whoami`	none

KDE Feature Summary

The following is a list of some helpful KDE utilities and the menus on which they appear.

Table 4 KDE Utilities and Corresponding Menus

Utility	Description
Main Menu	
kdehelp	KDE help system
kcontrol	KDE control center
kfind	File search utility
Applications Menu	
kedit	A simple text editor
kwrite	An advanced editor with syntax highlighting
Utilities Menu	
konsole	Terminal emulator
karm	Personal time tracker
kfloppy	Floppy disk formatter
kljettool	HP LaserJet admin tool
kplq	Printer queue administration
kmenuedit	Taskbar menu editor
kworldwatch	World time watch with map
kjots	Note-keeping utility
ark	Archive manager
kab	Address book
kcalc	Calculator
kdewizard	KDE setup wizard
khexdit	Hex dump editor
klipper	Clipboard manager
kmoon	Moon phase indicator
knotes	Sticky notes
kodo	Mouse tracker
kpackage	Software package manager
kpm	Process manager
kvt	Simple terminal emulator
Graphics Menu	
kfax	Fax preview program
kdvi	Tex preview program
kfract	Fractal generator
kghostview	PostScript previewer
kiconedit	Icon editor
kpaint	Drawing program
ksnapshot	Screen dump utility
kview	Picture previewer
Internet Menu	
kmail	Email client
korn	Email indicator
kppp	Internet dialup utility
krn	News reader
karchie	Archie client
kbiff	New mail indicator
kfinger	Network user information
knu	Network utilities
Multimedia Menu	
kmedia	Multimedia player
kmidi	MIDI file player
kmix	Sound mixer tool
kmid	Karaoke player
kscd	Audio CD player
System Menu	
arrange	Arranges desktop icons
kfontmanager	Font tool
kfmsu	File manager in super user mode
kikbd	International keyboard setup
kpager	Desktop switcher
ktop	System load monitor

Frequently Asked Questions

Q How do I add a new user?

A Use COAS from the KDE menu or type `lisa --user` at a command prompt. You can also type `useradd` or `adduser`.

Q How do I change my password?

A Use COAS user administration or, at a command prompt, type `passwd` and press Enter. Or you can type `passwd [`*`username`*`]` and then press Enter.

Q How do I access my CD-ROM?

A Use the KDE CD-ROM icon or, at a command prompt while you are logged in as root, type `mount /dev/cdrom /mnt/cdrom` and press Enter. Your CD-ROM is now mounted at /mnt/cdrom, and by changing to this directory you gain access to your CD-ROM.
Alternatively, you can change to /auto/cdrom, and your CD-ROM is automatically mounted in /auto/cdrom by the time you get back to a command prompt.

Q After my CD-ROM is mounted, how do I remove it?

A The CD-ROM will not eject while it is mounted. To eject it, use the KDE CD-ROM icon or type `umount /mnt/cdrom` at a command prompt.
If you accessed your CD-ROM from /auto/cdrom, simply back out of that directory and you should be able to remove your CD-ROM.

Q How do I access my floppy drive?

A Use the KDE floppy icon or type `mount -t type /dev/fd0 /mnt/floppy` at a command prompt. You can also type `mount -a /dev/fd0 /mnt/floppy`. Change to /mnt/floppy, and you have access to your floppy disk. If you do not want to mount your floppy disk and it is an MS-DOS–formatted floppy, you can use `mtools`. For example, you can list the directory of a floppy disk by typing `mdir a:` at the command prompt.
To copy, use `mcopy a:/[`*`filename`*`] [`*`destination_file`*`]` at the command prompt. To delete, use `mdel a:/[`*`filename`*`]`.
Alternatively, you can change to the /auto/floppy directory (just as you can mount and access your CD-ROM by changing to /auto/cdrom).

Q After my floppy is mounted, is it safe to remove it?

A No! Removing a floppy disk before it is unmounted can result in data loss. Make sure that you type `umount /mnt/floppy` before removing the floppy disk.
If you accessed your floppy from /auto/floppy, simply back out of that directory and you should be able to remove your disk.

Q How do I find out if my graphics card is supported by Xfree86?

A Read the OpenLinux hardware compatibility list in Appendix B, "Hardware Compatibility Lists," page 909, or online at `http://www.calderasystems.com/`. Xfree86.org maintains a list of cards and servers at `http://www.xfree86.org/`.

Q How do I search for a file on OpenLinux?

A Use `locate [`*`filename`*`]`.

Q How do I access my other partitions?

A `mount -t type /dev/hda1 /mnt` enables you to access that partition from `/mnt`.

Q How do I look at the contents of a file?

A Use one of the following commands:

- `cat [`*`filename`*`]`
- `less [`*`filename`*`]`
- `more [`*`filename`*`]`

Q How do I tell which executable will execute when I run a command?

A Use `which [`*`command`*`]`.

Q Where can I find information on a specific command?

A Use `man [`*`command`*`]`.

Q How do I gain a root shell while logged in as a normal user?

A Use `su` if you want to keep your current environment settings, or `su -` if you want to use the root user's environment settings. You will be prompted for the root password.

OpenLinux Support

Caldera Systems, Inc. does not provide support for the software accompanying this book.

Fee-based support for OpenLinux is available at 1-800-850-7779.

If there are problems with the content of the book, or defects in the CD, please visit our website at http://www.mcp.com/support

Linux Resources on the Internet

Linux How-Tos:

- `http://www.calderasystems.com/LDP/HOWTO/index.html`
- `http://metalab.unc.edu/LDP/HOWTO/`

Linux Magazines and Journals:

- *Linux Journal*: `http://www.linuxjournal.com/`
- *LinuxWorld*: `http://www.linuxworld.com/`
- *Linux Magazine*: `http://www.linux-mag.com/`

General Linux Information:

- Linux Online!: `http://www.linux.org/`
- Slashdot: `http://www.slashdot.org/`
- Fresh Meat: `http://www.freshmeat.org/`
- Linux Games: `http://www.linuxgames.com/`
- Linux user groups: `http://www.linux.org/users/groups/usa/index.html`

OpenLinux Resources:

- Caldera Systems home: `http://www.calderasystems.com/`
- Caldera Systems Support: `http://www.calderasystems.com/support/index.html`
- Caldera Systems Free Download page: `http://www.calderasystems.com/support/download.html`
- Caldera Systems Technical Notes: `http://www.calderasystems.com/support/techguide.html`
- Caldera Systems Online Documents: `http://www.calderasystems.com/doc/index.html`

Penguin created by Larry Ewing and logo created by Andreas Dilger

Special Edition Using Caldera OpenLinux

Allen Smart

Erik Ratcliffe

Tim Bird

David Bandel

Wilson Mattos

QUE®

A Division of Macmillan Computer Publishing, USA
201 W. 103rd Street
Indianapolis, Indiana 46290

Contents at a Glance

Special Edition Using Caldera OpenLinux

International Standard Book Number: 0-7897-2058-2

Library of Congress Catalog Card Number: 99-61629

Printed in the United States of America

First Printing: May 1999

01 00 99 4 3 2 1

Trademarks

All terms mentioned in this book that are known to be trademarks or service marks have been appropriately capitalized. Que cannot attest to the accuracy of this information. Use of a term in this book should not be regarded as affecting the validity of any trademark or service mark.

OpenLinux is a trademark of Caldera Systems, Inc.

Warning and Disclaimer

Every effort has been made to make this book as complete and as accurate as possible, but no warranty or fitness is implied. The information provided is on an "as is" basis. The authors and the publisher shall have neither liability nor responsibility to any person or entity with respect to any loss or damages arising from the information contained in this book or from the use of the CD or programs accompanying it.

Executive Editor
Jeff Koch

Acquisitions Editor
Gretchen Ganser

Development Editor
Maureen A. McDaniel

Managing Editor
Brice Gosnell

Project Editor
Sara Bosin

Copy Editor
JoAnna Kremer

Indexer
Heather Goens

Proofreader
Benjamin Berg

Technical Editors
Eric Richardson
Aron Hsiao
Ed Orcutt

Software Development Specialist
Dan Scherf

Interior and Cover Designs
Ruth Lewis

Layout Technicians
Brandon Allen
Darin Crone
Stacey Richwine-DeRome
Liz Johnston
Timothy Osborn
Staci Somers

Contents

IV Networking with OpenLinux

V X Window

VI Etc

About the Authors

Allan Smart currently works as the Director of Education Services at Caldera Systems, Inc. He graduated from Utah State University with a B.S. degree in computer science and subsequently earned an M.B.A. degree in the executive program at the Marriott School of Management of Brigham Young University. He has worked as an application developer, a systems engineer, a systems integrator, and a technical services director.

Erik Ratcliffe has been a Linux enthusiast since 1991 (starting with Linux kernel version 0.11). After playing with Linux as a hobby for five years, in 1996 he decided to leave his 12-year career in civil engineering to pursue a new career working with Linux at Caldera, Inc. He now works with Allan Smart in the Caldera Systems Education Services department; his current responsibilities include doing research and development for courseware and helping to pioneer the Linux certification effort. He is also studying computer science at Utah Valley State College.

Tim Bird has been working with Linux since 1993. He left Novell in 1995 to join Caldera, Inc., where he has been employed on various Linux programming projects. He has previously published articles in the *NetWare Technical Journal*. Tim received his master's degree in computer science from Brigham Young University in 1991. He currently works for Caldera Thin Clients, Inc. He and his wife and three children live in Orem, Utah.

David Bandel earned a master of aviation management from Embry-Riddle Aeronautical University in 1989 at Ft. Campbell, KY. He retired from 20 years in the Army in February 1996. While on active duty, he learned many of the basics of UNIX working on DEC 5000s running Ultrix and Sun SparcStations running SunOS 4. In 1993, he began dabbling with Linux, a hobby which quickly grew on him. Currently, David works for Custom Software Services, Inc. in Bellevue, WA, as the Senior Systems Technician. He installs and maintains systems for CSS and for their customers. He works on a wide variety of systems, maintaining Sparc Solaris, HP-UX, AIX, SCO Openserver, NT, and of course, Linux systems—most running CSS software, which uses Informix IDS and MSSQL Server databases. David also works as an independent networking consultant and writes for the *Linux Journal*. He can be reached at `dbandel@ix.netcom.com`.

Wilson Mattos is a Master Certified Novell Engineer (MCNE) and a Master Certified Novell Instructor (MCNI) with over five years of multiplatform enterprise networking experience. Besides being a Linux enthusiast for the past four years, in a recent partnership with Caldera Systems and the Kern County Superintendent of Schools, Wilson is assisting in the development of the first Linux authorized training courses and certifications.

Dedication

***Allan Smart**: To my wife Denise and our four children, Kelsey, Brittany, Ryan, and Natalie.*

***Erik Ratcliffe**: To my fiance, Brenda, for her patience and dedication. She not only allowed me to write when it would have been more entertaining to go out, but she also helped me get through some of my work at a time when I was feeling a wee bit overwhelmed. Behind every man is a good woman, and that's exactly what she is. This book (at least the portion I wrote) is for her.*

***Tim Bird**: To my loving wife Nadine, without whom this book could not have been written. I've neglected you too long, but I'll be home soon.*

***David Bandel**: Dedicated to my wife Silvia, our children—Lisa and Vanessa—and to the entire Linux community.*

***Wilson Mattos**: For my mom Maria, who has given me the world. A special thanks to my wife Christine who supports all my endeavors, and to Allan Smart for involving me in the writing of this book.*

Acknowledgements

Allan Smart: First and foremost, I thank my wife and best friend whose encouragement and support helped me see the finish line, and my kids, who put up with my absence and only occasionally asked, "Are we there yet?" Thanks to my parents, Ross and Darlene Smart, who taught me how to work and instilled in me a desire to always keep learning. This book wouldn't be what it is without the tremendous efforts of Erik, Tim, and David, who jumped into this project with unmatched enthusiasm. Many thanks to all those at MCP who made this book project possible—especially Jeff Koch, Gretchen Ganser, and Maureen McDaniel. They have been a pleasure to work with. I'd also like to acknowledge Ed Orcutt and Glenn Gunn, who selflessly offered technical assistance and support. And finally, a special thanks to Linus Torvalds and the many thousands of Linux developers and enthusiasts who have contributed and continue to contribute to the Linux movement and who make writing this kind of book possible.

Erik Ratcliffe: The work I did on this book would not have come together if it had not been for the considerable cooperation and patience of a number of people. First, I have to thank Gretchen Ganser, the coolest acquisitions editor anyone could ever hope to work with, for being not only calm in the face of adversity but also an all around nice person to talk to. I also need to thank Willy Wiegler from White Pine Software for his cooperation and a few long distance calls to chat about the book (so we can expect a Linux port of Cu-SeeMe soon, right? Maybe? Think about it?); Dev Mazumdar, President/CEO of 4Front Technologies for being the first to give me permission to use Open Sound System information in this book; Joyce Fowler of Adobe, Inc., for tolerating poor fax transmissions and incompatible graphics files, and for giving me permission to use screenshots of Acrobat Reader anyway; Brett Goodwin and Robin Mather of RealNetworks, Inc., for their help with screenshot permissions (are you seeing a pattern here yet?); jAY pETERSON (no, those are not typos) of WRNR in Annapolis, Maryland, not only for helping to run a way cool radio station but for allowing me to use a certain RealPlayer screenshot; Kathleen McVey for getting back with me on screenshot information for DataFellows's SSH Secure Tunnel & Terminal for Windows 95 (maybe in the second edition, eh? We'll be in touch); Stanley Jordan, Dead Can Dance, and Art Bell for keeping me company during some rather late nights (and early mornings); Allan Smart for living up to his last name by hiring me in the first place; the caldera-users mail list for being one of the most laid back, informative mail lists I could ever hope for (you *rock*); and Linus Torvalds, not only for creating one of the best operating systems around but also for jumping in to help me compile a 0.95a kernel a number of years ago (at a time when the maintainer of GCC felt it was more effective to chew me a new one for asking for help).

Tim Bird: As corny as it sounds, I'd like to thank Linus Torvalds for having the curiosity and interest to start a new OS from scratch, and for his incredible tenacity and leadership to carry it forth into the popular operating system that it is today. Although his technical skills are legendary, his ability to "herd cats" is even more important to the Linux movement. Thanks must also go to the fine people at Caldera who produce the most consistent, polished, and robust distribution of Linux available today. Also, although I can't pick out everyone of note, I'd like to mention a few folks from the KDE project with whom I am impressed: Torben Weis, Bernd Johannes Wuebben, Markus Wuebben, Matthias Ettrich, Kalle Dalheimer, and Roberto Alsina. It's a real disservice not to mention others as well, but that's the breaks. Much love and appreciation go to my family (Nadine, Amanda, Melanie, and Ryan) for putting up with my virtual absence for the last few months, and for helping me get the job done. Finally, I'd like to thank the fine people at Macmillan Computer Publishing for their assistance with this book, and for putting up with a newbie author like myself.

TELL US WHAT YOU THINK

As the reader of this book, *you* are our most important critic and commentator. We value your opinion and want to know what we're doing right, what we could do better, what areas you'd like to see us publish in, and any other words of wisdom you're willing to pass our way.

As an executive editor at Macmillan Computer Publishing, I welcome your comments. You can fax, email, or write me directly to let me know what you did or didn't like about this book—as well as what we can do to make our books stronger.

Please note that I cannot help you with technical problems related to the topic of this book, and that due to the high volume of mail I receive, I might not be able to reply to every message.

When you write, please be sure to include this book's title and author as well as your name and phone or fax number. I will carefully review your comments and share them with the author and editors who worked on the book.

Fax: 317.581.4663

Email: `opsys@mcp.com`

Mail: Executive Editor
Macmillan Computer Publishing
201 West 103rd Street
Indianapolis, IN 46290 USA

Introduction

In this chapter

In the beginning…

> "Hello netlanders,
>
> Due to a project I'm working on (in minix), I'm interested in the posix [*sic*] standard definition. Could somebody please point me to a (preferably) machine-readable format of the latest posix [*sic*] rules? Ftp-sites would be nice."
>
> **—Linus Torvalds, in a rather (at this point) historic message posted to the comp.os.minix newsgroup on July 3, 1991.**

A cliche statement following such a quote might read as follows: "It all started innocently enough…".

We will not say that, however, even though it is a true statement.

Profound shifts in ideology and technology tend to have rather humble beginnings. These shifts might start with a flash of cognition after months of heavy thinking, or they might start with a momentary brainwave that floated by while looking at a reflection in a cup of coffee. Or they might start with a Finnish college student's desire to figure out how to play with his new 386 computer.

The quote at the top of this page marks the beginning of what might end up being the most exciting, paradigm-redefining project to hit modern computing. It marks the germination of a project that grew into the operating system that is now known as Linux.

Created by Linus Torvalds, the Linux operating system has taken on a life of its own since its humble beginning in 1991, boasting a developer list that spans almost every country on the planet and a user base that is at least that extensive. Furthermore, there are currently no signs that its explosive growth is stopping—or even slowing. Every year that passes by produces a few million more Linux users. Estimates place the Linux user base somewhere in the ten million range as of late 1998.

WHY ARE SO MANY PEOPLE MOVING TOWARD LINUX?

Throughout the past few years (thanks to the efforts of commercial Linux businesses such as Caldera Systems), many major software and hardware companies have expanded their offerings to include Linux in one way or another. Corel, Sun, IBM, and Compaq are only a few of the corporations that not only acknowledge Linux as a viable operating system, but that have also joined the "revolution" by putting their hats in the Linux ring, so to speak.

Really, there are many possible answers to the question listed previously—some more probable than others. Perhaps it is a coincidence that all these people are picking up Linux now.

To trace it all back to a single incident would leave out many of the people and incidents that influenced the current Linux wave. So, to be fair, we are putting on our corporate hats and judging this wave by Linux's more practical merits.

STABILITY

Linux has proven itself to be one of the most stable operating systems available. Uptimes (the duration of time that a system stays running between reboots) for Linux systems tend to be astonishingly high. An uptime of a year or more is not uncommon, as many Linux system administrators are proud to boast.

FUNCTIONALITY

What do you want your Linux system to do? Actually, a better question might be "What do you want your server to do?" Linux can do just about anything you want to do with a server, from pretending to be a domain controller on a Windows network to acting as a name server or mail server.

Linux can also act as a powerful desktop system, providing an intuitive graphic interface and equivalents of most of the applications to which Microsoft Windows users have grown accustomed (in the case of application software, some applications such as WordPerfect and Corel Draw have even been ported to Linux). The K Desktop Environment (KDE), for example, provides a smooth migration from Windows to Linux by offering a look and feel that is similar to Windows as well as a suite of prepackaged Windows-like applications.

SUPPORT

In addition to being a commercially supported operating system, free support over the Internet has proven to be one of the greatest selling points for Linux. Imagine having a support team that literally covers the planet; you will start to see how powerful this feature is. At any point, any Linux user can tap into a wealth of Linux knowledge through the use of mail lists, Web sites, newsgroups, and freely downloadable documentation, often finding answers to their questions in mere minutes.

The commercial support that is offered to Linux users varies from company to company, but paid support options are available from many companies that specialize in Linux. Every level of support is available, from per-incident fee-based support to full 24-hours-a-day, seven-days-a-week support contracts for enterprise clients.

FREEDOM

The majority of a typical Linux system is not bound by restrictive licensing; if an administrator wants to allow a 200-machine network to access a Web server running on a Linux system, so be it. No extra per-machine licensing is incurred. In fact, depending on what kind of impact a company wants to take on support-wise, the operating system itself can be obtained free of charge and installed on unlimited numbers of systems (some Linux companies only support customers who paid for the software).

SECURITY

Any system administrator can tell you that there is no such thing as a secure system. This is one of those undeniable facts of system administration: Unless you lock up a system in a closet with no keyboard, no floppy drive, and no network connection, there is always some way to break in. Keeping up with security problems is vital for an operating system to remain viable in mission-critical installations.

Linux excels in this category, boasting minimal turnaround times for security fixes (quite often, when a security problem is discovered, patched versions of the affected Linux programs are available within a day). There have been cases in which Linux had fixes for security problems months before other commercial operating systems were fixed! The open source nature of Linux helps to facilitate this (*open source* meaning that the source code—the actual typewritten documents that a programmer produces when writing software—is available, unrestricted and editable by anyone who cares to do so).

THINGS HAVE CHANGED...A LOT

> "...It is NOT portable (uses 386 task switching etc.), and it probably never will support anything other than AT-hard disks, as that's all I have :-(."
>
> **—Linus Torvalds, in a message to the comp.os.minix newsgroup on August 25, 1991**

When it first started out, Linux only ran on 386 or higher Intel-based PCs. Today, Linux runs on a multitude of hardware platforms (and judging from the preceding quote, it can only be assumed that even Linus himself is surprised and delighted by this). These non-Intel platforms include Sun's Sparc, MIPS, Amigas, Apple's various offerings, Alpha-based systems, and even (oddly enough) hand-held digital assistants, just to name a few. Benchmarks on Linux systems, regardless of the platform, meet or exceed those of other operating systems on similar hardware. Furthermore, constant development is being done to keep Linux up to speed with advances in these systems.

No other operating system can boast the cross-platform support that Linux has today, and with players such as Intel and Silicon Graphics joining forces with entities within the Linux community, more cross-platform support is coming.

GET INVOLVED!

> "Do you pine for the nice days of minix-1.1, when men were men and wrote their own device drivers? Are you without a nice project and just dying to cut your teeth on a OS you can try to modify for your needs? Are you finding it frustrating when everything works on minix? No more all-nighters to get a nifty program working? Then this post might be just for you :-)..."
>
> **—Linus Torvalds, in a recruitment message to the comp.os.minix newsgroup on October 5, 1991**

The message from which this quote was taken is dated 1991, but the sentiment is just as valid today as it was then. Ask the preceding questions to yourself and see how you answer. Are you really willing to join the party and help out?

There is no invitation or application required; simply step up and help! This is not required, but if you are interested in contributing to Linux, you are more than welcome to do so. The vast majority of the programming that goes into Linux is done by volunteers. In fact, very few of the Linux developers are paid for any of the work they do on the operating system.

If you are a hardware guru, maybe you can write device drivers. If you are a documentation guru, write documentation. If you do neither but have Internet bandwidth, maybe you want to offer some Web space to a certain project, maintain a mail list for developers, or simply spend time on mail lists and newsgroups, helping others get started with Linux. Contributions to Linux operate on two levels now: the commercial level (handled well by commercial Linux companies) and a grass roots end-user level (handled by volunteers who feel an affinity for the freedom that Linux offers). No matter how many people are working on Linux, there is always room for more to join.

Don't Be Afraid to Learn Something New

Regardless of whether you want to be involved, the fact that you are reading this says that you are at least open-minded enough to give Linux a try. With this book, we hope to give you the tools that you need to migrate to Linux with as little pain as possible.

Note, however, that there is a learning curve with anything new. There was a time when you did not know how to use some other operating system either, but you learned and can now navigate your way around it with confidence. You will not be coddled in this transition (because that is contrary to the definition of this book series), but we will do our best to give you the information that you need. If there are serious problems with this book, we trust that you will let us know how it can be made better.

So, on behalf of all of us, welcome to Linux! We hope that you will find your experiences with this operating system as exciting and inspiring as we have.

Conventions Used in This Book

This book uses the following typeface conventions:

- New terms appear in *italics*.
- All code in the listings appear in `computer font`.
- Many code-related terms within the text also appear in `computer font`.
- Placeholders in code appear in *`italic computer font`*.

- When a line of code is too long to fit on one line of this book, it is broken at a convenient place and continued to the next line. A code continuation character (➥) precedes the continuation of a line of code. (You should type a line of code that has this character as one long line, without breaking it.)

Special design features enhance the text material:

- Notes
- Tips
- Cautions

Note

Notes explain interesting or important points that can help you understand important concepts and techniques.

Tip

Tips are little pieces of information that help you in real-world situations. Tips often offer shortcuts or information to make a task easier or faster.

Caution

Cautions provide information about detrimental performance issues or dangerous errors. Pay careful attention to Cautions.

PART I

Introduction to OpenLinux

CHAPTER 1

What Is OpenLinux?

In this chapter

To understand what OpenLinux is, one must first have an understanding of what Linux is, and possibly a little background on how Linux systems evolved to what they are today.

Linux is a variant of the UNIX operating system. It must be made clear that Linux is not UNIX, though; it is its own operating system, with its own nuances, its own quirks, and its own special features. It was written from the ground up by hundreds of different developers that span most of the countries on this planet, with the majority of the development taking place over the Internet.

The original idea behind Linux germinated in the early 1990s, at the Helsinki University of Technology in Finland, by a Swedish student named Linus Torvalds. What began in 1991 as a project to provide an alternative to the Minix operating system became somewhat of a movement when the first ALPHA grade Linux systems—generally in the form of a *root* and a *boot* disk—made their way to the Internet. Back then the numbers of Linux users could have been counted in the thousands, but that soon changed.

Note

One of the most confusing–and pointless–arguments that has ensued within the Linux community involves how to pronounce Linux. Really, however you pronounce it is fine, but the official pronunciation sounds like "lint-tux" without the Ts. This seems to come from the way that Linus Torvalds pronounces his first name, which provided the basis for the Linux name itself.

Within a few years, the Linux development team (having expanded to include not only driver/kernel developers, but also software developers and enthusiasts who worked feverishly to port open-source UNIX software to Linux) had gained a significant amount of mindshare.

Soon, what was considered a typical Linux system grew to the point of being unwieldy and difficult to maintain. Eventually, groups of people started pooling their efforts to create what are known as Linux *distributions*, or predefined sets of software packaged with the Linux operating system. These were typically distributed on disks and accompanied by some sort of installation utility. Early distributions such as SLS and Slackware quickly became popular among Linux enthusiasts for their relative ease of installation and frequent updates. By coincidence, the prices of CD-ROM drives dropped at about the same time that these early distributions were gaining popularity, and CD-ROMs quickly became the preferred (almost standard) media for Linux distributions. Today, distributions that are made to be installed from disks are rare.

For a while it seemed that everyone wanted to make their own Linux distribution. For the most part, these distributions differed only in the sets of software that they included. As time passed, the various distributions diversified their offerings, sometimes adding software written for the distributions themselves (such as packaging utilities and graphic interfaces) in an effort to differentiate themselves from the rest. Some offered subscriptions, where you get quarterly updates for a set yearly fee; others added technical support and moved in a more commercial direction. In time, even commercial software packages that had been ported to Linux were included, adding to Linux's commercial viability.

Most of the original distributions actually still exist, but they are mostly used by hobbyists and in academic scenarios. There is currently only a small handful of actual commercially produced and supported Linux distributions, OpenLinux being one of them.

Tip

Various Web sites that contain more information on the history and development of Linux are available (such as `http://www.linux.org`). See Appendix D, "How to Find Other Linux Information," if you want to locate other sources of Linux history.

Caldera Systems does not just sell OpenLinux; it also has a high-end system that is targeted for developers and resellers. So what is the difference? It is not very easy to differentiate between the two without listing the software that was included with one but not the other. Therefore, the difference lies mainly in the target market. OpenLinux has capabilities that are similar to those of the high-end reseller/developer system, but it is marketed mostly to users of other operating systems who are migrating to Linux.

Special attention was made to usability and functionality in OpenLinux. For instance, the desktop environment, although not a clone of Windows95/98/NT, is probably familiar enough to make migration from Windows systems relatively painless—at least from a *graphic user interface* (*GUI*) standpoint. The sharp edges that plague many other Linux distributions have been smoothed down to make OpenLinux more usable, yet power users who like command prompts still have access to the guts of the system, just as they always have.

HOW DOES OPENLINUX COMPARE TO OTHER LINUX DISTRIBUTIONS?

If you end up participating in online Linux discussions through mail lists, newsgroups, or Internet relay chat (IRC) channels, or even if you just read Linux publications such as *Linux Journal*, there is one term you will undoubtedly see repeated: Linux community.

Despite the incredible evolution Linux has experienced over the last few years, there is still a very real sense of community surrounding Linux and its users. The spirit of sharing and helping others without asking for anything in return is still prevalent and has even won the Linux community an award or two for providing the best technical support in the computer industry. The majority of Linux users believe that by sharing with others, they will ultimately be rewarded in other ways down the road somewhere. The same applies to commercial distributions of Linux: What goes around comes around, so supporting commercial distributions of Linux results in the production of more contributions to Linux development.

In some realms of the Linux community, the term *community* can be stretched a bit. Arguments over whose distribution is better have been elevated by some to the level of religion. This has proven to be somewhat unhealthy for Linux in general, especially when articles that are not favorable to one distribution or another are written. A rather vocal minority of Linux users have tended to respond with an unfair degree of venom, causing yet more bad press, and creating a snowball effect.

It is with this in mind that we say that you must not read the following as implying anything detrimental toward any particular Linux distribution. Comparisons made here are just that—comparisons. OpenLinux users are members of the Linux community, and as members they acknowledge that part of what makes Linux so great is that there is variety, and that whatever helps one distribution will ultimately help others. The differences give users choices, and choice is what differentiates Linux from the rest of today's popular operating systems. This is something to celebrate, not something to be used to fuel fires.

SLACKWARE

The first Linux distribution was the SLS distribution from Soft Landing Software in Canada. It provided convenient sets of packages that were able to be installed in any combination, precompiled, and ready to run. SLS offered a reduction in the steps that were previously required to install software on Linux systems—search for the source code, download it, extract it, compile it, and hope it installs and works correctly—and saved so much time and effort that many people had no problem with its $150 price tag.

However, it was still rather unfriendly to install, especially from the standpoint of someone migrating to Linux from a DOS background. The next major distribution answered many of the complaints that people had about SLS by simplifying the installation and offering a package management system (called `pkgtool`).

Slackware was that distribution.

For installation, instead of running a command-line program and passing the names of the package sets to be installed (SLS's installation method), Slackware offered a full-screen, menu-driven interface. It enabled the user to browse the package sets that were available for installation, and went the extra mile by offering users the capability to select/deselect individual packages within those sets.

One of its biggest boosts to the Linux distribution world was the management of installed packages. Using plain tarred/compressed archives, the `pkgtool` program did a fair job of making the installation and removal of software packages more painless. The main problem that occurred—and still occurs because Slackware hasn't really changed much in this regard—is that some files from individual packages are inevitably left behind when packages are removed. Without a database that keeps track of where all the installed files are (such as those used by `RPM` and `dpkg`), it is impossible to know how to cleanly remove files after they are installed. Regardless, Slackware's package management system does a good job, considering that it just uses ordinary archive files and not a special archive format such as `RPM` and `deselect`.

Slackware uses a BSD-style initialization scheme. The benefit of this is a more simplistic system for loading services at boot time. A drawback of BSD initialization is that the user does not have very much control over the services that are being started up. For instance, in

SysV initialization you can have a different set of services set to start with different *runlevels*, not unlike the runlevel menu you sometimes get when a Windows 95 system becomes corrupted (Safe Mode with Networking, Safe Mode without Networking, and so on are all runlevels). You can not do this with BSD initialization; therefore, you can not do this with distributions such as Slackware. Some users do not want to have that much control over their system startup, however. As with many other aspects of Linux, personal preference reigns supreme when considering such issues, and there is really no right or wrong.

Depending on the circles you walk in, a major cause for concern among some Linux users is that the maintainer of the Slackware distribution adamantly refuses to join the *Linux Standard Base* project (or *LSB*). Membership in LSB is not forced on anyone, and nobody (not even the members) is required to adhere to the standards set by the project, so this might not be a monumental thing. But the aim of LSB is to make Linux less of a moving target for commercial developers; therefore, many consider this project to be essential to the future commercial viability of Linux. To date, Slackware is the only major Linux distribution to reject LSB.

Regardless of the varying opinions of its package management system or the maintainer's stance on the LSB project, Slackware is favored by many as the most "traditional" of the Linux distributions. Nostalgia and inertia (keeping what is familiar on one's system) seems to be doing a good job of keeping this distribution alive, not to mention the fact that it is typically quite current with its software versions and technical fortitude. It provides its user base with consistency and an unflinchingly familiar installation system from version to version.

RED HAT

In the early days of Caldera, a Linux package called Caldera Network Desktop was sold. This system was essentially Red Hat's version 2.1 distribution with some commercial enhancements that provided NetWare connectivity and a graphical drag-and-drop desktop, among other things. Some of the early development of Red Hat's RPM packaging utility and some of the graphic administration utilities were originally produced with financial help from Caldera, primarily for the release of Caldera Network Desktop (of course, Red Hat used these updated utilities in their distribution as well).

This particular system was only released once. After version 1.0 was sold for a few years, Red Hat and Caldera amiably parted ways. Since then, Red Hat has gone on to become one of the most popular Linux distributions available. Many of the utilities that were used in their early distributions (including the RPM packaging utility and some of the graphic administration utilities) have persevered and are still included in their distributions today. There have been a few gyrations with their system in their tenure as a Linux distributor (for instance, additions such as a graphic installation have been tried and subsequently dropped for one reason or another), but the look of the distribution has remained somewhat consistent.

What differentiated Caldera from Red Hat in the early days were the target markets pursued by each company: Red Hat tended to stay more on the cutting-edge with software updates, and was therefore more appealing to individual users, hobbyists, and hackers. Caldera tended to be more conservative and focused on stability over innovation, at the expense of its software being a step behind distributions such as Red Hat. The main reason for this is that Caldera wanted to put more emphasis on technical support and providing a solid system for VARs and administrators to build mission critical systems on. Certain entities occasionally shied away from Red Hat's distribution, although it was stable, because of the cutting-edge nature of the software included with it.

Now, Red Hat and Caldera Systems are targeting similar markets. Both are seeking out enterprise clientele, and both are focusing on making Linux a commercially viable alternative to other mainstream operating systems. Both have free offerings and commercial offerings, and both provide technical support. Even the services they use to back up their Linux offerings (enterprise level support and training, for example) are comparable.

The main difference between the actual distributions lies in both administration and the desktop. Red Hat still uses the graphic administration utilities that were originally developed back when they and Caldera were partners, whereas OpenLinux uses a character based, all-in-one system called `lisa` (Linux Installation and System Administration). It is worth noting that Red Hat has recently adopted a system called `Linuxconf` as an alternative system administration package. This new package is quite extensible and powerful, but it has received mixed reviews among Red Hat's users; therefore, many users stick with the original graphic configuration utilities. OpenLinux does not use `Linuxconf`, but in the near future there will be a new administration system produced by Caldera Systems that will cover similar functionality to that of `Linuxconf` while eliminating some of the negative features of that system.

For the desktop, Red Hat uses a window manager system called fvwm95. Window managers provide the look and feel of the X Window system; items such as buttons, windows, and backgrounds are controlled by window managers. The fvwm95 window manager provides an interface that is familiar to Windows users, but possibly without all the Windows drag-and-drop functionality. Configuration is not all that simple, either, because it requires many customizations to text editors and configuration files. OpenLinux's desktop system—known as *KDE* (the *K Desktop Environment*)—provides not only some of the look and feel of the Windows interfaces, but also provides the drag-and-drop capabilities that are missing from fvwm95.

Note

Red Hat plans to adopt an add-on system referred to as *GNOME* (the *GNU Network Object Model Environment*) as an enhancement to the X Window environment that they currently use. GNOME is not a window manager, but instead adds drag-and-drop capabilities to existing window managers as well as application integration through the *Object Request Brokerage Architecture* (*ORB*). Similar functionality can be found in KDE; GNOME merely separates these elements from the window manager, enabling users to use whatever window manager they want.

In both distributions, ease of installation is taken very seriously. Red Hat has made a name for itself with its almost completely automatic installation. If you have a modern PC, chances are that most (if not all) of your hardware, from your mouse to your video card, can be detected at the time of installation. Most of your hardware can be detected by OpenLinux's installation as well, but you have to press Enter a few more times.

For the system administrators out there, both distributions use SysV initialization, which more closely matches AT&T's SysV UNIX (see Chapter 12, "System Initialization Under OpenLinux," for more information on SysV initialization).

SuSE

SuSE is a Linux distribution that has proven to be quite popular in Europe and is enjoying ever-growing success in the U.S. It uses a SysV initialization scheme, which puts it in line with distributions such as OpenLinux. It also uses `RPM` as its package management mechanism. Most of the administration centers around a utility called `YAST` (Yet Another Setup Tool), which handles package maintenance and upgrades, user administration, and a number of other essential administration tasks.

Other than the initialization scheme and the administration tools, the main difference between OpenLinux and SuSE (and other distributions for that matter) is that SuSE's distribution strives to be more *voluminous*, meaning that it tends to carry more packages than OpenLinux. This is not a drawback in and of itself; it is just that Caldera Systems has narrowed its package selection in the interest of strengthening the testing of the included packages. With fewer packages, testing on the packages that are left in can be more thorough.

At the time of this writing, SuSE's distribution of Linux is the most popular distribution in Europe. The bulk of the development on the distribution is performed at SuSE's headquarters in Germany, but offices in the U.S. and elsewhere have been created mostly to help with software distribution and support.

SuSE also uses KDE as its graphic environment.

Debian

Originally started as the *Free Software Foundation*'s (*FSF*) official distribution of Linux, the Debian project has since broken off from the FSF and become a sovereign entity. However, it has not dropped its adherence to the FSF's licensing. In fact, of all the top Linux distributions, the Debian distribution is by far the most devoted to the FSF's *GNU Public License*, or *GPL* (*GNU*, by the way, is a recursive acronym that stands for *GNU's Not UNIX*). They are so devoted that they only allow "pure" GPL software to be included in their distribution.

Instead of `RPM`, Debian uses a package management system known as `dpkg`. The general idea behind `dpkg` is similar to that of `RPM`, but there are some extra features that enhance dependency checking for package installation and removal, and some other features that offer convenient package updating mechanisms.

In addition to running on Intel x86 and Pentium platforms, Debian has been ported to other systems such as Sun's SPARC machines and StrongArm (currently used in systems such as Corel's NetWinder machines). There is also a port to the Alpha platform available.

This distribution is highly regarded in the sovereign software world as being one of the most stable and technically sound distributions of Linux. Unfortunately, it is also regarded as being one of the most unfriendly distributions for new Linux users from a usability and installability standpoint. This is understandable because technical quality was the main focus of the development team when the system was pieced together. Because of the level of technical Linux savvy required to install and use this distribution, Debian is aimed at experienced Linux users and developers.

Much like OpenLinux, Red Hat, and SuSE, fee-based technical support is available for Debian, but only in the form of corporate support contracts (the others offer lower priced end-user support as well as corporate support contracts). Free support, as usual (and as applicable to all the available Linux distributions), is available on the Internet through mail lists and newsgroups.

YES, THERE ARE OTHERS

Just when you think all the distributions have been made, another one pops up. These distributions all have their own focuses, each one being created to fill a perceived gap.

For instance, there is a new distribution in the works called Stampede that is optimized from top to bottom to run on Pentium-based systems. Another distribution called Mandrake takes KDE and installs it on top of current Red Hat distributions to overcome the philosophical issues that Red Hat has with distributing KDE (however, recent editions of Mandrake have been customized so extensively that they are almost not capable of being referred to as Red Hat derivatives anymore).

Some distributions that were meant as alternatives years ago are still around as well. One popular example is MCC, which was meant to provide a nice, small distribution of Linux (as opposed to the large, ever-expanding distributions that typically ship on CD-ROMs). Momentum is still there, at least in sufficient amounts to keep these distributions going.

To compare OpenLinux to these distributions would not only take up another chapter or two; it is also not a very worthwhile task. The comparisons given earlier cover distributions that are either in a market similar to that of OpenLinux or have enough history with Linux to warrant a comparison. But as many experienced Linux users can tell you, a year is a long time in this business, so the next edition of this book might have some different comparisons to offer.

THE LINUX STANDARD BASE PROJECT (LSB)

One of the biggest complaints that software vendors have about Linux is that it appears to be a "moving target." If you had the gumption to do so, you might update your systems to the latest version of the C library (libc, or glibc), the latest ALPHA grade kernel, or the latest BETA test versions of software on a weekly (sometimes even daily) basis. Some people actually do this, and it is those people who, innocently enough, have given Linux this moving target stigma.

Note

There is absolutely nothing wrong with updating a Linux system in this manner. An explanation of how Linux got this image was warranted, however.

This can be fun for a hobbyist or a casual tinkerer, but serious users and developers tend to shy away from systems that change weekly. This fear tends to bleed over into the corporate IT world—the same world that has to use the software that vendors are trying to keep working under Linux.

For instance, say a developer ported a software package to one Linux distribution that happened to use the latest version of the GNU C library (glibc2, also known as libc version 6 in some circles). The application might work great on that Linux distribution, but when moved to another distribution that uses an older C library (say, libc version 5), some essential pieces of the library are missing that might prevent the software from running. This implies that a whole slice of Linux users will probably not purchase that software package, or will ring up significant hours of technical support trying to get the software vendor to help with installation.

All in all, it is not a situation in which many vendors want to find themselves. It is situations like this that can prevent a company from porting their software to Linux.

To address this concern, a group was assembled under the umbrella of the Linux Standard Base project to discuss how to develop a solid, stable platform with known, established binaries and libraries with which software developers can reliably port their software. This group is not centered around any particular Linux distribution—far from it, actually. There is representation from at least the top five prominent Linux distributions (Slackware being the main exception), some Linux hardware vendors, and volunteers who are driven by the idea of slowing down the moving target syndrome described earlier.

The LSB project will also address compatibility issues between the various Linux distributions by settling on a common set of binaries, libraries, and directory layouts that have been the source of many cross-distribution problems in the past. Hopefully, in the end, software developed or packaged for one Linux distribution will simply plug into another distribution with a minimum of hassles, if any at all.

Anyone who wants to contribute mindshare to this project is encouraged to participate. There are mail lists and Web pages that cater to the LSB project and that are open to the general public. Observers are nudged toward lurking on the mail lists, though, in an effort to keep the signal to noise ratio low. For this reason, ideas and concerns need to be submitted to committee members instead of the mail lists. Everyone is encouraged to follow the discussion and consider becoming an official part of the effort, though. Be sure to check the LSB Web page for more information on this project (the address for this Web page, along with addresses for other essential Web pages that concern Linux, are available at the end of this book in Appendix D).

How Does OpenLinux Fit in with Other Networked Environments?

Many people within the Linux community want to establish Linux as a viable alternative to other graphic desktop operating systems. This is a good cause to support. Linux has proven itself as a highly stable end-user operating system, and with graphic interfaces such as the one provided by the K Desktop Environment (which is covered in Part II, "Using OpenLinux"), migration from other non-Linux operating systems is becoming easier and easier. In addition to that, commercial software companies such as Corel have targeted Linux as the plate on which their bread and butter (office software) can be served, and so far their porting efforts have gone over quite well with the Linux community in general.

However, to simply look at Linux as a replacement for other graphic operating systems is like looking at a fire truck and considering using it to pick up your sister at the airport. There are many, many other features of Linux that go way beyond simple desktop interaction, and many people think that this is where Linux shows its true colors. To ignore these features is to ignore the size and functionality (not to mention the misuse) of the fire truck mentioned earlier.

Networking is where the most power resides within Linux. No other operating system to date has offered the connectivity features that Linux offers at the price tag that Linux holds. Similar functionality might cost you literally a few thousand U.S. dollars with other variants of the UNIX operating system. With Linux, it is all included "in the box."

TCP/IP Networks

Whether it is a simple dial-up PPP connection to an Internet provider or a server that sits at the center of your company and serves up Web pages, FTP downloads, and peripheral pools, Linux is a hands-down winner over the current alternatives. It offers full IPv4 support (even IPv6), including the capability to do the following:

- **Forward network packets**—Can make it a nice gateway system to the Internet
- **Masquerade network packets**—Provides the capability to use only one valid IP address to give access to networks, such as the Internet, to an entire company
- **Tunnel network packets**—Creates a pipeline using IP that permits other IP packets, or even non-IP packets such as IPX packets from NetWare, to pass across the connection in encapsulated form
- **Alias IP addresses**—Hosts multiple addresses on one network interface, which is useful when providing virtual hosting services
- **Filter network packets**—Packet filtering firewall capabilities are contained within the Linux kernel, just waiting to be implemented

Also, special things you can do with TCP/IP—such as remote configuration *a la* DHCP and bootp—are possible with OpenLinux. FTP services, Web services, NFS file system sharing, mail (POP, SMTP), USENET news, and even video conferencing can be done either with software that is included with OpenLinux or with a few items that are freely downloadable from the Internet.

Basically, if it can be done with TCP/IP, it can be done with OpenLinux. See Part IV, "Networking with OpenLinux," for a series of chapters that address these features in more detail.

Intranets

Intranets—small versions of the Internet available solely within a closed network such as one found within a company—are quite popular nowadays. The capability to use one set of tools to access both intra- and extra-company network services such as mail and document distribution is smart from an administration standpoint. Also, services that are popular on the Internet typically offer, in one form or another, inexpensive or free client software; this makes the choice economical as well. Web browsers, news readers, mail readers, and other client software can be used for Internet access as well as for accessing intra-company network services.

All you need to create an intranet complete with the major services that everyone has come to depend on from the Internet is included with OpenLinux. There is the Apache Web server, sendmail for mail transportation, and POP3 for mail downloading (as well as IMAP for those who want to leave all mail on central mail servers). There is also INN for news servers, BIND for name resolution services, and even IP masquerading features to help your company/group get the internal systems on the intranet out to the Internet.

TCP/IP services are not the only network services offered by OpenLinux, though. Linux fits in well with heterogeneous networking scenarios, combining different protocols for file and print sharing services into one cooperative system; each networking system is capable of sharing the services of another, as you will soon see.

NetWare Networks

Yes, OpenLinux can connect to NetWare networks. This includes NDS as well as bindery services. Starting with the Linux NetWare client (originally developed with the Caldera Network Desktop system, and now available free of charge to Linux users), Caldera Systems has continued its NetWare line with the addition of NetWare Cross Platform Services (NCPS) for Linux. With this package, Linux jumped into the Novell server business with the capability to offer Novell file and print services.

The right to port such items to Linux was obtained primarily because of Caldera Systems' close relationship with Novell (`http://www.novell.com`). This is not just because Caldera Systems and Novell share the same home state in the U.S.; it is also because Novell wants to work with a business-oriented Linux company, and Linux is Caldera Systems' primary business focus.

Authoritative information on NetWare for Linux is available later in this book in Chapter 33, "NetWare and OpenLinux."

MICROSOFT WINDOWS NETWORKS

With the popularity of Windows systems comes the popularity of Windows Networking via the *Session Message Block* (*SMB*) protocol. This networking scheme allows connections to be browsed, established, and then dropped using simple graphic interfaces on the Windows system. The networks themselves are dynamically built and updated through a series of "elections" between computers on the network, with a new election being held every time another computer signs on.

In most Windows networks, a machine running Windows NT sits at the center of the network, acting as a source for passwords and home directories for client machines on the network. These central machines are known as *Domain Controllers*, and to date the Domain Controller specifications are known only to Microsoft (the rest of the SMB protocol specification is public knowledge). Domain Controllers are quite powerful, and their pivotal role as the centerpiece of the network makes them appealing to administrators. It is much easier to maintain one computer (the Domain Controller) than to maintain password files and such on each individual client machine on the network.

This type of networking is thankfully not limited to machines running Windows. A number of years ago, a protocol suite called Samba was developed by a gentleman named Andrew Tridgell that offered simple file sharing based on the SMB protocol. The project has taken on a life of its own, adding support for the *Common Internet File System* (*CIFS*), and recently taking on features that enable it to emulate Domain Controllers to a certain extent. Samba has been given support by major hardware vendors (for instance, DEC, Silicon Graphics, IBM), has outperformed other SMB implementations using Ziff-Davis's NetBench benchmark, and is now capable of being a domain client (obtaining authentication from a Domain Controller running on Windows NT). There are many more features of Samba that make it a worthy (if not superior) addition to any Windows network, but those are best left to the Samba Web pages (referenced in Appendix D) and to Chapter 34, "Microsoft Windows and OpenLinux."

SUMMARY

The network items listed here are not to be considered a complete list of the networking features available on OpenLinux. The fact is, there are lots of items that were not included in the list (and some are not even covered in this book). Items such as AppleTalk, SPX, AX.25, and a few others can be found documented on the Internet on their various Web and FTP distribution sites listed at the end of this book. This chapter covered what we believe to be the most common items and the ones that have been requested the most.

Remember, UNIX systems (and variants of UNIX, such as Linux) heavily emphasize file systems. If something can sit on a file system, odds are that it can be shared on a network.

Consequently, if a Samba share is accessible on a Linux file system, it can probably be shared right back out one way or another through NetWare, NFS, FTP, or any of a number of other routes. Creativity is the key when networking with a Linux system.

As for Linux distributions, keep in mind that there is room enough for all of us. Each distribution brings something different to the table, and in most cases what makes one distribution special can just as easily be installed on another distribution without violating any licensing. This is what makes Linux such a wonderful operating system. It is open, it is available to everyone, and nobody can steal it or make it proprietary. Commercial add-ons such as Caldera Systems' NetWare client that were created for one Linux distribution can typically be purchased (or, in the case of the NetWare client, downloaded free of charge) and installed on a different distribution with few or no problems. The LSB project will help to ensure that the compatibility that enables this to happen is carried into future distributions of Linux, and that the existing compatibility problems that might prevent this from succeeding will soon be eliminated.

For more information on some of the items listed in this chapter, refer to the following:

- To get started with using KDE, jump to Chapter 3, "Introduction to the Desktop (KDE)."
- For information on using NetWare for Linux, see Chapter 33.
- For information on how to put Samba to work for you, check out Chapter 34.

CHAPTER 2

INSTALLING OPENLINUX

In this chapter

Obviously, in order to use Linux, you must first have it installed. In the not too distant past, installing Linux was quite a challenge for many, but the method of installing Linux has evolved dramatically over the past few years. Gone are the days of having to build a set of install disks, or even of using install floppies that come in a box. With the advent of a system BIOS that supports a bootable CD-ROM, OpenLinux can be installed with a single CD-ROM. In fact, with the release of OpenLinux 2.2, a method of installing Linux directly from within Microsoft Windows is now available. Although many of the core components of any Linux distribution are very much the same, however, the method of installation is much different.

The development of the Linux kernel—and of many of the utilities that are used with Linux—is vendor neutral. In other words, all Linux vendors use the same source code, though modifications can be made and patches applied. However, the method of installation and the method of creating an installation CD-ROM differ dramatically between Linux vendors. The OpenLinux installation CD-ROM is created using a process known as *self-hosting*. Self-hosting is the process of applying commercial engineering practices to the open-source development model. Instead of a collage of many pieces that only looks good from a distance, OpenLinux is a complete system of source code and libraries that matches all the included binaries. The installation CD-ROM can be regenerated by completely compiling everything from the source.

One of the distinctly unique features of OpenLinux is the new installation procedure. This new procedure greatly simplifies the installation process. Even if you are brand new to Linux, you can easily complete the installation process using the newly created graphical installation procedure that is part of OpenLinux.

INSTALLATION REQUIREMENTS

Before beginning the installation steps, you'll want to take a minute and assess your system hardware. The following are crucial to a successful installation:

- Adequate disk space
- Sufficient RAM
- CD-ROM access

ADEQUATE DISK SPACE

The requirements for disk space vary depending upon the end objective of the system you are installing, but as a general rule of thumb, you'll want 500MB of free disk space. That, of course, is a minimum; in order to install the complete set of recommended packages and have enough disk space for your own data, you'll want to have at least 1GB of disk space available for installation. OpenLinux is installed into a separate partition on a hard drive. If you're unfamiliar with the concept of partitions, don't panic—the new method of installing OpenLinux handles partitioning rather painlessly.

Sufficient RAM

Of course, the more RAM your system has, the more responsive it is. However, for the purpose of discussion in this chapter, it's helpful to know the minimum requirements for a successful installation. You need a minimum of 16MB of RAM in order to complete the new graphical installation.

Note

An installation can be completed with only 8MB of RAM if you use the non-graphical method. This method requires that you perform a few manual steps during the installation process. See the section "Installing with `lisa`," later in this chapter, for details.

CD-ROM Access

In order to install OpenLinux, you need either a CD-ROM drive on your system or access to a CD-ROM drive via a network connection. The easiest method of installing OpenLinux is via a CD-ROM drive on the system.

Note

The installation can be completed by copying the contents of the CD-ROM to the hard drive and specifying the hard drive as the install source; at some point, though, you'll need access to a CD-ROM in order to prepare for that method of installation.

Selecting an Installation Method

The best method of installation depends on the state of the system that is to be installed. The first objective of an OpenLinux installation is to prepare the hard drive. The hard drive must be partitioned correctly for a successful installation. Partitioning can be accomplished with any of the installation methods that are offered with OpenLinux, but the easiest method of partitioning is via the Partition Magic routine that comes with OpenLinux. An installation can be initiated in one of three ways:

- Installing from Windows
- Installing via a bootable CD-ROM or floppy disk
- Installing with the old `lisa` method (via floppy)

The option to use Partition Magic to partition your hard drive is only available if you install OpenLinux with the first option, via Windows.

Note

You'll need a minimum of two new partitions, one for the Linux installation and one to be used as virtual memory (swap space).

The new graphical installation is aptly named *LIZARD*, as in *Linux Install Wizard*. It is used in the first two aforementioned options, but the `lisa` utility (Linux Install and System Administration) is used for the old method of installation.

INSTALLING FROM WINDOWS

Installing OpenLinux from within Windows (95, 98, or NT) is great for someone who is new to Linux. This method works well with systems that are already loaded with Windows and need to be partitioned for dual boot purposes. From a working Windows environment, complete the following steps:

1. Insert the OpenLinux CD-ROM. A simple multimedia presentation is shown, and then the OpenLinux installation and information main menu is displayed (see Figure 2.1). The following options are presented:
   - Install a Windows program group of utilities to prepare for OpenLinux installation.
   - Browse the contents of the OpenLinux CD-ROM.
   - Visit the Caldera Systems Web site (an Internet connection is required).
   - View a multimedia presentation. A fun Caldera commercial in AVI format is included in this section.
   - Register your copy of OpenLinux.
   - Learn more about products from Caldera Systems.
   - View contact information for Caldera Systems.

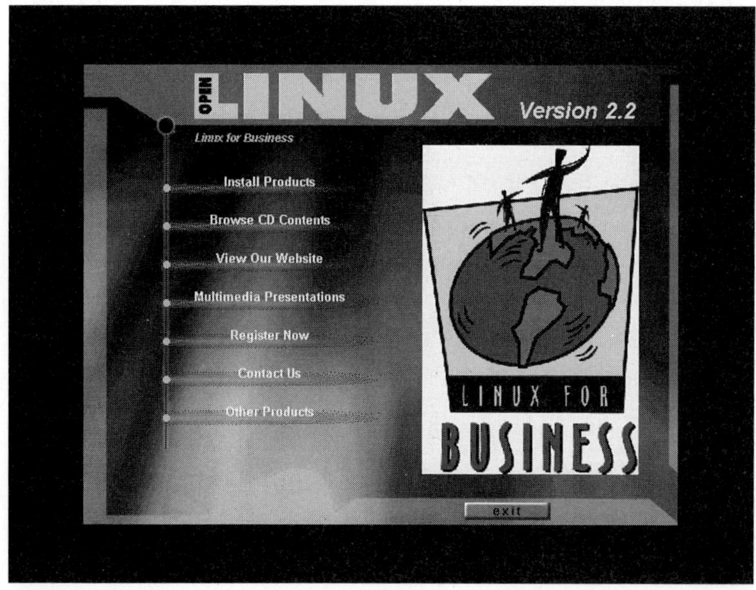

Figure 2.1
Installation of OpenLinux from Windows can be started from this main menu.

2. After you have explored any desired options from the main menu, select Install Products to begin the installation process. A screen is displayed with the following options:
   - Full Install Preparation
   - Partition and Launch Linux Install
   - Create Floppy Install Diskettes
   - Install Boot Magic

   Selecting the first option begins the installation of the Windows components of OpenLinux. This option installs the utilities that are necessary to perform the other listed options. These utilities can be accessed at any time from within the Windows program group in which they are installed. Select the first option, Full Install Preparation. The screen shown in Figure 2.2 is displayed.

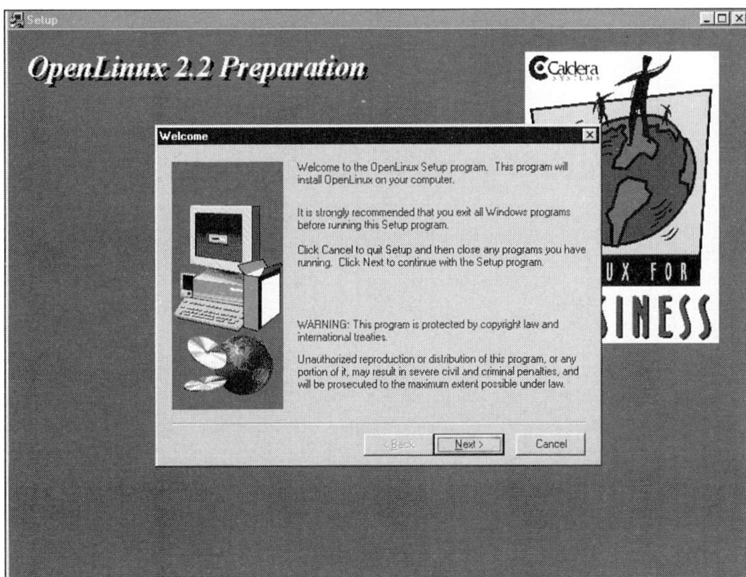

Figure 2.2
OpenLinux 2.2 Install Preparation Screen.

3. It is strongly recommended that you exit other applications before proceeding with this step. Select Next when you are ready.
4. Review the License agreement and select Yes to continue.
5. Select a destination directory to install the OpenLinux program group. The default directory is C:\Program Files\OpenLinux.
6. Select the Program Folder. The default folder is OpenLinux.
7. OpenLinux creates a program group, as shown in Figure 2.3.

Figure 2.3
The OpenLinux Windows tools program group.

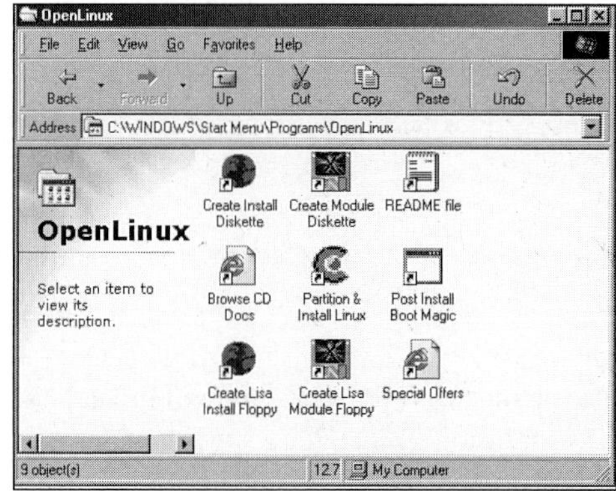

8. Select Partition and Launch Linux Install from the main menu (see Figure 2.1, earlier in this chapter).
9. OpenLinux creates the Partition Magic Caldera Edition program group and runs the Partition Magic routine.
10. In order to run Partition Magic and partition your hard drive, the system boots into DOS mode. This can only be accomplished if you remove any bootable CD-ROM or disk. Therefore, a dialog box is shown, prompting you to remove the CD-ROM.
11. Partition the hard drive so that you have a minimum of two new partitions, one for Linux and one for the swap space.

Note

Remember to remove the CD-ROM when you are prompted to do so. If you fail to do this, and your system supports and is configured for a bootable CD-ROM drive, the system will boot using the CD-ROM and will not complete the steps that were started previously.

Note

The screen goes blank once or twice during this process. This is normal behavior–don't be alarmed. This step is part of the process of booting into a safe environment to partition your hard drive.

After this procedure is complete, the installation of OpenLinux into the newly created partitions begins. See the section "The LIZARD Installation Steps," later in this chapter, for details.

Note

If you are installing OpenLinux tools to a system that is preloaded with Windows NT, you must create a boot disk to launch the Partition Magic partitioning utility. Just follow the onscreen instructions to complete this step.

INSTALLING FROM CD-ROM OR FLOPPY DISK

If you are already comfortable with the concept of partitioning a hard drive and you don't need to save any data to an existing partition on your hard drive, this is the option for you. This method bypasses the convenient steps of partitioning your hard drive from within Windows, but still follows the same set of steps that are outlined in the "The LIZARD Installation Steps" section.

INSTALLING WITH `lisa`

On the remote chance that the new LIZARD install method fails to work properly, you can revert to the old method of installing OpenLinux—using the `lisa` utility. You must first create a boot floppy in order to install via `lisa`. This can be accomplished by running the program from Windows to create a `lisa` installation floppy (refer to Figure 2.3). After you've created this installation floppy, just use it to boot your system. For the details of the steps that are required with this method of installation, see the Caldera Systems Web site at the following URL:

`http://www.calderasystems.com/doc/openlinux/english/install.html`

THE LIZARD INSTALLATION STEPS

Whether you've started the installation from within Windows or have booted directly from the CD-ROM or the installation floppy, the LIZARD installation steps are the same. Initially, a system startup screen is displayed (see Figure 2.4).

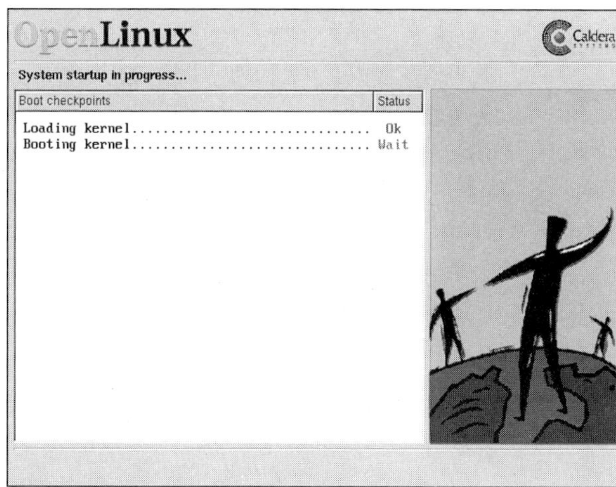

Figure 2.4
The OpenLinux system startup screen.

This system startup screen displays information about the system as it boots. This process actually performs an automated probing step to determine the hardware configuration of your system. This way, you don't have to know exactly what Ethernet card or video card you have—the auto-probing sequence determines this for you. The installation source is also determined at this stage of the installation process. If an OpenLinux CD-ROM is not detected in a local drive, the location of an installation source other than a local CD-ROM drive is attempted. If a local CD-ROM drive is not detected, the installation routine probes for an *NFS* (*network file systems*) drive or an *SMB* (*Samba*) share, or it looks for the needed files on another partition of a local hard drive.

After this phase of the installation is complete, an animated screen with the Caldera Systems logo is displayed; the process then begins, displaying the first of a series of screens where user input is required. The following selection screens are displayed:

- Language
- Mouse
- Installation target
- Package
- Keyboard (model & layout)
- Video card
- Monitor
- Video Mode (resolution & color depth)
- Set root password
- Add additional users and passwords
- Networking options
- Time Zone setting
- Installation entertainment

LANGUAGE SELECTION

The very first option is to select the language of choice. This causes subsequent steps of the installation to be displayed in the desired language. The language options are as follows:

- English
- Deutsch
- Francais
- Italiano

MOUSE DETECTION

The mouse is automatically detected when it is moved within the text window that is displayed on this screen. The three major options are as follows:

- PS/2
- Logitech Serial
- Microsoft Serial

INSTALLATION TARGET

The partition in which Linux is to be installed is selected at this stage of the installation process. Three options are displayed as follows:

- Entire Hard disk
- Prepared partitions
- Custom (Expert Only)

The first two options are, for the most part, self-explanatory: The first option uses the entire hard disk, and the second option uses the partitions that were prepared by the Partition Magic step. If you did not complete this step, and you are comfortable with the concept of partitioning a hard disk, you can select the Custom (Expert Only) option. It's really nothing more than a graphical version of the `fdisk` utility.

PACKAGE OPTIONS

At this stage of the installation, you must choose which set of packages to install. As a matter of simplification, only three options are presented. You can choose from the following three options:

- The minimum set
- All recommended packages
- All packages

Tip

The number of options that are displayed here might differ because several other predefined options have been considered. The key is to select the option that best suits your needs. If you're not certain, select the All recommended packages option.

Note

The installation of the selected package set begins immediately after you select Next on this screen. Package installation continues as you complete the rest of the installation options. A status bar is displayed in the lower-left corner of the screen with each subsequent dialog screen.

Note

You might notice some delay in responsiveness as package installation occurs. Of course, this is dependent upon your system configuration.

KEYBOARD (MODEL AND LAYOUT)

Keeping the default model (Generic 101) and layout (U.S. English) works fine for most people, but of course, you want to select the keyboard layout that matches your hardware and desired language.

VIDEO CARD

The installation program actually detects the video card that is used in your system. This is accomplished with an auto-probing routine that is run in a simple mode. When this screen is displayed, your video card is displayed at the top of the screen. The amount of video RAM initially defaults to 256K. If you happen to know the amount of video RAM on your video card you can manually select it. Otherwise, you can select Probe to have the auto-probing routine conduct a more in-depth investigation as to the amount of video RAM your video adapter has.

Note

Note that the more in-depth probe can cause your system to hang, and you might have to reboot your system. This is not a common occurrence, but this is left as a manual step so that you can bypass the more in-depth probe the second time if the auto-probing routine *does* cause your system to hang.

Tip

Select Probe to auto-detect the amount of video RAM. This takes about five seconds. When this is complete, a dialog box appears with the following message: `Probing is complete and apparently successful.`

MONITOR

The purpose of this step is to determine the horizontal and vertical refresh rates for your monitor. If you're not familiar with these settings for your monitor, you need not worry. An extensive database of monitors has been compiled to simplify this step. Just scroll down the list to find the manufacturer of your monitor. After you locate the appropriate manufacturer, simply click on the associated plus sign to see a listing of the monitor models. Selecting a model from the displayed monitor list sets the appropriate refresh rates for you. If you don't find your monitor in the prebuilt database, you can select one of the generic options at the beginning of this list or you can enter the refresh rates for your monitor in the selection boxes that are provided.

Caution

Be very careful to not select refresh rates that go beyond the capability of your monitor. Doing so can cause damage to your monitor. *Do not select refresh rates that are greater than those supported by your monitor*!

VIDEO MODE (RESOLUTION AND COLOR DEPTH)

The resolution and color depth are selected at this point. This is mostly a matter of preference. The higher the resolution, the smaller the font and the more you can fit on the screen at once. This can always be adjusted after the installation is complete.

Note

You can test the settings that you have selected for your display by clicking the Test button. The screen goes blank momentarily as the X Server switches to the desired resolution. If the selected options don't seem to work correctly, click the Back button and try an alternative selection.

SET ROOT PASSWORD

Enter the password for the root user. Because of the multiuser nature of Linux, setting passwords for individual users is a must. Make sure that you select a password for the root user that cannot be easily guessed or calculated by unwanted intruders. You must enter the password twice to confirm the spelling.

ADD ADDITIONAL USERS AND PASSWORDS

At this point in the installation, you can enter as many additional user accounts as you want. You must enter the usernames and set initial passwords for them.

NETWORKING OPTIONS

At this stage of the installation, a screen that offers the following three networking options is displayed:

- No Networking
- DHCP Networking
- Statically defined networking

NO NETWORKING

Select this option if you do not plan to connect this machine to a network or if you don't happen to have the network information that is required to complete the network setup.

Note

Select this option for dial-up connections to the Internet. Configuring your system for this setup is covered in Chapter 24, "Connecting to an ISP."

DHCP NETWORKING

Select this option if you want this machine to automatically configure networking at bootup by acquiring an IP address from a DHCP server.

STATICALLY DEFINED NETWORKING

Select this option if your system is to be assigned its own static IP address, and if it will be part of a local area network. This option requires several pieces of information, including IP addresses for the following items:

- Netmask
- Gateway
- Name Server
- Host Name

Note

If the system is connected to a network during the installation process, network information is automatically determined by the contents of network traffic packets.

TIME ZONE SETTING

The correct time zone setting can be determined by moving your mouse pointer across the world map to the appropriate location. You can also select the correct time zone using the drop-down combo box.

INSTALLATION ENTERTAINMENT

After you have completed the selections that make up each of the previous screens, you can enjoy a game of tetris while the installation of the selected package set completes. When all the selected packages are installed, the status bar in the lower-left hand corner displays `100%`, and the Finish button displays in black lettering instead of gray. Selecting Finish boots the machine to the newly installed OpenLinux system.

LOGGING IN TO THE NEWLY INSTALLED SYSTEM

After the installation steps are completed, a graphical login interface is displayed. You need to remember the passwords that were created during the installation. You can log in to the system by entering a user ID and its associated password. An initial KDE introduction screen is displayed the first time you log in (see Figure 2.5).

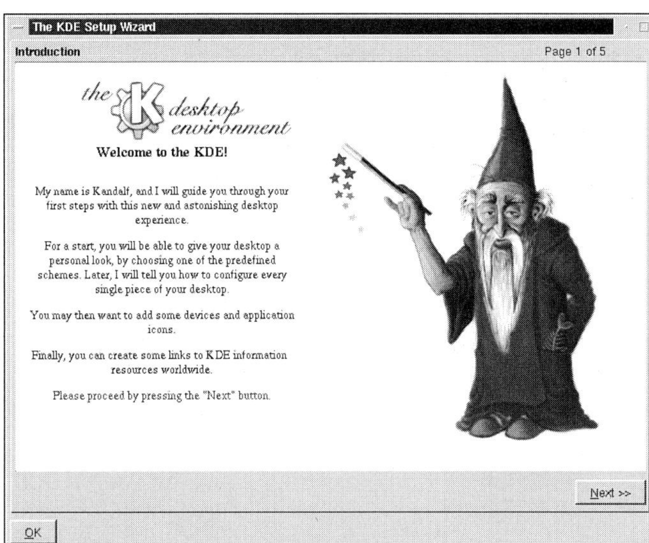

Figure 2.5
The initial KDE setup screen.

The wizard Kandalf walks you through a few simple setup steps to customize your K Desktop Environment (KDE). Just answer the questions, and you're all set. Your OpenLinux system is now up and running.

SUMMARY

If you've ever installed previous versions of Linux, you'll really come to appreciate the simplicity and ease of use of the new LIZARD installation. The simplest installation method is to have an existing Windows environment do most of the work for you. Just let the dialog box pop up in Windows, and then follow the steps from there. The bootable CD-ROM or installation floppy is almost as easy. The trick is to get your hard drive partitioned as you want it, and then just complete the installation steps. For more information, see the following chapters:

- See Chapter 3, "Introduction to the Desktop (KDE)," for more information on the desktop environment.
- See Chapter 4, "Navigating the Desktop," for information on the desktop layout and menu structure.
- See Chapter 5, "Customizing Your Desktop Environment," for information on how to configure the desktop environment to your liking.
- See Chapter 20, "Boot Loader," for more information on the boot loader and how to configure your system.

PART II

USING OPENLINUX

CHAPTER 3

Introduction to the Desktop (KDE)

In this chapter

WHAT IS KDE?

KDE stands for the *K Desktop Environment*. The name is a pun on CDE (Common Desktop Environment), which was a popular desktop system for many UNIX platforms. KDE provides some of the same functionality for a graphical environment that is found in other popular operating environments, such as Macintosh OS or Windows 98. However, it also provides some unique features of its own to enhance your graphical work environment.

KDE is a complete desktop environment, as opposed to being just a window manager or launch bar. There are several capable window managers for Linux, including olwm, fvwm, afterstep, and others. However, KDE provides much more functionality than a simple window manager.

GRAPHICAL BASICS

With Linux, as with many UNIX operating systems, the graphical environment is provided by multiple user-level programs. This is in contrast to, for example, Windows 98, where the graphical environment is part of the operating system kernel, and is, essentially, one service. With Linux, the graphical environment is usually split into three or more pieces:

- The X Window System
- A window manager
- A launch bar, or a desktop

The X Window System (XFree86 in OpenLinux) handles the screen and low-level graphics for graphical applications. The X Window System also provides network transparency for programs. That is, when a program is written for X Windows, its interface can be displayed remotely on another machine connected via the network, and that machine's mouse and keyboard are used for input. This is done without any special work on the part of the application programmer.

A window manager provides for managing the size and location of windows on the screen. This program controls much of the look and feel of a program as well as of the background screen itself. For example, the window manager controls the color of the window borders, the buttons that are part of the window title bar, and the backdrop of the screen, among other things. The window manager can also support virtual windows—which are a way of supporting more screen area for applications than there is actual screen space on the video monitor—and some pop-up menus associated with program windows and the screen backdrop.

A launch bar provides a simple way to start graphical applications by clicking their icons instead of typing their names.

KDE IS A GRAPHICAL DESKTOP

KDE runs on top of the X Window System (that is, it is an X program) and provides a built-in window manager, as well as the capabilities to launch other graphical applications.

(Thus, it provides the first two items in the preceding list.) However, KDE is also much more than this.

KDE provides a framework for applications to work together in useful ways to provide the end user with a rich object-oriented environment. For example, KDE enables you to do the following:

- Put icons on the desktop to mount and unmount removable disks (such as floppies).
- Browse the file system graphically.
- Associate applications with files of a particular type (so that when you click a file, it automatically loads the correct application).
- Create a desktop printer icon, to which you can drag files to print them.

None of these are features of a window manager or launch program by itself. The value of KDE is that it simplifies many tasks that a user has to perform by providing a graphical environment that simulates something more familiar to the user. In other words, KDE provides a desktop metaphor, which is a way of displaying and manipulating documents, directories, and programs in a manner that is more intuitive and appealing than typing commands at a shell prompt.

A more exhaustive list of KDE features is discussed in the section "KDE Capabilities" later in this chapter.

KDE Applications

The KDE system includes not only the desktop, but a whole host of applications and utilities to go along with it. In the default distribution of KDE, there are more than 80 programs, ranging from games to system utilities to full-blown applications (such as a word processor). Each of these programs is useful in its own right; in addition, however, the KDE applications can interoperate with each other to make certain operations easier. For example, you can drag a package file from the file manager to the package manager to view the contents of the package and install it.

KDE Is a Project

Besides being a graphical desktop, KDE is also a huge project. The KDE project provides a complete applications development framework and many guidelines and resources for the development and use of KDE programs.

Thousands of developers, spread around the world, work on various aspects of the KDE system, including programming, documentation, translation, all kinds of testing, and packaging. The KDE Web site is located at `http://www.kde.org/`.

This Web site contains many resources for both users and developers of KDE. For example, the Web site provides online documentation in many languages. Also, users can participate in mailing lists to receive or give assistance in working with KDE. For developers, there are application style guides, automated tools for constructing KDE applications, bug and feature wish lists, and more.

The KDE project is devoted to a philosophy of ease-of-use, consistency, and quality for graphical applications in the Linux world.

Competing Desktop Projects

As with many projects in Linux, KDE is by no means the only one of its kind. Another project, GNOME, has similar goals. KDE was started first, and has progressed quickly into a stable and highly usable platform–which is why Caldera chose to include it in OpenLinux. However, GNOME is also progressing rapidly.

Although a few malcontents try to create contention between the two groups, by and large the developers of each of these projects share a friendly rivalry–a healthy competition that encourages both teams to do their best.

If you want to check out the GNOME desktop, see their Web site at `http://www.gnome.org/`.

STARTING KDE

In most installations, if you have used the LIZARD installation program, KDE starts automatically when you start your machine. If you installed using the `lisa` program, you need to configure the X Server for your machine before you can run KDE. If you have not done this, follow the instructions in Chapter 37, "Configuring X", first, and then return to this section.

After X is configured, you start KDE by typing `kde` at the console prompt. Chapter 6, "KDM," provides instructions on configuring your machine to start automatically in graphical mode, if it does not do this by default.

The first time KDE starts, you are presented with a series of dialog boxes that enable you to configure a desktop and windowing theme, as well as to create some basic desktop items for immediate use.

A *desktop theme* is a group of settings that control the basic layout of different desktop items and how they work. KDE has support for looking and behaving like several popular desktop environments, including MacOS, Windows, and BeOS.

After selecting a theme, click the Next button and proceed through the dialog boxes to create various desktop items. This includes floppy and CD-ROM icons for your desktop, a printer icon, and a few other things.

This set of dialog boxes only appears once, but you can easily mdoify the look and feel of your desktop or create additional desktop items by following the instructions in chapter 5, "Customizing your Desktop Environment". Chapter 5, explains in detail the items that you can place on your desktop and how they work. When you are done with the KDE wizard program, click the OK button at the bottom of the window to proceed.

Tip

It is possible to switch back and forth between the console prompt and the graphical desktop (for example, between character mode and graphical mode); so you might want to put KDE in the background at the console prompt (if you start KDE manually) by using the following shell `&` option:

```
[root@thunder]$ kde &
```

BASIC DESKTOP ELEMENTS

When KDE first appears, it displays the desktop in the default configuration, shown in Figure 3.1. There are three basic screen components to be aware of: the Desktop, the Panel, and the Taskbar.

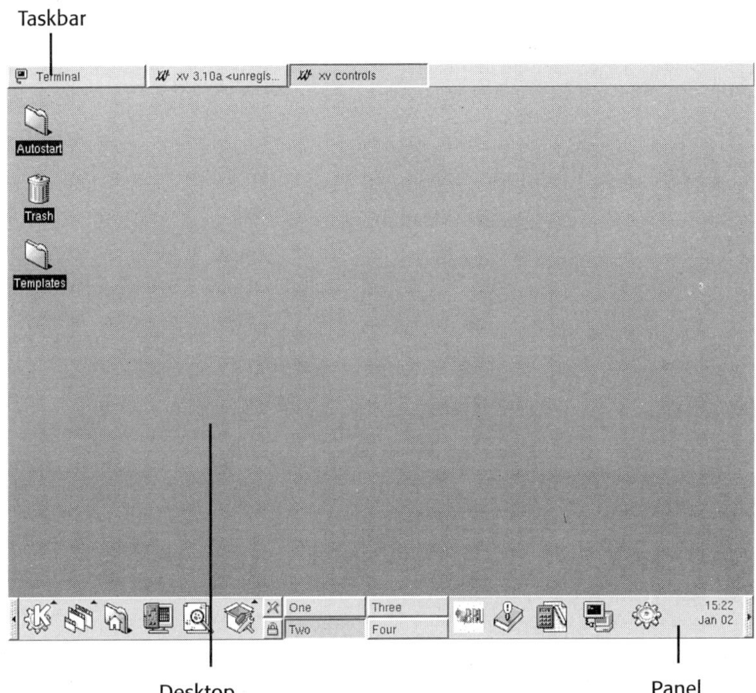

Figure 3.1
The default KDE desktop configuration.

These three main components of KDE are described in the following sections by way of introduction. In Chapter 4, "Navigating the Desktop," a much more thorough description of how to navigate and manipulate the main components and other parts of KDE is presented.

THE DESKTOP

The Desktop is the main working area of the KDE environment. This is the background behind all the other components that run on the screen. In the Desktop area, you place icons for programs, documents, and devices that you work with frequently. This makes these items readily available for access and manipulation. Think of the Desktop area in the same way that you think of an actual desktop, where you keep documents and tools handy to accomplish whatever tasks you are currently working on.

Besides what you see onscreen, KDE actually provides additional desktop space in which to run programs. There are four virtual desktop areas provided by default. A *virtual desktop* is another screen to which you can switch to run applications or to perform work.

Conceptually, you can think of the four different desktops as being part of a single large virtual screen—one that is bigger than your video monitor can display. Each virtual desktop enables you to see one fourth of this larger screen at a time. You can easily move programs and windows between virtual desktops. The extra space provided by virtual desktops gives you more room for your running programs, which enables you to leave application windows open and spaced apart, and therefore ready to use, instead of minimized or overlapped. Virtual desktops also enable you to organize the tasks that you are currently working on by placing related program windows on the same virtual desktop.

THE PANEL

The Panel has icons for important KDE functions, as well as for frequently used programs. One item on the Panel is particularly important; it is the Application Starter button, which is located (by default) on the left side of the Panel. It is the icon with a large 3D *K*. From this button, you can access a menu that lists all the KDE applications. Furthermore, this menu provides access to several other aspects of the KDE system, including the online help system, the KDE Control Panel, and more. Figure 3.2 shows the contents of the default applications menu for KDE.

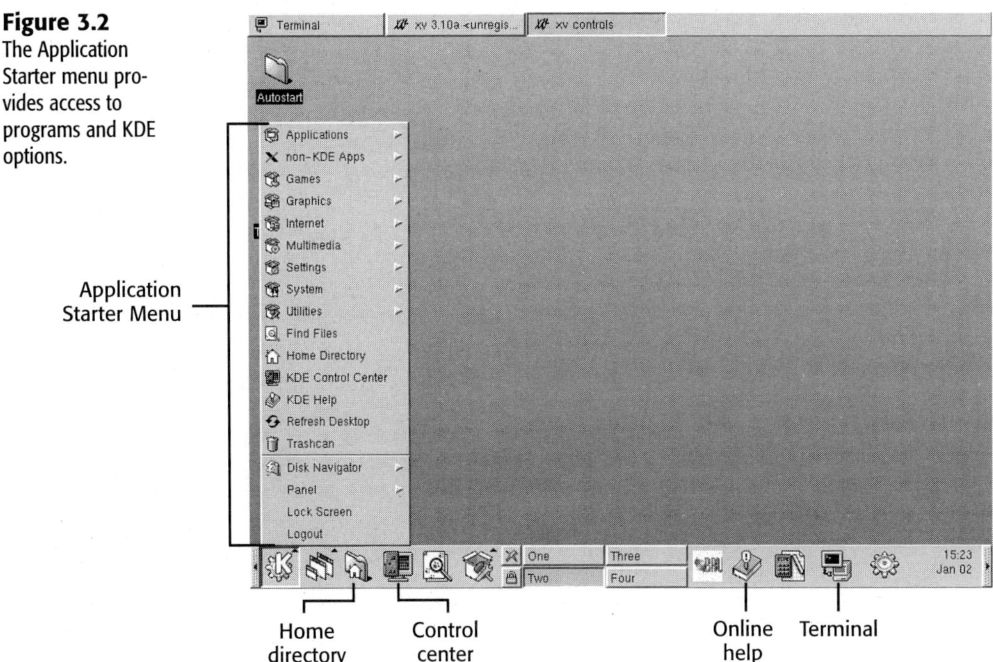

Figure 3.2
The Application Starter menu provides access to programs and KDE options.

THE TASKBAR

The Taskbar shows the programs that are currently running in KDE. Clicking a program in the Taskbar takes you immediately to that program.

RUNNING PROGRAMS

Probably the first thing you want to do after you've started KDE is run some applications. KDE's philosophy is that you can directly manipulate all the objects in the system, whether they are files containing documents to work on, programs that you run, or devices that you control.

LAUNCHING AN APPLICATION

You can start a program in KDE through several different mechanisms. To launch a program, you can do any of the following:

- **Single-click on a button on the Panel**—Several useful programs are provided by default on the Panel. For example, the default Panel provided in OpenLinux includes icons for a virtual terminal emulator, the KDE help program, a calculator, and the Netscape Web browser, among other things.
- **Single-click an item on the Desktop**—By default, there are only three items on the Desktop (the desktop Trashcan and the Templates and Autostart folders), but hopefully after you've used KDE for a while, you will have placed your favorite programs here, ready to use. Customizing the Desktop (that is, putting your applications and documents on it) is covered in Chapter 5.
- **Select a program from the Application Starter menu**—Click on the big K, and follow the menus to the program you want to run.
- **Click an item to launch it**—Inside a file manager window, click an item to launch it.

You can also run a program the old way, by opening a terminal window and typing its name at the shell prompt.

ESSENTIAL PROGRAMS

A few oft-used programs are described here to get you started.

First, the terminal program `kvt` enables you to open a window and access a regular command line shell environment. A button for `kvt` is provided on the Panel, with a small monitor in the icon.

Online help is available by clicking the icon of a book on the Panel. The online help includes a getting-started guide, as well as an index for accessing help for all the KDE applications on your system.

You can browse the file system, or access the World Wide Web using a file manager window. To start a file manager window showing the contents of your home directory, click the folder with the little house on it on the Panel.

STOPPING KDE

To stop KDE, open the Application Starter menu and select the Logout menu item. This ends your KDE session, takes you out of graphical mode (that is, it stops your X Server), and returns you to a shell prompt.

When KDE exits, it closes all the applications that are currently running. Many of the KDE applications remember from one session to the next their current positions, contents, and other attributes. When you restart KDE later, these applications are restored to their former state, just as you left them, enabling you to continue right where you left off. For non-KDE applications, or for applications in which saving the state is not possible, you are warned before KDE exits that you might lose your work, and you are shown a list of the applications. This enables you to save your work and exit those applications cleanly, if you need to, before ending your KDE session.

KDE CAPABILITIES

As stated previously, KDE provides much more than just a graphical window manager or launch environment. It provides many integrated features that are designed to make it easier to work in a graphical environment.

Finding Out More About the KDE Project

KDE is as much a project about a philosophy of UNIX ease-of-use as it is about developing KDE programs themselves. For additional information about the motivations of the KDE developers, and how you can participate, see the online help page "What is the K Desktop Environment?". Open a help window by clicking on the help button on the Panel, and follow the top link in the page that is displayed.

First and foremost, KDE provides an object-oriented environment in which to work. Instead of composing and typing commands at a shell prompt, you manipulate the objects on your system via the desktop or file manager windows. In KDE, you treat things as objects that can be accessed, manipulated, or combined by directly touching or moving them (clicking or dragging them). For example, to work on a document, just click the document and it opens with the correct application for working on that kind of file. To print a document, you drag the document and drop it onto a printer icon. To examine the contents of a floppy, click the floppy device on your desktop. (Neither a printer icon nor a floppy device is on the Desktop by default, but you will see how to add these in Chapter 5.)

This object orientation is provided by a sophisticated file typing system, as well as rigourous adherence (on the part of application authors) to standards that allow KDE applications to interact in intelligent ways.

KDE enables you to control a whole range of options to customize the appearance and functionality of the desktop. You can change the appearance of many things—the desktop backgrounds, the titlebar buttons, or the icons for the individual file system items themselves. You can also change the behavior of KDE to suit your tastes by adjusting such things as the focus policy (which determines how windows become selected) or the default application for certain type of files. Finally, you can alter the contents of the Desktop itself—or the Panel or applications menu—to match the set of programs or files that you use on a day-to-day basis.

KDE allows for completely graphical configuration of all these aspects. This is in stark contrast to other window managers in Linux, where you often have to edit text files by hand and restart the window manager to accomplish the same thing.

Another important aspect of KDE is that it provides a single framework for application development. You can run non-KDE applications in the KDE environment. However, all KDE applications share a highly consistent look and feel. All the KDE applications use the Qt graphical library to provide similar looking and functioning buttons, menus, controls, and other window items. Nevertheless, the KDE team has put together application style guidelines as well to help make sure that KDE applications look and behave consistently. For example, all KDE applications have a menu item located on the right side of the main application menu for accessing the program's online help. All the online help follows a consistent layout and style. Similar icons are used across all the KDE applications for buttons with similar functionality. Although these might seem like small things, when taken in the aggregate this uniformity contributes to your ability to easily use KDE applications because you don't have to relearn interface details from one application to the next.

Another—often overlooked—facet of the KDE project is the complete support for internationalization of all KDE programs. Support for multiple languages is built right into KDE from the ground up, with documentation and online help files available in many languages.

Finally, because of the massive effort that has gone into KDE, there are numerous applications already available for it. The KDE and Qt libraries provide a foundation for rapid development of new applications that conform to KDE requirements. KDE applications are rich in functionality, there are many of them available, and more are being developed every day.

OTHER DESKTOPS

Although KDE is the recommended desktop environment for your OpenLinux system, another desktop and several other window manager systems are provided as well. These are available for backward compatibility with previous versions of OpenLinux, or simply for those who prefer them. If you have a machine with limited processing speed or memory, you might want to use one of these options instead of KDE.

SUMMARY

This chapter provided an overview of the K Desktop Environment, KDE. KDE is more than just a window manager or a program launch bar—it is a comprehensive graphical environment that includes many applications and utilities.

You can start and stop KDE, and launch a few basic applications, to get started with this graphical environment. The three main components of KDE are the Desktop, the Panel, and the Taskbar.

KDE provides an object-oriented framework in which to work, and includes several features that make working with programs, files, and directories easier in a graphical environment.

For additional information, please see the following chapters:

- The next few chapters of this book describe various features and applications of KDE, and how to use them. Chapter 4 contains information on basic KDE usage, and Chapter 5 has information about configuring KDE.
- Chapters 6, 7, "KDE Applications," and 8, "Koffice," cover additional features and programs of KDE.
- KDE runs in conjunction with the X server on your system. Several chapters in Part 5 of this book cover configuring and customizing X. In particular, see Chapter 37 to get X initially set up on your machine.

CHAPTER 4

Navigating the Desktop

In this chapter

Chapter 3, "Introduction to the Desktop (KDE)," provided a brief introduction to the KDE graphical environment. This chapter goes in-depth about all the different icons, menus, and functions in KDE, and how to use them to your advantage.

Each window in KDE has borders and a title bar (with buttons and a menu) for manipulating that window (for example, for moving it around the screen or resizing it). KDE applications follow certain conventions for how their menus, button bars, and other attributes appear onscreen and behave. Behind the windows for the running programs, the main screen of KDE consists of three components: the Desktop, the Panel, and the Taskbar. The final major integral component of KDE is the file manager. The Desktop and the file manager work together to create the object-oriented experience provided by KDE. All these different elements are described in the sections that follow.

You might notice that there is a lot of redundancy in KDE; there are often two or three ways to accomplish the same thing. This is done to make the Desktop as easy to use as possible. When there are multiple ways to do something, just pick the one with which you are the most comfortable, and use it (that is, don't try to remember everything—you don't need to).

The Basics of Navigation

Before describing the different parts of the KDE system, it's good to get a few basic topics out of the way. Because it is a graphical system, almost everything can be manipulated using the mouse (or some other pointing device). Within KDE, a single click using the left mouse button selects or launches an item.

Note

If you are coming from a Windows environment, you might need to get out of the habit of double-clicking an item to launch it. If you do this with KDE, you'll launch the program twice, which can be both slow and annoying!

Almost everything in KDE has a *context menu*, which is accessed by clicking the object with the right mouse button. The context menu usually includes ways to customize or manipulate that specific item. Even the Desktop itself has a context menu, which enables you to customize it. Try right-clicking various things you see onscreen right now to see the different context menus that are available.

Some other buttons or items accept a right or middle click to perform an alternative action, instead of the default one. For example, if you click the maximize button on a window's title bar with the left mouse button, KDE maximizes the window to full screen. However, if you click it with the right or middle mouse button, KDE maximizes the window horizontally or vertically only, respectively.

How to Middle-Click with a Two-Button Mouse

If you only have a two-button mouse, you might be wondering how to click something with the middle mouse button. When you configure the mouse under X (using `XF86Setup`), you can select an option called Emulate3Buttons. When this option is set, you can simulate a middle mouse button press by pressing both the left and right buttons simultaneously.

See Chapter 37, "Configuring X," and Chapter 38, "Dissecting the XF86Config File," for more information about this and other X configuration options.

Often, to manipulate items onscreen you drag them from one area to another (for example, from the file manager to the Desktop). To drag a single item, click and hold the left mouse button on the item, and move the mouse to the location at which you want to drop the item. To drag multiple items, use the left mouse button to draw a rectangle around the items, and then release it. The items in the rectangle are shaded to show that they are selected. Now you can drag the whole group by dragging any one of the selected items.

KDE provides pop-up help (called *tooltips*) for most items in the system. Tooltips are available for items on the Desktop, in the Panel, and on the Taskbar, as well as for the icons in the button bars of almost all KDE applications. To view a tooltip, just move the pointer over an item about which you are curious, and leave it there for a few seconds. A short description of the item is displayed in a yellow box. Move the pointer off the item to get rid of the tooltip. (These tooltips are very similar to the ToolTip feature available in Microsoft Windows.)

Finally, there are keyboard shortcuts (key combinations) that you can use—instead of the mouse—to perform some common KDE operations. Menu items in the currently selected window can often be accessed with accelerator keys (use the Alt key with the key for the underlined letter in the menu). Other Desktop or window manager functions are available as well (for example, to switch between programs, use Alt+Tab). In this chapter, keyboard shortcuts are described in the section that covers that particular operation. Furthermore, a list of keyboard shortcuts is presented in Table 4.3, later in this chapter.

PROGRAM WINDOWS

Programs running under KDE all have a similar look and feel. KDE includes a window manager system that provides each window with a border and title bar, which can be used to manipulate that window.

Figure 4.1 shows a sample window (in this case, a file manager window), and indicates the different screen elements that you can use to manipulate that window.

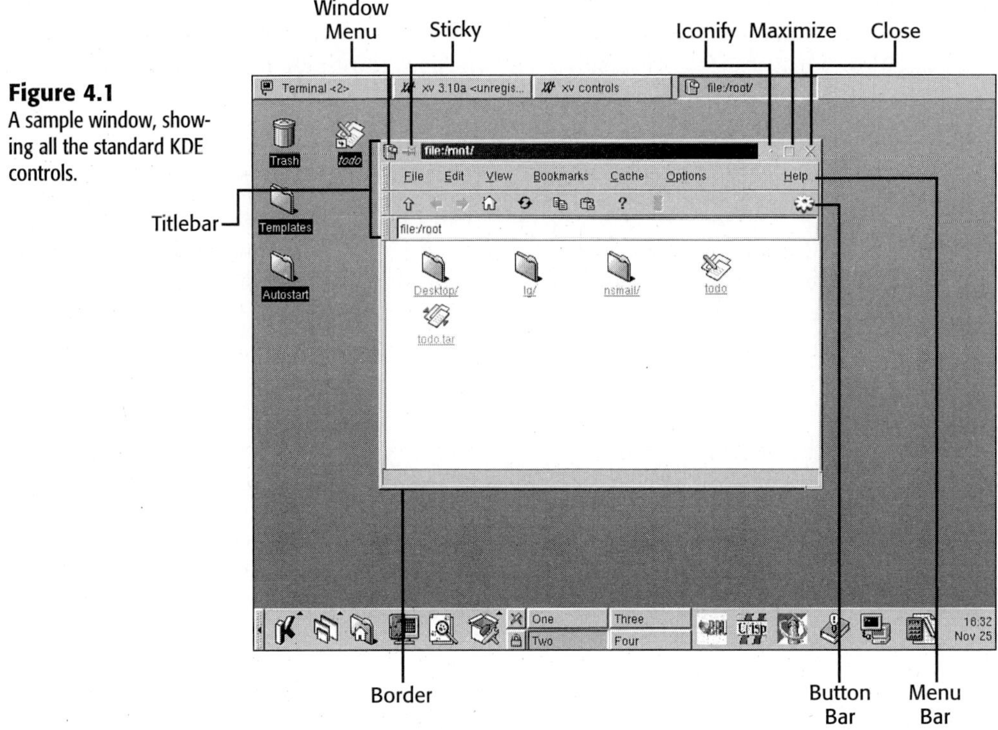

Figure 4.1
A sample window, showing all the standard KDE controls.

THE BORDERS OF THE WINDOW

When the mouse is over the border of a window, the mouse cursor changes to an image, indicating that you can stretch that edge of the window in the indicated direction (either straight up and down, straight left and right, or diagonally at the corners). To resize a window, select the edge of the window with the mouse and drag it to the position you want.

THE TITLE BAR

The title bar of a window shows a description of the window contents, if one is available, or just the name of the program to which this window belongs. If the description is too long to fit in the title bar, it scrolls back and forth so that you can see it. This feature is configurable in the KDE Control Center, or from the applications menu, under Windows, Title bar, via the Title animation option. You can move a window by clicking in the title area of the title bar and dragging.

Also included in the title bar are several buttons to manipulate the window, including a button to access the window menu.

The buttons have the following meanings:

- **Close**—This button closes this window. If it is the main window for the application, clicking this button has the effect of terminating the application (and thereby closing all its other windows as well).

- **Maximize/Restore**—This button makes the window as big as the entire usable screen area, or restores it to its original size. If you click it with the right mouse button, the window only expands horizontally, and if you click it with the middle mouse button, the window only expands vertically.
- **Iconify**—This button eliminates the window from the screen, leaving an entry for it in the Taskbar. Click the entry in the Taskbar to deiconify (or restore) the window.
- **Sticky**—This button, with the image of a push-pin, anchors the window to the background. If the window is stuck in this manner, when you switch to another virtual desktop this window stays in position. This is handy for moving a window to another desktop (by sticking it, switching desktops, and unsticking it), or for windows that you want visible no matter what virtual desktop you are on (such as a window containing a clock or a sticky note).

Note

You can configure the buttons on the title bar, selecting which buttons to show and which side of the title bar they are located on. To adjust button settings, select Settings, Windows, Buttons from the Application Starter menu (described shortly), and click the appropriate option for each button. Configuring the title bar buttons is discussed in greater detail in Chapter 5, "Customizing Your Desktop Environment."

The Window Menu

The window menu has a list of operations that you can perform on a window. These functions are essentially redundant with what you can do to the window using the border and other title bar buttons. The window menu is accessed by clicking the icon of the application, at the left edge of the title bar, as shown in Figure 4.2. You can also access the window menu by pressing Alt+F3 when the window is selected.

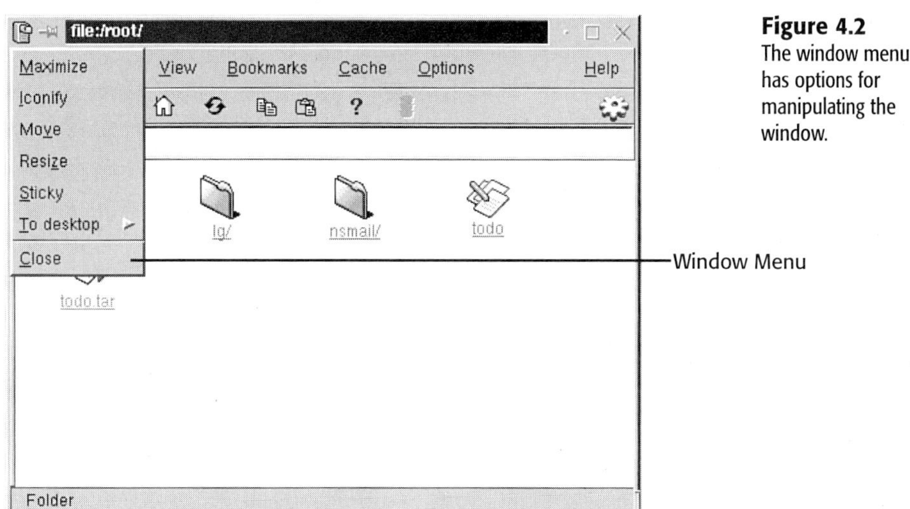

Figure 4.2
The window menu has options for manipulating the window.

The following options are on the window menu:

- **Maximize/Restore**—This performs the same operations as the Maximize/Restore button.
- **Iconify**—This performs the same operation as the Iconify button.
- **Move**—This is the same as dragging the window. If you select this option, the window frame changes to a transparent rectangle that you can move around with the mouse. Click the mouse button to drop the window in its new position.
- **Resize**—This is the same as dragging the border at the lower-right corner.
- **Sticky**—This performs the same operations as the Sticky button.
- **To desktop**—This enables you to move this window to a particular virtual desktop, without switching there yourself. Select the desktop to which you want to move the window, and the window is moved there.
- **Close**—This performs the same operation as the Close button. You can also close the currently selected window using the Alt+F4 keyboard shortcut.

APPLICATION CONVENTIONS

Each KDE program can have different window contents and layout, depending on what the program does. However, most KDE programs share similar attributes and have some display elements in common.

At the top of a KDE application is usually the main application menu bar. When a menu bar is present, a Help menu is always located on the far right side of the bar. Help is always available for an application by selecting Help, Contents, or by pressing the F1 key. An Exit option, to terminate the application, is usually located at the bottom of the first menu (usually the File menu) on the menu bar.

If the application has a button bar, it appears directly below the menu bar. Additional bars, specific to the application, might follow that. When a bar has a speckled left edge, it means that you can "tear off" the bar and reposition it as a separate window outside the main application window. To do this, click on the handle (the speckled edge) and drag the bar away from the window. You can then resize the bar or move it around to the position with which you are the most comfortable. Figure 4.3 shows the file manager with its button bar removed, resized, and placed to the right of the main window. Compare this to the image in Figure 4.2 to see the difference.

You can put the bar back in place by dragging it over the main application window, approximately where you took if from. You can also position a bar at the bottom of the application window instead of the top. Some bars can be positioned at the side of the window as well.

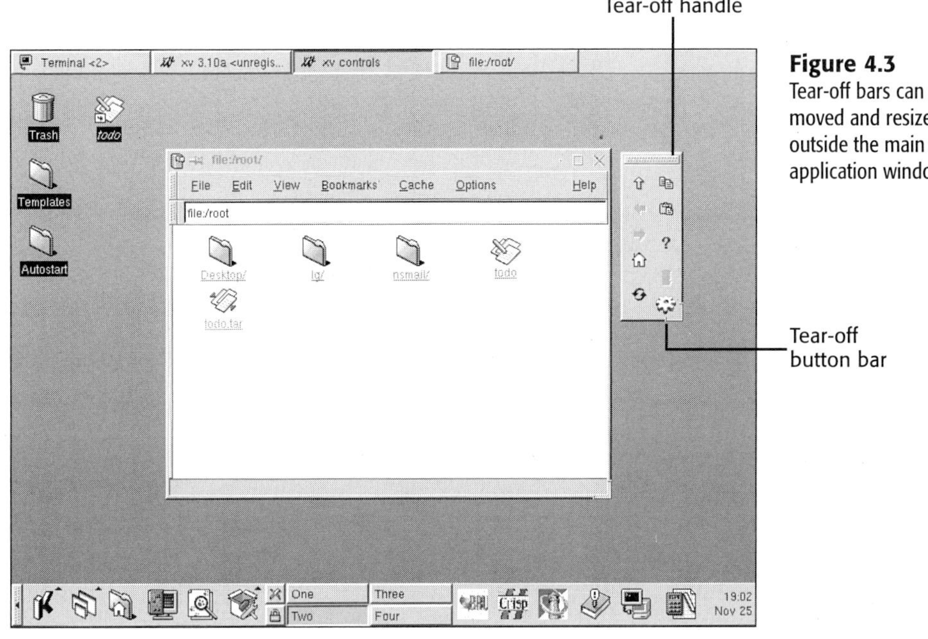

Figure 4.3
Tear-off bars can be moved and resized outside the main application window.

Many applications that have a main window provide a context menu for the window or its contents. Click inside the window with the right mouse button to view the context menu. This menu often contains options that are accessible via a menu on the main menu bar of the application. Sometimes, however, using the context menu is the only way to access a particular feature of the program.

Here is a summary of the operations that you can perform on a window under KDE. As you can see, there are many ways to perform most of these tasks.

To move a window, do one of the following:

- Drag a window by its title.
- Select move from the window menu.
- Use the Alt key and drag, with the mouse anywhere in the window.

Use any of the following methods to resize a window:

- Drag the borders of the window.
- Select Resize from the window menu.
- Use the Maximize/Restore button.
- Select Maximize or Restore from the Taskbar context menu.

Use one of the following methods to iconify a window:

- Use the Iconify button.
- Select Iconify in the window menu.
- Select Iconify in the Taskbar menu for this window.

Use one of the following methods to deiconify a window:

- Click on the window entry in the Taskbar.
- Click on the window entry in the Window List (see the Window List entry in the next section).

Use one of the following methods to move a window between virtual desktops:

- Use the Sticky pin.
- Select To Desktop on the window menu.
- Select Onto current desktop on the Taskbar menu for the window.

Use the following method to move a tear-off bar:

- Grab the bar by the handle, and then move it and resize it as you choose.

THE PANEL

The KDE Panel is displayed, by default, at the bottom of the screen (see Figure 4.4). It usually contains the following items:

- The applications menu
- The window list button
- The disk navigator menu
- Desktop control buttons
- Program and menu buttons
- A clock

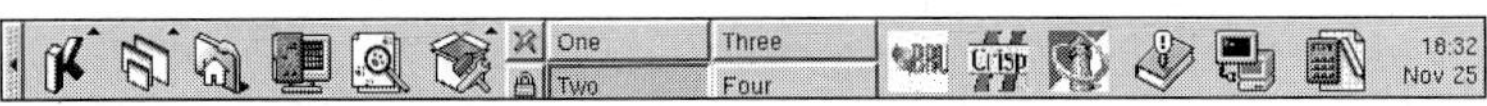

Figure 4.4
The Desktop Panel has several frequently used items.

Note that the icons on the panel that indicate menus have a small triangle in their upper-right corner. In Figure 4.4, the applications menu, window list, disk navigator menu, and utilities menu have these triangles, indicating that they pop up lists (or menus) when clicked.

Clicking other items on the Panel launches the indicated program, performs their function, or takes you to the indicated virtual desktop.

THE APPLICATION STARTER MENU

The button for the Application Starter menu has an icon with a big K, and is usually on the far left side of the Panel. On this menu (or its submenus) are all the KDE programs, as well as options for configuring the KDE system and the Panel itself. It also has links to other items, such as your home directory or the online help program. A sample Application Starter menu is shown in Figure 4.5.

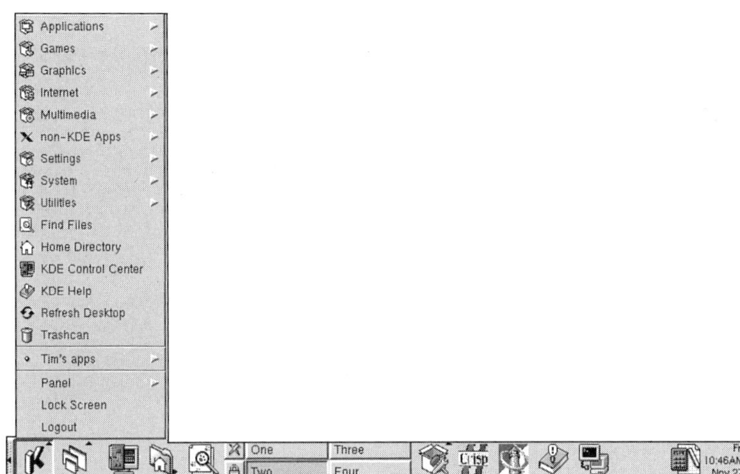

Figure 4.5
You can launch programs or configure the Panel from the Application Starter menu.

Although the distinction is not visible, the Application Starter menu actually consists of three different menus: the system application menu, your personal application menu, and a short Panel menu. By default, your personal application menu is empty, but you will learn how to fix that in Chapter 5.

Many of the items on the Application Starter menu are also on the Panel itself as individual icons. Those that appear on both the Starter menu and the Panel are described later in this section.

To open this menu, click on the Starter menu button. You can also open this menu at any time by using the Alt+F1 keyboard shortcut. The following sections list the items on the Applications Starter menu, roughly sorted by type.

PROGRAM GROUP MENUS

The following program groups are available in the default KDE Applications Starter menu:

- Applications
- Games

- Graphics
- Internet
- Multimedia
- Non-KDE Apps
- Settings
- System
- Utilities

Program groups help you organize the programs on your system. There are far too many KDE applications to put them all on the Desktop or the Panel itself, so they are organized into groups and subgroups on the KDE applications menu. Follow the menu items to find the application you want, and click on the application name to launch it.

You can customize the Starter menu by adding items to it, removing items from it, or rearranging the items on it. The default program groups hold KDE applications or well-known X applications. You can also put other applications on the menu. Usually these appear under a personal menu item called Personal. Chapter 5 discusses how to customize the applications menu in this way.

SPECIAL PROGRAMS

Some special programs are on the main menu itself, instead of under one of the program groups listed previously. All these programs also have buttons on the Panel bar, in the default OpenLinux Panel configuration:

- Find Files
- KDE Control Center
- KDE Help

These programs are described in the section "Programs and Menus on the Panel," later in this chapter.

SPECIAL LOCATIONS

Some of the items on the main menu show you the contents of specific directories, such as the following:

- Home Directory
- Trash can

The Home directory menu item opens a file manager window with your home directory as the current directory. The Trash can item shows you the contents of the Trash can, which you can also access by clicking on the Trash icon on the Desktop. Manipulating the items in the Trash can is discussed in the section "The Desktop" later in this chapter.

OTHER OPTIONS

Other options on the main menu perform specific functions:

- Refresh Desktop
- Panel
- Lock Screen
- Logout

The Refresh Desktop option is used when the contents of the Desktop have changed, or when something else changes that affects the appearance of the Desktop (for example, when you modify a file type to change the icon for a file). Select Refresh Desktop to cause the Desktop window to re-examine its contents and their associated types, and to update the Desktop display.

The Panel submenu is used to configure the Panel itself. The Panel configuration menu contains the following items:

- Add Application
- Add Disk Navigator
- Add Window list
- Configure
- Edit Menus
- Restart

These options are further discussed in the section "Configuring the Panel" in this chapter, as well as in Chapter 5.

The Lock Screen and Logout items perform the same functions as their counterpart buttons on the Panel itself (described momentarily).

WINDOW LIST BUTTON

The Window list button on the Panel enables you to see a list of all the windows for the currently running programs. This is similar to the Taskbar, except that this list includes the virtual desktop names, and the windows are sorted by virtual desktop. Also, the list is wide enough to display the full title of the program, which is often not possible on the Taskbar. A sample window list is shown in Figure 4.6. The active window is shown with a border around its icon. If there is no active window, a bullet is shown in front of the current virtual desktop.

Like the Taskbar or the virtual desktop buttons, the window list can be used to quickly switch to a different program window or desktop. Just click on the window title to select that window, or click on the desktop name to switch to that desktop.

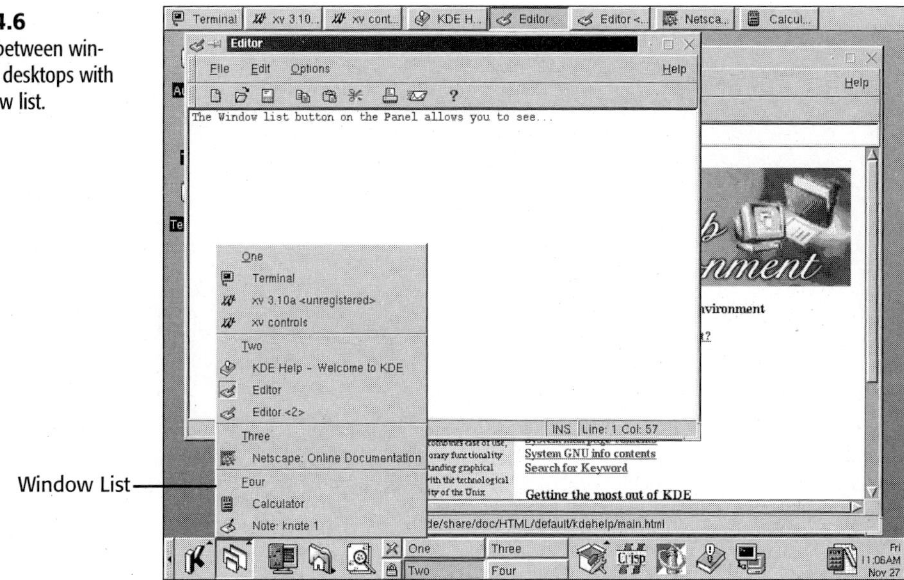

Figure 4.6
Navigate between windows and desktops with the window list.

DISK NAVIGATOR MENU

The Disk Navigator menu has entries that enable you to quickly browse to an item in your file system, or to access an item (directory or program) that you have recently used.

This menu consists of the following three different parts:

- Shared directory list
- Personal directory list
- Recently accessed directories or files (programs)

To browse to a location in your file system, open the Disk Navigator menu, and select the appropriate menu items to reach the location you need. Each menu item corresponds to a directory or file on your system. To open or launch an individual file, select the file from the appropriate menu. To open a file manager window in a directory, click the Open folder option at the top of the menu for that directory. You can also open a terminal window with the current working directory set to the selected directory by clicking the Open folder option while holding the Shift key.

When you launch a program or open a folder using the Application Starter menu, Panel, or Disk Navigator menu, a new entry is made for that item in the Recent section of the Disk Navigator menu. Thus, to access an item that you have recently used, open the Disk Navigator menu and select the corresponding item in the Recent section of the menu.

Configuring the Disk Navigator menu is discussed in the section "Configuring the Panel" later in this chapter.

DESKTOP CONTROL BUTTONS

A group of buttons on the Panel enables you to quickly switch to a virtual desktop, lock the screen, or end your KDE session. The desktop control buttons are shown in Figure 4.7.

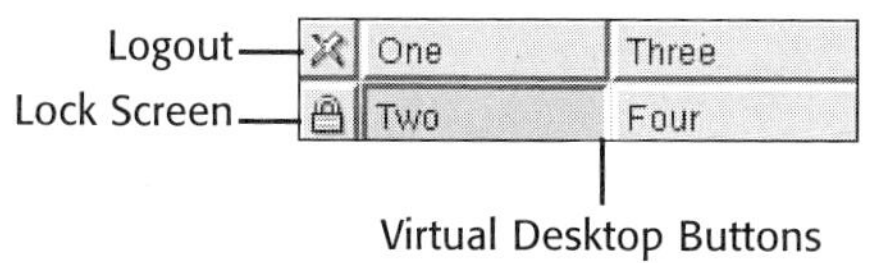

Figure 4.7
The Desktop control buttons.

SWITCHING BETWEEN VIRTUAL DESKTOPS

A *virtual desktop* is another virtual screen to which you can switch to run additional programs. Virtual desktops are discussed in greater detail in Chapter 3, but essentially they enable you to have more open windows than is normally feasible on your physical screen. To switch to a particular virtual desktop, click on the Desktop control button with the target desktop name.

The desktop that you are currently on is shown in the button group as a depressed button. The names of the virtual desktops can be customized using the Panel configuration dialog box (discussed shortly).

You can also switch between virtual desktops using the Ctrl+Tab keyboard shortcut. Hold the Ctrl key down, press Tab to cycle through the list of desktop names, and then release the Ctrl key to switch to the selected desktop.

LOCKING THE SCREEN

The Lock Screen button enables you to lock the KDE screen so that no one can use it in your absence. The Lock Screen button is shown with a padlock icon on it. You can use this if you have to leave your computer for a short time and you have sensitive or private information on the screen—or if you just don't want people to use the machine while you are gone. When you select this, the screen is blanked (or the screen saver is started) so that no one can see what is on it. If you press a key or move the mouse, a prompt appears, asking for your password. After the correct password is entered, the Desktop is restored and you can resume working.

Tip

It is especially important to lock the screen when you leave your computer if you are currently logged in as root, or if you have programs running with root privileges. If someone uses your computer as root, they can do great damage or install programs to allow them continued access to your machine at a later time.

ENDING YOUR KDE SESSION

The Logout button, shown with an X on it, ends your KDE session. If there are applications running that cannot be completely restored the next time you run KDE, you are warned before the session is ended. In this case, KDE displays a list of each running program that might not be restored correctly, along with the nature of the problem. At that point you can choose to go ahead with the logout or cancel the operation. If you select Cancel, go to each program that was listed and save your files, if necessary, and exit that program. After you have done this, you can proceed with the logout by clicking the button again.

PROGRAMS AND MENUS ON THE PANEL

You can use the Panel to launch many different programs, or to access individual menus (program groups) from the Application Starter menu. In OpenLinux, several programs are automatically placed on the Panel for you. You can add additional programs or menus by following the instructions in Chapter 5.

A few special programs and utilities are described here because they are central to using KDE. Many others are described in subsequent chapters (Chapter 7, "KDE Applications," and Chapter 8, "Koffice") in this book. The following programs are mentioned in the sections that follow:

- KDE help
- KDE Control Center
- Find Files Utility

ACCESSING ONLINE HELP WITH KDE HELP

Clicking on the Help button on the Panel brings up the KDE online help system. KDE's help system can be used to access not only the online help for KDE and its applications, but also other native OpenLinux help mechanisms.

The help program is called `KDE Help`. Figure 4.8 shows the default startup screen for the help system. This screen is the starting point for accessing the different online help resources available from this program.

ACCESSING KDE AND APPLICATION HELP PAGES Each KDE application provides its own set of help pages. These pages are available by selecting the Help, Contents menu item from the main menu of the application, or by pressing F1 in the application for which you need help. When you do this, the `KDE Help` program is started, with the help pages for that specific application displayed.

On the other hand, when you launch `KDE Help` using the Help button on the Panel (or from the Application Starter menu), it shows the main help page instead. To get to the main help page when you are running `KDE Help` from an application, click on the `Help Contents` button on the button bar, which has the icon of an open book with a question mark (refer to Figure 4.8).

Figure 4.8
`KDE Help` is used to access all kinds of help information.

The structure of the help pages for an application is usually a table of contents with links to individual help topics, where each major section of the help is on its own page. All the help pages for KDE and its applications are in HTML format. Thus, the `KDE Help` program works just like a Web browser to view these pages. Select a link on a help page to view that topic, and use the forward and back links on the `KDE Help` button bar to review or revisit pages that you have already seen. Also, use the Next, Previous, and Table of Contents links (located at the top and bottom of every page) to navigate through individual help pages.

Besides the help for KDE itself, the main help page provides a master index of the help for all the KDE applications. Follow the KDE application help index link from the main help page to see this index.

ACCESSING MAN AND INFO PAGES `KDE Help` can also be used to access Linux man pages and GNU info pages. These pages provide documentation and usage information for the bulk of the command-line utilities, C functions, and development tools on your OpenLinux system. Following the links provided on the main help page takes you to an index of man pages or an index of info contents. You can also type a path to the page you want directly into the location line at the top of the help window.

This means that you can use `KDE Help` as a substitute for the man and info commands when you are using KDE. For example, while you are writing a C program, you can keep a `KDE Help` window open and use it to look up man pages for the C functions that you use in the program. One extra advantage of using `KDE Help` instead of man is that `KDE Help` shows items in the SEE ALSO section of a man page as hypertext links, which enables you to navigate to related man pages quickly and easily.

Use the syntax `man:topic` to access Linux man pages. For example, to look up the man page for the Linux `cat` command, type `man:cat` into the location line and press Return. To access info pages, put the info topic in parentheses and use it with the `info:` prefix. For example, to look up information on using the GNU debugger, `gdb`, type `info:(gdb)` in the location line of `KDE Help`.

SEARCHING FOR HELP You can also search through these three different information sources, using the search page for `KDE Help`. To get to this page, either select the Search for Keyword link on the main help page, or select File, Search from the `KDE Help` menu. Enter the term for which you want to search in the dialog box that appears, and select the information categories to be searched. Then press the Submit Search button and KDE performs the search and shows a list of help pages that contain your search words.

KDE CONTROL CENTER

Another program you can start from the Panel (or the applications menu) is the KDE Control Center. This is the central configuration utility for KDE and many of its components. Use of the Control Center is discussed in Chapter 5.

`Find Files` UTILITY

The `Find Files` utility enables you to find files on your system using a number of different search criteria. After you have found a file (or set of files), it enables you to manipulate it in various ways. Use of this utility is described in more detail in Chapter 7.

THE PANEL CLOCK

The clock on the Panel appears on the right edge of the Panel bar, and shows the current time and date. By default, the clock displays the time in 24-hour format, but you can change it to use 12-hour format (or a special format known as *Internet beats*, described later) in the Panel Configuration dialog box.

CONFIGURING THE PANEL

You can change the location, size, and other options of the Panel and Disk Navigator (and the Taskbar, discussed next) using the Panel configuration dialog box. Also, you can adjust the positions of the items on the panel, or remove and add items on the Panel, by accessing individual item context menus.

PANEL CONFIGURATION DIALOG BOX

The Panel configuration dialog box is available on the Applications Starter menu, under Panel, Configure, or on the Panel context menu, under Configure. Right-click on an empty area of the Panel to access the Panel context menu.

The Panel Configuration dialog box, shown in Figure 4.9, enables you to select the location of the Panel and Taskbar, as well as the size of the icons in the Panel. Other options are available as well. This dialog box has four pages, which can be accessed using the Panel, Options, Desktop, and Disk Navigator tabs.

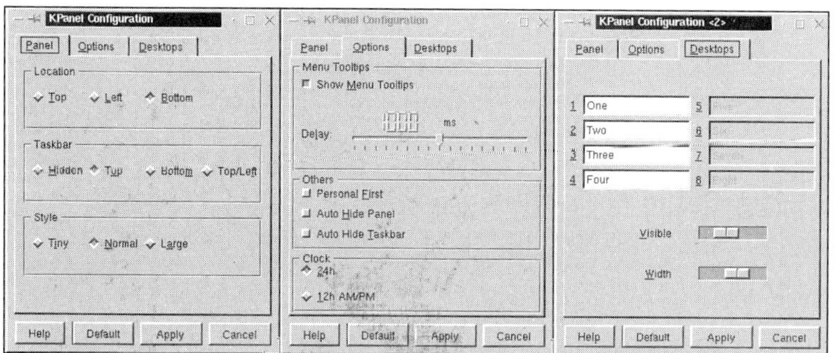

Figure 4.9
The Options and Disk Navigator pages of the Panel configuration dialog box.

On the Panel page of the dialog box, select the location for the Panel and Taskbar, and then choose the icon style for the Panel. The Tiny option uses small icons and shrinks the height of the Panel. The Normal and Large options use large icons, but with different Panel heights.

The Options page of this dialog box enables you to adjust items relating to the Applications Starter menu, the auto-hide feature of the Panel and Taskbar, and the clock.

To turn off the tooltips (pop-up help boxes) for the items in the Application Starter menu, or to adjust the delay before tooltips are displayed, adjust the Menu Tooltips settings. To make your personal application menu (Personal) appear before the system application menu (KDE's program groups) on the applications menu, select Personal First in the Others settings.

To make it so that the Panel or Taskbar disappears automatically, and then reappears when the mouse is moved to the edge of the screen where it is hiding, select the Auto Hide Panel or Auto Hide Taskbar options on the page, and adjust the delay and speed settings for each of these bars. The Delay setting controls how long a bar stays onscreen without interaction before it is hidden, and the Speed setting controls how fast the bar appears and disappears.

The Animate Show/Hide option (and Speed) controls whether (and how fast) the Panel bar slides off the screen when the left or right handle is clicked.

To select whether the clock displays time in 12- or 24-hour format, click the appropriate option at the bottom of the Options page. Also, you can choose to show the time in Internet beats (see accompanying sidebar for explanation).

What are Internet Beats?

Internet beats is a special worldwide measure of time that is independent of time zone or location. It was invented recently by the Swatch company of Switzerland to relieve the burden of constantly recalculating the time in order to communicate time references with others on the Internet. For example, when it is @319 in Los Angeles, it is also @319 in New York, London, Paris, and Hong Kong. Thus, a time expressed in Internet beats is universal and easily communicated to others around the world.

There are 1000 Internet beats in a 24-hour day; each beat is equivalent to 1 minute 26.4 seconds of time.

For more information about Internet beats, see the following Web page:

`http://www.swatch.com/internettime/internettime.phtml`

The Desktops page of the dialog box enables you to customize how many virtual desktops KDE has, as well as to set the desktop names and the widths of their buttons on the Panel. To change the number of desktops, move the Visible slider. The number of desktops changes in increments of two. To change the name of a virtual desktop, type a new name in the box for that desktop. To change the width of the desktop buttons on the Panel, move the Width slider.

Finally, the settings on the Disk Navigator page of the dialog box enable you to customize the Disk Navigator menu. The options in the History section of this dialog box enable you to control the entries in different sections of the menu. For example, to add or remove items from the Personal section of the Disk Navigator menu, click the Edit Personal button. A file manager window opens, and you can add or remove items in the directory that is shown ($(HOME)/.kde/share/apps/kdisknav) Other options in this dialog box enable you to configure how many entries (folders or files) are displayed in the Recent section of the Disk Navigator menu.

Using settings in the Options part of the dialog box, you can select which sections of the Disk Navigator menu to show. For example, you can turn off the Shared or Personal sections of the Disk Navigator menu to shorten the menu or customize it to your preferences. Also, for menu and submenu items that refer to directories and files, you can control whether to show hidden files (dot files) and whether to ignore case when sorting the menu items.

The Disk Navigator menu enables you to open a terminal window in a particular directory. To configure the terminal program used for this, enter the program executable name in the Terminal application field.

After making any changes to the Panel, Disk Navigator, or Taskbar settings, click the Apply button to have the changes take effect, or click Cancel if you change your mind. The Default button restores the settings on a particular page to their default (factory shipped) settings.

ADJUSTING ITEMS ON THE PANEL

To move an item on the Panel, or to remove an item from the Panel, use the options on the context menu for that item. Right-click on an item, and the context menu appears (see Figure 4.10). To move an item, select the Move option on this menu, and drag the item to the desired position on the Panel. Other buttons on the panel shift to make room for the item when you drop it.

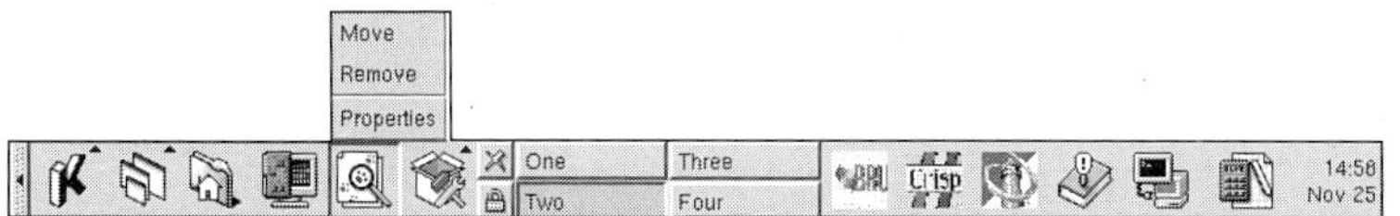

Figure 4.10
The Panel item context menu pops up when you right-click an item on the Panel.

Configuration of the Panel contents involves adding items to the Panel, or customizing the behavior of the individual applications on the Panel. Adding items to the Panel is performed via the Panel, Add application option on the Applications menu. Customizing the appearance and behavior of an application on the Panel is performed using the Properties option on the item context menu. Both of these topics are discussed in Chapter 5.

On either side of the Panel are handles with little arrows. These handles are used to hide or show the Panel bar. When the Panel is hidden this way, three mini-icons appear in the Taskbar: one for the Application Starter menu, one for the window list, and one for the disk navigator menu. This way, even if the panel is hidden you still have access to these items.

RESTART OPTION

After making adjustments to the Panel or Application Starter menu contents, it might be necessary to restart the Panel program in order for the changes to take effect. To restart the Panel, select Panel, Restart on the Starter menu, or choose Restart from the Panel context menu.

THE TASKBAR

The Taskbar shows the windows for the programs running under KDE. You can use the Taskbar to get an idea of the programs you already have running, or to switch quickly to another window. When you select a window on the Taskbar, KDE switches to the virtual desktop that contains that window (if necessary) and selects that window.

You can switch between windows on the current virtual desktop using the Alt+Tab keyboard shortcut. Hold down the Alt key, and press Tab to cycle through the list of windows. Release the Alt key to select the indicated window.

You can also call up the window menu for a window listed on the Taskbar by clicking on the window's entry with the right mouse button. The following options are available on this menu:

- **Maximize/Restore**—Maximizes or restores the window, without switching to it.
- **Iconify/Deiconify**—Iconifies or deiconifies the window.
- **Sticky**—Makes the window sticky (see the previous section "Program Windows" for information on this option).
- **Onto current desktop**—Moves the window to the current desktop. This is a handy way to move programs between virtual desktops.
- **Iconify other windows**—Iconifies all the other windows on the screen, leaving the selected window alone. This is useful for quickly uncluttering a screen with many windows and leaving one open to work with.
- **Close**—Closes the window.

THE DESKTOP

The Desktop is the main work area for the KDE environment. You can put any item from the file system on the Desktop. This includes programs, documents, and other types of files. However, you can also put special entries on the Desktop, including printers and devices, which you can then directly manipulate from the Desktop. Finally, you can also put references to remote documents on the Desktop, which you can then access as if they were local files.

In this section, some of the special folders and icons on the Desktop are discussed, and additional Desktop capabilities are described. To fully understand the capabilities of the Desktop, you need to read both this section and the next major section, "Manipulating Files and Directories."

DEFAULT DESKTOP ICONS

By default, the Desktop contains only three items—the Trash can, the Templates folder, and the AutoStart folder. You can add new items to the Desktop by dragging them to the Desktop from a file manager window, or by creating them using the New menu of the Desktop context menu. A sample Desktop is shown in Figure 4.11.

THE TRASH CAN

The Trash can is a special folder that holds items that you have discarded via KDE. To store files in the Trash can, do one of the following:

- Drag them from the Desktop or a file manager window onto the Trash icon on the Desktop.
- Select Move to Trash from the context menu of the item.
- Select the item in a file manager window, and then select Move to Trash from the Edit menu.

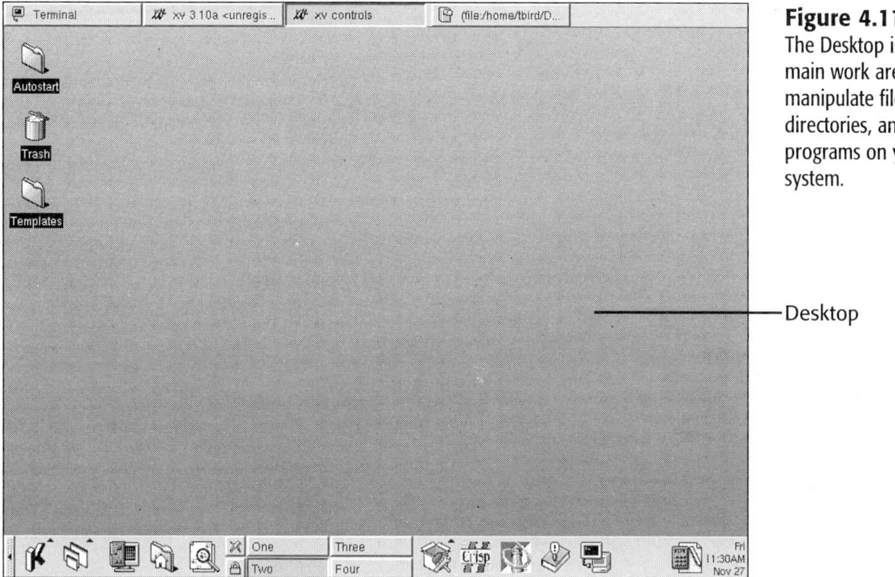

Figure 4.11
The Desktop is your main work area to manipulate files, directories, and programs on your system.

You can tell by looking at the Trash icon whether there is anything currently in the Trash. If there are no files or directories in the Trash, the icon is shown with the Trash lid closed. If there are things in the Trash, the lid is open and you can seem some rubbish inside.

To retrieve something from the trash, just open the Trash window by clicking on the Trash icon, and then drag the item you want to recover from the trash window to the Desktop or to another file manager window.

If you use the Trash can frequently, periodically remove its contents to free up disk space. Before doing so, you might want to examine the contents of the Trash to make sure that you are not deleting anything important. To remove the contents of the Trash can, select Empty Trash Bin from the context menu of the Trash can on the Desktop. All the contents of the Trash are then discarded.

Caution

Note that not all the files that you delete are stored in the Trash can—only those that you drag to the Trash on the Desktop or that you move to the Trash from the KDE file manager. If you delete a file by hand, by using the `rm` command for example, it is not stored in the Trash directory and there is no way to recover it. Also, if you choose the option Delete instead of Move to Trash in the file manager, you cannot recover the file.

The Trash window is really just a file manager window, displaying the contents of the special directory $(HOME)/Desktop/Trash, where items are stored when you move them to the Trash can.

THE TEMPLATES FOLDER

The Templates folder holds templates for creating new items in KDE. By default, this folder contains several kdelnk files, which are special files used by the KDE system. However, you can add your own files, directories, and kdelnk files here as well. Anything you put in this directory appears on the File, New submenu of the file manager program main menu. This enables you to create duplicates of the item in other directories using the file manager or Desktop New menu. kdelnk files are discussed in Chapter 5 (getting tired of hearing that yet?), but a template can be any file or directory (tree) worth duplicating.

To create a template, just drag the item that you want to duplicate into the Templates folder.

For example, if you have a standard makefile that you use to start each new development project, you can place it in the Templates folder. Then, whenever you need a copy of that makefile, just select File, New, Makefile from the file manager main menu and the file is copied from the Template folder to the current directory of the file manager. A directory (with files and subdirectories) can also be a template. Putting a directory tree in the Templates folder is an easy way to replicate the whole directory tree (with a complete, predetermined structure and files) any time you need to.

THE AUTOSTART FOLDER

The AutoStart folder holds programs that you want KDE to run automatically every time it starts. Most KDE programs do not need to be placed in this directory because they can retain their state between KDE sessions. To have a KDE program running the next time you start KDE, just leave it running when you exit KDE, and it is restarted automatically. However, for non–KDE-aware applications, or for KDE applications that you don't necessarily have running at the end of your session, you can have them start automatically by placing them (or links to them) in this directory.

MANIPULATING DESKTOP ITEMS

The main purpose of the Desktop is to hold files, directories, programs, and other items in a place where it is easy to access and manipulate them. Although it is possible to perform the same operations on these items from a file manager window (opened to the directory where they actually reside), the Desktop provides a more convenient place to keep things that you use on a day-to-day basis.

DECIDING WHERE TO PUT THINGS

You can launch programs or documents from the following five locations:

- From a file manager window, directly from the directory in which the item actually resides
- From the Desktop
- From the Panel (if you have made a kdelnk file for the item)

- From the Application Starter menu (if you have made a kdelnk file for the item)
- From the Disk Navigator menu

There is no simple rationale for deciding which items to put on the Desktop versus which to put in the Panel or Application Starter menu. You need to decide for yourself what is the most comfortable arrangement of items for your work habits.

DESKTOP VERSUS FILE MANAGER

The Desktop is similar to a special file manager window. Many of the same principles for manipulating Desktop items apply to manipulating items in the file manager. Following are the major differences between a normal folder displayed in the file manager versus the Desktop:

- **The items on the Desktop are positionable**—That is, you can move the items on the Desktop into new positions, and they will stay there. With a regular file manager window, the items are always displayed in sorted order.
- **The Desktop has no border, menus, and so on, like a file manager window does, and is always in the background**—This means that the Desktop is always available to work with, no matter what other windows you have open.
- **The Desktop itself has a different context menu than the file manager window does**—This is largely because the file manager enables you to change the directory that is being displayed (that is, you can `cd` to another directory), whereas the Desktop does not.

Other than these differences, the Desktop behaves very much like a regular file manager window. The items in both can be launched with a single click. Furthermore, the items in both have similar context menus when the item is clicked on with the right mouse button.

In fact, the Desktop actually is a real directory. Open your home directory in the file manager by clicking on the Home Directory icon in the Panel, and then click on the Desktop folder in the file manager window that appears. Note that the Desktop directory in the file manager window has the exact same contents as the Desktop—they are just not arranged the same way.

MOVING THINGS AROUND

To add an item to the Desktop, open the file manager to the directory containing the item that you want to add, and then drag the item from the file manager window onto the Desktop. To move something to a different position on the Desktop, just drag it to the new position. When you move an item on the Desktop, notice that it snaps to an invisible grid. Desktop items can only be placed in certain positions, so that the icons are always lined up in neat rows and columns.

Note

To change the spacing of the icons on the Desktop, select Settings, Desktop, Desktop Icons on the Application Starter menu, and adjust the numbers for the Horizontal Root Grid Spacing and Vertical Root Grid Spacing. To control the color of the text for the icons on the Desktop, adjust the Transparent Text for Desktop Icons and Icon foreground and background color settings in this same dialog box.

LAUNCHING OR OPENING ITEMS ON THE DESKTOP

To launch or open an item, *single*-click the icon for that item.

KDE recognizes several different types of items, and handles them differently depending on what type they are (see Table 4.1).

TABLE 4.1 SUMMARY OF DIFFERENT KINDS OF ITEMS RECOGNIZED BY THE DESKTOP

Kind of Item	Definition or Examples
Program	An executable binary or script
Folder	A directory
File	Documents, images, and other files
Device	Mountable file system device (such as CD-ROM or floppy)
URL	Remote item (such as WWW page or FTP file)
Trash can	A special directory to hold discarded items

Note

There is another special kind of item called a *MimeType*, whose use is discussed in Chapter 5. MimeType files are only used in special directories, not on the Desktop or in most file manager windows.

LAUNCHING A PROGRAM When you launch a program item, the program runs on the current virtual desktop. The current directory for the program is set to the directory from which you started KDE.

OPENING A FOLDER When you open a folder, the file manager is run, with the folder directory contents shown in the file manager window. The files and subdirectories (folders) in the directory you open are displayed using icons that represent their different types. More information about the file manager display is presented in the section "Navigating the File System with `kfm`" later in this chapter.

OPENING A FILE When you click a file item, KDE uses internal rules to decide what application to run with that file. If no other program is associated with a file, the file can be opened with KDE's default text editor, KEdit. In some cases, you might be prompted to type in the program with which you want to open the file.

If the program with which you want to open the file is different than the one KDE uses, you can indicate your preference either by dragging the file or specifying the program in the Open with dialog box. To open the file with a program that is on the Desktop or the Panel, or in an open file manager window, drag the file and drop it on the program's icon. To enter the name of the program to run, right-click the file, select Open with from the file's context menu, type the name of the program into the dialog box, and click OK.

OPENING A DEVICE When you click a device, KDE first checks to see if the device is mounted. If not, KDE tries to mount the device, using the parameters configured in the device properties. If the device is mounted successfully, or was already mounted, the top level directory (mount directory) of that device is displayed in a file manager window. For example, a CD-ROM device normally has a mount directory of /mnt/cdrom. If you click a CD-ROM device entry on the Desktop, it mounts the CD-ROM (if it is not already mounted) and displays /mnt/cdrom in a file manager window.

OPENING A URL When you click on a URL item on the Desktop, the referenced item is retrieved from its remote location and acted on accordingly. If it is a WWW page or FTP directory, it is displayed in a file manager window. For other kinds of remote objects, KDE determines the file type and opens the file with an appropriate application. For example, if you click on a URL item which refers to a remote image file, KDE downloads the image and displays it with an image viewing program (if one has been configured).

DESKTOP ITEM CONTEXT MENUS

Items on the Desktop can also be manipulated using their context menus. The Desktop item context menu has different options, depending on the type of item that is being manipulated. The context menu for a document file is shown in Figure 4.12.

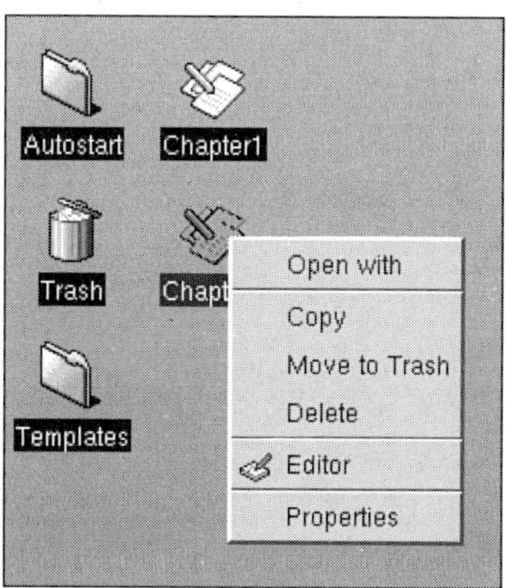

Figure 4.12
Manipulate an item, or launch it differently, with the item context menu.

Most items on the Desktop have the following options on their context menus:

- **Open with**—This option enables you to type in the program to be run with this file. A small dialog box appears. Type the name of the program, and click OK. If you can't remember the name of the application, you can use the Browse button to search through the Application Starter menu to find the application.
- **Copy**—This option copies the item. The item is marked to be copied to another location.
- **Move to Trash**—This option moves the item to the Trash can. The item can be recovered later, if necessary.
- **Delete**—This option deletes the item.
- **Add to Bookmarks**—This option adds the item to the bookmark list. You can then quickly access this item at a later time by selecting in the list. Right-click the Desktop and select Bookmarks, or click Bookmarks in the file manager menu, to access the bookmark list.
- **Properties**—This option configures the properties of this item.

There might be other options on the context menu of the item, depending on its type. These options enable you to perform operations on that item which are specific to its type. Table 4.2 shows some of the per-type options on the item context menus.

TABLE 4.2 PER-TYPE OPTIONS ON ITEM CONTEXT MENUS ON THE DESKTOP

Type	Option	Operation
Folder	New View	Opens the folder in a new file manager window. On the Desktop, this does the same thing as clicking on the folder. In a file manager, this opens a new window instead of changing the contents of the current window.
Trash	Empty Trash Bin	Discards the contents of the Trash can
File	(list of programs associated with this file)	Opens the file with the selected program. For example, a GIF file has the Image Viewer associated with it. Thus, Image Viewer shows up as an item on the context menu for GIF files. If you select the Image Viewer option on the menu, the program runs with the GIF as an argument.
Device	Mount	Mounts the device
	Unmount	Unmounts the device

If a Desktop entry that is a Device is set up properly, there is a graphical indication of whether the device is mounted. Usually this is a small green dot to the bottom right of the device icon. If this dot is present, the device is mounted.

For a Device, there might be multiple mount options in the context menu, if the device can be mounted with different file system types.

THE DESKTOP CONTEXT MENU

The Desktop context menu appears when you right-click unused space on the Desktop. It provides options for creating new Desktop items, jumping directly to a bookmarked item, configuring the settings of the Desktop, or accessing other Desktop features.

The following options are on the Desktop context menu, which is shown in Figure 4.13:

- **New menu**—This menu enables you to create a new item on the Desktop. It is an alternative to dragging items to the Desktop. The items in the New menu are the items in the Templates folder, which consists of kdelnk files by default. The use of kdelnk files to create special types of Desktop items is discussed in the next chapter. To create a new item on the Desktop, select New from the Desktop context menu and then choose from the list of items. Enter or edit the name of the item in the dialog box that appears. Click OK, and the item appears on the Desktop.

  After placing a kdelnk file on the Desktop, you probably want to customize its properties (its appearance and behavior). To do this, access the properties dialog box by right-clicking the item and selecting Properties from the context menu. Detailed information about kdelnk and the various properties you can adjust is presented in Chapter 5.
- **Bookmarks menu**—This menu provides a list of bookmarks that you have created using the file manager. To go directly to a bookmarked file or site, just click the bookmark in the list. You can also edit the bookmark list. Selecting Bookmarks, Edit Bookmarks from the menu opens a file manager window that shows the bookmarks. Use the file manager to add or remove items in this directory (which adds or removes items in the bookmarks menu). To create a submenu in the bookmark list, create a subdirectory (new folder) in the bookmarks directory.
- **Help on Desktop**—This option starts the online help program, `KDE Help`.
- **Execute command**—This opens a command window, where you can enter a single one-line command. You can use this window to quickly enter and execute a command, without having to start up and shut down a whole terminal window. No output from the command is displayed, so any kind of interactive or informational command (for example, `lisa` or `ls`) cannot be used here. However, for some actions, this is handy.

  (You can also open the command window using the keyboard shortcut Alt+F2.)
- **Display properties**—Use this option to configure Desktop parameters such as color, font, behavior, and so on. Complete coverage of customizing the Desktop settings is provided in Chapter 5.
- **Refresh Desktop**—Selecting this option causes KDE to redisplay the items on the Desktop. If new types have been defined or the icons for types have been modified, this causes the display to be updated with the new icons.
- **Unclutter window**—Use this option to move the currently open windows so that they overlap as little as possible.
- **Cascade windows**—Use this option to move windows so that they overlap with each other in a consistent way.

- **Arrange icons**—This lines up the icons on the Desktop. It places the icons starting at the top left of the Desktop screen, and moves down in columns and to the right.
- **Lock screen**—Hides the Desktop and requires a password to restore it. This performs the same operation as the Lock Screen button on the Panel or the Lock Screen option on the Application Starter menu.
- **Logout**—This ends the KDE session. Selecting this is the same as clicking the Logout button on the Panel.

KDE Keyboard Shortcuts

Table 4.3 shows the different keyboard shortcuts for navigating within the KDE environment, including windows and virtual desktops.

Table 4.3 Keyboard Shortcuts for the Desktop

Shortcut	Operation
Ctrl+Tab	Switches between virtual desktops
Alt+Tab	Switches between windows on the current desktop
Alt+left mouse button	Moves the window
Alt+F1	Opens the Applications menu
Alt+F2	Opens the Command line window
Alt+F3	Opens the Window menu
Alt+F4	Closes the window
F1	Opens the Online Help (for current program)

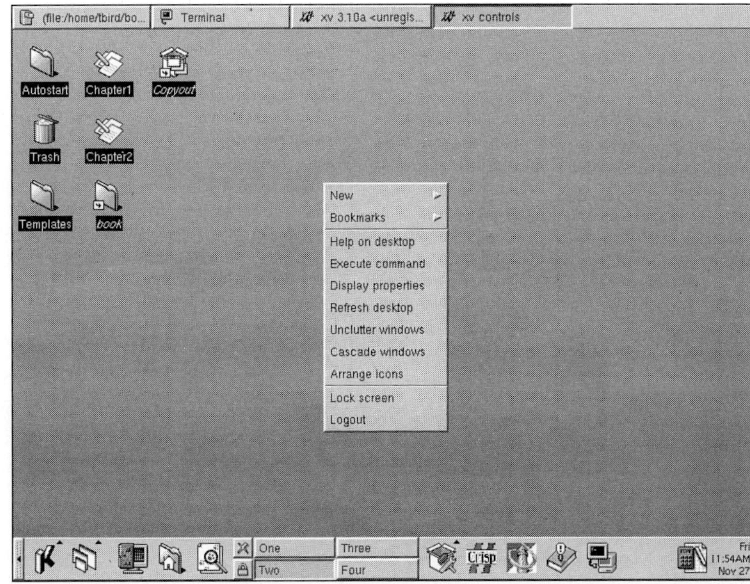

Figure 4.13
Use the Desktop context menu to access Desktop-related functions.

MANIPULATING FILES AND DIRECTORIES

The file manager, `kfm`, is such an integral part of KDE that it deserves special discussion here rather than in Chapter 7, where other KDE applications are discussed. This section covers how to use `kfm` to manipulate files and directories, as well as to navigate remote file systems and view World Wide Web pages.

INTRODUCTION TO THE FILE MANAGER

`kfm` is different from other file managers that you might have encountered because it treats all the objects that it browses in a very consistent manner. `kfm` is really a generic browser, capable of viewing not only file and directory listings, but other things as well. The way `kfm` achieves this is by using *uniform resource locators* (*URLs*) for all the paths that it browses and by converting everything it displays into HTML pages. Thus, besides being a file system browser and manager, `kfm` is also an FTP client, a World Wide Web browser, and an archive file contents viewer.

LOCATION TRANSPARENCY

Because all the separate things that `kfm` can browse are treated the same, it enables you to perform operations conveniently, without regard for the location of the item you are manipulating. For example, you can drag links from a World Wide Web page onto your Desktop, where you can click them at any time to call them up. You can do the same thing for FTP directories, placing them on your Desktop just like folders. When you click a file on a remote FTP site, `kfm` launches it or opens it as if it were a local file. The only difference is that it might take longer as `kfm` downloads the file to your system to operate on it.

In another example, you can drag files directly from a remote FTP site (in a folder in `kfm`) directly to another KDE application running on your Desktop. For example, you can drag a package file on an FTP site directly to the package manager program to view the package information and install it on your system.

This kind of seamless interaction between remote and local objects makes it easier to access and manage the things you work with on a day-to-day basis.

ACTIVE MANIPULATION

`kfm` is not just a viewer, however. It is also a manager that can be used to adjust and actively manipulate the objects it is browsing. For example, it uses the KDE file typing system to determine how to launch programs and documents. It recognizes file types on both local and remote files, so it knows what icons to display and what context menus to present to manipulate the items. When you launch a remote file, KDE downloads the file and starts the correct application. You can drag an item from one file manager window to another to make a copy of the item or to make a link to the item. Finally, on your local file system, `kfm` enables you to manipulate the file system attributes of the item (such as the owner and the permissions), with an easy, graphical dialog box.

To get started with the file manager, some user interface elements are described first. The subsequent sections cover specific tasks you can perform with `kfm`.

NAVIGATING THE FILE SYSTEM WITH `kfm`

To start the file manager, click on any directory folder or on the Home Directory button on the Panel. The file manager is started and displays the contents of the directory you selected in its main window. This is referred to as the browser area of the window. Usually, this is the only area in the main window. However, there is also a tree view, which shares the space in the main window with the browser area when it is exposed. Figure 4.14 shows the file manager with both the browser area and the tree view exposed.

THE BROWSER AREA

The browser area is usually filled with the contents of the current directory. The items in the directory have icons identifying their file type. You can change the view of the directory contents using options on the View menu. The four basic display types (corresponding to options on the View menu) are as follows:

- **Icon View**—Shows the directory contents as large icons in a grid.
- **Text View**—Shows a detailed listing of files and directories, as well as their file system attributes.
- **Long View**—Shows the same file details at the Text View, but also includes mini-icons to indicate the file type.
- **Short View**—Shows just the filename and mini-icon in a multi-column view.

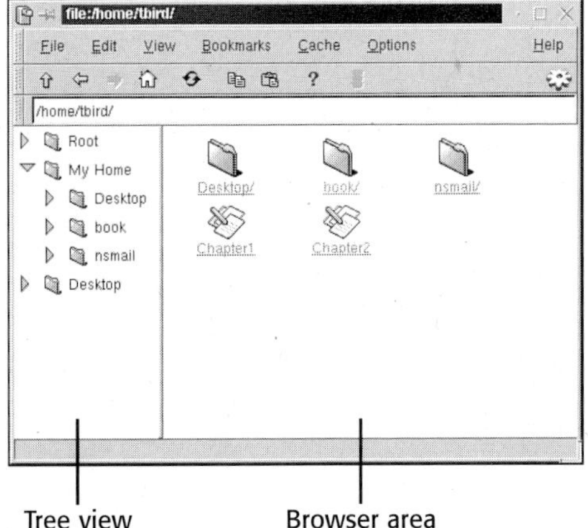

Figure 4.14
Use the file manager to browse files and directories on your system, and remote sites on the Internet.

Normally, hidden files (those that start with a dot) are not shown in the listing. To see these files in the listing, select View, Show Hidden Files from the menu.

Other options to control the view of the browser area are also available, and are described subsequently.

There are a number of ways to navigate to other directories in the file manager. To move to a subdirectory, simply click the folder or directory name in the browser window. To move to the parent directory, click the up arrow in the file manager button bar. To switch between directories that you have already visited, use the forward and back arrows on the button bar, or select a link on the history page or bookmark menu.

To show the history page, select the Cache, Show History menu item. This page contains a list of recently visited items, including items visited in previous file manager sessions.

To switch to an item in the bookmark list, select it in the Bookmarks menu.

Finally, you can type the location to which you want to jump in the location bar at the top of the file manager window, or in a pop-up Open Location dialog box. You can access this dialog box by selecting the File, Open Location menu item, or by using the keyboard shortcut Ctrl+L. When you type in the location, you can specify it as either a regular directory path or as a URL. Use the file prefix for locations within your local file system.

THE TREE VIEW

The other pane of the file manager window area is the Tree View. By default it is hidden, but you can expose it by dragging the splitter bar on the left side of the main window to the right, or by selecting View, Show Tree in the file manager menu.

The Tree View has three top-level directories, corresponding to different places to begin browsing the file system:

- **The Root folder**—Corresponds to the root of the entire file system.
- **The folder My Home**—Corresponds to your home directory.
- **The Desktop folder**—Enables you to begin navigating with the folders currently on your Desktop.

The Tree view only shows directories, not individual files or links. To expand or collapse a directory, click the blue arrow to the left of the directory name. When a directory is collapsed, the arrow points to the right; when it is expanded the arrow points down. To make the browser window jump to a directory in the Tree view, click the directory name.

PERFORMING MANAGEMENT TASKS

This section describes all the different management tasks you can perform with the file manager. This includes such things as getting information about a file; moving, copying, and removing files; and changing various attributes of a file, such as its name, ownership, and permissions.

GETTING INFORMATION ABOUT A FILE

The most basic management task is simply finding out information about a file. Information can be obtained in a number of different ways.

First, the status bar shows the size and type of the item that is currently under the mouse pointer. To see this information, move the mouse over the items in which you are interested.

You can also see detailed file information by selecting either Text View or Long View from the View menu. This shows the name, permissions, owner, group, size, and date of each item in columns across the screen.

The icons in the browser window indicate the type of each item, as recognized by KDE. KDE provides a large set of different icons to identify files of different types. By convention, a directory has a folder as its icon, a documents file often has a piece of paper in its icon, and a program often has a gear. A link is usually indicated with a small arrow in the lower left corner of the icon, and archives, packages, or groups have boxes in their background. Over time, you will learn these conventions and begin to easily identify, by the icon, the types of files you are looking at.

SELECTING ITEMS

Certain management actions can be performed by directly manipulating the items in the browser window. There are multiple ways to select more than one item to manipulate.

To select an item without launching it, hold down the Ctrl key and click the item. The item is shaded to indicate that it is selected. To add items to the selection, or to remove items that are already selected, use Ctrl+*click* as well. You can also select a group of items by dragging a rectangle around them.

Finally, if you have a large number of items and it is awkward—or impossible—to select them with a rectangle, you can select them using a name and wildcard specification. To do this, choose Edit, Select from the menu (or use the Ctrl+S keyboard shortcut), and type a filename or wildcard specification into the Select files dialog box. Click OK, and files matching your specification are selected.

MOVING AND COPYING FILES

The easiest way to move or copy files from one part of your file system to another, or to make links to a file, is to select and drag them. You can drag files between two open file manager windows, between the file manager window and the Desktop (and vice versa), or from the file manager window to a folder icon (either on the Desktop or in another file manager window).

When you drop the item, you are presented with a menu with three options: Copy, Move, and Link. Select one of these options, and the operation is completed. For operations that can take a long time, a status window pops up to inform you of the progress of the operation.

You can also copy files (but not move or link them) by selecting them, and then choosing the Copy option from either the Edit menu or the context menu for the files. This marks the items for copying. Now browse to the location where you want to copy the files, and select Paste from either the Edit menu or the context menu of the directory in which you want to copy the files.

Note

Using the Copy and Paste menu options requires only one file manager window to be open. If your screen is cluttered, or if there is some other reason why it might be awkward or time-consuming to have two file manager windows open, this method of copying files can be very useful.

Sometimes it is hard to decide which of the possible actions (Copy, Move, or Link) is the most appropriate. This is especially true when you start working with special KDE files and directories, such as the Desktop itself or the Templates or AutoStart directories. Some of the following suggestions might seem obvious, but here are some rules of thumb to help you decide:

- **Only select Copy if you really want to create another copy of the item**—This is rarely what you want to do with executable programs and scripts. It might or might not be what you want with documents and other files, depending on the circumstances. Remember that having multiple copies means that modifications to one copy won't affect the other. Although it is possible to put real documents in the Desktop directory, most people just put links there, or put files there only temporarily.
- **Only select Move if you want to change the location of the original item**—This is rarely what you want to do with a program or script. Programs are usually located in bin directories on the path, and moving them makes them inaccessible for command-line use.
- **For a kdelnk file, you usually copy it or link it**—Sometimes, moving a kdelnk file from its original location results in it no longer working correctly. For example, MimeType kdelnk files only have meaning in a mimelnk directory. Don't move kdelnk files out of special directories unless you understand the ramifications of them not being there.

Note

Here's one final tip about moving and copying files: Use the Desktop as a staging area for manipulating files. The Desktop itself is a directory, and it is always available in the background. An easy way to get a file from one place to another is to Copy, Move, or Link it to the Desktop; change the directory in the file manager; and then Move the item where you want it (back into the file manager).

REMOVING FILES

To remove a file from your system, you have two options—delete the file or move it to the Trash can. Deleting the file completely erases it from your system. There is no way to recover the file. Moving it to the Trash moves the file to the Trash directory, which means that it still takes up space in your file system, but that you can recover it if you need it in the future.

To delete a file, select the file (or files), and then choose the Delete option from either the Edit menu or the context menu for that item. To move it to the Trash can, choose the Move to Trash option (from either of these menus), or drag the item from the file manager window to the Trash icon on the Desktop.

LAUNCHING FILES

Launching a file from the file manager is exactly the same as launching it from the Desktop window. You can either click the item, drag the item on top of a program, select Open with from the context menu of the item, or select one of the programs listed in the context menu.

If you single-click the item, KDE determines an appropriate course of action, depending on the file type. If KDE cannot determine a default program for the file, KDE prompts you for a program with which to open the file.

MODIFYING FILES AND DIRECTORIES

KDE makes it very easy to manipulate the attributes of an item in the file system by providing a simple graphical dialog box to manipulate an object's properties. To access this dialog box, select Properties from the item's context menu. The dialog box has different tab pages, depending on the item type. But the first two tab pages of the dialog box, General and Permissions, are common to all types.

RENAMING A FILE To rename a file, select Properties from the file's context menu. When the dialog box opens, you are on the General page of the dialog box. Edit the Name field, and click the OK button.

CHANGING OWNERSHIP AND PERMISSIONS To change ownership and permissions on a file, access the Properties dialog box, and select the Permissions tab (see Figure 14.15).

To modify the permissions of an item, click the check boxes in the Access permissions section of the dialog box. To change the owner or group of the file, use the controls under Ownership.

CHANGING OTHER PROPERTIES Depending on the type of object you are modifying, the Properties dialog box might have additional tabs for adjusting more properties. Many of these are discussed in Chapter 5.

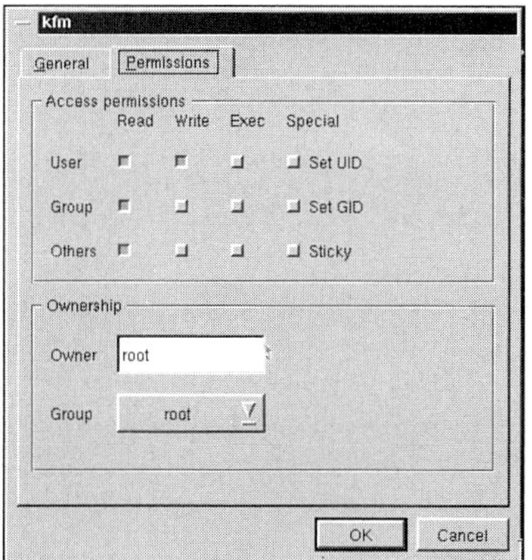

Figure 14.15
Click the check boxes to change permissions.

CHANGING DIRECTORY PROPERTIES One set of properties that is discussed here is on the Dir page of the Properties dialog box, available for directories. This page enables you to customize the icon and background of the directory. These changes can be applied to an individual directory, or to all the directories in the system.

To change these attributes for a directory, select Properties on the context menu for that directory. For a directory listed in the file manager window, right-click it to access the context menu. If the directory you want to change is the current directory, right-click anywhere in the file manager window, and then select Properties.

Now select the Dir tab, and click the icon button. The Select Icon dialog box appears. You can switch between the system icon gallery and your own personal icon gallery using the drop-down list at the top of the dialog box. Notice that there are several icons of folders with different colored tabs in the system icon gallery. You can use these to color-code your document folders, just like you do in the real world. Click the icon you want, and click OK. You can decide whether you want to use this icon for just this directory or for all directories. Select either the Apply or Apply Global buttons to do so.

The other attribute of a directory that you can customize this way is the background image. This image shows up behind the directory listing in the file manager window. Access the context menu, Properties, Dir tab again, and select an image from the drop-down list.

These background images on the drop-down list are located in the /opt/kde/share/wallpapers directory. To add a new wallpaper file to the list, place an image file in this directory.

NAVIGATING THE WEB

The file manager operates not just on local files. It is also a generic World Wide Web browser. To go to a Web page, click on a URL item, or enter the URL for the page in the location bar of the file manager.

To navigate, use the same techniques as you do with a normal Web browser: Click links and use the forward and back buttons in the button bar. Reload a page using the reload button. Access the history list by selecting Cache, Show History. You can also access things in the file manager's cache by selecting Cache, Show Cache.

To go to a bookmarked site, click the item in the Bookmarks menu. To add the current page to the bookmarks, select Bookmarks, Add Bookmark. If you have submenus in your bookmark list, you can select Add Bookmark for the menu on which you want the site to be placed.

Editing the bookmarks is discussed in the section "Panel Configuration Dialog Box," earlier in this chapter. To save a link in a Web page on the Desktop, drag the link from the file manager window to the Desktop. To save the current page to the Desktop, back up one page, and drag the link from the previous page to the Desktop. If you don't have a link to drag (for example, you got to a site by typing it in instead of following a link), you can make an entry on the Desktop by following these steps:

1. Select Bookmarks, Add Bookmark to add the page to the bookmark list.
2. Now select Bookmarks, Edit Bookmarks to show the Bookmarks folder
3. Drag the item from the Bookmarks folder to the Desktop.

LOOKING INSIDE TARS

To view the contents of an archive (TAR) file, click the file. You can operate on individual files and directories inside the archive, just like you do in a normal directory.

USING SPECIAL BROWSER VIEWS

The file manager has a couple of extra features for viewing directories that you might want to use: the capability to show images in a directory as thumbnails and the capability to customize a directory listing with HTML. The thumbnail feature is a powerful mechanism that enables you to use the file manager as an image manager and organizer. The HTML view feature enables you to work with local Web data, and to see it as if you were accessing it via a Web server. Also, it allows you complete control over the directory display for certain directories, which you can use for security or aesthetic reasons.

THUMBNAIL VIEW The file manager can interpret the images in a directory and show them as thumbnails in the browser window, instead of displaying regular icons. This feature enables you to browse through directories of image files and see the image for each file, which can be very helpful when working with lots of images.

To see how this feature works, log in as root and open a file manager window to /opt/kde/share/wallpapers. Select View, Show Thumbnails from the menu. The first time you use this feature in a directory, it takes some time to generate the thumbnail images. The images are stored in a hidden directory called .xvpics so that the display can be quicker on subsequent accesses.

HTML VIEW Another special feature of the file manager is the capability to customize the view of a directory with an HTML page. By default, the file manager generates its own HTML page of the directory contents, and displays that. However, you can override the page generated internally by `kfm` with your own page, so that whenever the directory is displayed by the file manager, your page is displayed.

You can use this feature to provide whatever look and feel you want for the directory. For example, you can change the background of the directory or the color of the text, or you can lay out the files in some custom arrangement. This feature also enables you to display only the contents you want.

To see how this feature works, open a file manager window to the location /home/httpd/html, and make sure that the menu item HTML View is checked in the View menu. Instead of the directory contents, you see the default home page for your machine. To see the directory contents instead of this page, select View, HTML View to turn this feature off.

When this feature is on, the file manager looks for files with the names index.html and .kde.html. If either of these is found, they are displayed instead of the internal HTML file listing generated by `kfm`. To create your own directory contents view, create an HTML file that you want to display, and then place it in the directory under either index.html or .kde.html.

This feature is on by default. If you are looking at a folder with HTML files that you want to manipulate, you might want to turn it off.

SPECIAL FEATURES OR TIPS

The file manager has a couple of other features that serve as handy shortcuts for common operations.

MISCELLANEOUS HANDY SHORTCUTS

To open a terminal window with the current directory the same as the file manager, select File, Open Terminal, or use the keyboard shortcut Ctrl+T. This is handy when you get to a directory and discover that you need to perform some complex action there. Instead of opening a terminal window and navigating there manually, just type Ctrl+T.

To open a folder in a new file manager window instead of the current file manager window, click it with the middle mouse button.

To open a new file manager window with the same current directory as the current window, click the gears icon in the toolbar (located on the right of the toolbar).

Sometimes, you need to perform a file manipulation for which you just don't have permissions. In this case it is possible to start a terminal window, `su` to root, and execute the commands by hand. However, to make it more convenient to overcome this situation, and to enable you to continue operating using a graphical file manager, KDE provides a way to launch a file manager with superuser (root) privileges.

To do this, select System, File Manager (Super User Mode) from the Application Starter menu. A special terminal window starts up and prompts you for the root password for your machine. Enter it, and a file manager with root privileges starts. To remind you that you are operating with special privileges, the handle of the menu bar in the file manager window is shown in bright red.

You can use this file manager window to perform operations that require root privileges. When you drag files between file manager windows of both types (root and regular user) onscreen, the window that performs the copy, move, or link operation is the destination window (the window being dropped on). This means, for example, that you cannot drag a file to which you don't have permissions from a root file manager window to a non-root file manager window. You can, however, perform this drag the other way around.

`kfm` KEYBOARD SHORTCUTS

The file manager provides several keyboard shortcuts for common or significant operations. Many of these are listed in the file manager menus, next to the item that they perform. However, Table 4.4 shows a list of some of the important keyboard shortcuts available for `kfm`.

TABLE 4.4 `kfm` KEYBOARD SHORTCUTS

Shortcut	Operation
Alt+Left arrow	Moves back in history
Alt+Right arrow	Moves forward in history
Alt+Up arrow	Changes to parent directory
Arrow keys	Move among the icons (directory view)
Arrow keys	Scroll in the indicated direction (on WWW pages)
Return	Opens a file/directory
Esc	Shows the context menu for the current file
Space	Selects/Unselects file
Page Up/Down	Scrolls by pages
Ctrl+N	Open a new file manager window
Ctrl+T	Opens a terminal window in the current directory
Ctrl+L	Changes the location (current directory)
Ctrl+F	Finds files
Ctrl+W	Closes window
Ctrl+X	Moves selected file to the Trash can
Ctrl+S	Selects files by filename and wildcard
Ctrl+A	Selects all files in the current directory

Shortcut	Operation
Ctrl+C	Marks files for copying (Copy)
Ctrl+V	Pastes marked files to the current directory
F2	Finds a word or phrase in the page
F3	Finds the next occurrence of the same word or phrase

CONFIGURING THE `kfm` BROWSER

Because `kfm` is a browser, it has many of the same options you find in a regular browser. Some of these are presented here very briefly. The configuration of `kfm` is done by selecting Options, Configure Browser (or Options, Configure File Manager) from the menu. The options on the pages of these dialog boxes enable you to customize browser-specific settings, such as the use of an Internet proxy, or more general file manager settings such as the font characteristics and colors for the display area of the file manager window.

PROXY SERVER

You can configure the file manager to use a proxy server in order to access the World Wide Web. This is a server that acts on behalf of your browser, requesting pages for it on the Web, that it then transmits to your machine. When configured to do so, the browser uses a proxy without you ever noticing any difference in the way you enter URLs or follow links on the Web.

Many businesses use proxy servers as a security measure to make it more difficult for an outsider to intrude on their network. Sometimes, a proxy server is configured to keep a copy of each document that it retrieves, so that subsequent accesses by you or others for the same document can be performed faster. Your network administrator or Internet service provider will tell you if you use a proxy for your Internet access and, if so, they will provide you with the information you need to configure the browser to use a proxy server.

To have `kfm` use a proxy server, select the Proxy page of the Browser Setting dialog box, check the Use proxy box, and enter the proxy address and port in the boxes provided. To avoid using the proxy for a specific server, enter the server name or address into the field No Proxy for.

HTTP AND USER AGENT SETTINGS

Use the HTTP tab to enter accepted languages and accepted character sets. The values of these fields are used as part of HTTP headers that are sent to the Web server, and can affect what documents are returned and their formatting. If you click on the Assume HTML button, the file manager assumes that a document coming from the server is HTML when no other MIME type is provided by the server.

The User Agent page enables you to configure the User Agent field that is transmitted to specific Web servers on HTTP requests. Some Web servers respond differently, depending on the User Agent value transmitted by the client (for example, some Web servers send pages that are formatted differently if they detect that a Netscape browser is being used). You can use this option to force certain servers to recognize `kfm` as a different (specific) browser. The default entry causes the user agent string Konquerer/1.0 to be sent to all Web servers.

Unless you understand these settings, it is recommended that you leave them alone.

BROWSER APPEARANCE

Other pages of the Configure File Manager dialog box enable you to adjust aspects of the page display for the browser.

To change the fonts used by the browser, modify the settings on the Fonts page of the dialog box.

To change the color of text and links displayed by the browser, select the Colors tab, and then click on a button. Choose a new color for that item from the Select Color dialog box. To have the cursor change when it is over a link, check Change cursor over link.

The last page of this dialog box, Other, has a few miscellaneous settings that don't fit anywhere else. To have the settings on the View and Options menus activated on a per-URL basis, instead of globally for all URLs, select the Allow per-URL settings option. When this is active, you can save the file manager settings for a particular directory by right-clicking the directory window, and then selecting Save settings for this URL. The next time you visit the directory, the file manager will display the directory using the settings that were previously saved.

To have the tree view of the file manager window update as you browse the file system in the browser area of the window, select Tree view follows navigation.

Finally, you can enter the name of a terminal program to be used with `kfm`. This is the program that is started when you select File, Open Terminal from the file manager menu.

SUMMARY

This chapter has covered a lot of territory with regard to navigating and using KDE. First, basic concepts of mouse and keyboard usage were presented, including selecting and dragging items with the mouse, accessing context menus with a right-button click, and using accelerator keys and keyboard shortcuts.

The different parts of the window frame, including the title bar and buttons, were explained, as were the major parts of the Desktop environment itself. The Desktop environment consists of three main components: the Panel, the Taskbar, and the Desktop background. Through these components, you launch and control the programs and files that make up your everyday work session.

The most important programs and files that make up KDE were described, including the online help program and the KDE control center. These were presented in the context of the Application Starter menu and the Panel launch bar. Many configuration options are available for customizing the items on the various menus and on the Panel.

Finally, the file manager was presented, which is KDE's general purpose file system and Internet (Web and FTP) browser. Its use for both browsing and file and directory management was described.

You may want to examine the following chapters for additional information related to the topics discussed here:

- Chapter 5 contains information about configuring and customizing KDE for your everyday use.
- The different KDE applications and programs that are available for your use are presented and described in Chapter 7 and Chapter 8.
- The chapters in Part 5 of this book describe many different configuration options and features of the X Window system, which is the graphical environment in which KDE runs. In particular, see Chapter 37 for details about getting your X Window system up and running before you run KDE. Also, see Chapter 39, "Customizing X," for other important configuration settings.

CHAPTER 5

CUSTOMIZING YOUR DESKTOP ENVIRONMENT

In this chapter

This chapter digs into the heart of KDE to explain how things work underneath its pretty veneer. You will learn the concepts and the detailed information that will enable you to make your own objects and customize their behavior and appearance. This chapter also covers in detail all the different settings that are available in configuring KDE—from Desktop background colors to window button layout and event sounds.

Accessing KDE Configuration Directories

Throughout this chapter references are made to the KDE configuration directories. Here's a note on the nomenclature used in this chapter to refer to these directories. The system directories for KDE are located under /opt/kde on an OpenLinux system. As you learn more about KDE, you will see that a mirror image of this directory structure also appears in each user's home directory, under $(HOME)/.kde. This directory tree contains personal customizations to KDE for that user. In general, files placed in the system KDE directories affect all users, whereas items placed in a personal KDE directory affect just one user. In this chapter, when referring to a directory that can exist under either tree, the prefix $(KDEDIR) is used. For example, the following directory reference

```
$(KDEDIR)/share/icons
```

means that either the directory /opt/kde/share/icons or $(HOME)/.kde/share/icons can be used–in this case, to hold icon files for use by KDE.

OVERVIEW OF FILE TYPING

At the core of the object-oriented model of KDE is the file typing system. KDE uses file typing to assign attributes to the files, directories, and devices in your file system. This allows KDE to display intuitive icons that tell you, visually, what kind of file something is. Also, it allows KDE to present you with context menus and property dialog boxes that are specific to the object on which you are working.

There are two basic levels of file typing. First, KDE uses information intrinsic in the file system to determine the basic class of an object. The major object classes are as follows:

- Program
- File
- URL
- Device
- Folder (directory)

KDE can distinguish between programs, folders, and files using information from the file system. However, to further distinguish objects, KDE uses MIME types and kdelnk files. This represents a second, more detailed, level of file typing. These two facilities allow KDE to assign each object an appearance and behavior in the system, and to make associations between objects to control how objects interact.

MIME Types

MIME is an acronym for *Multipurpose Internet Mail Extension*. It is a worldwide standard for assigning a type to an item in an email message or on a Web page. When a World Wide Web browser downloads a file from a Web site, the Web server indicates the type of the file that is using the MIME standard. The browser then displays or handles the file according to its type.

KDE uses this same system, but it assigns MIME types to the files on your local hard drive. It does this using `MimeType` kdelnk files.

The MIME standard uses a two-part naming scheme to indicate the type of an object. The first part of the name indicates a general class of object, and the second indicates a specific type, or file format, for the object. In the MIME specification these are referred to as the type and subtype of the object.

The standard set of MIME classes are as follows:

- application
- audio
- image
- text
- video

KDE adds another type, `inode`, which it uses to define different types of items in the file system.

A full MIME type consists of one of these classes, followed by a specific type or file format (the MIME subtype). For example, the MIME type for a file with a GIF image in it is the string image/gif.

kdelnk Files

KDE uses kdelnk files to hold information about other files on the system. kdelnk files are used in two different ways. `MimeType` kdelnk files are used to define MIME types, thereby assigning attributes to a whole class of files on your system. The other kdelnk files refer to specific programs or devices on your system; the other kdelnk file types are as follows:

- Application
- Device
- Link

These correspond to the program, device, and URL file classes mentioned earlier.

The Templates directory, discussed subsequently, contains every kind of kdelnk file. Figure 5.1 shows a snapshot of the kdelnk files in the Templates directory.

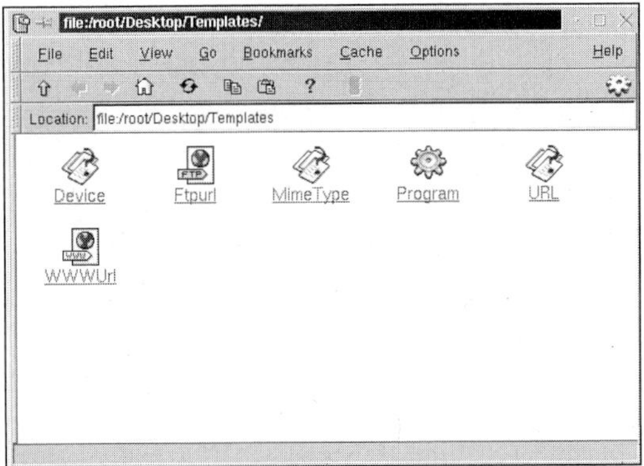

Figure 5.1
The Templates directory holds all the different kinds of kdelnk files.

Note

You don't normally see the .kdelnk extension. When the file manager displays the contents of a directory, it hides the .kdelnk extension of the files. This is done to avoid cluttering up the display, and to make the files appear more natural. However, its drawback is that sometimes when you are looking at a directory with the file manager, it is difficult to tell whether an item is a kdelnk file or just a regular file.

Note that the file Ftpurl.kdelnk and the file WWWurl.kdelnk in the Templates directory are both of kdelnk type Link. Don't confuse the name of the kdelnk file with its kdelnk type. For example, in Figure 5.1, the file Program.kdelnk has the kdelnk type of Application. You will give the kdelnk files that you create all kinds of different names.

So now you know how they look internally. Listing 5.1 shows the MimeType.kdelnk file for the GIF image type. This is located on your OpenLinux system at /opt/kde/share/mimelnk/images/gif.kdelnk.

LISTING 5.1 CONTENTS OF GIF.KDELNK FILE

```
# KDE Config File
[KDE Desktop Entry]
Type=MimeType
MimeType=image/gif
Icon=image.xpm
Patterns=*.gif;*.GIF;
Comment=Gif images
Comment==Imágen GIF
...
```

Because it is plain ASCII text, it is possible to edit a kdelnk file by hand. But it is much more convenient, and less error prone, to modify a kdelnk file using the graphical dialog boxes in KDE. Note that the kdelnk file in Listing 5.1 indicates its own kdelnk type (MimeType), the MimeType that it is defining (image/gif), and an icon to assign to that type (image.xpm), in addition to some other things. Notice also that the Comment is available in several different languages. Listing 5.1 shows only the English and Spanish translations of the Comment, but there are many more.

To manipulate the fields in a kdelnk file, use the Properties dialog box, which is accessible by selecting Properties from the file's context menu. Because kdelnk files are regular files on your file system, their Property dialog boxes have the same first two tab pages (General and Permissions) that all other files do. However, the other tabs in the Property dialog box depend on the which type of kdelnk file it is.

MimeType.kdelnk Files

MimeType.kdelnk files are used to define MIME types on your system. Each MIME type is defined by a single kdelnk file. These files must reside in special directories in order for them to be recognized by KDE.

A MIME type is assigned to a file by one of two methods:

- By using a filename pattern
- By matching part of the file's contents

A MimeType.kdelnk file is used to define a MIME type using the first method, a filename pattern.

Typing a File by Filename Pattern

The special properties of a MimeType.kdelnk file are listed on the Binding page of the Property dialog box. To see an example of these properties, open the directory /opt/kde/share/mimelnk/image in a file manager window, and right-click the file gif (the .kdelnk extension is hidden). Then select Properties from the context menu, and click the Binding tab. You see a dialog box like the one in Figure 5.2.

The fields on this page define the MIME type image/gif. They indicate how to recognize files of that type, and how to display and launch them. The following fields can be set:

- **Pattern**—This field specifies a filename pattern using wildcards. Files that match this pattern are assigned the indicated MIME type. In the example in Figure 5.2, any file ending in .gif or .GIF is assigned the MIME type image/gif.
- **Comment**—This field defines a short string to describe the type. This string appears in the file manager status line when the mouse is over an item of this type.
- **Mime Type**—This is the actual MIME type being defined. It needs to be a two part name, conforming to MIME standards.
- **Default Application**—This drop-down box can be used to define a default application for files of this type.
- **Icon**—This field defines the icon that is used whenever a file of this type is displayed (in a file manager window, on the Desktop, or on the Panel).

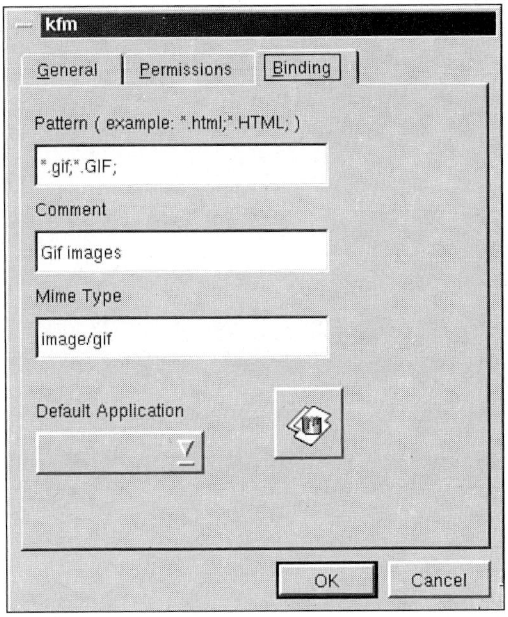

Figure 5.2
The Binding tab of a MimeType.kdelnk file defines a MIME type.

TYPING A FILE BY CONTENT

The second method of defining a MIME type has nothing to do with kdelnk files, but it is described here for the sake of completeness.

If a filename pattern just won't suffice to identify a file, you can also use the contents of a file to determine its type. Sometimes, it is preferable to not give every file of the same type a special extension or name component. For example, maybe you write lots of Python programs, but don't want to use the extension .py for all your scripts for purely aesthetic reasons. But you still want to be capable of assigning a special icon to python scripts so that you can recognize them in the file manager. You can do this by defining the MIME type for python files based on their content, instead of on their filename.

To indicate a file's MIME type by its content, put an entry in the magic file. This is a special KDE file normally found at $(KDEDIR)/share/mimelnk/magic.

For details of how the entries of the magic file look, see the system version of the file at /opt/kde/share/mimelnk/magic. Basically, each entry specifies a set of content tests, and the MIME type that is to be assigned to files that match those constraints. The content tests are bytes or strings of letters and offsets in the file where they are to occur.

The magic man page has details on the syntax used for the content tests in this file.

Application.kdelnk Files

A kdelnk file of type Application is used to define an executable program on your system. Although KDE can launch applications without kdelnk files, the Application.kdelnk file provides KDE with additional information about the application, which helps it integrate the application into the KDE system.

For this section, examine the properties of the file /opt/kde/share/applnk/Utilities/kpackage.kdelnk. Open a file manager window to the Utilities directory, right-click the file kpackage_(.kdelnk), and select Properties.

The properties of an Application.kdelnk file tell KDE how to launch the application, which icon to assign to it, and which types of files it works with.

The following fields are on the Execute page of the Properties dialog box:

- **Execute**—This is the program to execute when this kdelnk file is launched (clicked or dropped on).
- **Working Directory**—This specifies the directory that the program is to run in when it is launched.
- **Icon**—This indicates the icon that is used to display this application, on the Desktop, Panel, or in a KDE menu.
- **Swallowing on Panel: Execute**—This is the line to execute when the kdelnk file is dragged and dropped on the Panel.
- **Swallowing on Panel: Window Title**—This is the title of the application window that the Panel is to swallow. The Swallowing on Panel feature of KDE is discussed later in this chapter.
- **Run in Terminal**—If this option is selected, the program is run in a terminal window. This allows launching text-based programs in KDE. The terminal window closes as soon as the program exits.
- **Terminal Options**—This is used to pass any options required by the terminal program to run the program.

The Execute line supports the macros shown in Table 5.1, which are expanded when the application is launched. Some of the macros only apply when the program is launched with another file, such as when a file is dropped on this one.

Table 5.1 Macros for the Application Execute Line

Macro	Replacement
`%f`	Full filename path.
`%n`	Filename, just the name part.

continues

TABLE 5.1 CONTINUED

Macro	Replacement
%d	Directory part of the filename. Concatenating %d and %n yields the value of %f.
%k	Path to this kdelnk file.
%c	Name of application (often used for the title bar caption). This is the value of the Name field. This can be defined in different languages, to allow the title bar of the application to have a translated title.
%u	URL for filename.
%i	Expands to `-icon <icon>`, where `<icon>` is the filename of the icon for this program. The filename for the icon is determined by the icon that is selected for the Icon button of this dialog box.
%m	Expands to `-miniicon <icon>`, where `<icon>` is the filename of the mini-icon for this program, if one is defined.

Note

The %k option is interesting because it enables you to indicate to an application the kdelnk file that was used to execute it. This enables you to use the kdelnk file for both KDE configuration data and application-specific configuration data, if the application supports it.

For this to work, the application must be capable of reading its own configuration data out of the file, without being confused by the regular kdelnk fields. To set this up, place configuration data in the kdelnk file for the application, and use the %k option on the Execute line with whatever argument the application requires to specify its configuration file.

An example might help clarify how these macros are used.

Suppose a kdelnk file is created for the program xv. The file is /home/tbird/Desktop/xv.kdelnk, and the fields are set as follows:

- **Execute**—`/usr/X11R6/xv %f %d %n --useconfigfile %k -c "%c" %u %i`
- **Working directory**—`/home/tbird/images`
- **Icon**—`script.xpm` (a gear)
- **Run in terminal**—Not checked
- **Comment**—XV Image Program
- **Name**—XV
- **Handled Type**—`image/jpeg`

Now, if the file /tmp/picture.jpeg is dropped on the icon for this file on the Desktop, the following line is executed:

```
/usr/X11R6/bin/xv /tmp/picture.jpeg /tmp/ picture.jpeg --useconfigfile /home
/tbird/Desktop/xv.kdelnk -c "XV" file:/tmp/picture.jpeg -icon script.xpm
```

This example shows almost all the macros being used at once. This is only for demonstration purposes, and is unlikely to be useful in practice (that is, `xv` doesn't support all these different options).

The fields on the Application page of the Property dialog box are as follows:

- **Binary pattern**—These are the filename patterns of the binaries that this kdelnk file runs. If this kdelnk file is in an `applnk` directory, the icon selected for this file is displayed for the indicated binaries, wherever they are encountered in the file system. If this field is left blank, the icon is only displayed for this kdelnk file.

  For example, if the xv.kdelnk file in the previous example has the pattern xv in its Binary pattern field, the gear icon is used for both the xv.kdelnk file and for the file /usr/X11R6/bin/xv (and for any other file named xv in the file system).
- **Comment**—This string appears as the ToolTip for this file (on the Desktop, Panel, or Application Starter menu).
- **Name**—This name is displayed in menus, such as the Application Starter menu or the context menu of other files.
- **Handled file types**—These boxes aren't labeled, but they specify the types of files that this program can handle. The box on the left has the MIME types that this application handles, and the box on the right has the list of defined MIME types.

  If this kdelnk file is underneath the applnk directory (described in a moment), this application name appears in the context menus of files of the indicated types. More than one program can be assigned to handle the same MIME type. This means that a file's context menu might have multiple programs to choose from when launching it.

  For example, in the file xv.kdelnk you can indicate that it handles files of type image/x-bmp. In this case, xv (the value of the Name field) appears as an option in the context menu of all BMP image files on your system.

Link.kdelnk Files

These are probably the simplest kdelnk files. Basically, for a Link.kdelnk file, specify a URL and an icon to represent it. Link.kdelnk files are used for both WWW pages and FTP sites.

When you drag FTP objects or WWW links from a file manager window, `kfm` automatically creates Link.kdelnk files for you, and selects the correct icon type (either WWW or FTP).

Device.kdelnk Files

Device.kdelnk files are used for devices that represent removable media (such as CD-ROMS, floppies, Zip drives, and so on). They enable you to put icons for such devices on your Desktop, making it possible to mount and unmount using simple mouse clicks. Also, the icons for a Device.kdelnk file show the status of the removable device, so you can tell if it is safe to remove the physical media (such as the floppy) from the device.

The special properties for this kind of kdelnk file are as follows:

- **Device**—This is the path to the device. This matches the device name used in the configuration file /etc/fstab.
- **Readonly**—This indicates that the device needs to be mounted read-only.
- **Mount Point**—This specifies the directory in the file system in which the file system from the device is to be mounted. This is usually /mnt/floppy for floppies, or /mnt/cdrom for CD-ROM drives.
- **File Systems**—These list the file system types that this device supports. For floppies, this is usually msdos or ext2; for CD-ROM devices it is iso9660. You can list more than one, separated by commas. If more than one is listed, they appear as separate `Mount` options in the context menu for this device.
- **Mounted Icon**—This is an icon representing the device when it is mounted. It has a green dot in the corner. Icons for most of the common removable devices (3 1/2 disks, 5 1/4 floppies, CD-ROM, Zip drives) are in the system icon gallery.
- **Unmounted Icon**—This is an icon that represents the device when it is unmounted. It is the same as the mounted icon, but without the green dot.

SPECIAL DIRECTORIES

There are several special directories that KDE uses to hold kdelnk files or icon files, where they have special meaning. For each of these special directories, there is both a system directory and a personal directory. When files are placed in these directories, they are recognized by KDE and are subsequently usable on the system. Obviously, you can place kdelnk files or icon files anywhere in your file system, but KDE treats them specially (as noted in the sections that follow) when they appear in these directories.

MIMELNK DIRECTORY

The mimelnk directory tree holds the MimeType.kdelnk files used by KDE to define MIME types. The system mimelnk directories are in the /opt/kde/share/mimelnk directory.

Within this directory, there are subdirectories for the major MIME types, and files in each of those directories for the MIME subtypes. For example, the file that defines the MIME type image/gif is /opt/kde/share/mimelnk/image/gif.kdelnk.

Technically, it is not critical that kdelnk files be placed in a subdirectory matching the MIME major type. However, for a MimeType.kdelnk file to have any effect, it *must* reside underneath a mimelnk directory. They have no meaning to KDE anywhere else in the file system.

The personal mimelnk directory is $(HOME)/.kde/share/mimelnk.

The applnk Directory

The applnk directory holds the kdelnk files that appear on the Application Starter menu. The items in the system menu are under the /opt/kde/share/applnk/ directory.

The items on your personal menu are in $(HOME)/.kde/share/applnks/.

Subdirectories under the applnks directory correspond to program groups (submenus) on the applications menu.

The icons Directory

The icons directory holds the icons that are referenced by the kdelnk files on your system and displayed by the various parts of KDE when presenting file system objects.

These icon galleries show up in the Select Icon dialog box, which appears whenever you select an icon by clicking the icon button in a kdelnk Property dialog box. The drop-down list in the Select Icon dialog box enables you to choose icons from either the system icon gallery or from your personal icon gallery.

The system icon gallery is in /opt/kde/share/icons, with mini-icons in the directory /opt/kde/share/icons/mini.

Your personal icon gallery is in the $(HOME)/.kde/share/icons and $(HOME)/.kde/share/icons/mini directories.

The format of icon files and tips for creating new icons are discussed in the section "Making Your Own Icons" later in this chapter.

Templates

This directory holds items that show up on the file manager and Desktop New menus. It also holds kdelnk files that you can use to create new kdelnk entries anywhere in the system. (Refer back to Figure 5.1 to see the contents of the templates directory.)

Tip

Although you can create kdelnk files anywhere you want using templates, there are some constraints. MimeType.kdelnk files only have an effect in a mimelnk directory, so there's no point in creating them anywhere else. Other kdelnk files are primarily for direct manipulation of programs, devices, and URLs, so usually you will create them in an applnk directory or on the Desktop. Only icons in the special icons directories show up in the Select Icon dialog box. Furthermore, files must reside in the Templates directory in order to show up in the file manager and Desktop New menus.

CREATING NEW ITEMS ON YOUR DESKTOP

Now that all the theory behind file typing and kdelnk files is out of the way, it's time to put it to use. In this section you learn how to create various items on your Desktop that you will use in your day-to-day work.

Creating new items for your Desktop and menus is essential to establishing a convenient work environment. This is really where KDE shines, and where the power of KDE can be used to enhance your graphical experience. For example, I've been using graphical environments with Linux for years, but it wasn't until I started using KDE and created a CD-ROM device that I finally got past mounting the CD-ROM file system by hand. With KDE, I no longer have to remember the syntax of the mount command—or any of its obscure options—every time I mount a drive.

By following the instructions in the sections that follow, you can set up easy-to-use items on your Desktop and menus, and start to enjoy the higher productivity that GUIs are supposed to provide.

CREATING A PROGRAM ENTRY

The easiest way to make a program entry on the Desktop is to drag a program from a file manager window to the Desktop and select Link from the drag options menu. However, you can also make a program entry on the Desktop by creating a kdelnk file for the program. Creating a kdelnk file is the preferred method because it enables you to control much more of the behavior and appearance of the program on your Desktop.

To create an Application.kdelnk file for a program on your Desktop, follow these steps:

1. Right-click an open area of the Desktop to bring up the Desktop context menu.
2. Select New, Program from the context menu. You are prompted to edit the filename of the kdelnk file for this program.
3. Enter the name of the program, but do not remove the .kdelnk extension from the filename.
4. Click OK, and the file (without the .kdelnk extension) appears on your Desktop.

Now edit the properties of this item by following these steps:

1. Select Properties from the context menu of the kdelnk file you just created.
2. Select the Execute tab of the dialog box.
3. In the Execute field, enter the name of the actual program executable.

You can also enter any parameters with which you want to run the program, or use the macros shown in Table 5.1 to provide additional configuration options for the application. If you plan on dropping files on top of this icon, to run them with this application, use the `%f` macro.

If the program needs to run in a particular directory, or if it is more convenient to run it in a certain directory, enter that directory in the Working Directory field.

To assign an icon to this file, click on the icon button and select an icon from the dialog box that appears. In this dialog box, you can choose an icon from either the system icon gallery or your personal icon gallery.

If the program is a text-mode program, check the Run in terminal box, and enter any required options in the Terminal Options field. On the Application page, enter a description of this program in the Comment field, and enter the name of the program in the Name field.

For a kdelnk file that you plan to leave on the Desktop, you can leave the other fields on the Execute and Application pages blank. These fields are discussed in other sections of this chapter. (The Swallowing on Panel fields are discussed in the section "Adding a Live Application Window to the Panel". The Binary Pattern field and handled-types lists on the Applications page are described in the sections "Assigning an Icon to a Single File" and "Associating an Application with a File Type," respectively.)

To use your new entry, click its icon on the Desktop. If it makes sense, drag a file and drop it on the icon for this entry. The program you specified starts, with the file that you dropped as one of its arguments.

CREATING A DEVICE ENTRY

One of the most useful things you can do with KDE is put entries to represent removable devices right on your Desktop. Then you can and mount and unmount the devices quickly and easily from your graphical environment by clicking the icons for them on your Desktop.

Unfortunately, it is difficult to preinstall these device entries because different people have different devices that they might want to mount. Therefore, they are not set up by default in OpenLinux, so few people know about them. However, the instructions in this section show you exactly what you need to do to set this up—and it's not difficult.

This section covers creating CD-ROM and floppy devices on your Desktop, but the same steps can be used to set up device entries for other removable media such as ZIP drives or others.

Caution

Don't confuse the device entry on your Desktop with a Linux device entry in the file system. Linux device files are special entries in the file system (which almost always reside in the /dev directory). The device entry on your Desktop is a kdelnk file that refers to one of these Linux devices. In the discussions that follow, you don't directly manipulate (drag or create) any Linux device files. You just type one of their names into the appropriate dialog box as part of setting up the KDE device entry.

See Chapter 9, "Understanding the Linux File System," for more information on Linux device files.

CREATING A CD-ROM DEVICE ON THE DESKTOP

Creating a CD-ROM device on your Desktop is fairly straightforward. Basically, it involves creating a kdelnk file on the Desktop and modifying its properties so that it represents the physical device in question.

To create a CD-ROM device on the Desktop, follow these steps:

1. Select New, Device from the Desktop context menu.
2. Change the filename of the kdelnk file to cdrom.kdelnk in the dialog box that appears. The CD-ROM device appears on your Desktop.

Follow these steps to edit the properties of this file:

1. Select Properties from the context menu of the file.
2. Select the Device tab.

   If you are the super user (root), all fields in this dialog box are available to edit. If you are a regular user, you can only edit the Device, Mounted Icon, and Unmounted Icon properties. For the device entry to work for a regular user account, the device must have an entry in the configuration file /etc/fstab that defines the other fields that are required to mount the device.
3. Enter the Linux device filename for the device. This might be something such as /dev/cdrom, or a more specific device name. This name matches the device name for the CD-ROM found in the file /etc/fstab. You might want to check the Readonly checkbox, but for a CD-ROM this is not required because it can't be mounted writable anyway.
4. If you are the root user, enter the Mount Point for the device. For an OpenLinux system, this is usually the directory /mnt/cdrom.
5. Leave the Filesystems field set to the value Default.
6. Now select icons for the CD-ROM. There are two icons to select because the icon changes on the Desktop to indicate whether the CD-ROM device is currently mounted. Two icons in the system icon gallery, called cdrom_mount.xpm and cdrom_unmount.xpm, are specially drawn to represent CD-ROM devices. These icons both show a CD-ROM device, but one has a green dot to indicate that the CD-ROM is mounted. These icons are recommended, but you can select any two icons you want. It helps, however, if the icons match except for some visual indication for when the device is mounted.

   A complete entry for a kdelnk file for a CD-ROM device is shown in Figure 5.3. This figure shows the settings on the Device page of the Properties dialog box for this item.

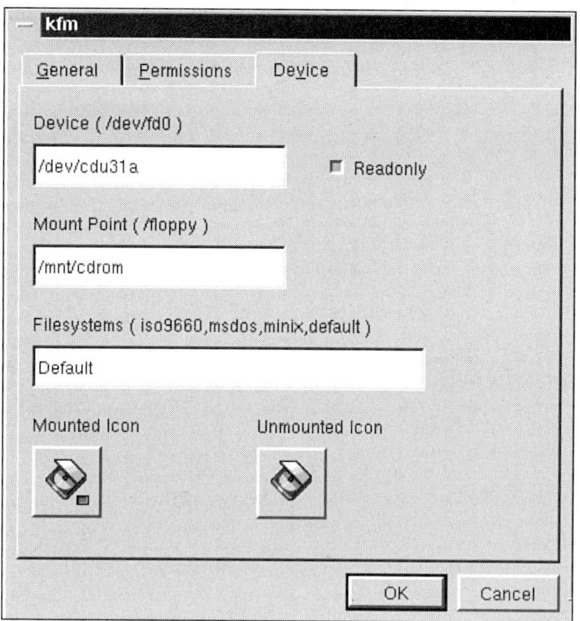

Figure 5.3
Enter the settings for a CD-ROM device for your Desktop.

If you are a regular user, you cannot set the Readonly, Mount Point, and Filesystems fields in this dialog box. In fact, you might not be capable of mounting the device at all unless you are allowed to by the configuration file /etc/fstab. It is up to the system administrator (who might be you) to decide if non-root users are allowed to mount file systems, and which ones they are allowed to mount. With a CD-ROM device, it is usually safe to allow non-root users to mount and unmount the device.

7. Click the OK button when you have finished entering the data.

To mount or unmount the CD-ROM device using this entry on the Desktop, right-click the icon, and select the appropriate option on the context menu. To see the root directory of the file system for the device (the mount directory), click the icon. If necessary, the device is mounted, and then KDE opens a file manager window with the contents of the mount directory displayed.

If KDE tries to mount the CD-ROM but determines that you don't have sufficient permissions to do so, it presents an error message describing the problem and aborts the operation. To avoid this problem, the system administrator can grant permission for users to mount the CD-ROM device by editing the file /etc/fstab. As root, open this file and add the option `user` to the CD-ROM mount options. A sample /etc/fstab file with this modification is shown in Listing 5.2. The last line of this file has the entry for the CD-ROM device.

LISTING 5.2 /ETC/FSTAB WITH OPTION TO ALLOW USERS TO MOUNT CD-ROM DEVICES

```
/dev/hda3 / ext2 defaults 0 1
/proc /proc proc defaults 0 0
/dev/hda2 none swap defaults 0 0
#
/dev/fd0 /mnt/floppy msdos defaults,noauto,user 0 0
#
/dev/cdu31a /mnt/cdrom iso9660 ro,noauto,user 0 0
```

CREATING A FLOPPY DEVICE ON THE DESKTOP

Creating a floppy device is almost identical to creating a CD-ROM device. The main difference lies in the values for the different property fields that you fill out for the entry. However, one important additional feature of floppy device entries is the capability to specify multiple file system mount options. This is discussed in the steps that follow.

To create a floppy device entry on the Desktop, follow these steps:

1. Select New, Device from the Desktop context menu.
2. Change the name of the file to floppy.kdelnk.
3. Select Properties from the context menu of the resulting Desktop item.
4. Select the Device tab.
5. For a floppy, you usually set the Device field to /dev/fd0 and the Mount Point field to /mnt/floppy.
6. For the Filesystems field, you can leave the value as Default, or you can specify a single or multiple file system type. For multiple file system types, separate the entries by commas. Specifying multiple file system types is handy if, for example, you have some floppies formatted for MS-DOS (msdos), and some formatted for Linux (ext2).

   When you have multiple entries in the Filesystems field, they show up as separate options in the context menu for the device, so you can select which type of floppy to mount. An example of this is shown in the floppy context menu in Figure 5.4.
7. Finally, select the Mounted Icon and Unmounted Icon for the floppy, and click OK to save your changes.

To see the contents of a floppy, insert a disk into the floppy drive and click the floppy icon on your Desktop. To mount or unmount the floppy, select the appropriate option from the context menu for the floppy device. If you have made modifications to the contents of the floppy (by adding, removing, or editing the files on it), make sure to unmount the floppy device before removing the floppy from the drive. Otherwise, you might lose the changes you have made.

If you want regular users to be capable of mounting floppies, you can make a modification to the /etc/fstab file, similar to those that were described for CD-ROM devices in the last section. (A sample entry which enables users to mount and unmount floppy devices is shown on the fifth line of Listing 5.2.)

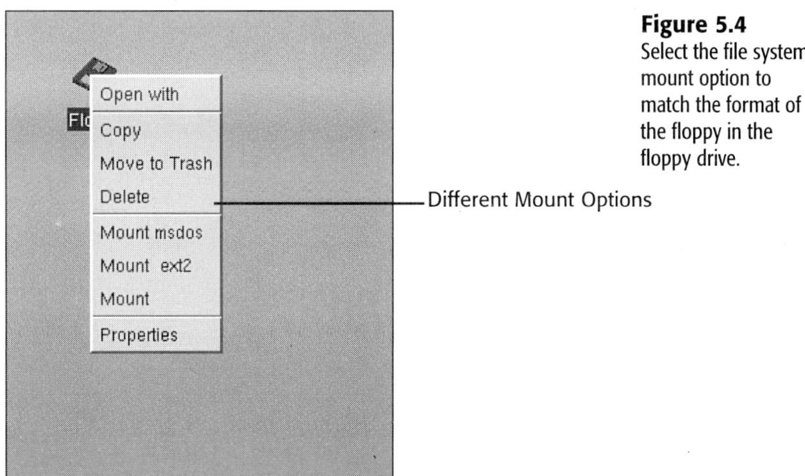

Figure 5.4
Select the file system mount option to match the format of the floppy in the floppy drive.

CREATING A PRINTER ON THE DESKTOP

Another very useful entry to have on your Desktop is an icon for a printer. You can have an icon to represent each printer on your system, or more than one icon for one printer to represent different ways of submitting jobs to that printer.

To create a printer icon on the Desktop, you create an Application.kdelnk file and configure it to run a program that submits jobs to your printer. For this section, it helps to have some familiarity with the various programs on your OpenLinux system that are used for printing files. Two programs that are discussed here are the basic printer command `lpr` and a PostScript formatting command, `mpage`. For the examples that follow, it is assumed that your OpenLinux printing system is configured and operational (meaning that the `lpd` print daemon is running).

USING THE BASIC PRINTER COMMAND `lpr`

A basic printer entry enables you to submit files and documents to the printer without any additional or special formatting.

To create the kdelnk file for a basic printer command, follow these steps:

1. Select New, Program from the context menu of the Desktop.
2. Change the name of the file in the dialog box that appears to something such as Printer.kdelnk. If you have more than one printer, you might give the file some name to identify the printer, such as Laserjet.kdelnk.
3. Edit the properties of the printer entry by selecting Properties from the context menu for the item.
4. Select the Execute tab of the dialog box.

5. For the Execute field, enter the name of a command which will print files on your system. For basic printer output, enter `lpr %f`. The `%f` macro is needed to supply the filename to print to the `lpr` program. When you drag a file and drop it on the icon for this kdelnk file, its filename is substituted for the `%f` macro in the `Execute` line when KDE runs the program.

   You can enter other options for the `lpr` program in the `Execute` line, if you want. See the `lpr` man page for details on the options that you can use with `lpr`. For example, if your system has multiple printers, or if you are making a kdelnk file for the non-default printer, you can use the `-P` option of `lpr` to specify which printer to use.
6. Click the icon button, and then choose an icon for the printer.
7. On the Application page of the Properties dialog box, enter a Comment and Name for this kdelnk file. The Comment appears in a ToolTip for this file, and the Name appears in any menus in which this kdelnk entry is used.
8. Click the OK button to save your changes.

To use the printer entry on the Desktop, simply drag a file from the Desktop or an open file manager window and drop it on the printer icon.

USING ADVANCED FORMATTING WITH mpage

Besides doing basic printing, you can do more advanced formatted printing using a KDE Desktop entry. For example, the `mpage` program formats documents with multiple pages per sheet, for PostScript printers. If you want to print program listings that are formatted two pages per sheet (as I usually do), you can use `mpage` as the program for a Desktop printer entry and have that icon on your Desktop for easy access.

To create a printer entry for producing formatted output on your printer, follow the steps described in the previous section, "Using the Basic Printer Command `lpr`," except for these modifications to the following steps:

1. In step 2, use a kdelnk filename that represents this entry (for example, 'laser_mpage')
2. In step 5, substitute the following command for the Execute field on the Execute page of the Properties dialog box:

   ```
   mpage -2 -Pps %f
   ```

   Make sure that the `mpage` command you use directs its output to a PostScript printer entry on your system. By default in OpenLinux, the printer entry `ps` is defined to accept PostScript files (and reformat them, if necessary, if you have a printer that does not natively accept PostScript documents).
3. Also, in step 6 modify the Comment and Name fields to describe this entry.

After you have modified and saved the properties, drag a file to the entry you have defined on the Desktop. The file is printed in two-page per sheet format. See the man page for `mpage` for additional formatting options to use with this command.

CREATING A URL ON THE DESKTOP

The easiest way to create a URL entry on your Desktop is to use the file manager to browse to a page containing a link to the URL, and then drag the link from the file manager window to the Desktop. In this case, KDE creates a Link.kdelnk file for you automatically and assigns all its properties. If you want to customize the properties (such as the kdelnk filename or the icon), do so in the Properties dialog box for the kdelnk file.

To create a URL on the Desktop without browsing to it, select New; then choose URL, Ftpurl, or WWWUrl, from the context menu of the Desktop. Change the name of the kdelnk file in the dialog box that appears, and then modify the properties for the URL in the Properties dialog box.

MAKING YOUR OWN ICONS

The ultimate customization of your Desktop system is to create your own icons to represent the folders, documents, and programs that you are using. KDE makes it very easy to add your own icons to the system and use them for the different windows and menus that KDE displays.

You can use any X paint program to create icons. The format for large icons is 32×32 color XPM files. For mini-icons, the format is 16×16 color XPM files. Mini icons have the same name as the large icon, but reside in the icons/mini directory.

If you place the icon files you create in your personal icon directories (usually $(HOME)/.kde/share/icons and $(HOME)/.kde/share/icons/mini), they are automatically displayed in the Select Icon dialog box when the personal gallery is selected.

In order to produce a good-looking icon, you might want to start with an existing KDE icon from the system gallery. If you are ambitious (or are just a good artist), you can publish your icons for the rest of the world to use. The KDE Web site provides a style guide for KDE icons at `http://www.kde.org/icon-style.html`, and also gives guidelines for icon creation and specifies the color palette that is to be used for all official KDE icons.

KDE provides a special program, the Icon Editor, for creating and editing icons. This program has several features specifically for working with icon files rather than other image files. These features, and the program itself, are discussed in Chapter 7, "KDE Applications," in the section on graphics programs. To start the icon editor, select Graphics, Icon Editor from the Application Starter menu.

CUSTOMIZING THE APPLICATION STARTER MENU AND PANEL

The Application Starter menu and the Panel can be customized by adding or removing entries from them, or by rearranging their contents. Also, you can adjust the properties of the items in these two places just as you can adjust the properties of the items on your Desktop.

The items that appear in the Application Starter menu and the Panel are defined by kdelnk files. Therefore, before you add an item to either of these places, you must find an existing kdelnk file or create a kdelnk file for that item.

The same principles for editing the properties of kdelnk file apply to editing the properties of items in the Application Starter menu or the Panel.

ADDING AN ITEM TO THE APPLICATION STARTER MENU

The menu items on the Applications Starter menu are defined by Application.kdelnk files in the applnk directory (either the system applnk directory or your personal one).

If you are placing an item on the menu that already has a kdelnk file defined, you can copy the kdelnk file from its current location to the applnk directory. However, if you need to create a new kdelnk file, you can create it directly in the applnk directory. This process is described in the paragraphs that follow.

As was mentioned previously, the Application Starter menu can *only* have kdelnk files on it. It does no good to copy a regular file or program into the applnk directory because these are ignored by KDE.

To add an item to the applications menu, start the file manager, and then select Edit, Applications. The directory $(HOME)/.kde/share/applnk, which is your personal applnk directory, is displayed in the file manager window.

File Manager applnk Merging

When you open the file manager to your personal applnk directory, you see the items that make up the personal portion of the Application Starter menu. But you also see the directories and files that make up the system portion of the menu. This can be quite confusing because these system items are not actually in the applnk directory shown in the location line of the file manager.

The file manager treats the applnk and mimelnk directories specially, merging the contents of the system and personal directories so that it is easier to manipulate the objects in them. However, be aware that you can only modify the system objects if you are logged in as the root account. Even though the system items are shown in your personal applnk directory when you are logged in as a regular user, you cannot change these items unless you switch to the root account.

To add an existing kdelnk file to this directory, drag it to the file manager window, and then select Copy from the drag options menu. To create a new kdelnk file, select File, New, Program from the file manager menu.

Now edit the properties of the kdelnk file to customize its behavior. Repeat this process for additional entries that you want to appear on the menu. When you are done, select Panel, Restart on the Application Starter menu. The Taskbar and Panel might momentarily disappear as the Application Starter menu reconfigures itself with your additions.

Open the Application Starter menu, and you see an entry called *Personal* (unless you have renamed it). This is your personal menu. The kdelnk files that you just placed in your applnk directory appear as menu options under this menu.

To add submenus to your personal application menu, create subdirectories in your applnk directory. You can place additional kdelnk files in these subdirectories to populate the corresponding submenus on the Application Starter menu. Always remember to restart the Panel when you are finished making changes to have the changes take effect.

Tip

A quick way to add a lot of items to your personal menu is to run Appfinder. This is a special program that scans your system for many common Linux applications, and puts them on your personal menu automatically. To run Appfinder, select System, Appfinder from the Application Starter menu. A window opens and shows each application for which Appfinder scans, and indicates which ones it finds and adds to your personal menu.

USING THE MENU EDITOR

There are actually two ways to manipulate items on the Application Starter menu. One way is to use the file manager to move items around directly in the applnk directory, as was described in the previous section. The other method is to use the menu editor, kmenuedit.

To open the menu editor, select Panel, Edit Menus on the Application Starter menu. Figure 5.5 shows the menu editor window with both a personal menu and a system menu displayed.

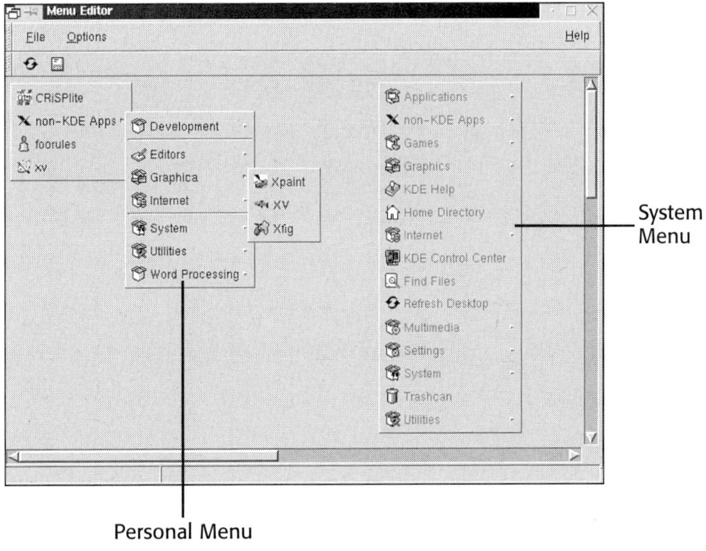

Figure 5.5 The Menu Editor for the Application Starter menu.

If you are logged in as root, you can edit both your personal menu and the system menu. If you are logged in as a regular user, both menus are displayed, but the system menu is grayed out and you cannot edit it.

You work in the menu editor through direct manipulation of the menu items, either by dragging them or by accessing their context menus (with a right mouse click).

To open or close submenus, click the submenu name. To copy a menu item from one menu to another, drag it using the mouse. To move a menu to a new position in the same menu, drag it using the middle mouse button. To cut, copy, paste, or delete a menu item, select the corresponding option on the context menu for that item.

To create a new menu item, you can do one of two things:

- Drag a kdelnk file to the menu editor window and drop it on the menu on which you want it to appear.
- Create a new item with the menu editor.

To create a new menu item, select New from the context menu of an item on the menu. A new entry, EMPTY, appears (positioned immediately above the already existing item in the menu). Now change the properties of the new menu item by selecting Change from the context menu of the item. First change the item type to the correct type, change the Name of the item (to something other than EMPTY), and then modify other attributes as appropriate for the type.

When you select Change from the context menu of an item in the menu editor, the Change dialog box is displayed. This dialog box shows the same fields for the menu item that appear in the Property dialog box of the corresponding kdelnk file. One difference is that the Change dialog box enables you to specify the type of the item. Some types correspond to regular kdelnk file types. However, some types are special types that are specific to the menu editor. The special types are as follows:

- **Separator**—Used to define a menu separator bar.
- **Submenu**—Used to define a submenu.
- **Swallow**—This is actually an Applications.kdelnk file, but the Swallow and Application pages are displayed in the Change dialog box instead of the Execute and Application pages. Swallowing an item on the Panel is discussed in the later section "Adding a Live Application Window to the Panel."

Use the Change dialog box to modify the settings of any of the items in your menus. You can also give your personal menu a different name. To do so, select Options, Change Menuname from the Menu Editor main menu.

If you want to discard your changes and start over, select File, Reload from the menu, or click on the Reload button in the button bar. To save your changes, select File, Save, or click on the Save button in the button bar. The Panel is restarted and your modifications appear in the Application Starter menu.

Adding an Item to the Panel

The easiest way to put an item on the Panel is to drag the kdelnk file to the Panel and drop it in the position in which you want the item to appear. Other items shift to make room for the new item when you drop it.

You can also add items from the Application Starter menu directly to the Panel. This is handy because the Application Starter menu often has entries for all the different items that you want to add. To add an item from the Application Starter menu to the Panel, select Panel, Add Application on the Starter menu, and follow the menus to the item that you want to add.

Use the Move and Remove options on the context menu of an item on the Panel to move it to a different position on the Panel or to remove it from the Panel, respectively. This topic is covered in additional detail in Chapter 4, "Navigating the Desktop."

Adding a Live Application Window to the Panel

If you have a program that can display meaningful status in a very small window, you can have it run with its live window displayed on the Panel. The is called *swallowing* the window, and is a special feature of the Panel.

To do this, you enter information in the Swallowing on Panel fields of the item that you want to place on the Panel, and then drag the kdelnk file to the Panel.

Enter the program to execute in the Execute field under Swallowing on panel. Also, enter the name of the window title that the Panel is to swallow after the program has started. This is required for the Panel to identify which window on the screen to swallow.

For example, one candidate for swallowing on the Panel is `xbiff`. `xbiff` is a program which indicates with a small mailbox icon whether you have unread email in your mailbox.

`kbiff` **Versus** `xbiff`

KDE includes a program called `kbiff` to provide even more functionality than `xbiff`, so you probably don't need to use `xbiff` this way in real life. However, `xbiff` is a good program for this example because it is simple and provides a service via a window small enough to swallow on the Panel.

For a description of `kbiff`, see Chapter 7.

To have the `xbiff` icon displayed as part of the panel, perform the following steps:

1. Make an Application.kdelnk file for `xbiff` by selecting New, Program from the Desktop context menu, and entering `xbiff.kdelnk` as the filename.
2. Configure the properties of the xbiff.kdelnk file by selecting Properties from the context menu of the file and selecting the Execute tab of the dialog box.
3. Enter `xbiff` in the Swallowing on Panel: Execute field.
4. Enter `xbiff` in the Swallowing on Panel: Window Title field.
5. Drag the file to the Panel.

Instead of adding an `xbiff` application button to the Panel, KDE runs `xbiff` and places its main window on the Panel. This is a real live application window. When `xbiff` notices that you have received new mail, the icon in the window changes to alert you to this fact.

CHANGING THE APPEARANCE AND BEHAVIOR OF FILES ON YOUR SYSTEM

KDE enables you to change the appearance and behavior of the files on your system, using MIME types. The appearance of the file is its icon, as assigned by the MIME type. The behavior of the file is the program (or set of programs) that the MIME type associates with the file. These settings determine what happens when you click on the file to open it, or when you open it with one of the programs listed in the file's context menu.

To change the icon or to launch behavior for a file (or set of files), you first need to define the MIME type for the file.

DEFINING A NEW MIME TYPE

To define a new MIME type, you create a MimeType.kdelnk file in your personal mimelnk directory and modify its properties to specify the means to identify files of the new type and how KDE is to treat them.

Before you begin, you need to have an idea what MIME type you want to define. If your end goal is to define a special icon or file association for README files, you might want to define the MIME type text/README to be used with these files. You might want to examine the directories and files in the system mimelnk directory to see examples of existing MIME types and how they are organized. Which MIME type you define determines the subdirectory under the mimelnk directory in which you place your MimeType.kdelnk file.

To create a MimeType.kdelnk file in your personal mimelnk directory, open a file manager window and select Edit, Mime Types from the menu. The directory $(HOME)/.kde/share/mimelnk is displayed in the file manager window. You see both the personal and the system directories and files for defining MIME types in this directory. (See the sidebar "File Manager applnk Merging" earlier in this chapter for an explanation of this combined view.).

If you are logged in as root, browse to the subdirectory where you want to create your MimeType.kdelnk file. If the directory you need does not exist, you might need to create it, with a name corresponding to the first part of the MIME type that you intend to create. For example, if you were defining MIME type text/README, you might create a directory called text in your personal mimelnk directory (if it didn't already exist), and create the file README.kdelnk in it. If you are a regular user, you must create the directory by hand in a terminal window. The merging of the system and personal directories interferes with normal file manager functionality in the mimelnk directory.

If you only plan to make a few MimeType.kdelnk files, you can actually just place them directly in the mimelnk directory, if you want, without creating the appropriate subdirectory. Although this is not recommended, it does not adversely affect the operation of the MimeType.kdelnk files you create.

After you are in the appropriate directory, follow these steps to create a new MIME type:

1. Select File, New, MimeType from the file manager menu.
2. In the dialog box that appears, change the name of the file from MimeType.kdelnk to a filename that corresponds to the second part of the MIME type you are defining. For example, if you are defining the MIME type text/README, name the file README.kdelnk.
3. Edit the properties of this file to define the new MIME type. Open the context menu of the file by right-clicking the file, and select Properties. Then select the Binding tab.
4. In the Pattern field, enter the pattern that will be used to identify files of this type. (For example, for README files, you might enter the pattern `README*;`.)
5. Enter a comment to associate with these files in the Comment field.
6. In the MIME type field, enter the actual MIME type string that you are defining (text/README, in this example).

ASSIGNING AN ICON TO A FILE TYPE

To specify an icon for the new file type, click the icon button and choose an icon from the dialog box that appears. Then select OK to save your changes to the kdelnk file.

ASSIGNING A DEFAULT APPLICATION FOR A FILE TYPE

To select the default application for a file type, select an entry from the Default Application drop-down list. If the application you want to use is not listed, follow the instructions in the section "Associating an Application with a File Type." Then return and follow these instructions to select the default application.

ASSIGNING AN ICON TO A SINGLE FILE

When you edit the MIME type for a file, it alters the icon for all files of that type. This might be a more general change than you want to make. If you want to assign an icon for a single file, you have two different options, depending on the type of file.

If the file whose icon you want to change is a program, you can avoid defining a MIME type—just for that one file,—by using an Application.kdelnk file instead. To use an Application.kdelnk file to assign an icon to a program file, follow these steps:

1. First, find or create an Application.kdelnk file for the program to which you want to assign an icon. Place it in your personal applnk directory.
2. In the Properties dialog box for the kdelnk file, on the Application page, enter the filename for the program in the Binary Pattern field.
3. On the Execute page, click the icon button and select an icon for the program.
4. Click OK to save your changes.

For a non-program, to assign the icon for a single file, you also use an Application.kdelnk file—but in a non-traditional way. In this case, you make a kdelnk file to serve as a "wrapper" for the file that you want to customize. Follow these steps to assign an icon to a single non-program file:

1. Create an Application.kdelnk file in the location at which you want the icon for the file to appear (on the Desktop, in a file manager window, and so on). Do this by selecting New, Application from either the Desktop context menu or the file manager main menu.
2. Enter the name of the file in the box that appears (leaving the .kdelnk extension).
3. Select Properties in the context menu of the item that appears, and select the Execute page of the dialog box.
4. Select an icon for this file by clicking the icon button.
5. In the Execute field, enter the application with which you want to open this file, along with the hardcoded filename. This is the equivalent of hard-coding the default application for the file.
6. In the Name and Comment fields on the Application page of the dialog box, enter the filename and a description of it.
7. Click OK to save your changes.

The kdelnk file is displayed with the icon that you selected, and you can launch (open) the file by clicking on it, just as you might if it were the real file.

Creating a wrapper in this way has its drawbacks. For example, the context menu for the icon displayed on the Desktop is not the same as for the original item. Also, dragging the kdelnk file is not the same as dragging the real file for which it is a wrapper. However, if all you want to do is get KDE to display a particular icon for a single file and specify a launch behavior for the file, this technique gets the job done.

ASSOCIATING AN APPLICATION WITH A FILE TYPE

When you associate an application with a file type, that application is listed in the context menu for files of that type. There might be multiple applications associated with a single file type, which means that the context menu might have many programs listed on it.

When this is the case, you can make one of the associated applications the default application for that type of file. For example, if you always want to run the WordPerfect word processing program when a WordPerfect document is clicked, associate the application WordPerfect with the MIME type for WordPerfect documents (if one was defined), and make it the default application for that type.

DETERMINING THE MIME TYPE OF THE FILE

The first step in associating an application with a file type is finding out what type of file you are dealing with. You can see a description of the type of a file in the status bar of a file manager window when you position the mouse cursor over the file. Sometimes, you can determine the type in which you are interested by looking at the complete list of MIME types. A list of defined MIME types is shown on the Applications page of the Properties dialog box for any Application.kdelnk file. For example, to see this list, select Properties from the context menu of the file /opt/kde/share/applnk/Kfind.kdelnk.

Then click the Application tab and look in the list box in the lower right corner of the dialog box.

As a last resort, you might need to actually examine the system MimeType.kdelnk files, in the system mimelnk directory, to determine if a MIME type is already defined for the file in which you are interested.

If a MIME type is not defined for your file, create one by following the instructions in the section "Defining a New MIME Type" earlier in this chapter.

FINDING OR CREATING AN APPLICATION.KDELNK FILE

After you have the MIME type for the file with which you want to associate a program, the next step is to find (or create) an Application.kdelnk file for the program.

If the program you are associating is on a KDE menu (either the system menu or your personal menu), the Application.kdelnk file already exists for it. In this case you can probably find the kdelnk file under the system or your personal applnk directory. If you are the system administrator and want to make the association for all the users on the system, edit the kdelnk file in the system applnk directory. Otherwise, modify the kdelnk file in your personal applnk directory.

If you need to create a kdelnk file for the application, follow the instructions in the section "Adding an Item to the Application Starter Menu." The kdelnk file must be under an applnk directory in order for it to be associated with a file type.

MAKING THE ASSOCIATION

After you have the MIME type and the Application.kdelnk file, it is very simple to make the association. Follow these steps:

1. Edit the Application.kdelnk file by selecting Properties from its context menu, and then selecting the Application page of the dialog box.
2. Find the MIME type in the list in the lower-right corner of the dialog box, and click the button with the arrow pointing left. This adds the MIME type to the list of Handled file types, shown in the lower left of the dialog box.
3. Click OK to save your changes.

Now open the context menu of a file of the indicated MIME type, and make sure that this application is listed.

To make this application the default application (the one that is used when a file is single-clicked), edit the MimeType.kdelnk file for that type, and change the Default Application setting on the Bindings page of the Properties dialog box for the kdelnk file.

CUSTOMIZING YOUR SYSTEM WITH THE CONTROL CENTER

The KDE Control Center enables you to customize many aspects of your KDE system. You can access the Control Center by clicking the Control Center icon on the Panel, or by selecting KDE Control Center from the Application Starter menu.

To navigate to an individual page of settings in the Control Center, follow the items in the tree view on the left side of the control panel window (see Figure 5.6). The tree view shows categories of configuration modules for your KDE system. Click a category to see the modules (individual configuration dialog boxes) for that category.

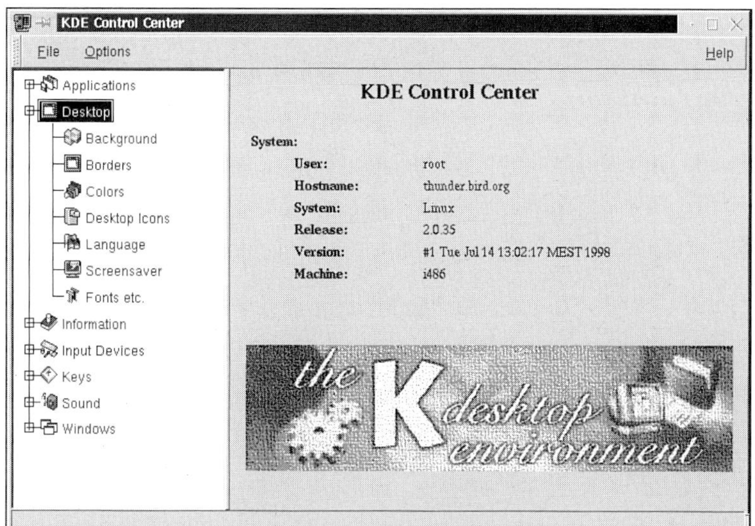

Figure 5.6
Use the Control Center to customize your KDE system.

The categories and configuration modules also appear on the Application Starter menu. You can access an individual configuration dialog box by selecting Settings on the Application Starter menu and navigating to the desired configuration dialog box.

Configuring the Desktop Attributes

One of the nice things about KDE is the vast number of items that are configurable. KDE enables you to configure many different aspects of the Desktop and Window appearance, including background images, icon appearance, fonts, and so on. Also, you can control in minute detail how the Desktop and windows behave. That is, how they respond to the mouse, how windows are loaded and activated, and what screen saver is used when your Desktop is inactive. These options and more are described in the sections that follow.

To configure the appearance and behavior of the Desktop, select one of the configuration dialog boxes underneath the Desktop category in the Control Center tree list. The Background, Colors, Desktop Icons, and Fonts dialog boxes enable you to customize the appearance of the Desktop, whereas the Borders, Language, and Screensaver dialog boxes enable you to configure the behavior of the Desktop.

Changing the Desktop Background

To change the background color or image of the Desktop, select Desktop, Background in the Control Center tree list. The dialog box that appears has four main areas:

- A list of (virtual) desktop names
- A preview monitor
- A color selection area
- A wallpaper selection area

Each virtual desktop in KDE can have its own background settings. This enables you to easily identify the virtual desktop you are on from its appearance. The first thing you need to do to change the background is select the virtual desktop that you want to change from the Desktop list.

For each desktop, you can choose a background consisting of either a single color, a two-color pattern, or a background image. If you choose a background image, you can configure how the image is displayed, or you can choose several images and cycle between them automatically.

As you make modifications to your selections, the preview monitor displays the background that results from your settings. Figure 5.7 shows the Background dialog box in the KDE Control Center.

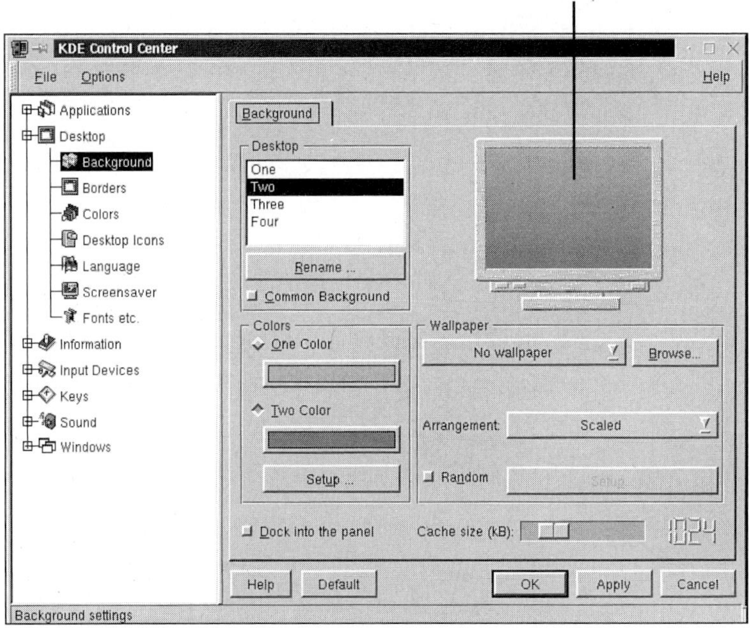

Figure 5.7
Select colors or wallpaper for the background of each virtual desktop in the Background dialog box.

SELECTING A COLORED BACKGROUND To put a single color or a simple two-color pattern on the background, select No wallpaper from the Wallpaper drop-down list. There are several different options for colored backgrounds:

- A single color
- A two-color horizontal gradient
- A two-color vertical gradient
- A two-color pattern

For a single-color background, choose the One Color option in the Colors area and click on the top color button. Then choose a color from the Select Color dialog box. You can choose one of the preset system colors, or you can select a specific color, either by typing in HSV or RGB values or by clicking on the hue and brightness areas in the upper right corner of the dialog box.

For any of the two-color backgrounds, select the Two Color option, select a second color, and click the Setup button. Select one of the following three options on this dialog box:

- Blend colors from top to bottom
- Blend colors from right to left
- Use pattern

If you select Use pattern, click a name in the Pattern name list. The preview area shows you each pattern as you select it. When you are done with your selections on the Setup dialog box, click OK (or Cancel).

SELECTING A BACKGROUND IMAGE To put an image on the background of a desktop, select an image file from the drop-down wallpaper list. By default, this list shows the image files located in /opt/kde/share/wallpapers, but you can browse and select an image file from a different location if you want.

After selecting an image, decide how you want the image arranged on the background. There are several different options, which are provided in the Arrangement list in the dialog box. Following is the meaning of each option:

- **Tiled**—Repeat the image vertically and horizontally, starting in the upper-left corner.
- **Mirrored**—Repeat the image vertically and horizontally, but flip some of the images top to bottom or left to right.
- **Center Tiled**—Repeat the image vertically and horizontally, starting in the center of the screen. This is a better tiling option for large images.
- **Centered**—Display the image in the center of the screen. The rest of the background is shown using the color settings.
- **Centered Brick**—Same as Centered, but cover the colored portion of the screen with a brick pattern.

- **Centered Warp**—Same as Centered, but cover the colored portion of the screen with a radiating line pattern.
- **Centered Maxpect**—Same as Centered, but enlarge the picture to fill as much of the screen as possible without changing its aspect ratio. That is, don't stretch the image more in one direction than another. This preserves the original look of the image.
- **Scaled**—Stretch the image to fill the whole screen.

SELECTING MULTIPLE IMAGES FOR THE DESKTOP Instead of having just a single image for a background, you can choose to have the Desktop cycle through multiple images. When you choose this option, KDE picks a new image to display after a specified interval, which keeps the background changing over time. Use the following steps to configure this feature:

1. To turn on this feature, select the Random option in the Wallpaper section of the dialog box.
2. Click the Setup button to select the files to use and to configure other settings for this option. The Random mode setup dialog box appears.
3. Now specify a set of files to use. In order to cycle through images, KDE needs to know the list of images to use. To cycle through all the files in a particular directory, select Pick files from directory and enter the directory name in the field at the top of the dialog box. To use a specific set of images, deselect the Pick files from directory option and enter the filenames in the Desktops list at the bottom of the dialog box. To add an item to the list, select an item on the wallpaper list in the Background dialog box, and then click the Add button in the Random mode setup dialog box.
4. Enter the interval between images in the Timer Delay in seconds field. This is the amount of time each image in the list (or directory) will be displayed onscreen.
5. Select the In order option if you want the images displayed in sequence, in the order shown in the list. If this option is left unselected, the images are shown in random order.
6. Click OK to save the setting in the Random mode setup dialog box, and OK or Apply to save the settings in the Background dialog box.

MISCELLANEOUS BACKGROUND OPTIONS There are a couple of other options available when configuring the backgrounds that are described here for completeness. These include adjusting the memory consumption of the background image, using the same background for all desktops, and docking the background dialog box on the Panel.

Under certain circumstances, the background image for the screen is kept in memory so that it can be refreshed quickly as the background is exposed during your KDE session. This is done if you select a non-tiled background (centered or scaled) or a colored background with more than a single color. If you are low on memory, you might want to use a single-color background or adjust the amount of memory that KDE uses to save the background image. There is a tradeoff—the more memory you allow, the quicker your Desktop background can update, but at the expense of other applications on your system. Select an amount of memory for the background image by dragging the Cache size slider. The number at the right of the slider changes to show you the amount of memory KDE uses for caching the background image.

If you prefer not to have a different background for each virtual desktop, select the Common Background option in the Desktop area of the dialog box. The items in the Desktop list are grayed, and the settings you choose for the background are applied to all the virtual desktops. You can change the names of the virtual desktops using the Background dialog box. To do so, select the virtual desktop whose name you want to change, and then click the Rename button and type a new name for the desktop.

If you want quick access to this configuration dialog box from the Panel, you can select the Dock in Panel option. This adds the dialog box to the Panel dock. Click on this item in the Panel to launch a window with display dialog boxes, including the Background dialog box.

CHANGING THE WINDOWS COLOR SCHEME

The Colors dialog box is used to change the color scheme for the windows of KDE and other graphical applications that you run.

A color scheme consists of twelve color selections for different parts of a program window and a contrast setting. The window preview area shows all the different parts of windows that are affected by the color scheme. As you make selections or adjust settings, the preview area changes to reflect the settings so that you can see how your new colors will look. Figure 5.8 shows the Colors dialog box of the Control Center.

To pick a predefined collection of color settings, just pick a scheme from the Color Scheme list.

To change one of the twelve color settings, either choose the name of the window part from the drop down list in the Widget color area or click the window part in the preview area. The window parts in the drop-down list are organized into five groups:

- Inactive window title bar
- Active window title bar
- Menu and border
- Regular window contents
- Selected (highlighted) window contents

All these parts have a foreground (text) and background color, with two additional colors being used for title bar blends (gradients).

After you have selected a window part, change the color for that part by clicking the color button and selecting a color from the dialog box that appears.

After making your selections, choose a contrast setting by dragging the Contrast slider bar between Low and High. The Contrast setting adjusts the colors used for the highlight and shadow of the three-dimensional frames around KDE interface elements. You can see the effect of the Contrast setting in the window preview area when you drag the Contrast slider.

After all your selections are made, click OK or Apply to save your settings (see Figure 5.8).

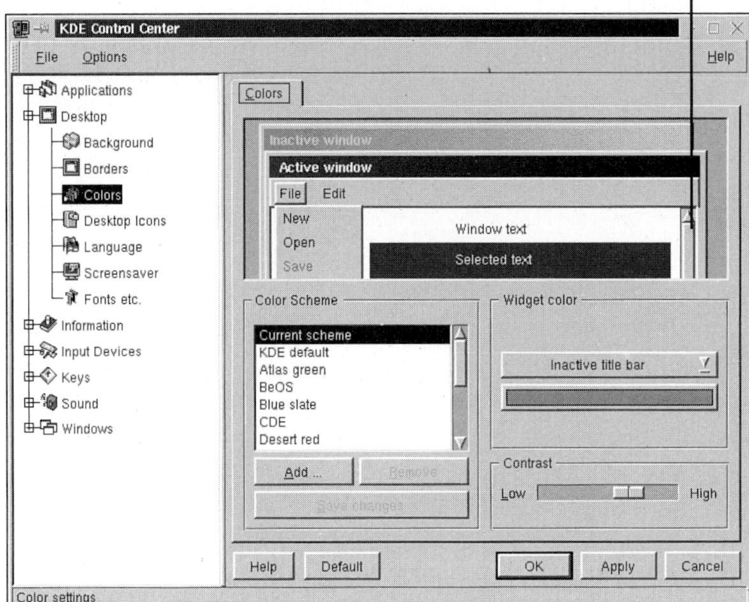

Figure 5.8
Customize window and text colors using the Colors dialog box.

If you switch between color schemes frequently, you might want to manipulate the color scheme list. To add the current collection of color settings to the list, click the Add button and type a name for your color scheme. To remove a color scheme, highlight a scheme in the list and click Remove. You can only remove color schemes that you have created, not any system color schemes.

Desktop Icons

The options on the Desktop Icons dialog box enable you to adjust the spacing of the icons on the Desktop and the way the text appears underneath the icons. Adjusting these settings can have a big impact on the overall readability of the items on the Desktop. Open this dialog box by selecting Desktop, Desktop Icons in the Control Center tree list, or by selecting Settings, Desktop, Desktop Icons from the Application Starter menu.

To change the spacing of the icons on the Desktop, enter numbers in the Horizontal Root Grid Spacing and Vertical Root Grid Spacing fields, or adjust the numbers with the scroll buttons. These numbers represent the distance between icons on the Desktop. Increasing the space between the icons makes it easier to read long entry names on the Desktop, and makes the Desktop appear less cluttered. However, it also increases the space each icon consumes on the Desktop, and makes it so that fewer icons can fit there.

You also use this dialog box to control the way that the text underneath each icon (the entry name) appears. Choose the color of the text by clicking the Icon foreground color button and choosing a color in the dialog box that appears. To make it so that the text is written directly on the Desktop background, select the Transparent Text for Desktop Icons option. This gives the text a transparent background. On a solid or uniform background, this looks good. However, if you have a busy, high-contrast image for the background, this can make the icon text very difficult to read. To make the icon text have a solid background color, deselect this option and choose a background color by clicking the Icon background color button.

DESKTOP FONTS

The Desktop Fonts dialog box enables you to customize the fonts used by the Desktop and the file manager for their text display. It also enables you to change the graphical look of the Desktop to match Windows 95, as well as the application menu bar placement.

There are five different Desktop text items whose fonts can be selected. These are listed in the box on the left side of the dialog box:

- **General**—This refers to almost all KDE text, including the text in the taskbar, menus, buttons, tabs, titles, and filenames.
- **Fixed**—Default fixed text font used by applications.
- **Window title**—The text in the window title bars.
- **Panel button**—The text for the virtual desktop buttons.
- **Panel clock**—The text for the clock on the Panel.

To change the font for one of these items, select it and choose a typeface, style (bold or italic), size, and character set for the desired font. Sample text at the bottom of the dialog box changes to reflect your choices. When you are done, click OK or Apply to save your changes.

To change the way graphical controls in KDE and its applications are displayed, check the Draw widgets in the style of Windows 95 box, and click Apply. Checkboxes, radio buttons, drop-down lists, menus, and other control elements (widgets) are now drawn and behave in a way similar to Windows 95.

To change the location of menu bars to the style used on Macintosh, select the menu bar on top of the screen. When this is selected, the menu bar for the current application is shown at the top of the screen instead of inside the application window. When you switch to a different application, the menu bar switches as well. This can save screen space when several applications are onscreen at once because the menu bars are not displayed for each application window separately.

CHANGING THE BEHAVIOR OF THE DESKTOP

The Borders dialog box of the KDE Control Center enables you to adjust whether you can switch between virtual desktops with mouse movement, and how windows are aligned next to each other and to the screen borders.

USING ACTIVE DESKTOP BORDERS By default, each virtual desktop in KDE acts like a self-contained screen. When you move the mouse to the edge of the screen, it just stops and doesn't allow you to go any further. However, with active Desktop borders, when you move the mouse to the edge of the screen, KDE automatically switches you to the virtual desktop that is logically adjacent to the current one in that direction. This is useful for switching desktops solely with mouse movement, and for directly dragging a window from one virtual desktop to another.

To switch between desktops by moving the mouse off the screen, select the Enable active Desktop borders option.

When this option is selected, it is possible to bump the mouse and switch desktops without intending to. To solve this problem, KDE allows you to set a switch delay, which causes the cursor to pause at the edge of the screen before switching desktops. Adjust the Desktop switch delay using the slider on this dialog box.

USING WINDOW MAGIC BORDERS Window magic borders is a KDE feature that helps you move windows so that they line up with each other or with the edge of the screen. Basically, it creates a *snap zone* where, if the edge of a window is placed, the window is moved to be immediately adjacent to the other object.

You can adjust the size of the snap zone for other windows or for the screen edge (or the edge of usable screen space, if you have the Taskbar or Panel enabled), using the Magic Border sliders.

SELECTING DEFAULT AND BACKUP LANGUAGES FOR THE DESKTOP

The Language dialog box allows you to select up to three languages for KDE applications. Messages for KDE applications have been translated to many languages, but not every message is available in every language yet. This dialog box enables you to specify the order in which to search for messages for your KDE applications. For example, suppose you select

Spanish, French, and German as your first, second, and third languages. Then when a KDE application tries to print a message, it first looks for the Spanish translation of the message. If a Spanish message cannot be found, KDE looks for a French message, and then for a German message.

CHOOSING A SCREEN SAVER

The Screensaver dialog box of the Control Center enables you to select a screen saver for your system and customize its settings. You can configure global options, such as the time before the screen saver kicks in, as well as options specific to the individual screen saver that you choose.

The Screensaver dialog box is divided into three major areas (see Figure 5.9):

- A preview monitor
- A screen saver list
- Some general screen saver settings

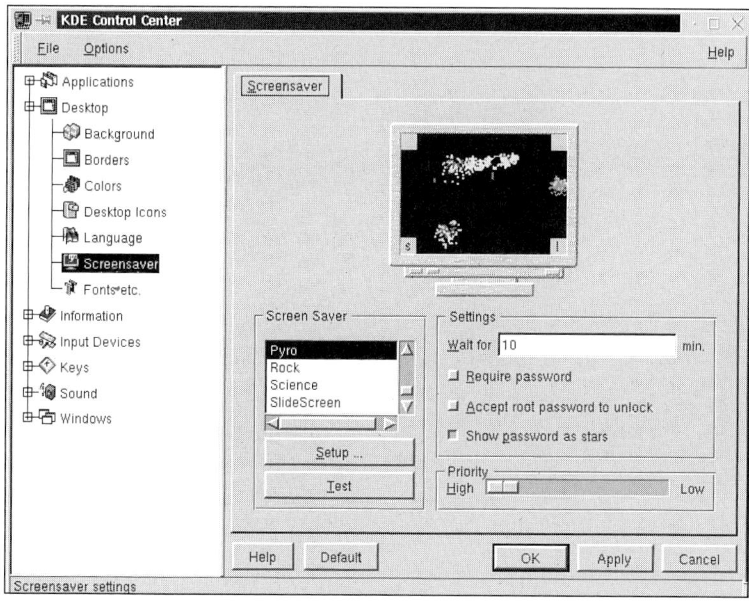

Figure 5.9
The Screen Savers dialog box enables you to pick a screen saver and adjust its settings.

To choose a screen saver, select the screen saver from the Screen Saver list. To customize the screen saver you have chosen, click the Setup button and edit the entries in the dialog box that appears. Each setup dialog box includes a preview window so that you can see the effect of your settings before you accept them.

To configure the amount of time before the screen saver starts, enter the number of minutes in the Wait for field of the dialog box. If you want the screen saver to lock the screen when it is activated so that a password is required to regain access to your machine, select the Require password option. You can also select whether you want KDE to echo password characters as stars as they are typed by selecting the Show password as stars option. If this option is not selected, the characters of the password are not echoed at all when the password is typed. To allow the use of the root password as well as your regular user password to unlock the screen, select the Accept root password to unlock option.

The Priority setting controls how much processor time is devoted to the screen saver when it is active. (This corresponds to the Linux *nice* value of the screen saver process). If you want the screen saver to run at a higher priority than other processes on your machine (so that the animation is smooth, for example), drag the slider to High. If you want other processes to have priority, slide it to Low.

To test the screen saver settings on the full screen, click the Test button.

The KDE screen saver system supports the capability to immediately start the screen saver—or lock the screen—by placing the mouse pointer in a corner of the screen and leaving it there for five seconds. This behavior is customized using the preview monitor in this dialog box.

The preview monitor has four gray rectangles in the corners. To set the action for a particular corner, right-click the gray rectangle for that corner and select one of the following options:

- **Ignore**—Do nothing when the mouse is in this corner.
- **Save**—Start the screen saver.
- **Lock**—Start the screen saver and lock the screen, requiring a password to regain access to KDE.

If you choose either Save or Lock, a letter appears in the rectangle to indicate your selection.

After adjusting the screen saver settings, click OK or Apply to save your changes.

WINDOWS

Another set of options that control window appearance and behavior can have a dramatic effect on the overall look and feel of your Desktop. The options are found in the dialog boxes in the Windows category in the Control Center.

The options in this category enable you to customize the appearance and behavior of application windows, including the button layout and other title bar characteristics, as well as aspects of the window manager, such as the placement policy for new windows. There are even options for fine-tuning the mouse and keyboard bindings, enabling you to adjust every action you perform with these input devices so that the behavior of the system is completely customized to your preferences.

CHOOSING WHICH BUTTONS TO DISPLAY IN WINDOW TITLE BARS

The Buttons dialog box enables you to choose which buttons to use on the title bar, and which side of the bar to put them on.

There are five different title bar buttons that you can adjust: Minimize, Maximize, Sticky, Close, and Menu. You can choose to position each button on the left or right side of the title bar, or to leave the button off the bar.

To select a position for each button, click one of the options for that button. You are allowed to put no more than three buttons on one side of the title bar. As you change the settings, the preview bar at the top of the dialog box displays how the title bar looks with those settings.

Buttons stack automatically on each side of the bar, with the buttons lower on the list on the outside of each edge. This supports the most common button placement preferences.

Click OK or Apply when you are done.

SELECTING OTHER TITLE BAR ATTRIBUTES

The title bar dialog box enables you to select the text alignment for the text in window title bars, the background appearance of title bars, and a few other related attributes.

To set the text alignment, choose one of the options (Left, Middle, or Right) in the Title Alignment section of the dialog box.

Title bar backgrounds can be displayed in one of four ways, using the following title bar appearance options:

- Shaded vertically
- Shaded horizontally
- Plain (single color)
- Pixmap (image)

The first two options display a gradient of colors in the indicated direction. The colors used for the gradients are the ones configured in the Desktop, Colors dialog box of the Control Center. The Plain option displays just a single color for the title bar background. The Pixmap option enables you to select a pixmap to tile on the background of the title bar. When this option is selected, you click on the Active pixmap and Inactive pixmap buttons to select which image files to use.

The Mouse action setting determines what operation to perform on the window when the left mouse button is double-clicked on a title bar. Most of the items in the list of actions are options from the window menu, which have been discussed before. However, the Shade and Unshade options are only available here.

The Shade option eliminates the content area of a window, leaving only the title bar. You can think of it as operating the window like a window shade. If this option is selected, when a title bar is double-clicked, the window rolls up. Double-click the title bar again to unroll the window (restore it).

Finally, the Title Animation setting controls whether a title that is too long for the title bar slides back and forth so that all of it can be seen. If you set the title animation value to 0, no animation occurs. Otherwise, titles that don't fit slide back and forth, with the speed depending on the value of the setting.

SETTING WINDOW MANAGER POLICIES

Settings in the Windows, Properties dialog box of the Control Center enable you to adjust window manager policies. These policies affect the appearance of windows when they are moved and resized, as well as how windows are maximized, placed, and selected (receive focus) by the window manager.

The options in the top part of this dialog box determine how windows look while they are being moved or resized, and how the Maximize operation works on a window. During a resize or move operation, you can choose to have windows appear with their contents intact, or as transparent rectangles. When windows are drawn with their contents during these operations, it requires more time to update the display during the move or resize operation. If you are on a slow machine, this can result in the operation appearing choppy or jerky.

To display the contents of windows during move or resize operations, select the appropriate options on this dialog box. However, if you want faster (smoother) performance for move or resize operations, deselect these options.

If you choose to display contents in resizing windows, you can also choose to have windows update their contents while they are being resized, using the Resize animation setting. Use the slider to specify a speed. If you select a value other than None, when you resize a window its contents are redrawn *while* it is being resized. This gives you a visual indication of how the program will lay out the window contents at various window sizes, so you can select the best size. However, it also makes the resize operation slower, and it can be choppy-looking.

Customizing the Mouse

The settings on the Windows, Mouse dialog box of the Control Center enable you to completely customize how the mouse interacts with KDE window elements. For each mouse button, you can configure the action to perform when that button is clicked on different window elements of both active and inactive windows.

The different window elements for which you can customize behavior are as follows:

- Active window title bar and frame
- Inactive window title bar and frame
- Inactive inner window
- Entire window (including the inner window, title bar, and frame)

For active inner windows, mouse clicks are delivered to the application without interpretation. For other window elements, the Mouse dialog box is used to configure what action to perform on the window element for the indicated mouse click.

The following actions are defined on the different drop-down lists in the dialog box:

- **Activate**—Makes the window the currently active window.
- **Raise**—Brings the window to the foreground.
- **Lower**—Pushes the window to the background. These options, when used alone, allow you to raise or lower a window without affecting its active status.
- **Operations menu**—Displays the window options menu.
- **Toggle raise and lower**—Switches the window between foreground and background on the display.
- **Pass click**—After performing other window manager actions, delivers the mouse event to the program that owns the window as well. This allows a single click to perform both a window operation and an application function. For example, a single click can activate a window and also set the text cursor position in an editor.
- **Move**—Moves the window by dragging it.
- **Resize**—Resizes the window by dragging an edge.

These mouse actions are shown in various combinations in the lists in the dialog box. Different actions are applicable to different window elements and window states (active or inactive). The action list for each mouse button and window element combination has options that are appropriate for that combination. For example, all the mouse operations on Inactive window elements include the Activate action.

Use the settings on the dialog box to configure the actions you prefer for each of the mouse operations shown.

CONTROLLING MISCELLANEOUS BINDINGS AND HANDLING WINDOWS

The settings on the Advanced dialog box control a few miscellaneous keyboard and mouse bindings and enable you to customize how the window manager treats special windows. This gives you great flexibility in handling special situations required for certain types of windows.

The top part of the dialog box enables you to customize the Ctrl+Tab and Alt+Tab key accelerators. Normally, when you press Ctrl+Tab, KDE switches you to the next virtual desktop. Deselect the option Ctrl+Tab walks through desktops to turn this feature off.

In KDE, the Alt+Tab key combination switches between application windows. By default, it only switches between windows on the current desktop. To have Alt+Tab switch between windows on all the desktops, deselect the option Alt+Tab is limited to current desktop. When you use Alt+Tab, you can configure it for one of the following two modes:

- **KDE mode**—A dialog box shows you the icons for the windows as you Alt+Tab through them.
- **CDE mode**—As you Alt+Tab, the windows are activated, but no dialog box is shown.

Select one of these modes to use for Alt+Tab switching.

The second part of this dialog box enables you to configure the KDE window manager to handle certain windows in a special way. This is useful for special types of windows in certain situations. For example, you can specify that the window for a clock program is to automatically be stuck to the background when it starts up. This causes the clock to appear in the same position on each virtual desktop, without you having to manually make the window sticky each time you run the program.

The following is a list of the options for special handling that the window manager can perform on a window:

- **Have tiny decorations**—This option makes it so that the window appears with no title bar. That is, the window is only shown with a frame. This is useful for windows that you don't need to manipulate (move, iconify, and so on) very frequently. It reduces the overall screen real estate used by such windows.
- **Have no decorations**—This option shows the window without any decorations (no title bar and no frame). Be careful with the use of this option because it makes windows very hard to manipulate. For some windows, however, this improves the way they look on the screen.
- **Never gain focus**—When this option is used, the window can never become the active window. You cannot click the window to activate it or Alt+Tab to the window. This is useful for windows that are purely informational.
- **Start as Sticky**—This starts the window as sticky, which means that it appears in the same position on every virtual desktop.

- **Be excluded from session management**—When this option is used, the window is ignored during KDE shutdown. This means that KDE does not complain about the window during the logout, which makes the logout operation smoother. This is useful for non-KDE application windows that you know contain no unsaved data that might be lost during a shutdown.

In order to assign special handling to a window, select one of the special handling options, and then add the title or class of the windows that are to be handled in that way to the lists shown.

INPUT DEVICES AND KEYS

Using the dialog boxes under the Input Devices and Keys categories, you can configure many settings for the keyboard, as well as a few mouse characteristics. In the area of keyboard settings, KDE allows you to customize a great many details about your keyboard, including how to handle international keyboards (that is, the exact codes produced by every key on your keyboard). Also, you can use the dialog boxes in the Keys categories to configure the keyboard shortcuts used for the Desktop and KDE applications.

CONFIGURING KDE FOR INTERNATIONAL KEYBOARDS

The International Keyboard dialog box enables you to configure KDE to support one or more keyboard mappings. These settings enable you to use other keyboards, besides American ones, with KDE and its applications. To do this, you must use the International Keyboard program. This program starts by default, and is usually shown docked in the Panel. If you need to start the International Keyboard program by hand, select System, International Keyboard Layout from the Application Starter menu.

SELECTING AND SWITCHING TO AN INTERNATIONAL KEYBOARD To switch to an international keyboard setting, you need to select the keyboard maps you want to use, adding them to the Keyboard maps list on the General page of the dialog box. A keyboard map is a set of codes that are transmitted by the keyboard, and the characters to which they correspond in a particular language. Several keyboard maps have been defined for many different language/keyboard combinations. To add a keyboard map to the list of maps you want to use, click the Add button next to the list, and select an appropriate keyboard map from the list that appears.

When the International Keyboard program is active, you can switch between the keyboard maps listed by clicking on the International Keyboard program icon in the Panel or by using a special key combination. To select the key combination to use to switch keyboard maps, select an option in the Switch list, and then click Apply to save your changes.

To actually switch keyboard maps, press the key combination that you selected in the Switch list.

Typing Alternate Characters Some keyboard maps allow more than one character to be assigned to an individual key on the keyboard. This is useful when you are using a language with more characters than there are keys on the keyboard. These extra character assignments are called alternate symbols. To configure the key used to type alternate symbols, select an option in the Alt Switch list, and click Apply to save your changes.

To type an alternate symbol, press and hold down the alternate switch key you chose, and then press the appropriate key on the keyboard.

Changing Attributes of the International Keyboard Indicator When you are using the International Keyboard program, an indicator for the program is displayed, normally on the Panel (docked). This indicator shows the currently selected keyboard map (as an abbreviation), and indicates the status of the caps lock and alternate state, under certain conditions.

To change the appearance of this indicator, modify the settings on the Style page of the International Keyboard dialog box. You can change the colors used for the text of the indicator and the background colors used to indicate caps lock and alternate states, and you can adjust the font used for the indicator.

Normally, the International Keyboard program indicator is positioned on the Panel. To configure the indicator somewhere else on the screen, click the StartUp tab and deselect the Docked option. Then select a screen location from the Place list.

You can exit the International Keyboard program, or reconfigure it, at any time by right-clicking the International Keyboard indicator, and selecting Quit, or Setup, respectively.

Adjusting Keyboard Settings

The Keyboard dialog box under the Input Devices category in the Control Center enables you to configure a few minor things about the keyboard. These include whether the keyboard repeats when a key is held, and the keyclick volume. Your hardware might not support the capability to adjust the keyclick volume.

To adjust these settings, select the appropriate options on the Keyboard dialog box.

Changing Shortcut Keys

KDE allows you to modify the key combinations used for keyboard shortcuts for applications and for the Desktop itself. This enables you to customize the key sequences for operations such as Open, Cut, and Paste, and for Desktop actions such as switching between virtual desktops or raising and lowering windows.

The keyboard shortcuts are configured using the Standard Keys and Global Keys dialog boxes, under the Keys category in the Control Center. The Standard Keys dialog box configures common keyboard shortcuts used by many different KDE applications, and the Global Keys dialog box configures keyboard shortcuts used by the Desktop and window manager of KDE.

These dialog boxes operate in a similar way. To change the key shortcut for an action, follow these steps:

1. Select the action from the action list.
2. Select the custom key.
3. Select the key modifiers to use with the key by selecting some combination of Shift, Ctrl, or Alt.
4. Click the button to the right of the modifier checkboxes, and press the key on the keyboard that you want to use.

To revert to the original shortcut setting, select the Default key option.

On the Global Keys dialog box, you can save a set of customizations and give it a name by clicking the Add button in the Key scheme area of the dialog box. This enables you to switch between sets of keyboard shortcut definitions quickly by selecting an entry on the Key scheme list.

SETTING MOUSE BEHAVIOR

The options on the Input Devices, Mouse dialog box settings enable you to configure both the acceleration characteristics of the mouse and the mouse button mapping. The acceleration settings enable you to adjust how the mouse responds to quick and slow movement, which can reduce hand strain while using the mouse. The button mappings are used if you need to switch the way the mouse buttons are recognized by KDE if you are left-handed.

MOUSE ACCELERATION Mouse acceleration is used to enable you to more quickly move the mouse to a distant part of the screen, while still allowing precise positioning of the mouse pointer during small mouse moves. Mouse acceleration saves you from having to move your hand a long distance to move the mouse a corresponding long distance on the screen. With mouse acceleration, when you move the mouse quickly, the pointer moves a longer distance across the screen. When you move the mouse slowly, the mouse moves in standard increments.

Two settings control the mouse acceleration. The Acceleration setting determines how fast the mouse moves when it is accelerated, and the Threshold setting controls how fast the mouse must be moving before it is accelerated. Drag the sliders to configure these settings, and then click the Apply button. After setting these values, experiment with them by moving the mouse around the screen, manipulating menus, and positioning the mouse over items. You can restore the original settings, if you need to, by clicking the Default button and then clicking OK or Apply.

MOUSE BUTTON MAPPINGS The Button mapping option enables you to decide which buttons are assigned to the different mouse actions. If you select the left handed mapping, the actions are switched so that the right mouse button is used to launch things and the left button is used to pop up context menus.

SOUND

Two dialog boxes in the Control Center enable you to adjust the sounds in your KDE system. The Bell dialog box enables you to adjust the sound made by the ASCII bell character. The System Sounds dialog box enables you to associate sounds with various KDE system events.

ADJUSTING THE SOUND MADE BY THE BELL CHARACTER

The Bell dialog box enables you to adjust three characteristics of the sound made by the bell character when it is emitted by a program.

The three settings are the Volume, Pitch, and Duration of the tone. Adjust these settings to your liking, and click the Test button to hear the sound that you have configured.

The bell sound is usually generated by the internal speaker of your computer (not via a sound card and external speakers), which is usually not a very flexible piece of hardware. Often, hardware limitations make it impossible to configure one or more of the bell sound characteristics (often, changing the volume is not supported). If changing a setting appears to have no effect, it is probably due to hardware limitations of your system.

Click OK or Apply to save your changes.

ASSIGNING SOUNDS TO SYSTEM EVENTS

The System Sounds dialog box enables you to specify the sounds that are to be played when certain events occur in KDE. For this to work, the sound system (sound device) for your OpenLinux system must be configured and operating.

To turn on the KDE event sound system, click the Enable System Sounds box. To add files to the list of sounds for your system, drag WAV files from a file manager window to the Sounds list.

To associate a sound with a particular event, select it in the Events list, and select a sound in the Sounds list.

To preview a sound, use the Test button to play a sound in the list.

After you have made your changes, click OK or Apply to save them.

OTHER CONTROL CENTER DIALOG BOXES

There are other items in the Control Center which are either covered in other chapters of this book, or are not related to configuring and customizing KDE.

The Desktop Manager dialog box under the Applications category is covered in Chapter 6, "KDM." The Panel configuration dialog box is covered extensively in Chapter 4.

The items in the Information category are used for displaying the status of various system components, and are not related to customizing KDE.

THE FONT MANAGER

The font manager enables you to customize the fonts used by KDE applications. Basically, it enables you to trim down the list of fonts in the KDE font selection dialog box. It is fairly common to have many X11 fonts on your system, only some of which are really very useful. By selecting only a few useful fonts with the Font manager, you can reduce the list of fonts in the font dialog box. Therefore, when you select a font inside a KDE application, instead of having a long list of X11 fonts to choose from you see a shorter list of the just the fonts you actually want to use.

To start the font manager, select System, Font Manager from the Application Starter menu. The font manager window has three dialog pages. The first page of the dialog box shows a list of all the available X11 fonts and a list of the currently selected X11 fonts to be used with KDE. To add an X11 font to the list that KDE uses, select it in the Available X11 Fonts list and click the Add button. To remove a font, select it in the Fonts made available to KDE list and click the Remove button.

The other two pages of this dialog box, the Font Explorer and the Raw X11 Font List, enable you to experiment with and examine X11 fonts to see which ones you want to use with KDE.

Not all KDE applications use the KDE font selection dialog box. Some still let you select directly from a list of all X11 fonts. The behavior of these applications is not altered by the settings you make in the font manager.

SUMMARY

This chapter covered customization and configuration of your KDE system. This includes making new entries on your Desktop and on the Panel and Application Starter menus. You add items to the Desktop using the drag-and-drop techniques or by using the New option on the Desktop context menu. You add applications to the Application Starter menu by creating kdelnk files in the appropriate applnk directory on your system.

Step-by-step instructions were provided for creating several special types of entries on your Desktop, including programs, devices, links to Internet documents, and printers. Using kdelnk files to define these and other items in your system enables you to make an easy-to-use, object-oriented work environment for your daily use.

You can also modify the KDE file typing system by adding new MIME types to customize the appearance and behavior of the files and programs on your system. These are added either to the system or to your personal mimelnk directory.

Also, the different configuration dialog boxes in the KDE Control Center were discussed.

These dialog boxes enable you to customize many aspects of the KDE system, including the Desktop appearance and behavior, the appearance and operation of program windows, and many keyboard, mouse, and sound settings.

For further information related to this topic, refer to the following chapters:

- Chapter 4 discusses basic KDE components and navigation. Many of the basic navigation and keyboard shortcut features described in Chapter 4 can be modified through configuration options in the KDE Control Center.
- Chapter 7 and Chapter 8, "Koffice," describe KDE applications that are affected by the settings described here.
- Chapter 39, "Customizing X," describes several customizations you can make to your X Window system. Many of these customizations are similar to options that are described here.
- In order to use sound with your KDE system, you might need to install a sound driver for the OpenLinux kernel. See Chapter 18, "Kernel Modules," or Chapter 42, "Multimedia," for information about installing sound support in the kernel.

CHAPTER 

KDM

In this chapter

Normally, when you start OpenLinux, the system presents a graphical login prompt. When you successfully enter your name and password,KDE starts and you can begin working in your desktop environment. However, in prior versions of OpenLinux, and with many other Linux distributions, the default startup mode is to present a character-based login prompt. This is also true of OpenLinux 2.2 if you install using `lisa` instead of LIZARD (see Chapter 2, "Installing OpenLinux"). When you install with `lisa`, your OpenLinux system presents a character-based login prompt and, after logging in, you are left at a console shell prompt. To start graphical operation, you must type `kde` and wait for the X system and KDE to take the screen and initialize.

KDM is the *KDE Desktop Manager* and is used to provide a graphical login directly into KDE. KDM enables you to bypass this interaction with character mode. Instead, when your system boots it goes directly into graphical mode, and you are presented with a graphical prompt for your name and password.

This is the same functionality that is provided by the X session manager, XDM, except that KDM has several notable improvements. One major difference is that KDM can be configured using graphical dialogs. Also, KDM supports multiple session types, and the capability to show a list of allowed users. Finally, a user can shut down the system directly from the KDM dialog box (if KDM is configured to allow it).

KDM allows you to customize the login process for your OpenLinux box, to simplify it or enhance it either for yourself or for others (such as your spouse or children) who might use your Linux machine.

How KDM Works

In this section, you will learn how KDM fits into the overall initialization process on your machine. If you have installed using `lisa`, you will need to configure certain parameters on your system to use KDM during system startup. Also, other scripts can be edited to provide complete customization of the initialization process.

The OpenLinux Initialization Process

In order to understand how KDM works, you need to understand a little about how your OpenLinux system initializes. Chapter 12, "System Initialization Under OpenLinux," covers the initialization process for OpenLinux, including a discussion of runlevels. This won't be covered in detail here, but the following list shows the sequence of programs that are run during this process, without KDM (this is the sequence of initialization steps that are performed when you have installed with `lisa` instead of LIZARD):

1. **`LILO`**—The boot loader (usually `LILO`) runs, enabling you to select an OS option.
2. **`vmlinuz`**—The kernel loads and runs. This is usually the file vmlinuz in the root directory.
3. **`init`**—After initializing its own drivers and internal state, the kernel runs `init` as the first, or root, process. All other processes in your OpenLinux system are descendents, in one way or another, of `init`.

4. **rc scripts**—init reads the file /etc/inittab, and determines the default runlevel. Based on the runlevel, it runs a series of rc scripts in one of the directories under /etc/rc.d. Normally, the default runlevel is 3, which brings up the machine in multiuser, networking, character-based mode.
5. **getty, login, bash**—init also starts a getty process for each virtual console. The getty process issues the character mode login prompt, and waits for input. When a name is entered, getty transfers control to login. If a valid name and password are entered, login starts a shell (usually bash) for the user.
6. **kde**—When you want to start your graphical environment, run kde, which is a script that runs xinit.
7. **xinit, kdeinitrc**—Behind the scenes, a program called xinit is run, which handles client and server options for X, your graphical environment. Unless you have made customizations to your system, xinit usually runs /etc/X11/xinit/kdeinitrc to prepare your system for starting X client software, and for X itself.
8. **X**—The X server is loaded by xinit, and your machine switches into graphical mode.
9. **startkde**—kdeinitrc usually runs startkde as its last step. startkde runs a whole series of processes that make up your KDE system. At this point, the Desktop, Panel, window manager, and file manager are all running and available for use. In addition, several other daemons are running in the background to support your KDE session.

When KDM is configured to run on your system (which is the default configuration for most users), the sequence of actions that init takes to start up your system are slightly different. getty processes are still run to accept login input on the character-mode virtual consoles. However, kdm is also run to start the X system and provide a graphical login.

The flow of control when KDM is installed is as follows (note that the first few steps are the same):

1. **LILO**
2. **vmlinuz**
3. **init**
4. **rc scripts**—The default runlevel is 5, which brings up the machine in multiuser, networking, X session mode. A different set of rc symlinks is used in this case. However, for OpenLinux the set of rc scripts used in runlevels 3 and 5 is identical.
5. **getty, login, bash**—These are loaded as with runlevel 3. However, the default login prompt that is shown to the user comes from virtual console 7, the graphical login displayed by kdm.
6. **kdm**—init starts kdm directly, when runlevel 5 is specified in /etc/inittab (after you have set it up). kdm uses the information in the file /opt/kde/config/kdm/xdm-config to specify its behavior and startup parameters.
7. **X**—The X server is loaded by kdm, and your machine switches into graphical mode.

8. **`Xsetup_0`, `GiveConsole`**—Behind the scenes, `kdm` runs the scripts `/usr/X11R6/lib/X11/xdm/Xsetup_0`, and `/usr/X11R6/lib/X11/xdm/GiveConsole`. `Xsetup_0` invokes `kdmdesktop`. At this point, a graphical login screen is presented to the user.
9. **`Xsession`**—When a valid name and password are entered into the login screen, the script `/usr/X11R6/lib/X11/xdm/Xsession` is run with a parameter indicating what type of session to start. If the user chose to run a KDE session, `startkde` is run.
10. **`startkde`**—`startkde` starts the KDE programs that comprise the desktop system.

MODIFICATIONS TO CONFIGURE KDM

If you installed OpenLinux using `lisa` instead of LIZARD, you need to modify /etc/inittab to enable KDM as the default login mechanism for your machine. You must be logged in as root in order to make this change.

CHANGE INITTAB FOR RUNLEVEL 5

Change the file /etc/inittab to start in runlevel 5 instead of runlevel 3 by default.

Tip

Basically, the `init` program uses the runlevel to determine the appropriate set of processes to start on your machine when it boots up. Runlevel 3 is used to have the `init` process start your machine in character-based mode, and runlevel 5 is used to start it in graphical mode. Chapter 12 describes the different runlevels in more detail.

`cd` to the /etc directory. Now, edit the inittab file, and change the line containing `initdefault`, so that the default runlevel is 5. (Change the 3 to a 5.)

Save your changes, and quit the editor.

Now, switch to runlevel 5 by typing `telinit 5`. If your machine does not switch to graphical mode, reboot.

TROUBLESHOOTING THE KDM SETUP

There are a couple of ways to diagnose and troubleshoot `kdm` if something goes wrong with the setup. First, because you are in X, you can always switch to a text-mode console using the Ctrl+Alt+F1 key combination (or some other Ctrl+Alt+F*x* combination, for the virtual console of your choice). Error messages from `kdm` are posted to the file /etc/X11/kdm/xdm-errors.

If you have trouble, switch your default runlevel in /etc/inittab back to 3 so that you can at least boot normally. Then try logging in as root and running `kdm` by hand (that is, from the character shell prompt). Watch the output on the virtual console, and look in the xdm-errors file for clues as to what part of the process is failing.If you need to, you can put additional programs in the script `/etc/X11/kdm/Xsetup_0` to give you control or status information during the startup sequence. This script is executed during the startup sequence for `kdm` itself, and can be used to start other diagnostic programs for use when KDM is active.

Disabling KDM

If you want to boot your OpenLinux system into a character-based login screen, you might want to disable KDM. To disable KDM as root, edit the file /etc/inittab and change the default runlevel from 5 to 3, on the line of the file that includes the keyword `initdefault`.

Using KDM

If everything is set up correctly, a screen similar to the one in Figure 6.1 appears (excepting, of course, for that handsome tbird user icon). This happens every time you enter runlevel 5, which is every time you start your machine.

Figure 6.1
KDM login screen.

Select one of the user icons shown, or type a username into the Login field of the dialog box. If you want, select the type of session you want from the Session Type list. You can choose between `kde`, `fvwm`, and `failsafe` modes.

Enter a password, and press Enter or click on the Go! button. You are logged in to the system, and KDE starts with the desktop for the user account you selected.

To shut down the system from this dialog box, click on the Shutdown button, and select one of the following options on the shutdown dialog box:

- Shutdown
- Shutdown and restart
- Exit `kdm`

The shutdown option shuts down OpenLinux (not just `kdm`) completely. You need to reboot your machine by turning it off and back on again. The option Shutdown and restart shuts OpenLinux down, but then reinitializes the machine so that it reboots again automatically. Select Exit `kdm` to end the `kdm` program. This is normally not very useful because under most configurations `kdm` immediately restarts and presents you with another login screen.

Tip

If you are not the root user, you need to type the root password into the text entry box on the Shutdown dialog box in order to shut down the machine.

KDM CONFIGURATION

You can configure almost everything about the KDM screen, from the background to the fonts for the text of the dialog box. You can adjust KDM settings using options in the KDE Control Center.

To open the Control Center, click the Control Center button on the Panel, or select KDE Control Center on the Application Starter Menu. In the Control Center, click the Applications category, and select the Login Manager dialog box.

There are several different pages of options for the desktop manager on this dialog box, including Appearance, Fonts, Background, Users, and Sessions.

The settings on each of these pages of the dialog box are described in the following sections. After you have adjusted the settings on the different pages of the dialog box, click OK to save the settings. They will be used the next time `kdm` presents the login screen.

THE APPEARANCE PAGE

The Appearance page of the Desktop Manager configuration dialog box enables you to adjust the string used to greet users of your machine, as well as the logo, the style of controls, and the language for the login screen.

At the top of the login screen, `kdm` displays a greeting string. To customize this string, enter a new phrase in the Greeting string field of the dialog box. If you use `HOSTNAME`, in all capital letters, as part of the string, `kdm` substitutes the name of your machine in place of the `HOSTNAME` string. This is handy in circumstances where you allow remote users to access your machine over the network because they can identify which machine they have attached to. (See Chapter 40, "Controlling X Resources," for information on how to use the `xhost` program to enable users to access your machine remotely.)

To change the logo on the login screen, click the logo button, and select a new image using the Select Icon dialog box. There are several icon (and image) galleries to choose from. Switch to a new gallery directory by selecting it from the drop-down list at the top of the Select Icon dialog box. When you select an image in the Select Icon dialog box and click OK, the image is copied from whatever gallery it is in to the directory /opt/kde/share/apps/kdm/pics.

You can also set the image file for the logo by typing the full path for the file into the KDM Logo field, or by dragging an image file and dropping it on the logo button.

Caution

If you change the logo, make sure that it fits in the login dialog box. The login screen does not resize automatically. If the logo is too large, it forces other fields off the dialog box, making it impossible to type in a name and password (and essentially making it impossible to use the dialog box to log in to the machine).

The default image used for the logo is /opt/kde/share/apps/kdm/pics/col_logo.xpm, which is a 100×110 color xpm image file. Choose a logo that is approximately this same size, or smaller.

To change the style of the window controls used by `kdm`, select an option from the GUI Style list. The Motif option shows lists and radio buttons (in the Shutdown dialog box) in a style that is probably familiar to most UNIX users. The Windows option causes `kdm` to show these items using the same style as Windows 95.

Finally, to change the language used for the buttons and list items on the login screen, select a language from the drop-down Language list.

The Fonts Page

The Fonts page of the Desktop Manager dialog box enables you to choose the font that is used for the messages and labels on the login screen.

There are three different categories of messages that can be adjusted:

- **Greeting**—Select this to set the font for the string at the top of the login dialog box, which welcomes users to your system. Usually, this is configured with a fairly large font size to set it off from the rest of the dialog box.
- **Fail**—Select this option to adjust the font for the login failure message. The failure message, usually `Login failed`, appears when an invalid account name and password are specified in the login dialog box. This string appears briefly in the lower-left corner of the dialog box. By default, this font is bold so that the user will notice it.
- **Standard**—This is the font used by all other dialog box messages, including field and button labels, list elements, and user names.

To change the font for one of these categories of messages, select the category from the drop-down list, and click the Change Font button. Choose options on the Select Font dialog box that appears, and click OK. A sample string using the font characteristics that you have selected is shown on the Font page of the dialog box.

The Background Page

On the Background page of the dialog box, you can select the characteristics of the background window used for the login dialog box. You can select either a solid color, a gradient, or an image file to be displayed as the background on the login screen.

To use an image on the background of the login screen, select an image from the wallpaper list. You can choose to have the image tiled, centered, or scaled on the screen. The login dialog box is centered on the screen when it is displayed, so a small image might be covered up if you choose to center it.

To have a solid color as the background of the login screen, select None in the wallpaper area. Then choose a color by clicking the top color button and selecting a color from the dialog box that appears. To use a gradient as the background, select either the Horizontal Blend or Vertical Blend options, and set the colors for the gradient using both color buttons in the dialog box.

As you make your selections, the preview monitor shows how the background screen looks with the new settings.

THE USERS PAGE

The Users page of the dialog box enables you to select which, if any, user images are presented in the login dialog box presented by `kdm` (see Figure 6.2).

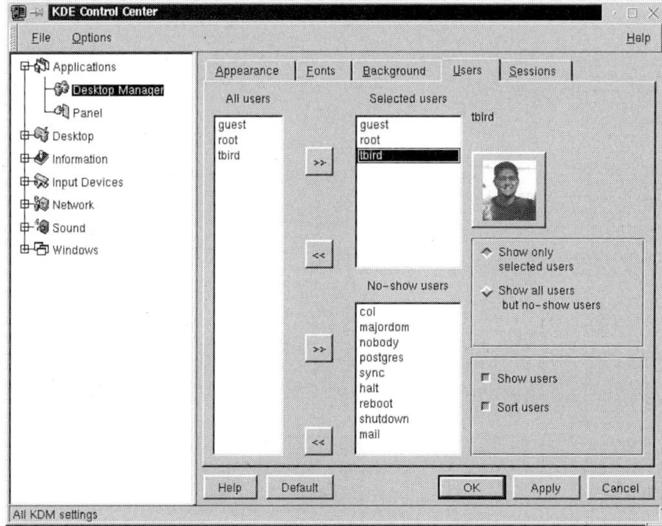

Figure 6.2
Edit the user options for the Desktop Manager with the Users page of this dialog box in the Control Center.

There are three lists that control which users appear in `kdm`: all users, selected users, and no-show users. To move users from one list to another, click the >> and << buttons. A user can only be on one list at a time.

Which of the lists are used is determined by the options on the right side of the dialog box. Select one of the following options:

- Show only selected users
- Show all users but no-show users

The list of users indicated by your selection is shown in the login dialog box the next time it is shown.

You can select the image to be shown for each user that appears in the dialog box. First, select the user whose image you want to define. Then click the image button and select an image from one of the galleries in the list; or drag an image and drop it on the button. A copy of the image is placed in the following directory: /opt/kde/share/apps/kdm/pics/users.

The image has the same name as the user, with the .xpm extension. For example, the image filename for the tbird user account is tbird.xpm.

The default images for root and other users are 62×63 color XPM files, but KDE doesn't appear to be too finicky about the exact dimensions of the image files.

To have the users who are displayed in the login dialog box sorted alphabetically, select Sort Users. If this option is not selected, the users are displayed in the order in which they are encountered in the password file of the machine.

Finally, for security reasons, you might not want to show the user list at all. To prevent the user list from appearing, deselect the Show Users option. This is really only a consideration for `kdm` if the machine that you are configuring allows remote X access or will be placed in a open area for public use.

How is exposing your user account names a security risk?

You might wonder how exposing just the names of your users, without their passwords, constitutes much of a security risk. In order to break into your machine, a cracker must determine both an account name and a password. If a cracker knows the names of users on your system, it makes that part of their task much easier. Often, especially in a true multiuser configuration, users cannot be counted on to create difficult-to-guess passwords. Given this, it's much better to hide the account names so that the cracker has to guess two things instead of just one.

The Sessions Page

The Sessions page of the dialog box enables you to configure aspects of the shutdown feature of the Desktop Manager, as well as customize the session list in the login dialog box.

Controlling Shutdown Operations

The upper part of the dialog box enables you to control who is allowed to shut down your OpenLinux machine from the login dialog box, and from where they can do it. Also, you can specify the exact commands to be run to shut down and restart the machine.

The following options are on the Allow to Shutdown list:

- **None**—No one is allowed to shut down the machine from the login dialog box.
- **All**—Anyone can shut down the machine.
- **Root Only**—The shutdown operations are only available if the last logged in account was root.

- **Console Only**—The shutdown operations can only be performed by a user who is physically at the machine (not by a remote user).

Also, the commands used to shut down the machine can be specified. To set the command used to shut down (and halt) the machine, type a command in the Shutdown field of the dialog box. To set the command used to shut down and restart the machine, enter a command in the Restart field of the dialog box. The commands default to `/sbin/shutdown` and `/sbin/reboot`, respectively, if these fields are left empty.

MANAGING THE SESSION LIST

A session under X consists of a set of graphical services made available to you and the X environment in which they run.

`kdm` can be used as the session manager for other types of X sessions, in addition to a `kde` session. The list of sessions is presented in the login dialog box, and the user can select one during the login process. For example, if you want to sometimes use the `fvwm` window manager (which is included in your OpenLinux system for the purpose of backward compatibility), you can add an `fvwm` session to the session list.

By default, OpenLinux provides the sessions `kde` and `failsafe`. If a user selects the `kde` session, KDE and its supporting programs are launched when the user logs in. The `failsafe` session provides only a single xterm and is used primarily in emergency situations, when the rest of the system is damaged and does not come up properly.

To add a new session value to the list, enter a name in the New Type field, and click the Add button. To remove a session from the list, select it in the Available types list, and click the Remove button.

Each session value on the list needs to have a corresponding entry in the case statement in the file /etc/X11/xdm/Xsession. Look at the existing entries in the file to see how these entries are formatted. Basically, the section in the Xsession file for the new case you are adding should perform the operations necessary to start the window manager for the session you are defining. The `Xsession` file is a shell script. If you need more information on modifying this or other shell scripts on your system, please refer to Chapter 13, "Customizing Your Shell Environment," which has a section on shell programming.

SUMMARY

In this chapter, you learned about the K Desktop Manager, which provides your OpenLinux system with its graphical login prompt.

The modifications necessary to get KDM working on your system (if it was not configured by default) were presented. Several KDM configuration options were also discussed.

The following chapters cover material related to the Desktop Manager:

- Chapter 5, "Customizing Your Desktop Environment," covers navigating items in the KDE Control Center. Several of the configuration options for `kdm` are similar to options that can be configured for KDE in general, and similar techniques are used to adjust them.
- Chapter 12 discusses the startup process of OpenLinux. Setting up KDM involves modifying the initialization process, and this chapter gives additional details on how this process works.
- Several chapters in Part V of this book, "X Window," cover additional details about setting up and configuring X. In particular, Chapter 39, "Customizing X," discusses configuration files for X.
- Chapter 40 has sections that cover `xdm` and X session management. `xdm` is a non-KDE program that performs the same functionality as `kdm`.

CHAPTER 7

KDE Applications

In this chapter

Along with the basic Desktop and file manager, KDE provides a wealth of programs and applications for your use. These range from small utilities to full-blown office productivity applications. This chapter describes in detail some of the important KDE applications that are included in OpenLinux. The KDE suite of office applications are covered in Chapter 8, "KOffice."

As the KDE project progresses, more and more applications become available. It's impossible to cover every aspect of every application, but most of the applications that are included with OpenLinux are at least mentioned so that you are aware of their existence. Most applications include at least a limited amount of online help that you can see at any time by selecting Help, Contents on the menu, or by pressing the F1 key. For non-critical applications, this chapter focuses only on concepts, tips, and tricks that are not mentioned in the online help. If you have any questions about using a particular program, be sure to check the online help for that application.

One thing you need to know about KDE is that it is a work in progress. Some KDE programs are fully functional, and are essentially complete. Other programs are not quite finished, and are missing some functionality. For a program to be included in OpenLinux, it must at least be stable under normal circumstances, and it must support some basic functionality for its intended use. That is true of all the programs that are described in this chapter. Although a program might not be entirely polished, if it is included in OpenLinux, it does *something* useful.

You can usually see what the general maturity level of a program is by looking at version number in the About box. The application About box is available by selecting the appropriate About option on the Help menu. If the version number is less than one, the program is not complete yet. If the program is missing functionality that you need, you might want to check on Caldera's Web site or the KDE Web site to see whether a newer version of the program has been made available. To see a list of packages that have been updated for your OpenLinux distributions, examine the following page on the Caldera Web site:

`http://www.caldera.com/support/download.html`

To see the current versions of all the KDE applications, look on the following page on the KDE Web site:

`http://www.kde.org/applications.html`

Almost every KDE application is available on the Application Starter menu. If you want to place an application on the desktop Panel, or on the Desktop itself, detailed instructions are provided in Chapter 5, "Customizing Your Desktop Environment." Basically, you just open a file manager window to the system applnk directory (/opt/kde/share/applnk) and drag the kdelnk file for the application to either the Panel or the Desktop.

Note

Because KDE and its programs are available in several different languages, the name of a KDE program, as it appears in the KDE menus or elsewhere, might be different than the name of the actual program binary. Throughout this chapter, you might see the same program referred to by both its (translatable) program name and its executable filename.

For example, the terminal emulation program is called `Terminal` in the menus and in its title bar. However, the actual program binary name is `kvt`.

CORE APPLICATIONS

This section discusses the core system programs and utilities that are central to KDE. These are applications that are related to the KDE system itself, as opposed to applications or programs that perform their own isolated function.

These core applications and utilities are found on the main area of the Application Starter menu and on the Applications and System submenus of that menu.

APPLICATIONS COVERED ELSEWHERE

Many of these, like the file manager, are covered extensively in other chapters of this book. To avoid unnecessary duplication, this chapter merely includes a reference to the chapter in which the following programs are covered. However, other core KDE programs are discussed here in detail.

Table 7.1 shows references for some of the core programs that are covered elsewhere in this book.

TABLE 7.1 CORE PROGRAMS DISCUSSED IN OTHER CHAPTERS

Application	Reference
File manager	Page 77
File manager (Super User Mode)	Page 56
Menu Editor	Page 111
KDE help	Page 62
KDE Control center	Page 118
`Appfinder`	Page 110
`Fontmanager`	Page 137
International Keyboard	Page 133
`kpackage`	Page 351

USING THE FIND FILES UTILITY

The Find Files utility enables you to search for files or directories on your file system using a number of different search criteria.

Figure 7.1 shows the Find Files dialog box before it has been used to find some files. When files are found that match the selected criteria, they are shown in a list that appears at the bottom of the dialog box. The files in the list can then be manipulated a number of ways, using menu options or the buttons on the button bar of the utility. (Figure 7.2, later in this chapter, shows the `find` utility with a list of found files.)

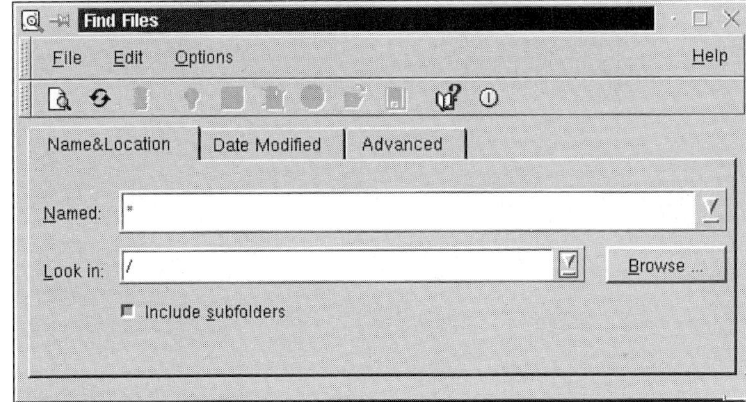

Figure 7.1
Use the Find Files utility to search for files using a variety of criteria.

FINDING FILES AND DIRECTORIES

The `find` utility scans your file system and tries to match each item it sees with the criteria you have specified on the pages of the `find` dialog box. To use this utility, first enter the search criteria on the pages of the dialog box, and then click the Start Search button; or select File, Start search in the `find` utility menu.

When you enter or select multiple criteria using the pages of the `find` dialog box, the criteria combine. This means a file must match *all* the criteria that you specify in order for it to be displayed in the match list. It is easy to forget which options you have entered or selected on the different pages of the dialog box; it is therefore easy to select options that conflict with each other. When starting another search with the dialog box, reset the options on the Date Modified and Advanced pages of the dialog boxes by clicking the New Search button (with the two circular arrows) on the button bar.

If your search is taking too long, you can cancel it by clicking the Stop Search button, which has a stoplight as its icon.

SEARCHING BY FILENAME AND LOCATION The most common type of search that you use with this utility is by filename or wildcard specification. To do this, enter the filename or expression in the Named field. A list of previously used names or expressions is available in a drop-down list, which you can access by clicking on the control at the right of the field.

You also need to specify a location to search. You can search the whole file system by entering a slash in the Look in field of the dialog box. Unfortunately, this takes a long time because the utility scans the entire hard disk. If you know which subdirectory to look under, you can considerably shorten the time it takes to search by entering the appropriate subdirectory name in this field.

You can also select whether to look in just the indicated directory, or in the directory and all its subdirectories, by clicking the Include subfolders checkbox.

You can use either a simple filename (for example, index.html) or a wildcard expression in the Named field of the dialog box. Standard shell wildcards are allowed. Table 7.2 shows how characters are matched in a wildcard expression.

Table 7.2 Characters Used in Wildcard Expressions

Expression	Matches	Example	Match	Non-match
char	The indicated character	a.html	a.html	b.html aa.html a.txt
*	Zero or more of any character	*.html	abc.html	abc.txt
?	One of any character	??.html	ab.html	a.html
[*chars*]	One of the indicated characters	[abc].html	a.html	ab.html d.html
[*char-char*]	One of the characters in the indicated range	[a-zA-Z] .html	a.html B.html	$.html
[^*chars*]	One character *not* in the indicated set	[^xyz] .html	a.html	x.html

For example, to search for HTML files in the directory /home/httpd/html (and all its subdirectories), follow these steps:

1. In the Named field, enter `*.html`.
2. In the Look in field, enter `/home/httpd/html`.
3. Select Include subfolders.
4. Click the Start Search button.

The results of this search are shown in Figure 7.2.

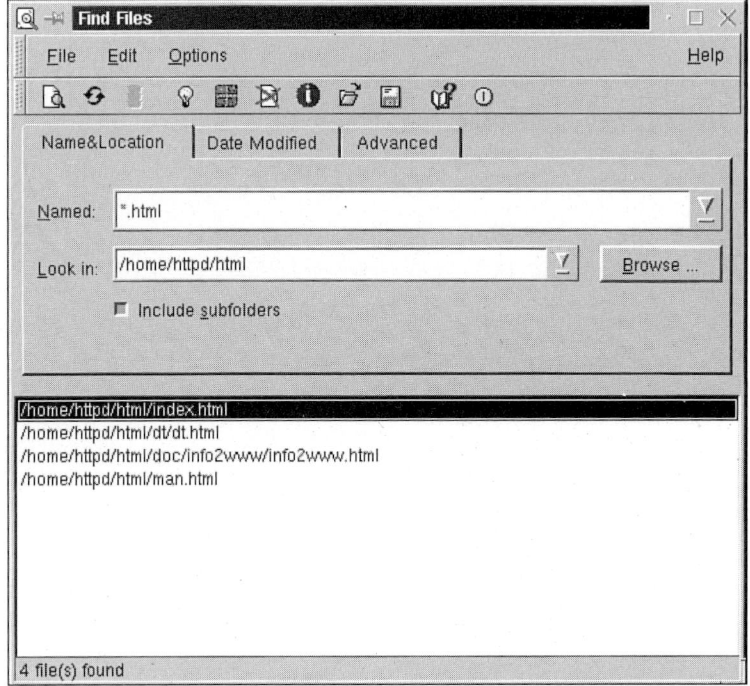

Figure 7.2
Results of a simple search.

SEARCHING BY OTHER CRITERIA You can also perform searches using other criteria, including the date of last modification, the file size, what the file contains, and the type of file it is.

Using the options on the Date Modified page of the dialog is especially useful for finding files that have changed during some particular time frame. You can specify the time frame either as a range of dates or as a number of months or days relative the current date. For example, to find all the files in your home directory that you have worked on in the last two months, use the following steps:

1. Click the Name&Location tab.
2. In the Named field, enter `*`.
3. In the Look in field, enter ~ (to specify your home directory).
4. Select Include subfolders.
5. Click the Date Modified tab.
6. Select Find all files created or modified.
7. Select During the previous [*blank*] month(s), and enter `2` into the months field.
8. Click the Start Search button.

Use the options on the Advanced page of the dialog box to find files using other criteria. To find files of a given type, select a file type from the drop-down list labeled Of type. Because this type is combined as a search criteria with the filename specification on the

Name&Location page of the dialog box, make sure that the two entries don't conflict. For example, if you search for files of type Gzip, with a filename specification of *.txt, you probably will not match any files.

To find files that contain a specific phrase, enter the word or phrase in the Containing Text field.

Some Broken Features of the `find` Utility

The Find Files utility is one of those KDE programs that is useful but not quite complete. As of this writing, there are several things that don't work with the utility. For example, searching does not work for many of the types on the Of type list. That is, when you select one for your search criteria, the utility might not find any files at all, even if there are some that match that type. The types that appear to work are the ones that can be determined from the file's attributes, rather than by its extension.

Also, the feature that is used to find files by the text they contain does not work. These problems might be fixed by the time this book is printed, but if you experience difficulty with either of these features, it is probably not because you are doing something wrong.

To find files of a particular size, use the Size is controls. Select one of the comparison options, At least or At most, and then enter a size in Kilobytes to match against. This is very handy for finding the files in your file system (or in a particular subdirectory) that are consuming the most space.

MANIPULATING MATCHED FILES

When the files are displayed, a number of operations can be performed on them. To operate on a single file, just click it. To operate on a set of files in the list, click the files on which you want to operate, or click and drag the cursor over the files to select them. To remove a file from the selected list, click or drag on the file that is already selected.

To open a file or directory, or to launch a program, double-click its entry in the list. You can also select the item and then select File, Open from the Find Utility menu or click the Open button on the button bar.

Using menu options or buttons, you can delete selected items, store them in an archive, change the properties of an item, or view the contents of the directory that contains them.

When you add the files to an archive, you are prompted for the name of the archive. If the archive does not exist, it is created—otherwise the files are added or updated in the existing archive. By default, TAR archives are supported, but the online help for the `find` utility shows you how to add support for additional kinds of archives. To use the TAR archive type, make sure that the filename you enter when you create the archive ends in the extension .tar.

SAVING THE LIST OF MATCHING FILES

Finally, it might be useful to save the list of matching files for future use. Click on the Save Search Results button to save the file list to a file. To change the file where the list is saved, select Options, Preferences, and click the Saving page of the dialog box; then adjust the settings on the page. You can choose to save the list in plain text or HTML format.

Other preferences (Archivers) are not configurable via the Preferences dialog at this time. However, you can adjust the Archivers preferences by editing the file ~/.kde/share/config/kfindrc. See the online help for details.

`kedit`—KDE'S BASIC TEXT EDITOR

`kedit` is KDE's basic text editor. Although it is not intended to be a replacement for full-function editing programs, it supports all the basic operations that are needed for simple text editing—and it is easy to use. You can use it to compose email or to edit, view, or print simple text files. To work with more complicated documents, including documents with formatted text and embedded images, figures, and tables, use the full-blown word processor, KWord, instead. KWord is covered in Chapter 8. If you are editing programs or scripts, consider using one of the powerful programmer editors, `kwrite`, `XEmacs`, or `vi`, instead.

To start `kedit`, select Applications, Text Editor from the Application Starter menu. Also, `kedit` is the default application for most types of text files on your system. Therefore, when you click a text file, the file is opened with `kedit` automatically.

Most of the features in `kedit` work as you might expect them to. You can open files, create a new file, make selections with the mouse and cut, copy, and paste them, and perform a number of other operations.

To spell check your document, select Edit, Spellcheck from the menu. The Spellcheck dialog box appears, and your document is scanned for misspelled words. Each misspelled word that is found is shown in the dialog box. The dialog box might show a replacement word and a list of suggestions. To replace the misspelled word, select a word on from the list of suggestions or type a new spelling in the Replacement field, and then click Replace. Click Replace All to replace all occurrences of the word in the document. Click Ignore to ignore this instance of the word or click Ignore All to ignore every instance of the word in the document. Click Add to add the word to your private word list (in the file .ispell_*language* in your home directory). To discontinue spell checking your document before you reach the end, you can select Stop or Cancel. Clicking Stop preserves the changes that you have already made, and clicking Cancel aborts any changes you have made.

Note

The spell checker in `kedit` requires that the `ispell` program and an accompanying word file be installed. If these are not installed on your system, you can install them easily from the CD. Log in as root, make sure that the OpenLinux CD-ROM is mounted, and look in the directory /mnt/cdrom/Packages/RPMS. You need to install the `ispell` program package and the package that contains the word files for your languages. You can use `rpm` to do this (see Chapter 15, "Software Package Management," for detailed instructions on installing packages).

To print the current document or the current selection in the document, click on the Print Document button or select File, Print from the menu Then select options in the dialog box that appears.

To mail the current document, click on the Mail Document button, or select File, Mail from the menu, enter an email address and subject line in the dialog box that appears, and then click the Mail button in the dialog.

When you have finished editing or viewing the file, save your work by choosing Save or Save as from the File menu, or just Exit.

A few other items are also worth mentioning here:

- Change the word-wrap column or turn word wrapping on or off using the settings in the Kedit Options dialog box. Select Options, Kedit Options to see this dialog box.
- To toggle auto-indenting (auto-indent moves the cursor to the same column under the start of the previous line when you press Enter), select Options, Auto Indent.
- To reformat the paragraph that the cursor is in, press Ctrl+J. This combines lines and wraps words so that the text is well-formed within the current wrap margins.

`kwrite`—The KDE Programmer's Editor

Another editor that comes with the KDE system is `kwrite`. This is similar to `kedit`, except that it has some special features for working with program source code files. These features include the following:

- Support for bookmarks
- Options for advanced kinds of text selection
- Commands and options to control source code indentation
- Word wrap and tab handling
- Syntax highlighting

These features allow for much more convenient manipulation of source code text; they are described briefly in the sections that follow.

To start `kwrite`, select Applications, Advanced Editor from the Application Starter menu.

Using Bookmarks

You can use the bookmarks feature of `kwrite` to help switch quickly between different areas of the source code on which you are working.

To set a bookmark, select Bookmarks, Set Bookmark from the menu and choose a bookmark number. Or, select Bookmarks, Add Bookmark, and the next available bookmark number is used. As you assign bookmarks, they are added to the bookmarks menu. To clear all bookmark assignments, select Bookmarks, Clear Bookmarks.

To go to a bookmark, press Alt and the bookmark number, or select the bookmark in the bookmarks menu.

ADVANCED KINDS OF SELECTION

To select a region of text, drag the mouse over the text while holding down the left mouse button.

To control the kinds of text selection that are performed in `kwrite`, select Options, and configure the select options in the dialog box that appears. The following select options are available:

- **Persistent Selections**—Continue to keep text selected, even when other text is being edited.
- **Multiple Selections**—Allow multiple regions of text to be selected at the same time. This only works if you also select Persistent Selections so that previously selected text stays marked when you make a new selection.
- **Vertical Selections**—Use vertical, or columnar, selection when the region is more than one line. Usually, a text selection includes all the text on the lines in the marked block. This option makes it so that just the text inside the rectangular region of the block is selected. This option can also be toggled directly on the Options menu, or by using the F5 keyboard shortcut.
- **Delete on Input**—Replace the selected text with newly typed characters.
- **Toggle Old**—When used with Persistent and Multiple selections, toggle nested selections. That is, when making a new selection, deselect any previously selected text, and vice versa.

CONTROLLING SOURCE CODE INDENTATION

To indent a block of text, select the text (as described previously), and select Edit, Indent from the menu. To unindent a block, select Edit, Unindent.

To have `kwrite` automatically indent the next line of text to match the current line when you press return (or when the line wraps), select Options, Options, and select the Auto Indent option in the dialog box that appears.

To back up a line to match the indentation of the previous line when using backspace at the beginning of a line, select the Backspace Indent option in the same dialog box.

SETTING TAB, WRAP, AND OTHER TEXT HANDLING OPTIONS

The tab and wrap settings in the Options dialog box enable you to adjust several aspects of `kwrite` tab and word wrap handling.

To configure tab handling, set the Tab Width in the dialog box. To have `kwrite` replace tabs with an appropriate number of spaces, as they are typed, select the Replace Tabs option.

To configure word wrapping, set the value for the wrap margin in the Wrap Words At field, and select the Word Wrap option. Select Wrap Cursor if you want the cursor to obey the wrap margin when you move it with the arrow keys on the keyboard. Without this setting, the cursor might be positioned outside the area that is defined by the wrap margins.

A few miscellaneous text handling options are also available in the Options dialog box. These are as follows:

- **Remove Trailing Spaces**—Remove blank spaces at the end of a line when it is modified.
- **Auto Brackets**—Automatically enter the matching closing brace, bracket, or parenthesis when an opening one is typed.

USING AND CONFIGURING SYNTAX HIGHLIGHTING

One important feature of a good programmer's editor that is supported by `kwrite` is the capability to alter the appearance of items in source code, depending on the type of each item. This is called *syntax highlighting* because it relies on the editor to recognize the syntax of the programming language and to highlight different text items in the source code for that language accordingly.

Different programming languages support different types of syntactical items. When you open a document in `kwrite`, it tries to automatically determine the appropriate highlighting scheme to use for that file, based on the extension or file type of the document. To select a specific highlighting scheme, select Options, Set Highlight from the menu, and choose an appropriate language from the list.

You can alter the appearance of individual items for a particular scheme by following these steps:

1. Select Options, Highlight to access the highlight configuration dialog box.
2. Select the scheme to be edited on the Highlight drop-down list.
3. Select an item on the Item list.
4. Deselect the Default option in the Item Style area of the dialog box.
5. Configure the appearance of the selected item using the options in the Item Style and Item Font areas of the dialog box.
6. Repeat steps 3–5 for the items you want to customize.
7. Click OK to save your changes.

GAMES

Numerous games come with the KDE system. They come in a wide variety, ranging from classic strategy games to board games and card games. There are even a few arcade-style action games. This section highlights some of the games that come with KDE, and provides a short description of each one. These games are found under the Games menu on the Application Starter menu.

STRATEGY GAMES

KDE provides several strategy games, which are games in which you use your intellect to solve a puzzle created by the computer.

In KBlackBox, there are several balls hidden inside a black box. You are allowed to shoot laser rays into the box, which can be reflected or absorbed by the balls in the box. You decide where to shoot rays into the box, and the ray either emerges from another point on the outside edge of the box, or doesn't emerge at all. Based on shooting several rays into the box, you deduce the location of the balls in the grid of the box. The object is to correctly determine the positions of the balls using the fewest possible rays.

Minesweeper is a classic game of mines and flags, familiar to Windows users. In this game, the computer places several mines on a grid. You click the cells in the grid to uncover the squares that do not contain mines. When a square is uncovered, if it is next to other mines (horizontally, vertically, or diagonally), the number of mines it is next to appears in the square. Using this information, you try to deduce where the mines are and place flags to mark them in order to avoid clicking on those squares. In this game, the object is to uncover every empty square, without hitting a mine, using the clues provided.

SameGame is an interesting game of strategy in which you are presented with balls of different colors. When you click on a ball of a particular color, that ball and all the balls of the same color that are adjacent to it are removed from the board. Your score is increased, depending on the number of balls in the group that you remove. The larger the group, the higher your score is for removing that group. When a group is removed, the balls on top of that group fall down, making new groups as the colored balls fall next to each other. The object is to remove the balls in a way such that the largest possible groupings can be removed, to achieve the highest score. An extra bonus is given if all the balls are removed from the board.

In Sokoban, the object of the game is to move a set of crates (that look like crystals) into their correct positions in a warehouse—on top of the green circular pads. The tricky thing is that you can only push a single crate at a time. You also can't pull a crate. Furthermore, the crates are large enough to block your path. Although it seems simple enough, it is very easy to move a crate into a position that makes it impossible to win the level. The game provides several different skill levels, and you can bookmark your spot in the game and return to it later.

BOARD GAMES

KDE provides a few board games, as well, to enable you to pit yourself against the computer or against another opponent.

Abalone is a reproduction of a popular six-sided board game, played by two opponents. Each player has several pieces that can be combined and moved in order to push the opposing player's pieces off the board. When one player has pushed six of the other player's pieces off, that player wins. This is a tricky game to learn, but it is quite fun. Unfortunately, you can only play against the computer, not another human opponent.

Tip

Pay particular attention to the instructions for moving the pieces in the online help (see page 2, "Rules of the Game"). The moves that are allowed are not complex, but several different mouse actions are used for different types of moves, and it's easy to get confused about how to accomplish the move you want to make.

Konquest is a game of intergalactic takeover. This game requires multiple (human) players, and involves sending fleets of ships to take over neutral and opponent planets, and to protect planets that you have already captured. Planets have different strengths and production capacities, and the object is to build your empire (and to eventually conquer the whole galaxy) by strategically capturing planets and increasing your fleet.

Reversi is a game involving two-colored discs. Each player tries to capture the discs of the other player by sandwiching them between the discs of their color. When a piece is captured, it is turned over (changed to the color of the new owner). Players take turns playing pieces and capturing their opponent's pieces until the board is full or until no one can take a turn. The player with the most pieces at the end of the game wins.

Card and Tile Games

Card and tile games provide an interesting way to pass the time and strategize against the computer.

Patience provides several different versions of solitaire card games. With these games, the object is generally to combine, rearrange, and take cards off of several stacks. If you can successfully uncover all the cards in the stacks (or rearrange the cards according to a particular pattern), you win the game. Patience supports nine different solitaire games. This includes the widely known versions of solitaire that most people are familiar with, as well as a few other tricky versions. See the online help for the rules for each game.

Poker is a popular card game played with hands (sets) of cards. The object is to create the highest valued hand to beat your opponents.

Mahjongg and Shisen-Sho are tile games. In these games, the computer lays out a pattern of tiles, and the object is to remove the tiles in pairs. Only certain tiles can be removed at any step, and the trick is to remove pairs of tiles without getting stuck. In Mahjongg, only tiles on the outside edge and top of a pile can paired and removed. In Shisen-Sho, tiles on the outside that are connected in certain ways can be removed. For each of these games, hints are available, and you can undo a move if you need to.

ARCADE GAMES

Finally, there are a few action games to test your reflexes and your quick thinking.

Asteroids is the classic space-ship shoot-em-up in which you move your ship through a treacherous asteroid field, breaking apart and destroying the rocks in the field. When you clear an asteroid field, you move to the next level. Higher levels have more asteroids to clear. In general, try to avoid breaking too many asteroids into small chunks at once, or it is very difficult to survive.

In SnakeRace, you move your snake and eat apples in order to escape each level. As you eat, your snake's length, your score, and the difficulty increases. You snake is constantly moving, and the object is to avoid obstacles, including other snakes, and clear the level of apples. You can create your own levels for this game—see the online help for details.

Smiletris is an interesting variation on the famous Tetris game. Blocks that are composed of different icons fall, and you must position each block so that the icons in the falling block line up with the icons that are already on the screen. When they do, the icons that are on top of each other crack and eventually disappear, and you score points. The object is to get as many points as possible before the screen fills up with blocks.

KDE also provides the venerable Tetris action-strategy game of falling blocks. This game is so well-known that it seems unnecessary to describe it here. To play this game, select Sirtet (Tetris spelled backwards) from the Games menu.

GRAPHICS

In the Graphics program group, there are several programs that are related to viewing and manipulating images or special document formats. Use the programs in this group to express your creativity or to work with files that are otherwise inaccessible.

GRAPHICS VIEWING AND MANIPULATION PROGRAMS

KDE provides several programs for viewing and working with image files. This includes a general purpose paint program and the special purpose icon editor, for creating and manipulating image files and icons, respectively. A powerful image viewing program is provided as well.

PAINT

The Paint program, `kpaint`, is a basic drawing program. It enables you to create or edit images in a variety of different formats. At the time of this writing, it still had a few rough edges (it is beta quality), but you can use it to produce images, or just to doodle. Figure 7.3 shows the main drawing window of `kpaint`.

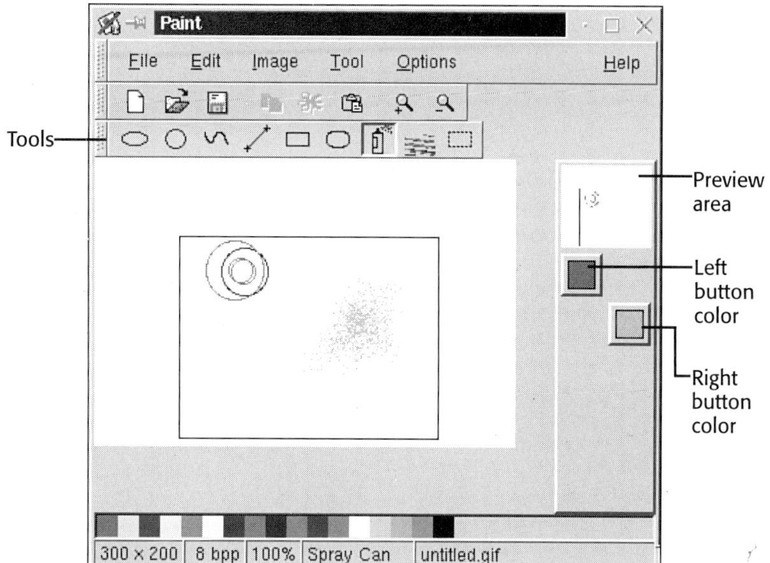

Figure 7.3
`kpaint` is a general-purpose drawing program.

To begin using `kpaint`, start it by selecting Graphics, Paint from the Application Starter menu. You can choose to edit an existing image, or you can create a new image. Select either Open or New on the File menu to start working. When you choose File, New, you are asked to enter the size of the image that you want to create (its height and width in pixels). If you need to, you can change the size of the image later, but it is better to start with the right size now if you know it.

To edit the image, select a tool from the tool bar or from the Tool menu, and select a color to work with. The following tools are available:

- Ellipse
- Circle
- Freehand pen
- Line
- Rectangle
- Rounded box
- Spraycan
- Text
- Selection box

All these tools draw the indicated item, except for selection box, which enables you to select a region on the image to cut, copy, or move.

To select a color, click on the colored buttons in the preview area, and then select a color from the dialog box that appears. The upper-left button corresponds to the left mouse button, and the lower-right button corresponds to the right mouse button. After your colors are selected, you can draw using your tool with either the left or right mouse button, using the color for that button.

You can adjust the line and fill attributes of the tools in the Tool Properties dialog box. Select Tool, Tool Properties to see this dialog box. You can adjust the line thickness and whether the outside line for an object is drawn solid or dashed. Also, you can select whether to fill in objects and, if so, what fill pattern to use.

A few special features are also available on the different menus of the program. To resize the image, select Image, Resize, and enter a new height and width in the dialog box that appears. If you stretch or shrink the image, some of the original image quality might be lost. You can also edit the palette of the image by selecting Image, Edit Palette. When you change a color in the palette of the image, all the pixels of that color are changed to the new color. To control the image format that is used to save the file, select File, Image Format, and choose a file format in the dialog box that appears.

Be sure to save your image out when you finish editing it.

Tip

If you are serious about graphics, consider using the GNU Image Manipulation Program (GIMP), which is a high-end drawing and image manipulation program. This is not a KDE program, but it provides a complete environment for professional quality image editing. It is installed by default in OpenLinux, and you can start it by running GIMP from a terminal window.

This large program requires a substantial amount of setup, and installs a whole tree of special files in your home directory the first time it is run. See online help for GIMP for more information about running it.

ICON EDITOR

The Icon Editor is similar to the paint program, except that has special features for working with images that are to be used as icons.

Figure 7.4 shows a screen shot of the Icon Editor being used to create a folder icon for a directory that contains Perl scripts.

The following list describes several of Icon Editor's special features for working with icon files:

- When you select File, New to create a new icon, you are given the option to create an icon from scratch or to create one from a template. If you select Create from Template, you can choose an icon to start with from a list of KDE standard icons. This helps you to make your icons look the same as other icons in the KDE system.

  To add or remove icons from the templates list, select Options, Configure, and then click the Templates page of the dialog box and use the buttons there to manipulate the list.

- The Icon Editor always saves its images as XPM files, which is the format used by KDE for icons.
- The palette used by the editor is a special one that was defined by the KDE organization for use with icons. You can add custom colors, if needed, to your icons; if possible, however, stay with the preselected system colors. Using the system colors helps make your icons look consistent with other KDE icons, and it helps your overall KDE system use as few colors in X as possible.
- Because icon files are small, often you want to work on individual pixels to fine-tune the image for the icon. Therefore, the icon editor includes an option to turn on (or off) a grid which helps delineate each pixel in the image. Click on the Toggle Grid button, or select Options, Toggle Grid from the menu to control this grid.
- Because it is very common for icons to have transparent backgrounds, the eraser in the icon editor erases to clear instead of to a fixed color.

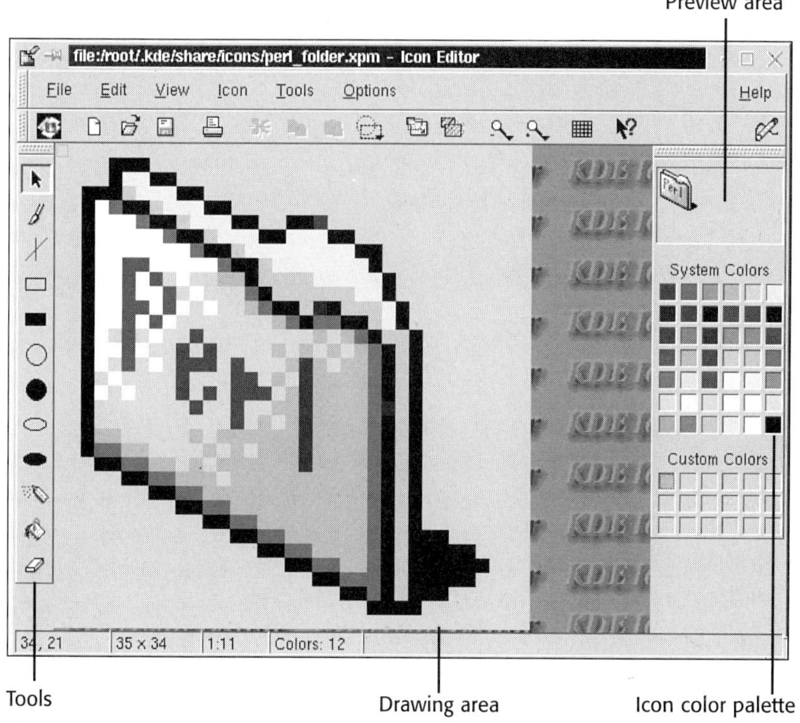

Figure 7.4
The Icon Editor is used to create or customize KDE icons.

If you need to edit or create icons for your KDE system, the Icon Editor is written specifically for this purpose.

IMAGE VIEWER

The Image Viewer program (`kview`) is a fairly straightforward tool for viewing image files on your system. You can start the program by right-clicking an image file in a file manager window and selecting Image Viewer from the context menu that appears. Or just left-click an image. (For most image file types, `kview` is defined as the default application). Also, you can start `kview` by selecting Graphics, Image Viewer from the Application Starter menu.

After it is started, the main window of `kview` shows the currently selected image. You can open additional images by selecting File, Open from the menu, or by dragging image files from a file manager window to the main window of `kview`. To see a list of the currently loaded images, select Images, List from the menu. Click a file in the list to see it in the `kview` window.

Besides just showing images as they normally appear, you can also use `kview` to experiment with an image, showing it at different sizes, with certain changes made to it, or as the background of the current window.

To see an image in different sizes, use options on the Zoom menu. For large images, select Edit, Full Screen to see the adjusted image as the only thing on the screen (that is, not inside the `kview` window). Press Esc to return to your normal Desktop screen. To see an image rotated or flipped, choose an appropriate option on the Transform menu.

There are several different manipulations that you can make to an image. You can select an area of the image by dragging a rectangle around it, and then crop the image to that rectangle. You can adjust image attributes (such as the image brightness) using options on the Filter menu.

Options on the To Desktop menu enable you to see how the image looks as the background of the current desktop. Select Tile, Max, or Maxpect to see the image placed as the background. The Maxpect option stretches the image to the size of the screen, while preserving the aspect ratio (the relationship between the height and width of the image).

Finally, options on the image list dialog box enable you to configure `kview` to show the images in the list as a slide show in the image window.

VIEWING DVI, FAX, AND POSTSCRIPT DOCUMENTS

KDE provides a few different programs that enable you to view documents that are in special formats.

The DVI Viewer program enables you to examine documents that are in TeX DVI format. The Fax Viewer program enables you to view documents that are in a special binary format received by a fax machine. The PS viewer enables you to examine PostScript documents. Each of these programs has a few special options for working with their particular document type. For example, the fax viewer supports different FAX encoding formats. Also, the DVI and PostScript viewers enable to you add bookmarks to certain pages. All these programs enable you to adjust the magnification of the documents, and to perform other adjustments that are appropriate for viewing documents of the respective types.

SPECIAL GRAPHICS PROGRAMS—SNAPSHOT AND FRACTALS GENERATOR

The Snapshot program is a very handy utility for taking screen or window snapshots and saving the images as files. In fact, this program was used to generate most of the KDE figures in this book.

When you launch the Snapshot program, it takes a picture of the whole screen at the time that it is launched, before its window appears. The preview area in the snapshot window shows a reduced version of this image. If what was onscreen is exactly what you wanted a snapshot of, you can save the image now by entering a file path, selecting the file format, and clicking the Save button. However, if you want to get an image of a different screen, or of a particular window, use the options in this dialog box to take another snapshot. To see a full-size version of the current snapshot, click the preview area (see Figure 7.5).

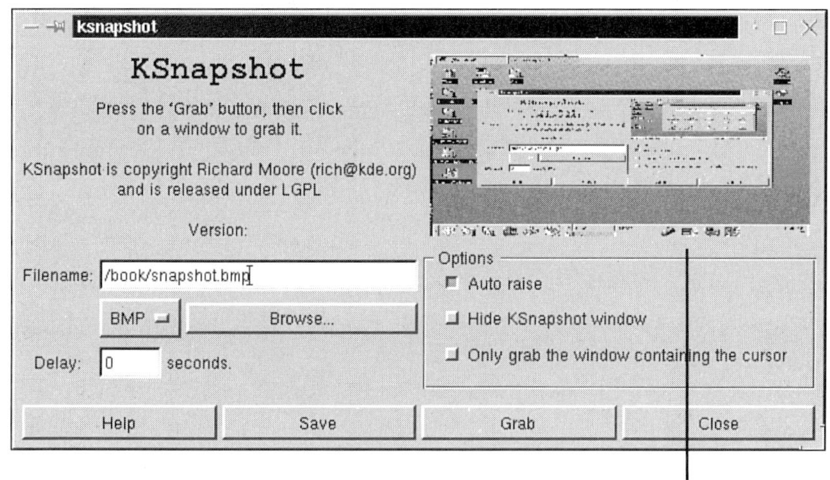

Figure 7.5
`ksnapshot` is handy for grabbing images of the screen and windows.

Fractals Generator is a program that is used to view various regions of two different fractals. A fractal is a special kind of image that is created by assigning colors to a region of space based on a mathematical formula. The interesting thing about a fractal is that it has similar kinds of detail at varying levels of magnification, or zoom, of the image. To see the details of a particular area of the image, drag a rectangle around the area that you want to magnify.

Note

Computer programmers are always interested in technical curiosities, such as fractals. This explains why the Fractal Generator program is included with KDE. It's there for no other reason than for you to play with these interesting mathematical figures, while pondering your place in the Universe.

MULTIMEDIA

The programs in the Multimedia group on the Application Starter menu enable you to work with sounds and music—and with devices that are related to sounds and music, such as a CD player. In the future this group might also include programs for working with video and other types of multimedia files.

The three main types of players that are provided with KDE 1.1 are the CD Player, a MIDI player, and a sound player (called the Media Player). In addition to these programs, there is a sound mixer panel, which enables you to adjust the input and output volume of many different sound elements on your system.

Note

In order for any of these programs to work, your sound system must be installed and operational. In order for sound to work, you must load the appropriate sound drivers for your system with the Linux kernel. For information about configuring the sound drivers on your system, see Chapter 18, "Kernel Modules," and Chapter 42, "Multimedia."

PLAYING CDS WITH THE CD PLAYER

The CD Player program enables you play CDs and organize and access information about your CDs so that you can better enjoy them. It is easy to use, but it also has several advanced features for playing CDs on your system.

Figure 7.6 shows the main window of the CD Player. In the center of the CD player window is the status display, which shows information about the play time, the volume, the name and number of the current track, and the CD title. You can toggle the play time to show time elapsed or time remaining on the current track or on the whole CD using the large button to the left of the status display. Underneath the status display is a slider, which controls the CD volume. Use this and the controls on the sound mixer panel (described shortly) to control the volume of the sound output by the CD.

Figure 7.6
The CD Player main window.

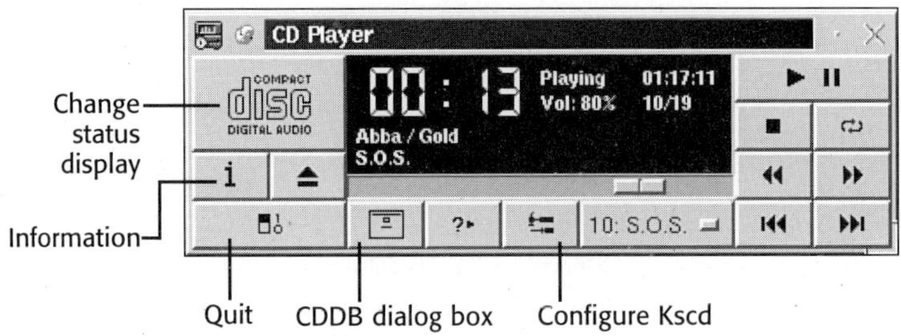

The main play controls are located to the right of the status display in the window; they are modeled after the buttons you see on a normal CD player panel. Many of these buttons are probably familiar to you; they perform functions such as play/pause, stop, fast forward, and so on. If you need to determine what a button does, position the mouse cursor over the button; a tooltip pops up, indicating the function for that button. The Play/Pause button toggles the CD between playing and pausing.

A few other controls are also available to provide additional features. These include the following:

- **Change status display**—Toggle the status display between different time measurements.
- **Information**—Access information on the Web about the CD that is currently playing or about its artist. This includes touring information for when the artist is in concert, links to CD vendors on the Internet, and music information sites.
- **Eject**—Eject the CD.
- **Quit**[md Exit the CD player program (like the Off button on a CD player).
- **CDDB dialog box**—Pop up the CD Database dialog box, which enables you to enter information about the CD, including the artist, title, and track descriptions for each track. You can save this information to a local database so that when you play the CD later the player can present the information in the status display and the track list.

  You can also upload this information to a Web-based national database of CD information (described shortly).
- **Random play**—Have the player play the CD tracks in a random order.
- **Loop CD**—Have the player start again at the first track after the last track is played.
- **Configure Kscd**—Open the configuration window. Some of the configuration options are described next.
- **Track Selection list**—Shows the currently selected track. Choose another track in the list to play that track.

CONFIGURING THE CD PLAYER

The CD Player supports a number of configuration options that have to do with its appearance, operation, and interaction with the World Wide Web. To open the configuration dialog box, click the Configure Kscd button (with the tools on it) in the CD Player window.

To configure the colors that are used for the status display, change the LED Color and Background Color on the Kscd Options page of the dialog box. To configure the Linux device that is used to play CDs, set the value of the CD-ROM Device on this same page. Normally, this is /dev/cdrom, and is set up automatically for you during OpenLinux installation.

The options at the bottom of this page control docking and automatic playing and stopping options, as well as whether tooltips are shown.

To configure the Web browser that is used for showing sites that are accessed using the information button, deselect the option. Use `kdm` as Browser, and enter another browser program in the text field under Use Custom Browser. The UNIX mail command field is used to specify the command that is used to send mail to an external CDDB site.

USING AN EXTERNAL CD DATABASE (CDDB)

One very nice feature of the CD Player is its capability to interact with a Web-based CDDB site, which is a site that provides information about artists and titles, as well as track descriptions for various CDs. This information is kept in a large database, which is queried automatically by the CD Player.

When you put a CD in the CD-ROM device, the CD Player reads the CD and determines a special identifier that is unique to that CD. It uses this identifier to look up information about the CD in your local CDDB or in an external CDDB on a site on the Internet. To configure the CD Player to do this, select the option Enable Remote CDBB on the CDDB page of the Kscd configuration dialog box. Other options on this page enable you to configure whether your Internet access is via a proxy server, and what CDDB servers to connect to for this information. By default, the server `www.cddb.com` is used.

To configure the directory where your local CDDB information is stored, enter a local directory path in the CDDB Base Directory field.

Finally, if no information about your CD can be found on the Web, you might want to enter it yourself and submit it to a CDDB organization so that others can use it. Click the CDDB button on the player to access a dialog box for entering your own CD information. In this dialog box, you can enter the title, artist, and track information for the currently loaded CD. When you finish, you can save the information to your local CDDB, or you can upload the information, via email, to an external CDDB site. Configure the email address to which to send your submissions using the Send CDDB submissions to list.

PLAYING MUSIC (MIDI) FILES WITH THE MIDI PLAYER

MIDI files are files that consist of sequences of notes and which instrument to play each note on. Most frequently, MIDI files contain music, which can be played on your sound card.

To play a MIDI file, use the file manager to find the file on your system, or on the Web, and then left-click the file. Normally, MIDI files have an extension of .mid. The MIDI Player loads and plays the file. Or, follow these steps:

1. Select Multimedia, MIDI player to start the MIDI Player program (`kmidi`).
2. Click the Open Playlist button (it has an eject symbol on it).
3. Browse to find the file you want to play.
4. Select the file, and click the Add button to add this file to the playlist.
5. Repeat steps 4 and 5 until you have the list of songs you want to play.
6. Click OK, and then use the controls in the MIDI Player window to play the songs.

The rest of the controls in the MIDI Player window are similar to those that are used for the CD Player, including status display, volume control, Play/Pause, and so on. If you experience problems, examine the contents of the information window by clicking the Information button (next to the playlist button).

PLAYING SOUND (WAV) FILES WITH THE MEDIA PLAYER

The Media Player program in KDE is used to play sound files in the WAV format.

To play a WAV file, use the file manager to find the file on your system, or on the Web, and then click the file. The Media Player loads and plays the file. Normally, WAV files have an extension of .wav. A few WAV files might be located on your system in the directory /opt/kde/share/sounds.

Or, open the Media Player and select File, Open, and then choose a file to play using the Open File dialog.

To play the file, use the buttons in the Media Player window.

When a Media Player window is already open, you can play a sound file by dragging it from a file manager window and dropping it on the Media Player window.

CONTROLLING THE VOLUME OF SOUND ELEMENTS

The Sound Mixer Panel provides controls for adjusting the volume of several different sound channels on your system, as well as adjusting the left/right balance, treble, and bass of sound output by the sound card.

To adjust the volume of a particular sound channel, open the mixer program by selecting MultiMedia, Sound Mixer Panel on the Application Starter menu. The dialog box for the sound mixer, shown in Figure 7.7, appears.

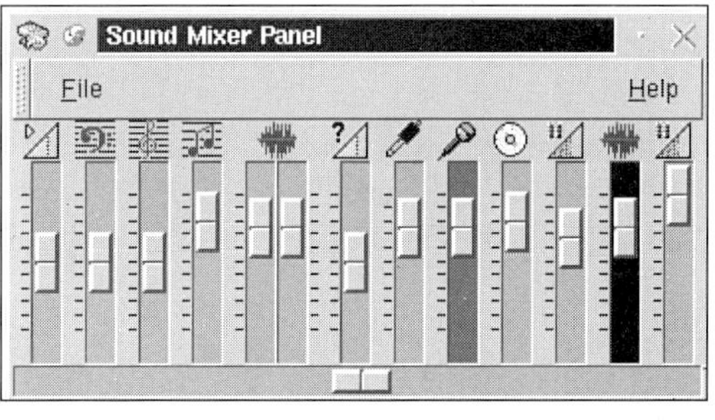

Figure 7.7
The Sound Mixer Panel is used to adjust volume and sound settings for your system.

Each slider in the dialog box controls a different sound element or attribute. For example, there are different controls for adjusting the volume and balance of the CD, MIDI, and WAV sound channels. (The MIDI channel is referred to as `Synth` and the WAV channel is referred to as `Pcm` in the tooltips of the dialog box.) A master volume control is located on the far left side of the dialog box. A master balance (or pan) control is positioned horizontally at the bottom of the dialog box.

To adjust the volume for a channel, drag the slider for that channel. To adjust the balance for all channels, drag the panning slider right or left. To adjust the balance for an individual channel, right-click on the slider for that channel and select Split from the context menu that appears. The slider splits into two sliders, and you can adjust the left and right volumes independently. To mute a channel, use the Mute option on the context menu for that slider.

To make something a recording source, select RecSource from the slider context menu for that channel.

The background color of the sliders changes to reflect the state of the channel, as follows:

- **gray**—Regular settings
- **black**—Channel is muted
- **red**—Channel is a recording source

A few options, including hiding the main menu and allowing docking, can be configured using options on the File menu or in the Options dialog box (accessed via File, Options).

NETWORKING

KDE provides several programs for working with your local network or the Internet. Actually, most KDE programs are Internet-ready because they can act on remote files as well as local ones (using URLs). However, most programs that are explicitly related to networking are listed in the Internet program group on the Application Starter menu.

The networking programs in KDE cover a wide range of Internet services, including surfing the World Wide Web, reading and responding to email, and accessing many other services and features of the Internet. These different tasks are described in the sections that follow.

CONFIGURING DIAL-UP INTERNET ACCESS

The program `Kppp` is used to configure the settings that are required for dial-up Internet access, and to actually connect to the Internet through a dial-up account. PPP is a protocol that is used to connect to an Internet Service Provider (ISP). Its use is discussed briefly in Chapter 24, "Connecting to an ISP." In that chapter, see the section "Dial-up PPP Accounts" for a discussion of the parameters that are required to establish a connection with an ISP via a modem.

To configure `Kppp`, click the Setup button on the main dialog box. The `Kppp` Configuration dialog box appears. Create a new account using the controls on the Accounts page of the setup dialog box. Click New, and a dialog box appears, asking you for information such as the ISP name (connection name), phone number, type of authentication, and various TCP/IP configuration parameters (address, DNS server, Gateway, and so on.) Your ISP provides you with the information necessary to fill out these fields when you set up your account with them.

Besides connection information, you might also need to configure `Kppp` with information about your serial line and modem. The settings for these items are located on the Device and Modem pages of the `Kppp` configuration dialog box. Most of the time, the default settings on these screens work fine. See Chapter 24 for more information about setting up PPP to work on your OpenLinux system.

When you start `Kppp`, a dialog box appears, asking you to select an ISP to which to connect (in a drop-down list), and asking for your Login ID and Password. Select the account and enter the information, and then click the Connect button. Your modem dials, and you are connected to the Internet through your service provider.

BROWSING THE WORLD WIDE WEB

Two important programs that are not listed in KDE's Internet program group are the file manager, which can act as a World Wide Web browser, and Netscape Communicator, which includes a Web browser. The file manager is listed in the `System` program group and Netscape Communicator is available in the Applications program group.

The file manager program is described extensively in Chapter 4, "Navigating the Desktop." Netscape Communicator is not a KDE application, so it is not covered here. However, it provides extensive online help. Please refer to that online help for additional information about using it to browse the Web.

SEARCHING FOR FILES ON FTP SITES

Use the Archie client to search for files on FTP sites on the Internet. Archie is a protocol for accessing databases that describe FTP sites and the files they contain. Using KDE's Archie client, you can search these databases using a number of different criteria. Start the Archie client by selecting Internet, Archie client on the Application Starter menu.

Note

As the World Wide Web becomes more and more popular, other, older Internet services, such as Archie, are being moved to this new medium. Archie is still valuable for searching certain collections of FTP archives, but increasingly the same functionality is available using Web search engines.

To search for a file, follow these steps:

1. Enter the search expression in the Search Term field in the main window. This can be the exact filename for which you are searching, or it can be a substring or a regular expression.
2. Select Settings, Searchmode, and choose the mode that matches the type of search term you are using.
3. Select Settings, Archieserver, and choose a server to use for the search.
4. Actually start the search by selecting Query, for Filename in the menu. The status line at the bottom of the Archie client window shows the progress of the search. When it says `Success`, the search is complete (although it is possible that no files were found).

After a search is complete, the list of matching files is displayed in a list on the screen. To see details about a file on the list, click its entry in the list, and the fields at the bottom of the window are filled in for that entry.

To download a file or access the directory that it is in, right-click the entry in the file list, and then select the appropriate option on the context menu that appears.

RECEIVING NOTIFICATION OF NEW MAIL

If you are interested in receiving notification when mail arrives on your system, use the program `KBiff`. This is a flexible program that periodically examines your mailbox and changes its icon on the screen to indicate the status of your mail.

Why "Biff"?

You might wonder where the name "Biff" comes from. In the 1980s a few pranksters forged newsgroup postings under the name BIFF (`BIFF@BIT.NET`), and it caught on as a term used to refer to an annoying style of email that utilized all uppercase letters, intentional misspellings, and other oddities that were looked down upon by the Internet crowd at the time. From there, "Biff" was popularized as the name of an email notification program in the Berkeley versions of UNIX. `xbiff` and `kbiff` continue this (somewhat amusing) legacy.

To start `KBiff`, select Internet, Biff from the Application Starter menu. A setup dialog box is displayed. Normally, you can just select an appropriate profile (inbox is selected by default), and click OK to proceed. `KBiff` then displays an icon to represent your email status either on the Panel or in a program window somewhere on the screen. However, you can also configure the settings of `KBiff` before proceeding.

`KBiff` supports multiple profile definitions. A profile consists of a set of mail-checking options, new mail actions, and mailboxes to check. The mail-checking options include the following items, which are configured on General page of the Setup dialog box:

- **Poll (sec)**—Amount of time in seconds between polls of the mailboxes for this profile
- **Mail client**—The program to use to check for mail
- **Dock in Panel**—Shows the status icon docked in the Panel, instead of as a separate window
- **Use session management**—Starts `KBiff` again with the same configuration the next time KDE starts
- **Status icons**—The icons that are used to indicate various states of your incoming mailbox

For each profile, you also configure a set of actions to perform when mail arrives. The following actions can be configured to occur when `KBiff` detects that new mail has arrived:

- **Run Command**—Runs the indicated program. Enter your own command into the field below this option.
- **Play Sound**—Plays a sound file.

- **System Beep**—Beeps.
- **Notify**—Pops up a notification dialog box, indicating the mail status.

To configure the set of mailboxes to monitor, click the Mailbox tab; use the controls on the page to manipulate the mailbox definitions on the list on the left side of the dialog box. Multiple mailbox definitions can be defined. For each mailbox definition, select the type of mailbox or mail protocol, and enter the information that is appropriate for that type in the fields on the dialog box. Then click the Add button (the button with the mailbox icon, under the mailbox definition list) to add that entry to the list.

READING AND SENDING ELECTRONIC MAIL

One of the most important features of the Internet is email. KDE provides a full-featured email client, which you can use to read email, manage email messages, and compose and send outgoing email.

To run the mail client, select Internet, Mail client from the Application Starter menu. The first time you run the program as a particular user, you are asked to configure a few settings, including the identity and mail account information for that user. For the identity, fill in the following fields on the Identity page of the dialog box:

- **Name**—A name you want to appear in mail headers (not your account name, but a real name).
- **Organization**—Normally, this is the name of your company.
- **Email Address**—The address for the From: line in the email header.
- **Reply-to Address**—The address to which responses are to be sent (often the same as the Email Address).
- **Signature File**—A file containing a message that is added to every message you send. It's important to set this, even if it refers to an empty file. If this field is left blank, `Kmail` asks you to select a signature file every time you compose a message.

`Kmail` automatically configures the Name and Email address, based on your user account settings, so you might not need to change those. It also configures your mail account settings for a local mailbox. If you are using a different email configuration (for instance, if your email account resides on your Internet Service Provider's machine or on some other external machine), adjust the settings on the Network page of the dialog box before proceeding.

The mail client main window (the reader window) is shown in Figure 7.8. Use this window to read and respond to email messages, and to manage your mail by marking or flagging it, organizing it into folders, or deleting it.

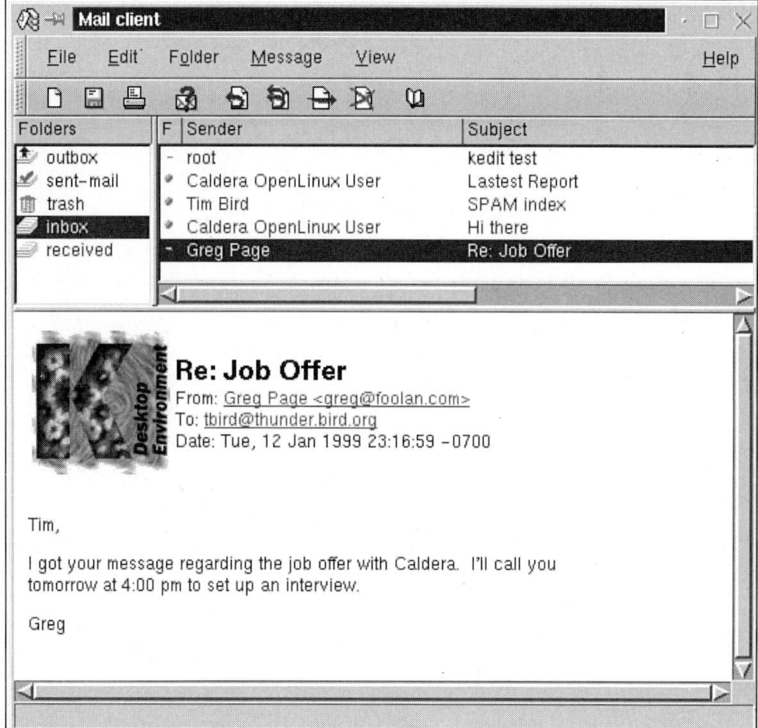

Figure 7.8
Use the mail reader window to read and manage email.

The mail reader window consists of three main areas, or panes. The folders pane, at the top left of the window, has a list of email folders in which your messages are stored. The message list, at top right, has a list of information from the header of each message in the currently selected folder. The message window shows the currently selected message. The relative sizes of these three panes can be adjusted by dragging the splitter bars between the panes.

READING EMAIL

To read a message, just select the folder from the folder list and the message from the message list, and the message is displayed in the message pane. To view the message in a separate window, double-click the message in the list.

To view additional messages, the message list can be navigated with the mouse, with the options on the Message menu, or via the keys indicated on the Message menu (without Alt or Ctrl modifiers). The set of keystrokes provided by `Kmail` matches the keys used in other popular character-based email programs for Linux.

The marks in the left-most column of the message list indicate the status of a message. There are marks to indicate that the message is new or unread, that you have replied to or forwarded the message, or that it is a message that you sent or are composing to send at a later time. You can use these marks to remind you which messages you are working on, and which you have already responded to. To flag a message with a particular mark, select Message, Set Status, and choose the status of the message from the menu.

You can adjust the column widths of the message list by dragging the edge of the column headings. To sort the messages in the list by a particular column, click that column heading.

You can also adjust the display of the message itself in the message pane, using options on the View menu. These options control what set of header fields are shown with the message (and their arrangement) and how attachments are displayed with the message. For example, attachments are usually shown as icons at the bottom of the message. For certain types of attachments, it is better to view them inline with the email message, rather than as icons. To view text attachments inline with the email message, select View, Inlined Attachments from the menu.

To open an attachment, click on the icon for the attachment in the message pane. To save an attachment, or to view it in a separate window, right-click on the icon for the attachment; select the appropriate option from the context menu that appears.

To print a message, select File, Print from the menu, and the current message is sent to the printer. You can also save a message to a file using the File, Save as menu option.

MANAGING MAIL AND FOLDERS

Use the folders in the folder list to keep track of your different messages and to organize them.

By default, the folder list consists of the following folders:

- **inbox**—This is where incoming mail is stored.
- **outbox**—When you have partially written messages, or messages that you have postponed sending, they are stored here. You can continue editing them and send them at a later time.
- **sent-mail**—By default, `Kmail` keeps a copy of the mail that you have sent in this folder, so you can refer back to it.
- **trash**—This folder is used to hold messages that you have deleted. Empty this folder to actually remove the messages from your system.

You can create additional folders to organize your email messages. To do so, select Folder, Create from the menu, and type the name of the folder in the dialog box that appears; click OK.

To move a message from one folder to another, select the first folder, and then drag the message that you want to move from the message list and drop it on the entry for the second folder in the folder list.

To delete a message, select it and either drag it to the trash folder or press the Delete key. The message is moved to the trash folder. Periodically empty the trash folder to permanently get rid of unwanted messages (and free up the disk space they consume). You can also empty the contents of other folders as well: Select a folder, and then select Folder, Empty from the `Kmail` application menu.

To remove a folder and all its contents, select the folder, and then choose Folder, Remove from the menu. You are asked to confirm the removal. Click OK to proceed.

COMPOSING AND SENDING EMAIL

To compose a new email message, click on the compose button or select File, New Composer from the menu. If you are responding to or forwarding an email, select a message and choose one of the following options in the Message menu (or click the corresponding button on the button bar):

- **Reply**—Send a message to the author of the selected email.
- **Reply All**—Send a message to the author of the selected email, and to all the other recipients of the email.
- **Forward**—Send the selected message to another person. You can send the message unaltered, or you can add additional comments before forwarding the message.

When you select one of these options, the composer window appears, and you can create (or edit, in the case of Forward) your message (see Figure 7.9).

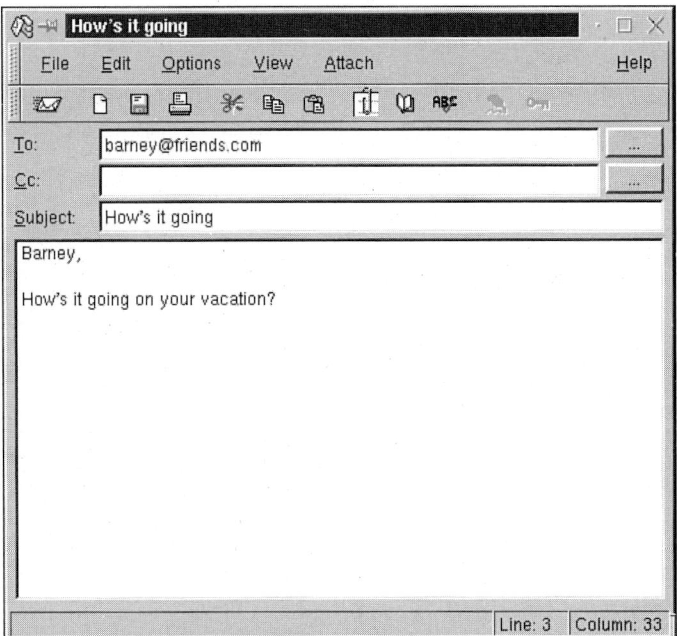

Figure 7.9
`KMail` Composer window.

To send an email, enter the address of the recipient in the To line at the top of the composer window. Click on the button to the right of an address line to access the `Kmail` address book. In the address book, you can store the email addresses of persons with whom you communicate frequently.

Also, enter a description of your message in the Subject line of the composer window.

You might need to edit other fields that are not shown on the dialog box for the message header. For example, you might want to send a blind copy (using the BCC address line) to someone, or you might want to alter the apparent source (From line) of the message. To make other header fields appear in the composer dialog box, access the View menu, and select the fields that you want to appear.

Enter your message in the message pane of the window. Use options on the Edit menu to manipulate your text. To insert a whole file into the message, select File, Insert File. To spell check a document, select Edit, Spellcheck from the menu.

Finally, to add attachments to a message, click the Attach button, or select Attach, Attach from the menu, and select a file in the browser that appears. After you select a file, you are asked to indicate the Mime type for the file, as well as its name, description, and encoding. Normally, you can just leave these fields alone (or just enter a description). However, if necessary, adjust these fields and then click OK to attach the file to the message. Use the options on the Attach menu to add additional attachments, or to remove, save, or change the properties of attachments, before sending your message.

Click the Send Message button—or select File, Send—to send your message to the indicated recipients. If you are interrupted while composing a message, you can save the message and finish editing it later. Select File, Send later, and your message is placed in the outbox folder. When you are ready to finish the message, select the message in the outbox folder, and select Message, Edit from the menu. The message is loaded into a composer window, and you can continue where you left off.

AUTOMATICALLY FILTERING EMAIL

Another nice feature of `Kmail` is the capability to automatically place mail in a particular folder, or to just delete it (send it to the trash), depending on the contents of the message. This is called filtering, and it is handy for organizing your mail and avoiding email from people with whom you don't want to communicate.

To configure email filtering, select File, Filter from the `Kmail` menu. The Filter Rules dialog box appears. This dialog box consists of a list of rules, as well as some controls that are used to configure each rule. A rule consists of matching criteria for a message and the action to take when a message is matched. In order to define a filter rule, follow these steps:

1. Click the New button. An empty rule (shown with angle brackets) appears in the rule list.
2. Select the empty rule in the rule list.

3. Enter the matching criteria using the controls at the top right of the dialog box. To do this, select a part of the message to examine, a matching operation, and a value to match.

   For example, to match messages with a subject line containing the word *KDE*, select the message part *Subject*, the matching operation *contains*, and enter the word `KDE` in the text field.

4. For complicated matches, you can also select a Boolean operation (`and`, `unless`, or `or`), and specify a second matching criteria. For a simple match, select ignore as the Boolean operation, and leave the other matching criteria fields blank.
5. Select an action to perform for matching messages. For now, the only actions allowed are transfer, skip rest, and nothing. To put matching messages in a particular folder, select the action transfer, and then pick the folder from the list that appears. For example, to ignore messages, just select the trash folder.
6. Select the action skip rest on the second action line.
7. Click OK to save your changes.

After the filter rules are in place, when `Kmail` examines your mailbox for incoming messages, it analyzes each new message according to the rules and performs the actions that you have specified.

READING AND PARTICIPATING IN INTERNET NEWSGROUPS

The News client program (`krn`) enables you to subscribe to and read Internet newsgroups. You must have access to an Internet News server in order to use this program. Your Internet service provider or system administrator can provide you with information about a news server that you can access in order to read news.

Start the News client by selecting Internet, News client from the Application Starter menu. Configure the news server by selecting Options, NNTP Options, and then entering the server name in the NNTP Server field. If you need to log in to that server in order to access it, enter the name and password for your news account on the server machine in the appropriate fields in this dialog box, and then select the Authenticate option.

After you are connected to the news server, a tree view of the available groups is shown in the News client window. There are two lists: a list of subscribed groups, and a list of available groups. Click a group to see the articles (messages) in that group.

The article window appears, and you can browse the messages in a group. Marks in the article window indicate the status of the messages for that group. You can read messages, respond to messages, and post new messages to the selected newsgroup.

Some newsgroups have a very high message turnover rate. In order to avoid using too much space on your drive, `krn` expires messages in a newsgroup after a certain period of time. This time can be adjusted by selecting Options, Expire options, and changing the values in the dialog box that appears.

NETWORK UTILITIES

The Network Utilities program is a graphical front end for various network diagnostics and information utilities on your system. Specifically, it provides access to the following utilities: `ping`, `traceroute`, `host`, `finger`, and `mtr`.

See Chapters 21–23 for information about setting up TCP/IP networking, diagnosing network problems, and related programs. Also, see the man pages for each of these individual command-line utilities for descriptions of their features and uses.

The online help for the Network Utilities program also has some good overviews of these functions.

UTILITIES

The Utilities program group on the Application Starter menu contains administration utilities for working with different aspects of your system. The Utilities group also includes some small personal productivity programs. Some of the utilities that are provided by KDE are described elsewhere in this book because they relate to a specific OpenLinux component or subsystem. For example, the use of `kpackage` is discussed in Chapter 15, and the menu editor is discussed in Chapter 5.

Brief mention of the other utilities in this group is made here.

SYSTEM UTILITIES

There are system utilities on the Utilities submenu of the Application Starter menu. These include programs to view and manipulate archive files or binary data files, as well as programs for working with floppy disks and printers. A very good process management tool is available as well.

MANIPULATING ARCHIVE AND BINARY FILES

The Archiver program is used to create and manage archive files. The archive file can be in one of several different formats, including tar, gzipped tar, or zip. To open an existing archive file, click the file in a file manager window. Or select Utilities, Archiver from the Application Starter menu to start the Archiver program, and select File, Open from the program menu.

To create a new archive, follow these steps:

1. Select File, New from the menu.
2. Browse to the location where you want to create an archive file.
3. Enter an archive filename, including extension, in the location line of the file browser dialog box. The extension is used by the Archiver program to determine the type of archive to create.
4. To add files to the archive, drag them from a file manager window (or the Desktop) to the Archiver window.

To extract an archive, select File, Extract To from the menu, and enter a destination directory. To extract an individual file, select it in the file list, and select Edit, Extract from the menu. You can add additional files to an archive or update the files in an archive by dragging them from a file manager window to the Archiver window.

The Hex Editor program is useful for showing a hexadecimal dump of a file. You can use this to examine the exact contents of a binary file, or to edit a specific hex byte in a file. The main window of the Hex Editor shows the contents of the file that you have open, with the address of the bytes, a hex dump of bytes (in 16-bit word format), and a column of ASCII characters for the bytes. To edit an individual byte, click it in the hex area and type a new hexadecimal value.

WORKING WITH PRINT QUEUES AND PRINTERS

The Printer Queue program enables you to examine and manipulate the jobs that are waiting to be printed in the different printer queues on your system. Also, you can control some basic operations on the print queues.

When Printer Queue is started, it displays a screen, showing the jobs that are currently queued for the default printer on your system. Also, the status of the printer and its queue are shown at the bottom of the screen. You can select a job in the job list and remove it (delete the job from the print queue); or you can move it to the top of the job list by clicking the appropriate button at the bottom of the dialog box. You can also perform both of these operations by right-clicking a job in the list, and then selecting the appropriate item in the context menu that appears.

You can select which print queue to monitor by selecting one from the drop-down list at the top of the dialog box. By default, OpenLinux configures your machine with `ps` and `lp` print queues. You can modify the print queue configuration by editing /etc/printcap, or by running the `lisa` administration tool. See Chapter 14, "Printing," for more information about how to configure printers and print queues on your machine.

By default, the Printer Queue program does not automatically update the contents of the job list. You can click the Update button to manually update the list. However, to have Printer Queue automatically update the list at periodic intervals, select Config, Auto update from the menu, and adjust the slider to control the update frequency. Then click the Auto button at the bottom of the job list dialog box. One other nice feature of the Printer Queue program is that you can drag a file from a file manager window, or from the Desktop, to the job list, and the file is sent to the printer (it shows up in the print queue).

If you have a Hewlett Packard LaserJet printer, you can use the HP LaserJet Control Panel program to control various settings on the printer. This includes the paper size and orientation, as well as printing control options such as number of copies, lines per page, resolution, and so on.

FORMATTING FLOPPIES

The `KFloppy` program is used to format floppies. To use it, insert a floppy to format in the floppy drive. Then start the `Kfloppy` program, select the formatting options you want (including density and file system type), and click the Format button.

MANAGING RUNNING PROCESSES

Finally, the Process Management program (`kpm`) is an exceptionally handy tool for managing the running processes on your Linux system. It is basically a graphical equivalent of the character-based `top` command. However, it is much easier to use, and provides some additional features to help you analyze and compare the running processes on your system. To see the list of running processes on your system, start the Process Management program by selecting it from the Utilities menu. A window like the one that is shown in Figure 7.10 is displayed.

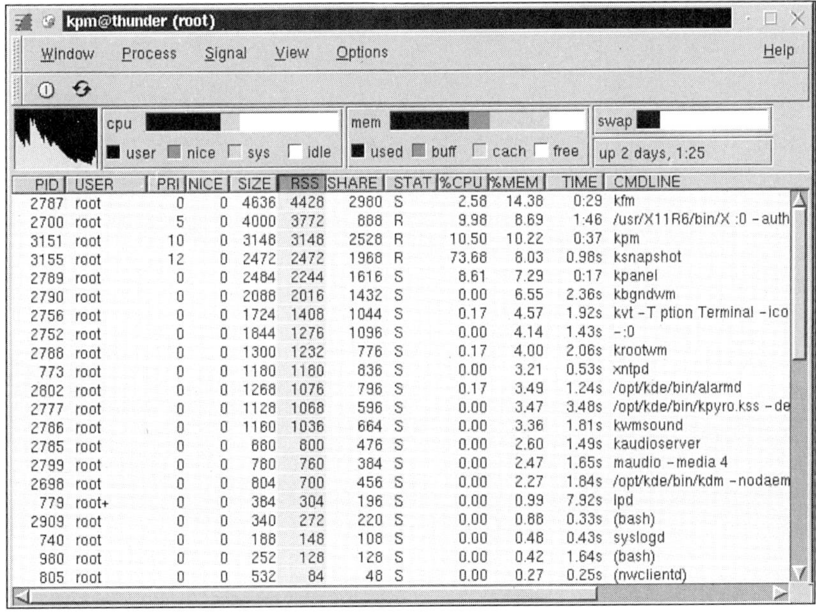

Figure 7.10
Process Management window.

The main window of `kpm` shows a chart and several bar graphs to indicate past and current CPU usage, memory usage, and swap space (disk) usage. Also, a list of processes is displayed in the main area of the window. Each line in the list corresponds to a single process, and shows various pieces of information about the process.

By default, all the processes on the system are shown. You can choose to see only a subset of processes by selecting the appropriate option on the View menu.

The headings of each column in the process list indicate different pieces of information for the processes. You can customize the list of headings (to see specific pieces of information) by selecting a preset group of fields (User, Jobs, or Memory fields) from the View menu, or by adding and removing individual fields from the list of fields that are to be displayed. Either select View, Select Fields from the menu and check the fields that you want to display or right-click the heading line in the process list, and choose Remove field or Add field. To get more information about what each field means, right-click the field and select Help on field.

One of the most useful things you can do with the process list is sort it by a particular field. This enables you to more easily detect processes that are using extreme amounts of memory, disk space, or processor cycles. Also, you can compare processes to see which ones use more resources than others. To sort the processes by the value of a particular field, click the field heading in the process list. Clicking the heading again toggles the sort order between ascending and descending order.

You can also use `kpm` to manipulate the processes on your system, either adjusting their scheduling priority, sending them a signal, or terminating them. Select a single or multiple processes in the process list, and then select the appropriate item in the Process menu, or right-click the selected items and choose an option from the context menu that appears.

Caution

Although you can send arbitrary signals to a running process using `kpm`, be careful when you do this. Most programs exit cleanly when they are sent the Terminate signal. For some processes, the Hangup signal is used as a normal method of restarting the process with new configuration parameters. However, be careful using `kill` or other (fault-oriented) signals, which most often terminate a process without giving it a chance to clean up and exit gracefully. You can potentially lose data or put the system into an unstable state if you are reckless about sending signals to the running processes on your system.

One last interesting bit of information that you can retrieve about a process is its list of open sockets. This information can be used to troubleshoot networking problems with a network service or daemon. Select a process, and then choose Process, Socket Info from the menu to see the sockets open by that process.

PERSONAL PRODUCTIVITY PROGRAMS

Some KDE applications are just small programs for managing bits of information or tracking personal items. They are described briefly in the following paragraphs.

The Address book enables you to enter and organize information (including addresses) for personal contacts.

The Calculator enables you to perform mathematical calculations. It is a full-functioned scientific, statistical, and programmer's calculator. Click on the kCalc button in the calculator window to configure the appearance of the result display and the numeric precision, and to select the calculator mode.

To see a history of items that you have cut or copied, use the Cut&Paste history program. This enables you to retrieve items from previous cut or copy operations. When it is run, this program docks on the Panel. To retrieve an older cut or copy buffer, click the clipboard icon on the dock and select the appropriate buffer; then select Paste in the application in which you want to put the text.

The `KJots` program enables you to create and manipulate notes or memos. Use this program to keep track of miscellaneous information. You use it by creating a book, and then creating pages in the book and entering your notes onto the pages. You can scroll through the pages in a book, or you can save a book out as a file.

Use the `KNotes` program to write notes to yourself and stick them as windows on the screen (kind of like paper Post-it notes.) However, `KNotes` also enables you to set an alarm on a note (to remind you to do whatever is in the note at a certain time), or to mail or print the notes that you create. After `KNotes` is started, it docks in the Panel. To create a new note, click on the icon in the dock. To manipulate a note, or to adjust `Knote` settings, right-click a note and select the appropriate option on the context menu that appears.

The Personal Time Tracker program (`karm`) helps you keep track of the amount of time you are spending on different activities. enter an activity name by selecting Task, New from the menu. After entering the different activities that you work on during the day, select one from the activity list and click on the Start Clock button to start timing that activity. As you switch activities during the day, select the activity that you are pursuing at the moment in the activity list. The number of hours and minutes that you spend on each activity are shown in the column to the left of the activity list.

Another personal productivity application is `KOrganizer`. This is an appointment book and to-do list organizer. This program is documented in Chapter 8, even though it is not an official part of the KOffice project, because `KOrganizer` is a full-featured productivity application like the others included in KOffice.

TERMINAL EMULATORS

KDE provides two different terminal emulation programs for use in working with command-line shells in your graphical environment. Terminal (`kvt`) is the main terminal emulation program. `Konsole` is a new terminal emulator that was written from the ground up, and that uses a few different techniques for managing multiple terminal sessions using one window.

To use `kvt`, select Utilities, Terminal from the Application Starter menu. The terminal window opens, and you can start working at the shell prompt inside the window. Use the scrollbar to see material that has scrolled past the window.

Caution

Don't confuse the scrollbar for the terminal window with scrolling features of a program that is running in the window. The `kvt` scrollbar can only be used to see material that was on the window at some point in time but that has now scrolled off. To scroll a document in, for example `vi`, use the cursor positioning keys specific to `vi`.

You can adjust several aspects of the terminal window, including the position of the scrollbar, the font and size of the window, and a color scheme (foreground and background colors) for the window, to customize it to your preferences. Use the settings on the Options menu to do this. You can also choose from a preset list of font sizes by selecting Options, Font size.

To make more screen real estate available, you can hide the menu bar by selecting Options, Hide Menubar.

To make these settings permanent so that new terminal windows will use them when they are started, select Options, Save Options from the menu.

To exit the terminal program, select File, Exit from the menu, or just type `exit` at the shell prompt inside the terminal.

SUMMARY

In this chapter, many of the KDE applications were presented. Some of these were covered in detail, whereas for others only a cursory overview was presented. KDE applications range in functionality from core applications, such as the file manager, to games, graphics, and multimedia applications, to network programs and utilities.

OpenLinux provides a wealth of prebundled KDE applications, and more will certainly be developed as the KDE project advances. These applications provide a set of services that make your system useful for a variety of end user tasks. This includes the following activities:

- **Working with documents**—Find files and documents using the `find` utility. Use `kedit` to view and edit simple text files, and `kwrite` to write and edit program files and other documents. Various viewers are available for special document formats (DVI, Fax, and PostScript).
- **Entertainment and diversion**—KDE provides many strategy and action games. Paint and graphics programs enable you to express yourself or experiment with interesting phenomena. There are players for audio CDs as well as for sound and music files.
- **Internet access**—The mail reader enables you to read and compose email, and to communicate with others on the Internet. The file manager acts as a browser to access the Web. The newsreader enables you to interact with news groups, and other KDE utilities enable you to manage your Internet access or perform network functions.

- **System management**—Some of the utilities in KDE enable you to manage various parts of your system, including manipulating the packages on your system, configuring KDE itself, adjusting printer settings, or formatting floppies.
- **Personal assistance**—Some programs, such as the calculator, the memo program (`kjots`), or the personal time tracker, work to enhance your productivity.

Because KDE applications cover such a broad range of functionality, it's hard to confine the list of related chapters. However, you might want to see the following chapters for additional information:

- See Chapter 4 for information about working in KDE, including launching programs with the Application Starter menu and Panel.
- See Chapter 8 for information about KDE's productivity suite of applications (word processor, spreadsheet, and so on.)
- Chapter 18 has information about loading sound drivers in the kernel, which is required for most KDE multimedia programs to work.
- Chapters 21, "Understanding TCP/IP Fundamentals," 22, "Network Administration," and 25, "Email Setup," discuss setting up your network and your mail service, which is related to the Internet programs that are described here.
- Most importantly, don't forget to look in the online help for an application if you need help using it. Do this by selecting Help, Contents from the application menu, or by pressing F1 at any time.

CHAPTER 8

KOffice

In this chapter

This chapter introduces you to KOffice, the office productivity suite for KDE. KOffice is an ambitious project to create a full-scale suite of office productivity applications that are powerful, easy-to-use, completely free, and available with source code.

The following packages are officially part of the KOffice project:

- **KWord**—Word processor
- **KPresenter**—Presentations package
- **KSpread**—Spreadsheet
- **KIllustrator**—Drawing program
- **KFormula**—Formula editor
- **KChart**—Charts and graphs editor
- **KImage**—Image viewer

Another program, KOrganizer, is not an official part of KOffice, but it is covered here because it is a full-featured personal productivity application, like the other KOffice programs.

At the time of this writing, the KOffice programs were not considered ready for release to the public as stable, completed applications. Think of this chapter as a preview of the functionality that will be included with these programs when they are ready to actually ship.

One major feature of KOffice is its use of an *object request broker* (*ORB*) to allow integrated functionality of the different applications. This is called OpenParts or KOM, and is a technology that supports placing documents or objects of one application inside a document of another.

It allows the embedded object to be edited and manipulated in place in the containing document, which makes it easier and more convenient to work with compound documents (documents with multiple kinds of data or objects). OpenParts is similar to Microsoft's COM/OLE in this regard.

All the KOffice applications support OpenParts, which means that they can interact with each other in order to produce complex nested documents.

The KOffice programs that are described in this chapter are not on the OpenLinux CD that comes with this book because they were not stable at the time that this book went to press. However, some of the programs are actually useful right now, and they will certainly have improved by the time you read this. These programs are progressing at a rate that can make them stable and ready for a 1.0 release sometime in the second half of 1999. The descriptions here are based on software binaries that were released in October of 1998.

Even though the KOffice suite is not included with this CD, you can probably obtain it either from Caldera's FTP site or by following the links on the KOffice Web site, which is located at `http://koffice.kde.org/`.

Follow the Download Binaries link, and then follow exactly the instructions to download and install the files on your system.

KWORD

KWord is the word processing application in KOffice. This program enables you to create and edit formatted documents. KWord is a full-blown word processor that includes several features that are normally found only in high-end desktop publishing applications.

STARTING `KWord`

Start KWord by opening a terminal window and typing `kword`. The `kword` program is actually a shell script that starts the mico ORB (`micod`), if one is not already running, and then runs `kword.bin`. The ORB is used if you embed an object from another KOffice program into your word processing document.

When you start KWord, it asks you to choose a template document with which to start. The templates come in two different categories: You can select a word processing template or a desktop publishing template. The difference between these two template types will become apparent in the section "Using Frames." For now, just select a basic word processing template.

When you have selected a template, the main KWord editing window appears. It looks similar to the window in Figure 8.1.

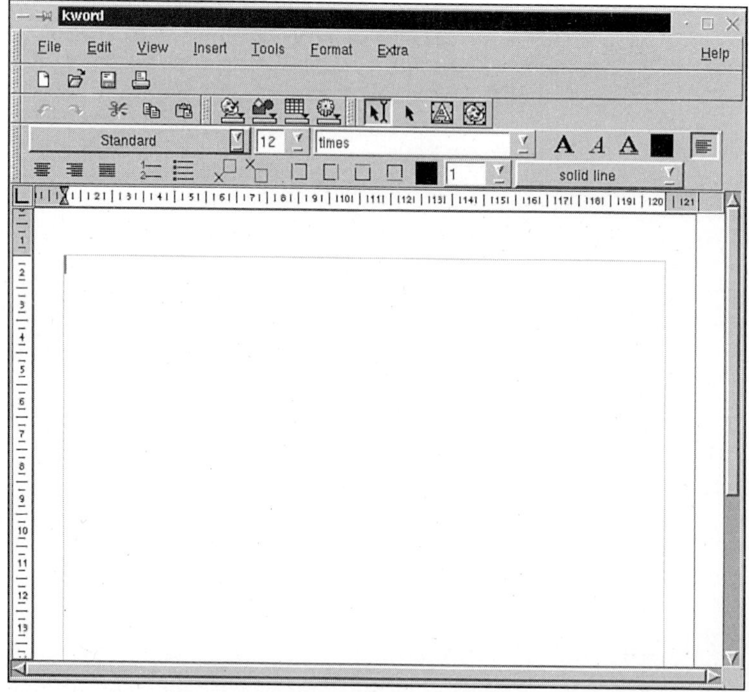

Figure 8.1
Use `kword` to create and edit formatted documents.

BASIC OPERATION

To edit your document, enter text in the main document window and use the options on the Edit menu to cut, copy, and paste buffers, as well as to perform other operations.

To change the style of the text that you enter, select Format, Font or Format, Color and configure the settings in the dialog boxes that appear. Or click the corresponding buttons on the button bar. For example, you can change the font, font size, color, and style (bold, italic, or underline). You can also adjust the alignment of the text to be left-justified, centered, right-justified, or blocked.

Use the subscript or superscript buttons to enter simple formulas or chemical equations (such as $a^2+b^2=c^2$ or H_20). For complex formulas, use KFormula, which is described in a later section of this chapter.

To put borders around your text, select Format, Paragraph, and then click on the Borders tab and define the border characteristics for your paragraph; or use the border buttons on the button bar.

KWord also supports numbered and unordered (bulleted) lists. Click on the appropriate button on the button bar to enable either of these list types. Then, as you type, each new line receives a number or bullet accordingly. To change the numbering scheme or bullet symbol, select Format, Paragraph, and then click on the Numbering tab and modify the settings to match your preferences.

To save or print a document, use the appropriate options on the File menu. When you save a document, it is saved in an XML format, which is a plain ASCII format that you can examine with a regular text editor if you want to.

ADJUSTING PAGE SETTINGS

To set page margins, indentation, and tabs, directly manipulate the items on the ruler bars at the top and side of the document window. Drag the page borders to adjust margins, or drag the first line or paragraph indent marks to configure paragraph indentation. To define a tab position, click on the tab symbol in the upper-left corner to select the type of tab stop you want to define, and then click on the ruler where you want that tab stop to be placed.

You can also adjust margins by selecting Tools, Page from the menu; this opens the Page Layout dialog box. In this dialog box, you can edit the page margins or configure the page for multiple columns. You can also change the unit of measurement of the ruler bars to inches from the default millimeters.

USING STYLES

A *style* in KWord is a combination of configuration settings—including font, size, color, indentation, and so on—that represents a particular part of a document (such as a heading or a list item). This combination of settings is given a name (the style name). After a style is defined, when you are working with your document, you can select the style to apply all the settings for that style at once.

To apply a style, select it from the style list in the button bar. To define a new style or to edit existing styles, select Extra, Stylist, and then select options on the Stylist dialog box for managing the list of styles. When adding or editing styles, use the Style Editor dialog box. In this dialog box, click the buttons to access dialog boxes in which you can define the font, color, spacing and indenting, alignment, borders, and type of numbering to use (for lists) for the style.

USING FRAMES

Normally, a word processor works with pages of text and graphics, with text that wraps at margins and flows from one page to the next as it is entered.

KWord supports a more general mechanism for handling the layout of word processing data, known as *frames*. Text that is entered in KWord flows from frame to frame instead of from page to page in the document. The frames can be positioned in a variety of ways and configured to support more complex page layouts than are otherwise allowed with a simply page-based system.

When you choose a word processing template, KWord initializes with frames that correspond to page boundaries, so KWord operates like a regular word processor. However, you can also start KWord by selecting a more complex frame layout (on the DTP tab of the templates dialog box), or you can create and manipulate the frames for your document while you are working.

To create a new frame, select Tools, Create Text Frame (for text), or Tools, Create Picture Frame (for a picture); then drag a rectangle in the document, and place it where you want the frame to be.

A dialog box appears, asking for the configuration for this frame. You can either make this a standalone frame, where the text from this frame does not flow into any other frame, or you can choose to connect the frame to an existing set of frames in the document. Text flows from frame to frame within connected frames in a set.

Also, choose how you want text to interact with frames that intersect this one. You can select one of the following options:

- Don't run around other frames.
- Run around the rectangle of intersecting frames.
- Run around the contents of intersecting frames.

Using these options, you can control how the text and graphics in your document interact to give it a high-quality, professional looking layout.

To manipulate existing frames, select Tools, Edit Frames, and then click the frame that you want to manipulate. Drag the frame border by the handles to resize it, or reposition the frame by dragging it. Or right-click the selected frame, select Properties, and adjust the frame characteristics.

To return to normal word processing mode, select Tools, Edit Text, and then click the frame in which you want to continue working.

INSERTING GRAPHICS OR OTHER OBJECTS

You can insert graphics or other objects into your documents in one of two ways:

- Put them inline with the text in a frame.
- Define a new frame for them.

To add an object inline inside a frame, position the cursor where you want the item to appear, and then select the appropriate item on the Insert menu. Then select the file that contains the picture, clip art, or table that you want to insert.

For pictures, you can automatically create a new frame to hold the object, and insert the picture in the frame by selecting Tools, Create Picture Frame; then draw a rectangle in the document window in which you want the new frame to appear, and select an image file for the frame.

EMBEDDING ANOTHER KOFFICE OBJECT IN A DOCUMENT

To place an object from another KOffice program in the document, follow these steps:

1. Position the cursor where you want the object.
2. Select Insert, Object from the menu (or click on the Insert Object button on the button bar).
3. In the dialog box that appears, select the KOffice program that provides the type of object you want to embed. Your menu and button bars change to those of the selected KOffice program.
4. Select File, Open, and open the file for the object that you want to embed.

After you finish working with the embedded object, click on another part of the document window to restore the menu and button bars for KWord. You can switch between editing your KWord document and the embedded object at any time.

KPRESENTER

The KPresenter program is used to create and manipulate presentations, outlines, or slide shows (similar to the PowerPoint program offered by Microsoft). After a presentation is defined, KPresenter can be used as a viewer for actually showing the presentation. KPresenter is one of the most mature of the KOffice programs, with a high level of functionality and many advanced features.

The KPresenter main window is shown in Figure 8.2.

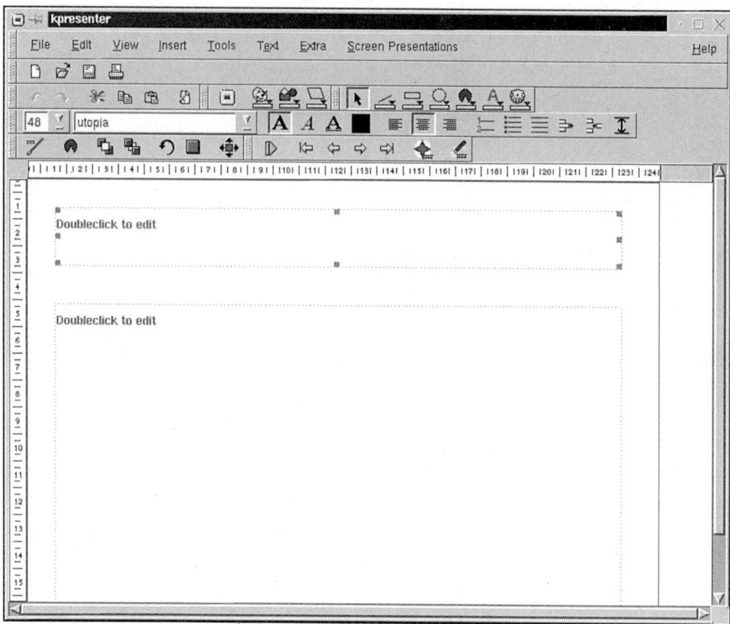

Figure 8.2
Use KPresenter to create presentations.

CREATING A PRESENTATION

To start KPresenter, type `kpresenter` at a terminal prompt. You are asked to select a basic template for the pages for your presentation. A template consists of a default background and a few default page elements (with predefined element styles) to give your presentation pages a consistent look.

To define your presentation, add new objects and new pages, and edit the objects on the pages to reflect the information that you want to present.

ADDING OBJECTS TO THE PAGE

There are several different objects that you can add to a page, including the following:

- Line
- Rectangle
- Circle or ellipse
- Pie/arc/chord
- Text
- object

To add an object to the page, select Tools and pick the type of object from the menu. Then use the mouse to create the object (or the rectangle that holds the object) on the page.

If the element that you are creating is a KOffice object, select the appropriate KOffice program, and then use the menus to load the object that you want to embed in your presentation.

After you have created objects of the chosen type, switch back to selection mode by choosing Tools, Mouse from the menu.

Each object has different attributes, or properties, that you can adjust to affect the appearance of the object. When an item is selected, right-click the object to pop up a context menu of operations to perform with that object.

To adjust the properties of an object, select options on this context menu, or choose Properties on the context menu, and adjust the settings in the dialog box that appears. This includes things such as the rotation of an object, the shadow for an object, and the line and fill settings for the object.

For the rotation of an object, select a preset angle of rotation or enter a specific number of degrees of rotation. For the shadow of an object, select the shadow color, the direction of the shadow, and the shadow distance in the Shadow configuration dialog box.

To resize objects, select them and drag the appropriate handle until the objects are the desired size.

For some types of objects, you modify their properties using menu options on the Text or Extra menus, or by clicking the buttons on the button bar.

For example, there are numerous settings that can be used to control the layout and configuration of text inside text objects.

To actually edit the text in a text object, double-click the text object. For other text attributes, use the options on the text menu to configure the font, size, style, color, and alignment of the text. Text objects can consist of regular text, numbered lists, or bulleted lists, which KPresenter handles intelligently.

To define a bulleted list, including the symbols that are used for bullets in different levels of the list, follow these steps:

1. Double-click a text object to select it.
2. Select Text, Text Type, Unsorted list.
3. Select a depth (1st level, 2nd level, and so on).
4. Choose the characteristics for the bullet for that level, including font, color, size, and so on. Note that the Symbol font has good characters for use as bullets.
5. Repeat steps 3 and 4 to define bullets for different depths.
6. Click OK.
7. Type the lines of text for each entry in the list.

To increase or decrease the level of an entry in the list, position the text cursor in that line of the list and select Text, Increase Depth, or Text, Decrease Depth from the menu. The indentation and bullet symbol (if applicable) are adjusted accordingly.

ADDING PAGES AND EXTERNAL OBJECTS

To add a new page to the presentation, select Insert, Page, and then select whether to put the page before or after the current page. A page, which has the objects defined by the template that was used to create the presentation, is inserted.

To adjust page characteristics, select either Extra, Page Background, or Extra, Page Layout. In the Page Background dialog box, select the type of background (either colored, picture, or clipart) and configure the settings for that type of background. To apply the change to just the current page, click Apply. To apply it to all the pages in the presentation, click Apply Global.

To add an external object to the current page, select Insert and choose an appropriate object type from the list. The following objects are available:

- **Picture**—Insert a graphic image.
- **Clipart**—Insert a windows metafile graphic (vector graphic).
- **Autoform**—Insert an element used for constructing form diagrams (arrow heads and connecting lines).

COMPOSING WITH MULTIPLE OBJECTS

When several objects are on a page, you can arrange them with respect to each other or combine them (overlaying some on top of others) to achieve the visual effect you want. To align a set of objects, follow these steps:

1. Select multiple objects.
2. Choose Extra, Text Alignment.
3. Select how you want the objects aligned.

When multiple objects overlap each other, you can raise or lower objects, relative to others on the screen. For example, if you want some text to appear in front of an ellipse, define a text object and an ellipse object, and then lower the ellipse so that it is behind the text object (or raise the text object so that it is above the ellipse).

DISPLAYING A PRESENTATION

After you create a presentation, you probably want to show it to someone. You can print your presentation to paper, slides, or transparencies, depending on the display capabilities at the location where you are presenting. However, if there is a computer present, you can make your presentation using the KPresenter program itself. In fact, KPresenter supports several additional features for enhancing your live presentation, including the capability to

animate aspects of your presentation or to draw on your presentation pages while you are presenting in order to highlight or point out important text or pictures.

To display a presentation using KPresenter, select Screen Presentations, Start from the menu. KPresenter takes over the full screen and shows each page of your presentation in sequence. To move from page to page (or to step through animations that you have defined) click the left mouse button or hit the spacebar. Press Esc to terminate the presentation.

During the show, you can use the mouse to draw on the pages of the presentation by switching to drawing mode. To switch to drawing mode, press the right mouse button, and select Drawing mode. Now draw on the page with the mouse. This is useful for highlighting a word or phrase, or for pointing out an item on the page. To revert back to switching mode for the mouse, right-click the screen again and select Switching mode.

Before starting the presentation, you can choose the pen size and color by selecting Screen Presentations, Choose Pen, and selecting options in the dialog box that appears.

Assigning Animation Effects

There are numerous effects that you can use during your presentation to make it animated and more interesting.

With animations, each page of the presentation is displayed in sequence. A number of steps can be defined for each page. Each element on a page can be assigned an effect that will occur at a particular step. As you proceed through the presentation, all the elements that are configured to animate at each step do so. The transitions between pages can also be configured.

You can assign and edit effects while you are creating the presentation, but it is easier to do so after you have everything in place, using the presentation structure viewer.

To see the structure viewer, select Screen Presentations, Open presentation structure viewer. The structure viewer window is shown in Figure 8.3.

The structure viewer window consists of the three following panes:

- **Element tree**—Shows all the different pages and objects in the presentation: Click a page to expand or contract its object list. Select the page or object that is to be configured. The configuration buttons for the type of object you select become active, and you can adjust the properties of that object.
- **Properties page**—Shows the properties of the selected object.
- **Step chart**—Shows which objects are onscreen at a particular step in the presentation.

To assign an effect, select an object in the element tree, click the Assign Effect button, and then choose an effect from the dialog box that appears. If you select a text element, you can also choose an object-specific effect. For now, the only text-specific effect that you can choose is Paragraph after paragraph, which makes each item of a text list appear at different steps in the presentation.

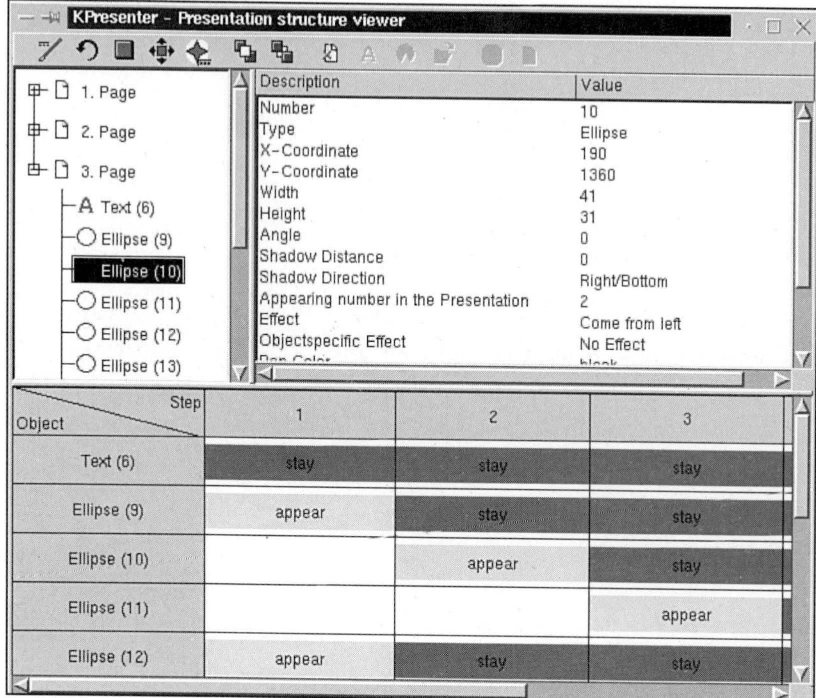

Figure 8.3
Use the Presentation structure viewer to adjust page elements and effects.

KSPREAD

KSpread is the spreadsheet program of KOffice. It is used to work with mathematical formulas and equations, to calculate complex results, and to test the different numbers that lead to those results.

Basically, a spreadsheet consists of a grid of cells, each of which can contain text (for labels, buttons, explanations, and so on), numbers, or formulas (see Figure 8.4).

BASIC OPERATION

The cells in the spreadsheet are referenced using a coordinate system, with a letter followed by a number. To enter the data for a cell, select the cell and type the data into the field at the top of the spreadsheet.

Text and numbers are entered normally. When formulas are entered they are preceded by an equal sign. KSpread automatically calculates the result of the formula every time the spreadsheet changes.

For example, if you enter the value `10` in cell A1 and `20` in cell A2, enter the formula `=A1+A2` (case is important) in cell A3; the value `30` is shown in cell A3. If you then change the value in either cell A1 or A2, the value in A3 changes automatically.

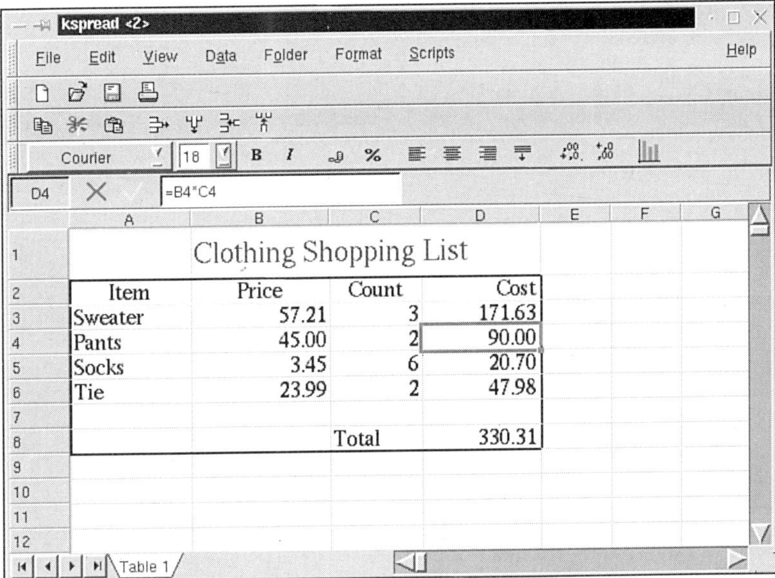

Figure 8.4
KSpread, the KOffice spreadsheet application.

To select a cell, click it with the mouse. To select a block of cells, drag over them with the mouse. To select a whole row or column in the spreadsheet, click the row or column header. You can cut, copy, or delete the selected cells, or you can change their appearance and format in the spreadsheet. When you paste cells, their formulas are automatically updated to reflect the new position in the spreadsheet.

To add or remove an entire row or column from the spreadsheet, select a row or column and click the appropriate buttons on the button bar.

To add additional pages to the spreadsheet, select Folder, New Table. You can select different pages, or tables, of the spreadsheet using the tabs at the bottom of the spreadsheet window.

CHANGING THE APPEARANCE AND FORMAT OF THE SPREADSHEET

You can adjust the width of columns and the height of rows in the spreadsheet by dragging the edge of a column or row header at the top or side of the spreadsheet grid.

The format for a cell, or for a block of cells, can be adjusted by selecting it, right-clicking it with the mouse, and selecting Layout from the context menu that appears. You can configure the following settings on the pages of the Layout dialog box that appears:

- Borders for the block of cells, including line style, thickness, and color for each of the edges
- Number format, including precision and negative value format
- Text and cell background color
- Font, font size, and style

Some of these options are also available via buttons on the button bar.

EMBEDDING AN OBJECT FROM ANOTHER KOFFICE PROGRAM

To embed an external object in the spreadsheet, select Edit, Insert, Object, and then select the program for the other object type. The menus change to those of the other KOffice program, and you can open the file that you want to embed in the document.

ADVANCED FORMULAS

Eventually, KSpread will support the use of a scripting language to define advanced functions that can be used in formulas for cells in your spreadsheet. The options under the Script menu enable you to edit the scripts that define these functions. The scripting language that is used to define functions is Python.

As of this writing, very few functions are available. However, you can see the scripts that are used for the current version of KSpread in the directory /opt/kde/share/apps/kspread/scripts. If you want more information about this powerful capability, consult the online help for KSpread or go to the KOffice Web site (`http://koffice.kde.org/`) to see if information about the scripting capabilities of the various KOffice applications is available.

Tip

> Work is progressing at adding scripting capabilities to other KOffice programs as well. The language that is being used for this is Python. If you are not familiar with Python, be aware that it is a powerful, concise, object-oriented language with very clean syntax.
>
> To find out more about Python, visit the Python Web page at `http://www.python.org/`.

KILLUSTRATOR

KIllustrator is the program in KOffice that is used to create and edit vector graphics images. These are images that are composed of lines, colors, and editable objects, and that are often referred to as *clip art*.

Vector graphic images are manipulated differently than image files are. Image files are pixel-based, with each part of the image having no defined connection to the pixels around it. With vector graphics, however, there is a relationship between the items in the picture; for instance, if you drag the edge of a box, the other lines and the inside pattern of the box are adjusted to match.

Figure 8.5 shows the main KIllustrator window.

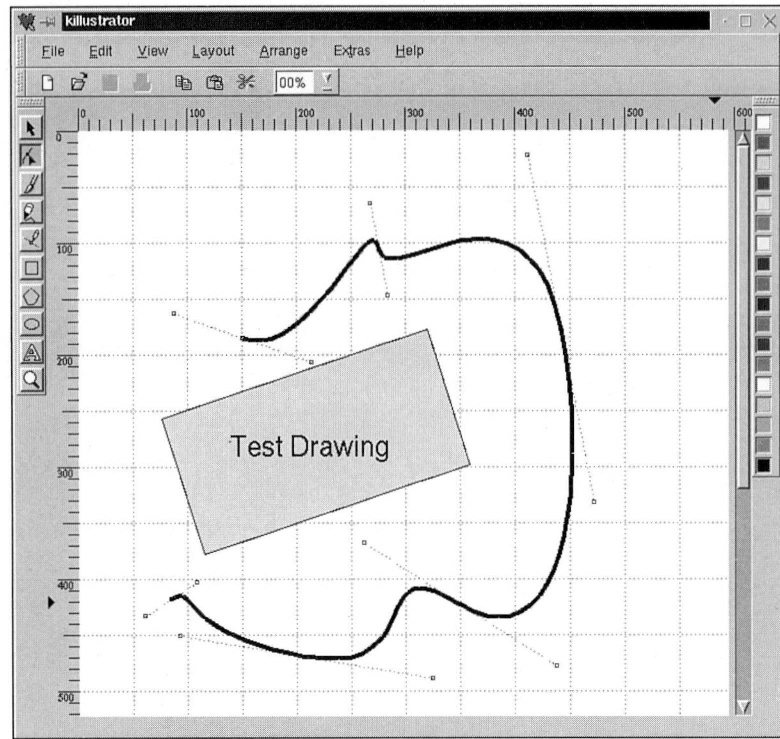

Figure 8.5
KIllustrator is a vector drawing program.

CREATING A DRAWING

To create a new image, select File, New from the menu. A blank page is displayed, along with a color palette and tools for drawing different items.

You can change the view to include a grid—or to include rulers to show your position—by selecting options on the View menu. Select Layout, Set up Grid to adjust grid spacing and to configure whether new items are to align with the grid when they are drawn.

DRAWING OBJECTS

Create new objects in the drawing window by first selecting a tool, and then drawing the item with that tool. Some tools are also available for manipulating the objects that are already in the drawing, rather than creating new objects.

The following tools are available:

- **Selection**—Used to select an object or group of objects to manipulate. Click a single object to select it individually, or drag an invisible rectangle around a set of objects to select them as a group.
- **Edit point**—Used to directly manipulate the points of an object. Select an object with the selection tool, and then select this tool and drag the points of an object.

- **Freehand line**—Draw a freehand line in the drawing.
- **Polyline**—Enter multiple straight connected line segments. Click with the left mouse button to define the points for the line segments. End a polyline by clicking with the right mouse button instead of the left mouse button.
- **Bezier curve**—Enter curved line segments. Click to set a point position, and then click to set the curve handle (length and angle). Repeat for subsequent curve points. Click with the right mouse button to end the curve.
- **Rectangle**—Draw a rectangle. Drag in the drawing area to create a rectangle. To create a square, hold Ctrl while you are drawing. For rectangles with rounded corners, draw the rectangle, and then select the Edit points tool and drag a corner point of the rectangle.
- **Polygon**—Draw a closed polygon.
- **Ellipse**—Draw an ellipse. To draw a circle, hold Ctrl while drawing.
- **Text**—Enter text. Click where you want the left edge of the text to be, and then start typing.
- **Zoom**—Change the zoom of the window. Draw a rectangle to zoom in on that part of the drawing.

MODIFYING AN OBJECT'S PROPERTIES

After an object is drawn, you can select it and cut, copy, or delete the object, or you can edit its properties. Select the object or set of objects that you want to manipulate, and then select Edit, Properties. Different pages of the dialog box enable you to adjust different properties of an object:

- **Line properties**—Use settings on this page of the dialog box to adjust the color and thickness of the lines in an object. Also, select whether lines are solid or dashed, and what, if any, arrow tips to use on line segment ends.
- **Fill properties**—Use this dialog box to configure the inside color or pattern for closed shapes. Select no color, solid (single color), a pattern, or a gradient, and then configure the settings to match your selection.
- **Font**—The Font tab is only available for text objects, and is used to configure the font, size, and style of the text in the text object.

You can also modify several aspects of an object through direct manipulation. If you select one or more objects, square handles appear. Drag the object to a new position on the page, or drag one of these handles to resize the object.

Click on the selected object again, and the handles change to rotation handles. Also, a rotation center is displayed as a small circle in the center of the object. Drag the center marker to a new position (if desired), and then drag a corner to rotate the selected objects about that center.

You can also perform similar operations using the dialog boxes that are accessible via the Arrange, Transform menu.

ARRANGING AND GROUPING OBJECTS

Various other features of KIllustrator enable you to arrange the way that objects are drawn on the page, and to control whether they are grouped together for operations. Furthermore, an advanced feature called Layers enables you to work with multiple overlapping drawings to compose the final image you want to create.

The items on the page are drawn in a specific order, back to front. When items overlap, the object on top covers up any objects behind it. To change an object's level on the page, use options on the Arrange menu. You can raise or lower objects until they occur in the desired draw order to yield the visual effect that you want.

You can group items together by selecting them and choosing Arrange, Group. Now, you can operate on the items as if they were a single object, for moving, resizing, and rotating them, as well as for adjusting their properties and duplicating them.

After you finish manipulating the objects, you can leave the objects grouped together, or you can ungroup them (using Arrange, Ungroup) to edit the properties of an individual item in the set.

When drawing with KIllustrator, sometimes it is useful to isolate a set of objects in a drawing to a separate plane (or layer) of the drawing. This enables you to work with some objects independently of others, or to reuse parts of drawings (such as backgrounds) separately from the rest of your artwork.

Use the Layers dialog box to create new layers and to manipulate layers in your drawing. To access the Layers dialog box, select Layout, Layers from the menu.

A list of layers is shown in the Layers dialog box. Click on the buttons to add or remove layers, or to reorder the layers for viewing. Click on the icon that is next to a layer to control whether the layer can be seen, drawn on, or printed. Make sure that the selected layer in the layer list can be drawn on so that you can work with your drawing.

KFORMULA

The KFormula program is a formula editor for KOffice. Whereas KWord includes the capability to do basic subscripting and superscripting to write very simple mathematical formulas, KFormula goes way beyond these simple capabilities.

To properly render a complex mathematical formula is a complicated task because the size of a symbol in the formula depends on the size of the items it surrounds. KFormula supports entering and editing formulas in an easy-to-use WYSIWYG (What You See Is What You Get) format. KFormula keeps track of the relationships between objects in a formula so that it can manipulate parts of the formula in an intelligent fashion. For example, when the equation inside an integral changes size, the integral symbol is automatically adjusted accordingly.

Figure 8.6 shows the KFormula main window.

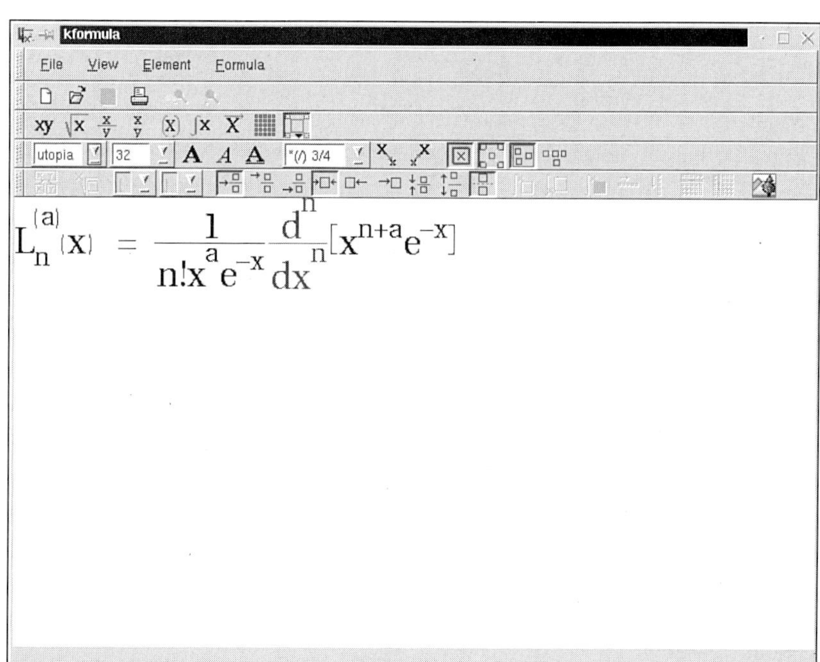

Figure 8.6
Use KFormula to create professional looking mathematical formulas.

To create a formula, select File, New. A formula consists of elements in the formula window, which have spatial relationships with each other.

FORMULA ELEMENT RELATIONSHIPS

The elements in a formula have the following three types of relationships:

- **Peer**—An element precedes or follows another element.
- **Child/parent**—An element is a child or parent of another element.
- **Index**—An element is an index of, or is indexed by, another element.

When you create a formula, you start with one empty element (a red square) that you expand into the formula that you desire. The way you add to the formula is to add peer, child, and index elements to it, and to fill empty elements with text, numbers, and symbols that define the formula. When you add something, the relationship that the new element has—and its position relative to other elements in the formula—depends on what element is currently selected in the formula.

To select an item in the formula, click the item. The currently selected element is shown in red. If the element you have selected is a container (a parent element), that element's children are shown in blue.

If you select a non-empty element, you can add a peer or index to the formula. If you select a square (an empty element), you can convert the element into a parent/child element grouping or add an index.

Note that you cannot add a parent to an existing group; therefore, you must define your formula from the outside in. That is, you need to define the outermost symbols and expressions of the formula first, and convert (empty) child elements into more complex expressions, working inward. It is helpful to write the formula down on paper before laying it out with the formula editor. You might even want to number the symbols and expressions of the formula so that you can enter them in the correct order.

ADDING ELEMENTS TO A FORMULA

The elements you can add to a formula are as follows:

- **Plain text**—This is used for text, numbers, and symbols that don't depend on anything else in the formula for their size (such as = or +). For example, use a plain text element for variable names (such as `x` and `y`), function names (such as `cos` or `tan`), and numbers.

  When inserting text, add peer elements at logical breaks in the text. For example, enter `x+y` as three elements (`x`, `+`, and `y`), and not as the string `x+y`. This last element cannot be used to add an index to `x` to make it into x^2, for example.
- **Root**—This is used for square (and other) roots, and is a container element.
- **Fraction**—This container element converts the element that it replaces into two children, separated by a fraction bar.
- **Vertical space**—This is similar to a fraction, but without the bar.
- **Bracket block**—This nests an element inside brackets. You can choose the style of brackets to use (parentheses, angle brackets, square brackets, and so on) by selecting an existing bracket element and choosing the new bracket style from the drop-down list on the button bar.
- **Integral**—This container element precedes its child element with a integral sign.
- **Symbol**—This allows an arbitrary symbol to be used with a child element.
- **Matrix**—This container supports multiple rows and columns of child elements. When you define a matrix, you select the number of rows and columns, and also whether you want to have lines to divide the child elements.

To add a container or peer element to the formula, highlight an element that is already in the formula, select Element, Add Element, and choose an element type from the menu. The new element is added to the formula following the highlighted element.

To convert an empty element into a text element, select it and start typing. Or, click the Change to simple text button on the button bar.

To convert an empty element to some other (parent/child) element group, select the appropriate item from the Element, Add Element menu, or click it on the button bar.

To add an index to an element (empty or not), highlight an element that is already in the formula, select Element, Add Index to, and choose the position (one of the four corners) at which the index is to be placed.

Manipulating Elements

When an item is selected, the buttons that are used to manipulate that item become active on the button bar. For example, if you select an integral symbol, the integral sign is shown in red, the child elements of the integral are shown in blue, and functions for working with integrals become active in the button bar.

Many functions are available only on the button bar (such as integral upper and lower limits, for instance), so it is important to note which buttons are available when you have selected an item.

Adjusting Element Attributes

Some of the main attributes that you can adjust for an element are its font, alignment, and spacing. When you define fractions and matrices, you can define the amount of space between the rows to give the best appearance in the formula.

To change these attributes, select an element and use the appropriate button bar controls to configure them.

Adjusting Element Sizes

In order to provide the most flexibility, KFormula enables you to change the size of elements in a unique modal fashion. To change the size of an element, first select the sizing mode; then select an element, and either increase or decrease its size.

The following sizing modes are available, and can be used alone or in combination:

- Change active element size
- Change index size
- Change children size
- Change peer size

Click on the buttons on the button bar to select the set of modes that you want to use. These modes express relationships among elements, and are useful for keeping related items in proportion to each other as you resize them.

For example, to increase the size of an element and all its children, select the modes Change active element size and Change children size, and then select the element and click the Increase size button.

To decrease the size of the indexes of an element, without changing the element itself, deselect Change active element size, and select Change index size; then select the element and click the Decrease size button.

When you are through working with your formula, save it or print it using the options on the File menu.

KCHART

The KChart application, shown in Figure 8.7, enables you to make basic charts and graphs, based on data that you enter or retrieve from another application. This program is used to allow embedding of charts and graphs in KOffice documents.

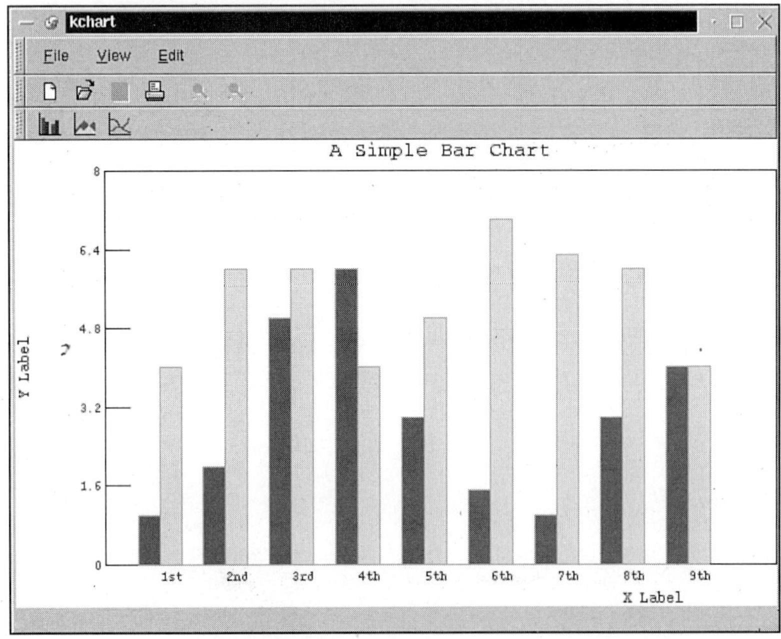

Figure 8.7
Use KChart to create charts and graphs to embed in other KOffice applications.

Select File, Open to open an existing chart data file, or select File, New to create a new chart.

To enter data for the chart, click Edit, Edit data, and then fill in the data for an item in a row of the chart. Edit the chart column labels by entering text in the column headings of the data table.

To format the data as a bar chart, area chart, or line graph, click the appropriate button on the button bar.

KIMAGE

KImage is an image file viewer. For viewing or manipulating images, it is not as full-featured as Kview, which is the regular KDE image viewer. Kview is described in Chapter 7, "KDE Applications." However, KImage can be used to embed an image in another KOffice application (see Figure 8.8).

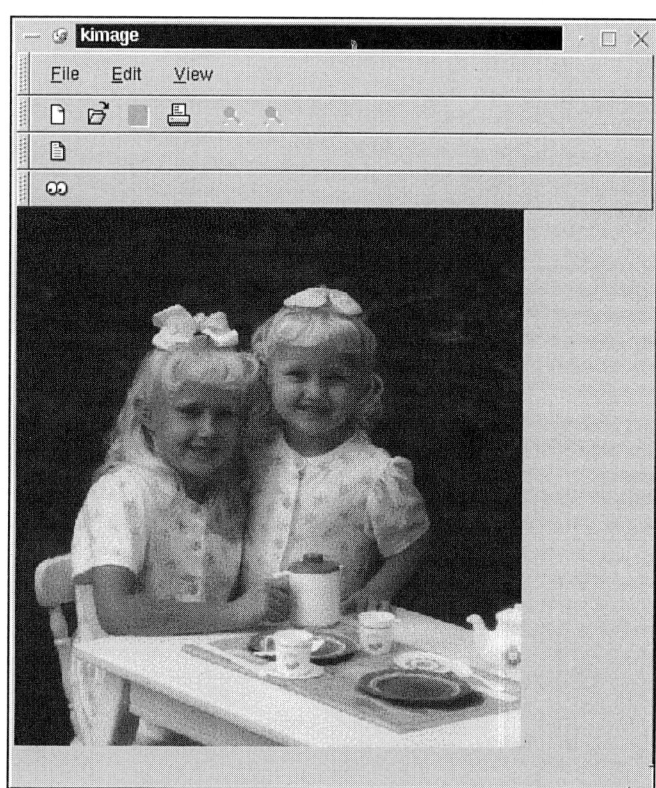

Figure 8.8
KImage is used to embed images in other KOffice documents.

Select File, Open to open an image for use with KImage. A few operations are available in the Edit and View menus.

KORGANIZER

KOrganizer is an appointment and task list manager. This powerful program enables you to keep track of appointments and meetings, and to manage your daily tasks.

When you start KOrganizer, the program shows you a screen with your appointments and to-do list (see Figure 8.9).

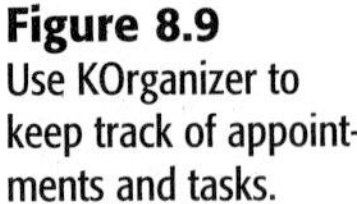

Figure 8.9
Use KOrganizer to keep track of appointments and tasks.

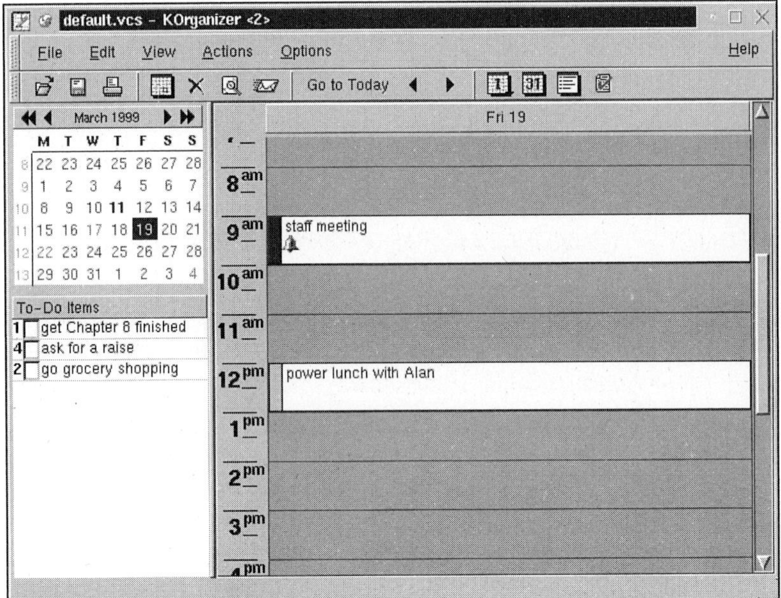

When you start KOrganizer, it shows the view that you were using when you exited the program. The default view (a one-day view) consists of the following screen areas:

- **Month calendar**—This shows a month's worth of days in calendar format. By default, the current day (today) is selected. Click on another day to see the appointments for that date. Click on the arrows at the top of the calendar to move forward or back by months or years.

  Dates on the calendar are shown in different colors to represent different things. A gray background indicates the current date. Red dates are holidays or other notable dates. Days with appointments are shown in blue.
- **To-Do lists**—A list of tasks is displayed in the lower-left corner of the screen.
- **Appointment schedule**—The main area of the screen shows the appointments that you have scheduled for the selected day.

Several different views of your schedule and task list are available. Select an option on the View menu, or click one of the view buttons on the button bar, to see a different view. The following views are available:

- **List**—Shows one day of appointments as a list instead of as an hourly chart. This is handy to see a summary of your appointments for the day.
- **Day**—Shows the appointments for one day.
- **Work Week**—Shows the appointments for five days (Monday through Friday) on a chart.

- **Week**—Shows seven days of appointments on a chart.
- **Month**—Shows a month's worth of appointments on a calendar grid. Days from more than one month can be shown—the grid covers several weeks (possibly into the next month).
- **To-Do list**—Shows the To-Do list filling the entire window.

Creating and Managing Appointments

To make an appointment in KOrganizer, right-click in the schedule area of the window, and select New Appointment from the context menu that appears. You can also select Actions, New Appointment, or click the New Appointment button on the button bar. Any of these options opens the New Appointment dialog box.

Entering Appointment Information

In the New Appointment dialog box, enter appropriate information for the appointment. You can enter a summary description of the appointment and select the starting and ending times for the event (to the nearest 15-minute interval), or you can enter a detailed description of the event using the fields that are provided.

To schedule an alarm for this event, check the Reminder box and enter a time (and select the time units). This time interval indicates the time at which you want to be notified of the event. By default, an alert message appears and a beep sounds at the alarm time you specify. However, you can also indicate a sound (WAV file to play) or specify a program to run at the alarm time by clicking the buttons on the dialog box.

To enter a recurring event (such as a weekly meeting), click the Recurring event button. The Recurrence tab of the appointment dialog box is no longer gray, and you can click it and select options to configure the frequency of the event. You can also select an end date and any exception dates on which the appointment will not occur.

To select one or more keywords for this event, click the Categories button at the bottom of the General page of the dialog box. In the dialog box that appears, select a category and click the Add button. You can add items to or remove items from the list of categories for this event, or you can create your own new categories using the fields in this dialog box.

The options on the Details page of the appointment dialog box are used for scheduling meetings and keeping track of attendees. These options can be ignored for non-meeting events. Enter the name and email address of each attendee, and select a role and status for the attendee. Click the Request Response option if you want to send email to the attendees for the meeting.

The appointment dialog box can be used to cycle through appointments for the entire day, and it can be used to edit or delete them (using the arrow and delete buttons on the button bar of the dialog box). When you finish editing the appointment information, click the Save and Close button on the button bar.

After you have saved the appointment, you might need to select View, Update for the appointment to appear in the schedule list. If you have created a meeting event, you can send email to the attendees of the meeting by selecting Actions, Mail Appointment.

MANAGING APPOINTMENTS

Right-click an appointment in the schedule chart to open a context menu of options for that appointment. You can edit, delete, or toggle the alarm for the appointment using these options.

You can use the mouse to modify the start and end times and the date of an appointment directly on the main screen of KOrganizer. To change the start or end time of an appointment, drag the top or bottom edge of the appointment box. To move the appointment to another time, click in the center of the appointment box and drag it to a new position in the schedule chart. To move an appointment to the same time on another day, click in the handle on the left edge of the appointment and drag it from the schedule chart to a day on the month calendar. Or, if you are in one of the week views, you can drag the appointment by the left edge to another day of the week—it stays at the same time. The mouse cursor changes to show which type of drag you can perform for a particular part of the appointment box.

MANAGING TO-DO LISTS

You can also use KOrganizer to manage a list of To-Do items that carry over from day to day. In the To-Do list, create a new item by right-clicking and selecting New To-Do. Double-click the blank entry that appears in the list, and enter a description of the item.

Change the priority of an item by clicking the priority number to the left of the item. Click the checkbox next to an item to mark it as completed. You can edit or remove individual items by right-clicking them and selecting Edit To-Do or Delete To-Do from the menu that appears. To remove completed list items, select the option Purge Completed from this same menu.

USING MULTIPLE CALENDARS OR OTHER CALENDAR PROGRAMS

When you finish working with your appointments, save your calendar data by selecting File, Save (or Save As). One unique attribute of KOrganizer is that it enables you to work with multiple independent calendar files.

To close the current calendar and start with a new, blank calendar, select File, Close from the menu. To open a different calendar file, select File, Open from the menu and choose another calendar file. You can also merge dates from multiple calendars; open one calendar (to start), and select File, Merge, and then enter or browse to a second file with appointments that you want to merge into the first calendar.

The calendar files are saved using a format called vCalendar, which is imported and exported by many other calendar programs (including many Windows programs). This is an ASCII text file format, which you can examine (and edit) outside of KOrganizer if you want to (although this is not recommended). To use a calendar file from another calendar program, export the data from the other program in vCalendar format (see the instructions for that program to learn how to do this), and then open the file in KOrganizer.

Finally, KOrganizer can be used with a 3Com PalmPilot (handheld computer) to synchronize appointments and To-Do lists between your desktop and handheld computers. See the KOrganizer online help for information about the Linux software components and configuration that are required to do this.

SUMMARY

In this chapter the various programs that make up the KOffice productivity suite of applications was presented. Although these programs are not yet finished, they show great promise as very sophisticated and powerful applications that will enhance the productivity of KDE and OpenLinux users.

For more information about the topics discussed here, see the following chapters:

- Chapter 3, "Introduction to the Desktop (KDE)," gives an overview of the KDE project (of which KOffice is a part) and its goals.
- Chapter 4, "Navigating the Desktop," contains introductory material for working with KDE windows and interface elements, many of which are used by the KOffice applications.
- Chapter 7 describes other KDE programs, some of which provide functionality that is similar or complementary to the programs in KOffice.

PART III

OpenLinux System Administration

CHAPTER 9

Understanding the Linux File System

In this chapter

THE LINUX FILE SYSTEM STRUCTURE

The Linux file system is very similar to the standard UNIX file system layout, but of course there are some minor differences. The key to understanding the Linux file system is to first understand the underlying structure. A more in-depth discussion on the internal workings of the Linux file system and the methodology used in handling files is covered in Chapter 19, "Disk Drives and File Systems." The Linux directory structure, which is very similar to UNIX or DOS, is designed as a tree hierarchy. At the top level is the main directory, often times referred to as the *root directory* (or the *system root directory*). It is the only directory at this level. All other directories are referenced in relation to the root directory. The root directory is denoted as the / (forward slash) directory.

Note

Don't confuse the top level root directory (/) with the /root directory. The /root directory is a subdirectory of the / directory.

The root directory contains a small set of subdirectories and files. Remember that the /root directory is a sub directory of the / directory, and is the home directory of the root user. The root user, or *superuser*, is described in more detail in Chapter 10, "Users, Groups, and Permissions."

Note

In Linux, the forward slash is used in denoting paths to specific directories. DOS uses the backslash (\).

One important thing to keep in mind when examining the inner workings of a Linux file system is the fact that the entire Linux system is addressed under one large directory tree spanning one or more hard drives, disks, CD-ROM drives, and so on. This means different hard drives or partitions are not accessed as separate drive letters as they are with DOS. Instead, all partitions are *mounted* to subdirectories that reside under the root file system directory (/). In order to access files on a secondary hard drive or partition, simply change to the directory to which the partition is mounted. Mounting and unmounting of partitions is discussed in detail in Chapter 19.

Note

Unlike a DOS file system, where you must map a drive letter to a specific partition or disk drive, in Linux all hard drives and partitions appear to the user as one file system or directory hierarchy.

Essentially, every part of your Linux system—including the hardware in your computer—resides on your file system in the form of files. Even the hardware devices are accessed as files. Of course, these aren't typical files and they can't be viewed like a simple text file; but as files, things such as modifying access to a specific device becomes a much simpler task.

Devices are one of the more unique file types in Linux. They are discussed in more detail in the last section of this chapter.

THE LINUX FILE SYSTEM STANDARD (FHS)

The OpenLinux file system hierarchy is based on, for the most part, the *File System Hierarchy Standard* (*FHS*). In the Fall of 1993, an effort began to restructure the file and directory layout of Linux. This project began as the *File System Standards*, or *FSSTND*, project. After several iterations as the FSSTND project, the scope was widened to include issues that were general to other UNIX-like operating systems. In view of this expanded focus, the project was renamed the File System Hierarchy Standard (FHS).

Many people have contributed to this effort, but the primary person behind it is Daniel Quinlan. As of this writing, the most current version of the FHS documentation was version 2.0, dated October 26, 1997. It can be obtained from `ftp://tsx-11.mit.edu/pub/linux/docs/linux-standards/fsstnd`. Dan also currently serves as the chairman of the steering committee for the Linux Standard Base Organization (`www.linuxbase.org`). It is the goal of the Linux Standard Base group to develop and promote a set of standards that increase the compatibility between Linux distributions. This enables independent software vendors to port and develop applications to a common Linux environment without worrying about compatibility issues between Linux distributions.

FHS OVERVIEW

Whereas the File System Hierarchy Standard contains a great level of detail concerning what the Linux file system should and shouldn't be, its primary objective is to provide a consistent and standardized file system. This standardized file system can be defined into two orthogonal categories:

- **Shareable versus non-shareable files**—This category consists of files that can be shared between several hosts and files that are specific to just one particular host. For example, data from a specific database application can be shared between hosts, whereas device lock files are not shared.
- **Static versus variable files**—This category includes static files such as documentation, application binaries, and libraries that do not change without system administrator intervention. Any files that do change without system administrator intervention are considered variable data files. The /var/log/messages file is an example of a data file that changes without any system administrator intervention.

Shareable data files need to be located in a directory structure that can be mounted as a read-only file system. An example of how these two categories might be summarized is depicted in Table 9.1. This table is a generalized example and does not necessarily apply to all possible implementations of a FHS-compliant system.

TABLE 9.1 GENERALIZED EXAMPLE OF FHS-COMPLIANT DIRECTORY LAYOUT

	Shared	Non-shared
Static	/usr /opt	/etc /boot
Variable	/var/mail /var/spool/news	/var/run /var/lock

FHS SPECIFICATIONS FOR THE ROOT DIRECTORY

As was outlined in the first section of this chapter, the root directory is the first and only directory at the top level of the tree hierarchy. As such, special considerations are warranted for the root directory. The FHS document states, "The contents of the root file system should be adequate to boot, restore, recover, and/or repair the system." In order to accomplish that goal, the root file system must contain the essential components to boot the system, the essential tools to repair the system, and the essential utilities to back up or restore the system while still keeping the root file system as small as possible. A small root file system is less prone to file system errors and lends itself to easier maintenance if something were to go wrong.

DEFAULT DIRECTORY LAYOUT

A typical installation of OpenLinux creates the root directory with the following files and directories:

```
[root@redrock /]# ls -CF
NetWare/    bru/        initrd/         mnt/        sbin/       vmlinuz
auto/       dev/        install@        opt/        tmp/
bin/        etc/        lib/            proc/       usr/
boot/       home/       lost+found/     root/       var/
```

Directories are denoted with a trailing forward slash and symbolic links have a trailing `@` symbol when files are listed with the `F` option. Following is a closer look at each of these directories.

/NETWARE

This directory is used as an automatic mount point for NetWare volumes as part of the NetWare client. The automatic mounting of NetWare volumes and NDS trees is discussed at length in Chapter 33, "NetWare and OpenLinux."

/AUTO

This directory is used to configure devices to automatically detect and mount removable media when loaded. For example, the CD-ROM drive can be configured to be automatically mounted after a CD-ROM is detected in the drive. This differs slightly from configuring the /etc/fstab file. The /etc/fstab file is used to predefine and, with the proper option, automatically mount a given device—but it does not detect changes when a removable medium has changed.

/BIN

The /bin directory contains system and user utilities. They are commonly referred to as binaries because most utilities are compiled code, although some utilities in the /bin directory are actually shell scripts. Hence the directory name, bin.

/BOOT

This directory contains crucial components for the boot process. If these files are moved or modified, you must rerun the map installer portion of `LILO` to re-establish a proper boot setup. See Chapter 20, "Boot Loader," for more details on the boot loader and the use of files contained in this directory.

/BRU

The /bru directory contains the components of a commercial add-on program for tape backups and restores. This directory is not defined as a part of the File System Hierarchy Standard, but it meets the criteria of what is required for backup and restore capability.

/DEV

The /dev directory is where all the device definitions reside. The drivers themselves are in the /usr directory, but the definition of a specific device is in this directory. Devices are discussed in detail at the end of this chapter. There are no subdirectories in the /dev directory.

/ETC

The /etc directory might have been more aptly named the config directory because it contains configuration files and subordinate directories of system configuration data. It is important to be familiar with and understand the files in this directory. These files are crucial in the day-to-day operation and maintenance of your system. Whether it is a simple task, such as adding a user, or a more complicated task, such as configuring domain name resolution service, configuration files in /etc must be modified.

/HOME

This is the directory that is used for user data. For example, each new user has a directory in the home directory when their account is activated. Upon logging in, a user is located in their home directory. If someone named Natalie were a newly added user, her home directory might be aptly named /home/natalie.

/INITRD

This directory is used in association with the requirement of initial ram disk for some system configurations. For example, if a system is comprised of a SCSI controller with SCSI CD-ROM and hard drive, the default system configuration uses loadable modules for SCSI support. In order for the hard drive to be recognized as the system boots, a ram disk is first initialized, which enables the loading of the module that supports the SCSI adapter and allows the boot process to continue. Loadable modules are discussed in detail in the chapter on system initialization.

INSTALL@

This is a symbolic link to the directory in which install scripts and files are located, /var/lib/LST.

/LIB

Common libraries are stored in this directory. Different applications can make use of the same shared library. For example, the C programming code library set is stored in this directory.

/LOST+FOUND

File system utilities to correct system errors store data (lost inodes) in this directory when attempts to fix the errors are unsuccessful, or when files become truncated.

/MNT

This directory is used for the default mount points for other file systems. For example, by default the CD-ROM device mounts to /mnt/cdrom. The disk drive mounts to /mnt/floppy. It is not required to use this directory for mount points.

/OPT

The /opt (options) directory is the directory in which add-on applications are installed. For example, the Netscape Communicator and Navigator packages are installed in the /opt directory. To comply with the File System Hierarchy Standard, all third-party applications install to this directory.

/PROC

The /proc directory is actually a special file system. It contains detailed information about processes that are currently running, as well as specific information about hardware configurations. It's commonly referred to as a *process information pseudo-file system*. It acts as an interface to kernel data structures. For example, the /proc/interrupts file contains information about which interrupts are being used. This is covered in more detail in the section, "Examining Key Directories."

/ROOT

This directory is the home directory of the root user. By default, the root user logs in to this directory. Only files specific to the root user are stored in this directory. As noted earlier, this directory is not to be confused with the / directory, which is commonly referred to as the root directory.

/SBIN

The /sbin directory contains system utilities or binaries. Utilities for partitioning a hard drive, checking the integrity of a file system, creating a new file system, and shutting down or rebooting the system are all stored in this directory.

/TMP

Temporary files are stored in this directory. Often, applications need to use temporary files with certain functions or when installing. These temporary files are stored in the /tmp directory.

/USR

The /usr directory is intended for shareable, read-only data. It is the major section of the file system, but it can be configured to reside on a secondary machine. The majority of documentation is located in the /usr/doc directory. The complete source tree for the Linux kernel is located in the /usr/src directory.

/VAR

The /var directory is set up to hold variable data. It contains spool directories for mail, news, print jobs, and other files, as well as other administrative files. All data logged by specific processes are stored in the /var directory.

VMLINUZ

The vmlinuz file is the kernel that is booted by default. Whereas not exactly equivalent, this file can be thought of as the COMMAND.COM file that DOS needs in order to boot.

EXAMINING KEY DIRECTORIES

Whereas all the directories serve a purpose, a few are worth a closer look. The /etc directory contains several directories and files that are crucial to the successful operation of the system. Almost all configuration files reside in the /etc directory. Understanding devices, what they are, and how they work is best accomplished by exploring the /dev directory. As was mentioned previously, the /proc directory is actually a special type of file system.

THE /ETC DIRECTORY

A listing of files and directories in the /etc directory follows:

```
# ls -F /etc
HOSTNAME        gpm-root.conf    magic          protocols
X11/            group            mail.rc        psdevtab
XF86Config      group-           mailcap        pwdb.conf
adjtime         group.rpmorig    makedev.d/     rc.d/
aliases         host.conf        man.conf       resolv.conf
```

```
aliases.db           hosts                mediaprm             rpc
amd.localdev         hosts.allow          mgetty+sendfax/      samba.d/
amd.localdev         hosts.allow          mgetty+sendfax/      samba.d/
at.deny              hosts.deny           modules/             securetty
bruhelp              httpd/               motd                 security/
brusmartrest         identd.pid           mta/                 sendmail/
brutab               inetd.conf           mtab                 sendmail.cf
cron.d/              inetd.conf.orig      mtools.conf          sendmail.cw
crontab              inittab              named.boot           services
csh.cshrc            ioctl.save           named.conf           shadow
dhcpd.conf           isdn/                ntp.conf             shadow-
dosemu.conf          issue                ntp.drift            shells
dosemu.conf.sample   issue.net            ntp.keys             skel/
dosemu.users         ksh.kshrc*           nwdsmgr@             slip/
drums.o3             ld.so.cache          nwdsmgr.english/     smbpasswd
drums.sb             ld.so.conf           pam.d/               smbusers
exports              lilo.conf            passwd               std.o3
fdprm                lilo.conf.backup     passwd-              std.sb
fstab                lilo.conf.tmp        passwd.rpmorig       sysconfig/
ftpaccess            localtime@           pcmcia/              syslog.conf
ftpconversions       login.defs           porttime             system.cnf
ftpgroups            logrotate.d/         ppp/                 termcap
ftphosts             lpd.conf             printcap             vga/
ftpusers             lpd.perms            printcap.ori         visix.apps
getty.conf           lst.cnf              profile              yp.conf
gettydefs            lst.cnf.rpmorig      profile.ksh*
[col@train1 /etc]$
```

The /etc directory contains both directories and configuration files. Each of the directories contains configuration files for a specific area. Table 9.2 lists the subdirectories of the /etc directory and a description of each.

TABLE 9.2 SUBDIRECTORIES OF THE /ETC DIRECTORY

Subdirectory	Description
X11	Contains configuration data for the X Window server as well as several window managers.
cron.d	Details on when to automatically run specific routines are outlined in this directory.
httpd	Configuration files for the setup and operation of the Apache Web server.
isdn	Configuration files for the operation of an ISDN interface.
logrotate.d	Configuration files for how and when to rotate log files.
makedev.d	Contains makefiles for the creation of devices. Each file has the parameters for the creation of a specific type of device such as hard drives, serial ports, or CD-ROMS.

Subdirectory	Description
mgetty+sendfax	Configuration files for the use of mgetty as the interface on a serial port. The mgetty routine has special features for handling things such as dial-up connections and fax transmissions.
modules	The list of modules to be automatically loaded is maintained in this directory.
mta	This directory contains information on what is being used as the mail transfer agent, and how it is configured.
nwdsmgr.english	NetWare directory services manager, English version.
pcmcia	Configuration files for the operation of PCMCIA devices.
ppp	Configuration files for the setup and operation of a PPP interface.
rc.d	This directory, the run-time configuration directory, contains system initialization scripts. These routines are categorized by runlevel.
samba.d	Configuration files for the setup and operation of Samba are stored here. Samba is the network protocol (SMB) that enables the interface of Linux to a Windows network.
security	Security features for things such as user limits are maintained in configuration files in this directory.
sendmail	Specific items regarding the operation of sendmail can be fine-tuned by modifying the configuration files stored in this directory.
skel	The default files for each new user are stored in this directory. Each time a new user is added, these skeleton files are copied into their home directory.
slip	Configuration files for the setup and operation of the SLIP (serial line IP) interface.
sysconfig	This directory contains configuration files and subdirectories for the setup of system configuration specifics. For example, the Ethernet configuration files are stored in the network-scripts subdirectory.
vga	The configuration file for the svgalib is stored in this directory.

Besides the subdirectories listed in Table 9.2, there are many other configuration files in the /etc directory. Some of the most commonly modified configuration files and some of the more important ones to be aware of are listed in Table 9.3.

TABLE 9.3 COMMONLY MODIFIED CONFIGURATION FILES

Configuration File	Description
HOSTNAME	This file contains the fully qualified domain name (FQDN) of your system. The FQDN is the machine name plus the domain name. For example, if your machine name is hook and your company domain is fish.net, your FQDN is hook.fish.net.
XF86Config	This file contains all the necessary configurations to enable the X Server to function. It is described in detail in Chapter 38, "Dissecting the XF86Config File."
aliases	All email aliases are maintained in this file. An aliases database file (aliases.db) is built from the entries in the aliases file by the `newaliases` utility.
crontab	This file is the cron table set up for the automatic running of system routines. A cron table can also be established for individual users.
dosemu.conf	This is the configuration file for the DOS emulator.
exports	This file acts as the control list for clients who want to access the system via NFS.
fstab	This is the file system table. Entries in this file are made to predefine specific devices, file systems, mount points, and mount options.
ftpaccess	Controlling access to the FTP server is configured in this file.
group	The definition of groups and users that belong to these groups is determined by the configuration of this file. The primary purpose of a group is for access control to a set of files and directories. For example, a development group can be established and permission set in such a way that only members of this group can access files and directories belonging to this group. See Chapter 10 for more details.
hosts	This file is used to define a system name and domain in combination with a specific IP address. This file needs to always contain an entry for the local loopback device (127.0.0.1). It might also contain an entry for an IP address, if the machine is connected to a network.
hosts.allow	This file defines which other machines (hosts) are allowed to access this machine.
hosts.deny	This file defines which other machines (hosts) are not allowed to access this machine.
inetd.conf	A configuration of services that are started by the INETD TCP/IP super server.
inittab	This is the table that contains definitions for init processes.
issue	This file contains the text that is displayed before logging in. In other words, the message shown right above a login prompt.
lilo.conf	This file contains configuration information for the LILO boot manager. It is covered in detail in Chapter 20.
motd	This is the *message of the day* file. The system administrator can put any text in this file that is to be shown to all users upon logging in to the system.

Configuration File	Description
passwd	This file contains crucial user information for individual login accounts. At one time the password was stored in this file—hence the file name passwd. However, passwords are now encrypted and stored in the /etc/shadow file.
printcap	The definition for all system printers, whether local or remote, is stored in this file.
profile	This file contains systemwide environment and startup scripts. This includes such things as the default setting for the $PATH environment variable as well as other environment settings.
resolv.conf	Configuration of how Domain Name resolution is to occur is defined in this file.
securetty	This file contains a list of ports (tty devices) that are allowed to log in to the system as the root user. By default, only the system virtual consoles are predefined.
sendmail.cf	This is the sendmail configuration file. Do not modify it unless it's absolutely necessary and you make a backup copy beforehand.
sendmail.cw	Machine name aliases are entered in this file. For example, if your machine name is hook.fish.net, adding an entry for just fish.net allows `sendmail` to recognize your email as user@fish.net as opposed to user@hook.fish.net.
services	A definition of the networks, services, and the associated port for each protocol that are available on this system. For example, Web services (http) are assigned to port 80 by default.
shadow	Encrypted passwords for user accounts are stored in this file.
shells	This file contains a list of shells that are available with OpenLinux.
syslog.conf	This file contains the definition of how logging is to take place on this machine. For example, all mail messages are logged in /var/log/mail by default.
system.cnf	This is an OpenLinux specific configuration file. It is maintained by external scripts and is not normally modified directly.

Many of these configuration files can be modified and maintained by graphical utilities. However, it's important to note that these utilities are merely that—utilities to make it easier to maintain these files. The best understanding of these files will come when you are comfortable in editing these files directly. Of course, this requires an understanding of the purpose and syntactical layout of each configuration file. Some configuration files are self-documenting; that is, they contain comments throughout the file that describe syntax and purpose. The /etc/dosemu.conf file is an example of this type of configuration file. Other configuration files require referencing an online manual page or other documentation file. For example, the man page for the /etc/passwd file is the best reference for a succinct description of how this file layout works.

THE /DEV DIRECTORY

The /dev directory is the directory in which all device definitions are stored. The majority of the devices are either block devices or character devices; however, other types of devices can be created. As a general rule of thumb, block devices can be thought of as devices that store or hold data, and character devices can be thought of as devices that transmit or transfer data. For example, devices for the diskette drive, hard drive, and CD-ROM are all block devices, whereas the devices for serial ports, mice, and parallel printer ports are all character devices. There is some sort of naming scheme for devices, but you pretty much have to memorize device names in order to reference them correctly. The common block devices are listed in Table 9.4, and the common character devices are listed in Table 9.5.

Note

CD-ROM drives that are neither IDE nor SCSI have a proprietary device name. This type of CD-ROM has its own interface card and a unique device name.

TABLE 9.4 COMMON BLOCK DEVICES

Device Type	Device Name	Description
Disk drive	/dev/fd0	This is the floppy disk drive. The DOS equivalent is drive letter A:.
IDE	/dev/had	An IDE device jumpered as the master device on the primary controller.
	/dev/hdb	An IDE device jumpered as a slave device on the primary controller.
	/dev/hdc	An IDE device jumpered as a master device on the secondary controller.
	/dev/hdd	An IDE device jumpered as a slave device on the secondary controller.
SCSI	/dev/sda	The first SCSI hard drive.
	/dev/sdb	The second SCSI hard drive.
	/dev/sdc	The third SCSI hard drive.
	/dev/scd0	The first SCSI CD-ROM drive.
	/dev/scd1	The second SCSI CD-ROM drive.
CD-ROM	/dev/gscd	A GoldStar CD-ROM drive.
	/dev/sonycd	A Sony CD-ROM drive.

Table 9.5 Common Character Devices

Device Type	Device Name	Description
Mouse	/dev/psaux	PS/2 style bus mouse
Parallel ports	/dev/lp0	The first parallel port
	/dev/lp1	The second parallel port
Serial ports	/dev/ttyS0	The first serial port
	/dev/ttyS1	The second serial port
	/dev/ttyS2	The third serial port

Define a device by specifying a type, such as block or character, and a major and minor number. The major number is used to categorize a device and the minor number is used to identify a specific device type. For example, all IDE devices connected to the primary controller have a major number of 3. Master and slave devices, as well as individual partitions, are further defined by the use of a minor number. Listing the IDE hard drive devices displays the major and minor numbers. These are the two numbers preceding the date in the following display:

```
# ls -l /dev/hd*
brw-r-----    1 root     operator   3,   1 Aug 19 02:22 hda1
brw-r-----    1 root     operator   3,  10 Aug 19 02:22 hda10
brw-r-----    1 root     operator   3,  11 Aug 19 02:22 hda11
brw-r-----    1 root     operator   3,  12 Aug 19 02:22 hda12
brw-r-----    1 root     operator   3,  13 Aug 19 02:22 hda13
brw-r-----    1 root     operator   3,  14 Aug 19 02:22 hda14
brw-r-----    1 root     operator   3,  15 Aug 19 02:22 hda15
brw-r-----    1 root     operator   3,   2 Aug 19 02:22 hda2
brw-r-----    1 root     operator   3,   3 Aug 19 02:22 hda3
brw-r-----    1 root     operator   3,   4 Aug 19 02:22 hda4
brw-r-----    1 root     operator   3,   5 Aug 19 02:22 hda5
brw-r-----    1 root     operator   3,   6 Aug 19 02:22 hda6
brw-r-----    1 root     operator   3,   7 Aug 19 02:22 hda7
brw-r-----    1 root     operator   3,   8 Aug 19 02:22 hda8
brw-r-----    1 root     operator   3,   9 Aug 19 02:22 hda9
brw-r-----    1 root     operator   3,  64 Aug 19 02:22 hdb
brw-r-----    1 root     operator   3,  65 Aug 19 02:22 hdb1
brw-r-----    1 root     operator   3,  74 Aug 19 02:22 hdb10
brw-r-----    1 root     operator   3,  75 Aug 19 02:22 hdb11
brw-r-----    1 root     operator   3,  76 Aug 19 02:22 hdb12
brw-r-----    1 root     operator   3,  77 Aug 19 02:22 hdb13
```

The major number for both hda and hdb devices is 3. Of course, the minor number changes for each specific partition. The definition of each major number category can be examined by looking at the contents of the /usr/src/linux/include/linux/major.h file. The devices.txt file also documents major and minor numbers. It is located in the /usr/src/linux/Documentation directory. This file defines the major numbers (outlined in Table 9.6).

Note

The same major number can be used for different device types. For example, a block device can use the same major number as a character device. Major numbers can be used in this manner because the device type is the distinguishing factor. In other words, devices are categorized by device type first, and then by major numbers, and finally by minor numbers.

TABLE 9.6 MAJOR NUMBER ASSIGNMENT

Major Number	Device Type	Description
0	Unnamed Devices	Reserved as null device number
1	Character	Memory devices
1	Block	RAM disk
2	Character	Pseudo TTY masters
2	Block	Floppy disks
3	Character	Pseudo TTY slaves
3	Block	The primary IDE, MFM, and RLL interface
4	Character	TTY devices
5	Character	Alternative TTY devices
6	Character	Parallel printer devices
7	Character	Virtual console capture devices.
7	Block	Loopback devices
8	Block	SCSI disk devices
9	Character	SCSI tape devices
9	Block	Metadisk (RAID) devices
10	Character	Non-serial mice
11	Character	Raw keyboard device
11	Block	SCSI CD-ROM devices
12	Character	QIC-02 tape devices
12	Block	MSCDEX CD-ROM callback support
13	Character	PC speaker
13	Block	8-bit IDE/MFM/RLL controller
14	Character	Sound card devices
14	Block	BIOS hard drive callback support
15	Character	Joystick
15	Block	Sony CDU-31A/CDU-33A CD-ROM

Major Number	Device Type	Description
16	Character	Non-SCSI scanners
16	Block	GoldStar CD-ROM
17	Character	Chase serial card
17	Block	Optics Storage CD-ROM
18	Character	Chase serial card—alternative devices
18	Block	Sanyo CD-ROM
19	Character	Cyclades serial card
19	Block	Double compressed disk
20	Character	Cylcades serial card (alternative devices)
20	Block	Hitachi CD-ROM
21	Character	Generic SCSI access
22	Character	Digiboard serial card
22	Block	Secondary IDE hard disk/CD-ROM controller
23	Character	Digiboard serial card—alternative devices
23	Block	Mitsumi proprietary CD-ROM
24	Character	Stallion serial card
24	Block	Sony CDU-535 CD-ROM
25	Character	Stallion serial card—alternative devices
25	Block	First Matsushita (Panasonic/Soundblaster) CD-ROM
26	Character	Quanta WinVision frame grabber
26	Block	Second Matsushita (Panasonic/Soundblaster) CD-ROM
27	Character	QIC-117 Tape devices
27	Block	Third Matsushita
28	Character	Stallion serial card (card programming)
28	Block	Fourth Matsushita
29	Block	Aztech/Orchid/Okano/Wearnes CD-ROM
30	Character	iBCS-2 compatibility devices
30	Block	Phillips LMS CM-205 CD-ROM
31	Character	MPU-401 MIDI
31	Block	ROM/flash memory card
32	Character	Specialix serial card

continues

TABLE 9.6 CONTINUED

Major Number	Device Type	Description
32	Block	Phillips LMS CM-206 CD-ROM
33	Character	Specialix serial card (alternative devices)
33	Block	Third IDE hard disk/CD-ROM controller
...		...
64-119		Unallocated
120-127		Local/Experimental Use
128-239		Unallocated
240-254		Local/Experimental Use
255		Reserved

Almost all devices are created by default at installation time. However, you can always create a device, if need be, by using the `mknod` command. Devices are created with this utility by supplying the device to be created, the device type (block or character), and the major and minor numbers. For example, the entry for the first serial port, COM1 in DOS, displays as follows:

```
# ls -l /dev/ttyS0
crw-rw----    1 root      uucp    4,  64 Aug 19  02:22  ttyS0
```

If this file is accidentally deleted, it can be easily recreated. Notice that the first letter in the preceding display indicates the file type. In this case, it is a character device. This device can be recreated as follows:

```
# mknod ttyS0 c 4 64
```

For the most part, you rarely have to recreate devices, but if you use Linux long enough you'll have to create a device at some point. A complete set of scripts is installed in the /etc/makedev.d directory for the easy rebuilding of any or all devices. Running /sbin/makedev rebuilds the entire set of devices. You can test this by setting the environment variable `$DESTDIR` to the destination at which you want the devices to be created. For example, if you want the devices to be created in the /test-devices directory, do the following:

```
# mkdir /test-devices
# cd /test-devices
# mkdir dev
# mkdir etc
# cd etc
# mkdir makedev.d
# cd makedev.d
# cp /etc/makedev.d/* .
# export DESTDIR=/test-devices
# makedev
```

The /test-devices/dev directory now contains the newly created devices.

THE /PROC DIRECTORY

As was previously mentioned, the /proc directory is actually a unique file system. Listing the files is this directory doesn't really give you any clues that there is anything unusual about this directory—until you take a closer look at the file sizes. All the files and directories have a file size of 0, with two exceptions: kcore and self. A directory listing looks similar to the following:

```
dr-xr-xr-x   3 root     root            0 Dec  6 01:13 1
dr-xr-xr-x   3 root     root            0 Dec  6 01:13 2
dr-xr-xr-x   3 root     root            0 Dec  6 01:13 21
dr-xr-xr-x   3 root     root            0 Dec  6 01:13 22
dr-xr-xr-x   3 root     root            0 Dec  6 01:13 23
dr-xr-xr-x   3 root     root            0 Dec  6 01:13 24
dr-xr-xr-x   3 root     root            0 Dec  6 01:13 3
dr-xr-xr-x   3 root     root            0 Dec  6 01:13 360
dr-xr-xr-x   3 bin      root            0 Dec  6 01:13 362
dr-xr-xr-x   3 root     root            0 Dec  6 01:13 373
dr-xr-xr-x   3 root     root            0 Dec  6 01:13 376
dr-xr-xr-x   3 root     root            0 Dec  6 01:13 387
dr-xr-xr-x   3 root     root            0 Dec  6 01:13 4
dr-xr-xr-x   3 root     root            0 Dec  6 01:13 412
dr-xr-xr-x   3 root     root            0 Dec  6 01:13 418
dr-xr-xr-x   3 daemon   root            0 Dec  6 01:13 425
dr-xr-xr-x   3 root     root            0 Dec  6 01:13 437
dr-xr-xr-x   3 root     root            0 Dec  6 01:13 439
dr-xr-xr-x   3 root     root            0 Dec  6 01:13 445
dr-xr-xr-x   3 root     root            0 Dec  6 01:13 460
dr-xr-xr-x   3 nobody   65535           0 Dec  6 01:13 465
dr-xr-xr-x   3 root     root            0 Dec  6 01:13 5
dr-xr-xr-x   3 root     root            0 Dec  6 01:13 525
dr-xr-xr-x   3 root     root            0 Dec  6 01:13 526
dr-xr-xr-x   3 root     root            0 Dec  6 01:13 527
dr-xr-xr-x   3 root     root            0 Dec  6 01:13 528
dr-xr-xr-x   3 root     root            0 Dec  6 01:13 529
dr-xr-xr-x   3 root     root            0 Dec  6 01:13 530
dr-xr-xr-x   3 root     root            0 Dec  6 01:13 56
dr-xr-xr-x   3 root     root            0 Dec  6 01:48 860
dr-xr-xr-x   3 col      users           0 Dec  6 01:48 861
dr-xr-xr-x   3 col      users           0 Dec  6 01:48 862
dr-xr-xr-x   3 root     root            0 Dec  6 01:48 875
dr-xr-xr-x   3 root     root            0 Dec  6 01:48 876
dr-xr-xr-x   3 root     root            0 Dec  6 01:50 891
dr-xr-xr-x   3 root     root            0 Dec  6 01:50 892
-r--r--r--   1 root     root            0 Dec  6 01:13 cmdline
-r--r--r--   1 root     root            0 Dec  6 01:13 cpuinfo
-r--r--r--   1 root     root            0 Dec  6 01:13 devices
-r--r--r--   1 root     root            0 Dec  6 01:13 dma
-r--r--r--   1 root     root            0 Dec  6 01:13 filesystems
-r--r--r--   1 root     root            0 Dec  6 01:13 interrupts
-r--r--r--   1 root     root            0 Dec  6 01:13 ioports
-r--------   1 root     root     33558528 Dec  6 01:13 kcore
-r--------   1 root     root            0 Dec  3 18:12 kmsg
-r--r--r--   1 root     root            0 Dec  6 01:13 ksyms
-r--r--r--   1 root     root            0 Dec  6 01:13 loadavg
-r--r--r--   1 root     root            0 Dec  6 01:13 locks
```

```
-r--r--r--    1 root      root            0 Dec  6 01:13 mdstat
-r--r--r--    1 root      root            0 Dec  6 01:13 meminfo
-r--r--r--    1 root      root            0 Dec  6 01:13 modules
-r--r--r--    1 root      root            0 Dec  6 01:13 mounts
dr-xr-xr-x    2 root      root            0 Dec  6 01:13 net
-r--r--r--    1 root      root            0 Dec  6 01:13 pci
dr-xr-xr-x    2 root      root            0 Dec  6 01:13 scsi
lrwxrwxrwx    1 root      root           64 Dec  6 01:13 self -> 889
-r--r--r--    1 root      root            0 Dec  6 01:13 stat
dr-xr-xr-x    5 root      root            0 Dec  6 01:13 sys
-r--r--r--    1 root      root            0 Dec  6 01:13 uptime
-r--r--r--    1 root      root            0 Dec  6 01:13 version
```

Each of the numbered directories correspond to an actual process ID. Looking at the process table, you can match processes with the associated process ID. For example, the process table might indicate the following for the Web server:

```
# ps ax ¦ grep httpd

460     ?     S     0:00 httpd -f /etc/httpd/apache/conf/httpd.conf
```

Details of this process can be examined by looking at the associated files in the directory for this process, /proc/460. You might wonder how you can see details of a process that has a file size of 0. It makes more sense if you think of it as a window into the kernel. The file doesn't actually contain any data; it just acts as a pointer to where the actual process information resides. A listing of the files in the /proc/460 directory looks similar to the following:

```
-r--r--r--    1 root      root            0 Dec  6 21:21 cmdline
lrwx------    1 root      root           64 Dec  6 21:21 cwd -> [0303]:2
-r--------    1 root      root            0 Dec  6 21:21 environ
lrwx------    1 root      root           64 Dec  6 21:21 exe -> [0303]:43066
dr-x------    1 root      root            0 Dec  6 21:21 fd
pr--r--r--    1 root      root            0 Dec  6 21:21 maps
-rw-------    1 root      root            0 Dec  6 21:21 mem
lrwx------    1 root      root           64 Dec  6 21:21 root -> [0303]:2
-r--r--r--    1 root      root            0 Dec  6 21:21 stat
-r--r--r--    1 root      root            0 Dec  6 21:21 statm
-r--r--r--    1 root      root            0 Dec  6 21:21 status
```

Even though the files appear to be of size 0, examining their contents reveals otherwise:

```
# cat status
Name:   httpd.apache
State:  S (sleeping)
Pid:    460
PPid:   1
Uid:    0       0       0       0
Gid:    0       0       0       0
VmSize:     1332 kB
VmLck:         0 kB
VmRSS:       688 kB
VmData:      300 kB
VmStk:        20 kB
VmExe:       376 kB
VmLib:       592 kB
SigPnd: 00000000
```

```
SigBlk: 00000000
SigIgn: 80000000
SigCgt: 0000466b
```

The man page for proc describes each of the files associated with a running process ID in detail.

The files in the /proc directory act very similar to the process ID subdirectory files. For example, examining the contents of the /proc/interrupts file displays something like the following:


```
# cat interrupts
 0:   27222899   timer
 1:       3152   keyboard
 2:          0   cascade
 9:     450448   eth0
12:       4477   PS/2 Mouse
13:          1   math error
14:      15198 + ide0
15:          0 + ide1
```

Each of the numbers down the left-hand column represent an interrupt that is in use. Examining the contents of the file dynamically gathers the associated data and displays it to the screen. Most of the /proc file system is read-only; however, some files allow kernel variables to be changed. This provides a mechanism to actually tune the kernel without recompiling and rebooting.

The `procinfo` utility summarizes /proc file system information into a display similar to the following:

```
# /usr/bin/procinfo

Linux 2.0.35 (root@buildmeister.caldera.com) (gcc 2.7.2.3) #1 [train2]

Memory:      Total        Used        Free      Shared     Buffers      Cached
Mem:         30884       20332       10552       10840        8900        5292
Swap:         66492           0        66492

Bootup: Thu Dec 03 18:12:23 1998    Load average: 0.00 0.00 0.00 3/38 895

user  :       0:00:19.69   0.0%  page in :    10886  disk 1:    6791r  3742w
nice  :        0:00:00.00   0.0%  page out:      6089
system:        0:00:34.14   0.0%  swap in :         1
idle  :   2d  7:42:19.82 100.0%  swap out:         0
uptime:   2d  7:43:13.61         context :  1083993

irq  0:  20059365 timer                  irq  8:         0
irq  1:         4 keyboard               irq  9:    326636 eth0
irq  2:         0 cascade [4]            irq 10:         0
irq  3:         0                        irq 11:         0
irq  4:         0                        irq 12:         0
irq  5:         0                        irq 13:         1 math error
irq  6:         2                        irq 14:     10515 ide0+
irq  7:         0                        irq 15:         0 ide1+
```

SUMMARY

The Linux file system is very similar to any other operating system, although you'll find the most similarities to other UNIX file systems. The directory structure is based on the same concept as others, as well—a system root directory with subdirectories in a tree-like hierarchy.

- See Chapter 13, "Customizing Your Shell Environment," for more information on how shells are used in Linux.
- See Chapter 19 for further information on how to add additional partitions and how to make then accessible.
- See Appendix A, "Commonly Used Commands," for a list of common commands used in Linux and how they are used in navigating the Linux directory structure.

CHAPTER 10

Users, Groups, and Permissions

In this chapter

USER ACCOUNTS

Because Linux is a multiuser system, the task of adding and maintaining user accounts is common in Linux system administration. Upon a successful installation of OpenLinux, two user accounts are configured: the root user and a normal user. These two user accounts represent the two basic types of users that are configurable with Linux.

Note

The concept of users, groups, and permissions is probably very familiar to those of you who are accustomed to multiuser environments, including NT systems.

The first type, the *root user*, is unique for several reasons. First and foremost, it is the only user account with systemwide privileges. Other accounts can be set up as an exact clone of the root user account, but it is strongly discouraged. For the most part, the root user account needs to be one of a kind.

The second type, a *normal user* account, is the type of account that is set up for each individual user. This type of account differs only in respect to access privileges and home directories. You'll examine this more closely in the subsequent sections of this chapter, which discuss groups and permissions.

Logging in to a Linux system is done in one of three ways: at the console, via a serial connection such as a terminal, or via a network connection. For some, the term *logging in* is a foreign term. If you fall into that category, think of it as authenticating a user to the server. The primary purpose for logging in, or authenticating yourself, is to establish access rights to a given set of files, directories, or services.

ROOT USER/SUPERUSER

The root user, often called the *superuser*, is the user that has the rights and privileges to perform any task or view any file on the system. He or she is, in essence, the all-powerful system administrator—hence the name superuser. There is nothing that the superuser can't do.

That being the case, it's very important that the root user account is closely guarded. Obviously, the password to the root user account is of primary importance when considering system security. The root password will only be given to those authorized to log in as root, and it needs to be changed periodically. The root user account is only used when performing system administration tasks, or when performing a task that can only be done as the superuser. In other words, it's best to perform as many tasks as possible as an individual user and only use the superuser account when it is absolutely necessary.

System administration tasks are performed from the superuser account. For example, the following list summarizes some of the duties and privileges of a system administrator:

- Has complete access to all files and directories regardless of owner and permissions.
- Controls user account administration.

- Performs system maintenance tasks such as file housekeeping.
- Halts the system when necessary.
- Sets up initial user passwords.
- Changes passwords when necessary.

NORMAL USERS

Normal user accounts are accounts that are set up for individual users. Each user has his or her own account. This does not mean that system utilities and server application software can't be shared; it means that it's easier to maintain and administer a system in which each individual user has an account.

Note

It is good system practice to have a separate account for each individual user. Avoid accounts that are shared, if possible.

VIRTUAL CONSOLES

By default, six virtual consoles are available. Each virtual console is accessed via the function keys at the console keyboard. After the system boots, the login prompt that is presented is on console one. Five additional consoles, that is, login prompts, are available by pressing the Alt key in conjunction with function keys F2–F5. Table 10.1 describes the virtual console configuration.

TABLE 10.1 VIRTUAL CONSOLE CONFIGURATION

Key Sequence	Description
Alt+F1	First Virtual Console [Default]
Alt+F2	Second Virtual Console
Alt+F3	Third Virtual Console
Alt+F4	Fourth Virtual Console
Alt+F5	Fifth Virtual Console
Alt+F6	Sixth Virtual Console

Toggling from one console screen to another is just a matter of pressing the Alt key and the desired function key.

SERIAL CONNECTIONS

Login sessions are also available via a serial port. For example, dumb terminals can be connected via an RS-232 interface. This can be one or two serial ports (COM1 and COM2 in DOS) typically found on PC systems, or via an add-on multiport card. Many multiport cards are supported in Linux, including Cyclades, Digiboard, and Stallion. Modifying the /etc/inittab file with the appropriate entries allows logins via any available serial connection.

NETWORK LOGINS

A very common method of logging in to a Linux server is via a network connection. In fact, a Linux server functions quite nicely as a standalone, monitorless box for specific services. For example, it is quite common to find a Domain Name Server (DNS) running on an appliance-like, Linux-based machine. Servers like this, without a monitor and keyboard, need only an occasional check via a remote login session. The most common way of connecting to a Linux server via a network link is with the `telnet` utility. A network connection can also be made with utilities such as `rlogin` or `slogin`.

ACCOUNT SETUP

Adding and deleting users is simple, but understanding the files involved with user account management is a bit more complex. Many utilities have been written to manage the data files associated with user accounts, including the default `useradd` utility, but the key to managing user accounts is to understand the underlying configuration files.

KEY CONFIGURATION FILE

The key file used in user account setup and configuration is the /etc/password file. This file is a simple ASCII text file, but it's crucial to the multi-user concept of Linux. Upon a successful installation, the contents of the /etc/passwd file resemble the following:

```
root:x:0:0:root:/root:/bin/bash
bin:x:1:1:bin:/bin:
daemon:x:2:2:daemon:/sbin:
adm:x:3:4:adm:/var/adm:
lp:x:4:7:lp:/var/spool/lpd:
sync:x:5:0:sync:/sbin:/bin/sync
shutdown:x:6:11:shutdown:/sbin:/sbin/shutdown
halt:x:7:0:halt:/sbin:/sbin/halt
mail:x:8:12:mail:/var/spool/mail:
news:x:9:13:news:/var/spool/news:
uucp:x:10:14:uucp:/var/spool/uucp:
operator:x:11:0:operator:/root:
games:x:12:100:games:/usr/games:
gopher:x:13:30:gopher:/usr/lib/gopher-data:
ftp:x:14:50:FTP User:/home/ftp:
man:x:15:15:Manuals Owner:/:
majordom:x:16:16:Majordomo:/:/bin/false
postgres:x:17:17:Postgres User:/home/postgres:/bin/bash
nobody:x:65534:65534:Nobody:/:/bin/false
col:x:100:100:COL User:/home/col:/bin/bash
natalie:x:101:100:OpenLinux User:/home/natalie/bin/bash
ryan:x:102:100:OpenLinux User:/home/ryan/bin/bash
brittany:x:103:100:OpenLinux User:/home/brittany/bin/bash
kelsey:x:104:100:OpenLinux User:/home/kelsey/bin/bash
```

Each line represents one user. The information for each user is separated into seven colon-delimited fields. The description of each of these fields is listed in Table 10.2.

TABLE 10.2 FIELD DESCRIPTIONS OF THE /ETC/PASSWD FILE

Field	Description
1	The first field is the username or login ID.
2	The second field is the password field. A lowercase x in this field indicates that shadow passwords are in use. The actual encrypted passwords are stored in a separate file for security reasons.
3	The number in this field is the User ID number. This is used to identify a unique user account. No two user accounts can have the same number.
4	This field is the Group ID (GID) field number. This number is used to create logical user groups.
5	This field is a comment field. It commonly contains the user's full name.
6	The sixth field is used to identify where in the file system hierarchy a user is to be placed upon logging in to the system. User accounts are typically configured to use the /home directory.
7	This field is used for the configuration of the default shell. The default shell is the bash shell.

New user accounts can be added by directly editing the /etc/passwd file, but passwords must be created using the `/usr/bin/passwd` utility. This utility is required because it creates the proper encryption.

PASSWORDS

Access to any account is controlled with a password. Shadow passwords are used by default with OpenLinux.

Note

Shadow passwords are passwords that are stored in a separate file. This file, the /etc/shadow file, adds an additional level of security.

Before the advent of shadow passwords, the password—albeit encrypted—was stored in the /etc/passwd file. The /etc/passwd file is readable by any user on the system, but it can only be modified by the root user. It has to be readable by all users for certain applications. However, this presents a problem because it means that anyone can see the encrypted password. With the powerful machines of today, it has become easier to crack the encryption of even well-chosen passwords. In order to combat this potential threat, the concept of shadow passwords was defined. By storing the password in a separate file, the /etc/shadow file, it became possible to keep the /etc/passwd file readable to all accounts but make the encrypted passwords themselves only readable to the root user. You'll take a closer look at this in the "Permissions" section later in this chapter.

Caution

Use the pwconv and pwunconv utilities to convert the /etc/passwd file to or from shadow enabling.

The /etc/shadow password file looks similar to the following:

```
root:Rb3mAtGdwFMDE:10568:0:-1:7:7:-1:1073897392
bin:*:10542:0::7:7::
daemon:*:10542:0::7:7::
adm:*:10542:0::7:7::
lp:*:10542:0::7:7::
sync:*:10542:0::7:7::
shutdown:*:10542:0::7:7::
halt:*:10542:0::7:7::
mail:*:10542:0::7:7::
news:*:10542:0::7:7::
uucp:*:10542:0::7:7::
operator:*:10542:0::7:7::
games:*:10542:0::7:7::
gopher:*:10542:0::7:7::
ftp:*:10542:0::7:7::
man:*:10542:0::7:7::
majordom:*:10542:0::7:7::
postgres:*:10542:0::7:7::
nobody:*:10542:0::7:7::
col:pbHeht8NUW842:10573:0:-1:7:7:-1:1073897392
natalie:jEFpY1Zqm18E.:10576:0:-1:9:-1:-1:1073897392
ryan:hBcIkjWnhFk/o:10576:0:-1:7:-1:-1:1073897392
brittany:oCtbTK7DjDye2:10576:0:-1:9:-1:-1:1073897392
kelsey:dDJLXtAbiJVaM:10576:0:-1:7:-1:-1:1073897392
```

Much like the /etc/passwd file, the /etc/shadow file consists of single-line entries with colon-delimited fields. The first field is the user account name and the second field is where the encrypted password is stored.

ADDING USERS

User accounts can be added by directly editing the /etc/passwd file or by using a utility such as useradd. Default characteristics for each user account are defined by the settings in the /etc/login.defs file, as follows:

```
###
# Password aging controls: (used by useradd and pwconv)
#
# Maximum number of days a password may be used:
# (-1 = no password changes are necessary)
PASS_MAX_DAYS -1

# Minimum number of days allowed between password
# changes:
PASS_MIN_DAYS 0

# Number of days warning given before a password expires:
PASS_WARN_AGE 7

# Number of days till account is closed after password
```

```
# has expired:
PASS_INACTIVE -1

# Force expiry at given day: (in days after 70/1/1,
# -1 = don't force)
PASS_EXPIRE -1

###
# Default values for useradd
#

# default group:
GROUP 100

# user's home directory: (%s = name of user)
HOME /home/%s

# default user shell:
SHELL /bin/bash

# directory where the home directory skeleton is located:
SKEL /etc/skel

###
# Min/max values for automatic gid selection in groupadd
#
GID_MIN 100
GID_MAX 60000
```


The useradd utility does not create the /home directory of the new user by default, but given the correct parameter, the home directory is created. For example, using useradd to create an account for someone named natalie, with the following parameters, creates both the /etc/passwd entry and the home directory:

```
# useradd -m -d /home/natalie natalie
```

A new directory, /home/natalie, is created and populated with copies of the default files in the /etc/skel directory. The /etc/skel directory contains the following files:

```
.bash_logout
.bashrc
.cshrc
.inputrc
.kshrc
.login
.logout
.profile
.profile_ksh
.seyon/
lg/
```

Running useradd with the -D option displays the default characteristics of user accounts:

```
# useradd -D
GROUP=100
HOME=/home/%s
SHELL=/bin/sh
```

```
SKEL=/etc/skel
PASS_MIN_DAYS=0
PASS_MAX_DAYS=-1
PASS_WARN_DAYS=7
PASS_INACTIVE=-1
PASS_EXPIRE=-1
```

These are the parameters that you saw previously, as defined in the /etc/login.defs file. They can be easily changed by merely modifying the entries in the /etc/login.defs file.

DELETING OR DISABLING USERS

A user account can be disabled by simply modifying the entry for a given user in the /etc/passwd file. For example, you can disable the account for the user natalie by changing the password field as follows:

```
natalie:x123:100:100:OpenLinux User:/home/natalie:/bin/bash
```

After this change is made, the account cannot be accessed. The original password is still intact in encrypted form in the /etc/shadow file, but it is not referenced due to the modification to the /etc/passwd file. Modifying the /etc/passwd entry back to its original state once again enables this account. The entry in the /etc/passwd file is as follows:

```
natalie:x:100:100:OpenLinux User:/home/natalie:/bin/bash
```

Completely removing the entry from the /etc/passwd file disables the user account as well, but it's a bit more difficult to restore the account if the need presents itself.

Note

Disabling or deleting a user account does not remove any data in the user's home directory. If you want to remove the contents of the /home/directory, you must specifically use the `rm` command.

GROUPS

The purpose of a *Group Identifier* (*GID*) is to logically group resources or files to members of a given group. For example, source code files might need to be shared between users in the engineering department. By creating an engineering group and adding the appropriate members to this group, the files can be shared among the engineering department, but secure from others accessing files that they can't see. It is the same with other departments or groups: Files can be shared in the accounting, sales, or service departments without the risk of unauthorized users accessing the data.

CREATING A GROUP

Groups are created by adding an entry to the /etc/group file. A default listing of this file is as follows:

```
root::0:
wheel::10:
bin::1:bin,daemon
```

```
daemon::2:bin,daemon
sys::3:bin,adm
adm::4:adm,daemon
tty::5:
disk::6:
lp::7:daemon,lp
mem::8:
kmem::9:
operator::11:
mail::12:mail
news::13:news
uucp::14:uucp
man::15:
majordom::16:
database::17:
games::20:
gopher::30:
dip::40:
ftp::50:
users::100:
nobody::65534:
```


Each line of the /etc/group file indicates one group. You'll notice that many of the predefined groups correspond directly to a specific service. For example, the `lp` group is for printer services. A description of the format of the /etc/group file is listed in Table 10.3.

TABLE 10.3 FIELD DESCRIPTIONS OF THE /ETC/GROUP FILE

Field	Description
1	The first field is the name of the group. For example, this might be `eng` for the engineering group or `acct` for the accounting group.
2	This is the password for the group. It is typically not used, but it can be set.
3	This is the Group ID (GID) number. User accounts that are default members of this group have this number in their /etc/passwd entry.
4	The last field is the list of user accounts associated with this group.

Each user account must belong to at least one group. The default group in OpenLinux is `users`. The associated group identification number (GID) is 100.

Note

Inclusion in the default group occurs by the group ID number (GID) being present in the /etc/passwd entry for each user. The user account names do not have to be present in the /etc/group file to be included in the default group.

ADDING USER ACCOUNTS TO A GROUP

There is no limit to the number of groups to which a user can belong. However, inclusion in groups beyond the initial default group is only accomplished by adding the user account name to the list of user account names in the /etc/group file. A user account can be added to a specific group by simply adding their username to the last field of the group entry in the /etc/group file. After the user account is added, access to shared files in that group is granted. An entry in the /etc/group file with several members (user accounts) is similar to the following:

```
eng::100:kelsey, brittany, ryan, natalie
```

Each of the user accounts listed in the last field of the preceding example are all members of the eng group.

The groupadd command can be used to add new groups to the /etc/group file. The general syntax is straightforward:

```
groupadd -g GID groupname
```

The -g GID parameter assigns the group ID to the new group. For instance, the following command creates a new group called eng and assigns it group ID 201:

```
groupadd -g 201 eng
```

REMOVING USER ACCOUNTS FROM A GROUP

Removing a user from a specific group is accomplished by removing the username from the list in the /etc/group file. Doing this does not remove data or change permissions—it only excludes a specific user account from accessing files that are inclusive to a specific group.

OTHER UTILITIES

To obtain a listing of all the groups to which you are assigned, use the groups command: To obtain a listing on yourself, simply execute groups with no parameters; to obtain a listing on someone else, execute groups with a user's name as a parameter.

The shadow password suite that comes with OpenLinux includes a useful utility called gpasswd. This utility helps to manage the /etc/group and /etc/gshadow files.

The syntax for adding a user to a group is as follows:

```
gpasswd -a username group
```

To remove a user from a group, the following syntax is used:

```
gpasswd -d username group
```

PERMISSIONS

There are three levels of permissions to files and directories in Linux. These levels correspond to the following three categories:

- Owner
- Group
- Other

Each level, or category, has associated privileges. These privileges come in the form of three permissions: read permissions, write permissions, and execute permissions.

All three levels—Owner, Group, and Other—have read, write, and execute permissions.

In order for the set of permissions for the owner and group to work, the file must have an indicator as to who is the owner and to which group the file belongs. Each file or directory has an owner *property* (sometimes referred to as the *user property*) and a *group property*. The owner, or user, property is set to the user account name of the person who owns the file. The group property works in a similar fashion: The group property contains the group name to which the file belongs. Examining the following long listing of the /etc/passwd file makes more sense of this:

```
#ls -l /etc/passwd
-rw-r--r--  1  root  root     695   Dec 7 12:48 passwd
```


Here's a closer look at what this information means. The key elements are depicted in Figure 10.1. In the listing of the /etc/passwd file, you can see that the owner is root, and that the group is set to root as well. This can be a little confusing because the owner and the group are set to the same value. This happens often with system files. Just remember that the owner setting corresponds to the /etc/passwd file and the group setting corresponds to the /etc/group file.

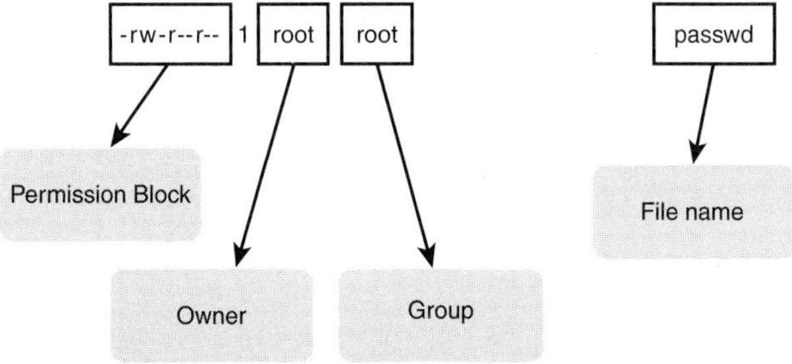

Figure 10.1
Specific characteristics of the /etc/passwd file.

The first set of dashes and letters represent the file type and permissions for this file. They are broken down into four logical groups. The first character indicates the file type. The next nine placeholders represent the permissions of each of the three levels: owner, group, and other. Each of these three levels uses three places to set permissions. For example, if you want to allow read, write, and execute privileges to the owner of a file, the letters *rwx* are present in positions 2–4. Figure 10.2 depicts the permission options for owner, group, and others.

CHANGING PERMISSIONS

The access rights for any given file can be modified by using the change mode (`chmod`) command. In order to change the access rights, you must specify the following three elements:

- The level (owner level, group level, or other level) to modify
- The permission (read, write, or execute) to modify
- The file or files to modify

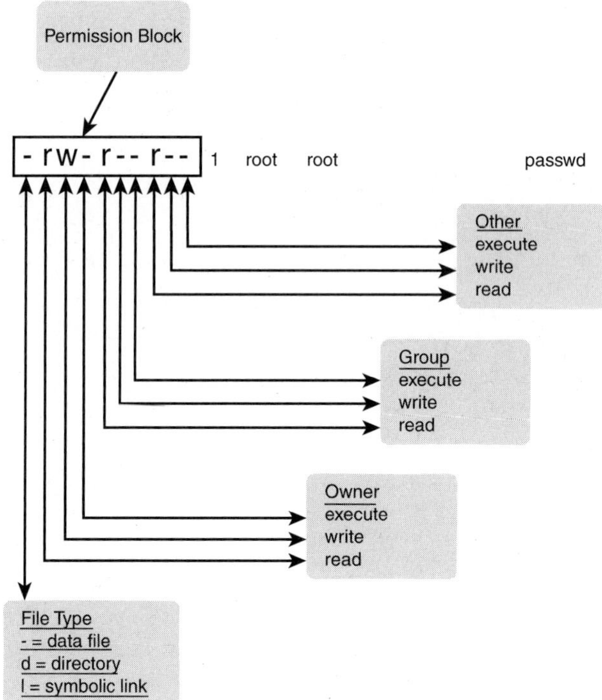

Figure 10.2
Detailed description of file permissions.

Table 10.4 lists the level options that can be used with the `chmod` command. The access rights or permissions that can be modified at each level are summarized in Table 10.5.

TABLE 10.4 OPTIONS WITH `chmod` COMMAND

Option	Level	Description
u	Owner	Owner of a file
g	Group	Group to which the user belongs
o	Other	All other users
a	All	Can replace `u`, `g`, or `o`

Permission	Description
r	Sets read permission
x	Sets execute permission
w	Sets write permission
s	Sets group or user ID to the owner of the file while the file is being executed

For example, adding write privileges for the group can be done be by running `chmod` as follows:

```
# chmod g+w /etc/passwd
```

Examining the permissions of the /etc/passwd file after the modifications shows the following:

```
# ls -l /etc/passwd
-rw-rw-r--  1  root  root    695   Dec 7 12:48 passwd
```

If the permissions to the /etc/passwd file are set for read, write, and execute for everyone (owner, group, and other), the file looks like the following:

```
#ls -l /etc/passwd
-rwxrwxrwx  1  root  root    695   Dec 7 12:48 passwd
```


Changing User or Group Ownership

As you learned earlier in this chapter, the key to the concept of permissions is the fact that a file has both an owner indicator and a group indicator. The `chown` utility changes the owner indicator, and the group indicator is changed by the `chgrp` utility. Only the superuser can change the ownership of a file.

Caution

Never change the owner indicator or the group indicator of any system file such as the /etc/passwd file. Only data files to be shared as part of a logical group are to be modified in this way. Modifying system files might render certain services unusable.

The owner indicator of a file can be modified as follows:

```
# chown natalie /tmp/testfile
# ls -l
-rwxr--r--   1 natalie     users          11 Dec 26 04:14 testfile
```

The group indicator of a file can be modified as follows:

```
# chgrp eng /tmp/testfile
# ls -l
-rwxr--r--   1 natalie     eng          11 Dec 26 04:14 testfile
```

Tip

The chown command can be used to modify both the owner indicator and the group indicator by specifying both and separating them with a period:

```
chown natalie.eng testfile
```

SUMMARY

In this chapter you've learned about the multiuser nature of Linux. This is one feature that distinguishes Linux from DOS. There are two types of users: the root user (superuser) and normal individual users. The root user has access rights to all files. Normal user accounts are limited to accessing files that they either own or that belong to the same group as that particular user. Permissions are granted based on user and group settings.

For further information on related topics, refer to the following chapters:

- See Chapter 9, "Understanding the Linux File System," to learn more about the directory hierarchy and the default location of individual user accounts.
- See Chapter 13, "Customizing Your Shell Environment," to learn more about how to modify the shell environment for individual users.
- See Chapter 42 to learn more about the importance of proper system security and methods of implementing security features.

CHAPTER 11

Running DOS Programs

In this chapter

The DOS emulator system in OpenLinux is called DOSEMU. This system enables you to create a DOS environment either at a console prompt or in an X window, where you can run DOS programs in your Linux environment.

Many old DOS programs still perform their functions very well and are useful for performing a variety of tasks. This includes many legacy applications and games. DOSEMU enables you continue to use the DOS programs that you need, without requiring that you reboot your system to do so.

When you create a DOS session under Linux, some special rules apply, but some special features are available as well. For example, some graphical DOS programs won't run inside a window under X. Most character-based DOS programs run under X. At the console prompt, almost all DOS programs run well, even in graphics modes. Many of your favorite old DOS games can be played quite effectively in DOSEMU.

One interesting feature of DOSEMU under Linux, which is usually not available on other operating systems that support a DOS box, is the capability to run the DOS environment over a remote terminal session. Therefore, even users with only telnet access or dumb terminal access to your Linux machine can also run (character-based) DOS programs.

Also, because DOSEMU can be run under the X window system, you can run multiple programs simultaneously in different windows onscreen, and you can use the remote display capabilities of X to allow remote workstations to run DOS programs.

This chapter provides an introduction to DOSEMU and discusses configuring DOSEMU for optimal use. It also provides a few troubleshooting tips for working with DOSEMU.

BASIC DOSEMU USE

You can start DOSEMU either at a shell prompt or in X. To start a DOS session at a console prompt, make sure that you are logged in as root, and then type `dos`. Several messages scroll by, and you are left at a DOS command prompt. From here you can immediately start running DOS commands and programs.

Caution

If you have a DOS formatted hard disk, you cannot see it as a drive in your DOS session in the default configuration of DOSEMU. This is explained shortly, and instructions for remedying this situation are described later in this chapter, in the section called "Configuring DOSEMU".

The default environment that is provided by Caldera for DOSEMU runs DR DOS (a competitor to MS-DOS that is owned by Caldera) in the DOSEMU session. If you want to, you can run another version of DOS, such as MS-DOS or PC DOS. However, this requires that you have a licensed copy of one of these programs and that you install it for use with DOSEMU. Caldera provides a license to use DR DOS as part of their OpenLinux distribution, so you can avoid having to do this.

A few of the commands and programs that comprise DR DOS are available for your use. Two drive letters are available where these and other files are found:

- **C:**—The C: drive is an emulated drive, or hard disk image, which contains the DR DOS system. This includes the code to boot up the DOS session, the `COMMAND.COM` shell, and a few of the utilities and programs that make up DR DOS. (Later in this chapter, you will see how to customize DOSEMU so that the drive letters can refer to other emulated drives or the actual hard drives on your system.)
- **L:**—The L: drive refers to the Linux file system. You can browse through the files on this drive using normal DOS commands (`cd`, `dir`, and so on). Files and directories with names longer than 11 characters (the maximum in DOS) are shortened, and odd characters are substituted in the filenames to distinguish them from other entries with similar names.

  Because you are in DOS, you use backslash instead of slash as the path delimiter for the filenames you use (even on this Linux drive). For example, to access file /tmp/README in Linux, you use the path `L:\TMP\README` in a DOSEMU session.

To run a DOS program, browse to the program on the C: or L: drive, and type the name of the program at the DOS prompt.

When DOSEMU is running, it is just another process on your Linux machine. You can switch to another console prompt (to continue working in Linux) using the Alt+*function key* shortcut. To switch back, use the appropriate Alt+*function key* for the virtual console at which you originally started `dos`.

To run a DOS session in X, use the `xdos` program. To start DOSEMU in a window while you are running KDE, make sure that you are logged in as root, and then type `xdos` in a terminal window. A window with the title "DOS in a BOX" is displayed, with a DOS session inside it (and with the cursor waiting at the DOS command prompt).

This provides the same DOS environment as a console prompt (the C: and L: drives are available). However, there are some differences with regard to the types of programs you can run.

DOS programs that switch into graphics mode might not work with `xdos` because the machine is already in graphics mode under X, and `xdos` needs to do some very tricky things to share the screen with the X server. However, some programs can be run in this environment—when the graphics mode of X and the graphics mode required by the program do not conflict.

Also, because X handles the keyboard and mouse differently than the console, you might have difficulty with certain keyboard combinations (such as Alt and Ctrl combinations or function keys). Or you might have problems getting the mouse to work properly with your DOS program (if it supports the mouse). If you have problems, either switch to running the DOS session in console (non-X) mode, or see the "Troubleshooting DOSEMU" section later in this chapter.

When you have finished using DOSEMU, exit your DOS session by typing `exitemu`. This command terminates the session and returns you to the console prompt (or closes the `xdos` window).

CONFIGURING DOSEMU

The DOS session that is provided by DOSEMU is not exactly the same as running DOS. In fact, it's quite a technical feat to provide an operating environment under Linux that mimics your machine hardware closely enough to fool DOS and the programs that run on it so that they can work unmodified under Linux.

In order to get around problems caused by emulation, there are numerous DOSEMU configuration settings. This enables you to customize DOSEMU so that it works best with the programs that you need to run (and the hardware you need to emulate).

The main DOSEMU configuration file is /etc/dosemu.conf. Another file, /etc/dosemu.users, is used to control per-user customizations of DOSEMU, and is discussed in the section called "Allowing Non-Root Users to Run DOSEMU". The dosemu.conf file contains many comments to help you select the appropriate values for your system.

CONFIGURING DOSEMU DRIVES

When DOSEMU runs, it provides you with drives C: and L: for use in your DOS session. One of the most important things you might want to do with DOSEMU is use it to directly access your native DOS hard drives. There are several reasons to do this:

- If you have drives that are formatted for DOS on your system, but you access them through Linux emulation (via drive L:), the multiple layers of emulation that DOSEMU goes through make accesses to the disk slower.
- Depending on how a DOS program accesses the hard disk, the program might not work at all, when the drive is accessed via Linux redirection (explained shortly). This is especially true if a DOS program accesses the disk using low-level (BIOS) services. For example, you can't run a DOS disk repair program in DOSEMU unless you configure direct disk access.
- If you are using a compressed DOS disk, Linux might not be able to mount the hard disk, whereas DOSEMU can do so if it is given direct access to it.
- Finally, you might want to use a different bootup sequence for DOSEMU, to boot directly from your own disk instead of from the hard disk image provided by Caldera.

The C: drive that appears by default in DOSEMU is a fake (emulated) hard drive. It is actually a regular Linux file, located at /var/lib/dosemu/hdimage.drdos703.eval. The line in the configuration file that defines this disk for DOSEMU is as follows:

```
$_hdimage = "hdimage.drdos703.eval"
```

Inside this file hdimage.drdos703.eval is data that looks to DOSEMU like the sectors and cylinders of a real hard disk. TheDR DOS system is installed on this hard disk image. This includes DOS boot sectors, CONFIG.SYS and AUTOEXEC.BAT files, the COMMAND.COM shell, and a few of the utility and support programs for DR DOS.

You can create a similar file, for example/var/lib/dosemu/floppy.image, that contains data that looks to DOSEMU like a floppy disk. This floppy disk image would contain DOS boot sectors and other DR-DOS files as well. Use of this file is discussed in the section "Accessing Floppy Drives," later in this chapter.

Using `mtools` to Manipulate Disk Image Files

`mtools` is a set of utilities for directly manipulating DOS-formatted floppy drives and disk images. You can use `mtools` programs to access and manipulate a DOSEMU drive image file by defining it in the file /etc/mtools.conf.

Use the following lines to define `mtool` drives for the hard disk image provided by Caldera in OpenLinux, and for a floppy image that you create:

```
drive m: file="/var/lib/dosemu/floppy.image"
drive r: file="/var/lib/dosemu/hdimage.drdos703.eval" offset=32384
```

With these definitions, you can access the floppy drive image as drive M: and the hard drive image as drive R:, using `mtools` utilities. For example, to copy a new program into the EMUBIN directory in the hard drive image, without getting into DOSEMU, you can type

```
mcopy program.exe r:/emubin
```

Refer to the `mtools` man page for additional information about `mtools` utilities.

Additionally, some programs that are specific to DOSEMU are located in the directory C:\EMUBIN (inside hdimage.od). This includes EXITEMU.COM, which is used to quit DOSEMU, and LREDIR.EXE, which is used to redirect drives to the Linux file system.

Inside DOSEMU, the hard disk image operates just like a regular hard drive. You can copy files to C:, and the hdimage file stores them. However, the image is only set up to act like a very small (7MB) disk. To install programs or store lots of data, you'll need a larger disk. Use either the Linux file system or a physical hard drive for this.

USING `LREDIR` TO ACCESS OTHER LINUX FILE SYSTEM LOCATIONS

By default, the drive letter L: refers to the root of the Linux file system. This means that from inside DOSEMU you can access the files and directories using this drive letter. This is called a drive redirection, and it is created at the time that DOSEMU starts, using the `LREDIR` command in the AUTOEXEC.BAT file.

You can redirect additional drive letters to refer to other points in the Linux file system as well, or you can change the location to which L: refers. There are several reasons to do so:

- **Easier access**—Because of path limitations in DOS, long Linux filenames are translated to 11 characters, and often contain hard to type characters. Redirecting a drive to a position lower in the file system than the root enables you to bypass directories that are hard to type because of the name translation.

- **Shorter paths**—Also, it can be handy to have drive letters pointing to multiple places in the Linux file system because it makes it easier, in DOS, to manipulate files using shorter paths.
- **Familiar drive letters**—If you've been using DOS or another operating system that includes DOS (such as Windows 95), you might be accustomed to using a particular set of drive letters for certain disks. For example, you might be accustomed to accessing CD-ROM data on drive E:.

Use the `LREDIR` command to redirect a drive to a location in the Linux file system. For example, to redirect drive E: so that it refers to the directory /mnt/cdrom, at the DOS prompt type the following:

```
lredir e: linux\fs\mnt\cdrom
```

If you get a directory listing of E:\, you see the contents of this directory (the contents of the CD-ROM drive, when the CD is mounted in Linux).

Tip

If you want a redirection to occur every time you start DOSEMU, put the command to create it in the file C:\AUTOEXEC.BAT, in the DOS session.

Accessing Physical Hard Drives in DOSEMU

If you already have a drive that DOS can recognize (a drive formatted as FAT12 or FAT16), you can enhance the compatibility of DOSEMU with that drive if you allow DOSEMU to access it directly instead of via the Linux file system.

To set this up, use a `$_hdimage` directive in /etc/dosemu.conf that tells DOSEMU to use a Linux device file for disk access.

For example, the following line configures the second partition of the first IDE hard drive (/dev/hda2) to be a disk recognized by DOS:

```
$_hdimage = "/dev/hda2"
```

In order for this partition to be used by DOSEMU directly in this way, the device cannot be mounted under Linux. DOSEMU refuses to load the configuration setting in this case, due to possible corruption of the disk with the two operating systems accessing it simultaneously (and independently).

DOSEMU creates DOS disks for its session in the order that they appear in the `hdimage` line of the dosemu.conf file, starting with drive C:. For example, the following line would define the hard disk image as drive C: and a physical partition as drive D:

```
$_hdimage = "hdimage.drdos703.eval /dev/hda2"
```

ACCESSING FLOPPY DRIVES

The same techniques that are used for different types of disk access can be used with floppy disks as well. You can either have DOSEMU access the actual physical device for the floppy, via the Linux device file, or have DOSEMU use files as floppy disk images. To define a floppy drive for use in DOSEMU, use the `$_floppy_a` or `$_floppy_b` directives in the configuration file.

For example, the following line in dosemu.conf defines a floppy drive for DOSEMU that actually accesses the physical floppy drive on your system:

```
$_floppy_a = "threeinch"43
```

You can also use a file containing a floppy disk image to represent a floppy drive in DOSEMU. Use the `$_vbootfloppy` directive to do this. The next section, "Controlling the Boot Sequence," gives reasons for doing this.

When using the `$_vbootfloppy` directive with a disk image, specify the name of a bootable floppy image that you have created on your system. For example, to create a bootable floppy image using the DR DOS hdimage that is installed on your system, perform the following steps:

1. As root, start dosemu by typing `dos` (or `xdos`).
2. Format a new bootable floppy using the command (inside the DOS session) `format a: /s`.
3. Exit the dosemu session by typing `exitemu`.
4. Make an image of the floppy you just formatted with the command `dd if=/dev/fd0 of=/var/lib/dosemu/floppy.image`.
5. Make the file accessible from the /usr/lib/dosemu directory by creating a symbolic link to the file with the command `ln -s /var/lib/dosemu/floppy.image /usr/lib/dosemu/floppy.image`.

Now, with the floppy image defined, you can boot DOSEMU by placing the following line into `dosemu.conf`:

```
$_vbootfloppy = "floppy.image"
```

If you want, you can also define a CONFIG.SYS and AUTOEXEC.BAT file for this bootable floppy, and place some of the files from the hdimage (including LREDIR.EXE and EXITEMU.COM) in order to make the image useful.

CONTROLLING THE BOOT SEQUENCE

During the boot sequence of DOS inside DOSEMU, the boot sectors for DOS are read, and the statements in the files CONFIG.SYS and AUTOEXEC.BAT are executed. All these files are read from the hard disk image that is provided by Caldera. You might want to use a different set of bootup files for your DOSEMU sessions, or decide to boot DOSEMU using a different drive. Once again, several factors might influence your decision, including the following:

- If you have a complicated CONFIG.SYS or AUTOEXEC.BAT, you might want to use the same files for DOSEMU that you use when booting DOS outside of Linux. Doing so makes it easier to maintain these files.
- The hard disk image that is provided by Caldera is large (7MB) If you don't need a complete installation of DOS (all the utilities and programs), you can boot off a floppy boot image instead of the hard disk image and remove hdimage.drdos703.eval to save yourself this disk space.

  The file hdimage.drdos703.eval is available on the OpenLinux CD for you to reinstall. So unless you have customized it, you don't need to worry about deleting it from your system. Just reinstall the package `drdos-hdimage-eval-7.03-2.i386.rpm` if you need to restore it.
- In the rare event that you have a program that runs better with another version of DOS, you might want to boot that version instead of DR DOS.

You control the drive from which to boot using the `$_vbootfloppy` directive in the configuration file. If you use this directive, DOSEMU boots from the indicated floppy image (as drive A:). If you do not use this directive, DOSEMU tries to boot from the first drive listed with the `$_hdimage` directive (drive C:).

After you have selected a boot drive, make sure that the disk definitions (either floppy or hard disk) are present, and that the image or device you specify is bootable.

Note

Some hard drives on your system might be bootable, but not in a way that works with DOSEMU. For example, partitions that boot directly into a protected mode (that is, 32-bit) operating system, such as Windows 98 or NT, do not boot properly in DOSEMU. You need to select some other boot option (such as booting from another real drive, or from a drive image) in order for DOSEMU to start up correctly.

If you decide to boot from a real hard drive, DOSEMU uses that drive's CONFIG.SYS and AUTOEXEC.BAT files for the startup. This might cause a problem if the files contain statements (that is, load drivers or run programs) that don't work with DOSEMU. Therefore, DOSEMU can be configured to use different files in place of these files.

To configure DOSEMU to use a different file in place of CONFIG.SYS, use the `$_emusys` directive, followed by the filename extension to use. For example, if you use the following line in the configuration file

```
$_emusys = "EMU"
```

DOSEMU uses CONFIG.EMU, at the root of drive C:, in place of CONFIG.SYS. To do a similar thing with AUTOEXEC.BAT, use the `$_emubat` directive.

After you have configured DOSEMU to use these other files, make sure that the files exist at the root of the drive you use for booting, and that they contain statements that are appropriate for use in DOSEMU.

Finally, after adjusting the hard drive and floppy settings for DOSEMU, make sure that copies of important DOSEMU utilities (such as `exitemu` and `lredir`) are somehow available in your DOSEMU session. For example, if you don't have access to `exitemu`, you cannot cleanly terminate your DOSEMU session.

If you are no longer using the drive image provided by Caldera, you need to copy these files (from the EMUBIN directory in either image) to another drive that will be available when you run DOSEMU. To do this, you might need to temporarily configure DOSEMU to use both your physical drives and an emulated drive image, copy the files, and then edit the configuration to remove the references to the Caldera disk image.

ALLOWING NONROOT USERS TO RUN DOSEMU

By default, DOSEMU is installed in a way that only allows the root user full access to the hardware features of your machine and processor. If you are in a situation where you trust all the users on your system (or you *are* all the users on your system), you might want to enable nonroot users to run DOSEMU with full, unrestricted privileges. Be careful, though, and do this only if the DOS programs you want to run do not work properly with the regular dosemu settings because it introduces a security risk to your system.

The actual `dos` executable file can be changed to be setuid root, which means it will run as the Linux root account even if it is started by a nonroot user. Normally, if the `dos` program detects that it is running as a regular user, it allows the user to proceed, but it only allows a restricted set of DOSEMU capabilities to be used. However, you can configure it to run with full privileges with certain other accounts by making the actual dos program `setuid root`, and by defining the allowed accounts privileges in the file /etc/dosemu.users.

To change the DOS executable file to be setuid root, type the following command:

```
chmod +s /usr/bin/dos
```

The following line enables the user tbird complete access to the DOS session (which includes access to privileged IP addresses and other things):

```
tbird c_all unrestricted
```

Add a line such as this to dosemu.users for each nonroot user that you want to allow to use DOSEMU. Additional parameters, besides `c_all`, are also available to allow only a subset of privileges for a user. These are provided to enable you to have precise control over the security on your system.

See the online documentation, sections 2 and 7 of the file /usr/doc/dosemu-0.98.5/README.txt, for details on the different parameters that you can use when defining user privileges in DOSEMU.

PRINTING IN DOSEMU

To configure a printer for DOSEMU, use the `$_print` directive in the configuration file. You can choose to print to any printer that is supported by the Linux printing command `lpr`. (The printers that are supported by `lpr` are defined in /etc/printcap). For example, to have data which is output to LPT1 in the DOS session printed to the hp4lj printer via `lpr`, you use the following line in /etc/dosemu.conf:

```
$_printer = "hp4lj"
```

You can also configure the timeout period using the following line:

```
$_printer_timeout = (20)
```

In the preceding example, after 20 seconds of inactivity DOSEMU assumes that the print job is complete, and sends the data to the printer using the indicated command and options. If more data is received on the printer port in DOSEMU after the first job is completed, a new print job is started.

Tip

If your print jobs from DOSEMU are split into multiple fragments, your program might be taking too long to print. A long pause between outputting characters causes DOSEMU to think that the job is finished, and it ends the job and sends it to the Linux printer. To work around this, increase the timeout value that is used with the print directive to a value higher than the longest pause during printing of your DOS program.

The timeout value is expressed in seconds..

USING SERIAL PORTS

If you have a program in DOS that needs to use a serial port, you can define serial port emulation in DOSEMU to make these ports available inside the DOS session. The Linux serial ports are represented by devices in the /dev directory. In DOS, these were referred to as COM devices. DOSEMU enables you to emulate COM devices in the DOS session it provides, using mappings to the Linux serial port devices.

To allow DOS programs access to the serial ports on your machine, use the $_com*x* directive in the configuration file. For each serial port you define, specify the COM port to be simulated in the DOS session and the Linux device entry to be used.

For example, the following line makes the COM1 port (first serial port) available in DOSEMU:

$_com1 = "/dev/cua0"You can have DOSEMU redirect the serial devices as it translates them from Linux to the DOS session so that the physical serial devices appear at different locations. For example, even if data is going through the physical COM1 (cua0) serial port on your machine, you can have DOSEMU redirect this to make it look like it is going through some other serial port (for example, COM2) inside the DOS session.

Using a Mouse

To use a mouse with DOS programs, you have two choices in DOSEMU:

- Configure a serial port, as described in the previous section, and use a DOS mouse driver inside the DOS session. In this case, specify a $_mouse_dev value that matches a serial port you have defined using a `$_comx` directive. For example, to use a mouse on the first serial port, put the following lines in the dosemu.conf file:

  ```
  $_com1 = "/dev/mouse"
  $_mouse_dev = "com1"
  ```

  Now, inside the DOS session, load an appropriate DOS mouse driver, such as MOUSE.COM.
- Use an internal DOSEMU mouse driver, which emulates the mouse for programs inside the DOS session. Use lines such as the following to emulate a Microsoft mouse driver in the DOS session:

  ```
  $_mouse = "microsoft"
  $_mouse_dev = "/dev/mouse"
  ```

Use the program EMUMOUSE.COM (located in the EMUBIN directory) to control the aspects of the mouse emulation that are provided by the internal mouse driver in DOSEMU. You can run the program with no parameters to see a list of the options that you can use with it.

Preventing DOS from Hogging the System

In order to provide responsive hardware emulation, DOSEMU actually polls some devices and Linux services. This means that DOSEMU is running very fast and consuming lots of machine cycles, even when the DOS program inside it is not very busy or important.

Use the $`_hogthreshold` directive in the configuration file to control how much DOSEMU hogs the system when it is running. Specifying a high number causes DOSEMU to yield more often to other processes on the system. If you specify zero, DOSEMU runs as fast as it can. Depending on how critical the task is in the DOS process, you can adjust this. For example, if your Linux machine is running for personal use, and you want DOSEMU to run as fast as possible in order to run a game, use a line such as the following in dosemu.conf:

```
$_hogthreshold = (0)
```

Troubleshooting DOSEMU

Because DOSEMU emulates the hardware environment that is required to run DOS programs, and because the emulation is not perfect, you might occasionally run into DOS programs that just don't work right. This section provides some basic troubleshooting techniques for working out these problems.

The main areas of problems in DOSEMU have to do with the keyboard, the video, the DOS memory system, and direct access to device hardware.

KEYBOARD PROBLEMS

One of the most common problems that people have with DOSEMU is with the keyboard. This is especially true when running DOSEMU via `xdos`, under X. X captures and consumes many keystrokes that DOS programs expect to receive, including complex key combinations and modifiers. In particular, many games require the use of multiple simultaneously held-down keys in order to play them effectively.

If you have problems with the DOS keyboard, the first thing to try is running the session at the console instead of in X. If the problems continue, try changing the settings of the `$_keybint` and `$_rawkeyboard` directives in the configuration file. Both of these directives take an argument of either `on` or `off` to control whether they are in effect.

When `keybint` is on, it causes DOSEMU to simulate hardware keyboard interrupts into the DOS session. Some DOS programs (particularly *Terminate and Stay Resident* programs, or *TSRs*) grab the keyboard interrupt, and it is essential for these programs that the interrupts be generated in the correct way.

When the `rawkeyboard` setting is on, it causes DOSEMU to read the Linux keyboard values directly as they come from the physical keyboard, without translation by the Linux kernel. These values are then passed directly into the DOS session.

With `keybint` and `rawkeyboard` both on, you get the most accurate and compatible keyboard operation inside DOSEMU. However, this configuration also prevents you from switching virtual consoles (because the Alt+*function keys* are passed uncaptured into the DOS session).

Also, if the DOSEMU process terminates unexpectedly (is killed), it might leave the keyboard in an unusable state. If this happens, and your machine is on a network, you can possibly recover the keyboard by running the Linux command `kdb_mode -a` from a remote machine (logged in via `telnet` or some other remote shell). Otherwise, you might have to reboot or even physically reset your machine to restore the keyboard.

Because of these potential problems, the `rawkeyboard` setting is off in the default DOSEMU configuration file for OpenLinux.

VIDEO PROBLEMS

Although DOSEMU contains some code for supporting a few old video cards directly, the default mechanisms for DOSEMU to support graphics for DOS programs is to make the video card and its BIOS available inside the DOS session. This is done by allowing the DOS session access to the I/O ports on the video card, and mapping the memory region for the video BIOS into the DOS session memory space.

Following are a few different types of video problems that you might encounter:

- Cannot enter graphics mode at all
- Failure to run the correct video mode for the DOS program
- Problems with fonts in the xdos window

If you are running DOSEMU under X using xdos, it is highly unlikely that you can run most DOS programs in graphics mode. The few that work are mainly those which run in 320×200×256 (MCGA) mode. For more complex graphics modes, try running DOSEMU at the Linux console. If this does not work, use the additional measures that are described in the next section to customize the video handling in DOSEMU.

ADJUSTING VIDEO SETTINGS

When you encounter problems with DOS programs running in graphics mode, there are a few settings you can use to try to fix the problem. These settings are defined using the directives $_videoportaccess, $_console, $_graphics, and $_ports.

Try to fix the problems using the direct video port and BIOS settings instead of the older card-specific emulation settings (which are configured using the $_chipset directive). Although this is more of a security risk, the legacy emulation settings (such as trident, et4000, and so on) are for older cards, and some of them never worked well anyway. The direct video access settings, when used with a DOSEMU session running at the Linux console, are most likely to yield the correct results for your DOS programs.

If you have problems getting into graphics mode, or if some graphics modes do not work, it is possible that you need to alter the DOSEMU settings related to the I/O ports and BIOS for your video card.

The default video configuration for DOSEMU in OpenLinux uses the following settings:

```
$__video = "vga"
$_console = (0)
$_graphics = (0)
$_videoportaccess = (1)
$_vbios_seg = (0xc000)
$_vbios_size = (0x10000)
```

The $_videoportaccess directive tells DOSEMU to allow DOS programs (and the video BIOS) to access the normal set of VGA I/O ports directly. Depending on your video card, you might need to define other I/O ports that can be accessed directly. See the section "Allowing Direct Device Access" for an example of how to specify additional I/O ports for use in DOSEMU.

Depending on your video card, the BIOS for your card might appear at a different physical address than the default 0xc000, or it might have a different size than the default 64K. You can adjust the location and size of the video BIOS to account for your card, using the $_vbios_seg and $_vbios_size parameters to the video directive.

For example, the following lines instruct DOSEMU that the video BIOS is at 0xe000, and that it is only 32K:

```
$_console = (1)
$_graphics = (1)
$_videoportaccess = (1)
$_vbios_seg = (0xe000)
$_vbios_size = (0x8000)

$_
```

You might have to consult hardware documentation for your video card, or search the Internet, to obtain information about the specific I/O ports or BIOS for your video card.

Finally, on some machines, you might need to turn off video BIOS shadowing in order to get DOSEMU video access working. When your machine boots, you are normally given the option to enter setup mode, where you can control several hardware features of your machine. If you are having video problems with DOSEMU under Linux, reboot, enter this setup mode, and turn off video BIOS shadowing (or adjust the settings for it). Then reboot and try your program again.

This option (to shadow video BIOS) is available because it provides a performance increase under some operating systems that use the video BIOS. Turning this option off in the BIOS setup does not adversely affect Linux video performance (for example, under X) because X does not use the video BIOS.

RUNNING DOS PROGRAMS WITH SPECIAL OPTIONS

Some DOS programs support options that make them more compatible with standard VGA video modes. Historically, these types of options were provided because of incompatibilities between graphics cards. However, when a DOS program supports these options, you can use them to increase the compatibility of the program with DOSEMU.

For example, DR DOS's `EDIT.EXE` program normally modifies the VGA font at runtime in order to provide a better looking screen in text mode. However, when run in `xdos`, some screens in `EDIT` look wrong because these characters aren't altered correctly by DOSEMU.

`EDIT` supports the use of a command line option (`/N`) to use normal fonts instead. Thus, to solve this problem, either run `EDIT` in a DOSEMU session that is started at the console or use the `/N` command line option to force `EDIT` to run without modifying the font.

Other DOS programs might provide similar options to avoid doing funny things to the font or the display when they run. For example, many programs can be run in different video modes (resolutions, memory layouts, and color depths). You might try experimenting with your DOS program, or reading its documentation, to try to find a setting that works with DOSEMU.

ENHANCED MEMORY SERVICES

DOSEMU provides its own enhanced memory services for DOS sessions. This includes expanded and extended memory and support for DPMI. Therefore, DOS programs that require specific kinds of advanced memory management in order to run are normally supported by DOSEMU.

However, you can tune the configuration of these different memory systems, or turn them off, or adjust the position where expanded memory appears in the DOS session.

Because DOSEMU provides its own enhanced memory services, you do not need to run DR DOS's EMM86 or HIMEM inside the DOS session. However, for expanded memory in DOSEMU, you do need to load the memory manager driver EMS.SYS (located in the EMUBIN directory). To support expanded memory, add the following line to the CONFIG.SYS file in the DOSEMU session:

```
DEVICE=C:\EMUBIN\EMS.SYS
```

The regular DOS memory managers (EMM386 and HIMEM) are normally run from the CONFIG.SYS file of DOS during the bootup sequence. If you dual-boot, use the `$_emusys` directive (described earlier) to configure DOSEMU to use a different startup configuration file that excludes these programs (and includes EMS.SYS, if desired).

If a DOS application reports that it does not have enough memory to run, increase the amount of the appropriate memory type using one of the following directives:

- **`$_dpmi`**—DOS Protected Mode Interface (DPMI) services
- **`$_xms`**—Extended memory
- **`$_ems`**—Expanded memory

To configure the amount of memory for each of these, specify the amount of RAM in kilobytes after the appropriate directive in the configuration file. For expanded memory, you can configure not only the memory amount, but the location of the frame in DOS low memory where the expanded memory appears. If you have hardware or other items mapped into specific memory regions in the DOS session (see the next section), you can use this parameter to avoid conflicts between those items and the expanded memory frame.

ALLOWING DIRECT DEVICE ACCESS

Some DOS programs might require access to specific I/O ports, memory-mapped regions, or interrupts in order to communicate with a hardware device on your system. Normally, DOSEMU tries to allow Linux to handle the actual hardware devices on the system. Then DOSEMU emulates a device in the DOSEMU session by accessing the Linux services for that device. However, for some hardware, Linux might not be aware of it, or you might not have a Linux driver for it. Thus, there is no Linux service for the hardware that is available.

In this case, DOSEMU can be configured to allow access to specific ports and memory, and to reflect hardware interrupts directly into the DOS session without any extra handling.

Allowing this access is very dangerous from both security and stability perspectives because it bypasses the Linux kernel and allows the DOSEMU process (on behalf of a running DOS program) to access the hardware directly. Only do this if you understand the requirements of the DOS program that needs it and its relationship to the hardware that uses these ports, memory, or interrupts.

Use the following directives to accomplish this:

- **`$_ports`**—Enable access to specific I/O ports on your machine.
- **`$_hardware_ram`**—Enable access to specific physical memory blocks (or ranges).
- **`$_irqpassing`**—Pass through specific hardware interrupts into the DOS session.

For example, to allow I/O ports 0x1ce and 0x1cf to be accessed directly inside DOSEMU, you use the following directive in /etc/dosemu.conf:

```
$_ports = "0x1ce 0x1cf"
```

See the online DOSEMU documentation for information about using the `hardware_ram` and `irqpassing` directives.

Caution

The online documentation refers to `irqpassing` as `sillyint`, and to the Linux kernel module as `emumodule.o`. The functionality for this module is now built into the Linux kernel, and you no longer need to load it manually, so you can ignore this part of the documentation. It is now no longer necessary to load a separate module to support `irqpassing` in DOSEMU.

The specifics of which ports, memory, and interrupts are needed for what hardware is too large a subject to be covered here. However, be aware of this capability in case you need to use it for a DOS program or for a piece of hardware that is otherwise impossible to support. Consult the online DOSEMU documentation for more information about this topic.

USING THE ONLINE DOSEMU DOCUMENTATION

To see much more detailed information about DOSEMU and the configuration parameters that you can use to control it, examine the online documentation. The online documentation is in the directory /usr/doc/dosemu-0.98.5. There are several different files in this directory. The one that is most authoritative and up-to-date for end-user use is README.txt. Other files in this directory are either for use by DOSEMU developers or describe solutions to specific problems (such as running a Novell client in DOSEMU—see the file NOVELL-HOWTO.txt).

Note

Unfortunately, some of the DOSEMU online help files are formatted using a UNIX convention in which backspace characters are used to create bold text (or other effects). This might make them difficult to read with a normal editor. You can use the command `less` to view these files (with **bolding** intact), or use the following command to strip the extra characters from the file:

```
perl -pi -e "s/\x08.//g" README.txt
```

SUMMARY

In this chapter, DOSEMU was described as the system by which you can run DOS programs under Linux. Run `dos` at a shell prompt, or run `xdos` under X, to start a DOSEMU session. By supplying a preinstalled hard drive image to boot a DOS session with DOSEMU, Caldera makes it easy to use DOSEMU.

Many DOSEMU configuration parameters are available, which enable you to customize the behavior of DOSEMU so that your DOS environment is best adapted to your specific programs and hardware. You can customize the drives and bootup sequence of DOSEMU, as well as many other hardware emulation parameters. Also, you can configure DOSEMU for use by nonroot users on your OpenLinux system.

For additional information on subjects related to the material in this chapter, see the following chapters:

- Chapter 9, "Understanding the Linux File System," has information regarding Linux device files, which can be used by DOSEMU to reference real hard drives or serial devices on your system.
- See Chapter 14, "Printing," for information about configuring printers for your Linux system, as well as the commands you can use to print documents. These commands can be used to provide printing support for DOS programs in DOSEMU.
- Chapter 19, "Disk Drives and File Systems," describes in greater detail the concepts of disk partitions and file systems, and the Linux hard drive devices used to access them.

CHAPTER 12

SYSTEM INITILIZATION UNDER OPENLINUX

In this chapter

Caldera OpenLinux uses System V (SysV) style system initialization as opposed to BSD style initialization. These are the two primary methods of performing system initialization in the UNIX and Linux worlds. BSD uses a few large scripts to handle all system initialization. SysV makes use of runlevels and a group of initialization scripts. The initialization scripts are run to start and stop *daemons* (background processes) depending on the *runlevel* (also referred to as the *system state*). One script per daemon or process subsystem is kept in a centralized directory (to be examined in detail later). System V states range from 0 to 6 by custom, with each runlevel corresponding to a different mode of operation, and often even these states are not all used. Although SysV initialization seems more complex, particularly to those coming from the world of DOS and Windows, this appearance belies a flexibility not seen with BSD style initialization.

THE BOOT PROCESS

All x86-type computers boot in a similar manner. (The details will be glossed over here because a complete understanding isn't necessary for your purposes.) When a system is powered on, a chain of events that is referred to as booting the computer takes place. The term comes from an old saying, "to pull yourself up by your bootstraps." After receiving power initially, most (but not all) computers receive a "power good" signal from the power supply. The system then begins a self-check process known as the POST (power on self test). This test looks for any system problems that might make the computer nonfunctional, such as bad memory. An acceptable POST normally terminates in one "beep" from the built-in speaker. Two or more (and usually a maximum of eight) beeps indicate a specific problem and give an indication of where to look for the problem.

After the POST has completed successfully, a very small loader program is run. This loader program in turn runs another, larger loader that looks at all the acceptable places for other code to load and run. Normally, these places are the boot sector of the first floppy disk, the boot sector of the first hard disk, and possibly even the boot sector of a CD-ROM, depending on the particular computer. This can be changed in the computer's setup program, which is generally accessible by pressing a key (such as Delete, Insert, or F2) during the POST process.

When the system finds the first loadable code in one of the boot sectors of the bootable disks, it begins loading and running it. In the case of most Linux systems, this is LILO (Linux Loader). LILO is a boot loader that enables a user to choose different operating systems to run, or different Linux kernels to load. It can also pass optional arguments to the kernel or `init`. (See Chapter 20, "Boot Loader.")

LILO then begins loading the kernel. A detailed discussion of how the Linux kernel loads is beyond the scope of this book, but it is a multistage process. A Linux kernel is compressed on disk, and uncompressed as it loads into memory; the size of the kernel image on disk is not representative of the amount of RAM it occupies.

init: WHERE IT ALL BEGINS

After the kernel has been loaded into memory you have a running Linux system—but it isn't very usable because the kernel doesn't interact directly with the user or user space (see Chapter 13, "Customizing Your Shell Environment," for more details). The kernel runs one program: `init`. This program is responsible for everything else, and is referred to as the parent of all processes. The kernel then retires to its position as system manager, handling kernel space and all requests for resource access.

When `init` starts, it reads its configuration from a file called inittab, which stands for initialization table, located in the /etc directory. Any defaults in inittab are discarded if they've been overridden on the command line. The inittab file describes how `init` set up the system. See Listing 12.1 for the default OpenLinux inittab. Later you'll see how to override inittab defaults, why you might want or need to, and the specific effects of doing so.

Tip

The tab ending (as in inittab, fstab, mtab, and so on) indicates that the file is a table—usually a configuration table. In the case of inittab, it tells `init` how to initialize the system, much like config.sys in DOS.

LISTING 12.1 THE /ETC/INITTAB FILE

```
#
# inittab       This file describes how the INIT process should set up
#               the system in a certain run-level.
#
# Author:       Miquel van Smoorenburg, <miquels@drinkel.nl.mugnet.org>
#               Modified for RHS Linux by Marc Ewing and Donnie Barnes
#               Modified for COL by Raymund Will
#

# The runlevels used by COL are:
#   0 - halt (Do NOT set initdefault to this)
#   1 - Single user mode (including initialization of network interfaces,
#       if you do have networking)
#   2 - Multiuser, (without NFS-Server and some such)
#       (basically the same as 3, if you do not have networking)
#   3 - Full multiuser mode
#   4 - unused
#       (should be equal to 3, for now)
#   5 - X11
#   6 - reboot (Do NOT set initdefault to this)

#
# Default runlevel.
id:3:initdefault:

# System initialization.
si::sysinit:/etc/rc.d/rc.modules default
bw::bootwait:/etc/rc.d/rc.boot
```

continues

LISTING 12.1 CONTINUED

```
# What to do in single-user mode.
~1:S:wait:/etc/rc.d/rc 1
~~:S:wait:/sbin/sulogin

l0:0:wait:/etc/rc.d/rc 0
l1:1:wait:/etc/rc.d/rc 1
l2:2:wait:/etc/rc.d/rc 2
l3:3:wait:/etc/rc.d/rc 3
l4:4:wait:/etc/rc.d/rc 4
l5:5:wait:/etc/rc.d/rc 5
l6:6:wait:/etc/rc.d/rc 6
# Normally not reached, but fallthrough in case of emergency.
z6:6:respawn:/sbin/sulogin

# Trap CTRL-ALT-DELETE
ca:12345:ctrlaltdel:/sbin/shutdown -t3 -r now

# Action on special keypress (ALT-UpArrow).
kb::kbrequest:/bin/echo "Keyboard Request--edit /etc/inittab
➥to let this work."

# When our UPS tells us power has failed, assume we have a few minutes
# of power left.  Schedule a shutdown for 2 minutes from now.
# This does, of course, assume you have powerd installed and your
# UPS connected and working correctly.
pf::powerfail:/sbin/shutdown -h +5 "Power Failure; System Shutting Down"

# If battery is fading fast -- we hurry...
p1::powerfailnow:/sbin/shutdown -c 2> /dev/null
p2::powerfailnow:/sbin/shutdown -h now "Battery Low..."

# If power was restored before the shutdown kicked in, cancel it.
po:12345:powerokwait:/sbin/shutdown -c
➥"Power Restored; Shutdown Cancelled"
# Run gettys in standard runlevels
1:12345:respawn:/sbin/getty tty1 VC linux
2:2345:respawn:/sbin/getty tty2 VC linux
3:2345:respawn:/sbin/getty tty3 VC linux
4:2345:respawn:/sbin/getty tty4 VC linux
5:2345:respawn:/sbin/getty tty5 VC linux
6:2345:respawn:/sbin/getty tty6 VC linux

# Run xdm in runlevel 5
x:5:respawn:/usr/bin/X11/xdm -nodaemon
```

At this juncture I want to note that runlevels are just a convenient way to group together *process packages* via software. They hold no special significance to the kernel. All Linux kernels start the boot process the same way. It's only after `init` starts that you begin to use runlevels.

INITTAB SPECIFICS

Reading inittab, you'll be skipping any lines that begin with a # because these are ignored by `init` as comments. The rest of the lines can be easily read as many other typical UNIX-like configuration tables; that is, each column is separated by a colon (:) and can be read as follows:

- **id**—This first column is a unique identifier for the line. This can be up to four alphanumerics long but is typically limited to two. Older systems had a two alphanumeric limitation, and Caldera hasn't changed that custom.
- **runlevel**—The second column indicates for which runlevel(s) this row is valid. This column can be null or can contain any number of valid runlevels. If null, it is valid for all runlevels.
- **action**—This can be any number of things; the most common is respawn, but it can also be any one of the following: once, sysinit, boot, bootwait, wait, off, ondemand, initdefault, powerwait, powerfail, powerokwait, ctrlaltdel, kbrequest.
- **process**—The specific process or program to be run.

Each row in inittab has a unique identifier. Normally, this is something that is easily associated with the specific action performed. For example, a line that spawns a `getty` on the first serial port might use the identifier s1.

The runlevels are identified as 0–6 and A–C by default. Runlevels 0, 1, and 6 are special—do not change them carelessly. These correspond to system halt, maintenance mode, and system reboot, respectively. Changing runlevel 1, for example, can have far-reaching consequences. Note that to enter maintenance mode (state 1), you can pass `init` the argument `1` (via `telinit`) . As an alternative, you can use `S` or `s`. If you change what transpires for state 1, the same changes apply when `S` or `s` is passed. Runlevels 2–5, though, can be customized as desired.

PART III

CH 12

Note

Using `telinit` is the preferred method for passing commands to `init`, but it is not unusual to call `init` directly.

In OpenLinux, the command `runlevel` (found in /sbin) can be used to give you information about the current and previous runlevels. Executing this command outputs the previous runlevel and the present runlevel, for example, N 3. The N indicates that there is no previous runlevel, as might occur following a reboot. If you make a change to state 2, and then reissue the `runlevel` command, you'll see 3 2.

HANDS-ON `init`

Because doing illustrates better than just reading about it, try this on your system: As root (only root can tell `init` to change states), issue the `init` command. You receive a usage message telling you to pass `init` an argument consisting of a number from 0 to 6, the letters

A–C, S, or Q. Lower-case letters are syntactically equivalent to their uppercase counterparts. If you pass `init` anything other than legal values, you receive a usage message to that effect; therefore, if you do not receive it, you know that it is a legitimate value (as far as `init` is concerned).

Caution

Only attempt the following if you are certain that you can `telnet` into your system over the network.

If the system you are using is connected to a network and you can `telnet` to it from another machine, you might want to try to pass `init` the argument `8`, as in `init 8` (or `telinit 8` if you want). You see some messages about sending the TERM and KILL signals to programs, and then your virtual terminal stops responding. Go to the other system, `telnet` into your system, and type `runlevel` again; you will see 3 8. After you have confirmed that you actually did change to runlevel 8, change back to your previous runlevel. Your logins reappear on the screen.

The preceding exercise showed that although runlevels 7–9 are undocumented, they actually are available for use if needed. (What happened when you changed to state 8 will become clear later in the chapter.) These runlevels aren't used simply because it's not customary to use them. The customizable states for OpenLinux (2–5) are generally more than sufficient for anyone, and Caldera, by default, doesn't use runlevel 4, so it is available for your use.

`init` OBSCURITIES

Here's a look at the other letter arguments you can pass to `init`. The letters A–C are used when you want to spawn a daemon listed in inittab, but only on demand. Telling `init` to change to state C doesn't change the runlevel per se; it just performs the action listed on the line at which the runlevel is C.

Suppose that you want to put a `getty` on a port to receive a call, but only after receiving a voice call first (and not all the time). Further suppose that you want to be ready to receive either a data call or a fax call, and that when you get the voice message you'll know which you want. You insert two new lines in inittab, each with its own ID, and each with a runlevel such as A for data and B for fax. When you know which you need, you simply spawn the appropriate one from one of the following command lines:

```
?telinit A" or ?
telinit B?.
```

The appropriate `getty` is put on the line until the first call is received. When the caller terminates the connection, the `getty` drops because, by definition, on demand will not respawn.

The other two letters, S and Q, are special. As noted earlier, S brings your system to maintenance mode and is the same as changing state to runlevel 1. The Q is used to tell `init` to reread inittab. The inittab file can be changed as often as required, but will only be read under certain circumstances:

- One of its processes dies (do you need to respawn another?)
- On a powerfail signal from a power daemon (or the command line)
- When told to change state by `telinit`

The Q argument tells `init`, "I've changed something, please reread the inittab."

THE INITTAB FILE FROM TOP TO BOTTOM

Here's a look at the default inittab in Listing 12.2. It is the same as Listing 12.1, but has the lines numbered for easier reference. Within the actual inittab, lines beginning with a # sign are disabled and left as examples or explanatory remarks, or as examples for possible future use. Be sure to read the comments throughout. These comments might give you a hint as to how to effectively customize inittab. Most programs, such as `mgetty` or `efax`, that were meant to run from inittab come with examples in their documentation showing how to implement them.

LISTING 12.2 LINE NUMBERED INITTAB

```
#
# inittab      This file describes how the INIT process should set up
#               the system in a certain run-level.
#
# Author:      Miquel van Smoorenburg, <miquels@drinkel.nl.mugnet.org>
#              Modified for RHS Linux by Marc Ewing and Donnie Barnes
#                Modified for COL by Raymund Will
#

# The runlevels used by COL are:
#   0 - halt (Do NOT set initdefault to this)
#   1 - Single user mode (including initialization of
➥network interfaces,
#       if you do have networking)
#   2 - Multiuser, (without NFS-Server und some such)
#       (basically the same as 3, if you do not have networking)
#   3 - Full multiuser mode
#   4 - unused
#       (should be equal to 3, for now)
#   5 - X11
#   6 - reboot (Do NOT set initdefault to this)

#
# Default runlevel.
id:3:initdefault:

```


continues

LISTING 12.2 CONTINUED

```
# System initialization.
si::sysinit:/etc/rc.d/rc.modules default
bw::bootwait:/etc/rc.d/rc.boot

# What to do in single-user mode.
~1:S:wait:/etc/rc.d/rc 1
~~:S:wait:/sbin/sulogin

l0:0:wait:/etc/rc.d/rc 0
l1:1:wait:/etc/rc.d/rc 1
l2:2:wait:/etc/rc.d/rc 2
l3:3:wait:/etc/rc.d/rc 3
l4:4:wait:/etc/rc.d/rc 4
l5:5:wait:/etc/rc.d/rc 5
l6:6:wait:/etc/rc.d/rc 6
# Normally not reached, but fallthrough in case of emergency.
z6:6:respawn:/sbin/sulogin

# Trap CTRL-ALT-DELETE
ca:12345:ctrlaltdel:/sbin/shutdown -t3 -r now

# Action on special keypress (ALT-UpArrow).
kb::kbrequest:/bin/echo "Keyboard Request--edit /etc/inittab
➥to let this work."

# When our UPS tells us power has failed, assume we have a few minutes
# of power left.  Schedule a shutdown for 2 minutes from now.
# This does, of course, assume you have powerd installed and your
# UPS connected and working correctly.
pf::powerfail:/sbin/shutdown -h +5 "Power Failure;
➥System Shutting Down"

# If battery is fading fast -- we hurry...
p1::powerfailnow:/sbin/shutdown -c 2> /dev/null
p2::powerfailnow:/sbin/shutdown -h now "Battery Low..."

# If power was restored before the shutdown kicked in, cancel it.
po:12345:powerokwait:/sbin/shutdown -c "Power Restored;
➥Shutdown Cancelled"


# Run gettys in standard runlevels
1:12345:respawn:/sbin/getty tty1 VC linux
2:2345:respawn:/sbin/getty tty2 VC linux
3:2345:respawn:/sbin/getty tty3 VC linux
4:2345:respawn:/sbin/getty tty4 VC linux
5:2345:respawn:/sbin/getty tty5 VC linux
6:2345:respawn:/sbin/getty tty6 VC linux

# Run xdm in runlevel 5
x:5:respawn:/usr/bin/X11/xdm -nodaemon
```

Because you already know how to read a line (id:runlevel:action:process), here's a look at what each line does.

Skipping down to line 24, you see that the default runlevel is 3. After you have configured your X server, if you change the 3 to a 5, the system presents you with a graphical login screen when it boots.

Just below the default runlevel on lines 27 and 28, you'll see the system initialization script calls. Line 27 is run once when the system boots. From the name of the script, you can surmise that this script loads the default modules for the system (you'll look at the script later). Line 28 is also run only once on bootup, and because it is run as `bootwait`, other scripts will wait to run until this script has terminated. Therefore, while line 27 is executing, so is line 28. The reason these two can run simultaneously is because the `bootwait` script doesn't require anything from the `sysinit` script (`rc.modules`)—but other scripts further down will need the `bootwait` script to finish before they can run successfully.

On lines 31 and 32 are two scripts that run whenever you enter maintenance (single user) mode. You'll look at the `rc` script later. The `sulogin` program is a special program to make your system a little more secure by preventing anyone who has physical access to the machine from rebooting into single user mode and gaining access to the system without knowing the root password. Without this line, booting into single user mode presents a root shell to the user without prompting for a password. However, this does not prevent a sophisticated user from breaking in to the system if they have physical access to the machine. In fact, one of the ways to bypass `sulogin` is discussed at the end of this chapter in the "Emergencies" section.

Lines 34–40 are run when you change to the particular runlevel. Each runlevel change will run the `rc` script with an argument for the particular runlevel that is being entered. Remember that runlevels 7–9 are legitimate runlevels that can be used if necessary. If you want to make use of any of these non-standard runlevels, you need to add a line between 40 and 41 to accommodate because you almost certainly want to run this script if you are going to use any of these runlevels.

Line 42 is designed to present a root password prompt in case a machine doesn't properly reboot when it enters runlevel 6. This is only precautionary. At the time of this writing, I am unaware of any machine that doesn't correctly respond to a reboot command.

Line 45 traps the keyboard sequence Ctrl+Alt+Delete and performs a shutdown and reboot. If desired, this line can be modified to change the `-r` to `-h` to halt the system; or you can just remove the `-r` to bring the system into single user mode with a root prompt.

Line 48 traps the keyboard sequence Alt+Up arrow. Currently it echoes the notice that this needs to be configured before use. On a default Caldera setup with `bash`, this particular command sequence will be ignored. First, the key mappings need to be changed so that `bash` passes the sequence. When that is finished, simply change the process portion of the line, substituting the command that you want to run for the `echo` command.

Lines 54, 57, 58, and 61 will be of interest to those who have a UPS compatible with powerd, the power daemon. The power daemon can monitor the serial port and perform the actions as documented in inittab. The inittab is sufficiently coherent, so I'll not belabor it here.

Lines 65 through 70 spawn `gettys` to the virtual terminals (VTs). Note that in single user mode only one VT is available. If you want to save some memory, you can run fewer VTs (I suggest one) in state 5. If you decide to make use of unlisted runlevels, you need to add those levels to the ones listed. You can increase the number of VTs simply by adding more lines (with unique IDs, of course).

Notice that `ca`, `kb`, `pf`, `p1`, `p2`, and `po` run regardless of the runlevel. When the runlevel column is null, the process is run in every runlevel.

Finally, you see that runlevel 5 spawns XDM (X Display Manager). If you want to use KDM (the KDE Display Manager), simply change the `xdm` to `kdm` and change the `initdefault` to runlevel 5.

Note

If your system has a default runlevel other than 1, but your system boots into maintenance mode, the `rc.boot` script has detected a problem with a hard disk that requires you to manually run `fsck`. When finished, the system reboots and tries to enter multiuser mode again.

THE rc SCRIPTS

Under OpenLinux, you'll find all the system initialization scripts in /etc/rc.d. This subdirectory has more subdirectories, one for each runlevel: rc0.d–rc6.d and init.d. Within the /etc/rc.d/rc#.d subdirectories (where the # is replaced by a single-digit number) are symbolic links to the master scripts stored in /etc/rc.d/init.d (see Table 12.1). The scripts in init.d take an argument of `start` or `stop`, and occasionally of `reload` or `restart`.

TABLE 12.1 DIRECTORY LISTING STARTING AT /ETC/RC.D/

ⁱ/etc/rc.d				
init.d/	rc2.d/	rc5.d/	rc.boot*	unconfigured.sh.done*
rc0.d/	rc3.d/	rc6.d/	rc.local*	
rc1.d/	rc4.d/	rc*	rc.modules*	
rc.d/init.d				
amd*	inet*	named*	pcmcia*	serial.sample*
atd*	ipfwctrl*	netatalk*	postgres*	single*
bigfs*	ipx*	network*	reboot@	skeleton*
cron*	ipxripd*	news*	rmnologin*	skipped*
dhcpd*	keytable*	nfs*	rstatd*	sprayd*
functions*	local@	nis-client*	rusersd*	sybase*
halt*	logoutd*	nis-server*	rwalld*	syslog*

rc.d/init.d

httpd*	lpd*	ntp*	rwhod*	urandom*
iBCS*	mta*	nwclient*	samba*	

rc.d/rc0.d

K05ipfwctrl@	K35netatalk@	K50mta@	K70ntp@	K90named@
K05news@	K39rwalld@	K59atd@	K73ipxripd@	K95urandom@
K08iBCS@	K40rstatd@	K60cron@	K74ipx@	K98pcmcia@
K09samba@	K44dhcpd@	K60nfs@	K75syslog@	K99network@
K25httpd@	K45nwclient@	K65lpd@	K79nis-client@	S99halt@
K30diald@	K47rusersd@	K65postgres@	K80nis-server@	
K30logoutd@	K48rwhod@	K70amd@	K85inet@	

rc.d/rc1.d

K05ipfwctrl@	K35netatalk@	K50mta@	K70ntp@	K90named@
K05news@	K39rwalld@	K59atd@	K73ipxripd@	K95urandom@
K08iBCS@	K40rstatd@	K60cron@	K74ipx@	S01pcmcia@
K09samba@	K44dhcpd@	K60nfs@	K75syslog@	S99single@
K25httpd@	K45nwclient@	K65lpd@	K79nis-client@	
K30diald@	K47rusersd@	K65postgres@	K80nis-server@	
K30logoutd@	K48rwhod@	K70amd@	K85inet@	

rc.d/rc2.d

K05ipfwctrl@	K40rstatd@	K79nis-client@	S26ipx@	S92iBCS@
K05news@	K44dhcpd@	K80nis-server@	S30amd@	S98local@
K09samba@	K47rusersd@	K85inet@	S30ntp@	S99bigfs@
K25httpd@	K48rwhod@	K90named@	S35lpd@	S99rmnologin@
K30diald@	K50mta@	S01network@	S40cron@	S99skipped@
K30logoutd@	K60nfs@	S01pcmcia@	S41atd@	
K35netatalk@	K65postgres@	S05urandom@	S55nwclient@	
K39rwalld@	K73ipxripd@	S25syslog@	S75keytable@	

rc.d/rc3.d

S01network@	S26ipx@	S41atd@	S65netatalk@	S95news@
S01pcmcia@	S27ipxripd@	S50mta@	S70diald@	S98local@
S05urandom@	S30amd@	S55nwclient@	S70logoutd@	S99bigfs@

continues

TABLE 12.1 CONTINUED

rc.d/rc3.d				
S10named@	S30ntp@	S56dhcpd@	S75keytable@	S99rmnologin@
S15inet@	S35lpd@	S60rstatd@	S85httpd@	S99skipped@
S20nis-server@	S35postgres@	S61rwalld@	S91samba@	
S21nis-client@	S40cron@	S62rwhod@	S92iBCS@	
S25syslog@	S40nfs@	S63rusersd@	S95ipfwctrl@	
rc.d/rc4.d				
S01network@	S26ipx@	S41atd@	S65netatalk@	S95news@
S01pcmcia@	S27ipxripd@	S50mta@	S70diald@	S98local@
S05urandom@	S30amd@	S55nwclient@	S70logoutd@	S99bigfs@
S10named@	S30ntp@	S56dhcpd@	S75keytable@	S99rmnologin@
S15inet@	S35lpd@	S60rstatd@	S85httpd@	S99skipped@
S20nis-server@	S35postgres@	S61rwalld@	S91samba@	
S21nis-client@	S40cron@	S62rwhod@	S92iBCS@	
S25syslog@	S40nfs@	S63rusersd@	S95ipfwctrl@	
rc.d/rc5.d				
S01network@	S26ipx@	S41atd@	S65netatalk@	S95news@
S01pcmcia@	S27ipxripd@	S50mta@	S70diald@	S98local@
S05urandom@	S30amd@	S55nwclient@	S70logoutd@	S99bigfs@
S10named@	S30ntp@	S56dhcpd@	S75keytable@	S99rmnologin@
S15inet@	S35lpd@	S60rstatd@	S85httpd@	S99skipped@
S20nis-server@	S35postgres@	S61rwalld@	S91samba@	
S21nis-client@	S40cron@	S62rwhod@	S92iBCS@	
S25syslog@	S40nfs@	S63rusersd@	S95ipfwctrl@	
rc.d/rc6.d				
K05ipfwctrl@	K35netatalk@	K50mta@	K70ntp@	K90named@
K05news@	K39rwalld@	K59atd@	K73ipxripd@	K95urandom@
K08iBCS@	K40rstatd@	K60cron@	K74ipx@	K98pcmcia@
K09samba@	K44dhcpd@	K60nfs@	K75syslog@	K99network@
K25httpd@	K45nwclient@	K65lpd@	K79nis-client@	S99reboot@
K30diald@	K47rusersd@	K65postgres@	K80nis-server@	
K30logoutd@	K48rwhod@	K70amd@	K85inet@	

Key: terminating characters indicate:
/ = directory
** = executable script*
@ = symlink to a script
All symlinks in rc[1-6].d subdirectories are to scripts in the ../init.d directory.

The files in the /etc/rc.d/rc#.d directories all begin with either an `S` or a `K` for `start` or `kill`, respectively, a number that indicates a relative order for the scripts, and the script name—commonly the same name as the master script to which it is linked (found in init.d). For example, you might see S35lpd. This is a symbolic link to ../init.d/lpd and is used by `rc` to run the `lpd` script in init.d with the argument `start`, which starts up the line printer daemon. The scripts can also be called from the following command line:

```
/etc/rc.d/init.d/lpd start.
```

The nice part about SysV initialization is that it is easy for root to start, stop, and, in many cases, restart or reload a daemon or process subsystem from the command line simply by calling the script in init.d with the appropriate argument.

When not called from a command line with an argument, the `/etc/rc.d/rc` script determines what to run, and how, based on the previous and current runlevel. For example, if you are in runlevel 3 and change to runlevel 2, the `/etc/rc.d/rc` script uses the runlevel command as you did earlier, and looks at the differences in the two directories corresponding to the two runlevels to determine what to do. Any process subsystems that are running and that need to be stopped are stopped by calling the appropriate `kill` script; any that are not running that need to be started are started by executing the corresponding `start` scripts as explained previously. The `rc` script always runs the `Knn` scripts from lowest to highest, and then the `Snn` scripts (also in ascending order). This ensures that the correct daemons are running in each runlevel, and that they are stopped and started in the correct order. For example, don't start `sendmail` (mta) or the Apache Web server (`httpd`) before you start networking. By the same token, you'll want to stop `sendmail` and Apache before you stop networking.

Remember when you changed to runlevel 8? Well, because there is no subdirectory rc8.d, and therefore no scripts, when you changed states, no `init` scripts were started. Had you come from boot directly to runlevel 8, you would have had a problem. Only the kernel, `init`, and those daemons started via the `sysinit`, `boot`, or `bootwait` commands in the inittab would have been running.

For those who find hand editing links to add or delete scripts in any particular runlevel to be a tedious task—and for those who are just not comfortable doing it—there is a program called `tksysv`, available if you are running X. This program uses a graphical interface (using tcl/tk), reads the script names in /etc/rc.d/init.d, and displays them on the far left side of the application box. It also reads the links in each of the rc#.d subdirectories and displays them for each runlevel from left to right, with start scripts above and kill scripts below. You can add, delete, and even change the order of execution as you see fit (see Figure 12.1). The program also enables you to execute or edit the scripts.

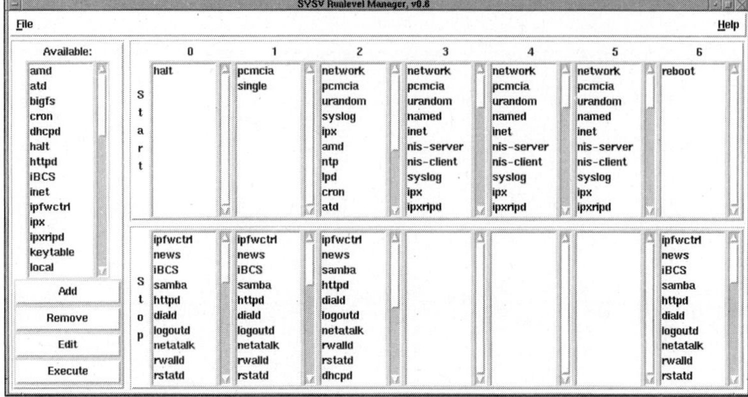

Figure 12.1
How `tksysv` looks onscreen.

THE STARTUP SCRIPTS

Here's a look at some of the startup scripts. This is a brief overview, and therefore is not intended to teach script reading. For more information, please refer to a book on shell scripting. The first startup script you'll look at is `/etc/rc.d/rc.modules` (see Listing 12.3). The line numbers don't appear in the actual script; they are for reference.

LISTING 12.3 THE `rc.modules` SCRIPT

```
#!/bin/sh
#
# Load default/additional modules
#
# $Id: rc.modules,v 1.10 1998/05/12 11:11:02 ray Exp $
#

# this script makes use of the following commands:
#   [
#   cat
#   echo
#   insmod
#   sed
#   uname
# (this is important for use on an 'initrd' :)

if [ -d /usr/bin ]; then
  PATH="/bin:/usr/bin:/sbin:/usr/sbin"
else
  PATH="/bin:/sbin"
fi

[ -n "$1" ] && Sep=.

PFX=/etc/modules
REL="`uname -r`"
VER="`uname -v`"
MODULE_LIST="$PFX/$REL/$VER$Sep$1"

```

```
30  if [ -n "$1" ] && [ ! -f "$MODULE_LIST" ]; then
31    MODULE_LIST="$PFX/$REL/$Sep$1"
32    [ -f "$MODULE_LIST" ] || MODULE_LIST="$PFX/$REL/$1"
33  fi
34
35  if [ "$1" = "default" ] && [ -f /etc/isapnp.conf ] &&
    ➥[ -x /sbin/isapnp ]; then
36    echo "Configuring ISA PnP cards..."
37    /sbin/isapnp /etc/isapnp.conf
38  fi
39
40  if [ -f "$MODULE_LIST" ]; then
41    [ -n "$1" ] && echo "Loading $1 modules..."
42    [ -z "$1" ] && echo "Loading additional modules..."
43    for m in `cat "$MODULE_LIST"` ; do
44      # check if module is already loaded
45      [ -r /proc/modules ] &&
46        [ "`sed -n 's/^'$m'[      ].*$/found/p'
     ➥/proc/modules`" = ?found" ] &&
47          continue
48      moduleopt=
49      for o in "$PFX/$REL/options/$m" "$PFX/options/$m"; do
50        [ -s "$o" ] && moduleopt="`cat $o`" && break
51      done
52      insmod $m $moduleopt > /dev/null 2>&1
53    done
54  fi
55
56  [ -n "$1" ] && exit 0
57
58  # load instructions inserted by third-party packages
        ➥would follow below...
```


Lines beginning with # are remarks (except the first line, which designates the program used to interpret the script) and will be ignored. Lines 17 through 34 perform some tests and initialize variables required by the rest of the script.

If necessary, lines 35 through 38 set up plug-and-play cards.

Lines 40 through 54 read through the modules list (normally found following /etc/modules), check for options needed by the modules (a separate file found in the same subdirectory), and load the modules listed therein (with any required options).

The next script you'll look at is a typical shell script that is found in /etc/rc.d/init.d and used to start a daemon or process subsystem. These scripts are linked from the various run-level directories (as discussed previously). The script in Listing 12.4 is representative of the others found with it.

LISTING 12.4 THE `mta init` SCRIPT

```
#! /bin/bash
#
# mta       This shell script takes care of starting and stopping
#           Mail Transfer Agents (e.g. sendmail).
#
#           Modified for COL by Raymund Will <ray@caldera.de> and
#           Olaf Kirch <okir@caldera.de>.

# Source network configuration
. /etc/sysconfig/network

# Source function library (and set essential variables).
. /etc/rc.d/init.d/functions

# Get the MTA variant we're supposed to start.
[ -n "$VARIANT" ] || exit 0
if [ ! -r /etc/mta/options/$VARIANT ]; then
    echo -n "WARNING: Mail Transfer Agent $VARIANT selected " >&2
    echo "but not installed." >&2
    exit 1
fi
. /etc/mta/options/$VARIANT

# See how we were called.
case "$1" in
 start)
  [ -e $SVIlock ] && exit 1
  [ ${NETWORKING} = "no" ] && exit 0

  # Start daemons.
  echo -n "Starting $DESCRIPTIVE: "
  #ssd -S -q -x $DAEMON -- $OPTIONS && echo -n " $VARIANT"
  ssd -S -x $DAEMON -n $VARIANT -- $OPTIONS
  echo "."
  touch $SVIlock
  ;;

 stop)
  [ -e $SVIlock ] || exit 0

  # Stop daemons.
  echo -n "Shutting down $DESCRIPTIVE: "
  ssd -K -p /var/run/$VARIANT.pid -n $VARIANT
  echo "?."
  rm -f $SVIlock
  ;;

 reload)
  [ -e $SVIlock ] || exit 0

  # Signal daemon.
  echo -n "Reloading $DESCRIPTIVE configuration: "
  ssd -K -s 1 -p /var/run/$VARIANT.pid -n $VARIANT -x $DAEMON
  echo "."
  ;;

```

```
57    *)
58     echo "Usage: $SVIscript {start|stop|reload}"
59     exit 1
60     ;;
61   esac
62
63   exit 0
```

Again, you'll ignore the comments. Lines 10 through 22 perform some tests and initialize variables and functions needed by the rest of the script.

Line 25 starts the typical initialization script sequence by looking at how the script was called—a `start`, `stop`, or, in some cases, `reload` or `restart` script. During bootup or a run-level change, the script knows (via the functions sourced in line 13) whether to append start or stop to the script name. The start/stop convention is used by all scripts in /etc/rc.d/init.d so that the script can be called manually by root at any time. Line 58 handles cases where an argument (`$1`) is not passed to the script.

EMERGENCIES

Editing inittab or any of the `rc` scripts requires some degree of caution. But even the best tests cannot simulate a complete system reboot, and a script that might appear to function properly after a system has initialized fails to execute, or worse, hangs during system initialization. The reasons are diverse, but usually involve getting things out of order.

For example, in Caldera's Network Desktop (which ran on a 1.2.13 kernel and used modules), I created a script to start the `kerneld` process early in the boot sequence. When I upgraded the system to Caldera's OpenLinux v1.0 (which ran a 2.0.25 kernel), I used the same script, tested it, and—when I was satisfied that all was well—rebooted the system. Much to my dismay, the boot process hung loading `kerneld`. I found out that with the newer `kerneld`, `kerneld` needed to know the hostname of the computer, which the system did not yet know. This has since been compensated for by putting the hostname discovery process early in the initialization sequence (in /etc/rc.d/rc.boot), but such things can happen to anyone. Something as simple as fat-fingering a key or forgetting to full-path something without declaring a `PATH` variable in a script can leave you in a lurch.

Fortunately, you can pass boot-time parameters to `init`. When the system boots and you see: `LILO:`, you can hit the Shift key and then the Tab key to see the kernel labels that are available for booting. You can then add a kernel label and follow it by any required parameters to boot the system. Any parameters the kernel needs are used and discarded, for example if you have more than 64MB of RAM, you need to pass that to the kernel in the form mem=96Mb (or however much RAM you have). If you pass the `-b` switch, the kernel doesn't use this but passes it on to `init`. The same goes for any single digit number or the letters s or q in either upper- or lowercase.

Tip

Use the `-b` option to boot into maintenance mode without running any scripts—for use when scripts might hang the system.

By passing any of the numbers or letters to `init`, you are overriding the defaults in inittab, as was stated earlier. Most of these numbers or letters do exactly what they might do if passed from a command line on a running system. But the `-b` argument is special. It is the emergency boot parameter. This parameter tells `init` to read the inittab. Except for some special exceptions, don't execute any of the commands, just drop into maintenance mode so no `rc` scripts will be executed. You can mount the system read-write and fix it. One exception to not executing any inittab commands is any process ID starting with ~, for example `~~` and `~1`. If you add or change any script with an ID beginning with ~, it is a good idea to check it as another ID first. You'll not find this feature in the man pages because it's undocumented.

Caution

The next paragraph discusses booting directly to a shell, which can cause irreparable corruption to the file system. This is a last resort option only!

If, however, despite your best efforts, you find that the boot process still hangs even with the `-b` option to LILO, or if you've forgotten the root password, don't despair. At the LILO prompt, you can pass the parameter `init=/bin/sh`. This argument will be used by the kernel itself. Remember that the kernel runs one and only one program before it goes into the background: `init`. By passing the preceding argument to LILO, the kernel runs a shell as its only program. This is very dangerous, but it enables you to mount the root file system (mount `-n -o remount,rw /`), change /etc/inittab or /etc/shadow, and then `sync` and reboot. In this case I recommend calling `sync` twice, and then remounting the root file system read-only and rebooting. Use this as a last resort before a reinstall because it can corrupt your disk, making a reinstall inevitable.

SUMMARY

This chapter covered how Caldera OpenLinux System V initialization works. You learned how the system gets everything set up and enters the default init runlevel, and that a runlevel is a software-implemented way to organize groups of process subsystems. You also learned where to look for the daemons or process subsystems that are stopped and started in each runlevel.

You learned how to pass arguments to change how the system initializes before the kernel begins to boot, for emergencies, or just to start in a runlevel other than the default. Also discussed in this chapter were methods to deal with problems that might occur during bootup and how to avoid them, or what to do if you can't avoid them.

For more information on the topics discussed here, refer to the following chapters:

- See Chapter 9, "Understanding the Linux File System," to learn more about subdirectories and how they work with the file system.
- See Chapter 13 to learn more about your login environment and shell scripts.
- See Chapter 17, "Building Custom Kernels," to learn more about installing a kernel.
- See Chapter 18, "Kernel Modules," to learn more about module loading and use.
- See Chapter 20 to learn more about LILO.

CHAPTER 13

Customizing Your Shell Environment

In this chapter

In this chapter, you'll take a quick look at shells and learn how shells interact with the kernel and the user. You'll also explore what an environment is in terms of Linux, and learn how to determine what it is and to change it.

You'll also take a quick look at shell programming. This chapter won't make you an expert on shell programming, but it will introduce you to the basics. (There are books devoted to the subject.)

WHAT IS A SHELL?

In order to explain what a shell is, you need to understand a few terms; you also need to understand how you interact with the system (both hardware and other software) as a whole. Previously, you learned that Linux sees everything as nothing more than files. Whether that file is ASCII text, binary instructions, a directory, or a special file that acts as a conduit to pass data to and from a piece of hardware, it is seen by the kernel as a file.

Looking at Figure 13.1, if you imagine that all the files on a disk go in the center circle—regardless of whether or not they represent hardware—it will be a little easier to understand what happens. After the kernel boots, it is in charge of everything in the center circle; all hardware and files are accessed through the Linux kernel. The area defined by the middle ring where the kernel lives is often referred to as *kernel space*. The outer ring is *user space*; the shell, all programs spawned by the shell, and the daemons operate in the user space. These programs access hardware and other files (*resources*) only by way of the kernel—this determination is made based on permissions. (Although the preceding is oversimplified and not completely technically accurate, it is sufficient for the purposes of this chapter.)

Figure 13.1
Simplified Linux system diagram depicting user, kernel, and resource space.

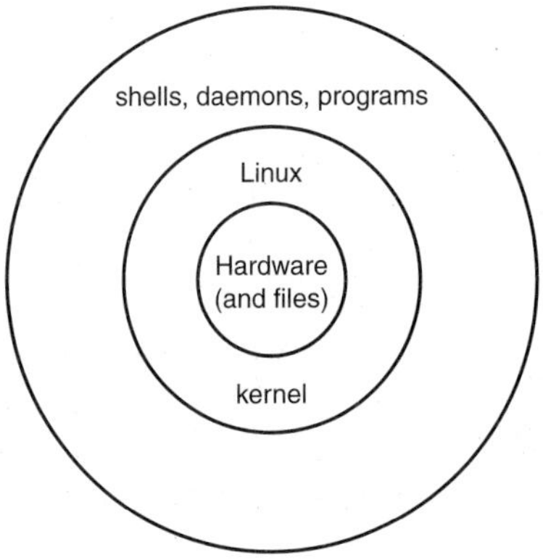

Relationship of the Linux kernel to hardware and programs

Step through this process slowly to ensure that you understand exactly how the system works. When the kernel boots, it sets up residence in a protected area of memory. The only way to access this memory, and the hardware beneath it, is through special *hooks* that facilitate that access. Some hooks are automatically built in, whereas others can be specified when you configure the kernel (see Chapter 17, "Building Custom Kernels"). You do not want, for example, to build the kernel without the hooks that it requires to interact with a console display and keyboard. Modules and programs grab onto the hooks that are designed for them and communicate with the kernel through them. Based on *permissions*—a combination of ownership and mode—the kernel decides whether to allow access to or communication with the file. (See the "File Permissions" section in Chapter 10, "Users, Groups, and Permissions.") A binary file doesn't become a program until the kernel permits it to be loaded into memory and executed. All normal programs run in user space (again, simplified for the purposes of this chapter).

After the kernel boots, it runs one, and only one, program: `init`. In Chapter 12, "System Initialization Under OpenLinux," you learned how `init` determines what to run. One of the programs that `init` runs is `getty`. On a standard system, `getty` then runs `login`, which causes a `login` prompt to be displayed on the console and certain virtual terminals (as determined by `inittab`). Because everything up to this point runs as a privileged process, access between the outer program layer and the inner hardware layer is unimpeded. Privileged processes run with a *user ID* (*UID*) of zero. Note that the user, root, has a UID of 0. So, when logged in as root, programs run as privileged processes unless modified by the permissions (suid, sgid) of the file (see Chapter 10).

When you sit down at the keyboard and type in your username, you are inputting data through `login`, a configurable program called by `getty`. It is `login`'s job to determine if the username/password pair you've input matches that of a valid system user as defined in `/etc/passwd` and related files. After `login` determines that the username/password pair defines a valid system user, it spawns the shell listed for that user in `/etc/passwd` as that user on the particular display where the login occurred.

So a shell is nothing more than a program running in user space that provides you with an interactive interface to the system (a *command prompt*) to input data or specify programs to run. The default shell on OpenLinux installations is `bash` (Bourne Again Shell). When the shell starts, a number of things happen. The shell determines how it was called and by what program (`login` or another shell). This in turn determines certain things regarding the shell's characteristics and which configuration files it loads. When called by `login`, the shell is called a login shell and begins by reading master configuration files in `/etc`. `login` itself has two configuration files: /etc/login.access, which matches `login` names with valid login locations, and login.defs, which can be used to call a universal environment file (not used in OpenLinux). Neither of these files are found on a default OpenLinux installation, but they can be added by the System Administrator to tailor the system. Another file that is present is /etc/security, which tells `login` which terminals are considered secure enough from eavesdropping for root to log in—but this only pertains to root.

The first configuration file called by a login shell is /etc/profile. Some of the other configuration files called are determined by whether the bash login shell was called as bash or via a symbolic link (sh). In OpenLinux, the default in /etc/passwd is /bin/bash; therefore, the files .bash_profile, .bash_login, .bashrc, and .profile, all located in the user's home directory, are called if they exist.

When a login shell exits it calls .bash_logout, if it exists. When an interactive shell that is not a login shell is started, it reads .bashrc, if that file exists, inheriting the environment (discussed as follows). Command-line options can be used to modify this behavior and have bash ignore its rc file or read a different one.

Note The environment variable SHLVL indicates whether a shell is a login shell. SHLVL=1 indicates a login shell, whereas higher numbers indicate a non-login shell. See the "Variables" section that follows to learn how to read environment variables.

When you enter input at the shell prompt and hit Enter, several things happen. The line is parsed, and each entry separated by white space (and not grouped by quotes) is read by the shell, interpreted if it's a shell special character, expanded if it's an alias, assigned a value in relation to its position on the command line, and executed. The shell first checks to see if what you typed is a shell built-in command. If not, it checks to see if it is an alias, and then a function. If it is none of these, the shell searches a predefined set of directories (PATH) for an executable file to run. (There is more on command-line processing, special characters, and aliases later in this chapter.)

TYPES OF SHELLS

Before you continue to a discussion of shell environments, it might interest you to know that a number of shells exist for Linux. Each of these shells has certain characteristics, but each is classified under one of two trees: the Bourne shell or the C shell family.

THE BOURNE SHELL

The Bourne shell is the oldest of the modern shells. It was designed for ease of use and to facilitate scripts. By default, most scripts you see on a Linux system use bash, a successor to the Bourne shell. For the purpose of this text, the environment and scripts are discussed in terms of bash. Some of the shells available for Linux systems that fall under the Bourne shell family include another Bourne successor, ksh, the Korn shell (implemented in OpenLinux as pdksh); ash, a shell similar to bash but with a smaller footprint, ideal for boot floppies; kiss, another simple shell interpreter, but with only rudimentary built-in commands—also ideal for boot or rescue disks; and zsh, a shell which more closely resembles the Korn shell.

THE C SHELL

The C shell was originally created to overcome the Bourne shell's limitations (such as support for numeric computations). It appealed to advanced users, and to users more familiar with C programming language syntax. The C shell provides a friendly interface but is considered more difficult to script for, particularly for those who are not comfortable with C syntax. Environment variable syntax varies significantly, and scripts written for the Bourne shell family do not normally run on a C shell, and vice versa. C shell (`csh`) successors include `tcsh`, which is recommended over `csh` for those who want to use this type of interface.

For those who enjoy exploring shells and shell programming, a number of other interfaces also exist for Linux, some with built-in support for languages; these include `es`, which has support for Scheme; `flin`, an interface that uses color and simple syntax; and `lsh`, which boasts DOS-compatible commands. Some half dozen other shells are also available.

INTERACTIVE SHELL USE

Most people use their chosen shell interactively. You'll decide what you want to do (start a word processor, list the directory, perform system administration tasks, and so on) and perform it from a shell. `bash` does have some nice features that you'll want to explore before you go much further.

I've been accused of being lazy, and to a degree that's true. I don't like typing long command sequences or directory paths into the command line. If I want to traverse six subdirectory levels, I don't want to type every character. I want to type `cd` and just go there. But the next best thing to a single keystroke is having the shell read my mind (or more accurately, choose intelligently among alternatives)—and it can, in a shell sort of way. If you start to type a path or filename, and that path or filename is unique among the choices available, you can press the Tab key, and the shell fills out the rest of the unique portion of that name. If the choices are not unique, that is, if a range of choices are available, you hear a beep (if your speaker is working), which indicates that ambiguous choices are present. If you press the Tab key a second time, you are presented with the possible options from which to choose—unless there are a large number, in which case you can choose whether you want to see all the options. Often, just one more character makes the selection unique again.

Another feature that is of interest is the command history. This is saved in a file called .bash_history and shows each command you've typed in. The file grows to a predetermined size, and then discards older command lines as newer ones are added. The default is 500 lines. Typing `history` shows you all the commands that `bash` remembers. (This might exceed the maximum allowable history file size, and will be truncated when the shell exits.) You can also use `fc -l` which, by default, shows you the last 17 commands. The most common use of the `fc` command is in the form `fc -s` *`xx`*, where *`xx`* (any number of letters can be used) searches backward in the history for the first command starting with *`xx`* and executes it. When saved to disk (when the shell exits), this command history makes shell scripting easy. Just cut and paste commands that worked properly into the script.

`bash` makes cut and paste simple, particularly for those in the X Window Environment, because this technique works between application boxes on the screen. Text can be highlighted using the mouse: Just place the cursor at the beginning of the area to be highlighted, press and hold the left mouse button, and drag. Text can also be highlighted using the keyboard: Position the cursor and press and hold the Shift key while using the up and down arrow keys to highlight text. Then, use the middle mouse button—or both the left and right mouse buttons simultaneously on two-button mice—to paste the highlighted text.

Most commonly, the up arrow is used to scroll backward through the history buffer until the desired command is found—which can then be changed if necessary—and executed by pressing Enter.

DEFAULT SHELL ENVIRONMENT

As mentioned previously, when you log in and get a shell, a number of things happen: Certain files are read, some variables are set, perhaps even a program or two are run. Most of what happens sets up your *default environment*. This environment is set via the previously mentioned files. A few, however, such as `$HOME` (a notation indicating a user's home directory; under `bash`, this can also be abbreviated as a tilde [~]); and `$SHELL` (which is the shell login called) are obtained from `/etc/passwd`, as is the UID.

> **Note**
>
> `login` allows arguments following the login name. For example, `login: dbandel -- norc` allows `dbandel` to log in and prevent reading of rc files such as .bashrc or .cshrc. Other options are also available.

VARIABLES

Listing 13.1 shows a sample `/etc/profile`. As you can see, one of the first things set is `PATH`. Custom dictates that environment variables are always uppercase. You can always see how a particular environment variable has been set by using `echo`, which tells the shell to echo whatever follows to the screen. Any variable can be referenced by prefixing it with `$`. Therefore, you can type `echo $PATH` to find out what your `PATH` environment variable is set to.

LISTING 13.1 A SAMPLE MASTER PROFILE

```
# /etc/profile: system-wide .profile file for bash(1).
PATH="/usr/bin:/bin:/usr/X11R6/bin:/usr/games:~/bin"
PS1="\\$ "
ROOTSYS=/opt/root
export PATH PS1 ROOTSYS
ulimit -c unlimited
umask 022
PATH="$PATH:/usr/local/bin:/opt/bin:$ROOTSYS/bin"
export PATH
```

Looking at Listing 13.1, you see the `PATH` variable being set a second time. This time, however, you see that the first part of the variable is a reference to the currently set variable. To avoid replacing the entire contents of the old variable `PATH` with the new value, or to avoid retyping a possibly long value to insert another directory into the `PATH`, you can use the following shortcut:

```
VAR=kludge:bar, VAR=$VAR:baz
```

This gives you the same result as typing `VAR=kludge:bar:baz`. If `VAR=$VAR:baz` is written as only `VAR=baz`, you lose the `kludge` and `bar`.

One other thing I want to explain at this time is the `export` line. This line is designed to make sure that the variables it references are available to all the subshells and programs that the current shell runs. When you type in a line to run a program, for example `vi`, your shell searches all the directories in the order that they are listed in the `$PATH` variable and runs the first executable that it finds called `vi`. Whenever a program is called, it normally performs a `fork()` and then an `exec()`. This detaches the program from the current shell and runs it in its own shell with its own environment. When this happens, the subsequent program inherits certain characteristics from the calling shell (its parent). What it inherits are exported environment variables. So, if the program you start is another shell and you have not exported an environment variable (such as `PATH`), it is not available to the new (child) shell. Although this gives a great deal of power and flexibility to the shell, what ensues can be a frustrating experience for new Linux users as the new shell returns the message `command not found` for commands that the parent shell had no problem finding.

If you want to see all the environment variables that are available, `bash` has a built-in command to help you: `set`. By itself, `set` displays your environment. (See Listing 13.2 for a sample output.) If you run a shell other than `bash`, the external command `env` might be the only way to see your environment. `set` can also be used to set an environment variable, as in `set VAR=kludge`—but why type four characters (three letters and a space) unnecessarily? Thus, common usage is to not use it. But it does suggest a complement: `unset`. You can use `unset` if you want to eliminate a variable, rather than just setting it to a null value. For example, if you have an environment variable `DISPLAY=:0.0`, and you change from an X window running on F7 to a non-graphic virtual terminal on F1 (by pressing Ctrl+Alt+F1), you might need to get rid of this variable. Some programs, when they start, look for the environment variable `DISPLAY` and use its value to determine if or where to run a graphic—instead of non-graphic—version. If the `DISPLAY` environment variable is present, the program fails with an ugly error message. This might even happen if `DISPLAY` is set to null (that is, `set DISPLAY`). To avoid this, you can simply type `unset DISPLAY`, and the variable will no longer exist.

LISTING 13.2 SAMPLE OUTPUT FROM set

```
BASH=/bin/bash
BASH_VERSINFO=([0]="2" [1]="01" [2]="1" [3]="1" [4]="release"
➥[5]="i486-pc-linux")
BASH_VERSION='2.01.1(1)-release'
COLUMNS=79
DIRSTACK=()
DISPLAY=LOCALHOST:0.0
EUID=1000
GROUPS=()
HISTFILE=/home/dab/.bash_history
HISTFILESIZE=500
HISTSIZE=500
HOME=/home/dab
HOSTDISPLAY=LOCALHOST:0.0
HOSTNAME=lnb1
HOSTTYPE=i486
IFS='
'
LINES=56
LOGNAME=dab
MACHTYPE=i486-pc-linux
MAILCHECK=60
OLDPWD=/home/dab/docs
OPTERR=1
OPTIND=1
OSTYPE=linux-gnu
PATH=/usr/local/bin:/usr/bin:/bin:/usr/bin/X11:/usr/games:
➥/usr/local/jdk116_v5/bin:/opt/root/bin:/usr/local/vnc
PIPESTATUS=([0]="0")
PPID=233
PS1='\s-\v\$ '
PS2='> '
PS4='+ '
PWD=/home/dab
ROOTSYS=/opt/root
SHELL=/bin/bash
SHELLOPTS=braceexpand:hashall:histexpand:monitor:history:
➥interactive-comments:emacs
SHLVL=2
TERM=xterm
UID=1000
USER=dab
WABIDIR=/home/wabi
WINDOWID=25165844
XFCE_LANG=en
_=set
```

Another important variable that you might want to know about but won't see using `set` is `umask`. This term stands for *user mask*, and is used to determine what permissions are applied to new files. The `umask` command by itself returns a three digit octal number. This number is the inverse of the octal number used by `chmod` to set a file's mode (for more on `chmod`, see the "File Permissions" section of Chapter 10). The most common `umask`s are `002` and `022`. A `umask` of `022` sets the mode of newly created directories and executable files to

755 (777-022), and other files to 644 (666-022). Assuming that the file kludge doesn't exist in your current directory, and that you have rights to write in that directory, typing `touch kludge` creates a regular file kludge with mode 644 (assuming a `umask` of 022).

Aliases and Functions

Beyond variables, two other important things that affect your environment and can be set up automatically in your configuration files are aliases and functions. Aliases known to your system can be seen by typing the word `alias` at the command prompt. Some common aliases are `which`, `z`, `h`, and `j` (see Listing 13.3). Aliases are declared by use of the `alias` command. For example, if you want your directory listings to show up in color, you might want the following included in your .bashrc file:

```
alias ls="ls --color=auto"
```

Now, any time you enter the `ls` command, it will be as if you typed `ls --color=auto`. Some people, to be safe, alias `rm="rm -i"` to prevent them from accidentally deleting something that they don't mean to delete. Unfortunately, if they ever log on to a system without this alias, they almost always unintentionally delete something. Therefore, an alias can be a double-edged sword. Of course, if you don't want this crutch, you can always remove it with `unalias`. An alias always takes precedence over an executable unless it is called via its full path (that is, `/bin/ls`). Aliases are not exported, but this is not a problem because they are usually only useful in a shell. Normally, aliases are declared in your .bashrc file and are available for each subshell spawned.

Listing 13.3 Sample Output from `alias`

```
# ~/.bashrc: executed by bash(1) for non-login shells.

ROOTSYS=/opt/root
export ROOTSYS

PATH=$PATH:/usr/local/jdk116_v5/bin:$ROOTSYS/bin
export PATH

PATH=$PATH:/usr/local/vnc
export PATH
WABIDIR=/home/wabi
export WABIDIR

alias ls="ls --color=auto"

TERM=xterm
export TERM

. .profile

. .functions

/usr/games/fortune
echo
```

Whereas an alias is generally a short command substitution, a function can be a single command or an entire multiline program. Listing 13.4 shows an example of a file called .functions. This file is called from the .bashrc file (Listing 13.3). As you can see, its syntax is similar to that of a shell script (discussed in a later section), and has the following form:

```
name () {statements ; }
```

Any functions can be seen from the current shell via `typeset` or `declare`. This shows your entire environment, including functions. To see functions only, use the `-f` option with either command. See Listing 13.5 for a sample output (notice that the output shows the alias expanded `ls` call). Functions exist in the current shell, and are an exception to the rule that commands are executed with `fork()` and `exec()`.

LISTING 13.4 EXAMPLE OF .FUNCTIONS

```
# This is a file with a function

 cdd ()
{
    if [ $# = 1 ]; then
        cd $1;
        ls -aF;
    else
        echo "function requires an argument";
    fi
}
```

Functions always execute in the current shell. Functions can supposedly be exported by using `declare -x` *name*, but I've had poor results with this method. As with aliases, though, if the .functions file is called from the .bashrc file (as in Listing 13.5), the functions will be available each time a new shell is spawned.

LISTING 13.5 SAMPLE OUTPUT FROM `declare` OR `typeset`

```
declare -f cdd ()
{
    if [ $# = 1 ]; then
        cd $1;
        ls --color=auto --color=auto -aF;
    else
        echo "function requires an argument";
    fi
}
```

One thing you might have noticed is the way that the .function file is called in .bashrc. The command is preceded by a solitary period (.). This is a synonym for `source` (which can be substituted for `.` but rarely is) and tells the shell to run the command or file in the current shell—that is, to "source" the file. This causes `exec()` to run without a `fork()`, in a manner similar to functions.

CUSTOMIZING YOUR ENVIRONMENT

By using what you've learned previously, you can see that it is a fairly simple task to customize your environment. From within your own home directory, just change or add those things that you want, export them if necessary, and you're off. Additions and changes can be made from a command line as well as from .bashrc (which I suggest you source from .bash_login for login shells). Just type the command at a command prompt as you list it in the rc file. This is a great way to experiment.

Take a look at your environment by typing `set` (or `declare` if you're also using functions). If you look down the list, you'll see something interesting: a UID. This is how the system knows who I am, and what my permissions are. Great! If you change this, you can become root. Sound too easy? A few environment variables have been set with the `-r` option—they're read-only. You can't `set` them, and you can't `unset` them. They're permanent when declared, and the system has also exported them. Your system administrator can also `set` environment variables as read-only in files in `/etc`. In certain circumstances, this might be necessary.

If you decide to set a variable from scratch, such as `PATH`, and it is very long, breaking it up into several lines might be desirable. But how do you do that, when hitting the Enter key executes the line? If the last character in the line is a backslash (\), the shell does not execute the line, but waits for more input until you enter a line not terminated by a backslash. You might also notice that your command prompt has changed. This is a signal to you that the shell is awaiting further input. You can see the continuation prompt as the environment variable `PS2`. `PS1` is your primary command prompt, and it can also be customized. You can change your prompt as follows:

```
export PS1="$USERNAME@$HOSTNAME \$ "
```

This gives you the prompt `me@myhost $ `. You can also change this to always show your present directory (pwd) by using the following:

```
export PS1='`pwd` '
```

This brings up the next point. You have four sets of punctuation to work with. Until this last example, I deliberately stayed with examples that needed only double quotes (""); but there are also single quotes ('') and grave quotes (``). The grave quotes are the quote marks normally found on a 102-key keyboard in the upper left corner below the Esc key, and to the left of the 1/! key. A shifted grave quote gives you a tilde (~). So when do you use which? The rules are as follows:

PART III

CH 13

- **Use double quotes to pass what's inside the quotes to the command, but allow variable substitution**—That is, `echo "$HOME"` gives you `/home/username`. You need to use double quotes whenever you have a single argument that contains white space (as defined by your IFS environment variable, usually Space+Tab+Newline). For example, `cd /etc/modules/`uname -r`/`uname -v`` gives you the error `bash cd: /etc/modules/2.0.35/#1: No such file or directory`. Note that the entire name of the directory is `#1 Thu Jul 23 12:41:51 PDT 1998`, but `cd` stopped reading when it reached the first space—between the 1 and the T. So, for this to work properly, you need to surround the argument to `cd` with quotes: `"/etc/modules/`uname -r`/`uname -v`"`.

- **Use single quotes to pass what's inside the quotes to the command, but do not allow variable substitution**—That is, `echo '$HOME'` gives you `$HOME`. This is handy if you need to pass `$HOME` to the next command through a pipe without it being expanded first. You'll need to use this technique in your last command prompt example (shown previously).
- **Use grave quotes to pass what's inside the quotes to the command, after executing (with variable substitution) the command inside the quotes**—That is, ``echo `pwd` `` gives you `/home/username`.

So the command line required in the previous paragraph, ``export PS1='`pwd` '``, is a single quote, then `pwd` surrounded by grave quotes, a space (for aesthetics), and the closing single quote. By doing this, when you read the environment variable `PS1`, you'll see `` `pwd` ``. Each time you get a command prompt, it executes `pwd` and displays it. If you use double quotes instead of single quotes around the argument, you see something such as `PS1=/home/username`, and the variable does not update each time you change directories. Experiment with it.

You're probably asking, "But what if I need to use a quote inside a quote?" No problem. I said you had four sets of punctuation, and this is the fourth. But to tell the shell that the quote you're about to use is not part of the open/close quote sequence, you escape it by preceding it with a backslash (\). In fact, the backslash can be used to escape any character the shell can interpret, such as `$`, `*`, and so on. So, ``` `echo \$HOME` ``` produces `$HOME`. Some newer texts might tell you that the grave quotes have been replaced by $(command), as in ``` `echo $(pwd)` ```; however, common usage is still grave quotes, and this is the syntax you'll see on scripts in OpenLinux.

SHELL PROGRAMMING (SCRIPTS)

When you're comfortable with the command-line interface, you'll find yourself performing some tasks repeatedly. Personally, if I have to do something more than twice, I'll write a quick script to handle it for me. When you learn how to do this, you have a really powerful ally at your side.

However, writing scripts also necessarily entails a few more steps. For one thing, because you'll save them (probably in a scripts directory), you'll want to be able to reuse them. You might also find that you'll want to have `cron` run them late at night, or when the system is idle, or just daily so that you don't have to remember to do it yourself. But when you get to this level of sophistication, you'll need to ensure that your scripts are written to compensate for certain conditions, including the shell to use, and the proper environment.

The previous discussions and examples all revolved around one shell, `bash`, but you know that other shells exist: `csh`, `pdksh`, and so on. Scripts written and tested on one shell might very well not work on another. Additionally, when `cron` runs a script for you, it really doesn't know about your specific login environment. So, again, the script might fail—but it doesn't need to.

SOLVING THE SCRIPT COMMAND DILEMMA

Solve the first problem, that of the correct shell, first. On Linux, all files have a "magic number" as determined by the contents of the first two bytes of the file. The `file` program reads these two bytes and determines what type of file you have. If you expect `file` to return the fact that the file is a shell script and executable, two things must happen. The first (in Chapter 10, see "File Permissions") is to ensure that when it is saved, the execute bit is set: `chmod a+x` *`scriptname`*. The second is to begin every script the same way:

```
#!/bin/bash
```

The combination #! as the first two characters in a file ensures that the file is seen by the system as a shell script. The rest of the line is the full path to the program needed to execute the statements in the script. This can be `/usr/bin/perl`, `/usr/bin/awk`, `/usr/bin/sed -f`, and so on. Now, whether run from a C shell or from `cron`, the system always uses the correct program to execute the code.

ADDRESSING THE SCRIPT ENVIRONMENT QUANDARY

The second problem you need to overcome is the shell environment. We've discussed the environment as it applies to a logged-in user, and any script or program run by a logged-in user inherits all exported environment variables in the parent shell. But if `cron` runs the script, how will the environment look? If you start with the assumption that any environment that `cron` or any other user might have either doesn't exist or is wrong, your scripts will work correctly. That means explicitly declaring any environment variables that you want your script to know about. This also prevents manipulation of your script by unethical users.

There are two rules I always use when writing scripts:

- If I need an environment variable, I declare it.
- If I call a program, I call the full path to the executable (to ensure that the script can find it and to prevent `cron` from running a trojan horse). As an added precaution, you'll want to write temporary files that you will subsequently read from to a protected directory, and not `/tmp`, for security reasons.

Earlier I showed you how to get the contents of a variable. You did this by prefacing the variable with a `$`. Suppose that you have the variable `KLUDGE='this '`, and another variable `BAR='that'`, and that you want to combine these two and add a word in between. If you type `echo $KLUDGEAND$BAR` you see `that` printed on the screen. This is not what you wanted. The shell thought the first variable was `KLUDGEAND`, not `KLUDGE`. To get around this problem, use `{}` to surround the variable:

```
echo ${KLUDGE}AND${BAR}
```

This time you get the correct output:

```
this AND that
```

Another sticky issue that you run into with scripts, and particularly with those that you run non-interactively, is how to handle output. For this, you have *redirectors*. Normally, the system takes commands and input from stdin (the standard input), or the keyboard. This is device 0. You then see output on the screen, also known as stdout (the standard output, or device 1). But you also have a third channel. This is known as stderr (standard error, device 2). It would be nice if you never needed stderr—but such is not life.

REDIRECTION

The system ordinarily shows stderr on the screen when you are working interactively. However, with a script that runs when no one is around, and with stdout—if any—that goes to a file, you need to deal with stderr or the system administrator will wonder why the console has error messages when he looks at it in the morning. But first, let's cover how you're going to deal with getting just stdin and stdout redirected.

In order to have the normal output from the script redirected to a file so that you can see the results later, use a redirector (>). If you enter `ls > direct`, you create a file called direct in the current directory, and in that file are the results of the ls command. If you then enter `ls -l > direct`, you overwrite the previous file direct with a new file direct that contains a long listing of the directory. But that's not what you wanted. You wanted to append the results of the second command to the file. For that, you use >>. So entering `ls -l >> direct` leaves what's already in the file intact and adds this new listing to the bottom.

I want to point out that `ls > direct` is the same as entering `ls 1> direct` because you are redirecting stdout (device 1) to the file. In order to include stderr (device 2) in the file so that it has somewhere to go, you can do the following:

```
`ls > filename 2>&1`
```

What this says is that you want to send a directory listing to *filename* and, by the way, any error messages are to be included with the listing. You can also send them their own separate ways, as in the following example:

```
`ls > filename 2> /dev/null
```

This sends the listing to *filename* but dumps any error messages on the floor.

Similarly, you can redirect input, such as cat < *filename*. Input and output redirection can also be combined:

```
cat < filename 2>&1 nextfile
```

Those of you who are keeping score on this have probably noticed that you have >, >>, and <, but you don't have <<. The doubled input redirector does have a legitimate role. Assume that you want to get a file every morning from an FTP site. Because this is repetitious, you'll write a script. `out ftp client` automatically logs you in because you created a .netrc file, but you need to send input to the `ftp` prompt to `cd` into a new directory (pub), to make sure you are in binary mode, to get the file, and to terminate `ftp`. That part of the script looks like this:

```
ftp ftp.server.com <<EOF
cd pub \n
binary \n
get file \n
bye \n
EOF
```

What you are going to do is read from the file as input to the command until you reach the `EOF`. The `\n` is a new line. So you can see that you have some very powerful allies with scripts.

FINAL SUGGESTIONS

Before the end of this chapter, I want to make some suggestions to give your scripts a professional touch. Just following the first line, but before you begin declaring your environment and executing code, it's a good idea to include a few commented lines about the script. Lines that begin with a `#` are not treated as commands by the script, but are ignored as comments. Here, near the top of the file, add a few things such as the name, date, and purpose of the script. Many times I've looked at a script and wondered who did this kludgy hack, and there at the top was my own name. I had no one to blame for this but myself (and perhaps insufficient quantities of coffee or a lack of sleep).

I also recommend that you put comments throughout the script. This will help you troubleshoot it later (or just figure out what you did in the first place). Script changes need to be noted and dated as well, both at the top and in the body. There's no such thing as a script with too many comments. Finally, make use of variables. If you use a path or filename, for example, more than once in a script, assign it to a variable near the top of the script. That way, when you need to change something you can change the variable, and all references are changed—and you won't miss one.

SUMMARY

In this chapter, you learned what happens when you log in to your shell and that there are different kinds of shells. You learned how to determine what your interactive shell environment is, how to view it, and how to change it. You learned the difference between aliases and functions and how to implement each, as well as how to customize your environment. Finally, you learned a few basics about shell scripting. For more information on shells, refer to the following chapter:

- Chapter 10 discusses file permissions. The more you know about file permissions, the easier it is to work with shells.

CHAPTER 14

PRINTING

In this chapter

Printing under Linux is similar to printing under other operating systems, with one major exception: You control the entire process from beginning to end, giving you the capability to customize the printing process to fit your exact needs.

Unfortunately, this usually translates into added confusion and complication—especially for people who are more used to DOS/Windows print systems, which generally allow printing as soon as a driver is loaded from a disk and the system is restarted.

In Linux (and most of the other UNIX variants), the process is totally visible. You set up a print queue, you create a filter if your print jobs need to be translated from one print language to another (such as translating from PostScript to PCL so that HP LaserJet printers can process the print job), and you specify the final destination for the print job, be it remote or local (see Figure 14.1). All these steps are done in print setups on non-Linux operating systems as well; you just do not see it as openly as on a Linux system.

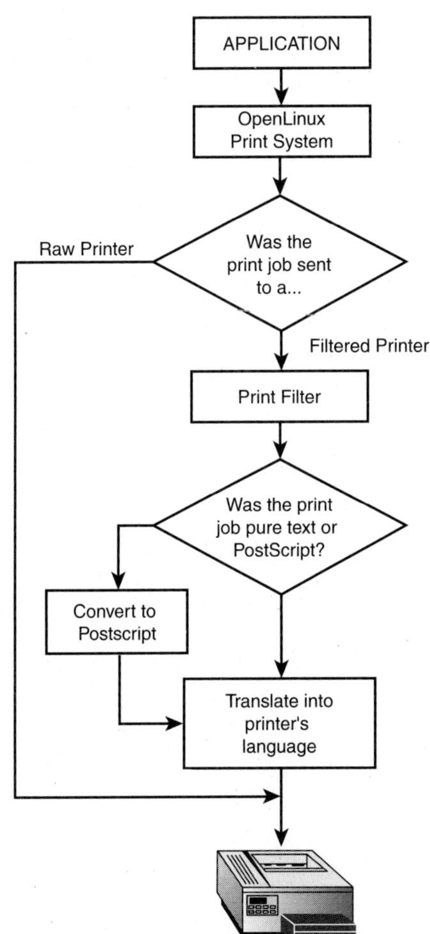

Figure 14.1
Path of a print job.

OpenLinux's printing system is built on a package called *LPRng*, which is an enhanced version of the system used by Berkeley Software Distribution's version of UNIX. At the center of this system is a program called `lpd` that maintains the spooling of print jobs in the print queue. This program temporarily holds on to print jobs until the printer associated with the print queue is free to process the job; at that point, `lpd` sends the print job to the printer and clears the job from the queue.

Details on how to set up print queues are given later in this chapter. For now, an overview of using an existing print system is given.

PRINTING WITH lpr

LPRng (as well as its predecessor from BSD) uses a binary called `lpr` to send print jobs to print queues. This is the equivalent of DOS's `print` command, but it offers greatly enhanced control over such items as banner pages, the number of times the print job will be printed, special functionality for binary files, and a slew of other options that help to control the final printouts.

The syntax for `lpr` is quite extensive, but in general the following syntax is used (check the man page for `lpr` to see all the options offered):

```
lpr -Pprinter [-b] file-to-print
```

For example, to print out the /etc/printcap file to a printer called `ps`, the following command can be executed:

```
lpr -Pps /etc/printcap
```

Like most Linux utilities, `lpr` can be used as a filter of sorts, accepting *standard output* (*stdout*) from the command line or console just as easily as if it were being sent an actual file. For instance, the following command captures the output from `cat` and pipes it through `lpr` instead of sending the output to the console, essentially mirroring the printout from the preceding command line:

```
cat /etc/printcap ¦ lpr -Pps
```

This functionality can also be used to print data that is not contained in files. For example, to capture a printout of the partition information on the computer, the following command works nicely:

```
fdisk -l ¦ lpr
```

Simple redirection of files works with `lpr` as it does with any filter:

```
lpr -Pps < /etc/printcap
```

The utility in using this method is sometimes questionable because it is the same as the first example (given earlier) but with an extra character (<). However, the functionality is there.

As indicated in the upcoming sections of this chapter, more than one print queue can be used on one machine. This extends beyond just the hardware level; not only can more than one printer be connected to the computer, but more than one print queue can be assigned to each printer—each queue treating the print jobs that it receives differently. The `-Pprinter` parameter allows for the specification of an exact print queue to which to send a print job.

If there is no print queue specification indicated on the `lpr` command line, an environment variable called `PRINTER` is checked. This environment variable needs to point to the printer to be used by default (see Chapter 13, "Customizing Your Shell Environment," for details on setting environment variables). What is referred to by this variable is a string that matches one of the print queue names in /etc/printcap, which is the file that houses all the print queue configurations. This file is covered in the "Setting up Printers" section later in this chapter.

If there is no printer specified on the `lpr` command line and there is no `PRINTER` environment variable set, the first print queue entry in /etc/printcap is used for the print job.

When the print job is sent, a few things happen. First, a copy of `lpd` is started to handle the print job. There is a reason for this: The instance of `lpd` that loads when the system is first started is really only meant to sit in system memory and wait for incoming print job requests. When a request is received, the original `lpd` spawns copies of itself to handle each print job, leaving itself alone to continue to watch for incoming print requests.

Next, some files are created in the selected print queue that contain control information on the print job (these are the files that start with `cf`, indicating that they are control files) and contain the actual data to be printed (these files start with `df`, which indicates that they are data files). Other files are created during the actual spooling procedure as the print data is being collected, but in the end there will only be `cf` and `df` files created for each print job that is waiting in the print queue.

When the printer is ready to accept another print job, the next print job in line is opened, filtered (if a print filter is specified in /etc/printcap), and then sent out to the printer through the appropriate printer device in the /dev directory. At that point, if everything worked out well, the job will print. After the job is printed, the control and data files are removed from the queue.

On occasion there is a need to specify that the print job you are sending is, in fact, a binary file. Such is the case with some versions of WordPerfect for Linux; if the print job is not specified as being binary, the print job either does not print or produces erratic results. The `-b` parameter to `lpr` remedies this nicely. It is good to keep that in mind when specifying data from applications such as word processors and spreadsheets; if there are problems, specify the print output from the application as being binary and the problems might disappear.

SETTING UP PRINTERS

When you set up a printer configuration in an `lpr/lpd` based print system, what you are actually setting up is a print queue. This print queue acts as a first-in/first-out holding cell for incoming print jobs (see Figure 14.2). When a job comes in, it enters at the back of the line, and as the jobs in front of it are processed and consequently dropped from the queue, the new job moves up in the line. The order of incoming print jobs is maintained until all jobs in the queue are printed and erased, or until a system administrator intervenes and moves the order of jobs around (more information on that can be found in the "Managing Print Queues" section later in this chapter).

This process is known as *spooling*, and the settings assigned to a print queue in an `lpr/lpd` system such as LPRng determine how spooling is to be handled within each print queue.

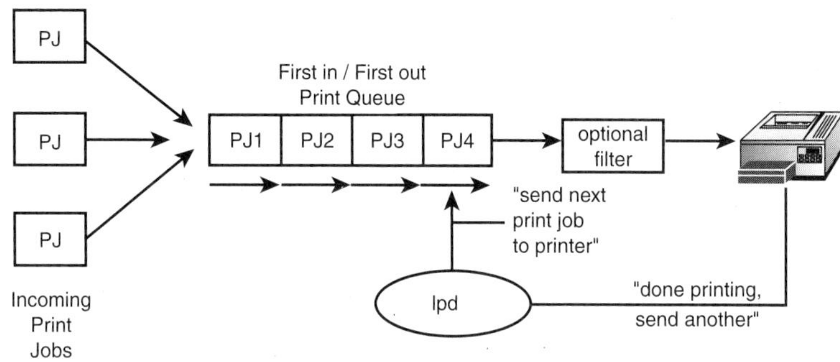

Figure 14.2
Print spooling.

The configuration of the print queue/spooling system is stored in a file called /etc/printcap. This file contains information such as the following:

- The location on your file system where you want to spool print jobs
- The name and location of your print filter (if one is used)
- The printer to which you are going to send print jobs
- Alternative printer entries that are set up to handle print jobs differently
- Various other commands that will be addressed later in this chapter

Fortunately, you only really need to know a handful of configuration items to get a solid, effective print configuration going.

Caution

You must be logged in as root to configure print services. Only an individual possessing system administrator—or *superuser*—status can create, modify, or delete system-level services such as print systems.

LOCAL PRINTERS

As with the Berkeley implementation of the `lpd` spooler, the difference between a print server and a print client is indicated by the configuration of `lpd` itself. In other words, the same software package used to set up a print server on your local system can be used as a client to connect to a remote print server that is also running some version of `lpd`. Also, after you set up a print configuration locally—regardless of whether it is for a printer on your machine or for a printer pointed to on another machine—you can serve print services from your machine to others on your network (see Figure 14.3).

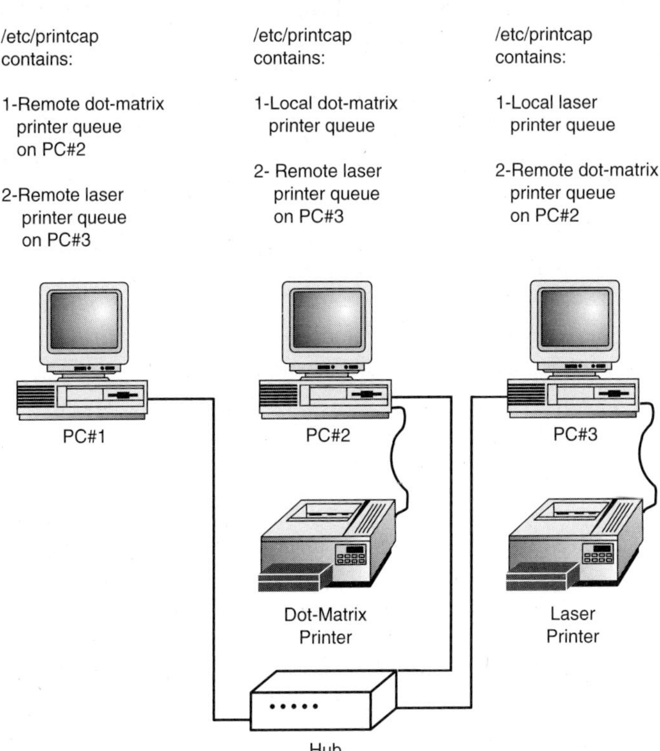

Figure 14.3
A sample networked printer scenario.

SETTING UP THE /ETC/PRINTCAP FILE

Listing 14.1 is an example of a typical BSD printcap file (many Linux systems still use this type of print system).

LISTING 14.1 SAMPLE /ETC/PRINTCAP FILE FOR LOCAL PRINTERS

```
lp
        :lp=/dev/lp1
        :sd=/var/spool/lpd/lp
        :mx#0
        :sh
```

```
7  ps
8        :lp=/dev/lp1
9        :sd=/var/spool/lpd/ps
10       :mx#0
11       :if=/var/spool/lpd/ps/filter
12       :sh
```

Note

Readers who are familiar with the Berkeley implementation of `lpd` might notice a difference in the syntax of LPRng's /etc/printcap file. With LPRng, you do not need to have `:\` at the end of each line. If you are more comfortable putting the characters in, go ahead; LPRng simply ignores them.

Examine the contents of this file more closely. You see that there are two chunks of configuration information here. Each one is actually for a different printer queue. Each treats the print jobs it receives differently.

If you look closely, you can also see that the only real difference between the two queues is the title associated with each, and the line that starts with `:if=` in the `ps` queue. This is the line that specifies a print filter; therefore, the `ps` queue is for print jobs that require some sort of special processing before being sent to the printer. The other queue, `lp`, does not have this line, so print jobs that are sent there must already be in a format that the printer understands. Both /etc/printcap entries in Listing 14.1 have the same `:lp=` line. This line tells where to send print jobs locally; that is, to which printer port on your system the print entry sends print jobs.

A full breakdown of the lines in this file is in order. Because the `ps` entry contains everything the `lp` entry has and then some, `ps` is used as the example.

The first line in each entry—lines 1 and 7—is where you specify all the names by which the /etc/printcap entry can be called. There can be more than one name in this line, as long as all the names are separated by a pipe character (|). For instance, say the `ps` section of this /etc/printcap file is associated with an HP LaserJet 5L printer connected to a server called `rumble`; conventional procedures indicate that `ps|rumble-lj|HP LaserJet 5L` is a good set of names (*`general name|server-printertype|brand and model`*).

Lines 2 and 8 indicate which device to send print jobs to on your system. The device /dev/lp1 is a rather common device used for standard printer ports on modern PCs. Occasionally the printer port is located on /dev/lp0, but this is not as common. Generally speaking, one or the other is probably the one you will be using; devices numbered higher than that are quite uncommon unless multiple printers/parallel ports are installed on your system.

For printers connected to serial ports, the serial port device needs to be specified here instead of an `lp#` device. If this is the case, you must also specify at least a `:br` line to indicate the baud rate of the serial connection. The possible values for `:br` are 50, 75, 110, 134.5, 150, 200, 300, 600, 1200, 1800, 2400, 4800, 9600, 19200, and 38400. Indicating a speed higher than the speed at which the printer prints is considered to be a bad idea; be safe and stick with the appropriate baud rate used by the serial port. The number is specified by a pound sign (#) followed by the baud rate, such as `:br#19200`.

Line 9 indicates in what directory the print queue is located. The queue is where print jobs spool. When you send multiple print jobs one after the other (or if your printer is networked and you are spooling print jobs from others on your network), this is the directory where the print jobs are spooled before being sent to the printer. Print jobs are processed in the order they are spooled in unless an administrator moves the jobs around manually in the queue. Utilities that enable this kind of shuffling of print jobs are covered in the "Managing Print Queues" section later in this chapter.

The `mx#` lines (lines 4 and 10) specify the maximum size of an acceptable print job. If it is set to 0, there is no size limit imposed. The 0 value is usually used unless there is a serious need to limit job sizes.

As stated earlier, line 11 specifies the print filter location and filename (in this example, `/var/spool/lpd/ps` is the path and filter is the name of the filter file). Any special processing or translation that needs to be done to the print job before it is sent out to the printer needs to happen within this filter. The name and path to the filter is not set in stone anywhere, but the syntax used here is fairly standard and probably needs to be adhered to for consistency across systems.

A typical (simple) print filter for an OpenLinux system might look like Listing 14.2.

LISTING 14.2 SAMPLE FILTER FILE

```
#!/bin/sh

# Specify the language ghostscript should translate#  PostScript into
➥ (run 'gs -h' to see device list)
DEVICE=ljet4

# The maximum resolution for the printer
RESOLUTION=600x600

# The paper size - a4 or letter
PAPERSIZE=letter

# If an EOF (end of file) character is required
#  after print jobs, put in a 1; otherwise, ignore
SENDEOF=

# Determine the correct paper size
#
if [ "$PAPERSIZE" = "a4" ]; then
  T=A4
else
  T=US
fi

# If the print job is pure text, use
```

```
#  either nenscript or enscript to
#  convert the plain text to PostScript
#
if [ -x /usr/bin/nenscript ]; then
        nenscript -T$T -ZB -p-
else
        if [ "$T" = "US" ]; then
           T="Letter"
        fi
        enscript -M $T -Z -p -
fi |

# If the value of the DEVICE variable
#  is "PostScript", do nothing to the
#  print job and send it to the printer
#
if [ "$DEVICE" = "PostScript" ]; then
        cat -

# Otherwise, send the data - now in
#  PostScript format - through the
#  ghostscript interpreter to be converted
#  into the language specified in DEVICE above
else
        gs -q -sDEVICE=$DEVICE \
           -r$RESOLUTION \
           -sPAPERSIZE=$PAPERSIZE \
           -dNOPAUSE \
           -dSAFER \
           -sOutputFile=- -
fi

if [ "$SENDEOF" != "" ]; then
        printf "\004"
fi

exit 0
```

This sample filter does the following:

- If plain text is piped into the filter, it is converted into PostScript (by the `nenscript` text-to-PostScript converter if it is installed; otherwise, it converts it using `enscript`, which performs the same task). The output is piped through an interpreter called `ghostscript` (specified as `gs` in the script because that is its executable name), which takes the PostScript data and translates it into a specific printer language (specified in Listing 14.2 as `ljet4` or LaserJet 4 PCL language). After that, the formatted/translated print job is sent to the print queue to be printed.
- If the data that is being piped through the filter is PostScript already, it is sent straight to the `ghostscript` interpreter for translation. If the printer specified at the beginning of the filter is PostScript (indicating that the printer has PostScript handling capabilities built into the hardware), the PostScript data the filter receives or creates bypasses `ghostscript` and is sent right back out of the filter and on to the printer (the `cat -` line does this).

Be sure to set a filter like this to be executable before using it (see Chapter 10, "Users, Groups, and Permissions," for details on permissions).

Note that this is just one example of a print filter. The possibilities of what can be used here are almost limitless. Simple filters such as the previous one are fine for basic usage, but some situations might require something a bit more sophisticated. For instance, print jobs might have to be formatted for wide carriage printers, for ledger paper, or for check printing. Covering all the options might require a complete book in itself.

The best thing to do for a filter is to start small and simple, and then work up to more complexity from there. Also, a number of print filter packages that might warrant an evaluation (such as LPRng's `lpf` and various free offerings on the Internet such as `apsfilter` and `magicfilter`) are available.

`:sh`, which is a rather simple configuration item, suppresses the use of *headers* on print jobs. This is more of a paper saving item than anything else. Note that headers are not the same as banner pages, like those that are printed with many printers that are networked with hardware such as HP JetDirect cards. These banner pages must be disabled in the network card's hardware; they can not be disabled from within /etc/printcap.

That should be sufficient for dealing with a basic /etc/printcap file that covers one non-filtered and one filtered local printer configuration. Note that the directories for the print queue set up by default with OpenLinux are located in /var/spool/lpd, so all that needs to be set up after /etc/printcap is created are the specific subdirectories of /var/spool/lpd for each print queue containing an `:sd=` line.

CREATING THE QUEUE (FILES AND DIRECTORIES)

With Berkeley's `lpd` package you had to set these items up manually, including the log files that were used for each print queue. With LPRng, however, you do not need to do this.

LPRng ships with a utility called `checkpc` that can build all these items for you. It takes the information entered into your /etc/printcap file and makes your print queue directories and logs automatically, right down to the ownership and permissions on the individual files. All you need to do is ensure that the information in /etc/printcap is correct for your print configuration and run the following command:

```
checkpc -f
```

What you will see is similar to the output shown in Listing 14.3.

LISTING 14.3 OUTPUT FROM `checkpc -f`

```
[root@trident /root]# checkpc -f
 LPRng version LPRng-3.2.3
 Get_perms: permissions entry '/etc/lpd.perms'
 Get_perms: permissions entry '/usr/etc/lpd.perms'
 Cannot open '/usr/etc/lpd.perms' - No such file or directory
 Get_perms: permissions entry '/var/spool/lpd/lpd.perms.trident'
Cannot open '/var/spool/lpd/lpd.perms.trident' -No such file or directory
```

```
 LPD lockfile '/var/spool/lpd/lpd.lock.trident'
  Checking directory: '/var/spool/lpd'
   checking file '/var/spool/lpd/lpd.lock.trident'
 Truncating LPD log file '/var/spool/lpd/lpd.log.trident'
 Checking /var/spool/lpd/lpd.log.trident
➥file '/var/spool/lpd/lpd.log.trident'
checkpc: Warning - cannot open '/var/spool/lpd/lpd.log.trident'
 lp: Checking printer 'lp'
 lp:  Checking directory: '/var/spool/lpd/lp'
 lp: directory stat '/var/spool/lpd/lp' failed -No such file or directory
 lp: Printer 'lp' spool dir '/var/spool/lpd/lp/' needs fixing
 lp:  Checking directory: '/var/spool/lpd/lp'
checkpc: Warning - creating '/var/spool/lpd/lp'
checkpc: Warning - changing ownership '/var/spool/lpd/lp'
 lp:   checking file '/var/spool/lpd/lp/control.lp'
 lp:   checking file '/var/spool/lpd/lp/status.lp'
 lp:   checking file '/var/spool/lpd/lp/log'
checkpc: Warning - owner/group of '/var/spool/lpd/lp/control.lp'
➥are 0/2, not 2/2
checkpc: Warning - owner/group of '/var/spool/lpd/lp/status.lp'
➥are 0/2, not 2/2
checkpc: Warning - owner/group of '/var/spool/lpd/lp/log'
➥are 0/2, not 2/2
 lp:  Need to fix 'lp' files, control dir '/var/spool/lpd/lp/log'
checkpc: Warning - changing ownership '/var/spool/lpd/lp/control.lp'
checkpc: Warning - changing ownership '/var/spool/lpd/lp/status.lp'
checkpc: Warning - changing ownership '/var/spool/lpd/lp/log'
 lp: Checking log file '/var/spool/lpd/lp/log'
 lp:    'log' file 0 bytes long: no truncation
 [root@trident /root]#
```

The items in bold text indicate where changes are made to match the configuration in /etc/printcap. Actions such as directory creation, log file creation, and ownership changes are performed when the `checkpc` program detects that there is an inconsistency in your print queue setup (which is understandable here because there was no existing print queue when `checkpc` was executed).

REMOTE/NETWORKED PRINTERS

The syntax is quite different for *basic remote* (also known as *networked*) printer configurations, usually because you are sending generic text and/or PostScript output to the remote printer and letting the remote print queue worry about any special filtering requirements. The server end has a setup similar to the one described in the "Local Printers" section of this chapter.

Note There is no special syntax in /etc/printcap to specify if a printer is to be served to others on a network; after a local printer is set up and operational with LPRng, anyone else on the network with `lpr` printing capabilities will be able to access it, unless it is otherwise configured.

Listing 14.4 is an example of what a simple remote printer entry looks like.

LISTING 14.4 SAMPLE /ETC/PRINTCAP FILE FOR A REMOTE PRINTER

```
remote
        :mx#0
        :rm=server.domain.com
        :rp=ps
```

Two lines are being introduced here: the `:rm=` and `:rp=` lines. As might or might not be evident by the letters used to label the lines, `rm` stands for *remote machine* (not to be confused with the `rm` command, which erases files and directories) and `rp` stands for *remote printer*. These lines were added in place of the `:lp=` line because remote printers do not require the specification of local printer ports (there is an exception to this that will be addressed later in this chapter).

Note that the printer on the remote machine needs to be set up on its own `lpr/lpd` print system for this to work. In other words, if `server.domain.com` is a machine running Windows 95 and you do not have the `ps` printer on that machine set up with some kind of Windows 95 port of `lpd`, the preceding printer entry is useless; `lpd` systems speak to `lpd` systems and nothing else.

As was mentioned earlier, remote print queues are typically expected to perform any formatting/filtering that might be required to successfully print incoming jobs. It is for this reason that there is no `:if=` line in the remote queue entry in Listing 14.4. Filters on the remote print server's end do not have to be any different from print filters on a local printer. Remember, the same software is used to set up print servers and print clients; so, after a local printer is set up on a print server, it is ready to be used by remote clients on a network. Simply use the preceding syntax to forward all printing to a remote printer.

LOCAL FILTERING FOR REMOTE PRINTERS—OPTION I (FILTER REDIRECTION)

What happens if there is no filter running on the remote print server end? This is actually becoming a common occurrence with the popularity of network cards for printers. In these cases, printers simply accept print jobs and expect the format of the job to be sufficient for getting it printed using whatever graphics language the printer uses. In other words, the printer is not connected to a server, it does not have any built-in filtering capabilities, and, basically, if you do not format/filter your print jobs before sending them on their way, you will fail to get printouts.

For these situations, you must perform some minor trickery to spool and filter your print jobs locally. Keeping in mind the logic of the print filter in Listing 14.2, some sleight of hand with the `lpr` command enables you to illustrate one way of accomplishing this.

Because filtering must be done locally and the print job needs to be sent to a remote queue, you must set up both a local and a remote queue to accomplish this. Listing 14.5 is a good example of how an /etc/printcap file looks.

Listing 14.5 Sample /etc/printcap File for Local Filtering of Remote Print Jobs

```
ps
        :lp=/dev/null
        :sd=/var/spool/lpd/ps
        :mx#0
        :if=/var/spool/lpd/ps/filter
        :sh

remote
        :mx#0
        :rm=server.domain.com
          :rp=ps
```

At this point, nothing seems to be especially exciting or different. The `:lp=` line points to /dev/null because there is not a local printer in this case—a local queue is being used for filtering of remote print jobs. There is one print queue that filters and one print queue that sits on `server.domain.com`.

So where does the redirection happen? The trick occurs within the filter itself.

In Listing 14.2 you see a number of places where there is a -. These are actually routes out of the filter. They sit in place of filenames, and they simply say, "Send whatever came into this filter right back out now that I have done my magic." What needs to happen at each of these portions of the filter is a redirection to the remote queue in /etc/printcap.

As indicated earlier, the `lpr` command offers a command line parameter `-P`, after which you can indicate a specific queue from the /etc/printcap file to which to send the print job. Using this, the filter can capture the output from each one of the command lines using -, and then send the output to the remote queue.

Listing 14.6 is the revised version of the filter in Listing 14.2, with the necessary changes for local filtering applied.

Listing 14.6 Sample Filter File Altered for Local Filtering of Remote Print Jobs

```
#!/bin/sh

DEVICE=ljet4
RESOLUTION=600x600
PAPERSIZE=letter
SENDEOF=

if [ "$PAPERSIZE" = "a4" ]; then
  T=A4
else
  T=US
fi
```

continues

LISTING 14.6 CONTINUED

```
if [ -x /usr/bin/nenscript ]; then
nenscript -T$T -ZB -p- ¦ lpr -Premote
else
if [ "$T" = "US" ]; then
T="Letter"
fi
enscript -M $T -Z -p - ¦ lpr -Premote
fi ¦
if [ "$DEVICE" = "PostScript" ]; then
cat - ¦ lpr -Premote
else
gs -q -sDEVICE=$DEVICE \
-r$RESOLUTION \
-sPAPERSIZE=$PAPERSIZE \
-dNOPAUSE \
-dSAFER \
-sOutputFile=- - ¦ lpr -Premote
fi

if [ "$SENDEOF" != "" ]; then
printf "\004"
fi

exit 0
```

Every route out of this filter now pipes to the remote queue specified in /etc/printcap. Print jobs are sent through this filter, they get processed based on the setting in the DEVICE line at the top of the filter, and then they are sent out to the remote queue. If the remote printer is busy, the print jobs are spooled locally until the printer is ready.

LOCAL FILTERING FOR REMOTE PRINTERS—OPTION II (BOUNCE QUEUES)

Although this is not overly complicated, it is actually a lot of trickery to get something like this set up. However, it is the only way to get local filtering for remote printing set up on Berkeley `lpd` systems. As luck would have it, the LPRng package on OpenLinux provides a slightly shorter method for accomplishing this task.

One of the nicest features offered by LPRng is the *bounce queue* setting (specified with a `:bq=` line in /etc/printcap). This enables the print system to filter outgoing print jobs before they are sent to the remote queue. This can be considered a shortcut to achieving the same results as the method just described.

Listing 14.7 is an example of an /etc/printcap file that uses this feature.

Listing 14.7 Sample /etc/printcap Utilizing a Bounce Queue

```
ps
        :lp=/dev/null
        :sd=/var/spool/lpd/lp
        :mx#0
        :bq=ps@server.domain.com
        :if=/var/spool/lpd/lp/filter
        :sh
```

Here you see that the `:bq=` line is pointing to the same printer that was configured as a remote printer earlier, but the syntax used to point to it has changed slightly: `remoteprinter@remotemachine` is the syntax used with the `:bq=` line. The same `:lp=` line is included and is pointing to /dev/null, there is a spool directory just as there was before, there is no limitation on print job size, header pages are suppressed, and there is a filter specified. The main difference between this local filtering scheme is that the original print filter specified in Listing 14.2 is utilized instead of the altered one from Listing 14.6. This is because the redirection with bounce queues is specified within the `:bq=` line, and is therefore not required within the filter using `lpr` parameters.

Raw Printers

There will come a time when, as an administrator of a print server, you will want to have some sort of raw printing functionality. *Raw printing* means the capability to send a print job straight through the Linux print system without it being altered or processed in any way—just spooled. This functionality is important if you want certain non-Linux systems on your network to be capable of sending print jobs formatted on their systems and having them print correctly. Raw printing allows systems such as Windows to create print jobs using native Windows printer drivers, and then to send them—undamaged and unprocessed—through a Linux machine and straight out to the printer. This is important because it is quite often simpler to have a native printer driver running on one of these non-Linux machines than it is to have something general such as an Apple LaserWriter driver.

Note

The Apple LaserWriter printer was one of the first PostScript printers ever produced. Drivers written for it are guaranteed to produce quality PostScript output, so it has become somewhat of an industry standard PostScript driver for systems such as Windows and Macs. The fact that the LaserWriter printers have been around for so long has helped to entrench it as an established medium for producing PostScript through print systems.

Accomplishing this task is not always the simplest thing to do with a Linux print system. Plain print queues (such as the `lp` queue in Listing 14.1) that do not do any filtering are not the same as raw print queues. There is still some processing done on the data being passed between the server and the printer, and some of that processing can render print jobs that are created with native Windows (or other) printer drivers unprintable. In this situation, a pure, raw print queue that does absolutely nothing to the print job data before it hits the printer is needed.

LPRng has the capability to do this. A few minor tweaks to the `lp` queue from the sample /etc/printcap file in Listing 14.1 will do the trick (see Listing 14.8).

LISTING 14.8 RAW /ETC/PRINTCAP QUEUE

```
1  raw¦raw printer for Windows clients
2      :rw
3      :sh
4      :lp=/dev/lp1
5      :sd=/var/spool/lpd/raw
6       :fx=flp
```

Walk through the file to learn what is being said.

The `:rw` line (line 2) says to open the print device for reading *and* writing, rather than just for writing. Smart printers, such as modern laser printers, can send information back to the systems that are sending print jobs. Opening the device for reading as well as for writing enables this information to get back to the systems where the print jobs originated, allowing such items as print queue monitors to work from the client end. Without this item, there would be a one-way communication going from the client to the server, forbidding any monitoring to be done from the client end. After sending a print job, therefore, nothing short of prayer and a trip to the printer itself would indicate if the print job went through.

As with the queue examples in Listing 14.1, line 3 suppresses headers from printing. Line 4 points to the printer device.

As for line 5, always create a new print spool directory for each print queue. It is not essential, but it is a good practice to get into.

The field in line 6 specifies the types of data that the printer can handle. The letter following the `=` sign indicates the data types:

- `f` indicates ordinary format, nothing special.
- `l` indicates binary format.
- `p` indicates a special format that is produced by the `pr` formatting program (which splits print jobs into pages).

The "raw printer for Windows clients" name is quite intentional here. As was mentioned earlier, the primary use for a queue like this is with Samba (covered in Chapter 34, "Microsoft Windows and OpenLinux"). The combination of the raw pass-through capabilities of this queue along with the read/write functionality provide a seamless print system for Windows clients. Print Manager and other vendor-specific print queue monitors do not know the difference between a Samba printer shared through a queue like this and a printer connected to another Windows machine. The easier an administrator can make life for his/her Windows clients, the better—at least one queue like this needs to be set up if Samba is going to be used.

Detailed configuration of Samba is offered later, but the actual print configuration is addressed here (refer to Chapter 34 for the rest). When there is a raw print queue set up, edit the default Samba configuration file /etc/samba.d/smb.conf and add the following line to the [printers] section of the file:

```
print command = lpr -b -P%p %s
```

Note

You might have to copy the smb.conf.sample file in /etc/samba.d over to smb.conf if there is no existing smb.conf file.

Following the syntax discussed earlier, the combination of this command and the information that Samba replaces for `%p` and `%s` (printer and data stream, respectively) provides the final touch to the Samba print configuration. After this edit is complete, stop and start both the `lpd` daemon and Samba itself:

```
/etc/rc.d/init.d/lpd stop
/etc/rc.d/init.d lpd start
/etc/rc.d/init.d/smb stop
/etc/rc.d/init.d/smb start
```

At this point, Windows clients will be able to connect to the raw print queue just like they connect to any other shared printer. Please refer to Windows's documentation for details on printer connection and networking instructions.

MANAGING PRINT QUEUES

As an administrator of an OpenLinux server, you must have the capability to enforce a certain amount of control over your print system. This control goes beyond simple settings for maximum print job sizes—it goes into actual queue management and troubleshooting, both of which are primarily administrator tasks (although there are some things that can be done at a user level).

LPRng provides what are considered to be traditional BSD style queue administration tools: `lpq`, `lprm`, and `lpc`.

Note

Those who are more familiar with SysV print systems will note the lack of such items as `lpadmin` and `lpstat`. Odds are, however, that by using combinations of `lpg`, `lprm`, and `lpc`, you will find functionality similar to that of these utilities.

PEEKING INTO QUEUES WITH `lpq`

The `lpq` utility is rather simple in nature. It merely produces a printout of the latest status of a print queue. If there are jobs stacked up, it shows which jobs are there and what each job's number is, as well as its position in the queue (see Listing 14.9).

LISTING 14.9 OUTPUT FROM `lpq`—ONLY ONE QUEUED PRINT JOB

```
1  [erat@rumble ~]$ lpq
2  Printer: lp@rumble  'PostScript'
3   Queue: 1 printable job
4   Server: pid 716 active
5   Unspooler: pid 717 active
6   Status: printed all 670 bytes at 09:24:07
7   Rank    Owner/ID                Class Job  Files                Size Time
8  active  erat@rumble+715         A   715 /etc/printcap        670 09:24:07
9  [erat@rumble ~]$
```

In line 2, you see that the information listed pertains to the `lp` print queue in /etc/printcap (also known as PostScript, which means that the title of the printcap entry contains at least `lp¦PostScript` as a name). Line 3 states that there is only one printable job in the queue, and lines 4 and 5 give process information on the `lpd` server associated with the print job. Line 6 gives a current status on the spooling of the print job; and line 8 gives detailed information on the print job itself, including the owner, the filename, the size, and the time it was sent to the printer. If more than one print job waits in the queue, numeric ranks are assigned to each job and the preceding report might more closely resemble Listing 14.10.

LISTING 14.10 OUTPUT FROM `lpq`—MULTIPLE QUEUED PRINT JOBS

```
[erat@rumble ~]$ lpq
Printer: lp@rumble  'PostScript'
 Queue: 14 printable jobs
 Server: pid 728 active
 Unspooler: pid 764 active
 Status: printed all 670 bytes at 09:29:40
 Rank   Owner/ID                Class Job  Files                Size Time
active  erat@rumble+735           A  735 /etc/printcap        670 09:29:32
2       hugh@rumble+737           A  737 /home/hugh/kludge     13240 09:29:33
3       doris@rumble+739          A  739 /etc/fstab           420 09:29:33
4       bennie@rumble+741         A  741 /home/bennie/bar    1200 09:29:34
5        george@rumble+743          A  743 /home/george/notes 58663 09:29:34
```

The jobs preceding the active job on top are given a number that corresponds with their positions in the print queue. Print queues are *FIFO*s (first-in, first-out buffers), so as one job is printed the others following it are moved up to take the printed job's place. And so it goes until the print queue is empty.

Note that the previous listings only point to one print queue. If more print queues exist in /etc/printcap, a few options are available to view their contents as well. First, you can specify a specific queue on the `lpq` command line using the same syntax that is used by `lpr—Pprinter` (see Listing 14.11).

LISTING 14.11 OUTPUT OF `lpq -l -Praw`

```
[erat@rumble ~]$ lpq -l -Praw
Printer: raw@rumble  'winprint'
 Queue: no printable jobs in queue
 Status: aborting operations on job erat@rumble+749 at 09:35:18
 Status: server finished at 09:35:18
[erat@rumble ~]$
```

The `-l` tells `lpq` to give more detail in its printout. It is similar in scope to the same parameter used by the `ls` command to give more information on the contents of a directory.

Likewise, if a report of all the print queues set up in /etc/printcap is desired, the `-all` parameter can be used; the `-l` parameter is assumed when specifying `-all` (see Listing 14.12).

LISTING 14.12 OUTPUT FROM `lpq -all`

```
[erat@rumble ~]$ lpq -all
Printer: lp@rumble  'PostScript'
 Queue: no printable jobs in queue
 Status: printing 'root@rumble+627', closing device at 08:47:55
 Status: printing 'root@rumble+627', finished  at 08:47:55
 Status: subserver status 'JSUCC' for 'root@rumble+627' at 08:47:55
 Status: server finished at 08:47:55

Printer: nofilter@rumble
 Queue: no printable jobs in queue
 Status: printing 'erat@rumble+595', closing device at 08:43:07
 Status: printing 'erat@rumble+595', finished  at 08:43:07
 Status: subserver status 'JSUCC' for 'erat@rumble+595' at 08:43:07
 Status: server finished at 08:43:07

Printer: raw@rumble  'winprint'
 Queue: no printable jobs in queue
 Status: kludge: Print_job: job 'erat@rumble+595', cannot open data file
➥'/var/spool/lpd/lp/dfA595rumble.fish.net' at 08:43:17
 Status: subserver status 'JABORT' for 'erat@rumble+595' at 08:43:17
 Status: aborting operations on job erat@rumble+595 at 08:43:17
 Status: server finished at 08:43:17
[erat@rumble ~]$
```

Here you see some interesting data. It seems that the last print job sent to the `raw` print queue failed to be processed because of a missing data file. Errors such as this one (which aborted the print job with a `JABORT` status) might indicate queue directory ownership/permission problems, or simply an abnormally aborted print job from the server end. When having problems printing to a specific queue, sometimes the output from `lpq` can be useful in the debugging process.

DELETING PRINT JOBS WITH `lprm`

As the name might indicate, `lprm` is a utility that removes print jobs from the print queue. This can be run by users as well as by the system administrator, as can `lpq`. Certain functions are still reserved for superusers, but operations on a user's print stack can be altered by the owner of the stack whether the owner is a user or not. No single user can remove other users' print jobs unless the remover is the system administrator.

> **Caution**
>
> **The `lprm` utility is a very trusting one, and therefore does not warn you that important print jobs might be deleted by its use. So be sure of what you want to do with `lprm` before executing it.**

When invoked without parameters, `lprm` deletes the last print job sent to the printer by the user who invoked `lprm`. This is the default behavior for both users and the system administrator. Various command-line parameters offer extended functionality to allow print job deletions to be more specific:

- `lprm` *`username`*

  This deletes all the print jobs sent by the user matching *`username`*. Note that this is reserved for the system administrator.

- `lprm 157`

  This removes print job number 157 from the print queue. If the print job is not owned by the user executing `lprm` and the user is not the system administrator, this fails. Only the user who owns print job 157 and the system administrator can delete this print job.

- `lprm all`

  Removes all the print jobs on the default print queue that were sent by the person invoking `lprm`. Another similar command for users follows:

- `lprm -`

  When executed as a user, all print jobs sent by that user are deleted from the default printer; when invoked by the system administrator, however, it deletes all the print jobs for the default queue, period.

- `lprm all all`

  Removes all print jobs on all print queues sent by the user who invoked `lprm`. When executed by the system administrator, this deletes all print jobs on all queues regardless of who sent them.

Combinations of these commands are possible, of course. For instance

```
lprm username all
```

deletes all print jobs sent by the user matching *username* on all print queues.

You can see that the possibilities are extensive when deleting print jobs. Clearly, care must be taken when flipping back and forth as a user and system administrator; because similar syntax performs drastically different tasks with this utility, be sure of who you are logged in as before executing any `lprm` command. If you are not careful, you might inadvertently delete a job you did not intend to delete.

Taking Control with `lpc`

The `lpq` and `lprm` utilities offer some administration capabilities for users, but there are certain tasks that are absolutely reserved for system administrators. Managing the order of a print queue, the capability to kill and print daemons, the capability to enable or disable a print queue, and the capability to redirect print jobs are but a few of the things that can be done with `lpc`, the system administrator's print control utility.

Among the items just listed, there is also a capability to run `lpq` and `lprm` from within `lpc`. It is the one true control center for all print activities on your system.

When invoked, all that is shown is a command prompt that looks similar to the following:

```
lpc>
```

From there, the ? key can be pressed to get a screenful of help items, descriptions, and syntax for each included.

Commands are entered at the `lpc>` prompt. For instance, when getting a status listing on all the print queues, the output resembles Listing 14.13.

Listing 14.13 Output from the `status all` Directive Within `lpc`

```
lpc>status all
 Printer       Printing Spooling Jobs  Server  Slave Redirect Status/Debug
lp@rumble        enabled  enabled  0    none    none
nofilter@rumble enabled  enabled  0    none    none
raw@rumble       enabled  enabled  0    none    none
lpc>
```

With a listing like this, you can see in an instant which print queues are disabled, whether any redirection is enabled, whether there is a server machine involved with the queue, and how many print jobs are currently spooled for each.

Taking down a print queue is as simple as stopping the queue from processing any more jobs:

```
lpc> stop nofilter@rumble
```

Redirecting print jobs to different printers is fairly straightforward as well:

```
lpc> redirect nofilter@rumble other-ptr@other-svr
```

To hold all print jobs on a print queue that were sent by user `erat`, use the following command:

```
lpc> hold lp@rumble erat
```

To disable printing from a certain print queue, the following can be executed:

```
lpc> disable lp@rumble
```

To enable the queue again, use the following command:

```
lpc> enable lp@rumble
```

This is fairly simple, to say the least. The collective commands offered by `lpc` are quite intuitive and will not pose too many difficulties for budding system/print administrators.

The syntax for these items, as well as for others that might prove to be useful for problem resolution, are available by invoking `lpc` with the `-h` parameter. The items mentioned previously will give a general idea of the functionality of this utility.

SUMMARY

The underlying setup of LPRng is quite stable and rarely—if ever—needs tweaking. In fact, the *RFC* (*request for comment* document) that defines how BSD printing is supposed to work is adhered to more strongly by LPRng than by many commercial implementations of the BSD `lpr/lpd` print spooling system. However, there might be a time when you want to alter a timeout value, direct print output through a different port, or change various operational parameters that affect filtering or logging. To do these things, there is a system-wide configuration file called /etc/lpd.conf that can be altered. The need to do so is rare (to date, we have not heard of anyone having to do anything to this file beyond leaving it on the hard drive intact), but the file still needs to be mentioned.

Also, one hears every now and then about remote servers that do not want to accept print jobs from some Linux systems. In these cases, odds are that there is a file on the remote system called hosts.lpd that houses the names of machines that are allowed to print to the server. Fully qualified domain names must be used in such files (for example, `rumble.fish.net` is okay, but plain `rumble` is not). Nine out of ten times, if there is a complaint from a remote print server, it is because of something that is missing from this file.

As always (with just about any troubleshooting activity), be sure to refer to the logs for the system you are debugging when problems arise. In each print queue directory, there is a log file that tells what the queue has been up to and what the results of each print job have been. These log files are your best friends when printing problems occur. Also, the much maligned and well trusted /var/log/messages file is a good source of information, as are the commands listed earlier (such as `lpq` and `lpc`). Even the `lpr` utility can help; it offers a `-D`*`debuglevel`* parameter that can show you more of what is happening when print jobs are being sent out. A combination of all the preceding needs to be employed when tracking down anomalies in print systems.

Nobody will argue with you when you say that printing on Linux can be a trying experience. There is much more to think about than most new Linux users are accustomed to. Just try to remember that simple is better, and follow the previous examples as much as possible before delving into man pages and HOWTO documents. On probably 90 percent of all Linux systems, the print setup is the same; only the filter differs, and then it is mostly because the printer being used needs different parameters for `ghostscript` to get successful printouts.

For more information about Linux and printing, see the following chapters:

- See Chapter 10 for more information on ownership and permissions on files and scripts.
- See Chapter 13 for more information on shell scripting and setting environment variables.
- See Chapter 34 for more information on setting up Samba so that Windows users can connect to your OpenLinux print server.

CHAPTER 15

SOFTWARE PACKAGE MANAGEMENT

In this chapter

INTRODUCTION TO PACKAGE MANAGEMENT

This section will introduce you to the basic concepts of package management, which is the fundamental means for you to install and manage software on your OpenLinux system.

WHAT IS PACKAGE MANAGEMENT?

The *package management system* is the part of your Linux system that enables you to install, uninstall, and manage the software on your machine. If you are familiar with Windows 95, this is similar to the `Add/Remove Programs` option in the Windows Control Panel.

Almost all distributions of Linux include some kind of package management system. The most popular of these is the *Red Hat package manager* (RPM), and this is the system used by OpenLinux. RPM enables you to perform the basic tasks of installing and uninstalling packages. You can also use it to perform other important management tasks related to packages, such as analyzing the disk space used by certain software or verifying that the files that belong to a particular package have not been deleted or corrupted.

MORE THAN JUST AN INSTALL PROGRAM

Although RPM is the primary installation program for your Linux system, it is also much more than that. Most of the things that you will install on your system are available in package format, which means that you will use RPM to install virtually all the software that you use. (Exceptions to this are discussed in the Section "Working With TAR Files"). Under some other operating environments, such as Windows, each component you add to the system comes with its own installation program. Sometimes an uninstall program is provided as well, but sometimes it is not. In contrast to this, RPM provides a single uniform installation and uninstallation mechanism for all the software for your system. RPM keeps track of all kinds of information about the packages that are installed on your system in a special package database. RPM uses the information in the database to uninstall a package so that it can remove all traces of the package cleanly from your system. However, the information in the package database can also be used for many other management tasks, which are described in the following section.

THINGS YOU CAN DO WITH A PACKAGE MANAGER

Following is a list of some of the tasks that you can perform to manage the software on your OpenLinux system:

- Examine the contents of a package before you install it to see how much space it will take up on your hard drive, what files it contains, and where they will be placed in your file system.
- Check to see if you have the necessary libraries or other files that are required for a new software package to run.

- Check to make sure that a new package won't conflict with one already installed on your system.
- Examine the procedure used to install a package, and verify that it doesn't do anything to corrupt your system or defeat your system security.
- Verify that a package comes from a reliable, trusted source.
- Analyze the size of installed packages.
- Verify that a package's files have not been corrupted or deleted.
- Find out other information about a package, such as where the software in it originally came from, or what restrictions there are on using or redistributing it.
- Upgrade to a newer version of software while preserving all your customizations to the software's configuration files.
- Surprisingly, there is much more that you can do with RPM.

Note

RPM is the name of the package management system, but there are actually several different programs that can be used to manage your packages. There is a program called `rpm` that is used to manage packages from the shell command line. This same program is used to create a package (described in Chapter 16, "How to Build/Rebuild a Package"). Unfortunately, a package file itself is often referred to as an RPM because its filename ends in the extension .rpm. This overloaded use of the acronym can (and does) cause a lot of confusion. In this book, the package management system is referred to as RPM (all caps), the command line utility as `rpm`, and a .rpm file as a package.

What Is a Package?

A *package* is a special file that contains the directories and files that are part of a particular piece of software or system component. It also contains additional information about the software, which is used by the package manager. There are actually two different kinds of packages: binary and source. A *binary* package contains software components that have already been built and are ready to use. This is the kind that you normally install on your system. A *source* package contains the source code and other items used to build the corresponding binary package. Source packages are provided in the event that you want to modify—and recompile—a program yourself.

Binary package filenames end in the suffix .rpm, whereas source package filenames end in the suffix .src.rpm. The use and manipulation of source packages is covered in Chapter 16, so it is not covered here. From now on in this chapter, wherever there is an unqualified reference to a package, it is a reference to a *binary* package.

WHAT'S IN A NAME?

A binary package has a filename that looks similar to the one shown in Figure 15.1.

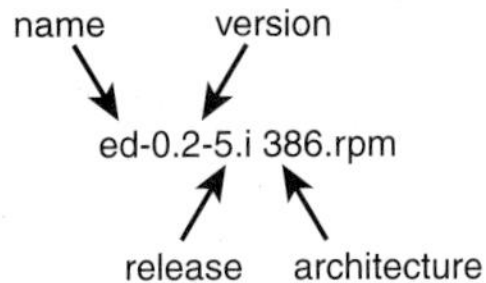

Figure 15.1
Anatomy of a package filename.

The first part of the filename is a short string that identifies the package. After the name is the version number (in this case 0.2), which identifies the version of the *software* contained in the package. This is followed by the package release number (5). It is important to distinguish between the software *version*, and the package *release*: The version number is the version of the software that is provided by the package. In the example in Figure 15.1, it is `ed`, version 0.2. This number is set by the original author of the software, which is often a different person than the one who created the package for the software. The version number reflects the status of the software. The release number refers to the version of *this package* of the software. Sometimes, even if the original software inside the package has not changed, it is necessary to repackage it. The release number indicates which instance of the package this is.

After the release number is a short string which indicates the architecture for the package. Most packages contain software that has been compiled for a particular processor or machine architecture. For example, packages with programs compiled for Intel x86 or compatible processors include the architecture string `i386`. In some cases, the contents of a package are independent of any machine architecture (for example, a package that only contains icons, and not executable programs). In these cases, the architecture string `noarch` is used. Table 15.1 shows some common architecture strings.

TABLE 15.1 ARCHITECTURE STRINGS IN RPM FILENAMES

String	Processor
`noarch`	Any
`i386`	Intel x86, Pentium, and compatibles
`alpha`	DEC Alpha
`sparc`	Sun Sparc
`mips`	MIPS
`ppc`	PowerPC
`m68k`	Motorola 68000 family

Often, the files required for a piece of software are bundled into a single package. Sometimes, however, the files are provided in multiple separate packages. This is done to give you additional flexibility in installing only those parts of a program that you are actually going to use. When the software's files are separated in this manner, you can often tell from the package name what kinds of files are contained in the package. Table 15.2 shows a few naming conventions that will help you to identify packages that have files for particular uses.

TABLE 15.2 NAMING CONVENTIONS FOR PACKAGE FILENAMES

String	Package Contains...	Example
`static`	programs that have been statically linked with certain libraries	`nwutils-static`
`devel`	files required for developing new programs with this system	`slang-devel`
`devel-static`	files required for developing statically linked programs with with this system	`slang-devel-static`
`doc`	regular text documentation	`lilo-doc`
`doc-html`	documentation in HTML format	`povray-doc-html`
`doc-<format>`	documentation in the specified format	`povray-doc-ps`

Often, software that provides a library to be used by other programs comes as three separate packages:

- The main package provides the shared library that program binaries use to run.
- A development package provides the header files and programming documentation necessary to develop new programs that use the library.
- A static development package provides a version of the library that is ready to be statically linked to a new program.

Unless you plan to create or alter programs that use a particular library, you do not need to install the `devel` packages for that library.

PACKAGE CONTENTS

To understand how the package manager can support all the tasks listed previously, it is important to know what a package contains.

A binary package contains the following items:

- Files and directories for each file:
  - Ownership
  - Permissions
  - Checksum (MD5Sum)
  - File type (regular, configuration, or documentation)
- Description of the package
- The origin of the software in the package
- The version of the software
- A URL for the Web site (if any) for the software
- The build date and author of the package
- A package category
- The size of all the files in the package
- Dependency and conflict information
- Install and uninstall scripts

The core of a package is the files and directories that comprise the actual software or component in the package. The files in a package are divided into three different types: *configuration*, *documentation*, and *regular* files. The reason for this distinction is to allow more intelligent handling of these different types of files by RPM. For example, you can choose whether to install the documentation files for a package. Often, documentation takes up a lot of disk space, and if you are familiar enough with how to use a piece of software it might not be necessary to have the documentation installed. In a pinch, you can always go back and install the extra files if necessary.

Configuration files receive special handling during remove and upgrade operations. This is discussed more in later sections of this chapter, but the basic idea is to preserve configuration files, even when a package is no longer installed.

For each file in a package, other attributes are stored in the package and recorded in the package database upon installation. These attributes include the file owner and group, the permissions on the file, and a special checksum called the MD5SUM. The MD5SUM can be used to determine whether the contents of a file have changed even if the time, date, and size have not changed.

The Summary, Version, Size, and Description of the package provide information about the software or component that the package contains.

The Packager, Build Date, Build Host, and Release provide information that is helpful in tracking down problems with a package. The Distribution and Vendor show what product and company produced the package.

The Group indicates the general category of software. Packages are categorized by the type of software they contain into a hierarchy of Groups and Subgroups. This is done to enable you to view related packages more easily in the graphic management tools.

The Dependency information in a package is there to help you make sure that the software on your system has all the other libraries and components that are necessary for the package to run.

Although it comes in separate packages, the software on your system is inter-related, sometimes in not so obvious ways. Dependencies help keep track of the relationships between packages. For example, many packages include software that relies on shared libraries or interpreters (for example, `perl`) to run. If you remove the package that provides this required component, the dependent software stops working. The most dramatic example of this is the main system shared library, `libc`. In a default installation of OpenLinux, more than 200 of the installed packages contain software that stops working if `libc` is removed.

Packages that rely on other pieces of software, or which provide components that other pieces of software rely on, contain dependency information. Each package that relies on another component includes a *requires* entry for that component. A package that provides a required component includes a *provides* entry for that component. By matching up the requires and provides entries of the packages, the package manager can determine whether it is safe to install or remove a package.

For example, when you try to install a package, `RPM` examines your system to see if all the items required by the new package are present on your system. If not, you are warned about the missing items, and the installation is aborted. This gives you an opportunity to install all the necessary components to make sure that all your software runs smoothly.

Something similar happens when you try to remove a package. `RPM` determines if other packages are dependent on that package and warns you about the problem. By default, it does not proceed with the removal. If you determine that it is okay to proceed, you can override the dependency check and force the removal to occur.

Finally, a package might also include installation scripts. There are a total of four scripts that might be associated with a package. Two of the scripts are used for installation, and two are for uninstallation. The pre-install script is run before the files in the package are actually copied to your file system, and the post-install script is run after the files are copied. Similar scripts (preuninstall and postuninstall) are run when you uninstall a package. Most of these scripts are very short and involve steps such as updating the shared library cache for newly installed (or removed) libraries.

WHERE TO FIND PACKAGES

The packages that come with your OpenLinux system are provided on the OpenLinux CD-ROM, in the directory `/Packages/RPMS`. When you install OpenLinux, the installation program creates a list of the packages you selected to install, finds them on the CD-ROM, and uses `rpm` to install them. Additional packages are on the OpenLinux CD-ROM, ready to be installed with the package manager. Package files are also available from a variety of sites on the Internet, including Caldera's FTP site and many other sites that provide Linux software.

Increasingly, in addition to the Linux distribution vendors, the original authors of the software provide their software in package format. If you see a piece of Linux software that you want on the Internet, check the download area of the site that provides it. Frequently, you will find package files that you can install directly on your system using the package management system.

WORKING WITH `rpm`

Just to get acquainted with the `rpm` command, try using it to examine the contents of a package right now. The arguments to the `rpm` command fall into several major categories. The entire man page isn't reproduced here, but Table 15.3 shows a basic summary of the important options for `rpm`. Notice that some option letters have different meanings when combined with another main option.

TABLE 15.3 THE MOST FREQUENTLY USED OPTIONS FOR `rpm`

Option	Sub-option	Meaning
`-q`		query
	`-i`	show detailed package information
	`-l`	list all files
	`-d`	list only documentation files
	`-c`	list only configuration files
	`-f`	find which package owns a file
	`-p`	operate on a package file (as opposed to an installed package)
	`--scripts`	view install/uninstall scripts
`-i`		install
`-e`		erase (uninstall)
`-U`		upgrade
`-V`		verify a package installation
`-b`		build a package (covered in Chapter 16)

Make sure that the OpenLinux Installation CD-ROM is in the CD-ROM drive, and that it is mounted. If not, as superuser, mount it using the following command:

```
mount /mnt/cdrom
```

Now cd to the directory /mnt/cdrom/Packages/RPMS, and do a listing of this directory. You see more than 500 packages listed. Now, to examine the information about a package, use the following command:

```
rpm -qpi ed-0.2-5.i386.rpm
```

This shows a listing similar to the following:

```
should now read
Name        : ed                        Vendor: Caldera, Inc.
Version     : 0.2                 Distribution: OpenLinux 2.2
Release     : 5                     Build Host: knob.calderasystems.com
Install date: (not installed)       Build Date: Sat Apr  3 15:03:39 1999
Group       : Textprocessing/Editor Source RPM: ed-0.2-5.src.rpm
Size        : 93986
Packager    : rwp@lst.de (Roger Pook)
ed is a line-oriented text editor.  It is used to create,
display, modify and otherwise manipulate text files.  red
is a restricted ed: it can only edit files in the current
directory and cannot execute shell commands.
```

To see a listing of the files in this package, type the following:

```
rpm -qpl ed-0.2-5.i386.rpm
```

This prints a listing similar to the following:

```
/bin/ed
/bin/red
/usr/doc/ed-0.2
/usr/doc/ed-0.2/NEWS
/usr/doc/ed-0.2/POSIX
/usr/doc/ed-0.2/README
/usr/doc/ed-0.2/THANKS
/usr/info/ed.info.gz
/usr/man/man1/ed.1.gz
/usr/man/man1/red.1.gz
```

The ed package should already be installed on your system. You can find this out by querying the RPM database, instead of the package. Leave off the p option, and use just the package name (not the whole filename), as follows:

```
rpm -qi ed
```

In this case, the Install date will be set, indicating when the package was installed. If the package is not installed, rpm reports this to you:

```
[tbird@thunder]$ rpm -qi edsel
package edsel is not installed
```

Note

Sometimes it's tricky to remember when you need to specify the whole filename of the package, or just the name of the package (that is, ed-0.2-5.i386.rpm versus ed.) For software that is not installed, you refer to the package file itself (by full filename) to query it for information or to install it. For operations on packages that are currently installed on your system (operations such as query, verify, or remove), use just the package name.

INSTALLING NEW SOFTWARE

Now that you understand the basics of package management, you probably want to install some software. The first step is to figure out which package provides the software you need.

FINDING THE PACKAGE YOU WANT TO INSTALL

Unfortunately, there is so much software available for Linux that even if you know exactly what you want, you might have a hard time finding it.

USE THE PACKAGE NAME

Sometimes the package that contains your software is easily identifiable from its filename. The packages on the OpenLinux CD-ROM are in the directory /mnt/cdrom/Packages/RPMS, when the CD-ROM is mounted at /mnt/cdrom. So, if you are looking for `gimp` (a powerful image manipulation program), you can find the packages for `gimp` by simply listing the contents of that directory. Use wildcards or pipe the output of `ls` through `more`, or else you will be overwhelmed because there are almost 600 packages in this directory. Also, use the naming conventions shown in Table 15.2 to help you identify the packages that you need.

THE COMPLETE PACKAGE MANIFEST IS AVAILABLE

Sometimes you know the name of the program you want to install, but no package filename jumps out as the obvious one.

To solve this problem, Caldera provides a list of all the files provided for OpenLinux, with their associated packages. This list can be used to find out which package contains an individual file. The list is on the CD-ROM at /mnt/cdrom/col/data/pkgfiles.gz.

Note that the list is compressed (it contains more than 70,000 entries), so you have to use `zgrep` instead of `grep` to search through it. If you were looking for the package that contains the `ping` program, for example, you might use the following command:

```
zgrep ping /mnt/cdrom/col/data/pkgfiles.gz
```

Unfortunately, this produces a tremendously long listing. Also, the format of the listing might be confusing because the lines are very long (to accommodate long entries), and wrap to two terminal lines on a normal 80-column terminal. The format of each line is as follows:

```
filename    directory    package
```

You can further filter the list with `grep` to find only those entries that include the string `bin` (`ping` is a program that is located in one of the `bin` directories, such as `/bin` or `/usr/bin`). If you do this, you see that the package `netkit-base-0.11-3` contains the file you are looking for. For example

```
[tbird@thunder]$ zgrep ping /mnt/cdrom/col/data/pkgfiles.gz ¦ grep bin
[tbird@thunder]$ zgrep ping /mnt/cdrom/col/data/pkgfiles.gz ¦ grep bin
ping            /bin            netkit-base-0.11-3
```

The moral of this story is that you might have to use your knowledge of the file system, the likely elements of a package, or other clues to help you deduce which package contains the software that you want to install.

PACKAGE DESCRIPTIONS

A short one-line summary of each package is provided in the compressed file /mnt/cdrom/col/data/pkglist.gz. You can scan this file using `zcat`. The files pkgfiles.gz and pkglist.gz are intended to be useful for quick lookups. If you need to, you can also query individual packages to get their full descriptions.

INTERNET RESOURCES FOR FINDING A PACKAGE

If you are trying to find a particular software package on the Internet, you might want to visit one of the package indexing sites. There is a good site located at `http://rufus.w3.org/linux/RPM/`.

By following the instructions at this site (or at one of its many mirrors), you can see the contents of several thousand different package files located at various sites on the Internet.

Updates to the packages provided with OpenLinux are available on Caldera's FTP site, and are reported on its Web site. To see if a package has been updated, check out `http://www.calderasystems.com/support/download.html`.

Caldera also issues Security Advisories about the software in OpenLinux to alert customers to security problems that have been discovered in the software that is provided with OpenLinux. These advisories almost always specify an updated package that can be obtained immediately to correct the problem mentioned in the advisory. Caldera Security Advisories can be found on Caldera's Web site at `http://www.calderasystems.com/news/security/`.

The Freshmeat Web site is another online resource for tracking recent updates to software. You can access it at `http://www.freshmeat.net/`. Freshmeat is a fairly definitive guide to current releases of software available for Linux. Much of the software referred to on Freshmeat is provided as TAR files. Often, however, when a new release of software is mentioned on Freshmeat the software is made available as a package soon after.

Caution

When downloading RPM packages from the Internet, be sure to check which distribution of Linux they are intended to run with. Although many packages built for some other vendor's distribution of Linux run perfectly fine on Caldera's OpenLinux, it is wise to check the package information, file lists, and dependencies to make sure that the package will operate correctly with your system.

The section "Library Compatibility" later in this chapter discusses how to resolve some issues with programs that have been compiled for a Linux system with different shared libraries.

continues

continued

If you can find the software that you need in a package specifically built for OpenLinux, use it. However, you can also use packages built for other distributions of Linux (such as Red Hat or SuSE). When in doubt, try finding out by searching or participating in mailing lists or newsgroups related to that software; alternately, you can check to see if others have already tried the package with OpenLinux, and find out what success they have had.

DECIDING WHICH UTILITY TO USE

As is the case with many operations in Linux, there's more than one way to manage packages. Several different utilities that can manage packages exist on your OpenLinux system. The two preferred utilities are `rpm` for command line use, and `kpackage` for graphic use. `rpm` offers the capability to do more complex operations, whereas `kpackage` is easier to use. The descriptions in this chapter largely use the `rpm` command, but there is a short section at the end that discusses using `kpackage` as well.

SECURITY CONCERNS

With the large amount of software available for your Linux system, and with it coming from a variety of sources, you might start to wonder if all of it is harmless. When you add any piece of software to your system, you want to make sure that it will do what you expect it to, and no more. You can be fairly sure that the software packages on the OpenLinux CD-ROM can be trusted because they were built by the engineers at Caldera. If the site that you downloaded your package from is public and widely used, you also have some degree of assurance that the package is safe. However, if you are ever unsure of the software in a package, RPM includes two features that enable to you protect yourself.

First, you can verify that the installation itself will not do funny things to your system: You can use `rpm` to examine the exact scripts that will be executed to install the software. Because you install a package as the root user on your system, it is crucial that the scripts used during installation don't do strange things (such as installing trapdoors or Trojan Horses).

Second, you can use RPM to verify the source of a package in two ways. If a package is signed, and you have PGP installed, you can verify the package signature with a special `rpm` option. This enables you to validate that the package comes from where it says it comes from. Also, each package includes a whole-package checksum that can be verified against some public list to make sure that the package has not been tampered with. Caldera can tell you the checksum (MD5SUM) for any package provided with OpenLinux.

STEPS PERFORMED DURING AN INSTALLATION

The package manager completely automates the process of installing software on your system. In most cases you can type a single command and everything is done for you. Behind the scenes, however, there are quite a few steps to the installation process:

1. Check to make sure package is not already present.
2. Check to make sure package does not conflict with one already present.

3. Check to make sure that other files or components required by this package are present.
4. Run the preinstall script.
5. Copy the files and directories to the file system.
6. Correctly set the ownership and permissions on the files and directories.
7. Record the package information in the RPM database (in the files in /var/lib/rpm).
8. Run the postinstall script.

THE ACTUAL INSTALL

After all that explanation, the actual installation of the package is somewhat anticlimactic. Just make sure that you are root, and use the rpm command with the -i option and the filename of the package that you want to install:

```
[root@thunder]$ rpm -i /mnt/cdrom/Packages/RPMS/ytalk-3.1-1.i386.rpm
[root@thunder]$
```

That's it. There are no questions, and no output (when the installation is successful). This is as easy as software installation gets.

REMOVING A PACKAGE

Removing a package from your system is also very simple. Just use rpm with the -e option and the package name (not filename). For example, to remove perl-cgi (your default Web server), type something like the following:

```
 [root@thunder]$ rpm -e perl-cgi
removing these packages would break dependencies:
    perl-cgi is needed by kquery-0.9-2
```

Only root Can Perform Package Modifications on Your System
As with installation, you must be logged in as root to perform the remove operation. In general, this is true of any package operation that actually modifies the contents of your system, such as installing, removing, or upgrading packages. Regular users can perform other operations that are purely informational, such as querying or verifying packages. If you are logged in as a regular user and try to perform an operation with rpm that requires root privileges, you see an error message similar to the following:

```
failed to open //var/lib/rpm/packages.rpm
error: cannot open //var/lib/rpm/packages.rpm
```

In this example, rpm aborts the remove operation and informs you that there is a problem with removing perl-cgi because of dependencies.

DEALING WITH A DEPENDENCY PROBLEM

Apparently, another piece of software on the system needs perl-cgi in order to run. With RPM, you can't blindly mess up the software on your system.

There are two ways to deal with this type of problem. One way is to remove the package that is dependent on the one that you are trying to remove. In this case, kquery is a set of scripts that allow you to use RPM via KDE. These scripts require a particular perl module and are useless without it installed. If you are not planning on using this functionality, both the perl module and the scripts can be removed.

The other way to deal with this situation is to force the package to be removed, despite the dependency problem. Perhaps you do plan to install a different cgi module, or the same module at some later date. In this case, you can leave the kquery package installed and use the `--nodeps` option with `rpm` to force it to ignore dependencies when performing the remove. Both the `--nodeps` and `--force` options can be used during install, upgrade, or remove operations to continue despite dependency or other types of problems, respectively.

This example demonstrates how the dependency information helps you do the right thing with regard to your software. Whether you decide to remove the dependent package, force the removal of the original package, or just leave things as they are, `RPM` has enabled you to make an informed decision so that you won't run into problems later.

OTHER TYPES OF REMOVAL PROBLEMS

Because of the interrelated nature of the various system components, when you remove a package, `RPM` might not be capable of removing the directories that are owned by that package.

For instance, if you modify the file /etc/httpd/apache/conf/access.conf (by, for example, putting a small comment at the end of the file), and then remove the `perl-cgi` package, you get a list of messages similar to the following:

```
cannot remove /var/log/httpd/apache - directory not empty
cannot remove /home/httpd/html - directory not empty
cannot remove /home/httpd/cgi-bin - directory not empty
cannot remove /home/httpd - directory not empty
cannot remove /etc/httpd/apache/conf - directory not empty
cannot remove /etc/httpd/apache - directory not empty
```

There are three different causes for these messages. The directory /var/log/httpd/apache can't be removed because it contains `perl-cgi` log files. These log files are new and are not part of the `perl-cgi` package, even though `apache` created them. This is an important distinction to make. `RPM` only tracks files that it installed, and not ones that were created later, even if it is obvious (to a human, anyway) that the files belong to a specific package. This is actually the right and safe thing to do; `RPM` does not remove any files that it can't restore by reinstalling the package.

The /home/httpd directory (and some of its subdirectories) can not be removed because other packages have files placed there. Specifically, the OpenLinux package provides a default home page for the Web browser that is placed in these directories. Once again, it is appropriate for `RPM` to leave these files alone. You probably want to preserve any Web content that you have created even though you are removing the Web server.

Finally, the /etc/httpd/apache/conf directory (and its parent) are preserved because the file access.conf was modified. If you look in that directory, you can see that the modified file was saved with the filename access.conf.rpmsave.

Any configuration files that have been modified are saved by `rpm` with the extension .rpmsave. This is a valuable feature because it saves you from inadvertently removing a file that you have worked very hard to customize for your system. By saving the file with a special name, it is possible to restore the configuration later if you decide to re-install the package. If, however, you are really, really, *really* sure that you won't need this customized configuration file in the future, you can remove it manually.

Periodically—and especially after doing a lot of package management—it is worthwhile to check your system for configuration files that have been saved in this way. Use the command

```
locate rpmsave
```

or

```
find / -name "*.rpmsave"
```

to locate saved configuration files on your system. You need to know the reason each one is there, and make sure you keep the ones that you might need in the future.

UPGRADING A PACKAGE

You can use `rpm` to upgrade a package on your system, to get a later release of the package, or to get a newer version of software on your system. Upgrading a package is logically the same as removing the currently installed package and installing a new one. However, using the upgrade feature makes these steps a single operation. This enables you to avoid dependency and other file conflict problems that might arise if you do the steps separately. Use the `-U` (uppercase U) option with `rpm` to upgrade a package on your system.

HOW ARE CONFIGURATION FILES DEALT WITH?

You might recall that a package's files are categorized into three different types: configuration, documentation, and regular files. During a package upgrade the configuration files receive special handling.

It is impossible for `RPM` to know whether the configuration files used for the new version of software are the same (in location and format) as those used by the old version. Therefore, to be especially safe, during an upgrade `RPM` renames your old configuration files with the extension .rpmsave before installing new configuration files. You need to manually restore these files after an upgrade. If a change has occurred in the configuration file, you can now deal with it. Although this seems like a tedious process, it is the safest policy for `RPM` to have because it ensures that the software installed on your system is using configuration files that it can read and utilize.

Tip

It is a good habit to look for .rpmsave files after you have upgraded packages on your system, and to make sure that any customized configuration files that were saved are replaced into their proper files.

WORKING WITH TAR FILES

When software is not available in package format, the next most common form is in a TAR file. *TAR* stands for Tape Archive and refers to the original use of these files, which was to store, or archive, information on magnetic tapes. The term is now used for any bundle of files created with the `tar` command. In terms of package management, this section refers only to TAR files that contain software that you plan to use on your system.

A TAR file is similar to a package file in that it contains files and directories, along with their ownership, permission, size, and date information. However, because a TAR file doesn't include the additional information that a package does, you don't get nearly the same management benefits when you use a TAR file. They are often harder to install and more difficult to keep track of after they are installed. Therefore, try to find the software that you are looking for in package format first, and only rely on TAR files if you can't find what you want.

Often a TAR file contains binaries that can run directly on your system, but sometimes the TAR file contains the actual source code for the software—and you are expected to compile the program yourself.

Regular TAR files end in the extension .tar; however, it is more common to find compressed TAR files, which end in either .tar.gz or .tgz. The `tar` command is capable of dealing with either compressed or regular (uncompressed) TAR files.

The files and directories in a TAR file all share a common root directory. Therefore, after a TAR file is installed it is often necessary to perform additional steps to move some of the files from the common directory tree to places in your file system where they can do some good.

INSTALLATION STEPS

The first thing to decide when installing a TAR file is where to put it. Chapter 9, "Understanding the File System," describes the various parts of the Linux file system and where things need to go. Software that is provided as part of OpenLinux by Caldera is placed in the / and /usr main directory hierarchies. It is highly recommended that you place other software that you install into the /usr/local directory hierarchy. This keeps the software from a TAR file separate from the software provided by Caldera, which makes it easier to keep track of and remove later, if desired. If you are dealing with a TAR file that contains source code, place it under /usr/local/src. For any other file, you might want to place it in its own directory under /usr/local.

Before installing a TAR file, examine its contents, to see if it includes a root directory. If so, just extract it in /usr/local subdirectory. If not, first make a directory in which to extract the file, and then `cd` there before extracting the file.

The most common options used with the `tar` command are listed in Table 15.4.

TABLE 15.4 THE MOST FREQUENTLY USED OPTIONS FOR `tar`

Option	Sub-option	Meaning
`-t`		tell what's in a TAR file
`-c`		create a TAR file
`-x`		extract files from a TAR file
	`-v`	verbosely list files processed
	`-f`	used to specify the TAR filename
	`-z`	work with compressed TAR files

COMMON INSTALLATION AIDS

Because TAR files can include any conceivable arrangement of files, or require any sequence of installation steps, it is impossible to cover all the possible TAR installation issues. However, there are a few common conventions for dealing with TAR files.

Almost every TAR file contains a set of instructions in a README file at the root of its directory tree. It is best to read these instructions carefully, and to follow them to the letter.

Sometimes, TAR files that contain binaries have an installation program, which usually has a name that is easy to identify such as `install` or `setup`.

TAR files that contain source files often include a `configure` script (made by the GNU `autoconf` system). This is a script that tries to auto-detect information about your system, and to automatically configure the build environment for the source code so that you can compile it for your system. Sometimes you are required to make modifications to the .in files used by the `configure` script before running it. Often, you can pass arguments to `configure` to have it make customizations to the build environment. Sometimes other scripts or programs besides `configure` must be run to customize the build environment for a program.

After making customizations to the build environment, you next proceed to actually compiling the software. The software is almost always built using the `make` command (usually with no parameters). After the software is compiled, a `make install` command places the software into appropriate places in the file system, where you can begin to use it.

In summary

- Read the README
- Run `configure` (optional)

- Edit `make` file or run other scripts (optional)
- `make`
- `make install`

When you get to this stage, it's time to try to use the software. If you encounter problems along the way, be sure to read any FAQs or other documentation available for the software. Don't be afraid to ask for help from newsgroups or mailing lists where the software is discussed. You might be surprised at how helpful people will be if you've shown a good effort to try things yourself first.

LIBRARY COMPATIBILITY

This section describes how to overcome the problem of incompatibility between the programs and shared libraries installed on your system.

Most of the software that you install onto your OpenLinux system utilizes shared libraries. *Shared libraries* are files of shared sub-routines and functions that programs use to perform their operations. When a program is compiled to use shared libraries, as most are, the linker records information about the version number of the shared library with which the program needs to be run.

Inevitably, as you manage your software you will run into software that was compiled for different versions of shared libraries than what you have on your system. Luckily, there are straightforward ways of dealing with this problem.

HOW SHARED LIBRARIES ARE VERSIONED

First, you need to know how the versions of shared libraries are determined, and how they are expressed in the file system.

Library version numbers provide at least two, and sometimes three levels of versioning. For example, one instance of the `libc` shared library has version number 5.4.38. The major version of the software is the one that counts the most with regard to software compatibility. If you look in the `/lib` directory, you should see that `libc.so.5` is a symbolic link (a reference) to `libc.so.5.4.38`, and that libc.so.6 is a symbolic link to libc-2.1.so, which is the primary C shared library on your system. This is the single most important (and most widely used) library in the system.

The shared library system is maintained with the `ldconfig` command. Whenever a new shared library is installed on the system, `ldconfig` is run and a new entry is made in the file /etc/ld.so.cache. If one does not already exist, a symbolic link is created with the name of the library and its major version number, which references the actual shared library file—with the full version in its name. This all happens automatically when packages are installed via `RPM` because packages that install shared libraries have a postinstall script that runs `ldconfig` for you. If you have installed shared libraries from TAR files, you might need to run this command yourself so that the libraries are registered with the system.

USE OF ldd TO DISCOVER REQUIRED SHARED LIBRARIES

When a program is created, the linker records the versions of the shared libraries that it requires in the program file. You can examine which shared libraries an executable program needs by using the `ldd` command. For example, you can find out what shared library is used by `man` by typing `ldd /usr/bin/man`, which should result in the following output:

```
libc.so.6 => /lib/libc.so.6 (0x40019000)
/lib/ld-linux.so. => /lib/ld-linux.so.2 (0x40000000)
```

`man` is a fairly simple program. For a more interesting listing, try `ldd /opt/kde/bin/kdecode`. This command lists 12 shared libraries required by this KDE program.

If you determine that you have a shared library incompatibility problem, there are several ways to handle it.

If the library that is missing has a different major version number than the one your program needs, just find the package that provides the version of the library that you need and install it. If the major version numbers are different, the other software on your system will be unaffected by the addition of another library, even one of the same name.

Another solution is to create a symlink for the shared library name you need, link it to an existing shared library on your system, and hope that the library is compatible. This might work in some circumstances, depending on how extensively the library is used and what subroutines are referenced by the program. This is, however, a stopgap measure, and will only be used when you know (that is, have it on good authority) that the library versions in question are compatible for the purposes of the target program.

The recommended solution is to actually install the correct version of the shared library that you need and use the environment variable `LD_LIBRARY_PATH` to alter the shared libraries that are used by your program.

Programs are loaded in OpenLinux as follows: The runtime loader examines /etc/ld.so.cache to determine the correct shared libraries to load with the program. However, if `LD_LIBRARY_PATH` is set in the environment, the loader uses any libraries found in the specified directory first.

The steps to set this up for a specific program are somewhat involved, but not complicated. You want to run the one program you need with the special version of the shared library without affecting any other program running on the system. This is done by creating a wrapper script that sets up the shared library environment, and then executes the original program.

Following are the steps for setting this up, for the hypothetical program `/usr/bin/prog1`, which requires `libgoo.so.2.1.18`—and your system has the incompatible `libgoo.so.2.1.23`:

1. Obtain a copy of `libgoo.so.2.1.18`. The easiest way to do this is to scour the Internet for old packages or TAR files. Often, when incompatibilities such as this are discussed in online forums, pointers to libraries are mentioned.

2. Make a new directory to hold this compatibility library, separate from the library where `libgoo.so.2` normally resides. For example, create the directory /usr/lib/compat, and copy `libgoo.so.2.1.18` to it.
3. Make a symlink for the shared library with the major version number included. For example, `'ln -s libgoo.so.2.1.18 /usr/lib/compat/libgoo.so.2'`.
4. Save the `prog1` program by renaming it to something else: `mv /usr/bin/prog1 /usr/bin/prog1.real`
5. Create a wrapper script called `prog1`, which refers to the shared library. The script might look similar to the following:

```
#/bin/sh
export LD_LIBRARY_PATH=/usr/lib/compat
exec /usr/bin/prog1.real
```

6. Don't forget to mark the script as executable: `chmod a+x /usr/bin/prog1`

When you have done all this, you can run `prog1` and have it use `/usr/lib/compat/libgoo.so.2.1.18` instead of `/usr/lib/libgoo.so.1.23`.

MISCELLANEOUS ADMINISTRATION TASKS

There are numerous other administration tasks that you can perform with your package management system.

FIND OUT WHICH PACKAGE OWNS A FILE

Use the `rpm -qf` command to find out which package owns a file. This can be very useful when you find problems with the software on your system and need to find other related files. You must specify the full pathname to the file for `rpm` to find the matching package in the package database.

CUSTOMIZING THE FORMAT OF PACKAGE QUERIES

`rpm` enables you to customize the format of the output of queries that you make. You can create custom reports or use the output of `rpm` with other programs by specially formatting the query output. Use the `–queryformat` option to specify the format string for the query output. If you want each item listed on a separate line, be sure to include a newline character at the end of the line. Special tags in the format string are used to output a particular piece of information about a package or file.

For example, the command

```
rpm -qa --querytags "Package %-20{NAME} came from %{PACKAGER}\n"
```

shows a list of all the packages on your system, along with the name of the packager, in the format shown.

The command `rpm --querytags` shows you a list of the tags that you can use as part of a queryformat string.

ANALYZE DISK SPACE USED BY PACKAGES

When your disk space starts to get low, you can use the `rpm` command to find the packages that are using up all your disk space. For example, use the following commands to list how much space each package on your system is consuming:

```
rpm -qa --queryformat "%-30{NAME} %{SIZE}\n" ¦ sort
```

It can also be sorted by package size:

```
rpm -qa --queryformat "%10{SIZE} %{NAME}\n" ¦ sort -n
```

For a real shock, look at the `xemacs` packages and see how much room they take. If you don't use `emacs`, now is a good time to remove these packages and save yourself that disk space.

WORKING WITH kpackage

All the examples given so far have been with the `rpm` command line utility. However, you might find it easier to work with a graphical utility to manage the packages on your system. The KDE utility `kpackage` enables you to perform the most common package management tasks.

You can find `kpackage` on the KDE Applications Starter menu, under Utilities. By default, there is a Utilities menu on your desktop panel, which also includes `kpackage`. When you start `kpackage`, you see two frames of information. (Figure 15.2 shows the `kpackage` main screen.) On the left side is a listing of the packages installed on your system, organized by package category or group. You can expand or contract the groups or subgroups by clicking on the tree diagram. Categories are shown as folders, and individual packages are shown as open boxes. Beside each package is shown the disk space used by that package. This is handy for taking a quick look at the size of related packages.

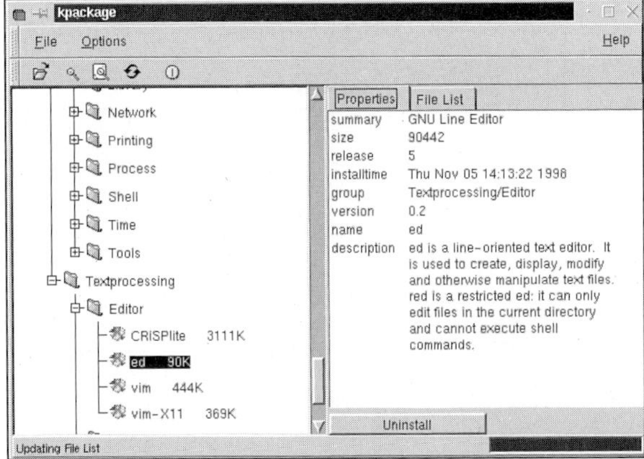

Figure 15.2
`kpackage`, with the ed package selected.

On the right side of the window is a frame showing details about the package you have selected. There are two tabs at the top, which show either some of the Properties of the package or the file listing for the package. Figure 15.3 shows `kpackage` with the file listing for the ed package. In the file listing, there is an icon beside each filename indicating the file's status. Question marks are shown by default and indicate that file verification has not been performed. If file verification is turned on, other marks appear in the file list.

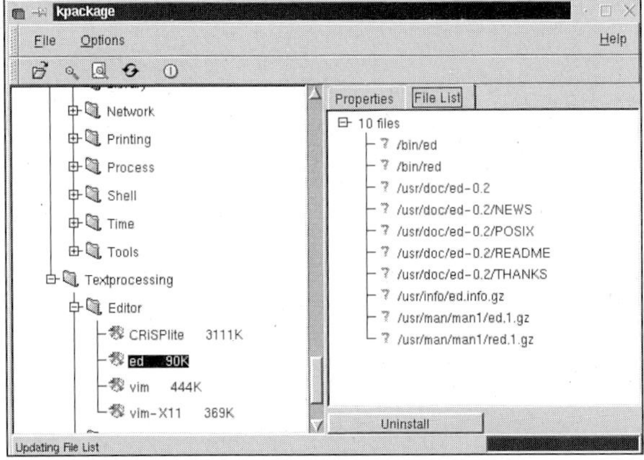

Figure 15.3
The file listing for `ed`.

The following sections show you how to perform various administration tasks with `kpackage`.

INSTALLING A PACKAGE

First, open the package that you want to install by using the File, Open menu option. If you are installing a package from the OpenLinux installation CD-ROM, use the location /mnt/cdrom/Packages/RPMS. Use the file browser to select the package you want to install.

After you select a package, the main window of `kpackage` switches to an install screen, which asks you for various options and provides you with the package details (or file list). Figure 15.4 shows the `kpackage` installation window.

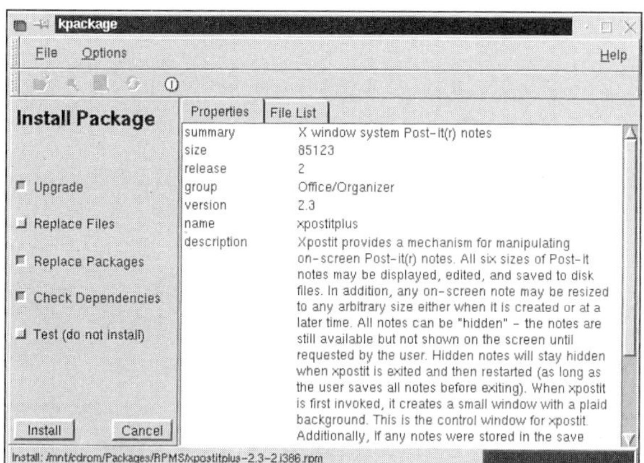

Figure 15.4
Use `kpackage` to install a package.

Removing a Package

Select the package in the package list window, and then click on the Uninstall button in the package detail window. You are prompted with a dialog asking you if you want to use scripts, check dependencies, or merely test if the package will uninstall cleanly. You can leave these at the default settings for most uninstall operations. Click on the Uninstall button and the package is removed (barring any difficulties, which `kpackage` will report to you).

Finding the Package for a File

Select File, Find File from the main menu and type the filename you want to find in the top box of the dialog box. You must provide the full filename, from the root of the file system, in order for the query to work. Click on the Find button and a list of packages that own this file is shown. Usually, only one package is shown. Figure 15.5 shows the dialog box used to find the package for a file.

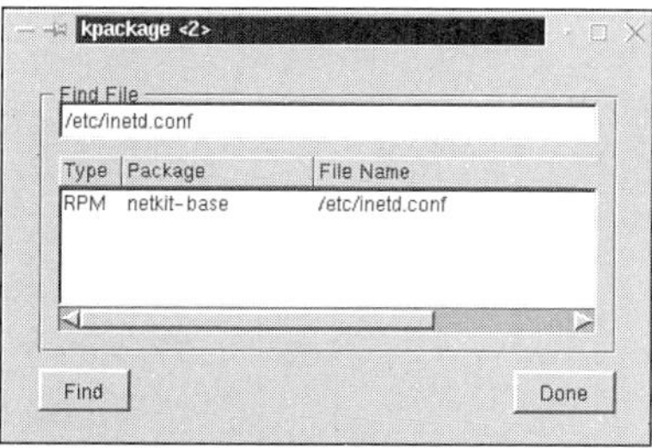

Figure 15.5
`kpackage` finds the package for the file you enter in the top line.

VERIFYING A PACKAGE'S FILES

To verify a package's file, select the `Options`, `Options` menu item, click the misc tab, and select the checkbox for Verify File List. Then select the package in the package list window, and select the File List tab. The list of the package's files will be displayed in the package detail window, with a mark by each filename. A green check mark means the file is okay. Other marks indicate problems with the file.

SUMMARY

In this chapter, the basic concepts and capabilities of the `RPM` package management system were presented. You have learned how to use the packaging tools on your system (including both `rpm` and `kpackage`) to install and uninstall software on your machine. Also, several other software management operations were presented.

If you can't find the software you need in package format, you might find it in a TAR file. This chapter briefly discussed some of the issues regarding TAR files and installing the software from them on your system.

Finally, a section of this chapter discussed how to resolve library incompatibility problems by writing wrapper scripts that used the `LD_LIBRARY_PATH` environment variable.

You might want to examine the following chapters, which cover topics related to the material presented here:

- Chapter 16 explains the process of creating packages, and covers in great detail the contents of packages and how some of the information in a package is generated and used.
- Part of Chapter 2, "Installing OpenLinux," discusses the packages (or sets of packages) installed by default on your OpenLinux system.
- Chapter 4, "Navigating the Desktop," presents information about launching and basic operation of KDE applications (of which `kpackage` is an example).

CHAPTER 16

How to Build/Rebuild a Package

In this chapter

This chapter describes the steps that are necessary for you to make packages of your own. If you like having everything built for you and you don't like to tinker, this chapter is probably not for you. But if you want to "look under the hood," and possibly even get your hands dirty modifying the source code for the software on your system, read on.

The capability to obtain and modify the source code for the software you run on Linux is what sets it apart from other operating systems. On many other systems, you are stuck with what the author of the software gave you. This is not the case with Linux. The capability to modify, maintain, and enhance the software on your system is one of the biggest attractions of Linux. Even if you don't personally enhance the software, that fact that it is available for anyone to do so is what leads to more robust, full-featured, and useful software for everyone.

There are many different reasons that you might want to modify the programs on your system. Sometimes, for example, there is a patch available for your software that no one has integrated into a package yet. By learning to rebuild packages, you can repair or upgrade the software yourself. Maybe you just have a desire to experiment with creating new features or making fixes to software yourself. If your ideas are good, you can submit the changes back to the original author of the software and watch as others use your enhancements. The reason that Linux has become so popular is that thousands of people have taken the time to make contributions to enhance the software and documentation. You can do this, too, but you must start by learning how to build and rebuild packages.

THE `build` PROCESS

The tool used to build packages is the same command line tool used to manage packages: `rpm`. This section gives an overview of the build process, starting with a little bit of history to explain why the packaging system works the way it does. (For a background introduction to RPM, see Chapter 15, "Software Package Management.")

PHILOSOPHY OF RPM

Before diving into the details of building packages, it helps to learn some of the philosophy behind the package manager as well as something about the development methods commonly used with open source software. Understanding how software is distributed and built without the benefit of package management will help you see what types of problems RPM tries to solve, and how it can best be used.

In the UNIX world, open source software has historically been distributed in the form of TAR files that contain the source code necessary to build the software on your machine. Sometimes these bundles of files include readily executable binaries. Often, however, you are expected to compile the software and install it yourself using the source files in the TAR. Because there are various versions of UNIX from different vendors, the software has to be written so that it can compile for many different OS versions and *platforms* (processors).

RPM is derived from this heritage of starting with source code from TAR files and, from that, producing working software. What differentiates RPM from other packaging systems is that it tries to automate the steps required to go from the author's original source code to a very easy-to-install package. This was done to make it easier to maintain a distribution of Linux, which might include hundreds or even thousands of packages. Therefore, although the automation provided by the package building system is essential to a distribution vendor (such as Caldera), it also provides some important benefits to the end users of the software—they can use the same automated steps to rebuild the software on their own machines.

WORKING WITH ORIGINAL SOURCES

One overriding philosophy of RPM is that it can be used to rebuild—from *original* sources obtained from the Internet—software that runs effectively.

Getting software to run on a particular machine or version of OS often requires that changes be made to the software. In order to help others who might want to use the software on similar machines, a developer makes changes, and then submits the modifications back to the original author of the software in the form of patches. The original author often includes the changes in the next release of the software. Sometimes, however, the author doesn't have the time or inclination to include new patches; therefore, subsequent releases of the software need to have the same set of patches applied in order to get them to compile again on the target platform.

You need to remember that Linux is just one (increasingly, the most popular one) of a breed of operating systems on which open source software is intended to work. Often, the author of the software doesn't run the same operating system or distribution of Linux that you do. Authors control what happens with the source code for their project and, because their priorities are different than yours, they might not integrate the changes that you need into subsequent releases. The way that RPM automates the process of applying patches and rebuilding source code makes it much easier to keep software up to date, even if the desired changes are never integrated by the original software author.

NO QUESTIONS = FLEXIBILITY AND EASE OF USE

"Ask me no questions, and I'll tell you no lies." This phrase aptly sums up the philosophy the authors of RPM have regarding the installation process. You might notice that RPM never asks any questions as it installs software on your system. RPM provides no facility to ask the user questions during package installation because users are notorious for not knowing the answers; furthermore, software developers are prone to asking questions that many users don't know the answers to!

Developing packages that install and run properly without any user feedback often requires extra work on the part of the package developer. However, one benefit of this is that packages can be installed from a wide variety of environments (text mode, graphic mode, over the Web, or an automated environment), without regard to user interface issues (that is, how questions are displayed or how input is obtained and relayed back to the install tool). This makes RPM extremely flexible in that it can be utilized with a number of front ends, and can be used for both interactive and unattended operation.

Although it makes the packager work harder, not asking questions generally results in easier-to-install packages for the end user—which is a good thing.

In the packages that you produce, you might really need to ask the user a question before the software can be properly configured to run; the correct way to deal with this is with a setup program that the user runs after installing the package. However, this is not encouraged. Rack your brain for ways to avoid asking questions to configure the software that you package; usually you can find ways to get the information you need without asking the user.

STEPS IN THE `build` PROCESS

The `RPM build` process includes four basic steps, which automate what a human might do to produce working binaries from a software base. These are referred to as *stages* of the `build` process:

1. **Prep stage**—Extract the source files from a TAR file and apply patches that are relevant for the target platform.
2. **Build stage**—Build the software by compiling the programs and (possibly) formatting the documentation.
3. **Install stage**—Install the software on your system.
4. **Packaging stage**—Bundle the files and directories for the software into a package.

This last step is unique to package management. Although automating the first three steps is great, it is the final step—creating a working package—that results in all the benefits of packages mentioned in Chapter 15.

Each of these stages is described in the sections that follow. For the examples in this chapter, you'll modify a small command line editor, `ed`, and repackage it with your changes. When you are finished you will have learned enough techniques to get you started modifying your own packages. Whether you make packages purely for yourself or share your packages with others, learning how to do it is a rewarding experience.

DIRECTORIES INVOLVED IN THE `build` PROCESS

The directories used by the `RPM build` process are underneath the directory /usr/src/OpenLinux. The following directories are used during the build process:

- **SOURCES**—This directory contains the source TAR files, patches, and icon files for the software to be packaged.
- **SPECS**—This directory contains the SPEC files for building packages. A SPEC file for a package contains information about the package as well as scripts that are used to automatically build the package from the files in the SOURCES directory.
- **BUILD**—The BUILD directory holds the source code for the software while it is being compiled and constructed (during the build process). Source files are extracted to subdirectories of the BUILD directory during the prep stage. Compiled program

binaries and configuration and documentation files are moved from this directory into the main file system during the install stage.

- **RPMS**—The resulting binary package is placed in a subdirectory underneath the RPMS directory when the package is finally assembled (during the packaging stage). There are subdirectories beneath RPMS that hold the packages for particular platforms. These subdirectories have the same name as the architecture string used in the package filename. (See Table 15.2 for a list of architecture strings.) Packages compiled for the Intel platform are placed in the i386 subdirectory.
- **SRPMS**—This directory holds the source `RPM` package that results from a `build`. This is a snapshot of all the materials required to produce the corresponding binary `RPM`.

The location of this directory tree can be overridden by setting the value of topdir in either usr/lib/rpm-2.5.5/rpmrc or ${HOME}/.rpmrc. These files can also be used to make other customizations to `RPM` for both normal package management and package building. See the file /usr/lib/rpmrc for examples of other options that can be set for the `build` process.

Caution

In order to perform the examples in this chapter, you need to access the directories listed in the preceding section. Normally, this means you need to log in as the root user (or use the `su` command to become root). The section "Creating Packages as a Regular User," later in this chapter, provides a few tips for building packages as a non-root user.

PREPARING THE SOURCE CODE

There are two routes you can take to building a package. `RPM` was actually designed with the concept of building programs from source code in mind. Occasionally, however, you encounter situations in which the source code for the software you want to package is not available. In this case, you start with a TAR file that has prebuilt binaries instead of a TAR file with source files. Then you proceed as usual, except that you have `rpm` do nothing during the build stage.

For most software you will be packaging, however, you will start with the source code. You usually start with source code from one of two sources: a TAR file or a source `RPM` package.

STARTING WITH A TAR FILE

A few hints for installing and building from a source TAR file are mentioned in Chapter 15, in the section "Working with TAR Files." In this chapter, it is assumed that you are comfortable with downloading a TAR file and extracting its contents. When you build a package, you use many of the same steps—such as running `configure` or `make`—that are used in building and installing the software by hand. In this case, however, you record the steps in scripts and automate the process with `RPM`.

After you find and obtain the TAR file that contains the software you want to package, place it in the SOURCES directory.

STARTING WITH A SOURCE RPM

If you want to rebuild the software for a package that is already in RPM format, you can start with the source RPM file for that package. The source RPM includes the SOURCE TAR files and the SPEC file (described later) for the software. It might also include patches or an image file (for the icon) for the package. The source RPM files for all OpenLinux software are provided on the OpenLinux Source CD-ROM, in the directory /mnt/cdrom/Packages/SRPMS, or from Caldera's web site at `ftp://ftp.caldera.com/pub/`. For the examples that follow, if you do not have the OpenLinux Source CD, download the source rpm for `ed` from Caldera's site, and install it using rpm, as described next.

The files ed-0.2.tar.gz and ed.gif are placed in the SOURCES directory, and the file ed-0.2.spec is placed in the SPECS directory.

The source packages provided with OpenLinux will rebuild into binary packages without any problems. As a quality assurance step, Caldera builds all the packages for OpenLinux on the exact same version of OpenLinux that they are included in. This is called *self-hosting* the package build and guarantees that the source packages provided with OpenLinux can be used by Caldera customers to re-create the actual software that shipped with the product.

Test Driving a Build with `ed`

With the `ed` sources installed on your system, you can proceed directly to building the binary package if you want to test it out right now. First, `cd` to the packaging area at /usr/src/OpenLinux, and then type the following:

```
rpm -ba SPECS/ed-0.2.spec
```

Watch as the various stages of the `build` take place. First, the files in ed-0.2.tar.gz are extracted into the BUILD directory. Then the `ed` program is compiled and installed on your system. Finally, a new ed-0.2-5.i386.rpm file is created from the installed files and placed in the RPM/i386 directory, and a new ed-0.2-5.src.rpm is placed in the SRPM directory.

Wasn't that easy?

In general, you will want two copies of the source directory tree while you are working on it: one copy of files to work on, and another copy with the original files that you can refer to and make patches against. These need to be constructed outside the RPM `build` area because that area is automatically used (files are deleted and overwritten) during the `build` process. If the two directory trees are parallel to each other, it is easier to make patch files from them.

To make two copies of the `ed` software, use the `tar` command to make the first copy and the `cp` command to make an exact duplicate. First, `cd` to /usr/local/src, and then extract the `ed` sources with the following command:

```
tar -xzvf /usr/src/OpenLinux/SOURCES/ed-0.2.tar.gz
```

The files in the TAR file are extracted into the directory ed-0.2. Now make a reference copy of the files in the directory ed-0.2.orig with the `cp` command:

```
cp -a ed-0.2 ed-0.2.orig
```

You are now ready to make some changes to `ed`.

MAKING PATCH FILES

After you make modifications to the software, you record those modifications in patch files. A *patch* contains a listing of the changes required to convert an old version of a file into a new version. Because the `build` process is automated, all the changes to be made to the original sources during the `build` must be recorded in patch files.

To make a patch file, use the `diff` command with two versions of the file—the original version and the version you have modified. Use the `-c` option with `diff` to format the output as a context diff, which is the best format for patch files.

Go ahead and change the main.c file for `ed` to include some minor modification to the usage help lines. First, `cd` to the directory /usr/local/src/ed-0.2; then use the command `chmod a+w main.c` to change the permissions on the main.c file so that it is world-writable. Open main.c in an editor and find the `usage()` routine, which starts at about line 135 in the file. Add a `printf` statement to this routine to output some new message. Listing 16.1 shows the first part of the `usage()` routine in this file. I added the line which reads, "Hey, I modified `ed`!" You can be more creative if you want.

LISTING 16.1 THE FIRST PART OF THE `usage()` ROUTINE IN ED-0.2/MAIN.C

```
void
usage (status)
    int status;
{
  if (status != 0)
    fprintf (stderr, "Try `%s --help' for more information.\n",
➥program_name);
  else
    {
      printf ("Hey, I modified ed!\n");
      printf ("Usage: %s [OPTION]... [FILE]\n", program_name);
      printf ("\
  \n\
```

Save your changes, and make a patch file that converts the standard, mundane `ed` into something with your own personal flair. Save the patch file in the SOURCES directory.

From the /usr/local/src directory, use the following command to make a patch file that records your modifications:

```
diff -c ed-0.2.orig/main.c ed-0.2/main.c
➥>/usr/src/OpenLinux/SOURCES/ed-main.patch
```

Note

It is fairly common to get the order wrong on the filenames with the `diff` command. *Backward* patch files might cause problems during the `build` process, so try to remember the correct order. `diff` uses the same file order as a `copy` or `move` command, with the old file as the source and the new file as the destination. Just remember that you want the patch to result in the second file, or destination.

THE SPEC FILE

When you build packages, you use special files, called SPEC files, to contain the information and scripts which automate the package building process itself, and the information and scripts that are bundled as part of the package. This second set of scripts is used on the user's system when the package is installed.

These two sets of information are intermingled in the SPEC file, without any distinction between them other than their names. However, it is important to remember which items are used on your system during the package `build` process, and which items are used on the end user's system during package usage.

The SPEC file for a package is located in the SPECS directory and needs to have a filename consisting of the name of the package, the version number, and the extension .spec. For example, the name of the SPEC file for `ed` is ed-0.2.spec. For SPEC files that are used to produce multiple packages, the base package name needs to be used for the filename.

A SPEC file includes two different kinds of entries: one-line *fields* and multiline *sections*. The one-line fields are placed at the top of the file in the header, and the sections follow. Most sections in the SPEC file contain Bourne shell scripts that run either during the package building process or on the end user's system during package installation or removal. However, the `%Description` section is just a series of text lines that describe the package. Listing 16.2 shows the SPEC file for the `ed` package, which is used for the examples in this chapter. This SPEC file has been simplified to shorten it for inclusion in this book. If you have installed the `ed` source `RPM`, you can look at the unedited version at /usr/src/OpenLinux/SPECS/ed-0.2.spec.

LISTING 16.2 THE SPEC FILE FOR `ed` (SIMPLIFIED)

```
Summary: GNU Line Editor
Name: ed
Version: 0.2
Release: 5
Group: Textprocessing/Editor
Copyright: GPL
Packager: rwp@lst.de (Roger Pook)
Icon: ed.gif
# URL: No WWW site found
Source0: ftp://prep.ai.mit.edu/pub/gnu/ed-0.2.tar.gz
# Patch: - optional -
# Provides: - optional -
```

```
# Requires: - optional -
# Conflicts: - optional -
BuildRoot: /tmp/ed-0.2
%Description
ed is a line-oriented text editor.  It is used to create,
display, modify and otherwise manipulate text files.  red
is a restricted ed: it can only edit files in the current
directory and cannot execute shell commands.

%Prep
%setup

%Build
./configure --prefix=/usr --exec-prefix=/
make CFLAGS="$RPM_OPT_FLAGS" LDFLAGS=-s

%Install
DESTDIR=$RPM_BUILD_ROOT; export DESTDIR
make CFLAGS="$RPM_OPT_FLAGS" LDFLAGS=-s install \
    prefix=$DESTDIR/usr exec_prefix=$DESTDIR/
gzip -9fn $DESTDIR/usr/info/ed.info

%Post
lisa --info install ed --section "Miscellaneous:" --entry \
  "* ed:(ed).                      The GNU line-oriented text editor."

%PreUn
lisa --info remove ed $1

%Files
%doc NEWS POSIX README THANKS
/bin/ed
/bin/red
/usr/info/ed.info.gz
/usr/man/man1/ed.1.gz
/usr/man/man1/red.1.gz
```


FIELDS IN THE SPEC FILE

Fields are indicated with the fieldname followed by a colon. A pound sign (#) indicates a comment in the SPEC file, either in the Fields header or in any of the sections.

Most of the fields are pieces of information that are just put into the package when it is built. However, some are used during the actual `build` process.

INFORMATIONAL FIELDS

Following are descriptions of the informational fields most commonly used in a SPEC file:

- **`Summary`**—A one-line description of the package.
- **`Name`**—The name of the package.
- **`Version`**—The version of the software in the package.

- `Release`—The release number of the package. This is what you modify if you make changes to the package (that is, when the original version of the software has not changed).
- `Group`—The *group* is a multipart (usually two-part) string used by package management utilities to organize the packages into a hierarchy. Table 16.1 shows the current list of groups used for OpenLinux packages supplied by Caldera. The parts of the group are separated by a slash. For example, the `ed` package is in the Textprocessing/Editor group.

TABLE 16.1 PACKAGE GROUPS USED IN OPENLINUX

Group	Sub-Group
Administration	Archiving
	Hardware
	Monitoring
	Network
	Printing
	Software
	System
	User
Applications	Emulators
Browser	FTP
	File System
	Graphic
	Information
	Mail
	News
	OnlineDoc
	WWW
Communication	ISDN
	Modem
	Network
	WWW
Emulators	Software
Libraries	
Multimedia	Audio
	Graphic
	Video

Group	Sub-Group
Networking	Utilities
Office	Database
	Organizer
	Publishing
	Spreadsheet
	Time
	Wordprocessor
Programming	Case
	Compiler
	Converter
	Debugger
	Environment
	Interpreter
	Library
	Tools
	VersionControl
Recreation	Action
	Amusement
	Network
	Simulation
	Strategy
Scientific	Fractal
	Math
	Modelling
	Presentation
	Simulation
Server	Boot
	Mail
	Network
	News
	Printing

continues

TABLE 16.1 CONTINUED

Group	Sub-Group
Server	Time
	WWW
	X11
System	Base
	Boot
	Compression
	Console
	Data
	Desktop
	File System
	Font
	Kernel
	Library
	Network
	Printing
	Process
	Shell
	Time
	Tools
Textprocessing	Editor
	Encoding
	Postscript
	TeX
	Tools

- `Copyright`—This indicates the copyright holder and/or the license that the software uses. Common values for the license are BSD, distributable, GPL, artistic, public domain, MIT, freeware, and shareware.
- `Packager`—This provides the name and email address of the person who built this package. In the case of packages that come with OpenLinux, this field is primarily for the use of Caldera to track package-related support issues. Please don't contact this person to get support for the software in the package. If you have questions about the software provided by a package, visit the site at which the software originated, or use other normal support channels.

- **`Provides`**—This lists the items that the package provides. The package automatically provides its own name and all the files that it contains (including shared libraries and interpreters), so these do not need to be explicitly listed.
- **`Requires`**—This lists the items that the package requires. If programs in the package require shared libraries or interpreters, `rpm` detects this automatically, and these items do not need to be explicitly listed.
- **`Conflicts`**—This lists conflicts that the package has. For instance, if this were a mail engine, it might conflict with sendmail because there can usually only be one mail engine on a machine. This information is used by `RPM` to prevent two conflicting packages from being installed on the same machine.
- **`%Description`**—This is a multiline description of the package. Actually, this is a section and not a field, but it fits better here because it is purely informational and is not used during package building.

FIELDS USED DURING PACKAGE BUILDING

The following fields are used during the `build` process:

- **`Icon`**—The GIF file that contains an icon for this package (used by graphical package management tools such as `glint`).
- **`Source`*n***—This is an URL for the source files for the software. The filename part is used by the `build` process, and the rest of the URL is for informational purposes. Note that `Source` is the same as `Source0` (the "0" is optional).
- **`Patch`*n***—These entries denote the filenames of the patch files used during the `build` process. `Patch` is the same as `Patch0`.

SECTIONS

Sections in the SPEC file begin with a section identifier, and continue until the next section identifier. The section identifiers start with a percent sign.

Note

Unfortunately, `rpm` uses a percent sign to indicate both section identifiers and directives in the `%Prep` and `%Files` sections, which can be confusing. Caldera capitalizes the first letter of section identifiers and leaves directive names in all lowercase to distinguish the two in their SPEC files.

Most sections in the SPEC file contain shell scripts that perform the actions required for that stage of the build process. If you are not familiar with shell scripting, you might want to refer to the "Shell Programming" section in Chapter 13, "Customizing Your Shell Environment."

SECTIONS USED DURING THE `build` PROCESS

The following sections are used during the build process:

- **`%Prep`**—This section contains a shell script to extract the source files and apply the patches. It is used during the prep stage.
- **`%Build`**—This contains a shell script to build (compile) the software. It is used during the build stage.
- **`%Install`**—This contains a shell script to install the software. This is used during the Install stage. (You can probably see a pattern emerging here!)
- **`%Files`**—This section contains a listing of the files and directories in the package.
- **`%Clean`**—This optional section contains a shell script to clean up after a package build.
- **`%Changelog`**—This contains changelog information about the SPEC file itself.

The `%Prep`, `%Build`, `%Install`, and `%Files` sections are discussed in greater detail in subsequent sections of this chapter.

SECTIONS FOR PACKAGE SCRIPTS

The following scripts are not used at build time; they are inserted into the package and used by the package manager on the end user's system when the package is installed, removed, or verified.

- **`%Pre`**—Contains a script run on the end user's system before installing the package files.
- **`%Post`**—Contains a script run on the end user's system after installing the package files.
- **`%Preun`**—Contains a script run on the end user's system before removing the package files.
- **`%Postun`**—Contains a script run on the end user's system after removing the package files.
- **`%Verify`**—Contains a script run on the end user's system to verify the package files. If empty, the default verification mechanism of `RPM` is used.

WHEN IN DOUBT, STEAL

With package management, as with many other things in open source software, reusing existing code is the key to making your life easy. Don't try to create SPEC files from scratch. Look at other packages' SPEC files and copy the parts you need.

To continue with your example of rebuilding `ed`, modify a few of the fields in the `ed` SPEC file.

First, change the `Release` number in the SPEC file to 6 so that the package you build doesn't get confused with the package that originally shipped with OpenLinux. Also, change the `Packager` field to your name and email address.

BUILDING A PACKAGE

Use the `-b` option with `rpm` to build packages. You can use other options with this command to perform only certain stages of the `build` process. This is useful for debugging the `build` process for a package. Table 16.2 lists the `build` options and the stages that they refer to.

TABLE 16.2 RPM BUILD OPTIONS

Option	Stage, or Action
`p`	Prep
`c`	Build (compile)
`i`	Install
`b`	Packaging (create a binary package)
`a`	all (build binary and source packages)
`l`	check file list
`--short-circuit`	skip preceding stages

Use `--short-circuit` to Save Yourself Time

Normally, when you specify a stage, all preceding stages are performed also. However, you can use the `--short-circuit` option to perform only that specific stage. This is useful when some of the stages in the `build` process take a long time to execute. These stages can be omitted during the development of the SPEC file and package to save time.

For example, to execute the prep and build stages of the `build` process for the `ed` package, change to the SPECS directory and type the following:

```
rpm -bc ed-0.2.spec
```

To execute the install stage of the `build` process without performing the prep and build stages, use the following command:

```
rpm -bi --short-circuit ed-0.2.spec
```

THE PREP STAGE

During the prep stage of the package build, the script in the `%Prep` section of the SPEC file is run. This script will extract the source files from the TAR file and apply patches in preparation for the actual compilation of the software.

During this stage, a directory is created under /usr/src/OpenLinux/BUILD; this is where the files are placed, and where other stages will operate. This is referred to as the *BUILD directory*. Usually the directory is created because the source TAR file includes a top-level directory. However, you can also create a directory yourself, using commands or directives in the `%Prep` section script.

Usually, when setting up the %Prep section, you examine the source TAR file to see whether it includes a top-level directory. This is a single directory (usually with the name of the software) that all the other files and directories are under when the files are extracted. If the TAR file doesn't include a single top-level directory, or uses one with a non-standard name, you might need to use special options with the %setup directive (described as follows) to get it to work.

You can use any commands you need to prepare the source files in the BUILD directory. However, there are two special directives that handle most of the actions that need to be performed. The %setup directive is used to extract the source files, and the %patch directive is used to apply patches.

These directives do the same thing that can be accomplished with regular commands in the shell script; however, it is better to use these directives because when %setup or %patch is used they reference the source file or patch file, respectively, by number instead of by filename. This reduces the number of times that the filenames appear in the SPEC file, making it easier to maintain. If these directives are used, when the SPEC file is modified to use different source or patch files, it only requires modifying the Source: and Patch: fields in the SPEC file header.

THE %setup DIRECTIVE: EXTRACTING THE SOURCE CODE

The default behavior of the %setup directive is to cd to the BUILD directory, extract the first source TAR file (indicated by the Source0: field in the SPEC file), and then cd into the BUILD directory. It also sets the ownership and permission of the files in the BUILD directory.

Following is the sequence of commands that the %setup directive performs when used with no options and a hypothetical source file (Source0:) of kludge-0.1.tgz:

```
cd /usr/src/OpenLinux/BUILD
rm -rf kludge-0.1
/bin/gzip -d /usr/src/OpenLinux/SOURCE/kludge-0.1.tgz
tar -xvvf /usr/src/OpenLinux/SOURCE/kludge-0.1.tgz
cd kludge-0.1
chown -R root .
chgrp -R root .
chmod -R a+rX,g-w,o-w
```

Note that by default, %setup removes the BUILD directory and all its contents. If you work with multiple source files and use multiple %setup directives, you need to use the -D option (described later) to suppress this behavior.

It is tempting to use the BUILD directory to actually work on the files for the package when you are making modifications and patches. This is a bad practice because these files get wiped out every time you build the package. Instead, keep your work directories elsewhere, or you risk inadvertently losing important work.

Notice that at the end of the prep stage, the current directory is the BUILD directory. The scripts for the other stages of the build process operate from this directory, unless you specifically change the directory in those scripts.

Normally, `rpm` expects the BUILD directory name to consist of the package name followed by the version number (for example, `ed-0.2`). If the TAR file specifies a different top-level directory for the source files, `rpm` gets confused. Use the `-n` option with the `%setup` directive to specify a different BUILD directory name.

Following are the options to the `%setup` directive:

- `-n name`—Specify the different name for the BUILD directory. This name will match the name of the root directory of the source TAR file, unless it doesn't have one. In this case, it can be anything you want, and you need to use the `-c` option.

  This name is used with the `rm` and `cd` commands of the setup script. If you use multiple `%setup` directives, this option, with the same name, needs to be included in each one.
- `-c`—Create the BUILD directory and change to it before extracting the contents of the source TAR file. This is useful for TAR files that have no single top-level directory.
- `-b #`—Extract the contents of source file # before changing into the BUILD directory. This is used to extract additional source files besides Source0. This option can be used with the same `%setup` directive that extracts Source0.
- `-a #`—Extract the contents of source file # after changing into the BUILD directory. This is used with additional source files besides the Source0, when TAR files don't have their own top-level directory.
- `-T`—Don't extract Source0 as part of this `%setup` directive. This is used when multiple `%setup` directives are used with either the `-a` or `-b` option.
- `-D`—Don't delete the BUILD directory before extracting the indicated source file. This is used when multiple `%setup` directives are used, and is critical. Make sure that this option is used in *all* subsequent `%setup` directives, after the first one.

THE `%patch` DIRECTIVE: APPLYING PATCHES

The `%patch` directive is used to apply patches to the source code after it has been extracted. The primary reason to use this directive instead of using the `patch` program directly is, once again, to make the SPEC file easier to maintain. This directive essentially runs `patch` with the appropriate patch file (as indicated by the number). If no number is specified, it is assumed to be 0:

- **#**—Indicates the number of the patch to apply. This is put directly after the `%patch` directive, as in `%patch1`.
- **`-p#`**—Passed as the `-p#` option to the patch program.

The -p option with this directive is passed directly as the -p option to the patch program. The patch program uses this option to strip path elements from the filenames in the patch file so that it can determine the correct file in the source tree to work on.

THE ed SAGA CONTINUES

In order to build a package with the new and improved ed program you've been working on, you need to add a few things to the SPEC file. For the sample modification to ed, edit the SPEC file for ed and add the lines necessary to apply the patch made earlier in this chapter.

Add a reference to your patch file, and add a %patch directive to the %Prep section of the file.

Here's how the patch reference will look:

```
Patch: ed-main.patch
```

This line will be added just under the Source0 line in the file.

You also need to add a %patch directive to the %Prep section of the SPEC file. Add this after the %setup directive, which extracts the source files for ed. The format for this is as follows:

```
%patch -p1
```

The -p1 option is used to strip the first element off the filename inside the ed-main.patch file. This patch file was made one directory above the location of the source file, but the patch is applied in the same directory as the source file. Therefore, one path element must be removed from the filename inside the patch file in order for patch to find the correct file to operate on.

Now test the prep stage of the build process by changing to the SPECS directory and typing the following command:

```
rpm -bp ed-0.2.spec
```

You might want to redirect the output to a file, or pipe it through more, so that you can review it.

THE BUILD STAGE

The build stage is where rpm actually compiles the software for your system, using the script in the %Build section. Often this script includes running programs such as configure, to set up the software build environment, and make, to actually compile the software.

No special directives are available for this section of the SPEC file. However, rpm sets several shell variables that have values that might be useful for this script.

The following shell variables are available for your use throughout the scripts in the SPEC file:

- **RPM_SOURCE_DIR**—Location of RPM SOURCES directory. This is /usr/src/OpenLinux/SOURCES by default, but can be overridden by configuration values in /etc/rpmrc or ${HOME}/.rpmrc.
- **RPM_BUILD_DIR**—Location of RPM BUILD directory. This is /usr/src/OpenLinux/BUILD by default. This can also be overridden.
- **RPM_DOC_DIR**—Location at which the document directory for this package is placed. The default value is /usr/doc.
- **RPM_OPT_FLAGS**—String of compiler options for producing optimized code for the target architecture (i386). This is often used with `make` during the compilation of the software.
- **RPM_OS**—String indicating the OS used during the `build` process.
- **RPM_ARCH**—String indicating the architecture during the `build` process.
- **RPM_ROOT_DIR**—Root directory used during all steps of the `build` process.
- **RPM_BUILD_ROOT**—Root directory used for the install and packaging stages of the `build` process.
- **RPM_PACKAGE_NAME**—The name of the package.
- **RPM_PACKAGE_VERSION**—The version of the software in the package.
- **RPM_PACKAGE_RELEASE**—The release of the package.

To perform the prep and build stages of the `build` process for the `ed` package, change to the SPECS directory and type the following:

```
rpm -bc ed-0.2.spec
```

THE INSTALL STAGE

During the install stage, the commands are run to actually install the software onto your system. At the end of this stage, the software will be installed on your system, compiled, formatted, and ready to run, exactly as it needs to be on an end user's system. The shell script to perform this is found in the `%Install` section of the SPEC file.

Tip

Don't confuse this install step with the operation an end user performs when they install the package on their system. The install stage happens when you build the package, and is not something the user does. Although both result in the files for the package being placed on a system, they are two different things. Essentially, as a packager you are installing the software on your machine the hard way (using `make` commands or copying files individually), so that the end user can install the software on their machine the easy way (using the package manager).

The files put in a package during the packaging state (described in the next section) are taken from their regular positions in the working file system. Their placement, ownership, and permissions are recorded in the package so that they will have those same attributes on the user's system when the package is installed. Thus, it is critical that the install stage sets up the files completely and properly.

DECIDING WHERE TO INSTALL THE SOFTWARE

For this stage, you might need to decide where to place the software in the file system. If the installation mechanism provided with the original software gives you an option of where to put things, use the guidelines discussed in Chapter 9, "Understanding the Linux File System," to make your decisions. The general rule of thumb is that if you plan to distribute the package for use by others, you need to package it as a vendor would, with configuration files going into /etc, executable files going into /usr/bin, and so forth. Software from packages is usually placed under the /usr directory hierarchy, not under /usr/local. /usr/local is usually reserved for things that are not packaged, but it's up to you.

Most software installs into specific predetermined areas of your file system. Often the original software author knows best, and it is good to follow his placement policy.

Often, the `%Install` section contains just a reference to `make install`, possibly with some options to indicate file location preferences. Sometimes additional commands are used to format documentation or install other components of the software. This is exactly what the `%Install` section in the `ed` SPEC file does. It uses `make`, with an `install` option, followed by a command to compress the ed.info file (refer to Listing 16.1).

USING `BuildRoot` TO PROTECT YOUR SYSTEM

Unless you are using the `BuildRoot` feature of `RPM`, when the install stage is finished, the software will function properly on your system and be completely operational. This ensures that the resulting package will work on the end user's system. However, this system of installing the package files onto your running system might present problems with developing the package and testing it, especially if the package is for essential system components. For example, when packaging an important shared library, if something goes wrong while debugging the packaging process, you might be left with a crippled system because the library is actually replaced during the `build` process.

For this reason, `RPM` provides a facility to install and package the files from a separate directory tree instead of from the (live) file system. The way to do this is using the `BuildRoot` field in the SPEC file.

The `BuildRoot` field in the SPEC file specifies a different directory tree from which the files need to be installed and packaged, instead of from the regular locations in the file system.

Using `BuildRoot` requires that the mechanism used during the install stage is capable of placing files in different locations than usual. Many `makefiles` do not support this capability, but virtually all the packages provided by Caldera use `BuildRoot`.

BACK TO ed

To try the install stage for the `ed` package, make sure that you are in the SPECS directory, and use the following command:

```
rpm -bi ed-0.2.spec
```

THE PACKAGING STAGE

During this stage, the package file (binary `RPM` file) is actually created. The files that were placed into your file system during the install stage are collected and placed into the package file, along with information from the SPEC file. Also, all the materials used to produce the package are collected and bundled together into a source `RPM` package, which can be used (with a similar set of tools and libraries) to reproduce the package at a later date.

The `%Files` section of the SPEC file lists the files and directories on your file system that will be put into the package. This will correspond with the files that were placed on your file system during the install stage of the `build` process. It would be nice if `rpm` figured out this list automatically, but this is not really possible. One reason is that you might not want to package all the files that were installed during the install stage; another reason is that because Linux is a multitasking system, it is extremely difficult to guarantee that `rpm` will detect the right file list automatically. However, if there is a mechanism for your software to determine the files that will be put into the package, you can use that mechanism to write the list to a file, and use the `-f` option to read that list for the `%Files` section.

The `%Files` section supports the following directives and options:

- **`%doc`**—Mark documentation files. These go in a directory under /usr/doc on the end user's system. Don't use this for man pages or other documents that have to reside in specific locations on the end user's system. Note that the paths listed with this directive are relative to the BUILD directory, not the regular file system. For example, in Listing 16.2, the NEWS file listed with the `%doc` directive refers to /usr/src/OpenLinux/BUILD/ed-0.2/NEWS, which will be placed on the user's system as /usr/doc/ed-0.2/NEWS when this package is installed.
- **`%config`**—Mark configuration files. These files get special handling during remove and upgrade operations on the user's machine.
- **`%dir`**—Indicates a directory. This causes `rpm` to package all the files in the indicated directory and all its subdirectories.
- **`-f`** ***`filename`***—The `-f` option used with the `%Files` section indicates to read the file list from a separate file. For example, the following line

  ```
  %File -f edlist
  ```

  reads the file list from the file /usr/src/OpenLinux/BUILD/ed-0.2/edlist, instead of from the SPEC file.

Caution

Be careful with listing directories in the file list. If an item in the file list is a directory, `rpm` interprets it as a `%dir` item, and reads all the files in it. This can end up placing a huge number of files (and not the right ones) in the package, if the directory is not correct.

At the end of this stage, there will be a binary package file in the RPM/i386 directory, and a source package file in the SRPMS directory, under /usr/src/OpenLinux.

`ed`, THE FINAL BUILD

From the SPECS directory, type the following command:

```
rpm -ba ed-0.2.spec
```

This will perform the entire `build` process and create new binary and source `RPM` packages for `ed`. The resulting packages will be as follows:

```
/usr/src/OpenLinux/RPMS/i386/ed-0.2-6.i386.rpm
/usr/src/OpenLinux/SRPMS/ed-0.2-6.src.rpm
```

If these files are there, you've successfully built your first package. Install the new `ed` package, and see if your changes are present by typing the following:

```
rpm -i /usr/src/OpenLinux/RPMS/i386/ed-0.2-6.i386.rpm
ed --help
```

If `ed` is already installed on your system, remove it with `rpm -e ed`; then try the preceding commands again.

PACKAGING MISCELLANY

This section has a few miscellaneous tips to help you debug the package building process. Also, some of the conventions used by Caldera for its packages are described. You might want to use similar techniques when you build packages—or you might want to avoid some of them—to increase the portability of your packages.

Finally, there are a few cautions about testing your packages on your own machine (the one used to build them), as well as some brief instructions for creating packages as a regular (non-root) user.

DEBUGGING THE `build` PROCESS

`rpm` executes the shell commands and scripts that it processes with the shell `set -x` option set. This means that in the output of `rpm`, commands that it executes are displayed with a plus sign in front of them. Output from these commands appears unmodified. You can use the output of `rpm` to determine what commands `RPM` is executing at each stage of the `build` process, for debugging purposes.

CALDERA SPEC FILE CONVENTIONS

Virtually all packages produced by Caldera use the `BuildRoot` feature of `RPM`. This means you can't just install the source `RPM` for a package, modify a few things, and rebuild it to get the software in the package installed on your system. For example, to make a quick patch, some people are accustomed to installing a source `RPM` on their system, running the prep stage of the `build` process, and then applying the patches and manually running the steps in the install stage. Because Caldera packages use `BuildRoot`, the software doesn't end up in the live part of the file system. With Caldera packages, you actually have to build the binary package and install it, or modify the SPEC file not to use `BuildRoot`, to do your own software patching.

USE OF `lisa` IN INSTALL/UNINSTALL SCRIPTS

Many of Caldera's packages use `lisa` (the installation and administration tool) to perform special operations during their postinstall or postuninstall scripts. For example, Listing 16.2 shows that the `ed` package uses `lisa` to install the `an` entry for `ed` into the info directory. Another common use of `lisa` is to create the symlinks for the SysV initialization system (that is, the symlinks for the various run levels, under /etc/rc.d).

The use of `lisa` makes packages not fully portable to other distributions of Linux because these do not have the `lisa` program installed. If you want to make a package that is completely portable to other distributions of Linux, you need to replace these references with commands that accomplish the same thing, or forego the feature that is being provided by `lisa` and simply remove the references.

TESTING YOUR PACKAGE

If you are not using `BuildRoot`, it can be difficult to test your package on the same system on which you are building it because the files for the software are installed on your system during the install stage. These can get confused with the files installed from the package when you are testing it.

You need to meticulously erase all traces of the software from your system before you do test installs of the package you have built. Otherwise, you risk using files left over from a build—not necessarily files that were installed from the package.

If you are not using `BuildRoot`, it is highly recommended that you test install the package on at least one other machine besides the one on which you built the package to verify that the file list is complete.

CREATING PACKAGES AS A REGULAR USER

All the discussion in this chapter has assumed that you can become the root user in order to build packages. However, you might not be able to do this. Packages can be built as a regular user. However, this requires using a ${HOME}/.rpmrc that specifies a different topdir instead of /usr/src/OpenLinux because regular users don't have permissions to access that directory or its subdirectories. Also, because a regular user doesn't usually have write access to the parts of the file system where files are normally installed, you need to use the `BuildRoot` feature for the install and packaging stages to work correctly.

SUMMARY

This chapter introduced you to package building, and stepped you through modifying and rebuilding a simple package that comes with your OpenLinux system.

All the source code for your OpenLinux system is available for you to modify and repackage if you want to do so. Packaging is really just the process of recording and automating the steps that you perform manually to build and install a program from source code on your system.

Use sources obtained from the Internet or a source package. Put information about the software, and shell scripts to build and install the software, into the SPEC file and actually create the package using the `rpm` command.

The techniques discussed here will enable you to refine or enhance the packages provided by Caldera, or to create your own packages of software, for your own or others' use.

For more information on the topics discussed here, refer to the following chapters:

- See Chapter 9 to learn more about directories and how they work with the file system.
- Chapter 13 has a section on shell programming. This is particularly relevant to building packages because most of the actions performed during the `build` process are the result of shell scripts in the SPEC file.
- Chapter 15 describes how to install and uninstall (and otherwise manipulate) packages using the `rpm` command. This chapter introduces many of the key concepts of packages discussed here.

CHAPTER 17

Building Custom Kernels

In this chapter

Building a custom kernel is not anything for the faint of heart, but it's not as intimidating as it might seem—after you successfully complete it once, that is. The key to successfully building a kernel is to understand each of the steps along the way and take the precautionary steps to recover from potential problems. It sounds more ominous than it really is, but after you've finished you'll be saying to yourself, "That wasn't so bad."

The Linux Kernel

The Linux kernel is similar to the engine for your car: Without the kernel, you're not going to get anywhere. It is the brain behind the software that controls your computer. It's easy to take for granted the aspects of how an operating system works, but it really is quite complex. Every aspect of the interaction between you and your computer is controlled, in some fashion, by the operating system. In everything from typing at the keyboard or moving your mouse to printing a file or accessing data across the network, the kernel plays a part.

Precautionary Prerequisites

Taking some precautionary steps when building a new kernel is strongly recommended. This enables you to recover in case the newly built and installed kernel fails to work properly. It doesn't take very long, and it can save you a great deal of time in the long run if things don't go as planned. The key is to make a copy of the current working kernel and provide a way for the boot loader to find it. The boot loader (LILO) provides a way for multiple boot images to be selected; it only takes three simple steps to accomplish this:

1. Make a copy of the current kernel.
2. Modify the boot loader configuration file to recognize the new kernel.
3. Reinstall the boot loader.

Note

If you haven't already done so, you want to seriously consider performing a complete system backup before proceeding with a kernel rebuild. It is not mandatory, but it is good system administration practice to archive your environment before making any kind of changes to it.

Copying the Kernel

The Linux kernel is stored in the main directory of the Linux file system and is named vmlinuz.

Note

The Linux kernel, vmlinuz, is similar to the COMMAND.COM file in DOS.

Copying the kernel can easily be done using the following command:

```
# cd /
# cp vmlinuz vmlinuz.orig
```

You now have both vmlinuz and vmlinuz.orig in the directory list. Of course, you can name the kernel anything you want, but vmlinuz is the default name for which kernel configuration scripts are programmed.

MODIFYING THE LILO CONFIGURATION

The LILO boot loader enables you to specify several boot images. An additional boot image can be added by inserting another image section in the /etc/lilo.conf file. See Chapter 20, "Boot Loader," for further information on LILO. An example of a simple, single-image LILO configuration follows:


```
# general section
#
boot = /dev/hda
install = /boot/boot.b
message = /boot/message
prompt

# wait 20 seconds (200 10ths) for user to select the entry to load
timeout = 200

#
# default entry
#

image = /vmlinuz
        label = linux
        root = /dev/hda1
        read-only
#
#
```

The four lines in the default entry section must be duplicated and modified in order for the second boot image to be available at boot time. The image line and the label entry must be changed to accomplish this correctly. The image entry must match the kernel name that was copied in the previous step: `vmlinuz.orig`. The label entry must be unique. This label is the unique identifier that enables you to select between the choices that are configured in the /etc/lilo.conf file. The newly created image section in the /etc/lilo.conf file might look similar to the following:

```
image = /vmlinuz.orig
        label = linux.orig
        root = /dev/hda1
        read-only
```

The complete /etc/lilo.conf is constructed as follows:

```
# general section
#
boot = /dev/hda
```

```
install = /boot/boot.b
message = /boot/message
prompt

# wait 20 seconds (200 10ths) for user to select the entry to load
timeout = 200

#
# default entry
#

image = /vmlinuz
        label = linux
        root = /dev/hda1
        read-only
#
#  The original kernel image
#

image = /vmlinuz.ori
        label = linux.orig
        root = /dev/hda1
        read-only
#
```

REINSTALLING THE BOOT LOADER (LILO)

After the /etc/lilo.conf file is configured to include the additional boot image, you must reinstall the boot loader in order for it to be an option at boot time. Use the following command:

```
# lilo
Added linux *
Added linux.orig
```

Note

The preceding steps apply if LILO is used as the boot manager. If another boot loader, such as System Commander, is used, the documentation for the loader needs to be referenced for setup instructions.

After this step is complete, you can reboot; both selection options are available at the LILO boot prompt. You can now boot to the original kernel even if the new kernel fails to boot the system. You must enter the label name of the desired boot image in order for it to boot. Display the available boot options (labels) by pressing the Tab key.

Tip

You can use the install floppy to boot to an existing Linux partition by supplying the parameter `boot root=/dev/{device_name}`. Just replace `{device_name}` with the actual partition name (such as `hda1, hda2, ...` or `sda1, sda2, ...`).

BUILDING A NEW KERNEL

One distinct advantage with Linux is the capability to truly recompile the complete operating system, rather than just reconfiguring some of the system parameters. Because Linux comes complete with all the source code, you can optimize the code for a specific hardware configuration as well as design the kernel. The steps to building a new kernel are as follows:

1. Change to the /usr/src/linux directory.
2. Configure the parameters.
3. Check dependencies.
4. Clean up extraneous files from any previous kernel builds.
5. Compile the kernel.
6. Compile the loadable modules.
7. Install loadable modules.
8. Reboot the system and try the newly built kernel.

GO TO THE KERNEL SOURCE DIRECTORY (STEP 1)

The source code for the Linux kernel is located in the /usr/src/linux directory. You must be in this directory when you are building a kernel—this is where all the necessary files are located for configuring and compiling a new kernel. You'll find that the Linux subdirectory in the /usr/src directory is only a symbolic link to the actual directory in which the source code is stored. For example, examining the details of /usr/src/linux reveals something similar to the following:

```
# ls -l /usr/src/linux
lrwxrwxrwx   1 root  root   12 Jan 12 09:35 /usr/src/linux -> linux-2.2.1
```

This link will change as later revisions of the kernel are installed. If you keep more than one revision of the kernel source tree on your system, just be sure to have the /usr/src/linux link pointed to the correct source tree when you are building a new kernel.

Note

You must be in the /usr/src/linux directory when you are running the `make` options.

CONFIGURE THE PARAMETERS (STEP 2)

This is the step in which you must select all the options that you want in the new kernel. Don't be intimidated by all the selections. The key to completing this step is to trust the default settings. If you come across a parameter that you don't understand, keep the default selection. There are actually three methods for creating the configuration file that is used in building a new kernel:

- `make config`
- `make menuconfig`
- `make xconfig`

Each of these options provides a method for configuring the desired parameters in building a kernel; however, they differ greatly in ease of use. Of course, this is all a matter of personal preference. Option number one is a simple, text-based, sequential script. It looks somewhat similar to the following:

```
# make config
rm -f include/asm
( cd include ; ln -sf asm-i386 asm)
/bin/sh scripts/Configure arch/i386/config.in
#
# Using defaults found in arch/i386/defconfig
#
*
* Code maturity level options
*
Prompt for development and/or incomplete code/drivers (CONFIG_
EXPERIMENTAL) [Y/n/?] y
*
* Loadable module support
*
Enable loadable module support (CONFIG_MODULES) [Y/n/?] y
Set version information on all symbols for modules (CONFIG_MODVERSIONS)
[Y/n/?]
```

The second option, like the first, is not dependent on an X Window environment, but it's not a sequential script. In other words, you have the capability to select options and make changes in any desired order. The main screen for `make menuconfig` looks somewhat similar to the following:

```
------------------------------ Main Menu ------------------------------
 | Arrow keys navigate the menu. <Enter> selects submenus --->.        |
 | Highlighted letters are hotkeys. Pressing <Y> includes, <N> excludes |
 | <M> modularizes features. Press <Esc><Esc> to exit, <?> for Help.   |
 | Legend: [*] built-in  [ ] excluded  <M> module  < > module capable  |
 | |-------------------------------------------------------------|    |
 | |      Code maturity level options  --->                      |    |
 | |      Loadable module support  --->                          |    |
 | |      General setup  --->                                    |    |
 | |      Floppy, IDE, and other block devices  --->             |    |
 | |      Networking options  --->                               |    |
 | |      SCSI support  --->                                     |    |
 | |      Network device support  --->                           |    |
 | |      ISDN subsystem  --->                                   |    |
 | |      CD-ROM drivers (not for SCSI or IDE/ATAPI drives)  ---> |    |
 | |      File systems  --->                                     |    |
 | |------.(+)---------------------------------------------------|    |
 |----------------------------------------------------------------|-  |
 |                  <Select>    < Exit >    < Help >                  |
 |--------------------------------------------------------------------|
```

The last option is by far the easiest to use, but you must be in the X Window environment to use it. The initial screen is displayed by running the following from a shell prompt:

```
# cd /usr/src/linux
# make xconfig
```

Initially, some necessary pieces are compiled, and then a dialog box is displayed (see Figure 17.1).

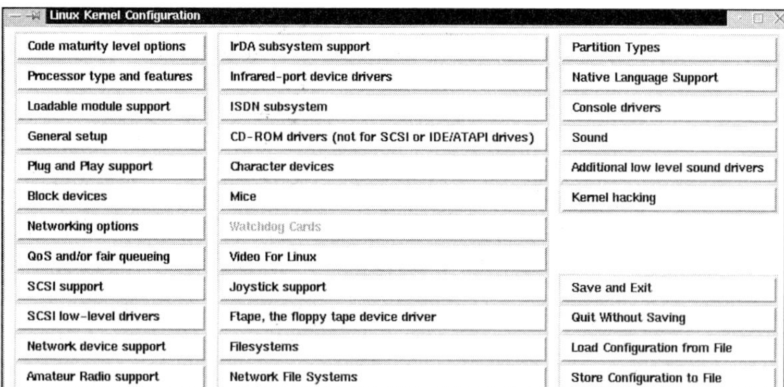

Figure 17.1
The X Window-based kernel configuration screen.

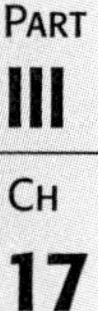

Click the desired category for a complete list of configurable options. For example, selecting the Network options category displays the dialog box that is depicted in Figure 17.2.

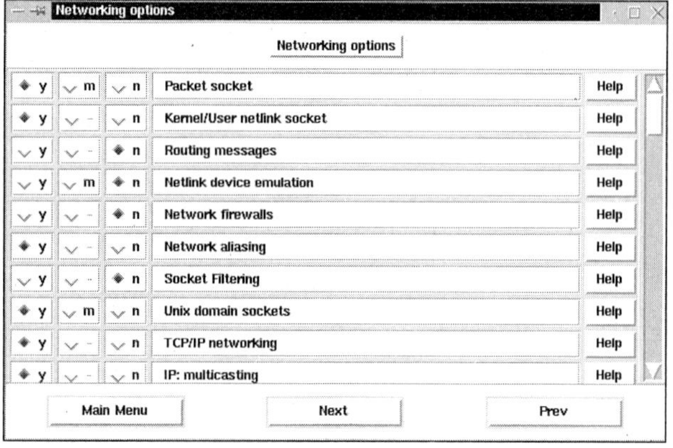

Figure 17.2
The Networking options dialog box.

Each listed option has two or three configurable settings: `y`, `m`, or `n`. The definition of these settings is described in Table 17.1.

TABLE 17.1 KERNEL CONFIGURATION SETTINGS

Settings	Value	Description
y	yes	Select this setting to include support for the corresponding option and build it directly into the kernel.
m	module	Select this setting to create a loadable module for the corresponding option. A module can be loaded or removed dynamically. Rebooting the system is not required.
n	no	Select this setting to disable any support for the corresponding option.

You'll find that some options are not available as modules, so the module option is not offered. Also, some options are dependent upon other options being enabled. If the setting choices are grayed out, the option upon which it is dependent has been set to No. Simply enabling the master option enables you to then select support for the dependent option.

Remember that there are many choices in a wide range of categories. If you're not familiar with what a particular option does, click the Help button for further information. If it's still not clear what a particular option does, leave the default setting.

The X Window-based kernel configuration program provides the capability to save and load previously saved configuration files. This can be quite handy when you're first learning to set kernel options.

SUMMARY OF KERNEL CONFIGURATION OPTIONS

Each of the preceding three options creates a file in the /usr/src/linux directory named .config. This file contains the parameter selections that are defined by the previous steps. In fact, if you really want to, you can hand-edit this file and make any desired changes, although that is not the recommended method of making changes.

> **Note**
>
> There is no .config file until after you complete the `make config`, `make menuconfig`, or `make xconfig` step for the first time. You might want to make a backup copy of this file before configuring subsequent kernel configurations. The original system default kernel configuration file can be found in the /usr/src/linux/arch/i386 directory.

As you can see from the category options that are listed in Figure 17.1, there is a wide range of selections, including some kernel configuration categories that have been added since the previous major kernel release. These new categories include the following:

- Processor type and features
- Plug and Play support
- QoS and/or fair queuing
- IrDA subsystem support

- Infared-port device drivers
- Video for Linux
- Joystick support
- Additional low level sound drivers

Check Dependencies (Step 3)

The `make dependencies` step is the step that checks the dependencies of the selections you made in the previous .config step. It ensures that the required files can be found, and it builds a list that is to be used in the compile step. This step actually starts off by compiling the `mkdep.c` program that is then run to complete this task. This only occurs the first time you run this script. You'll notice that as the program runs, it actually changes into the directory for each requested component. An excerpt from the `make dep` process might look similar to the following:


```
make[1]: Entering directory `/usr/src/linux-2.2.1/arch/i386/boot'
make[1]: Nothing to be done for `dep'.
make[1]: Leaving directory `/usr/src/linux-2.2.1/arch/i386/boot'
scripts/mkdep init/*.c > .depend
scripts/mkdep `find /usr/src/linux-2.2.1/include/asm /usr/src/linux-2.2.1
/include/linux /usr/src/linux-2.2.1/include/scsi /usr/src/linux-2.2.1/
include/net -follow -name \*.h ! -name modversions.h -print` > .hdepend
make _sfdep_kernel _sfdep_drivers _sfdep_mm _sfdep_fs _sfdep_net _sfdep_
ipc _sfdep_lib _sfdep_arch/i386/kernel _sfdep_arch/i386/mm _sfdep_arch/
i386/lib _sfdep_arch/i386/math-emu _FASTDEP_ALL_SUB_DIRS="kernel drivers
mm fs net ipc lib arch/i386/kernel arch/i386/mm arch/i386/lib arch/i386/
math-emu"make[1]: Entering directory `/usr/src/linux-2.2.1'
make -C kernel fastdep
make[2]: Entering directory `/usr/src/linux-2.2.1/kernel'
/usr/src/linux-2.2.1/scripts/mkdep acct.c capability.c dma.c exec_domain.
c exit.c fork.c info.c itimer.c kmod.c ksyms.c module.c panic.c printk.
c resource.c sched.c signal.c softirq.c sys.c sysctl.c time.c > .depend
make[2]: Leaving directory `/usr/src/linux-2.2.1/kernel'
make -C drivers fastdep
make[2]: Entering directory `/usr/src/linux-2.2.1/drivers'
/usr/src/linux-2.2.1/scripts/mkdep  > .depend
```

This step creates two files, .depend and .hdepend. These two files are used during the compile step. The contents of the .depend file look similar to the following:

```
init/main.o: \
   /usr/src/linux-2.2.1/include/linux/proc_fs.h \
   /usr/src/linux-2.2.1/include/linux/unistd.h \
   /usr/src/linux-2.2.1/include/linux/ctype.h \
   /usr/src/linux-2.2.1/include/linux/delay.h \
   /usr/src/linux-2.2.1/include/linux/utsname.h \
   /usr/src/linux-2.2.1/include/linux/ioport.h \
   /usr/src/linux-2.2.1/include/linux/init.h \
   /usr/src/linux-2.2.1/include/linux/smp_lock.h \
   /usr/src/linux-2.2.1/include/linux/blk.h \
   /usr/src/linux-2.2.1/include/linux/hdreg.h \
   /usr/src/linux-2.2.1/include/asm/io.h \
   /usr/src/linux-2.2.1/include/asm/bugs.h \
```

```
$(wildcard /usr/src/linux-2.2.1/include/config/pci.h) \
/usr/src/linux-2.2.1/include/linux/pci.h \
$(wildcard /usr/src/linux-2.2.1/include/config/dio.h) \
/usr/src/linux-2.2.1/include/linux/dio.h \
$(wildcard /usr/src/linux-2.2.1/include/config/zorro.h) \
/usr/src/linux-2.2.1/include/linux/zorro.h \
$(wildcard /usr/src/linux-2.2.1/include/config/mtrr.h) \
/usr/src/linux-2.2.1/include/asm/mtrr.h \
$(wildcard /usr/src/linux-2.2.1/include/config/apm.h) \
/usr/src/linux-2.2.1/include/linux/apm_bios.h \
```

Clean up Extraneous Files (Step 4)

The `make clean` step is nothing more than what its name implies. This step removes object code and other files that were created during a previous kernel compilation. An excerpt from the `make clean` process looks similar to the following:

```
make[1]: Entering directory `/usr/src/linux-2.2.1/arch/i386/boot'
rm -f tools/build
rm -f setup bootsect zImage compressed/vmlinux.out
rm -f bsetup bbootsect bzImage compressed/bvmlinux.out
make[2]: Entering directory `/usr/src/linux-2.2.1/arch/i386/boot/
compressed'
rm -f vmlinux bvmlinux _tmp_*
make[2]: Leaving directory `/usr/src/linux-2.2.1/arch/i386/boot/
compressed'
make[1]: Leaving directory `/usr/src/linux-2.2.1/arch/i386/boot'
rm -f kernel/ksyms.lst include/linux/compile.h
rm -f core `find . -name '*.[oas]' ! -regex '.*lxdialog/.*' -print`
rm -f core `find . -type f -name 'core' -print`
rm -f core `find . -name '.*.flags' -print`
rm -f vmlinux System.map
rm -f .tmp*
rm -f drivers/char/consolemap_deftbl.c drivers/video/promcon_tbl.c
rm -f drivers/char/conmakehash
rm -f drivers/sound/bin2hex drivers/sound/hex2hex
if [ -d modules ]; then \
        rm -f core `find modules/ -type f -print`; \
fi
```

Compile the Kernel (Step 5)

This is the step that actually compiles each piece of source code that is requested at the configuration step. Depending on the speed of your system, and to a certain extent on the selected components, this step might take awhile. As with the kernel configuration step, there are three methods of completing this step:

- `make zImage`
- `make zdisk`
- `make zlilo`

Each of preceding steps compiles a new kernel. The steps that occur after the kernel is compiled, however, differ.

`make zImage`

This is the standard step that does nothing more than compile a new kernel. If all components compile correctly, a new kernel can be found in the /usr/src/linux/arch/i386/boot directory. The new kernel is aptly named zImage. Of course, this is nothing more than a compiled kernel. You must configure the boot loader, that is LILO, to find the new kernel and boot. This is normally done by copying the `zImage` file to /vmlinuz, running `lilo` to reinstall a new boot loader, and then rebooting the system.

`make zdisk`

This method performs exactly the same task as the `make zImage` method, but after the compilation is complete, it automatically copies the newly built kernel to a floppy disk. This new disk can then be used to boot the system; the new kernel will then be active. This method is typically used to test a kernel with the system on which it was built, or it is used in testing the kernel on other hardware.

`make zlilo`

This is the recommended method of building and installing a new kernel. However, it is strongly recommended that you follow the steps that were outlined in the beginning of this chapter. This enables you to still boot the original kernel in the event that something fails to work. This method is exactly like the `make zImage` method, except that it automatically performs the steps that are manually outlined with it. In other words, after the compilation completes, the newly built kernel is copied to the / directory as vmlinuz (a backup copy is made of the original vmlinuz), and `lilo` is run to reinstall the boot loader (to recognize the new kernel).

Compile the Loadable Modules (Step 6)

This step compiles all the components as modules that were flagged as such in the configuration step. The modules must match the kernel with which they are intended to work. See Chapter 18, "Kernel Modules," for further information on working with loadable modules.

Install the Modules (Step 7)

This step copies all the newly compiled modules to the /lib/modules directory, where they are accessible for insertion into the kernel. Because modules must work with the kernel for which they were built, OpenLinux utilizes a special method of automatically loading modules at boot time. Currently, a manual step is required to have modules continue to load automatically at boot time. Again, see Chapter 18 to learn how to complete this task.

Reboot the System (Step 8)

This is the easy step is this process. Sometimes it takes a little faith that what you've configured will work, but if you've followed the steps in the "Precautionary Prerequisites" section, you can probably recover if your newly built kernel fails to cooperate.

Note

Make sure you either use the `make zlilo` option or that you manually run `/sbin/lilo` after you install the new kernel. Failing to do this, a common mistake, causes a kernel panic when you are attempting to boot because the boot loader is unable to find the newly built kernel.

SUMMARY

Building a new Linux kernel can seem quite ominous the first time you try it, but don't let that stop you. If you follow the outlined steps, you can recover if something doesn't work. With the safety net in place, you can have fun investigating the many, many possible kernel configuration options and build a kernel to suit your exact needs. For more information, check out the following chapters:

- See Chapter 18 for more information on how to use loadable modules as opposed to building support directly into the kernel.
- See Chapter 20 for more information on the boot loader (LILO) and how it works with the Linux kernel.
- See Chapter 29, "IP Masquerading," for more information on the kernel components that are required to configure for this capability.
- Chapter 30, "IP Firewalling," for more information on what is required in the kernel to enable this funcionality.

CHAPTER 18

Kernel Modules

In this chapter

In operating systems such as DOS (and in operating environments such as the many flavors of Windows), a kernel is incorporated to handle most of the low-level tasks that are expected of an operating system, such as interaction with the CPU, memory management, and so on. These kernels are supplemented with smaller chunks of code for those items that can not be compiled into the kernels themselves for whatever reason.

A good example of this is a driver for a piece of hardware. How could the operating system manufacturer know you were going to be using that particular piece of hardware on your system? Obviously, there is no conceivable way to know this information ahead of time, so mechanisms are put in place that allow these items to be loaded after the operating system is shipped and installed.

In DOS systems, these drivers and other loadable chunks of operating system code can be installed by adding lines to the CONFIG.SYS and/or AUTOEXEC.BAT files. In environments such as the various Windows offerings, there are .INI files that can accomplish this task. Other systems have their own methods for doing this, but in the end it all boils down to the same thing: Features and drivers can be added to the operating system after it has been shipped and installed.

Linux is no exception. As was indicated in Chapter 17, "Building Custom Kernels," recompiling the kernel is a viable option when adding hardware or enabling new features. In fact, if the items that are being added are (for lack of a better term) permanent, compiling support into the kernel is probably the best all-around option.

Kernel compilation is rarely required, however, because of the loadable module facilities that are included with modern Linux distributions. With modules, you can simply plug in the features or drivers that you want to include and leave out the rest. This saves on memory and enables you to add or remove features and drivers without recompiling the kernel. Another added benefit of the modularity of Linux kernels is that these items can be added or removed without even rebooting your Linux system (see Figure 18.1).

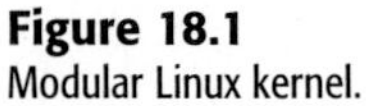
Figure 18.1
Modular Linux kernel.

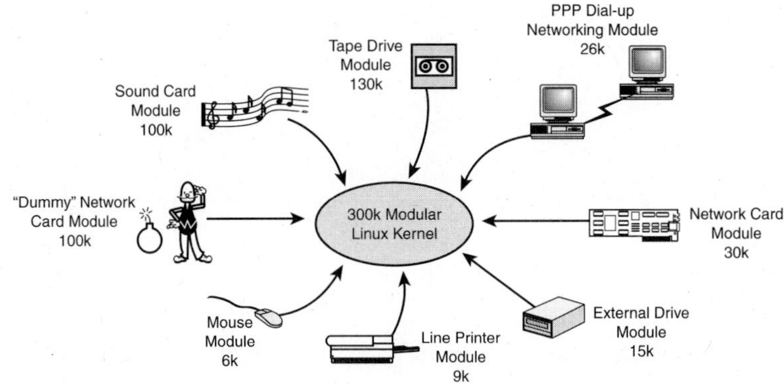

When a Linux kernel is compiled to include modular support for various optional drivers, the modules themselves are stored in a directory under /lib/modules, which matches the version number of the kernel with which they are associated. So if a version 2.2.1 kernel is compiled to use modules for some of its supported drivers, the modules are stored under the /lib/modules/2.2.1 directory. This way, if more than one version of the Linux kernel is compiled to include optionally loaded modules, the different kernels' modules are not mixed.

The classifications of modules are further broken down under /lib/modules/2.2.1 to group the modules into logical sets (see Listing 18.1). These sets are described fairly clearly by the names of the subdirectories in which they are contained.

Listing 18.1 Subdirectories Under /lib/modules/2.#.##

```
drwxr-xr-x   2 root     root         1024 Sep 28 15:11 block
drwxr-xr-x   2 root     root         1024 Sep 28 15:11 cdrom
drwxr-xr-x   2 root     root         1024 Sep 28 17:26 fs
drwxr-xr-x   2 root     root         1024 Sep 28 15:11 ipv4
drwxr-xr-x   2 root     root         1024 Dec  4 11:52 misc
drwxr-xr-x   2 root     root         1024 Sep 28 15:11 net
drwxr-xr-x   2 root     root         1024 Sep 28 15:11 scsi
drwxr-xr-x   2 root     root         1024 Sep 28 15:11 sound
```


The subdirectories contain the following items:

- **block**—Drivers for various block devices, such as IDE hardware (tapes, CD-ROM drives, removable drives), are stored here.
- **cdrom**—This subdirectory contains proprietary CD-ROM drivers (that is, drivers for CD-ROM drives that are neither IDE/ATAPI nor SCSI).
- **fs**—Modules that cover support for different file systems (NFS, ISO9660, and so on) are stored in this subdirectory.
- **ipv4**—This is the typical location of modules that offer TCP/IP networking services, such as those used for PPP and SLIP dial-up networking, IP masquerading, and IP aliasing (these are all discussed in Part IV, "Networking with OpenLinux").
- **misc**—When a module simply does not fit into any of the other categories, it goes here. The most common module stored here is the iBCS module (Intel Binary Compatibility System), which offers Linux users binary compatibility with some applications that were written to be run under SCO UNIX and other variants of their operating system. Also found here are modules for sound card drivers and PCMCIA hardware.
- **net**—Simply put, if there is a module that is compiled to support a network card, it is placed here.
- **scsi**—Various modules that are applicable to SCSI hardware, including drivers for SCSI interface cards, hard drives, CD-ROM drives, and SCSI generic devices such as CD writers and scanners.
- **sound**—Newer Linux kernels use a modularized version of the free OSS (Open Sound System) sound card driver (details on the commercial version are available in Chapter 42, "Multimedia"). This subdirectory contains all the modules that comprise the driver suite.

MODULE VERSIONS

By default, when recompiling a Linux kernel, all the modules that are to be loaded with the new kernel have to be recompiled as well. This can get to be a tedious process, especially if the system on which the kernel is being compiled uses legacy hardware. Compilation of the kernel can take a long time on slow hardware, so cutting down on the time required to do a compilation is desirable.

There is, however, a method by which modules can be reused without recompiling them; this option is available during the kernel configuration process (see Chapter 17, which goes into configuration in detail). If you activate the following option

```
Set version information on all symbols and modules
```

version information is set on all modules that will allow the modules to be loaded with any kernel that matches the version of the kernel against which the modules were compiled. In other words, a Linux kernel that is at version 2.2.1 loads modules compiled for 2.2.1 kernels as long as the symbols within the module are set at version 2.2.1 as well.

Note

Kernel modules essentially have two version numbers: one *internal* (referencing symbols within the module) and one *external* (referencing the version that the driver author assigned to the driver). It is the internal version number that is set to match the Linux kernel with which the module was compiled. This sets up the kernel/module association that prevents the module from loading on different versions of the Linux kernel.

This is a very useful feature, especially if the modules that are being used did not ship with the kernel sources (that is, iBCS, PCMCIA). Modules that are external to the kernel sources can be reused as long as the overall kernel version against which the module was compiled remains the same. Moving from a 2.2.1 kernel to a 2.0.36 kernel causes a 2.2.1 compiled module load to fail because the overall version of the kernel does not match the symbols within the module. In a case like this, the following error message is displayed:

```
Error: The module was compiled on kernel version 2.2.1.
       This kernel is version 2.0.36. They don't match!
       Check that the module is usable with the current kernel,
       recompile the module and try again.
```

Another error message that you might receive looks like the following:

```
Loading failed! The module symbols (from linux-2.2.1) don't match your
➥linux-2.0.36
```

Either way, the errors are descriptive enough to tell you what the problem is. Recompile the modules for the kernel (being sure to set versions on all the module symbols), and the modules load.

MODULE MANAGEMENT

Kernel modules can be loaded manually as well as automatically. Typically, a system administrator starts off manually loading modules until he becomes familiar with the process (and with which modules he really wants to load on a regular basis); he then moves on to loading modules automatically.

Familiarity is not the only reason to do this, however. Many modules require that special behavior-altering parameters be passed to them before they can load successfully. Without experimenting with these parameters and figuring out exactly which ones are needed, a few things might happen.

Sometimes the module might load with incorrect settings, such as those for the interrupt and I/O port. These two settings have not prohibited the older 3c509 Ethernet card driver from loading, which gives the appearance of successfully adding support for the card while actually just acting as a red herring.

Also, the autoprobing process might dramatically extend the time that is required to boot the system. A good example of this is the driver for SoundBlaster CD drives (sbpcd.o), which probes a rather long list of drives before giving up, thus adding a solid five to ten minutes to the time that is required to boot your system.

In most cases, without module parameters being passed, modules do not load at all. A solid example of this is the Sony CDU-31a driver (cdu31a.o), which does absolutely no autoprobing for hardware; therefore, it does not load unless it is told explicitly where your hardware can be found.

Caution

It is very important to make a distinction between boot parameters and module parameters. Module parameters are passed to a kernel module at the time that the module is loaded, and they only apply to kernel drivers that are compiled as modules. Boot parameters are parameters that are passed to the kernel itself to alter the behavior of drivers that are compiled directly into the kernel. Boot parameters are passed at the LILO boot prompt (or through LILO itself using the `append=` tag in /etc/lilo.conf). For more information regarding passing boot parameters with LILO, see Chapter 20, "Boot Loader."

Unfortunately, there is little or no consistency in the optional parameters from one module to the next, with the possible exception being module parameters for Ethernet cards—but even there some of the options differ from one module to the next. Therefore, getting to know the appropriate parameters for the modules that you are loading before automatically loading them can save you lots of grief. Refer to Appendix C, "Loadable Module Parameters," for information on the parameters that are offered on modules that ship with OpenLinux systems.

MANUAL LOADING

There are three utilities that are commonly used for manual module loading, unloading, and listing:

- **insmod**—Loads, or inserts, modules into the currently loaded/running kernel
- **rmmod**—Removes modules that are currently loaded
- **lsmod**—Lists the modules that are currently loaded

The syntax is fairly simple for each utility. To insert a module (for example, the bttv driver for BT848 based video capture cards), execute something like the following:

```
insmod bttv
```

To remove the module after loading it, run the following:

```
rmmod bttv
```

To get a verbose listing of what is going on when the module is being loaded, add the `-v` option:

```
insmod -v bttv
```

The output from this command resembles Listing 18.2.

LISTING 18.2 SAMPLE OUTPUT FROM `insmod -v`

```
[root@trident erik]# insmod -v bttv
Section 1: (.text) at 0x805ba50
Section 2: (.rel.text) at 0x8064100
Section 3: (.data) at 0x806121c
Section 4: (.rel.data) at 0x8064b68
Section 5: (.bss) at 0x806225c
Section 7: (.rodata) at 0x8061a50
Section 8: (.comment) at 0x8062247
Section 9: (.shstrtab) at 0x8064d78
Section 10: (.symtab) at 0x8064dd8
Section 11: (.strtab) at 0x80658d8
textseg = 0x805ba50
bss_size = 3208
last byte = 0x8062ee4
module size = 29844
versioned kernel: yes
versioned module: yes
ELF kernel
ELF module
[root@trident erik]#
```

The output is probably more interesting to kernel hackers and driver authors, but it is good to know how to get verbose listings in case strange errors are occurring when you are loading modules.

AUTOMATIC LOADING

There are three module autoloading methods available on OpenLinux systems:

- The modules are loaded by command lines that are added to the end of /etc/rc.d/rc.local.
- The "kmod" method, which loads modules on demand and unloads them when they are not needed anymore.
- The modules are loaded from a list in /etc/modules/2.#.## by a script.

By default, OpenLinux uses the third method, which is covered in this chapter.

In this method, a file residing in /etc/modules/*kernel-version#* contains a list of modules to load. Each module in this list is loaded by a script called `/etc/rc.d/rc.modules`. This script runs the `insmod` utility against each of the modules in the list. All this happens when the OpenLinux system is booted.

The file that contains the list of modules is named after the output of the following command:

```
uname -v
```

Note

If you are using OpenLinux 2.2 or higher, the module auto-load list no longer needs to be named from the output of the uname command above. You can simply name the file "default". Note that this will make the file kernel version independent (in other words, if your module list is named "default," an attempt will be made by your OpenLinux system to load all the modules in that list regardless of the version of the Linux kernel you are booting). If you tend to compile and boot multiple different Linux kernels and wish to have different sets of modules load with each one, follow the uname method detailed below.

This command produces a timestamp string on the currently loaded/running Linux kernel. A .default extension is added to the timestamp to complete the filename. For instance, if the output of running `uname -v` on the current kernel produced the following timestamp:

```
#1 Wed Mar 25 15:23:05 MST 1998
```

the resulting module list in /etc/modules/2.#.## is named

```
#1 Wed Mar 25 15:23:05 MST 1998.default
```

Note

This is just an example; your output from `uname -v` will be different.

Because of the way that the rc.modules script works with this file, there is no way any other kernel can load modules from this list except for the kernel that matches the timestamp after which the file is named. This way, different sets of modules can be loaded with different kernels. This is especially handy for people who enjoy experimenting with booting back and forth between different kernels (for instance, one stable kernel and one bleeding-edge

ALPHA grade kernel); each kernel has its own personal module autoload list that is never shared with the other versions of the kernel.

Whenever a kernel is compiled on an OpenLinux system, the module autoload list needs to be copied over (or renamed) to a file that matches the timestamp of the new kernel. The most common method for obtaining this timestamp is to boot the system with the kernel after it is compiled and then run the following command (replace `"#1 Wed Mar 25 15:23:05 MST 1998.default"` with the name of the existing module autoload list):

```
cp "#1 Wed Mar 25 15:23:05 MST 1998.default" "`uname -v`.default"
```

The single quotes that are used around `"uname -v"` are significant; use the single quotes that lean to the left—that is, the ones that are typically found on the tilde (~) key in the upper-left corner of the keyboard. Note that the single quote near the Enter key does not work. These single quotes tell the system to replace everything in between with the output of the command that is encased in the quotes. Therefore, the preceding command takes the existing module autoload list name and copies it over to a file built from the output of `"uname -v"`, and adds .default for the extension.

A slightly more complex method of obtaining the timestamp (but one that some favor because it does not require rebooting the computer) is to run the `strings` utility against the new kernel and search for distinctive characters (such as `1999`) using `grep`:

```
strings /vmlinuz ¦ grep 1999
```

Doing so produces the full timestamp—including some information that is unnecessary for the task. Using the timestamp, simply rename the existing file, choosing a name that matches the timestamp from the `#` to the end of the string, and add a .default extension to the end.

For example, if the previous command line produced

```
2.2.1 (root@trident.caldera.com) #11 Wed Feb 3 12:50:41 MST 1999
```

the command to rename the existing file might look like the following:

```
mv "#10 Mon Feb 1 12:33:00 MST 1999.default" "#11 Wed Feb 3 12:50:41
➥MST 1999.default"
```

With that done, when the computer is rebooted for the first time with the new kernel, the modules load just like they did with the former kernel.

The following is an example of a short module autoload list:

```
8390
ne
isp16
sbpcd
```

Because the rc.modules script loads these sequentially, it is essential to have modules in the proper order. For instance, in order for ne (the NE2000 Ethernet card driver) to load, the 8390 module must first be loaded, so 8390 appears before ne. Likewise, below that you see that the isp16 driver (which is a driver for a proprietary CD-ROM interface card) was needed before the sbpcd driver (which drives a number of proprietary SoundBlaster CD-ROM drives) could be loaded; therefore, isp16 preceded sbpcd. Not all sbpcd driven CD-ROM drives require that an isp16 driver be loaded, but this example helps illustrate that some drivers must be loaded before others.

In most cases, though, a module can be put anywhere in the autoload list and load correctly, as long as it is not dependent upon the existence of any other module or other preloaded kernel support. A good example of this is the Mitsumi proprietary CD-ROM driver (mcd)—it does not depend on any other drivers to load, so it can go anywhere.

What if there are parameters that must be passed to the modules? In the case of the ne module, parameters are absolutely required, at least to indicate an I/O port for the installed NE2000 card.

If parameters are required for any of the modules that are being loaded, they are typed up in text files that are named after the modules with which they are associated, and then they are placed in the /etc/modules/options directory.

Use the ne driver as an example; say that there is an NE2000 card at I/O port 0x320 and IRQ 11. To pass these parameters to an automatically-loaded ne module, create a file in /etc/modules/options called ne, which contains the following information:

```
io=0x320
irq=11
```

This file is read during boot time, and the parameters within are passed to the ne module at the time that it is loaded.

Each parameter (`io`, `irq`) needs to be on its own line. Settings within each parameter can be stacked and separated by commas, though, for cases where more than one device is being controlled by a module. In the case of the ne module, if there are two NE2000 cards in the system (a second one at I/O port 0x240 and IRQ 5, for example), the ne file in /etc/modules/options looks more like this:

```
io=0x320,0x240
irq=11,5
```

The first card that the computer sees needs to have its information listed first in each parameter line; the second card is listed after that, and so on. Some experimentation might be required for initializing items such as network cards in this manner, but the most that will be required is switching the order of the comma-delimited settings and rebooting the system until the order is correct.

MODULES NOT INCLUDED IN THE KERNEL SOURCES

Not all the modules that are considered to be part of a standard Linux system are included with the kernel source code. Some items—iBCS, ftape, and PCMCIA card services—are shipped external to the kernel sources but are included with almost every Linux distribution that is in existence today.

Under normal circumstances, there is no real reason to download, compile, and install an updated version of any of these packages. Occasionally, however, the need to do so arises. For instance, a new tape drive might be supported in the latest beta version of the `ftape` package, but it might not be supported in the version that shipped with OpenLinux. Likewise for PCMCIA hardware; occasionally a new card is supported only in a newer version of the `pcmcia-cs` package, so an upgrade is understandable.

It is always recommended that the package set that ships with OpenLinux be adhered to as long as is humanly possible. The assembly of packages on the CD are tested as a set, proven to work as a set, and are to be used as a set unless a serious need arises to break away and download updates. So be forewarned that—although there is little risk involved in performing an upgrade of any of these packages if you follow the directions—you are altering a tested, proven system; when you do so, you run the risk of having something not work exactly as it did before.

iBCS

The Intel Binary Compliance Standard (`iBCS`) package provides a number of items, including kernel patches, terminal definitions, hints, and (most importantly) a kernel module, all of which help provide the capability of running SCO and other SysV compiled applications on a Linux system. This was part of the Linux kernel source code a number of years ago, but it has since been moved out and has become its own entity. It has also matured significantly since its original inception. Applications such as WordPerfect and various Informix database packages that were compiled to run on SCO systems have been proven to run on Linux systems under iBCS emulation.

The following sections cover the definitive compatibility information for `iBCS`, lifted from the README file that is contained within the `iBCS` source code archive (author unknown).

SUPPORTED CPU ARCHITECTURES

- Intel 386/486/Pentium and compatibles
- Sparc

SUPPORTED BINARY FORMATS

- A.OUT (using standard Linux loader unless using BSD support)
- ELF (using standard Linux loader)
- COFF
- XOUT

SUPPORTED OS EMULATIONS

- Sparc Solaris
- i386 BSD (386BSD, FreeBSD, NetBSD, BSDI/386)—very alpha, very old. Effectively deprecated.

- SVR4 (Interactive, Unixware, USL, Dell and so on)
- SVR3 generic
- SCO (SVR3 with extensions for symlinks and long filenames)
- SCO OpenServer 5
- Wyse V/386 (SVR3 with extensions for symlinks)
- Xenix V/386 (386 small model binaries only)
- Xenix 286

SUPPORTED SUBSYSTEM EMULATIONS

- SYSV IPC
- /dev/socksys socket interface as used by the Lachman STREAMS based networking implementation
- BSD and Wyse V/386 system call socket interface
- /dev/spx STREAMS device
- XTI/TLI transports for TCP, UDP and related protocols—client only (outgoing connections). Accepting connections untested.

For the sake of simplicity, the terms SysV and SCO are used interchangeably in the remainder of this section, and are used to reference the preceding list (with the exception of Xenix 286 emulation; the reasoning for this will be apparent later).

The importance of this compatibility list is not lost to various SCO resellers and consultants. The capability to run existing applications with which clients are familiar on a Linux system enables resellers and consultants to install Linux in lieu of SCO. This significantly increases their profit margins, and at the same time increases the manageability of the system that is being installed. Remember, Linux is an Open Source operating system, so bug fixes can be distributed and implemented quickly. The long waits for bug fixes that are typical of other major commercial operating system companies simply disappear.

The main distribution location for the `iBCS` package is found at the following FTP site:

```
ftp://tsx-11.mit.edu/pub/linux/BETA/ibcs2
```

There, you find not only the latest version of `iBCS`, but also some "fake" shared libraries that are meant to emulate most of the basics of SCO's shared libraries. These fakes have been known to solve lots of problems with running modern SysV compiled applications. This is because most of the newer software that is compiled for SysV is dynamically linked, which means that the packages require the presence of certain shared libraries on your system before they can run.

It is questionable as to whether it is legal to place copies of SCO's shared libraries (more specifically, libc, libnsl, and protlib) on your OpenLinux system. We have not researched this, and are quite hesitant to suggest that it is okay even if the current license says that it is (licenses can change); so your best bet is to check the license for your copy of SCO and see if this is permitted. If so, many of your problems with running modern SCO applications on OpenLinux might be eliminated. Place the libraries in a directory called /shlib (you have to create this directory first) and you are set.

If you do not see any legal way to copy these libraries, the fake libraries might be of benefit. They are not perfect and there are some things they simply cannot do, but they are better than nothing.

Note

For what it is worth, OpenLinux ships with an RPM package that contains these fake shared libraries. These are sufficient if the fake libraries are desired; they do not seem to be updated frequently at all, so odds are that what is offered on the CD is the most recent set. If not, be sure to check the README.shlibs file on the iBCS distribution site for up to date information on how to install the latest versions of the fake libraries.

Even with a good set of shared libraries, some SCO applications might still not run under Linux. The applications that require the X Window system to run, for example, have proven to be a bit shaky in some situations. Regardless, the bulk of SCO applications can be run one way or another on OpenLinux using the iBCS package.

Compiling iBCS is not very difficult. If you perform the following steps, everything will compile correctly (use the ibcs-2.1-981105.tar.gz source code archive in the following examples:

1. As with most source code packages, the compressed archive needs to be copied to the /usr/src directory and extracted from there:

   ```
   cp ibcs-2.1-981105.tar.gz /usr/src
   cd /usr/src
   tar zxvf ibcs-2.1-981105.tar.gz
   ```

2. Change to the directory that was created when the source code archive was decompressed.
3. Because you are working with an Intel system, copy the CONFIG.i386 file over to CONFIG.
4. Load the new CONFIG file into an editor. Some lines need to be changed within.
5. There is an uncommented line in the CONFIG file that says

   ```
   SMP = yes
   ```

   This needs to be changed to say

   ```
   SMP = no
   ```

   if you are not running with multiple processors and SMP support compiled into the Linux kernel. If you are running multiple processors with SMP support, this line can safely be left as is.

Note

There is a reason why `iBCS` is set to compile the `iBCS` module for an SMP system by default: A non-SMP compiled `iBCS` module can load successfully to an SMP compiled Linux kernel, but will subsequently crash at some point after being `insmod`ed. However, an SMP compiled `iBCS` module does not load against a non-SMP kernel at all. It is safer for the `iBCS` module to be rejected by the kernel when it is inserted than it is to load the module and have the system crash afterward; therefore, the default is to compile `iBCS` for SMP systems.

6. The rule about setting version information on module symbols applies just as much to modules that are compiled outside the kernel source tree as it does within. Therefore, the line that says

   ```
   USE_VERSIONS = no
   ```

   needs to be changed to read

   ```
   USE_VERSIONS = yes
   ```

7. There might be some temptation to enable X286 emulation within the CONFIG file. Resist it. This support—for all intents and purposes—needs to be removed from the default package and offered as a patch. The x286emul capabilities of `iBCS` were all but abandoned a number of years ago. Because of this, it has not been updated very well to cover the new format of the a.out compiler packages that need to be installed on modern Linux distributions just to compile the support within `iBCS`. Unless there is a dire need to experiment with this emulation, just say "no" to x286emul.

8. The makefile in the top level `iBCS` source code directory is fine the way it is. Disregard any indications in the accompanying README file that the makefile has user-configurable options. They have all been relocated to the various CONFIG.*xxx* files.

9. There are some device files that SysV applications might require before they can run under `iBCS`. Unfortunately, the makedev system in OpenLinux does not include any facility to create these device files. Luckily, there is a `MAKEDEV.ibcs` script included with `iBCS` source code, which can make these devices for you. Simply execute either

   ```
   ./MAKEDEV.ibcs
   ```

   from the top level source directory or

   ```
   sh MAKEDEV.ibcs
   ```

   to run the script.

10. Compile `iBCS` by executing the following:

    ```
    make
    ```

    Manually copy the `iBCS` module over to its final destination:

    ```
    cd iBCSemul
    cp iBCS /usr/lib/modules/2.#.##/misc
    ```

Caution

> Executing `make install` installs `iBCS` (the module) to /lib/modules/2.#.##. You do not want to do this! The script that starts/loads `iBCS` in OpenLinux expects the module to be located in /usr/lib/modules/2.#.##/misc, so manually copy the ./iBCSemul/iBCS module to that location instead of running `make install`.

At that point, you are ready to load the module and start experimenting with SysV applications. To do so, the existing OpenLinux script that is contained within its `iBCS` package needs to be executed SysV-init style:

```
/etc/rc.d/init.d/iBCS start
```

If you have problems running your applications from other platforms, it is wise to check for solutions in the various hints, termcap customizations, and possible patches that ship with the source code to `iBCS`. These files can change from version to version, so cut-and-dried problem-to-solution mappings are not possible. The `iBCS` package is still considered to be beta software, so expect some experimentation if you plan to implement it.

ftape

Although they are not favored as an enterprise backup solution, floppy tape drives are quite popular in small businesses and homes. Mostly favored for their affordability, these devices provide a decent backup medium, albeit not as reliable as the more robust SCSI offerings such as DAT (Digital Audio Tape) devices.

Floppy tape drives—as indicated by their classification—share the floppy controller with floppy and disk drives. The `ftape` package (written by Claus-Justus Heine, `heine@math1.rwth-aachen.de`) strives to support these drives almost exclusively, with the possible exception of a few parallel port drives. Check the hardware compatibility listings in Appendix B, "Hardware Compatibility Lists," for lists of supported drives.

The main distribution site for the `ftape` package can be found at

```
http://www.math1.rwth-aachen.de/~heine/ftape/
```

Because new floppy (and parallel port) tape drives are released often, you might want to keep up with what the newest versions of `ftape` support. Occasionally someone will purchase a floppy tape drive and not have it work in OpenLinux by default (the hardware world moves rather fast), but the latest beta version of `ftape` might support it. Knowing how to update this package can prove to be useful if you are an owner—new or seasoned—of a floppy tape drive.

Compiling `ftape` for OpenLinux can be accomplished following these steps (ftape-4.03-pre-2.tar.gz is used in this example):

1. Download and copy the source code archive into /usr/src, and then decompress it:

   ```
   cp ftape-4.03-pre-2.tar.gz /usr/src
   cd /usr/src
   tar zxvf ftape-4.03-pre-2.tar.gz
   ```

2. Change to the directory in which the source code archive was decompressed.
3. The MCONFIG file in the top-level source code directory (to which you just changed) needs a few slight modifications:
   a. Comment out (add a # in front of) the line that reads

      ```
      BINDIR = $(PREFIX)/bin
      ```
   b. Create a replacement line that reads

      ```
      BINDIR = /bin
      ```
   c. By default, the CPU for which `ftape` is being compiled is 486 (as specified by the `CONFIG_M486=y` line). If you are not compiling this package to run on a 486, select the line that matches the CPU of the machine on which `ftape` is being compiled. All other `CONFIG_###` lines equal `n`.
   d. Uncomment `CONFIG_MODVERSIONS=y`. As has been mentioned a number of times, you always want versions set on module symbols.
   e. If you are running an SMP machine, uncomment the `SMP = 1` line. Otherwise, leave it alone.
   f. A number of options are given for various floppy (and other) controllers that are too extensive to go into here. Uncomment the `FDC_OPT` line that matches your hardware setup.
   g. In addition to that, a few items addressing bugs in GCC and a smattering of `ftape` compilation options are offered. Unless you feel the need to experiment, simply leave these lines alone.
4. There is a patches subdirectory off the top-level `ftape` source code tree that contains patches for various items that are found in different kernels. Some of these patches prevent bugs that might otherwise prevent `ftape` from doing its job well. These patches change from release to release, so the best thing to do is to check this directory in the version of the `ftape` source code you downloaded and extracted to see if there is anything that might affect your system. Do not be surprised if the directory is empty, though.

Note

If you patch the kernel, the kernel has to be recompiled afterward.

5. It is time to build the modules and associated utilities that comprise the `ftape` package. From within the top level `ftape` source code directory, execute the following:

   ```
   make
   ```
6. If no errors were encountered, execute

   ```
   make install
   ```

   to install everything in the locations that are specified in the MCONFIG file.

7. Odds are that the device files in /dev need to be created. To do this, run the following command:

   ```
   makedev --package ftape --all
   ```

   This generates the required qft#, nqft#, zqft#, nzqft#, rawft#, and nrawft# device files in the /dev directory.

Note

> The devices that start with an *N* are "non-rewinding" devices. If these devices are used to address your tape drive, the drive does not rewind the tape after finishing its job. Also, the devices with a *Z* in their names are devices that allow data compression.

8. There is a rather long sample script, called `insert`, in the modules subdirectory off the `ftape` source tree; this script tries to insert all the necessary modules in the `ftape` package (including the most important: ftape.o and zftape.o). You can use this script to load the necessary modules for floppy tape support, or you can use it as an example for writing your own autoload script. Otherwise, loading the modules using the method described in the first part of this chapter suffices, as does adding `insmod` entries to the end of /etc/rc.d/rc.local. Either way, load all the modules that are loaded in the `insert` script (examples of module parameters for the various `ftape` modules are included within).
9. Test the configuration by running a small backup. There are numerous backup software packages to choose from, but even running something such as

   ```
   tar cvf /dev/nqft0 /etc
   ```

   is sufficient.

If everything works, you have successfully installed `ftape` by hand. The biggest challenge at this point is finding a backup software package to suit your needs. Commercial packages such as `BRU` are good, as are free packages such as `amanda` and `taper`. Web search engines are perfect for locating these kinds of software packages.

Note

> Be sure to check Appendix C for details on module parameters for this package.

pcmcia-cs

The `pcmcia-cs` (PCMCIA Card Services) package offers drivers for PCMCIA chipsets and hardware (Ethernet cards, SCSI controllers, modems), mostly for laptop systems. It also offers beta quality support for CardBus, if it is compiled to do so.

One of the primary sources of confusion with this package is the fact that it is comprised entirely of modules, and therefore is not affected by the use of special boot parameters. So entering

```
ether=11,0x340,0,0,eth0
```

as a parameter when booting Linux does not pass any behavior altering information to the modules in the `pcmcia-cs` package (details on boot parameters and LILO are offered in Chapter 20).

In fact, regular module parameters that are passed in the manner that was detailed earlier in this chapter do not work either. The `pcmcia-cs` package uses its own set of configuration files for its modules, so in essence it is an island among the sets of modules. However, adjusting how the modules load and pass parameters to those modules are not overly complex tasks after you know where to look and what to edit.

The main distribution site for the `pcmcia-cs` package is located at the following FTP site:

`ftp://csb.stanford.edu/pub/pcmcia/`

There, you can find the most recent version of `pcmcia-cs`, pointers to configuration information for hardware that is not included in the default configuration files, and developer versions of the package (these are not for production systems—they are for testing purposes only). There is also extensive documentation included at that site in the form of the PCMCIA-HOWTO and the PCMCIA-PROG documents (the latter is intended for programmers).

The main Web site for Linux PCMCIA information is

`http://hyper.stanford.edu/HyperNews/get/pcmcia/home.html`

To build `pcmcia-cs` yourself, follow these instructions (pcmcia-cs-3.0.6.tar.gz is used in this example):

1. Download the `pcmcia-cs` package and extract it into /usr/src:

   ```
   cp pcmcia-cs-3.0.6.tar.gz /usr/src
   cd /usr/src
   tar zxvf pcmcia-cs-3.0.6.tar.gz
   ```

2. Configure the `pcmcia-cs` package in preparation for the actual compilation:

   ```
   make config
   ```

   This step runs a configuration script called `Configure` in the top level `pcmcia-cs` source code directory. It is generally safe to accept the defaults offered by the script (items such as the kernel source code directory and the compiler/linker names are okay as they are). But a few options for new and experimental features are offered, which you might or might not want to take advantage of.

   Listing 18.3 is sample output from `make config`.

LISTING 18.3 SAMPLE `make config` SESSION FOR `pcmcia-cs`

```
Linux PCMCIA Configuration Script

The default responses for each question are correct for most users.
Consult the PCMCIA-HOWTO for additional info about each option.
```

continues

PART III CH 18

LISTING 18.3 CONTINUED

```
Linux source directory [/usr/src/linux]:

The kernel source tree is version 2.0.35.
The current kernel build date is Wed Aug 19 12:57:30 1998.

Alternate target install directory []:
  Module install directory [/lib/modules/2.0.35]:
C compiler name [gcc]:
Linker name [ld]:
Compiler flags for debugging []:
Build 'trusting' versions of card utilities (y/n) [n]:
Include 32-bit (CardBus) card support (y/n) [n]:
Experimental interrupt probe code (y/n) [n]:

The PCMCIA drivers need to be compiled to match the kernel with which they
will be used, or some or all the modules might fail to load.
If you are not sure what to do, please consult the PCMCIA-HOWTO.

How would you like to set kernel-specific options?
    1 - Read from the currently running kernel
    2 - Read from the Linux source tree
    3 - Set each option by hand (experts only!)
Enter option (1-3) [1]:

Extracting kernel symbol versions...
Kernel configuration options:
    Symmetric multiprocessing support is disabled.
    Max physical memory in MB is 1024
    PCI BIOS support is enabled.
    Advanced Power Management (APM) support is disabled.
    SCSI support is enabled.
    Networking support is enabled.
     IPv6 support is disabled.
     Radio network interface support is disabled.
     Token Ring device support is enabled.
    Module version checking is enabled.
    PCMCIA IDE device support is enabled.
    DEC Alpha UDB target platform is disabled.
    /proc filesystem support is enabled.

Your module utilities are version 2.0.0.

System V init script layout (y/n) [y]:
Top-level directory for RC scripts [/etc/rc.d]:

X Windows include files not installed.
    If you want to build the 'cardinfo' PCMCIA control panel, you need
    to install the Forms Library, as well as the X Windows include files.
    See the HOWTO for details.
```

The kernel version and timestamp that are reported in the preceding capture might be different, but the rest of the script will closely resemble what you see.

In Listing 18.3, all the defaults were accepted except for the part that sets the kernel-specific options, at which time option one was selected (which reads settings from the currently running kernel). Note that if option two is selected (`Read from the Linux source tree`), the .config file /usr/src/linux, which contains kernel configuration settings, is required. If you have not previously run one of the kernel configuration routines to set options for a kernel recompilation, you do not have this file and therefore can not select option two. Selecting option one works well in most cases.

Option three—selecting each option by hand—simply prompts for settings for each of the kernel configuration options that are shown in Listing 18.3 (that is, SMP support, PCI BIOS support, and so on). No new configuration settings are offered if this option is chosen.

3. Compile the binaries and modules that make up the `pcmcia-cs` package:

   ```
   make all
   ```

4. Install all the binaries and modules in their proper places:

   ```
   make install
   ```

If an alternative directory was specified for installation during the `make config` step, the alternative directory becomes the equivalent of the root (/) directory during this installation step. Each subdirectory off the root directory that might have been affected (for example, /lib and some subdirectories off /etc) is duplicated off the alternative directory (that is, if a file was supposed to go in /etc/rc.d, it goes in /alternate-directory/etc/rc.d instead). This helps if the compiled binaries and modules are going to be packaged and moved to another system, or if there is no desire to overwrite an existing `pcmcia-cs` installation with a new version.

The configuration files for the `pcmcia-cs` package all reside in /etc/pcmcia (see Table 18.1).

TABLE 18.1 CONFIGURATION FILES FOR THE `pcmcia-cs` PACKAGE

Filename	Purpose
cdrom	Initialization script for PCMCIA CD-ROM device.
cdrom.opts	Contains configuration information for CD-ROM devices.
cis/	Directory containing CIS (Card Information Structure) information for various PCMCIA cards.
config	Main database of supported hardware and the modules associated with each device. Global, package-wide configuration information is stored here.
config.opts	Holds general configuration data for the `pcmcia-cs` package. Local configuration information is adjusted in this file, not the config file.
ftl	Initialization script for FTL flash memory cards (the only flash cards that are supported by `pcmcia-cs`).
ftl.opts	Contains configuration information for FTL flash memory cards.
`ide`	Initialization script for IDE adapters.
ide.opts	Holds general configuration data for IDE adapters.

continues

TABLE 18.1 CONTINUED

Filename	Purpose
`memory`	Initialization script for memory devices.
memory.opts	Contains configuration information for memory devices.
`network`	Initialization script for PCMCIA network hardware.
network.opts	Holds the networking (IP, IPX) information for PCMCIA network interfaces.
`scsi`	Initialization script for SCSI adapters.
scsi.opts	Contains configuration information for SCSI adapters.
`serial`	Initialization script for serial devices (such as modems).
serial.opts	Holds configuration data for serial devices.
Shared	Some scripting shared among all classes of supported PCMCIA devices.

Of all the files that are listed, only the .opts files need to be altered. Probably the main two files that will be worked with are the config.opts and network.opts files. The rest are typically fine in their default states.

The config.opts file is the one that is most often frequented. By default it is rather short, but it is the top-level configuration file for the entire `pcmcia-cs` package (see Listing 18.4).

LISTING 18.4 DEFAULT /ETC/PCMCIA/CONFIG.OPTS FILE

```
#
# Local PCMCIA Configuration File
#
# System resources available for PCMCIA devices
#
include port 0x100-0x4ff, port 0x1000-0x17ff
include memory 0xc0000-0xfffff, memory 0xa0000000-0xa0ffffff
#
# Extra port range for IBM Token Ring
#
include port 0xa00-0xaff
#
# Resources we should not use, even if they appear to be available
#
# First built-in serial port
exclude irq 4
# Second built-in serial port
#exclude irq 3
# First built-in parallel port
exclude irq 7
#
# Options for loadable modules
#
# To fix sluggish network with IBM ethernet adapter...
#module "pcnet_cs" opts "mem_speed=600"
#
# Options for Xircom Netwave driver...
#module "netwave_cs" opts "domain=0x100 scramble_key=0x0"
```

In this file you can set such items as memory address ranges (`include memory`), I/O port ranges (`include port`), excluded IRQs (`exclude irq`), and special parameters to be passed to the various modules (`module opts`), if necessary.

The best all-around resource to have handy when working with settings down to the `Options for loadable modules` line is the manual for the machine containing the PCMCIA hardware (which is, more often than not, a laptop). Memory address ranges, for instance, might have to be adjusted slightly if there is overlap with the machine's VGA address range. Likewise, if other devices within the machine are using certain IRQs for other, non-PCMCIA hardware, exclude those IRQs from the list of choices.

Options for loadable modules differ with each module. The best resources to have around for PCMCIA module parameters are the man pages for each module. There, all the information that is necessary to compile module option lines (like those in Listing 18.4) can be found.

The network.opts file contains much of the same information as the files in the /etc/sysconfig hierarchy, as well as the information that is typically contained within /etc/resolv.conf. Network fundamentals are addressed in Chapter 21, "Understanding TCP/IP Fundamentals," so it is best to defer descriptions of the IP addressing to that chapter. Just keep in mind that the network configuration information for PCMCIA Ethernet cards is referenced from /etc/pcmcia/network.opts in case anything needs to be changed.

One final note: The HOWTO document for PCMCIA acts as the documentation for the package; few—if any—other HOWTO documents act as official documentation for their associated subjects. This document comes with all `pcmcia-cs` source code archives and is available on Linux HOWTO Web sites that are mirrored all over the Internet. When in doubt, the PCMCIA-HOWTO has much more comprehensive information on topics related to this package and needs to be the single document to fall back on when PCMCIA questions that are not answered here arise.

SUMMARY

Anyone who has added a driver to another operating system (such as one that runs Windows) will undoubtedly appreciate the virtues of modular kernels. Although hardware is not "hot-swappable" with Linux (yet), drivers are, and the capability to remove, recompile, and reload drivers in Linux systems without completely restarting the system is one of Linux's strongest features.

This is especially useful when running in a multiuser environment. Restarting a multiuser system to load a new driver results in all the users being kicked off; however, the capability to unload and reload modules on-the-fly without restarting the system enables users to stay logged in. Also, when debugging problems with hardware drivers, it is quicker to unload a module and reload it with different settings than it is to change a setting in a startup file (such as CONFIG.SYS in the DOS operating system) and restart the system. Minutes turn into seconds when you remove the system restart step, enabling you to solve driver problems in a fraction of the time.

For more information on subjects related to those that are discussed in this chapter, refer to the following chapters:

- Chapter 12, "System Initialization Under OpenLinux," contains more information on how the startup procedure works on OpenLinux systems (and how to change it).
- Chapter 20 contains information on how the boot loader (LILO) can be used to pass settings to drivers that are built into the Linux kernel.
- Appendix B lists mappings that reference kernel modules to the hardware they support.
- Appendix C provides information on what you can do to change driver settings at the time the driver module is loaded.

CHAPTER 19

Disk Drives and File Systems

In this chapter

In this chapter you'll examine the requirements for adding or replacing hard drives, as well as the steps necessary for configuring them to work with Linux. Four basic steps are required to accomplish this:

1. Physically connect the new drive.
2. Partition the drive.
3. Create a new file system on the new partitions.
4. Mount the new file system.

HARD DRIVE INSTALLATION

Although installing new hard drives into a PC goes beyond the scope of this book, a few general rules might be worth reviewing. The two most common types of hard drives are IDE drives and SCSI drives. The key to installing an IDE drive is to make sure that jumpers are set correctly as either a master or slave device. Each IDE controller (many systems today have two IDE controllers directly embedded on the motherboard) can support two drives. One drive must be jumpered as the master device, and the other as the slave device.

SCSI drives must be connected to a SCSI adapter (typically a separate card), and there must be a terminating device on the SCSI chain. If you're adding a new hard drive to an existing SCSI environment, there is already a terminated device; make sure that the new hard drive is not terminated. Only one device on the SCSI chain will be terminated—this must be the last device on the SCSI chain.

Note

The Linux kernel automatically probes for new devices as they are added to the system.

After the new hard drive is installed, it is detected when Linux is booted—that is, of course, as long as it is installed correctly and there are no conflicts with other hardware components. However, if you are installing a new SCSI controller, you have to manually install the module for it. Module management is covered in detail in Chapter 18, "Kernel Modules." The presence of the new hard drive is displayed by the boot messages as they scroll by.

Note

You can review the boot messages at any time by running `dmesg`.

Also, the `sysinfo` command displays system information, including detailed information on each hard disk installed. For example, the following is taken from the output of the `sysinfo` command:

```
# sysinfo

Hard disk 1  : /dev/hdb
   Model     : Maxtor 7850 AV
   Serial No : J502E2KS
   Capacity  : 814 MB
   Cache     : 64 KB
   CHS (log) : 827 cylinders, 32 heads, 63 sectors
   CHS (phy) : 1654 cylinders, 16 heads, 63 sectors
```

Each installed hard drive will have a section similar to the one listed previously. As you can see, very detailed information about the hard drive is listed with `sysinfo`, including the hard drive make and model. If your newly installed hard drive is not detected, it is most likely a cabling or configuration issue. The key to detecting SCSI devices is to make sure that the SCSI controller is detected. After the SCSI controller is detected, all SCSI devices need to be found. If not, the problem is most likely one of incorrect termination or faulty cabling.

PARTITIONING THE HARD DRIVE

Partitioning the hard drive is done with the `fdisk` utility, which is very similar to the utility used on other operating systems such as DOS. A new partition can be created on the newly added hard drive by running `fdisk` and supplying the name of the device to be partitioned. For example, if the newly added drive is /dev/hdb, it can be partitioned as follows:

```
# fdisk /dev/hdb
```

After a partition is created, it becomes known to Linux by a unique device name and partition number. In the preceding example, the first partition on the drive hdb is referenced as `/dev/hdb1` in Linux.

In order to partition the new drive, you must know what the correct device name is in Linux. The system boot messages, as well as `sysinfo`, display the new device name. The device naming scheme for IDE drives is listed in Table 19.1. The naming scheme for SCSI drives is listed in Table 19.2.

TABLE 19.1 IDE DEVICE NAMES

Device Scheme	IDE Controller	Jumpering
/dev/hda	Primary	Master
/dev/hdb	Primary	Slave
/dev/hdc	Secondary	Master
/dev/hdd	Secondary	Slave

TABLE 19.2 SCSI DRIVE DEVICE NAMES

Device	Description
/dev/sda	First SCSI drive
/dev/sdb	Second SCSI drive
/dev/sdc	Third SCSI drive

Note Some drives might be removable devices, such as Jaz and Zip drives.

When the drive is accessible as a device under Linux it can be partitioned in preparation for creating a file system. Like with DOS, the utility for partitioning a hard drive is `fdisk`; however, the Linux version is much more powerful. The options available with the Linux version of `fdisk` are displayed in the Help menu as follows:

```
# fdisk /dev/hda

Command (m for help): m
Command action
   a   toggle a bootable flag
   b   edit bsd disklabel
   c   toggle the dos compatibility flag
   d   delete a partition
   l   list known partition types
   m   print this menu
   n   add a new partition
   o   create a new empty DOS partition table
   p   print the partition table
   q   quit without saving changes
   t   change a partition's system id
   u   change display/entry units
   v   verify the partition table
   w   write table to disk and exit
   x   extra functionality (experts only)

Command (m for help):
```

The steps for creating a new Linux partition are as follows:

1. Run `fdisk` on the new hard drive.
2. Examine any existing partitioning.
3. Create a new partition.
4. Select the partition type (primary or extended).
5. Select the partition number.
6. Select the beginning cylinder.
7. Select the ending cylinder or size.
8. Set the partition system ID.

9. Write the new partition table.
10. Reboot the computer to update the partition table.

Following is a closer look at each step.

STEP 1

Run the `fdisk` utility and specify which hard drive (by device name) you want to partition. The following is displayed on the screen:

```
# fdisk /dev/hda

Command (m for help): m
```

STEP 2

The letter *p* is used to display the current partition table, if any exists. If no partitions are present, the following is displayed onscreen:

```
Command (m for help): p

Disk /dev/hda: 32 heads, 63 sectors, 827 cylinders
Units = cylinders of 2016 * 512 bytes

  Device Boot    Start      End   Blocks   Id  System
```

If partitions are already configured, the following is displayed:

```
Command (m for help): p

Disk /dev/hda: 32 heads, 63 sectors, 827 cylinders
Units = cylinders of 2016 * 512 bytes

  Device Boot    Start      End   Blocks   Id  System
/dev/hda1            1       17    17104+  82  Linux Swap
/dev/hda2   *       18      827   816480   83  Linux Native
```

STEP 3

Create a new partition as follows:

```
Command (m for help): n
Command action
    e   extended
    p   primary partition (1-4)
```


STEP 4

Select a partition type. Unlike DOS, where only one primary partition is allowed, Linux supports a hard drive of all primary partitions, or any combination of primary or extended partitions:

```
Command (m for help): n
Command action
    e   extended
```

```
    p  primary partition (1-4)
p
Partition number (1-4):
```

STEP 5

Select the partition number. If this is to be the first partition on this drive, select 1:

```
Command (m for help): n
Command action
    e  extended
    p  primary partition (1-4)
p
Partition number (1-4): 1
```

STEP 6

Select the first cylinder number:

```
Command (m for help): n
Command action
    e  extended
    p  primary partition (1-4)
p
Partition number (1-4): 1
First cylinder (1-827): 1
```

STEP 7

Select the last cylinder number, or select the partition size in cylinders, megabytes, or kilobytes:

```
Command (m for help): n
Command action
    e  extended
    p  primary partition (1-4)
p
Partition number (1-4): 1
First cylinder (1-827): 1
Last cylinder or +size or +sizeM or +sizeK ([1]-17): 17
```

After the partition type, partition number, first cylinder, and last cylinder are set, the main `fdisk` prompt is displayed as follows:

```
Command (m for help):
```

STEP 8

Set the partition system ID. For a Linux file system, this is always type 83, Linux native:

```
Command (m for help): t
Partition number: 1
Hex code (type L to list codes): L

0 Empty         b   Win95 FAT32          75  PC/IX          a7  NEXTSTEP
1 DOS 12-bit FATc   Win95 FAT32 (LB      80  Old MINIX      a9  NetBSD
2 XENIX root    e   Win95 FAT16 (LB      81  Linux/MINIX    b7  BSDI fs
3 XENIX usr     f   Win95 Extended       82  Linux Swap     b8  BSDI swap
```

```
4 DOS 16-bit <32M  40 Venix 80286       83  Linux Native    c7  Syrinx
5 Extended          51  Novell?          85  Linux extended db  CP/M
6 DOS 16-bit >=32M 52  Microport        93  Amoeba          e1  DOS access
7 OS/2  HPFS        63  GNU HURD         94  Amoeba BBT      e3  DOS R/O
8 AIX               64  Novell Netware   a5  BSD/386         f2
➥DOS secondary
9 AIX bootable    65  Novell Netware    a6  OpenBSD         ff  BBT
a  OS/2 Boot Manag

Hex code (type L to list codes):
```

Enter type 83 for a Linux native, second extended (ext2) file system:

```
Hex code (type L to list codes): 83

Command (m for help):
```

Tip

Repeat steps 3–8 for each additional partition.

STEP 9

Write out new partition table information to the hard drive as follows:

```
Command (m for help): w
The partition table has been altered!

Calling ioctl() to re-read partition table.
Syncing disks.
```

After the new partition table is written to disk, reboot your system to ensure that the partition table is updated. The newly created partitions are now ready for a Linux file system.

Note

You can examine the existing partition of any drive by running `fdisk` with the option `-l`. For example, `fdisk -l /dev/hda` displays the existing partitions on the first IDE drive on the primary controller. You can display the partitions for all hard drives by just supplying the `-l` option without specifying any particular hard drive.

LINUX FILE SYSTEMS

Even though the newly added drive is now recognized by the operating system, it's not usable until it is partitioned and a file system is created on it. The default file system for Linux is the extended type-2 file system (ext2). Characteristics of an ext2 file system are listed in Table 19.3.

TABLE 19.3 SECOND EXTENDED (EXT2) FILE SYSTEM CHARACTERISTICS

Characteristic	Limit
Maximum file system size	4 terabytes
Maximum file size	2 gigabytes
Maximum filename length	255 characters
Minimum block size	1024 bytes
Default inode allocation	1 per 4096 bytes of partition space

The file system structure is built when the `make file system` utility (`mkfs`) is run. This utility is actually just a front-end program that calls subordinate routines for file system creation. When making an ext2 file system, the `mkfs` utility actually calls `mke2fs` to create the correct file system structure. After the file system structure is created, it cannot be modified without reformatting the partition, or—in other words—remaking a new file system with the `mkfs` utility.

Caution

The `mkfs` utility completely erases all data. You are not prompted to continue. It runs without any user interaction. Use it with caution.

The `mkfs` utility builds an ext2 type file system by default. The results of running `mkfs` are reported as follows:

```
#  mkfs /dev/hdb2
mke2fs 1.10, 24-Apr-97 for EXT2 FS 0.5b, 95/08/09
Linux ext2 file system format
File system label=
3024 inodes, 12096 blocks
604 blocks (4.99%) reserved for the super user
First data block=1
Block size=1024 (log=0)
Fragment size=1024 (log=0)
2 block groups
8192 blocks per group, 8192 fragments per group
1512 inodes per group
Superblock backups stored on blocks:
    8193 ....
Writing inode tables:  done
Writing superblocks and file system accounting information:  done
```

If you are installing an older hard drive, it is strongly recommended that you use `-c` the option to check for bad blocks as follows:

```
#  mkfs -c /dev/hdb2
mke2fs 1.10, 24-Apr-97 for EXT2 FS 0.5b, 95/08/09
Linux ext2 file system format
File system label=
3024 inodes, 12096 blocks
604 blocks (4.99%) reserved for the super user
First data block=1
```

```
Block size=1024 (log=0)
Fragment size=1024 (log=0)
2 block groups
8192 blocks per group, 8192 fragments per group
1512 inodes per group
Superblock backups stored on blocks:
    8193 ....

Checking for bad blocks (read-only test):  done
Writing inode tables:  done
Writing superblocks and file system accounting information:  done
```

When an ext2 file system is created, it builds a set of areas on the hard drive partition. These areas are commonly referred to as *block groups*. Each block group is segmented into several smaller sections. Figure 19.1 depicts the block group layout, and Table 19.4 describes each of the sections of a block group.

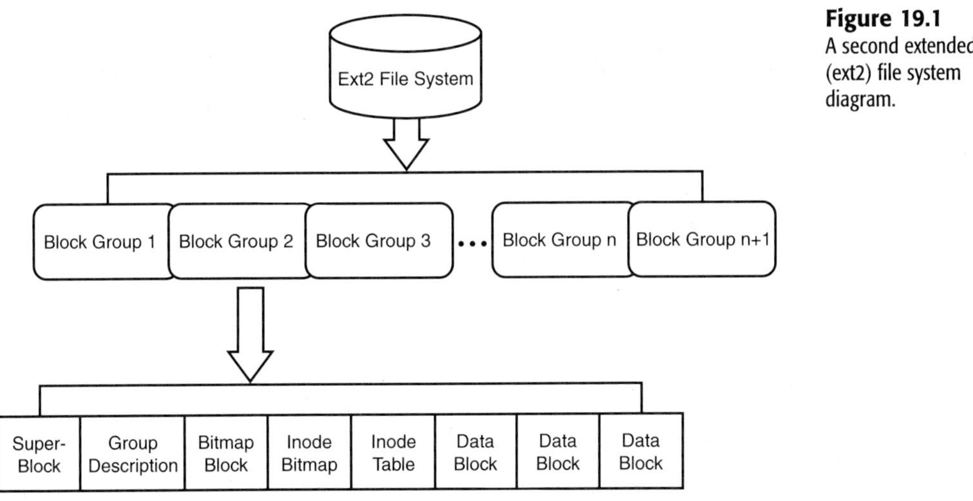

Figure 19.1
A second extended (ext2) file system diagram.

TABLE 19.4 BLOCK GROUP DESCRIPTION

Block Group Section	Description
superblock	Information about the entire file system is stored in the superblock. Each block group contains a superblock, but it is only a backup copy of the superblock in the first block group.
group descriptor	Information on each block group is stored here. Each block group contains a group descriptor, but they are all duplicates of the group descriptor block in the first block group. Pointers to the table of inodes reside here.
bitmap block	This is a map of bits indicating which blocks are in use.
inode bitmap	This is a map of bits indicating which inodes are in use.

continues

TABLE 19.4 CONTINUED

Block Group Section	Description
inode table	This is a table of inodes actually allocated to this block group.
data blocks	This is where the actual data is stored.

An *inode* is basically a pointer to a file; however, it contains pertinent information about the file. It stores information such as file permissions, ownership, date of last modification, and pointers to actual data blocks. An inode does not contain any file data. There is exactly one inode per file. An ext2 file system is built with a fixed set of inodes at creation time. By default, one inode is allocated for every 4096 bytes. This is not a literal mapping—it is only used as a general rule of thumb when establishing the block groups.

If a file is small enough, it fits entirely within the directly accessible blocks of a given block group. If not, an indirect method of linking blocks together is used to store all the data of a given file. This scheme allows a file to be as large as 2GB in size.

Note

The majority of files on a Linux system are small enough to be directly accessible.

MOUNTING FILE SYSTEMS

In order for a newly created file system to be accessible in Linux, it must be mounted. Whereas the requirement to mount a file system seems very user-unfriendly, it actually offers some powerful flexibility. Unlike a DOS environment where, in most cases, a drive letter represents a separate partition, Linux file systems can be logically grouped together so that they appear to be on one file system when in reality they aren't. This multipartition file system appears to the user as one directory hierarchy. For example, I can partition my hard drive into four primary partitions. Each partition can then be mapped to a specific mount point that is a part of the overall directory structure as is outlined in Table 19.5.

TABLE 19.5 SAMPLE MOUNT POINTS WITH SEPARATE PARTITIONS

Directory (Mount Point)	Physical Partition
/	/dev/hda1
/var	/dev/hda2
/home	/dev/hda3
/usr	/dev/hda4

Take the example of the /var directory. This is the directory in which incoming mail is located. With the /var directory on a separate partition, a system administrator does not have to be overly concerned about the incoming mail directory filling up and causing the system to halt because of the lack of disk space. In this scenario, the /dev/hda2 partition can completely fill up with incoming email, but the system continues to run because the /dev/hda1 file system is not full. Of course the mail will begin to bounce, but the system won't come to a halt. If, however, the /var directory is a part of the /dev/hda1 file system, the root file system can become filled with incoming mail and cause the system to halt due to a lack of disk space.

MANUALLY MOUNTING A FILE SYSTEM

File systems can be manually mounted by using the mount command. The mount command uses the following syntax:

```
mount -t filesystem device-name mount-directory
```

The command for manually mounting the CD-ROM is as follows:

```
mount -t iso9660 /dev/cdrom /mnt/cdrom
```

The actual CD-ROM device is referenced by the symbolic link /dev/cdrom.

The mount directory is similar in logic to a drive letter in an operating system such as DOS: It's a place to reference and access a drive. With Linux, however, the place of reference and access to a drive device is a directory no different from any other directory on the Linux file system. (In other words, you can change directories with the cd command to go to a mount directory to access the drive device mounted to it. With DOS, you type the letter of the drive with a colon to access the drive device.) For example, CD-ROM drives are often mounted to a /mnt/cdrom directory.

You can find a list of currently mounted file systems by executing the mount command without any options. You can generate a similar list by running the cat command on the /proc/mounts file.

Note

When you mount a device to a mount directory, anything that was in that directory is no longer accessible until you unmount the drive using the umount command. When you umount the directory, the previous contents are once again intact in the directory.

UNMOUNTING A FILE SYSTEM

The umount command is used to detach previously mounted file systems from their mount directories. The syntax used is similar to the mount command, but a typical command line can be much simpler. For instance, the following command unmounts a CD-ROM drive that was mounted using the example given earlier:

```
umount /mnt/cdrom
```

Note

If the unmounting procedure is to succeed, no one can be using the mount directory when you unmount a device or a mount directory. If anyone is accessing the mount directory, you get a busy device error, and the unmounting procedure fails. Be sure to back out of a mount directory before unmounting the device attached to it.

AUTOMATING THE MOUNTING PROCESS

The mounting process can be automated by configuring the file system table file (/etc/fstab). You can do this by adding the drive device in question to the automount file system table contained in the /etc/fstab file.

When you start the system, Linux mounts certain devices automatically. The /etc/fstab file contains the information about these devices that is necessary to have them mounted without interaction from the system administrator.

The /etc/fstab file offers two kinds of functionality. Entries in the fstab file can be configured to have specific file systems mounted automatically each time the system boots. Furthermore, by defining an entry in the /etc/fstab file, you don't have to supply the entire `mount` command when mounting a file system manually. For example, if your CD-ROM drive has its own entry in /etc/fstab that contains all the information necessary for it to mount, the following command can be used to mount the drive:

```
mount /mnt/cdrom
```

Each file system is described on a separate line in the /etc/fstab file. Each entry contains all the information that you type at the command prompt, as well as a few other options that change the way that the drive is mounted.

The entry in the /etc/fstab file for an ATAPI-IDE CD-ROM looks similar to the following:

```
/dev/hdc /mnt/cdrom iso9660 ro,noauto, 0 0
```

Each line entry has six space-delimited fields. The description of these fields is outlined in Table 19.6.

TABLE 19.6 FIELD DESCRIPTIONS OF THE /ETC/FSTAB FILE

Field	Description
`/dev/hdc`	The actual device name or partition to be mounted.
`/mnt/cdrom`	The mount point. When mounted, data on this file system is accessible via this directory name.
`iso9660`	The file system type. Hard drive partitions are of type ext2.
ro, noauto	Mount options: `ro`=read-only `noauto`=do not automount this file system.

Field	Description
`0`	Used by the `dump` command. `0`=don't back up this file system
`0`	Sets the order by which file system checks are done at reboot. `0`=don't run a check on this file system.

Note

For further information on valid values for each of the entries in the /etc/fstab configuration file, see the man page for fstab.

After the file system is mounted, it can be accessed via the mount point. In other words, the newly mounted file system appears to the user as just another directory in the file system hierarchy.

Summary

This chapter reviewed some of the general rules of installing a new hard drive and the required steps of configuring it for use in Linux. When installed and detected, a new hard drive must be partitioned and a new file system must be established in order for it to be accessible within Linux. The hard drive is partitioned using the `fdisk` utility, and a new file system is created by using the `mkfs` utility. The final step is to mount the newly created file system, either manually with the `mount` utility or automatically by configuring the /etc/fstab file.

For more information on the topics discussed here, refer to the following chapters:

- Chapter 9, "Understanding the Linux File System," gives more information on devices and how they are used.
- See Chapter 10, "Users, Groups, and Permissions," for further information on how to set or modify permissions for a given device.
- See Chapter 20, "Boot Loader," for details on how the boot loader works in conjunction with a hard drive.

CHAPTER 20

Boot Loader

In this chapter

WHAT IS LILO?

LILO, in simple terms, is a boot loader program. In reality, it's a collection of several programs and files. The two primary programs are the map installer and the boot. The map installer is the Linux program that places the necessary files in the proper location and records it in a map file. This location is then used at boot time to determine where to find the operating system. It is installed in the /sbin directory and is named `lilo`; therefore, it is often referred to as running `/sbin/lilo` or just running `lilo`.

The boot loader program is the program, installed by the map installer, that facilitates the loading of the operating system. It is run when the BIOS initiates it.

Of the several files that LILO uses, the /etc/lilo.conf file is the most crucial file to maintain. The other files are, for the most part, self-maintaining.

The boot loader is executed at an interim stage when the system BIOS is determining how to pass control to the operating system.

Note

The term LILO is derived by taking the first two letters of the words Linux Loader (LInux LOader).

LILO is a general-purpose boot loader package used on most modern Linux systems. With it, you can specify any number of installed operating systems to boot. You can also pass behavior-altering parameters to the Linux kernel. When you first start a system with LILO installed, you can enter such parameters or options and specify an operating system to load. You can also specify different partitions from which you want to boot your system.

LILO is configured and installed as part of the initial installation of OpenLinux. However, LILO, like every other component of OpenLinux, is packaged in RPM format. The files included in the LILO RPM are described in Table 20.1.

TABLE 20.1 THE LILO RPM FILES

Files	Description
/boot/boot.b	This is installed as the default boot sector.
/boot/chain.b	Used to boot a non-Linux operating system.
/boot/os2_d.b	Used to boot an OS/2 system.
/sbin/activate	Used to change the active flag of a given partition.
/sbin/lilo	The map installer program. It installs the boot loader to the place designated in the /etc/lilo.conf file.
/usr/doc/lilo-0.20/COPYING	This file contains the copying policy for LILO.

Extensive documentation for LILO is included on the CD in one of three RPMs: lilo-doc-0.20-1.i386.rpm, lilo-doc-dvi-0.20-1.i386.rpm, or lilo-doc-ps-0.20-1.i386.rpm. The only difference is the format of the documentation. The first one is plain text, the second is in `dvi` format, and the last one contains the documentation in `postscript` format. Werner Almesberger is the author of LILO as well as of the included documentation.

Operating systems have now evolved to the point where much of what they do is transparent to the user. However, transparent as the boot process is today, the boot strapping process still involves the same kind of steps that were required in the early days of computer development. The manual steps of flipping switches to boot a computer of yesterday have been replaced with the automated method of using the system BIOS and a boot loader to complete the boot process. In order to understand what LILO is and how it works, it is important to first know and understand what the CMOS and BIOS of a PC is, and how the boot sequence works.

BOOT STAGES

The first stage of the boot process is begun at power up by loading a program called the system *basic input/output system* (*BIOS*). This program uses settings that reside in the *Complementary Metal Oxide Semiconductor* (*CMOS*) to determine how to initialize hardware components and complete the first stage of the boot process. The system BIOS and the CMOS are included as part of your PC hardware.

The next stage of the boot process is begun as the BIOS passes control to the operating system. In essence, the BIOS is an operating system, but, as its name describes, it is only a very basic one. The CMOS contains several parameters based on the system hardware components and desired preferences, including a setting for the desired boot sequence. For example, a typical CMOS setting for the boot sequence might be `A, C`. This means that the BIOS first tries to pass control to the boot sector of the floppy drive (A:); if no boot sector is found there, it then tries to locate a valid boot sector on hard drive (C:). In simple terms, the boot sequence (see Figure 20.1) on a PC is as follows:

1. The power is turned on.
2. The system BIOS loads.
3. The BIOS, based on CMOS settings, determines where to look for a valid boot sector.
4. Control is passed to the *master boot record* (*MBR*).
5. The MBR passes control to the boot sector of the active partition.
6. The boot sector loads the operating system.

Each step of the boot sequence, or boot strapping process, initializes a minimal set of devices and builds upon the previous step.

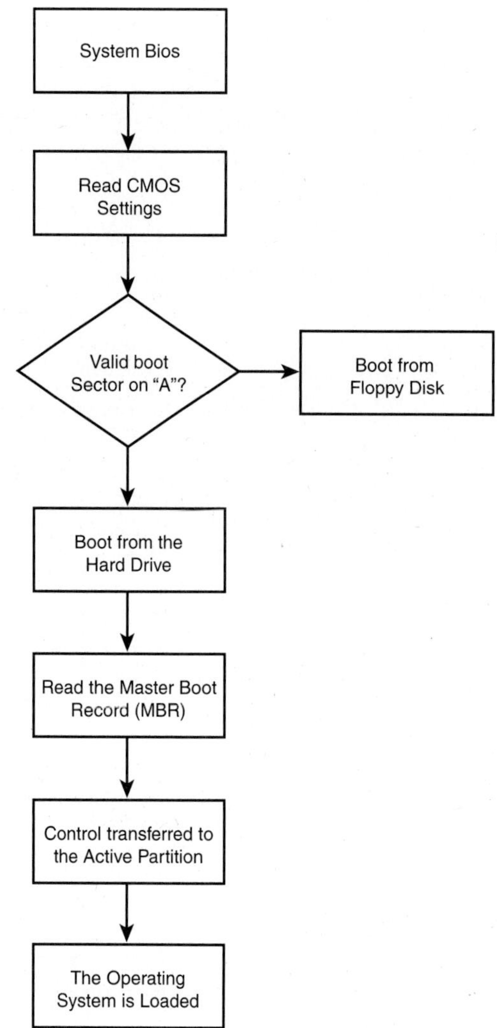

Figure 20.1
BIOS boot sequence.

How Does LILO Work?

LILO acts as an interim agent between the system BIOS and the operating system. It is a customizable program that enables the system BIOS to pass control to the Linux kernel. It is also quite good at managing the boot processes of operating systems other than Linux. After control is passed to the boot loader program, it begins a sequence of steps to determine where to find the operating system.

Linux does not depend on any specific file system. It uses a map file that contains information about the physical location of a given boot sector. This map file is normally stored as /boot/map. It is rebuilt each time you run the map installer.

Note

LILO can be configured to boot up to 16 different images or operating systems.

After LILO is installed, the boot loader portion must be capable of accessing certain areas of the system in order to work properly. These areas are listed in Table 20.2.

Table 20.2 System Areas Accessed by LILO

System Area	Description
The root file system partition	The data files that LILO needs to complete a successful boot are typically located in the root file system, usually in the /boot directory.
The boot sector	The boot sector contains the first part of the LILO boot loader. It, in turn, loads the second-stage loader. Both parts of the loader are typically stored in the file /boot/boot.b.
The kernel	The kernel is located and initiated by the second-stage loader. The default kernel is /vmlinuz.

LILO is not designed to know how to work with a given file system such as the second extended file system (ext2). Rather, it uses the physical location (cylinders, heads, sectors) of the required files to know how to proceed. This allows LILO to work with most file systems that are supported by Linux.

Disk Organization

In order to get a better picture of how this process works, it's helpful to understand the basic organization of a disk. The simplest case is that of the floppy disk. It is basically divided in to two sections—the boot sector and the data area. The boot sector itself is 512 bytes and is divided into several parts. A DOS boot sector is depicted in Figure 20.2.

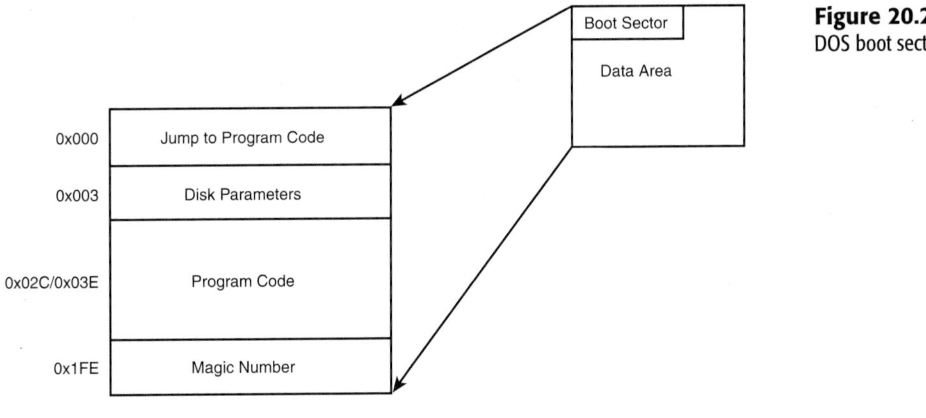

Figure 20.2
DOS boot sector.

LILO uses a similar boot sector, but it does not contain the disk parameters.

Caution

Installing LILO to the boot sector of a DOS file system makes the DOS data files inaccessible. This is because disk parameters are stored as part of a DOS boot sector, and a LILO boot sector does not contain disk parameters. Without the disk parameters, a DOS file system becomes inoperable.

The disk organization of a hard disk differs from that of a floppy because of partitioning. Figure 20.3 shows how a typical hard disk might look if partitioned using primary and extended partitions. Due to BIOS limitations, a hard disk can only be divided into four primary partitions. If more than four partitions are required, extended partitions must be used. The partition information for a given disk is contained in the partition boot sector. The partition boot sector is commonly called the master boot record (MBR).

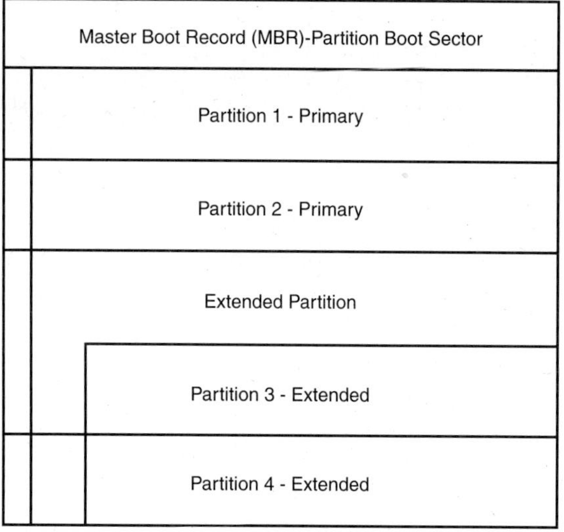

Figure 20.3
Typical partitioned hard disk.

The MBR or partition boot sector is structured as outlined in Table 20.3.

TABLE 20.3 MASTER BOOT RECORD STRUCTURE

Location	Description
0x000	Program code
0x1BE	Partition table
0x1FE	Magic number

LILO Locations

The LILO boot sector can be stored in the following locations:

- The boot sector of a floppy disk
- The MBR of the first hard disk
- The boot sector of a Linux file system on a primary partition on the first hard disk (recommended location)
- The boot sector of an extended partition on the first hard drive

Although there are many possibilities for how you can configure LILO, and though it often depends on your hardware, the third option is the recommended location for LILO. Installing LILO in the boot sector of the primary Linux file system partition on the first hard drive enables you to keep the MBR at the factory default setting.

Note

There is a misconception that you have to install LILO to the MBR in order to boot LINUX or to enable the system to boot multiple operating systems.

Booting Basics

With LILO installed to one of the four possible locations, your Linux system is ready to be recognized. As a point of reference, it might be helpful to compare the booting sequence for Linux with that of a traditional DOS system. A DOS boot sequence is depicted in Table 20.4.

Table 20.4 DOS Boot Sequence

Master Boot Record	Boot Sector Type	Operating System
DOS-MBR	DOS	COMMAND.COM

The recommend method of configuring LILO is to place the boot loader in the boot sector, sometimes referred to as the *superblock*. Such a configuration is depicted in Table 20.5.

Table 20.5 Linux Boot Sequence

Master Boot Record	Boot Sector	Operating System
DOS-MBR	LILO (boot loader)	Linux kernel (vmlinuz)

NOTE: In order for the MBR to pass control to LILO, the partition on which the Linux root file system resides must be marked as active.

LILO depends on the BIOS of the PC to load the following items:

/boot/boot.b

/boot/map

/vmlinuz (kernel)

boot sectors of all other boot images

startup message

Because of limitations in mapping methods of the system BIOS, large IDE drives typically require something such as *logical block addressing* (*LBA*) mode. This is a means of mapping a large drive with many physical cylinders to a logical set of fewer than 1023 cylinders.

Note

The system BIOS cannot access cylinders beyond 1024. This is due to an addressing limitation of the original algorithm used to manage access to hard drives. A newer algorithm, sometimes referred to as enhanced-BIOS, uses logical block addressing to overcome this limitation.

A map is built based on where the Linux kernel resides. LILO uses this to determine where the kernel is located on the physical disk. You might have to use the linear option with larger disk drives if LILO doesn't install successfully otherwise.

The LILO boot loader program consists of several stages, including the primary loader and the secondary loader.

As each phase of the LILO boot process completes, a letter in the word *LILO* is displayed on the screen until the LILO boot process completes. If the boot loader fails, the last letter of the word LILO can be used to debug what might have caused the problem. This is covered in detail later in this chapter in the "Troubleshooting" section.

As the LILO boot loader program runs, it displays data contained in the /boot/message file as a boot banner. Although this file is a simple text file and can be edited, it has embedded control characters for block characters, and making changes is a little more difficult than it looks.

BASIC CONFIGURATION

A simple installation of LILO requires the configuration of the basic pieces of the /etc/lilo.conf file and running the map installer. A sample configuration of the /etc/lilo.conf file is shown here:

```
# general section

boot = /dev/hda
install = /boot/boot.b
message = /boot/message
prompt
```

```
# wait 20 seconds for user to select the entry to load
timeout = 200

# default entry

image = /vmlinuz
label = linux
root = /dev/hda2
read-only

# additional entries
```

The lilo.conf file is quite simple. As is typical with most configuration files, lines beginning with a hash mark (#) are comment lines. The lilo.conf configuration file consists of three primary sections: the general section (sometimes referred to as the *global* section), the Linux image section, and the section for non-Linux entries. These sections are organized in this manner for readability only. The first image entry is the default system if no option is selected at the LILO boot prompt. This is discussed further in the section "Dual Booting," later in the chapter.

Table 20.6 describes what each line in the sample lilo.conf file does.

Table 20.6 Sample /etc/lilo.conf File

lilo.conf File Entry	Description
boot = /dev/hda1	The boot loader is installed to the boot sector, sometimes referred to as the superblock, of the first IDE drive.
install = /boot/boot.b	Installs the specified file as the new boot sector.
message = /boot/message	This is the file that contains the information that is to be displayed to the screen after LILO is run.
prompt	Forces the boot prompt to be displayed.
timeout = 200	The boot loader pauses 20 seconds waiting for operator input.
image = /vmlinuz	The name of the Linux kernel.
label = linux	This label (name) is displayed at the boot prompt if the Tab key is pressed. It is used to distinguish between options if more than one OS is available to boot.
root = /dev/hda1	The root file system resides on the first partition of the first IDE drive.
read-only	The root file system is mounted as read-only initially. It is remounted during the boot process as read-write.

The options available for the /etc/lilo.conf file correspond with the three major sections—general, Linux images, and other images. In fact, the options for other images actually apply to any bootable image. A comprehensive list of options for each of the three sections of the /etc/lilo.conf file is shown in Tables 20.7, 20.8, and 20.9.

TABLE 20.7 GLOBAL OPTIONS (GENERAL)

Option	Description
`backup=`*`filename`*	Copies the original boot sector to the specified file.
`boot=`*`boot_device`*	Uses the boot sector from the specified device.
`change-rules`	Defines partition type numbers.
`compact`	Reads several adjacent sectors in a single read request.
`default=`*`name`*	Image specified here is the default boot image. The first image listed in /etc/lilo.conf is the default if this option is omitted.
`delay=`*`tenths_seconds`*	The time delay, in tenths of seconds, before the default image boots.
`disk=`*`device_name`*	Sets non-standard parameters for the specified disk.
`fix-table`	Allows LILO to adjust 3D addresses in partition tables.
`force-backup=`*`filename`*	Same as the backup option, except an existing backup file is overwritten with this option.
`ignore-table`	Ignores partition tables that appear to be corrupt and allows LILO to install a boot sector.
`install=`*`boot_sector`*	Specified file is installed as the new boot sector.
`keytable=`*`table_file`*	The keyboard is remapped based on the settings in the specified file.
`linear`	Generates linear sector addresses instead of addresses using cylinders, heads, and sectors.
`map=`*`map_file`*	Uses the map file specified here. If not specified, /boot/map is used as the default.
`message=`*`message_file`*	The contents of this file are displayed as part of the LILO boot prompt. *The map installer must be rerun if this file is modified.*
`nowarn`	Warning errors are ignored and not displayed.
`prompt`	Forces the display of the boot prompt.
`serial=`*`parameters`*	Enables console control from a configured serial port.
`timeout=`*`tenths_seconds`*	The amount of time, in tenths of seconds, that the user is allowed to press a key before the default boot image is loaded.
`verbose=`*`level`*	Different levels of progress diagnostics can be selected.

TABLE 20.8 LINUX IMAGE OPTIONS

Option	Description
`append=`*`string`*	Appends options specified here to the string that is passed to the kernel. Typically used for hardware parameters such as a hard disk geometry.

Option	Description
`initrd=name`	The file specified here is used as the initial RAM disk.
`literal=string`	Similar to the append option, but the specified string replaces any previous options that are to be passed to the kernel.
`ramdisk=size`	Sets the size of the RAM disk.
`read-only`	The root file system is initially mounted as read-only.
`read-write`	Sets the root file system to mount as read/write.
`root=root_device`	Selects the device specified here as the root device.
`vga=mode`	Selects the display mode to be used when booting.

Table 20.9 General Per-Image Options

Option	Description
`alias=name`	Indicates a second name for this image.
`fallback=command_line`	The command line specified here is used if this image is selected to boot on a subsequent attempt to boot this image.
`label=name`	Assigns a name to the boot image for easy reference.
`lock`	Any command-line options added are recorded and used for subsequent boots until manually overridden.
`optional`	Omit this image when running the map installer if the main file is missing. Typically used with test kernels.
`password=password`	The password set here must be entered at the boot prompt in order for this image to boot.
`restricted`	Only works with the password option set. The password is only required if boot line options are added.
`single-key`	Allows an image to be booted by pressing a single key.

How to Install LILO

Installing LILO is really quite simple. The key to a successful installation of LILO is to create the configuration file correctly. After the configuration file is created, it's just a matter of running the map installer program. Modifications to the configuration file (/etc/lilo.conf) can be made at any time, but the map installer (/sbin/lilo) must be run each time changes are made in order for the changes to take effect.

Installing LILO

LILO is installed by logging in as the root user and running the map installer (`/sbin/lilo`). The map installer reads the configuration contained in the /etc/lilo.conf file and configures the boot loader based on directives contained therein. If the map installer is run using the sample /etc/lilo.conf file described in the previous section, the output is as follows:

```
# /sbin/lilo
 Added linux *
```

The word `linux` refers to the specified label. For example, if the label entry is

```
# default entry

image = /vmlinuz
label = linux2.0
root = /dev/hda2
read-only
```

the map installer reports the following:

```
Added linux2.0 *
```

The asterisk indicates that this image is the default operating system. This image is booted if no other option is selected at the LILO boot prompt. The map installer has several options, most of which can be implemented by configuring the /etc/lilo.conf file. See the man page on `lilo` for further details.

Note

If the kernel is rebuilt, the boot loader must be reinstalled in order to have the map rebuilt. This allows LILO to find the location of the newly built kernel.

The reason is simple: The kind of information written to the boot loader includes items such as a map of where the Linux kernel is located on your hard drive, and none of it is updated if you don't run the map installer.

UNINSTALLING LILO

The process by which LILO is to be uninstalled is completely dependent upon how LILO was installed. If LILO was installed in the recommended location (the boot sector, or *superblock*, of the Linux partition), LILO can be uninstalled by deleting, disabling, or overwriting the partition in which it resides.

If LILO was installed to the MBR, it takes a little bit more to disable LILO. The MBR of the hard drive is unaffected by changes to any partitions. As such, simply deleting or overwriting a partition has no effect on LILO.

In most cases, LILO can be uninstalled by running the map installer with the uninstall option as follows:

```
# lilo -u
```

When the map installer is run, a backup copy of the original boot sector is made. The uninstall option tries to restore the boot sector to its original state by removing the boot sector that was previously installed and replacing it with the original boot sector. This might not always work. It is completely dependent upon being capable of reading the file system in which the backup boot sector is stored. A factory default MBR can be restored by running the DOS version of `fdisk` with the appropriate parameter as follows:

```
fdisk \MBR
```

Note

OpenLinux includes the latest version DR DOS which can be used for the purpose of configuring the MBR.

Dual Booting

In addition to providing the means for booting a Linux kernel, LILO offers the added bonus of being capable of managing the booting of other, non-Linux operating systems. LILO offers the additional benefit of booting multiple versions of the same operating system. You might find yourself in a position in which you need to compile a customized version of the Linux kernel; using LILO, you can set up your old kernel to be booted in case the new one doesn't work for some reason.

It's actually quite easy to configure LILO to manage the boot process of other images. The most common occurrence of a dual booting situation is that of Linux and an operating system that comes preloaded on a PC. The steps for preparing such a system for Linux are as follows:

1. Run a defragmenting program.
2. Split the existing partition into two partitions.
3. Delete the second partition.
4. Create two new partitions from the existing free space.
5. Set one partition as Linux swap and the other as Linux native.
6. Install Linux.

The preceding steps are described in more detail in Chapter 2, "Installing OpenLinux," and in Chapter 19, "Disk Drives and File Systems." The last phase of the installation process enables you to configure LILO to boot all available operating systems. However, it is quite easy to modify the LILO configuration at any time to enable booting of other operating systems or other Linux kernel images. It takes only two simple steps. First, modify the /etc/lilo.conf file and add an entry for each additional operating system or image. Second, rerun the map installer. An example of a /etc/lilo.conf file with two Linux kernels and one non-Linux image is shown here:


```
# general section

boot = /dev/hda
install = /boot/boot.b
message = /boot/message
prompt
```

```
# wait 20 seconds for user to select the entry to load
timeout = 200

# default entry

image = /vmlinuz
label = linux
root = /dev/hda2
read-only

image = /vmlinuz.new
label  = linux.new
root = /dev/hda3
read-only

# additional entries
other = /dev/hda4
label = dos
table = /dev/hda
```

Reinstalling the boot loader by rerunning the map installer produces the following:

```
# /sbin/lilo
 Added linux *
Added linux.new
Added dos
```

The newly configured system is depicted in Table 20.10.

TABLE 20.10 LINUX BOOT SEQUENCE

Master Boot Record	Boot Sector	Operating System
DOS-MBR	LILO (boot loader)	Linux kernel (vmlinuz)
		Linux (vmlinuz.new)
		DOS

PARAMETERS

By default, LILO is configured to pause at a boot prompt. This is done for two basic reasons. First, because LILO offers the capability to manage the booting of several operating systems, it must pause long enough to offer the user a choice of which operating system to boot. If you press the Tab key at the boot prompt, a selection list of available boot images is displayed. The name displayed is the label name entered in the /etc/lilo.conf file for each available boot image.

Second, kernel parameters can be entered at the boot prompt. These command-line options are entered at the boot prompt, and multiple entries are delineated by spaces.

Note

Boot prompt options apply to kernel drivers only. Behavior of loadable modules is not altered by any boot prompt parameter.

Although several options can be entered at the boot prompt, only a few are presented here. A comprehensive list of all options is contained in the BootPrompt HOWTO document. This document, written and maintained by Paul Gortmaker, can be found on the OpenLinux installation CD as well as many other archive locations. These other archives are discussed in Appendix D, "How to Find Other Linux Information."

The boot prompt options are categorized into non–device-specific arguments and several hardware-specific ones. The hardware specific categories include SCSI devices, hard disks, CD-ROMs, and miscellaneous devices such as Ethernet adapters and sound cards.

Most boot prompt options have the following syntax:

```
name[=value1][,value2]...[,valueN]
```

The common non–device-specific boot prompt options are listed in Table 20.11.

TABLE 20.11 NON–DEVICE-SPECIFIC BOOT PROMPT OPTIONS

Boot Prompt Options	Description
`root=device`	Specifies an alternative root device. Most commonly used when the boot loader on the hard disk fails.
`single`	Boots the selected image into single user mode.
`reserve=base,size...`	Used to reserve specified IO ports. This prevents auto-probing of these addresses.
`debug`	Logs more verbose status messages.

NOTE: You can use the OpenLinux installation floppy to boot to the hard disk, if necessary, by entering `boot root=/dev/hda1` *at the boot prompt.*

TROUBLESHOOTING

Although LILO is quite easily installed, it's really quite a complex set of programs and routines. Fortunately, most of the process is transparent to the user. However, because of the level of complexity, it sometimes fails when trying to determine disk geometry or the location of key files. This section describes the types of error messages that LILO produces and how they can be used in debugging LILO failures. Both the map installer and the boot loader produce helpful messages for debugging purposes.

MAP INSTALLER

Two types of errors are reported by LILO—fatal errors and warning errors. As the name suggests, fatal errors are unrecoverable. Warning errors are just that, a warning that everything is not completely correct but that the map installer will still run. However, often a warning error is followed by a fatal error and the map installer fails. Using the `nowarn` option suppresses all warning errors. A comprehensive list of error messages is included in the LILO documentation RPM.

Fatal errors are typically caused by problems with the interpretation of disk geometry. One main objective of the map installer is to create the map of where the required components reside in order for it to work. If you recall, this is done by identifying the physical location on the hard drive rather than relying on a given file system.

BOOT LOADER MESSAGES

Three types of messages can be generated by the boot loader:

- Messages resulting from invalid boot prompt options
- Disk access error messages
- Progress or error messages

The first type is basically self-explanatory. The second type, disk access errors, is described in detail in the LILO documentation RPM. They are most often the result of some sort of media problem. For example, a 0×10 error commonly occurs when the boot loader cannot be read from the floppy disk. This is almost always corrected with a new disk.

The third type of message is either a progress status report as the boot loader proceeds and completes or an identification of an error if it stops at some point. As the boot loader proceeds, the word *LILO* is printed to the screen, one letter at a time. If, for some reason, LILO fails, the last letter displayed to the screen can be used as a clue as to why it might have failed. The letter *L* is displayed when LILO begins to run. If the letter *L* does not appear, it means that LILO was not found. If the LILO is completely spelled out, the boot loader completed successfully. Table 20.12 lists the descriptions of what failed if the boot loader stops before spelling out the word LILO.

TABLE 20.12 TROUBLESHOOTING THE LILO BOOT PROMPT

LILO Prompt Display	Description
L	The first stage boot loader started, but it was unable to load the second stage. This usually indicates a media failure.
LI	The first stage and the second stage of the boot loader have successfully run. This typically means that LILO cannot find the kernel.
LIL	Can't read the data from the map file. Usually caused by a media error.
LIL?	The second stage boot loader was loaded but at an incorrect address.
LIL-	The descriptor table is corrupt.
LILO	LILO has successfully completed.

Other Boot Loader Options

An alternative boot loader is LOADLIN. LOADLIN is a DOS-based boot loader program that boots Linux. Because it is DOS-based, your system must be configured to first boot to DOS and then run LOADLIN.EXE to switch to Linux. LOADLIN works well in situations in which a certain hardware component depends on a DOS driver to set a few proprietary registers before it is recognized by another operating system. Table 20.13 depicts the steps of the boot sequence using LOADLIN.

Table 20.13 LOADLIN Boot Sequence

Master Boot Record	Boot Sector Type	Operating System
DOS-MBR	DOS	COMMAND.COM
LOADLIN.EXE	Linux kernel	

Summary

In this chapter, the details of the boot process were covered. You should now feel comfortable with the concept of a boot loader and how it is used. LILO is the default boot loader used with Linux. The two key programs of LILO are the map installer (`/sbin/lilo`) and the boot loader. The map installer uses the LILO configuration file (/etc/lilo.conf) to determine how and where to install the boot loader. The boot loader is the program that is initiated during the boot process to determine where the Linux kernel resides.

For more information on the topics discussed here, see the following chapters:

- See Chapter 2 for further details on configuring LILO during the installation procedure.
- See Chapter 9, "Understanding the Linux File System," to learn more about the Linux File System hierarchy and the location of key configuration files.
- See Chapter 19 to learn more about additional hard drives and new partitions.

PART IV

NETWORKING WITH OPENLINUX

CHAPTER 21

Understanding TCP/IP Fundamentals

In this chapter

In this chapter you will look at networking basics as they apply to OpenLinux. This chapter lays the groundwork for a better understanding of the concepts covered in this and the next few chapters. You'll start with the Internet Protocol (IP) and see how Transmission Control Protocol (TCP), User Datagram Protocol (UDP), and Internet Control Message Protocol (ICMP) fit in. You'll see how to maximize usage of your available address space with subneting. Finally, You'll look at how to configure a network interface card (NIC).

INTERNET PROTOCOL

The Internet Protocol (IP) is defined in RFC791. This is the standard protocol used on the Internet. Most other protocols, such as TCP and UDP, *piggyback* on IP. It is the IP header that provides the information to get the rest of the packet to its destination. But the destination is assumed by IP to be local, so an IP packet travels the local network and is routed to the next local network by a gateway. The gateway and routers along the way make routing decisions based on the destination address contained within the IP header. When the IP packet arrives on the local network of the receiving machine it finds the recipient interface card.

IP PACKET HEADERS

Basically, an IP packet consists of a header and the data packet. This description is not going to go into great detail, but it is sufficient to say that the IP header contains the protocol of the information in the data portion of the packet, the source and destination addresses, and other information used by routers and destination host of the data. You'll take a more in-depth look at routing and addressing issues as they apply to OpenLinux in the "CIDR" section later in this chapter.

Note

Although the header contains a lot of information, the most important is where it came from (source address) and where it's going (destination address). After all, that's what IP is all about–routing messages.

The IP header has a very strict protocol. Certain information must appear in certain locations. This information is rewritten each time the header is processed. To ensure the integrity of the header, it includes a checksum; if the checksum is incorrect, or the packet cannot be handled because it is too large or is just not accepted by a router or host, it is dropped. They are also dropped if they begin to route circuitously and make too many hops. The number of hops left before the packet expires is called the *TTL* (*time to live*). The number is normally around 40. Each router that passes the packet decrements the counter. IP packets are not returned to the sender.

Note

The `traceroute` program takes advantage of the TTL by sending out 40 sets of three packets, setting the first set's TTL to one and incrementing each set's TTL until receiving a reply indicating that it reached the destination. As each packet expires, it is dropped and an ICMP packet is sent from the dropping router that `traceroute` uses to show the route to the destination.

IP DATA PACKET

The data portion of the IP packet can contain just about anything, including—but not limited to—application data, another IP packet (IP in IP), or a packet of another protocol (TCP, UDP, and so on). The two primary protocols contained in an IP packet are TCP and UDP. There are major differences between the two. UDP packets are small, and the sender has no way of knowing if the recipient actually received the packet. Any number of things can happen (as mentioned previously), or the packet can suffer a collision, and the sender will have no indication. It is for this reason that UDP is known as a connectionless protocol. Two-way communications are not considered vital. UDP is size constrained due to its connectionless status.

Some of the common services that use UDP include: SNMP (simple network management protocol), DNS (domain name service), RLP (resource location protocol), and TFTP (trivial file transfer protocol). You can see by looking through your /etc/services file that a number of services use both UDP and TCP. DNS queries on port 53 are generally UDP unless the response set is larger than a UDP packet is allowed to be. The information is then transmitted via TCP. (For more on ports and services, see Chapter 23, "Advanced Network Features.")

TCP, in contrast to UDP, creates a connection between the two computers in a special sequence of events involving the SYN/ACK bits. Every host "listens" for packets to arrive at particular ports. When one arrives for the host, it knows by the port which service to use to respond to the packet. If the packet is a UDP packet, it is passed directly to the application. If the packet that arrives is TCP, the listener (which is already waiting, or is spawned in response to the packet) goes on a *wait queue*; that is, the destination host hears a knock on the door and answers it. This listener passes back to the originating host a packet with the identification number sent by the original host plus one, and the SYN bit is set. This tells the originating host that "Okay, I'm here, so what do you want to talk about?" The originating host sees the SYN packet and increments the identification number again, and then sends a packet with the ACK (acknowledgment) bit set. Now the two hosts have established a connection and the destination host moves off the wait queue so that another listener can be spawned.

Some of you might recognize this SYN-ACK and remember that a particular denial of service attack takes advantage of hosts whose processes do not abandon the wait queue if they don't receive the ACK. The attacker sends the connection request with a forged header changing the source address. The SYN packet goes to a host that has no way to respond (because a host that requests a connection reply cannot refuse to ACK a SYN packet, but no other host can answer it). So by flooding a host with multiple connection requests with forged headers an attacker can fill the wait queue of the destination host.

But some of you might wonder why this doesn't happen more often due to collisions, lost packets, and so on. Well, it does. But normally, if something happens to a packet and a router sees a bad packet (or for whatever reason drops a packet), other things take place.

First, if a host requests a connection and no response (SYN) is received, it tries again. The same goes for the destination host. A second ACK packet is sent just in case the first packet somehow died.

But something else can also take place. Along the way a router or even the destination host for a packet might be able to read the packet, but might have to drop it. Perhaps the packet is too large (Ethernet commonly uses a maximum transmission unit (MTU) of 1500, but some hosts only accept 380); so an ICMP packet is generated.

ICMP

Internet Control Message Protocol packets exist at the same level as IP packets. Whereas TCP and UDP travel via IP, an ICMP packet is a host-to-host datagram and doesn't require IP—it has its own IP header. Most folks know ICMP for one particular type—the `ping` packet. In fact, there are several different types of ICMP packets, and some have a number of codes that correspond to those types.

The `ping` packet is a type 8 packet (as defined by RFC792). A host receiving a type 8 packet replies with a type 0 packet (`echo` reply). But a type 3 ICMP message belongs to the generic Destination Unreachable, which is further broken down into codes 0–5:

- Type 0 Echo Reply Message
- Type 3 Destination Unreachable Message
  - Code 0 = net unreachable
  - Code 1 = host unreachable
  - Code 2 = protocol unreachable
  - Code 3 = port unreachable
  - Code 4 = fragmentation needed and DF set
  - Code 5 = source route failed
- Type 4 Source Quench Message
- Type 5 Redirect Message
  - Code 0 = Redirect datagrams for the Network
  - Code 1 = Redirect datagrams for the Host
  - Code 2 = Redirect datagrams for the Type of Service and Network
  - Code 3 = Redirect datagrams for the Type of Service and Host

- Type 8 Echo Message
- Type 11 Time Exceeded Message
  - Code 0 = time to live exceeded in transit
  - Code 1 = fragment reassembly time exceeded
- Type 12 Parameter Problem Message
  - Code 0 = problem with option
- Type 13 Timestamp Message
- Type 14 Timestamp Reply Message
- Type 15 Information Request Message
- Type 16 Information Reply Message

ICMP also allows for MTU discovery, which is a way of finding out how large a packet can travel from one host to another without fragmentation. By utilizing the largest possible packet (up to 1500 bytes), you can speed up communications. However, when these large packets are fragmented, communications are substantially slowed. So ICMP allows those hosts that know how to do MTU discovery to self-tune their packet size to optimize performance. The Linux kernel does MTU discovery by setting the DF bit, and then adjusting the packet size downward when it receives ICMP type 3 code 4 messages.

NETWORK AND INTERNET ROUTING

Now that you have a basic understanding of TCP, UDP, IP, and ICMP, you need to understand how routing works. As you already know, packets are sent out with a particular destination in mind via a network interface. This interface is most commonly an Ethernet card, but can be a token ring card or modem, and so on. The important thing is that this device has an IP address (as found in the IP packet for source and destination) assigned to it. Often, the IP address, and therefore the device, has a name associated with it.

Each Ethernet device has a unique address burned into the card by the manufacturer. This hardware address is in the form of six hexadecimal numbers: 00:12:3a:bc:de:ff. A host learns its own IP address to hardware address through something known as Address Resolution Protocol (ARP) and maintains a cache with this pairing. ARP also learns and caches this address pairing for devices on its local network as it communicates with them. This cache maintains the addresses until they expire and are purged, and then has to learn them again the next time that communication is established. Often, ARP is used to tell a device what its address is, as with HP JetDirect print spoolers.

Note

IP addresses are assigned to communications devices. These are the devices that physically connect to the network, that is, Network Interface Cards (NICs), modems, HP JetDirect printer spoolers, and so on—not the computer. Each communications device (there can be several on one host) gets its own unique IP address and, if it is assigned a name, a unique name that corresponds to only that IP address.

So on a local network, cards communicate by their hardware addresses. If a hardware address to IP address is not held in cache, a host consults its routing table to see where it needs to send a packet. The routing table might say to leave it on the local network, and then broadcasts for the correct hardware address to add to its ARP cache for further communications; or, commonly, it finds out that it needs to send the packet to a gateway machine for further routing.

By way of definition, when I talk about a host being on a local network, I am talking about a host that is directly connected to the same wire or network segment. If you have to go through another host to get to your destination (gateway or router), the destination is not local. This even applies to machines that appear to belong to the same Class C address when subnetted via variable length subnet masking (VLSM) (as explained in the next section, "CIDR.") As you'll see, this can be as many as 254 hosts in the case of a full "Class C" network, but is often less. So ARP caches normally don't grow very large. Unless, of course, you are employing a host as a router with connections to several networks—then the ARP cache can grow quite large.

CIDR

CIDR, Classless Inter-Domain Routing, enables you to maximize use of the limited address space under the current implementation of the Internet Protocol version 4 (IPv4). After reading this section, even if you've never configured a computer for network communications before, you need to have a good understanding of these references to networking.

BACKGROUND

CIDR is the current trend in routing and has been for more than three years. This concept was introduced in 1993 to alleviate the shortage of Internet Protocol (IP) addresses until the next generation (IP version 6—IPv6, or IPng for IP next generation) arrives.

Currently in testing, IPng significantly expands the IP address space by several orders of magnitude. IPng also comes with its own security enhancements. Those desiring to participate in the future today might have the opportunity to do so because Linux has kernel-level support for IPng. Until IPng is deployed on a large scale, making the best use of what you have is what CIDR is all about.

To help you understand why you need CIDR at all, let's journey back in time to the late 1980s. IPv4, the protocol used by computers to find each other on a network, was in use then—but there really weren't many connections to the Internet, or even machines needing Internet connections. In fact, a good number of systems still relied on uucp, the UNIX to UNIX copy protocol, where machines called each other at predetermined times and exchanged email traffic. At that time, the IP-address pool seemed unlimited. That was before Mosaic, the first Web browser, appeared.

IP Routing Basics

Those who consider themselves well-versed in classful routing might want to skip ahead to the next section. Computers understand base 2 numbers (ones and zeros), and humans understand base 10 (0–9), so engineers worked out a compromise to give computers numbers while keeping it simple for use by humans. All computers on the Internet have a unique IP address, which can be represented by a string of ones and zeros. If that string is divided up into four sets of eight (octets), you get four numbers with a range from 0 (eight zeros) to 255 (eight ones), which are arranged in the form XXX.XXX.XXX.XXX. This arrangement is called dotted decimal notation and makes understanding the significance of each unique IP address a little easier for us humans.

Note

It is no coincidence that the dotted decimal notation is four pairs of 8 bits. The number 255 in hexadecimal is written 0xff and corresponds to one byte. So a netmask of 255.255.255.0 to us looks like ffffff00 to a computer. Hexadecimal numbers are prefixed with "0x" to prevent confusion.

These addresses were then further broken down into arbitrary classes A–D. Look at the first half of the first octet:

Class A = 0–127 (0000)	16,777,216 hosts per network
Class B = 128–191 (1000)	65,534 hosts per network
Class C = 192–223 (1100)	254 hosts per network
Class D = the rest (1110)	

The preceding numbers provide for a maximum of

127 Class A networks of 16,777,214 hosts each

64 Class B networks of 65,534 hosts each

32 Class C networks of 254 hosts each

The positions beginning from the left represent 128, 64, 32 and 16 (see Table 21.1). Furthermore, Class A uses only the first number as the network number, for example, 10.XXX.XXX.XXX; Class B uses the first two numbers as the network number, for example, 172.32.XXX.XXX; Class C uses three numbers as the network number, for example, 192.168.1.XXX; Class D is reserved for testing purposes. A network address can be thought of as having a network and host portions represented by numbers and XXXs, respectively. For a Class C address, the network portion consists of the first three octets with the host portion as the final octet.

TABLE 21.1 DECIMAL TO BINARY EQUIVALENTS

Decimal	Binary
0	00000000
128	10000000
192	11000000
224	11100000
240	11110000
248	11111000
252	11111100
254	11111110
255	11111111

The following concepts with respect to networking computers must be understood. Note that the definitions provided here are expanded and given to aid in understanding basic concepts for use in this chapter:

- **host address**—A unique address assigned to a communications device in a computer. If a computer has multiple communications devices (for example, Ethernet cards or modems), each of these devices has its own unique address. This means that a host (computer or router) can be multihomed, that is, it can have multiple IP addresses. This can also be artificially created by assigning different IP addresses to the same device (see IP aliasing).
- **network address**—The base (lower) address assigned to a network segment, depending on its netmask. This is the first host IP number on a subnet. For example, on the Class C network that extends from 192.168.1.0 to 192.168.1.255, the network address is 192.168.1.0.
- **broadcast address**—The upper address assigned to a network segment. In the preceding example, this address is 192.168.1.255. All hosts on the net will listen to packets sent to this IP address.
- **netmask**—A mask consisting of that portion of the IP address where all greater bits consist of ones (in base 2) and all lower bits consist of zeros—in other words, ones represent the network portion of the address, and zeros represent the host portion. For the preceding example, this mask is 255.255.255.0. If you want the netmask for a class B address, it is 255.255.0.0. That is, the portion of the IP address that doesn't change from host to host on the network is replaced by ones in binary.

With this introduction to IP addressing, and remembering that a decade ago almost no PCs participated in networking, it is easy to see why during the 1980s IPv4 seemed to have an endless supply of addresses, even though not all addresses can be assigned. Theoretically, if you could make use of all the usable IP addresses available, you'd have a maximum of approximately 500 million addresses; but if even 100 million hosts have IP addresses, that is extremely optimistic and insufficient for today.

Before leaving this section, I want to describe an experiment. This experiment will not work properly if performed in an environment with machines using only the Microsoft Windows IP stack because its implementation doesn't follow the rules that everyone else plays by. Therefore, you need to be on a UNIX or Linux machine with other UNIX or Linux boxes on your network. Type the following command:

```
ping -c 2 your_network's_broadcast_address
```

What you see in response is every UNIX box answering back with its IP address, and each reply following the first one has `(DUP!)` next to it, indicating that it is a duplicate reply to the query. The `-c 2` argument tells `ping` to send only two ping packets. The number of replies received depends on how many (non-MS) machines you have on the network. If this is performed from an MS Windows machine (95 or NT), you receive a reply from the local machine only.

What is the point of this little demonstration? If you change the netmask on a machine, for example from 255.255.255.0 to 255.255.0.0, you therefore change its network and broadcast addresses; even though nothing else changed (that is, it still has the same IP address and is still connected to the network the same way) it ceases to talk to its neighbors. In other words, this machine is now on another network and requires a gateway to talk to the other machines on the local net (all bets are off for the Microsoft machines).

VLSM

Although IP classifications A–D are still in common use in the networking world, those terms are obsolete according to RFC 1519. For the sake of clarity, I will continue to use them to explain how CIDR works and how you can implement it. Along with CIDR comes the concept of variable length subnet masking (VLSM).

Basically, with a Class address, you have a default subnet mask. For a Class C address, this default subnet is 24 bytes long, so if you put all ones in the first 24 bytes and zeros in the rest, you have 255.255.255.0. For class A and B, this is 255.0.0.0 and 255.255.0.0, respectively. This basically gives anyone assigned a full Class C address 256 unique addresses; two of these are reserved, one for network and one for broadcast addresses. Under classful addressing, you are limited to providing full Class A, B, or C addresses to those requiring IP addresses. With classless addressing, you can subnet these addresses quite simply. As stated previously, the network portion of the address is equivalent to that portion of the IP address corresponding in base 2 to all ones, and the host address to all zeros. This means that a Class C address looks like the following:

```
11111111.11111111.11111111.00000000 = 255.255.255.0
(128+64+32+16+8+4+2+1 in the first three positions and 0 in the last).
```

Again, note that this is 24 ones and 8 zeros, for a total of 32 positions.

Say you have one Class C address (192.168.1.0) available for use, but you have two offices with approximately 75 hosts at each location, one in New York and one in New Jersey. Although you can simply use the Class A address at each site with each office using unique numbers, you can't connect them together because machines in New Jersey can't find those in New York and vice versa. In order for a computer to find another computer on a network, it assumes that an address on its local network (the host portion where all the numbers are zeros) is directly connected to it, and that one on another network is reachable only by going through a gateway.

Note

A *gateway* is a machine (computer or router) that has two or more network addresses, at least one on the local network and one or more on other networks. A gateway sends any communications not destined for the local network to one of its other communications devices, depending on the information stored in its routing table.

Under classful routing, you need two (half-used) Class C addresses, one for each office, which wastes IP addresses. With CIDR, you can cut the Class C address into two different networks. To do this, extend your netmask by one more bit; this gives you two separate networks, whereas before you just had one. This changes your netmask from 255.255.255.0 or 24 ones (hereinafter referred to as /24) to 255.255.255.128, or a /25 network. Both of your new networks have this same netmask; all other rules remain the same. You now have one network with a network address of 192.168.1.0 and a broadcast address of 192.168.1.127. The other network uses a network address of 192.168.1.128 and a broadcast address of 192.168.1.255. Routing tables in the gateway machines take care of the rest.

In the same manner, you can continue slicing up your network into four, eight, sixteen, thirty-two, and so on, networks. In fact, starting at /8, you can slice and dice until you reach /30. Because you have 32 numbers to work with, a /32 represents just one address, and in this special case, there's no need for network or broadcast addresses. That also means a /31 represents two addresses, but because one is the network address and the other the broadcast address, this leaves you with no host addresses—an undesirable result.

Under this scheme, the first octet of the netmask remains 255, but after that you can change any of the other numbers. Instead of being restricted to 255 and 0, you might find yourself replacing the first zero in your netmask with any of 128, 192, 224, 240, 248, 252 or 254, except in the last octet. The network and broadcast addresses bind each subnet (see Table 21.2 for details). Now, any network can be referred to by its variable length subnet mask, or the number of ones in the host portion of the address from /8 to /32 (excepting /31). By extrapolation, each host can be referred to directly by its IP address and the VLSM notation, so that it is readily apparent what the network and broadcast addresses and netmask are.

TABLE 21.2 PARTIAL NETMASK AND VLSM NOTATION TABLE

255.255.0.0	= /16
255.255.128.0	= /17
255.255.255.0	= /24
255.255.255.128	= /25
255.255.255.192	= /26
255.255.255.224	= /27
255.255.255.240	= /28

For example, if someone tells you to assign your machine the number 192.168.0.50/27, you know that the network address is 192.168.0.32, the broadcast address is 192.168.0.63, and the netmask is 255.255.255.224. If you are still having problems visualizing how this translates, I've provided a table to assist you (see Table 21.3).

TABLE 21.3 CIDR TRANSLATION TABLE

Mask	A	B	C	networks	divisions at each multiple of:
.0	/8	/16	/24	1	none
.128	/9	/17	/25	2	128
.192	/10	/18	/26	4	64
.224	/11	/19	/27	8	32
.240	/12	/20	/28	16	16
.248	/13	/21	/29	32	8
.252	/14	/22	/30	64	4
.254	/15	/23	N/A	128	2
.255			/32	0	N/A

To understand how to read the chart, if you have a Class B address of 130.124.0.0, and want to subnet it into 8 networks, read down the networks column to find the first number equal to or greater than 8. This corresponds to .224. Substituting in the netmask gives you a netmask of 255.255.224.0. The divisions at each multiple of: column tells you where to apply network addresses. So the third number of the 130.124.X.0 network becomes 0, 32, 64, 96, 128, 160, 192, and 224. The broadcast addresses are one less, or 130.124.Y.255, where Y=31, 63, 95, 127, 159, 191, 223, and 255. You can refer to this as network 130.124/19. To calculate the maximum number of hosts available for use, use the formula 2^(32-X)-(2*Y) where X is the number under the A, B, or C column you're using, and Y is the corresponding number of networks. For the preceding example, 2^(32-19)-(2*8)= 8192 - 16= 8176 hosts, which equals eight networks of 1022 hosts each.

You will find more uses for classless addressing. CIDR can also give you a way to isolate departments in large organizations to provide better security (by implementing internal firewalls) and decrease traffic on any given network segment, reducing collisions and increasing response times.

STARTING NETWORKING UNDER OPENLINUX

To begin this portion of the chapter, here's a look at how networking starts on Linux in general terms. Next, you'll look specifically at OpenLinux.

Every Linux computer has a network built into it, regardless of any other devices it might have to communicate with the outside world. Every Linux box has as its address localhost, which maps to 127.0.0.1. This is necessary for certain multiuser applications to function. If you are in state 1 (single user or maintenance mode), even this network interface is inactive. But under all other conditions, you'll want to have this available. So first set up this host using the `ifconfig` utility as follows:

```
ifconfig lo 127.0.0.1
```

This creates the network device known as `lo`. To complete the network setup for `lo`, you need to tell the system just a little more about 127.0.0.1. For this you use the `route` command as follows:

```
route add -net 127.0.0.0
```

You can optionally tell the system its netmask and broadcast address, but because in this example you didn't, it assumes the defaults, which are netmask: 255.0.0.0, and broadcast: 127.255.255.255. If you don't understand why these are the defaults, review the "IP Routing Basics" section earlier in this chapter.

Because the OpenLinux kernel is a modular kernel, any NIC (network interface card) needs to have its module loaded during bootup. (To configure a modem, see Chapter 24 "Connecting to an ISP.") If, during installation, you told `lisa` about your NIC, this module was loaded when `init` ran the `/etc/rc.d/rc.modules` script. This script looks in a file called /etc/modules/`uname -r`/`uname -v`.default for the names of files to be loaded during system initialization. You can add to or delete from this list as you see fit.

After the module is loaded, you can configure your NIC. To ensure that the module is loaded, type `/sbin/lsmod`. This shows which modules are loaded. If the correct module for your NIC isn't loaded, you can, as root, use the `/sbin/insmod` command to load the module. For example, use `` `insmod tulip` `` to load the `tulip.o` driver. Note that a few modules depend on other modules being loaded first. Usually, it is the 8390 module. If you receive errors when trying to load your module, try the 8390 module first, and then try your module.

To configure your NIC, you do essentially the same thing as you did with `` `lo` ``, but this time call it `` `eth0` `` for an Ethernet device, or `` `tr0` `` for a token ring device.

Note

> Network devices, unlike all other devices that have a corresponding block or character special file in /dev, do not have such a file. Network devices are virtual devices, and are created in memory when the device is activated. Under the 2.2.x kernel you can create special files that can communicate as if they were network devices, but this is a special case.

You need to know your IP, netmask, and broadcast addresses. They are used as follows: `/sbin/ifconfig eth0 192.168.10.85 netmask 255.255.255.128 broadcast 192.168.10.127`, substituting the appropriate numbers for your host and network. Now the Ethernet device is active and can be reached by other hosts. But to respond to other hosts, particularly those off the local network, you'll need a few routing commands as follows: `/sbin/route add -net 192.168.10.0` for local routing, and `/sbin/route add default gw 192.168.10.90` for external routing. The `default` corresponds to 0.0.0.0 which means any unknown routes. The `gw` means this host is the gateway and therefore routes all packets destined for hosts not on this network to the next network segment.

All this is accomplished under OpenLinux by a series of scripts and configuration files. These files can be found under /etc/sysconfig. The first configuration file, /etc/sysconfig/network, is a very basic three line configuration file configured by `lisa` during installation; it says whether you want to set up networking, what you've told `lisa` your fully qualified hostname is, and the types of devices you want to configure. These can be changed by hand at any time, and will be effective during the next bootup or when the `/etc/rc.d/init.d/network` script is run by hand.

The scripts in /etc/sysconfig/network-scripts, specifically `ifcfg-eth0 (-lo, -eth1, -tr0)`, contain the configuration data for particular devices. You will never have to modify `ifcfg-lo`, but you might want or need to modify the others. These can be modified either by using `lisa` or by hand. The variables contained within these files are self-explanatory so I'll not go through them; rather, I'll just show you one (`ifcfg-eth0`):

```
#!/bin/sh
#>>>Device type: ethernet
#>>>Variable declarations:
DEVICE=eth0
IPADDR=192.168.0.1
NETMASK=255.255.255.0
NETWORK=192.168.0.0
BROADCAST=192.168.0.255
GATEWAY=none
ONBOOT=yes
#>>>End variable declarations
```

Although other scripts run to actually perform the setup, I'll leave reading the scripts, starting with `/etc/rc.d/init.d/network`, as an exercise for the reader. All the configuration you might need to change resides in the scripts mentioned in this chapter:

```
/etc/modules/`uname -r`/`uname -v`.default
/etc/sysconfig/network
/etc/sysconfig/network-scripts/ifcfg-eth0, and possibly one or two others.
```

You'll look at other network-related topics in subsequent chapters.

SUMMARY

In this chapter you learned the basics about IP, TCP, UDP, and ICMP. You also learned some basic concepts in networking and network routing of IP packets. You learned about classful and classless addressing for networks, and how VLSM can maximize a small IP pool. Finally, you learned how to initialize a NIC and set up basic routing for your host.

For more information on the topics discussed here, refer to the following chapters:

- See Chapter 18, “Kernel Modules,” to learn more about using kernel modules to activate your NIC.
- See Chapter 23 to learn more about configuring gateways in OpenLinux.
- See Chapter 24 to learn more about using modem devices to connect to the Internet.
- See Chapter 22, “Network Administration,” to learn more about administering a network in OpenLinux.

CHAPTER 22

NETWORK ADMINISTRATION

In this chapter

In this chapter you'll continue your look at networking. You'll perform some troubleshooting, see how to determine where any problems might lie, and discover some corrective measures. You'll also look at the network as a whole, with an eye to guidelines to determine if you have problems.

CHECKING THE NETWORK STATUS

Before you begin checking the external network, a good starting point is to make sure that the machine you've just configured is correctly set up. To do that, it is recommended that you check your /etc/hosts file. This file always contains a localhost entry and an entry for the machine. It is also a good idea to put any other hosts on the local network in this file if you do not have a DNS server on your network. This file can be edited by hand. Any warnings to use `lisa` can be safely ignored. The hosts file always has the following format:

```
# remarks begin with a "#" symbol and terminate with a <newline>.
# other entries are IP address, fully qualified name, alias
➥(or short name):
127.0.0.1     localhost
192.168.0.1     bar.baz.org     bar
192.168.0.2     foo.baz.org     foo
```

One of the advantages of maintaining a complete /etc/hosts file on at least one system is that errors such as giving two hosts the same name or IP address are minimized. This is especially true for systems using static rather than dynamic addressing. If one system is used as the master and copied to the other system, problems such as the ones mentioned previously can be reduced.

To test that your interface is working correctly, type `ping -c 5 192.168.0.2` (assuming you are working on the host `192.168.0.2`). If that doesn't work, the Ethernet card is not properly configured (see Chapter 21, "Understanding TCP/IP Fundamentals"). If it does work, try `ping -c 5 foo` to see if you get proper name resolution. If you don't, something is wrong in your /etc/hosts file. After you've assured yourself that your machine is networking, you can proceed to the next step.

NETWORK MEDIUM

Ethernet networks come in several different configurations. The most common today is 10Base, although 100Base is catching up. The 10 and 100 refer to the speeds that the network is capable of maintaining. However, the numbers are deceptive. You can surmise by looking at the numbers that a 100 megahertz circuit allows your host to communicate with another host at 10 times the speed of the 10Mhz circuit. Unfortunately, that's not exactly correct. Because of limitations of PCs, whereas the network circuit can support 100Mhz, a PC cannot normally exceed transfer speeds greater than that of a 20Mhz circuit.

After you've decided on 10 or 100Mhz for your circuit, you must decide which medium to use. A common medium is coax cable, or *thinnet*, which is often called *cheapernet* because of its lightweight price. But coax is also the least reliable of the common media and is only available in 10Mhz. This type of network is referred to as 10Base-2.

A higher priced medium is *UTP* (*unshielded twisted pair*). This cable looks similar to telephone cable and uses a similar modular plug. But the plug is an RJ-45 that has four pairs of connectors (as opposed to the telephone's RJ-11, which has only two connector pairs). These can be either 10Base-T or 100Base-T networks. For 10Base-T, cabling can be category 3 (Cat 3) or Cat 5. For 100Base-T, the cabling must be Cat 5. Also, you'll probably need a hub. Most mini-hubs sold in stores today have four or seven standard ports and one *uplink* port. This uplink port is wired backward so that it can be connected to another hub in one of the standard ports to daisy-chain hubs (if necessary). Without an uplink port, you'll need a cross-over cable to daisy-chain hubs. If you only have two computers to connect, it is possible to forego the expense of a hub by using a cross-over cable. This cable is made by reversing the wires on one end, swapping the 1–3 and 2–6 pairs. These can be purchased where mini-hubs or cables are sold.

A more expensive option is fiber-optic cable. Fiber-optic cable doesn't lose signal strength the way copper cable does. However, although attenuation isn't a major problem, fiber-optic cable is both costly and fragile. You'll need transceivers and AUI cables for the hosts, in addition to expensive fiber-optic hubs. Although this is a good solution for a network backbone (the server-to-server part of the network), it is probably overkill for the hosts.

After installing your network and configuring your network cards, you can try to communicate between the two hosts. The first test is to see if you can `ping` from one host to the next. You'll want to start by using the IP address of the other host:

```
ping 192.168.10.1
```

Substitute the IP address of the host you are trying to reach. If you don't get an immediate response, allow the command to run while you troubleshoot. Some PCMCIA Ethernet cards seem to need a "kick" to get them going; that is, starting a `ping` from the machine with the PCMCIA cards and allowing it to run for approximately ten seconds. Suddenly, all the `pings` return.

If you've chosen 10Base-2, the first thing you'll want to check is the terminators at each end of the wire. Sometimes, these do not make good electrical contact and can cause the network to fail. If you have an indicator light on the Ethernet card, you might check the one on the distant host to see if it is flashing. The host from which you are running the `ping` is flashing. If the distant host's Ethernet activity light is not flashing, nothing is reaching the card. Check the T connectors for a good electrical connection as well. This will permit you to communicate. If you're not communicating yet, you might have a bad cable or a bad or misconfigured Ethernet card.

If you're using a 10- or 100Base-T network, the easiest thing to do is to check the lights in the hub. These indicate whether the hub thinks it can communicate with the Ethernet card it is plugged into. These activity lights can also give you an indication of the amount of traffic flowing over the network. Some hubs use the activity lights to show different network conditions, depending on the hub. Consult the manual that came with the hub for details. Intelligent hubs, although expensive, give better indications of what is going on with the network—and they shut down "chatty" cards. That is, a card that is sending traffic for no reason can be identified, and the port shut off.

EXPANDING YOUR NETWORK

After you have the network functioning between two computers, you can easily add more hosts. The most difficult part is now over, and additions to the network are simply a matter of following the preceding steps. It is also easier to isolate the problem when you have several computers already networked because it is easy to tell if the problem lies with the network cable or within the host itself.

Local networking is probably the easiest to set up. After you have good connectivity locally, you'll almost certainly want to connect to the Internet. If you are using a modem to connect to an ISP, Chapter 24, "Connecting to an ISP," provides further information. This information is also applicable to internal ISDN modems. (External ISDN modems are normally more similar to cable modems, which are discussed later.) After you have one system connected to your ISP, all others can connect through it. See Chapter 29, "IP Masquerading," for details on setting this up.

Regardless of how you connect to the Internet, however, if you want any other systems to connect through your Internet connected host, you'll have to do the following two things:

- Have the Internet-connected host listed as the gateway for all the other hosts on the network. This can be easily added to /etc/sysconfig/network-scripts/ifcfg-eth0.
- Enable IP forwarding in your Internet connected system. This is accomplished for you if `/etc/rc.d/init.d/ipfwctrl` is run during system initialization, if /etc/sysconfig/network has `NETWORKING=yes`, and if /etc/sysconfig/network-scripts/ifcfg-eth0 has `ONBOOT=yes`. You'll also need to ensure that `ONBOOT=yes` and `ONBOOT_TWEAK=true` in your /etc/sysconfig/daemons/ipfwctrl file. You can check to see if IP forwarding has been activated using the following command:
  ```
  cat /proc/sys/net/ipv4/ip_forward
  ```
- If the result is `0`, IP forwarding is turned off; if it is `1`, IP forwarding is turned on. This feature is off by default in the 2.2.x kernels. You can manually turn this value on or off via /etc/rc.d/init.d/ipfwctrl, which issues the command `echo 1>/proc/sys/net/ipv4/ip_forward` to turn on IP forwarding or `echo 0` to turn it off (or you can do it manually).

If you are using a cable modem, you can do one of several things to connect to the outside world. A cable modem is nothing more than a router. Your cable modem provider, most likely believing the world revolves around Microsoft Windows, will probably want to connect one computer with Windows via a cable to the cable modem, and use software that will get an IP address dynamically via DHCP. You can mimic this setup by connecting the cable modem to one Ethernet card and running dhcpcd, the DHCP client daemon, to automatically get an IP address for the cable modem-connected Ethernet card; or you can connect through a mini-hub. If you use the mini-hub, you can use the cable provided by the cable modem company and connect it to the uplink port. If the uplink port is not available or is nonexistent, a cross-over cable is needed to run between the cable modem and the hub.

If you connect to the cable modem through the hub, only the host you want to use as the gateway runs the `dhcpcd` script (/etc/rc.d/init.d/dhcpcd). At this point, you actually have two separate networks running on the same wires. This will not cause any problems, but you might see a great deal of activity on the Internet connected activity light on the hub, depending on how your cable modem provider has set up the network. (See the IP aliasing section of Chapter 23, "Advanced Network Features," to configure one Ethernet card with multiple IP addresses or to install two Ethernet cards in the same host.)

Caution

There is one thing you need to be aware of regarding `dhcpcd`. If you configure a network address on eth0 and don't reconfigure `dhcpcd` to look at a configuration file containing a different interface, `dhcpcd` reconfigures `eth0`, and connectivity to the local network is lost.

By default, the `dhcpcd` software looks for configuration files in /etc/dhcpc. The default configuration file is called config. Other information can be found in hostinfo-eth0 and resolv.conf in the same directory. See Chapter 35, "ARP, BOOTP, and DHCP," for more details.

NETWORK RELATED FILES

The network related files you'll need to deal with on any given machine include, but are not limited to, the following:

- hosts
- resolv.conf
- nsswitch.conf

The /etc/hosts file is the first file generally consulted in regard to IP address to hostname lookup and vice versa. This file can be as small as two entries (localhost and the actual host name), or it can be very large. It is, however, much more efficient to run a name server or use NIS maps than to try to maintain a very large hosts file. You looked at the hosts file previously, and its simplicity doesn't warrant a second iteration.

The /etc/resolv.conf file tells the name resolver libraries where they need to go for information not contained in the hosts file. This always has at least one nameserver line, but preferably three. The resolver uses each in turn. More than the first three can be included, but anything beyond the first three will be ignored. Two lines that appear in the /etc/resolv.conf file are `domain` and `search`. But these are mutually exclusive options, and where both show up (as in the `lisa`-created file), the last one wins. So the `domain` entry, because it is first, for all intents and purposes might as well not exist. Other entries beyond the three discussed in this paragraph are listed in the man pages, but aren't often used.

The /etc/nsswitch.conf replaced the host.conf file present in OpenLinux 1.3 and earlier editions. The change is due to the inclusion of Sun-style resolver routines used in the glibc (libc6) libraries. A number of new options exist and are used here. Unless you have special requirements or make radical modifications to your system, the default OpenLinux file is adequate.

THE NETWORK LOAD

To understand a little about how Ethernet works, you need to know that Ethernet is based on the principle of *Carrier Sense Multiple Access/Collision Detection* (*CSMA/CD*). This means that the Ethernet card, when it is ready to send data, listens for a break in the traffic (if any) and sends out its packets, listening even as it does so. This is the way all the cards on the local network work, and they can all access the network and put packets on it at any time. If two cards begin to send packets at the same time, you get a collision of the packets from the two cards. These cards each detect the collision and stop transmitting packets for a random duration; then they listen and broadcast again. Collisions can result in corrupted headers, or *runts*, packets too small to be valid IP packets.

Token ring networks, on the other hand, work on the principle of collision avoidance. No machine is allowed to talk unless it has the *token*, which is passed around the network. When a machine that needs to talk receives the token, it sends packets. When it is finished (or when a predetermined amount of time has elapsed), it stops talking and releases the token.

Because of concerns about network efficiency, methods of measuring the efficiency of a network have been developed. These methods employ software to read the packet stream and then detect the load on the network, the number of collisions (for Ethernet), and other factors. Some of these software packages, provided with OpenLinux, are discussed later in this chapter. The provided packages might be modified by Caldera at any time without notice; therefore, some packages might not be present, and others that are not mentioned here might be present. Note that many other software packages exist; you only need to search on the Internet or at various sites which have Linux software in either source or RPM format to find something.

NETWORK PARAMETERS

Before continuing, take a minute to study the network parameters you need to know about, what they tell you about the condition of the network or network interface card (NIC), and some general numbers to keep in mind as you look at the output from various programs.

In general, you'll want to know about network throughput, how congested the network is, whether it's suffering from lack of bandwidth, and so on. Some programs provide a better clue for certain information than others do. If this is an area on which you need to focus for justifying new expenditures, and so on, try out the different programs to see if they meet your needs.

One thing to keep in mind is that at the network layers, numbers are often discussed in units of bits, whereas the programs might show you bytes. For example, an ISDN B channel has a rating of 64k or 56k for its throughput. If you use something to measure this throughput, you might see 8K or 7K as the actual throughput. Because a byte is 8 bits, 64k bits equals 8k bytes. Often, a little translation is required.

Also, you want to see low bandwidth utilization on a network. The higher the utilization, the more likely you are to have collisions. A high collision rate seriously degrades a network. Collision rates of more than 15 percent are considered high, and collision rates of more than 20 percent are debilitating. These rates rise as you get higher usage on the network. Many mini-hubs have an indicator light for collisions, and another to indicate more than 40 percent usage. You can be sure that when the 40 percent light starts flashing, the collision light is also flashing. The usage statistics on the network itself can be deceiving, though. A lower network usage can result in a higher collision rate, depending on the number of NICs on the network that are participating (waiting to transmit), and on the protocol being used (TCP versus UDP). For example, one NIC transmitting UDP packets can make better use of the network (with fewer collisions) than 200 NICs transmitting TCP packets. For this reason, raw usage numbers for a network can be deceiving. It is better to look at the numbers of runts and other errors.

MONITORING THE NETWORK

Monitoring the network can also give you the key to problems other than just raw network bandwidth consumption. It can also point to NICs that are going bad. Sometimes, NICs just stop transmitting when they malfunction. This is often not a big problem. The bigger problem comes when a NIC malfunctions and becomes chatty, spewing nonsense onto the network and consuming bandwidth for no reason.

SOFTWARE FOR NETWORK MONITORING

The preceding paragraphs discussed why monitoring the network is a good idea—but just how is it accomplished? Fortunately, this need is so common that a large number of tools exist to measure various parameters. In OpenLinux, it's more a question of finding the appropriate package to measure the parameters that you've decided are important. Unfortunately, because these programs are generally written by and for those with extensive network experience, the programs can be difficult to use, and the output even more difficult to understand. But gradually, that is changing.

`spray`

The first package that might be of interest is `spray`. This particular utility can help you see what kind of throughput your connection is capable of. This utility does, however, require the use of sprayd, the spray daemon, on the remote system. You can use `spray` to see how much throughput you are getting on a segment between two systems. This is particularly good for checking throughput on modem or ISDN lines. The following is a sample output taken from the man pages by Olaf Kirch:

```
$ spray -v -l 1500 -c 800 -r 2 marian
           sending 800 packets of length 1500 to marian...
                   in 19.53 seconds elapsed time,
                   91 packets rcvd by marian in 19.53 seconds,
                   709 packets (88.62%) dropped (0 locally, 709 en route)
           Sent:   40 packets/sec, 61.4 KBytes/sec
           Recvd:  4 packets/sec, 7.0 KBytes/sec
           RPC:    69.45 ms RPC round-trip time
```

This example shows 7K received by the far end of the link, giving us approximately 56k throughput. If this is a 64k link, one of the ISDN modems can be set up to pass 56k rather than the full 64k. It might also be a problem with the line itself not being capable of the full 64k.

Caution

One thing you must be careful of when using any kind of software like this is that it saturates the network. This will be extremely noticeable to anyone else trying to use the network at the same time. It also skews your results slightly. If this software is available for general use, you might experience inadvertent network denial of service, so use this and other routines that put high volumes of traffic on the network sparingly.

statnet

One program that doesn't put a load on your network is `statnet` (not to be confused with `netstat`, which you'll look at in the next chapter). This program reads from the kernel to gain information about network statistics. You'll see the percentage of different types of traffic passing over the network, including TCP, UDP, ARP, Appletalk, NetBEUI, SAP, ICMP, and so on.

traceroute

Yet another tool that network administrators find indispensable is `traceroute`. Whereas `ping` enables you to find out whether you can reach a host, `traceroute` provides you with information regarding the routing to a remote host. The output from `traceroute` can be most telling about where network connectivity is lost. If your network consists of numerous subnets, or you just want to see where you are losing connectivity with a distant host, `traceroute` can help. Each router along the way to the remote host will register, as well as round trip times to each router. This can give you an indirect idea about bandwidth usage along the route. Following is a quick look at some sample output:

```
traceroute to rim.caldera.com(207.179.39.2), 30 hops max, 40 byte packets
 1  stl-wa-pm39.netcom.net (165.236.128.73)  140.277 ms  150.917 ms
➥135.976 ms
 2  stl-wa-gw1.netcom.net (165.236.128.1)  142.078 ms  157.931 ms
➥139.358 ms
 3  h6-0-6-scl-ca-gw1.netcom.net (163.179.232.54)  182.799 ms
➥178.068 ms  379.222 ms
 4  pacbell.good.net (198.32.128.52)  185.372 ms  167.914 ms  169.422 ms
```

```
 5  san-jose.salt-lake.good.net (209.54.101.122)  262.96 ms  287.791 ms
➥289.459 ms
 6  inquo.salt-lake.good.net (209.140.5.2)  275.981 ms  287.835 ms
➥291.384 ms
 7  rim.caldera.com (207.179.39.2)  310.596 ms  346.228 ms  279.485 ms
```


nstat

Another program that dumps information regarding your network to a file or the screen (default) is `nstat`. Sample output is shown here. The cmu-snmp-utils RPM contains this program. This information is in a form that those who are comfortable with SNMP probably find familiar:

```
ipForwarding:           1
ipDefaultTTL:           64
ipInReceives:           266928
ipInHdrErrors:          0
ipInAddrErrors:         0
ipForwDatagrams:        0
ipInUnknownProtos:      0
ipInDiscards:           0
ipInDelivers:           1078
ipOutRequests:          280185
ipOutDiscards:          0
ipOutNoRoutes:          0
ipReasmTimeout:         0
ipReasmReqds:           0
ipReasmOKs:             0
ipReasmFails:           0
ipFragOKs:              0
ipFragFails:            0
ipFragCreates:          0

icmpInMsgs:             26
icmpInErrors:           0
icmpInDestUnreachs:     21
icmpInTimeExcds:        0
icmpInParmProbs:        0
icmpInSrcQuenchs:       0
icmpInRedirects:        0
icmpInEchos:            0
icmpInEchoReps:         5
icmpInTimestamps:       0
icmpInTimestampReps:    0
icmpInAddrMasks:        0
icmpInAddrMaskReps:     0
icmpOutMsgs:            15
icmpOutErrors:          0
icmpOutDestUnreachs:    15
icmpOutTimeExcds:       0
icmpOutParmProbs:       0
icmpOutSrcQuenchs:      0
icmpOutRedirects:       0
icmpOutEchos:           0
icmpOutEchoReps:        0
```

```
icmpOutTimestamps:       0
icmpOutTimestampReps:    0
icmpOutAddrMasks:        0
icmpOutAddrMaskReps:     0

tcpRtoAlgorithm:         0
tcpRtoMin:               0
tcpRtoMax:               0
tcpMaxConn:              0
tcpActiveOpens:          56861
tcpPassiveOpens:         0
tcpAttemptFails:         0
tcpEstabResets:          21
tcpCurrEstab:            6
tcpInSegs:               265873
tcpOutSegs:              278529
tcpRetransSegs:          72

udpInDatagrams:          594
udpNoPorts:              15
udpInErrors:             0
udpOutDatagrams:         904
```

SNMP

The final package you'll look at in this chapter is SNMP. This comes in the cmu-snmp RPM. Although you can use the programs in the cmu-snmp-utils RPM to read the output from snmpd directly, you'll find the `tkined` program in the scotty RPM to be a usable GUI interface. This chapter doesn't go into depth with SNMP because other texts covering the details of SNMP do the subject justice. If your network is large or complex, you'll most likely want to investigate how SNMP can help you. Support for both SNMP versions 1 and 2 is available.

The sample `tkined` screen shown in Figure 22.1 shows a typical network. This network was built by using the IP Discover tool, and then asking `tkined` to `Discover IP Network`. The network address was passed to `tkined`, and a few minutes later active nodes appeared. These nodes were then selected; some of them had their visual representations changed, and were moved around somewhat to be visually informative.

This software can monitor nodes and perform network troubleshooting. In fact, many of the things you've done in this chapter can be done from `tkined` (your monitoring station) over the network. If you have a network to administer, `tkined` is an asset with which you'll want to become familiar. This is sophisticated software, but fortunately, each set of tools has some help, albeit terse in many instances. This software assumes a level of familiarity with SNMP.

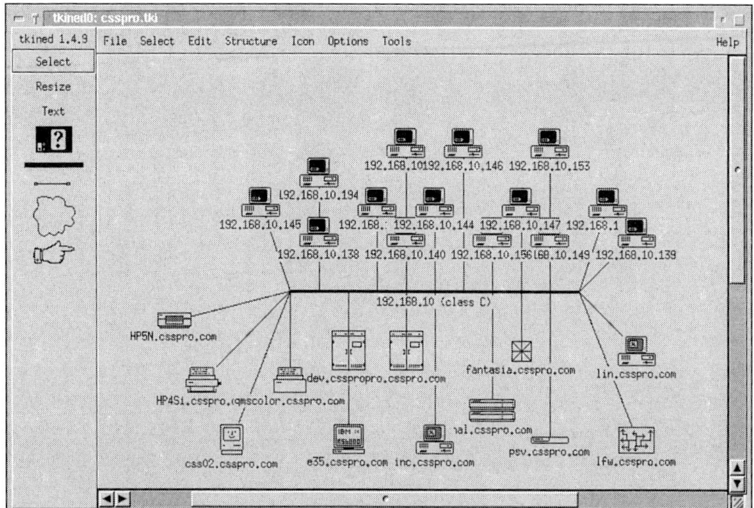

Figure 22.1
A sample `tkined` screenshot.

Summary

In this chapter, you learned how to configure a NIC and to check to see if it is working. You were introduced to the types of networks and media that are in use today. You took a quick look at those files that affect networking and the capability to find and connect to other hosts. You also learned about network monitoring, why it's important, and how to do it. For more information on networking, refer to the following chapters:

- Chapter 21 discusses basic IP networking concepts and routing.
- See Chapter 23 to learn more about how networking and network services work under OpenLinux.
- Chapter 24 discusses basic issues involved with connecting to the Internet via modem.
- See Chapter 26, "Domain Name Server (DNS)," to learn more about how name resolution occurs under OpenLinux.

CHAPTER 23

Advanced Network Features

In this chapter

In this chapter you'll continue your networking by looking at more advanced features of networking. You'll cover multihoming and IP aliasing. You'll also extend your understanding of how Linux deals with services and binding those services to IP addresses and ports. You'll follow that up with an examination of all network-related files.

INTRODUCTION TO ADVANCED NETWORKING

Before you get into the nitty-gritty of advanced networking, including how to multihome a host and put multiple IP addresses on a NIC, you need to be sure you have a good grasp of certain concepts, including how services work within Linux.

Tip

A *multihomed* host is a host with multiple IP addresses and names. This is done to allow one host to share resources between two or more organizations with different domain names.

Within Linux, you can have a lot of different things going on at one time. You can have telnet sessions to and from your host, World Wide Web, FTP, and more. Each of these is its own separate connection to an IP address and a port. The ports differentiate services, each of which uses a different *protocol*, or set of rules, and has a server (to discriminate from a host) that speaks that protocol.

This is the easiest way to explain it: Assume a host is like a house. The family living in this house is very large, and many of the family members speak different languages (as well as a common household language). They are all busy, but a number of them are doing their work in the living room. Between the living room and the front door is a very small vestibule. This vestibule can't hold very many people, so when someone comes knocking on the front door (the NIC), they know to use a special knock. The family members sitting in the living room respond only to their special knock. These knocks correspond to a port. So someone who wants to speak FTP knocks 21 times, and the family member who speaks FTP gets up to answer the door. But just to make sure that it is for him, when he arrives at the door, he knocks on the door himself for verification. When the person outside responds in kind to the reply knock, the family member who speaks FTP opens the door and begins the conversation, bringing the person outside into the living room with him and freeing the vestibule area for someone else.

Although this explanation is very simplistic, it is a fair representation of a connection request on an IP port. A subsequent response is returned to the client with the SYN bit set by the server listening on the port in the wait queue (vestibule). The client requesting the connection then replies (with the ACK bit set), which creates the connection, and moves the connection off the wait queue so that another server process can bind (listen on) the port.

When the conversation is finished, a simpler but similar disconnection ritual takes place. You'll take a closer look at this connect/disconnect process later in the chapter, in the section "Reading `netstat` Output."

MANAGING MULTIPLE IP ADDRESSES

Sometimes, you find yourself in a situation in which you need to have multiple IP addresses on a host. This often causes problems for inexperienced administrators. During the OpenLinux installation, you are asked for a name for the host. This question is asked regardless of the presence or absence of a NIC. If a NIC is installed, the installation routine also asks for a domain name. At this point, it is of no consequence that you call the name that you gave this host the hostname.

But now you need to have two network addresses on your machine. You're going to multihome your box because you have two different companies that share the box for the purpose of running a Web and FTP site. These two companies have different needs, so this is not a simple case in which you can configure a virtual server from which to run the two different companies. Because you can't bind two different servers to the same IP/port combination, you're going to add a second Ethernet card.

You run into the first problem during bootup. Somehow, you need to differentiate the cards so that you know which IP address to bind to which card. You can do this in /etc/lilo.conf with the following command:

```
append="ether=eth0,io=0x300,int=10 ether=eth1,io=0x220,int=11"
```

This can also be accomplished from a command line.

Now you can assign each Ethernet card its own IP address. You can either use `lisa` to do this or you can `cd` into /etc/sysconfig/network-scripts/ and edit the file ifcfg-eth1, including the information you need. (See Chapter 29, "IP Masquerading," for details on IP forwarding.)

Now that you have two separate Ethernet cards activated, you'll probably want to assign a name to each IP address. You can edit the /etc/hosts file and then insert the IP address, the name you want to associate with that IP address, and any aliases. Each part is separated by white space. (See Listing 23.1 for a simple /etc/hosts file.)

LISTING 23.1 SAMPLE /ETC/HOSTS FILE

```
127.0.0.1        localhost
192.168.0.1      foo.void.org      foo
192.168.0.2      bar.void.org      bar
192.168.0.3       baz.void.org      baz
```

A frequent misunderstanding arises at this point for inexperienced administrators. Because the name you assigned to this host is its hostname, and both Ethernet cards are in the same host, they must both have the same name. This can cause no end of confusion and problems when you can't connect to the correct server. It is not the host whose name you put next to the IP address, but the name that corresponds to the IP address. These are commonly one and the same; however, with multiple IP addresses on the same host, this is no longer true. Each unique IP address also needs to have a unique name assigned to it. Some server processes look in the hosts file for the hostname they are to bind to, and choose the first IP address corresponding to that hostname. This might, in fact, be the wrong IP address, and therefore cause clients to fail to connect if the second IP address is the only one bound by the service that you need. You'll look at this closer in the section on `netstat` that follows. So plan to assign each communications device that has a unique IP address, be it a NIC or modem, a unique name.

Note

For any communications device that gets its name dynamically, you do not have an entry in /etc/hosts.

IP ALIASING

You don't necessarily need to have two network cards to have two IP addresses on a single host. By using IP aliasing, you can assign multiple IP addresses to the same NIC. In order to do that, though, the Linux kernel must have been configured and built with that support. To find out if support is available, you can `cat/proc/net/alias_types`. A response of `type 2, name IP, n_attach 0` means that IP aliasing is available. With a modular kernel, a call to `` `insmod ip_alias` `` might be necessary to turn IP aliasing on. This module can be loaded automatically during system initialization by typing the following from a command line:

```
echo "ip_alias" >> /etc/modules/`uname -r`/`uname -v`.default
```

If the kernel doesn't support IP aliasing, you'll need to rebuild it with support. For more specific information on rebuilding the Linux kernel, see Chapter 17, "Building Custom Kernels." To include aliasing support, both the `CONFIG_NET_ALIAS` and `CONFIG_IP_ALIAS` options must be specified. The `CONFIG_NET_ALIAS` option is only yes or no, but the `CONFIG_IP_ALIAS` can be yes, no, or module. Also, `CONFIG_IP_ALIAS` depends on `CONFIG_NET_ALIAS`, and is not available without it.

ADDRESSING ONE NIC WITH TWO IP ADDRESSES

With two Ethernet cards in the host, assigning an IP address to each is a matter of specifying the address and device as arguments to `ifconfig`. Because only one Ethernet card gets two addresses, a way to specify which one you are addressing is necessary. The first address can be specified as usual. But to assign the second address, a modification to the device name is made. Specifically, you refer to the second address assignment for a particular card in the form `eth0:1`. This is substituted for the simple `eth0` that was used formerly. To refer specifically to the first IP address, change from `eth0` to `eth0:0`.

Caution

A number of Ethernet cards, when they are assigned multiple IP addresses, enter a mode known as *promiscuous mode*. During normal operation, a NIC listens for traffic only destined for itself. In promiscuous mode, a NIC listens to all traffic on the local net. This can make it susceptible to attacks directed at other hosts on the net. Most sniffers–and some network monitoring software–put the NIC into this mode to capture all network packets. This mode should never be used on firewalls or other sensitive hosts.

SERVICES AND PORTS

As you saw earlier, clients connecting to your host IP address request service on a port. These ports determine the protocols that are to be used during data exchange. Some 65,535 ports are available for use by either the system or the users. The first 1,024 ports might only be bound by root, and many have well-known services associated with them. Taking a look at a sample /etc/services file (Listing 23.2), you see the service name, port number with which the service is associated, the protocol (TCP or UDP) permitted for that service, and sometimes an alias. The *Internet Assigned Numbers Authority* (*IANA*) generally assigns both TCP and UDP protocols to each port, although some services use only one. But several services allow both UDP and TCP. For example, the domain service (DNS) on port 53 normally uses UDP when requesting and transferring name lookups, but if the name service request results in an answer that can't fit in a UDP packet, the servicing DNS host initiates a TCP connection.

LISTING 23.2 SAMPLE /ETC/SERVICES FILE

```
#$NetBSD: services,v 1.18 1996/03/26 00:07:58 mrg Exp $
#
# Network services, Internet style
#
# Note that it is presently the policy of IANA to assign a single
➥well-known
# port number for both TCP and UDP; hence, most entries here
➥have two entries
# even if the protocol doesn't support UDP operations.
# Updated from RFC 1340, ``Assigned Numbers'' (July 1992).  Not all ports
# are included, only the more common ones.
#
#from: @(#)services      5.8 (Berkeley) 5/9/91
#
tcpmux          1/tcp           # TCP port service multiplexer
echo            7/tcp
echo            7/udp
discard         9/tcp           sink null
discard         9/udp           sink null
systat          11/tcp          users
daytime         13/tcp
daytime         13/udp
```

continues

LISTING 23.2 CONTINUED

```
netstat         15/tcp
qotd            17/tcp          quote
msp             18/tcp          # message send protocol
msp             18/udp          # message send protocol
chargen         19/tcp          ttytst source
chargen         19/udp          ttytst source
ftp-data 20/tcp         # default ftp data port
ftp             21/tcp
ssh             22/tcp
ssh             22/udp
telnet          23/tcp
# 24 - private
smtp            25/tcp          mail
# 26 - unassigned
time            37/tcp          timserver
time            37/udp          timserver
rlp             39/udp          resource        # resource location
nameserver      42/tcp          name            # IEN 116
whois           43/tcp          nicname
domain          53/tcp          nameserver      # name-domain server
domain          53/udp          nameserver
mtp             57/tcp                          # deprecated
bootps          67/tcp          # BOOTP server
bootps          67/udp
bootpc          68/tcp          # BOOTP client
bootpc          68/udp
tftp            69/udp
gopher          70/tcp          # Internet Gopher
gopher          70/udp
rje             77/tcp          netrjs
finger          79/tcp
www             80/tcp          http    # WorldWideWeb HTTP
www             80/udp                  # HyperText Transfer Protocol
link            87/tcp          ttylink
kerberos 88/tcp         krb5    # Kerberos v5
kerberos 88/udp
supdup          95/tcp
# 100 - reserved
hostnames 101/tcp       hostname        # usually from sri-nic
iso-tsap 102/tcp        tsap            # part of ISODE.
csnet-ns 105/tcp        cso-ns  # also used by CSO name server
csnet-ns 105/udp        cso-ns
rtelnet         107/tcp         # Remote Telnet
rtelnet         107/udp
pop2            109/tcp         pop-2 postoffice        # POP version 2
pop2            109/udp
pop3            110/tcp         pop-3 # POP version 3
pop3            110/udp
sunrpc          111/tcp
sunrpc          111/udp
auth            113/tcp         authentication tap ident
sftp            115/tcp
uucp-path 117/tcp
nntp            119/tcp         readnews untp   # USENET News Transfer Protocol
ntp             123/tcp
```

```
ntp             123/udp                    # Network Time Protocol
netbios-ns      137/tcp                    # NETBIOS Name Service
netbios-ns      137/udp
netbios-dgm     138/tcp                    # NETBIOS Datagram Service
netbios-dgm     138/udp
netbios-ssn     139/tcp                    # NETBIOS session service
netbios-ssn     139/udp
imap2           143/tcp         imap       # Interim Mail Access Proto v2
imap2           143/udp
snmp            161/udp                    # Simple Net Mgmt Proto
snmp-trap 162/udp       snmptrap        # Traps for SNMP
cmip-man  163/tcp                       # ISO mgmt over IP (CMOT)
cmip-man  163/udp
cmip-agent      164/tcp
cmip-agent      164/udp
xdmcp           177/tcp                 # X Display Mgr. Control Proto
xdmcp           177/udp
nextstep  178/tcp       NeXTStep NextStep       # NeXTStep window
nextstep  178/udp       NeXTStep NextStep       # server
bgp             179/tcp                 # Border Gateway Proto.
bgp             179/udp
prospero  191/tcp               # Cliff Neuman's Prospero
prospero  191/udp
irc             194/tcp                 # Internet Relay Chat
irc             194/udp
smux            199/tcp                 # SNMP Unix Multiplexer
smux            199/udp
at-rtmp         201/tcp                 # AppleTalk routing
at-rtmp         201/udp
at-nbp          202/tcp                 # AppleTalk name binding
at-nbp          202/udp
at-echo         204/tcp                 # AppleTalk echo
at-echo         204/udp
at-zis          206/tcp                 # AppleTalk zone information
at-zis          206/udp
z3950           210/tcp         wais    # NISO Z39.50 database
z3950           210/udp         wais
ipx             213/tcp                 # IPX
ipx             213/udp
imap3           220/tcp                 # Interactive Mail Access
imap3           220/udp                 # Protocol v3
ulistserv 372/tcp               # UNIX Listserv
ulistserv 372/udp
#
# UNIX specific services
#
exec            512/tcp
biff            512/udp         comsat
login           513/tcp
who             513/udp         whod
shell           514/tcp         cmd             # no passwords used
syslog          514/udp
printer         515/tcp         spooler         # line printer spooler
talk            517/udp
ntalk           518/udp
```

continues

LISTING 23.2 CONTINUED

```
route           520/udp         router routed   # RIP
timed           525/udp         timeserver
tempo           526/tcp         newdate
courier         530/tcp         rpc
conference      531/tcp         chat
netnews         532/tcp         readnews
netwall         533/udp                         # -for emergency broadcasts
uucp            540/tcp         uucpd           # uucp daemon
remotefs 556/tcp        rfs_server rfs  # Brunhoff remote filesystem
#
webster         765/tcp                         # Network dictionary
webster         765/udp
#
# From ``Assigned Numbers'':
#
#>The Registered Ports are not controlled by the IANA and on most systems
#>can be used by ordinary user processes or programs executed by ordinary
#> users.
#
#> Ports are used in the TCP [45,106] to name the ends of logical
#> connections which carry long term conversations.  For the purpose of
#> providing services to unknown callers, a service contact port is
#>defined. This list specifies the port used by the server process as its
#> contact port. Although the IANA can not control uses of these ports it
#> does register or list uses of these ports as a convenience to the
#> community.
#
ingreslock      1524/tcp
ingreslock      1524/udp
prospero-np     1525/tcp                # Prospero non-privileged
prospero-np     1525/udp
rfe             5002/tcp                # Radio Free Ethernet
rfe             5002/udp                # Actually uses UDP only
#
#
# Kerberos (Project Athena/MIT) services
# Note that these are for Kerberos v4, and are unofficial.
#
klogin          543/tcp                 # Kerberos `rlogin'
kshell          544/tcp         krcmd   # Kerberos `rsh'
kerberos-adm    749/tcp                 # Kerberos `kadmin' (v5)
kerberos4 750/udp       kdc     # Kerberos (server) udp
kerberos4 750/tcp       kdc     # Kerberos (server) tcp
kerberos-master 751/udp                 # Kerberos admin server udp
kerberos-master 751/tcp                 # Kerberos admin server tcp
krbupdate 760/tcp       kreg    # BSD Kerberos registration
kpasswd         761/tcp         kpwd    # BSD Kerberos `passwd'
eklogin         2105/tcp                # Kerberos encrypted `rlogin'
#
# Unofficial but necessary (for NetBSD) services
#
supfilesrv      871/tcp                 # SUP server
supfiledbg      1127/tcp                # SUP debugging
#
# AppleTalk DDP entries (DDP: Datagram Delivery Protocol)
```

```
#
rtmp            1/ddp               # Routing Table Maintenance Protocol
nbp             2/ddp               # Name Binding Protocol
echo            4/ddp               # AppleTalk Echo Protocol
zip             6/ddp               # Zone Information Protocol

ase            7000/tcp            #Sybase server
ase_bkup       7010/tcp            #Sybase backup server
online1         1541/tcp            #Informix
srv_agent 1526/tcp          #Informix

swat            901/tcp             #Samba Web Administration Tool
```


Caution

The /etc/services file must not be changed lightly, and it rarely has services deleted or commented out. This file acts as a reference for all network related services, including those used by localhost–the host itself.

Deleting or commenting out services in this file might have far-reaching effects on the operation of the machine, even if it is operating as a standalone host and is not connected to any external network. This is because Linux often makes use of its own internal network, the one defined by the address `127.0.0.1` (belonging to the network `127.0/8`) that needs to always be available. Most often, services are added to /etc/services as you install things such as database servers, whose ports are not generally found in the baseline /etc/services file when it is loaded during system installation. Care must be taken to ensure that the same port numbers are not listed twice.

THE INET METADAEMON

If you look at the process table, you might see `httpd` running. You know from looking at the services file that `httpd` binds port 80. You also see that neither `ftp` nor `telnet` are running (at least, not unless someone is connected to the system). But if you haven't disabled that service, and someone does request it, the system knows to start up the appropriate server process. This is because you have given instructions to a daemon known as the inet metadaemon (inetd—the Internet daemon), or Internet "super server," that a request on a particular port corresponds to a particular service, and that it is to start that service. By examining /etc/inetd.conf, you can tell inetd what you want it to listen for, and what to do when it hears a request on a particular port.

Tip

By commenting out services in the /etc/inetd.conf file, you can deny those services. One of the most commonly denied is `finger`, due to its reputation as a security risk.

The /etc/inetd.conf file is the file that you use to enable or disable services on a port, and what actions to take for a particular port. This saves resources because now you don't have to have dozens of daemons running, waiting for a connection. So why not do this with all services, not just some? This is done simply because some daemons take so long to start that the TCP connection request can time out before a daemon starts to answer the request. An httpd server is a good example. Most httpd servers take so long to start, in fact, that it is common to see several running at any time. Furthermore, although I said that only one process can bind a port, only one is binding the port. If the httpd server is configured to always have five sessions ready for requests, six daemons appear in the process table. One is owned by root, and the other five are probably owned by "nobody"—or a similar user account with no privileges. These processes are started, but they aren't binding the port, as you'll see shortly.

The /etc/inetd.conf file is a fairly complex configuration file with seven fields (see Listing 23.3). The first field is the service name. This name must correspond to a service name listed in the first field of the /etc/services file. The second field is the socket type and corresponds to one of the following: `stream`, `dgram`, `raw`, `rdm`, or `seqpacket`, depending on whether the socket is a stream, datagram, raw, reliably delivered message, or sequenced packet socket. In general, TCP packets are stream, and UDP packets are datagram. When setting up a service in inetd.conf, these values need to be used unless instructions accompanying the software state otherwise.

LISTING 23.3 SAMPLE INETD.CONF

```
#
# inetd.conf      This file describes the services that will be available
#         through the INETD TCP/IP super server.  To reconfigure
#         the running INETD process, edit this file, and then send the
#         INETD process a SIGHUP signal.
#
# Version:        @(#)/etc/inetd.conf     3.10    05/27/93
#
# Authors:        Original taken from BSD UNIX 4.3/TAHOE.
#         Fred N. van Kempen, <waltje@uwalt.nl.mugnet.org>
#
# Modified for Debian Linux by Ian A. Murdock <imurdock@shell.portal.com>
#
# Modified for RHS Linux by Marc Ewing <marc@redhat.com>
#
#Further modified by Olaf Kirch <okir@caldera.com> for Caldera Open Linux
#
# <service_name> <sock_type> <proto> <flags> <user> <server_path> <args>
#
# Echo, discard, daytime, and chargen are used primarily for testing.
#
# To re-read this file after changes, just do a 'killall -HUP inetd'
#
# Note: builtin UDP services now silently drop packets from ports < 512.
echo     stream  tcp     nowait  root    internal
echo     dgram   udp     wait    root    internal
discard  stream  tcp     nowait  root    internal
```

```
discard dgram    udp     wait    root    internal
daytime  stream  tcp     nowait  root    internal
daytime dgram    udp     wait    root    internal
chargen  stream  tcp     nowait  root    internal
chargen dgram    udp     wait    root    internal
#time    stream  tcp     nowait  root    internal
#time    dgram   udp     wait    root    internal
#
# These are standard services.
#
ftp     stream  tcp     nowait  root    /usr/sbin/tcpd in.ftpd -l -a
telnet   stream  tcp     nowait  root    /usr/sbin/tcpd  in.telnetd
gopher   stream  tcp     nowait  root    /usr/sbin/tcpd  gn

# do not uncomment smtp unless you *really* know what you are doing.
# smtp is handled by the sendmail daemon now, not smtpd.  It does NOT
# run from here, it is started at boot time from /etc/rc.d/rc#.d.
#smtp    stream  tcp     nowait  root    /usr/bin/smtpd  smtpd
#nntp    stream  tcp     nowait  root    /usr/sbin/tcpd  in.nntpd
#
# Shell, login, exec and talk are BSD protocols.
#
shell    stream  tcp     nowait  root    /usr/sbin/tcpd  in.rshd
login    stream  tcp     nowait  root    /usr/sbin/tcpd  in.rlogind
exec     stream  tcp     nowait  root    /usr/sbin/tcpd  in.rexecd
talk     dgram   udp     wait    nobody.tty      /usr/sbin/tcpd  in.talkd
ntalk    dgram   udp     wait    nobody.tty      /usr/sbin/tcpd  in.ntalkd
#dtalk   stream  tcp     waut    nobody.tty      /usr/sbin/tcpd  in.dtalkd
#
# Pop and imap mail services et al
#
pop2    stream  tcp     nowait  root    /usr/sbin/tcpd ipop2d
pop3    stream  tcp     nowait  root    /usr/sbin/tcpd ipop3d
imap    stream  tcp     nowait  root    /usr/sbin/tcpd imapd
#
# The Internet UUCP service.
#
uucp     stream  tcp     nowait  uucp    /usr/sbin/tcpd  /usr/sbin/uucico -l
#
# Tftp service is provided primarily for booting.  Most sites
# run this only on machines acting as "boot servers." Do not uncomment
# this unless you *need* it.
#
#tftp    dgram   udp     wait    root    /usr/sbin/tcpd  in.tftpd
bootps  dgram   udp     wait    root    /usr/sbin/bootpd bootpd -i
#
# cfinger is for GNU finger, which is currently not in use in RHS Linux
#
finger   stream  tcp     nowait  root    /usr/sbin/tcpd  in.fingerd
#cfinger stream  tcp     nowait  root    /usr/sbin/tcpd  in.cfingerd
#
# Finger, systat and netstat give out user information which might be
# valuable to potential "system crackers."  Many sites choose to disable
# some or all of these services to improve security.
```

continues

LISTING 23.3 CONTINUED

```
#
#systat   stream  tcp     nowait  nobody  /usr/sbin/tcpd  /bin/ps -auwwx
#netstat stream  tcp     nowait  nobody  /usr/sbin/tcpd  /bin/netstat --inet
#
# Authentication
#
auth    stream  tcp    wait    root    /usr/sbin/tcpd in.identd -w -t120
#
# Samba web administration tool
swatstream      tcp    wait.400        root    /usr/local/samba/bin/swat
swat
# End of inetd.conf
```

The third field is the protocol type, and might include any of TCP, UDP, or RPC/TCP or RPC/UDP. This field also corresponds to the protocol type listed for the service in /etc/services.

The fourth entry is either `wait` or `nowait`. Generally, UDP is `wait`, and TCP is `nowait`. One exception to this is tftp, which, although it is a UDP packet, creates a pseudo-connection, and so must use `nowait` in order to avoid a race condition. The `wait` and `nowait` tell the server how to respond to packets received on the port. `wait` services are single threaded and remain on the wait queue until they terminate. `nowait` services establish a connection and move off the wait queue while they continue communications so that another server can bind to the port. This entry might also have an optional numeric argument appended following a decimal point, as in nowait.400. This specifies the maximum number of servers that can be spawned within a 60 second period. Without this option, the default is 40.

The fifth field specifies the user that the server is run as when invoked by inetd. This permits the flexibility to run a service as a user who is less privileged than root. The user field can also optionally specify a group in the form user.group. If no group is specified, the primary group of the specified user is used.

The last two fields are the program and program arguments. The flexibility of having two fields for the program is what makes it possible to invoke the TCP wrappers program with the actual server as the argument. The default entries in the example use tcpd, the TCP wrappers daemon, to call the actual daemon. (See Chapter 31, "TCP Wrappers.")

Tip

The two ways to protect services are via TCP Wrappers and with ipchains (see Chapter 30, "IP Firewalling," for details). Both include ways to offer the services to a restricted audience without stopping them completely or posing too great a security risk.

netstat

The best troubleshooting tool available for network related problems with any particular host is `netstat`. `netstat`, with no options, shows you the state of network connections. `netstat`, by default, resolves both IP addresses and service names through the standard resolver routines and the /etc/services file.

READING netstat OUTPUT

Let's walk through a sample `netstat` output (see Listing 23.4) from the command `netstat` with no options.

LISTING 23.4 REPRESENTATIVE netstat OUTPUT

```
Active Internet connections (w/o servers)
Proto Recv-Q Send-Q Local Address          Foreign Address        State
tcp        1      1 stl-wa37-31.ix.net:1061 dangle.wolfe.net:www   LAST_ACK
udp        0      0 stl-wa37-31.ix.n:domain *:*
udp        0      0 foo.void.org:domain     *:*
udp        0      0 localhost:domain        *:*
Active UNIX domain sockets (w/o servers)
Proto RefCnt Flags       Type       State         I-Node Path
unix  1      [ ]         STREAM     CONNECTED     875    @00000059
unix  1      [ ]         STREAM     CONNECTED     871    @00000057
unix  1      [ ]         STREAM     CONNECTED     1169   @00000069
unix  1      [ ]         STREAM     CONNECTED     96     @00000002
unix  1      [ ]         STREAM     CONNECTED     76     @00000001
unix  1      [ ]         STREAM     CONNECTED     861    @00000054
unix  1      [ ]         STREAM     CONNECTED     176    @00000006
unix  1      [ ]         STREAM     CONNECTED     147    @00000005
unix  1      [ ]         STREAM     CONNECTED     938    @00000062
unix  1      [ ]         STREAM     CONNECTED     132    @00000004
unix  1      [ ]         STREAM     CONNECTED     934    @00000061
unix  1      [ ]         STREAM     CONNECTED     117    @00000003
unix  1      [ ]         STREAM     CONNECTED     1170   /tmp/.X11-unix/X0
unix  1      [ ]         STREAM     CONNECTED     939    /tmp/.X11-unix/X0
unix  1      [ ]         STREAM     CONNECTED     935    /tmp/.X11-unix/X0
unix  1      [ ]         STREAM     CONNECTED     876    /tmp/.X11-unix/X0
unix  1      [ ]         STREAM     CONNECTED     872    /tmp/.X11-unix/X0
unix  1      [ ]         STREAM     CONNECTED     864    /tmp/.X11-unix/X0
unix  1      [ ]         STREAM     CONNECTED     177    /dev/log
unix  1      [ ]         STREAM     CONNECTED     148    /dev/log
unix  1      [ ]         STREAM     CONNECTED     133    /dev/log
unix  1      [ ]         STREAM     CONNECTED     118    /dev/log
unix  0      [ ]         STREAM                   107
unix  1      [ ]         STREAM     CONNECTED     97     /dev/log
unix  1      [ ]         STREAM     CONNECTED     77     /dev/log advance \d12
```

The first line of the `netstat` output always reminds you what you are looking at: Active Internet connections (w/o servers). This line changes depending on the option.

The second line contains the headers for the first section. The first column is `Proto`, for protocol, normally TCP or UDP, but can also be `raw`, and so on, as defined in the /etc/services file you looked at previously. The second and third columns are the `Revc-Q` and `Send-Q` (Receive Queue and Send Queue), respectively. This shows the number of bytes not copied by the user program connected to the socket, or the bytes not acknowledged by the remote hosts, respectively. After a TCP socket closes, it is common to see one byte not acknowledged by the remote host. This is because the connection is closed and the final ACK was not acknowledged.

The next two columns are local and foreign (remote) address, respectively. These are in the form of *address:port*. In the example, you see `stl-wa37-31.ix.net(com.com):1061` (the full domain name was truncated to fit in the space provided) connected to `dangle.wolfe.net:www`, which you know is port 80. Because TCP connects the server to the client, it sends on one port (in this case 80) and receives on another port (in this case 1061). The return port is not specifically set. This is a random port above 1024 that is not currently in use. On the first connection, the client tells the server which port it picked, and awaits the SYN packet from the server on that port. When the client receives the SYN packet, it returns an ACK, and the connection is complete—and data begins to be passed. The disconnection sequence that occurs when the connection is terminated is similar. This brings us to the last column; in this case, it says `LAST_ACK`. The client sends the `LAST_ACK` and, when the server receives it, drops the connection. Because no connection exists, no reply is possible. Hence, you will often see things like the first line.

The last column, the state of the connection, can be any of the following:

- `ESTABLISHED`
- `SYN_SENT`
- `SYN_RECV`
- `FIN_WAIT1`
- `FIN_WAIT2`
- `TIME_WAIT`
- `CLOSED`
- `CLOSE_WAIT`
- `LAST_ACK`
- `LISTEN`
- `CLOSING`
- `UNKNOWN`

Some of these correspond only to the server side, and others only to the client side, but a few correspond to both sides.

If you add the `-e` switch, you see one more column called User, which gives you the UID number of the user running the process that created this connection.

Starting the next section, you see Active UNIX domain sockets (w/o servers), and then a header line. The header line includes `Proto`, `RefCnt`, `Flags`, `Type`, `State`, `I-Node`, and `Path`.

Looking at each of the columns, `Proto` is for Protocol, as you saw previously. This protocol, however, is normally UNIX, for UNIX-type sockets.

The `RefCnt` column is a reference count of the number of attached processes; it is normally `1`, but can be `0`.

The `Flags` column is normally blank, but if the `RefCnt` is `0` and the corresponding processes are awaiting a connect request, the flag might be `ACC` for `SO_ACCEPTON`, meaning that the socket is ready to accept a connection. On occasion, other flags might show up, such as `W` for `SO_WAITDATA` or `N` for `SO_NOSPACE`.

The Type column is normally `STREAM`, but can also be `DGRAM`, `RAW`, `RDM`, `SEQPACKET`, `PACKET`, or `UNKNOWN`. These correspond to a stream (connection) socket, datagram (connectionless) mode, raw socket, reliably-delivered message, sequential packet, raw interface access packet, or unknown mode (for future expansion).

The State column shows the state of the socket; this can be `FREE`, `LISTENING`, `CONNECTING`, `CONNECTED`, `DISCONNECTING`, blank (no entry), or `UNKNOWN`. The final state (`UNKNOWN`), should not occur.

The `I-Node` column is not of general interest. It shows the I-Node that corresponds to the connection. However, this I-Node exists in /proc only when the connection is in use, so a search for this I-Node does not give the expected result.

The final column is `Path`, and it shows the process attached to the socket.

The preceding examples have not shown one of the most common connection states: `LISTENING`. This particular state is only shown by `netstat` when accompanied by the `-a` switch. Using this switch changes the first line in each of the section headers. Where before you saw Active Internet connections (w/o servers), you now see Active Internet connections (including servers). Likewise for the second section, which now reads Active UNIX domain sockets (including servers). This shows us a much longer list of servers because it includes those that are listening for connections (see Listing 23.5). Looking through the list, you can determine that some of the processes that are listening for requests do not have a daemon spawned to bind the port. This is because the inetd metadaemon is listening and is ready to spawn as daemon for those ports on demand, such as the telnet port.

LISTING 23.5 REPRESENTATIVE `netstat -a` OUTPUT

```
Active Internet connections (including servers)
Proto Recv-Q Send-Q Local Address           Foreign Address         State
tcp        1      1 stl-wa37-31.ix.net:1061 dangle.wolfe.net:www    LAST_ACK
tcp        0      0 stl-wa37-31.ix.n:domain *:*                     LISTEN
tcp        0      0 *:6000                  *:*                     LISTEN
tcp        0      0 *:1024                  *:*                     LISTEN
tcp        0      0 *:mysql                 *:*                     LISTEN
tcp        0      0 *:841                   *:*                     LISTEN
```

```
tcp        0      0 *:7101                  *:*                     LISTEN
tcp        0      0 *:2049                  *:*                     LISTEN
tcp        0      0 *:7100                  *:*                     LISTEN
tcp        0      0 *:printer               *:*                     LISTEN
tcp        0      0 bar.void.org:domain     *:*                     LISTEN
tcp        0      0 localhost:domain        *:*                     LISTEN
tcp        0      0 *:finger                *:*                     LISTEN
tcp        0      0 *:auth                  *:*                     LISTEN
tcp        0      0 *:exec                  *:*                     LISTEN
tcp        0      0 *:login                 *:*                     LISTEN
tcp        0      0 *:shell                 *:*                     LISTEN
tcp        0      0 *:telnet                *:*                     LISTEN
tcp        0      0 *:time                  *:*                     LISTEN
tcp        0      0 *:daytime               *:*                     LISTEN
tcp        0      0 *:discard               *:*                     LISTEN
tcp        0      0 *:sunrpc                *:*                     LISTEN
udp        0      0 stl-wa37-31.ix.n:domain *:*
udp        0      0 *:xdmcp                 *:*
udp        0      0 *:838                   *:*
udp        0      0 *:2049                  *:*
udp        0      0 *:1024                  *:*
udp        0      0 bar.void.org:domain     *:*
udp        0      0 localhost:domain        *:*
udp        0      0 *:ntalk                 *:*
udp        0      0 *:talk                  *:*
udp        0      0 *:time                  *:*
udp        0      0 *:daytime               *:*
udp        0      0 *:discard               *:*
udp        0      0 *:sunrpc                *:*
raw        0      0 *:1                     *:*
raw        0      0 *:6                     *:*
Active UNIX domain sockets (including servers)
Proto RefCnt Flags       Type       State         I-Node Path
unix  0      [ ACC ]     STREAM     LISTENING     179    /var/run/mysql.sock
unix  0      [ ACC ]     STREAM     LISTENING     109    /var/run/gpmctl
unix  0      [ ACC ]     STREAM     LISTENING     530    /dev/log
unix  0      [ ACC ]     STREAM     LISTENING     127    /tmp/.font-unix/fs7100
unix  1      [ ]         STREAM     CONNECTED     875     @00000059
unix  0      [ ACC ]     STREAM     LISTENING     143     fs7101
unix  1      [ ]         STREAM     CONNECTED     871     @00000057
unix  1      [ ]         STREAM     CONNECTED     1169    @00000069
unix  0      [ ACC ]     STREAM     LISTENING     189    /tmp/.X11-unix/X0
unix  1      [ ]         STREAM     CONNECTED     96      @00000002
unix  1      [ ]         STREAM     CONNECTED     76      @00000001
unix  1      [ ]         STREAM     CONNECTED     861     @00000054
unix  1      [ ]         STREAM     CONNECTED     176     @00000006
unix  1      [ ]         STREAM     CONNECTED     147     @00000005
unix  1      [ ]         STREAM     CONNECTED     938     @00000062
unix  1      [ ]         STREAM     CONNECTED     132     @00000004
unix  1      [ ]         STREAM     CONNECTED     934     @00000061
unix  1      [ ]         STREAM     CONNECTED     117     @00000003
unix  1      [ ]         STREAM     CONNECTED     1170    /tmp/.X11-unix/X0
unix  1      [ ]         STREAM     CONNECTED     939     /tmp/.X11-unix/X0
unix  1      [ ]         STREAM     CONNECTED     935     /tmp/.X11-unix/X0
unix  1      [ ]         STREAM     CONNECTED     876     /tmp/.X11-unix/X0
unix  1      [ ]         STREAM     CONNECTED     872     /tmp/.X11-unix/X0
unix  1      [ ]         STREAM     CONNECTED     864     /tmp/.X11-unix/X0
```

```
unix  1      [ ]         STREAM     CONNECTED     177      /dev/log
unix  1      [ ]         STREAM     CONNECTED     148      /dev/log
unix  1      [ ]         STREAM     CONNECTED     133      /dev/log
unix  1      [ ]         STREAM     CONNECTED     118      /dev/log
unix  0      [ ]         STREAM                   107
unix  1      [ ]         STREAM     CONNECTED     97       /dev/log
unix  1      [ ]         STREAM     CONNECTED     77       /dev/log
```

If you add the -v switch, you can find out about unsupported protocols on the system. The last few lines of output give us the following:

```
netstat: no support for `AF IPX' on this system.
netstat: no support for `AF AX25' on this system.
netstat: no support for `AF NETROM' on this system.
```

These lines show that this particular system does not have support for IPX, AX25, or NETROM compiled in.

Troubleshooting Services

One of the options to netstat that you can use to troubleshoot systems, and particularly multihomed systems, is the -n option. This option prevents the resolution of IP addresses and service names. With multiple IP addresses on a host, this shows at a glance which IP addresses have what services bound to them. If this is compared to the output without the -n option, any misconfiguration in address resolution becomes readily apparent. Some services bind to the first IP address that the name resolver returns as the corresponding name to IP address. But hosts on the network might be using DNS or a local hosts table that is different from the /etc/hosts or DNS resolution that the server is using—this option quickly shows you if this is the case.

The Routing Table

One final area that netstat shows is the routing table. With the -r option, netstat shows the kernel routing table. This can be combined with the -e option to provide a slightly different set of output parameters. To see all parameters, use -ee—you get a combination of both outputs (with and without the -e). Listing 23.6 shows the routing tables with and without name resolution, and with and without the -e switch.

Listing 23.6 Representative netstat Outputs

```
bash-2.01$ netstat -r
Kernel IP routing table
Destination   Gateway        Genmask         Flags   MSS Window  irtt Iface
stl-wa-pm39.net *            255.255.255.255 UH        0 0          0 ppp0
localnet        *            255.255.255.0   U         0 0          0 eth0
default     stl-wa-pm39.net 0.0.0.0          UG        0 0          0 ppp0
bash-2.01$ netstat -re
Kernel IP routing table
Destination     Gateway        Genmask       Flags Metric Ref    Use Iface
```

continues

LISTING 23.6 CONTINUED

```
stl-wa-pm39.net *               255.255.255.255 UH    0     0       0 ppp0
localnet        *               255.255.255.0   U     0     0       0 eth0
default      stl-wa-pm39.net 0.0.0.0         UG    0     0       0 ppp0
bash-2.01$ netstat -rn
Kernel IP routing table
Destination     Gateway         Genmask         Flags   MSS Window  irtt Iface
165.236.128.73  0.0.0.0         255.255.255.255 UH        0 0          0 ppp0
192.168.0.0     0.0.0.0         255.255.255.0   U         0 0          0 eth0
0.0.0.0        165.236.128.73  0.0.0.0         UG        0 0          0 ppp0
bash-2.01$ netstat -rne
Kernel IP routing table
Destination     Gateway         Genmask         Flags Metric Ref    Use Iface
165.236.128.73  0.0.0.0         255.255.255.255 UH    0      0        0 ppp0
192.168.0.0     0.0.0.0         255.255.255.0   U     0      0        0 eth0
0.0.0.0        165.236.128.73  0.0.0.0         UG    0      0        0 ppp0
```

The columns and meanings are assigned as follows:

- **`Destination`**—The destination network or host.
- **`Gateway`**—The gateway address. If not set, this is either `*` or `0.0.0.0`.
- **`Genmask`**—Netmask for the destination. This is the netmask for the interface, and is often `0.0.0.0` for the default route, `255.255.255.255` for a host, or the netmask for the network (see the TCP Fundamentals chapter).
- **`Flags`**—These are one or more of the following: `U`, indicating that the interface is up; `H`, indicating that the target is a host (the genmask is `255.255.255.255`); `G`, indicating the gateway for packets that are not destined for one of the hosts or networks listed in the table.
- **`Metric`**—Distance (normally a hop count) to the target. This parameter is not used by 2.2.x Linux kernels.
- **`Ref`**—Number of references to this route (also not used by Linux kernels).
- **`Use`**—Count of lookups for the route.
- **`MSS`**—Maximum segment size for this route (TCP connections only). `0` indicates that the default of 536 bytes hasn't been overridden.
- **`Window`**—The window size for connections over this route (TCP connections only). `0` indicates that the default has not been overridden. This is normally only used on AX.25 networks.
- **`irtt`**—Initial round trip time (TCP connections only). `0` indicates that the default of 300ms has not been overridden. Valid values run from 1–12000ms. Normally only used for AX.25 networks.
- **`Iface`**—Interface. Shows the interface to which this entry corresponds.

When troubleshooting network connectivity problems, `netstat` can often help you find the problem. By checking the routing table, you can verify if the default route has been properly set up or changed (if you are using demand dialing to the Internet). You can also ensure that your nameserver is working by not using the `-n` option. If `netstat` is unable to resolve names, the most likely culprit is the nameserver listed in /etc/resolv.conf (assuming that you've already checked to ensure that your default route is correctly set up).

RELATED NETWORK FILES

You've already looked at some of the network related files found on a Linux file system, namely the following: /etc/services, which resolves service names to specific port numbers; /etc/inetd.conf, which uses /etc/services to determine what service to start when a connection to a particular IP address/port is initiated; and /etc/hosts, an IP address to name resolution file.

Now you'll look at some of the other network related files found in any Linux system as well as one found only in Caldera's OpenLinux.

Under the older libc5 systems, you used a file called /etc/host.conf to determine the order and manner in which the resolver library resolves names to IP addresses. Normally, this is a two-line file, with the first line telling the resolver the order of lookup: This was usually hosts; bind, which meant to look in the /etc/hosts file first; use DNS; and a line that said `multi on`, which meant that if the first failed, it was to use multiple sources to resolve the name.

The newer glibc used by OpenLinux 2.x no longer uses the /etc/host.conf file. This has been replaced by a file called /etc/nsswitch.conf. This is the Name Service Switch Configuration file required by glibc, following the Sun Microsystems convention. This file specifies the databases and the lookup order to be used, not only for IP address resolution, but for other database lookups as well. Looking at a sample /etc/nsswitch.conf file (Listing 23.7), you see two columns separated by a colon. The first column is the database that is available to the NSS; the second column, which can consist of more than one entry, specifies the way lookups work for each database.

LISTING 23.7 SAMPLE NSSSWITCH.CONF FILE

```
# /etc/nsswitch.conf
#
# Example configuration of GNU Name Service Switch functionality.
# Information about this file is available in the `libc6-doc' package.

passwd:         compat
group:          compat
shadow:         compat

hosts:          files dns
```

continues

LISTING 23.7 CONTINUED

```
networks:       files

protocols:      db files
services:       db files
ethers:         db files
rpc:            db files

netgroup:        db files
```

The first column might be any of the following: `aliases` (used by `sendmail`), `ethers`, `group`, `hosts`, `netgroup`, `network`, `passwd`, `protocols`, `publickey`, `rpc`, `services`, or `shadow`. Note that most of these names look familiar. In fact, most have a corresponding file in /etc. Those services that are not used do not need to be listed.

The second column describes the lookup type. Each entry must have a corresponding library in /lib as follows:

```
/lib/libnss_compat.so.1
/lib/libnss_dns.so.1
/lib/libnss_nis.so.1
/lib/libnss_db.so.1
/lib/libnss_files.so.1
```

With the previous libraries, you can use `compat` (compatibility mode), `dns`, `nis` (Network Information Services—formerly Yellow Pages), `db`, or `files`. Conspicuous by its absence is `nisplus`—this means that you can not specify `nisplus` as a valid lookup type.

The database lookup type must match the particular service that you are using. For example, `compat` is applicable to `passwd`, `group`, and `shadow`, but not to `hosts`. Those that you specify with the lookup type of file also need to have a corresponding file in /etc, such as /etc/networks.

Most of the lookup types are self-explanatory:

- `files`—Use files in /etc
- `dns`—Use DNS lookup
- `db`—Use database files

The `compat` mode requires a little explanation. Under libc5, the /etc/passwd, /etc/group, and /etc/shadow files might have used entries with a plus sign (+) or minus sign (–) to include or exclude a user or netgroup, or a `+::::::` entry to signify that `nis` is to be used to complete the file. Under glibc, these are not included by default, but can continue to be used if you specify `compat`.

Tip

> Eliminating NIS-specific items such as netgroups, the + entries in password files, and so on, denies attackers an easy back door into your system. Also make sure that you're not running any `yp` services (`ypbind`, `yppasswd`) if you're not using NIS.

The sample file is devoid of any special fine tuning. But if you don't have an /etc/nsswitch.conf file, the following defaults are used:

- **passwd**—`compat`
- **group**—`compat`
- **shadow**—`compat`
- **hosts**—`dns [!UNAVAIL=return]` files
- **networks**—`nis [NOTFOUND=return]` files
- **ethers**—`nis [NOTFOUND=return]` files
- **protocols**—`nis [NOTFOUND=return]` files
- **rpc**—`nis [NOTFOUND=return]` files
- **services**—`nis [NOTFOUND=return]` files

Note the use of [STATUS=action] between the lookup types. The status can be any of the following: `SUCCESS`, `NOTFOUND`, `UNAVAIL`, or `TRYAGAIN`. They might be further modified by `!`, meaning NOT. The action might be either `return` or `continue`, which means if a `STATUS` value is true, perform the action. So on the hosts line, if `dns` is available but didn't return a value, the lookup exits without consulting the file (in this case, /etc/hosts). These `STATUS=action` modifiers help fine-tune the lookup. The default value for `SUCCESS` is `return`; for the rest, it is `continue`. But under some circumstances, you might not want to continue (or return).

A number of files listed in /etc/nsswitch.conf have either been discussed previously or, as in the case of /etc/networks, are self-explanatory. Little more can—or needs to be—said about /etc/networks than to show what one looks like:

```
localnet        192.168.0.0
void.org        192.168.0.0
```

Often, the file /etc/ethers is nonexistent, and is normally only needed when arp isn't sufficient. The /etc/ethers file is a hardware address to IP address (or hostname) resolution file. This file contains the six hexadigit hardware address (in the form `x:x:x:x:x:x` where `x=00` to `ff`) and its corresponding name (as found in /etc/hosts) or IP address. The /etc/protocols file lists the protocols and service numbers for IP packets. The service number is found in the IP header and is used to identify the protocol of the rest of the packet. The /etc/rpc file shows the program number that corresponds to the `rpc` program name.

The final network related file you'll look at is the /etc/resolv.conf file. This file is used by the resolver to determine which nameservers to use for DNS lookups, and what domains to check for a short hostname. This file has either a `domain` or `search` line. If both are included, only the last entry is used. Up to three nameservers can be specified. The resolver ignores anything beyond the first three. Nameservers are to be specified by IP address only.

CALDERA'S SYSTEM CONFIGURATION FILE

One file that Caldera uses that is not a part of most distributions is a file called /etc/system.cnf (see Listing 23.8). This file is created by `lisa` and is used to construct and change a number of files. Normally, this file is not changed by hand. A glance through it shows that all the information for network-related files and others are included in this one file. If hand edits are done to any file generated by `lisa`, those hand edits are subject to be overwritten when `lisa` is invoked. For this reason, `lisa` needs to be always used or never used, or hand edits to files affected by `lisa` need to have the corresponding entry edited in /etc/system.cnf. However, `lisa` is very sensitive to changes in the files it uses, so it is important to make any hand changes exactly as `lisa` would or the program might abort or produce unexpected results.

Caution

The use of `lisa` is an all or nothing deal. Use of `lisa` following hand edits of any system files might destroy the portions added by hand. The system.cnf file is usually the culprit.

LISTING 23.8 SAMPLE /ETC/SYSTEM.CNF FILE

```
# /etc/system.cnf The one and only central system configuration file
#
# Copyright (c) Ralf Flaxa, Linux Support Team Erlangen, 1993-1996
#
# This configuration file is parsed by all the automated configuration
# scripts and updated automatically. All information herein will be
# propagated automatically to the appropriate "normal" configuration
# files like /etc/hosts or /etc/fstab.
#
# Important notice !
# Please do not edit this file manually unless you really know what
# you are doing. Otherwise the automated configuration scripts might
# get confused or your configuration can be overwritten with wrong
# values. This can result in an inconsistent or unusable system.
#
# Information for configuration. Should be scanned by all scripts before
# doing any actions and wrote back after any modifications.
#
# $Id: system.cnf,v 2.11 1998/08/05 14:45:19 rf Exp $
#
#
# Setup:
#
CONF_SETUP_DISABLE_PNP=off
CONF_SETUP_USE_BOOTP=off
CONF_SETUP_USE_NETPROBE="off"
CONF_SETUP_NETPROBE_PROBES="hostname netmask gateway nameserver"
#
# Partitions:
```

```
#
CONF_PARTITIONS_ROOT=""
CONF_PARTITIONS_SWAP=""
CONF_PARTITIONS_OTHER=""
#
# Hostname:
#
CONF_FQ_HOSTNAME="baz.void.org"
CONF_NODENAME="baz"
#
# Language:
#
CONF_LC_CTYPE="ISO-8859-1"
# CONF_LANG="de_DE.88591" # not implemented yet
CONF_LANG="ISO-8859-1"
CONF_LST_LANG_SUPPORTED="us de fr it es pt"
CONF_LST_LANG="us"
#
# Timezone:
#
CONF_TIMEZONE="US/Pacific"
# CONF_KERNTZ_FLAG="l" # not implemented yet
CONF_KERNTZ_FLAG="u"
#
# Keyboard map:
#
CONF_KEYBOARD_MAP="us.map"
#
# Default Module List:
#
CONF_DEFAULT_MODULES=""
#
# Init setup:
#
# Time files in /tmp are kept.
CONF_INIT_TMP_TTL="forever"
# Set to yes if you want sulogin to be spawned on bootup
CONF_INIT_SULOGIN="no"
# Set to no if you want to be able to login over telnet/rlogin
# before system startup is complete (as soon as inetd is started)
CONF_INIT_DELAYLOGIN="yes"
#
# System resources set by init:
#
# Set/raise max number of files on bootup
CONF_INIT_MAX_FILES=2048
# Set/raise) max number of inodes on bootup (should be 3 * CONF_
➥INIT_MAX_FILES)
CONF_INIT_MAX_INODES=6144
#
#
# Floppy Device:
#
CONF_FLOPPY1_DEV=""
```

continues

LISTING 23.8 CONTINUED

```
CONF_FLOPPY2_DEV=""
#
# Mouse Device:
#
CONF_MOUSE1_TYPE="MouseMan"
CONF_MOUSE1_X_TYPE="mmseries"
CONF_MOUSE1_DEV="/dev/ttyS0"
CONF_MOUSE1_BUTTONS=""
#
# Modem Device:
#
CONF_MODEM1_TYPE=""
CONF_MODEM1_DEV=""
CONF_MODEM1_SPEED=""
CONF_MODEM1_FAXID=""
#
# Printer:
#
CONF_PRINTER1_TYPE=""
CONF_PRINTER1_DEV=""
CONF_PRINTER1_SPEED=""
CONF_PRINTER1_HOST=""
CONF_PRINTER1_NAME=""
CONF_PRINTER1_RES=""
CONF_PRINTER1_PAPER=""
#
# Sound:
#
CONF_SOUND1_STAT=""
CONF_SOUND1_TYPE=""
CONF_SOUND1_DEV=""
#
# CDROM:
#
CONF_CD1_DEV="/dev/hdb"
CONF_CD2_DEV=""
#
# Tape:
#
CONF_TAPE1_DEV=""
CONF_TAPE2_DEV=""
#
# Monitor:
#
CONF_MONITOR1_TYPE=""
CONF_MONITOR1_MAXRES=""
CONF_MONITOR1_BANDWITH=""
CONF_MONITOR1_FMAX_HOR=""
CONF_MONITOR1_FMAX_VERT=""
#
# Graphic Card:
#
CONF_GRAPHIC_CARD1_CHIPSET=""
CONF_GRAPHIC_CARD1_VIDEORAM=""
CONF_GRAPHIC_CARD1_CLOCKS=""
```

```
CONF_GRAPHIC_CARD1_MODES=""
CONF_GRAPHIC_CARD1_DEF_MODE=""
CONF_GRAPHIC_CARD1_FMAX=""
#
# X-Server:
#
CONF_X_SERVER1_TYPE="XF86_SVGA"
CONF_X_SERVER1_RESOL=""
CONF_X_KEYBOARD_MAP=""
#
# Local Daemons:
#
CONF_DAEMON_SERVICES=":amd:cron:httpd:mta:named:nfs:nwclient:rstatd:
➥syslog:"
#
# User Administration:
#
CONF_GROUP_DEFAULT="users"
CONF_HOME_DEFAULT="/home"
CONF_SHELL_DEFAULT="/bin/bash"
#
# First Ethernet Connection:
#
CONF_eth0_STAT="up"
CONF_eth0_DEV="eth0"
CONF_eth0_NAME="baz.void.org"
CONF_eth0_IP="192.168.0.3"
CONF_eth0_MASK="255.255.255.0"
CONF_eth0_NET="192.168.0.0"
CONF_eth0_BCAST="192.168.0.255"
#
# Second Ethernet Connection:
#
CONF_eth1_STAT=""
CONF_eth1_DEV=""
CONF_eth1_NAME=""
CONF_eth1_IP=""
CONF_eth1_MASK=""
CONF_eth1_NET=""
CONF_eth1_BCAST=""
#
# Router:
#
CONF_ROUTER1_IP="192.168.0.1"
#
# Nameserver:
#
CONF_DNS_DOMAIN="void.org"
CONF_DNS_SEARCH="void.org"
CONF_DNS_SERVER1_IP="192.168.0.1"
CONF_DNS_SERVER2_IP=""
CONF_DNS_SERVER3_IP=""
#
# Mail:
#
CONF_MAIL_SERVER1=""
```

continues

LISTING 23.8 CONTINUED

```
CONF_MAIL_TRANSPORT=""
CONF_MAIL_VISIBLE_NAME=""
CONF_MAIL_MORE_HOSTNAMES=""
CONF_MAIL_SMART_PATH=""
CONF_MAIL_SMART_USER=""
#
# News:
#
CONF_NEWS_SERVER1=""
CONF_NEWS_WHOAMI=""
CONF_NEWS_MAILNAME=""
CONF_NEWS_ORGANIZATION=""
CONF_NEWS_NNTPFEED=""
#
# NIS/YP Server:
#
CONF_NIS_DOMAIN=""
CONF_NIS_SERVER1_IP=""
CONF_NIS_SERVER2_IP=""
CONF_NIS_SERVER3_IP=""
#
# NFS Server:
#
CONF_NFS_SERVER1=""
CONF_NFS_SERVER1_PATH="/mnt/cdrom"
#
# Archie Server:
#
CONF_ARCHIE_SERVER1=""
#
# Network Daemons:
#
CONF_INET_DAEMONS=""
#
# SLIP Connection:
#
CONF_SLIP1_STAT=""
CONF_SLIP1_NAME=""
CONF_SLIP1_IP=""
CONF_SLIP1_DEV=""
CONF_SLIP1_SPEED=""
CONF_SLIP1_SERVER_NAME=""
CONF_SLIP1_SERVER_IP=""
CONF_SLIP1_LOGIN=""
CONF_SLIP1_PASSWD=""
#
# PPP Connection:
#
CONF_PPP1_STAT=""
CONF_PPP1_NAME=""
CONF_PPP1_IP=""
CONF_PPP1_DEV=""
CONF_PPP1_SPEED=""
CONF_PPP1_SERVER_NAME=""
CONF_PPP1_SERVER_IP=""
```

```
CONF_PPP1_LOGIN=""
CONF_PPP1_PASSWD=""
#
# UUCP Connection:
#
CONF_UUCP1_STAT=""
CONF_UUCP1_NODENAME=""
CONF_UUCP1_DEV=""
CONF_UUCP1_SPEED=""
CONF_UUCP1_PORT=""
CONF_UUCP1_FEEDNAME=""
CONF_UUCP1_POLL_PHONE=""
CONF_UUCP1_POLL_TIME=""
CONF_UUCP1_POLL_ACCOUNT=""
CONF_UUCP1_POLL_PASSWD=""
#
# FIDO Connection:
#
CONF_FIDO1_STAT=""
CONF_FIDO1_POINTNAME=""
CONF_FIDO1_POINTADDR=""
CONF_FIDO1_FEEDNAME=""
CONF_FIDO1_FEEDADDR=""
CONF_FIDO1_PORT=""
CONF_FIDO1_DEV=""
CONF_FIDO1_SPEED=""
CONF_FIDO1_POLL_PHONE=""
CONF_FIDO1_POLL_TIME=""
CONF_FIDO1_POLL_ACCOUNT=""
CONF_FIDO1_POLL_PASSWD=""
#
# LISA Modes:
#
MODE_USER="newbie"
MODE_QUERY="auto"
MODE_DEBUG="true"
CONF_INSTALL_MEDIUM="cdrom"
CONF_INSTALL_DEV="/dev/hdb"
CONF_INSTALL_PATH_SRC="col"
DIR_SOURCE="/mnt/col"
DIR_PKGS="/mnt/col/install"
CONF_INSTALL_ROOT="/dev/hda1"
DIR_TARGET="/"
```


SUMMARY

In this chapter you gained some insight into the more advanced aspects of networking, including working with multiple IP addresses on a host and the kinds of problems it can create. You learned how to put multiple IP addresses on one NIC. You also learned how a combination of IP addresses and ports are defined to unique services. You learned how the Internet metadaemon works and keeps resource usage to a minimum. Finally, you learned about `netstat` and all the different things it can show you about the state of your host and the services on it. You learned that `netstat` can be a help in troubleshooting connection problems with your host.

To learn more about networking, refer to the following chapters:

- See Chapter 21, "Understanding TCP/IP Fundamentals," to learn how IP communicates. The more you understand about IP, the better you'll understand the output of `netstat` and how to interpret it.
- See Chapter 22, "Network Administration," to learn about networking in general and network-related files. The more you understand about how hosts interact with files and the network, the easier it will be to troubleshoot network problems.
- See Chapter 26, "Domain Name Server (DNS)," to learn more about how systems find other hosts on the network, and how IP addresses and hostnames resolve.
- See Chapter 29 to learn how a private network can exist and access a public network.
- See Chapter 30 to learn more about how to protect a network, and how IP and services work and can be restricted.

CHAPTER 24

Connecting to an ISP

In this chapter

This chapter covers most aspects of what it takes to get connected to an *Internet service provider* (*ISP*). With the ever-increasing popularity of the Internet, this is an area that is evolving quickly. Connecting to the Internet has become quite commonplace for the home user. The pervasiveness of the Internet has made a connection to it basically a necessity, even for people who are somewhat new to personal computing. An OpenLinux system can be used as a personal workstation connected to the Internet or, perhaps more often, used as a gateway connection for a small to medium-sized local area network. See Chapter 29, "IP Masquerading," for more details on how an OpenLinux system can masquerade for an entire local area network.

ISP Connections

Connecting to an Internet service provider (ISP) can take several different forms. It was, at one time in the not too distant past, that direct connections were only available to educational institutions or large corporations. However, much has evolved over the past several years. In fact, no longer do individual users and small businesses have to only rely on dial-up connections; many direct connections are now available—and very affordable. Still, dial-up connections remain the most common method for individuals and small businesses to connect to the Internet. However, with the many dedicated connection options now available at a very affordable cost, look for a dramatic shift to more and more dedicated connections over the next few years. Some of the most common methods for connecting to an ISP are listed in Table 24.1.

Table 24.1 Common Methods of Connecting to the Internet

Method	Type	Provider	Hardware Requirements
PPP	Dial-up	ISP Local or National	Modem Analog Phone Line
Frame-Relay	Direct	Local Phone Company	Frame-relay card CSU/DSU Separate digital phone connection
ISDN	Direct	Local Phone Company	ISDN modem
DSL	Direct	Local Phone Company	Special Modem Analog phone line
Cable Modem	Direct	Local Cable TV provider	Cable modem
Direct PC	Dial-up Satellite Dish	ISP	Satellite dish Modem Analog phone line

Note

A *direct connection* to your ISP is one that is constantly attached. In other words, the need to dial an access number is not required.

The methods for connecting to the Internet go well beyond those that are listed in Table 24.1. However, this gives you a good idea of what is available at the low end, that is, reasonable *bandwidth* (connection speed) and low-cost alternatives. The connection costs for the options that are listed here range from $0.00 to approximately $200.00 a month. You are now probably asking yourself, was that a typo or did he really mean *zero*? Only time can tell if this will last, but as of this writing there were at least two Internet services offering access for free. The only catch that I've seen is that you have to tolerate some advertising; advertising is what enables them to offer their services to individuals for free. The two that I'm aware of are `www.juno.com`, which offers email only, and `www.netzero.com`, which offers both Web access and email.

As was mentioned previously, the most common method for connecting to an ISP is via a dial-up connection using PPP. However, with the cost of direct connections decreasing, the feasibility of switching to a non–dial-up method of connecting to the Internet is becoming much more within the realm of possibility for anyone, not just the Fortune (or fortunate) 500 corporations. Following is a closer look at what it takes to get a dial-up PPP connection going, as well as a look at the requirements for making a direct connection to the Internet.

Note

If you'd rather not understand the underlying concepts of how PPP works and what it takes to get a PPP connection established, skip to the section titled "Using kppp."

DIAL-UP CONNECTIONS WITH PPP

The most common method of connecting to the Internet, by far, is via a dial-up modem connection using the Point-to-Point Protocol. This is true for any operating system; PPP is the de facto standard for dial-up connections. Setting up PPP on Linux is slightly more involved than some other operating systems, but when you understand the basics, it's really quite easy to configure. Also, an understanding of PPP setup at the level of configuration files gives you much more insight into how it works. After a connection is established you are, for all intents and purposes, a node on the Internet. All other applications that are dependent upon an Internet connection, such as Web browsers, are then operational.

Caution

Be aware that after a connection to the Internet is established, you can not only access anything on the Internet, but others can see your machine as well. Take the necessary precautions to safeguard your system.

GETTING STARTED WITH PPP

PPP, or Point-to-Point protocol, is simply a means of establishing a network connection that allows normal IP (Internet Protocol) traffic. It actually supports many different protocols, but for the purposes of this book, you'll just look at it in the context of a establishing an Internet connection using IP Control Protocol (IPCP). PPP connections in Linux are established using the Point-to-Point Protocol daemon, pppd. It consists of the following three components:

- **Data link layer**—A method for encapsulating datagrams (packets) over serial links.
- **LCP (Link Control Protocol)**—Provides link control information over a serial link.
- **NCP (Network Control Protocol)**—Provides a method for establishing and configuring different network-layer protocols.

PPP SETUP STEPS

The setup steps for PPP are quite simple. The things that complicate the setup of PPP are usually the modem itself and the information required from your ISP. If you've ever worked with a modem before, you know that when they work they're great, but when they don't they can be most difficult to debug. Often it's just a matter of sending the appropriate setup string to the modem. If all goes well, you can skip the last step.

Following are the steps to take in the setup:

1. Gather prerequisite information.
2. Configure the chat script.
3. Configure the PPP options file.
4. Configure authentication files.
5. Configure other required network components.
6. Run `/usr/sbin/pppd`.
7. Troubleshoot the connection.

GATHERING PREREQUISITE INFORMATION

The most important prerequisite is to gather information about your Internet service provider. Having this information handy before you begin any configurations can save you much time and frustration. The pieces of information you need from your ISP are as follows:

- The local phone number to dial
- How your ISP assigns IP addresses (dynamic or static)
- The Name Server IP address (DNS)
- The authentication method used (Manual, PAP, CHAP)

The most difficult item to identify is the authentication method that is used; this is because many Internet service providers are accustomed to Windows users, and the software that they provide handles the authentication method transparently. Don't be surprised if the person you talk to at your ISP doesn't know what authentication method is used, especially if you're dealing with a large ISP that has a big customer service staff. The good news, though, is that many of these large ISPs document this kind of information on their Web site, and some even have the scripts and configuration files for Linux. The different authentication methods are listed in Table 24.2.

TABLE 24.2 PPP AUTHENTICATION METHODS

Authentication Method	Description
Manual	This method is just logging on to a system where a user ID and password are required. The trick here is building a script of expected strings and associated responses.
PAP	This stands for *Password Authentication Protocol*. Although it is a better method of password security than manual authentication is, it is still vulnerable to the same kind of attacks that plague any reusable password system.
CHAP	This stands for *Challenge Handshake Authentication Protocol*. This is the most sophisticated, and the most secure, method of authenticating PPP users. It does not use reusable passwords and it repeatedly reauthenticates PPP users.

Aside from the information gathered from your ISP, it's a good idea to double-check the configuration of your system. Support for PPP is built into OpenLinux by default. However, if you've rebuilt your kernel or made other system adjustments, it's a good idea to double check that the module for PPP is loaded. You might have to manually modify the module list to have modules load automatically. See Chapter 18, "Kernel Modules," for further details on how this is done. Examining the loaded module list can be done as follows:

```
# lsmod
Module:         #pages:  Used by:
nkfs                3          2
ipx                 3          5
psaux               1          1
misc                1    [psaux] 1
ppp                 5          0
slip                2          0
slhc                2    [ppp slip]      0
lp                  2          0
3c509               2          1
isofs               5          0
nfs                12          1
sg                  1          0
st                  6          0
sr_mod              4          0
sd_mod              4          0
scsi_mod           10    [sg st sr_mod sd_mod]   4
8390                2          0
```

The module ppp is listed in the left-hand column if it has been loaded. If you've built PPP support into the kernel rather than build it as a loadable module, it is not listed here.

CONFIGURING THE CHAT SCRIPT

The *chat script* is an automated method of talking with the modem. It is used to establish the connection with your ISP, in conjunction with your PPP settings. The chat script can be placed anywhere on the system, but it is recommended that you place it with the other PPP files in the /etc/ppp directory. Each line of the chat script is a simple combination of expected strings and strings to send, although there are a few exceptions. A sample chat script follows:

```
ABORT     BUSY
""        ATDT5551386
CONNECT   ""
```

Each line of the chat script represents an expect/send combination. Each pair of strings in the chat script must be separated by one or more spaces or tabs. It's a good idea to use white space in such a manner that the items line up in two columns.

Note

Enclose all strings that contain spaces in quotes to ensure the correct parsing of what is an expected string and what is a string to be sent to the modem. For example, to send the string "AT &S1 &C1" to the modem, it must be enclosed in quotes.

The expected string is placed in the left column and the string to be sent is placed in the right column. The first line of the preceding chat script is an exception. The string "ABORT" is not expected. It is used to identify cases in which the script is to be aborted. In this case, if the modem returns the string "BUSY", the chat script aborts. This allows the script to terminate without waiting indefinitely for a string that might never come.

Line two of the script just sends a dial string to the modem without waiting because there is no expected string. The third line causes the script to pause until the string "CONNECT" is received from the modem, and then continues with any remaining portion of the script; in this case, pppd completes the PPP connection. A more involved chat script might look similar to the following:

```
ABORT      BUSY
ABORT     "NO CARRIER"
ABORT     "NO DIALTONE"
""         ATZ
OK         "AT S0=0"
OK         ATDT5551386
CONNECT     ""
```

See the online man page for chat for further details and options.

CONFIGURING THE PPP OPTIONS FILE

The options for pppd are stored in the /etc/ppp/options file. When pppd runs, it looks in this file for the runtime parameters, including the method by which it interacts with the modem. The options that are used most frequently with pppd are listed in Table 24.3.

TABLE 24.3 LIST OF FREQUENTLY USED OPTIONS WITH PPPD

Option	Description
tty device	Specify which tty device the modem is connected to. The full pathname to the device that is used is typically specified. For example, the first COM port is /dev/ttyS0.
modem speed	Specify the baud rate that is to be used.
asyncmap *<map>*	Set the asynchronous character map. This map specifies which control characters cannot be successfully received over the serial line.
auth	Require the peer to authenticate itself before allowing network packets to be sent or received.
connect *<script>*	This parameter specifies how a connection is made via the serial port. This is typically a chat script called by the chat command.
crtscts	Set the flow control on the serial port to use hardware handshaking (RTS/CTS).
defaultroute	Set the default route to the PPP interface. The route is removed when the connection is dropped.
disconnect *<script>*	Run a script or executable after the connection has been terminated. For example, a script can be run to reset the modem after the connection is dropped.
escape xx, yy...	Specifies a list of characters that are to be escaped when transmitted. The list is specified as a set of hex numbers separated by commas.
file *<f>*	Read options from the file specified here. The default file is /etc/ppp/options.
lock	Specifies that pppd is to create a lock file when initiated to ensure exclusive access to the serial device.
mru	Set the maximum receive unit (MRU) in bytes. The default value is 1500. A value of 296 is recommended for slow links.
mtu	Set the maximum transmit unit (MTU) in bytes. The maximum value is typically set by the peer with the MRU setting, but can be controlled from the transmit end as well.
netmask *<netmask>*	Set the interface netmask in decimal dotted notation. For example, 255.255.255.0
passive	Sets pppd to wait passively for a valid LCP packet response. By default, if no valid LCP packet is returned on initial request, pppd just exits.
silent	Sets pppd to not transmit any LCP packets until a valid LCP packet is received.

For the complete list of options, see the man page for pppd. An example of a working /etc/ppp/options file follows:

```
connect "/usr/sbin/chat -f /etc/ppp/chat-script"
/dev/modem 38400
crtscts
defaultroute
noipdefault
```

In the preceding options file, the first two lines are the most important. The first line indicates how pppd is to access the modem line. In this example, a chat script is called via the `chat` utility, the script discussed in the preceding section. The second line defines what device to use. In this example, the device /dev/modem is used, but it might just as easily have been /dev/ttyS0 or /dev/ttyS1, depending on which serial port the modem is connected to.

> **Note**
>
> You must either use the actual device name in the /etc/ppp/options file or create a symbolic link to it and use the symbolic link name. A symbolic link is recommended for use in the options files. This enables changes to modem port without necessary changes to the options file. It's just a matter of changing the symbolic link.

The /dev/modem device is not created by default. It is only a symbolic link to the actual serial device to which the modem is connected. It can be created as follows:

```
# ln -s /dev/ttyS0 /dev/modem
```

The first COM port is usually `/dev/ttyS0` and the second COM port is usually `/dev/ttyS1`.

CONFIGURING AUTHENTICATION FILES

Authentication to the PPP server takes place in one of several ways, the most common being Manual, PAP, and CHAP (refer to Table 24.2). Manual authentication takes place by simply supplying a user ID and password to the PPP server. PAP and CHAP authentication require special files.

> **Note**
>
> Your Internet service provider will only offer one method of authentication. You only need to configure your system according to the authentication method used by your provider.

MANUAL AUTHENTICATION

Manual authentication of a PPP client to a PPP server is done by logging in to the PPP server and starting pppd. This method is completely dependent upon the chat script written to handle the interaction between the client and the server. No other configuration files are required. It works much like the normal process of logging on: The system presents a login prompt, you enter your user ID, the system responds with a password prompt, and you enter your password. The trick is to automate this process by configuring a chat script of expect and send strings. An example of this type of script follows:

```
ABORT      BUSY
ABORT     "NO CARRIER"
ABORT     "NO DIALTONE"
""         ATZ
OK         "AT S0=0"
OK         ATDT5551386
CONNECT     ""
login:   mylogin
ssword:  mypassword
```

The first part of the chat script remains the same. The last two lines represent the automated login steps. This is how it works: The chat script waits for the login: string, which is the expect string. When this is detected, the string "*mylogin*" (of course this is changed to the actual User ID) is sent back to the PPP Server. The same holds true with the password prompt and actual password. Notice that the expect string does not have to be a complete string. To avoid issues of whether or not the prompt is capitalized and so on, you can just place a unique portion of the string in the chat script.

PAP AUTHENTICATION PAP authentication is done by including the necessary information in the /etc/ppp/pap-secrets file. This means that you do not have to create the chat script to look for a login prompt and send the user ID and password information—this is all handled by the pap-secrets authentication protocol. Simply add the user ID and password to this file as follows:

```
# Client        Server        Secret
  mylogin         *         mypassword
```

Of course, *mylogin* and *mypassword* are changed to your user ID and password.

Note

With both PAP and CHAP authentication methods, you must add the an entry to the /etc/ppp/options files as follows:

```
name mylogin
```

where *mylogin* is your actual user ID.

CHAP AUTHENTICATION CHAP authentication works in much the same way as PAP authentication. The information to enable CHAP authentication is stored in the /etc/ppp/chap-secrets file. The format of the chap-secrets file is described in the comment files included at the beginning of this chapter as follows:

```
# Secrets for authentication using CHAP
# client        server  secret                  IP addresses
```

According to the AT&T WorldNet Users Reference Desk Web site (`http://204.127.237.208/wurd/software/dialers/linux.html`), the chap-secrets file needs to be set as follows for authenticating to AT&T WorldNet account:

```
# Secrets for authentication using CHAP
# client                  server  secret      IP addresses
999999999@worldnet.att.net   *    "password"    *
```

CONFIGURING OTHER REQUIRED NETWORK COMPONENTS

Besides the necessary PPP configuration files that you need to make operational, there are a couple of other files that you'll need to configure to have your Internet connection work correctly. First, the /etc/hosts file needs to contain an entry identifying your host name and IP address. If this machine is a standalone system (not connected to a network), add a line to your /etc/hosts file as follows:

```
0.0.0.0     yourmachine.yourdomain.com yourmachine
```

The IP address is set dynamically when you connect to your ISP using PPP. Of course, you'll want to set your machine name and domain to something more creative than *yourmachine.yourdomain*.com.

Also, a key piece of information gathered from your ISP is the IP address of the Domain Name Server (DNS). Set this value in the /etc/resolv.conf file as follows:

```
# possible entries are:
#
#       domain <domain>             Local domain name. If not present, the
#                                   gethostbyname syscall is used to
#                                   determine the local domain name.
#
#       search <list_of_domains>    Search list for hostname lookup.
#                                   The search list is normally determined
#                                   from the local domain name but it
#                                   can be set to a list of domains.
#
#        nameserver <ip_addr>       Define which server to contact
#                                   for DNS lookups. If there are
#                                   multiple nameserver lines (Max=3),
#                                   they are queried in the listed order.
#
#
domain caldera.com
search caldera.com
nameserver 207.179.18.1
```

RUNNING /usr/sbin/pppd

After everything is configured, you can try a PPP connection by simply running the pppd utility as follows:

```
# /usr/sbin/pppd
```

The pppd utility offers several options, each of which are described in the man page for pppd. A common option is the `detach` option. This option starts pppd in the foreground (a non-background job), which allows terminating the PPP session with a keyboard sequence (Ctrl+C). Starting pppd with this option can be done as follows:

```
# /usr/sbin/pppd -detach
```

In order to terminate the PPP process without using the `detach` option, you must know the process ID. However, the process ID is stored in the /var/run directory, or you can find it by examining the process table. You can check the status of a successful PPP connection by checking the available network interfaces with the `ifconfig` utility.

TROUBLESHOOTING THE CONNECTION

You can troubleshoot the PPP connection process by adding a couple of options in the /etc/ppp/options file. First of all, the `chat` utility produces more verbose output if you add the v option as shown in the following options file:

```
connect "/usr/sbin/chat -v -f /etc/ppp/chat-script"
/dev/modem 38400
crtscts
defaultroute
noipdefault
```

The second method of capturing more information about the PPP connection is to add debug statements to the /etc/ppp/options file as follows:

```
connect "/usr/sbin/chat -v -f /etc/ppp/chat-script"
/dev/modem 38400
crtscts
defaultroute
noipdefault
debug
```

By adding the debug statement to this file, the contents of all control packets are logged, in readable form, in the /var/log/messages file.

USING KPPP

A user-friendly, graphical method of configuring PPP is provided with KDE: kppp. This utility can be initiated from the desktop by clicking the K menu button and selecting Internet from the menu dialog. If you had trouble following the details in the previous section on configuring PPP, or if you don't really care to understand what happens behind the curtain (the configuration file details), don't worry. kppp offers a very simple and straightforward method of configuring PPP without editing all the necessary configuration files. Upon starting kppp from the menu, the dialog box shown in Figure 24.1 appears.

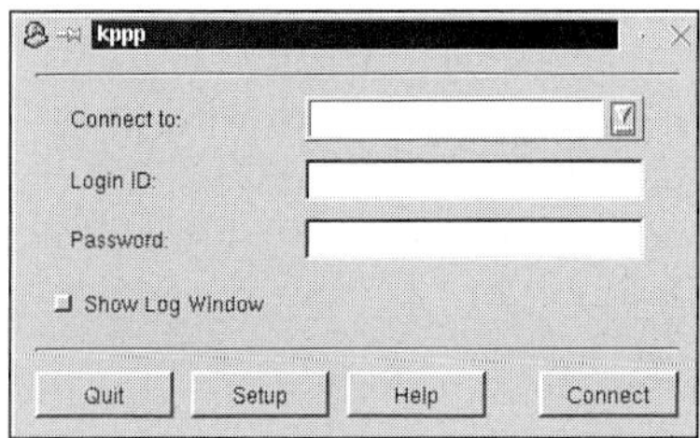

Figure 24.1
Initial kppp dialog screen.

Select Setup and create a new PPP connection profile. A new dialog box appears (see Figure 24.2).

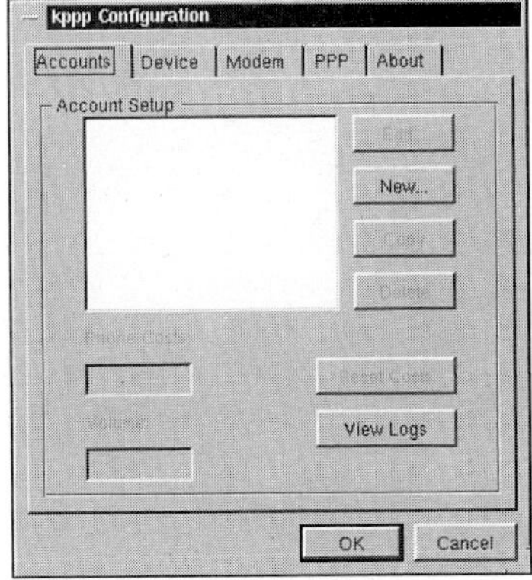

Figure 24.2
Kppp configuration screen.

Select New to create the new PPP profile. The dialog box shown in Figure 24.3 is displayed.

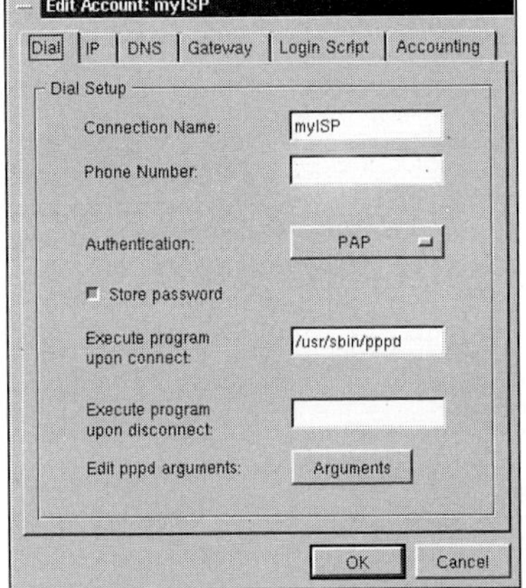

Figure 24.3
PPP account setup.

Enter a name for this PPP connection profile and add the information provided by your ISP. Most of the defaults will work, but be sure to check the following items:

- The phone number
- Dynamic or static IP assignment
- The IP address for the Domain Name Server (DNS)
- Authentication method
- The device (/dev/modem is the default)
- The program to execute upon connect (`/usr/sbin/pppd`)

When you have entered the required information, save this profile and enter your User ID and password information in the dialog box (shown in Figure 24.1) and click Connect. A screen similar to the one shown in Figure 24.4 is displayed.

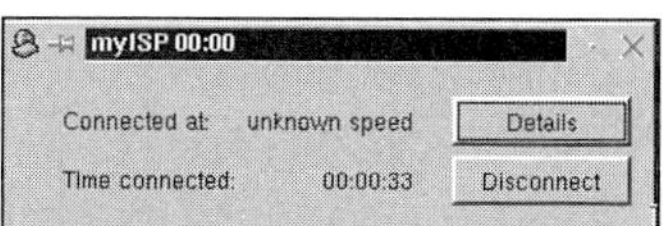

Figure 24.4
PPP connection status dialog screen.

You are now connected, via PPP, to your ISP. You can verify the status of your PPP interface by running the `ifconfig` utility with no parameters, as follows:

```
[root@train100 ppp]# ifconfig
lo        Link encap:Local Loopback
          inet addr:127.0.0.1  Bcast:127.255.255.255  Mask:255.0.0.0
          UP BROADCAST LOOPBACK RUNNING  MTU:3584  Metric:1
          RX packets:32 errors:0 dropped:0 overruns:0
          TX packets:32 errors:0 dropped:0 overruns:0

ppp0      Link encap:Point-to-Point Protocol
          inet addr:207.179.18.65  P-t-P:207.179.18.63  Mask:255.255.255.0
          UP POINTOPOINT RUNNING  MTU:1500  Metric:1
          RX packets:9 errors:1 dropped:1 overruns:0
          TX packets:11 errors:0 dropped:0 overruns:0
```


SUMMARY

By understanding the information in this chapter, you should feel comfortable with what PPP is and how it operates. You can probably also get PPP up and running. There are several options for connecting to an ISP, but PPP is still the most common method for individual users. For more information on topics discussed in this chapter, see the following:

- See Chapters 3–8 for more information on the K Desktop Environment and how it functions.
- See Chapter 22, "Network Administration," for more information on administrating a network environment.
- See Chapter 29 for further information on how IP Masquerading can be used in conjunction with PPP to enable a small network to access the Internet concurrently.

CHAPTER 25

Email Setup

In this chapter

Setting up electronic mail (email) services on an OpenLinux system is really quite simple. Depending upon what your objectives are, email can be operational upon completing the OpenLinux installation. However, that is not to say that email configuration and operation is simple by any means. The internals of email configuration and the process by which it works are quite complex. It is not the intent of this chapter to even begin to address all aspects of email, but rather only the basics of what email is, how it operates, and which components you might want to modify.

EMAIL—WHAT IS IT?

Email, in simple terms, is merely an automated way of delivering conventional mail. In fact, thinking of it in terms of the conventional mail that is delivered by the postal service can actually help you understand what email is and how it works. Conventional mail delivery can be thought of in three distinct parts: sending mail, receiving mail, and transporting mail between between one or more intermediate stations en route to its final destination. As a postal service customer, you are typically only involved in either sending mail or receiving it. The steps in between are, for the most part, transparent to you as a customer of the postal service. The postal service handles the intermediate steps of determining how your letter is to be handled and where it is to be delivered. After it is delivered, the recipient retrieves the letter from the mailbox.

HOW DOES EMAIL WORK?

Email works in much the same way as conventional mail does. Three distinct agents are involved in this process: the email client (sender), the mail transport agent, and the mail delivery agent (recipient). The email client is often referred to as the Mail User Agent (MUA) and the transport agent is often referred to as the Mail Transport Agent (MTA). Each of these agents, and their respective tasks, are listed in Table 25.1.

TABLE 25.1 ELECTRONIC MAIL COMPONENTS

Agent	Component	Description
User Agent (MUA)	Sender	Formats the message, addresses the message, and delivers the message to the Mail Transport Agent
Transport Agent (MTA)	Message Handler	Accepts messages from User Agents and other Transport Agents. Routes the message over appropriate network. Resolves aliases and forwarding.
Delivery Agent (DA)	Recipient	Delivers messages to destination accessible by recipient.

The sender of an email constructs a message, using an email client, and addresses it to a recipient. After the email client sends the message, the Transport Agent (TA) takes over the process. This is equivalent to dropping off your letter at the post office. Of course, the

Transfer Agent for email is nothing more than a sophisticated program, unlike the postal service, which has a host of employees and sorting machines and a fleet of vehicles. OpenLinux uses a program called `sendmail` as its Mail Transport Agent. Although other transport agent programs are available, `sendmail` is still the one that is most commonly used.

Note

`sendmail` was written by Eric Allman at the University of California, Berkeley, and is the most popular email Transport Agent on Linux and UNIX platforms.

The Transport Agent accepts the mail from a user agent, determines the address of the recipient, and delivers the message to the Transport Agent that services email for the recipient. The Delivery Agent is really nothing more than an email client or user agent. However, depending on the setup of incoming email for a given client, an additional component might be necessary. You can be logged in directly to the machine that acts as the email server and read your email on that system; or you can read your email on your desktop system using either Internet Message Access Protocol (IMAP) or Post Office Protocol (POP). You can find more information about these two protocols in the section "Delivery Agents."

User Agents

The User Agent is that aspect of email that involves you, individually, as either the sender of a message or the recipient of a message. This is typically the email client that is used to read incoming messages or to compose outgoing messages. The job of the User Agent is really quite simple. In the case of outgoing messages, it's just a matter of providing a method for you to compose a message, address the message to the desired recipient or recipients, and then sending the message on its way. Many email clients are available with Linux—both character-based clients and graphical, X Window-based clients. Outbound mail is operational by default after the OpenLinux installation is complete. The only setup that is required is the configuration of an account for each individual user. With a user account configured, you can log in and send email. Of course, you'll need to access an email client in order to complete that task. Choosing an email client is just a matter of preference, and although there is no default email client, there are several from which to choose. Table 25.2 lists some of the many email clients that are available with Linux.

Table 25.2 List of Email Clients Available with OpenLinux

Email Client	User Interface	Description
/bin/mail	Character	`mail` is an intelligent mail processing system that has a command syntax reminiscent of `ed`, with lines replaced by messages.
/usr/bin/elm	Character	Elm is an interactive screen-oriented mailer program that supersedes `mail` and `mailx`.

continues

Table 25.2 continued

Email Client	User Interface	Description
/usr/bin/pine	Character	`pine` is a screen-oriented message-handling tool. In its default configuration, `pine` offers an intentionally limited set of functions geared toward the novice user, but it also has a growing list of optional power-user and personal-preference features. `pinef` is a variant of `pine` that uses function keys rather than mnemonic single-letter commands.
/usr/bin/mutt	Character	`mutt` is a small but very powerful text-based program for reading electronic mail under Linux or UNIX operating systems, including support for color terminals, MIME, and a threaded sorting mode.
/usr/X11R6/ bin/xfmail	X Window	`XFMail` is an application for sending and receiving email under X. It's partially compatible with MH-style mailboxes but it does not require that any MH tools be installed on the system. `XFMail` supports POP and SMTP mail protocols and it has full MIME support.
Netscape Messenger	X Window	This is an email handler that is part of Netscape Communicator.

Character-Based Email Clients

A character-based email client is one that is not graphical in nature. In other words, it's not pretty but it is very functional for those who like to keep their hands on the keyboard rather than a mouse. Character-based email clients are typically ones that are used when a user is logged in directly to the system that hosts the email server.

Note

Some character-based email clients, such as `mutt`, have or are adding capabilities to use such protocols as IMAP, which enable the email client to retrieve messages from the email server without being directly logged in to it.

X Window–Based Email Clients

Many graphical email clients are available with Linux. Of course, user preferences and opinions vary, but the email client that is part of the Netscape Communicator might be the easiest to configure and use. Two basic components need to be configured to set up email with Netscape Communicator. In order to configure the necessary components of email, click on the Edit menu within the Netscape Navigator browser and then select Preferences. When the initial dialog box appears, select Mail & Newsgroups.

Note

Be sure to click on the arrow next to the heading Mail & Newsgroups in order to see the complete list of options within this category.

A list of the following options is displayed:

- Identity
- Mail Servers
- Newsgroups Servers
- Addressing
- Messages
- Copies and Folders
- Formatting
- Return Receipts
- Disk Space

Selecting Identity produces a screen similar to the one that is depicted in Figure 25.1.

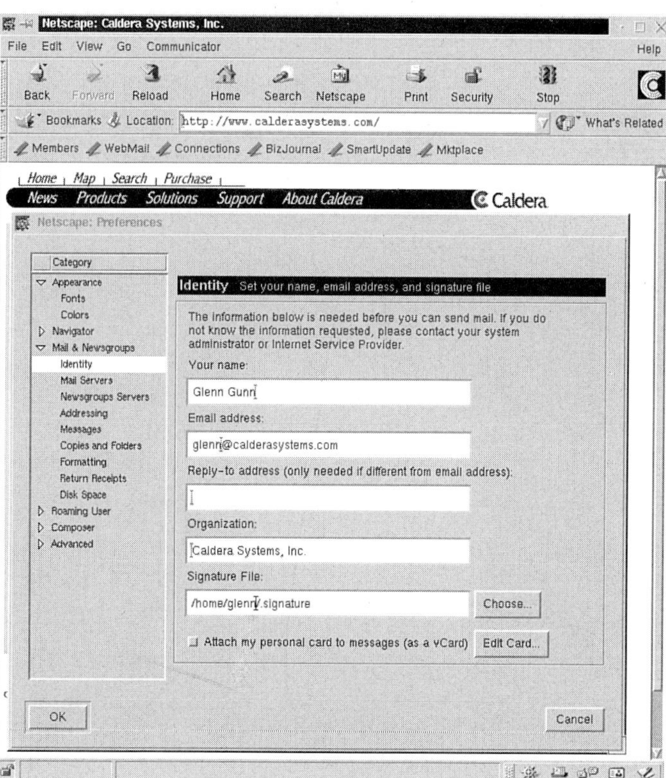

Figure 25.1 Identity setup for Netscape Communicator Mail Handling.

Enter the pertinent information in the appropriate fields and click OK. You are now ready to send email. You can send email by simply selecting Messenger from the Communicator menu on the Web browser and clicking the New Message icon.

The second component that needs to be configured is the Mail Server. Configuring this component enables the capability to receive email. Clicking Mail Servers in the Mail & Newsgroups category presents a screen that enables you to add or modify mail servers. Click Add to display the screen that is depicted in Figure 25.2.

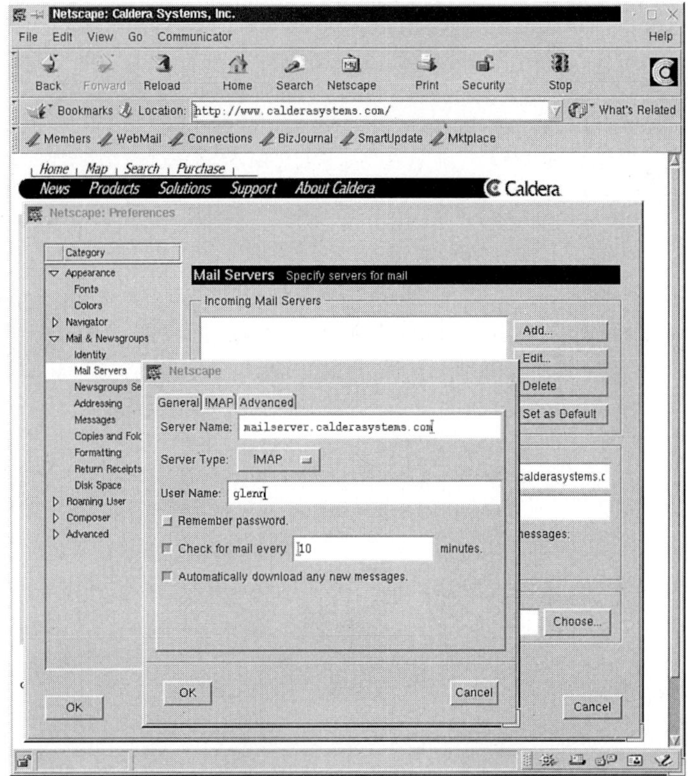

Figure 25.2
Mail Server setup for Netscape Communicator Mail Handling.

Add the host name, complete with the domain name, as the server name; also add your username. Your username is the same as the user ID that was created as your account name on the Linux server.

Note

The mail server must be set up to support IMAP in order for the mail handler in Netscape Communicator to receive email. See the "Delivery Agents" section toward the end of this chapter for details on how to set this up with OpenLinux.

MAIL TRANSPORT AGENT CONFIGURATION

Although email clients are getting more and more sophisticated and user-friendly, they remain the simplest part of the whole email process. The email client handles the step that is the equivalent of someone dropping off their letter at the post office or retrieving it from the mailbox in their front yard. In other words, it's the easy part. The mail transport agent, on the other hand, handles the most complicated aspects of email. In the conventional mail scenario, the MTA is the equivalent of the postal service. The postal service has to receive the letter, determine how it is to be routed, deliver it to the appropriate local office, and get it on the correct mail truck to be delivered. The transport agent for email works in a similar fashion. The MTA receives the email from an email client, determines how to route it, transports it to the appropriate MTA for the given recipient, and places it in a retrievable location for the addressee. The configuration of the MTA is complicated by the fact that it needs to be prepared to handle a number of system and network configurations. This is enough of the theory, however—here's a look at what is required with OpenLinux.

`sendmail` CONFIGURATION FILES

The primary configuration file for `sendmail` operation is the /etc/sendmail.cf file. Suffice it to say that this file is very complex and should only be modified if you are certain of the changes that you are making.

Note

As with all system administration, it is good practice to make a backup copy of this file before making any modification.

The sendmail.cf file can be modified in one of two ways: by editing it directly or by modifying the m4 configuration file and regenerating a new sendmail.cf file. The `m4` utility is a macro processor. Rather than having to know all the aspects of the sendmail.cf file, the m4 configuration file offers a method of identifying and configuring the desired components (in somewhat simpler terms), and then processing them with the `m4` utility to create a new sendmail.cf file.

Note

For more information on the `m4` utility, type `info m4` at a shell prompt. A comprehensive README document can also be found in the /usr/share/sendmail/cf directory.

M4 CONFIGURATION FILES

The m4 configuration file that is used to generate the default /etc/sendmail.cf is stored in the /usr/share/sendmail/cf/cf directory. The m4 configuration file used for OpenLinux `sendmail` setup is generic-col1.2.mc.

A new `sendmail` configuration file can be generated using this file as follows:

```
# cd /usr/share/sendmail/cf/cf
# m4 ../m4/cf.m4 generic-col1.2.mc > /etc/sendmail.cf
```

EMAIL MASQUERADING

The MTA can be configured to masquerade for other domain names. This can easily be accomplished by modifying the m4 configuration file with the needed features and regenerating the /etc/sendmail.cf file as follows:

```
# cd /usr/share/sendmail/cf/cf
# cp generic-col1.2.mc tempfile.mc
```

Add the following two lines to the end of this file:

```
MASQUERADE_AS(domain_name.com)
FEATURE(masquerade_envelope)
```

Then regenerate the file as follows:

```
# m4 ../m4/cf.m4 tempfile.mc > /etc/sendmail.cf
```

Of course, you'll want to replace the name *`domain_name.com`* with the host name for which you want to masquerade.

THE SENDMAIL.CW FILE

The sendmail.cw file needs to be modified to contain all the names by which your host can be recognized. For example, if your fully qualified domain host name was main.calderasystems.com, you'd want to add the following to the /etc/sendmail.cw file:

```
# sendmail.cw - include all aliases for your machine here.
calderasystems.com
```

This allows incoming mail to be correctly handled by `sendmail`. Otherwise, `sendmail` doesn't know what to do with email that is addressed to `me@calderasystems.com`. Email that is sent to `me@main.calderasystems.com` is handled by `sendmail` just fine by default.

THE /ETC/RC.D/INIT.D/MTA FILE

This file contains the script for initiating the startup of `sendmail` or any other MTA. To manually start or stop `sendmail`, do the following:

```
# /etc/rc.d.init.d/mta start

# /etc/rc.d/init.d/mta stop
```

In order to have `sendmail` start automatically at system boot, modify the `ONBOOT` line in the /etc/sysconfig/daemons/mta file as follows:

```
# /etc/sysconfig/daemons/mta
IDENT=MTA
DESCRIPTIVE="Mail Transfer Agent"
ONBOOT="yes"
VARIANT="sendmail"
```

The /etc/mta/options/sendmail File

The /etc/mta/options/sendmail file defines the actual binary that is used as the Mail Transfer agent and the options that are used when it is started up initially. The default settings are as follows:

```
# /etc/mta/sendmail/options
DAEMON=/usr/sbin/sendmail
OPTIONS="-bd -q5m"
```

Delivery Agents

The Delivery Agent is very similar to the user agent; it is merely a method of getting the actual message into the recipient's hands. For example, with conventional mail the recipient can walk out to the mailbox in his front yard or drive to the location of a post office box. Similarly, the recipient of email can use different methods of collecting his or her messages.

Note

The Mail Transfer Agent must be enabled to receive incoming mail with OpenLinux. This is done by modifying the /etc/sysconfig/daemons/mta file.

Setting up a POP Server

Post Office Protocol (POP) provides a way for end-users to retrieve their mail. It's very similar to you walking out to your mailbox, collecting the mail, walking back into your house, and sitting down and reading it. Using POP, email is delivered to the email client on your desktop when you say that you want to retrieve it. Often, the client desktop is configured to do this each time a dial-up connection is made or at a predetermined time interval. The mail is literally moved from the server to the client.

Setting up an IMAP Server

An IMAP server behaves much like a POP server, but with one major difference—the IMAP server does not literally transfer the email from the server to the client desktop. It basically creates a "map" for a given user that enables him to read the mail directly on the email server system. The advantages and disadvantages of IMAP versus POP are very similar to the advantages and disadvantages of central versus distributed processing.

Enabling POP and IMAP Services

Enabling either POP or IMAP service is a very simple task. Each of these protocols is predefined in the /etc/services file. The only real requirement is to install the IMAP RPM. This package contains the following files:

```
/etc/pam.d/pop+imap
/usr/man/man8/imapd.8c.gz
/usr/man/man8/ipopd.8c.gz
/usr/sbin/imapd
/usr/sbin/ipop2d
/usr/sbin/ipop3d
```

After the RPM is installed, the appropriate daemon is called when requests are detected for either POP or IMAP services on the respective ports, as defined in the /etc/services file. That's all there is to setting up both POP and IMAP services. After they are enabled, email clients can be configured to receive email via this server.

ALIASES

Aliases can be used in a number of ways. One of the most common uses of an alias is to handle different spellings or the complete name of a given person. An alias can also be used to set up generic names that don't necessarily point to a specific person. For example, an alias for `webmaster` can be set up to have all incoming mail directed to `Glenn`. The aliases file looks similar to the following:

```
#  This file lists the default mail aliases for Caldera OpenLinux.
#
#  Aliases in this file will NOT be expanded in the header from
#  Mail, but WILL be visible over networks or from /bin/mail.
#
#                      IMPORTANT NOTE:
#
#  After you make any changes to this file, you have to run
#
#       /usr/sbin/mta-switch newconfig
#
#  or the program `newaliases' (works for smail and sendmail).
#  Otherwise, the changes won't be visible to your MTA.
#

# Basic system aliases -- these MUST be present.
MAILER-DAEMON:  postmaster
postmaster:     root

# General redirections for pseudo accounts.
bin:            root
games:          root
ingres:         root
system:         root
toor:           root
news:           root
uucp:           root
operator:       root
ftp:            root
nobody:         root

# Well-known aliases.
manager:        root
dumper:         root
newsadm:        news
newsadmin:      news
usenet:         news
netnews:        news
gnats:          root
ftpadm:         ftp
ftpadmin:       ftp
ftp-adm:        ftp
```

```
# trap decode to catch security attacks
decode:         root

# Person who is to get root's mail
#root:          col
```

Adding an entry to the /etc/aliases file as follows directs all mail that is coming to `webmaster@calderasystems.com` to be sent to `glenn@calderasystems.com`:

```
webmaster:        glenn
```

Note

In order for changes to this file to take effect, you must run the `newaliases` utility.

SUMMARY

For the most part, email setup is preconfigured by default. However, the MTA must be enabled in order for incoming mail to be correctly recognized. This is accomplished by modifying the /etc/sysconfig/daemons/mta file by setting the `ONBOOT=` parameter to `yes`. You learned about the three major aspects of email—User Agent, Transport Agent, and Delivery Agent. The User Agent and the Delivery Agent are the simplest parts of the email process. The intermediate step that connects the two is the mail transport step. This step is the most complicated because of the many potential variables. For more information on email, see the following chapters:

- See Chapter 10, "Users, Groups, and Permissions," for information on how to set up new users. This step is required in order for email to work properly for a given user.
- See Chapter 21, "Understanding TCP/IP Fundamentals," for more information on TCP/IP fundamentals.
- See Chapter 24, "Connecting to an ISP," for information on how to establish a connection to an Internet service provider.

CHAPTER 26

Domain Name Server (DNS)

In this chapter

This chapter covers some aspects of DNS and BIND, and will help you get familiar with the terms; it will also help you get started using BIND in a limited fashion, sufficient for most home or small business networks. If you want to set up your own server, this chapter will be of some help, but this chapter is too short to make an expert out of you. If you need detailed information, several good books cover DNS and BIND.

You might not be familiar with DNS, but if you've ever surfed the Internet, you've made extensive use of it. Computers know how to find each other by means of their addresses, and specifically by an IP address, just as you can (usually) find the book store after looking up its address in the phone book. DNS is to computers what the phone book is to you. You don't remember Internet sites by their IP addresses, but by their names. But you don't know where the FOOBAZ bookstore is if you've never been there (or seen it in passing), so you need to look up the address. Similarly, when you want your Web browser to find `www.caldera.com`, your system uses DNS to look up the IP address.

On your OpenLinux system you have resolver libraries that know how to resolve names into IP addresses. In your /etc/nsswitch.conf (name service switch configuration) file you have a line that looks like the following:

```
hosts:          files dns
```

This line tells the resolver routines that when they are looking for hosts, they need to first consult the system's files; and if they don't find what they're looking for there, they need to perform a DNS lookup.

Note

> The nsswitch.conf file replaced the /etc/host.conf file when Linux moved from libc5 based systems to the new glibc (libc6). The nsswitch.conf file follows Sun Microsystems's lead and acts as a single reference for system database files for applications requiring this information.

The system files are /etc/hosts, where commonly accessed local network hosts might be listed. This lookup is faster than a DNS lookup. But if names that might change are included, you might wonder why the lookup failed to find what you were looking for. Therefore, refrain from putting any entries over which you have no control into /etc/hosts.

The resolver libraries, failing to find the address they seek in /etc/hosts, consult /etc/resolv.conf to find the IP addresses of machines known as *Domain Name Servers*, or just *nameservers* for short. Up to three, but not fewer than two, need to be entered in this file. Why two? In case one is down. But no more than three are consulted, so all nameserver entries beyond the first three are ignored.

WHAT IS BIND?

Several different DNS servers are available under different names. But the most common, and the one you'll find on your OpenLinux system, is the *Berkeley Internet Nameserver Daemon* (BIND). As of this writing, the current major version number was 8. Version 8 was a departure from the previous version, version 4. Aside from some security enhancements, version 8 changed the main configuration file from named.boot to named.conf; furthermore, it changed its syntax. Fortunately, a direct correlation exists between what is found in the new configuration file and the old, making upgrading fairly straightforward and easily scripted. In fact, a script called `named-bootconf` can be found on your OpenLinux system. (You'll look at this in the section "Moving from BIND 4.x to BIND 8.x," later in this chapter.) Also fortunate is the fact that the "zone files," which are discussed later, didn't change.

ABOUT DOMAINS

Before you go further, it is helpful to understand a little about domains. You've seen domain names before. They are in the form of bar.org, and contain at least two parts. Reading from the right, the "org" part is called a top-level domain. A number of top-level domains exist. In the United States, currently, are the following top-level domains:

- **.com**—Commercial entities (businesses)
- **.org**—Non-commercial organizations
- **.net**—Network affiliated organizations
- **.mil**—U.S. military branches
- **.gov**—U.S. government agencies
- **.edu**—Educational institutions
- **.int**—International organizations
- **.us**—The U.S. domain, which has each state as lower-level divisions

Additional top-level domains have been proposed, but have not yet been implemented.

In other countries, top-level domains are administered by the Internet authorities of those countries and include a two-letter country suffix. Some examples are as follows:

- **.uk**—United Kingdom
- **.ca**—Canada
- **.mx**—Mexico
- **.za**—Zud Africa (South Africa)

Within each of the countries a top-level domain structure, which is decided by the country's Internet authority, exists. These might or might not correspond to the top-level domains found in the US.

Below the top-level domain is the name of the institution or organization, which constitutes the actual domain name. For example, ibm.com, or ibm.co.uk. These examples are IBM's domain names in the US and the UK, respectively.

Some large domains also have subdomains. Very large institutions might have subdomains. For example, the army.mil domain, which has military bases all over the world, and which has very large units on those bases, might be further broken down into subdomains. Therefore, a large base such as Fort Bragg, North Carolina, will have a subdomain ftbragg.army.mil. Because Ft. Bragg is so large, this might be further divided based on units; for example the Corps Support Command at Ft. Bragg might have its own subdomain, coscom.ftbragg.army.mil, under the ftbragg subdomain. Finally, individual host computers have their own hostnames added to the domain name. So the hostname eagle1 becomes eagle1.coscom.ftbragg.army.mil. If this host exists, you can find out the IP address for this host via DNS (assuming that the host has a record in the DNS database).

For current information on domains, visit the Internet Assigned Numbers Authority domains page at `http://www.iana.org/top-level-domains.html`.

Root Name Servers

The existence of these top-level domains suggests a structure for DNS lookups. Each top-level domain is the top of a tree (an upside-down tree, that is). So when you do a lookup of caldera.com, a nameserver looks to the top-level domain name server for .com and is directed to a name server down the branches for caldera. The nameserver for Caldera listed in the top-level domain is one of the servers that are authoritative for the caldera.com domain; it can give the answer to the DNS server that is making the query.

Fortunately for all involved, this lookup at the top level doesn't have to happen often. Because this kind of activity can generate significant traffic, it causes delays in querying for domain name resolution. Each DNS server that queries a DNS server for a domain gets several pieces of information. In addition to the address resolution that is requested, each original query also returns a *time to live* (*TTL*) value. This TTL tells the querying DNS server how long to cache the records it received from the authoritative source. It saves the answers and uses them to respond to further queries until the TTL drops to zero, at which time it queries the authoritative source once again. These values are often as long as a week. You'll see this again later.

Types of DNS Servers

Despite anything you might read here or elsewhere, only two types of name servers are defined by the DNS specs—primary masters and secondary masters. The top-level DNS servers, called *Root Name Servers*, are just primary or secondary masters for the top-level domain; they only point queries to other primary or secondary masters that are authoritative for the second-level domain, the domain that you are looking up. You'll often see text that discusses primary and secondary nameservers (but not necessarily masters), forwarding name servers, caching name servers, and so on. These terms are related to the use or type of setup rather than to the role they play in the DNS hierarchy.

Note

The difference between primary masters and secondary masters is that the primary master has the master list for the domain, and the secondary masters perform a zone transfer to get the information to answer queries authoritatively. This design is to reduce administrative tasks to maintaining only one DNS server. You might see secondary masters referred to as *slaves*, and primary masters as only *masters*.

DNS servers can be set up to perform different roles. If you register a domain name with Internic.net, you are asked to provide at least two DNS servers, a primary and a secondary master. You might have chosen to administer these yourself, or you might have asked your Internet provider to do the honors. You must supply two, and it's better if these two are not on the same network.

If your provider is handling DNS resolution for your domain, all you need to do is provide them with the names of those hosts that you want to have registered. Not all hosts need to be registered, just those that you want to be available from outside—these are most likely your Web server, your FTP server, and your mail server. You can give your provider something like a hosts file, with host names and aliases. That is, you might give them something such as

```
192.168.100.2     foo.bar.org     www.bar.org
192.168.100.3     baz.bar.org     ftp.bar.org
```

and a note that 192.168.100.3 receives mail for bar.org.

Your provider, in return, gives you the addresses of the primary and secondary masters for DNS resolution for your host's /etc/resolv.conf files. This is true whether you or they host your DNS. However, if you host your own DNS, your internal hosts look at your DNS servers rather than your providers.

If you host your own DNS, either primary or primary and secondary masters, you need to learn more about DNS than this chapter can tell you. The same is also true if you're going to run a private network with full DNS because this requires the same level of knowledge. But if you only want to run a caching DNS server, you can do so under OpenLinux "straight out of the box". That is, OpenLinux already has the default files necessary for you to do this without knowing more. The system with the caching DNS server only needs to have /etc/resolv.conf pointing to your provider's DNS, and your other hosts pointing to your caching DNS servers.

BIND Files

The BIND v8 that comes on OpenLinux installs a number of files and builds a few others. First, the file called named is installed in /etc/sysconfig/daemons; `lisa` uses this to configure named for startup at boot. A named script is installed in /etc/rc.d/init.d, which has links for startup from runlevels 3–5. The installation utility also builds a /etc/named.conf file. This file is created from scratch on a new installation, or from /etc/named.boot if this installation is an upgrade.

Also installed are several files in /var/named for localhost lookups. These are created during the installation. Finally, in /usr/sbin, four files—named, named-boot, named-xfer, and ndc—are installed. These are the name server daemon, a perl script to convert named.boot to named.conf, an external zone file transfer program, and a name server daemon control program, respectively.

ndc—Nameserver Daemon Control

The program ndc helps an administrator control the nameserver daemon. After running, named caches hits until they expire. The ndc program provides a way to interface with the running nameserver daemon. With ndc, you can do things such as dump the cached database to a file. This does not clear the cache—it just allows you to look at the contents. It also enables you to trace queries and start a query log. The ndc interface can show you the status of the daemon or dump a statistics file. It can start, stop, or restart the daemon.

The ndc program itself is a shell script. The script works by sending different signals to named. These signals tell the daemon what to do. But remembering the different signals and what they mean is difficult, so the script gives you a simple means of controlling the daemon, with easy to remember terms. If you feel so inclined, take a look at the script. It isn't very long, and it can be educational.

Configuration Files and DNS Terms

The nameserver daemon uses a number of files. Some are read to provide an initial configuration and tell it where to find other needed files; others are read at startup and retained in memory for use in answering queries. The first of these files is /etc/named.conf (see Listing 26.1).

Listing 26.1 A Sample /etc/named.conf File

```
// generated by named-bootconf.pl

options {
        directory "/var/named";
        /*
         * If there is a firewall between you and nameservers you want
         * to talk to, you might need to uncomment the query-source
         * directive below.  Previous versions of BIND always asked
         * questions using port 53, but BIND 8.1 uses an unprivileged
         * port by default.
         */
        // query-source address * port 53;
};

//
// Boot file for name server
//
// type         domain                  source          file
zone "." {
        type hint;
        file "named.root";
```

```
};

// Zone boot information and daemon options are kept in other files
// (autoincluded from boot.zones)
//
// Name server zone boot file
// See named(8) for syntax and further information
//
// type        domain                    source        file
// (autoincluded from boot.options)
//
// Options for name server
// Use `bindconfig' to automatically configure this file
//
// type        domain                    source        file
zone "localhost" {
        type master;
        file "named.local";
};

zone "127.in-addr.arpa" {
        type master;
        file "named.rev-local";
};

// Custom configurations below (will be preserved)
```

The comments (followed by `//` to the end of the line) are fairly self-explanatory. The sections themselves each start with a statement and are surrounded by `{}` and terminated by `;`. Each substatement within a statement also ends with a `;`. The first statement, `options`, tells named where zone files are located. Other startup options, such as `query-source`, `listen-on port`, and more might also be included. In all, some 34 separate substatements within the options statement are possible, many of which only pertain to large sites with multiple zones and specific requirements.

Note

Zone files are databases that hold a table of hostnames/IP addresses for which the nameserver is authoritative, with one exception. This exception is the hints zone file (.), which is a list of root nameservers.

The next three statements in Listing 26.1 list zone files. These three zone files are all that are required for a caching name server. Sites that are authoritative for a zone have no fewer than two zone entries. All nameservers, including caching-only nameservers, are masters of their own domain, the domain defined by localhost. The applicable files (zone localhost and zone 127.in-addr.arpa) are always created when installing the `bind` package. Contents of the zone files are explained in the following sections.

Note

Zone files are made up of *resource records* (*RRs*). These resource records are named to IP mappings, one RR per mapping.

The newer BIND v8 has a number of other configuration statements. Many of these are new to v8. The various statements include `acl` (access control list), `include` (include files), `logging`, `key` (for authentication and authorization), and `server` (sets per server options). The options and logging statements might occur only once. Other statements might occur multiple times (see the section "Moving from BIND 4.x to BIND 8.x," later in this chapter).

ZONE DATABASE FILES

A set of zone files containing RRs is found by default in /var/named, although in the options statement in /etc/named.conf, any location can be chosen. Each zone file is listed as a statement in the named.conf file as shown in Listing 26.1.

A number of different RR types make up the zone files. Several that are of note are discussed later. A complete list of RRs in database (db) files includes

- **SOA record**—Admin data and info about this data's authority
- **NS record**—Name servers for this domain
- **A record**—Name to address mapping
- **PTR record**—Pointer for address to name mapping
- **CNAME record**—Canonical (alias) name
- **MX record**—Mail exchange record
- **TXT**—Textual information
- **WKS**—Well known services
- **HINFO**—Host information

START OF AUTHORITY HEADER

The *Start of Authority Header* (*SOA*) is the first entry in the db file. The SOA indicates that this nameserver is the best (authoritative) source for information in this domain. There can be only one SOA entry per db file. A sample SOA looks like the following:

```
bar.org. IN SOA  foo.bar.org.  dab.bar.org.  (
                     1998122300  ; Serial
                     10800       ; Refresh time -- 3 hours
                     3600        ; Retry -- 1 hour
                     604800      ; Expire -- 1 week
                     86400  )    ; TTL - 1 day
```

The first part of the entry, `bar.org.` (note the trailing .), indicates the domain to which this db file refers. The `IN` indicates Internet. The SOA indicates that this is the SOA record entry for this file. The entry `foo.bar.org.` is the host on which you created the file, and the entry `dab.bar.org` is the email address of the db file's contact. The address is converted from `dab.bar.org` to `dab@bar.org`.

Tip

One of the most common misconfiguration problems with nameservers has to do with the use of terminating periods (.) on entries. The rule is, if you don't want to have the domain name (bar.org) appended to the entry, remember to include the trailing period.

The parentheses permit the data that follows to span multiple lines. The opening parenthesis must be on the first line. Within the parentheses are various values that the nameserver passes to querying nameservers. The first is the serial number. Serial numbers are for secondary masters. They compare the current serial number with the one that they had when they downloaded the data. If the two are different, they download the new data. If the two are the same, they do not. This serial number can be any number that increments. One method is shown: the eight digit date plus a two digit trailing sequence number (it is unlikely you'll make more than 99 changes to the dbfile in one day). Note that a ; begins a comment and continues to the end of the line.

Tip

Remember to change the serial number and restart the nameserver (`ndc reload`) or your changes do not take effect.

The refresh time, retry time, and expire time are also for secondary masters. These tell the secondary that it needs to refresh its data (check the serial number and, if it is different, reload) at this interval in seconds. If the primary master is not available, it needs to retry every hour. If it cannot make contact for a week, the zone expires and the domain data needs to be flushed.

The TTL tells how long a nameserver that is not a secondary master is to cache the data. If your zone is static, longer times decrease the load on your nameserver. If you need to change the file often, you'll want to decrease this time; however, it causes a significant increase in queries because after this amount of time, nameservers must requery.

These four times—refresh, retry, expire, and TTL—give you a good indicator of how long it will take a DNS change to propagate through the Internet. Remember that in the instant before you did a restart, a secondary might have refreshed. If, just before the secondary came back to the primary to refresh (3 hours later), a foreign DNS query returned the old value with the TTL, it might be more than 27 hours from the change before the change propagates out. This is assuming, too, that the secondary had no problems connecting to the primary at its first refresh.

Tip

The entire SOA entry (minus comments and parentheses) can be put on one line, but it is best to follow the preceding template because the order of the values is important.

DB FILE ENTRIES

Each db file has entries that correspond to hosts in the domain. The first entries look like the following:

```
bar.org.    IN NS foo.bar.org.
bar.org.    IN NS baz.bar.org.
```

These entries are the name servers for this domain. Again, note the trailing . on each entry.

The next RR that is found in the db file is the A or address record. These appear as follows:

```
foo.bar.org.        IN A 192.168.0.1
;
baz.bar.org.        IN A 192.168.0.2
baz.bar.org.        IN A 192.168.10.90
;
baz2.bar.org.    IN A 192.168.0.2
baz90.bar.org.    IN A 192.168.10.90
```

There is nothing special with the first entry. The host baz either has two Ethernet cards, each on a different network, or one card with two addresses on different networks. This host is what's known as a multihomed host. You can use comments with blank lines to separate parts of the file. A good recommendation is to separate multihomed hosts from those with only one address. The same separation can be used for other sections. This just makes it easier to read and troubleshoot.

The last two are additional names that each map specifically to only one interface of the multihomed host. These entries are here because a lookup on baz.bar.org returns both addresses—you can't pick out the one that you want to `ping` specifically. Therefore, there are additional entries for each interface that are particular to only one interface. This is especially useful for routers that might have several NICs.

The next RR of interest is the CNAME. This is used to map aliases to A records as follows:

```
www.bar.org.    IN CNAME foo.bar.org.
ftp.bar.org.        IN CNAME baz.bar.org.
```

Note that, because host baz has more than one address, you'll want to either make sure that ftp is binding all addresses, or have `ftp.bar.org` point to a specific interface. As explained in Chapter 23, "Advanced Network Features," using the same name for multiple IP addresses can cause problems. For example, some services do not bind two addresses. They bind only one address. But which one? Likewise, clients looking to connect to that service sometimes connect and sometimes do not, depending on which IP address they get first in reference to their query. Such confusion needs to be avoided; you can only do so by assigning multihomed hosts unique names to each IP address.

The final RR you'll look at in this section is the MX, or mail exchange, address. This RR takes a little more explanation. A sample MX record looks like the following:

```
bar.org.    IN    MX    50    foo.bar.org.
bar.org.    IN    MX    100    baz.bar.org.
```

The records read as follows: For mail being sent to `user@bar.org`, `foo.bar.org` is the primary mail host, and `baz` is the secondary mail host. The numbers `50` and `100` indicate the priority for the mail hosts. The lower the number, the higher the priority. The numbers can range from `0` to `65535`, but in practice, the most common numbers tend to be `5`, `10`, `50`, and `100` for simplicity's sake. This allows MX hosts to be inserted before or after any existing entries without rewriting all the entries.

So if the primary mailhost is foo, but for whatever reason foo can't receive an email message, baz receives it. But because our mail host is foo, and that's where folks receive their mail, what happens to mail delivered to baz? Well, baz checks the MX records too and sees that foo is the primary mail host, so baz tries to send to foo. If there are more MX records, baz looks at the hostname and priority. The host baz does not resend mail to itself or an MX host with a higher or equal number; it only sends to those with a lower number. Eventually, though, foo comes back up and accepts the messages that baz has queued up.

The other RR types, HINFO, TXT, and WKS, are of little value to most sites, so they are not covered here. The important RRs for forward resolution have now been reviewed.

Reverse Resolution Databases

Up to this point, you've looked at RRs for forward resolution db files. But sometimes a lookup is needed on a reverse resolution. That is, you have an IP address, but don't know the host to which it belongs. Look at Listing 26.1, near the bottom of the listing, at the last two statements; the first refers to a zone localhost, and the substatements, not the filename, as named.local. This is your forward resolution database. The next one, with a statement zone 127.in-addr.arpa, tells named that this is a reverse lookup statement and to use this on any lookup for an IP address beginning 127.x.x.x. If you are master for bar.org and have a zone bar.org with filename named.bar.org, and the IP network is 192.168.0.0/24, your zone statement for the reverse resolution database is 192.168.0.in-addr.arpa, and your filename can be anything you want to call it—but named.rev-bar.org is nice and descriptive.

The reverse resolution db file is slightly different from the forward resolution database, but only in the RRs used within. The SOA is very similar and might look like the following:

```
0.168.192.in-addr.arpa.    IN SOA foo.bar.org.  dab.bar.org. (
1998122301 10800 3600 604800 86400 )
```

The only difference here is the use of the backward network portion of the IP address corresponding to the domain, and the use of the in-addr.arpa. suffix. This special suffix is required on all RRs in the reverse resolution database.

The rest of the RRs in the database are of the following form:

```
1.0.168.192.in-addr.arpa.    IN PTR foo.bar.org.
2.0.168.192.in-addr.arpa.    IN PTR baz.bar.org.
```

These two entries are PTR records and point from the reversed IP address annotation with the in-addr.arpa. suffix to the host name. This file also carries the NS records in reverse form as follows:

```
0.168.192.in-addr.arpa.    IN NS foo.bar.org.
0.168.192.in-addr.arpa.    IN NS baz.bar.org.
```

Again nothing unusual. The reverse address is that of the domain, just as the forward NS addresses were for the domain.

NAMED.ROOT DATABASE

The named.root database is a special database. This db file contains hints to the nameserver as to where to look for the root name servers on the Internet. Because these servers do change from time to time, this file needs to also be updated. A good rule of thumb for updating this is once a month. A script in the "`dig`" section that follows can be run to perform the update automatically.

MOVING FROM BIND 4.X TO BIND 8.X

For those of you already running BIND v4, Caldera has provided a `perl` script from the BIND maintainers. This script, written in Perl (so you'll need to have Perl loaded on your system), converts named.boot files to named.conf files. The old file is preserved, and everything is carried over. But the newer version 8 does allow certain statements that the version 4 doesn't know about. For instance, an access control list (acl) restricts access to the DNS server. This might be desirable if you want users who are querying from outside to receive a more restricted list of hosts than a user on the inside. So they might be pointed at different DNS servers, but each restricted from specifying the wrong one.

Because other files don't change, just named.boot to named.conf (as noted earlier in this chapter), the zone files don't need to change. The new named.conf is not particularly complicated. By comparing an old named.boot (Listing 26.2), to the newer named.conf (Listing 26.1), the differences become clear.

LISTING 26.2 SAMPLE NAMED.BOOT FILE

```
; Boot file for name server
;
directory /var/named
;
; type          domain                                      file
cache           .                                           named.root
primary         localhost                                   named.local
primary          127.in-addr.arpa                              named.rev-local
```

The directory became a substatement of the options statement. The listings under domain in Listing 26.2 became the names of zone files in the new zone statement. In the zone substatements, type cache became type hint, type primary became type master, type secondary became type slave. A new type, stub, which is similar to slave, was created. The stub doesn't transfer the entire zone from a master as a slave does; it transfers only the NS entries. So a type stub does not become authoritative for zone, but acts similar to a root server and points the query at one of the authoritative servers.

The file entry is also a substatement of the zone statement as can be seen in Listing 26.1. Because the files have such a 1:1 correlation, and only new statements and substatements appear in v8, normally only some adjustments are required to optimize the setup, such as changing a slave to a stub, including access control, and so on.

NAMESERVER TOOLS

A number of tools that are useful for debugging DNS are available in OpenLinux under the `bind-utils` package and the `fwhois` package. These tools are invaluable to administrators. Although some overlap exists between the tools, each has its advantages and disadvantages. The best way to compare them is to take a look at some of them.

nslookup

The `nslookup` program performs name server lookups. The program has two modes, interactive and noninteractive. There are two ways to enter interactive mode. The first way is to run `nslookup` with no arguments. The second way is to run `nslookup` with a hyphen (signifying input from the keyboard) and a nameserver. If `nslookup` is not given a name server to use, it consults the /etc/resolv.conf file and uses the first one listed. If you are running a nameserver on your system, the first line in /etc/resolv.conf is the localhost (127.0.0.1).

The `nslookup` program has eleven possible commands, two of which are the lookup name itself and the lookup name with a nameserver to use to perform the lookup. Other commands provide specific types of lookups or set options. The `set` command has 14 options that can be set. After they are set, these options remain in use until `set` is invoked to change them again. The most common of the `set` arguments is to set the querytype. Querytypes can be any of the valid RR types plus a few extras (`A`, `ANY`, `CNAME`, `HINFO`, `MX`, `PX`, `NS`, `PTR`, `SOA`, `TXT`, `WKS`, `SRV`, `NAPTR`). The `PX` option provides information regarding zone creation, zone contact, serial number, and TTL information—just slightly less information than the `SOA` option. The `ANY` option provides `PX` information plus nameservers, plus `SOA`. The `SRV` and `NAPTR` options provide information similar to the `PX` option, but specify the forward or reverse lookup databases respectively. The default is `A`.

When `nslookup` starts, it reports the DNS server that it will use for lookups and presents you with a prompt as follows:

```
bash-2.01$ nslookup
Default Server:  localhost
Address:  127.0.0.1
>
```

Each subsequent use reports the server again, so this information is omitted in subsequent examples.

Now, you'll take a look at some output. First, look at the default output (`querytype=A`) for the domain caldera.com. The following is the non-authoritative answer:

```
Name: - caldera.com
Address: - 207.179.18.1
```

Note that the first line tells you that the answer you've obtained is non-authoritative. This means that the information was provided from information that the current DNS server cached.

Now look at the output after setting the querytype to ANY. Following is the non-authoritative answer:

```
caldera.com     nameserver = caldera.caldera.com
caldera.com     nameserver = gw.caldera.com
caldera.com
        origin = caldera.caldera.com
        mail addr = root.caldera.com
        serial = 1998123001
        refresh = 3600 (1H)
        retry   = 900 (15M)
        expire  = 604800 (1W)
        minimum ttl = 21600 (6H)
caldera.com     internet address = 207.179.18.1
Authoritative answers can be found from:
caldera.com     nameserver = caldera.caldera.com
caldera.com     nameserver = gw.caldera.com
caldera.caldera.com     internet address = 207.179.18.1
gw.caldera.com  internet address = 207.179.18.252
```

Here again you see that the answer is non-authoritative. Following that, you see the nameservers for the caldera.com domain listed. Then comes the information from the SOA. Looking at the serial number, you can see that this is update 1 on 30 Dec 98. Because this domain is maintained by someone other than the author of this chapter, you can see that the serial numbering convention suggested earlier is a sound one from more than this author's point of view. Looking through the rest of this data, about the only information you don't have is the MX data.

Note

Setting the querytype each time by typing it out can be annoying at best, especially if your typing skills are not the greatest. But the querytype can be set by just using `q`, as in `set q=MX`.

So here's a look at that:

```
caldera.com    preference = 5, mail exchanger = caldera.caldera.com
caldera.com    nameserver = caldera.caldera.com
caldera.com    nameserver = gw.caldera.com
caldera.caldera.com    internet address = 207.179.18.1
gw.caldera.com    internet address = 207.179.18.252
```

Here you see the mail exchange with a preference of 5. Because no others are listed, this is the only address to which mail will go.

Tip

Normally, `nslookup` uses the search list specified in /etc/resolv.conf when trying to resolve names. Sometimes, this can return undesired results. Put a . on the end of domain queries, as in `nslookup caldera.com.`, to avoid this.

dig

The next program that is useful for debugging—and some other purposes—is `dig`. `dig` returns more information than `nslookup` does, and in a different form. The easiest way to show what `dig` can do for you is to give you a sample script used to update the named.root hint file, and then look at the output (see Listing 26.3).

LISTING 26.3 A NAMESERVER UPDATE SCRIPT, `hintupdt.sh`

```
#!/bin/bash
# Original script author unknown -- modified
#
# Update the nameserver cache information file once per month.
# This is run automatically by the following cron entry.
# 0 0 1 * * /usr/local/sbin/hintupdt.sh
(
echo "To: sysadmin <root@localhost>"
echo "From: system <root>"
echo "Subject: Root servers hint file update"
echo

export PATH=/usr/local/sbin:/sbin:/usr/sbin:/bin:/usr/bin:/usr/local/bin
cd /var/named

dig . @rs.internic.net > named.root.new

echo "The hint file (named.root) has been updated to contain"
echo "the following information:"
echo
cat named.root.new

chown root.root named.root.new
chmod 444 named.root.new
mv named.root named.root.old
mv named.root.new named.root
ndc restart
echo
echo "The nameserver has been restarted to ensure that the update
➥is complete."
echo "The previous named.root file is now called /var/named/
➥named.root.old."

) 2>&1 ¦ /usr/lib/sendmail -t
exit 0
```

The line that is of interest to you is the following:

```
dig . @rs.internic.net
```

This returns the output that is shown in Listing 26.4.

LISTING 26.4 `dig` LOOKUP OF ROOT SERVERS FROM `internic.net`

```
; <<>> DiG 8.1 <<>> . @rs.internic.net
; (1 server found)
;; res options: init recurs defnam dnsrch
;; got answer:
;; ->>HEADER<<-opcode: QUERY, status: NOERROR, id: 10
;; flags: qr rd; QUERY: 1, ANSWER: 0, AUTHORITY: 13, ADDITIONAL: 13
;; QUERY SECTION:
;;      ., type = A, class = IN

;; AUTHORITY SECTION:
.             5d6h47m12s IN NS  D.ROOT-SERVERS.NET.
.             5d6h47m12s IN NS  C.ROOT-SERVERS.NET.
.             5d6h47m12s IN NS  B.ROOT-SERVERS.NET.
.             5d6h47m12s IN NS  H.ROOT-SERVERS.NET.
.             5d6h47m12s IN NS  A.ROOT-SERVERS.NET.
.             5d6h47m12s IN NS  M.ROOT-SERVERS.NET.
.             5d6h47m12s IN NS  L.ROOT-SERVERS.NET.
.             5d6h47m12s IN NS  K.ROOT-SERVERS.NET.
.             5d6h47m12s IN NS  J.ROOT-SERVERS.NET.
.             5d6h47m12s IN NS  G.ROOT-SERVERS.NET.
.             5d6h47m12s IN NS  F.ROOT-SERVERS.NET.
.             5d6h47m12s IN NS  I.ROOT-SERVERS.NET.
.             5d6h47m12s IN NS  E.ROOT-SERVERS.NET.

;; ADDITIONAL SECTION:
D.ROOT-SERVERS.NET.    5w6d16h IN A    128.8.10.90
C.ROOT-SERVERS.NET.    5w6d16h IN A    192.33.4.12
B.ROOT-SERVERS.NET.    5w6d16h IN A    128.9.0.107
H.ROOT-SERVERS.NET.    5w6d16h IN A    128.63.2.53
A.ROOT-SERVERS.NET.    5w6d16h IN A    198.41.0.4
M.ROOT-SERVERS.NET.    5w6d16h IN A    202.12.27.33
L.ROOT-SERVERS.NET.    5w6d16h IN A    198.32.64.12
K.ROOT-SERVERS.NET.    5w6d16h IN A    193.0.14.129
J.ROOT-SERVERS.NET.    5w6d16h IN A    198.41.0.10
G.ROOT-SERVERS.NET.    5w6d16h IN A    192.112.36.4
F.ROOT-SERVERS.NET.    5w6d16h IN A    192.5.5.241
I.ROOT-SERVERS.NET.    5w6d16h IN A    192.36.148.17
E.ROOT-SERVERS.NET.    5w6d16h IN A    192.203.230.10

;; Total query time: 360 msec
;; FROM: foo to SERVER: rs.internic.net  198.41.0.6
;; WHEN: Fri Jan  1 06:43:30 1999
;; MSG SIZE  sent: 17  rcvd: 436
```

The `dig` program returns data in a format that is usable directly by the DNS server, making updates like this easy. Remarks are marked with `;;` by `dig`. The header section shows you the options that are set for this `dig` query, but not necessarily those that are used. The `HEADER` tells you that this was a query that returned no errors. The `authority` section provides a simplified (translated from seconds) readout of the expire time, the time after which the DNS server that obtained these results needs to stop using them. The `internic` expires its root servers at six weeks (604800 seconds).

Compare the following dig output for caldera.com to the output in the previous nslookup section. The dig lookup also defaults to querytype of A (see Listing 26.5).

LISTING 26.5 OUTPUT FROM A dig QUERY

```
 ; <<>> DiG 8.1 <<>> caldera.com
;; res options: init recurs defnam dnsrch
;; got answer:
;; ->>HEADER<<-opcode: QUERY, status: NOERROR, id: 6
;; flags: qr rd ra; QUERY: 1, ANSWER: 1, AUTHORITY: 2, ADDITIONAL: 2
;; QUERY SECTION:
;;      caldera.com, type = A, class = IN

;; ANSWER SECTION:
caldera.com.            3h47m17s IN A   207.179.18.1

;; AUTHORITY SECTION:
caldera.com.            4h58m30s IN NS  caldera.caldera.com.
caldera.com.            4h58m30s IN NS  gw.caldera.com.

;; ADDITIONAL SECTION:
caldera.caldera.com.    4h42m4s IN A    207.179.18.1
gw.caldera.com.         4h58m30s IN A   207.179.18.252

;; Total query time: 2 msec
;; FROM: foo to SERVER: default --127.0.0.1
;; WHEN: Fri Jan  1 11:19:19 1999
;; MSG SIZE  sent: 29  rcvd: 116
```

This provides the same basic information, just more of it and in a slightly different format. So whether you use dig or nslookup is a personal choice. But nslookup is less cluttered.

PART IV CH 26

dnsquery

The dnsquery program is similar to dig, shown in Listing 26.5, but returns the data in a slightly different format. It also returns a little more information than dig, but not as verbosely. Because it provides more information from the start, it has fewer options; therefore, it is, in some ways, less intimidating than dig and as easy as or easier than nslookup. Two sample outputs, one from the Caldera domain and one from the caldera host at caldera.com, are shown in Listing 26.6.

LISTING 26.6 TWO dnsquery RETURNS

```
foo# dnsquery caldera.com
;; ->>HEADER<<-opcode: QUERY, status: NOERROR, id: 58127
;; flags: qr rd ra; QUERY: 1, ANSWER: 5, AUTHORITY: 2, ADDITIONAL: 2
;;      caldera.com, type = ANY, class = IN
caldera.com.            3h9m41s IN NS   caldera.caldera.com.
caldera.com.            3h9m41s IN NS   gw.caldera.com.
caldera.com.            3h46m42s IN SOA  caldera.caldera.com.
➥root.caldera.com.
(
```

continues

LISTING 26.6 CONTINUED

```
                                        1998123001      ; serial
                                        1H              ; refresh
                                        15M             ; retry
                                        1W              ; expiry
                                        6H )            ; minimum

caldera.com.            3h19m41s IN MX  5 caldera.caldera.com.
caldera.com.            2h8m28s IN A    207.179.18.1
caldera.com.            3h9m41s IN NS   caldera.caldera.com.
caldera.com.            3h9m41s IN NS   gw.caldera.com.
caldera.caldera.com.    2h10m20s IN A   207.179.18.1
gw.caldera.com.         3h19m41s IN A   207.179.18.252

foo# dnsquery caldera.caldera.com
;; ->>HEADER<<-opcode: QUERY, status: NOERROR, id: 8858
;; flags: qr rd ra; QUERY: 1, ANSWER: 1, AUTHORITY: 2, ADDITIONAL: 2
;;      caldera.caldera.com, type = ANY, class = IN
caldera.caldera.com.    2h2m4s IN A     207.179.18.1
caldera.COM.            3h7m51s IN NS   caldera.caldera.com.
caldera.COM.            3h7m51s IN NS   gw.caldera.COM.
caldera.caldera.com.    2h2m4s IN A     207.179.18.1
 gw.caldera.COM.          3h17m51s IN A   207.179.18.252
```

Notice that the first query returns all information, including NS, MX, and all A entries that are applicable. The second query returned all the entries it found about the host caldera, including the host gw. If you can't see why, the host caldera has an RR that corresponds to caldera.com. Likewise, caldera.com corresponds to both host caldera and host gw.

host

If all you want to know is the IP address for a particular host name, the `host` program provides it in a clean format that is easily redirected to a file or run through `awk` for direct inclusion into a file such as /etc/hosts. Sample output of host caldera.caldera.com returns the following:

```
caldera.caldera.com         A         207.179.18.1
```

To change this, simply do something like the following:

```
host caldera.caldera.com ¦ awk '{print $3 "\t" $1 }' -
```

The `awk print` command reverses the order of the output and inserts a Tab character (`\t`) between them. This can be redirected and appended to `/etc/hosts` via >>.

Caution

The preceding example is only to be used for hosts over which you have control, or which you know will not change. Putting Caldera's hosts in your /etc/hosts file if you are not the domain administrator for Caldera is a bad idea.

whois

The last program you'll look at in this chapter is whois. Although it is not one of the BIND utilities, this program provides DNS-related information. Specifically, it provides information from the internic.net database regarding domain registration information. It is advisable to direct your query to the appropriate whois server. As of this writing, whois servers include the following:

- whois.internic.net
- whois.nic.gov
- whois.nic.mil
- whois.ripe.net
- whois.sunet.se
- whois.apnic.net
- whois.arin.net
- whois.funet.fi
- whois.nic.fr
- whois.nic.uk

A whois query on the caldera.com domain returns the following:

```
# whois -h whois.internic.net caldera.com

Registrant:
Caldera, Inc. (CALDERA-DOM)
   240 West Center Street
   Orem, UT 84057

   Domain Name: CALDERA.COM

   Administrative Contact, Technical Contact, Zone Contact:
      Roberts, John  (JR4265)  johnr@CALDERA.COM
      1-801-377-7687 (FAX) 1-801-377-8752
   Billing Contact:
      Cooper, Doug  (DC1630)  doug@CALDERA.COM
      (801) 226-1675

   Record last updated on 14-Jan-98.
   Record created on 04-Nov-94.
   Database last updated on 1-Jan-99 03:27:16 EST.


   Domain servers in listed order:

   NS.CALDERA.COM               207.179.18.1
   NS2.CALDERA.COM              207.179.18.252


The InterNIC Registration Services database contains ONLY
non-military and non-US Government Domains and contacts.
```

```
Other associated whois servers:
   American Registry for Internet Numbers -whois.arin.net
   European IP Address Allocations        -whois.ripe.net
   Asia Pacific IP Address Allocations    -whois.apnic.net
   US Military                            -whois.nic.mil
   US Government                          -whois.nic.gov
```

SUMMARY

In this chapter, you learned what DNS is and the role that BIND plays. You learned about the files that BIND uses and what they looked like. You learned how to use `ndc` to control named, the name server daemon that is the current name for BIND. You learned about zone files and what comprises them. Finally, you learned about some utilities that you can use to check your DNS server and see output from it. For more information on resolving DNS names see the following chapters:

- Chapter 21, "Understanding TCP/IP Fundamentals," discusses how IP in general works. The more you know about how computers communicate, the easier it is to understand the role that DNS plays in networking.
- See Chapter 22, "Network Administration," to learn more about administering a network, in which DNS plays a significant role.
- See Chapter 23 to learn more about diagnosing network problems and understanding how services connect to IP addresses and ports. The more you understand about how ports work, the easier it is to see how DNS communicates the information from DNS servers to clients.

CHAPTER 27

File Transfer Protocol (FTP)

In this chapter

The File Transfer Protocol (FTP) is quite simple to use but rather powerful in its capability to facilitate the transfer of files or data between two systems. With many networking protocols and file sharing systems designed and developed subsequent to the existence of FTP, it still stands as the most popular method for remotely transferring files. OpenLinux uses what is perhaps the most widely used version of FTP, `wu-ftp`, which was developed at Washington University in St. Louis (see `www.wu-ftpd.org` for more details).

FTP OVERVIEW

FTP is, by far, the most common method for transferring files between similar or dissimilar systems. FTP provides the capability to transfer any type of file between two systems. It is designed (see RFC 959) so that the two systems do not have to be the same. In other words, any operating systems that support TCP/IP and offer FTP services can exchange files. One of the systems acts as the server, and the other as the client. The format of the data, whether it's a text file, a database file, or a binary program, does not matter.

FTP service is based on the Transmission Control Protocol/Internet Protocol (TCP/IP) standard. FTP uses two entirely separate TCP sessions to complete a transfer of files. One session is commonly referred to as the Control Connection or Protocol Interpreter (PI) session, and the other as the Data Connection or Data Transfer Process (DTP). Figure 27.1 depicts the basic components of an FTP session.

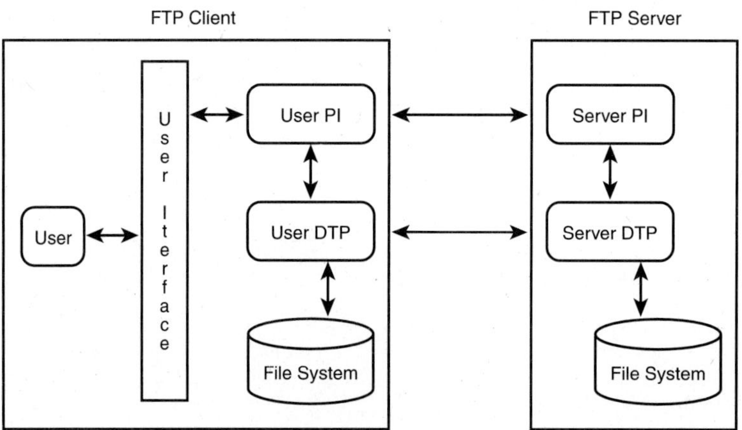

Figure 27.1
The Protocol Interpreter session is predefined to take place on port 21 and the Data Transfer process occurs on port 20. These ports are defined in the /etc/services file.

As long as the underlying TCP/IP network is in place and FTP services are configured, an FTP session can be established between two hosts. The FTP client initiates an FTP session by connecting to an FTP server. The server component must be configured and active whenever an FTP request is made from a client. By default, the FTP server is enabled with OpenLinux.

Caution

If your FTP server is active and your machine is accessible to anyone on the Internet, be aware that, by default, all users have access to the FTP server unless explicit changes are made to disable access.

This chapter examines the details of the FTP client and how to initiate an FTP session. You'll also look at the specifics of setting up an FTP server and the associated configuration files, including the configuration of an anonymous FTP server and how to control access to the server.

FTP Client

OpenLinux comes with a standard command-line FTP client. It's not the fanciest utility, but it gets the job done. Many other FTP clients are available for Linux, including the FTP client capability that is built into the Netscape Web browser. These FTP clients can be easier to use and offer a better user interface; however, an understanding of the command-line client not only gives you a better understanding of how the FTP service works, but also adds some additional features such as unattended or batch mode transfers.

Performing a file transfer via `ftp` as the client is a simple task. It basically consists of two steps:

1. Establish a connection to an FTP server.
2. Specify the file to either place on the server or download from the server.

Following is a closer look at each of these steps. First, in order to establish a connection to an FTP server, you must supply the server name. Many FTP sites have configured the machine name so that the first part of the name is set to `ftp`. For example, the Caldera Systems FTP server is aptly named `ftp.calderasystems.com`. Establishing an FTP session to this FTP server can be done as follows:

```
# ftp ftp.calderasystems.com

Connected to rim.caldera.com.
220 rim.caldera.com FTP server (Version wu-2.4.2-academ[BETA-17](1) Wed Aug 5 19
:49:36 MEST 1998) ready.
Name (ftp.calderasystems.com:allan):
```


After a connection is established, you must authenticate yourself to the FTP server. This can be done in one of two ways: as a normal user account or as an anonymous user. Unless you have an individual login account on the FTP server that you are accessing, you must authenticate yourself as an anonymous user.

Authenticating to the FTP server is done by supplying a username and password, or by giving the username *anonymous* (the name *ftp* works as well) with your email address as the password. As you might have guessed, you can enter anything you want as the password when connecting to an FTP server as an anonymous user. However, it is common courtesy to supply your email address when connecting in this way because it enables the system administrator of the FTP server to contact you if the need arises. Completing the connection to the FTP server is as follows:

```
Connected to rim.caldera.com.
220 rim.caldera.com FTP server (Version wu-2.4.2-academ[BETA-17](1) Wed
Aug 5 19:49:36 (MEST 1998) ready.
Name (ftp.calderasystems.com:allan): anonymous
331 Guest login ok, send your complete email address as password.
Password:
230-
230-                    Welcome to the Caldera FTP site!
230-                            ftp.caldera.com
230-
230-                  "Extend Your Systems to the World!"
230-
230-This site is provided as a public service by Caldera, Inc.  This
230-server is located in Orem, Utah, USA; use in violation of any
230-applicable laws strictly prohibited.
230-
230-For comments on this site, please contact <ftpmaster@caldera.com>.
230-=====================================================================
230-**All file transfers are logged. If you object to this, logout now.**
230-=====================================================================
230-
230 Guest login ok, access restrictions apply.
Remote system type is UNIX.
Using binary mode to transfer files.
ftp>
```

The connection is complete when the `ftp>` prompt is received. It is at this point that file transfers can be initiated. This interactive method also provides the capability to perform several other tasks during an FTP session. The commands that are available within an FTP client session can be displayed by entering `help` (a question mark displays the same list) at the `ftp>` prompt as follows:

```
ftp> help

!               debug           mdir            sendport        site
$               dir             mget            put             size
account         disconnect      mkdir           pwd             status
append          exit            mls             quit            struct
ascii           form            mode            quote           system
bell            get             modtime         recv            sunique
binary          glob            mput            reget           tenex
bye             hash            newer           rstatus         tick
case            help            nmap            rhelp           trace
cd              idle            nlist           rename          type
cdup            image           ntrans          reset           user
chmod           lcd             open            restart         umask
close           ls              prompt          rmdir           verbose
cr              macdef          passive         runique         ?
delete          mdelete         proxy           send
```

A brief description of each of these commands is listed in Table 27.1.

Table 27.1 FTP Client Command Listing

Command	Description
`!`	Escape to the shell
`$`	Execute macro
`account`	Send account command to remote server
`append`	Append to a file
`ascii`	Set ASCII transfer type
`bell`	Beep when command completed
`binary`	Set binary transfer type
`bye`	Terminate FTP session and exit
`case`	Toggle `mget` upper- and lowercase ID mapping
`cd`	Change remote working directory
`cdup`	Change remote working directory to parent directory
`chmod`	Change file permissions of remote file
`close`	Terminate FTP session
`cr`	Toggle carriage return stripping on ASCII gets
`delete`	Delete remote file
`debug`	Toggle/set debugging mode
`dir`	List contents of remote directory
`disconnect`	Terminate FTP session
`exit`	Terminate FTP session and exit
`form`	Set file transfer format
`get`	Receive file
`glob`	Toggle metacharacter expansion of local file names
`hash`	Toggle printing # for each buffer transferred
`help`	Print local help information
`idle`	Get (set) idle timer on remote side
`image`	Set binary transfer type
`lcd`	Change local working directory
`ls`	List contents of remote directory
`macdef`	Define a macro

continues

TABLE 27.1 CONTINUED

Command	Description
`mdelete`	Delete multiple files
`mdir`	List contents of multiple remote directories
`mget`	Get multiple files
`mkdir`	Make directory on the remote machine
`mls`	List contents of multiple remote directories
`mode`	Set file transfer mode
`modtime`	Show last modification time of remote file
`mput`	Send multiple files
`newer`	Get file if remote file is newer than local file
`nmap`	Set templates for default filename mapping
`nlist`	List contents of remote directory
`ntrans`	Set translation table for default filename mapping
`open`	Connect to remote FTP
`prompt`	Force interactive prompting on multiple commands
`passive`	Enter passive transfer mode
`proxy`	Issue command on alternative connection
`put`	Send one file
`pwd`	Print working directory on remote machine
`quit`	Terminate FTP session and exit
`quote`	Send arbitrary FTP command
`recv`	Receive file
`reget`	Get file restarting at end of local file
`rstatus`	Show status of remote machine
`rhelp`	Get help from remote server
`rename`	Rename file
`reset`	Clear queued command replies
`restart`	Restart file transfer at byte count
`rmdir`	Remove directory on the remote machine
`runique`	Toggle store unique for local files
`send`	Send one file
`sendport`	Toggle use of `PORT` command for each data connection

Command	Description
`site`	Send site specific command to remote server. (Try `rhelp site` or `site help` for more information.)
`size`	Show size of remote file
`status`	Show current status
`struct`	Set file transfer structure
`system`	Show remote system type
`sunique`	Toggle store unique on remote machine
`tenex`	Set tenex file transfer type
`tick`	Toggle printing byte counter during transfers
`trace`	Toggle packet tracing
`type`	Set file transfer type
`user`	Send new user information
`umask`	Get (set) umask on remote side
`verbose`	Toggle verbose mode
`?`	Print local help information

Some commands act as toggle switches between two different FTP session parameters. For example, by default the FTP download mode is set to binary. By entering the command `ascii`, the transfer mode is changed from binary to ASCII. Another example of a toggle type command is `prompt`. The `status` command displays the current settings. The default settings are as follows:

```
ftp> status
Connected to localhost.
No proxy connection.
Mode: stream; Type: binary; Form: non-print; Structure: file
Verbose: on; Bell: off; Prompting: on; Globbing: on
Store unique: off; Receive unique: off
Case: off; CR stripping: on
Ntrans: off
Nmap: off
Hash mark printing: off; Use of PORT cmds: on
Tick counter printing: off
```


Downloading Files via an FTP Session

As you saw in the previous section, it's quite simple to establish a connection with an FTP server. Use the following steps to downloading files via FTP services:

1. Establish an FTP session by connecting to an FTP server.
2. Authenticate yourself as an anonymous user by supplying the login `anonymous` and your email address as a password.

3. Navigate the FTP directories to locate the desired files.
4. Initiate the download process.
5. Close the FTP session and exit.

After a connection is established, the next step is to locate the desired files. Navigating through an FTP site is very similar to navigating around a Linux file system at a shell prompt (see Chapter 9, "Understanding the Linux File System"). The commands are the same for listing files and changing directories. After the files that are to be downloaded are located, it's just a matter of setting the download parameters and initiating the transfer. In the following sample FTP session, the complete set of QT development utilities is downloaded:

```
ftp> ls
200 PORT command successful.
150 Opening ASCII mode data connection for /bin/ls.
total 22
drwxr-xr-x  10 root     root          1024 Mar 13  1998 .
drwxr-xr-x  10 root     root          1024 Mar 13  1998 ..
d--x--x--x   9 root     root          1024 Jan  2 16:07 .private
d--x--x--x   7 root     root          1024 Dec 19 23:35 .virtual
d--x--x--x   2 root     root          1024 Oct 21 19:45 bin
d--x--x--x   2 root     root          1024 May 20  1997 etc
d-wx-wx-wt   3 root     root          1024 Dec 30 12:52 incoming
drwxr-xr-x   2 root     root          1024 Feb 15  1997 lib
drwxr-xr-x   2 root     root         12288 May 15  1997 lost+found
dr-xr-xr-x  16 root     root          1024 Dec 23 15:41 pub
-r--r--r--   1 root     root           593 Mar 13  1998 welcome.msg
226 Transfer complete.
ftp>
ftp> cd /pub/OpenLinux/contrib/RPMS
250 CWD command successful.
ftp>ls qt*
200 PORT command successful.
150 Opening ASCII mode data connection for /bin/ls.
-r--r--r--  1 root root   643562 Dec  7 16:43 qt-1.42-1.i386.rpm
-r--r--r--  1 root root  2646588 Dec  7 16:43 qt-1.42-1.src.rpm
-r--r--r--  1 root root   662655 Dec  7 16:43 qt-devel-1.42-1.i386.rpm
-r--r--r--  1 root root  1203320 Dec  7 16:44 qt-doc-html-1.42-1.i386.rpm
-r--r--r--  1 root root   596047 Dec  7 16:44 qt-examples-1.42-1.i386.rpm
-r--r--r--  1 root root   138712 Dec  7 16:44 qt-tutorial-1.42-1.i386.rpm

226 Transfer complete.
ftp> prompt
Interactive mode off.
ftp> mget qt*
local: qt-1.42-1.i386.rpm remote: qt-1.42-1.i386.rpm
200 PORT command successful.
150 Opening BINARY mode data connection for qt-1.42-1.i386.rpm (643562
bytes).
226 Transfer complete.
643562 bytes received in 6.71 secs (94 Kbytes/sec)
local: qt-1.42-1.src.rpm remote: qt-1.42-1.src.rpm
200 PORT command successful.
150 Opening BINARY mode data connection for qt-1.42-1.src.rpm (2646588
```

```
bytes).
226 Transfer complete.
2646588 bytes received in 27.6 secs (94 Kbytes/sec)
local: qt-devel-1.42-1.i386.rpm remote: qt-devel-1.42-1.i386.rpm
200 PORT command successful.
150 Opening BINARY mode data connection for qt-devel-1.42-1.i386.rpm
(662655 bytes).
226 Transfer complete.
662655 bytes received in 6.39 secs (1e+02 Kbytes/sec)
local: qt-doc-html-1.42-1.i386.rpm remote: qt-doc-html-1.42-1.i386.rpm
200 PORT command successful.
150 Opening BINARY mode data connection for qt-doc-html-1.42-1.i386.rpm
(1203320 bytes).
226 Transfer complete.
1203320 bytes received in 10.6 secs (1.1e+02 Kbytes/sec)
local: qt-examples-1.42-1.i386.rpm remote: qt-examples-1.42-1.i386.rpm
200 PORT command successful.
150 Opening BINARY mode data connection for qt-examples-1.42-1.i386.rpm
(596047 bytes).
226 Transfer complete.
596047 bytes received in 5.3 secs (1.1e+02 Kbytes/sec)
local: qt-tutorial-1.42-1.i386.rpm remote: qt-tutorial-1.42-1.i386.rpm
200 PORT command successful.
150 Opening BINARY mode data connection for qt-tutorial-1.42-1.i386.rpm
(138712 bytes).
226 Transfer complete.
138712 bytes received in 1.37 secs (99 Kbytes/sec)
ftp>quit
221 Goodbye.
[allan@caldera allan]$
```

Note

Commands that deal with multiple files, such as `mget`, `mput`, and `mdelete`, take wildcards for parameters. For example, the command `mget qt*` gets all the files that begin with the letters *qt*.

SERVING FILES VIA FTP

As with many of the services that are available with OpenLinux, the FTP server is configured as operational by default. This means that files can be served to anyone who has access to the system. Access to the system is only offered to users with previously set up accounts. See Chapter 10, "Users, Groups, and Permissions," for more details on user account setup.

FTP SERVER OVERVIEW

The FTP server is a program (often referred to as a daemon) that starts up at boot time and waits for any FTP requests. The system initialization process (see Chapter 12, "System Initialization Under OpenLinux") runs a script called `inet`. The `inet` process serves as a master program for all Internet protocols, including FTP services. Having one main program that functions in this fashion makes the system more efficient and easier to maintain. The initialization script, `/etc/rc.d/init.d/inet`, starts a program (for die-hard Linux or

UNIX people, it's a daemon) called inetd. This program reads the configuration file /etc/inetd.conf and sets up the configured services. FTP service is one of the protocols that is configured as enabled by default in the /etc/inetd.conf file. The entry for FTP service in the /etc/inetd.conf file is as follows:

```
ftp    stream    tcp    nowait    root    /usr/sbin/tcpd in.ftpd -l -a
```

After the inetd (inet daemon) program is running, it listens for incoming requests for all preconfigured services as defined in the /etc/inetd.conf file and the /etc/services file. If a request for FTP service is detected (defined by the appropriate port), a program to service that request is spawned. The program that is spawned is the one that is defined in the /etc/inetd.conf file. In the case of FTP services, it's the program `in.ftpd`. For further information on the /etc/inetd.conf file, see the man page for inetd.

The primary purpose of an FTP server is to offer files to remote users. These users might be local to an organization, or they might be anonymous users somewhere on the Internet. Access to an FTP archive, or to any files via FTP, is controlled by a user account. For users with previously configured accounts, accessing files via FTP is allowed by default. You merely have to supply a user account and password. After a user is authenticated to the FTP server in this fashion, he can access any files on the system that he has rights to. The default directory is the user's home directory, as specified in the /etc/passwd file. The standard set of packages that is installed with OpenLinux includes one called `anonftp`. This package contains all the components to set up an anonymous FTP server.

ANONYMOUS FTP

Anonymous FTP is arguably the most common use of FTP services. Countless FTP archives exist all around the globe. Each of these sites offers access to unknown users to connect to the server and download files of their choice. Most software companies offer demo programs via FTP. Some FTP sites even offer the capability to place files on the FTP server system. For example, the Caldera FTP site has an incoming directory where many programmers have contributed software packages for the use and benefit of others.

If an incoming directory is set up on your FTP server, it is good practice to configure it so that the system is protected from malicious acts. For example, it is strongly recommended that the incoming directory reside on its own partition. This way, if the incoming directory becomes full—either accidentally or maliciously—it does not impact the rest of the system. Also, setting up the incoming directory as write-only enables you to monitor the content that has been placed there. After the files have been determined to be okay, that is, there are no offensive or inappropriate files, they can be moved to a location to which all anonymous users can have access. Most FTP sites call this the contrib area of the FTP site.

Tip

If you offer incoming FTP services, place the incoming directory on its own partition to avoid filling up the root file system. Also, set the permissions on the directory so that it's write-only; this way, you can avoid having all FTP users see inappropriate material, if someone has maliciously placed any in the incoming directory.

The anonymous FTP RPM contains the following files:

```
/home/ftp
/home/ftp/bin
/home/ftp/bin/gzip
/home/ftp/bin/ls
/home/ftp/bin/tar
/home/ftp/bin/zcat
/home/ftp/etc
/home/ftp/etc/group
/home/ftp/etc/passwd
/home/ftp/pub
/usr/doc/anonftp-3.1
/usr/doc/anonftp-3.1/README
```

Installation of this package sets up everything that is required to make anonymous FTP service available. As was mentioned earlier in this chapter, in order to connect to an FTP server, you must have a user account. Even with anonymous FTP service, a user account is required. However, rather than creating a new user account for this purpose, one is already created in the /etc/passwd file. Of course it is appropriately named `ftp`. It's actually a special type of user account that differs from the typical user accounts that are found in the /etc/passwd file. The entry for the `ftp` account in the /etc/passwd file is as follows:

```
ftp:x:14:50:FTP User:/home/ftp:
```

It is the user account entry in the /etc/passwd file that allows a connection to the FTP server by anonymous users. Even though the user account entry is `ftp`, the user ID `anonymous` is accepted when connecting to the FTP server. In fact, many people mistakenly think that the user ID `anonymous` is the only one that works.

Controlling Access

Access to the FTP server can be controlled in one of four ways:

- Removing or commenting out the FTP user in the /etc/passwd file
- Adding a user to exclude to the /etc/ftpusers file
- Removing the class of user from the /etc/ftpaccess file
- Shutting down the FTP server

The /etc/ftpaccess file is used to configure access to the FTP server. Upon initial installation, the contents of the this file are as follows:

```
class    all    real,guest,anonymous   *

email root@localhost

loginfails 5

readme  README*    login
readme  README*    cwd=*

message /welcome.msg            login
```

```
message .message                  cwd=*

compress        yes               all
tar             yes               all
chmod           no                guest,anonymous
delete          no                guest,anonymous
overwrite       no                guest,anonymous
rename          no                guest,anonymous

log transfers anonymous,real inbound,outbound
shutdown /etc/shutmsg

passwd-check rfc822 warn
```

Each of the entries defined in this file is described in detail in the man page for `ftpaccess`. The entries in the /etc/ftpaccess file control not only who can access the FTP server, but what they can do after a connection is made.

Tip

To disable access to the FTP server to all real accounts on the system, remove the entry for `real` in the class line of the /etc/ftpaccess file.

The /etc/ftpusers file is used to control which users do not have access to the FTP server. By default, the following entries are placed in the /etc/ftpusers file:

```
root
bin
daemon
adm
lp
sync
shutdown
halt
mail
news
uucp
operator
games
nobody
```

If a username is included in the /etc/ftpusers file, that user cannot access the FTP server. If a connection to the FTP server is attempted with one of the user names included in this file, the following message is returned:

```
# ftp ftp.kcpartners.com
Connected to ftp.kcpartners.com
220 router.kcpartners.com FTP server (Version wu-2.4.2-academ[BETA-17](1)
Wed Aug 19 02:55:52 MST 1998) ready.
Name (kcpartners.com:col): ftp
530 User ftp access denied.
Login failed.
Remote system type is UNIX.
Using binary mode to transfer files.
ftp>
```

SHUTTING DOWN THE FTP SERVER

The `ftpshut` command can be used to discontinue FTP service at a given time. It provides a means of notifying users that the FTP server is temporarily shut down and that they can try again later. The `ftpshut` command creates a file in the /etc directory called shutmsg. When an attempt to connect to the FTP server is made, the FTP server checks for the existence of this file. If it is found, the following message is displayed:

```
# ftp router
Connected to router.kcpartners.com.
500 router.kcpartners.com FTP server shut down -- please try again later.
ftp>
```

Note

You must remove the /etc/shutmsg file in order to re-establish FTP service after issuing a `ftpshut` command.

FILE PLACEMENT

Because the FTP server is enabled by default for anonymous user access, placing files for FTP access is a simple step. The default directory structure for anonymous FTP access is configured in such a way that simply placing files in the /home/ftp/pub directory will suffice. Note that the other two directories within the /home/ftp directory, /home/ftp/bin and /home/ftp/etc, are not accessible when connecting via FTP. Place all publicly accessible files under the /home/ftp/pub directory or a subdirectory tree structure within /home/ftp/pub.

Note

Remember to set all files on the FTP server with permissions of read-only. The directory permissions for /home/ftp/pub are set this way by default.

SUMMARY

This chapter covered the basics of FTP operations. You should feel comfortable with what FTP is and how it operates, and be able to access an FTP server as a client as well as perform simple system administration on an FTP server. Controlling access to the FTP server can be done in one of several ways, but the /etc/ftpaccess configuration file is the most powerful way of differentiating between FTP users. See the /usr/doc/wu-ftpd-2.4.2b17 directory for further documentation on the FTP software. Refer to the following chapters for more information:

- See Chapter 9 to learn more about the directory hierarchy.
- See Chapter 10 to learn more about user accounts and setting permissions on files and directories.
- See Chapter 21, "Understanding TCP/IP Fundamentals," to learn more about the underlying protocol that is prerequisite to FTP operation.

CHAPTER 28

The Web Server

In this chapter

One of the most basic, yet important, services that is available for use with OpenLinux is the Web server. The Web server provides you with the capability to set up your own Web site (or multiple Web sites), where you can publish your own information, process data, or serve some community in which you are interested.

OpenLinux ships with the most popular Web server available today, the Apache Web server. In this chapter, you will learn how Apache works, and you will learn about many of the different features that you can configure on it. Serving Web pages is, at its core, a very simple operation; however, there are numerous modifications and extensions that you can make to the basic Web server configuration, which you can use to customize the Web site that you create.

OVERVIEW OF OPERATION

Before diving into the configuration of the Apache Web server, it helps to get a basic understanding of its operation on your machine. A Web server responds to requests that are made to it, using the *Hypertext Transfer Protocol* (*HTTP*). This protocol is a simple one that primarily allows clients to request documents from a server. The HTTP protocol also allows clients to provide information back to the server for interactive operations. Because the Web server uses this protocol, the actual server daemon program is called `httpd.apache` (and is located in /usr/sbin).

By default, Apache is installed and operational when you install OpenLinux. In fact, it is probably running right now on your system. To verify that it is, start a browser under X and open this address by typing the following into the location line for the browser:

```
http://localhost/
```

If Apache is running on your machine, you see a page of links to documentation for your OpenLinux system. Although you are accessing information on your local box, you are actually going through the network—accessing your local Web server—to see it. The basic sequence of operations performed by the browser and server is as follows:

1. The browser opens a connection to the server that is listed in the URL (in this case localhost). This involves looking up the address of the machine, based on its name, and using TCP/IP port 80 if none is specified.
2. The browser sends a `GET` request to the server with the path to the document that it wants to retrieve. In the preceding case, the path is just `/`, which is the root directory.
3. The server translates the requested path into a path in its local file system. By default, OpenLinux uses a document root of `/home/httpd/html` for the Web server; therefore, the requested path `/` is translated into the path `/home/httpd/html/`.
4. The server evaluates the path to see if any security or other restrictions apply to that path. If so, the server might request that the user enter his name and password in order to see the document, or it might reject the request immediately (depending on the access control settings for the document in question).

5. If the path indicates a regular file, the server returns the file to the client, indicating the file type as part of the response. The file type is returned in MIME format as part of the response header. (MIME types are discussed in Chapter 5, "Customizing Your Desktop Environment," and later in this chapter.)
6. If the path indicates a directory (as it does in the current example), the server can do one of several things: Look for a specially named file in the directory (usually index.html) to return to the client; generate a directory listing of the directory as an HTML page, and return that to the client; or return an error to the client.
7. If the path indicates a special program, called a `CGI` script, the server might run the program and return the output of the program to the client.
8. After the server finishes sending the data to the client, and after the client receives it, the client and server terminate their connection.
9. At this point, the server usually makes an entry in a log file about the request.

The Web server is started automatically at the time that you boot your machine. The following steps describe how the Web server begins operation when it is started:

1. The Web server begins operation when an `rc` script is run by the `init` daemon. See Chapter 12, "System Initialization Under OpenLinux," for an explanation of the `init` process and the different `rc` scripts that run during system startup.
2. The Web server reads its configuration file and configures many of its internal settings, including its name and address, the location of the documents that it serves to requesting clients, security settings, the location and format of log files, and numerous other things.
3. The server changes its privileges from root to some less privileged user account on the system to reduce the risk of someone using the Web server to break into your machine to access private documents.
4. The Web server binds to an address (or multiple addresses) on your machine.
5. The Web server starts several child processes to handle actual requests from clients and begins receiving and responding to requests.

BASIC CONFIGURATION

Although the Web server is essentially a mechanism to transfer files from your machine to another (the client) on the network, it is a surprisingly flexible piece of software.

It supports many options for changing its name, address, and performance characteristics. You can specify multiple directories from which to serve documents, and you can apply different document and directory handling options, security settings, and access rights to each. You can also control how errors are returned to the user, where and how log files are written, and how the server assigns types to files that it returns.

INTRODUCTION TO CONFIGURATION

Before presenting all the different configuration options for Apache, this section first covers some basic items, such as where the configuration files are located and the default values (in OpenLinux) for some important Web server settings. It also presents an overview of the types of options that are available for configuring the Web server.

There are too many different directives, options, and modules in Apache to list them all in this chapter. Instead, the most common customizations to the Web server are presented here. Detailed online documentation has more information about each directive; furthermore, it covers the other modules and features of Apache. The online documentation for the Apache Web server is available in the package `apache-docs-1.3.1-2.i386.rpm`, which is not installed by default. To install it, log in as root, and then mount the `cdrom` and install the package using the following commands:

```
mount /mnt/cdrom
rpm -i /mnt/cdrom/Packages/RPMS/apache-doc*
```

The documentation is installed in the directory /home/httpd/apache/doc/manual. To view it, open a browser to that location and follow the links to the topic in which you have an interest.

APACHE CONFIGURATION FILES

The Apache configuration files are located in the directory /etc/httpd/apache/conf. If you look in this directory, you see several files that control different aspects of the Web server's behavior and functionality.

The base directory for the Web server configuration files is specified in the file /etc/httpd/apache/conf/httpd.conf, using the `ServerRoot` directive. When the Web server is started by the initialization scripts, the path to httpd.conf is specified on the command line of the server (httpd.apache), and the other configuration files are determined from there.

There are five basic configuration files in the configuration directory. These files, and their usual contents, are described in Table 28.1. The most common configuration changes for Apache are made in first three files listed in the table (httpd.conf, srm.conf, and access.conf).

TABLE 28.1 WEB SERVER CONFIGURATION FILES

File	Contains
httpd.conf	General server configuration settings.
srm.conf	Request processing directives, including error responses, directory indexing options, and script handling. This file basically defines the document tree (*name space*) that is visible to the outside world, as well as how the server delivers information from that tree to remote clients. The structure of the document tree doesn't necessarily match the directory structure of your local file system.

File	Contains
access.conf	Per directory options, including access control and security restrictions.
mime.types	MIME file type definitions for different file extensions.
magic	MIME file type definitions based on file contents.

Historically, the .conf files hold the different types of information that are described in Table 28.1. However, any Web server directive can be put in any of the three .conf files, and the Web server will interpret it correctly. The three .conf files are processed in the following order: httpd.conf, srm.conf, and access.conf. Additional configuration files (particularly those that are related to security) might be present in the actual document tree that is processed by the server. These files are described in greater detail in the sections "Defining Options Using a File in the Current Directory" and "Adding Security to Your Web Site" in this chapter.

There might be other files in the configuration directory that end in -dist or -dist-win. These files are provided as examples of the original versions of the configuration files, as distributed by the Apache organization (with settings for UNIX and Windows machines, respectively).

Modifying the names and locations of configuration files used by the server is discussed in the section "Global Server Options."

Note

If you have followed some of the examples in previous chapters of this book (or if you have reinstalled or upgraded the Apache package), you might see configuration files with the extension .rpmsave. For a description of how these files are used by the package manager, see Chapter 15, "Software Package Management." Don't worry about them for now.

LOCATION OF LOG FILES

Log files are configured by default to be written in the directory /var/log/httpd/apache. There is a symbolic link to this location at /etc/httpd/apache/logs, which enables you to access this directory more quickly from the configuration directory. Log file options are discussed later in this chapter in the section "All About Logging."

DEFAULT DOCUMENT DIRECTORY

The default document directory for Apache on your OpenLinux system is /home/httpd/html. This means that when you put any file in this directory, or in subdirectories of this directory, remote users can see the file.

Other directories are also configured, by default, to be available through the Web server to the outside world, including the following directories:

- /home/httpd/cgi-bin
- /home/httpd/icons
- /home/httpd/apache/icons
- /home/httpd/cgi-bin
- public_html under each user's home directory (for example, /home/tim/public_html)

All these directories appear at different locations in the directory structure (name space) that is visible to the outside world. This is explained in the section "Defining the Document Name Space."

TYPES OF CONFIGURATION DIRECTIVES

At this point, before a detailed presentation of server configuration directives, it is useful to categorize the different options for the server.

Table 28.1 showed the different files that are used to hold configuration information for the Web server. The configuration data falls into roughly four major categories (represented by the files mentioned in the table).

There are global server directives, which control aspects of the server such as its address, the user and group account it runs as, and logfile formats and locations. Also, there are numerous options for tuning the performance and responsiveness of the server, and for setting timeouts and limits used by the server for its network connections.

Another category of directives has to do with how the server handles requests. The server provides a whole tree of documents to the outside world. Certain directives define this tree, including the location of the main document directory and other directories that the server provides. Furthermore, these directives control how the items in the tree are presented to clients (whether they are returned as files, as directory listings, or as output from programs in the document tree). You can configure many aspects of the directory listings that are provided by the server, and you can control how documents are selected and manipulated before they are returned to the user.

A third category of directives has to do with controlling access to the items that are returned by the file server. There are directives to limit access to clients that are making requests from certain locations, as well as directives to limit access to users who supply specific name-and-password combinations to the Web server. Other options control how the access limitations are applied and what options are allowed when files and directories are processed by the server.

Finally, there is the file typing system of the server. The server uses a system called MIME typing (*MIME* stands for *Multipurpose Internet Mail Extensions*) to communicate to the client the type of data that it is returning in each of its documents. This allows the client to handle the data more intelligently (for example, if the server identifies a document as a sound file, the client can load a sound program to play the file when it is received). There is a set of directives for defining the type of each file, based on its filename extension. Also, file types can be defined based on the content of the file.

It is important to distinguish between the different types of directives for several reasons. First, it helps you keep related directives near each other, and in the correct file. Some directives—such as those for defining file types—must reside in the correct file in order for the server to process them correctly. Another reason to distinguish the directives has to do with their scope. Some directives apply to the whole server and specify either general server behavior or apply to every document returned by the server. Other directives, however, can be applied to specific directories or files in the document tree. For example, you might have a part of your Web site where only authorized users can view documents, and another part for the general public. The per directory configuration options enable you to completely customize the different areas of your Web site to suit your individual needs.

Restarting the Server to Experiment with Your Changes

As you make modifications to the Web server configuration, you probably want to restart the server and access the documents on it to see the effect of your changes. You can stop and restart the Web server directly using the `httpd` script in the initialization system.

To stop the server, as root, type

```
/etc/rc.d/init.d/httpd stop
```

To restart the server, as root, type

```
/etc/rc.d/init.d/httpd start
```

Another way to do this is to send the running server a SIGHUP signal, which causes the main process of the server to terminate its children, reread the configuration files, and–if all goes well–restart child processes with the new configuration. To do this, use the following command:

```
kill -s SIGHUP `cat /var/run/httpd.pid`
```

Note the backquotes in the command. The drawback of this method is that if there is any problem with the modifications to the configuration files, the server just exits without any message. When the initialization script is used to restart the server, the server reports any problems it encounters with the configuration files, enabling you to fix them and restart it.

Global Server Options

The global server options control how the server interacts with the network and the host machine. Also, many options are available to control the performance of the server.

The directives for these options are in the file /etc/httpd/apache/conf/httpd.conf.

Changing Server Configuration Files

If, for one reason or another, you need to change the names or locations of the server configuration files, you can do so using the `ServerRoot`, `ResourceConfig`, `AccessConfig`, `TypesConfig`, and `MimeMagicFile` directives.

The `ServerRoot` directive specifies a base directory below which the configuration files are stored. Any filenames that are specified with the other directives, that do not start with a slash, are appended to the `ServerRoot` path. This makes it possible to leave all the other filenames alone and just switch the server to use another configuration directory. The default value for `ServerRoot` in OpenLinux is /etc/httpd/apache.

The most common reason to change the configuration filenames is when you are running more than one Web server. Obviously, the configuration of the servers must be different for the Web servers to respond on different addresses and serve different documents. You can decide whether you want to keep all the configuration files in /etc/httpd/apache/conf and change the names for the other files, or if you just want to make another directory (for example, /etc/httpd/apache2/conf), keep all the filenames the same, and change the value of `ServerRoot`.

The following list shows the default values for the other configuration file directives:

- **`ResourceConfig`**—conf/srm.conf
- **`AccessConfig`**—conf/access.conf
- **`TypeConfig`**—conf/mime.types
- **`MimeMageFile`**—None, but there's a magic file at conf/magic

If you use these directives, place them in the file httpd.conf. These directives are not present in the default httpd.conf file for Apache that is provided with OpenLinux. Often, even if directives are not used by the default configuration files, they are explained and shown in comments in the files—this is not true of these directives.

For example, to change the name of the access configuration file, edit httpd.conf and add a line such as the following:

```
AccessConfig conf/myaccess.conf
```

CHANGING THE ADDRESS OF THE SERVER

There are three directives that are used to control the address of the server. Often, your machine has only one IP address, and you use that address with the server. If you have multiple IP addresses, you might want the Web server to respond to requests on any of the machine's addresses. In these cases you can leave the configuration of the address for your server alone.

However, if your machine has multiple IP addresses, you might want to have it respond on only one of them. You can then run another instance of the Web server on a different address, to serve a different set of pages to clients. This enables you to make it appear, to the outside world, as if your machine were actually two (or more) different Web sites. This feature is called *virtual hosting*, and is a rather complex subject (which is covered in greater detail later in this chapter).

However, to simply change the address or port used by the server, use one of the following directives: `BindAddress`, `Listen`, or `Port`.

Use `BindAddress` when you want to specify either a single address or all addresses on your machine to which the server is to respond. You can specify any of the following:

- `*`—Respond on all IP addresses for the machine.
- **`address`**—Respond on just this IP address.
- **`name`**—Respond on the address that corresponds to this hostname (the name must be a fully qualified Internet domain name).

Only one `BindAddress` can be specified per server, and the directive doesn't enable you to specify the port that is to be used for service (use the `Port` directive for this). The `Listen` directive, on the other hand, can be used multiple times, and does enable you to specify the port as part of the address. This allows more precise control over the exact set of addresses on which the server will respond. Use of the `Listen` directive is discussed in greater detail in the "Virtual Hosting" section of this chapter.

To change the TCP port that is used by the server, use the `Port` directive. The default port used by Web servers is port 80. If you change the port, users are required to either type it in as part of the URL to access your site, or to follow a link, which includes the port number, to your site. Changing the port number can be useful in restricting access to your site to some set of pages and links that are internal to your local network. If you use a nonstandard port, it is difficult for someone coming from the outside to guess which port your server is on, and therefore more difficult for an unauthorized user to access your server.

For example, if you change the port to 8093, users are required to type something such as the following in their browsers to acccss your sitc:

```
http://www.foo.com:8093/somedir/somepage.html
```

Certain ports on your OpenLinux system are reserved for use only by the root account, for security reasons. If you choose a port lower than 1023, you cannot start the server as a user other than root. This prevents ordinary users on your machine from starting servers to handle well-known networking services (which might enable them to trick unsuspecting clients into giving them privileged information). This restriction is usually not a problem because the server is normally started as root during the bootup of the machine (by the initialization scripts). However, if you use a different initialization sequence, be aware of this restriction.

Changing the Account Used by the Server Process

When the Web server first starts, it is usually running as root. This allows it to access privileged configuration information and to open the restricted networking ports (if it is configured to do so). However, after the server is all set up, it is unwise for it to continue to run as root—the root account has access to every file and directory on the system. Because the Web server provides a conduit for remote users to access files and directories on your system, it is very dangerous for the Web server to run as root.

Therefore, the Web server changes its user and group account shortly after startup. Use the `User` and `Group` directives to control the way the Web server runs (which user and group account on your system it uses) during normal operation. By default, the Web server is configured to run as user nobody and group -1 (which doesn't correspond to any real group on your OpenLinux system). Note that you can specify the values for these either by name or by account number (preceded by a pound sign).

The user and group you that specify need to be accounts with limited access to the resources on your machine in order to prevent remote clients from accessing sensitive or private material. If you change the accounts that the server uses to run, you must make sure that the server can still access the documents it needs to serve. You might need to modify the owner, group, or permissions on files and directories in the Web document tree after changing these settings. See Chapter 10, "Users, Groups, and Permissions," for additional information on this topic.

For example, if you want the Web server to run as a special Webmaster account, perform the following steps:

1. Create a user account with the name Webmaster.
2. Edit the file httpd.conf, and change the user directive to read

   ```
   User Webmaster
   ```
3. Make sure that all the files you want the Web server to provide to remote clients are readable (or executable, if applicable) by the Webmaster account.

Modifying the Server Performance Characteristics

The Web server that is provided with OpenLinux is configured by default for minimal Web use. It is basically configured to serve as a help server or small LAN server. However, Apache is capable of acting as the server for a full-blown high-traffic Web site. Some of the options that are discussed in this section enable you to configure the server for higher performance, or to tune it to best match the traffic that you expect.

Handling High Server Loads Gracefully The `StartServers`, `MinSpareServers`, and `MaxSpareServers` directives affect the way in which the Web server prelaunches child processes to handle high request traffic at startup and runtime.

`StartServers` indicates the number of child processes that the server starts when it first initializes. Because the server responds automatically to the load that is placed on it, it is rarely necessary to adjust this value.

`MinSpareServers` and `MaxSpareServers` are used to configure the number of *idle* child processes that are started by the server during runtime, in order to handle *load spikes* (sudden increases in request traffic). If extra (or *spare*) child processes are already present when a sudden burst of requests comes in, the server can avoid the overhead of starting the child processes, which allows it to respond to the requests more quickly. This makes the server more responsive than it might otherwise be under heavy, fluctuating loads. Because these spare processes essentially do nothing until a load spike occurs, and because they do take up valuable memory and add overhead to your system, be careful about setting these numbers very high.

Periodically, the main Web server process checks to see how many spare servers are present. If the number is greater then `MaxSpareServers`, some child processes are terminated. If it is less than `MinSpareServers`, some child processes are started, at a rate of one per second.

By default, Caldera configures these numbers as `MinSpareServers 1` and `MaxSpareServers 2`. This is adequate for a machine with incidental Web use (such as for local help pages or a small number of clients). However, if you make your machine into a real Web site and expect lots of traffic, increase these numbers to the originals that are shown in the configuration file: `5` and `10`, respectively.

`MaxClients` indicates the maximum number of clients that the server can support simultaneously. This limits the number of child processes that the Web server creates to respond to client requests, and is mainly intended to limit the server and keep it from exhausting all the resources on your machine in case of server malfunction or outside attack.

Supporting Persistent Client Connections Through `KeepAlive` In the original HTTP protocol specification, every request that was made to a server required a separate new connection to the server. The complexity of Web pages and Web sites has grown, however, and it is now very common for a single page, as viewed by the client, to consist of many different files and images. To avoid the overhead of establishing (and terminating) a connection for each individual file requested by the client, newer versions of the HTTP protocol provide for *persistent* (multirequest) client connections. This feature is called `KeepAlive`, and it is configured in Apache with the following directives: `KeepAlive`, `MaxKeepAliveRequests`, and `KeepAliveTimeout`.

Use of `KeepAlive` greatly reduces the overhead of clients accessing your site (and thus greatly increases the performance of your server). Normally, you do not need to modify these settings. However, use of the `KeepAlive` feature might enable malicious users to tie up your Web server with bogus connections, which can disrupt your service. The `KeepAlive` directives enable you to tune whether the server supports persistent connections, how many requests a client can make on a single connection, and how long a connection remains open before it is terminated automatically by the server.

`KeepAlive` support is on by default. To turn off support for this feature, change the setting of `KeepAlive` to Off in the httpd.conf file.

Set the value of `MaxKeepAliveRequests` to control how many requests a client can make on a single connection. After this number of requests, the server closes the connection, and the client must make a new one to continue downloading documents.

Use `KeepAliveTimeout` to control how long the server keeps a connection open when the client has not made a request on it. By default, connections are left open for 15 seconds so that if the user selects another page on the same site (within a short period of time), they can continue using the same connection. Be careful about making the timeout too long because higher timeout values tend to make the server connection table fill up, and might result in other clients not being able to connect.

CHANGING THE SERVER NAME

Sometimes, the server returns information about itself to the client that the client can use on subsequent requests. For example, when the server returns a directory listing to a client, it includes a self-referencing link (URL) on each column heading so that the client can sort the listing by the contents of that column. Several directives are available to control what information is used for this link, as well as other pieces of server information.

To set the name of the server, use the `ServerName` directive. This name needs to match the actual hostname of your machine. You can't just make up a name here because the client must use this name in a URL to access your machine.

When self-referencing links are constructed by the server, it can use either the value specified by `ServerName` or the value that is currently being used by the client to access your machine. The reason for using the value that is supplied by the client is that in cases in which the client provides a shortened name or an alias, it is better to continue having the client use that name. This is done to avoid confusing the user, or to avoid requiring the client to log in to your machine again (because the name is different) when you have security turned on.

The `UseCanonicalName` directive controls this feature. To have the server use the name that is supplied by the client, set `UseCanonicalName` to Off. Note that the value of the `SERVER_NAME` environment variable that is passed to `CGI` scripts is also affected by this setting.

A few other directives are used to provide information about your server to clients, on certain server generated pages (primarily error response or directory listing pages). To set the email account for the server administrator, use the `ServerAdmin` directive. For example, to set the email account to Webmaster, use a line such as the following:

```
ServerAdmin Webmaster@www.yourserver.com
```

Use the `ServerSignature` directive to specify an information line to be included with server-generated documents, using one of the following options:

- **`Off`**—Don't include server information on error pages.
- **`On`**—Show server name, version, and address.
- **`EMail`**—Include an email link (for the email address specified by `ServerAdmin`) in the signature line.

Defining the Document Name Space

This section discusses the document name space, and the ways in which you can modify it.

Testing Configuration Options

When you make modifications to the options for the document name space and for request processing settings, test them out by restarting the server (see previous sidebar), loading a browser, and trying to access an item that is affected by your modification. For example, if you modify directory indexing options, try to access an affected directory using a browser right away.

One important thing that you need to do, to make sure that you see the right results, is to reload the document in your Web browser. When you access a URL that you have looked at before, some browsers use their local cache and display the results for the last page they retrieved from the server. This can be confusing, making you think that your changes did not take effect. In some extreme cases, you might need to clear the cache of the browser in order to see exactly which documents the server is responding with for your request.

The directives in the srm.conf configuration file define the document tree (or name space) that the Web server presents to the clients that access it. Also, it defines how the items in the document tree are processed by the server. There are four basic types of processing that the server can perform on an item requested by a client:

1. If the item referenced by the client's URL is a file, the server simply returns the file to the client.
2. If you have enabled the *server side includes* (*SSI*) feature, the server might do additional processing of the file. This is also referred to as *server-parsed HTML* because it makes the server read the file and process it (parse it) on each request.
3. If the client's URL refers to a directory, the server does one of three things: returns a specially named file (usually index.html) to represent that directory; generates a listing for the directory and return that to the client; or returns a failure message to the client.
4. Finally, if the item is a special program called a `CGI` script, the server runs the program and returns its output to the client.

The structure of the document tree that is visible to clients is a logical structure that does not necessarily match the layout of the file system of your machine. The Web server takes requests from the server and translates the path in the URL of the request to a path in your local file system, using rules that you define. The server has a main document root (by default /home/httpd/html) at which the main document tree resides. This is configured using the `DocumentRoot` directive in srm.conf. Additional directories can be logically grafted into this tree using the `Alias` directive. If a directory contains `CGI` scripts, the `ScriptAlias` directive is used to make that directory accessible.

The default settings for the name space of the Web server (without comments and intervening directives from srm.conf) are shown in Listing 28.1.

LISTING 28.1 DEFAULT NAME SPACE FOR THE DOCUMENT TREE SERVED BY THE WEB SERVER

```
DocumentRoot /home/httpd/html
UserDir public_html
Alias /icons/ /home/httpd/icons/
Alias /icons.apache/ /home/httpd/apache/icons/
ScriptAlias /cgi-bin/ /home/httpd/cgi-bin/
```

With these definitions, the following URL translations (and actions) are performed by the server:

- **`http://server/man.html`**—Translated to /home/httpd/html/man.html, and file is returned to the client.
- **`http://server/icons.apache/bomb.gif`**—Translated to /home/httpd/apache/icons/bomb.gif, and the file is returned to the client.
- **`http://server/`**—Translated to /home/httpd/html/, which is a directory. Because there is a file called index.html in this directory, it is returned to the client (see the description of the `DirectoryIndex` directive). If directory indexing is on, and this file is not present, the server generates a listing of this directory and returns it to the client.
- **`http://server/cgi-bin/rpm_query`**—Translated to /home/httpd/cgi-bin/rpm_query. Because this is in a `ScriptAlias` directory, the program is run and its output is returned to the client.
- **`http://server/~tim/page1.html`**—Translated to /home/tim/public_html/page1.html, and the file is returned to the client (if the user tim is defined and the page is present).

Table 28.2 summarizes the different directives and their effect on the logical document tree, as seen by clients.

TABLE 28.2 NAME SPACE DIRECTIVES

Directive	Refers to
`DocumentRoot`	Main document tree
`Alias`	Other directories logically grafted into the tree
`ScriptAlias`	Directories containing `CGI` programs
`UserDir`	Directories for individual user pages

These directives are discussed in detail next.

To change the location of the main document tree, edit the value of `DocumentRoot` in srm.conf. By default, all files and directories under the directory that you specify are made available to remote clients. Be careful, with any of these directives, to make sure that private or sensitive data on your system does not reside underneath these directories. There are options (listed later in this chapter in the section "Per Directory Options") to keep the Web server from following symbolic links to other parts of your file system from the document tree.

To set an `Alias`, you need to provide the "fake" name that the clients will use to access the directory, and the real directory name on your file system for the directory. The same is true of `ScriptAlias` values.

For example, you can use the following `Alias` statement to make files in the /usr/share/data/jpeg directory available from your Web site:

```
Alias /images/ /usr/share/data/jpeg/
```

So if the client accesses

```
http://www.yourserver.com/images/alien.jpg
```

the server translates this to the following path:

```
/usr/share/data/jpeg/alien.jpg
```

`ScriptAlias` values are also specified using a fake name and a real directory name. However, when an item is referenced in a `ScriptAlias` directory, the server tries to execute the resulting filename and returns the output of the program to the user.

By default, the directory /home/httpd/cgi-bin is defined as a `ScriptAlias` directory, and is where `CGI` scripts are stored on your OpenLinux system.

Use the `UserDir` directive to control whether individual users are allowed to publish pages from your machine, and to control where the Web server reads their pages from.

When a user page is requested (using the `~user` syntax in a request URL), the server combines the path part of the URL with the value of the `UserDir` directive. If a single directory name is specified with the `UserDir` directive, that directory is combined with the user's home directory, as specified in the /etc/passwd file. If a path is specified with `UserDir` and starts with a slash, the URL path is combined with the path (and username) directly.

For example, if the directory public_html is used (this the default value), the requested URL

```
http://www.server.com/~tim/subdir/file.html
```

translates to the file system path

```
/home/tim/public_html/subdir/file.html
```

Use the `disable` or `enable` option with `UserDir` to allow or disallow user pages on an individual account basis. The `UserDir` directive can be used multiple times to establish the correct set of available directories. See the examples in Table 28.3 to learn how the Web server translates requested paths, depending on the settings of `UserDir`.

TABLE 28.3 UserDir TRANSLATION SAMPLES

Directives	URL	Translation
UserDir public_html	http://server/~tim/subdir/file.html	/home/tim/public_html/subdir/file.html
UserDir /usr/web	http://server/~tim/subdir/file.html	/usr/web/tim/subdir/file.html
UserDir /usr/web/*/www	http://server/~tim/subdir/file.html	/usr/web/tim/www/subdir/file.html
UserDir disable UserDir enable david allan UserDir public_html	http://server/~tim/subdir/file.html	File not found
UserDir disable UserDir enable david allan UserDir public_html	http://server/~allan/subdir/file.html	/home/allan/public_html/subdir/file.html

FILE PROCESSING DIRECTIVES

When a client requests a file from the server, the server transfers the document to the client. In the process, however, the server might perform additional operations on the file. For example, the server tries to indicate to the client the type of file it is transferring so that the client knows what to do with it. Also, the server can indicate an encoding and language for the document. Some browsers can automatically decode documents to make handling them easier on the client side. Finally, the server can tell a client that a file has moved and indicate the new location for it. In this case, the client usually automatically loads the document from the new location, avoiding an error for the remote user.

All these operations can make the file handling between the client and server easier for the end user. The different directives to control these features are described in the sections that follow.

DEFINE FILE TYPES

The server indicates the type of file that it is returning to the client using a special header in the response. The type is expressed as a MIME type. This standard is discussed more in Chapter 5; furthermore, Chapter 5 contains more details about the syntax of a MIME file type.

Basically, the server uses two files to define the file types on your system: mime.types and magic. The mime.types file assigns a MIME file type based on the extension of the file. The magic file can be used to assign a MIME type to a file based on its contents. To add a MIME type definition, add a line to the file mime.types, or use the `AddType` directive in any of the .conf server configuration files. The lines in the mime.types file have the following format:

```
type/sub-type    extension [extension2 ...]
```

For example, the definitions for a few video file formats are as follows:

```
video/mpeg          mpeg mpg mpe
video/quicktime     qt mov
video/x-msvideo     avi
```

Note that types which have not been formally approved by a standards body are indicated with an `x-` preceding the subtype part of the type name. If you define your own types, follow this convention to avoid conflicting with new types that will be defined in the future.

The `AddType` directive has a similar syntax. The following line adds a new file type for files with the extension .mdoc:

```
AddType text/x-mydoc mdoc
```

In situations in which you cannot use file extensions to identify the files on your system, you can use content-based file typing. This system tries to identify a file's type based on whether small strings or sequences of bytes can be found in the file at particular offsets. These matching rules are defined in a file called the magic file.

Content-based file typing is not turned on in the default Web server configuration files. Use the directive `MimeMagicFile` to specify the magic file for content-based file typing. For example, to use the default magic file (/etc/httpd/apache/conf/magic) for content-based file typing, add (or *uncomment*) the following line in srm.conf:

```
MimeMagicFile conf/magic
```

To modify the magic file to support additional file types based on content, see the magic man page, which describes the syntax that is used for defining entries in this file.

DEFINING ENCODINGS AND LANGUAGES

Some browsers are capable of doing more intelligent handling of a file if they know the file's *encoding*. The encoding of a file is the way the file is formatted, and includes things such as whether the file is compressed and which character set is used for the file.

You can define encodings for files using the `AddEncoding` directive, which defines a MIME encoding based on the extension of the file. The default encodings that are specified in srm.conf are as follows:

```
AddEncoding x-gzip gz
AddEncoding x-compress Z
```

Content-based encodings can also be defined in the magic file. See the previous section for a description of this file.

Unless you have a good understanding of how encodings are interpreted by browsers, you probably need to leave these definitions alone.

The Web server can indicate the language of a file to the client, using definitions that are created using the `AddLanguage` directive. This feature can be used by add-on server modules to select the correct file to deliver to a client based on its language preference (this is called content negotiation). Use the `AddLanguage` directive to assign a language code to a file, based on a portion of the file's name. For example, the following lines define the file page.en.html as an English HTML file:

```
AddFileType    text/html       html
AddLanguage    en    .en
```

REDIRECTING CLIENTS TO MOVED FILES

The Web is a dynamic place. Web sites undergo constant revision and maintenance to keep up with new developments and needs. Because of this, it is very common for files to be moved around in the document tree (or even to other Web sites). The Web server is capable of notifying a client of a new location for a file by sending the client a redirect response.

This is beneficial for a few reasons. When a browser receives a redirect response from a server, it usually loads the document automatically from the new location. This makes it easier for the user to deal with the transition of documents to their new locations. Also, some automated link-following software can actually use this information to adjust the links that deal with referencing pages so that they are up to date.

To redirect a client to a file's new location, use the `Redirect` and `RedirectMatch` directives. With both of these directives, you specify a filename or path in the document tree that is no longer present (or that you no longer want to serve), and you specify a URL with the new location for that path. In the case of `RedirectMatch`, you can specify a wildcard expression in the filename (or path) to match. You can also specify a status with these directives, which indicates a code that is to be returned to the client in the redirect response. This code tells the client what type of problem was encountered with the original path.

Following are a few examples of redirection:

- `Redirect /images http://www.server.com/icons.apache`
- `Redirect temporary /dir1/dir2 http://www.server`
- `Redirect permanent /company_a http://www.companyb.com/subsidiary_company_a`
- `Redirect gone /old_files`
- `RedirectMatch (.*)\.gif$ http://www.server.com$1.jpg`

Most of these examples are self-explanatory. The arguments `temporary`, `permanent`, and `gone` tell the server which type of error code to return to the client. In the last example, when the client tried to access a file with the extension .gif, it was automatically redirected to a file of the same name, but with the extension .jpg on `www.server.com`.

DIRECTORY INDEXING OPTIONS

When a directory is referenced (instead of a file), the Web server tries to return a page to represent the directory. This is called the *directory index*. Several settings in srm.conf control which file is used for static—or fixed—directory indexing and how dynamic directory indexes are generated.

SPECIFYING A DIRECTORY INDEX FILE

The simplest way to respond to a directory request is with a static file. Use the `DirectoryIndex` directive to indicate to the server which file in the directory is used to represent this directory on your Web site.

For example, the default value for `DirectoryIndex` is index.html. With this setting, if the following URL is requested

```
http://server/dir1/
```

the server looks for the file:

```
/home/httpd/html/dir1/index.html
```

If it is present, the file server returns that file to the client. If not, a dynamic directory listing can be generated, which is discussed in the next section.

GENERATING DIRECTORY INDEXES

When the server cannot find a static directory index file, it has the capability to generate a dynamic listing at the time of a client request. There are many options to control the format of this dynamically generated listing.

Dynamic directory indexes are allowed or disallowed using the `Options` directive. The `Options` directive supports many different directory-handling settings, and is covered more extensively in the section on per directory options, but the `Indexes` setting for this directive is discussed briefly here.

To turn on dynamic index generation for the entire Web server, add the following line anywhere in srm.conf:

```
Option +Indexes
```

You can also achieve the same effect, but in a somewhat more controlled fashion, by finding the lines in access.conf that define options for the document root directory, and then adding `Indexes` to the `Options` line there.

Several directives enable you to control the page that is generated by the server.

CONTROLLING THE DIRECTORY LISTING PAGE

There are two basic formats for the directory listings that are generated by the server: simple and fancy. The simple directory listing shows the entries in the directory as a bulleted list, with each name being a link to the file or directory it represents. The fancy directory index shows a multicolumn list of files, and is described in greater detail later in this chapter.

Several directives are available to control the listing page that is generated by the server. Among the main directives that affect both simple and fancy listings are `IndexIgnore`, `IndexOptions`, `HeaderName`, and `ReadmeName`. Other directives, which mainly control fancy indexing, are discussed later.

EXCLUDING FILES FROM THE DIRECTORY LISTING To exclude files from the directory listing, use the `IndexIgnore` directive. This is useful for situations in which the directory contains superfluous—or private—files that you don't want clients to see. After the directive, place the list of files to ignore. This list is space separated, and can contain filenames and wildcard expressions. For example, to hide README files and text files, you can use the following line:

```
IndexIgnore README* *.txt
```

Multiple `IndexIgnore` directives can be used. Each one adds items to the list of things to ignore for the directory listings that are generated by the Web server.

> **Caution**
>
> Don't confuse the use of `IndexIgnore` with real security access control (discussed later, in the section "Adding Security to Your Web Site"). Although this option prevents certain files from being listed in directory indexes, the files can still be retrieved if the remote user accesses them by their exact name.
>
> Some crackers are good guessers, or can find out the filenames using some other means. For data that must be kept secure, use access control and secure Web server features—not just the IndexIgnore option.

ADDING A PREAMBLE OR POSTAMBLE TO THE PAGE To add a preamble or postamble to the directory listing page, use the `HeaderName` and `ReadmeName` directives, respectively. When a filename is specified with these directives, the Web server first looks for a file with the indicated name and the extension .html in the directory where the listing is being generated. If that file is found, it is included in the directory listing page as HTML. If the file is not found, the Web server looks for the filename (without an extension) and includes it as plaintext, if it is found.

For example, to add the contents of the file list_header.html as the preamble to the directory listing page, use the following `HeaderName` directive:

```
HeaderName list_header
```

Using Fancy Indexing

Fancy indexing provides a much "fancier" display of the contents of a directory. For example, the fancy directory listing shows directory entries as a multicolumn list. Each row displays the name, icon, date of last modification, size, and description for a directory entry. The icons in this listing are selected according to the file type, and can be customized extensively. The description is defined using an `AddDescription` directive, or by examining the files for their HTML titles. The other pieces of information come from the file system itself.

This section describes these and other options that are available for customizing the format of the fancy indexes produced by the Web server.

To turn on fancy indexing, place the following line in your srm.conf file:

```
IndexOptions FancyIndexing
```

Setting File Icons One of the things that you can control about the fancy directory listing is the icon used to represent each entry in the directory. Because some browsers are not configured to support graphics, you can also set a text string to be used in place of the icon (called an *alt*, or alternate, *string*).

The icon files that are used for the directory entries can be assigned by file extension, file type, or encoding type. Use the following directives to accomplish this:

- **`AddIcon`**—Assign an icon by file extension. If the file's type can be determined using a MIME type, it is better to use `AddIconByType` instead so that you can place all the type-related directives in one place (in the mime.types file).
- **`AddIconByType`**—Assign an icon by MIME file type. The type is determined by the settings in the mime.types configuration file.
- **`AddIconByEncoding`**—Assign an icon by MIME encoding. File encoding types are defined by `AddEncoding` directives, usually in the file srm.conf.
- **`AddAlt`**—Assign alt string by file extension.
- **`AddAltByType`**—Assign alt string by MIME file type.
- **`AddAltByEncoding`**—Assign alt string by MIME encoding.
- **`DefaultIcon`**—Specifies the icon to use, when no other icon can be found for this entry.

The syntax for the `Add...` directives is as follows:

```
<directive> <icon> <match> [<match2> ...]
```

For any of the `AddIcon...` directives, for the icon field you can specify either just the icon filename, or a combination of alt string and icon filename. This enables you to bypass use of the `AddAlt...` directives, if you want. The icon filename is expressed as a path relative to the Web server document tree, not relative to your local file system. Also, an `AddIcon` directive can use the string `^^DIRECTORY^^` to match directory entries. The following example shows several different icon assignment lines. Some of these overlap in functionality, but they are shown for illustrative purposes:

```
AddIcon /icons.apache/binary.gif .bin .exe
AddIcon /icons.apache/text.gif .txt
AddIconByType /icons.apache/text.gif text/*
AddAltByType "TXT" text/*
AddIconByType (TXT,/icons.apache/text.gif) text/*
AddIconByType (HTM,/icons.apache/layout.gif) text/html
AddIconByEncoding (CMP,/icons.apache/compressed.gif x-compress x-gzip
AddIcon (DIR,/icons.apache/folder.gif) ^^DIRECTORY^^
DefaultIcon /icons.apache/unknown.gif
```

Note

The icon directives are processed in the order that they occur in the srm.conf file. The Web server uses the first match that it finds as the icon for a file. Therefore, place more specific directives earlier in the file in order for the matching to work.

You can, of course, add your own icon files if you want to completely customize the look of the directory listing pages. The icons need to be in .gif or .jpg format and reside in a directory somewhere in the document tree. The default icons provided with Apache are in the directory /home/httpd/apache/icons, and are 20x22 8-bit color GIF files. These icons use very few colors (a good idea) and a transparent background.

USING DESCRIPTIONS The `Description` column in a fancy directory listing has a short description of each entry. The Web server determines the value for this field based either on `AddDescription` directives used in server configuration files, or on the title of the document, if it is an HTML file.

Use the `AddDescription` directive to add a description for an entry. For example, the following line adds a description for the file foo.txt at the root of the document tree.

```
AddDescription "foo text file" /foo.txt
```

The server can automatically add descriptions to the directory listing, based on the title of HTML documents in the directory. Add the `ScanHTMLTitles` option to the `IndexOptions` directive in srm.conf to have the server do this. Note that this causes the server to read each HTML file in the directory and parse out the HTML title every time the directory is read. This takes a relatively long time, and should not be used on busy Web sites.

Controlling Columns and Directory Formatting The IndexOptions directive enables you to control several other aspects of the fancy directory listing. Table 28.4 shows the options you can use, and their effect on the listing page.

Table 28.4 Options to Control Fancy Directory Listings Using IndexOptions

Option	Meaning
IconHeight=pixels	The Web server includes the height of icons in the IMG tag used in the directory index page. This can speed up processing of the page by client browsers.
IconWidth=pixels	The Web server includes the width of icons in the IMG tag used for directory indexes.
IconsAreLinks	This makes the icons part of the link to the entry, so the user can click on either the entry name or the icon to access it.
NameWidth=n¦*	Indicates the width of the filename column. If * is used, the column is sized automatically.
ScanHTMLTitles	The server scans HTML files for their titles, to be used in the Description column.
SuppressDescription	Hide the Description column.
SuppressLastModified	Hide the Last Modified column.
SuppressSize	Hide the Size column.
SuppressColumnSorting	Do not make the column headings links that can be used to sort the listing by that column.
SuppressHTMLPreamble	Do not precede the file specified by HeaderName with the standards HTML preamble (HTML, HEAD, and so on). This allows you more flexibility in controlling the page output with the header file.

Customizing Error Messages

The Web server automatically generates error message responses for certain error conditions. However, you can customize the error response for your Web site to provide your own messages (and look and feel) to remote clients when things go wrong.

Use the ErrorDocument directive to customize the error response for a particular error condition. This directive can be used multiple times, to specify a response for each different error code that the server generates. Common error codes used by the Web server are shown in Table 28.5.

Table 28.5 Common HTTP Error Codes

Error Code	Summary	Meaning
400	Bad Request	The request from the client was malformed.
401	Unauthorized	Client must provide a name and password to access the item. Note that the error response for this code can not be customized because the client automatically displays a login prompt (and not the returned page) when it receives this error from the server.
402	Payment Required	Access to the requested item requires that the client provide some kind of payment.
403	Forbidden	Client is not allowed to access the item. Providing a name and password does not help.
404	Not Found	The server did not find a document or directory matching the URL submitted by the client.
500	Fatal Error	The server encountered some unresolvable condition, and could not fulfill the request.
501	Not Implemented	The server does not support the requested functionality.
502	Temporary Overload	The server cannot service the request due to high load. It can possibly service the request at a later time.

The error document can be specified in several ways. First, you can specify just a string to return to the user as the value for the `ErrorDocument`. You can also refer to a local file to return a static error page, or to a `CGI` script to generate one at the time of the request. Using a `CGI` script enables you to customize the response to exactly match your situation because the script can examine information about the client, its request, and the local file system at the time that the request is made. Finally, you can also specify an external document as an error response.

For each `ErrorDocument` directive, specify the error code, and then the item with which you want the server to respond for that error. Following are some examples of `ErrorDocument` lines:

```
ErrorDocument 400 "Hey, you sent invalid request."
ErrorDocument 402 http://www.subscribe.com/pay_me.html
ErrorDocument 500 /fatal.html
ErrorDocument 404 /cgi-bin/missing.pl
```

Configuring Settings on a Per Directory Basis

When you use the configuration directives for controlling file information, directory indexing, error responses, and authorization (discussed later) in either srm.conf or httpd.conf, they apply to the entire document tree that the Web server provides. However, you can also apply these directives to specific directories and files on your system.

There are a few different reasons that the server supports per directory customizations in this way. First, you might want to have some directories on your Web site available to the general public, whereas other files and directories are restricted to a specific set of users. Besides security-specific directives, many other directives have important security ramifications. For instance, you usually do not want the general public to see the contents of the directories in your document tree. Therefore, it is customary to disable directory indexing for the part of your document tree that is accessible to any remote user. You might still want, however, to allow indexing for users within your organization.

Sometimes the content of a Web site is maintained by different organizations in a company. In this case, they might have different policies and conventions for controlling their part of the site. For example, one department might use server-parsed HTML files for some of their content, whereas another might not. Because server-parsed HTML files require extra processing by the server, it is wise to limit its use to only the part of the document tree that needs it.

The use of per directory settings allows for fine-grained control over the presentation, handling, and access control of the server document tree.

Per Directory Options

Some of the main options that can be configured on a per directory basis are controlled with the `Options` directive. This directive enables you to set many policies with regard to directories:

- **`All`**—All options except for `MultiViews`
- **`ExecCGI`**—Execution of `CGI` scripts is allowed.
- **`FollowSymLinks`**—The server follows symbolic links in this directory. This can be a potential security risk.
- **`Includes`**—Server-side includes (server-parsed HTML) are allowed.
- **`IncludesNOEXEC`**—Server-side includes are allowed, but certain directives are not processed (`#exec` and `#include`).
- **`MultiViews`**—Allows the server to select a document that best matches the client's request when the requested file does not exist. This is referred to as content-negotiation, and is covered in the online manual on at `file:/home/httpd/html/doc/manual/content-negotiation.html`.
- **`SymLinksIfOwnerMatch`**—Allows the server to follow a symlink if the target of the link and the link have the same owner ID.

Note

Most of the options in this list have important security consequences. For example, allowing any kind of execution by the Web server (for example, use of `ExecCGI` and `Includes`) might lead to situations in which unauthorized users can allow remote clients to run dangerous programs or scripts. Consult the online documentation for each of these options for information about the security ramifications before using them on a multiuser system.

In addition to the settings that are configured using the `Options` directive, many other directives can be used on a per directory basis. These include directives for the following:

- File content handling
- File indexing options
- Error response settings
- Authorization and access control (security) settings

In fact, although many of the directives that have been discussed so far have been presented in the context of the server configuration files, many are more appropriately placed in a per directory area of access.conf. If you need to determine whether a particular directive can be applied on a per directory basis, see the online documentation. For each directive, the documentation indicates the contexts in which the directive can be used.

DEFINING OPTIONS FOR A SPECIFIC PART OF THE DOCUMENT TREE

Options that apply to a specific part of the file system are defined by placing their directives within a section of the access.conf file or in a special file called .htaccess.

A section in the access.conf file is defined by an opening and closing directive. For example, to apply certain options to only the objects in the directory /home/httpd/icons, you can declare a section in access.conf such as the following:

```
<Directory /home/httpd/icons>
Options Indexes
IndexOptions FancyIndexing SuppressDescription SuppressSize
</Directory>
```

There are several different section directives that can indicate the set of objects to which they apply based on different criteria:

- ***<Directory>***—Matches objects based on the directory where they reside
- ***<Files>***—Matches objects based on their filenames
- ***<Location>***—Matches objects based on the URL path used to access them.

Each of these directives is used by placing the target path or filename inside the angle brackets. Then the desired directives, which apply to the indicated object set, are declared, followed by a matching close-section directive (*</Directory>*, *</Files>*, and *</Location>*, respectively).

You can also use the directives `<DirectoryMatch>`, `<FilesMatch>`, and `<LocationMatch>`, which take a regular expression as their argument instead of a simple string; this results in even more flexibility in defining a target object set. A few examples follow:

- **`<Directory /home/httpd/icons>`**—Declares a section for specifying settings in the icons directory.
- **`<FilesMatch "*\.txt$">`**—Declares a section that applies to files that end in .txt.
- **`<Location /private>`**—Declares a section that applies to objects referenced using the URL prefix `http://server/private`. With the default document root, this means files and subdirectories under /home/httpd/html/private.
- **`<LocationMatch ".*www*">`**—Declares a section that applies to anything with `www` as part of the path portion of the URL (including both files and directories).

DEFINING OPTIONS USING A FILE IN THE CURRENT DIRECTORY

Instead of defining per directory settings in the configuration files, you can also define the settings in a special file in the directory in which you want the settings to apply. This is useful in the event that you move directories around. Instead of having to modify the pathname in the configuration files, the configuration follows the directory to its new location automatically because the file resides in the directory.

Also, you might want to generate some directives (such as `AddDescription`) automatically. There are cases in which it is unwise to allow an end-user program to modify the server's general configuration files, but where modification of per directory configuration files can be allowed.

The default filename for per directory settings is .htaccess. You can modify the name that is used for this file using the `AccessFileName` directive. Basically, .htaccess files can contain any directive that you can place in a *`<Directory>`* section in the configuration files.

In order to avoid certain security problems, the Web server provides an extra facility to limit the options that are allowed in a .htaccess file. Specifically, each *`<Directory>`* section in the server configuration file needs to include an `AllowOverride` directive that controls which classes of directives can be used in .htaccess files. The following classes of directives can be specified (one or more of them) as arguments to the `AllowOverride` directive:

- **`All`**—.htaccess files can contain any per directory directive.
- **`AuthConfig`**—Allow the use of directives which control authorization (user-based security).
- **`FileInfo`**—Allow directives that deal with file types, encodings, languages, and error responses.
- **`Indexes`**—Allow directives related to directory indexing.
- **`Limit`**—Allow directives related to host-based security.
- **`Options`**—Allow use of the `Options` or `XBitHack` directives.
- **`None`**—Do not allow .htaccess files to be used to define per directory options.

For example, to allow for the use of .htaccess files under the directory /home/httpd/www but limit users to controlling directory indexing and host-based security, you add the following entry to access.conf:

```
<Directory /home/httpd/www>
AllowOverride Indexes Limit
</Directory>
```

SECTION ORDERING

There might be overlaps between the sets of files that are specified by different section directives and the .htaccess file. When this happens, the options are accumulated from the sections that apply, in the order that the sections are processed. This means that the last section that is processed determines the settings.

Sections are processed in the following order:

1. `<Directory>` and .htaccess files. Within this group, sections are ordered by directory name length from shortest to longest. .htaccess files are processed after `<Directory>` sections for matching directories.
2. `<DirectoryMatch>`
3. `<File>` and `<FileMatch>`
4. `<Location>` and `<LocationMatch>`

The result of the "shortest to longest" part of the first rule is that the options for a directory apply to that directory and all its subdirectories, until another section (with a longer directory path) overrides them.

In the case of duplicate entries within each category (for example, two `<Directory>` sections with the same directory name), the sections are processed in the order in which they occur in the configuration files. The configuration files are read in the following order: httpd.conf, srm.conf, access.conf.

ALL ABOUT LOGGING

One of the nice things about the Web server is that you can configure it, via server log files, to provide all kinds of information about itself and the operations that it is performing. By default, the Web server logs each request that it fulfills and each error that it encounters in the access log and the error log, respectively. However, you can create additional logs of server activity and customize the format of each log entry.

There are five basic types of logs that the Web server can produce:

- Transfer log
- Agent log
- Referer log

- Error log
- Script log

Each of these logs is described in detail in the sections that follow.

TRANSFER LOG

The main kind of log is referred to as a *transfer* log or *access* log. With a transfer log, an entry is made for each response that the server sends. Multiple logs of this kind can be created, using either of the `TransferLog` or `CustomLog` directives.

The simplest way to create a transfer log is to just specify the log filename using the `TransferLog` directive. If no `LogFormat` directive has been used to set the format of the log entries, the log is created and formatted using the Common Log Format. This log format includes most of the basic information about a request and is used by several different Web servers. Several log analysis tools are available on the Internet, all of which work with this format to do statistical analysis of the traffic that is handled by your Web server.

CUSTOMIZING LOG FORMATS Instead of using the Common Log Format, you can also customize the format of the log entries for transfer log files. If you configure the server to produce multiple transfer logs, you can separate the information about the requests into different logs, making it easier to write your own custom log analysis tools.

The `LogFormat` directive is used to define the format string used to output log entries. The format string can contain literal characters as well as conversion specifiers. The conversion specifiers are replaced with information about the request when the log entry is made. Table 28.6 shows the conversion specifiers that are available for use in log format strings.

TABLE 28.6 LOGFORMAT CONVERSION SPECIFIERS

Specifier	Translates to
%h	Client hostname or IP address.
%l	Client identity (if identd information is available from the client).
%u	Username (if user logged in).
%t	Time of day, in [day/month/year:hour:minute:second:zone] format.
%(t_format)t	Time in the specified format. See the strftime man page for the syntax of the format string.
%r	The client request line. This is usually put in quotes because it includes spaces.
%s	Status code for the request.
%>s	Last status code for the request. For requests that get redirected, %s specifies the status of the original request, and %>s specifies the status of the final request (after redirection).

continues

TABLE 28.6 CONTINUED

Specifier	Translates to
%b	Number of bytes in the returned item.
%f	Filename.
%{VAR}e	Value of environment variable VAR.
%{Header}i	Value of request header line Header.
%{Header}o	Value of response header line Header.
%{Var}n	Value of note "Var" from a server module.
%p	Server port.
%P	Process ID of the child that handled the request.
%T	Number of seconds it took to handle the request.
%U	The URL path requested.
%v	Server name.

The Common Log Format uses the following format string:

`"%h %l %u %t \"%r\" %s %b".`

Listing 28.2 shows sample entries from an access log using the Common Log format.

LISTING 28.2 SAMPLE ACCESS LOG USING COMMON LOG FORMAT

```
200.251.107.134 - - [24/Dec/1998:17:06:38 -0700] "GET/ HTTP/1.1" 200 3304
200.251.107.134 - - [24/Dec/1998:17:06:40 -0700] "GET /moro1s.jpg
➥HTTP/1.1" 200 26625
192.168.1.3 - - [24/Dec/1998:17:23:31 -0700] "GET /robots.txt
➥HTTP/1.0" 404 163
203.93.18.173 - - [24/Dec/1998:17:37:29 -0700] "GET / HTTP/1.0" 200 3304
203.93.18.173 - - [24/Dec/1998:17:37:33 -0700] "GET /moro1s.jpg
➥HTTP/1.0" 200 26625
203.93.18.173 - - [24/Dec/1998:17:37:33 -0700] "GET /blueball.gif
➥HTTP/1.0" 200 326
203.93.18.173 - - [24/Dec/1998:17:37:45 -0700] "GET /redball.gif
➥HTTP/1.0" 200 326
192.168.1.2 - - [24/Dec/1998:22:17:57 -0700] "GET /starcraft/
➥HTTP/1.1" 200 3003
192.168.1.2 - - [24/Dec/1998:22:17:59 -0700] "GET /starcraft/topban1.gif
➥HTTP/1.1" 200 6780
192.168.1.3 - - [25/Dec/1998:06:56:37 -0700] "GET /david/ball.gif
➥HTTP/1.0" 200 1135
203.93.18.173 - - [25/Dec/1998:14:05:01 -0700] "GET/tim HTTP/1.0" 301 173
```

Many of the conversion specifiers can include a status indicator to conditionally show the value for that specifier. The status indicator follows the `%` and consists of a comma-separated list of status codes (optionally preceded by `!`). If the request results in the indicated status codes, the value for the specifier is included in the log entry. Otherwise, the specifier is replaced with a dash in the log entry.

Following are some example conversion specifiers with status indicators:

- **%404f**—Logs the filename that the server tried to open when it encountered error 404, `Not Found`.
- **%!200,304,302r**—Logs the request for anything not returning a valid status.
- **%302{Referer}i**—Logs the value of the Referer header in the request when the URL is redirected.

To specify a log format, use the directive `LogFormat`, followed by the format string in quotes and a name for that format. If no name is provided, the format string is used as the default format for subsequent logs defined in the configuration file. The following log formats are defined in the default Web server configuration files:

```
LogFormat "%h %l %u %t \"%r\" %>s %b \"%{Referer}i\" \"%{User-Agent}i\""
➥combined
LogFormat "%h %l %u %t \"%r\" %>s %b" common
LogFormat "%{Referer}i -> %U" referrer
LogFormat "%{User-agent}i" agent
```

Using Client Host Name Lookups By default, the server logs the address, but not the hostname, of requesting clients when the %h conversion specifier is used in a log format string. Use the `HostNameLookups` directive to make the server log the hostname instead of the address.

When `HostNameLookups` is configured to On, the logging software in the server tries to determine the hostname of the requesting client by doing a DNS lookup using the client's IP address at the time of the request. This adds a considerable amount of overhead for each request that the server processes, so the feature is defaulted to Off. For low traffic sites, it is usually all right to turn this on.

Tip

If you have `HostNameLookups` turned off, you can use the program `logresolve` (located in /home/httpd/bin/) to process logs and convert IP addresses to hostnames after the fact. This is usually much more efficient than adding the hostname at the time of each request because `logresolve` doesn't have to look up the same IP address over and over again. However, `logresolve` might not be able to determine some hostnames accurately because some clients might change their name or address between the time of their request and the time that `logresolve` is run.

To resolve the IP addresses in a log file, use `logresolve` with the target log file as standard input and the processed log file as standard output. For example, log in as root, switch to the directory /home/httpd/bin, and type the following:

```
./logresolve </var/log/httpd/apache/access_log >/tmp/log_with_names
```

DEFINING ADDITIONAL LOGS You can define as many transfer logs as you want. When combined with custom log formats, this enables you to divide your log information among different files, which might make it easier to process with log analysis tools.

To define additional logs, use the `CustomLog` directive. Each `CustomLog` directive needs to be followed by the name of the log file and a log format string or name (as defined by a `LogFormat` directive). For example, an agent log (described next) can be defined with the following directives:

```
LogFormat "%{User-agent}i" agent
CustomLog /var/log/httpd/apache/agent_log agent
```

AGENT AND REFERER LOGS

Besides the transfer log, you can define additional log files to record information about the requests that your server handles. Two other commonly used logs are called the *agent log* and the *referrer log*. An agent log is used to record information about the client browser (user agent) that is used to make requests of your system. This information is useful because it enables you to develop a profile of the types of users who are visiting your site. The referrer log is used to record information about what page referred the client to your site (that is, what page held the link that the client followed to get to one of your pages). This is useful for determining how users are getting to your site, which might help you advertise or promote your Web site more effectively.

These logs are defined using the `AgentLog` and `RefererLog` directives, respectively.

You can define a log, using `LogFormat` and `CustomLog`, to record the same information that goes into either the agent log or the referrer log. In fact, use of the `AgentLog` directive is now deprecated. However, when you use the `RefererLog` directive to create a referrer log, it allows you one additional capability that the `Customlog` method does not—you can use the `RefererIgnore` directive to eliminate a specific set of referrers from the log.

For example, if you use the following line

```
RefererIgnore www.companyb.com
```

no record of references from companyb's Web site is included in your log. This can help reduce the size of your log and help you pinpoint new entries in the referrer log.

ERROR LOG

The *error* log is a special log that records server status—usually error—events. Use the `ErrorLog` directive to set the output location for the log. This can include a filename, a pipe to another program, or the syslog daemon. The default definition of the error log is as follows:

```
ErrorLog /var/log/httpd/apache/error_log
```

To specify a pipe to another program, use a vertical bar in front of the program specification, as follows:

```
ErrorLog |/usr/local/bin/page_me_at_home.pl
```

To output the error log records to the syslog daemon, use an argument of `syslog`, as in

```
ErrorLog syslog
```

You can use the `LogLevel` directive to control the verbosity of the error log. Table 28.7 shows the list of available log levels and their descriptions.

TABLE 28.7 ERROR LOGGING LEVELS

Level	Description
`emerg`	Emergency—system is unusable
`alert`	Action needs to be taken immediately
`crit`	Critical condition
`error`	Error
`warn`	Warning conditions
`notice`	Normal, but important, event
`info`	Information message
`debug`	Debugging messages

The levels in the table are shown in order of decreasing event importance. If `LogLevel` is not defined, the level `error` is used. The default value of `LogLevel` used in OpenLinux is `warn`.

SCRIPT LOG

The server supports another special log specifically to aid in debugging `CGI` scripts. This is the *script* log. A script log holds information about the parameters, input, and output to a `CGI` script when the script fails. Debugging `CGI` scripts has historically been difficult because the server silently discards the context of the request and output of the script. The script log is a fairly recent addition to the Web server, which makes debugging scripts much easier.

To define a script log, use the `specify the log name with the ScriptLog` directive. When a `CGI` script runs on your system and fails, the following information is logged:

- Time of the failure
- Request line from the client
- HTTP status code
- `CGI` script filename

- An error message, if the script failed to run
- HTTP headers received in the request
- HTTP headers produced by the `CGI` script
- CGI script standard output
- CGI script standard input

Using this information, you can probably track down problems with the `CGI` script in question. Many problems with `CGI` scripts come from improperly formatted response headers.

Note that a script log is intended for debugging use only. It creates overhead that is not appropriate for a Web server in production use. Also, because of the amount of information logged on each failed request, a script log can get quite large. To avoid problems caused by an oversized script log file, the `ScriptLogLength` and `ScriptLogBuffer` directives enable you to limit the maximum size of the script log and the size of an individual request buffer, respectively.

ADDING SECURITY TO YOUR WEB SITE

One of the most common customizations that Webmasters make to their site is adding security. This is particularly important for your site if you are only serving documents for use inside your own organization. Adding security enables you to limit access to clients with specific addresses or hostnames, or to require users to authenticate themselves to the Web server by providing a user name and password.

If you are new to security, the following definitions will help you as you follow the descriptions in this chapter:

- **Authorization**—The process of determining if a client is allowed to access your Web site.
- **Access control**—The process of allowing or preventing access to specific Web site objects, based on the authorization of a client.
- **Host-base authorization**—Controlling access to your Web site based on the location (host name or IP address) of the client.
- **User-based authorization**—Controlling access to your Web site based on the identity of a user.
- **Authentication**—The process of determining the identity of a remote user. This involves having the user provide a name and password, which only an authorized user will know.

Authorized Access Versus Secure Communications

This section of the chapter deals with the authorization and access control aspects of your Web site security. Another key ingredient in the overall security of your Web site is secure communications (that is, encryption). If you have private or sensitive data on your Web server, it does little good to create strict authorization and access controls if you subsequently allow the server to send the data to the client in the clear. The section "Using Apache with SSL," later in this chapter, describes the use of *Secure Sockets Layer* (*SSL*) to provide a secure communications channel between the server and its clients, to complement the security features that are discussed here.

The process of adding authorization and access control to your Web site is not complicated, and the paragraphs that follow will help you set up your own security for your Web site.

In general, the directives discussed here are used as per directory options in one of the sections in the access.conf configuration file. This enables you to customize the security for your Web site by individual directory, file set, or location path.

In this section, the directives are discussed as if they were applied to the entire document tree (Web site). However, remember that these settings can be customized on a per directory basis. As with other per directory options, you can also place security-related directives in .htaccess files, in the directories that you want to secure.

Note

If you decide to place the security control directives in a .htaccess file, make sure that the `AllowOverride` settings that apply to the directory you are working with enables you to do so. It will support `AuthConfig` for user-based security directives and `Limit` for host-based security directives.

HOST-BASED AUTHORIZATION

Restricting access to your site by client host location is fairly simple. Use the `allow` and `deny` directives to indicate the host names or addresses of clients that are allowed or denied access to your site, respectively. You can also use the `order` directive to control what to do with hosts that are not covered by the `allow` and `deny` rules and to control the order in which the rules are evaluated.

For the `allow` and `deny` directives, specify the host location as a fully qualified host name or a domain name part (starting with a .) to match every host in the domain. For example

- **`deny foo.baddudes.net`**—Denies access to the specific host that is named.
- **`deny .baddudes.net`**—Denies access to all hosts from domain baddudes.net

You can also use a host location of `all` to allow or deny access by all hosts.

To specify an IP address, just put the address after the directive. To refer to a whole network of hosts, use one of the following syntaxes to express the network address and netmask:

- ***a.b.c.***—Example: `allow 207.179.18.` This implies a 24-bit mask because of the use of three address digits. Other whole-digit mask sizes are supported.
- ***a.b.c.d/masksize***—Example: `allow 207.179.18.128/25`. This example uses a 25-bit mask.
- ***a.b.c.d/m.n.o.p***—Example: `allow 207.179.18.160/255.255.255.248`. This example uses an explicit mask.

After you have decided which hosts to explicitly allow or deny, you need to decide how to handle the rest of the hosts in the world.

There are two different approaches that are supported by the server in defining host-based authorization. One is based on the principle of including every host that is not specifically excluded by the `allow` and `deny` directives, and the other is based on the principle of excluding every host that is not specifically included. The `order` directive indicates which of these approaches is used by the server. The way to remember how this directive works is as follows: "The last rule wins." These approaches are defined by specifying arguments to the `order` directive, as follows:

- **`order deny,allow`**—Process the `deny` rules, followed by the `allow` rules. In cases where the rules conflict, the `allow` rules override the `deny` rules. For hosts not covered by any rule, allow access.
- **`order allow,deny`**—Process the `allow` rules first, followed by the `deny` rules. In cases where the rules conflict, the `deny` rules override the `allow` rules. For hosts not covered by any rule, deny access.

Following are some examples to clarify the use of these directives:

```
order deny,allow
deny from all
allow from .foo.com
```

This only allows hosts in the domain `foo.com` to access to your site.

```
order allow,deny
allow from .foo.com
```

This accomplishes the same thing as the previous example.

```
order allow,deny
allow from all
deny from .baddudes.com
deny from .spammer.net
```

Allow all hosts except those from the domains baddudes.com and spammer.net to access your site.

User-Based Authorization

The second method of authorization is based on user identification. The attractive thing about host-based authorization is its simplicity and non-intrusiveness. With host-based authorization, the process of authorizing clients does not affect the user at all. User-based authorization, on the other hand, requires that a user enter a name and password to access your Web site. This is more secure and reliable than host-based authorization, but requires more administration work on your part and imposes some inconvenience on the users who access your site.

To establish user-based authorization, you must define user accounts for your Web server. Each user account consists of a name and password. You can also create groups and assign users to them to ease the administration burden of working with sets of users. After users and groups are created, you specify the access allowed for the different accounts to the objects on your Web site.

After the server is configured to user-based authorization, the sequence of events between the server and a client goes something like this:

1. The client requests a document.
2. The server responds that the document requires authorization, and indicates an authorization realm and type.
3. The client browser prompts the user for a name and password, including the realm name in the prompt.
4. The client requests the document again, this time sending the name and password to the server, in the format requested.
5. The server verifies the name and password and grants the access indicated by its configuration. If the verification is successful and the access is allowed, the server sends the document to the client.
6. On subsequent requests, the client includes the name and password automatically (that is, the user is not prompted for the name and password again during the session).

Defining Users and Groups To define users and groups for use with user-based authorization, you need to create some new files. This section describes how to create these files, as well as how to add and remove entries from them in order to manipulate the accounts on your system. The files described here are flat text files. The server can use other file formats to define user and group accounts, but text files are very simple to manipulate and suffice for almost all uses.

The format of the user file is very simple. Each line of the file consists of a user name, a colon, and an encrypted password string. The user account file needs to be located outside the document tree; otherwise remote clients can download the file and use the information in it to try to crack your system. In the following examples, the file /etc/httpd/apache/conf/htuser is used.

Use the program htpasswd (located in the directory /home/httpd/bin) to create the file to hold user accounts, and to add user accounts to the file. You create the file when you add the first user account to it by using the -c parameter. For example, to create a file with the user tim in it, login as root and cd to the directory /etc/httpd/apache/conf. Then type the following command:

```
/home/httpd/bin/htpasswd -c htuser tim
```

You are prompted for the password for tim twice. The password is encrypted and placed in the file. You can cat the file if you want to see its contents.

To add additional users, use the same command, but without the -c option. To remove a user, just edit the file with a text editor and remove the line for that user. Add a few users now to the htuser file, using the htpasswd command.

You can also define a group file to enable you to manage sets of users more easily. Each line in a group file consists of a group name, followed by a colon and a space-separated list of user names. To create and modify this file, just use a normal text editor. For example, to define a group file with one group in it, start an editor and enter the following line:

```
admin: tim ron fred
```

Of course, you need to substitute names that you entered in your user file for the accounts listed here. Save the file out as htgroup in the directory /etc/httpd/apache/conf.

The user and group files are specified to the server using the AuthUserFile and AuthGroupFile directives. If the filenames you use with these directives do not start with a slash, they are appended to the end of the ServerRoot value. To define the files that you just created, enter the following in an appropriate section in access.conf:

```
AuthUserFile conf/htuser
AuthGroupFile conf/htgroup
```

SETTING THE AUTHORIZATION REALM AND TYPE The authorization realm is used to tell the client what authorization system they are logging in to. In some complicated systems, a Web server might use a backend (non-local) authentication system to validate users. In this case, the server needs to tell the client what system it is using so that the user can enter the correct name and password. Also, you might define different areas of your Web site with different user accounts and access privileges. Using the authorization realm, you can tell the user which part of the site they are logging in to—again, so they can enter the correct name and password.

Set the authorization realm string for the server using the AuthName directive as follows:

```
AuthName "Main Document Tree"
```

The authorization type specifies the format of the items passed between the client and server during the authorization. This is specified using the `AuthType` directive. The Web server supports both `Basic` and `Digest` authorization. `Digest` is a fairly new authorization format that not all browsers support. Unless you have reasons to do otherwise, use the value `Basic`.

CONFIGURING ACCESS CONTROL The last part of the whole user-based authorization system is actually defining the access control on a per user or per group basis. The `require` directive is used for this.

The `require` directive tells the server to require a particular account in order to grant access to the object on the server. The `require` directive can be used in three different ways: with the `user`, `group`, and `valid-user` options. These options are used as follows:

- **`require user`** ***`username`*** **`[`*****`username2`*****` ...]`**—Allow the listed users to access the Web site.
- **`require group`** ***`groupname`*** **`[`*****`groupname2`*****` ...]`**—Allow the users in the listed groups to access the Web site.
- **`require valid-user`**—Allow all users that are defined in the user account file to access the Web site.

Listing 28.3 shows an example with all the directives required to set up user-based authorization, in the context of a /private directory.

LISTING 28.3 EXAMPLE OF USER-BASED AUTHORIZATION DEFINITION

```
<Directory /private>
AllowOverride None
Options Index
AuthUserFile conf/htuser
AuthGroupFile conf/htgroup
AuthName "private files"
AuthType Basic
require user tim ron
require group admin
</Directory>
```

The first two directives in Listing 28.3 (`AllowOverride` and `Options`) disable .htaccess usage and allow directory indexing in the private directory. They are not required parts of user-based authorization, but are presented for illustration purposes.

For this example to work, you need to use the files created earlier in this chapter (htuser and htgroup), with the user accounts tim and ron defined and the group account admin defined. Also, make the directory /home/httpd/html/private, and put some private files there.

Try to access the directory by opening a browser and entering a URL such as the following:

```
http://server.com/private
```

You are prompted with a dialog box with the phrase *private files* in it, asking for a name and password. If you enter valid information for tim, ron, or any of the users in the group admin, you are allowed to see the directory.

VIRTUAL HOSTING

With the explosion of interest in the Internet and the resulting increase in the number of Web sites, it is increasingly common to see a single machine acting as the server for more than one Web site. When multiple Web sites are provided on the same machine, it is referred to as *virtual hosting*. This section describes the different virtual hosting options that are available with the Apache Web server and shows examples of some basic virtual host setups.

There are a few different ways to provide more than one Web site from a machine. One way is to run multiple copies of the Web server, one for each site. However, this can be prohibitive in terms of machine resources. Supporting 20 Web sites requires 20 instances of the Web server, which means that your machine probably runs 60–120 processes (or more) just for serving Web documents. Fortunately, Apache supports the capability to use a single server to serve multiple Web sites, using the `VirtualHost` directive.

There are two methods of supporting virtual hosts with a single server. One is based on using multiple IP addresses—one for each Web site—and the other is based on supporting multiple host names on (usually) one IP address. These are called *IP-based* and *name-based* virtual hosting, respectively. A minor variant of IP-based virtual hosting is port-based virtual hosting, where only the port part of the address differs between virtual hosts.

The procedures and settings that are required to set up virtual hosting using these different methods are discussed in the sections that follow. Here are a few criteria you can use to select one of the virtual hosting methods:

- **Does your machine have more than one IP address?**

  If your machine has multiple IP addresses, and particularly if it already has an IP address for each Web site you want to configure, use IP-based virtual hosting.

  If your machine doesn't have multiple IP addresses, consider whether you can add them. Although configuring multiple IP addresses on a machine is not difficult (see Chapter 23, "Advanced Network Features," for more information on this process), you need to consider whether you have enough addresses for the sites you want to host.

- **How many Web sites do you plan to host?**

  If you plan to run two or three Web sites on a single machine, using two or three IP addresses for IP-based virtual hosting is probably all right. However, if you plan to set up many Web sites, you probably need to use name-based virtual hosting. This requires more effort in terms of configuring the name server, but consumes fewer IP addresses (which are quickly becoming a precious commodity).

- **Do all your sites need to use the default HTTP port (80)?**

  If you are doing multiple internal sites (or sites that are interrelated, and are *not* linked to from the outside), you can set up virtual hosting using the same IP address, but with multiple ports. This option is simple to set up, but requires that your Web authors use the port number that you choose as part of the links in the documents that they create; therefore, there is some extra work in that area of your site maintenance.

- **Does your system have multiple host names assigned to it?**

  If you have multiple names that resolve to the same IP address, you need to use name-based virtual hosting. This requires local as well as remote clients to resolve the different names for your machine successfully; furthermore, it usually requires that you have control over the DNS name server for your domain.

- **Do you want to rigidly separate the Web sites?**

  You might have a situation in which the security requirements or administration requirements of your Web sites are dramatically different. For example, if you have one Web server that runs as a privileged account (for example, to allow remote administration of the machine through a Web interface), you might want to run it separately from your main Web site server to decrease the risk that a misconfiguration of the main server might compromise your overall machine security. In this case, you probably want to set up virtual hosting with multiple separate Web servers.

Running a Single Server on Multiple IP Addresses

One way to configure your machine with multiple Web sites is to use a different IP address for each site. This is called IP-based, or address-based, virtual hosting; it easy to set up, after you have your machine configured with multiple IP addresses.

There are a couple of different ways to configure your box with more than one IP address. If you have multiple networking cards (for example, two Ethernet cards), each card has its own IP address. You can also assign more than one IP address to a single network card, using a feature of Linux called *IP aliasing*. See Chapter 23 for a description of IP aliasing and how to set it up on your machine. For the rest of this section, it is assumed that you have already set up and tested the IP addresses that you plan to use for your Web sites.

To configure the Web server to listen to multiple addresses and respond differently to each one, use the `<VirtualHost>` directive. You use the `<VirtualHost>` directive to declare a section (much similar to a *`<Directory>`* section) in one of your server configuration files. As part of the `<VirtualHost>` directive itself, you specify an address to match. Inside the virtual host section, you specify the settings that are to be used when that address is used by clients to access the server. For clients that access the server using some other address, the main server settings (outside any `<VirtualHost>` section) are used.

A simple virtual host setup, for a machine with addresses 192.168.1.1 and 192.168.1.2, is shown in Listing 28.4.

LISTING 28.4 A SIMPLE EXAMPLE OF IP-BASED VIRTUAL HOSTING

```
...
BindAddress *
Port 80
DocumentRoot /home/httpd/html
ServerName site1.com

<VirtualHost 192.168.1.2>
DocumentRoot /home/httpd/site2
ServerName site2.com
...
</VirtualHost>
```

In this example, the server binds to address 0.0.0.0:80 (because of the `BindAdress *` and `Port 80` directives). This means that it receives TCP requests on port 80 for all the IP addresses on the machine. When the server receives a request, it determines which address the request was received on. If the address is 192.168.1.2, the server responds with a document from the document tree under /home/httpd/site2. Otherwise (when the request is received on address 192.168.1.1), the server responds with a document from /home/httpd/html. In this example, clients access the two different Web sites as `http://site1.com/` and `http://site2.com/`.

Inside a `<VirtualHost>` section, you place directives to control all the aspects of the server that are specific to the particular site that you are defining. This includes directives to do the following:

- Define the document name space.
- Control document and script handling.
- Define directory indexing options.
- Set log file options.
- Perform access and authorization control.

For example, to define per directory options for site2, you add a `<Directory>` section, nested *inside* the `<VirtualHost>` section shown in the example in Listing 28.4.

For each virtual host you define, you need to at least define a new `DocumentRoot`. You need to also set up transfer and error logs that are specific to that site, using appropriate log directives. It is up to you to decide what other customizations to make for each Web site (that is, inside each virtual host section) that you define.

You specify the IP address for a virtual host in the `<VirtualHost>` directive itself. This can include a port number, which is separated from the IP address by a colon. The server must be listening on the address that you specify. In certain complex situations, you might need to tell the server to listen to specific address and port combinations, using some combination of `BindAddress`, `Port`, and `Listen` directives. Use of `BindAddress` and `Port` was discussed earlier in this chapter. The `Listen` directive allows more precise control over the addresses that are used by the Web server. The example in Listing 28.5 uses the `Listen` directive to specify three separate addresses to listen to, and for subsequent mapping to virtual hosts.

LISTING 28.5 AN EXAMPLE OF IP-BASED VIRTUAL HOSTING, USING COMPLEX ADDRESSING

```
Listen 192.168.1.1:80
Listen 192.168.1.1:8080
Listen 192.168.1.2:80

<VirtualHost 192.168.1.1:80>
...
</VirtualHost>
<VirtualHost 192.168.1.1:8080>
...
</VirtualHost>
<VirtualHost 192.168.1.2:80>
...
</VirtualHost>
```

By default, any client access to the machine on an address that is not matched by a virtual host directive is handled using the directives outside any virtual host statement. To make the definitions for the sites more consistent, you can use the keyword `_default_` in place of the IP address in a `VirtualHost` directive, and place the settings for alternative Web site access inside that virtual host section. This can be important in complex virtual hosting configurations. For example, Listing 28.6 accomplishes the same thing as Listing 28.4, when only two IP addresses are used.

LISTING 28.6 USING `_default_` WITH VIRTUAL HOSTING

```
...
BindAddress *
Port 80

<VirtualHost 192.168.1.2>
DocumentRoot /home/httpd/site2
ServerName site2.com
...
</VirtualHost>

<VirtualHost _default_:*>
DocumentRoot /home/httpd/html
ServerName site1.com
...
</VirtualHost>
```

RUNNING A SINGLE SERVER WITH MULTIPLE DNS NAMES

IP-based virtual hosting is fine if you have multiple IP addresses that you can configure on your machine. However, if you are hosting many sites, you might not obtain all the addresses you need. Also, you might have a machine that already has more than one name assigned to a single IP address. In these cases, you need to use name-based virtual hosting.

The principles in name-based virtual hosting are basically the same as those for IP-based virtual hosting. In this case, however, the server also uses the hostname in the client's request to determine which virtual host to use for the request. Name-based virtual hosting can be used with a single IP address or with multiple IP addresses.

To set this up, use the `NameVirtualHost` directive to indicate which addresses are being used for name-based virtual hosts. Then, inside the `<VirtualHost>` sections for that address, indicate a name (or set of names) to match using the `ServerName` and `ServerAlias` directives. When the server tries to match the incoming request to a virtual host section, it examines the hostname sent by the client and matches it against these names. Listing 28.7 shows an example of name-based virtual hosting. This example shows the server supporting two site names on address 192.168.1.1.

LISTING 28.7 AN EXAMPLE OF NAME-BASED VIRTUAL HOSTING

```
Listen 192.168.1.1:80
NameVirtualHost 192.168.1.1:80

<VirtualHost 192.168.1.1:80>
DocumentRoot /home/httpd/html
ServerName www.server.com
ServerAlias www www.server.com
</VirtualHost>

<VirtualHost 192.168.1.1:80>
DocumentRoot /home/httpd/site2
ServerName www2.server.com
</VirtualHost>
```

Note the use of the `ServerAlias` directive in the first virtual host definition. If a client request contains either the name `www.server.com` or just `www`, the first host definition is used. Use of `ServerAlias` is useful to allow clients on the local network to use short alias names instead of fully qualified domain names, in conjunction with name-based hosting.

RUNNING MORE THAN ONE WEB SERVER ON THE SAME MACHINE

Another way to run more than one Web site on a machine is to load multiple instances of the Web server on the machine. Instead of using `<VirtualHost>` directives, you configure each server with its own set of configuration files, making sure that the servers do not interfere with each other.

Making a Set of Configuration Files for Each Server

In this setup, each server needs to have its own set of startup and configuration files. The startup file is the initialization script `/etc/rc.d/init.d/httpd`. This file can be edited to add a second and subsequent invocation lines for a server, when the script is run at system boot. To do this, duplicate the commands in the `start)` and `stop)` sections of the case statement in this file, and edit them to reflect the additional servers that you want to start. See Chapter 12 for more information about OpenLinux initialization scripts.

The directives for adjusting the configuration files were discussed earlier in this chapter. Basically, you want to configure each server with its own set of configuration files, using the `ServerRoot` and `ResourceConfig`, `AccessConfig`, `TypeConfig`, and `MimeMagicFile` directives to accomplish this. Note that it is likely that you will want to share the MIME typing files. If you create a new configuration directory, you might want to use file system links so that the files mime.type and magic are shared between the two directories.

Other settings that are specific to each server instance need to be placed in the appropriate configuration file for that server.

Binding Each Server to Its Own Address or Port

In order for the servers to run without interfering with each other, they need to use different addresses—or at least different ports. Use the `BindAddress`, `Port`, and `Listen` directives in each server's httpd.conf to establish the IP address and TCP port used by that server.

Other Per Instance Configuration Variables

There are a few other configuration variables that you must change for subsequent instances of the server in order for the different server processes not to interfere with each other. These include the values set by the `ScoreBoardFile`, `LockFile`, and `PidFile` directives, as well as log file locations (set by `TransferLog`, `ErrorLog`, `CustomLog`, and so on).

Using Apache with SSL

Earlier in this chapter, authorization and access control were discussed as two important aspects of you Web site security. This section deals with another aspect of security: making the communications between the clients and your Web server private. This is done by encrypting the communications between the clients and the server, using the *Secure Sockets Layer (SSL)* protocol.

This section gives an overview of the mechanisms that are used for secure communications, as well as providing some information about the `mod_ssl` modification to Apache, which allows it to function as a secure Web server. This section also discusses some of the creation and manipulation of special data files that are used for secure communications.

The availability of SSL for use with your Web server creates some interesting dilemmas for governments that want to control encryption to avoid having it fall into the hands of foreign entities that they want to spy on. This topic is discussed as well.

OVERVIEW OF SECURE COMMUNICATIONS CONCEPTS

SSL is a protocol that was originally defined by Netscape Communications Corporation to allow two machines communicating over TCP/IP to encrypt the information sent between them. After a communication session is secured in this way, the two machines can exchange private or sensitive information without worrying about eavesdroppers or other interlopers stealing or using the information. This is an essential feature for Web servers used for e-commerce because they often require the transfer of personal, confidential information, such as credit card numbers or account codes.

PUBLIC-PRIVATE KEY SYSTEMS

To encrypt the packets that travel between two machines, the machines must understand a common encryption algorithm, and must exchange some information which allows one machine to decrypt (unscramble) what the other one encrypts. The parts of the security information that are used to encrypt or decrypt data are called keys.

Encryption is performed by making a modification to the information at one location, using a key. The information is then transmitted to another location, where a key is used to restore the information to its original form (decrypt it). In a simple system, the key used to encrypt the information is the same key that is used to decrypt it. This is called a private key system because the contents of the key must be kept secret for the information to be kept secret. However, private key systems present a problem because the key must be somehow transmitted securely to the new location. SSL uses a special kind of encryption, called a public-private key system, as a part of the overall system it uses to allow secure communications sessions.

A discussion of the mathematical details of public-private keys is outside the scope of this short section. However, in a such a key system, two keys are used for the encryption/decryption process, and one of them (called the public key) can be made freely available to anyone without damaging the security of the communications between the two machines. This solves the problem of secure key distribution, inherent to private key systems.

CERTIFICATES—VERIFYING WHO IS AT THE OTHER END OF A SECURE SESSION

Another issue that is related to secure communications is whether to trust the Web server with which you are communicating. Although a Web server might send a client a key so that the server can communicate securely with the client, it is possible that the client might be talking to the wrong Web server (for example, the server might provide a credit card number to some fake server run by con artists). When a public-private key system is used, it is also possible to transmit some additional information, called a *certificate*, which describes the Web server and the organization behind it.

This certificate can be electronically "signed" by a trusted agency. There are various agencies that research both the organization that is running the Web site and the information in the certificate, and then sign the certificate—for a price. Client browsers have a list of trusted agencies, which they use to verify the signature on a certificate. The use of a signed certificate allows a client to verify that it is communicating with the server that the user intends it to (that is, that the server is actually run by the organization that the user expects).

When you set up a secure Web server, you must create a public-private key pair and a certificate for use with the server. If you want to run a secure Web site for public use, you must also get your certificate signed by one of these trusted agencies.

USE OF SECURE `httpd—https`

When communicating with a secure Web server, the client uses a different protocol, called HTTPS (or Secure HTTP), instead of HTTP. As the name implies, it is similar to HTTP, but with security added to it.

To access a secure Web server, a user must specify the URL with the `https` protocol identifier, as follows:

```
https://www.server.com/cgi-bin/process_credit_card
```

One of the most common mistakes that new administrators of secure Web servers make is failing to use the correct protocol type (`https`) in URLs that refer to the secure Web site. Whereas the default TCP port for the HTTP protocol is port 80, the default port for HTTPS is 443. When a browser tries to access a secure server at the wrong port, the browser appears to hang, and eventually times out.

This can be disconcerting to end users, so take special care to test all the URLs that you create and which link to your secure site.

CREATING A SECURE WEB SERVER USING `mod_ssl`

Because of governmental export restrictions in the U.S., Caldera does not provide secure Web server functionality with OpenLinux. (OpenLinux is sold worldwide, and the U.S. government does not allow certain kinds of encryption to be shipped outside the U.S.) Unfortunately, this means that you have to do a bit of legwork in order to obtain, build, and install the secure Web server functionality for Apache.

Note

Indeed, because of the funkiness of the U.S. government restrictions in this area (and because this book might be sold abroad), I can't even include some automated mechanism on the CD in this book (such as an RPM SPEC file, for instance), that might make this process easier for you.

There are a couple of different options for adding SSL to Apache. The one described here—which is recommended—is called `mod_ssl`. It consists of a set of patches and a special module for use with the Apache source code. It uses a cryptography library that provides SSL functions called SSLeay.

OBTAINING SOURCES

To build Apache with `mod_ssl`, you need sources from at least three places (and maybe four, depending on what you plan to use it for). Examine the following Web sites, and follow the links to an appropriate download area, to obtain the source code you need.

If there are U.S. mirrors for the download areas listed on the respective Web sites for these software pieces, use those instead. For each download URL, the current software version as of this writing is shown. Check in the indicated download directory of each software piece for newer versions, and download them as appropriate.

APACHE SOURCE CODE For the Apache source code itself, either use the source code on the OpenLinux CD or obtain the latest release from the Apache organization download area.

The Apache organization Web site is at

```
http://www.apache.org/
```

To install the source code from the OpenLinux Apache source RPM, log in as the root user, make sure that the OpenLinux CD is mounted, and type the following command:

```
rpm -i /mnt/cdrom/Packages/SRPMS/apache-1.3*
```

The Apache source TAR file is installed in the directory /usr/src/OpenLinux/SOURCES.

To obtain the latest release of Apache from the Apache organization, download the source tar file from the following location:

```
ftp://ftp.apache.org:/apache/dist/apache_1.3.3.tar.gz
```

SSLEAY SOURCES SSLeay is an essential cryptographic library for programs using SSL, including a secure Web server. The SSLeay Web site is at

```
http://www.ssleay.org/
```

The SSLeay library can be obtained by downloading the latest version at

```
ftp://ftp.psy.uq.oz.au/pub/Crypto/SSL/SSLeay-0.9.0b.tar.gz
```

RSAREF SOURCES If you live in the United States, you need to obtain an additional source file in order to use certain encryption algorithms that are patented in the U.S. (and some other countries) by RSA Data Security, Inc.

The library that provides these algorithms is called rsaref, and is used in conjunction with SSLeay. There are restrictions on exporting it outside the United States, and you must obtain the source code for it from RSA itself.

To obtain the source code for rsaref, read the file at

`ftp://ftp.rsa.com/rsaref/README`

and follow the instructions in the file. Basically, you have to follow a temporarily created link in the dist directory to download the file rsaref20.tar.Z.

The license for the library is at

`ftp://ftp.rsa.com/rsaref/info.reply`

Note that rsaref can be used to create a secure Web server, but that you cannot charge for rsaref or the secure Web server you create, or for any services based on the secure Web server. You can, however, use the secure Web server created with rsaref internally in a commercial setting.

Obtaining a Commercial Secure Web Server

If this whole process sounds complicated and, legally, a little bit dicey, you can opt to obtain, from a commercial supplier, a secure Apache Web server that is prebuilt and ready to run. There are several commercial versions available, which run on OpenLinux. Following are three of the more popular versions and their suppliers:

- **Stronghold, by C2Net**
  `http://www.c2.net/products/stronghold`
- **Raven SSL, by Covalent**
  `http://raven.covalent.net/`
- **Red Hat Secure Web Server, by Red Hat**
  `http://www.redhat.com/product.phtml/WB2000`

`mod_ssl` SOURCES `mod_ssl` is a set of patches for Apache that allows it to use the SSLeay library. Also, `mod_ssl` provides a special module that adds additional functionality related to processing client and server security data.

The `mod_ssl` Web site is at

`http://www.engelschall.com/sw/mod_ssl/`

The `mod_ssl` TAR file can be obtained at

`ftp://ftp.engelschall.com/sw/mod_ssl/mod_ssl-2.1.4-1.3.3.tar.gz`

NOTES ON BUILDING THE SOURCE At the `mod_ssl` Web page, Ralf Engelschall (the primary author of `mod_ssl`) provides detailed instructions for installing and building all the required components. The Web page to examine is `http://www.engelshcall.com/sw/mod_ssl/distrib/mod_ssl-SNAP/INSTALL`

Download this document, print it out, and follow it exactly. If you are in the United States, follow the US instructions. For the `--prefix` argument to the `./configure` script for `mod_ssl`, use either `/usr/local/apache` or `/opt/apache`.

When you are finished with the instructions, the Apache software is installed in a subdirectory under the directory that you chose as the argument to `--prefix`. You can run the secure Apache from that location (highly recommended), or you can install the software over the top of your existing OpenLinux Apache files. To do the latter, you need to perform, by hand, the commands listed in the `%Install` section of the apache.spec file. If you have installed the Apache source RPM, this file is located at /usr/src/OpenLinux/SPECS/apache.spec.

PREPARING SPECIAL FILES REQUIRED FOR SECURITY

Several special files are required by the server in order for it to operate in secure mode. During the course of the build, you probably made a server key file and certificate using the (patched) makefile in the Apache source directory. However, you can make these files manually at a later time—and some of them require special processing by a trusted agency (a Certificate Authority) in order for your Web site to be used correctly by the general public.

The following files are used for server security:

- **A server key file**—This file contains a public and private key which are used by the server for encryption and decryption operations.
- **A certificate file**—This file specifies that the key and Web site are run by a certain organization. If this certificate is signed by a trusted agency, the user can trust that the Web site is indeed run by the indicated organization.
- **A certificate signing request**—This file contains information from the certificate, as well as information about the key. It is intended to be sent to a trusted agency (called a Certificate Authority) for signing.

All these are made when you run the command `make certificate` in the Apache source directory. Each of these files is described in greater detail in the paragraphs that follow.

THE PUBLIC/PRIVATE KEY PAIR

The public/private key pair is saved in the file server.key by default. This file contains the keys that are used to perform encryption by the server.

The private key of the public/private key pair needs to be protected at all times. For this reason, during the creation of the key, you are asked to enter a pass phrase to encrypt the key file. When the key file is encrypted, you are required to enter this pass phrase every time the server starts in order for the server to access the file. Although this can be annoying, it is very dangerous to leave the private key unencrypted on the disk without a pass phrase.

Use the `SSLCertificateKeyFile` directive in the server configuration file httpd.conf to specify the key file that is to be used for secure operations.

The Server Certificate

The server certificate file contains information about the organization that runs the Web site. The server certificate file is transmitted to the client when a secure session is set up, and the client tries to use it to verify that the site is legitimate. This file is sometimes called an X.509 file because that is the name of the standard that defines the format used for this file.

In order for the certificate to be accepted by the client, it must be digitally signed by a Certificate Authority (CA). Each major browser that supports SSL has a list of trusted certificate authorities whose signatures it accepts. When a browser sees a certificate signed by a CA that it does not know about, it usually provides the information about the CA and the certificate to the user, and asks if it is to proceed. It is then up to the user to determine if she can trust that the site to which she is connecting is valid.

The certificate file to use is specified in the server configuration file using the `SSLCertificatFile` directive.

The Certificate Signing Request

In order for your site to be trusted by clients, you need to have your certificate signed by a trusted agency that operates as a Certificate Authority. To have the certificate signed by a Certificate Authority, create a *certificate signing request* (*CSR*) and send it to the authority with some documentation and some money.

There are several agencies that act as certificate authorities, which involves verifying the information in the certificate and digitally signing it. The price that they charge for their service is in exchange for the cost of researching the information in your CSR and taking on the liability of certifying your Web site.

The following are two popular Certificate Authorities:

- **Thawte Digital Certificate Services**

  `http://www.thawte.com/`
- **Verisign, Inc.**

  `http://www.verisign.com/`

Both of these companies accept certificate signing requests generated by the `mod_ssl` package, for use with Apache with `mod_ssl`. When you make your server key file and certificate, you also make a certificate signing request. The information required for this request must match exactly the company name, registered domain name, and other details that are required by the Certificate Authority, in order for them to process your request. Also, the file is automatically encoded in a special format. Detailed information on pricing, and instructions for creating the CSR and submitting it and the required accompanying documentation to the Certificate Authority, are available on the Web sites of the respective companies.

In order to test your server, or to run your server internally in your organization, you can act as your own Certificate Authority and self-sign your certificate. This is also referred to as *self-certifying*. The browsers that connect to your server won't recognize your signature as one from a valid Certificate Authority, but users can manually accept the certificates on their browsers after seeing an error message.

For internal use, you can eliminate the error message on the client by adding a Certificate Authority file to the client's browser. The steps involved in doing this are beyond the scope of this section, but see the online `mod_ssl` documentation for more information.

After you receive a certificate signed by a real Certificate Authority, you substitute it for the self-signed one by copying it over the old file, or by modifying the value of the `SSLCertificateFile` directive.

SPECIAL SECURITY DIRECTIVES

The security directives to control `mod_ssl` are added to the Apache documentation that is installed when you build the secure Web server—you can examine them in-depth there. However, a few security directives are worth highlighting here, to give an overview of their use.

Use the `SSLCipherSuite` directive to control which algorithms are allowed for secure sessions. Unless you are a security expert, you probably need to leave these settings alone.

Use the `SSLSessionCache` directive to indicate whether to support an interprocess cache of SSL session information (and if so, what the filename for it is to be). Because secure sessions require substantial setup, and because client requests can be served by multiple server child processes, use of a session cache to share information between child processes can speed things up considerably. Use the value `none`, to turn off the session cache, or `dbm:` followed by the path of a file to use as the session cache.

Use the `SSLLog` and `SSLLogLevel` directives to create logs to hold SSL-specific information.

Finally, SSL and X.509 certificates can also be used by the server for authenticating clients—much as the server certificate is used by the client to authenticate the server. Use the following directives to set up client authentication using client certificates: `SSLCACertificatePath`, `SSLCACertificateFile`, `SSLVerifyClient`, `SSLVerifyDepth`, and `SSLRequire`.

MAKING SURE YOU ARE LEGAL

In their infinite wisdom, agencies of the U.S. government have created regulations that make it a crime to export certain strong encryption software from the United States. This is ostensibly done with the intent to prevent strong encryption capabilities from falling into the hands of unfriendly governments and terrorists. The actual result of this situation, however, is that most good encryption software development is now done in other countries and imported to the U.S., rather than vice versa. Encryption software that is imported to the U.S. cannot be exported from the U.S.—even to the original author of the software!

Furthermore, the company RSA Data Security, Inc. has a U.S. patent on certain public-private key encryption algorithms used in SSL. Therefore, if you plan to use RSA algorithms, in the U.S., you must obtain code and permission from RSA to do so. You must not, under any circumstances, ship the code that you obtain from RSA, or the libraries or server that you create with code obtained from RSA, outside the U.S.

If you are operating in the U.S., you need to abide by these laws (export controls and RSA's encryption patents) or you will face stiff penalties.

If you just plan to use Apache with `mod_ssl` as a secure Web server at your organization, you are probably all right. If, however, you plan to distribute the Web server or a machine containing it overseas, check with an attorney to determine what the applicable U.S. export and patent laws are and to make sure that you are in compliance with them.

SUMMARY

This chapter discussed the Apache Web server that is provided with OpenLinux. You are now familiar with the basic configuration files and directives necessary to customize your Web site. Many options are available for adjusting the performance, behavior, and operation of the Web site. Also discussed was security, via authorization, access control, and encrypted communication via SSL. See the following chapters for more information:

- To understand how the server interacts with the document directory tree, you might want to read Chapter 9, "Understanding the Linux File System," and Chapter 10, which cover the Linux file system and user, group, and file permissions, respectively.
- Chapter 12 contains information about the initialization system of OpenLinux. This system includes the script that runs the Web server during system startup.
- See Chapter 23 for information on IP aliasing, which might be required for IP-based virtual hosting. Also, see Chapter 26, "Domain Name Server (DNS)," for information about assigning names to your machine, which is also usually required for virtual hosting.
- The Apache documentation can be installed from the OpenLinux CD and referenced online using a Web browser. See the instructions on page *xx* of this chapter for installation instructions. Use this documentation for additional descriptions and details regarding specific server configuration directives and optional modules.

CHAPTER 29

IP Masquerading

In this chapter

What is it?

In a nutshell, IP masquerading enables you to provide access to a TCP/IP network outside your own through a single server using a single IP address.

The "single IP address" statement is what makes this so significant. With a block of IP addresses, any network can contain multiple machines, each with its own legitimate IP address, and have a gateway machine provide each machine behind it with access to other networks (see Figure 29.1).

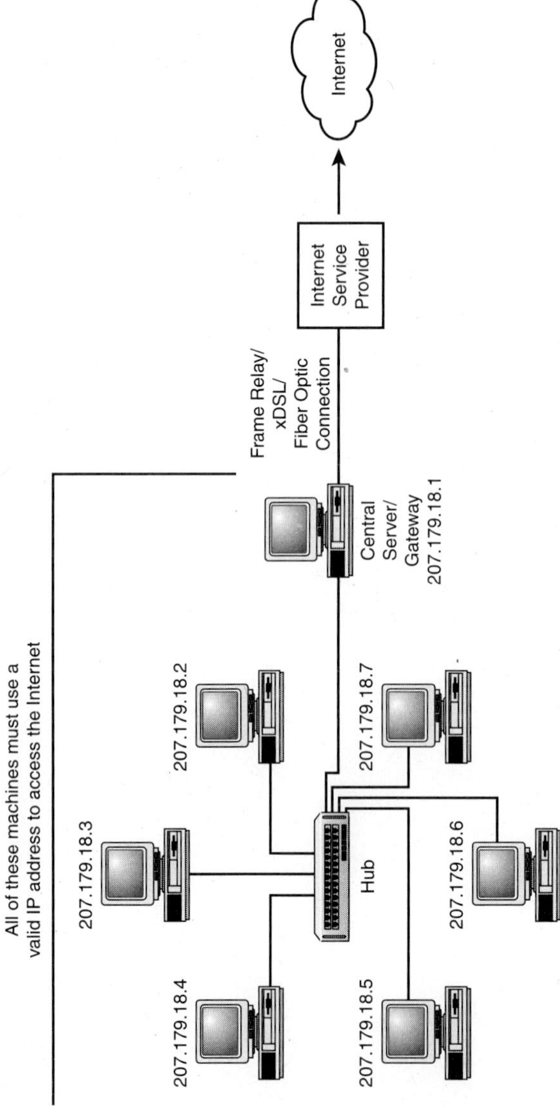

Figure 29.1
Network with a block of IP addresses.

There is a common networking scheme that does not follow this recipe, however: home and small business networks, most of which do not have legitimate blocks of IP addresses to work with, and most of which only have dial-up access to other TCP/IP networks, in particular the Internet (see Figure 29.2).

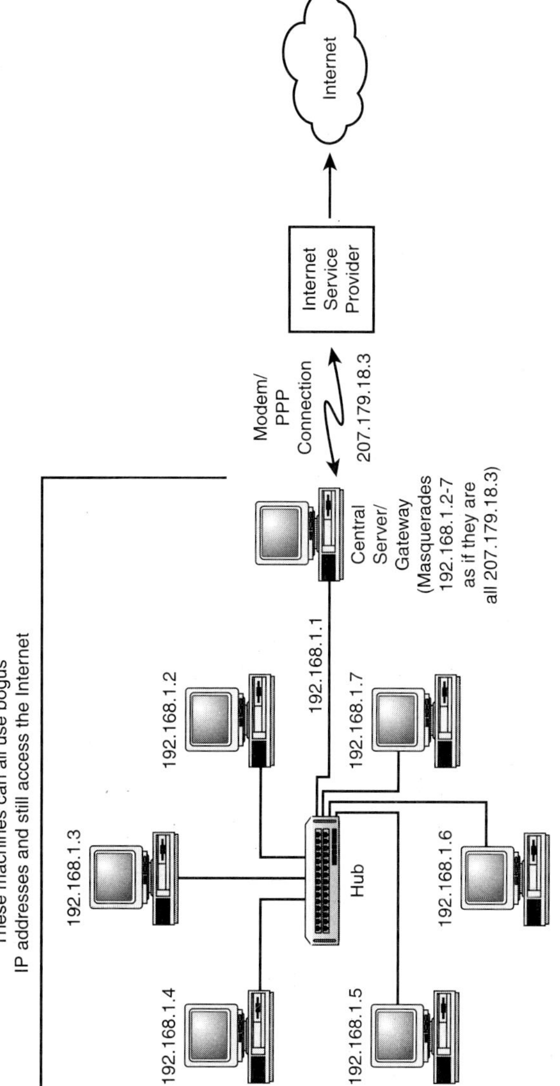

Figure 29.2
Network with one IP address and IP masquerading.

Using IP masquerading, a home or small business network can offer all connected machines access to an outside network such as the Internet using a single IP address on a single server machine. All Internet-bound network packets are masqueraded as if they were being sent from the server that is running IP masquerading. The server maintains the information necessary to route the returning network packets back to the machines that are supposed to receive them.

Note that although IP masquerading is commonly seen on servers connected to the Internet through a modem via PPP, there is nothing that says that you cannot do the same thing using Ethernet connections to the Internet. For example, a company might want to have a training room full of computers networked to the Internet, but they might not want to give up a whole block of IP addresses for the task. If you give the machines bogus IP addresses and masquerade them through one machine, only one IP address is necessary.

REQUIRED KERNEL COMPONENTS

The Linux kernel that ships with OpenLinux is precompiled with everything you need to utilize IP masquerading. All that needs to be done to implement it is to load some kernel modules and set up some simple firewall rules.

For those who want to compile their own kernels, following is the list of items that need to be compiled into the kernel in order for IP masquerading to work (the names are listed as they are seen during a `make config` or `make menuconfig` procedure):

- Prompt for development and/or incomplete code/drivers
- Enable loadable module support
- Networking support
- Network firewalls
- TCP/IP networking (see Chapter 21, "Understanding TCP/IP Fundamentals," for details on setting up TCP/IP network interfaces on OpenLinux)
- IP: forwarding/gatewaying
- IP: firewalling
- IP: masquerading (EXPERIMENTAL)
- IP: ipautofw masquerade support (recommended)
- IP: ICMP masquerading (recommended)
- IP: always defragment (recommended)
- Dummy net driver support (recommended)

Of course, there are other options that you compile in as either modules or built-in support; the preceding list is just for masquerading features. See Chapter 17, "Building Custom Kernels," for more information on recompiling Linux kernels.

SETUP

IP masquerading is accomplished though the packet filtering firewall capabilities of modern Linux kernels. When an outgoing network packet hits the firewall machine (the server with IP masquerading set up on it), the firewall rewrites elements of each package to make them look as if they are emanating from the firewall and not the machine behind the firewall. The return packets are modified to go back to the machine that sent the original outgoing packets. The machine on the Internet to which the packets were sent thinks that they were sent from the firewall machine, and the host behind the firewall thinks that the return packets were sent from the machine on the Internet. To both ends of the transaction, there seems to be nothing odd going on at all.

There are some services that cannot be accessed without special handling. The following modules were made for just such services. These modules are all offered on default installations of OpenLinux:

- **`ip_masq_ftp.o`**—Gives the machines on your network the capability to use the FTP file transfer protocol (in non-passive mode) through the server that is doing the masquerading.
- **`ip_masq_irc.o`**—Gives the capability to use Internet Relay Chat (IRC) clients through the masquerading server.
- **`ip_masq_quake.o`**—To participate in three-dimensional Internet gore-fests as typified by the game "Quake," you must use this module.
- **`ip_masq_raudio.o`**—Allows masqueraded machines behind your server to receive audio and video streams over the Internet through Real Networks clients.
- **`ip_masq_vdolive.o`**—Permits audio/video streams used by the various VDO-Live clients to pass through the masquerading server.

Chapter 18, "Kernel Modules," details how to automatically load modules every time your system boots. If you want to use any (or all) of these modules, please refer to that chapter for details on how to load them.

Some services that do not have special kernel modules written for them can be handled through special port forwarding configurations, but that topic is best left for the next chapter, "IP Firewalling."

The first thing that you need to do is to create a network with bogus IP addresses. The blocks of addresses allocated in RFC 1597 as being reserved for private networks were listed in Chapter 21, but they are duplicated here in Table 29.1.

TABLE 29.1 PRIVATE NETWORK ADDRESS BLOCKS

Class	Address Start	Address End	Mask
A	10.0.0.0	10.255.255.255	8
B	172.16.0.0	172.31.255.255	16
C	192.168.0.0	192.168.255.255	24

Unless there are literally hundreds of computers to be set up on the network, odds are that the Class C block is the one that is used.

The `ipchains` utility is used to set up the forwarding rules for IP masquerading. The following syntax is used:

```
ipchains -P forward DENY
ipchains -A forward -j MASQ -s startIP/mask -d 0.0.0.0/0
```

The first command denies everything from being forwarded through the firewall (a security measure). In the second command, replace *`startIP`* with the beginning IP address from Table 29.1 for the class of addresses you are using, and replace *`mask`* with the corresponding mask value.

For example, if a Class C address block is being used by the computers on the network, the following commands are used:

```
ipchains -P forward DENY
ipchains -A forward -j MASQ -s 192.168.0.0/24 -d 0.0.0.0/0
```

In most cases, this is all that needs to be done to set up the firewall rules. Combined with the modules listed earlier, most of the common Internet services are covered by this configuration.

```
One thing that is important to note about IP masquerading is that, for the most
part, it is
a one-way street. You can go from the machines on your network out to the
Internet, but without special packet forwarding rules, you cannot get into the
systems behind the masquerading server from the Internet.
```

What does this mean? It means that a machine that has a bogus IP address and is sitting behind a masquerading server cannot serve Web pages out on the Internet, nor can it accept direct FTP connections from the outside, nor telnet, nor ssh/secure transactions, and so on.

The next chapter deals with how to set up special firewall rules to enable such services to be accessible from the outside. Barring that, services that are to be accessible from outside your network probably need to be set up on the same server machine that is running IP masquerading.

SUMMARY

In this chapter, you saw how to set up a server machine running OpenLinux to act as a gateway to an external TCP/IP network (such as the Internet) using a single valid IP address. You also learned how to allow special services such as streaming audio and video through the small firewall that lies at the base of the masquerading configuration.

You are encouraged, however, to expand on this knowledge, at least in the area of firewalling. The firewall rules used to set up IP masquerading do not provide much in the way of protection from outside attacks. They merely provide a thin shield for a set of networked machines behind the firewall, making direct access to the machines from the outside more difficult.

Any way you approach IP masquerading, though, it is a useful service to implement on networks that are tight with their free IP addresses. At this point, all Class C IP address blocks in the current IP specification (IPv4) are gone—having been procured by companies and Internet providers—and are typically distributed only when a serious need is presented or a chunk of money is exchanged, or both. Until the new IPv6 specification (the next generation of IP addressing) is implemented and we all have our own personal block of IP addresses, masquerading is the best all around choice for saving these precious addresses, not to mention the money required to procure them.

Refer to the following chapters for additional information on the subjects discussed in this chapter:

- See Chapter 18 for information on how to automatically load kernel modules such as those listed in the "Setup" section.
- See Chapter 21 for more information on setting up TCP/IP network interfaces.
- See Chapter 30 for more information on setting up firewall rules.

CHAPTER 30

IP Firewalling

In this chapter

This chapter discusses a little about firewalls in OpenLinux—what they are, how they work, and how to begin building one. Although this chapter will not make anyone an expert on firewalls, it does introduce the basic concepts.

The term *firewall* comes from the firewall that is used in cars (and other motorized vehicles), which protects the occupants in the cabin from a fire in the engine compartment. A firewall on a network protects both users and the data that is behind it on the local network from the savagery of the Internet (or extranet). It can also be used to prevent users on the local network from connecting to prohibited sites, and it can be used to compartmentalize the internal network.

Tip

Some people learn too late that a firewall does not protect against insiders. Internal firewalls can be used to isolate departments so that damage is not widespread; for example, it can be used to protect accounting from engineering, and engineering from sales, each of which likely has little or no business browsing through files that belong to the others.

INTRODUCTION TO FIREWALLS

Basically, there are two kinds of firewalls in Linux. Each of these two basic types has two subtypes. The two basic types are *packet filters* and *proxy* firewalls. The packet filter firewalls can be one of the following types:

- **Forwarding**—It is in this type of packet filter firewall that decisions are made whether to forward or not.
- **Masquerading**—These firewalls rewrite the source and destination addresses.

Proxy firewalls can be one of the following types:

- **Standard**—With this type of proxy firewall, a client connects to a special port and is redirected to out through another port.
- **Transparent**—With this firewall, the client doesn't use a special port, but the firewall software proxies the connection through transparently.

This chapter deals primarily with packet filtering firewalls. The information in this chapter is designed to complement and round out the information in Chapter 29, "IP Masquerading."

PACKET FILTERS

Packet filtering firewalls work on the following principle: The information that is needed to make a decision about what to do with a packet is contained in the header. The header contains information regarding the source and destination addresses, time to live (TTL), protocol, and much more. It also contains a header checksum that recounts the size of the payload and whether the header has been corrupted. In all, some thirteen separate fields of information are contained in an IP header, some of which contain multiple pieces of information. For complete details, refer to RFC 791 (available from `http://www.rfc-editor.org/rfc.html`).

Note

IP does not check the payload other than to tell if the payload is the correct size. The transport control protocol (TCP) is responsible for ensuring the integrity of the data payload.

OpenLinux uses `ipchains` to provide packet filtering. To implement a packet filtering firewall, decisions must be made regarding the types of packets to address specifically, and what to do with those packets when they are encountered.

The `ipchains` software permits a number of different criteria to be applied to packets. The criteria can be applied to incoming packets, outgoing packets, or packets that will pass through the firewall. These decisions can be based on where the packets came from by address, where they are going by address, or where they are going by port. Different rules can be applied, depending on whether these are TCP packets, UDP packets, or ICMP packets. Finally, for any packets that are not specifically addressed, the overall policy determines the fate of the packets.

PROXY FIREWALLS

Proxy firewalls work differently than packet filters do. All traffic is received on the firewall, whether it is incoming or outgoing. But proxies redirect permitted traffic through the firewall by rewriting the headers. To be redirected, the traffic has to log in to the firewall. In fact, much of the discussion in the preceding section is applicable to a proxy. The difference is subtle; because packet filtering software is rewriting the headers when it is masquerading, it is difficult to explain that there is a difference between a transparent proxy and a masquerading (packet filter) firewall. But the main difference is that the proxy redirects (locally) the traffic that is arriving at one interface and leaving by another, and a packet filter normally does not redirect traffic. Looking at it from a different perspective, proxies work higher up in the OSI model than packet filters.

Note

Any router, gateway, or host that transports a networking packet from one network to another rewrites the header. But this rewriting doesn't alter the source or destination addresses; it only alters-the TTL and checksum, and–on occasion–the total length and fragment offset (among others), if the packet needs to be fragmented to continue. When header rewriting is discussed in this text, it refers mostly to address rewriting.

The *Open Source Interconnect* (*OSI*) model is one of the popular models that is used to explain how packets move from the Application layer to the Physical layer (it might not be completely accurate, but it's a good theoretical paradigm nevertheless). The seven layers are used to explain where certain software works. For the purposes of this text, it is only important to note that the level where each works is different, and that this is one of the distinguishing characteristics between proxies and packet filters.

But this difference is important. Proxies are more overhead intensive, but they can inspect entire packets more thoroughly. They also tend to be a little more difficult to set up initially.

WHICH TO USE?

Packet filtering firewalls and proxying firewalls perform similar functions. They act as shields to protect trusted network segments from untrusted ones. In this regard, each works equally well. Both require monitoring and occasional reconfiguring; both, if they are misconfigured, provide only a false sense of security; and both, when implemented in a methodical, well-thought-out manner, can provide a modicum of security.

> **Tip**
>
> If you remember that the only secure system is the one that is not assembled and powered on (and therefore not of much use, either), you'll have a more realistic idea of what firewalls can buy you: time to react to an attack. It remains your responsibility to reconfigure the firewall to protect against this attack. I want to emphasize that: A firewall buys you time to react to an attack.

Basically, the decision to use packet filtering or proxying comes down to an individual decision, and might be based on the prior experiences of those who are involved in maintaining the firewall. If you are implementing a firewall and have worked with proxies before and are comfortable with them, by all means, continue. The use of one type doesn't preclude use of the other. Some proxies that are designed to work specifically with Web (HTTP) traffic can complement a packet filter nicely. For example, the use of `junkbuster` to block particular Web sites or advertising banners is often easier than writing packet filtering rules to deny or reject the banner sites. Conversely, `ipchains` rules can be created solely for the purpose of logging traffic, and can be used in conjunction with a proxy to track specific kinds of traffic. So the best option might be to mix and match, depending on your overall objectives and level of comfort.

From a security standpoint, therefore, neither is better. The one place in which `ipchains` might tip the balance is in situations in which you want to rewrite the *Type of Service* (*TOS*) field to optimize traffic flow.

> **Tip**
>
> You can use `ipchains` to modify the TOS field to specify one of minimum delay, maximum reliability, maximum throughput, or minimum cost.

PHYSICAL CONFIGURATIONS

When discussing physical configurations, you need to look at both the hardware and the software as it applies to the firewall. Remembering that one of the reasons the firewall exists is to protect the trusted network from the untrusted network, this host must necessarily be both the funnel for network traffic that is moving between the two networks, making it a possible choke point, and the focus for those who are looking to penetrate your security. If they want to come in, they've got to pass through here first.

THE FIREWALL HOST

You need to consider the type of host you want to install. You can install a firewall that has only one interface, and that uses that interface for both trusted and untrusted connections; but you'll want to consider whether this is wise, taking into account the cost of a second interface versus the weakened security posture that this configuration entails. It is better to have a host with two interfaces, which completely isolates one network from the other. With this configuration, bypassing the firewall becomes more difficult.

> **Note**
>
> A host that isolates an untrusted network from a trusted network using two interfaces–one for each network–is termed a *Bastion Host*.

The question of how powerful a system needs to be depends on your decisions; if you are going to use the firewall to connect two 10Mb Ethernet cards, and if you plan to use packet filtering and no proxies, an 80486-33 processor with 16MB RAM is sufficient for low to moderate traffic loads. However, if you plan to use 100Mhz Ethernet cards in a high traffic route, this CPU will not be able to keep up with the demand and you'll experience significant packet loss.

THE FIREWALL KERNEL

In building a firewall, you'll need to reconfigure the kernel. Several parameters must be set in the kernel to permit packet filtering. Some of these are subjective and are based on your hardware; one must be turned off; others are required. For more information on building a custom kernel, see Chapter 17, "Building Custom Kernels." The first parameter follows:

```
CONFIG_EXPERIMENTAL=y
```

As of this writing, the 2.2 kernel has not been released. One of the items that the kernel hackers plan to review is the experimental status on a number of the kernel parameters. When it is reviewed, the experimental status will, most likely, better reflect reality. Therefore, enabling this is a judgement call, although you might need it for some drivers.

It is strongly recommended that you consider compiling the kernel as a *monolithic* kernel as opposed to a *modular* kernel (for more information on building a custom kernel, see Chapter 17). This is an exception to the rule, "Always build a modular kernel." The reasoning behind this is that anyone can build a module. If someone manages to crack your security, they'll want access again. Rather than amateurishly adding a user with root privileges, they can drop a loadable module on your system, have it inserted, and then erase the other traces of entry. Although this is extreme and a rather sophisticated way to go about it, it might enable nearly undetectable access to your system. So kernel modules can be dangerous. On the other hand, anyone this sophisticated can, most likely, easily find other means to enter the system. Unfortunately, to enable things such as IP port forwarding and some other parameters, module support is required. If you don't see a parameter that you need, it might either be experimental or only available as a module.

In other sections, give careful thought to the parameters that you install. You need to support your hardware (disk drives), the file system, Ethernet drivers, other communications drivers (modems, ISDN devices, and protocols such as PPP), and ELF formats. But sound and other unnecessary parameters need to be disabled.

Note

If this is a home network or part of a small, low-profile business with low bandwidth, you might not need or want to go to the extremes detailed in this chapter. Only you can perform a proper risk assessment for your situation.

With the other sections appropriately set, the section that needs to be detailed is "Networking Options." Although it is not the last section in the kernel configuration, it is certainly the most important for the purposes of this chapter.

NETWORKING OPTIONS

The Linux 2.2.x kernel adds significant complexity to the networking options section from the 2.0.x kernels. The additional options can be daunting, and the help is not always helpful. Plan to spend some time getting acquainted with this section. Items that are of interest are highlighted here; some of these items are required, others are recommended, and still others are optional.

Caution

Items that are marked as not recommended have the potential for weakening your firewall. If you know that you won't use it, don't install it.

The following parameter is required for programs such as `tcpdump`:

```
CONFIG_NETLINK=                    recommended
```

This first kernel parameter is required for such programs as `tcpdump`. However, `tcpdump` puts your Ethernet card in promiscuous mode:

```
CONFIG_PACKET=                        not recommended
```

The following parameter requires devices with major number 36 to communicate. If this option is chosen, `Routing messages` needs to also be chosen, as does `IP: firewall packet netlink device`, which can be used to warn of possible attacks:

```
CONFIG_NETLINK=                    recommended
```

Use of the following parameter requires /dev/route to be created with major 36 so that you can read routing information:

```
CONFIG_RTNETLINK=                     optional
CONFIG_NETLINK_DEV=                     required
```

The following is required for packet filters or masquerading, but not for proxy firewalls:

```
CONFIG_FIREWALL=                      required/optional
```

The following is only required to configure an Ethernet card with multiple IP addresses; it might put your NIC into promiscuous mode:

```
CONFIG_NET_ALIAS=                  not recommended
CONFIG_FILTER=                      not recommended
CONFIG_UNIX=                       required
CONFIG_INET=                       required
CONFIG_IP_MULTICAST=               optional
```

To use TOS, verbose route monitoring, or large routing tables, this is required. The next six parameters depend on this one:

```
CONFIG_IP_ADVANCED_ROUTER          optional
CONFIG_IP_MULTIPLE_TABLES          optional
CONFIG_IP_ROUTE_MULTIPATH          optional
CONFIG_IP_ROUTE_TOS                  optional
CONFIG_IP_ROUTE_VERBOSE              recommended
CONFIG_IP_ROUTE_LARGE_TABLES          optional
```

Following is the network address translation parameter for routers:

```
CONFIG_IP_ROUTE_NAT                  recommended/required
```

The next two parameters depend on this one:

```
CONFIG_IP_PNP                      not recommended
CONFIG_IP_PNP_BOOTP                  not recommended
CONFIG_IP_PNP_RARP                  not recommended
CONFIG_IP_FIREWALL                  required
```

The following parameter requires a device with major 36 and minor 3, plus a program to read the device:

```
CONFIG_IP_FIREWALL_NETLINK          optional
```

Only choose this parameter for firewalls, but *always* choose it for firewalls. It is required for masquerading. For non-masquerading firewalls, packet filters act on the first packet only, and others are passed on. Hosts receiving fragments cannot reassemble them without the first packet, and therefore are discarded in time. However, some hosts—most notably Microsoft Windows and NT—are susceptible to "big `ping`" attacks, even if they only receive the last packet. Choose yes for this option:

```
CONFIG_IP_ALWAYS_DEFRAG              recommended/required
```

The following parameter is required for `ipchains` REDIRECT targets and for transparent proxys; otherwise, it is not needed. If in doubt, include

```
CONFIG_IP_TRANSPARENT_PROXY          optional/required
```

The following is required for masquerading firewalls:

```
CONFIG_IP_MASQUERADE               optional/required
```

This is required only if you chose `CONFIG_IP_MASQUERADE` in the preceding example and want to masquerade ICMP. Without this, `ping` does not work. Furthermore, MS `traceroute`, which uses ICMP rather than UDP, also does not work:

```
CONFIG_IP_MASQUERADE_ICMP          optional/recommended
```

This parameter requires the ipmasqadm program. The next three options depend on enabling this. The following requires kernel module support:

```
CONFIG_IP_MASQUERADE_MOD            optional/required
CONFIG_IP_MASQUERADE_IPAUTOFW        optional
CONFIG_IP_MASQUERADE_IPPORTFW        optional
CONFIG_IP_MASQUERADE_MFW            optional
CONFIG_IP_ROUTER                optional
```

The following also requires kernel module support:

```
CONFIG_NET_IPIP               optional
```

The following is useful for multicast, or if the remote end is a Cisco router:

```
CONFIG_NET_IPGRE                optional
CONFIG_NET_IPGRE_BROADCAST        optional
```

The following requires CONFIG_IP_MROUTE:

```
CONFIG_IP_MROUTE                optional
CONFIG_IP_PIMSM_V1                optional
CONFIG_IP_PIMSM_V2                optional
CONFIG_IP_ALIAS               not recommended
```

This is needed only if you are directly connected to more than 256 hosts; ARPD is also required:

```
CONFIG_ARPD                   optional
```

The following requires CONFIG_SYSCTL and CONFIG_PROC_FS, as well as putting a 1 in /proc/sys/net/ipv4/tcp_syncookies:

```
CONFIG_SYN_COOKIES                recommended
CONFIG_INET_RARP                not recommended
CONFIG_IP_NOSR                    recommended (highly)
CONFIG_SKB_LARGE                optional
CONFIG_IPV6                   optional
CONFIG_IPV6_EUI64               optional
CONFIG_IPV6_NO_PB               optional
```

The ipchains program currently only works for IP, not IPX:

```
CONFIG_IPX                  not recommended
CONFIG_IPX_INTERN              not recommended
CONFIG_SPX                  not recommended
CONFIG_ATALK                  not recommended
CONFIG_X25                  not recommended
CONFIG_LAPB                  not recommended
CONFIG_BRIDGE                  optional
CONFIG_LLC                  not recommended
CONFIG_ECONET                  optional
CONFIG_ECONET_AUNUDP          optional
CONFIG_ECONET_NATIVE          not recommended
CONFIG_WAN_ROUTER              optional
CONFIG_NET_FASTROUTE          DO NOT USE
```

The following is of limited availability:

```
CONFIG_NET_HW_FLOWCONTROL         optional
```

Following is an alternative to `CONFIG_NET_HW_FLOWCONTROL`, if you think that your system will be saturated by high volume traffic:

```
CONFIG_CPU_IS_SLOW                optional
```

Sixteen options depend on the following parameter, but are omitted for the sake of brevity:

```
CONFIG_NET_SCHED                  not recommended
```


SOFTWARE CONSIDERATIONS

After the kernel is built, you can look over the system for software that isn't required for operation. Extraneous software needs to be removed. This is especially true of compilers, games, and other unnecessary software. The use of the X Window software is discouraged because this binds to port 6000 and 6010. If you feel that it is needed, consider using `ipchains` to deny output on the untrusted network side. This includes `nfs` and other services that are not used or needed. If an intruder breaches the firewall, it doesn't make sense to provide tools to use or services to activate.

What you probably want to have is software—such as `ipmasq`—to help manage the `ipchains` rules. This program might or might not be included on the OpenLinux CD, but it is worth downloading and installing if you have many rules to track. The secure shell (`ssh`) program is also highly recommended. Running TCP wrappers on ports that are not forwarded and not used (normal services do not run on a firewall), as well as using `tripwire` to watch files, is a good idea. Another good program to add to your arsenal is a Perl program called `courtney`. This program watches for port scans.

OTHER CONSIDERATIONS

A firewall is not to be considered a normal network host, and it is not to be treated like one. This system should not enable normal users to log in or share files or directories on the network. The need to use good passwords for the accounts on the firewall, along with the necessity of using of shadow passwords, goes without saying. What might need to be said is that the firewall is not to have the same password as any other host on your network. The fact that the host is broken because the attacker broke the password should not automatically provide access to other hosts on the internal network.

This host needs to also be physically separated from the rest of the hosts, and placed in a secure area where unauthorized individuals cannot gain physical access to it. Any machine to which a knowledgable individual has access can be "broken", often in minutes. The case needs to be locked, and access to the system setup password must be protected.

PORT FORWARDING

Port forwarding is redirecting a connection from one host to another; this is what proxy firewalls do well. If you connect from host foo to host bar on port 80, and that port is redirected—by software—to host baz on port 80, host foo thinks it's connected to host bar on port 80 even though it is actually accessing host baz on port 80. Host baz sees a connection from host bar. This can work in either direction, permitting inside clients out and outside clients in—but in a controlled environment. Either way, all connections appear to be to and from host bar.

The `ipchains` software does not do port forwarding. Although one of the `ipchains` targets is REDIRECT, this target is for local redirection, not redirection to another host. If you use `ipchains` and want to do port forwarding, you'll need to use `ipportfw`. The `ipmasqadm` program is a useful wrapper to `ipportfw`. Outside connections coming in might require redirection, particularly if the internal (trusted) network is being masqueraded.

A SIMPLE PACKET FILTERING FIREWALL

The next few sections step you through building a very simple firewall with `ipchains`. This firewall is not adequate for use as is—you'll need to determine if this is what you need. But it does give you a good idea about how to plan and implement a simple firewall, including how to write the `ipchains` rules. In the real world, it's just not this easy; this is only a chapter, although it deserves a book.

To begin, you'll need to know something about the network from which you're connecting, and about the network to which you're connecting. The following assumptions are valid for the rest of this section:

- **Internal (trusted) Network**—209.191.169.128/25
- **External (untrusted) Network**—209.191.169.0/25
- **Bastion host**—foo, with foo1/foo2 interfaces, 209.191.169.1/209.191.169.129.

PLANNING

You can start from one of two general policies. The overall policy can be either "Permit everything that is not specifically prohibited" or "Prohibit everything that is not specifically permitted." Because the latter is easier, your general firewall policy will be "Prohibit."

The network is set up internally as trusted, and no services will be run from inside for now. All the services that the company wants to provide to the Internet will reside on the untrusted network: anonymous FTP, HTTP, and so on. You might see the untrusted portion of the company's network referred to as the DMZ, the demilitarized zone, in some textbooks. This is because it is similar to the front lines in a battle; if the bad guys are going to show their faces, this is where they will try to penetrate. This has the disadvantage of having more hosts to monitor for intrusions, but it has the advantage of not allowing an intruder into your internal net via port forwarding.

Because this network is considered low risk, the decision has been made to run mail on the firewall, with a pop server for users to get mail whether they are at the office or home (`imap` will not be run for security reasons). The `smtp` and `popd` services will later be moved inside via port forwarding. DNS will be run from inside, but will only service the internal network. Primary DNS will be provided externally by the Internet provider.

Allow internal clients to use standard services on the Internet, except `nntp`. The following summarizes the policy you're going to implement:


```
Summary:
Default policy: prohibit
Anon FTP: external (deny incoming in to the firewall)
http: external (deny incoming in to the firewall)
ssh will be used: deny incoming telnet
smtp: firewall (future: port forward to internal machine)
popd: firewall (future: port forward to internal machine)
DNS: internal (no external access)
also stop incoming pings
```

`ipchains` GENERAL

In order to understand how to proceed with `ipchains`, you need to understand how `ipchains` works. The next few sections walk you through some of the finer points. Most `ipchains` text makes the assumption that all packets run through the *chains*, or list of rules. In fact, however, `ipchains` only sees a packet if that packet is the first or only packet. Subsequent packet fragments do not traverse the chains. The reason for this is simple—a host cannot reassemble the fragments into a packet until it has the first packet. If this packet is denied, the others time out and are dropped.

Tip

When you think *chain*, think of a logically grouped list of rules. Each rule in a chain is a test to apply against the IP header for a match.

The chains contain rules, numbered from one. As you will see, some rules can be referred to either by rule specification or by rule number.

A *rule specification* is the set of conditions that the packet must meet—the test. The same basic rule can exist in multiple chains, so the chain argument is normally required.

There are seven variations on the `ipchains` command line. The first six contain a command as the first argument. All six variations accept options as a final argument.

The commands are as follows (all commands are preceded by a hyphen):

- **`-A` (append)**—This takes a chain name and a rule specification as mandatory arguments.
- **`-D` (delete)**—This takes a chain name and a rule specification as mandatory arguments.
- **`-C` (test/check)**—`-s`, `-d`, `-p`, and `-i` are required. This takes a chain name and a rule specification as mandatory arguments.

- **-I (insert)**—An extension of append, but is placed ahead of the rule that is referenced.
- **-R (replace)**—An Insert and Delete. This takes as mandatory arguments a chain name, a rule number, and a rule specification.
- **-D (delete)**—This takes as mandatory arguments a chain name and rule number (this is a variation on the preceding delete command, where the rule number is known).
- **-F (flush)**—Delete all rules.
- **-Z (zero)**—Zero counters.
- **-N (new)**—Create a user-defined chain. This requires a chain name but otherwise works on all chains.
- **-X (delete a user-defined chain)**—This requires a chain name, and the chain must be empty, but otherwise works on all chains.
- **-P (policy)**—This takes as mandatory arguments a chain and a target.
- **-M (masquerade)**—This requires the following mandatory arguments:
  - **-L**—List
  - **-S**—Set tcp, tcpfin, udp

  The masquerade command, as opposed to the MASQ target, requires either `-L` or `-S`. The `-S` command requires three arguments: the `tcp` (TCP session), `tcpfin` (TCP session after receiving a FIN packet), and UDP timeout values in seconds.
- **-h (help)**—The seventh variation on the `ipchains` command line is `help`, which takes no commands, only accepts one option, and optionally accepts one argument.

  This option lists the usage argument (it can take the argument `icmp` to provide a list of ICMP code and type names that it knows can be used as arguments).

`ipchains` OPTIONS

A number of options are available for `ipchains`. These include some options to save mistyping a second rule when it is the same as the first but in the opposite direction, as well as a way to reverse the meaning of a parameter. Where address masks are specified, the mask can be of either of the following types: `/N` or `N.N.N.N`. Addresses can also be hostnames. Ports can be either numbers or service names.

The `-b` option enables you to specify one rule with a source and a destination address, but to have `ipchains` also build a rule with the addresses reversed.

The `!` can be used with a number of options to reverse the meaning. The options include the following:

- **`-p proto`**—Protocol. Can accept `!` (as in `-p ! icmp` to match all but `icmp` messages); or it can accept `all` to match all protocols.
- **`-s address`**—Source address. Can optionally take `!`, a netmask, or a port. Note that an address of 0/0 matches all addresses and is the default if `-s` is not specified. Because

ICMP doesn't use ports, you can follow `-s` with either an ICMP name, as listed by `ipchains -h icmp`, or a type number. If you use a name, you cannot also use `-d code`.

- **`-d address`**—Destination address. Same criteria as for `-s`. If you use `-s` and specify an ICMP type number, you can use `-d` and specify the code.
- **`-i name`**—Interface name. Can accept `!`. Also accepts a `+` suffix on the interface name to signify all interfaces of that type; that is, `ppp+` is all PPP interfaces (ppp0–pppN).
- **`-j target`**—Target for rule (user-defined chain name or special value), if it matches. If special value is `REDIRECT`, port can be included.
- **`-m mark`**—Number to mark on matching packets.
- **`-n`**—Numeric output of addresses and ports. By default, `ipchains` tries to resolve them.
- **`-l`**—Log matching packets. These are logged by the kernel.
- **`-o`**—Output matches to netdev, the userspace device.
- **`-t` and `xor`**—Masks for TOS field. Used to manipulate the TOS field.
- **`-v`**—Verbose mode. Outputs the interface address, rule options (if any), TOS masks, and packet and byte counters.
- **`-x`**—Expand numbers. When packet and byte counters are displayed, do not use the abbreviations K, M, or G, but display all zeros.
- **`-f`**—Second and further fragments. Can be preceded by `not`.
- **`-y`**—Matches TCP packets that have the SYN bit set. Can be preceded by `!`.

The following are valid ICMP types and subtypes (indented under the main type):

```
echo-reply (pong)
destination-unreachable
    network-unreachable
    host-unreachable
    protocol-unreachable
    port-unreachable
    fragmentation-needed
    source-route-failed
    network-unknown
    host-unknown
    network-prohibited
    host-prohibited
    TOS-network-unreachable
    TOS-host-unreachable
    communication-prohibited
    host-precedence-violation
    precedence-cutoff
```

```
source-quench
redirect
      network-redirect
      host-redirect
      TOS-network-redirect
      TOS-host-redirect
echo-request (ping)
router-advertisement
router-solicitation
time-exceeded (ttl-exceeded)
      ttl-zero-during-transit
      ttl-zero-during-reassembly
parameter-problem
      ip-header-bad
      required-option-missing
timestamp-request
timestamp-reply
address-mask-request
address-mask-reply
```

Table 30.1 lists the values that you need to use if you want to implement routing priorities based on the Type of Service (TOS).

TABLE 30.1 TOS MASKS

TOS Name	Value	Sample Uses
Minimum Delay	0x01 0x10	`ftp`, `telnet`, `ssh`
Maximum Throughput	0x01 0x08	FTP-data
Maximum Reliability	0x01 0x04	`snmp`, DNS
Minimum Cost	0x01 0x02	`nntp`, email

The TOS is only usable if you compiled support into the kernel (`CONFIG_IP_ROUTE_TOS`).

The `-o` option requires kernel support (`CONFIG_IP_FIREWALL_NETLINK`) and a device with major 36 and minor 3.

BUILT-IN CHAINS

The three built-in chains in `ipchains` are input, forward, and output. Other user-defined chains can be created and destroyed; these three, however, cannot be destroyed, and must always contain at least one rule. By default, these rules are all `DENY`.

As packets are received, they traverse these chains, rule by rule, in the following order: input, forward, output. They continue in the chain until a match is encountered. When a match is encountered, the chain is interrupted until the target is evaluated. If no target exists, the chain continues with the next rule.

A rule does not have to have a target. Perhaps you want to know how many packets match a certain rule. As the rule is matched, the rule counter is incremented. Combined with the counter for the chain, you can see how many of the packets that traversed the chain matched any particular rule.

If there is a target, `ipchains` evaluates the target. The target can either be a user-defined chain name or a special value. If it is a user-defined chain name, `ipchains` immediately transfers to that chain and begins traversing it. If no matches are found in the user-defined chain, `ipchains` returns to the chain that sent it, and continues with the next rule in the chain.

Tip

Think of user-defined chains as subroutines, and of the targets sending them as `GOSUBS`.

If there is a target and it is not a user-defined chain name, it must be one of the following special values:

- **`ACCEPT`**—This match is okay; jump to the next chain.
- **`DENY`**—Quietly drops the packet on the floor.
- **`REJECT`**—Same as **`DENY`**, but generates an `ICMP destination not reachable` response.
- **`MASQ`**—Masquerade: Forward and user-defined chains only.
- **`REDIRECT`**—Input and user-defined chains only; performs local redirection.
- **`RETURN`**—Jumps immediately to the end of the chain.

Tip

Think of the special values as a `GOTO`. This terminates the current chain and either starts on the next packet (`DENY`, `REJECT`) or sends the packet to the next built-in chain (or the calling chain, if you've jumped to a user-defined chain).

USER-DEFINED CHAINS

User-defined chains provide a way to group rules logically. These chains are called from built-in chains as targets. At any point in the chain, you can call a user-defined chain. When a user-defined chain terminates with no matches, it returns to the next argument in the calling chain.

When creating user-defined chains, names can be up to eight characters long. Names are lowercase because uppercase is not used, but is rather reserved for future use. The name cannot be one of the built-in names or special values.

HOW `ipchains` WORKS

When `ipchains` looks at an IP header, the following occurs, in this order:

- **`checksum` performed**—The packet is accepted and passed or denied and dropped.
- **`sanity check`**—This step looks for malformed packets and drops them.
- **`input chain`**—If it is not `DENY` or `REJECT`, continue to the next step.
- **`demasquerade`**—Responses to masqueraded hosts have address rewritten; otherwise, skip.
- **`routing`**—Sends the packet to `local process` or `forward chain`.
- **`local process`**—The interface changes to `lo` and, if it is destined for a local process, traverses the output and input chains; otherwise, it only traverses the output chain where the local process handles it.
- **`local`**—If the packet went through the local process, but did not originate locally—that is, if it came from a remote host but was processed locally for forwarding (proxy processing, port forward, and so on)—and the final destination is remote, `local` sends it to `forward chain`; otherwise it is sent to `output chain`, where, if it is not `DENY` or `REJECT`, it is passed to the localhost.
- **`forward chain`**—This is the chain for all packets that are using this host as a gateway to another remote host.
- **`output chain`**—This is for all the packets that are leaving this host.

> **Note**
>
> The preceding description of `local process` is confusing; but if you think of HOST and LOCALHOST as two different hosts, it makes more sense. To go from HOST to LOCALHOST, you must traverse all the rules (except `forward`), leaving HOST and entering LOCALHOST, and then going the other way for processes that are destined for remote hosts.

SIMPLE FIREWALL POLICIES

Now you're ready to get down to specifying what you want to filter. There are a few things to keep in mind. While you are making changes to rules, you can change /proc/sys/net/ipv4/ip_forward from 1 to 0 to turn off forwarding. This prevents things from slipping through while you're making changes. This is also the first place to look if nothing is passing through your firewall when you expect it to.

> **Caution**
>
> If you change all the built-in chain policies to `DENY` or `REJECT`, make sure that you do not specify rules that require lookups. Use IP addresses, not host names.

Keep in mind, also, that rules are matched in order. The first rule to match with a special value terminates that chain (except as explained previously), so be careful about which rules come first. Take a look at the following rule: `ipchains -I input 1 -j REJECT` (insert, as the first rule, `REJECT`). Because this rule has no `-s`, it applies to all addresses. Furthermore, because it has no `-i`, it applies to all interfaces. Finally, with no `-p`, it applies to all protocols. Essentially, this rule rejects everything, even messages from localhost.

So to start, always keep your policies simple and build on them from there.

WHAT TO FILTER AND WHERE

Sometimes you need to think about not only what you want to filter, but where. Suppose you don't want to answer `ping` packets for any host. You can handle this in two ways—but only one makes good sense. The first way is to deny or reject `echo-requests` as follows:

```
ipchains -A input -s echo-request -j DENY
```

The second way is to deny or reject the `echo-response` before it goes out:

```
ipchains -A output -s echo-response -j DENY
```

Although both of these work, they have very different effects. You probably want to use the first method. Normally, your first response is correct. But be aware that both of these prevent the sender from receiving a reply. If the `ping` packet happens to be a `big-ping` and is being sent to a vulnerable host inside your network, the first method works (if you compiled `CONFIG_IP_ALWAYS_DEFRAG`). The second method does not.

WHAT NOT TO FILTER

Some administrators believe that ICMP packets are not that important. They equate `icmp` with `ping`. Unfortunately, a number of other important network messages use ICMP. The destination-not-reachable messages travel this way, so you won't receive them. Although TCP normally times out, these ICMP messages still need to be passed. Your OpenLinux system, for example, uses ICMP messages to set the maximum transmission unit (MTU). For Ethernet, this is normally 1500 for maximum throughput. Fragmenting causes more delays than dropping the MTU. So Linux sets the Don't Fragment (DF) bit. If a host or router needs to fragment the packets, it can't because the DF bit is set, so it drops the packet and sends an ICMP message. Linux drops the MTU and tries again until it can pass packets. If you don't accept ICMP messages, your connections with some hosts might be excruciatingly slow.

Most administrators are also aware that DNS uses UDP, and they want to block TCP on port 53 (the DNS port). But when DNS needs to do a zone transfer or other large data transfer, it switches to TCP.

The bottom line is this: If you experience network problems after implementing certain rules, back the rules out until you stop experiencing the problem, and then reimplement them one at a time, with logging turned on, until you can isolate the problem.

Implementing the Policies

Now all that's left is to implement the policies. Declare a few variables because this reduces errors. Follow these steps:

1. Use the following names, which are similar to the ones in the previous summary:

```
foo1int=209.191.169.1/25      # this is eth0
foo2int=209.191.169.129/25    # this is eth1
fooall=209.191.169.0/24    # so you can specify both subnets
```

2. Stop pings that come from outside:

```
ipchains -A input -s echo-request -i eth1 -j DENY #incoming
➥pings from outside denied
```

3. Now pass all traffic from inside out (except nntp):

```
ipchains -A input -s foo1int ! 119 -d 0/0 -i eth0 -j ACCEPT
```

4. Block those pesky services that are a common security problem or that you just don't want, such as `telnet`, `ftp`, `http`, and `imap`:

```
ipchains -A input -i eth1 -s 0/0 -d fooall 23 -j DENY
ipchains -A input -i eth1 -s 0/0 -d fooall telnet -j DENY
ipchains -A input -i eth1 -s 0/0 -d fooall 80 -j DENY
ipchains -A input -i eth1 -s 0/0 -d fooall imap -j DENY
```

Note

In the previous step, you really don't need to specify `eth1` because if it came from `eth0`, you've already accepted it previously and, therefore, you won't get the chance to deny it.

5. Be sure to accept DNS (on `foo1int` only), `ssh`, and returns on most upper ports (and on both networks) as well as `smtp` and `pop-3`:

```
ipchains -A input -p all -s 0/0 -d foo1int domain -j ACCEPT
ipchains -A input -p tcp -s 0/0 -d fooall 22 -j ACCEPT
ipchains -A input -p tcp -s 0/0 -d fooall 1024:5999 -j ACCEPT
ipchains -A input -p tcp -s 0/0 -d fooall 6010: -j ACCEPT
ipchains -A input -p tcp -s 0/0 -d fooall 25 -j ACCEPT
ipchains -A input -p tcp -s 0/0 -d fooall pop-3 -j ACCEPT
```

6. Verify that localhost packets are okay:

```
ipchains -A input -i lo -j ACCEPT
```

7. Block the rest:

```
ipchains -P input DENY
```

8. You want to forward both ways—the input rules are taking care of most of the work:

```
ipchains -P forward ACCEPT
```

9. Make some optimizations:

   - Minimum delay for Web, `telnet`, and `ssh` traffic:

   ```
   ipchains -A output -p tcp -d 0/0 80 -t 0x01 0x10
   ipchains -A output -p tcp -d 0/0 telnet -t 0x01 0x10
   ipchains -A output -p tcp -d 0/0 22 -t 0x01 0x10
   ```

- Maximum throughput for FTP-data:
  `ipchains -A output -p tcp -d 0/0 ftp-data 0x01 0x08`
- Maximum reliability for `smtp`:
  `ipchains -A output -d tcp -d 0/0 smtp 0x01 0x04`
- Minimum cost for `pop-3`:
  `ipchains -A output -d tcp -d 0/0 pop-3 0x01 0x02`
- To finish up (if you got this far, just let it go), enter the following rule:
  `ipchains -P output ACCEPT`

There's just one more rule that you might want in order to stop IP spoofing (by someone from the outside who is pretending to be you). No one should connect to the external interface, claiming to be from the inside. The following rule enables you to log these attempts and reject them:

```
ipchains -I input 1 -i eth1 -s foo1int -l -j REJECT
```

Testing the Policies

The easiest way to test the policies is to make up a few cases that you do and don't want to get through and use the `ipchains` check option (`-C`). You'll probably want to use the `-v` option to get a verbose listing of the check. This tells you if the packet is passed. Remember that the `-C` option requires `-s` with address and port, `-d` with address and port, `-p`, and `-i` in addition to the chain name.

Often, enabling logging for some rules can help. This needs to be used judiciously or you will have very large logs, very quickly. One rule at a time is a good idea.

Monitoring

Remember to look through the logs from time to time, particularly if you put in rules that are designed to detect attacks. Furthermore, just in case someone does break in, you might want to have a trusted internal host doing your syslogging for you.

`tcpd`, `tripwire`, `courtney`, and all the other tools don't do any good if they are not properly used and checked. The first thing an attacker does is look for these things. Time is what your firewall is buying you. However, time works *for* the attacker and *against* you. The best time to catch an attack is before the penetration occurs, when your network is being probed. To enter, an attacker must find your weaknesses. This way, you will have warning. It might not be much, though.

Under Attack

After you've been probed or attacked, you need to have a plan to deal with the situation: Do you allow it to continue in an attempt to track it, or do you stop it cold? Do you alert the authorities? (It *is* a crime.) Do you have the authority to contact the police? If not, who does?

These—and many more—questions are all part of a good network security policy. But it is just as important to practice what you'll do when the time comes. Note that I said *when*, not *if*. Some Internet sites that carry tools for crackers are a constant source of new exploits, so finding out how the attacker entered, if possible, is essential to preventing a recurrence.

NETWORK SECURITY POLICY

Possibly the greatest failing of most companies is the lack of a coherent network security policy. A good policy explains clearly the network policy, penalties for violation of the policies, and enforcement guidelines (what happens to violators). This policy must apply to all—equally. A synthesis of this policy (two or three sentences) needs to be posted on Web and FTP sites to warn guests.

But the document should not focus on the prohibitive/punitive side. Rather, a good policy needs to cover the actions that are to be taken, as well as when and by whom, when your security is at risk. Furthermore, it needs to cover a reasonable timeline for the eventuality that someone, somewhere will at least attempt to penetrate your security. When an attack is discovered, what actions are taken? This includes discovery of the attempt after the fact as well as during an ongoing attack. A number of responses are possible in each situation, but because time is often the key element, those who are involved must know their part. In many larger companies, emergency response teams have been designated. A good reference is RFC-2196, "Site Security Handbook". All current RFCs are available from `http://www.rfc-editor.org/rfc.html`.

SUMMARY

In this chapter, you learned about what a firewall is, the different kinds of firewalls that are available for Linux, and how they work. You also learned how `ipchains` works and how to set it up. Then you looked at some things that you can do with `ipchains` via some of the rules. For more information on firewalls, refer to the following chapters:

- Chapter 17 discusses how to build a custom kernel. The more you understand about which options you do and don't need in your kernel, the better it can support your firewall.
- See Chapter 23, "Advanced Network Features," to learn more about services and how they work. Understanding services helps you decide how to build your ipchains rules.
- See Chapter 29 to learn how to masquerade a network and use it to hide your internal network. The more you know about how to hide your system and network configuration from an attacker, the more secure it will be.

CHAPTER 31

TCP Wrappers

In this chapter

This chapter deals with a security tool that will help you detect and aid in preventing intrusions and intrusion attempts, and to track intruders back to their source.

On the intrusion early warning and prevention side, you'll look at TCP wrappers—what they are, how they work, and how to configure this facility. Because of the nature of TCP wrappers, it is expected that the reader already has a firm grasp of /etc/inetd.conf, what it contains, and its file format. (For more information on inetd.conf, see Chapter 23, "Advanced Network Features.")

WHAT ARE TCP WRAPPERS?

A *wrapper* is something that is put around something else to protect it or modify its environment. TCP wrappers are put around server programs to help protect the host from exploit via that program, or to track abusers as they access the programs in an attempt to circumvent security safeguards. Although not a foolproof method of preventing intrusions, TCP wrappers do provide good early warning—via system logging—of possible intrusion attempts, and they are one more piece of the puzzle used to prevent subsequent intrusions and to track intruders back to their source.

Perhaps a better way to explain what TCP wrappers are is to explain what they aren't. TCP wrappers aren't a program that can be run around every process on the machine—they are only effective for some programs run by the inetd metadaemon. Processes with which TCP wrappers are only partially effective, or totally ineffective, include the `r` commands (for example, `rlogin`, `rsh`) and `udp` based services. Unless the `r` services are absolutely vital (for most, better substitutes exist), they need to be shut off by commenting out the line that calls them in /etc/inetd.conf, and then sending a SIGHUP to inetd.

HOW TCP WRAPPERS WORK

The TCP wrappers program is called in place of the actual service that it is to protect. There are two different methods for implementing TCP wrappers. The first is to simply replace the actual program with tcpd (the TCP wrapper daemon). Because this is a rather limited usage, and because the second method is more flexible, this chapter looks exclusively at the second implementation method—to have either the inetd metadaemon call tcpd for every invocation of a daemon, or to use tcpd within the /etc/hosts.allow file for certain patterns.

Some of the functionality of TCP wrappers is based on compile-time options. If you desire or require any of this functionality that is not built by default, you'll need to recompile, and turn the features on (or off). One of the default compile-time features is `PARANOID`. With this turned on, TCP wrappers perform name-to-address lookups via DNS and compare them to address-to-name lookups for the client that is requesting the connection. If this check fails, TCP wrappers assume that the client is trying to fool (*spoof*) you as to his true identity; in that case, the connection is dropped. Some sites might want to recompile to include this functionality.

The daemon provided in the Caldera OpenLinux distribution has been compiled without the PARANOID option because other rules can then run. Because PARANOID immediately drops the connection if the forward and reverse names don't match, it doesn't allow other rules to fire.

Another reason not to include PARANOID is that many hosts connected to the Internet do not have DNS listings, so the reverse lookups fail. They also fail if the primary and secondary DNS servers happen to be offline. So unless you have a compelling reason to include PARANOID, it's probably better not to, and to handle those suspect connections in another manner.

Another related function has to do with source-routing. TCP wrappers can be compiled to disallow host address spoofing by ignoring source routing information provided by the client. (This is not effective for udp-based services.)

A final compile-time option is RFC 931 lookups. This uses the ident daemon running on the remote machine. Because few PCs run the ident daemon, turning this feature on results in response times in excess of 10 seconds (the default timeout) for those clients. This feature is also not effective for udp-based services.

The OpenLinux version of tcpd does not use most of the compile-time options. Although this is always subject to change, the package is compiled in a way that is most useful to the most users, that is, without PARANOID, RFC 931 lookups, or ignoring source routing. Other packages (such as ipchains—see Chapter 30, "IP Firewalling") or the 2.2.x kernel itself have features that can be activated to prevent IP spoofing and ignore source routing. If you still insist on having these features compiled into tcpd, however, consult Chapter 16, "How to Build/Rebuild a package."

TCP wrappers uses the syslog facility to log captured information pertaining to client:daemon connections. You'll look at the specifics of this configuration in the following sections.

Implementing TCP Wrappers

You can begin to use the TCP wrappers daemon by finding the line in /etc/inetd that looks similar to the following:

```
telnet          stream  tcp     nowait  root    /usr/sbin/in.telnetd
➥  /usr/sbin/in.telnetd
```

Change it to look like the following:

```
telnet          stream  tcp     nowait  root    /usr/sbin/tcpd
➥  /usr/sbin/in.telnetd
```

inetd starts tcpd, and when tcpd has logged the client:daemon request—and has satisfied any conditions—it starts the telnet daemon.

Note

inetd needs to be signaled to reread the /etc/inetd.conf file by sending the SIGHUP signal after each change.

At this point, you have a log of all connection attempts to the telnet port. You can do this for every service started by inetd that you are not denying in inetd.conf simply by using tcpd as the target and making the argument the service daemon (as shown previously).

Sometimes, however, this might not be the real intention. For example, say you want to log all attempts to connect to services, but don't want to provide certain services, such as telnet. You just want to use the logging facilities to provide early warning of intrusion attempts. For this, look at your /etc/hosts.allow and hosts.deny files.

Originally, tcpd required both hosts.allow and hosts.deny for full functionality. Although this option is available for those wanting to use it, you can now consolidate everything into /etc/hosts.allow and maintain only one file. This one-file-fits-all configuration (looked at later in this chapter) is enabled by ensuring that tcpd is compiled with the PROCESS_OPTIONS turned on (this is the default with OpenLinux). Some syntax, specifically in the shell commands used by the two different methods (with and without hosts.deny), is different. So blindly combining the two files into one can produce unexpected results, and is not recommended.

Tip

As rules are being written, remember that the first match terminates the search, so subsequent rules are not processed.

The format for the hosts.allow file is as follows:

```
daemon(s) : client(s) : option : option ...
```

Each line is a colon-separated list. Start with any daemons that you are interested in protecting, followed by a client list, and then any number of options you need, with each option separated by a colon. If any option uses colons within the option (as in a `PATH` statement), the colons that are not used as column separators must be protected by a backslash (\). Also, every line, including the last line in the file, must be terminated by a newline or it will not be executed.

Start by taking a look at valid values for each of the columns.

DAEMONS AND WILDCARDS

The daemon list is a list of daemons separated by white space and/or commas. It is only the daemon name itself as it is on the system, that is, in.telnetd. In the case of multihomed hosts, the form daemon@host is acceptable to differentiate one bound NIC from another. Wildcards are also acceptable. Valid wildcards include the following:

- **`ALL`**—Universal match (all daemons/hosts).
- **`LOCAL`**—Matches hosts whose name do not contain a dot, as in the hosts foo or baz.
- **`UNKNOWN`**—Matches any user whose name is unknown, or any host whose name or address is unknown.
- **`KNOWN`**—Matches any known user, and any host whose name and address are both known.
- **`PARANOID`**—Matches any host whose name does not match its address.

Note that KNOWN and UNKNOWN are subject to the vagaries of DNS. When said service is unavailable, these wildcards might not match properly. Likewise, with PARANOID, if DNS is not available, the hostname does not match an address.

Clients, Patterns, and Hostnames

The client list is a list of host name(s), host IP address(es), patterns (see next paragraph), or wildcards to be matched.

Patterns can take one of the following forms: leading or trailing dot.

If you have the following hosts table in your system (foo)

```
192.168.0.1  foo.void.org  foo
192.168.0.2  bar.void.org  bar
192.168.0.3  baz.void.org  baz
```


you can specify as a hostname .void.org, and match foo, bar, or baz at .void.org. If you omit the leading ., only the (non-existent) host void.org is matched. Likewise, if you specify 192.168.0. as a host, you match all hosts that have an address beginning with 192.168.0.

Forms and Operators

You can also use a network/netmask form to match a range, as in 192.168.0.0/255.255.255.128. This matches 192.168.0.0 through 192.168.0.127. So an individual host can be singled out by using a specific host address and a netmask of 255.255.255.255.

The final pattern match possible is of the form @ and the netgroup name (valid for clients only). Note that this form is only available if you are running NIS. The netgroup name is case sensitive.

One operator is possible for use in either daemon or client lists: EXCEPT. Exercise caution if EXCEPT is to be nested. An argument in the form a EXCEPT b EXCEPT c translates as (a EXCEPT (b EXCEPT c)).

Two basic options that you'll want to use are ALLOW and DENY. You will look at more advanced options later.

Rules

You now have enough information to create some basic rules:

- `ALL : LOCAL, .void.org EXCEPT dab@bar.void.org : ALLOW`
- `ALL EXCEPT in.telnetd : dab@bar.void.org : ALLOW`
- `in.ftpd : ALL : ALLOW`
- `ALL : ALL : DENY`

These rules allow any host from void.org, unless it is the user dab connecting to you from bar.void.org in an attempt to use any of the services (maybe he's attempted a telnet exploit from here, so you disallow him telnet via rule 2). Everyone is allowed ftp access. Anyone else attempting to connect to any other service is denied. The order of most of the preceding rules above is unimportant because they don't overlap. However, if rule 4 is moved up, all rules following it become academic.

Additional options with any of these rules can include shell commands, network options, lookup options, and miscellaneous options. Two commands enable you to run shell commands as options: spawn and twist.

The spawn command enables you to run a shell command as one of your options, and does not interfere with client/server communications because all stdin, stdout, and stderr are directed to /dev/null. A common usage for this is described in the man pages as follows:

```
spawn (/path/to/safe_finger -l @%h ¦ /usr/bin/mail root) &
```

The preceding command mails root the results of a safe_finger on a connecting system (character expansion is explained later). The preceding can be used with DENY as an option to booby-trap services not offered to outsiders. Be careful not to use this on the in.fingerd daemon—you can finger a host that fingers you, that you then finger back, ad infinitum (or until one of you runs out of resources). In the preceding example, you might want to add a rule 3 that is similar to the following:

```
in.telnetd : dab@bar.void.org : spawn (/usr/sbin/safe_finger -l @%h \
        ¦ /usr/bin/mail root) & : DENY
```

This tells root when dab@bar.void.org has been attempting to use telnet again. Add this just after the second line in your hosts.allow file.

> **Note**
>
> Note that long lines can be broken into two lines by making the last character of the first line a \ (as in the preceding example).

A second way to invoke a shell command is to use twist. The difference between spawn and twist is that spawn sends all communications to /dev/null, whereas twist sends all communications back to the client. This can be used to substitute a different command for the usual one:

```
in.ftpd : ... : twist /bin/echo 421 Message to client
```

twist must be the last option on the line. Instead of invoking the ftp daemon, the previous line sends a 421 Message to client to any client matching the in.ftpd rule.

Other options include: keepalive, linger, rfc931, banner, nice, setenv, umask, and user. These are used as follows:

- **keepalive (no arguments)**—The server periodically sends a keepalive packet to the client. If the client does not respond, the server terminates. This is useful for users who turn off their machines while still connected to the server.
- **linger *<number of seconds>***—Length of time the kernel is to continue to try to send undelivered data to the client after a connection is closed.

- **rfc931 [*timeout in seconds*]**—Perform RFC 931 username lookups. Only valid for TCP. If the client is not running IDENT or a similar RFC 931 service (as is the case with many PCs), noticeable connection delays can result. Timeout is optional; if it is not specified, compile-time default is used.
- **banners </*some*/*path*>**—Look in */some/path/* for a file with the same name as the daemon process (for example, in.telnetd for the telnet service), and then copy its contents to the client. This option uses character expansion within the file (explained as follows). Banners only work with TCP connections.
- **nice [*number*]**—Change the `nice` value from its default of 10.
- **setenv <*name value*>**—Used to set environment variables for those daemons that don't reset their environment on startup. The *value* is subject to character expansion.
- **umask < *octal* >**—Similar to the shell `umask` variable.
- **user <*user*[.*group*]>**—Sets the daemon's user and, optionally, the group.

Character Expansion

The following character expansions can be used as noted previously:

- **%a (%A)**—The client (server) host address.
- **%c**—Returns client information depending on what's available. Can be a user@host or IP address, or just an IP address.
- **%d**—The daemon process name (for example, in.telnetd)
- **%h (%H)**—Client (server) hostname or IP address.
- **%n (%N)**—Client (server) hostname (or `unknown` or `paranoid` if not available).
- **%p**—Daemon process ID.
- **%s**—Server information: daemon@host or IP address, or just a daemon name, depending on available information.
- **%u**—Username (or unknown).
- **%%**—Expands to single `%`.

Miscellaneous Concerns

There are, however, some problems with implementing tcpd for all services. As noted earlier, `r` commands and `udp` won't work effectively—if at all—and neither will RPC-based services (indicated by `rpc/tcp`) work. Another stopping point comes from the use of `wait` instead of `nowait` with services. A service using `wait` lingers on the queue for other connections. TCP wrappers log only the first connection request (the one that spawned the service), but not any subsequent ones while the same service is still alive. So a second connection can occur with no logging for daemons already sitting on the wait queue.

Do not use TCP wrappers with the Apache Web Server. Apache has the TCP wrappers functionality built into it. Use of tcpd in this case is redundant. The Apache configuration is similar to tcpd, so it will be understandable to anyone already familiar with tcpd.

tcpdchk

`tcpdchk` is a utility that enables you to see what kind of syntax errors you've made while creating your /etc/hosts.allow file. The utility has several options, including `-d`; this option enables you to start from a directory other than /etc, create your hosts.allow file, and then test against that file before replacing the one that you are currently using. The `-d` option reads the hosts.allow file in the current directory (rather than in /etc). Obviously, this option is somewhat limiting if you are already in /etc.

By using the `-v` option, you can see every line that `tcpdchk` is reading, and how it operates. See Listing 31.1 for a sample output.

LISTING 31.1 SAMPLE `tcpdchk` TEST OUTPUT

```
# tcpdchk -v
Using network configuration file: /etc/inetd.conf

>>> Rule /etc/hosts.allow line 1:
daemons:  ALL
clients:  .void.org EXCEPT dab@bar.void.org
option:   ALLOW
access:   granted

>>> Rule /etc/hosts.allow line 2:
daemons:  ALL EXCEPT in.telnetd
clients:  dab@bar.void.org
option:   ALLOW
access:   granted

>>> Rule /etc/hosts.allow line 4:
daemons:  in.telnetd
clients:  dab@bar.void.org
option:   spawn (/usr/sbin/safe_finger -l @client_hostname ¦
➥/usr/bin/mail root) &
option:   DENY
access:   denied

>>> Rule /etc/hosts.allow line 5:
daemons:  in.ftpd
clients:  ALL
option:   ALLOW
access:   granted

>>> Rule /etc/hosts.allow line 6:
daemons:  ALL
clients:  ALL
option:   DENY
access:   denied
```

If tcpdchk is having trouble finding your /etc/inetd.conf file, -i path/to/inetd.conf can be used.

Finally, the -a option checks for any ALLOWs that aren't explicitly declared, that is, which daemons can be started by a client as a result of omitting a statement to specifically ALLOW them.

tcpdmatch

The tcpdmatch utility enables you to test specific examples against your configuration files. Again, tcpdmatch enables you to test against a hosts.allow file in your current directory by specifying the -d option. It also recognizes the -i/path/to/inetd.conf if tcpdmatch has trouble finding it.

The syntax for tcpdmatch is as follows:

```
tcpdmatch daemon[@server] [user@]client
```

The server option is for multihomed hosts, and the user is for specific users at a client.

See Listing 31.2 for sample tpcdmatch output.

LISTING 31.2 FOUR SAMPLE tcpdmatch OUTPUTS

```
# tcpdmatch in.telnetd bar
warning: bar: hostname alias
warning: (official name: bar.void.org)
client:   hostname bar.void.org
client:   address  192.168.0.2
server:   process  in.telnetd
matched:  /etc/hosts.allow line 1
option:   ALLOW
access:   granted

# tcpdmatch in.telnetd dab@bar
warning: bar: hostname alias
warning: (official name: bar.void.org)
client:   hostname bar.void.org
client:   address  192.168.0.2
client:   username dab
server:   process  in.telnetd
matched:  /etc/hosts.allow line 4
option:   spawn (/usr/sbin/safe_finger -l @bar.void.org |
➥ /usr/bin/mail root) &
option:   DENY
access:   denied

# tcpdmatch in.ftpd rim.caldera.com
client:   hostname rim.caldera.com
client:   address  207.179.39.2
server:   process  in.ftpd
matched:  /etc/hosts.allow line 5
```

continues

LISTING 31.2 CONTINUED

```
option:    ALLOW
access:    granted

# tcpdmatch in.telnetd rim.caldera.com
client:    hostname rim.caldera.com
client:    address  207.179.39.2
server:    process  in.telnetd
matched:   /etc/hosts.allow line 6
option:    DENY
access:    denied
```

SUMMARY

In this chapter you learned what TCP Wrappers are and how to implement them. You learned about the flexibility you have in their implementation, and that some of this flexibility is based on compile-time options. You also learned which options are compiled into the OpenLinux version of tcpd. You learned how to booby trap services in inetd.conf, and even how to send messages back to the client. For further information, refer to the following chapters:

- See Chapter 23 to learn more about services and inetd.conf.
- See Chapter 30 to learn more about alternative strategies to protect your network and services. The more complementary tools you use, the better your overall network security posture will be.

CHAPTER 32

Sharing Files via NFS

In this chapter

As soon as you have more than one computer on a network, certain conveniences become apparent. It is nice to sit down at any system on the network and have access to the same mail, the same files, and the same programs. It is even better if instead of having to put every single file on all the computers, the files can be shared. This saves disk space as well.

The original implementation for the capability to share files and directories over the network was developed by Sun Microsystems. Called the *Network File System*, or *NFS*, it allowed directories to be mounted from one computer to hosts across the network. This system also allowed any computer that understood NFS to mount or share its file system seamlessly with other hosts, whether they were other UNIX flavors, or even Macintosh or PC systems. From this was born the concept of "the network is the computer."

PREPARATION FOR NFS

The Linux kernel can be configured to permit or deny the use of NFS. In order for NFS operations to be permitted, they must be configured into the kernel. In the older 2.0.x kernels, one parameter, `CONFIG_NFS_FS`, must be either `y` (yes) or `m` (module). On the 2.2.x kernels, two parameters must be considered, and a third is optional.

The newer kernels can support only mounting NFS directories from other systems, can support making directories on the local machine available to other machines (called exporting), or can do both. The third parameter has to do with exporting a local file system for mounting locally. Sun supports this on Solaris, so the option is available to allow Linux to export a file system, such as /export/home, and mount it on /home.

To configure systems to mount NFS directories, you must choose either yes or module for `CONFIG_NFS_FS`. If you want to have the capability to export directories, `CONFIG_NFSD` must be either yes or module. You can, of course, choose both. The optional argument, that of `CONFIG_NFSD_SUN`, is probably only of interest to those who are comfortable with the Sun way of configuring NFS file systems. This option is not recommended because it makes administration more complex. Unless you have good reason not to, modules are recommended for NFS. This permits you to unload the module and stop use of NFS if you need to, and it makes the kernel smaller and faster.

PLANNING NFS MOUNTS

The time to think about NFS directories is prior to installing your first system. You might not think that you will need it, but as soon as you add a second host to the local network, you'll be glad you did. Rearranging everything after the fact makes it much more difficult because you might have files scattered across several machines in "common" directories.

So which directories make sense to share via NFS and which do not? Looking at the file structure, some are obvious. You probably want to share /home because this is where users keep not only their files, but also their personal configurations. If they have their $HOME directory following them from machine to machine, when they log in, every machine looks and feels the same, making them more comfortable and productive.

This applies to mail as well. Depending on how you're handling mail, it might also make sense to export the mailhub's /var/spool/mail directory to each machine.

Often, in larger installations where it is important to maintain a consistency of applications across a network, the /usr directory is exported. But this poses some interesting problems, which are addressed in the next few paragraphs.

PREPARING THE FILE SYSTEMS

In the previous paragraphs you looked at those file systems that you want to share—but what about those you don't want to share? In fact, this constitutes a large number of directories. You need to have all the files necessary to boot a system on that system (excluding network computers that NFS-mount their entire root directory structure). That means that /bin, /boot, /dev, /etc, /lib, /sbin, and /var are not to be exported—at least not in their entirety.

Caution

Never export the /proc file system. Doing so puts your entire system at risk from anyone with malicious intent that might gain access to your network. Additionally, only the local machine needs any information contained within.

Also notice that in the preceding example you considered /usr in its entirety as an NFS. But within /usr, you have /usr/local. Normally, /usr/local is where files specific to a local host's installation are maintained. So how do you deal with that? The best recommendation here is to move the local directory from /usr to another location (such as the root directory or under /var) and put a symlink in /usr that points to it.

Another problem that you might encounter in exporting a file system such as /usr is that it includes /usr/X11R6. This becomes a problem only if you are running X servers on different machines. It is very likely that these different machines have different hardware (video cards and monitors). Therefore, any symlink in /usr/X11R6 from X to a specific X server needed for one machine might be pointing to the wrong X server executable for another machine. The previous paragraph (as well as Chapter 37, "Configuring X") points out this problem and suggests a solution. Because you are not NFS exporting /etc, it is safe (and indeed prudent) to make the symlink /usr/X11R6/X point somewhere such as /etc/X11/X first, with /etc/X11/X then pointing to the correct X server binary for that particular host. This entails ensuring that the needed binaries for the different hardware exist in the exported directory.

The final problem that might need to be addressed concerns those software packages that use the flexlm licensing scheme. When these packages are installed, a license file is installed in a subdirectory of /etc called flexlm/licenses. Although copying these licenses to each machine is an obvious solution, it allows more copies of the software to run than the number of licenses that are owned. So within /etc, you might want to export flexlm so that only that number of copies of the software that you own can be run at any given time.

Note that below /var, you might have other subdirectories that it makes sense to share. Consider a number of factors, including whether or not the directories (or any subdirectories) contain dynamic information that is applicable only to the local host—particularly information that might confuse other hosts, such as lock files, temporary files, and so on. Fonts, for example, although they can be exported, need to be shared by other, more appropriate methods, such as via a font server, as discussed in Chapter 39, "Customizing X."

REQUIRED CONFIGURATION FILES AND PROGRAMS

Simply wanting to start using NFS and exporting the file system will not give you the results you want. The way NFS is shared across a network is slightly more complicated. Several different configuration files and programs are involved. You'll see in the following sections which programs are involved, and which configuration files are needed.

PROGRAMS FOR NFS

Before looking at the specific programs involved in NFS, a few words regarding how NFS is implemented are in order. NFS uses *RPC*, *remote procedure calls*, in order to work. This is because different systems that might use NFS might have different system calls. RPC levels the field, making calls across the network and allowing each system to interpret the calls and translate them into local system calls.

In order to use RPC, the first program run must be `/sbin/portmap`. This program maps each port that is used by an RPC program to the specific daemon. So as each RPC daemon is started, it contacts the portmapper to register itself. If the portmap daemon dies or crashes, it is necessary to stop and restart all RPC daemons. Generally, RPC daemons use UDP over IP for communications because UDP is more efficient than TCP on a local network and results in less traffic. However, NFS on Linux can work via TCP if necessary.

One program that is useful for examining what the portmapper knows about is `rpcinfo`. This program provides you (or anyone else who can query your hosts, for that matter) with information regarding your hosts (see Listing 32.1).

LISTING 32.1 OUTPUT OF `rpcinfo -p foo`

```
program vers proto   port
    100000    2   tcp    111  portmapper
    100000    2   udp    111  portmapper
    100003    2   udp   2049  nfs
    100003    2   tcp   2049  nfs
    100005    1   udp    869  mountd
    100005    2   udp    869  mountd
    100005    1   tcp    872  mountd
    100005    2   tcp    872  mountd
```

Hosts that do not support NFS over TCP do not have the corresponding entries.

In OpenLinux, Caldera has opted to use the naming convention that has become common in recent years: renaming daemons such as nfsd and mountd that use RPC as rpc.nfsd and rpc.mountd, respectively.

This brings up two more programs with which you need to be concerned: rpc.nfsd, which is the NFS daemon, and rpc.mountd, which is the mount daemon for NFS. As was stated earlier, these must be started after the portmapper in order to register themselves. These two programs are the two that actually do all the work in serving the exported directories to clients.

The `nfsd` program has a number of arguments that can be passed to it. Some of the more notable ones include `-d call` and `-f`, which are usually used together to debug `nfsd` in the foreground. The `-l` option allows `nfsd` to log transfers, and is particularly useful when used with the `-R`, or public root option, and `-p`, for promiscuous mode. These enable you to provide a public NFS server at which you can log transactions, just like FTP. The public root option requires a corresponding entry in the /etc/exports file (see the example under "Restricting Mount Access" that follows). The port number that NFS uses (2049 by default) can be changed by using the `-P #` option. Finally, you can allow clients that mount your directories to re-export them by specifying the `-r` option. Other options are available, but are of limited value.

Caution

When allowing re-export of a directory, be sure that you do not permit re-entry into the exported directory, or NFS locks up. That is, if host foo is exporting /usr and host bar has a directory /usr/X11R6, do not export /usr/X11R6 to mount under /usr on host foo, and then mount /usr on host bar. Because this is a circular reference, it cannot be resolved and results in a "cat chasing its tail" situation.

The `mountd` program, like the `nfsd` program, enables you to troubleshoot using the `-d` and `-f` options to put the program that is in the foreground in debug mode. It also has a corresponding `-r` option to re-export imported mounts. The program can also be put into promiscuous mode with `-p`, or have its port number specified with `-P #`. Normally, `mountd` uses a random port below 1024 (one not already reserved). This can be changed by specifying the port on the command line or in the /etc/services file.

Note

If you are using modules, although the daemons might be started, you cannot share directories if the nfsd.o module is not loaded. Furthermore, if the nfs.o module is not loaded, you cannot mount directories. This can result in an RPC error on the client that the program is not registered, the same as if the portmapper were started after the RPC daemons on the server.

One final program that is of interest is the `showmount` program, which shows you what it believes are file systems mounted on other hosts. This program does little more than read the /etc/rmtab file, which is a table of remotely mounted directories. However, the information contained in this file, and therefore the information returned by `showmount`, might be totally inaccurate. Although entries are made in /etc/rmtab, they are often not removed, giving a false sense of what is exported.

CONFIGURATION FILES

A number of configuration files affect the NFS programs. The first is /etc/hosts.allow. Earlier, you saw that `rpcinfo` enables anyone with access to your network to find out which RPC programs you are running and on which ports. To prevent this, you can disallow hosts that will not be using your RPC services from accessing the portmapper. The following lines in /etc/hosts.allow restrict clients:

```
portmap: .bar.org : allow
portmap: ALL : deny
```

These two lines permit all the hosts in the domain bar.org to connect.

Note

The order in which these lines appear is important. The first match is the one that determines acceptance or denial, so put the more specific ones first. If the `portmap: ALL: deny` line is first, it denies everyone, and the line to allow `.bar.org` is never even considered.

Similar lines can be used to restrict access to rpc.mountd and rpc.nfsd. (See Chapter 31, "TCP Wrappers," for more information.)

The next file to look at is the /etc/fstab file. This file is used on the client machines to determine which NFS directories from which NFS servers to mount where. Lines in /etc/fstab look like the following:

```
server:/exported/directory    /mount/point    nfs    options,rsize=8192,etc
```

You'll note that this format is different from standard mounts in that the two final arguments are not included. Also note that white space separates the various arguments, so no white space can appear in the options, or else `mount` stops reading the options at that point. The options that are available to the `mount` command for NFS mounts are different from the standard options. The options for NFS mounts are principally concerned with network behavior, and therefore modify the defaults. Two values that are of interest are the read and write size (`rsize=` and `wsize=`). By default, the value is 1024 bytes. This can be changed in the kernel source, but it is easier to do using these variables. Increasing the size to 8192 improves performance.

Another option that is of interest is `intr`. This option is only valid with the default hard mount, and permits operations on NFS files to be interrupted. Without this, a program would continue trying forever to access the file system. This option needs to always be used with hard mounts, which are the best. If the network is unreliable, a better option might be to specify `soft` as an option. With a soft mount, NFS operations time out, rather than try forever, if a `server not responding` message is received.

More options that are of interest are `port=`, `mountport=`, `mountprog=`, `nfsprog=`, and `tcp`. These options can be used to change the default port number (which is 0, telling `mount` to query the portmapper); they can also change the `mountport` from its default of 2049, the `mountprog` from its default of 100005, the `nfsprog` from its default of 100003, and, finally, they can change an argument to use TCP instead of UDP.

Although these are not all the options that are available, the rest are fairly specialized and of little interest. For more information, see the NFS man page. Naturally, all these are available from a command line to the `mount` command because the /etc/fstab file is little more than default arguments when none are given.

DEFINING THE METHOD OF SHARING

Now that you've looked at a large part of the NFS process, you're going to look at the /etc/exports file. Other files and programs, even the programs that provide NFS services, pale in comparison. You've seen how to deny access to NFS. You've seen how to mount NFS. But the /etc/exports is the heart and soul of the NFS process. This is, without a doubt, the most important file because it defines the method of sharing, whether clients can read and write or read only, how to respond when the user root is the file system user on the client, and so on. This file does far more than just list those directories that other hosts can mount—it controls what they are permitted to do to the file system while it is remotely mounted.

When thinking about a directory that is listed in /etc/exports, it helps to remember that that directory and all the files in it belong to the kernel that is running on the server where the file system actually resides. What you are doing is permitting an extended kind of FTP access to the client that is requesting to mount the file system. This client is being provided with a listing of all the files and subdirectories that it is permitted to see, and that it can read from and possibly write to, in this file system. But it still belongs to the server that is exporting it. So the NFS server (and the kernel controlling the disk) permits or doesn't permit operations based on the permissions granted, implicitly or explicitly, in /etc/exports.

As a very simple example, you might see something similar to the following:

```
/home   (rw,no_root_squash)
/cdrom  (ro)
```

This particular server is giving all the hosts that can access it the capability to mount the /home directory read-write; furthermore, if the user is root, root has all the privileges of the root user on the NFS server itself, that is, root is not to be "squashed." Never use something as simple as the preceding in any environment other than perhaps a private home network of two computers so that any member of a family can access their home directory.

RESTRICTING MOUNT ACCESS

Most probably, one of the first things you'll want to explore is how to keep those unwanted or unknown hosts from mounting your directories. Expanding on the example in the preceding paragraph, assume that you have the following four hosts:

- A domain called bar.org
- Two subdomains, accounting and engineering
- Four hosts: acctpay and acctrec in accounting, and CAD and CAM in engineering.

The /etc/exports file enables you to specify wildcards of the form `*.bar.org` as follows:

```
/home          *.bar.org(rw,no_root_squash)
```

However, if you do this, none of the four hosts in your organization can mount /home because the `.` is not expanded by the wildcard `*`. So you either have to specify something similar to

```
/home          *.accounting.bar.org(rw,no_root_squash)
/home          *.engineering.bar.org(rw,no_root_squash)
```

or, more simply,

```
/home          *.*.bar.org(rw,no_root_squash)
```

Note also that if you had a host foo.bar.org, it is unable to access /home based on this example. In general, the easiest way to specify a range of hosts that are permitted access on an IP network is to substitute the network_address/netmask pairing. So if you want to allow access for hosts with addresses 192.168.0.1–192.168.0.62, you can substitute `192.168.0.0/255.255.255.192` for `*.bar.org` in the preceding examples.

Occasionally, you'll want to export a directory, but not a subdirectory. By default, all subdirectories are exported. But if you have a subdirectory under /home called /home/private that you don't want other hosts to access, you can deny them access to that subdirectory without affecting any of the others:

```
/home            *.bar.org(rw,no_root_squash)
/home/private    *.bar.org(noaccess)
```

The `noaccess` option denies clients access to the files or subdirectories of /home/private. The subdirectory private still shows up, but nothing more than the `.` and `..` are seen.

In the paragraphs that discussed `nfsd` and `mountd`, you learned that you can make a public NFS server by specifying the `-R` option. To fully implement this option, two separate entries are required in /etc/exports:

```
/usr/share/apache/htdocs    =public
/usr/share/apache/htdocs    (ro,root_squash)
```

Despite the fact that `root_squash` is the default in the preceding case, prudence dictates specifying it explicitly. Furthermore, you won't want to export a directory to the world in read-write mode. This can leave you open to numerous problems, both from a security as well as a legal standpoint.

SUMMARY

In this chapter, you learned about factors that you need to take into account in deciding which directories you might want to share via NFS. You also learned about the programs that affect sharing files via NFS, and in which order they need to start. You learned about the configuration files that are involved, as well as some of the more important options that give NFS great flexibility. You learned how to define what the client is permitted to do when the file system is mounted, and how to share only portions of a file system. For more information on mounting file systems, refer to the following chapters:

- Chapter 9, "Understanding the Linux File System," discusses what file systems are and what types of files are found in each major subdirectory. This can help you plan which directories you'll want to export via NFS, and how you want to export them.
- Chapter 10, "Users, Groups, and Permissions," discusses file permissions. The more you know about file permissions, the more you'll understand about how clients interact with exported directories because the rules remain the same.

CHAPTER 33

NetWare and OpenLinux

In this chapter

NetWare and OpenLinux

This chapter reviews the client and administrative utilities for NetWare that are included with OpenLinux 1.3. The utilities enable you to access and manage NetWare resources in a network environment where NetWare and OpenLinux coexist. Utilities are available for both bindery services and NDS.

First you will learn about the utilities that allow client access to NetWare servers and NDS. Next you will learn about the NDS administrative utilities. Finally, you will learn about the Bindery-based administrative utilities. Figure 33.1 shows the sample NDS tree that is used in the examples throughout this chapter.

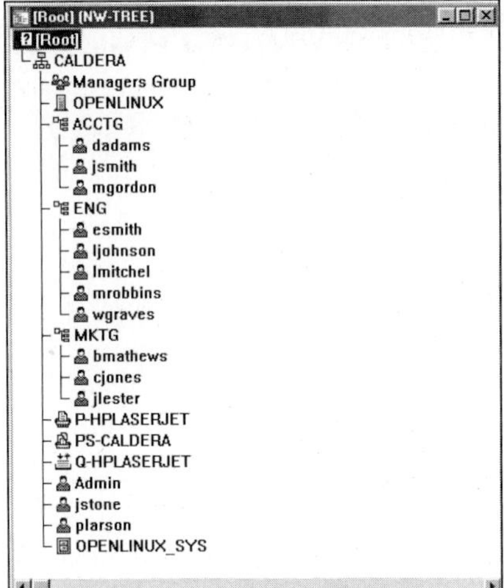

Figure 33.1
Sample NDS Tree used in this chapter.

NetWare Client Utilities

The NetWare client utilities available with OpenLinux enable Linux users to access NetWare file and print services from the Linux environment. This section reviews each of the available utilities and provides examples of how to use them. The available NDS and bindery based NetWare client utilities are shown in Table 33.1.

TABLE 33.1 OVERVIEW OF NETWARE CLIENT UTILITIES

Client Utilities	Use
`nwlogin`	Log in to a NetWare Tree (NDS) or Server (bindery)
`nwdelqjob`	Delete print jobs in a NetWare print queue
`nwmsg`	Configure client options for broadcast messages
`nwmount`	Mount a NetWare volume
`nwpasswd`	Change NetWare password

Client Utilities	Use
nwprint	Print to a NetWare print queue
nwqstat	Display NetWare print queue status
nwsend	Send messages to a NetWare client
nwwhoami	Display current connection information
xnwmanageq	Display NetWare print queue status (X Window based)
xnwprint	Print to a NetWare print queue (X Window based)
nwlogout	Log out of a NetWare Tree (NDS) or Server (bindery)

In order to access and utilize NetWare resources from OpenLinux, your Kernel must have ipx support and the NetWare client daemon (nwclientd) must be running. (For information on building ipx support in your kernel, see Chapter 17, "Building Custom Kernels." For information on autostarting the nwclientd daemon, refer to Chapter 12, "System Initialization Under OpenLinux.")

Configuring NetWare Client Settings

Accessing NetWare resources requires that you log in to either an NDS tree or a NetWare Bindery Server. Set up your NetWare client preferences in order to facilitate login and use of resources. NetWare client preferences are configured via environment variables and can be set up in your Linux environment scripts (that is, `.bashrc`). Table 33.2 shows the environment variables that can be used to configure the NetWare client.

Table 33.2 NetWare Client Configuration Environment Variables

Environment Variable	Purpose
NWCLIENT_PREFERRED_SERVER	Preferred server to use when logging in (if not set, client uses first NetWare server that replies to GET_NEAREST_SERVER request)
NWCLIENT_PREFERRED_TREE	Preferred NDS Tree to use when logging in (if not set, client uses NDS tree of first NetWare server that replies to GET_NEAREST_SERVER request)
NWCLIENT_DEFAULT_NAME_CONTEXT	Default NDS context to be used by client when logging in and accessing NDS resources (if not set, client uses [ROOT] of NDS Tree to login. Because no users exist in the [ROOT] of the NDS Tree, the client attempts to find the user in the context of the server the user is using to authenticate. After logging in, client still points to [ROOT] of NDS Tree)
NWCLIENT_DEFAULT_USER	Default users to log in as (if not set, client prompts for username)

If you are using bash as your shell, and you use the admin account in the O=CALDERA context to log in, you can set the preferences for the sample NDS Tree by adding the following lines to .bashrc:

```
export NWCLIENT_PREFERRED_TREE="NW-TREE"
export NWCLIENT_DEFAULT_NAME_CONTEXT="O=CALDERA"
```

LOGGING IN TO NETWARE

nwlogin is a command line utility used to log in or authenticate to both NDS- and bindery-based NetWare networks. The following syntax is used (Table 33.3 shows the possible command line options for the nwlogin utility):

```
nwlogin [OPTIONS]
```

TABLE 33.3 COMMAND-LINE OPTIONS FOR nwlogin

Option	Description
-b	Force a bindery-based login
-h	Display command help
-n	Attempt NDS-based login (default)
-p <PASSWORD>	Specifies password in command line
-s <SERVER>	Specify server to log in or authenticate to
-t <TREE>	Specify NDS Tree to log in to
-u <USER>	Specify user to log in as
-l <LINUX USER>	Specifies which Linux user you want to log in

If you want to log in to an NDS Tree named NW-TREE as the NetWare user jsmith in the context OU=ACCTG.O=Caldera, issue the following command:

```
nwlogin -t NW-TREE -u .jsmith.acctg.caldera
```

If you have set up your client properties as described previously, you do not need to specify a tree or use a distinguished username. Instead you can simply log in by issuing one of the following two commands:

```
nwlogin -u jsmith
```

```
nwlogin
```

If you do not specify a username in the command line with the -u option and you have not set up the NWCLIENT_DEFAULT_USER environment variable, you are prompted for a username as shown in Figure 33.2.

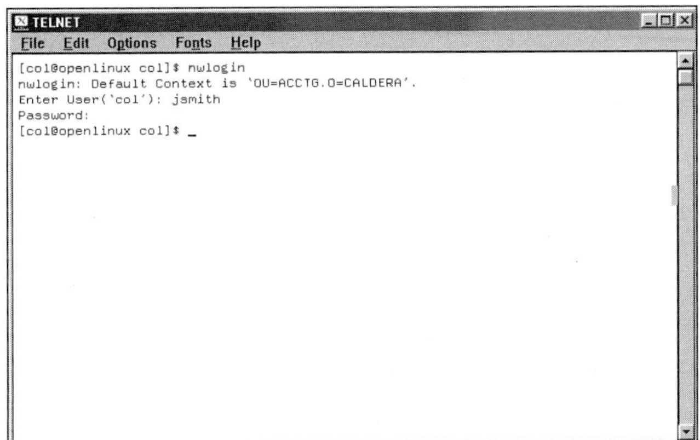

Figure 33.2
Sample Login Session for NetWare User jsmith.

If you are logged in to Linux as root, you can use `nwlogin` to establish a NetWare connection for another Linux user with the `-l` option. If you want to log the Linux user col in to the sample tree with the NetWare account jsmith in the OU=ACCTG.O=CALDERA context, issue the following command:

```
nwlogin -l col -u .jsmith.acctg.caldera
```

Note

The client preferences used during login with the `-l` option are the ones for root, and not for col; however, the client preferences used when the col user is using NDS resources are those of col.

When a Linux user logs in to NDS or a bindery server, the login session is valid for any terminal that the Linux user is logged in to. If the user has multiple telnet sessions open on the OpenLinux server, all sessions for that user are considered logged in to NetWare and can use NetWare resources.

If a user logs in to NDS or a bindery server, and then logs out of Linux, the Linux server keeps the user's NDS or bindery connection open; the next time that the user logs in to Linux, the NDS or bindery connection will still be usable. This is true as long as the `nwclientd` daemon is not stopped or restarted.

Viewing Current NetWare Connections

You can use the NetWare client for Linux to log in to multiple NDS Trees and bindery servers simultaneously. The `nwwhoami` utility enables a user to view all current NetWare connections. The utility does not have any command-line parameters associated with it. To view your NetWare connections, issue the following command:

```
nwwhoami
```

LOGGING OUT

When you no longer need a NetWare connection, log out. In order to log out from an NDS Tree or NetWare bindery server, you can use the `nwlogout` utility. The following syntax is used (Table 33.4 shows the possible command-line options for the `nwlogout` utility):

```
nwlogout [OPTIONS]
```

TABLE 33.4 COMMAND-LINE OPTIONS FOR `nwlogout`

Options	Use
`-a`	Log out of all NDS Trees and NetWare Servers
`-h`	Display command help
`-s <SERVER>`	Log out from Server (Bindery)
`-t <TREE>`	Log out from Tree (NDS)

Because the NetWare client enables you to log in to multiple NDS Trees and Bindery servers simultaneously, during logout you must specify which server or tree you want to log out of.

If you want to log out from the NW-TREE NDS Tree, issue the following command:

```
nwlogout -t NW-TREE
```

By issuing the previous command you are logged out of the NW-TREE and all associated servers. However, you remain logged in on all other NDS Trees and Bindery servers.

If you want to log out from all NDS Trees and Bindery servers at once, you can issue the following command:

```
nwlogout -a
```

This command disconnects you from all NetWare resources (NDS and Bindery based).

THE NETWARE AUTOMOUNTER

The NetWare client (`nwclientd`) enables you to access both NDS and Bindery based objects via the Linux file system. The `/NetWare/` directory is called the automount path. After you log in, you can navigate through an NDS directory tree or through NetWare server resources by using simple `cd` commands in the /NetWare/ directory.

As you can see in Figure 33.3, you can navigate through both the NDS Tree contexts as well as through the NetWare file systems by changing directories in the NetWare automount path. You can also navigate through bindery servers and volumes by changing to the /NetWare/bindery/ directory in the NetWare automount path.

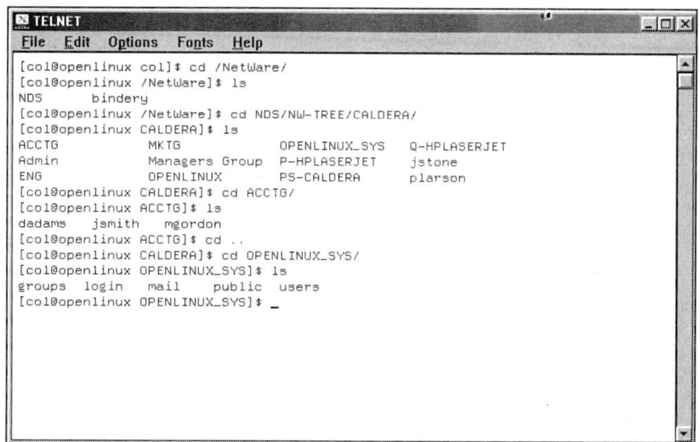

Figure 33.3
Navigating through the NW-TREE NDS Tree via the NetWare Automount path.

Printing to NetWare Print Queues

All printing utilities that are described in this section can use environment variables as previously explained in the "Configuring NetWare Client Settings" section. The relevant variables for printing are shown in Table 33.5.

Table 33.5 Environment Variables Used by the Printing Utilities

Environment Variable	Function
`NWCLIENT_PREFERRED_SERVER`	Used by printing utilities to specify NetWare server that holds the print queue when not specified by the `-s` option
`NWCLIENT_PREFERRED_QUEUE`	Used by printing utilities to specify print queue object to be used by default when not specified by the `-q` option

The two utilities available for printing from OpenLinux to NetWare print queues are `nwprint` and `xnwprint`. The following syntax is used (Table 33.6 shows the possible command-line options for the `nwprint` and `xnwprint` utilities):

```
nwprint [OPTIONS]
xnwprint [OPTIONS]
```

Table 33.6 Command-line Options for `nwprint` and `xnwprint`

Options	Description
`-q <QUEUE NAME>`	NetWare Print queue to be used
`-s <SERVER>`	NetWare server where queue resides
`-b <PATH>`	NetWare Automount path of bindery queue object to print to
`-n <PATH>`	NetWare Automount path of NDS queue object to print to
`-p <PRINTSERVER>`	Print Server object that will service print job

continues

TABLE 33.6 CONTINUED

Options	Description
`-# <NUMBER>`	Number of copies to be printed
`-l <NUMBER>`	Number of printable lines per page
`-t <NUMBER>`	Number of spaces to expand each tab
`-w <NUMBER>`	Number of printable columns on a page
`-f <FORMNAME>`	Name of NetWare print form to use (form must exist in NetWare container object)
`-j <JOBNAME>`	Name of job that appears on banner page
`-u <NAME>`	Name of user that appears on banner page
`-c`	Inserts carriage return before each line feed
`-N`	Suppresses banner page from printing
`-h`	Display command help

Printing three copies of a file called myfile to the Q-HPLASERJET NetWare print queue in the O=CALDERA context can be accomplished with the following command:

```
nwprint -s OPENLINUX -q .Q-HPLASERJET.CALDERA -# 3 myfile
```

Note

You must specify the distinguished name of an NDS print queue. The distinguished name used can be type-full or type-less.

You can also print using a NetWare automounted path for the Q-HPLASERJET print queue in the sample NDS Tree by issuing the following command:

```
nwprint -n /NetWare/NDS/NW-TREE/CALDERA/Q-HPLASERJET myfile
```

Note

When using the NetWare automounted path, you can specify the NDS print queue or the NDS printer object.

CHECKING PRINT JOB STATUS

Checking the status of your print jobs can be accomplished with the `nwqstat` or `xnwmanageq` utilities. The following syntax is used (Table 33.7 shows the possible command-line options for the `nwqstat` and `xmanageq` utilities):

```
nwqstat [OPTIONS]
xnwmanageq [OPTIONS]
```

TABLE 33.7 COMMAND-LINE OPTIONS FOR nwqstat AND xnwmanageq

Options	Description
-q <QUEUE>	Name of print queue
-s <SERVER>	NetWare server where queue resides
-b <PATH>	NetWare automounted path of bindery queue object
-n <PATH>	NetWare automounted path of NDS printer or print queue object
-h	Displays command help

To view the status of Q-HPLASERJET in the O=CALDERA context using the NetWare automount path, issue the following command:

```
nwqstat -n /NetWare/NDS/NW-TREE/CALDERA/Q-HPLASERJET
```

The previous command shows you a listing of print jobs currently in the print queue in the order in which they will be printed.

The xmanageq utility enables you to get a graphical view of the jobs in the print queue as shown in Figure 33.4. This utility also enables you to delete print jobs if you have the appropriate NDS rights.

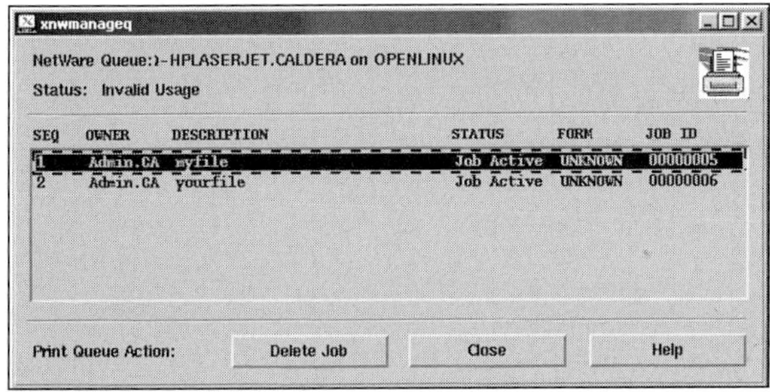

Figure 33.4
The xmanageq utility screen.

DELETING JOBS FROM A PRINT QUEUE

The nwdelqjob utility enables users to delete print jobs that they submit to a NetWare print queue. By default, users can only delete their own print jobs. If you have the appropriate NDS rights, however, you can use this utility to delete other users' print jobs. The following syntax is used (Table 33.8 shows the possible command-line options for the nwdelqjob utility):

```
nwdelqjob [OPTIONS] <JOB ID>
```

TABLE 33.8 COMMAND-LINE OPTIONS FOR nwdelqjob

Options	Description
-q <QUEUE>	Name of print queue
-s <SERVER>	NetWare server where queue resides
-b <PATH>	NetWare automounted path of bindery queue object
-n <PATH>	NetWare automounted path of NDS printer or print queue object
-h	Displays command help

In order to delete a job, you must identify the job ID returned when you submitted the print job. If you do not know the job ID, you can find it by using the `nwqstat` or `xnwmanageq` utilities to view the jobs in the print queue.

You can also delete print jobs using the `xnwmanageq` utility described in the previous section.

To Delete job number 012311 from the NetWare print queue Q-HPLASERJET using the NDS automounted path, for example, issue the following command:

```
nwdelqjob -n /NetWare/NDS/NW-TREE/CALDERA/Q-HPLASERJET 012311
```

CHANGING NETWARE PASSWORDS

You can change your NetWare password with the `nwpasswd` utility. This utility is used for both NDS and Bindery services. The following syntax is used (Table 33.9 shows the possible command-line options for the `nwpasswd` utility):

```
nwpasswd [OPTIONS]
```

TABLE 33.9 COMMAND-LINE OPTIONS FOR nwpasswd

Options	Description
-h	Display command help
-p <PASSWORD>	Specifies the new password in the command line (this option can only be used by a user with supervisor object rights in NetWare)
-s <SERVER>	Bindery server to change password in
-t <TREE>	NDS tree to change password in
-u <USER>	Specify the user whose password is to be changed (this option can only used by a user with supervisor object rights in NetWare)

Changing your NetWare password in the sample NDS Tree can be accomplished by issuing the following command:

```
nwpasswd -t NW-TREE
```

You are asked to enter your old password, and then to enter your new password twice.

NetWare Client Message Options

The NetWare client for OpenLinux enables you to specify whether you want to receive broadcast messages sent by users, administrators, or system messages. Client message options are set for each server to which you are attached. The following syntax is used (Table 33.10 shows the possible command-line options for the `nwmsg` utility):

```
nwmsg [OPTIONS] none¦system¦all
```

Table 33.10 Command-line Options for nwmsg

Options	Description
`-h`	Display command help
`-a`	Modifies message options for all connections
`-s <SERVER>`	Modifies message options for specified server only

Setting your NetWare client to receive messages from all sources can be accomplished by issuing the following command:

```
nwmsg -a all
```

To receive messages from the system administrator only for the OPENLINUX NetWare server, you can issue the following command:

```
nwmsg -s OPENLINUX system
```

The previous command only modifies the message option for the OPENLINUX server. All other connections remain unchanged. The `nwwhoami` utility displays the message options set for each server to which you are connected.

You can configure your NetWare client to not receive any messages from any system to which you are attached. If you want to do so, issue the following command:

```
nwmsg -a none
```


Administration Utilities for NDS

OpenLinux 1.3 ships with several utilities that enable you to administer a NetWare NDS Tree. This section reviews each of these utilities. Table 33.11 contains a brief overview of each utility.

Table 33.11 Overview of NDS Administration Utilities

Utility	Use
`nwdsaddtrust`	Give an NDS Object rights to a NetWare directory or file
`nwdsattrs`	List attributes of an NDS object class

continues

TABLE 33.11 CONTINUED

Utility	Use
`nwdscreate`	Create an NDS object
`nwdsmodify`	Modify values of an NDS object
`nwdsrm`	Delete an NDS object
`nwdssetspace`	Set directory size restriction for a NetWare directory
`nwdsshowspace`	Show directory size restriction for a NetWare directory
`nwdsshowtrust`	Show trustee assignment and rights for NetWare directories
`nwdsvalues`	Show values for attributes of an NDS object
`xnwdstrustees`	Give an NDS object rights to a NetWare directory or file
`nwpasswd`	Change password for an NDS user

MAKING FILE AND DIRECTORY TRUSTEE ASSIGNMENTS

The two utilities available to manage directories and file trustee assignments for NDS objects are `nwdsaddtrust` and `xnwdstrustees`. The following syntax is used (Table 33.12 shows the possible command-line options for `nwdsaddtrust`. Table 33.13 shows the possible command-line options for the `xnwdstrustees` utility):

```
nwdsaddtrust [OPTIONS]
xnwdstrustees [OPTIONS]
```

TABLE 33.12 COMMAND-LINE OPTIONS FOR `nwdsaddtrust`

Options	Description
`-o <OBJECT>`	Object being made a trustee and receiving rights
`-p <PATH>`	Directory or file trustees assignment is being added to
`-r [RWCEMFA]`	Rights to assign to new trustee. The possible rights are: R = Read W = Write C = Create (only applicable for directories) E = Erase M = Modify F = File scan A = Access control
`-h`	Displays command help

To make the user jsmith in the OU=ACCTG.O=CALDERA context a trustee of the OPENLINUX_SYS:groups\acctg directory, and to assign read, write, and create rights, issue the following command:

```
nwdsaddtrust -o /NetWare/NDS/NW-TREE/CALDERA/ACCTG/jsmith -r [RWC] -p /NetWare/
➥NDS/NW-TREE/CALDERA/OPENLINUX_SYS/groups/acctg
```

If jsmith is already a trustee of the acctg directory, his rights will be overridden by the new assignment.

The `xnwdstrustees` utility gives you a graphical interface for managing trustee assignments for NetWare files and directories.

Table 33.13 Command-line Options for `xnwdstrustees`

Options	Description
`-p <PATH>`	Directory or file to which trustees assignment is being added
`-h`	Displays command help

To make the user jsmith in the OU=ACCTG.O=CALDERA context a trustee of the OPENLINUX_SYS:groups\acctg directory, and to assign read, write, and create rights, issue the following command:

```
xnwdstrustees -p /NetWare/NDS/NW-TREE/CALDERA/OPENLINUX_SYS/groups/acctg
```

The command brings up the graphical interface shown in Figure 33.5.

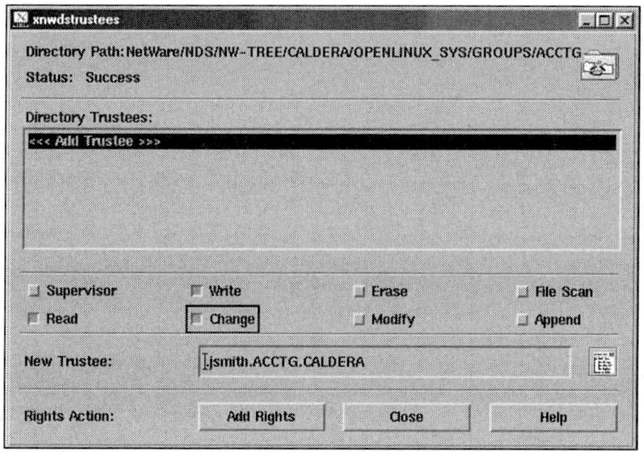

Figure 33.5
The `xnwdstrustees` Utility window.

After the window comes up, you need to perform the following steps to accomplish the desired results:

1. Click Add Trustee in the Directory Trustees window.
2. Click the search icon next to the New Trustee field.
3. Navigate the NDS Tree to find jsmith.
4. Click jsmith and choose OK.

5. Choose the rights that you want to give jsmith by clicking the appropriate checkboxes (treat the Change option as the Create right).
6. Click the Add Rights button.

After you have performed these steps, the same command that brought up the graphical interface can be used to modify or remove the rights assigned to jsmith.

VIEWING NETWARE DIRECTORY AND FILE TRUSTEE ASSIGNMENTS

The `nwdsshowtrust` utility can be used in one of two ways. You can use it to show directories and files on a server of which the specified object is a trustee, or it can be used to list all trustees of a specific directory or file. The following syntax is used (Table 33.14 shows the possible command-line options for the `nwdsshowtrust` utility):

```
nwdsshowtrust [OPTIONS]
```

TABLE 33.14 COMMAND-LINE OPTIONS FOR nwdsshowtrust

Options	Description
`-o <OBJECT PATH>`	Specifies the object NetWare automounted path whose rights are being checked (must be used with the `-s` option)
`-s <SERVER>`	Specifies the NetWare automounted path of the server where you want to see an object's rights (must be used with the `-o` option)
`-p <PATH>`	Specifies the path of the directory for which to list trustee assignments (used without `-s` or `-o` options)
`-h`	Displays command help

You can see which directories on the server OPENLINUX the user jsmith in the OU=ACCTG.O=CALDERA container is a trustee of and what his rights are by issuing the following command:

```
nwdsshowtrust -o /NetWare/NDS/NW-TREE/CALDERA/ACCTG/jsmith -s /NetWare/
➥NDS/NW_TREE/CALDERA/OPENLINUX
```

A list of objects that are trustees of the OPENLINUX_SYS:groups\acctg directory can be retrieved by issuing the following command:

```
nwdsshowtrust -p /NetWare/NDS/NW-TREE/CALDERA/OPENLINUX_SYS/groups/acctg
```

The `xnwdstrustees` utility can also be used to view the trustees of a directory. Use it as follows:

```
xnwdstrustees -p /NetWare/NDS/NW-TREE/CALDERA/OPENLINUX_SYS/groups/acctg
```

In addition, the `xnwdstrustees` utility can be used to make rights assignments changes and to add new trustees.

VIEWING ATTRIBUTES OF AN NDS OBJECT

The `nwdsattrs` utility enables you to view the NDS attributes for an object class by specifying an existing object. The following syntax is used:

```
nwdsattrs -o <PATH>
```

The `<PATH>` option is the NetWare automounted path of an NDS object.

You can view the attributes for an Organization object by pointing to the O=CALDERA container. To accomplish this, issue the following command:

```
nwdsattrs -o /NetWare/NDS/NW-TREE/CALDERA
```

The results of this query are shown in Figure 33.6

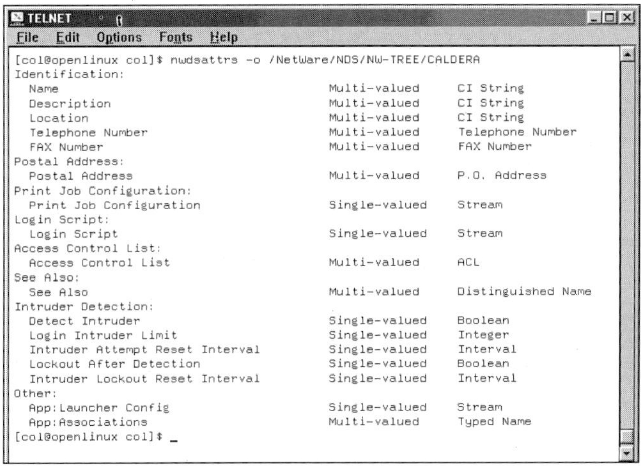
TELNET
File Edit Options Fonts Help
[col@openlinux col]$ nwdsattrs -o /NetWare/NDS/NW-TREE/CALDERA
Identification:
Name Multi-valued CI String
Description Multi-valued CI String
Location Multi-valued CI String
Telephone Number Multi-valued Telephone Number
FAX Number Multi-valued FAX Number
Postal Address:
Postal Address Multi-valued P.O. Address
Print Job Configuration:
Print Job Configuration Single-valued Stream
Login Script:
Login Script Single-valued Stream
Access Control List:
Access Control List Multi-valued ACL
See Also:
See Also Multi-valued Distinguished Name
Intruder Detection:
Detect Intruder Single-valued Boolean
Login Intruder Limit Single-valued Integer
Intruder Attempt Reset Interval Single-valued Interval
Lockout After Detection Single-valued Boolean
Intruder Lockout Reset Interval Single-valued Interval
Other:
App:Launcher Config Single-valued Stream
App:Associations Multi-valued Typed Name
[col@openlinux col]$ _

Figure 33.6
NDS Attributes for an Organization object.

PART IV

CH 33

VIEWING VALUES FOR NDS OBJECT ATTRIBUTES

The `nwdsvalues` utility can be used to display the values of NDS object attributes for a specified object. The following syntax is used (Table 33.15 shows the possible command-line options for `nwdsvalues`):

```
nwdsvalues [OPTIONS]
```

TABLE 33.15 COMMAND-LINE OPTIONS FOR nwdsvalues

Options	Description
`-o <PATH>`	NetWare automounted path for NDS object being queried
`-a <ATTRIBUTE>`	Attribute of object being queried
`-h`	Displays command help

To view the "Telephone Number" attribute value for user jsmith in the OU=ACCTG.O=CALDERA container, issue the following command:

```
nwdsvalues -o /NetWare/NDS/NW-TREE/CALDERA/ACCTG/jsmith -a "Telephone
➥Number"
```

Note

Remember to enclose any attribute or object name that contains spaces in double quotes.

CREATING AN NDS OBJECT

The utility used to create NDS objects is `nwdscreate`. The following syntax is used (Table 33.16 shows the possible command-line options for `nwdscreate`):

```
nwdscreate [OPTIONS] [ATTRIBUTE VALUE]
```

TABLE 33.16 COMMAND-LINE OPTIONS FOR nwdscreate

Options	Description
-p <PATH>	NetWare automounted path of container where object will be created
-o <NAME>	Name of object that will be created
-t <CLASS>	NDS object class to be created. Possible classes are AFP Server, Computer, Directory Map, External Entity, Group, List, Message Routing Group, NCP Server, Organizational Role, Organizational Unit, Print Server, Printer, Profile, Queue, User, and Volume
-H <PATH>	NetWare automounted path to HOME DIRECTORY (only applicable for user objects)
[ATTRIBUTE]	Mandatory attribute(s) for object being created. The mandatory attribute for the user object is `Surname`
[VALUE]	Value for the mandatory attribute
-h	Displays command help

Note

Object types that contain spaces must be enclosed in double quotes (for example, "Print Server")

You can create a user object called john in the O=CALDERA container with the following command:

```
nwdscreate -p /NetWare/NDS/NW-TREE/CALDERA -o john -t User -H /NetWare/
➥NDS/NW-TREE/CALDERA/OPENLINUX_SYS/users/john Surname Doe
```

Notice that there is a specified value for the mandatory attribute `Surname` and that a home directory for the user john is being created at the same time as the account is being created.

You can also specify non-mandatory values during account creation by entering them in the command line. Remember to enclose any attributes or values that contain a space in double quotes.

Modifying NDS Object Attribute Values

You can change the values of an NDS object's attributes with the `nwdsmodify` utility. The following syntax is used (Table 33.17 shows the possible command-line options for `nwdsmodify`):

```
nwdsmodify [OPTIONS]
```

Table 33.17 Command-line Options for nwdsmodify

Options	Description
-o <PATH>	NetWare automounted path of object to be modified
-a <ATTRIBUTE>	Object attribute to be modified
-v <VALUE>	Value for the attribute being modified
-s <SYNTAX>	Attribute syntax for the attribute (the attribute syntax is the field type in NDS. It can be found using the `nwdsattrs` command. Figure 33.6 shows the syntax for each container object attribute in the rightmost column)
-c <OPERATION>	Defines what the command will do with the specified attribute and value. The possible values for <OPERATION> are as follows:
	a = add
	d = delete
	r = replace
-h	Displays command help

Note

All options (except -h) are required for the `nwdsmodify` command.

You can add the telephone number property value for the user jsmith in the OU=ACCTG.O=CALDERA container with the following command:

```
nwdsmodify -o /NetWare/NDS/NW_TREE/CALDERA/ACCTG/jsmith -a "Telephone
➥Number" -v "801-555-1212" -s "Telephone Number" -c a
```

Note

Remember to enclose any single item that contains spaces, such as "Telephone Number," in double quotes.

Changing NDS User Passwords

A NetWare user with administrative privileges can change another user's password with the nwpasswd command explained previously. The following syntax is used:

```
nwpasswd -t <TREE> -u <USER>
```

Note that with the nwpasswd command the NDS distinguished name for the user must be used. After the command is issued, you are asked to enter the new password twice.

Change the password for user jsmith in the OU=ACCTG.O=CALDERA container with the following command:

```
nwpasswd -t NW-TREE -u .jsmith.ACCTG.CALDERA
```

You can use type-full or type-less distinguished names to specify the user.

Deleting NDS Objects

You can delete any NDS object with the nwdsrm utility. The following syntax is used:

```
nwdsrm -o <PATH>
```

The <PATH> is a NetWare automounted path for the object being deleted. Container objects can only be deleted if there are no subordinate objects in the container.

You can delete the username john in the O=CALDERA container by issuing the following command:

```
nwdsrm -o /NetWare/NDS/NW-TREE/CALDERA/john
```

Note

The command is performed and you are returned to a command prompt—there is no confirmation. After an object is deleted, it cannot be undeleted. If you delete an object and you need it back, your only option is to restore that object from an NDS backup. Be careful to restore only the objects you need, and not all of NDS, because you might corrupt your tree.

Home directories are not deleted when a user object is deleted. You must manually delete home directories after deleting user objects.

Setting Directory Size Restrictions

Directory size limits can be placed on NetWare directories with the nwdssetspace utility. The following syntax is used (Table 33.18 shows the possible command-line options for nwdssetspace):

```
nwdssetspace [OPTIONS]
```

Table 33.18 Command-line Options for nwdssetspace

Options	Description
`-d <PATH>`	NetWare automounted path for directory where restriction is to be set
`-b <BLOCKS>`	Directory size limitation specified in number of 4K blocks
`-k <KILOBYTES>`	Directory size limitation specified in number of Kilobytes
`-m <MEGABYTES>`	Directory size limitation specified in number of Megabytes
`-h`	Displays command help

To set a directory size limit of 30MB for the OPENLINUX_SYS:groups\acctg group directory, you can issue the following command:

```
nwdssetspace -d /NetWare/NDS/NW-TREE/CALDERA/OPENLINUX_SYS/groups/
➥acctg -m 30
```

Viewing Directory Size Restrictions

The size restrictions placed on a NetWare directory can be viewed with the `nwdsshowspace` utility. The following syntax is used:

```
nwdsshowspace -d <PATH>
```

The `<PATH>` is specified via the NetWare automounted path of the directory being queried.

Bindery-Based Administrative Utilities

OpenLinux 1.3 includes utilities that enable you to manage bindery-based NetWare servers. This section reviews each of these utilities in detail. Table 33.19 shows a brief description of each available utility.

Table 33.19 Overview of Bindery Administration Utilities

Utility	Use
`nwboaddtrust`	Give a NetWare bindery object rights to a NetWare directory
`nwbocreate`	Create a new NetWare bindery object
`nwboprops`	List the properties of a NetWare bindery object
`nwborm`	Removes an object from the NetWare bindery
`nwbosetspace`	Set a disk quota for a specific NetWare bindery directory
`nwboshowspace`	Show the disk quota for a specific NetWare bindery directory
`nwboshowtrust`	Display NetWare Bindery object's rights for NetWare directories
`nwbpadd`	Adds a value to a property of a NetWare bindery object

continues

TABLE 33.19 CONTINUED

Utility	Use
`nwbpvalues`	List all values of a property of a NetWare bindery object
`xnwboadmin`	Manage NetWare bindery objects
`xnwbocreate`	Create NetWare bindery objects
`xnwborights`	Give a NetWare bindery object rights to a NetWare directory
`xnwborightsDD`	Give a NetWare bindery object rights to a specified NetWare directory
`xnwbotrustees`	Manage trustees of a NetWare directory
`nwpasswd`	Change a NetWare bindery user's password

ASSIGNING NETWARE FILE SYSTEM RIGHTS TO BINDERY OBJECTS

`nwboaddtrust` and `xnwbotrustees` are the two utilities available to make NetWare bindery objects trustees of directories or files, and to make rights assignments. The following syntax is used (Table 33.20 shows the possible command-line options for `nwboaddtrust`. Table 33.21 shown the possible command-line options for `xnwbotrustees`):

```
nwboaddtrust [OPTIONS]
xnwbotrustees [OPTIONS]
```

TABLE 33.20 COMMAND-LINE OPTIONS FOR `nwboaddtrust`

Options	Description
`-o <OBJECT>`	Object being made a trustee and receiving rights
`-p <PATH>`	Directory or file to which trustees assignment is being added
`-r [RWCEMFA]`	Rights to assign to new trustee. The possible rights are as follows:
	R = Read
	W = Write
	C = Create (only applicable for directories)
	E = Erase
	M = Modify
	F = File scan
	A = Access control
`-h`	Displays command help

To make the user jsmith in the NetWare bindery for server OPENLINUX a trustee of the SYS:groups\acctg directory, and to assign read, write, and create rights, use the following command:

```
nwboaddtrust -o /NetWare/bindery/OPENLINUX/objects/jsmith -r [RWC] -p
➥/NetWare/bindery/OPENLINUX/volumes/SYS/groups/acctg
```

If the user jsmith is already a trustee of the acctg directory his rights will be overridden by the new assignment.

TABLE 33.21 COMMAND-LINE OPTIONS FOR xnwbotrustees

Options	Description
-p <PATH>	Directory or file to which trustees assignment is being added
-h	Displays command help

The xnwbotrustees utility gives you a graphical interface for adding trustees and making rights assignments to files and directories.

To make the user jsmith in the OPENLINUX server NetWare bindery a trustee of the SYS:groups\acctg directory, and to assign read, write, and create rights, use the following command:

```
xnwbotrustees -p /NetWare/bindery/OPENLINUX/volumes/SYS/groups/acctg
```

The command brings up the graphical interface shown in Figure 33.7.

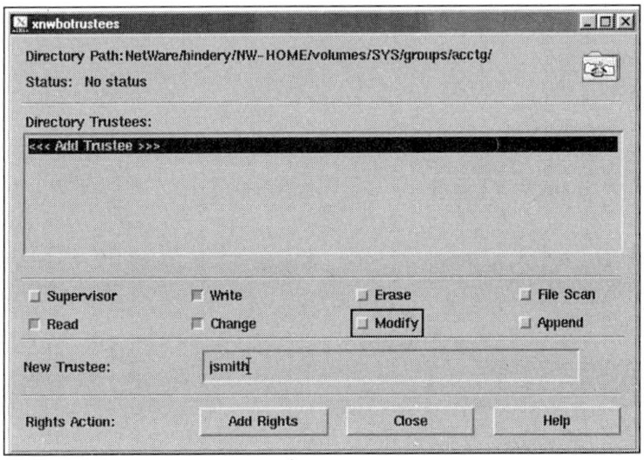

Figure 33.7
The xnwbotrustees Utility window.

After the window comes up, you need to perform the following steps to accomplish the desired results:

1. Click on Add Trustee in the Directory Trustees window.
2. Type the username in the New Trustee field.
3. Choose the rights that you want to give jsmith by clicking on the appropriate check-boxes (treat the Change option as the Create right).
4. Click the Add Rights button.

After you have performed these steps, the same command that brought up the graphical interface can be used to modify or remove the rights assigned to jsmith.

VIEWING NETWARE FILE SYSTEM TRUSTEES ASSIGNMENTS AND RIGHTS

The `nwboshowtrust` utility can be used in one of two ways. You can use it to show directories or files on a server of which the specified object is a trustee, or you can you can use it to list all trustees of a specific directory or file. The following syntax is used (Table 33.22 shows the possible command-line options for the `nwboshowtrust` utility):

```
nwboshowtrust [OPTIONS]
```

TABLE 33.22 COMMAND-LINE OPTIONS FOR nwboshowtrust

Options	Description
`-o <OBJECT PATH>`	Specifies the object NetWare automounted path whose rights are being checked (cannot be used with the `-p` option)
`-p <PATH>`	Specifies the path of the directory for which to list trustee assignments (cannot be used with the `-o` option)
`-h`	Displays command help

You can see what directories on the server OPENLINUX the user jsmith is a trustee of and what his rights are with the following command:

```
nwboshowtrust -o /NetWare/bindery/OPENLINUX/objects/JSMITH
```

To see which bindery objects are trustees of the SYS:groups\acctg directory on the OPENLINUX NetWare server, issue the following command:

```
nwboshowtrust -p /NetWare/bindery/OPENLINUX/volumes/SYS/groups/acctg
```

The `xnwbotrustees` utility can also be used to view the trustees of a directory. You can do this with the following command:

```
xnwbotrustees -p /NetWare/bindery/OPENLINUX/volumes/SYS/groups/acctg
```

In addition, the `xnwbotrustees` utility can be used to make rights assignments changes and to make new trustee assignments.

VIEWING NETWARE BINDERY OBJECT PROPERTIES

The `nwboprops` utility enables you to view the properties for a specified bindery object. The following syntax is used:

```
nwboprops -o <PATH>
```

The `<PATH>` is a NetWare automounted path for the bindery object you are querying.

To view the attributes for user object jsmith in the OPENLINUX NetWare server bindery, issue the following command:

```
nwboprops -o /NetWare/bindery/OPENLINUX/objects/JSMITH
```

Viewing NetWare Bindery Object Property Values

You can view a bindery object's property values with the `nwbpvalues` utility. The following syntax is used (Table 33.23 shows the possible command-line options for the `nwbpvalues` utility):

```
nwbpvalues [OPTIONS]
```

Table 33.23 Command-line Options for nwbpvalues

Options	Description
-o <PATH>	NetWare automounted path for NetWare bindery object being queried
-p <PROPERTY>	Property of object being queried
-h	Displays command help

To view the Surname property value for user jsmith in the OPENLINUX NetWare server bindery, issue the following command:

```
nwbpvalues -o /NetWare/bindery/OPENLINUX/objects/JSMITH -p Surname
```

Creating a NetWare Bindery Object

Two utilities that can be used to create bindery objects are `nwbocreate` and `xnwbocreate`. The following syntax is used (Table 33.24 shows the possible command-line options for `nwbocreate`):

```
nwbocreate [OPTIONS]
xnwbocreate
```

Table 33.24 Command-line Options for nwbocreate

Options	Description
-s <PATH>	NetWare automounted path of server where object will be created
-o <NAME>	Name of object that will be created
-t <TYPE>	NetWare bindery object type to be created. Type is an integer between 1 and 3. Possible types are:
	1 = User
	2 = Group
	3 = Print Queue
-H <PATH>	NetWare automounted path to HOME DIRECTORY (only applicable for user objects)
-h	Displays command help

You can create a user object called john in the OPENLINUX NetWare server bindery with the following command:

```
nwbocreate -s /NetWare/bindery/OPENLINUX -o john -t 1 -H
➥/NetWare/bindery/OPENLINUX/volumes/SYS/users/john
```

Notice that you are creating a home directory for the user john at the same time that the account is being created.

The `xnwbocreate` utility gives you a graphical interface for adding a NetWare bindery object. The following syntax is used:

```
xnwbocreate -s <SERVER> -t <TYPE>
```

The `<SERVER>` and `<TYPE>` follow the same rules as `nwbocreate` (see Table 33.24).

To create a user object named mary in the OPENLINUX NetWare server bindery, issue the following command:

```
xnwbocreate -s /NetWare/bindery/OPENLINUX -t 1
```

When the graphical interface appears, use the following steps to achieve the desired results:

1. Type the username in the `New User Name` field.
2. Type the Home Directory path in the `Home Directory Path` field. Note that this path is relative to the server, and not to the NetWare automounted path; therefore, a sample home directory path for mary is sys/users/mary.
3. Click the Create button.

MODIFYING BINDERY OBJECT PROPERTY VALUES

The two utilities available to modify property values of a bindery object are `nwbpadd` and `xnwboadmin`. The following syntax is used (Table 33.25 shows the possible command-line options for the `nwbpadd` utility):

```
nwbpadd [OPTIONS]
xnwboadmin -o <PATH>
```

TABLE 33.25 COMMAND-LINE OPTIONS FOR nwbpadd

Options	Description
`-o <PATH>`	NetWare automounted path of object to be modified
`-p <PROPERTY>`	Object attribute to be modified
`-v <VALUE>`	Value for the attribute being modified
`-t <TYPE>`	Option for the property being added. Valid types are as follows:
	SET = Add value to property specified with the `-p` option (can only be used in properties of type SET)

Options	Description
-t <TYPE>	STRING = Is used as literally as the new value for the property specified with -p option (can only be used in properties of type ITEM)
	SEGMENT = Hexadecimal value to be translated and stored as a byte stream value
	You can view the property type by using the nwboprops command and looking at the third column
-h	Displays command help

Note: All options (except -h*) are required for the* nwbpadd *command.*

To modify the Surname property value for the user jsmith in OPENLINUX NetWare server bindery, issue the following command:

```
nwbpadd -o /NetWare/bindery/OPENLINUX/objects/JSMITH -p SURNAME -t
➥STRING -v Smith
```

The graphical utility xnwboadmin enables you to add and edit values for bindery object properties of a specified object.

To edit the properties of jsmith in the OPENLINUX NetWare server bindery, issue the following command:

```
xnwboadmin -o /NetWare/bindery/OPENLINUX/objects/JSMITH
```

When the graphical utility comes up, you can select the property that you want to edit and make the changes using the Edit Property Value field, and then clicking on the Add Value button.

Changing Bindery User Passwords

A NetWare user with supervisor privileges can change another user's password with the previously explained nwpasswd command:

```
nwpasswd -s <SERVER> -u <USER>
```

To change the password for user jsmith in the OPENLINUX NetWare server bindery, issue the following command:

```
nwpasswd -s /NetWare/bindery/OPENLINUX -u jsmith
```

In addition to changing a user's password, you can also remove a bindery user's password with the nwnulpaswd utility with the following syntax:

```
nwnulpaswd -o <PATH>
```

The <PATH> is a NetWare automounted path for the bindery object.

DELETING BINDERY OBJECTS

The utility used to delete bindery objects is nwborm. The following syntax is used:

```
nwdsrm -o <PATH>
```

The <PATH> is a NetWare automounted path for the object being deleted.

You can delete a user named john from the OPENLINUX NetWare server bindery by issuing the following command:

```
nwborm -o /NetWare/bindery/OPENLINUX/objects/JOHN
```

Note

The command is performed and you are returned to a command prompt—there is no confirmation. After an object is deleted, is cannot be undeleted. If you delete an object that you need back, your only option is to restore the entire bindery.

Home directories are not deleted when a user object is deleted. You must manually delete home directories after deleting user objects.

SETTING DIRECTORY SIZE RESTRICTIONS

The nwbosetspace utility is used to set size limitations on NetWare directories. The following syntax is used (Table 33.26 shows the possible command-line options for the nwbosetspace):

```
nwbosetspace [OPTIONS]
```

TABLE 33.26 COMMAND-LINE OPTIONS FOR nwbosetspace

Options	Description
-d <PATH>	NetWare automounted path for directory where restriction is to be set
-b <BLOCKS>	Directory size limitation specified in number of 4K blocks
-h	Displays command help

To set a directory size limit of 400KB for the SYS:groups\acctg directory on the OPENLINUX server, issue the following command:

```
nwbosetspace -d /NetWare/bindery/OPENLINUX/volumes/SYS/groups/acctg -b 100
```

VIEWING DIRECTORY SIZE RESTRICTIONS

The nwboshowspace utility is used to display directory size restrictions placed on a NetWare directory. The following syntax is used:

```
nwboshowspace -d <PATH>
```

The <PATH> is a NetWare automounted path to the directory being queried.

Granting NetWare File System Rights Bindery Objects

The two utilities that enable you to grant NetWare file system rights to a bindery object are `xnwborights` and `xnwborightsDD`. The following syntax is used (Table 33.27 shows the possible command-line options for the `xnwborightsDD` utility):

```
xnwborights -o <OBJECT PATH>
xnwborightsDD [OPTIONS]
```

Table 33.27 Command-line Options for xnwborightsDD

Options	Description
`-o <OBJECT PATH>`	NetWare automounted path to which bindery object rights will be granted
`-p <PATH>`	NetWare automounted path of directory of file where rights will be granted
`-h`	Displays command help

Both utilities are graphical and allow granting file system rights to a specified bindery object. The `xnwborights` utility enables you to grant and modify rights to multiple locations on the file system by selecting the server and volume where rights will be granted.

The `xnwborightsDD` utility enables you to grant or modify rights of a specified object to a specified directory or file.

To grant or modify rights for user jsmith in the OPENLINUX NetWare server bindery for multiple directories or files, issue the following command:

```
xnwborights -o /NetWare/bindery/OPENLINUX/objects/JSMITH
```

After the graphical utility comes up, you need to perform the following actions:

1. Select a server (note this must be the bindery server where the user exists).
2. Navigate the file system by clicking on the search button next to the New Trustee Directory field.
3. Make your rights assignments and click OK.

Granting or modifying the rights that user jsmith has to the SYS:groups\acctg directory can be accomplished with the following command:

```
xnwborightsDD -o /NetWare/bindery/OPENLINUX/objects/JSMITH -p
➥/NetWare/bindery/OPENLINUX/volumes/SYS/groups/acctg
```

After the graphical utility comes up, you can modify the rights by clicking on the appropriate radio buttons and clicking on the Modify Rights button.

Note

Treat the Change option as the Create right for both of the previously listed utilities.

SUMMARY

As you have seen in this chapter, OpenLinux provides a wide array of utilities to enable you to manage NetWare networks (both NDS-based and bindery-based) via the OpenLinux shell and X Window interfaces. Using these tools, a network administrator can manage NetWare networks across TCP/IP based networks such as the Internet as long as one OpenLinux server has IPX access to the NetWare environment.

For more information on the topics discussed in this chapter, refer to the following chapters:

- For additional information on making the nwclientd daemon autostart during system bootup, see Chapter 12.
- To learn about customizing your environment to facilitate NetWare client configuration as explained in this chapter, see Chapter 13, "Customizing Your Shell Environment."
- For more information on configuring your Linux Kernel to support the IPX protocol, see Chapter 17.
- For the latest NetWare client updates and patches for OpenLinux, visit Caldera Systems' FTP Site at: `ftp://ftp.calderasystems.com/pub/netware/`.

CHAPTER 34

Microsoft Windows and OpenLinux

In this chapter

Today's networking environment is normally a heterogeneous mix, consisting of various UNIX servers and workstations, the seemingly inevitable Microsoft NT server, Microsoft Windows desktops, and so on. As much as some of us want the Microsoft operating systems to completely disappear, it appears that they will continue to challenge connectivity and information sharing for some time to come. Fortunately, the Linux community is rife with programmers whose level of frustration has prompted them to write programs that overcome the obstacles that Microsoft has erected in an effort to deny users connectivity options (except on their terms). One such program is called Samba. This chapter attempts to introduce Samba in the most expeditious manner possible. Because the subject of Samba is enough for its own book, this chapter highlights a few common basic configurations and some of the new features in version 2.0.x.

In the UNIX world, there is NFS, the Network File System, which allows heterogeneous file systems to be shared among hosts (see Chapter 32, "Sharing Files via NFS"). As part of its quest to dominate the industry, Microsoft decided to eschew NFS in favor of its own flavor of file sharing. This chapter explains how to cope with that decision.

SAMBA

Samba is a set of programs that allow UNIX and UNIX-like operating systems (including Linux) to communicate with Microsoft hosts. Microsoft uses a superset of the LanManager protocol—NetBIOS, which was developed by IBM and is sometimes referred to as the Common Internet File System (CIFS). The Microsoft version is called NetBEUI. The foundation for the LanManager protocol is *server message blocks* (*SMB*); this is where Samba derived its name. The Samba team, headed by Andrew Tridgell, in Australia, managed to take what little public information is available (because Microsoft does not release protocol information) and reverse engineer what NetBEUI does; they then mimicked that to allow communication with Microsoft hosts on their terms.

Note

Throughout the text, three terms appear: NT hosts (workstation, standalone, or member server, or Primary or Backup Domain Controller–PDC or BDC, respectively) running the NT OS, Win9x hosts, and Microsoft hosts. The first two references (NT or Win9x hosts) are specific to the OS that is running on the host; the third (Microsoft hosts) refers to either. The distinction is required because of the way that each participates in the networked environment. (For more information, see the "Network Environments" section that follows.)

SAMBA PROGRAMS

Some of Samba's suite of programs run as daemons and offer services; others are client programs that perform specific tasks. These programs include the following:

- `smbd`—The Samba daemon provides SMB services to clients.
- `nmbd`—The NetBIOS Name server daemon provides NetBIOS over IP naming services to clients to allow the UNIX host to appear in the Network Neighborhood.

- **smbclient**—A client utility that allows FTP-like access to SMB resources on the network.
- **swat**—Samba Web administration tool. This tool configures the smb.conf file.
- **testparm**—A sanity checking tool for the smb.conf configuration file.

You'll look at these programs and more in this chapter. The focal point, however, is swat because proper swat configuration is not intuitively obvious. Furthermore, improper setup can result in anything from an inability to run swat to an insecure server because anyone on the network can run swat and overwrite the smb.conf file.

Caution

You must protect your smb.conf file (and, by extension, your swat binary). This file defines what access is permitted to individuals using the Samba services to access your OpenLinux host. Because smbd runs as root, an improperly configured smb.conf can give any user coming in root privileges. The smbd program overrides all security settings and permissions that the user has as a standard UNIX user.

THE SAMBA WEB ADMINISTRATION TOOL

The Samba 2.0 release introduced a new program to assist in setting up and administering Samba, the Samba Web administration tool (swat). This tool is a boon to those who need Samba, but who do not have time to devote to its complexity. Samba configuration options go on for pages, and some settings conflict with others. To save you a very steep learning curve, you need to get swat properly set up.

GETTING READY TO RUN swat

There are two ways to run swat on your system. The first (and preferred) method uses inetd to launch swat when your Web browser is pointed at the correct port on your OpenLinux host. The second method requires that you are running a Web server. Although almost any Web server will do, this text describes setting up swat for secure access from an Apache Web server. If you want to use other Web servers, you'll need to research how to set it up and how to restrict access.

RUNNING swat FROM INETD

In order to run swat from inetd, you'll need to take care to configure several things. Some of these might already be taken care of for you during installation of the Samba RPM; but just in case you want to troubleshoot a setup or install from source, the process is explained here. The first step involves /etc/services and /etc/inetd.conf files. As root, you'll need to add the following line to /etc/services:

```
swat    901/tcp
```

This line assigns port 901 as a TCP connection to the program swat.

Then, according to the Samba documentation, you'll need to add the following to inetd.conf:

```
swat      stream   tcp     nowait.400    root      /path/to/swat swat
```

This line tells inetd, the Internet metadaemon, to spawn `swat` as a TCP stream (as root). The documentation also suggests the `nowait.400` option. This permits `swat` to be spawned up to 400 times per minute. Without this option, the default is 40—which is probably sufficient. You might want to have tcpd, the TCP Wrappers program, spawn `swat`. In this case, your entry might look similar to the following:

```
swat      stream   tcp     nowait        root     /usr/sbin/tcpd      /path/to/swat
```

Feel free to add a `.100`—or any number of your choosing—as the maximum number of instances of `swat` that can be spawned during a given 60 second period.

Note

In the preceding examples, */path/to/swat* needs to have the correct value substituted. This binary is most likely located in /usr/bin, although it might be located in /usr/sbin. Use the `locate` command to find `swat`.

The Samba utilities are "pam aware"; that is, they make use of the *password authentication modules* (*pam*) that are found in /etc/pam.d. These control what is required to access certain programs. The particular file that you need to verify is samba. This file contains several lines. However, to run `swat`, they must appear as follows:

```
auth     required        pam_unix_auth.so
account  required        pam_unix_acct.so
password required        pam_unix_passwd.so
session  required        pam_unix_session.so
```

If any of the preceding lines say `pam_deny.so`, you'll be unable to start swat.

Caution

The inetd process requires a hangup signal, following the editing of the /etc/inetd.conf file, and before it responds to queries on the newly inserted line. Any time you see a reference to sending a SIGHUP to a process, this is what they are talking about. You can do this by using one of the two following syntaxes: `kill -1` *pid* or `kill -HUP` *pid* (substituting the process id number for *pid*).

An alternative to looking up the pid is to use `kill -HUP `/sbin/pidof` *inetd*`` ` `` (substituting the name of the program for the name *inetd*).

You are now ready to access `swat`. Just fire up your Web browser and enter `http://localhost:901` in the location bar as the *uniform resource locator* (*URL*) and hit Enter. You are prompted for a username and password. Enter `root` as username, and root's password. (Note that you can use your system's hostname or any IP address that corresponds to the host, including 127.0.0.1, but the specific hostname and IP that belong to that hostname can, and probably need to be, blocked by `ipchains` for security; see Chapter 30, "IP Firewalling.")

If you enter any other valid username/password pair at the prompt, you'll get the swat screens, but some of the options are not available. The Commit Changes button does not appear because only root can make changes to smb.conf, and the capability to start and stop the smbd and nmbd daemons is not available.

If, when swat is started, a smb.conf file does not exist, swat opens with some default values.

Caution

If you have a hand-configured smb.conf file that you want to preserve, either make a copy of it or don't use swat. The swat program reads what it can (comments are not preserved) and rewrites the file in its own format; includes and copy statements are lost.

RUNNING swat FROM THE APACHE WEB SERVER

Configuring swat to run from the Apache Web server is a little more involved and requires more attention to detail—otherwise, you'll compromise the security of your system. With that in mind, if you're already running Apache and feel comfortable configuring it, the following steps will help guide you through.

First, create a directory called swat below your Apache document root. Copy the contents of the samba/swat directory to the Apache document swat directory. The subdirectories that are to be copied are help, images, and include. Copy the binary swat to your cgi-bin directory.

In the swat directory below Apache document root, create a file called .htaccess. In this file you'll want to put the following:

```
AuthName "swat restricted"
AuthType Basic
AuthUserFile /etc/swat.users
require valid-user
```

Next, you'll want to create the authorized user file. This is done with the following command:

```
htpasswd -c /etc/swat.users root
```

You'll be prompted for a password. The file is created with a user root and a hashed password inside.

Note

You want to ensure that only root can write to this file. Also, passwords that are used in this file need to be strong passwords to prevent your system from being compromised.

Finally, in your Apache access.conf file, find the line that begins AllowOverride and make sure that it is set to AuthConfig. Then just SIGHUP your server. (For Apache 3.1.x, use the apachectl command with the restart argument.)

Now you can access swat with your Web browser by pointing it at `http://localhost/swat/cgi-bin/swat`.

Caution

Regardless which of the two methods you chose previously, be aware that the passwords are being sent over the network in the clear unless you have set up your Apache server with ssl, and unless you have swat in the ssl document root. You might want to restrict this directory with a hosts.allow/hosts.deny entry to prevent administration over untrusted routes.

RUNNING swat

After you start using swat, you can quickly become spoiled. Nearly anything that you can do from a command line to configure smb.conf, including reloading nmbd and smbd and getting the status of Samba, can be done using this tool (see Figure 34.1). You can also access all the man pages for Samba, which open in a separate browser window.

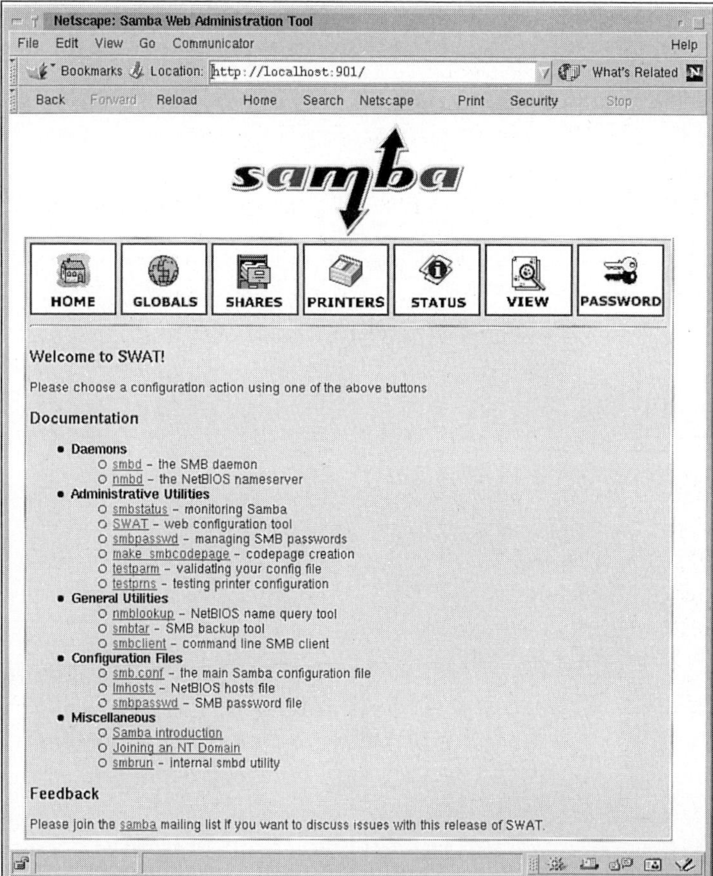

Figure 34.1
The swat home page.

When you start swat for the first time, you'll be prompted for a username/password pair. Use root unless you only want to view the smb.conf file because only root can change it. swat opens on its home page as shown in Figure 34.1. As you can see, this is principally a documentation page. The various links point to man pages, but don't actually run any of the programs. Each of the graphical links across the top of the swat page (Home, Global, Shares, Printer, Status, View, and Password) invoke a page dedicated to that purpose.

Note If you leave swat but do not close your Web browser, you can reenter swat and not be prompted for a password. This is normal behavior. After you exit your Web browser, you are once again prompted for a password when you enter.

When you start Samba, if you have no smb.conf file, Samba starts with all defaults. If you look at the View page, you see exactly what will be written. This file is written each time you click Commit Changes, Create Share, or Create Printer. If you leave a page (Globals, Shares, or Printers) without committing the changes, they will be lost. A default smb.conf file with no changes looks similar to the following:

```
# Samba config file created using SWAT
# from localhost (127.0.0.1)
# Date: 1999/01/09 13:06:14

# Global parameters
```

As changes from the default are made and committed, the file is written. You still need to send a SIGHUP to the smbd and nmbd daemons for the changes to take effect.

Caution Currently, swat does not create a backup file when it starts, so it is wise to have a copy of your current smb.conf file before starting swat.

NETWORK ENVIRONMENTS

You can have essentially two different network environments. The first is an NT server environment in which one NT server acts as a Primary Domain Controller. The PDC and any Backup Domain Controllers act in a way that is similar to Network Information Services (NIS) masters and slaves; they also provide user network logons and grant permissions within the NT Domain.

Note An NT Domain has no relation whatsoever to the IP address domain that is normally referred to when networking IP is discussed. This text makes use of the term *NT Domain* to describe the Microsoft idea of a domain, and just *domain* to describe IP networking.

The second type of network is a peer network. No PDC exists on this type of network; all machines are standalone. Although they can share information among themselves, directory and file sharing is performed on a share by the machine and can be restricted in any manner by the user of the host.

NT SERVER AS PDC ON A LOCAL NETWORK

When you are running Samba on a network with a PDC, you want to pay attention to certain settings. Within an NT Domain, hosts have a pecking order. Microsoft hosts all have hard-coded values for their OS level, and so on. These define the way a Microsoft host acts as it enters and leaves the NT Domain.

When a new host that uses SMB enters a network, it looks at the other hosts on the network. If no other system outranks it, it triggers a phenomenon known as a *browser war*. That is, it challenges the other systems that are present on the network to determine which host is to be the browse master (this can be turned off in Samba). This also happens when a host that acted as the browse master leaves the network. But because a Samba host isn't a Microsoft host, it doesn't have a hard-coded value.

Caution

A Samba server can be set up to outrank any machine on the network and win (hands down) all browser wars. However, this can be a very bad idea, particularly in an NT Domain. Although a Samba server is capable of wresting control of the domain from the PDC, this can cause all manner of erratic browsing behavior among Microsoft hosts.

ENTERING AN NT DOMAIN

One feature that has been introduced in the Samba 2.0.x version is the capability to enter an NT Domain. The procedure is simple.

First, the hostname by which the Samba server will be known within the NT Domain (which does not need to correspond to its DNS hostname) must be entered into the PDC in Server Manager for Domains. Enter this host as a standalone server or as a workstation.

The rest of the steps are performed from the Samba server. Note that for the purpose of this text, NTDomain is the NT Domain name, PDC is the NetBIOS name of the PDC, and BDC is the NetBIOS name of the Backup Domain Controllers.

Stop all Samba daemons and make the following entries in your smb.conf file (if you use `swat`, you must choose the Advanced View at the top of the Global page):

```
Security = Domain
Workgroup = NTDomain
Password Server = PDC BDC(s)
encrypt passwords = yes
```

You might also want to set the Wins server. This particular variable requires either the IP address or DNS name (not the NetBIOS name) of the WINS server.

Then run the following command:

```
smbpasswd -j NTDomain -r PDC
```

If it is successful, the message `Joined domain NTDomain` appears. This creates a file in the Samba private directory with a suffix of .mac (for Machine).

More setup needs to be done to this host, but it is now visible in the Network Neighborhood, and shares are made available on the host.

One final step remains in order for users to log in to the Samba server, and that is to create a Samba password. This is done by using the `smbpasswd` program, and passing the argument `-a` to add a user in addition to the username of the user that is being created. You'll then be prompted for a password. This addition fails if the user does not exist as a valid Linux user on the system.

Tip

To reduce administrative burdens, you can have new users dynamically created as they attempt to access shares on the Samba server by adding the following to the Global parameter `add user script: /usr/sbin/useradd %u`.

Shares still remain to be created, but the preceding procedure prepares a Samba server for use in an NT domain.

Tip

Another administrative timesaver comes in the form of the `UNIX password sync` parameter on the Global page, under Advanced View. Setting this to `true` updates the UNIX password each time the NT password is changed.

PDC on a Distant Subnet

On some occasions you might find that your Samba server is connected to a subnet with no PDC or BDC on the local subnet. That is, traffic on the local network must pass through a gateway to reach the PDC or a BDC. If this is true, the Samba server is on a *broadcast isolated network*. The NetBIOS protocol is a broadcast protocol; that is, the local network browse master sends broadcast traffic to all hosts on the local net to update its browse lists, and as hosts enter the network they broadcast their presence. But NetBIOS won't pass through a gateway—broadcasts are isolated to the local network. So hosts on a broadcast isolated network have names of the local machines, but not ones on other subnets.

Enter local browse masters. These hosts act as browse masters for the local subnet and know the location of the domain master browser—normally the PDC. In order to allow the Samba server to act as a local browse master, you need to set the Preferred Master setting to `true`. The Samba server also needs to know the IP address (or DNS name) of the WINS server. Upon restarting the nmbd daemon, the Samba server forces a browser election (browser war). Set this to 65 to win all elections. By default, the OS level is 0, but all the parameters that are discussed in this paragraph are available on the Global page, under Basic View. You might also want to set the WINS support parameter to Yes if no other WINS server exists on the local subnet.

Caution

Never set the WINS support to Yes on a subnet with a Microsoft WINS server. This Samba server needs to be the only WINS server on the subnet, or erratic browsing behavior results.

PEER NETWORK WITH MICROSOFT HOSTS (NT AND WINDOWS 95/98)

This configuration is the default for Samba. If no changes are made, only shares need to be added; otherwise, Samba can be used as is. However, from this starting point it is almost certain that some changes will be made. For example, Windows NT 4 with Service Pack 3 or 4 and Windows 95 with the OSR2 updates or Win98 require the use of encrypted passwords. Some common changes of interest are discussed in the following sections.

All that is required from here is to set up shares and printers. You might also tell Samba to act as a WINS server for the Win95/98 machines and NT workstations, and for standalone servers.

OPENLINUX AS A PDC SUBSTITUTE

The Samba team has been working to implement Samba as an NT PDC replacement. As of this writing the code is still experimental, but it is included.

Caution

This setup is not to be used in a production environment yet because some users report that the Samba code has corrupted the SAM databases (the databases that are used by NT, and that permit logins and grant permissions). Consider this the ALPHA code.

However, in the expectation that these bugs will be fixed, a short recipe for creating a Samba PDC and allowing hosts to enter its domain is presented. This recipe is subject to change. Think of the Samba documentation that comes with the package as authoritative.

Make the following changes in the Global section of `swat` (some of these parameters can be found on the Advanced View page):

`workgroup`—*SAMBA* (substitute the name of your choice for your domain)

`encrypted passwords`—Yes

`domain logon`—Yes

`domain master`—Yes

`preferred master`—Yes

`security`—`User` (if you are using another SMB server, this can be changed to `server`, but then you'll also need to fill in the `password server` = value with an IP address or DNS name)

Additionally, you might want to add the following:

`wins support`—Yes

`logon script`—`%U.bat`

In order to use the logon scripts, you'll also need to create a share to keep the netlogon scripts, as follows:

[netlogon]

`path`—`/path/to/netlogon`

`writable`—No

`guest`—No

The preceding can be added easily in the Shares section of `swat`.

Then you'll need to create machine entries in the Samba server. This is equivalent to creating entries in the Server Manager for Domains:

```
smbpasswd -m NetBIOSname
```

(This is the NetBIOS name of the machines that will enter the SAMBA domain.) You are prompted for a password. Use the password `machine`.

You'll also need to create, if you haven't already, some logins with `smbpasswd` (as previously discussed).

Now restart (SIGHUP) smbd.

On the Microsoft host, go to Start/Control Panel/Networking and change the domain to *SAMBA* (substitute the name from `workgroup =`). Do not select Create an Account. When you select OK, you see the following message: `Welcome to the` *`SAMBA`* `Domain`.

Now reboot. On NT Workstations, the time that you press Ctrl+Alt+Del to the time at which you receive the login box should be less than 20 seconds (or else something is probably wrong). You see three text boxes labeled Name, Password, and Domain.

SHARING DIRECTORIES

Sharing directories is a fairly straightforward affair with Samba. The `swat` utility makes setting them up not much more difficult than selecting almost any name for the share and reviewing some of the parameters, such as the path. Most selections don't require any extraordinary measures, and if you want a particular option, it's just a matter of selecting it. However, there are one or two parameters that can cause problems—these are noted later. In addition, one share name, Homes, has a special significance for Samba and is also explained. The Share section is broken down by functional areas that correspond to the sections that follow.

BASE OPTIONS

After naming a share, it is created with default values and written to smb.conf. For all except the special Homes share, the path defaults to /tmp and the comment is blank. These can be changed as you desire.

> **Caution**
>
> Shares define an area below which a user cannot leave unless wide links is Yes (default). Within that share, the user has whatever privileges Samba is told to grant. These privileges can exceed what the user has when logging in as an OpenLinux user.

SECURITY OPTIONS

The security section deals with the permissions that users have to read, write, and create files, and so on. Guest permissions and the identity of the guest are also here. If guest only is chosen, all users are forced to be the guest account user when accessing this share.

This is also the place to allow or deny host access to the share. This option works in a fashion that is similar to the /etc/hosts.allow hosts.deny.

The `revalidate` option can be used to force users to log in to the share each time they access it.

The most confusing parameter in this section deals with create mask, which is a synonym for create mode. The value to insert here is the value that you use in a `chmod` command.

LOGGING OPTIONS

The logging option serves several purposes. In addition to logging access to the share, it also enables or disables the capability to see, via `smbstatus`, whether anyone is accessing the share. Leave this parameter set to Yes.

TUNING OPTIONS

The default max connections `0` means unlimited connections. The number is enforced via locks.

The two sync variables, which default to No, require some explanation. Many Windows applications, including the Windows 98 Explorer, confuse flushing a buffer with doing a `sync to disk`. Under Linux, a `sync to disk` normally suspends the client process until the buffers are written to stable storage. Having a large number of Windows applications that are allowed to do syncs to disk when they mean to flush a buffer can seriously degrade performance; hence the No default for `strict sync`.

The `sync always` option has to do with whether a `sync to disk` call returns before the write is finished. The Samba server then follows the client's lead for syncs. If this is set to Yes, `strict sync` must be Yes; otherwise, `sync always` is ignored.

FILENAME HANDLING

The file handling defaults are sufficient for most environments with NT 4 and Windows 95 or better. Environments that still have DOS or Windows 3.1 might have to look into various filename handling routines to ensure that clients can read and access files properly.

This section also deals with how to map differences between the Microsoft OS files, such as hidden and system files, and UNIX files (dot files). Because a one-to-one correlation does not exist, administrators can choose how different types of files are to be handled.

BROWSE OPTIONS

The only browse option is whether a share is browsable. Windows NT has a default method for hiding shares. Any share name that ends with `$` is hidden and does not show up in a browse list. With Samba, any share can be hidden just by setting the browsable option to No.

LOCKING OPTIONS

The parameters in this section, by default, protect shares that are set to read-write. The parameters are also set to enable fast operations in which they don't interfere with actual locking (blocking locks). But for some shares that are read-only, tremendous performance increases can be realized by setting `fake oplocks` to Yes.

Caution

Before changing locking options on shares or files, make sure that you understand what the implications are. Setting `fake oplocks` to Yes on read-write shares can cause file corruption, with several clients writing to the file at the same time.

Some parameters can be changed, depending on the network. For example, on a reliable network, leaving `oplocks` (opportunistic locks) set to Yes increases speed. However, on an unreliable network, you'll want to forego the speed so that files aren't locked by clients that become disconnected.

MISCELLANEOUS OPTIONS

The miscellaneous section deals with a myriad of problem options that impact various areas or that don't clearly belong to any of the previously mentioned areas. This can be as simple as whether the share is available, or whether symlinks are to be followed.

Among the options that bear consideration is the `wide links` option. This controls whether areas outside the share are permitted. If `wide links` is Yes (default), a symlink to another part of the system outside the share is followed. This is combined with the `follow symlinks` option (default is Yes), which permits or denies the use of symlinks to files. The `wide symlinks` option, when set to No, prevents users from following a symlink if it changes directory to outside the share. But setting the `follow symlinks` option to Yes enables a user to read a file anywhere on the system. The difference is subtle and often confusing, especially because the two are implemented separately. Note that setting `follow symlinks` to No slows down filename lookups.

The other parameters that are of interest are the four `exec` options. These options execute programs as the user logs in or out, whether as the user or as root. Consideration needs to be given regarding the security risk or necessity of running a program either as the user or as root. For example, the `mount` (and `umount`) command might need to be run as root unless you have an entry in the /etc/fstab file for that mount, permitting the user to perform the action.

HOMES SHARE

The Homes share is a special share. When it is implemented, each user accessing the Samba box has his username compared to /etc/passwd for his home directory. That user's home OpenLinux home directory is made available as a share, but other users' home directories do not appear. This can provide users with a directory that is "safe" from the prying eyes of other Samba users. It might be prudent to give users a subdirectory to use to avoid naming convention problems between Linux and Microsoft clients. This is one share that does not default to /tmp; rather, it automatically defaults to the user's home directory.

SHARING PRINTERS ACROSS THE NETWORK

Printing within Linux tends to be one of the most difficult things for novice users to set up—and it is extremely difficult to understand. This text assumes that you can set up and print files from your OpenLinux host. If printing from OpenLinux cannot be accomplished, Samba does not help because it adds yet another layer of complexity. However, when you can print from OpenLinux, printing from Samba is simple.

To begin, printers can be connected in one of three ways for use on the network. They can be connected directly to a port on the OpenLinux host, in which case they use the OpenLinux print daemon and print spool. They can be connected directly to a Microsoft host, and that host can share the printer on the network, in which case the Microsoft host is spooling jobs for the printer.

The third way of connecting has two variations. The printer is connected to the network via a print spooler. This can be an HP JetDirect card, an IBM print spooler, or another print spooler. The key is that the printer itself is identified as a host with its own IP address (and possibly a DNS entry). This third way is considered to work as one of the two preceding options: Either a Microsoft host has this printer set up as part of its print spooler, or the OpenLinux host acts as the print spooler. So you are back to treating printers as though they are spooled by OpenLinux or by a Microsoft host. (For more information on setting up printers under OpenLinux, refer to Chapter 14, "Printing").

From a UNIX (Linux) perspective, printers are owned by the server that acts as the print server. This print server is in charge of formatting documents for the specific printer. The print server receives the document to print as either ASCII text or generic PostScript, formats it for the specific printer via its filter, and prints the document. Alternatively, it can receive a document that is formatted by the client for the printer and, by use of the `-b` binary switch, the server can pass the document untouched to the printer.

Enter Microsoft print spoolers. Despite the widespread use of the server to format the document for the specific printer to which it was spooling, Microsoft decided to force the clients to always know what printer they were printing to, and to have the spooler act like a UNIX print spooler that was always invoked with the `-b` switch. Although this reduced the load on the print spooler, it added complexity by forcing clients to know specifically about every printer on the network to which they might be printing. In an effort to reduce administrative burdens, Microsoft print spoolers that are shared on the network can communicate to other Microsoft hosts (but not to UNIX hosts) what kind of printer driver is needed when the client connects for the first time. In version 2.0.x, Samba also permits this kind of communication (see the section "Printing Options").

So to print using Samba shares on an OpenLinux box, you can choose one of two avenues. You can set up each client that is to connect to a printer on a Samba share to print natively to the printer (using a specific Microsoft driver for the printer); or you can set up all clients to use a generic Passthrough PostScript driver, and allow them to print to any Samba client and any printer identically, regardless of the printer type.

THE PRINTERS SHARE

The Printers share is a special share that is similar to the Homes share. This share needs to be created on the Printers page and can only be removed on the Printers page. After it is created, the Printers share only appears on the Printers page.

The Printers share is created by default with `path = /tmp` and `print ok = Yes`. If the global default for `load printers` has not been changed from Yes to No, after the Printers share is created, all printers in /etc/printcap show up in the list of print shares. They can be identified by the `*` in front of the share name. If you delete the Printers share or turn off the Global `load printers` option, these printer shares no longer appear. The printer shares that are identified with `*` cannot be deleted from Samba—they can just made not to appear.

If changes are made to the Printers share, the changes are global for all the printers that are marked with an asterisk. If you choose one of the printcap printers (ones with an asterisk) and make a configuration change that applies to that printer only, a new section under Printers is created with the name of that printer (without the asterisk) in the smb.conf file. That printer now also appears in the Printers list in `swat`, without the asterisk. You'll notice that in the View page this printer now has its own entry. If that share is subsequently deleted, it reverts to showing up with an asterisk and has the Printers defaults. If the Printers share is deleted, this print share without the asterisk remains. In other words, when it is created as a share by itself, it behaves as if it were created from the `swat` Printers page. Otherwise, it has an asterisk and is only an appendage to the special Printers share.

Tip

When setting up printers, the most common printing problem is that the spool directory does not have the proper permissions. These directories are world writable with the `sticky` bit set, that is, `chmod 1777 spool`.

Going through the functional areas that are available under printing, you'll see that there are a few differences from the Shares functional areas. Again, some of these options are only available from the `swat` Advanced View page.

BASE OPTIONS

These options are no different from the Base Options in Shares: a comment field for identification, and a path for the spool directory.

SECURITY OPTIONS

Only four options are available, but they are important. The first, `guest account`, is only of interest if Guest ok is set to Yes. The default `guest account` is nobody, and this account can be so restricted that printing isn't possible. You might want to change this to the account ftp or to another account set up for the purpose of printing.

Tip

Make sure that your `guest account` has enough privileges to print before looking elsewhere.

LOGGING OPTIONS

Read the entry under Shares called Logging Options. You'll find this in `swat` in the Shares section, Advanced View, between the Security Options and Tuning Options.

TUNING OPTIONS

The only option here, `min print space`, defaults to `0`, meaning that a user can always print. But this might become a problem on a system with low disk space and large print jobs.

PRINTING OPTIONS

This section is specific to printers. The first option, `print ok`, must be Yes for all print shares. Many of the other options are for commands. These depend on your system. OpenLinux uses Lprng, so the commands for Lprng need to be used, although the defaults in `swat` work.

The last two options are probably of interest to those with extensive Microsoft hosts on their network. The `printer driver` must be the name that the Microsoft hosts are expecting. If you don't know, don't fill it in—let one of the Microsoft machines provide you with a list, and you can copy the printer driver from that list. It must be an exact match, case and all. The next option, `printer driver location`, must be a share that you set up called

PRINTER$, where the printer drivers (copied from a Microsoft host or from the Microsoft CD-ROM) are located.

BROWSE OPTIONS

This option controls whether the printer share can be seen in the Network Neighborhood.

MISCELLANEOUS OPTIONS

The few options that are available here are the same as those that are found in the Shares section under Miscellaneous Options.

RESTRICTING ACCESS TO SERVICES

The Samba server configuration is extremely flexible. It can make use of UNIX NIS groups for access control, giving certain users read-only access, others read-write access, some users admin access, and still others no access. It can also force all users to be treated as members of the guest account (which is, by default, the UNIX user nobody) or as another special user. It can force users to belong to a certain group. All these options and more are part of the Shares page, in the Security Options section under Advanced View. Specifically, these options are `valid` and `invalid users`, `admin users`, `read list`, `write list` (which is both read and write), `force user`, and `force group`.

By making use of these advanced options, very tight control can be maintained over users' connections to any given share. There is also an option on the Global page to set a root directory to something other than the default of /.

Caution

If you set the root directory, you'll need to make sure that everything that is required to run the Samba server, plus binaries and all the libraries that are used by users, are copied below this new root directory. This functions the same as the FTP `chroot` command.

VARIABLES AVAILABLE TO SAMBA

If you've followed along in `swat` and looked at any of the default entries on the Advanced View pages, you've seen variables in the form `%X`, where `X` is one of many upper- or lowercase letters. These variables can be used to extend the flexibility of Samba. Following is a list of the variables and a short explanation of each:

- **%S**—The name of the current service, if any.
- **%P**—The root directory of the current service, if any.
- **%u**—Username of the current service, if any.
- **%g**—Primary group name of `%u`.
- **%U**—Session username (the username that the client requested, not necessarily the same as the one received).

- **%G**—Primary group name of %U.
- **%H**—The home directory of the user (%u).
- **%v**—The Samba version.
- **%h**—The Internet hostname (DNS) on which Samba is running.
- **%m**—The NetBIOS name of the client machine.
- **%L**—The NetBIOS name of the server. This enables you to change your configuration based on what the client calls you. Your server can have a dual personality.
- **%M**—The Internet name (DNS) of the client machine.
- **%N**—The name of your NIS home directory server. This is obtained from your NIS auto.map entry. (Without NIS, this is the same as %L).
- **%p**—The path of the service's home directory, obtained from your NIS auto.map entry. The NIS auto.map entry is split up as %N:%p.
- **%R**—The selected protocol level after protocol negotiation. It can be CORE, CORE-PLUS, LANMAN1, LANMAN2, or NT1.
- **%d**—The process ID of the current server process.
- **%a**—The architecture of the remote machine. Only some are recognized, and those might not be 100 percent reliable. It currently recognizes Samba, WfWg, WinNT and Win95. Anything else is UNKNOWN.
- **%I**—The IP address of the client machine.
- **%T**—The current date and time.

Samba Global Variables: A Quick Review

Listing 34.1 shows all the Global configurations and their defaults. The most commonly changed variables are on the Basic View page, but many more that are often needed are hidden. The list can be overwhelming, especially when you take into account that the Printers section has more than 25 values, and Shares has more than twice that many. In total, more than 190 configurable parameters exist. Some settings are mutually exclusive of others. Some modify or depend on others.

Tip

Global configurations apply to all shares, including special shares, unless they are overridden within the share listing.

Listing 34.1 Comprehensive Global Variables Listing with Defaults as Created by swat

```
workgroup = WORKGROUP
netbios name =
netbios aliases =
```

```
server string = Samba 2.0.0beta5
interfaces =
bind interfaces only = No
security = USER
encrypt passwords = No
update encrypted = No
use rhosts = No
map to guest = Never
null passwords = No
password server =
smb passwd file = /usr/local/samba/private/smbpasswd
hosts equiv =
root directory = /
passwd program = /bin/passwd
passwd chat=*old*password* %o\n *new*password* %n\n *new*password* %n\n *changed*
passwd chat debug = No
username map =
password level = 0
username level = 0
unix password sync = No
log level = 1
syslog = 1
syslog only = No
log file =
max log size = 5000
timestamp logs = Yes
protocol = NT1
read bmpx = Yes
read raw = Yes
write raw = Yes
nt smb support = Yes
nt pipe support = Yes
announce version = 4.2
announce as = NT
max mux = 50
max xmit = 65535
name resolve order = lmhosts host wins bcast
max packet = 65535
max ttl = 259200
max wins ttl = 518400
min wins ttl = 21600
time server = No
change notify timeout = 60
deadtime = 0
getwd cache = Yes
keepalive = 300
lpq cache time = 10
max disk size = 0
max open files = 10000
read prediction = No
read size = 16384
shared mem size = 1048576
socket options =
stat cache size = 50
```


continues

LISTING 34.1 CONTINUED

```
load printers = Yes
printcap name = /etc/printcap
printer driver file = /usr/local/samba/lib/printers.def
strip dot = No
character set =
mangled stack = 50
coding system =
client code page = 850
stat cache = Yes
domain groups =
domain admin group =
domain guest group =
domain admin users =
domain guest users =
machine password timeout = 604800
add user script =
delete user script =
logon script =
logon path = \\%N\%U\profile
logon drive =
logon home = \\%N\%U
domain logons = No
os level = 0
lm announce = Auto
lm interval = 60
preferred master = No
local master = Yes
domain master = No
browse list = Yes
dns proxy = Yes
wins proxy = No
wins server =
wins support = No
kernel oplocks = Yes
ole locking compatibility = Yes
smbrun = /usr/local/samba/bin/smbrun
config file =
preload =
lock dir = /usr/local/samba/var/locks
default service =
message command =
dfree command =
valid chars =
remote announce =
remote browse sync =
socket address = 0.0.0.0
homedir map =
time offset = 0
unix realname = No
NIS homedir = No
panic action =
comment =
path =
alternate permissions = No
```

```
revalidate = No
username =
guest account = nobody
invalid users =
valid users =
admin users =
read list =
write list =
force user =
force group =
read only = Yes
create mask = 0744
force create mode = 00
directory mask = 0755
force directory mode = 00
guest only = No
guest ok = No
only user = No
hosts allow =
hosts deny =
status = Yes
max connections = 0
min print space = 0
strict sync = No
sync always = No
print ok = No
postscript = No
printing = bsd
print command = lpr -r -P%p %s
lpq command = lpq -P%p
lprm command = lprm -P%p %j
lppause command =
lpresume command =
queuepause command =
queueresume command =
printer name =
printer driver = NULL
printer driver location =
default case = lower
case sensitive = No
preserve case = Yes
short preserve case = Yes
mangle case = No
mangling char = ~
hide dot files = Yes
delete veto files = No
veto files =
hide files =
veto oplock files =
map system = No
map hidden = No
map archive = Yes
mangled names = Yes
mangled map =
```


continues

LISTING 34.1 CONTINUED

```
browseable = Yes
blocking locks = Yes
fake oplocks = No
locking = Yes
oplocks = Yes
strict locking = No
share modes = Yes
copy =
include =
exec =
postexec =
root preexec =
root postexec =
available = Yes
volume =
fstype = NTFS
set directory = No
wide links = Yes
follow symlinks = Yes
dont descend =
magic script =
magic output =
delete readonly = No
dos filetimes = No
dos filetime resolution = No
fake directory create times = No
```

SUMMARY

In this chapter, you learned how to set up `swat` to configure Samba using your Web browser. You saw how `swat` was logically arranged to assist you in creating shares for both file and print services. You also saw how you can specify restrictions on users, groups, and read-write permissions, as well as how to force all users who are connecting to a share to become a certain user or a guest or belong to a particular group. For more information on Samba, refer to the following chapters:

- Chapter 14 discusses setting up the /etc/printcap file under OpenLinux. When printing works properly under OpenLinux, getting printing to work under Samba is much easier.
- See Chapter 10, "Users, Groups, and Permissions," to learn more about how user permissions are granted under OpenLinux, and therefore how they are granted under Samba. File permissions play a crucial role in both file sharing and printing under Samba.

CHAPTER 35

ARP, BOOTP, AND DHCP

In this chapter

This chapter is about setting up machines to provide other systems on the local network with an address when they boot. In today's networking environment, it's often a better idea to configure user workstations to obtain an address as they enter and leave the network, rather than going through the trouble of setting every machine up with a permanent IP address. You might want to do this for various reasons:

- Networks tend to be fairly dynamic.
- Hosts come and go.
- Network addresses change along with service providers.
- Your internal requirements are constantly changing.

Any number of things influence address changes on your network. Changing a handful of servers is no big task. Changing several hundred workstations, though, can be a daunting task. Then there are the laptops that are on the road during the changeover: Tracking them down can take days, or even weeks.

Or perhaps you need dynamic address resolution because you have diskless clients. One common diskless client you might encounter is the HP JetDirect Print spooler. The external print spoolers can only be configured dynamically. For this, several tools are at your disposal: address resolution protocol (ARP), bootstrap protocol (BOOTP), and dynamic host configuration protocol (DHCP). In the next few sections you'll find out about each of these protocols, what they offer, and their drawbacks.

ARP

The address resolution protocol was the first protocol to handle client requests for address information. This is the oldest and least secure method of handling address resolution. It was designed to provide address resolution for diskless clients. It also provided the mechanism for booting over the network. ARP can still be used, but it has fallen out of favor. When booting a diskless client via ARP (when the ARP daemon provides the address), the job of transferring the file system from the server to the client becomes the job of tftpd, the trivial file transfer daemon—unless you are using the Linux kernel, RARP, and NFS solution. If you know anything about `tftp`, you'll remember that it is the one service in /etc/inetd.conf that is almost universally disabled. The `tftp` daemon is considered a security risk, and is extremely difficult to control. Very few sites will use it, and those that do generally do so because they are using old hardware that cannot be updated to newer protocols. `tftp` is not secure because it does not use authentication, and therefore must rely on other programs (such as TCP Wrappers) to provide a modicum of security.

But all this doesn't mean that ARP is not usable. One of the more common tasks for ARP is to configure the new equipment that is entering the network. Several network spoolers can use ARP resolution when they enter a network. The HP JetDirect print spoolers, among others, can be configured with ARP. All you need is the hardware address of the spooler's Ethernet card. This is in the form of six pairs of hex numbers, and is provided with the spooler's documentation. When these numbers are entered into the ARP table via `arp`, the spooler is configured.

First plug in the spooler. After it is connected to the network, you can enter the following command into your OpenLinux system at the command line:

```
arp -s hostname hwaddress temp
```

The hostname is resolved normally; that is, a lookup is performed in /etc/hosts or DNS for the corresponding IP address (the IP address can be used, but it is better to use the hostname). The hardware address is then supplied. This address is in the form 00:00:FF:FF:FF:00. This address will have been supplied with the spooler. The final argument, `temp`, tells ARP to put the address in the kernel's ARP cache temporarily instead of permanently. Temporary entries time out and are refreshed or replaced each time the host talks to the hosts on the network (see Listing 35.1).

LISTING 35.1 OUTPUT OF THE `arp` COMMAND (WITH NO OPTIONS AND WITH THE `-a` OPTION)

```
# arp
Address                  HWtype  HWaddress           Flags Mask            Iface
bar.void.org             ether   00:00:C0:34:BF:D0   C                     eth0
baz.void.org             ether   00:00:A0:01:02:3D   C                     eth0

# arp -a
bar.void.org (192.168.0.3) at 00:00:C0:34:BF:D0 [ether] on eth0
baz.void.org (192.168.0.2) at 00:00:A0:01:02:3D [ether] on eth0
```

Note that the two outputs are different, but because you're only looking at Ethernet interfaces, the same information is presented. As you `ping` or otherwise access other hosts from your system, the system (in this case the host foo.void.org) learns the accessed machine's hostname/hardware address combination and uses them for communication. Because these other hosts are subject to being down, the entries in the ARP cache time out; however, they are refreshed with each communication. You'll only have ARP entries for hosts on your local network.

tftp

It is good to know a little bit about `tftp`. If you have a choice, though, you'll want to use `nfs root` rather than `tftp` to mount a root file system over the network. The most compelling reason is that NFS is not only more secure, but also more robust. Some basic information is provided here, but the details of the implementation of `tftp` are left up to the reader.

Caution

If you decide to use `tftp`, remember that tftpd does no authentication. You can configure `ipchains` to block spoofing and to block requests on the `tftp` port from all but local addresses. This deters threats from outside, but does little to protect against inside threats.

The `tftp` daemon expects to find the files that it needs to serve to its client in /tftpd subdirectories, one per IP address. So, for the network outlined in Listing 35.1, each subdirectory in /tftpd looks like the following: /tftpd/192.168.0.2 and /tftpd/192.168.0.3. These directories contain the file system for each machine.

Note

The Linux kernel provides support for both RARP and BOOTP to mount the root file system via NFS. This is an option for all systems. Some systems, however, include RARP or BOOTP support directly in the Boot ROM image. The kernel support can be used in lieu of the hosts support if you want to use NFS instead of `tftp` (see the BOOTP section that follows for more details).

BOOTP

Following ARP and `tftp`, BOOTP offers a slightly more advanced way to handle requests for address resolution from clients. Sun Microsystems machines can use BOOTP to find out who they are. To implement BOOTP, you need to run the BOOTP daemon, bootpd. The configuration file for this daemon is found in /etc, and is called bootptab. The /etc/bootptab is highly configurable and offers more choices (as well as better security) than ARP does. Although BOOTP can still use `tftp` when mounting a directory, it offers the advantage of allowing newer `tftp` daemons that can do a `chroot` (change root) to the directory that contains the IP addresses of the clients that are to be served. This adds to the overall security of the server. Also, with BOOTP, gateway servers can be set up so that gateways don't become obstacles to address resolution, as is the case with RARP.

Linux also allows a native client-side implementation of BOOTP from within the kernel—as it does with RARP—that allows the use of NFS instead of `tftp` for mounting a file system. The advantage of using NFS over `tftp` is security. To better understand how NFS works, see Chapter 32, "Sharing Files via NFS."

SETTING UP `nfsroot` VIA BOOTP OR RARP IN OPENLINUX

If you've decided that the way to proceed is to use the Linux kernel and BOOTP or RARP support to run a workstation `nfsroot`, you have a few things to prepare. For the purpose of this text, it is assumed that you're not using any built-in Ethernet ROM image from which to boot, but that you are using the Linux kernel support.

Note

If you set up a kernel to configure the system via RARP or BOOTP (described as follows), and no server is set up to respond to ARP or BOOTP requests on the network, booting of the Linux kernel hangs until these protocols have timed out–approximately two minutes.

To implement this solution, the Linux kernel must be rebuilt. The client kernel must be built with `CONFIG_IP_PNP=y` and either `CONFIG_IP_PNP_RARP=y` or `CONFIG_IP_PNP_BOOTP`, or both must be selected (as well as compiling in Ethernet and NFS support). The server must be built with `CONFIG_INET_RARP` if you are using RARP to respond, or if you have a daemon that responds to BOOTP requests. This includes bootpd or DHCPD (discussed in the section "DHCP"). The DHCPD solution is much cleaner, and it is recommended. The server must also run NFS as a server, and it must have exported the /tftpd directory.

First, you must construct the file system for the client that you plan to boot. The server that responds to the BOOTP requests is the best choice for simplicity's sake. A complete file system must be constructed under /tftpd/*ip_address* because this is the default location in which Linux looks for the root file system. This location can be altered from a command line or `LILO`, but for this text, a floppy will be used that cannot be passed command-line or `LILO` parameters.

After the root file system is in place on the server, a kernel must be built to accommodate the hardware of the machine that is to be booted. Copy the kernel image to a floppy using `dd if=/path/to/kernel.img of=/dev/fd0 conv=sync bs=512 ; sync`. Because this floppy wants to boot from the root partition of the machine where the kernel image was built, you'll need to modify this image slightly. You'll need to tell it to boot from an NFS mount, so this is what you'll need to put in the kernel. But there's a trick to this; the kernel expects a device for booting. To put the device reference into the kernel, it must exist on the machine that you are using to alter the kernel. Fortunately, this is not difficult. Just issue the command `` `mknod /dev/boot255 c 0 255` ``. This creates a special character device for reference to write to the kernel. The kernel knows when it sees this device that the device is bogus and really refers to an NFS mount. Now, to alter the kernel, issue the command `` `rdev /dev/fd0 /dev/boot255` ``. When the disk drive stops turning, you are almost ready to reboot the machine. You can also remove the /dev/boot255 device because it won't be needed again.

If you've already set up your server to respond to BOOTP or RARP requests, you can now use this floppy to boot your machine. If you haven't yet set this up, but you've decided to use BOOTP as implemented by DHCP, the next section will fill you in.

DHCP

DHCP is a client/server service in the true form of the term. It requires a server, which is the DHCP daemon (dhcpd), to run from one or more hosts on the network that provide addresses to systems as they enter and leave the network. It also requires a DHCP client daemon (dhcpcd), running on machines that are requesting an IP address. Be aware that, although you might have several servers running dhcpd, they cannot be offering the same or an overlapping range of addresses; the address range offering must be unique to each DHCP server.

The DHCP daemon, as implemented by Linux, is capable of handling both requests for BOOTP and DHCP configuration. Use of the new DHCP server is recommended in lieu of bootpd. Given its flexibility, there is little reason to run bootpd.

The configuration file for dhcpd is /etc/dhcpd.conf. This file is referred to as the configuration file for dhcpd for the remainder of the chapter. As of the writing of this chapter, two versions of dhcpd are available. They are both similar in many regards, although some differences are present. The differences do not matter for the purposes of this chapter, but those of you who are making extensive use of DHCP probably want to read the documentation pertaining to the DHCP server that you are running.

When you have the DHCP server running, it, of course, doles out addresses as established in its configuration file. It records the addresses that are assigned in a file called dhcpd.leases. This file is normally found in /var/dhcpd, but it can be configured to appear almost anywhere on the system. This file contains data on all the leased addresses so that DHCP doesn't duplicate addresses (see Listing 35.9 and the discussion in the "New DHCP Clients" section that follows for details). As leases are provided or renewed, entries are made in the file. When the file grows to a predetermined size (based on the server's configuration), a copy is made as dhcpd.leases~, and a new dhcpd.leases file is created with the expired entries removed. This copy is made before the alteration is done so that if the server crashes during the process, it has all the information that is necessary for it to start up again.

The DHCP server isn't difficult to set up, and it affords administrators the capability to provide dynamic address resolution for hosts on the network. As with many services, more than one DHCP daemon can be run on a network, but the range of addresses that each offers cannot overlap with another DHCP server. So a network with up to 30 hosts can be subnetted to accommodate up to 62 hosts, and two DHCP servers can each serve one half of the network, in case one server goes down. For many networks that don't have hosts entering and leaving often, this backup might not be necessary. If addresses are provided in a network environment for a week or longer at a time, an outage of several hours might not matter. On the other hand, networks that require a short renewal time because hosts are entering and leaving the network often (for example, in a production environment that works on hosts and performs operations for fewer than 30 minutes at a time, and then unplugs and connects the next one), and where an hour's down time might adversely affect operations, a backup might be necessary.

Although a simple configuration for DHCP is easy to do, many complex setups can also be handled by DHCP. Because the range of situations is very large in scope, this text restricts itself to more mundane configurations and leaves it to administrators with more complex needs to research the man pages and documentation pertaining to the particular DHCP server that they have installed.

Configuring DHCPD

The dhcpd.conf file can be considered to be comprised of several different sections. These sections might apply to all the sections that follow them, or just to the section in question. Often this is obvious. The global parameters section, of course, applies globally (although global parameters can be overridden within a section, if necessary). Other sections are more difficult to figure out. The trick comes in understanding that this file is constructed in a fashion similar to a C program. That is, it makes extensive use of braces ({}) to enclose parameters. These braces can be nested so that subsections are enclosed within a section. How these braces are paired is important to the section as a whole. It is important to understand that sets of braces cannot overlap—one set must be contained completely within another.

Throughout the configuration file, white space—in the form of new lines, or tabs—can be used for readability. The DHCPD parser ignores these. White space in the form of spaces must separate parameter names, but comma-separated lists do not require spaces (although the practice is common for ease of reading).

Caution

Unlike most services, when a change is made to dhcpd.conf, the DHCP daemon must be stopped and restarted for the changes to take effect. Sending a SIGHUP to the server might not be enough for it to reread the file. A simple call to '/etc/rc.d/init.d/dhcpd stop' and a corresponding call with the `start` argument is sufficient.

Within the dhcpd.conf file, lines within sections might begin with the word *option*, or they might just begin with a declaration, followed by its arguments. Options describe various services or network configurations for clients. Declarations provide specific information about how the DHCP server works or what it provides. This distinction will become clearer as you see examples of declarations and options.

Global Parameters

The parameters that are common to all the hosts that are to be served are included within this section. This section usually contains most of the options statements for the network. Some 62 total options exist; however, a few of them are not specified in the configuration file, even though they are used by the DHCP server. That leaves more than 48 configurable options, not counting vendor-specific extensions. For most, the order does not matter—but for a few it does. For example, netmask must come before routers.

The options are normally given in the configuration file by name, but the configuration numbers can also be used, if they are known. Options that specify IP addresses might also specify host names, if those host names resolve to one and only one IP address. For strings, the string data must be quoted with double quotes (see Listing 35.2).

LISTING 35.2 SAMPLE GLOBAL PARAMETERS FOR DHCPD.CONF FILE

```
server-identifier foo.void.org;
option domain-name "void.org";
option domain-name-servers foo.void.org;
option subnet-mask 255.255.255.0;
option broadcast-address 192.168.10.255;
option routers 192.168.10.90;
option ntp-servers foo.void.org, sol.void.org;
default-lease-time 604800;
max-lease-time 2419200;
```

Looking at Listing 35.2, the first global parameter specifies the DHCP server. The name must resolve to one and only one IP address, as was mentioned earlier. The first option specifies the domain name, and because this is a string value, it requires double quotes. Most of the options are self-explanatory. Options and declarations that accept more than one value have the values listed in order of priority from highest to lowest.

Note

The semicolons that terminate each option or declaration are required. Remember, a new line and tabs can be used to make the configuration file more readable, so the DHCP parser needs to know where a line ends.

SUBNET STATEMENT

Every DHCP server must have a subnet statement. This statement tells the server which subnet it is serving. Inside is the range of addresses that are available, as are any options or declarations that are different from the global section. The subnet statement displays all the options and declarations that pertain to it in braces (see Listing 35.3).

LISTING 35.3 A SAMPLE SUBNET STATEMENT

```
subnet 192.168.10.0 netmask 255.255.255.0 {
  range 192.168.10.191 192.168.10.250;
  option netbios-name-servers 192.168.10.30;
  default-lease-time 1209600;
}
```

In Listing 35.3, the subnet statement specifies the network address and netmask of the network with which you are working. Then, in braces, options and declarations define parameters that are specific to this subnet. Global options apply, except where they are explicitly overridden. For example, the default-lease-time that is shown here overrides the default-lease-time that is given in the global section. The time is given in seconds; therefore, the time 1,209,600 is equal to two weeks.

One of the most important declarations within the subnet statement is the range declaration. This tells the DHCP server the range of addresses that are in the pool, ready to be assigned to clients. The numbers are inclusive, so this DHCP server can assign the numbers ending 191 up to and including 250.

The option for netbios-name-server is the address that corresponds to the Microsoft NT WINS server, indicating that the clients that are being served include Microsoft Windows desktops.

Shared Network Statement

A shared network statement is used to group two or more subnets. If each department is assigned a subnet of 30 hosts, but a department grows too large and requires two subnets, these two subnets might be grouped together and served by the same DHCP server (see Listing 35.4).

Listing 35.4 A Sample Shared Network Statement

```
shared-network MARKET-NET {
    option domain-name  market.void.org ;
    option routers 192.168.1.1;
    subnet 192.168.1.0 netmask 255.255.255.224 {
        range 192.168.1.3 192.168.1.30;

        option routers 192.168.1.2
    }
    subnet 192.168.1.32 netmask 255.255.255.224 {
        range 192.168.1.35 192.168.1.62;
        option routers 192.168.1.33;
    }
}
```

In Listing 35.4 you can see that the shared network has its own domain name below void.org of market.void.org. This domain name only applies to the two subnets that are grouped within the shared network statement. Likewise, the router 192.168.1.1 is probably the gateway to the Internet, or at least to anything beyond the two subnets here.

Each subnet has a range declaration as required, and also a router which looks as though it provides connectivity between the two subnets (that is, 192.168.1.2 and 192.168.1.33 are two interfaces in the same host).

Group Statement

Sometimes it becomes necessary to group hosts together for some reason. Perhaps the hostsso group shares something in common (for instance, maybe the same server holds the file system for nfs root mounting). Each group statement contains group-specific declarations and options, plus two or more other statements. These other statements are typically host statements that identify specific hosts, and these statements contain host specific parameters (see Listing 35.5).

LISTING 35.5 SAMPLE GROUP STATEMENT

```
group {
    filename  zImage.nfs.boot ;
    next-server foo.void.org;
        host bar {hardware ethernet 00:00:3c:b2:08:15; }
        host baz {hardware ethernet 00:00:4f:ef:12:a5; }
}
```

In Listing 35.5 you can see that the group statement requires no parameters; because groups are only meant for the DHCP server internally, no reference outside the group statement is ever needed. You can have as many group statements as you want. You can have other groups that use other filename declarations or next-server declarations, and so on. The filename declaration tells the DHCP server to point to the hosts that are listed below to the file that is named in quotes for booting. The next-server tells the DHCP client where to look for the root file system. Finally, the host, which takes the hostname as an argument, includes the required declarations for the host. These are the hardware type (Ethernet) and the hardware address.

Tip

To get the hardware address from a NIC, you can boot from a modular kernel image such as the one that is provided with OpenLinux. Look for a line similar to the following:

```
Jan 15 18:18:00 foo kernel: eth0: Digital DC21041 Tulip at 0xb800, 21041
mode, 00 00 c0 83 c0 d0, IRQ 10
```

The part of the line that reads `00 00 c0 83 c0 d0` is the hardware address for the NIC. All that's required is that this set of six octets (six bytes) have colons substituted for the spaces.

Given the fact that setup is more detailed—that is, you must also have the NIC address—these statements are not used except where they are required. If a NIC is changed in any of these hosts, you must remember to change the hardware address in the configuration file.

Although group statements are normally used for hosts, as in the previous example, the group statement can be used to group nearly anything: shared networks, subnets, even other groups. Its usage is determined by your specific requirements.

CONFIGURING DHCPD FOR BOOTP

The final configuration step involves configuring hosts that make BOOTP queries rather than DHCP queries. Just as with the preceding host declaration in the group statement, you'll need to know the hardware address of the NIC that is requesting configuration information. In fact, the declaration for BOOTP hosts is almost identical to the host declaration in the previous group statement (compare Listing 35.5 to Listing 35.6).

LISTING 35.6 SAMPLE BOOTP ENTRY

```
host tazfoo {
  hardware ethernet 08:00:09:ed:8e:0d;
  fixed-address tazfoo.void.org;
}
```

In Listing 35.6, the host statement is the same as the preceding host statement for groups, but it requires a resolvable host name or IP address. If a host name is used, it must resolve to one and only one IP address.

Caution

One major difference between BOOTP and DHCP is that DHCP has lease times. When a BOOTP client receives an address, that address is assumed by default to have a duration of infinity. That is, the BOOTP host will use that address for as long as it is running. See the following section for two ways to avoid this problem.

Two methods can be used to prevent BOOTP clients from retaining their addresses until the next shutdown. The availability of these methods depends on the DHCP server you are using. Check the documentation. The first method is with a declaration that might be used in the global section: `dynamic-bootp-lease-length time_in_seconds`. This declaration forces BOOTP hosts to reacquire their addresses during the period that is specified in this declaration. The second method is with the following declaration: `dynamic-bootp-lease-cutoff` *`date`*. The date is in the following form:

```
W YYYY/MM/DD HH:MM:SS
```

It can be read as follows: `W` is the day of the week from zero to six (Sunday to Saturday); the `YYYY/MM/DD` and `HH:MM:SS` are self-explanatory as to their parameters. Note, however, that the time expressed is interpreted as Greenwich Mean Time (GMT), also referred to as Universal Coordinated Time (UTC)—not local time. This declaration might appear as part of the global section or as a declaration under individual host statements.

Caution

Despite the use of these parameters, BOOTP clients do not renew their leases. The clients require a reboot or a shutdown and restart of their networking subsystems to regain the lease. The DHCP server just refuses to recognize the lease. Some clients might stop using the lease, but you should not depend on this.

DNS AND DHCP

Throughout the text, examples using DNS or other types of resolution have been used for many parameters. However, for pure DHCP clients, DNS resolution becomes a problem. Because the addresses that can be given to any one client cannot be foreseen, they cannot be entered into the DNS table. Several solutions to this problem are being worked on. Some commercial DNS packages that can merge information from the dhcp.leases file into the database are available. But the DNS package that is currently offered in OpenLinux and the DHCP server do not presently talk to each other.

The solution for the moment, at least with the packages that are provided, is to use the DHCP server to assign specific addresses. The DHCP server can provide static addresses by including host statements within subnets. These host statements are identical to those that are used in the host statements in the BOOTP example. This method is a tradeoff between configuring hosts individually and allowing full dynamic address assignment. It permits the use of DHCP for systems that don't speak BOOTP, while permitting the micro-management of IP addresses à la BOOTP. Then, when address changes need to take place, they can be done once in the DNS files; as leases expire (or the hosts are restarted), the addresses update.

CONFIGURING DHCP CLIENTS

OpenLinux does not provide the DHCP client daemon (dhcpcd) to obtain a dynamic IP address from a DHCP server (that is, it is not offered as of this writing; but check the distribution, including the contribs folder). However, one can be obtained from `ftp://sunsite.unc.edu/pub/Linux/system/network/daemons/dhcpcd*`. This client is easily set up. Configuration is normally performed by Caldera's administration utility.

Caution

The dhcpc daemon reconfigures any interface that it is called against. Ensure that dhcpcd is configured to run against only those interfaces to which you want a dynamic address given.

Looking in /etc/sysconfig/network-scripts, the file that is of interest to you is ifcfg-eth0 (or ifcfg-eth1, if your system is so configured). Within this file is a parameter called `BOOTPROTO`. This parameter is one of the following: `none`, `bootp`, or `dhcp`. Naturally, the `dhcpc RPM` must be installed for DHCPC to work.

After dhcpcd is started, /etc/dhcpc, a directory that is created during installation of the dhcpc RPM, is populated with two files. These files are resolv.conf (see Listing 35.7) and hostinfo-eth0 (see Listing 35.8). The information in these files comes from the server. This information will be used by dhcpcd in future messages to the server (explained as follows) to try to obtain the same IP address each time the system is restarted on the network.

LISTING 35.7 SAMPLE /ETC/DHCPC/RESOLV.CONF FILE

```
domain void.org
nameserver 192.168.10.61
```

As you can see in Listing 35.7, this looks exactly like the resolv.conf file in /etc. The difference is that this file is changed based on the information received from the DHCP server. The old values are compared to the new, and if the new values are changed, the old values are discarded.

LISTING 35.8 SAMPLE /ETC/DHCPC/HOSTINFO-ETHO FILE

```
LEASETIME=604800
RENEWALTIME=302400
REBINDTIME=529200
IDPADDR=192.168.10.195
NETMASK=255.255.255.0
BROADCAST=192.168.10.255
ROUTER=192.168.10.90
```

This file is used during the span of the lease, and it is used if the host is restarted to attempt to reacquire the lease. The `leasetime` is the time (in seconds) of the lease. The `renewaltime` is when the first renewal will be attempted. Note that this is at 50 percent of the leasetime. It will tries again at 75 percent (half the 50 percent value), and again at 87.5 percent (another half). The `rebindtime` variable is `529200`, which corresponds to 87.5 percent of the leasetime, or the third retry to renew the lease. At this point, dhcpcd reinitiates the discovery process (as outlined later).

The rest of the file is self-explanatory; the router line is the gateway. The behavior of this DHCP client is fairly standard in regards to renewal and rebind times. Other parameters can be included if they are provided from the DHCP server, but they are primarily networking options.

If you are using a Linux DHCP server, you should have no trouble obtaining a lease. If you are using another DHCP server, one that requires that a hostname be sent to it, you might need to make some changes to /etc/dhcpcd.conf to enable this behavior. Specifically, you can specify that dhcpcd send a hostname by specifying this either on the command line or in the /etc/dhcpcd.conf file via the `-h` *`hostname`* argument.

OpenLinux also provides the BOOTP client (bootpc). As seen previously, this client can also be used, but it must be configured in the DHCP or BOOTP server first.

DHCP Messages and Overview of the DHCP Process

The following paragraphs attempt to describe the process that DHCP clients and servers go through when negotiating DHCP leases. This is a summary of RFC 1541, which is authoritative and is subject to becoming obsolete if a new RFC that pertains to DHCP is released in the future.

NEW DHCP CLIENTS

When a new DHCP client enters a network, it sends out a DHCPDISOVER message. This broadcast message is an attempt to locate DHCP servers on the subnet, or to locate a DHCP relay that is connected to the subnet.

All DHCP servers respond to DHCPDISCOVER messages with DHCPOFFER. The DHCP client looks at the DHCPOFFER messages in the order in which they arrive. The first response is examined. The client has two options: Send a DHCPREQUEST or DHCPDECLINE message.

If a client believes that a parameter it received in a DHCPOFFER is incorrect (the network address is on the wrong subnet, for example), it sends a DHCPDECLINE and continues to the next DHCPOFFER. If all DHCPOFFERs are declined, it rebroadcasts a DHCPDISCOVER message.

After a client is satisfied with a DHCPOFFER, it sends a DHCPREQUEST to the appropriate server (implicitly declining offers from all other servers), requesting that the DHCPOFFER be accepted by the server.

When the DHCP server receives the DHCPREQUEST, it has two options. The server can send a DHCPACK with configuration parameters and commit this information to the dhcpd.leases database, or it can send a DHCPNAK, indicating the reason for refusal (address already in use, and so on).

A DHCPNAK back to a client results in the client restarting the process from DHCPDISCOVER. A DHCPACK that is received by the client results in the client committing the configuration and communicating on the network via its newly received address.

Listing 35.9 shows what the DHCP server commits to its dhcpd.leases file after the client sends a DHCPOFFER that is accepted by the server. This entry takes place just prior to the DHCPACK message being sent to the client.

LISTING 35.9 SAMPLE DHCPD.LEASES ENTRY

```
lease 192.168.10.224 {
        starts 0 1999/01/17 19:34:02;
        ends 0 1999/01/24 19:34:02;
        hardware ethernet 00:00:c0:83:c0:d0;
        uid 01:00:00:c0:83:c0:d0;
        client-hostname "TMT";
}
```

Based on previous text, this file is simple to read. The lease statement line contains the IP address as a parameter. The declarations inside the statement contain detailed information about the lease. The start time (this date and time is read the same as the dynamic-lease-bootp-cutoff date) indicates that the lease started (or was renewed) on Sunday, 17 Jan 1999, at 19:34:02 GMT. The lease ends on Sunday, 24 Jan 1999, at 19:34:02 GMT. The hardware address is self-explanatory. The uid is a string that the client sent and that it will use to identify itself in future communications (DHCPREQUEST or DHCPRELEASE messages). Clients are now supposed to send their hardware addresses preceded by a number. Some older clients do not do this, instead sending an arbitrary string. The final declaration is optional and might not be sent by all DHCP clients. Some clients send a client-host declaration, and others send on a host name declaration. If a declaration is sent, it is duly recorded.

Continuing Leases

Three things might occur during the course of a lease: A client might remain connected to the network, the client might be gracefully shut down, or the client might crash. Each of these carries with it different consequences. The two disconnection scenarios, a graceful shutdown and a crash, might each also carry with it two possibilities when the client reconnects.

In the case of a graceful shutdown, many clients send a DHCPRELEASE message to the DHCP server. This is not required, so it is not universally employed. If such a message is sent, the IP address is immediately returned to the pool. If the client does not send this message, the results are the same as a crash—the lease remains until expiration, until it is removed by the server, or until it is re-leased by the same client.

Some clients record the information that they receive in the DHCPACK from the server and make use of this information again as if they never left the network. In the case of a graceful shutdown (regardless of whether a DHCPRELEASE message was sent), or in a crash with a client that remembers the information from the previous connection, things work as they do with a client that remains connected.

For clients that remain connected, at a predetermined time in the lease (generally the halfway point), the client will attempt to renegotiate the lease with the server from which it obtained the lease. If that fails, it uses the time to the end of the lease to recompute a value using the same algorithm to try again. This process continues until the lease expires, at which time the client must release the address and start the discovery process over again.

But for those clients that either remain on the network or remember previous information, the process explained previously for new clients is short-circuited. In this case, clients skip the discovery process and begin with the DHCPREQUEST message. If the client has moved to another subnet, it receives a DHCPNAK from the server and starts over with the discovery process. Otherwise, the server uses the uid information that it receives in the DHCPREQUEST message, along with the IP address that the client is requesting to verify that this client was the last one to have the requested address. If so, the lease might be re-leased to that client via a DHCPACK.

SUMMARY

In this chapter, you learned the basics about how ARP, BOOTP, and DHCP work. You learned how to set up both DHCP servers and clients for basic operations. You learned how DHCP servers and clients negotiate address assignments. For more information on dynamic networking, refer to the following chapters:

- Chapter 23, "Advanced Network Features," discusses different files that pertain to networking, and how they fit together. This will help you understand where DHCP fits into the networking process.
- See Chapter 26, "Domain Name Server (DNS)," to learn more about name resolution. This will help you understand how DHCP and DNS work together.
- See Chapter 32 to learn how to set up and configure an NFS server so that it can serve a root file system to clients.

CHAPTER 36

Setting Up a Sample Network

In this chapter

Probably one of the most exciting moments for new OpenLinux users is when their first network is successfully implemented. OpenLinux, as illustrated elsewhere in this book, works great as a desktop system, but to limit it to desktop use is like purchasing a Ferrari just to drive back and forth to the grocery store. Linux is a fantastic operating system for networking; you are cheating yourself if you do not at least try networking with it—even just between two machines—just to see what it is like.

One of the fastest growing uses of Linux seems to be in home networking. It is common to find more than one computer in a home, so this is somewhat understandable. The classic *SneakerNet*, in which data was transferred by copying it to a disk and carrying the disk to another machine, is no longer acceptable to most people with multiple computers, and it is a waste of resources. Resources such as printers, disk drives, and even Internet access can be shared across a network, and the cost of setting it all up is rather low (an average low-end Ethernet card for a PC can cost around $25, and the cabling that connects the machines is even less expensive—you will learn about hardware shortly).

This chapter discusses setting up a small network at home. However, the principles and concepts are not unique to home use; you can take these instructions into your office and use them to set up a network server there. Furthermore, with the way that OpenLinux is licensed, you can take your CD-ROM in and use it to set up all the other machines on the network as well without incurring any extra costs or per-seat restrictions. It is a win-win situation for everyone involved.

HARDWARE

Network hardware covers quite a range of possible network connections. There are items that cover networking over frame relay, or through the same cable that gives you television services, *digital subscriber lines* (*DSL*), or even satellite dishes. There are router boxes and firewall boxes, and nowadays there are embedded Web server machines, some of which even run Linux. There are watchdog boxes that monitor your network and make sure that the server is rebooted if it appears to have crashed. There are multiport serial devices that set up dial-in connections through the use of modems. There are as many different types of networking hardware devices as there are types of networks, and the list continues to grow.

Despite the many different types of hardware that are available for networks, for the sake of simplicity only the three most basic, most essential kinds are discussed here: network cards, cabling, and hubs.

NETWORK CARDS

Naturally, each computer that is going to be networked has to have its own network card. There are many different kinds of network cards, but the ones most commonly used are of the Ethernet variety. The quality of these cards run the gamut from $25 NE2000 clones all the way up to major name brand offerings that can transfer data ten times as fast as the low end clones, and then some. Find out what others who have networks either at home or at work recommend.

Unless you are doing really serious data transfers over your network, you will be just fine with the low-end NE2000 clones. These come in a few different varieties, the most common being 10Base-T, 10Base-2, and 10Base-T/2. As indicated by the classification of the card, it is capable of transferring ten megabits of information at any given time. The *T*, *2*, and *T/2* at the end of the classification indicate the cabling that is required by the card.

CABLING

Computers with network cards are pretty much useless unless they are connected with network cables. 10Base-T cards use what is known as Cat.5 twisted pair cabling. This kind of cabling has what look like telephone plugs at each end; because it does not permit direct card-to-card connections between computers, it is typically used in conjunction with a hub (hubs are discussed a bit later). A special kind of twisted pair cable called a *reverse pair cable* permits direct connections, though, and is commonly used to connect one hub to another or one computer directly to another computer. The use of a hub is much more common. Networks that use these cards tend to be arranged in a star topology around a central location at which the hub resides (see Figure 36.1).

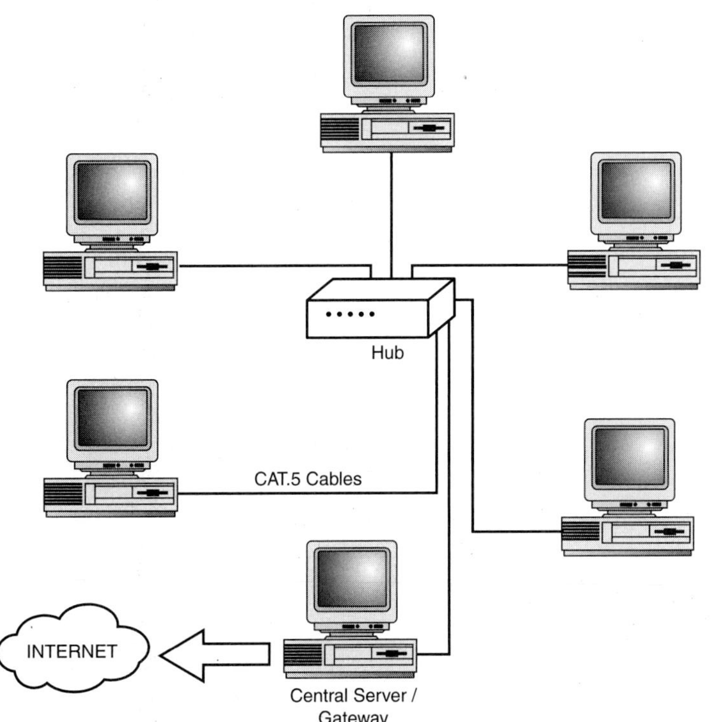

Figure 36.1
A 10Base-T network scheme.

10Base-2 cards use coaxial cable similar to those used with cable TV. Instead of having what look like phone plugs at the ends, these cables have what are called *terminators*—little metal devices that terminate the line by looping the wiring back into the cable. The cables themselves are connected to the network cards with small tees. Networks that use these types of cables tend to be strung together in one long line, with each computer joining the connection at the tee in the back of the network card (see Figure 36.2).

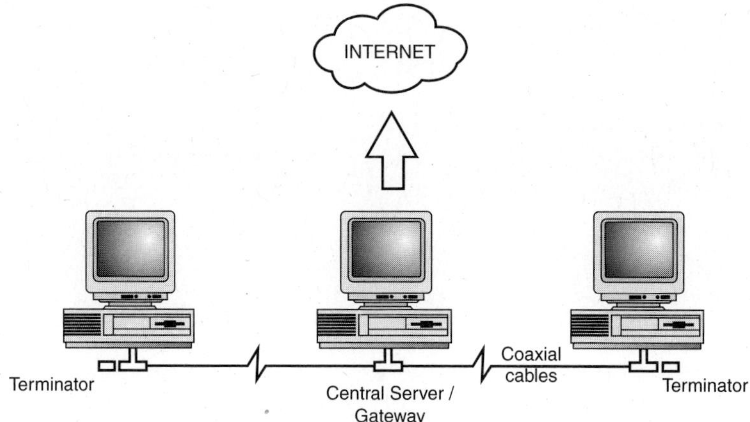

Figure 36.2
A 10Base-2 network scheme.

The drawback to using this kind of cabling with 10Base-2 cards is that for each cable coming into the computer's room from the previous system, another cable has to go out of the room for the next system. The benefit to using twisted pair cabling with 10Base-T cards is that only one cable is is needed to connect the computer in the room.

What about 10Base-T/2 cards? They simply have jacks on the back that can handle both types of cables.

Hubs

Hubs are small boxes that can accommodate a number of different network cable connections, but they are primarily used to connect computers containing 10Base-T cards. Among their benefits, they can act as the central connection point for all systems on a network, or they can help to split the network connections into more easily manageable chunks (see Figure 36.3). For instance, if there are multiple rooms with multiple computers in each, it makes more sense to take one cable into each room and give each its own hub than it does to have multiple cables coming out of each room going to a central hub.

Hubs can also act as traffic cops by helping to monitor network traffic for packet collisions.

A typical four- or eight-port hub can cost anywhere from $40 to more than $100, depending on the brand and the features. Again, unless you are planning on passing around bandwidth-intensive network traffic, stay inexpensive. Buying features can be fun, but if you never really use the features you are wasting your money.

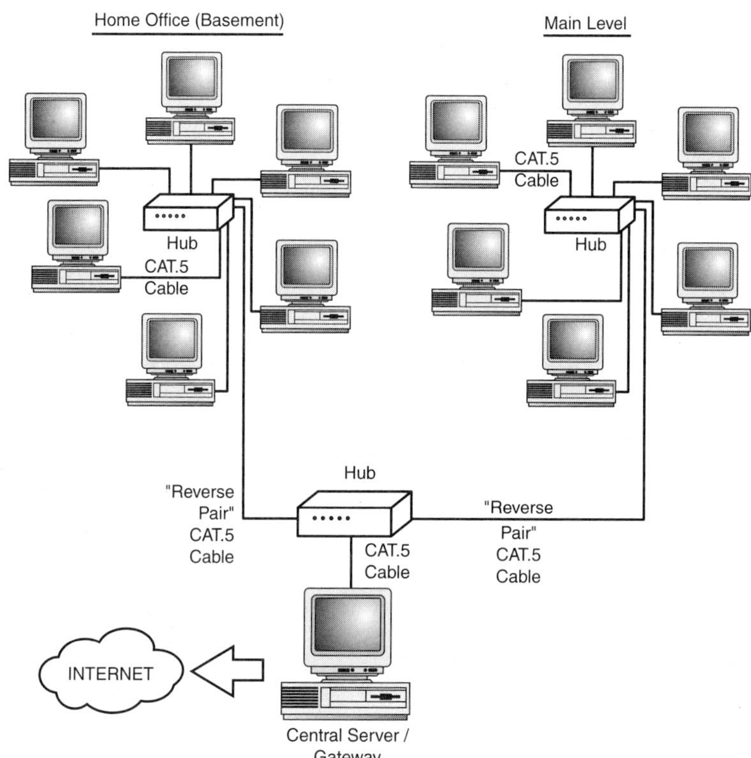

Figure 36.3
Another 10Base-T network scheme.

Caution

There is hardware available for 100Mb networking if you are interested. Be careful about mixing bandwidths if you are using a hub, though; if you have 10Base-T or 10Base-2 (or 10Base-T/2) cards, do not purchase a 100Mb hub to connect them. Mixing bandwidths in this manner does not work without special, expensive switching hubs. If you plan on eventually moving to a 100Mb network, it might be cheaper in the long run for you to simply go 100Mb right from the start.

ASSUMPTIONS

The following sample network consists of five computers: four PCs running various operating systems (including Windows NT and OpenLinux) and one Mac. All are connected via 10BaseT/2 Ethernet cards through a small 10BaseT hub with twisted pair cabling.

TABLE 36.1 ASSUMPTIONS FOR YOUR SAMPLE NETWORK

Computer Name	IP Address	Type	O/S Used
rumble.fish.net	192.168.1.1	PC	OpenLinux
gefilte.fish.net	192.168.1.2	PC	Windows 95
go.fish.net	192.168.1.3	PC	Windows NT
silver.fish.net	192.168.1.4	Apple	System 7.5
tuna.fish.net	192.168.1.5	PC	OpenLinux

Note: fish.net is being used as an example only. If your network is going to be connected to the Internet, please register your own domain name and do not use fish.net. Of course, if fish.net is not taken…

All systems are connected via TCP/IP, plus various other protocols that allow the connection of networked drives. For the sake of brevity, only the TCP/IP setup is addressed here. Also for the sake of brevity, it is assumed that the names of the OpenLinux systems were assigned when the systems were installed. For the Windows and Mac systems, the assumption is made that they already have names as well.

Each system has the equivalent of a *hosts* file that contains all the preceding addresses plus the localhost address. A DNS server can work on this network as well, but it is a bit excessive for a network of this size.

The format of the file is actually quite consistent across the various platforms. Each one will resemble Listing 36.1.

LISTING 36.1 SAMPLE HOSTS FILE

```
127.0.0.1     localhost
192.168.1.1  rumble.fish.net  rumble
192.168.1.2  gefilte.fish.net gefilte
192.168.1.3  go.fish.net       go
192.168.1.4  silver.fish.net  silver
192.168.1.5  tuna.fish.net    tuna
```

This file has different locations depending on the system in question:

- For OpenLinux, it is /etc/hosts.
- On WindowsNT, the file is most likely \WINNT\SYSTEM32\DRIVERS\ETC\HOSTS.SAM.

- The file for Windows 95 is \WINDOWS\HOSTS.SAM.
- The Hosts file for the Mac is in the System Folder.

Rumble.fish.net—the server—is set up to dial out to the Internet. It has IP masquerading set up, so the other computers on the network can use it as an Internet gateway (see Chapter 29, "IP Masquerading," for more details).

Rumble's Linux kernel was precompiled with the necessary protocol support (TCP/IP, PPP), IP forwarding/gatewaying, and everything required for IP masquerading support.

Note

You must be logged in as root to perform the OpenLinux configurations detailed in this chapter. The ownerships and permissions on the files that will be edited require superuser status; therefore, plain users cannot perform any edits.

THE INDIVIDUAL SYSTEMS

The tuna.fish.net system (which runs OpenLinux) is used as an example. As detailed in Chapter 21, "Understanding TCP/IP Fundamentals," the TCP/IP configuration for OpenLinux is held in the /etc/sysconfig/network-scripts directory. The configuration for each network interface is contained in its own separate file within this directory. The Ethernet configurations are held in the ifcfg-eth# files (starting with ifcfg-eth0). Assuming that tuna.fish.net only has one Ethernet interface, Listing 36.2 shows the contents of its ifcfg-eth0 file.

LISTING 36.2 SAMPLE /ETC/SYSCONFIG/NETWORK-SCRIPTS/IFCFG-ETHO FILE

```
#!/bin/sh

#>>>Device type: ethernet
#>>>Variable declarations:
DEVICE=eth0
IPADDR=192.168.1.5
NETMASK=255.255.255.0
NETWORK=192.168.1.0
BROADCAST=192.168.1.255
GATEWAY=192.168.1.1
ONBOOT=yes
#>>>End of variable declarations
```

Note the gateway specification. It is pointing to the IP address used by rumble.fish.net, which is the server that will eventually be connecting to the Internet. All computers that will be given access to the Internet through rumble need to have it specified as the gateway system; otherwise, no Internet access will be possible.

Also note the netmask, network, and broadcast addresses. These are used on all computers on the network. In fact, the only address that changes per machine on a typical network is the IP address; all the rest of the addresses are shared among all computers on the same subnetwork.

When discussing addresses, it is important to note that some sort of name server is required for Internet usage (your hosts files only cover address conversion on the local network). Because Internet navigation will be common on this network, the ISP's name servers need to be used when addresses outside the local network are requested. These addresses are entered in various locations on the various systems (for instance, in the Network setup under Control Panel on Windows systems, and in the MacTCP extension on the Mac); but on OpenLinux, they are entered in the /etc/resolv.conf file. Assuming the IP address for the ISP's nameservers are 192.168.100.100 and 192.168.100.101, Listing 36.3 illustrates the OpenLinux systems' /etc/resolv.conf files (including rumble's):

LISTING 36.3 SAMPLE /ETC/RESOLV.CONF FILE

```
search fish.net
domain fish.net
nameserver 192.168.100.100
nameserver 102.168.100.101
```

The search and domain lines contain the domain name that you are using on your network.

Recall the discussions on SysV initialization in Chapter 12, "System Initialization Under OpenLinux." When networking changes are made on the OpenLinux systems, you can use the `/etc/rc.d/init.d/network` SysV initialization script to restart the networking. This causes the changes to take effect without rebooting:

```
/etc/rc.d/init.d/network stop
/etc/rc.d/init.d/network start
```

THE SERVER

When all computers on the network are set up with their proper addressing, it is time to set up the IP masquerading rules on rumble. The sample rules in Chapter 29 work here because the same bogus IP address set used in that chapter is being used here:

```
ipchains -P forward DENY
ipchains -A forward -j MASQ -s 192.168.0.0/24 -d 0.0.0.0/0
```

These lines need to be placed in rumble's /etc/rc.d/rc.local file. There are also some modules that you might want to load from the module auto-load file that enable certain processes that are destined to the Internet to work correctly through a server that is masquerading IP addresses. These modules were discussed in Chapter 29 as well, and the module auto-load list was covered in Chapter 18, "Kernel Modules."

The following lines can be added to the module auto-load list to load all the IP masquerading add-on modules:

```
ip_masq_cuseeme
ip_masq_ftp
ip_masq_irc
ip_masq_quake
ip_masq_raudio
ip_masq_vdolive
```

At this point, the server machine can be restarted to load the masquerading rules; as with networking changes, however, most people favor immediate gratification over waiting for a system to start all over again. Simply execute the `ipchains` commands manually to load the masquerading rules, and then run the `insmod` utility on each of the module names you added to the module auto-load list.

Of course, this is all for naught if there is no Internet connection on rumble, so a reliable dial-up connection to an Internet provider is required. For this network, a simple PAP authenticated PPP connection (by far the most common method used today with ISPs) is assumed. Following the instructions listed in Chapter 24, "Connecting to an ISP," a pap-secrets file and an options file are created in the /etc/ppp directory. For this example, the following is assumed for the dial-up Internet account:

```
Username: myname
Password: mypass
ISP phone number: 555-1111
Address is allocated: dynamically
Modem port: /dev/ttyS1 (the same as COM2 under DOS/Windows)
```

With these assumptions, the pap-secrets and options file looks like that shown in Listing 36.4.

LISTING 36.4 /ETC/PPP/PAP-SECRETS

```
# Secrets for authenticating using PAP
# client      server        secret        IP addresses
myname           *            mypass
```

Because this file contains sensitive information such as the password required by the ISP, it should only be readable and writeable by the root user. Because the file was created by root, the only thing that is required for this security measure is a change in the permissions to the file:

```
chmod 600 /etc/ppp/pap-secrets
```

Following this change, the options file looks like Listing 36.5.

LISTING 36.5 /ETC/PPP/OPTIONS

```
connect "/usr/sbin/chat -f /etc/ppp/chat-script"
/dev/ttyS1 115200
modem
crtscts
defaultroute
noipdefault
user myname
```

With this options file, PPP uses the second serial port as the modem device (locked in at 115,200 bps), reads modem control messages, uses hardware handshaking (crtscts), sets the modem device as the default network route when connected, negotiates a dynamically allocated IP address, and uses `myname` to start the authentication process after connecting.

As you can see in the first line, the `chat` utility is being executed and a file called chat-script, which contains the parameters that chat uses to connect to the ISP, is passed to it. With a PAP authenticated login, all that needs to be done is to make a successful modem connection; PAP takes it from there.

Listing 36.6 shows what the chat-script file contains.

LISTING 36.6 /ETC/PPP/CHAT-SCRIPT

```
ABORT     BUSY
""     ATDT5551111
CONNECT     ""
```

That covers the basic PPP dial-up configuration.

Earlier it was mentioned that the same addresses (except for the actual IP address of any particular system's Ethernet card) are shared among all the computers on the network. This is true, but there is one small modification to the rule: rumble is the gateway machine for the other computers, but it is not using its Ethernet card as a gateway to the Internet—it's using the modem via PPP—so *it has no gateway*.

Caution

You cannot have your system gating through an Ethernet card and through a modem at the same time; if you are using PPP and a modem to gate out to the Internet, do not specify an Ethernet gateway. Replace any address in the `GATEWAY=` line with `none`.

MISCELLANY

Some odd items that are set up on a per-client basis on non-Linux systems are set up on a system-wide basis on Linux systems. For instance, things such as the address of the ISP's news server and the masquerading of outgoing mail (making it look as though it's emanating from the ISP, and not from your personal machine) are typically handled on a systemwide basis. This is not necessarily a bad thing; this way, you can set/change one setting and all the applicable client programs you use will utilize the new setting.

By far, the most popular item set in this manner is the domain used for outgoing email. Chapter 25, "Email Setup," addresses configuration issues and schemes used with sendmail; the m4 configuration system discussed in that chapter is used to accomplish masquerading a domain name.

Simply put, the following two lines are added to your system's .mc file:

```
MASQUERADE_AS(isp-domain.net)
FEATURE(masquerade_envelope)
```

Afterward, a new /etc/sendmail.cf file is created as follows:

```
cp /etc/sendmail.cf /etc/sendmail.cf.backup
m4 ../m4/cf.m4 yourmcfile.mc > /etc/sendmail.cf
```

Note that you must have the `sendmail-cf` package installed to do this (see Chapter 15, "Software Package Management," for information on package management). After performing this step, sendmail needs to be stopped and started again as follows:

```
/etc/rc.d/init.d/mta stop
/etc/rc.d/init.d/mta start
```

With that done, all outgoing email is sent as `username@isp-domain.net`. To change the domain name that is used, change the `MASQUERADE_AS()` line in the system's .mc file and recompile the /etc/sendmail.cf file.

Setting up systems to read news from a remote NNTP host is another common change to OpenLinux systems. Luckily, it requires fewer steps than masquerading mail addresses.

The address of a remote NNTP news server is typically stored in an environment variable called `NNTPSERVER`. Setting this with the `bash` shell is fairly simple:

```
export NNTPSERVER=news.isp-domain.net
```

Using the C shell (`csh`), the command looks more like the following:

```
setenv NNTPSERVER news.isp-domain.net
```

The command can be placed in the appropriate rc file in a user's home directory (.profile or .cshrc, respectively) to set the variable automatically every time a shell is started; or it can be placed in one of the main shell configuration files in /etc (profile or csh.cshrc, respectively) to have the variable set systemwide when the system is started.

Summary

In this chapter, you learned how to set up a basic home network. The knowledge used to set up this network was covered in the chapters that comprise Part IV, "Networking with OpenLinux." Hardware was discussed at some length, as were the general design criteria of a small home network. Note that there is no hard, fast rule about how a network must be arranged, nor is there anything saying that 10Base-2 is always better or worse than 10Base-T. Go with what works for you and your network arrangement.

Naturally, every possible service that can be implemented on a network was not covered in this chapter. That is what the rest of the book is for; this chapter merely assembled some of the knowledge in previous chapters to help you to build a base on which these other services can be added. After the network is up and running, adding another service to it can be as simple as executing an RPM command with the OpenLinux CD-ROM mounted.

For more information on the topics discussed here, refer to the remainder of the chapters in Part IV. Start with the following chapters:

- See Chapter 14, "Printing," to learn more about setting up printing services—local and remote—on your network.
- See Chapter 34, "Microsoft Windows & OpenLinux," for information on setting up Windows file sharing on your network.
- See Chapter 24 for information on alternative methods of giving your network Internet access.

PART V

X Window

CHAPTER 37

Configuring X

In this chapter

In this chapter, you will look at using the different configuration utilities that are available for X. You'll start by looking at `SuperProbe`, and then `XF86Setup` and `xf86config`, and, finally, `xvidtune`.

One of the more difficult and potentially damaging (to your hardware) things you'll do is configure your X Server. The X Server is one of two pieces you need to set up to have a *graphical user interface* (*GUI*) on your system. Few users these days care to use a system that presents them with a command-line interface; therefore, configuring an X server is one of the tasks you'll need to perform for systems that are destined to be workstations. But this is only one of two tasks that you'll need to perform to put a GUI on your OpenLinux system. In fact, this is the harder task. Because a default window manager is set up for you, you merely need to refine its configuration. (You'll look at window managers in subsequent chapters.)

ABOUT THE X SERVER

The X Server is the *server piece* that needs to run on the local machine. The window manager is the *client piece* and can be run locally or on another machine. Although this arrangement might seem counterintuitive, a closer look shows us that this makes sense. The X Server controls the monitor, video card, and mouse. The X server passes information about the mouse's position on the screen, and about key press/key release events, to the window manager. The window manager customizes what you see on the screen and what happens when key events are passed to it. The window manager is the program with which you interface; the server just serves the client up to you like a network server serves files, and so on, to you. The client/server model enables you to run the client from almost anywhere, whereas the X Server typically runs on the local machine.

Earlier it was mentioned that setting up an X Server is potentially damaging to your hardware. This is true. Selecting settings that exceed the capabilities of the monitor or video card can damage either or both. For this reason, it is important that you find out some information regarding your hardware before setting up the X Server. With any luck, your hardware will be listed in the server configuration files, and good values will be known for them. If not, you'll need to do a little searching, or select values you are sure do not exceed the capabilities of your hardware. Anyone who tells you that software cannot damage hardware has never fried a monitor or video card.

Caution

The majority of today's monitors (the decidedly more damage-prone part) go into a sleep mode if pushed beyond their rated limits—but don't let that fact lull you into a false sense of security. You can burn out your monitor exceeding its capabilities.

USING SuperProbe TO FIND INFORMATION

After you've looked for all the available information regarding your hardware—video card, monitor, and mouse—you need to ensure that you have the correct information (or more information, if you feel that the little bit that is supplied with your hardware is insufficient). So here's a look at `SuperProbe`, which is a configuration utility designed to assist you.

ABOUT YOUR VIDEO CARD

`SuperProbe`—hopefully—tells you something about your video card. This utility is not a panacea. In fact, it won't work for a number of cards. For the cards it works with, however, it can give you good information. You can take a look at the kind of cards `SuperProbe` can help you with by typing `SuperProbe -info`. The following general information is displayed:

- SuperProbe version and date
- Video hardware
- SVGA Chipsets and Vendors
- Graphics Coprocessors and Vendors
- RAMDACs

More cards and chipsets are added at each program update. But although `SuperProbe` probes the cards in the system, it is not infallible. Because it directly accesses the hardware, it must be run as root. As soon as it is invoked, you see a warning that this software can *hang* the machine because probed hardware can be put in an unstable state. If you have run-of-the-mill daughterboards in your system, you will not experience problems. The problems come with cards that make use of the video area of memory or, occasionally, with PCI cards.

The three pieces of information that are obtained from running this program against a Diamond Stealth 64 PCI are as follows:

- **First video**—Super-VGA
- **Chipset**—S3 Vision864 (PCI Probed)
- **Memory**—2048 Kbytes
- **RAMDAC**—S3 86C716 SDAC 15/16/24-bit DAC w/pixel-mux w/clock-PLL (with 6-bit wide lookup tables, or in 6-bit mode)

`SuperProbe` has options to restrict probes for any one or more of these parameters. If your system has problems, an in-depth read of the man page on `SuperProbe` is in order. Problems with `SuperProbe` are actually fairly rare, and don't warrant a detailed discussion here.

This is more than enough information for configuring your video card as long as it is listed in the cards database, as this one is. Cards that are not listed in the cards database normally use either the VGA or SVGA server. A card requiring the SVGA server might look like the following from a Diamond Stealth 3D 2000 Pro:

```
First video: Super-VGA
       Chipset: S3 ViRGE/DX (PCI Probed)
       Memory: 4096 Kbytes
       RAMDAC: Generic 8-bit pseudo-color DAC
               (with 6-bit wide lookup tables [or in 6-bit mode])
```

Note the lack of detailed information regarding RAMDAC. Although identified as an S3 Virge/DX chipset, this Diamond Stealth 3D 2000 Pro is not supported by the S3/Virge server. When you run the configuration program XF86Setup (discussed in a later section), and get to the video card selection screen and select this Diamond Multimedia card, the program selects the SVGA server for you. This is because several companies, including Diamond Multimedia, refuse to provide sufficient information regarding their cards—so programmers cannot write drivers for these cards without paying Diamond for the privilege. Furthermore, because Diamond refuses to cooperate with the Linux community, they won't write a driver. It is best to avoid these companies and their proprietary products. Although it is unusual for a video card to be damaged by exceeding its or the monitor's capabilities, it is possible.

About Your Monitor

Now you need some information regarding your monitor. Often, it is more difficult to find this information. Many manufacturers provide user manuals that tell you how to plug in and turn on the monitor, but nothing about the frequency ranges for the horizontal and vertical frequencies that you'll need. But often, with new monitors, you can get an idea from the programming functions found on the front panel. Review the various screens. You're looking for a set of two numbers, the first in the range of 31 to perhaps as high as 82, and the second generally 40 or 50 to 100. Very large, high quality monitors can often have a larger range of values. But you need to be very careful with this. Selecting a frequency beyond that of which your monitor is capable can result in a fried flyback transformer. You can hear this condition because it is often accompanied by a high-pitched whine coming from the back of the monitor just before the screen goes dark for good. Again, newer monitors often go into sleep mode if they are asked to exceed their maximum sync rates—but don't count on it.

Caution

If you hear a high-pitched whine coming from the back of your monitor, *shut it off immediately*. Your monitor's flyback transformer is in the throes of death. Do not count on protective circuitry to save your investment.

The numbers you find might or might not be accompanied by video sizes such as 1024×768 or 1280×1024. Note that you'll usually see higher frequencies listed by the slightly smaller screen sizes. That is, 1024×768 might show a horizontal sync of 62.5kHz and a vertical sync of 69Hz, whereas 1280×1024 only shows 63.9kHz and 59Hz. This is normal. So you know that you can select up to at least 64k as your horizontal sync and, most likely, 90Hz for your vertical sync (other selections might have shown 75Hz for horizontal sync, but a range of

50–90 is common). If you can find something in the user manual regarding the maximums, such as 1280×1024 at 60Hz, this corresponds to known safe values for the horizontal and vertical sync rates.

ABOUT YOUR MOUSE

The final piece of information you need concerns the mouse. Mice come in several varieties: bus mice, serial mice (probably the most common), and PS/2 mice. These can either have one of their own devices or be /dev/ttyS0, /dev/ttyS1 (commonly referred to by their DOS names of `COM1` and `COM2`), or /dev/psaux for the PS/2 mice. You might want to use /dev/mouse, and as long as /dev/mouse is a link to the correct device, this is acceptable. When you have an idea about those two items, the mouse type, and its connection, you are ready to forge ahead.

XFree86, as well as most commercial X servers, now also support optical mice, trackballs, and the Intellimouse, as well as the older Logitech mice and Inport mice. Several of these have their own special device, such as /dev/atibm, /dev/logibm, or /dev/inportbm for several of the bus mice, and so on. Most serial port mice take one that is from /dev/ttyS0 through /dev/ttyS3. The PS/2 type mice, all of which can be recognized by the PS/2 labeling on the end, connect to /dev/ps2.

Tip

The file /dev/mouse can be a symbolic link to any one of the preceding mice devices for convenience. The root user can do this by changing directories to /dev and issuing the command `ln -s <device> mouse`, where *`<device>`* is the specific mouse device, such as psaux, ttyS0, atibm, and so on.

CONFIGURING USING XF86Setup

Probably the easiest way to configure your X Server is to use the `XF86Setup` utility. This utility walks you through a complete X server setup in a graphical mode. `XF86Setup` is not restricted solely to configuring the X server; it can also be used to reconfigure it while X is running.

With that said, you can start `XF86Setup`. After it has started, do not touch the mouse until the mouse is configured and you've applied the changes—otherwise you might need to start over again. The first screen you'll see is the one shown in Figure 37.1, the initial splash screen. To continue, simply hit the Enter key; you'll get an instruction screen regarding mouse configuration (see Figure 37.2). Use the Page Up and Page Down keys to view the entire set of instructions. The main keys to remember are Tab (to move between fields), the arrow keys (to change selections), and the space bar or Enter key (to highlight the selection).

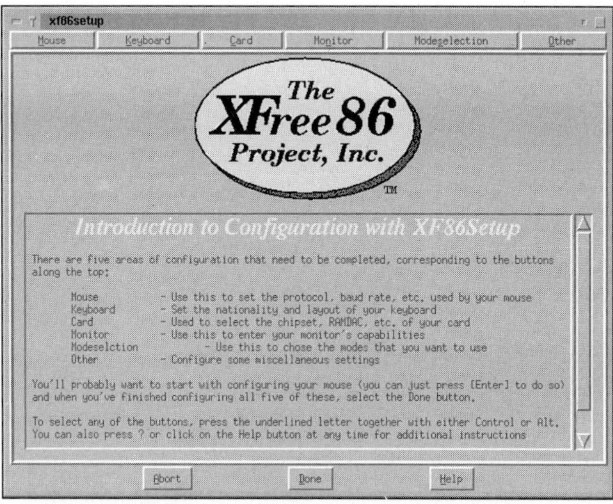

Figure 37.1
XFree86 Splash Screen.

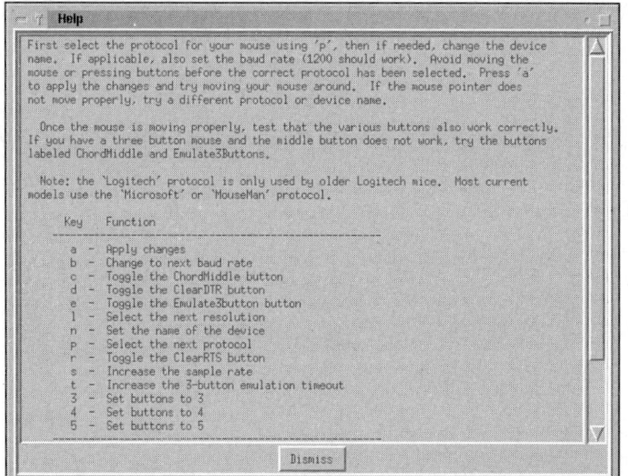

Figure 37.2
Initial instructions.

To leave the initial instruction screen, hit Enter and you'll be on the Mouse configuration screen (see Figure 37.3). Using the Tab key or the *P* key, change the current selection to your mouse type (protocol) and press the spacebar or Enter key. Tab to your mouse device (or use the *N* key) and either enter the correct device via the keyboard, or Tab to the selection field and use the up and down arrow keys to find your device; then use the Enter key to make it the active selection. When you're happy with your choices, you can hit the *A* key to apply the changes. At this point, you can try to use the mouse. If the mouse behaves erratically (jumps around the screen randomly or clings to the upper left corner of the screen and only jumps occasionally across the top of the screen), you've misconfigured it. Most likely, all you need to change is the protocol—if you selected the wrong device, nothing happens (and you can remedy that by choosing the correct device). You can try to use the keyboard again to select the protocol—the *P* shortcut key takes you to the first box, and subsequent presses of the *P* key continue through the selections. If the keyboard does not respond, you can start over by using the sequence Ctrl+Alt+Backspace, which terminates the X server. Otherwise, choose a different protocol and press the *A* key again to apply the changes and try the mouse once again. If the device you have chosen does not seem to work, but you are sure that it is the correct device, you might need to check that the appropriate module are loaded to activate the device.

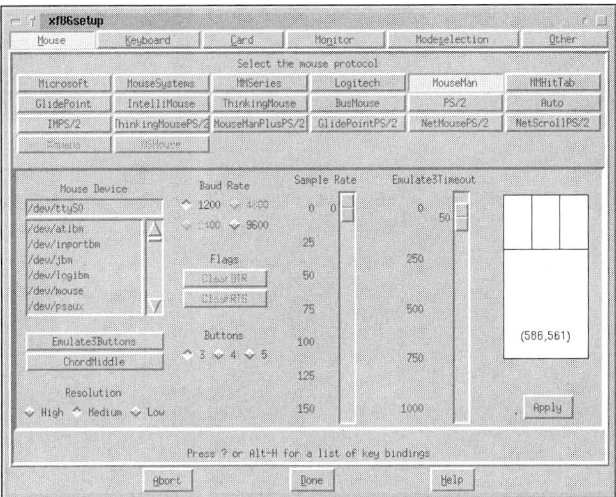

Figure 37.3
Input device configuration screen.

Tip

`/sbin/lsmod` shows you the loaded modules. For PS/2, you need to use `/sbin/insmod misc` and `psaux`, in that order. For serial ports (`COM1` and `COM2`), you need to use `/sbin/insmod serial`.

Bus mice require their own appropriate modules and might require a kernel recompile if not included in the default kernel.

When the mouse is working, you can use it to change any other options on the screen and apply them.

With your mouse configured, you can continue to the next screen to configure the keyboard (see Figure 37.4). Keyboard selection is relatively simple, and the keyboard graphic helps show the keyboard layout. If any options (such as changes to the location of the Ctrl key, and so on) are desired, they can also be made here and applied immediately.

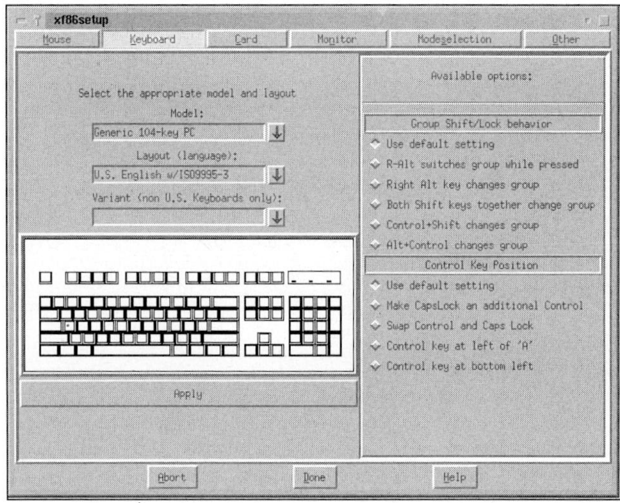

Figure 37.4
Keyboard configuration screen.

Your next screen is the Card List screen. By default, you enter the Card List screen first (see Figure 37.5), but `XF86Setup` remembers where you were, so if you were on the second (Detailed Setup) screen (see Figure 37.6) when you left last time, you'll return there. From the Card List screen you can select the card that you have in your system from a list of hundreds. Note that if you choose a card and do not have the appropriate X server installed, a warning appears below the card list telling you which server to install.

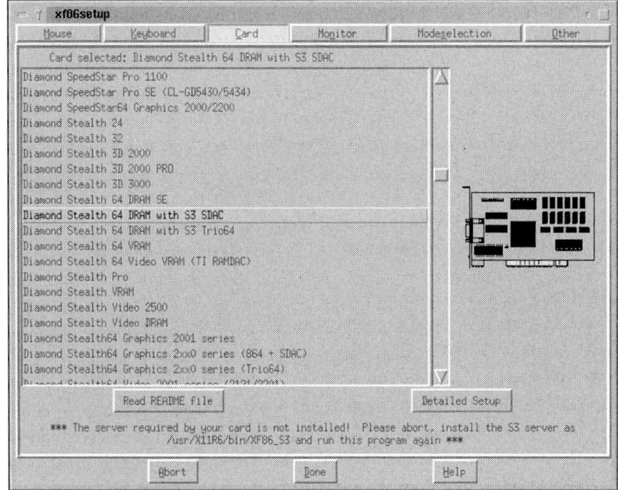

Figure 37.5
Video Card List screen.

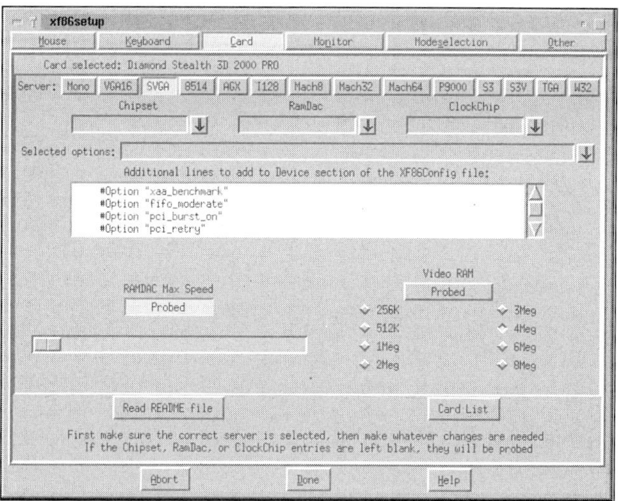

Figure 37.6
Video Card Detailed Setup screen.

Switching to the Detail Setup, you can view and change (if necessary) any information that is displayed. Normally, this is not necessary. Use care here because these selections override the generic setup information and, if they are wrong, can cause problems. Unless you find it necessary or just want to bypass probing, leave the default values. You might want to select the amount of video RAM, but most of the other settings are fine.

Your next screen is the Monitor screen (see Figure 37.7). If you are certain of the valid values for your monitor, particularly the Horizontal sync value, these can be entered manually in the boxes next to Horizontal and Vertical. Otherwise, select the appropriate monitor from the list inside the screen. Note that the values in the boxes increase as you go down the list.

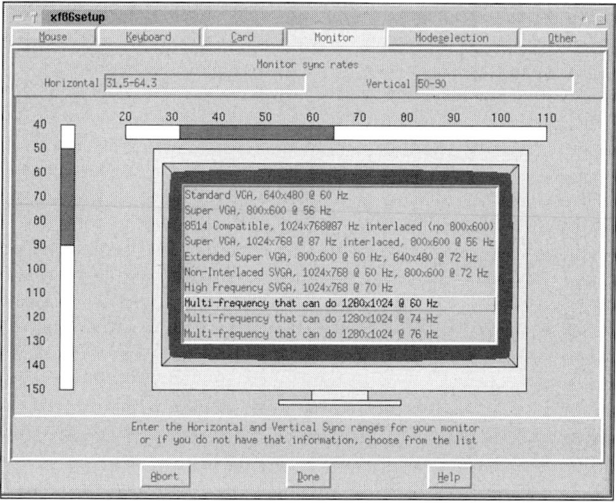

Figure 37.7
Monitor selection screen.

Caution

If in doubt about a monitor's capabilities, choose a less capable monitor selection than you have. If you overestimate the monitor's capabilities, you might have to buy a new monitor. Remember that the danger signal is a high-pitched whine coming from the monitor.

Continuing on to the Modeselection screen, you can select the default screen mode and color depth (see Figure 37.8).

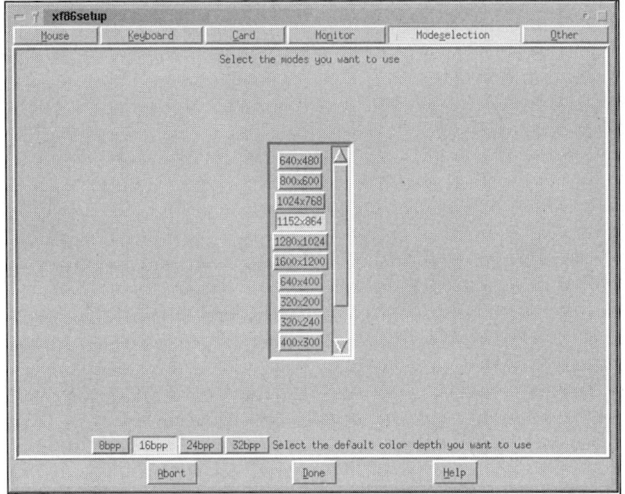

Figure 37.8
Select the modes and default color depth you want to use.

A word is needed here regarding color depth versus screen size. The 8, 16, 24, and 32 stand for the number of *bits per pixel* (*bpp*). These correspond to 256 colors; 65,536 (64k) colors; 16 million colors (16,777,216); and 4,294,967,000 colors, respectively. Often, you'll see the terms *pseudocolor* and *true color* applied to the 16 and 24bpp values. Note that 8, 16, 24, and 32bpp convert to 1, 2, 3, and 4 bytes, respectively (eight bits per byte), and that the video RAM in your card is measured in bytes. You can take the screen size you want to use and multiply the two numbers (which are the number of pixels horizontally and vertically), and then multiply by the number of bytes (1–4) to arrive at the amount of video RAM required to display your selected mode and color depth. This is a little easier to see in table form (only the most commonly-used sizes are displayed). Table 37.1 shows the amount of video RAM required for several different display modes at various color depths.

Table 37.1 Video RAM Requirements

Screen Size	Pixels	Color Depth: 8bpp	Color Depth: 16bpp	Color Depth: 24bpp	Color Depth: 32bpp
640×480	307,200	300KB	600KB	900KB	1.2MB
800×600	480,000	470KB	940KB	1.41MB	1.82MB
1024×768	786,432	768KB	1.54MB	2.31MB	3.08MB
1152×864	995,238	972KB	2.0MB	2.92MB	3.9MB
1280×1024	1,310,720	1.28MB	2.56MB	3.84MB	5.12MB
1600×1200	1,920,000	1.88MB	3.75MB	5.63MB	7.5MB

You can see that a video card with 512k memory only enables you to see a 640×480 or 800×600 pixel screen at 8bpp or 256 colors. Likewise, a 1Mb card permits you to see a maximum of 6400×480 at up to 24 bpp, 800×600 at up to 16bpp, or either 1024×768 or 1152×864 at only 8bpp. A 4Mb card gives you even more choices, but for extremely large modes and high color depths, you'll need an 8MB card.

Note

Regardless of the RAM on your video card, screen painting slows down at higher color depths. Although this is dependent on your display card, the more bits per pixel, the more time that is required to render the colors. With slow cards, the screen painting might be quite noticeable.

Your final screen, the Other screen, enables you to set those options that don't pertain to any of the previous screens (see Figure 37.9). Most of these can be left in their default state—the first two selected and the final three deselected. If you have a special setup, you might want to change these. The first box enables you to kill the X Server via the key sequence shown. The second box allows the video mode to be changed by using the Ctrl+Alt++ key sequence (using the numeric keypad plus sign key). All defined video modes can be cycled through. The third selection is only of interest if you are debugging the X server and don't want the X server to trap signals. However, as is stated in the note that accompanies this option (see the line following the third check box in Figure 37.9), selecting this might prevent the X Server from exiting the way it is supposed to. It still exits, but it does not properly clean up after itself. The next two check boxes permit operations from remote hosts. Normally, you won't want video modes switched from remote hosts unless this station is going to be run remotely. The same goes for the final selection.

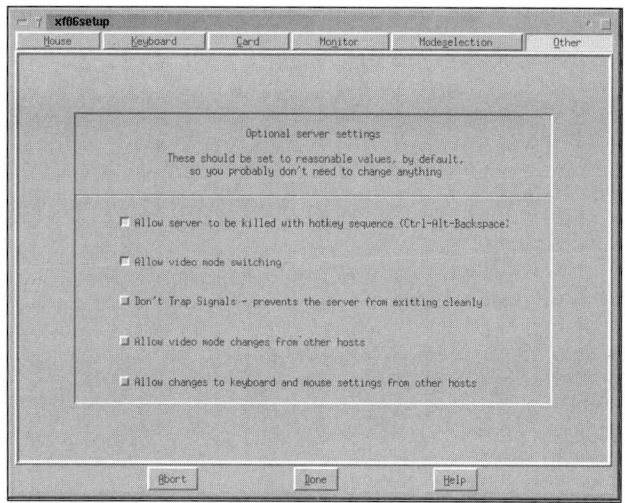

Figure 37.9
The Other screen from `XF86Setup`.

When you are finished, selecting Done again provides you with another prompt (see Figure 37.10). This is an advisory screen. Selecting OK produces the screen shown in Fig 37.11.

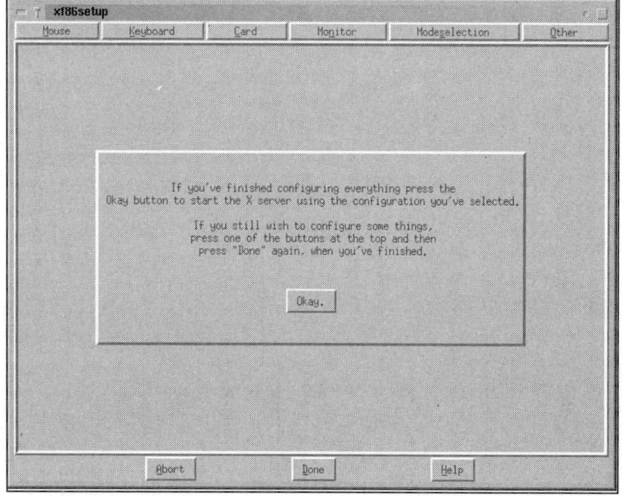

Figure 37.10
End of configuration screen.

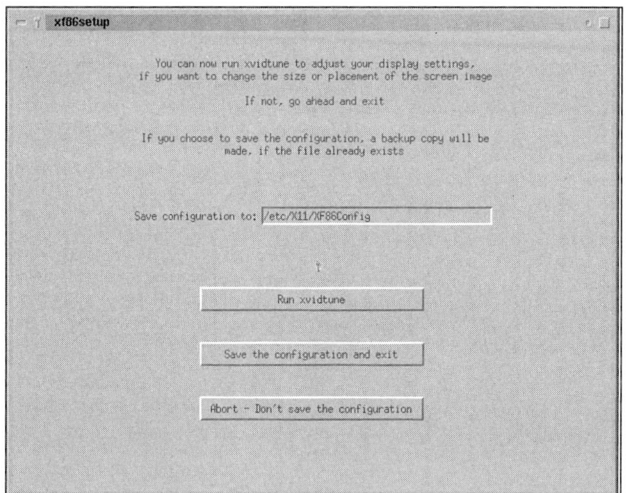

Figure 37.11
Save configuration screen.

At this point, you can safely choose the Save the Configuration and Exit option. Because default values are used, however, when certain screens appear, they can be shifted to one side (or *squashed*); therefore, selecting Run `xvidtune` enables you to make fine-grained changes to your configuration file. But `xvidtune` can also be run from an xterm box command line. (You'll look at `xvidtune` later in this chapter in another section.

CONFIGURING USING xf86config

An alternative method of configuring your X Server is through the use of `xf86config`. This command-line program walks you through the same basic steps as `XF86Setup`. This program requires just slightly more knowledge of your hardware than `XF86Setup`, however. We'll go quickly through this one.

When `xf86config` starts, two startup screens containing information that is important to running this program are displayed. The program can be aborted at any time via the Ctrl+C sequence.

The third screen requests that you select your mouse protocol type by number from the list presented on the screen.

The next question concerns `ChordMiddle`, which is required with some mice to enable the middle mouse button. Choose this only if the middle button doesn't work without it.

You are then asked if you want to Emulate3Buttons, which is a way to allow two-button mice to emulate three-button mice by interpreting a (near) simultaneous left/right mouse button press as a middle mouse button press. Three-button mice do not require this option.

Note

It is probably obvious that you won't need to select Emulate3Buttons when you already have a three-button mouse. This option is only to allow two-button mice to use a (near) simultaneous press on both buttons at once to simulate the missing middle mouse button.

Finally, you are asked which device the mouse is connected to. Most commonly this is /dev/mouse if you have a symlink, /dev/psaux for PS/2 mice, or either /dev/ttyS0 or /dev/ttyS1 for mice that are connected to the first or second `COM` port.

The keyboard questions come next, asking if you want to use the newer XKB convention or the older `xmodmap` to remap keyboard keys from the defaults. If you answer Yes, you are given a selection list to choose from. If none of the first nine fit, six more are presented. Then a language layout selection list that is comprised of 21 choices appears (18 on the first screen, with three final choices on the second screen).

The next question (which is only asked if you didn't answer Yes to the preceding question) involves alternative keyboard bindings for the Alt keys to enable certain foreign language characters. The choices are Yes and No.

The monitor section follows, first with an informational screen, and then with a list of ten common monitor horizontal sync rates—or you can enter your own. Recall the previous cautions about selecting monitor refresh rates that are higher than your monitor is capable of.

The vertical sync range comes next, with four common choices or an option to enter your own.

Three optional free-form questions ask for the monitor definition identifier, vendor name, and monitor model.

Upon completion, you enter the video card selection. If you answer Yes, you are presented with more than 24 screens and 417 separate cards from which to choose. After your card is chosen, `xf86config` displays the information that it intends to write to the X Server configuration file.

Then you're presented with five choices regarding the server you want to run. Normally, the fifth choice—the server in the card definition—is the best option.

The amount of video RAM on the card is the next question, with standard answers available as well as a fill in the blank.

The three free-form card definition, vendor, and model questions follow.

Next comes the RAMDAC type question, followed by the Clockchip line question. These can be bypassed by answering `q` if they don't apply or aren't known.

The next question explains probing for clock chips. If your card definition says don't probe, or you're unsure, do not permit probing. This can hang the machine. Just continue on.

On the next screen, `xf86config` presents you with a list of modes for each color depth it believes your card is capable of, based on the answers that you supplied previously. Make any changes, and then select 5 to save the changes for later writing to the file and continue.

The last screen verifies that you now want to write the file to disk and request verification of its location.

xvidtune

After you have a working X server (from either `XF86Setup` or `xf86config`), you might find that you need to tune the sync frequencies slightly to prevent the screen from appearing stretched, squashed, shifted left or right, shifted up or down, or wrapped. Note that `xvidtune` does not help a mode that is out of sync—that is, you can't see a picture because the image is a series of (two or more) bars, or it appears as diagonal lines on the screen. If the server comes up this way, you can use the Ctrl+Alt++ key sequence to try to find a mode that does work. You can then manually eliminate modes that don't work (see Chapter 38, "Dissecting the `XF86Config` File").

The `xvidtune` program can be run (as you saw) either from `XF86Setup` as the last step, or directly from a command line. If it is run from a command line, `xvidtune` provides some limited information on the command line regarding what it believes to be valid horizontal and vertical sync ranges (`hsync` and `vsync`, respectively). It then shows you a standard disclaimer regarding use of the program and the developers' liability for damage (none) resulting from the use of the program (see Figure 37.12).

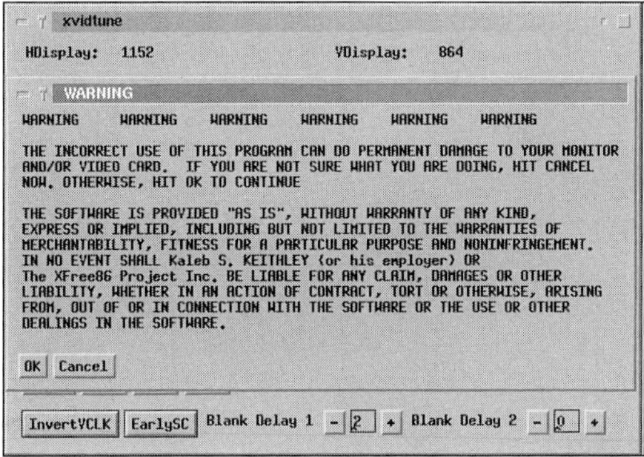

Figure 37.12
`xvidtune` warning screen.

Figure 37.13 shows you how the `xvidtune` program looks when it is running. Some of the controls, in this case the InvertVCLK and other buttons on the bottom row, are not available for all X Servers and card definitions. When you examine modelines in the next chapter, you'll see the numbers listed on this screen again, strung out in a row in groups of four corresponding to the numbers that are running vertically here, starting with 1152 and 864.

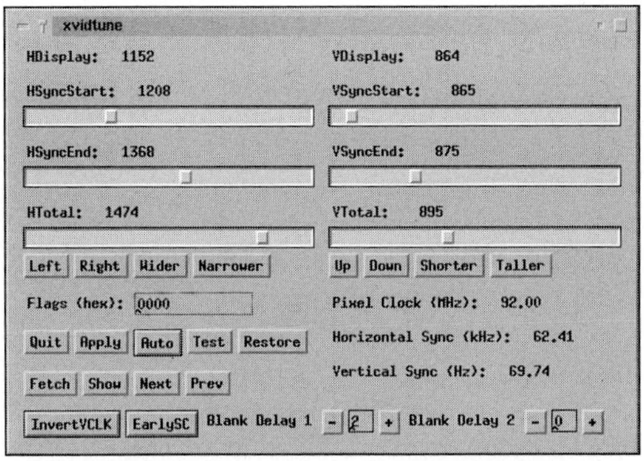

Figure 37.13
Main `xvidtune` screen.

You can make adjustments to the various horizontal and vertical bars if you use the buttons (such as Left, Right, and Taller), and then Test or Apply them. You can also see each adjustment as you make it by selecting Auto first.

The Show button only works when `xvidtune` is called from an xterm box command line because the output goes to `stdout`. In your case here, a modeline is shown:

```
"1152x864"      92.00    1152 1208 1368 1474     864  865  875  895
```

As you can see, all the numbers come directly from the `xvidtune` display.

Leave `xvidtune` running and cycle through each mode that is available for your current color depth. You can repeat this process for each color depth by starting the server in the different color depths and cycling through the modes using the Ctrl+Alt++ key sequence.

Note

The easiest way to start the X server from a command line other than the default mode is to pass the color depth on the command line. However, for a script such as `startx`, a special syntax is required: `startx — -bpp 16`, where you substitute valid values for the 16, such as 8, 15, 16, 24, or 32. The X server only starts up if a good combination of display modes, color depths, and RAM can be found for your video card and monitor.

Your X Server is now tuned and ready for use from a command line, or you can configure `xdm` to present you with a graphical login at bootup so that none of your users ever need to see a command line prompt.

SUMMARY

In this chapter, you learned about gathering information regarding your video card, monitor, keyboard, and mouse, and about one utility to gather information about your video card—`SuperProbe`. You also learned two different ways to configure your X server: `XF86Setup` and `xf86config`. You also saw how to fine-tune your X server using the `xvidtune` program. For more information on X servers, refer to the following chapters:

- Chapter 38 discusses the XF86Config file in more depth. Understanding this file helps you further tune your X server.
- Chapter 40, "Controlling X Resources," discusses configuring the X server after it is running, and how it calls a particular window manager. It also shows you how to keep a graphical screen running when no one is logged in.

CHAPTER 38

DISSECTING THE XF86CONFIG FILE

In this chapter

In a perfect world, there would be no need to give details on the contents of the /etc/XF86Config file. Truth be told, we are almost there—the current need to manually alter this file is minimal to nonexistent for most users. However, there are going to be times when a specific setting or two needs to be changed for one reason or another. Quite often when this happens it is not worth the effort to go through the configuration process á la `XF86Setup` or the `XF86Config` program just to make one or two small changes. In many cases, it is simpler and quicker to edit the /etc/XF86Config file manually.

At first glance, the /etc/XF86Config file might look a bit intimidating. There are, in fact, portions of the file that deserve this stigma. But only power users are likely to ever bother tinkering in those areas; the bulk of installations of the X Window system only need to worry about the simpler, more straightforward sections.

It will hopefully become clear as you browse through this chapter which areas apply to which crowd. A fair amount of information is included here regarding the contents of the X Window system configuration file, but occasionally some knowledge of hardware (and access to hardware documentation) has to be assumed. It is simply too broad a task to cover all the internals of video hardware just to explain how XF86Config is structured. If you come across an area that sounds too complex to be dealt with, taking into account your existing knowledge of video hardware, by all means *avoid changing anything in that section of XF86Config*! When it comes to tinkering with the X Window system configuration, it is always best to err on the side of caution than to try something that you do not understand.

SECTIONS

In the early days of the X Window system on Linux, the XF86Config configuration file was rather obtuse and was not broken into logical configuration groupings. This made for quite a bit of confusion because configuration items can reside just about anywhere within the file and still be set correctly.

Recent versions of the X Window system for Linux have broken XF86Config into logical sections to address this issue. The result is a much more readable, more easily parsed configuration file.

All the sections within XF86Config adhere to a very basic format:

```
Section "Name"
    Subsection "SubName"
    ...
    ...
    EndSubsection
    Subsection "SubName"
    ...
    ...
    EndSubsection
EndSection
```

Not all sections contain subsections, but when they do, they adhere to the preceding format.

The standard set of sections within this file are titled Files, Module, ServerFlags, Keyboard, Pointer, Monitor, Device, Screen, and Xinput (which this chapter does not go into here, for reasons that are explained later). Each section is explained as follows, including *tags* (options that require parameters to be passed to them) and *flags* (settings that are activated by the presence of a single word), what they do, and some suggestions regarding why to—or why not to—use them.

Note that for a tag or flag to be seen by the X Window server when it is started, it must be uncommented. The character that starts a comment line in XF86Config is the usual # symbol. Any line that is preceded by this character is ignored by the X Window server. For example, the following

```
# DefaultColorDepth 16
```

is ignored, whereas

```
DefaultColorDepth 16
```

is not.

Also, unless otherwise indicated, all parameters that are to be passed to tags in any given section (or subsection) of XF86Config must be enclosed in double quotes. For example, to set the Microsoft serial mouse protocol for a serial mouse, in the Pointer section there is a tag that reads like this:

```
Protocol "Microsoft"
```

Note that only the parameter—not the tag itself—is enclosed in quotes.

There is one last thing that you need to know: If you see, listed in this chapter, a tag or a flag that you want to enable, but it does not appear in your copy of /etc/XF86Config, simply add it using a text editor. Just be sure to put the tag or flag in its proper section when doing so.

THE FILES SECTION

The Files section specifies font path information for the X Window server, as well as information regarding the RGB database for color translations.

The following descriptions cover the various tags and flags that are offered in this section.

`RgbPath` *`path`*

This tag specifies the location of the RGB database that is used by the X Window system. This database maps red/green/blue color values (specified as bytes 0–255, where 0 means 100 percent shade and 255 means 0 percent shade) to color names that are used within applications. For example, following is a snippet of the /usr/X11R6/lib/X11/rgb.txt file from OpenLinux:

```
230 230 250            lavender
255 240 245            lavender blush
255 240 245            LavenderBlush
```

```
255 228 225            misty rose
255 228 225            MistyRose
255 255 255            white
  0   0   0            black
 47  79  79            dark slate gray
 47  79  79            DarkSlateGray
```

The byte values along the left-most columns represent red, green, and blue values, respectively. The names to their right are English versions of the colors that are produced by the three shades specified to the left.

None of this needs to be altered by users; however, it might be useful to know where to find these values and color names.

`FontPath` *path*

There is one of these for every directory that contains fonts for X, the path enclosed in double-quotes. Each font directory contains the various .pcf, .snf, and .bdf files that contain the fonts (generally, these are compressed with `gzip`, making the extensions .pcf.gz, .snf.gz, and .bdf.gz); the `mkfontdir` command needs to be run against the directory to create the fonts.dir file that is used to map fonts to their filenames.

A font server path can be set in lieu of an actual path on the hard drive. The path to the font server is specified as follows:

```
local_path,tcp[or udp]/hostname:port
```

For instance, if there is a font server residing at host tuna.fish.net and listening on TCP port 6200, and if there are some (but not many) fonts residing locally in /usr/X11R6/lib/X11/fonts/misc, there might be a FontPath line that resembles the following:

```
FontPath /usr/X11R6/lib/X11/fonts/misc,tcp/tuna.fish.net:6200"
```

This uses fonts in /usr/X11R6/lib/X11/fonts/misc if there are any; if not, the font server running on tuna.fish.net is accessed.

`ModulePath` *path*

Some services (such as hardware drivers) are available to the X Window system in the form of loadable modules. These are not unlike the modules that the Linux kernel can load, but they are intended for use only by the X Window system. This tag points to the path where these extra modules are stored.

In OpenLinux systems the default module path is `/usr/X11R6/lib/modules`. If one of the modules is needed, it is loaded in the Module section of XF86Config, which is described in the following section.

THE MODULE SECTION

This section is where optional, dynamically loadable modules are specified for loading. Currently supported modules are the following:

- xf86Elo.so (which is used for Elographics touch-screens)
- xf86Jstk.so (which is used for joystick support; might not be included with OpenLinux)
- xf86Summa.so (used for SummaSketch digitizer tablets)
- xf86Wacom.so (the Wacom IV protocol, used with some Wacom digitizer tablets)

OpenLinux also includes modules that offer PEX extensions (which are extensions that enable extended capabilities to render 2D images of 3D geometric objects) and XIE extensions (the X Imaging Extensions, which aid in image translation and color mapping functions that can be used with PEX). They are the pex5.so and xie.so modules, respectively.

Note

Additional modules can be added at any time, so this list might have expanded since this description was written.

```
Load module_name
```

This is the only tag that is available in this section of XF86Config. This tag specifies one of the aforementioned modules for loading. Replace `module_name` with the module that you want to load. For example, if you want to load the PED and XIE extension modules, you need to have the following in this section:

```
Load "pex5.so"
Load "xie.so"
```

As was indicated earlier, there are no other tags or flags allowed within the Module section of XF86Config.

THE SERVERFLAGS SECTION

The ServerFlags section accepts a slew of unclassifiable, behavior-changing flags for the X Window server that you are using.

The following descriptions cover the flags that are available in this section of XF86Config.

```
NoTrapSignals
```

This causes the X Window server to terminate with a core dump when a fatal signal is encountered. Without this, the server gives an error and exits cleanly.

Use this only when debugging debilitating problems with X Window servers—it is useless for anything else. The resulting core dump file can be run through a debugger to trace what lead to the fatal signal. For normal operation, do not set this flag.

DontZap

The key sequence Ctrl+Alt+Backspace provides a quick way to kill an X Window server. This is most commonly used when the server settings somehow get reworked and the monitor does not agree with them (the tell-tale squeal emanating from the back of the monitor is a dead giveaway that this might have happened).

If you specify `DontZap` in this section of XF86Config, the capability to use the Ctrl+Alt+Backspace sequence is eliminated.

It is not recommended that you set this option. If anything bad happens as a result of a misconfiguration, you definitely want a hotkey sequence that kills the X Window server quickly; otherwise, serious hardware damage might occur.

DontZoom

The key sequences Ctrl+Alt+KeyPad+/- can flip the display to the next/previous resolution specified for the screen in XF86Config. (There is a Modes line in the Screen section, which is described later in this chapter, that specifies all the available screen resolutions. These are the resolutions that are scrolled through, in order from first to last.) Specifying `DontZoom` eliminates the capability to do this.

Unless there are applications that require these two key sequences, it is recommended that you leave this option out.

DisableVidModeExtension

The `xvidtune` utility, covered in Chapter 37, "Configuring X," uses VidMode extensions that are disabled when this flag is uncommented. Essentially, this enables `xvidtune` to run and view settings, but none of the settings for the X Window server can be changed.

Because `xvidtune` can be dangerous to hardware if it is used by someone who does not know what they are doing, it might be wise to set this flag after getting a solid X Window server configuration up and running.

AllowNonLocalXvidtune

True to its name, setting this flag allows the `xvidtune` client to be run from a nonlocal machine. It is questionable why anyone might want to enable something like this at all.

It is recommended that you leave this flag out.

DisableModInDev

By default, input device settings can be changed on-the-fly using such utilities as `xset`. Setting this flag prevents these settings from being changed on-the-fly.

Unless you want to lock your current configuration settings and not risk having them changed on you, you probably don't want to set this flag.

`AllowNonLocalModInDev`

Setting this flag allows nonlocal machines to change settings to your input devices. Again, it is questionable why anyone might want to offer such a service.

It is recommended that you leave this flag out.

`AllowMouseOpenFail`

By default, if the pointer device that is configured in XF86Config cannot be initialized upon startup, the X Window server bombs out with an error and you are returned to the command prompt almost immediately. Setting this flag enables the server to fully start, and thus enables you to work—but without a mouse.

With no mouse, it is rather difficult to move around in a GUI, so it is probably wise to leave this flag out.

THE KEYBOARD SECTION

Keyboard settings are held in this section. Everything from how the NumLock key is handled to what kind of keyboard mappings will be used is stored in this section.

The following descriptions cover the various tags and flags that are offered in this section of XF86Config.

`Protocol` *`protocol`*

This specifies the protocol that is used, either Standard or Xqueue. Xqueue is really not meant for Linux systems, so choose Standard here.

`AutoRepeat` *`delay_value rate_value`*

This sets the keyboard auto-repeat rates within the X Window system. The default setting that is specified for OpenLinux systems is a delay value of `500` (that is, the delay timing between when you start holding down a key and when the characters start repeating) and a rate value of `5`. If this is insufficient for your needs—if the delay is too short or the rate is too fast—increase or decrease the delay and rate values to suit your needs.

In general, these settings are left alone. If you do end up making changes, do not enclose the values in double quotes for this tag.

`ServerNumLock`

Some older X Window applications (those compiled for Release 5 versions of the X Window system) require special handling of the NumLock key. When `ServerNumLock` is enabled and the NumLock key is activated, a different set of key mappings are set on the number pad, enabling the application to act more appropriately.

Modern (Release 6) applications do not really require this flag to be set, so it is recommended that you do not set it.

`Xleds` *`LEDs`*

This tells which of the LED settings (NumLock, Caps Lock, or Scroll Lock) can be changed by users. Each of the LEDs is assigned a number between 1 and 3—where 1 is NumLock, 2 is Caps Lock, and 3 is Scroll Lock. The LEDs that users are allowed to change or remap are specified after the `Xleds` tag, each one separated by a space.

By default, none of the LEDs are changeable by users; in other words, the NumLock key lights up the NumLock LED, the Caps Lock key lights up the Caps Lock LED, and so on.

Unless there is a desire to use these LEDs for other purposes, it is recommended that none of the LEDs be made available to change; so leave this tag out.

`LeftAlt` *`mapping`*, `RightAlt` *`mapping`*, `RightCtl` *`mapping`*, AND `ScrollLock` *`mapping`*

The names of these keys need to be descriptive enough to locate them on the keyboard. The default X Window mappings of these keys are as follows:

```
LeftAlt     Meta
RightAlt    Meta
RightCtl    Control
ScrollLock  Compose
```

The optional remappings are

```
Meta
Compose
ModeShift
ModeLock
ScrollLock
Control
```

Basically, if there is no real need to change the default mappings for these keys, do not use these tags to change them. They work fine with X Window applications as is.

`VTSysReq`

The default key sequence to switch from the console in which the X Window system is running (tty7 by default, or the seventh console) to another virtual console is Ctrl+Alt+F*n*, where F*n* is the F-key that corresponds to the virtual console to which you are switching. If this flag is set, the default key sequence changes to Alt+SysRq+F*n*, which more closely matches SysV behavior.

If you are migrating from a SysV environment and want to keep a familiar key sequence for switching between terminals, set this flag. Otherwise, do not.

`XkbDisable`

This flag disables the XKB server extensions. By disabling XKB, the X Window server resorts to using `xmodmap` key bindings instead. This flag was required by some applications that did not like XKB taking over the keyboard (Wabi for Linux was one of them).

There is rarely any need to disable XKB. In fact, it is highly recommended that you do not set this flag.

`XkbRules` *`rules_file`*, `XkbModel` *`model`*, `XkbLayout` *`layout`*, `XkbVariant` *`variant`*, AND `XkbOptions` *`options`*

Here, things can get a bit tricky. This grouping is intentional because it components are typically configured as a group. All together, these tags tell the X Window server what kind of keyboard and overall keyboard mappings are to be used.

The first tag—`XkbRules`—specifies a rule file in /usr/X11R6/lib/X11/xkb/rules that contains information for the remaining four lines. The default file is called xfree86, but there is also a rule file for SGI systems. Being an OpenLinux user, stick with the xfree86 rule file.

Within the associated xfree86.lst file in the same directory, you see items that can be filled in for the remaining tags in the preceding example, along with brief explanations of what each stands for.

Listing 38.1 is a sample xfree86.lst file. Note the headings in the file (indicated by the preceding `!` characters) and how they neatly map out to the previously listed tags (`model`, `layout`, `variant`, and `options`).

LISTING 38.1 SAMPLE XFREE86.LST FILE

```
// $TOG: xfree86.lst /main/2 1997/06/13 06:29:00 kaleb $
//
//  Rules descriptions for XFree86
//  Copyright 1996 by Joseph Moss
//
//$XFree86:xc/programs/xkbcomp/rules/xfree86.lst

! model
  pc101         Generic 101-key PC
  pc102         Generic 102-key (Intl) PC
  pc104         Generic 104-key PC
  dell101     Dell 101-key PC
  everex    Everex STEPnote
  flexpro    Keytronic FlexPro
  microsoft     Microsoft Natural
  omnikey101     Northgate OmniKey 101
  winbook    Winbook Model XP5
  jp106         Japanese 106-key
  pc98         PC-98xx Series

! layout
  us         U.S. English
  en_US         U.S. English w/ISO9995-3
  be         Belgian
  bg         Bulgarian
  ca         Canadian
  cs         Czechoslovakian
  de         German
```

continues

LISTING 38.1 CONTINUED

```
  de_CH        Swiss German
  dk        Danish
  es        Spanish
  fi        Finnish
  fr        French
  fr_CH        Swiss French
  gb        United Kingdom
  hu        Hungarian
  it        Italian
  jp        Japanese
  no        Norwegian
  pl        Polish
  pt        Portuguese
  ru        Russian
  se        Swedish
  th        Thai
  nec/jp    PC-98xx Series

! variant
  nodeadkeys    Eliminate dead keys

! optional
  grp            Group Shift/Lock behavior
  grp:switch        R-Alt switches group while pressed
  grp:toggle        Right Alt key changes group
  grp:shift_toggle     Both Shift keys together change group
  grp:ctrl_shift_toggle Control+Shift changes group
  grp:ctrl_alt_toggle    Alt+Control changes group
  ctrl            Control Key Position
  ctrl:nocaps        Make CapsLock an additional Control
  ctrl:swapcaps        Swap Control and Caps Lock
  ctrl:ctrl_ac        Control key at left of 'A'
  ctrl:ctrl_aa         Control key at bottom left
```

There is an alternative method for doing this, though. To understand how to follow it, you must first check out the subdirectories under /usr/X11R6/lib/X11/xkb:

```
compat
compiled
geometry
keycodes
keymap
rules
semantics
symbols
types
```

Now, look at the tags that can be used in place of the five that were just covered:

```
XkbCompat <compatibility_file>
XkbGeometry <geometry_file>
XkbKeycodes <keycodes_file>
XkbKeymap <keymap_file>
XkbSymbols <symbol_file>
XkbTypes <types_file>
```

A number of the names of these tags resemble names of subdirectories under /usr/X11R6/lib/X11/xkb for a reason: Those directories contain the files that each of these tags can point to.

The default values that the X Window server uses with these tags are as follows:

```
XkbCompat      "default"
XkbGeometry      "pc"
XkbKeycodes      "xfree86"
XkbKeymap      none
XkbSymbols      "us(pc101)"
XkbTypes     "default"
```

With the exception of the `XkbKeymap` tag, each of the preceding tags defaults to the filename that is enclosed within the quotes. Each of these files resides in the subdirectory that matches the name of the tag. The only slight exception to this is shown in the value of the `XkbSymbols` tag: It points to an us file in the symbols subdirectory, but calls on the pc101 settings within that file. Similar parameters can be entered for other tags as well (for instance, `xfree86(us)` is passed to `XkbKeymap` in the XF86Config file that ships with OpenLinux).

The first five tags are preferred over the latter six tags for configuring the XKB settings because the latter six tags require a certain degree of knowledge about how the X Window server you are using works with keyboard mappings. It is highly recommended that the files that can be referenced by these six tags not be altered unless you know what you are doing! Altering these files is not covered here; you merely learn how to reference them.

When you first set up your X Window system using XF86Setup or XF86Config, these tags are set for you. It is recommended that you do not change them unless it is absolutely necessary.

THE POINTER SECTION

The Pointer section is where the mouse configuration on your X Window system is held. Certain additional settings can be activated within this section as well, as can functional settings that are required to make the mouse operational (such as serial port settings for serial mice).

The following descriptions cover the tags and flags that are offered in this section of XF86Config.

`Protocol` *`mouse_type`*

This specifies the type of mouse that is being used. Table 38.1 lists the currently offered valid mouse protocols.

TABLE 38.1 AVAILABLE MOUSE PROTOCOLS

Protocol	Description
Auto	Might (or might not) auto-detect your mouse. Can be used to detect most PnP compatible mice (including busmice, PS/2 mice, and serial mice).
BusMouse	Protocol for busmice and InPort mice (such as Logitech's, Microsoft's, and ATI's).
GlidePoint	ALPS GlidePoint serial mouse protocol ALPS.
GlidePointPS/2	ALPS GlidePoint PS/2 mouse protocol.
IntelliMouse	Driver for newer mice with wheels in lieu of a third button (that is, Logitech MouseMan Plus, and, of course, the Microsoft IntelliMouse). If a mouse with a wheel does not work with this protocol, try setting it up as a three-button mouse with one of the three-button protocols that follow. If your mouse is an ASCII MieMouse this protocol might work, but only with the serial version (see the NetMousePS/2 protocol for the PS/2 version). This protocol is also known to work with Logitech MouseMan+ and FirstMouse+ mice when in serial mode.
IMPS/2	Microsoft IntelliMouse PS/2 mouse protocol.
Logitech	For older Logitech serial mice.
Microsoft	For most Microsoft and compatible (that is, new Logitech) serial mice. Most new two-button mice use this protocol.
MMHitTab	Protocol for MMHitTab-compatible serial mice.
MMSeries	Protocol for MMSeries-compatible serial mice.
Mouseman	Some NEW Logitech serial mice (such as the TrackMan Marble) use this. It can also be used to drive some generic three-button serial mice.
MouseManPlusPS/2	For use with Logitech MouseMan+ PS/2 and FirstMouse+ PS/2 mice.
MouseSystems	Generic three-button serial mouse protocol. If this does not work on your three-button generic mouse, try Mouseman.
NetMousePS/2	Genius NetMouse and NetMouse Pro PS/2 mouse protocol. If this does not work with your NetMouse or NetMouse Pro, try the IntelliMouse protocol. This protocol is also known to work with ASCII MieMouse PS/2 mice.
NetScrollPS/2	Genius NetScroll PS/2 mouse protocol.
OSMouse	Standardized protocol that allows the operating system's mouse protocols to be used. This is utilized by the OS/2 and SysV r.3 ports of the X Window system, but it is not used with Linux.
PS/2	The default PS/2 protocol.
SysMouse	Standardized protocol similar to OSMouse. Used by the FreeBSD port of the X Window system, but is not used under Linux.
ThinkingMouse	Kensington Thinking Mouse serial mouse protocol.

Protocol	Description
ThinkingMousePS/2	Kensington Thinking Mouse PS/2 mouse protocol.
Xqueue	Typically not used under Linux. Standardized protocol used by such operating systems as SysV and PANIX.

`Device` *`device_file`*

This is where the actual hardware device in the /dev directory is specified for the mouse that is being used.

During a typical OpenLinux installation, a symbolic link called mouse is made in the /dev directory that points to the device file that is used by the mouse. For instance, if a serial mouse is specified during installation as being connected to the first serial port (COM1 under DOS/Windows, which is /dev/ttyS0 under Linux), a symbolic link called mouse is made in the /dev directory that points to /dev/ttyS0.

With this in mind, it is usually sufficient to specify `/dev/mouse` as the parameter for this tag. Otherwise, the actual hardware device needs to be specified directly. See Chapter 9, "Understanding the Linux File System," for more information on what kinds of devices are offered for mice.

`Port` *`device_file`*

This is the exact same thing as the `Device` tag. Use one or the other, but not both.

`BaudRate` *`rate`*

Here is where the actual baud rate for serial mice is specified. The default value (if nothing else is specified) is 1200 baud. Not all serial mice support higher baud rates, so do not change this value from the default unless you have solid knowledge that the mouse that is being used can work with the higher rate.

If you plan to use this tag, do not enclose the parameter in quotes.

`Buttons` *`number_of_buttons`*

This specifies how many buttons are on the mouse. The default value is three. Note that wheels on mice are to be counted as buttons, just like the buttons that typically surround them.

If you plan to use this tag, do not enclose the parameter in quotes.

`Emulate3Buttons`

This flag specifies that you want your two button mouse to simulate a third, middle button when both buttons are pressed simultaneously. Three-button mouse users do not specify this because there is no need to simulate a third button when a perfectly functional third button already exists.

`Emulate3Timeout` *`timeout_value`*

This tag specifies how long the X Window server is to wait to determine if both of the two buttons on a two-button mouse were pressed in a manner fitting for the `Emulate3Buttons` flag. The default value is 50 milliseconds.

You might want to increase this if you are having problems timing the button presses so that they are close enough to be read as a simultaneous action. Do not enclose the parameter in quotes if you do.

`ChordMiddle`

This flag is typically required for three-button mice in order to get the middle button functioning properly, sending the correct mouse events through the X Window server. If you have a three-button mouse that is using a three-button mouse protocol, set this flag.

`SampleRate` *`rate`*

If you are using a Logitech mouse, it might be possible to use this tag to adjust the rate at which mouse events are sent to the X Window server. Not all Logitech mice support this, however—mostly it is used by the MouseMan series.

If in doubt, do not worry about using this tag. If you plan to use it, do not enclose the parameter in quotes.

`Resolution` *`counts_per_inch`*

This sets the resolution of the mouse's movement. The higher the value, the smoother the mouse movement is (and the more resources it will take to use).

This feature is not supported by all mice, so it is safe to leave it out. If you use this tag, do not enclose the parameter in quotes.

`ClearDTR` AND `ClearRTS`

These flags clear the Data Terminal Ready (DTR) and Request To Send (RTS) signals on the serial port if you are using a MouseSystems or compatible serial mouse. If you are using another kind of mouse, do not use these flags.

`ZAxisMapping X`, `ZAxisMapping Y`, AND `ZAxisMapping` *`negative_button positive_button`*

Some mice, such as the Microsoft IntelliMouse, ship with a wheel instead of a third, middle button. This wheel defaults to using the Z axis, but it can be redefined, using either `ZAxisMapping X` or `ZAxisMapping Y`, to use the X axis or the Y axis.

Alternatively, two buttons on the mouse can be defined to use the Z axis, where one button indicates negative movement and the other indicates positive movement (specified by `ZAxisMapping`).

These options are often left out of XF86Config because there are few applications that currently take advantage of them in any useful way; but they are there if you want to experiment. If you use this tag, be sure to not enclose the parameters in quotes.

THE MONITOR SECTION

In this section, items such as supported frequency ranges and mode lines for various screen resolutions are specified. Be forewarned, though: This section gets somewhat technical, so a fair amount of knowledge of video hardware and monitors is required to understand some of these tags.

The following descriptions cover the tags that are offered in this section of XF86Config.

`Identifier` *`identification_string`*, `VendorName` *`vendor_name`*, **AND** `ModelName` *`model_name`*

Each of these strings (with the parameters enclosed in double-quotes) is freeform and does not change the behavior of the X Window server in any way.

There can be multiple monitor specifications given within XF86Config. The actual monitor section that is used is specified in the active Screen section, which is described later in this chapter. The string that is contained in the preceding Identifier tag is the one that is used by the Screen section to determine which monitor entry is to be used. The last two tags are optional and are only used for your reference.

`HorizSync` *`horizontal_frequency_range`* **AND** `VertRefresh` *`vertical_frequency_range`*

These two tags list, respectively, the horizontal and vertical ranges of frequencies (or comma-delimited lists of specific horizontal and vertical frequencies) that are supported by your monitor. These values are probably listed in your monitor's documentation, in the technical specifications section. By default, the values that are specified here are in kHz unless the numbers or ranges are followed by MHz or Hz.

Caution

It is vitally important that the exact supported frequencies–whether they are ranges or specific individual frequencies–are listed accurately in these tags. If a range or individual frequency that is too high is specified in either of these tags, there is a chance that permanent damage can be inflicted on your monitor (most modern monitors shut off if a rogue frequency is encountered, but not all do). Double, triple, quadruple check these values before even thinking about starting up the X Window system after changing them.

You might be one of those people who simply cannot find their monitor's documentation, and no information can be found with which educated guesses can be formed regarding frequency ranges. It is always better to err on the side of safety, so if you have a multifrequency monitor that supports SVGA graphics (most monitors that are sold from clone manufacturers fit this category), you might—repeat, *might*—be safe trying a horizontal range of 31–38kHz and a vertical range of 50–90kHz. These are generally safe, educated guesses, but because they are guesses, there is no guarantee that using these ranges will not hurt your monitor. So, be careful if you want to try these frequencies.

Caution

Be prepared to shut off your monitor quickly if any strange noises emanate from it after starting the X Window system. If this happens, shut off the monitor and hit Ctrl+Alt+Backspace to kill the server before turning the monitor on again. After you have a workable screen again, check over the frequency settings that are specified in this section and make any necessary changes to stop the problem. Note that it is safer to decrease the frequency ranges than it is to increase them.

`Gamma` *`gamma_value`*

Some X Window servers offer gamma correction for monitors. Not all do, however. If you are using one that does (check the man page for your X Window server for details) and you require gamma correction, the values can be specified in this tag. Generally, however, this is left out.

`Modeline ...` AND `Mode ...`

The core of the monitor configuration lies with the video modes. These lines are mercifully built by default (using `XF86Setup` or `XF86Config`) up to resolutions such as 1800×1440 at certain frequencies. However, unlike other operating systems and operating environments that lock you into a certain set of screen resolutions, odd resolutions such as 1269×1058 (this is a guess, of course) are not uncommon with the X Window system. Many factors are taken into account when forming the video mode lines that permit these resolutions.

Note

Unfortunately, the process of manually calculating your own video mode timing information is rather complex and requires extensive knowledge of how video images are presented on your monitor. The requirement of "rolling your own" configuration disappeared when `XF86Setup` and `XF86Config` were implemented within modern X Window systems, so the manual configuration procedure is not covered here. There is a document available on the Internet that details how to make these video mode configurations manually; check Appendix D, "How to Find Other Linux Information," for details on where to get it.

First, take a look at a typical video mode line:

```
# 1024x768 @ 76 Hz, 62.5 kHz hsync
Modeline "1024x768"    85     1024 1032 1152 1360   768  784  787  823
```

In order, the elements that make up this line (after the `Modeline` tag) are as follows (corresponding values from the preceding sample line are indicated in parentheses):

- The name of the mode (`1024×768`). This string is used in the Screen section that follows, in the `Modes` line.

- The mode description, which consists of four parts:
  - The dot clock rate for the mode (85).
  - The horizontal timings, broken down into the following:
    The horizontal resolution (1024)
    The horizontal sync start (1032)
    The horizontal sync end (1152)
    The horizontal sync total (1360)
  - The vertical timings, broken down into the following:
    The vertical resolution (768)
    The vertical sync start (784)
    The vertical sync end (787)
    The vertical sync total (823)
- A list of possible flags are listed in Table 38.2. Check the monitor's documentation to learn whether any of these can be used; do not just try them out without knowing if they work!

TABLE 38.2 Modeline FLAGS

Flag	Description
Composite	Specifies composite sync
+CSync, -Csync	Specifies composite sync polarity
DoubleScan	Doubles each scan line
HSkew *pixels*	Sets the number of pixels the display is to be skewed to the right
+Hsync, -Hsync	Specifies the horizontal sync polarity
Interlace	Indicates that the mode is interlaced
+Vsync, -Vsync	Specifies the vertical sync polarity

With the exception of the previously listed Modeline flags, the xvidtune utility, which is covered in Chapter 37, can set these values. For example, Figure 38.1 shows how xvidtune looks for a mode line that is similar to the example listed previously.

Alternatively, the Modeline tags can be broken down into clearly labeled chunks using the Mode tag. The sample Modeline that was given earlier looks like the following if it is broken down within a Mode tag:

```
Mode "1024x768"
    DotClock 85
    HTimings 1024 1032 1152 1360
    VTimings 768 784 787 823
    Flags ""
EndMode
```

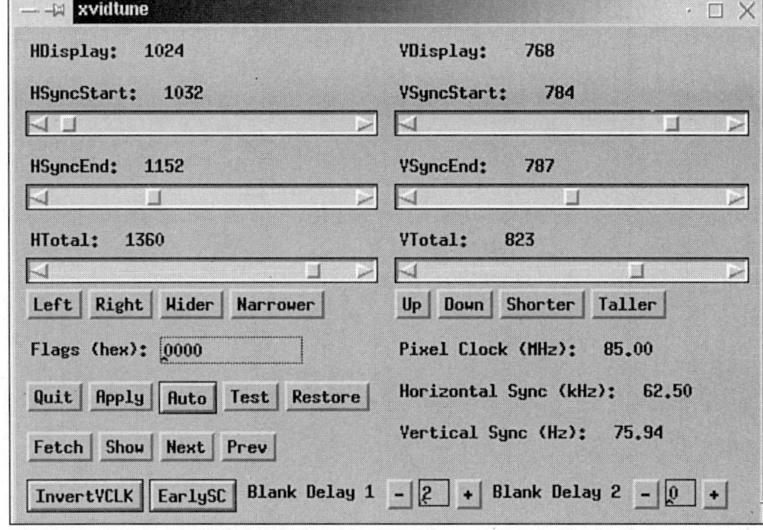

Figure 38.1
Sample `xvidtune` screen for 1024×768 `Modeline` example.

The information is the same, but it is formatted in such a way that it is much simpler to follow. This kind of formatting has to be done after server configuration (using `XF86Setup` or `XF86Config`) is complete because the default format for video mode definitions is the former `Modeline` method, not the `Mode` method.

As was stated earlier, the default XF86Config file has many canned video modes that are already configured and ready to use. Each requires a specific horizontal and vertical frequency pair to be usable. When the X Window server is started—when you execute `startx` or `kde`—it goes through each of the video modes; the ones that do not operate within the specified horizontal and vertical frequencies, which are set in the `HorizSync` and `VertRefresh` tags, are discarded. Only the video modes that are supported by the monitor are used. Once again, the importance of entering the correct supported horizontal and vertical monitor frequencies needs to be stressed. An incorrect setting can make the X Window server think that a certain video mode is supported by your monitor even if it is not; the result can be permanent damage to your monitor.

The Device Section

Your video card settings are held in the Device section. As with the Monitor section, there can be multiple configurations set for multiple video cards. Only the video card configuration that is referenced by the active Screen section that follows is used. A fair amount of knowledge of your video card is required to understand some of these tags.

The following descriptions cover the tags that are offered in this section of XF86Config. Please note that these are not the only tags that are allowed within XF86Config's Device section. Each X Window server allows additional tags to be entered. For instance, the XF86_SVGA server allows a `TextClockFreq` tag that allows specification of a text console clock to be used in situations in which the X Window server does not properly restore the text console when exiting. The S3 server also has a number of server-specific tags that are not meant to be used within an `Option` tag (which is described later). The man page for your X Window server can provide rather extensive server-specific information that can be implemented and, therefore, is well worth perusing when you are tinkering within the Device section of XF86Config.

`Identifier` *`identification_string`*, `VendorName` *`vendor_name`*, AND `BoardName` *`board_name`*

The same basic idea that is behind the first tags in the Monitor section also applies here. These are freeform strings that are used to identify this particular video card configuration. The Identifier string is referenced in the Screen section of XF86Config to determine which video card configuration is to be used. The last two tags are optional and are only used for your reference.

`ChipSet` *`chipset`*

In most cases, the X Window server probes for the actual chipset in your video card and finds it. However, this does not always work reliably, in which case you need to specify the chipset using this tag. For the actual names of the chipsets that the server recognizes, see the man page for the X Window server that is used on your system.

`Ramdac` *`RAMDAC`*

Like the video card's chipset, the RAMDAC that is used on the card is typically auto-detected by the X Window server upon startup. If this detection procedure fails and the RAMDAC is not found correctly, it can be specified using this tag.

`DacSpeed` *`speed`*

It is quite rare that the speed of the RAMDAC chip (usually printed on the chip itself, in MHz) needs to be specified. On the rare occasion that the server default speed does not match the RAMDAC speed (I know of no specific cases where this scenario applies), the speed of the RAMDAC can be specified here.

`Clocks` *`supported_dotclocks`*

When the X Window server first starts, one of the things that it probes for is a list of supported dotclocks (in MHz). Typically, this operation is successful, but sometimes it is not; when this happens, chaos can ensue.

This tag has caused quite a bit of grief for no small number of Linux users. Depending on your video card chipset, some servers want to probe for these clock settings and do not fully start if the clocks are already specified with a `Clocks` tag. Others start, probe, and find the clocks, only to cause problems with the monitor that is being used (some monitors do not fare well during the dotclock probing phase). The former is more common than the latter, however.

One case in which a `Clocks` tag is absolutely forbidden is with Cirrus Logic video cards; if a `Clocks` tag is in XF86Config under the section where the Cirrus Logic card configuration resides, the server either does not start at all or it locks up the console.

Your best bet is to not include a Clocks tag unless you are told to do so or the monitor cannot handle the probing process.

`ClockChip` *`clock_chip`*

This tag is used for specifying programmable clock generator chips. Because these are not supported by all X Window servers (check the man page for your server to see if it supports them), and because not all cards use them, it is safe to leave this out.

`ClockProg` *`command`* `[textclock]`

With programmable clock generators like those that were just mentioned, this tag can specify a command to be run during the server initialization phase to set dotclocks on the clock chip. The optional textclock setting after the command that is to be run says that the same command needs to be run to restore the text mode clock before the server terminates completely when the X Window system is shut down. Unless you have a programmable clock generator on your video card and you need to program dotclocks for it, leave this out.

`Option` *`string`*

There are a number of optional settings offered by the various X Window servers. Check the man page for your particular server to see what these options are. It is highly recommended that you do this, even if you think everything is running okay, because within the man page there might be optimizations that are not enabled by default or there might be obscure bug fixes that can be implemented.

If there is a server-specific option that you want to implement, use one of these `Option` tags to specify it. There can be more than one `Option` tag within any specific video card configuration in XF86Config.

`VideoRam` *`kilobytes_of_RAM`*

Although the number of kilobytes of video RAM is typically detected when the X Window server starts, occasionally the entirety of it is not detected; in such a case, you can specify the actual amount with a VideoRam tag. Remember, it is specified in kilobytes, not megabytes.

`BIOSBase` *`address`*

In the rare case in which a video BIOS address must be specified (for instance, some onboard video setups use a BIOS starting address other than the default 0×C0000), the actual address can be specified here, in hexadecimal (preceded with 0x). This is typically not required.

`MemBase address`

The base address of the linear frame buffer within video cards can be specified with this tag. The only X Window servers that really use it are the P9000, S3, Mach64, Mach32, and TGA servers. Even then, it is used only when linear frame buffering is activated.

`IOBase address`

This tag can be used to specify the video card's I/O base address. It is quite rare that this is required. It is really only used by the AGX server and with the Viper PCI video card in the P9000 server.

`DACBase address`

This tag can be used to specify the RAMDAC's I/O base address. It is rare that this is required.

`POSBase address`

This is used to specify the I/O base address for the video card's POS. This is typically not required, so you can safely ignore it.

`COPBase address`

If the video card has a coprocessor, this tag can be used to specify its I/O base address. Such things are typically detected automatically by the X Window server, though, so it is usually safe to ignore this.

`VGABase address`

If the location of the VGA video base address is required (this is highly unlikely because it is usually auto-detected by the X Window server), this tag allows it to be specified.

`Speedup selection`

Some X Window servers include coding that enables certain "speedup" functionality with certain video chipsets. The man page for each X Window server will indicate if this tag is even used and, if so, what the optional selections are (for example, the XF86_SVGA server offers `none` and `all` as the selections, and does not break it down any further).

The Screen Section

This section puts a lot of what was previously configured together into one cohesive system. It assembles the video card and the monitor configurations, and then it sets the video modes that are to be used with the various color depths that are offered. Note that there can be multiple configurations within this section.

The following descriptions detail the tags that are available within this section of XF86Config.

`Driver driver_name`

This tag tells what kind of X Window server is being used. Consequently, it also tells which of the various configurations within the Screen section are to be used (only one X Window server can be used and, depending on which one is started, the applicable Screen subsection is used).

For example, if the XF86_SVGA server is being used and there are multiple subsections within Screen, the one that specifies svga as the driver with this tag will be the one that is used.

Table 38.3 details the parameters that are available for this tag.

TABLE 38.3 DRIVER TAG PARAMETERS

Parameter	Description
`Accel`	For any of the accelerated, non-SVGA servers (for example, Mach64, S3, P9000)
`Mono`	For the mono drivers in the XF86_Mono and XF86_VGA16 servers
`SVGA`	For the XF86_SVGA server
`VGA2`	For the 2bpp drivers in the XF86_VGA16 server
`VGA16`	For the 4bpp drivers in the XF86_VGA16 server

`Device string`

Remember the Identifier string in the Device section (used for the video card)? This is where the string is duplicated—letter for letter—for the video card configuration that is to be used.

`Monitor string`

The Identifier string in the Monitor section for the monitor that is to be used with this Screen configuration needs to be specified here.

`DefaultColorDepth bits_per_pixel`

One of the most often requested pieces of X Window configuration information, this tag sets the default color depth with which the server will operate (8 indicates 8bpp, or 256 colors; 16 indicates 16bpp, or 65k colors; and so on). This takes the place of the `-bpp` command-line parameter that can be passed when the X Window system is started from a command line.

By default, unless it is told otherwise, the X Window system uses an 8bpp color depth. Do not enclose the parameters in quotes if you use this tag.

`ScreenNo screen_number`

In a multiheaded (that is, multimonitor) configuration, the order of the various Screen subsections determines, by default, how the screens are to be numbered. If each of the subsections contains a `ScreenNo` tag that forces a different numbering system, the default numbering is overridden.

Currently, stable multiheaded configurations for XFree86 are being slated for the 4.0 release of XFree86. Some support is offered today, but it is not completely stable; avoid it unless you want to experiment. Because of its experimental nature, it is not covered in this book.

If you use this tag, do not use quotes around the parameters.

`BlankTime time_in_minutes`

This tag sets the timeout for inactivity before the screen is blanked. The default time is `10` (meaning 10 minutes). This can be changed here, and it can even be overridden with the `xset` command while the X Window system is running.

Do not use quotes around the parameters for this tag.

`StandbyTime time_in_minutes`

If a VESA DPMS monitor is being used, this tag—along with an `Option` parameter called `power_saver`, which is specified in the appropriate preceding Device section—can enable the monitor to go into "standby" mode after the specified number of minutes of inactivity pass by. The default value is `20` (indicating 20 minutes).

Do not use quotes around the parameters for this tag.

`SuspendTime time_in_minutes`

This tag expands on the preceding `StandbyTime` tag for VESA DPMS monitors, and it sets the amount of inactivity in minutes that are to pass before putting the monitor in "suspend" mode.

The default value is `30` (indicating 30 minutes). As with the `StandbyTime` tag, the `power_saver` option needs to be set in the appropriate Device entry.

Do not use quotes around the parameters for this tag.

`OffTime time_in_minutes`

This expands on the last two tags for VESA DPMS monitors by specifying the amount of inactive time to wait for before shutting down the monitor completely. The `power_saver` option needs to be set for this tag to work as well.

Do not use quotes around the parameters for this tag.

```
SubSection "Display"
```

There is no parameter to be passed with this one. Each of these subsections specifies settings for each individual color depth with which the X Window server can operate. All the text that starts with a `SubSection "Display"` label is considered to be enclosed within the same subsection until an `EndSubSection` label is encountered.

Table 38.4 details the tags that are allowed within Display subsections.

TABLE 38.4 TAGS ALLOWED WITHIN DISPLAY SUBSECTIONS

Tag	Description
`Depth` *`bits_per_pixel`*	Indicates what color depth this subsection applies to. Optional depths are 8, 15, 16, 24, and 32. Note that not all color depths are supported by all X Window servers. Also, note that there are no quotes used around parameters to this tag.
`Weight` *`RGB_values`*	Tells what RGB weighting is to be used at 16bpp color depths. Not all servers support this, so be sure to check the man page for the X Window server that you are using to see if this is available. Do not use quotes around parameters to this tag.
`Virtual` *`x_width y_width`*	The X Window system allows what are known as virtual desktops, or graphic work areas that are much bigger than the display area of the monitor that is being used. For instance, a monitor that is running an 800×600 display can use a desktop that is much larger, such as 1024×768, and scroll around it by dragging the mouse to the edges of the display. Although this tends to have a dizzying effect after a while, some people really like using virtual desktops. If you are one of those people, you can specify the X and Y values (for example, `1024` and `768` for a 1024×768 virtual desktop) using this tag. If the Virtual tag is not used, the maximum resolution that is configured in the `Modes` line (see the following) is used. Do not use quotes around parameters to this tag.
`ViewPort` *`x_coord y_coord`*	If a virtual desktop is being used, this tag allows the setting of the default upper-left corner coordinates to be adhered to when the X Window system is first started. If this is not specified, the display is centered within the virtual desktop. Do not use quotes around parameters to this tag.
`Modes` *`list_of_modes`*	All those `Modeline` tags used in the Monitor section come into play here. The names of the modes that are to be offered with this color depth are specified here. The first mode name is the one that the X Window system uses when it first starts; the rest can be scrolled through using the Ctrl+Alt+NumPad+/- sequence. Be sure to specify the mode that you want to use as the first one in the list, and be sure to enclose each mode name in double-quotes (that is, "1024×768" "800×600" "640×480") and not all in one set of quotes.

Tag	Description

`Visual` *`visual_type`*	Each of the various color depth offer default visual types to be specified here. They are as follows:
	
	For 1bpp:
	`StaticGray`
	
	For 4bpp:
	`StaticColor (default)`
	`StaticGray`
	`GrayScale`
	`PseudoColor`
	
	For 8bpp:
	`PsuedoColor (default)`
	`StaticGray`
	`GrayScale`
	`StaticColor`
	`TrueColor`
	`DirectColor`
	
	For 16 & 32bpp:
	`TrueColor`

`Option` *`string`*	Some X Window servers offer options that can be specified using this tag within the Screen section. Not all do, though. Be sure to check the man page for the X Window server that is being used to see if there are any options that can be set here.
`Black` *`red green blue`*	If you are using the VGA2 driver of the XF86_Mono server, the values that make up the color `black` can be set here. The values range from 0 to 255—from 100 percent shade to 0 percent shade, respectively. Do not use quotes around parameters to this tag.
`White` *`red green blue`*	The same idea and theory that are behind the `black` tag apply here, but to the color `white`. Do not use quotes around parameters to this tag.

The Xinput Section

The Xinput section is used for storing configuration information on the additional devices that are specified in the Module section at the beginning of the chapter. Because these devices are not hard-coded and new devices can be added at any time, it is not a good idea to list parameters here. As with X Window server-specific parameters, it is best to refer to man pages for this kind of information. Specifically, near the end of the man page for XF86Config you can find the various specific configuration tags that are offered for these modules.

SUMMARY

The first reaction that most people have when they see the incredibly long list of configuration options for X Window servers is astonishment; intimidation usually follows close behind. Neither of these should be experienced, though. The bulk of X Window systems nowadays—probably around 90 percent of them—never need any tinkering after the initial setup is created with either `XF86Setup` or `XF86Config`. Of the remaining ten percent, probably eight percent make up people who just want to play, and the remaining two percent have honest requirements that they need to enable in their configurations just to get things going.

Regardless of which camp you are in, it is always good to know how to get around this file. After its contents have been demystified a bit, setting and changing parameters in tags and enabling options by adding and removing flags is a piece of cake. Nobody expects everyone to know the ins and outs of how video mode lines are created, so try not to feel like you are missing vital information if you do not understand such things. Retain what you understand, and feel free to do some experimentation if you feel up to it (be careful in the Monitor section, though!). You can learn more by experimenting than by reading, so if there seems to be a feature listed here or in the man page for your X Window server that you want to try, go ahead and try it. As long as you heed warnings when they are given and as long as you lend at least half an ear to the little voice that says to back off when you get too close to the fire, everything will be fine.

The following chapters can provide information that relates to or expands on topics discussed here:

- See Chapter 37 for more information on the `XF86Setup` and `XF86Config` utilities.
- See Chapter 40, "Controlling X Resources," for information on setting up access rights to use resources on your X Window system.
- See Part II, "Using OpenLinux," for primers and explanations of valuable features in KDE, the graphic environment OpenLinux uses in the X Window system by default.

CHAPTER 39

Customizing X

In this chapter

Among the darker secrets of Linux, the X Window client and X server are some of the most difficult to fathom. This is in part due to the origins of today's X Window system, as well as the use by Caldera of files designed to hide this complexity from beginners. Unfortunately, this combination makes it difficult to explain all the intricacies in one chapter. However, the information in this chapter will help you begin to understand how you can customize the client side of the X server/client architecture.

Tip

Whenever you see a reference to client/server architecture, you have an implied networking environment. This means that, although you normally see the X server and X client (window manager) on the same machine, they don't have to be set up that way.

But unlike most client/server architectures, the X server runs on the local machine, whereas the client can be run on most any machine on the network.

As you've probably surmised from the information in the first paragraph of this chapter, several different programs work together to bring you the *graphical user interface* (*GUI*) that you see on your screen when X is active. In Chapter 37, "Configuring X," you configured the files to run the X server that controls the keyboard, the video display (including monitor and video card), and the mouse. In this chapter, you'll look at the default configurations for the X clients, the window managers, and how to change the defaults to personalize your window environment. You'll also look at the files that affect the X environment.

DEFAULT SETTINGS

When you install the graphical environment on your system, you install a large number of programs from the X11 packages. Depending on which packages you install, you might or might not have all the programs that are discussed in this chapter on your system. But because a great deal of them are required if you install X, almost all of them are at your disposal. If you find that you are missing some files you want to have, you can always install them later.

STARTING YOUR GRAPHICAL INTERFACE

Basically, there are four ways to start the X server:

- `X`—This method starts the X server itself, but without any options, it does not start any client programs. This method should only be used by root, and only with the desired options.
- `startx`—This is the preferred method for a user to start an X session from the command line.
- `xinit`—This is a configurable method that is designed to be used as part of a script. Normally, this is used at larger sites as part of a tailored login process.

- `xdm`—This method was designed to provide a complete graphical interface to X, including a graphical login screen. This needs to be started by root, and is run from /etc/inittab in runlevel 5 (see Chapter 12, "System Initialization Under OpenLinux," for more information on runlevels and inittab).

Although each of the preceding methods has valid uses, you will want to determine which one is best for your particular situation. Just as each has its advantages, each has drawbacks. You'll get a sense for each in the following paragraphs.

X is normally symbolically linked to the actual X server binary that is used by the local machine.

When you configured the X server in Chapter 37 (a necessary prerequisite), the setup program created the link for you. So executing X is the same as executing the corresponding server binary. Both are located by default in /usr/X11R6/bin.

Caution

If you are exporting or importing /usr or /usr/X11R6 as an NFS mount, be sure to change the symbolic link/usr/X11R6/bin/X to point first to an intermediate link that is not imported or exported, such as /etc/X11/X, which will then point back to the correct X server in /usr/X11R6/bin. Also ensure that the correct X server binary is available for use because it is unlikely that a large number of machines will be identical or will remain identical over time. This technique works even if you are using an NFS root file system or tftp because /etc is always machine-specific.

Starting the X server from a command line is a valid option only for root. To permit a non-privileged user to start the X server directly, you need to make the actual binary SUID or SGID; however, this is not recommended because it poses a security risk. Normally, X is not called without some options. Because X only points to the server binary, and the server binary controls only the video, keyboard mapping, and mouse, this option is rather useless by itself. Calling the X server directly provides you with no window manager or X program to run. All you see on the screen is a gray mesh pattern and an *X* that you can move around with the mouse. Mouse button presses do not net any activity. Some of the standard options that are used when X is called directly include, but are not limited to, the following:

- A display number in the form of :*X*, where *X* can be any number. If a display number is not specified, the default display of :0 is assumed.
- A fontpath in the form of `fp /path/to/fonts`. Multiple paths are in the form of a comma separated list (with no white space), as in `fp /path/to/fonts,/path/to/more/fonts`.
- A query, as in `-query` *<hostname>*, where *<hostname>* is the name of a host on the network that is running `xdm`.
- A screen resolution in the form of `-bpp <#>`, where `<#>` is any valid color depth expressed in bits per pixel, such as 8, 16, or 24. Invalid resolutions are ignored.

startx

The most common method for a nonprivileged user (for more information on privileged and nonprivileged users, see Chapter 10, "Users, Groups, and Permissions") to start an X session from a command line is via `startx`. This program is a shell script that is installed by default on OpenLinux systems. This script, found in /usr/X11R6/bin, can be modified by the system administrator. As it is installed, the script sets up some variables and executes `xinit` (see Listing 39.1).

LISTING 39.1 THE startx SCRIPT

```
#!/bin/sh
# $XConsortium: startx.cpp,v 1.4 91/08/22 11:41:29 rws Exp $
# $XFree86: xc/programs/xinit/startx.cpp,v 3.0 1994/05/22 00:02:28
➥dawes Exp $
# This is just a sample implementation of a slightly less primitive
# interface than xinit.  It looks for user .xinitrc and .xserverrc
# files, and then system xinitrc and xserverrc files, or else lets
➥xinit choose
# its default.  The system xinitrc should probably do things like
# for .Xresources files and merge them in, startup up a window manager,
# and pop a clock and several xterms.
# Site administrators are STRONGLY urged to write nicer versions.

userclientrc=$HOME/.xinitrc
userserverrc=$HOME/.xserverrc

if [ -f /etc/X11/wmconfig/xinitrc ] ; then
    sysclientrc=/etc/X11/wmconfig/xinitrc
else
    sysclientrc=/etc/X11/xinit/xinitrc
fi

if [ -f /etc/X11/wmconfig/xserverrc ] ; then
    sysserverrc=/etc/X11/wmconfig/xserverrc
else
    sysserverrc=/etc/X11/xinit/xserverrc
fi

clientargs=""
serverargs=""
if [ -f $userclientrc ]; then
    clientargs=$userclientrc
elif [ -f $sysclientrc ]; then
    clientargs=$sysclientrc
fi

if [ -f $userserverrc ]; then
    serverargs=$userserverrc
elif [ -f $sysserverrc ]; then
    serverargs=$sysserverrc
fi

whoseargs="client"
while [ "x$1" != "x" ]; do
```

```
    case "$1" in
        /''*¦\.*)   if [ "$whoseargs" = "client" ]; then
                clientargs="$1"
            else
                serverargs="$1"
            fi ;;
        --)     whoseargs="server" ;;
        *)      if [ "$whoseargs" = "client" ]; then
                clientargs="$clientargs $1"
            else
                serverargs="$serverargs $1"
            fi ;;
    esac
    shift
done

# do an exec
-> don't leave startx in memory during X session
exec xinit $clientargs -- $serverargs
```

The `startx` script, as presented, is sufficient for most installations. However, you are encouraged to modify this script or write your own to suit your environment.

Tip

> The `startx` script passes arguments through to the program that is used to start the X server, but the method for doing so is not intuitive. It requires you to first send an end of arguments signal (`--`) to `startx`, before sending arguments that are to be passed through. For example, assuming that the X server normally starts in 256 colors (bpp 8) and that you want it to start in 65k colors (bpp 16), the command line looks like this: `startx -- -bpp 16`.

For more information on the complete sequence of events that follows the initialization of the `startx` script in a default OpenLinux setup, see the "Configuration Files" section that follows.

`xinit`

Using `xinit` is a legitimate way for a user to start the X server, but unless the system administrator has reconfigured either the systemwide script or the system administrator or user have installed the appropriate script (see the "Configuration Files" section that follows) in the user's home directory, this method is unlikely to produce the desired result. Use of `xinit` is normally reserved for larger sites that require special setups based on factors such as the user's privilege level (for example, professors versus students), and so on. Then, as different users are created in their respective classes, they copy into their $HOME directory files to configure `xinit` when it is run. Because no .xinitrc file is provided in the users' $HOME directories by default, calling `xinit` runs the following:

```
xterm -geometry +1+1 -n login -display :0
```

This runs the Xserver, an xterm, and nothing else. Although a window manager can be run from the xterm, exiting the xterm terminates the session, regardless of the window manager.

The final way to have a graphical interface is to have one at all times. The xdm program facilitates just that. Short for X Display Manager, xdm can only be run by root, and starts a graphical login screen. The xdm program allows for much more than just putting a graphical login on the screen. It is also the best way for clients to run remotely. The X Display Manager manages not only local displays, but also clients querying it via the network. In fact, if one or two servers are created to be X display managers, and no one will be using those specific machines, they only need to run xdm—they don't need to run an X server.

Of all the ways to run a graphical user environment, xdm is the one of the most powerful and flexible—but that power and flexibility come at the price of complexity. The xdm configuration files, which you will look at more closely in Chapter 40, "Controlling X Resources," are among the most complex single program configuration files in OpenLinux.

CONFIGURATION FILES

Many programs in OpenLinux that are started from a command line or by a script have configuration files. Some look only for systemwide configuration files in standard locations, such as /etc, or in the program's own configuration directory. But some, and particularly those run by users, look first (and in the case of xinit *only*) for a configuration file in the user's $HOME directory so as to provide the user with a consistent, user-tailored interface. The following section deals with the two ways users normally start an X session: via xinit and startx.

XINITRC

The xinit program, as explained previously, is a legitimate way for users to start an X session.

However, under OpenLinux, xinit is not configured to be called directly by the user. With no preconfiguration, calling xinit to start the X server results in an X server running with a gray mesh screen and one xterm window (as noted previously). However, without a window manager running, the xterm becomes not much more than a fancy VT with smaller letters. In order to do much more, each user who wants to run xinit from the command line needs to build either his own .xinitrc file in his $HOME directory or a link to the sample provided as /etc/X11/xinit/xinitrc (see Listing 39.2).

LISTING 39.2 THE DEFAULT /ETC/X11/XINIT/XINITRC FILE

```
#!/bin/sh
# $XConsortium: xinitrc.cpp,v 1.4 91/08/22 11:41:34 rws Exp $

userresources=$HOME/.Xresources
usermodmap=$HOME/.Xmodmap
sysresources=/usr/X11R6/lib/X11/xinit/.Xresources
```

```
sysmodmap=/usr/X11R6/lib/X11/xinit/.Xmodmap

# merge in defaults and keymaps

if [ -f $sysresources ]; then
    xrdb -merge $sysresources
fi

if [ -f $sysmodmap ]; then
    xmodmap $sysmodmap
fi

if [ -f $userresources ]; then
    xrdb -merge $userresources
fi

if [ -f $usermodmap ]; then
    xmodmap $usermodmap
fi

# start some nice programs

twm &
xclock -geometry 50x50-1+1 &
xterm -geometry 80x50+494+51 &
xterm -geometry 80x20+494-0 &
exec xterm -geometry 80x66+0+0 -name login
```


Looking at the script, you can see that a number of variables (`userresources`, `usermodmap`, `sysresources`, and `sysmodmap`) are set, and then checked to see if they exist; if so, they are merged with the system files. Then `twm`, a rather Spartan window manager, and three `xterms` are run along with a clock. The system xinitrc file is not executed by default if $HOME/.xinitrc does not exist. So to run the preceding, a $HOME/.xinitrc file has to be created as a link or a script that sources the system xinitrc file.

The Default `startx` Configuration

When a user runs the `/usr/X11R6/bin/startx` script from a command line in a default OpenLinux installation, a series of events occurs. To understand what happens and how to modify the default behavior to add and change menu items, and so on, follow the logic and look at a few scripts. You've already seen the `startx` script itself in Listing 39.1. First, the script looks in the user's $HOME directory for an .xinitrc and an .xserverrc file. If the .xinitrc file is found, it is the one that is used when X starts. For the purposes of this text, you'll assume that the file does not exist because, by default, it doesn't. To prevent its use in a production business environment, you might want to comment out the `userclientrc=$HOME/.xinitrc` line or substitute a safe value. The .xserverrc file contains arguments to the X server, such as `-bpp 16`, to start the server in 65K color mode.

The script then continues to look for xinitrc files in other locations. Again, for the purposes of this discussion, you'll look at /etc/X11/wmconfig/xinitrc because this is installed in a default OpenLinux installation with X. The xserverrc file isn't installed by default, but it can be added by root. Most of the script just tests for the existence of files and assigns them to certain variables. These are then passed as arguments to `xinit`. On a standard OpenLinux installation, `xinit` is started with the xinitrc found in Listing 39.3.

LISTING 39.3 THE /ETC/X11/WMCONFIG/XINITRC FILE

```
#!/bin/sh

XINIT_DIR=${XINITDIR:-/etc/X11/xinit}
sysresources=$XINIT_DIR/.Xresources
userdefaults=$HOME/.Xdefaults
userresources=$HOME/.Xresources

# export OPENWINHOME and HELPPATH
export OPENWINHOME=/usr/openwin
export HELPPATH=$OPENWINHOME/help

# get and export WINMGR
if [ -r $HOME/.wmconfig/rc.config ]; then
    WINMGR=${WINMGR:-$(get_val -f $HOME/.wmconfig/rc.config WINMGR)}
fi
WINMGR=${WINMGR:-$(get_val -f /etc/X11/wmconfig/rc.config WINMGR)}
WINMGR=${WINMGR:-fvwm}
export WINMGR

# echo "Window manager is $WINMGR"

# merge in defaults and keymaps
if [ -x /lib/cpp ]; then
    XRDB=xrdb
else
    XRDB="xrdb -nocpp"
fi

for res in ${sysresources}* $userresources $userdefaults ; do
    if [ -f $res ]; then
        $XRDB -merge $res
    fi
done

xsetroot -solid SteelBlue
# check for space on /tmp and $HOME and for write access
#  error exit, if not
space_tmp=`df /tmp ¦ xargs ¦ cut -d" " -f11`
space_home=`df $HOME ¦ xargs ¦ cut -d" " -f11`

if [ $space_tmp -lt 50 ]; then
    echo Not enough free disk space on /tmp
    exit 1
fi

if [ $space_home -lt 30 ]; then
    echo Not enough free disk space on $HOME
    exit 1
fi
```

```
testfile=FVWM_$$.testfile

if ! echo TEST_TEXT >/tmp/$testfile 2>/dev/null ; then
    echo "Have no write permissions for /tmp"
    exit 1
fi
rm -f /tmp/$testfile

if ! echo TEST_TEXT >$HOME/$testfile 2>/dev/null ; then
    echo "Have no write permissions for $HOME"
    exit 1
fi
rm -f $HOME/$testfile

test "$(whoami)" = "root" &&
test -f /usr/share/lgtypes/needs_update &&
test -x /usr/sbin/rebuild_lgtypes &&
    /usr/sbin/rebuild_lgtypes

# start the window-manager and redirect output to a file (appending)
# some applications are started by the window manager itself
exec $WINMGR >> $HOME/.xerrors 2>&1
```


PARSING xinitrc

The xinitrc script checks first to see if $HOME/.wmconfig/rc.config exists, and it looks for a variable WINMGR; if it is not set there, it looks for the same variable in /etc/X11/wmconfig/rc.config. If it doesn't find it there either, it falls back to fvwm. The script then merges in any global Xresources and the user's .Xdefaults or .Xresources. System administrators can modify the global resources in /etc/X11/xinit/.Xresources for use by all users. After the resources are set, the root X window is set to solid steel blue. The xinitrc script then checks to ensure that the /tmp and $HOME directories have sufficient free space and are writable by the user. The script continues with its housekeeping by checking to see if the user who is logging in is root, and if some looking glass type files need rebuilding. Finally, the window manager is started.

THE SYSTEM.FVWMRC FILE

For the purposes of this text, assume that the WINMGR variable was not changed.

If this variable has been changed, it's left to the reader to determine the correct system rc file that is to be read and interpreted, depending on the window manager that is used. However, most look similar to the one you are examining here. When fvwm starts, it looks for a $HOME/.fvwmrc file. If a system administrator wants to retain the default system.fvwmrc file, links to it can be put in the user's home directory as .fvwmrc. If the user does not have .fvwmrc in $HOME, fvwm uses /etc/X11/fvwm/system.fvwmrc (see Listing 39.4).

LISTING 39.4 A PORTION OF THE /ETC/X11/FVWM/SYSTEM.FVWMRC FILE

```
divert(-1)
################################################################
##########
#  system.fvwmrc: collate global and specific macro definitions and apply
#                 them onto the window manager configuration
#
[miscellaneous macro information deleted]
#
dnl the two following lines are for console testing ...
ifdef(`HOME',`',`define(`HOME', esyscmd(`echo -n $HOME'))')
ifdef(`FVWMDIR',`',`define(`FVWMDIR',`/usr/X11R6/lib/X11/fvwm')')

divert(0)dnl
ifelse(syscmd(test -r /etc/X11/wmconfig/rc)sysval, 0,
    `define(`WinMgr',`Fvwm1')sinclude(/etc/X11/wmconfig/rc)',
dnl else
# Start an xmessage box ...
Function "InitFunction"
    Exec      I  dnl
printf "Window manager not configured\nPlease install the package
➥'wmconfig' dnl
\nPress any mouse button to quit Fvwm" ¦ dnl
        xmessage -file - -center -font 10x20
EndFunction
Mouse 0 A A Quit
```

The system.fvwmrc file in Listing 39.4 has had a large block of informational text deleted, but the important parts remain. The syntax might look extremely odd because it is designed to be interpreted by m4, a macro language interpreter. The most important portion is the line `` `define(`WinMgr',`Fvwm1')sinclude(/etc/X11/wmconfig/rc) ``, which sends m4 to the first of many scripts that dynamically build the users' menus each time they log in. Looking in the /etc/X11/wmconfig directory, you see a number of scripts. Among them is `rc`, the master script that calls all others.

FOLLOWING M4

It takes some time to get accustomed to the m4 language. The `rc` script is not heavily commented, but it contains enough comments and references to other files that it is easy to see what is added, and where. In the appropriate places, it also checks to see if the user has changed any of the defaults and saved them for subsequent logins. These changes are maintained in $HOME/.wmconfig/rc.config. Before `rc` calls any other scripts, it sets up a few variables, such as the `ExecPath`, which is the path that is searched for executables to dynamically build menus. In the following list, you'll see the order in which the m4 scripts are called from rc, as well as what they do. Although it is somewhat brief, this list will give you a good idea of where to look to make specific changes to menus, and to mouse and keyboard key bindings:

- **Fvwm1.M4**—This is the first script that is called by `rc`. It creates some definitions for use by m4 to build the menus, and initializes some window manager specific variables, such as default colors. `Fvwm1.M4` includes `Common.M4`.
- **Common.M4**—This script sets up the common portion of the window manager with default menu buttons. These default buttons are links to those executables that anyone can reasonably expect to find on an OpenLinux installation. `Common.M4` includes `WmConfig`.
- **WmConfig**—This script does a lot of processing to build or rebuild the menus. This is called when a restart or change of window managers takes place from a menu selection.

The `rc` script takes over again, this time checking the user's $HOME directory for .wmconfig/rc.config to see if the `LGDESKTOP` variable is overridden. If not, desk is folded in as one of the menu items. The `rc` script continues by setting the `PixmapPath` and `IconPath` environment variables. Then it reads the following scripts in order:

- **rc.options**—Sets up default window colors, textures, fonts, and other window aesthetics.
- **rc.styles**—Sets up default window styles and icons.
- **rc.functions**—Sets up mouse functions such as click, double-click, and click and drag.
- **rc.menus.prep**—This is listed in the `rc` script, but it is a leftover, and is not used.
- **rc.menus**—Used to build the menus.
- **rc.bindings**—Defines the mouse bindings for clicks with left, middle, and right mouse buttons and keyboard bindings.
- **rc.goodstuff**—The `fvwm` Goodstuff menu items.
- **rc.modules**—Window module configuration.
- **desk**—The looking glass desktop.

The files that can safely be changed without losing edits include the rc.options, rc.styles, rc.functions, rc.menus, and rc.bindings. The rc.goodstuff and rc.modules can have things commented out, but they cannot be added to or changed easily because they are specially written programs.

The `rc.menus` script uses the `EXECPATH` environment variable from the `rc` script and searches the path for executables. These executables are compared against the list of files in rc.menus.exclude and are excluded if they are present in this file; otherwise they are added to the "Applications/Other Applications" section (see Listing 39.5).

Given the degree of difficulty in interpreting m4 scripts, Listings 39.5 and 39.6 are a completed menu built from the preceding scripts, with `WHARF_PLACEMENT="none" set`.

LISTING 39.5 COMPLETE fvwm, MENU WITH COMMENTS (THIS FIRST SECTION COMES STRAIGHT FROM THE rc SCRIPT)

```
#
#   Window manager configuration file
#
#     Module path and paths to the icons
#
ModulePath  /usr/X11R6/lib/X11/fvwm:/etc/X11/wmconfig
PixmapPath  /usr/share/data/pixmaps/desktop/:/usr/share/data/pixmaps/
IconPath    /usr/share/data/bitmaps/

As indicated, this part comes from rc.options
########################################################################
# rc.option:
#    set up the colors, window look and misc. stuff
#
# OK some people like bright clear colors on their window decorations.
# These people, I guess would mostly be from nice sunny/good weather

#  places such as California.
#

# COL/CND default color set
StdForeColor     Black
StdBackColor     #d3d3d3

HiForeColor     Black
HiBackColor     #5f9ea0

StickyForeColor     Black
StickyBackColor     #5f9ea0

PagerBackColor     #5c54c0
PagerForeColor     orchid

MenuForeColor     Black
MenuBackColor     gray
MenuStippleColor SlateGray


#
#  fonts settings
#
Font        -adobe-helvetica-medium-r-*-*-12-*-*-*-*-*-*-*
WindowFont    -adobe-helvetica-bold-r-*-*-10-*-*-*-*-*-*-*
IconFont fixed

#
#  focus stuff
#
AutoRaise -1
ClickToFocus

#
#  icon stuff
#
```

```
# Auto Place Icons is a nice feature....
# This creates two icon boxes, one on the left side, then one on the
# bottom. Leaves room in the upper left for my clock and xbiff,
# room on the bottom for the Pager.

     IconBox   0 -70  -1  -1
     IconBox -64   0  -1 -70

# If you uncomment this, and make sure that the WindowList is bound to
# something, it works pretty much like an icon manager.
#SuppressIcons

# StubbornIcons makes icons de-iconify into their original position on
# the desktop, instead of on the current page.
#StubbornIcons

# With AutoPlacement, icons will normally place themselves underneath
# active windows. This option changes that.
StubbornIconPlacement

# If you want ALL your icons to follow you around the desktop (Sticky),
# try this
StickyIcons

# Don't change to an icon when using Alt+Tab to page through open windows
CirculateSkipIcons

# mwm-style border reliefs (less deep than default fvwm) ?
MWMBorders

#
#  MWM emulation for fvwm1
#
# My feeling is that everyone should use MWMDecorHints and
# MWMFunctionHints because some applications depend on having the window
# manager respect them

# MWMFunction hints parses the function information in the MOTIF_WM_HINTS
# property, and prohibits use of these functions on the window.

# Appropriate portions of the window decorations are removed.
MWMFunctionHints

# MWM is picky about what can be done to transients, and it was
# keeping me from iconifying some windows that I like to iconify, so here
# is an override that will allow me to do the operation, even though the
# menu item is shaded out.
MWMHintOverride

# MWMDecor hints parses the decoration information in the MOTIF_WM_HINTS
# property, and removes these decorations from the window. This does not
# affect the functions that can be performed via the menus.
MWMDecorHints
```

continues

LISTING 39.5 CONTINUED

```
# These are affect minor aspects for the look-and-feel.
# Sub-menus placement mwm-style?
MWMMenus
# Maximize button does mwm-inversion thing
MWMButtons


#
#  misc. stuff
#
#  If you don't like the default 150 msec click delay for the complex
#  functions change this and uncomment it.
ClickTime 150

#  OpaqueMove has a number (N) attached to it (default 5).
#  if the window occupies less than N% of the screen,
#  opaque move is used. 0 <= N <= 100
OpaqueMove 30

# flip by whole pages on the edge of the screen.
EdgeScroll 100 100

# A modest delay before flipping pages seems to be nice... (try 750ms)
# I thresh in a 50 pixel Move-resistance too, just so people
# can try it out.
EdgeResistance 100000 50


#
#  window placement
#
#  RandomPlacement prevents user interaction while placing windows
RandomPlacement

# SmartPlacement makes new windows pop-up in blank regions of the screen
# if possible, or falls back to random or interactive placement.
SmartPlacement

# With SmartPlacement, windows will normally place themselves over icons.
# Uncomment this to change that.
# StubbornPlacement

# NoPPosition instructs fvwm to ignore the PPosition field in window
# geometry hints. Emacs annoyingly sets PPosition to (0,0)!
NoPPosition

#
#  window decoration
#
DecorateTransients

#
#  set up the virtual desktop
#
DeskTopSize 2x2
```

```
#
#  define some special buttons for the title bar
#


# default Buttons for MWM
ButtonStyle 1 50x22
ButtonStyle 4 50x50
ButtonStyle 6 22x22

ButtonStyle : 3 4 50x35@1 65x65@0 35x65@0 50x35@1
ButtonStyle : 5 4 50x65@1 35x35@1 65x35@1 50x65@0

ButtonStyle : 2 14 25x15@1 15x25@1 40x50@1 15x75@1 25x85@1 50x55@0
55x60@0 75x85@185x75@0 55x50@0 85x25@0 75x15@0 50x40@1 25x15@0

This section comes from rc.styles
########################################################################
# rc.styles:
#    Set the decoration styles and window options
#
# Order is important!!!!
# If compatible styles are set for a single window in multiple Style
# commands, the styles are ORed together. If conflicting styles
# are set, the last one specified is used.

# These commands should command before any menus or functions are
# defined, and before the internal pager is started.

# change the default width.
Style "*" BorderWidth 4, HandleWidth 4, Icon window3d.xpm

Style "Fvwm*"       NoTitle, Sticky, WindowListSkip
Style "FvwmPager"   StaysOnTop
Style "Pager"       NoTitle, Sticky, StaysOnTop, WindowListSkip
Style "FvwmBanner"  StaysOnTop
Style "GoodStuff"   NoTitle, HandleWidth 3, Sticky, WindowListSkip
Style "AddonStuff"  HandleWidth 3, Sticky, WindowListSkip
Style "*clock"      NoTitle, BorderWidth 0, StaysOnTop, WindowListSkip
Style "coolmail"    NoTitle, WindowListSkip
Style "perf"        NoTitle, Sticky
Style "xbiff"       NoTitle, WindowListSkip
Style "xload"       NoTitle, BorderWidth 0, WindowListSkip
Style "xman"        NoTitle
Style "Minitabx11"  StaysOnTop
Style "Wharf"      NoTitle, Sticky, WindowListSkip, StaysOnTop, NoHandles
Style "Banner"     NoTitle, NoHandles, WindowListSkip, Sticky, StaysOnTop

#
# Icon assignments
#
Style "xterm*"      Icon xterm-linux_3d.xpm
Style "*XSpread*"   Icon Chart.xpm
Style "Manual*"     Icon manpage_blue_3d.xpm
Style "*emacs*"     Icon Moviemaker.xpm
Style "*mail*"      Icon Mail2.xpm
```

continues

LISTING 39.5 CONTINUED

```
Style "*man"         Icon xman3d.xpm

Style "Appointment" Icon datebook.xpm
Style "GoodStuff"   Icon Moviemaker.xpm
Style "Seyon"          Icon FAX.xpm
Style "Terminal"    Icon FAX.xpm
Style "Tgif"          Icon CAD.xpm
Style "animate"        Icon Animator.xpm
Style "arena"       Icon earth_3d.xpm
Style "ghostview"   Icon WordProcessing2.xpm
Style "lisa*"       Icon install_3d.xpm
Style "lyx"        Icon DTP.xpm
Style "matlab"        Icon math4.xpm
Style "ml"        Icon Mail2.xpm
Style "netscape*"   Icon netscape_3d.xpm
Style "perf"        Icon Moduleplayer.xpm
Style "plan"        Icon calendar.next.xpm
Style "rxvt"        Icon TextEditor.xpm
Style "seyon"          Icon FAX.xpm
Style "tb"            Icon Game2.xpm
Style "tgif"          Icon CAD.xpm
Style "workman"     Icon CompactDisc.xpm
Style "xanim"          Icon Animator.xpm
Style "xbiff"       Icon mail1.xpm
Style "xcalc"       Icon Calculator.xpm
Style "xclipboard"  Icon Database.xpm
Style "xconsole"    Icon C.xpm
Style "xedit"       Icon DTP.xpm
Style "xfig"        Icon pixmap.xpm
Style "xfractint"   Icon Fractal.xpm
Style "xgraph"        Icon graphs.xpm
Style "xlock"       Icon Moduleplayer.xpm
Style "xmag"        Icon Reader.xpm
Style "xmahjongg"   Icon dragon.xpm
Style "xmgr"        Icon Chart.xpm
Style "xpaint"        Icon xpaint.xpm
Style "xpostit"        Icon postit_3d.xpm
Style "xv"         Icon xv.color.xpm
Style "xvgr"        Icon graphs.xpm
Style "xwatch"      Icon C.xpm

From the rc.functions script
##########################################################################
# rc.functions:
#    Now define some handy complex functions
#

# This one moves and then raises the window if you drag the mouse,
# only raises the window if you click, or does a RaiseLower if you
# double-click

Function "Move-or-Raise"
    Move     "Motion"
    Raise    "Motion"
    Raise    "Click"
```

```
    RaiseLower    "DoubleClick"
EndFunction

# This one maximizes vertically if you click (leaving room for the
# GoodStuff bar at the bottom), or does a full maximization if you double
# click, or a true full vertical maximization if you just hold the mouse
# button down.

Function "Maximize-Func"
    Maximize    "Motion" 0 50
    Maximize    "Click" 100 100
    Maximize    "DoubleClick" 0 100
EndFunction

# This one moves or (de)iconifies:
Function "Move-or-Iconify"
    Move     "Motion"
    Iconify    "Click"
EndFunction

# This one resizes and then raises the window if you drag the mouse,
# only raises the window if you click, or does a RaiseLower if you
# double-click

Function "Resize-or-Raise"
    Resize     "Motion"
    Raise    "Motion"
    Raise    "Click"
    RaiseLower    "DoubleClick"
EndFunction

# This one this quits fvwm and handles the autosave
# desktop functionality

Function "Quit"
    Quit    "Immediate"
EndFunction


From the rc.menus script -- where the menus are built
#########################################################################
# rc.menus: menu templates, see /usr/doc/wmconfig* for documentation
#           /etc/X11/wmconfig/Common.m4 for macro definitions
#
Popup "Terminals"
    Title   "Terminals"
    Exec    "Xterm"     xlaunch xterm
    Exec    "Color Xterm"     xlaunch xterm-color
    Exec    "Kterm"     xlaunch kterm
    Exec    "ShellTool"     xlaunch shelltool
    Exec    "CmdTool"     xlaunch cmdtool
    Exec    "Rxvt"     xlaunch rxvt
    Exec    "X3270 (IBM)"     xlaunch x3270
EndPopup
```


continues

LISTING 39.5 CONTINUED

```
Popup "Shells"
    Title   "Shells"
    Popup   "&Terminals"     Terminals
    Nop     ""
    Exec    "Xterm (&6x13 font)"    xlaunch xterm -fn 9x15 -sb -sl 1000 \
-j -ls -fn 6x13
    Exec    "Xterm (&7x14 font)"    xlaunch xterm -fn 9x15 -sb -sl 1000 \
-j -ls -fn 7x14
    Exec    "Xterm (&9x15 font)"     xlaunch xterm -fn 9x15 -sb -sl \
1000 -j -ls -fn 9x15
    Nop     ""
    Exec    "&Color Xterm (6x13 font)"     xlaunch xterm-color -fn 9x15 \
 -sb -sl 1000 -j-ls  -bg grey80 -fg darkblue -fn 6x13
    Exec    "C&olor Xterm (7x14 font)"     xlaunch xterm-color -fn 9x15 \
 -sb -sl 1000 -j-ls  -bg grey80 -fg darkblue -fn 7x14
    Exec    "Co&lor Xterm (9x15 font)"     xlaunch xterm-color -fn 9x15 \
 -sb -sl 1000 -j-ls -bg grey80 -fg darkblue -fn 9x15
EndPopup

Popup "Screensaver"
    Title   "Screensaver"
    Exec    "Ant"     xlaunch xlock -nolock -nice 0 -mode ant
    Exec    "Ball"     xlaunch xlock -nolock -nice 0 -mode ball
    Exec    "&Bat"     xlaunch xlock -nolock -nice 0 -mode bat
    Exec    "B&lank"     xlaunch xlock -nolock -nice 0 -mode blank
    Exec    "Bl&ot"     xlaunch xlock -nolock -nice 0 -mode blot
    Exec    "Bom&b"     xlaunch xlock -nolock -nice 0 -mode bomb
    Exec    "Bouboule"     xlaunch xlock -nolock -nice 0 -mode bouboule
    Exec    "Bou&nce"     xlaunch xlock -nolock -nice 0 -mode bounce
    Exec    "Braid"     xlaunch xlock -nolock -nice 0 -mode braid
    Exec    "Bug"    xlaunch xlock -nolock -nice 0 -mode bug
    Exec    "Cartoon"     xlaunch xlock -nolock -nice 0 -mode cartoon
    Exec    "Clock"     xlaunch xlock -nolock -nice 0 -mode clock
    Exec    "Crystal"     xlaunch xlock -nolock -nice 0 -mode crystal
    Exec    "Daisy"     xlaunch xlock -nolock -nice 0 -mode daisy
    Exec    "Dclock"     xlaunch xlock -nolock -nice 0 -mode dclock
    Exec    "Demon"     xlaunch xlock -nolock -nice 0 -mode demon
    Exec    "Drift"     xlaunch xlock -nolock -nice 0 -mode drift
    Exec    "Eyes"     xlaunch xlock -nolock -nice 0 -mode eyes
    Exec    "Flag"     xlaunch xlock -nolock -nice 0 -mode flag
    Exec    "&Flame"     xlaunch xlock -nolock -nice 0 -mode flame
    Exec    "Forest"     xlaunch xlock -nolock -nice 0 -mode forest
    Exec    "Fract"     xlaunch xlock -nolock -nice 0 -mode fract
    Exec    "&Galaxy"     xlaunch xlock -nolock -nice 0 -mode galaxy
    Exec    "Geometry"     xlaunch xlock -nolock -nice 0 -mode geometry
    Exec    "G&rav"     xlaunch xlock -nolock -nice 0 -mode grav
    Exec    "&Helix"     xlaunch xlock -nolock -nice 0 -mode helix
    Exec    "H&op"     xlaunch xlock -nolock -nice 0 -mode hop
    Exec    "H&yper"     xlaunch xlock -nolock -nice 0 -mode hyper
    Exec    "Ico"     xlaunch xlock -nolock -nice 0 -mode ico
    Exec    "Ifs"     xlaunch xlock -nolock -nice 0 -mode ifs
    Exec    "Image"     xlaunch xlock -nolock -nice 0 -mode image
    Exec    "Julia"     xlaunch xlock -nolock -nice 0 -mode julia
    Exec    "&Kaleid"     xlaunch xlock -nolock -nice 0 -mode kaleid
    Exec    "Laser"     xlaunch xlock -nolock -nice 0 -mode laser
```

```
    Exec    "&Life"     xlaunch xlock -nolock -nice 0 -mode life
    Exec    "Life1d"     xlaunch xlock -nolock -nice 0 -mode life1d
    Exec    "Life3d"     xlaunch xlock -nolock -nice 0 -mode life3d
    Exec    "Lightning"     xlaunch xlock -nolock -nice 0 -mode lightning
    Exec    "Lisa"     xlaunch xlock -nolock -nice 0 -mode lisa
    Exec    "Lissie"     xlaunch xlock -nolock -nice 0 -mode lissie
    Exec    "Loop"     xlaunch xlock -nolock -nice 0 -mode loop
    Exec    "Marquee"     xlaunch xlock -nolock -nice 0 -mode marquee
    Exec    "&Maze"     xlaunch xlock -nolock -nice 0 -mode maze
    Exec    "Mountain"     xlaunch xlock -nolock -nice 0 -mode mountain
    Exec    "Nose"     xlaunch xlock -nolock -nice 0 -mode nose
    Exec    "Pacman"     xlaunch xlock -nolock -nice 0 -mode pacman
    Exec    "Penrose"     xlaunch xlock -nolock -nice 0 -mode penrose
    Exec    "Petal"     xlaunch xlock -nolock -nice 0 -mode petal
    Exec    "Puzzle"     xlaunch xlock -nolock -nice 0 -mode puzzle
    Exec    "&Pyro"     xlaunch xlock -nolock -nice 0 -mode pyro
    Exec    "&Qix"     xlaunch xlock -nolock -nice 0 -mode qix
    Exec    "&Random"     xlaunch xlock -nolock -nice 0 -mode random
    Exec    "Ro&ck"     xlaunch xlock -nolock -nice 0 -mode rock
    Exec    "Roll"     xlaunch xlock -nolock -nice 0 -mode roll
    Exec    "Ro&tor"     xlaunch xlock -nolock -nice 0 -mode rotor
    Exec    "Shape"     xlaunch xlock -nolock -nice 0 -mode shape
    Exec    "Sierpinski"   xlaunch xlock -nolock -nice 0 -mode sierpinski
    Exec    "Slip"     xlaunch xlock -nolock -nice 0 -mode slip
    Exec    "&Sphere"     xlaunch xlock -nolock -nice 0 -mode sphere
    Exec    "Spiral"     xlaunch xlock -nolock -nice 0 -mode spiral
    Exec    "S&pline"     xlaunch xlock -nolock -nice 0 -mode spline
    Exec    "Star"     xlaunch xlock -nolock -nice 0 -mode star
    Exec    "Strange"     xlaunch xlock -nolock -nice 0 -mode strange
    Exec    "S&warm"     xlaunch xlock -nolock -nice 0 -mode swarm
    Exec    "Swirl"     xlaunch xlock -nolock -nice 0 -mode swirl
    Exec    "Triangle"     xlaunch xlock -nolock -nice 0 -mode triangle
    Exec    "Tube"     xlaunch xlock -nolock -nice 0 -mode tube
    Exec    "Turtle"     xlaunch xlock -nolock -nice 0 -mode turtle
    Exec    "Voters"     xlaunch xlock -nolock -nice 0 -mode voters
    Exec    "Wator"     xlaunch xlock -nolock -nice 0 -mode wator
    Exec    "Wire"     xlaunch xlock -nolock -nice 0 -mode wire
    Exec    "&Worm"     xlaunch xlock -nolock -nice 0 -mode worm
    Exec    "Worl&d"     xlaunch xlock -nolock -nice 0 -mode world
EndPopup

Popup "Screenlock"
    Title   "Screenlock"
    Exec    "Ant"     xlaunch xlock -nice 0 -mode ant
    Exec    "Ball"     xlaunch xlock -nice 0 -mode ball
    Exec    "&Bat"     xlaunch xlock -nice 0 -mode bat
    Exec    "B&lank"     xlaunch xlock -nice 0 -mode blank
    Exec    "Bl&ot"     xlaunch xlock -nice 0 -mode blot
    Exec    "Bom&b"     xlaunch xlock -nice 0 -mode bomb
    Exec    "Bouboule"     xlaunch xlock -nice 0 -mode bouboule
    Exec    "Bou&nce"     xlaunch xlock -nice 0 -mode bounce
    Exec    "Braid"     xlaunch xlock -nice 0 -mode braid
    Exec    "Bug"     xlaunch xlock -nice 0 -mode bug
    Exec    "Cartoon"     xlaunch xlock -nice 0 -mode cartoon
    Exec    "Clock"     xlaunch xlock -nice 0 -mode clock
```


continues

LISTING 39.5 CONTINUED

```
Exec    "Crystal"    xlaunch xlock -nice 0 -mode crystal
Exec    "Daisy"    xlaunch xlock -nice 0 -mode daisy
Exec    "Dclock"    xlaunch xlock -nice 0 -mode dclock
Exec    "Demon"    xlaunch xlock -nice 0 -mode demon
Exec    "Drift"    xlaunch xlock -nice 0 -mode drift
Exec    "Eyes"    xlaunch xlock -nice 0 -mode eyes
Exec    "Flag"    xlaunch xlock -nice 0 -mode flag
Exec    "&Flame"    xlaunch xlock -nice 0 -mode flame
Exec    "Forest"    xlaunch xlock -nice 0 -mode forest
Exec    "Fract"    xlaunch xlock -nice 0 -mode fract
Exec    "&Galaxy"    xlaunch xlock -nice 0 -mode galaxy
Exec    "Geometry"    xlaunch xlock -nice 0 -mode geometry
Exec    "G&rav"    xlaunch xlock -nice 0 -mode grav
Exec    "&Helix"    xlaunch xlock -nice 0 -mode helix
Exec    "H&op"    xlaunch xlock -nice 0 -mode hop
Exec    "H&yper"    xlaunch xlock -nice 0 -mode hyper
Exec    "Ico"    xlaunch xlock -nice 0 -mode ico
Exec    "Ifs"    xlaunch xlock -nice 0 -mode ifs
Exec    "Image"    xlaunch xlock -nice 0 -mode image
Exec    "Julia"    xlaunch xlock -nice 0 -mode julia
Exec    "&Kaleid"    xlaunch xlock -nice 0 -mode kaleid
Exec    "Laser"    xlaunch xlock -nice 0 -mode laser
Exec    "&Life"    xlaunch xlock -nice 0 -mode life
Exec    "Life1d"    xlaunch xlock -nice 0 -mode life1d
Exec    "Life3d"    xlaunch xlock -nice 0 -mode life3d
Exec    "Lightning"    xlaunch xlock -nice 0 -mode lightning
Exec    "Lisa"    xlaunch xlock -nice 0 -mode lisa
Exec    "Lissie"    xlaunch xlock -nice 0 -mode lissie
Exec    "Loop"    xlaunch xlock -nice 0 -mode loop
Exec    "Marquee"    xlaunch xlock -nice 0 -mode marquee
Exec    "&Maze"    xlaunch xlock -nice 0 -mode maze
Exec    "Mountain"    xlaunch xlock -nice 0 -mode mountain
Exec    "Nose"    xlaunch xlock -nice 0 -mode nose
Exec    "Pacman"    xlaunch xlock -nice 0 -mode pacman
Exec    "Penrose"    xlaunch xlock -nice 0 -mode penrose
Exec    "Petal"    xlaunch xlock -nice 0 -mode petal
Exec    "Puzzle"    xlaunch xlock -nice 0 -mode puzzle
Exec    "&Pyro"    xlaunch xlock -nice 0 -mode pyro
Exec    "&Qix"    xlaunch xlock -nice 0 -mode qix
Exec    "&Random"    xlaunch xlock -nice 0 -mode random
Exec    "Ro&ck"    xlaunch xlock -nice 0 -mode rock
Exec    "Roll"    xlaunch xlock -nice 0 -mode roll
Exec    "Ro&tor"    xlaunch xlock -nice 0 -mode rotor
Exec    "Shape"    xlaunch xlock -nice 0 -mode shape
Exec    "Sierpinski"    xlaunch xlock -nice 0 -mode sierpinski
Exec    "Slip"    xlaunch xlock -nice 0 -mode slip
Exec    "&Sphere"    xlaunch xlock -nice 0 -mode sphere
Exec    "Spiral"    xlaunch xlock -nice 0 -mode spiral
Exec    "S&pline"    xlaunch xlock -nice 0 -mode spline
Exec    "Star"    xlaunch xlock -nice 0 -mode star
Exec    "Strange"    xlaunch xlock -nice 0 -mode strange
Exec    "S&warm"    xlaunch xlock -nice 0 -mode swarm
Exec    "Swirl"    xlaunch xlock -nice 0 -mode swirl
Exec    "Triangle"    xlaunch xlock -nice 0 -mode triangle
Exec    "Tube"    xlaunch xlock -nice 0 -mode tube
```

```
    Exec    "Turtle"     xlaunch xlock -nice 0 -mode turtle
    Exec    "Voters"     xlaunch xlock -nice 0 -mode voters
    Exec    "Wator"     xlaunch xlock -nice 0 -mode wator
    Exec    "Wire"    xlaunch xlock -nice 0 -mode wire
    Exec    "&Worm"     xlaunch xlock -nice 0 -mode worm
    Exec    "Worl&d"     xlaunch xlock -nice 0 -mode world
EndPopup

Popup "Strategy"
    Title   "Strategy"
    Exec    "&Gypsy Patience"     xlaunch xpat2
    Exec    "&Mine Sweeper"     xlaunch xmine
    Exec    "&Backgammon"     xlaunch xgammon
    Exec    "S&pider"     xlaunch spider
    Exec    "&Sokoban"     xlaunch xsok
    Exec    "&Four in a row"     xlaunch xvier
    Exec    "GNU &Chess"     xlaunch xboard
    Exec    "&Risk"     xlaunch risk
    Exec    "Ci&vilization"     xlaunch civ
    Exec    "XCubes"     xlaunch xcubes
    Exec    "XDino"     xlaunch xdino
    Exec    "Xmball"     xlaunch xmball
    Exec    "Xmlink"     xlaunch xmlink
    Exec    "XRubik"     xlaunch xrubik
    Exec    "XSkewb"     xlaunch xskewb
    Exec    "XChomp"     xlaunch xchomp
EndPopup


Popup "Billard"
    Title   "Billard"
    Exec    "&Cannon"     xlaunch xcannon
    Exec    "Ca&rrom"     xlaunch xcarrom
    Exec    "C&urling"     xlaunch xcurling
    Exec    "&Hockey"     xlaunch xhockey
    Exec    "P&ool"     xlaunch xpool
    Exec    "&Snooker"     xlaunch xsnooker
EndPopup


Popup "Games"
    Title   "Games"
    Popup   "&Strategy"     Strategy
    Popup   "&Billard"     Billard
    Nop     ""
    Exec    "&Flight simulator"     xlaunch acm
    Exec    "&Jewel Box"     xlaunch xjewel
    Exec    "XB&last"     xlaunch xterm -exec xblast
    Exec    "X&trojka"     xlaunch xtrojka
    Exec    "&Pac Man"     xlaunch xpacman
    Exec    "Xhe&xtris"     xlaunch xhextris
    Exec    "X&lander"     xlaunch xlander
    Exec    "Xconq"     xlaunch xconq
    Exec    "Koules"     xlaunch xterm -e xkoules
    Exec    "Xpanex"     xlaunch xpanex
    Exec    "Xshogi"     xlaunch xshogi
```

continues

LISTING 39.5 CONTINUED

```
    Exec    "Xtriangles"     xlaunch xtriangles
    Exec    "Scavenger"     xlaunch scavenger
    Exec    "Spellcast"     xlaunch spellcast DISPLAY
    Exec    "NetMaze"     xlaunch netmaze
    Exec    "X&tetris"     xlaunch xtetris
    Exec    "XEvil"     xlaunch xevil
    Exec    "Galaga"     xlaunch xgal
    Exec    "XPilot"     xlaunch xpilot
    Exec    "XBoing"     xlaunch xboing
    Exec    "Block Out"     xlaunch xbl
EndPopup

Popup "Help"
    Title   "&Help on Linux and this distribution"
    Exec    "&Information Homepage" \
   xlaunch browser /usr/doc/html/index.html
EndPopup

Popup "Text and Publishing"
    Title   "Text and Publishing"
    Exec    "L&yX (WYSIWIM TeX)"     xlaunch lyx
    Exec    "X&wpick (Screen shot)" \
   xlaunch xwpick /home/dbandel/xwpick.gif
    Exec    "X&fig (Vector graphic)"     xlaunch xfig
    Exec    "&Tgif"     xlaunch tgif
    Exec    "&Gv"     xlaunch gv
    Exec    "G&hostview"     xlaunch ghostview
    Exec    "Graphical ViM"     xlaunch gvim
    Exec    "Xelvis"     xlaunch xelvis
    Exec    "XJed (Multi buffered)"     xlaunch xjed
    Exec    "&aXe"     xlaunch axe
    Exec    "TextEdit"     xlaunch textedit
    Exec    "X&edit"     xlaunch xedit
EndPopup

Popup "Software Development"
    Title   "Software Development"
    Exec    "Xx&gdb"     xlaunch xxgdb
    Exec    "X&wpe"     xlaunch xwpe
    Exec    "&Qt dialog editor"     xlaunch dlgedit
    Exec    "&Fdesign"     xlaunch fdesign
    Exec    "&XEmacs"     xlaunch xemacs
    Exec    "&Ddd"     xlaunch ddd
    Exec    "X&events"     xlaunch xterm -e xev
    Exec    "E&ditRes"     xlaunch editres
EndPopup

Popup "Internet Connectivity"
    Title   "Internet Connectivity"
    Exec    "&Seyon (Fax)"     xlaunch seyon -modem /dev/modem
    Exec    "&FtpTool"     xlaunch ftptool
    Exec    "X&gopher"     xlaunch xgopher
    Exec    "Xar&chie"     xlaunch xarchie
    Exec    "&News reader"     xlaunch xrn
    Exec    "&Amaya"     xlaunch amaya /usr/doc/html/index.html
```

```
    Exec    "&Netscape"     xlaunch netscape /usr/doc/html/index.html
EndPopup

Popup "Productivity Tools"
    Title   "Productivity Tools"
    Exec    "&Time planner"     xlaunch plan
    Exec    "M&L (Mail Tool)"     xlaunch ml
    Exec    "Xmh"     xlaunch xmh
    Exec    "X&fMail"     xlaunch xfmail
    Exec    "&Coolmail"     xlaunch coolmail
    Exec    "XMailbo&x"     xlaunch xmailbox
    Exec    "&Xfm (File Manager)"     xlaunch xfm
    Exec    "&Tree Browser"     xlaunch tb
    Exec    "&Post It!"     xlaunch xpostit
    Exec    "&Grok (Database)"     xlaunch grok
EndPopup

Popup "System administration"
    Title   "System administration"
    Exec    "&KPackage"     xlaunch kpackage
    Exec    "XF&86Setup"     xlaunch --su xterm-color -T XF86Setup \
-e XF86Setup
    Exec    "Mouse con&fig"     xlaunch xmseconfig
    Exec    "&Perfmeter"     xlaunch perf -geometry +0+0 -cpu \
-load -context
    Exec    "&XLoad"     xlaunch xload
    Exec    "Cpu&state"     xlaunch xcpustate
    Exec    "X&vidtune"     xlaunch xvidtune
    Exec    "X&osView"     xlaunch xosview -net 0 -l
    Exec    "XSysInfo"     xlaunch xsysinfo
    Exec    "XWatch"     xlaunch xwatch /home/dbandel/.xerrors
    Exec    "XIsp"     xlaunch xisp
    Exec    "PCMCIA CardInfo"     xlaunch cardinfo
    Exec    "&Glint"     xlaunch glint
    Exec    "Kernel config"     xlaunch --su "cd /usr/src/linux ; \
 make xconfig"
EndPopup

Popup "Amusement"
    Title   "Amusement"
    Exec    "&Workman (CD)"     xlaunch workman
    Exec    "&XplayCD"     xlaunch xplaycd
    Exec    "Xm&play"     xlaunch xmplay
    Exec    "&JukeBox"     xlaunch jukebox
    Exec    "Xmpe&g"     xlaunch xmpeg
    Exec    "&Oneko"     xlaunch oneko
    Exec    "Xm&ountains"     xlaunch xmountains
    Exec    "X&tartan"     xlaunch xtartan
    Exec    "X&fractint"     xlaunch xterm -font fixed -e xfractint -share
    Exec    "&Cute teddy"     xlaunch xteddy
EndPopup

Popup "Graphics"
    Title   "Graphics"
    Exec    "&Gimp"     xlaunch gimp
    Exec    "X&fig"     xlaunch xfig
```

continues

LISTING 39.5 CONTINUED

```
    Exec    "&Tgif"     xlaunch tgif
    Exec    "&ImageMagick"     xlaunch xgetfile -title "Select\a\file\
for\ImageMagick" \¦ xargs -r display
    Exec    "X&paint"     xlaunch xpaint
    Exec    "X&v"     xlaunch xv
    Exec    "Gnu&plot"     xlaunch xterm -e gnuplot
    Exec    "X&mag"     xlaunch xmag
    Exec    "&Animate"     xlaunch xgetfile \
 -title "Select\a\file\for\animate" \¦xargs -r animate
    Exec    "XAnim"     xlaunch xgetfile\
 -title "Select\a\file\for\xanim" \¦ xargs-r xanim
    Exec    "RasMol"     xlaunch xterm \
-e rasmol/usr/X11R6/lib/X11/rasmol/1crn.pdb
    Exec    "MpegPlay"     xlaunch xgetfile \
-title "Select\a\file\for\mpeg_play" \¦xargs -r mpeg_play
    Exec    "Scene Editor"     xlaunch sced
    Exec    "Xmorp&h"     xlaunch xmorph
    Exec    "Xm&Gr (Graphs)"     xlaunch xmgr
    Exec    "X&wpick"     xlaunch xwpick /home/dbandel/xwpick.gif
    Exec    "XbmBro&wser"     xlaunch xbmbrowser
    Exec    "&Bitmap"     xlaunch bitmap
    Exec    "&Pixmap"     xlaunch pixmap
    Exec    "X&colormap"     xlaunch xcmap
    Exec    "Xcolor&select"     xlaunch xcolorsel
EndPopup

# This menu is invoked as a submenu - it allows you to quit
# or restart the window manager
Popup "Exit-Desktop"
    Function "&Quit Desktop"     Quit
    Restart "&Restart fvwm"     fvwm
EndPopup

Popup "Background"
    Title   "Background"
    Module  "&Blue points"     WmConfig
BACKGROUND=xpmroot/usr/share/data/pixmaps/background/blue_point.xpm
    Module  "&Mesh steelblue"     WmConfig BACKGROUND=xsetroot \
-bg SteelBlue -mod 1616
    Module  "Mesh slate&gray"     WmConfig BACKGROUND=xsetroot \
-bg SlateGray -mod 1616
    Module  "Mesh lightslateg&ray"     WmConfig BACKGROUND=xsetroot \
-bg LightSlateGray-mod 16 16
    Module  "&Plain steelblue"     WmConfig BACKGROUND=xsetroot \
-solid SteelBlue
    Module  "Plain &slategray"     WmConfig BACKGROUND=xsetroot \
-solid SlateGray
    Module  "Plain &lightslategray"     WmConfig BACKGROUND=xsetroot \
-solidLightSlateGray
    Module  "&Fishtank"     WmConfig BACKGROUND=xfishtank
    Module  "&Xearth"     WmConfig BACKGROUND=xearth
    Module  "Other background ..."     WmConfig BACKGROUND=xv -ncols 32 \
-root -rmode 3-quit %getfile%
EndPopup
```

```
Popup "Fonts"
    Title   "Fonts"
    Module  "Standard font"     WmConfig WM_FONT=%getfont%
    Module  "Window font"     WmConfig WINFONT=%getfont%
    Module  "Icon font"     WmConfig ICONFONT=%getfont%
EndPopup

Popup "Window manager"
    Title   "Window manager"
    Restart "Switch to &fvwm"     fvwm
    Restart "Switch to &afterstep"     afterstep
    Restart "Switch to &twm"     twm
    Restart "Switch to &olwm"     /usr/openwin/bin/olwm
    Restart "Switch to ol&vwm"     /usr/openwin/bin/olvwm
EndPopup


Popup "Default WM"
    Title   "Default WM"
    Module  "Default to &fvwm"     WmConfig WINMGR=fvwm
    Module  "Default to &afterstep"     WmConfig WINMGR=afterstep
    Module "Default to &twm"   WmConfig WINMGR=twm
    Module "Default to &olwm"  WmConfig WINMGR=/usr/openwin/bin/olwm
    Module "Default to ol&vwm" – WmConfig WINMGR=/usr/openwin/bin/olvwm
EndPopup

Popup "Clocks"
    Title   "Clocks"
    Exec    "OpenWin clock"     xlaunch /usr/openwin/bin/clock
    Exec    "Afterstep clock"     xlaunch asclock
    Exec    "Xclock"     xlaunch xclock
    Exec    "XDaliclock"     xlaunch xdaliclock
    Exec    "Moonclock"     xlaunch moonclock
EndPopup


Popup "Misc"
    Title   "Misc"
    Popup   "&Terminals"     Terminals
    Popup   "&Clocks"     Clocks
    Nop     ""
    Exec    "&Calculator"     xlaunch xcalc
    Exec    "X&man"     xlaunch xman
    Exec    "&Hman"     xlaunch hman
    Exec    "&TkMan"     xlaunch tkman
    Exec    "Cli&pboard"     xlaunch xclipboard
    Exec    "XCept"     xlaunch xcept
    Exec    "XCDroast"     xlaunch xcdroast
    Exec    "FSshowfont"     xlaunch fsshowfont
    Exec    "Console"     xlaunch xconsole
    Exec    "XCut&sel"     xlaunch xcutsel
    Exec    "Xe&yes"     xlaunch xeyes
    Exec    "Xlogo"     xlaunch xlogo
    Exec    "&Kill"     xlaunch xkill
    Exec    "X&Tar"     xlaunch xtar
    Exec    "X&Biff"     xlaunch xbiff
```

continues

LISTING 39.5 CONTINUED

```
    Exec     "X&Fontsel"     xlaunch xfontsel
EndPopup

Popup "Demos"
    Title    "Demos"
    Exec     "&Mxp (Mandelbrot)"     xlaunch mxp
    Exec     "X&Gc"     xlaunch xgc
    Exec     "X11 &Performance"     xlaunch x11perf -all -time 1 -repeat 2
    Exec     "&Ico"     xlaunch ico -softdbl -faces -bg grey80 \
-colors red green blueyellow gray
EndPopup

Popup "GS Placement"
  Title "GS Placement"
  Module "horizontal &top"  WmConfig GOODSTUFF_PLACEMENT=horizontal_top
  Module "horizontal &bottom"  WmConfig GOODSTUFF_\
PLACEMENT=horizontal_bottom
  Module "vertical &left"  WmConfig GOODSTUFF_PLACEMENT=vertical_left
  Module "vertical &right"  WmConfig GOODSTUFF_PLACEMENT=vertical_right
  Module "&disable"  WmConfig GOODSTUFF_PLACEMENT=none

EndPopup

Popup "GS Buttons"
    Title    "GS Buttons"
    Module   "&More... button off"     WmConfig `GS_MORE_BUTN'=off
    Module   "Swallow as&clock off"     WmConfig `GS_SWAL_ASCK'=off
    Module   "Swallow x&load on"     WmConfig `GS_SWAL_XLOD'=on
    Module   "Swallow &perf off"     WmConfig `GS_SWAL_PERF'=off
    Module   "&Admin button off"     WmConfig `GS_ADMN_BUTN'=off
EndPopup

Popup "GoodStuff"
    Title    "GoodStuff"
    Popup    "GS &Placement"     GS Placement
    Popup    "GS &Buttons"     GS Buttons
    Module   "GS &Font"     WmConfig GS_FONT=%getfont%
EndPopup

Popup "Wharf placement"
    Title    "Wharf placement"
    Module   "horizontal &top"     WmConfig WHARF_PLACEMENT=horizontal_top
    Module   "horizontal &bottom" \
   WmConfig WHARF_PLACEMENT=horizontal_bottom
    Module   "vertical &left"     WmConfig WHARF_PLACEMENT=vertical_left
    Module   "vertical &right"     WmConfig WHARF_PLACEMENT=vertical_right
    Module   "&disable"     WmConfig WHARF_PLACEMENT=none
EndPopup

Popup "Snap to edge"
    Title    "Snap to edge"
    Module   "Do &not snap to edge"     WmConfig EDGESNAP=0
    Module   "Snap below &10 pixels"     WmConfig EDGESNAP=10
    Module   "Snap below &25 pixels"     WmConfig EDGESNAP=25
    Module   "Snap below &50 pixels"     WmConfig EDGESNAP=50
```

```
    Module  "Snap below 1&00 pixels"    WmConfig EDGESNAP=100
EndPopup

Popup "Window colors"
    Title   "Window colors"
    Module  "&Default"    WmConfig COLORSET=0
    Module  "&Alternate"    WmConfig COLORSET=1
    Module  "More &blue"    WmConfig COLORSET=2
    Module  "After&Step style"    WmConfig COLORSET=3
EndPopup

Popup "Autoraise windows"
    Title   "Autoraise windows"
    Module  "&500 ms"    WmConfig AUTORAISE=500
    Module  "&750 ms"    WmConfig AUTORAISE=750
    Module  "&Off"    WmConfig AUTORAISE=-1
EndPopup

Popup "Focus policy"
    Title   "Focus policy"
    Module  "&Click-to-focus"    WmConfig WM_FOCUS=CLICK
    Module  "&Sloppy-focus"    WmConfig WM_FOCUS=SLOPPY
    Module  "&Follow-focus"    WmConfig WM_FOCUS=FOLLOW
EndPopup



Popup "Miscellaneous"
    Title   "Miscellaneous"
    Module  "Kill button o&ff"    WmConfig USEKILL=false
    Module  "Mwm emulation o&ff"    WmConfig MWMEMUL=false
    Module  "Flip pages by &Mouse and Pager"    WmConfig FLIPTIME=500
    Module  "Workplace button is &right"    WmConfig WORKPLBTN=3

EndPopup

Popup "Config"
    Title   "Config"
    Popup   "&GoodStuff"    GoodStuff
    Popup   "&Wharf"    Wharf placement
    Module  "Enable autosave topics"    WmConfig AUTOSAVE=false
    Popup   "&Snap to edge"    Snap to edge
    Popup   "&Window colors"    Window colors
    Popup   "&Autoraise windows"    Autoraise windows
    Popup   "&Focus policy"    Focus policy
    Popup   "&Background"    Background
    Popup   "&Fonts"    Fonts
    Popup   "&Default WM"    Default WM
    Popup   "&Miscellaneous"    Miscellaneous
    Module  "Disable Looking Glass"    WmConfig LGDESKTOP=off
EndPopup

Popup "Other modules"
    Title   "Other modules"
    Module  "Animate"    Animate
    Module  "Audio"    Audio
```


continues

LISTING 39.5 CONTINUED

```
    Module  "Banner"     Banner
    Module  "FvwmAudio"     FvwmAudio
    Module  "FvwmBacker"     FvwmBacker
    Module  "FvwmBanner"     FvwmBanner
    Module  "FvwmClean"     FvwmClean
    Module  "FvwmDebug"     FvwmDebug
    Module  "FvwmIconBox"     FvwmIconBox
    Module  "FvwmIdent"     FvwmIdent
    Module  "FvwmSave"     FvwmSave
    Module  "FvwmScroll"     FvwmScroll
    Module  "FvwmWinList"     FvwmWinList
EndPopup

Popup "Desktop"
    Title   "Desktop"
    Popup   "&Background"     Background
    Popup   "&Screensaver"     Screensaver
    Popup   "Screen&lock"     Screenlock
    Popup   "&Window manager"     Window manager
    Exec    "Start &Looking Glass"     xlaunch lg
    Module  "Start &GoodStuff"     GoodStuff
    Module  "Start Whar&f"     Wharf
    Popup   "&Other modules"     Other modules
EndPopup
```

Listing 39.6 shows the section built dynamically by the m4 macro using the EXECPATH environment variable, and subtracting those programs that are found in rc.menus.exclude.

LISTING 39.6 THE M4 MACRO AND THE EXECPATH ENVIRONMENT VARIABLE

```
Popup "Other"
    Title   "Other applications"
    Exec    "gimptool"     xlaunch gimptool
    Exec    "gtk_config"     xlaunch gtk_config
    Exec    "vrweb_mesa"     xlaunch vrweb_mesa
    Exec    "xispid"     xlaunch xispid
    Exec    "xtank"     xlaunch xtank
    Exec    "kappfinder"     xlaunch kappfinder
    Exec    "kappfinder_restart"     xlaunch kappfinder_restart
    Exec    "kaudioserver"     xlaunch kaudioserver
    Exec    "kbanner_kss"     xlaunch kbanner_kss
    Exec    "kbat_kss"     xlaunch kbat_kss
    Exec    "kbgndwm"     xlaunch kbgndwm
    Exec    "kblankscrn_kss"     xlaunch kblankscrn_kss
    Exec    "kblob_kss"     xlaunch kblob_kss
    Exec    "kbouboule_kss"     xlaunch kbouboule_kss
    Exec    "kcmbell"     xlaunch kcmbell
    Exec    "kcmdisplay"     xlaunch kcmdisplay
    Exec    "kcminfo"     xlaunch kcminfo
    Exec    "kcminput"     xlaunch kcminput
    Exec    "kcmkpanel"     xlaunch kcmkpanel
    Exec    "kcmkwm"     xlaunch kcmkwm
    Exec    "kcmlocale"     xlaunch kcmlocale
    Exec    "kcmsamba"     xlaunch kcmsamba
```

```
Exec    "kcmsyssound"    xlaunch kcmsyssound
Exec    "kcontrol"    xlaunch kcontrol
Exec    "kdehelp"    xlaunch kdehelp
Exec    "kdm"    xlaunch kdm
Exec    "kdmconfig"    xlaunch kdmconfig
Exec    "kdmdesktop"    xlaunch kdmdesktop
Exec    "kfind"    xlaunch kfind
Exec    "kflame_kss"    xlaunch kflame_kss
Exec    "kfm"    xlaunch kfm
Exec    "kfmclient"    xlaunch kfmclient
Exec    "kfmexec"    xlaunch kfmexec
Exec    "kfmsu"    xlaunch kfmsu
Exec    "kfmsu2"    xlaunch kfmsu2
Exec    "kfmwarn"    xlaunch kfmwarn
Exec    "kfontmanager"    xlaunch kfontmanager
Exec    "kforest_kss"    xlaunch kforest_kss
Exec    "khop_kss"    xlaunch khop_kss
Exec    "kioslave"    xlaunch kioslave
Exec    "klaser_kss"    xlaunch klaser_kss
Exec    "klines_kss"    xlaunch klines_kss
Exec    "klissie_kss"    xlaunch klissie_kss
Exec    "klock"    xlaunch klock
Exec    "kmenuedit"    xlaunch kmenuedit
Exec    "kpanel"    xlaunch kpanel
Exec    "kpolygon_kss"    xlaunch kpolygon_kss
Exec    "kpyro_kss"    xlaunch kpyro_kss
Exec    "krdb"    xlaunch krdb
Exec    "krock_kss"    xlaunch krock_kss
Exec    "krootwm"    xlaunch krootwm
Exec    "kscience_kss"    xlaunch kscience_kss
Exec    "kslip_kss"    xlaunch kslip_kss
Exec    "kstartondesk"    xlaunch kstartondesk

Exec    "kswarm_kss"    xlaunch kswarm_kss
Exec    "kvt"    xlaunch kvt
Exec    "kwm"    xlaunch kwm
Exec    "kwmcom"    xlaunch kwmcom
Exec    "kwmpager"    xlaunch kwmpager
Exec    "kwmsound"    xlaunch kwmsound
Exec    "kpat"    xlaunch kpat
Exec    "maudio"    xlaunch maudio
Exec    "startkde"    xlaunch startkde
Exec    "unpack"    xlaunch unpack
Exec    "kabalone"    xlaunch kabalone
Exec    "kasteroids"    xlaunch kasteroids
Exec    "kmahjongg"    xlaunch kmahjongg
Exec    "kmines"    xlaunch kmines
Exec    "kpoker"    xlaunch kpoker
Exec    "kreversi"    xlaunch kreversi
Exec    "ksame"    xlaunch ksame
Exec    "kshisen"    xlaunch kshisen
Exec    "ksnake"    xlaunch ksnake
Exec    "ktetris"    xlaunch ktetris
Exec    "kdvi"    xlaunch kdvi
Exec    "kfax"    xlaunch kfax
Exec    "kfract"    xlaunch kfract
```


continues

LISTING 39.5 CONTINUED

```
    Exec    "kghostview"    xlaunch kghostview
    Exec    "kpaint"    xlaunch kpaint
    Exec    "kview"    xlaunch kview
    Exec    "cddaslave"    xlaunch cddaslave
    Exec    "kmedia"    xlaunch kmedia
    Exec    "kmid"    xlaunch kmid
    Exec    "kmidi"    xlaunch kmidi
    Exec    "kmix"    xlaunch kmix
    Exec    "kscd"    xlaunch kscd
    Exec    "kscdmagic"    xlaunch kscdmagic
    Exec    "workman2cddb_pl"    xlaunch workman2cddb_pl
    Exec    "kdecode"    xlaunch kdecode
    Exec    "kmail"    xlaunch kmail
    Exec    "knu"    xlaunch knu
    Exec    "korn"    xlaunch korn
    Exec    "kppp"    xlaunch kppp
    Exec    "kppplogview"    xlaunch kppplogview
    Exec    "krn"    xlaunch krn
    Exec    "kde"    xlaunch kde
    Exec    "karm"    xlaunch karm
    Exec    "kcalc"    xlaunch kcalc
    Exec    "kedit"    xlaunch kedit
    Exec    "kfdformat"    xlaunch kfdformat
    Exec    "kfloppy"    xlaunch kfloppy
    Exec    "khexdit"    xlaunch khexdit
    Exec    "kjots"    xlaunch kjots
    Exec    "kljettool"    xlaunch kljettool
    Exec    "kmkdosfs"    xlaunch kmkdosfs
    Exec    "kmke2fs"    xlaunch kmke2fs
    Exec    "knotes"    xlaunch knotes
    Exec    "kzip"    xlaunch kzip
    Exec    "kpackage_dpkg_ins"    xlaunch kpackage_dpkg_ins
    Exec    "kpackage_dpkg_rm"    xlaunch kpackage_dpkg_rm
EndPopup

Popup "Applications"
    Title   "Applications"
    Popup   "&Productivity"    Productivity Tools
    Popup   "&Graphics"    Graphics
    Popup   "&Text and Publishing"    Text and Publishing
    Popup   "&Software Development"    Software Development
    Popup   "&Internet Connectivity"    Internet Connectivity
    Popup   "&Amusement and Recreation"    Amusement
    Popup   "S&ystem administration"    System administration
    Popup   "&Miscellaneous"    Misc
    Popup   "&Demos"    Demos
    Popup   "&Other applications"    Other
EndPopup

# This menu is the main menu
Popup "Workplace"
    Title   "Workplace"
    Nop     ""
    Popup   "&Applications"    Applications
    Nop     ""
```

```
    Popup   "&Shells"     Shells
    Nop     ""
    Popup   "&Games"     Games
    Nop     ""
    Popup   "&Desktop"     Desktop
    Nop     ""
    Popup   "&Config"     Config
    Nop     ""
    Popup   "&Help on Linux"     Help
    Nop     ""
    Popup   "&Exit Desktop"     Exit-Desktop
EndPopup

# This defines the most common window operations
Popup "Window Ops"
    Title   "Window Ops"
    Function     "Move"          Move-or-Raise
    Function      "Resize"     Resize-or-Raise
    Iconify      "(De)Iconify"
    Raise        "Front"
    Lower        "Back"
    Stick    "(Un)Stick"
    Function      "(Un)Maximize"    Maximize-Func
    Nop      ""
    Close        "Quit an app"
    Nop      ""
    Refresh     "Refresh Screen"
    Restart "Restart fvwm"     fvwm
EndPopup

# A trimmed down version of "Window Ops", good for binding to decorations
Popup "Window Ops2"
    Function      "Move"          Move-or-Raise
    Function       "Resize"     Resize-or-Raise
    Iconify      "Iconify"
    Raise        "Front"
    Lower        "Back"
    Stick    "(Un)Stick"
    Nop      ""
    Close        "Quit"
EndPopup


########################################################################
# One more complex function - couldn't be defined earlier because it used
# pop-up menus
#
# This creates a motif-ish sticky menu for the title-bar window-ops
# pop-up
# Menu acts like normal twm menu if you just hold the button down,
# but if you click instead, the menu stays up, motif style

Function "Window-Ops-Func"
    Popup   "Click"     Window Ops2
    Popup   "Motion"     Window Ops2
    # Motif would add
```

continues

LISTING 39.5 CONTINUED

```
    Close    "DoubleClick"
EndFunction

This section comes from the rc.bindings script
##########################################################################
#    rc.bindings:
#    This defines the mouse and keyboard bindings
#
#
#   Context can be one or a combination of:
#     A   - any
#     R   - root window
#     W   - application windows
#     I   - Icon window
#     S   - window sides
#     F   - window frames
#     T   - title bar
#    0-9  - title bar button #
#
#   Modifier can be one or a combination of:
#     A   - any
#     N   - no modifier
#     M   - meta
#     S   - shift
#     C   - control
#    1-5  - X11 modifiers mod1 through mod5
#

#   First, for the mouse in the root window
#    Button 1 gives the Workplace menu
#    Button 2 gives the Window Ops menu
#    Button 3 gives the WindowList (like TwmWindows)
#

#      Button     Context Modifi      Function
Mouse 1          R        A       PopUp "Workplace"
Mouse 2          R         A           PopUp "Window Ops"
Mouse 3           R        A       WindowList

# Now the title bar buttons
# Any button in the left title-bar button gives the window ops menu
# Any button in the right title-bar button Iconifies the window
# Any button in the rightmost title-bar button maximizes
# Note the use of "Mouse 0" for AnyButton.

#      Button     Context Modifi      Function
Mouse 1          1      A          Function "Window-Ops-Func"
Mouse 2          1      A          Delete
Mouse 3          1      A          Function "Window-Ops-Func"
Mouse 1          4     A         Function "Maximize-Func"
Mouse 2           4     A     Maximize 100 0
Mouse 3           4     A     Maximize 0 100
Mouse 0          6      A         Iconify
# Now the rest of the frame
# Here I invoke my complex functions for Move-or-lower, Move-or-raise,
# and Resize-or-Raise.
```

```
# Button 1 in the title, with any modifiers, gives move or raise
# Button 2 in the title, with any modifiers, maximizes like olwm double-
# click
# Button 3 anywhere in the title-bar does a raise-lower
Mouse 1         T    A    Function "Move-or-Raise"
Mouse 2         T    A    Maximize 0 100
Mouse 3         T    A    RaiseLower


# Button 1 in an icons gives move for a drag, de-iconify for a click,
# Button 2 in an icon, w/ any modifiers, gives de-iconify
# Button 3 in an icon, w/ any modifiers, pops up window ops
Mouse 1         I    A    Function "Move-or-Iconify"
Mouse 2         I    A    Iconify
Mouse 3         I    A          PopUp "Window Ops"


# Button 1 in the corner pieces or sides gives resize or raise
# Button 2 in the corners or sides gives the window ops menu
# Button 3 in the corners or sides gives move and raise for a drag,
#          raise for a click
Mouse 1         FS    A    Function "Resize-or-Raise"
Mouse 2         FS    A    Function "Window-Ops-Func"
Mouse 3         FS    A    Function "Move-or-Raise"


# Button 3 in the window, with the Modifier-1 key (usually alt or
# diamond) gives Raise-Lower. Used to use control here, but that
# interferes with xterm
Mouse 3          W       M       RaiseLower


# Click on optional kill button destroys the application
Mouse 1         2    A    Close

#
#  Now some keyboard shortcuts.
#
#  You get all possible key symbol out of /usr/X11R6/include/X11/
#  keysymdef.h by stripping off the `XK_' prefix
#


#  Move in the virtual desktop with keypad arrow keys and control key
#
Key Left RTSF    C    Scroll -100 0
Key KP_Left    A    C    Scroll -100 0
Key KP_4    A    C    Scroll -100 0
Key Right    RTSF    C    Scroll +100 +0
Key KP_Right    A    C    Scroll +100 +0
Key KP_6    A    C    Scroll +100 +0
Key Up         RTSF    C    Scroll +0   -100
Key KP_Up    A    C    Scroll +0   -100
Key KP_8    A    C    Scroll +0   -100
Key Down    RTSF    C    Scroll +0   +100
Key KP_Down    A    C    Scroll +0   +100
```

continues

LISTING 39.5 CONTINUED

```
Key KP_2    A    C    Scroll +0   +100

# press control-shift and arrow key to scroll by 1/4 of a page
Key Left RTSF    CS    Scroll -25 +0
Key KP_Left    A    CS    Scroll -25 +0
Key KP_4    A    CS    Scroll -25 +0
Key Right    RTSF    CS    Scroll +25 +0
Key KP_Right    A    CS    Scroll +25 +0
Key KP_6    A    CS    Scroll +25 +0
Key Up        RTSF    CS    Scroll +0  -25
Key KP_Up    A    CS    Scroll +0  -25
Key KP_8    A    CS    Scroll +0  -25
Key Down    RTSF    CS    Scroll +0  +25
Key KP_Down    A    CS    Scroll +0  +25
Key KP_2    A    CS    Scroll +0  +25

# move the cursor with arrow keys and control and meta key pressed
#  shift is the `fine tuning' key as above
Key Left RTSF    MC    CursorMove -10 +0
Key KP_Left    A    MC    CursorMove -10 +0
Key KP_4    A    MC    CursorMove -10 +0
Key Right    RTSF    MC    CursorMove +10 +0
Key KP_Right    A    MC    CursorMove +10 +0
Key KP_6    A    MC    CursorMove +10 +0
Key Up        RTSF    MC    CursorMove +0  -10
Key KP_Up    A    MC    CursorMove +0  -10
Key KP_8    A    MC    CursorMove +0  -10
Key Down    RTSF    MC    CursorMove +0  +10
Key KP_Down    A    MC    CursorMove +0  +10
Key KP_2    A    MC    CursorMove +0  +10

# move by 1% of the screen size with additional shift key
Key Left RTSF    SMC    CursorMove -1 +0
Key KP_Left    A    SMC    CursorMove -1 +0
Key KP_4    A    SMC    CursorMove -1 +0
Key Right    RTSF    SMC    CursorMove +1 +0
Key KP_Right    A    SMC    CursorMove +1 +0
Key KP_6    A    SMC    CursorMove +1 +0
Key Up        RTSF    SMC    CursorMove +0 -1
Key KP_Up    A    SMC    CursorMove +0 -1
Key KP_8    A    SMC    CursorMove +0 -1
Key Down    RTSF    SMC    CursorMove +0 +1
Key KP_Down    A    SMC    CursorMove +0 +1
Key KP_2    A    SMC    CursorMove +0 +1


# Keyboard accelerators
Key F1        A    M    Popup "Workplace"
Key F2        A    M    Popup "Window Ops"
Key F3        A    M    Module "WindowList" FvwmWinList
Key F4        A    M    Iconify
Key F5        A    M    Move
Key F6        A    M    Resize
Key F7        A    M    CirculateUp
Key F8        A    M    CirculateDown
```

```
Key F9          A       M       Delete
Key F10         A       M       Close


# Some M$ alike keyboard bindings. Sorry, but this will help
#  some people to get free from Billy Boy
Key Tab         A    M    CirculateUp
Key Tab         A    SM    CirculateDown
Key Escape    A    M    Module "WindowList" FvwmWinList

Key space    I    A    Iconify
Key Return    I    A    Iconify

# Keyboard accelerators for menus
Key h         A    MS    Popup "Help"
Key s         A    MS    Popup "Shells"
Key a         A    MS    Popup "Applications"
Key g         A    MS    Popup "Games"
Key d         A    MS    Popup "Desktop"
Key t         A    MS    Popup "Terminals"
Key c         A    MS    Popup "Config"
Key p         A    MS    Popup "Productivity Tools"
Key f         A    MS    Popup "Graphics"
Key x         A    MS    Popup "Text and Publishing"
Key v         A    MS    Popup "Software Development"
Key i         A    MS    Popup "Internet Connectivity"
Key r         A    MS    Popup "Amusement"
Key y         A    MS    Popup "System administration"

This section comes from the rc.goodstuff script
#########################################################################
#  Definitions used by the goodstuff module
#
#  Module GoodStuff
#


# Layout: specify rows or columns, not both
# Geometry: really likes to pick its own size but giving a position is OK

#
# Colors and font
#
*GoodStuffFore Black
*GoodStuffBack #c0b0b0
*GoodStuffFont -adobe-helvetica-medium-r-*-*-10-*-*-*-*-*-*-*

#
#  Swallowed apps
#
*GoodStuff - "" SwallowModule "FvwmGoodStuffPager" FvwmGoodStuffPager 0 0
*GoodStuff - ""     Swallow "asclock"       xlaunch asclock -24 \
-shape -position+5000+5000
*GoodStuff - ""     Swallow "perf"       xlaunch perf -cpu -disk \
-fn 6x12 -col1 "\#FF0000"-col2
"\#0000FF"          -col3 "\#00FF00" -col4 "\#00c000" -bgcolor "\#e0d8d8"
```

continues

LISTING 39.5 CONTINUED

```
*GoodStuff Admin install_3d.xpm Exec "" \
xlaunch --su xfp/usr/X11R6/lib/xf-control-panel/Admin
#
# Define the buttons to use.....
#
*GoodStuff Xterm xterm-linux_3d.xpm     Exec "xterm"    \
xlaunch xterm -sb -sl 250-ls -fn 6x13
*GoodStuff WWW earth_3d.xpm     Exec "" \
xlaunch browser /usr/doc/html/index.html
*GoodStuff XEmacs dtp.xpm     Exec ""       xlaunch xemacs
*GoodStuff Gimp Paint4.xpm     Exec ""       xlaunch gimp
*AddonStuff Plan calendar.next.xpm     Exec "plan"       xlaunch plan
*AddonStuff LyX DTP.xpm     Exec "LyX"       xlaunch lyx
*AddonStuff Filetree Game2.xpm     Exec "tb"       xlaunch tb
*AddonStuff XfMail Mail2.xpm     Exec "XFMail"       xlaunch xfmail
*AddonStuff Grok-DB Database.xpm     Exec "grok"       xlaunch grok
*AddonStuff Kcalc Calculator.xpm     Exec ""       xlaunch kcalc

*AddonStuff PPP DFUe.xpm     Exec ""       xlaunch kppp
*AddonStuff CD-Player CompactDisc.xpm     Exec ""       xlaunch kscd
*AddonStuff TGif bullwinkle_3d.xpm     Exec ""       xlaunch tgif
*AddonStuff Search icon_help_3d.xpm     Exec ""       xlaunch helptool
*AddonStuff Info info_2_3d.xpm Exec "" xlaunch kdehelp /usr/info/dir
*AddonStuff Man xman3d.xpm Exec "" xlaunch kdehelp "man:\(index\)"
*GoodStuff More... Multiview.xpm    Module "Other Apps" AddonStuff

#
# Calculated adddon geometry etc.
*AddonStuffRows 2
*AddonStuffBack #c0b0b0
*AddonStuffFont -adobe-helvetica-medium-r-*-*-10-*-*-*-*-*-*-*

#
#  Wharf customization
#

#

# Animate Wharf's folders + compression into one icon
*WharfAnimate
*WharfAnimateMain

# Create a pullout "Folder" as the first button on Wharf
*Wharf AfterStep AFstep.xpm Folder
  # Include all desired icons for this initial Folder here
  # The first listed will be closest to Wharf upon expansion
  # The last will be furthest
  # This first will shut down AfterStep
*Wharf Shutdown shutdown.xpm Quit
  # Lock the display and use a random screensaver from the modelist
*Wharf xlock KeysOnChain.xpm Exec "-" xlaunch xlock -modelist "braid \
 flame grav pyroqix rock spiral spline swarm worm" -mode random \
-duration 0 -allowroot -usefirst
  # Close the Folder
*Wharf ~Folder
```

```
  # Add a "Beat"iful little timepiece
  # MaxSwallow it in order to fit the full button
*Wharf asclock nil MaxSwallow "asclock" asclock -12 -shape \
-position -1-1 &
  # Check for mail ... this time only use a regular Swallow in order
  # to capture the application in a 48x48 frame
*Wharf xbiff   nil   Swallow "xbiff" xbiff -bg "#8e8a9e" \
-fg "#00003f" -geometry45x45-1-1 &
  # Examine your computer's load
*Wharf xload nil  Swallow "xload" xload -nolabel -hl black \
-bg "#8e8a9e" -geometry48x48-1-1 &
*Wharf xload nil  Exec "" xterm -ut -T top -e top &
  # Open up an xterm
*Wharf xterm monitor.xpm   Exec "-" xterm -geometry 80x25 -sl 256 \
-sb -ls -T'xterm@afterstep.org' &
  # Start up GNU Emacs
*Wharf emacs text.xpm Exec "-" emacs &
  # Create amazing art with the freeware masterpiece, The GIMP
*Wharf gimp 3dpaint.xpm Exec "-" gimp &
  # Read some mail
*Wharf pine writeletter.xpm Exec "-" xterm -T "pine" -e pine &
  # Surf the web
*Wharf Netscape netscape3.xpm Exec "-" netscape &
  # Swallow a pager to quickly get an outlook on your virtual desktop
  # Click on the different "desks" to change in between them
*Wharf pager nil SwallowModule "Pager" Pager 0 0
  # Recycle your AfterStep session (Restart)
*Wharf Recycler  recycler.xpm  Restart " " WINMGR

This section comes from the rc.modules script
##########################################################################
# rc.modules: common window manager module configuration
#
#

#
# Fvwm1 window identifier
#
*FvwmIdentFont -adobe-helvetica-medium-r-*-*-12-*-*-*-*-*-*-*


#
# Fvwm1 pager
#
*FvwmPagerBack #b0a0a0
*FvwmPagerFont -adobe-helvetica-bold-r-*-*-10-*-*-*-*-*-*-*
*FvwmPagerFore black
*FvwmPagerGeometry -54+4
*FvwmPagerHilight LightGrey
*FvwmPagerSmallFont 5x8

*FvwmGoodStuffPagerBack #b0a0a0
*FvwmGoodStuffPagerFont none
*FvwmGoodStuffPagerFore black
*FvwmGoodStuffPagerGeometry -1000-1000
*FvwmGoodStuffPagerHilight LightSlateGrey
```

continues

Listing 39.5 continued

```
*FvwmGoodStuffPagerSmallFont 5x8


#
# Fvwm1 window list
#
*FvwmWinListAction Click1 Iconify -1,Focus
*FvwmWinListAction Click2 Iconify
*FvwmWinListAction Click3     Module  "FvwmIdent"     FvwmIdent
*FvwmWinListBack #b0a0a0
*FvwmWinListFont -adobe-helvetica-bold-r-*-*-10-*-*-*-*-*-*-*
*FvwmWinListFore Black
*FvwmWinListGeometry +0-1
*FvwmWinListUseSkipList

#
# Clean modules: perform action after some time focus loss
#
*FvwmClean 900 Iconify 1

#
# Stuff to do at start-up
#

Function "StartupFunction"
    Exec    "I"     xlaunch lg
EndFunction


Function "RestartFunction"
    Exec    "Immediate"     xlaunch --one background-$DISPLAY xv \
-ncols 32 -root-rmode 3 -quit /usr/share/data/jpeg/blue.jpg
    Module  "Immediate"     FvwmPager 0 0
EndFunction

Function "InitFunction"
    Function  "Immediate"     RestartFunction
    Function  "Immediate"     StartupFunction
EndFunction
```

These two listings, after being created, are stored in /tmp as fvwmrca, with the pid number of fvwm.

As you can see, executable files that are added to the `EXECPATH`, in this case /usr/X11R6/bin, /opt/kde/bin, and /usr/openwin/bin, and that are not included in rc.menus.exclude, are added automatically. The `EXECPATH` variable can be adjusted in the `rc` script.

Troubleshooting and Customizing

The explanation about how the menus are dynamically created should give a good hint about where to look for problems if executables are added to the `ExecPath` but do not show up the next time a user logs in.

The place to look is the user's $HOME directory. If the user has installed a .xinitrc or .fvwmrc file (or .steprc if you're using AfterStep), these files short-circuit the system files.

You've also seen indications of other files that can be used to customize the user's environment. These are .Xresources, .Xmodmap, and .Xdefaults.

xsetroot/xset

The `xsetroot` and `xset` programs enable you to change the visual appearance or other behavior of your graphical environment on-the-fly. Often these programs are called by other scripts or rc files to set up your visual environment at startup. These tools are meant for use by users—or by user scripts—to change the X server after it is running.

The `xsetroot` program manipulates the root window and is usually used to change the background color or to put a bitmap image on the root window. Used without any arguments or with the `-def` option, `xsetroot` resets the root window to the default—which is normally a Grey mesh. But `xsetroot` also enables you to change your cursor to whatever bitmap you want the cursor to look like when it is outside of any window. This can be a bitmap file you've created, or it can be one of the standard cursor names.

The `xset` program is used to control all the aspects of the X server's behavior that the user can control, other than the root window. The `xset` program enables you to manipulate the bell and key click volume and duration, or to turn them off. The `xset` program also enables you to specify which keys are auto repeating, how soon they begin to auto repeat, and at what rate. Other parameters that `xset` enables you to control include the mouse and monitor. For the mouse, only the acceleration and threshold can be set. For the monitor, however, a number of parameters can be set. These parameters include DPMS (Energy Star) features, as well as pixel colors, screen blanking, and blank interval. One other area that `xset` controls is the font path for the fonts that are used by the X server. This aspect is dealt with in more detail in the next section, "Installing Fonts." If `xset` is called without any options, a usage message shows valid options. If you want to find out what settings your system is currently using, the `-q` option shows you a complete output (see Listing 39.7).

LISTING 39.7 OUTPUT OF `xset -q`

```
Keyboard Control:
 auto repeat:  on    key click percent:  0   LED mask:  00000000
 auto repeat delay:  500    repeat rate:  30
 auto repeating keys:  00ffffffdffffbbf
             fa9fffffffdfe5ff
             7f00000000000000
             0000000000000000
 bell percent:  0   bell pitch:  400    bell duration:  100
Pointer Control:
 acceleration:  2/1    threshold:  4
Screen Saver:
 prefer blanking:  no    allow exposures:  yes
```

continues

LISTING 39.7 CONTINUED

```
 timeout:  0      cycle:  600
Colors:
 default colormap:  0x23    BlackPixel:  0   WhitePixel:  65535
Font Path:
/usr/X11R6/lib/X11/fonts/misc:unscaled,/usr/X11R6/lib/X11/fonts/7
5dpi:unscaled,/usr/X11R6/lib/X11/fonts/100dpi:unscaled,/usr/X11R6
/lib/X11/fonts/Type1,/usr/X11R6/lib/X11/fonts/Speedo,/usr/X11R6/l
ib/X11/fonts/misc,/usr/X11R6/lib/X11/fonts/75dpi,/usr/X11R6/lib/X
11/fonts/100dpi,/opt/wp8pre1/shlib10/fonts/,tcp/femur:7100
Bug Mode: compatibility mode is disabled
DPMS (Energy Star):
 Standby: 1200    Suspend: 1800    Off: 2400
DPMS is Disabled
```

INSTALLING FONTS

New fonts can be added to the fonts that are already available by installing them in one of the recognized formats, adding them to another directory or their own directory, and performing a few steps to make them available for use. The recognized formats are PCF, SNF, PFA, PFB, SPD, and BDF by XFree86, but other servers might not recognize all formats. Because most X servers that are available for Linux recognize PCF, this is the recommended format for OpenLinux systems. Utilities such as `bdftopcf` are available for changing formats. The current version of XFree allows for compression of the font files with `gzip` to save space, but some commercial X servers do not. Complete the following steps to install new fonts:

1. Convert the fonts to a recognized format (preferably pcf).
2. If desired, `gzip` the fonts to save space.
3. Copy or move the fonts into one of the existing font directories, or create a new directory for them. Fonts are installed by default below /usr/X11R6/lib/X11/fonts in directories indicative of their group: 100dpi, 75dpi, Speedo, Type1, and so on.

If the newly installed fonts are scalable fonts, you must make the appropriate entry in the fonts.scale file (or create a new one). Format for the file is as follows:

- The first line is the number of fonts in the file.
- Subsequent lines are composed of two columns separated by white space. The first column contains the name of the font in the directory. The second column contains the name of the font name pattern in its full form. Font name patterns have each element of the name preceded by a hyphen. Elements can be filled in, or they can be null. Font elements, in order of appearance, are foundry, family, weight, slant, slant width, additional style, pixel size, point size, x resolution, y resolution, spacing, average width, registry, and encoding.
- If an installed font is to be aliased with a new name, a fonts.alias file needs to be created or added to. It has the same format as the fonts.scale file. In both the fonts.scale file

and fonts.alias file, a ! at the beginning of a line indicates a remark. From within the directory with the new fonts, run the program `mkfontdir`. This program creates the file fonts.dir from the files in the directory, plus the fonts.alias and fonts.scale files. The `xset` program is used to inform the Xserver of the new fonts. If a new directory was added to hold the fonts, `xset` is used with either the `+fp` or `fp+` option, followed by the full pathname to the new fonts' directory. If the fonts were added to a directory that is already known to the X server, this step can be skipped. Finally, the command `` `xset fp rehash` `` tells the X server to reread the fonts.dir files so that it knows about the new fonts.

- Fonts that are installed by `lisa` or `rpm` are already configured and ready for use. The previous steps are only for adding individual font files and making them immediately available.

REMOTE VERSUS LOCAL FONTS

An X server has access to those fonts on the local system with no further configuration.

However, an X server can also connect to and use fonts on a remote host. In order to do this, the remote host's fonts have to be set up in the manner that was discussed in the preceding list. A font server such as `xfs` must then be run on the remote host for the local host to connect to. Because fonts consume considerable disk space, and because it is desirable for an organization to maintain a uniformity of appearance in applications, font servers are often set up by administrators. To add a font server to the font path, specify the protocol/host:port, adding it to the font path as follows:

```
xset fp+ tcp/fontserver:7100.
```


Note

Font paths are always relative to the machine on which the X server is running, which might not necessarily be the machine on which the program that will be using the fonts is located. The fonts that are to be displayed must be available to the X server that will display the font. Often, client programs also need access to the fonts.

KEYBOARD MAPPING

In general, your default keyboard mapping comes from the X Server setup that was performed in Chapter 37. But if, for some reason, the default configuration for your keyboard is not the way you want it and you can't or don't want to use XF86Setup as root to change it globally, you'll need to use the `setxkbmap` program.

setxkbmap

`setxkbmap` enables you to set your entire keyboard to a particular set of definitions. To see how your keyboard is set up by the X server by default, you can look in the /etc/XF86Config file written by either XF86Setup or xf86config. The keyboard section of this file shows you how your default keyboard is set up (see Table 39.1). The lines that begin `Xkb` are the same options and use the same arguments as `setxkbmap`. Several of the arguments must be surrounded by quotes, or `setxkbmap` terminates with errors. For example, to set the keyboard to use the menu key as the compose key, you can set the symbols option to us(pc104compose)—but you are required to surround the argument with double quotes.

TABLE 39.1 KEY/VALUE PAIRS OF THE KEYBOARD SECTION OF THE /ETC/XF86CONFIG FILE

Section	Keyboard
Protocol	"Standard"
AutoRepeat	500 30
LeftAlt	Meta
RightAlt	Meta
ScrollLock	Compose
RightCtl	Control
XkbKeycodes	"xfree86"
XkbTypes	"default"
XkbCompat	"default"
XkbSymbols	"us(pc101)"
XkbGeometry	"pc"
XkbRules	"xfree86"
XkbModel	"pc104"
XkbLayou	"en_US"

To rebuild the kbdmap, you can call `setxkbd` without any options. However, if you call it with the `-v` argument, you'll see what keymapping is being installed (see Table 39.2).

TABLE 39.2 OUTPUT OF `setxkbdmap -v`

Component	Output
Keycode	`xfree86`
Type	`complete`
Compat	`complete`
Symbol	`en_US(pc104)`
Geometry	`pc(pc104)`

If you are interested in the various symbols, types, geometries, and so on that are available on your system, they are /usr/X11R6/lib/X11/xkb and its directories. You can compose your own keymaps, but those that are supplied are usually more than sufficient. The `setxkbmap` program makes it easy to change your keyboard to a mapping, such as Spanish (es), or to any of the other symbol tables or geometries that are found in the xkb directories.

xmodmap

If you don't need to completely redefine your keyboard—for example, if you just want to change the mapping on one key, and only for yourself—the `xmodmap` program is the easy way to do it. If you create an .Xmodmap file in your $HOME directory, you can modify your .xinitrc to run `xmodmap` with .Xmodmap as the configuration file. When `xmodmap` is called with no arguments, it returns the modifier keys and a description of how they are mapped (see Table 39.3).

TABLE 39.3 `xmodmap` OUTPUT WITH NO ARGUMENTS

Component	Output
`xmodmap`	Up to 2 keys per modifier (keycodes in parentheses)
Shift	`Shift_L (0x32), Shift_R (0x3e)`
Lock	`Caps_Lock (0x25)`
Control	`Control_L (0x42),Control_R (0x6d)`
mod1	`Alt_L (0x40), Alt_R (0x71)`
mod2	`Num_Lock (0x4d)`
mod4	`Meta_L (0x73)`
mod5	`Scroll_Lock (0x4e)`

For example, if you are more comfortable with a keyboard that emulates a Sun keyboard, where the Caps Lock and left Control key are swapped, you can change them easily by putting the following in your .Xmodmap file:

- `remove Lock = Caps_Lock`
- `remove Control = Control_L`
- `reysym Control_L = Caps_Lock`
- `keysym Caps_Lock = Control_L`
- `add Lock = Caps_Lock`
- `add Control = Control_L`

The first two lines remove the keymappings that are currently on the Caps Lock key and the left Control key. The next two lines remap them, swapping the functions. The final two lines add the new keymappings for all programs to use. The Backspace and Delete keys can be swapped in a similar manner. If you want to add comments to your .Xmodmap file, use the `!` as the first character on the line. If you plan to do lot of work with remapping keys, you'll find that the `xmodmap` program has some drawbacks. In that case, you might want to check out `xkeycaps`, a graphical program that creates your .Xmodmap file. By running the program, you can remap any key by right-clicking on the key and selecting Edit Keysyms of Key. The `xkeycpas` program is available from `http://www.jwz.org/xkeycaps`.

FINAL RECOMMENDATIONS

Often, the way to make administration easier is to do things in advance. If files and links are installed in /etc/skel, they are propagated to user's $HOME directories when user accounts are created, saving considerable time later.

Among the files and links that you might want to include are the following:

- **.Xclients**—Used by some window managers for startup configuration.
- **.xinitrc**—As was explained previously, this can be linked to .Xclients to provide consistent startup.
- **.Xdefaults**—Provides some default user settings for colors, and so on, in some applications.
- **.Xresources**—Provides global user default settings for X widgets.
- **.Xmodmap and .xmodmap**—Provides user defined key mappings of rc files for various window managers, such as .xfcerc, .fvwmrc, .fvwm2rc, .steprc, .blackboxrc, and so on.

SUMMARY

In this chapter you learned about customizing your GUI interface, from changing the root window to adding more fonts and making them available, even across a network. You learned how to start the X server and window manager client, and you learned the difference between the two. You also learned how the GUI menu system, which you see when you start X in a default install environment, is built.

For more information on X, refer to the following chapters:

- Chapter 3, "Introduction to the Desktop (KDE)," discusses the KDE window manager.
- Chapter 5, "Customizing Your Desktop Environment," discusses how to add programs and shortcuts to your KDE desktop, and it covers using the Font Manager.
- Chapter 37 discusses how to set up the X server, and it gives you an idea of how the server differs from the client.
- Chapter 40 discusses interactions with the display, and having a permanent graphical environment to work in.

CHAPTER 40

Controlling X Resources

In this chapter

In this chapter, you look at some additional aspects of the X Server, with a focus on administration and security. You'll see how to configure xdm locally. Then you'll see how session management can save you keystrokes when you log in. You'll see how you can permit or prohibit the capability of others to write to your X screen. You'll also see how to implement security controls that can be shared with others to allow access to the X server.

xdm

The *X Display Manager*, or xdm, enables you to maintain a graphical login environment, either locally or on network machines. The xdm program is responsible for controlling or managing the display. It is separate from both the X Server and Window Manager. Before xdm can work, the X server must be configured and working properly. After you start the X server from a command line by entering startx, xdm can be used. Test xdm first by running it as root from a command line. When you are certain that all is well, edit /etc/inittab and change 3 to 5 in the line id:3:initdefault:.

Caution

Do not change the initdefault to 5 before testing to see that the X server works properly. If X is not properly configured, the X server enters a loop, and you have to telnet into the box, su to root, and change runlevels to break the cycle. Occasionally, holding Ctrl and hitting the *R* key also works (if this key sequence is set up).

The location for the xdm files is /etc/X11/xdm. By default, nine files are present: eight configuration files and one program. When xdm is run, other files are created. But the most important of the eight configuration files is xdm-config, the master configuration file. This file controls what other files are called. The default xdm-config is shown in Listing 40.1. The files that are found by default in the OpenLinux /etc/X11/xdm directory are: xdm-config, Xservers, Xaccess, Xsetup_0, GiveConsole, TakeConsole, Xresources, Xsession, and chooser (a program).

LISTING 40.1 A DEFAULT XDM-CONFIG FILE

```
! $XConsortium: xdm-conf.cpp /main/3 1996/01/15 15:17:26 gildea $
DisplayManager.errorLogFile:    /usr/X11R6/lib/X11/xdm/xdm-errors
DisplayManager.pidFile:         /usr/X11R6/lib/X11/xdm/xdm-pid
DisplayManager.keyFile:         /usr/X11R6/lib/X11/xdm/xdm-keys
DisplayManager.servers:         /usr/X11R6/lib/X11/xdm/Xservers
DisplayManager.accessFile:      /usr/X11R6/lib/X11/xdm/Xaccess
! All displays should use authorization, but we cannot be sure
! that X terminals will be configured that way, so by default
! use authorization only for local displays :0, :1, and so on
DisplayManager._0.authorize:    true
DisplayManager._1.authorize:    true
! The following three resources set up display :0 as the console.
DisplayManager._0.setup:        /usr/X11R6/lib/X11/xdm/Xsetup_0
DisplayManager._0.startup:      /usr/X11R6/lib/X11/xdm/GiveConsole
```

```
DisplayManager._0.reset:          /usr/X11R6/lib/X11/xdm/TakeConsole
DisplayManager*resources:         /usr/X11R6/lib/X11/xdm/Xresources
DisplayManager*session:           /usr/X11R6/lib/X11/xdm/Xsession
DisplayManager*authComplain:      false
```

xdm Global Variables

Going through the default file, you'll notice first that remarks begin with a `!`. The five lines that begin `DisplayManager.` are global configuration files. The first line writes an error log called `xdm-errors` to the directory /usr/X11R6/lib/X11/xdm. However, this particular directory is a symlink to /etc/X11/xdm, so the file shows up here. This file captures everything written to `stdout` and `stderr`, so you can troubleshoot problems by consulting this file. The second line specifies where to write the pid file. This file contains the pid for the `xdm` process that is running on the server. The third line tells `xdm` where to look for the keyfile. Although it is specified, this file isn't generally used, and its absence will not cause any errors. This file, if it is present, permits XDMCP-style authentication and contains two columns that consist of the display name and shared key. The key is DES encrypted. In order to take advantage of this feature, you'll need to recompile `xdm` to include DES support. This support is not included by default, due to encryption exportation restrictions. In all, five different access control mechanisms exist for X: host access, via `xhost`; MIT magic cookie, shared plain-text cookies via `xauth` and the Xauthority file; XDM authorization, the secure DES-based access control which uses private keys; SUN DES, based on Sun's secure `rpc` system; and MIT Kerberos, which uses Kerberos version 5 user-to-user.

The fourth line (DisplayManager) tells `xdm` which server file to use (see Listing 40.2). This file starts the X server.

Listing 40.2 Default Xservers File

```
# $XConsortium: Xserv.ws.cpp,v 1.3 93/09/28 14:30:30 gildea Exp $
# Xservers file, workstation prototype
# This file should contain an entry to start the server on the
# local display; if you have more than one display (not screen),
# you can add entries to the list (one per line).  If you also
# have some X terminals connected which do not support XDMCP,
# you can add them here as well.  Each X terminal line should
# look like:
#       XTerminalName:0 foreign
:0 local /usr/X11R6/bin/X
```

The line that starts the local server can have most of the options that are available to the X server. For instance, `-bpp 16` is perfectly legal. However, the `-broadcast` and `-query` options are not supported. The last DisplayManager line in the first section of Listing 40.1 is the line that tells `xdm` which clients it can see (access). The default filename is Xaccess. The default within Xaccess is to permit access to all local hosts via a broadcast, but this might be changed per the instructions in the file. This file only applies to environments that are using remote clients.

xdm DISPLAY VARIABLES

The next two sections of the xdm-config file set up certain defaults for displays that xdm manages.

Note

You've seen that display names are usually of the *family:name* variety. The family is assumed to be the default, that is, localhost. The display number, which contains a colon as the first part of the name, poses a problem. The xdm-config file uses a colon to separate the resource name from the filename for that resource. So when colons are required as part of the resource name, an underscore is substituted for each colon. Note also that the resource name has three parts that are separated by a .. This is only required when specific display names are involved.

The first two lines, `DisplayManager._X.authorize: true`, tell xdm that proper authorization must be used to connect to the display. If these lines are set to `false`, xdm does not require authorization. The next three lines that control DisplayManager resources for `:0`—`setup`, `startup`, and `reset`—point to the files that are responsible for setting up the display when xdm starts. When a user logs in, `startup` is run, and when the user logs out, `reset` is run. The Xsetup_0 file is shown in Listing 40.3.

LISTING 40.3 DEFAULT XSETUP_0

```
#!/bin/sh
# $XConsortium: Xsetup_0,v 1.3 93/09/28 14:30:31 gildea Exp $
xconsole -geometry 480x130+0+0 -daemon -notify -verbose -fn fixed
➥-exitOnFail
```

The Xsetup_0 file can be modified to include other things to be displayed on the default X screen.

Caution

Do not run programs that can shell out to a command prompt or execute other programs because they run as root, but are under the control of the user who is logging in. This is similar to giving all users root access; you don't want to do this because when they have root access they can do anything, including format your hard drive.

For example, you can add a line such as

```
/usr/X11R6/bin/xsetroot -solid darkblue &
```

which paints the root window a dark blue. Note the `&`, which backgrounds the process. This is required on all lines that are added to this file.

Tip

> The geometry argument can consist of two or four numbers. The first two, which are optional, are the number of pixels wide by the number of pixels high, as in 480×130. The second two numbers specify the position of the box on the screen. The first number specifies right or left positioning, and the second number represents the up or down position. When zeros are specified, they enable you to anchor the box to a corner. To anchor to the upper left corner, use +0+0; upper right –0+0, lower left +0–0, and lower right –0–0.

A favorite addition to the Xsetup_0 file is the following line:

```
/usr/X11R6/bin/xfishtank &
```

This puts a fishtank on the root window while `xdm` waits for a user to log in. However, this program does not terminate when a user logs in, so it must be killed. This is taken care of in the `GiveConsole` script, noted as follows. The `GiveConsole` and `TakeConsole` programs are shown in Listing 40.4.

LISTING 40.4 DEFAULT `GiveConsole` AND `TakeConsole` PROGRAMS

```
#!/bin/sh
# Assign ownership of the console to the invoking user
# $XConsortium: GiveConsole,v 1.2 93/09/28 14:29:20 gildea Exp $ #
# By convention, both xconsole and xterm -C check that the
# console is owned by the invoking user and is readable before attaching
# the console output.  This way a random user can invoke xterm -C without
# causing serious grief.
#'
chown $USER /dev/console

#!/bin/sh
# Reassign ownership of the console to root, this should disallow
# assignment of console output to any random users's xterm
# $XConsortium: TakeConsole,v 1.2 93/09/28 14:30:29 gildea Exp $ #
chmod 622 /dev/console
chown root /dev/console
```


These two programs perform complementary functions as users log in and out. They change the ownership of the `xconsole` to the user so that the xconsole is displayed on the screen during the user's session. If the change of ownership to the user fails, the `xconsole` line in Listing 40.2 forces the `xconsole` session to terminate. If a program is running that must be terminated when a user logs in, the command to kill that program must be put in the `GiveConsole` script before the console is `chown`ed, as follows:

```
kill `/sbin/pidof xfishtank`
```

If the program has a pidfile, the best method is to substitute the following so that the pidfile is properly cleaned up:

```
kill `cat pidfile`
```

The preceding line has the name of the actual pidfile that is substituted for *pidfile*. When processes run, they have a *process identification* (*pid*) number associated with them. (This can easily be seen by using the `ps ax` command.) This number is returned by the operating system when a program starts executing. Many programs capture this pid number and put it in a file named after the process. By `cat`ing the file, you know what the process number is. If you use `kill` with `cat pidfile` (in grave quotes as explained in Chapter 13, "Customizing Your Shell Environment"), you can kill the process very easily.

Other methods, such as using the `` `killall` `` command, also work. If this is not done, the program does not display on the user's screen, but it still consumes resources. When the user logs out and another instance of the program is started, two instances of the program reside in memory. This continues as users log in and log out—another instance of the program is run for each login. Eventually, the system runs out of resources (memory) and the X server crashes. Although using the aforementioned command solves the problem, it will most likely occur when a user is working on a project and will be very unhappy to lose hours of work.

LOCAL VARIABLES

The final section of the `xdm` config file has a slightly different format from the previous two sections. The specific display has an asterisk (*) substituted. This means the same as it does on a command line–any display. Dot separators between the parts are not required with this syntax. Listing 40.4 shows the default resources file that `xdm` uses. This file is used specifically to customize or set up the authentication (login) screen.

LISTING 40.5 DEFAULT XRESOURCES FILE

```
! $XConsortium: Xresources /main/8 1996/11/11 09:24:46 swick $
xlogin*login.translations: #override\
Ctrl<Key>R: abort-display()\n\
<Key>F1: set-session-argument(failsafe) finish-field()\n\
Ctrl<Key>Return: set-session-argument(failsafe) finish-field()\n\
<Key>Return: set-session-argument() finish-field()
xlogin*borderWidth: 3
xlogin*greeting: CLIENTHOST
xlogin*namePrompt: login:\040
xlogin*fail: Login incorrect
#ifdef
COLOR
xlogin*greetColor: CadetBlue
xlogin*failColor: red
*Foreground: black
*Background: #fffff0
xlogin*Foreground: black
xlogin*Background: white
#endif
XConsole.text.geometry: 480x130
XConsole.verbose:    true
XConsole*iconic:    true
XConsole*font:
Chooser*geometry:    700x500+300+200
```

```
Chooser*allowShellResize:    false
Chooser*viewport.forceBars:    true
Chooser*label.font:    *-new century schoolbook-bold-i-normal-*-240-*
Chooser*label.label:    XDMCP Host Menu  from CLIENTHOST
Chooser*list.font:    -*-*-medium-r-normal-*-*-230-*-*-c-*-iso8859-1
Chooser*Command.font:    *-new century schoolbook-bold-r-normal-*-180-*
```

Looking through the Xresources file, you can see that the top several lines (`xlogin*login.translations:`) are terminated by `\`, except the last. Because of the `\`, these lines are considered one line. They set some special keyboard functions to be available on the login screen.

The `#override` sets the keys that follow it to override any X defaults set up in the X server temporarily, but it doesn't replace them. Without the `#override`, the default X keymappings are replaced. The next line says that pressing the *R* (not case sensitive) while holding down the Ctrl key terminates the display. To restart the display, you'll need to restart `xdm`. The `F1` line means that if you use F1 instead of Enter to complete the login (that is, if you enter your password, and then hit F1), a special "failsafe" session can be started (see the explanation of the Xsession script that follows). The same failsafe session can also be started by holding down the Ctrl key and pressing Enter to complete your login. The final entry says that just pressing Enter completes the login normally. If you want to have special login session arguments sent to Xsession, you can add them here, or you can change one of the ones that is listed. For example, you might change one of the `(failsafe)` arguments to read `(kde)`, and modify the Xsession script appropriately (see the following example, in the section "Xsession"). If you want to make this the default login, enter `kde` in the parentheses on the last line, but be sure to change one of the `(failsafe)` entries to `()` so that you can enter a standard session.

The next few lines, which begin `xlogin`, define how the `xdm` login box that appears on the screen looks. This includes text, background colors, and so on. `CLIENTHOST` is a variable that will be replaced by the hostname of the machine. The `xlogin*namePrompt` is self-explanatory, as is the `xlogin*fail` text. The other variables are principally colors. Color names are as found in /usr/X11/R6/lib/X11/rgb.txt. Whereas the rgb.txt file gives the red, green, and blue intensity numbers in decimal from 0–255, the Xresources file uses the hexadecimal equivalents of 00–ff.

Caution

If the text or fonts that are specified are too large, the login box might not be displayed by `xdm`. Use caution when specifying fonts or large text values.

The final file that is specified by the xdm-config file is Xsession. This file controls what transpires when a username password pair results in a correct match. This script is run as the user who is logging in and gives the user a session. Listing 40.5 shows an Xsession script with an addition. The following lines

```
        kde)
                exec /opt/kde/bin/startkde
                ;;
```

have been added, and are discussed later.

LISTING 40.5 MODIFIED XSESSION SCRIPT

```
#!/bin/sh
# $XConsortium: Xsession /main/10 1995/12/18 18:21:28 gildea $

# redirect errors to a file in user's home directory if we can
for errfile in "$HOME/.xsession-errors" "${TMPDIR-/tmp}/xses-
➥$USER" "/tmp/xses-$USER"
do
        if ( cp /dev/null "$errfile" 2> /dev/null )
        then
                chmod 600 "$errfile"
                exec > "$errfile" 2>&1
                break
        fi
done

case $# in
1)
        case $1 in
        failsafe)
                exec xterm -geometry 80x24-0-0
                ;;
        kde)
                exec /opt/kde/bin/startkde
                ;;
        esac
esac

startup=$HOME/.xsession
resources=$HOME/.Xresources

if [ -f "$startup" ]; then
        exec "$startup"
elif [ -f "/etc/X11/wmconfig/xsessionrc" ]; then
        exec "/etc/X11/wmconfig/xsessionrc"
else
        if [ -f "$resources" ]; then
                xrdb -load "$resources"
        fi
        exec xsm
fi
```

This script is simple and robust. First it creates the xsession-errors file to capture errors, and then it checks to see if it was called with any arguments. You saw how to pass arguments previously, in the Xresources file, by declaring keyboard translations. This is where those arguments are acted on. This Xresources file has been modified to add the `kde` case, as noted previously. This enables you to start one of three sessions from `xdm`: standard (which normally starts `fvwm`), failsafe (which only starts an `xterm`), and KDE (which starts `kde`). It is very simple to add your own case; between the `case` and `esac` you add three lines: one to declare the case (`mycase`), a second line where you put `exec myprogram` (more lines can be inserted, but this is a minimum), and a final line with `;;` that terminates the case. Make sure that your program works properly before you make it the default. By changing your Xsession file to look like the preceding one, and by modifying your Xresources file to make `kde` the default (as explained earlier in this section), you can use `xdm` to start `kde`.

When Xsession runs, if the case arguments are not used, Xsession checks first for an .xsession file in the user's $HOME directory. If this is not found, it continues with this script or it runs the user's script. If this file runs to completion, the last program it runs is `xsm`, a session manager, which is explained in the following section.

Note

Unlike the other scripts in the xdm directory, this Xsession script is run as the user who has logged in. This makes Xsession a "safe" script because it is not run with root privileges.

The discussion of `xdm` in this chapter is far from comprehensive, but it will give you a good understanding of how `xdm` works. When you are armed with this knowledge, the manual pages and other documentation—which are often daunting and obtuse—will be easier to understand.

Session Management

When a user is logged in to X, the environment is referred to as a session. This session can be captured at any point and saved for future reference. For example, a user might have three basic sessions types: one that is for Internet use, where he is running a graphical FTP client, a Web browser, and mail; another that is used for word processing, with a word processor and a spreadsheet; and a third that is a graphical session with some graphics programs such as `GIMP` and `xv`.

Note

If you've modified your programs to run `kde`, you can ignore this section because `kde` has its own session manager.

By using `xsm`, an X session manager, the state of each of these sessions can be captured and restored. All that is required is to run `xsm`, open the applications you want to be a part of that session, and perform either a "checkpoint" or a save and exit. This writes information to the user's .xsession file.

Tip

Some applications are *session aware*. These applications can be saved (or checkpointed) with certain information, such as a starting file; then, when they are restored with `xsm`, that file is opened. Note, however, that this does not restore old information such as an "undo"–it merely opens the file that has been saved on disk, thus saving you the extra steps of opening the file.

When using `xsm`, don't use the .xsession file to start applications. The xsm file also needs to be the last line in the .xsession file so that terminating `xsm` terminates the session.

When it is first started, `xsm` looks for .xsmstartup in the user's $HOME directory. If it is not found, `xsm` falls back to /etc/X11/xsm/system.xsm (see Listing 40.6).

LISTING 40.6 DEFAULT SYSTEM.XSM FILE

```
! $XConsortium: system.xsm,v 1.5 94/12/27 17:57:25 mor Exp $
twm
smproxy
xterm
```

The `twm` line is provided as a default window manager. If you don't want to use `twm`, substitute your window manager of choice. Normally, a window manager is already running, and `twm` just fails to start because two window managers cannot be active at the same time.

The xsession manager works very well under some circumstances, but not well in others. Often, this depends on whether you are using session aware clients. The best way to use the session manager is as it is set up in the `xdm` Xsession file.

After `xsm` is running, you'll have a box with four buttons: Client List, Session Log, Checkpoint, and Shutdown (see Figure 40.1).

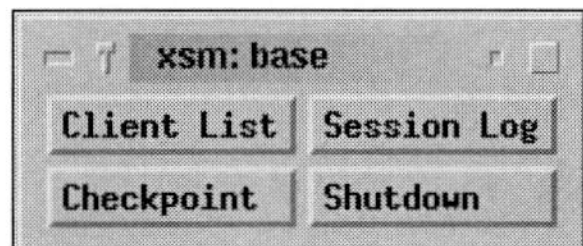

Figure 40.1
The xsm main application menu.

The Client List button shows you the list of session aware and non-session aware clients (see Figure 40.2).

The buttons are well-marked as to their functions. View Properties pops up a box that provides you with information about the X properties for the highlighted client. The Clone button creates another instance of the highlighted application. The Kill button kills the highlighted application, and Done closes the box. The Restart Hints button provides a drop-down selection for changing the client. Figure 40.2 shows clients in each of the four possible states.

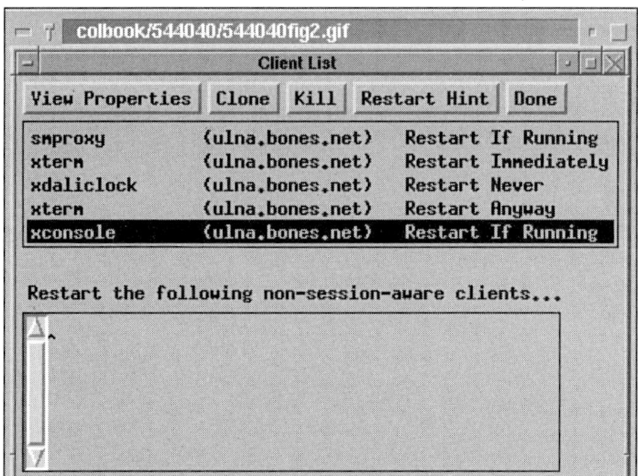

Figure 40.2
The Client List dialog box.

Returning to the main `xsm` application menu, the Session Log button shows a log of all applications that have been started, killed, and so on during the current session. The Checkpoint button enables you to either save the current state as the session that is running or create a new session. Finally, the Shutdown button enables you to close the session and select either With Checkpoint so that you can save the state of the session, or Immediately, with no save.

X SECURITY

Early in this chapter, you learned that `xdm` has five ways to implement security. Of these five, the most common is host access (using `xhost`). Host access is also the least secure. Recent versions of `xhost` are less tolerant of remote users trying to manipulate the host access table, but it is still fairly easy to work around this. This is discussed in some depth in the following sections.

This chapter also looks at one other security control, the `MIT-MAGIC-COOKIE`. This protection scheme also has some problems, but is slightly more secure than the host access method. The other methods, `XDM-AUTHORIZATION`, `SUN-DES`, and `MIT-KERBEROS`, are not discussed; `XDM-AUTHORIZATION` requires that you recompile X with the DES library, SUN-DES is not generally available except in a SUN environment, and Kerberos 5 is not generally implemented in Linux. The latter two are extremely secure, but they bring with them their own set of problems and configuration issues. For Kerberos, timed tickets require the use of a time protocol to keep hosts closely synchronized, and the Sun secure `RPC` protocol has not been ported to Linux.

xhost

The `xhost` program provides some rudimentary control for your X server display. When you start an X session, you open a display. By default, you are the only one who is allowed to write to this display. That is, another user cannot `telnet` or `rlogin` to the host you are working on, declare your display as the active display, and write directly to your screen.

Tip

Display names are composed of two parts: *family:name*. The most common family is the Internet host, and name is the display name, a two part display_number:screen_number, as in LOCALHOST:0.0, FOO:0.0, or 192.168.0.2:0.0. By convention, the hostname is in all uppercase, but this is not necessary for the Internet host family. The screen number can be left off, and it defaults to 0. If the family is left off, localhost is assumed. So the shortest display name is :0. Other families include DECnet, NIS, and Kerberos. Some of these family names are case sensitive.

That is, unless you permit it. You do so by using `xhost`. You can check this by executing `xhost` with no arguments. You'll get a response that looks like the following (baz has been given permission to write to the display):

```
access control enabled, only authorized clients can connect
INET:baz.bar.org
```

Or, it might look like the following (after executing `xhost +`):

```
access control disabled, clients can connect from any host
```

Hosts can be added to or removed from the access control list by listing them with a `+`, as in: `xhost + foo` (to allow access) or `xhost - foo` (to deny access to foo). If no hostname argument is given, it permits or denies access to all hosts.

Caution

The `xhost` program is not meant to be used as the primary means for securing access. The program is easily bypassed. Although `xhost` does not allow remote users to run the program and permit access, these controls are not secure.

`MIT-MAGIC-COOKIE-1` AND `xauth`

You read earlier that the `MIT-MAGIC-COOKIE` was not completely secure. This is because of the manner of implementation. But although it is not completely secure, this security method is better than the `xhost` method. The reason this method is not secure is because the default method of storing the cookies in the user's .Xauthority file makes it easy for others to read this file and the cookies in it. Furthermore, the cookies are sent across the network without encryption. So, like the host access method, this control method is only as good as the access control to the physical network.

The .Xauthority file holds the secret data that is used to access the X server. The `xdm` program generates the 128-bit cookies that are used for connection access. When clients want to connect, they pass a 128-bit cookie, unencrypted, to the server. If the cookies match, access is allowed. The `xdm` program is only involved once, when the cookie is generated. For all other purposes, the `xauth` program is used.

The `xauth` program can be run interactively or through scripts. The most important and commonly used commands deal with extracting a key to pass to a client and merging the key on the client into the appropriate file.

The authority file can be a centralized one, if so desired; just specify this with the `-f authfile` option. Other options to `xauth` include verbose (`-v`); quiet (`-q`), which is the opposite of verbose; ignore authority file locks (`-i`); and break authority file locks (`-b`).

Note

The environment variable `XAUTHORITY` is used as the filename to use in place of the .Xauthority file, unless the `-f authfile` option is used.

When `xauth` is started interactively, you get a prompt—`xauth>`—and you can enter commands. Either `help` or `?` provides a list of commands, most of which require an argument.

If you want to permit a client to connect, you can extract the record into a file. Two commands exist for extracting the cookie: `extract` and `nextract`. `nextract` provides a readable key that can be put in a file and emailed. The `extract` command is less usable because it produces a binary key with unprintable characters. The command syntax is identical for both:

```
nextract <filename> <displayname [...]>
```

The numeric keys can be extracted to a file or `stdout` (`-`).

This resulting file can then be sent to the client machine, and the reverse process can be used to merge or, if `nextract` was used, to `nmerge` the key into the client's Xauthority file. The syntax simply consists of `merge` or `nmerge` and the filename.

To remove old, expired, or unwanted cookies, the `remove` command is used. This is just the command `remove` followed by the display name.

Tip

To list the status of the Xauthority file, use `info`. To save changes when terminating the program, use `exit`. To ignore changes and terminate the program, use `quit`.

The easiest way to automate the process is to create a script as follows:

```
#!/bin/bash

a=$1
b=$2
if [ $# = 1 ] ; then
        b=$1
        a=`hostname`:0

else if [ $# != 2 ] ;  then
        echo  Usage $0 `hostname`:0 remoteclient  ; exit 0
fi
fi
xauth extract -$a  ¦ rsh $b xauth merge -
```

Name the script something such as `transauth` and make sure that it is executable (`chmod 755`). Note that `rhosts` must be set up in order to do this. A more secure way is via `ssh`.

Then call the script name with two arguments, the display name of the current machine (for example, foo:0), and the machine that is to receive the key. Note, however, that the script can be called with only the name of the machine that is to receive the key. Obviously, both machines have to be able to resolve the name of the other either through the /etc/hosts file or through DNS.

SUMMARY

In this chapter, you learned about `xdm` and how to set up and modify the default `xdm`. You also learned about session management and a tool to make session management easier. You also learned some basics about X security, and two methods for allowing remote access when necessary.

For more information on X Resources, refer to the following chapters:

- Chapter 37, "Configuring X," discusses setting up the X server. This is necessary before you can run `xdm`.
- Chapter 39, "Customizing X," gives you a good basis for understanding client seesions and user configurations. It also explains what happens when you log in with the default system files.

PART VI

ETC.

CHAPTER 41

ENCRYPTION

In this chapter

Picture sending out a private letter to someone through the U.S. Postal Service, written on a postcard. Everyone who comes across that post card can see it, right? Therefore, it does not require a major stretch of the imagination to understand why private letters are typically sent to their destinations sealed in envelopes. If the letter is delivered incorrectly, or if there is some other problem with delivery, the letter is sent back still sealed in the envelope. At no point was the privacy of that letter compromised (unless someone decided to rip the letter open and read it).

Now, picture email over the Internet, or even within a small network. At least one machine other than the sending machine receives that message; if you are talking about passing it to someone out on the Internet, numerous different machines are in the email's path. At each stopping point—and at a few points in between—it is entirely possible that someone can read that message. It is in plain text, after all, and is not sealed in anything. If there is a problem in the delivery and it ends up in another destination, odds are that the message was read before it was returned.

Put simply, email, by default, is not secure at all. Nor are file attachments that are sent via email. Even sensitive files sitting on a local machine that will never be passed through any network pipe are insecure if the machine is left unattended for any period of time.

Electronic documents, binary files, and anything else that can sit on a hard drive—and that need to be kept confidential—require some sort of envelope that can be sealed around them. Short of packing the computer in a large box and sealing it every time it goes unattended, there is only one technology that seems to provide a valid solution: encryption.

Not just any encryption will work, though. An encryption scheme known as *public key encryption* has almost become the de facto method for encrypting sensitive information. This scheme incorporates two keys: one private key, which you keep to yourself; and one public key, which you pass out to others. The public key—belonging to you or to someone to whom you want to send an encrypted file—is used to encrypt a file, and only the holder of the associated private key can decrypt it. A third key—the *session* key—is generated automatically and is used for encryption and decryption. Because it is handled automatically in the background, however, it is rarely credited for its involvement in the process.

The biggest problem with public key encryption systems is that they are resource intensive. The mathematics involved in decrypting an RSA encrypted message are tremendous—heads and shoulders above the single key method (in which each party has the exact same private key and no public key—the private key is used to encrypt and decrypt files), and significantly slower to process. DES and IDEA encryption systems are used for this kind of single key encryption scheme. The mathematics are not as intense with single key methods because there are no mathematical relationships to establish between any public and private keys. The single keys on both ends of the exchange match, so the extra math is not required.

Two encryption packages that incorporate public key encryption are *Pretty Good Privacy* (*PGP*) and *Secure Shell* (*SSH*). Both are available for UNIX variants such as Linux, as well as for other platforms (there are Windows and Mac versions of each). Although nothing short of disconnecting a computer and sticking it in a locked closet can keep your data safe from attack, using encryption in your every day operations drastically reduces the possibility of your data being compromised.

Pretty Good Privacy (PGP)

The primary use of PGP is file encryption. It does not set up secure channels between local and remote systems, nor does it use a server/client topology. It simply encrypts data to be shared with specific individuals, and it sets up criteria for determining data integrity on the receiving end of the file exchange. Although there are a number of interfaces for the various platforms to which PGP is available, PGP itself is command line driven. The list of parameters that can be passed to PGP is rather extensive; luckily the author, Phil Zimmerman, made it quite simple to perform the most common tasks.

The process of encrypting a file follows. First, a random 128-bit session key is created using the IDEA encryption algorithm. Then, the entire file is encrypted using the IDEA session key (this is the single key method). PGP then encrypts the session key—not the file that was just encrypted with IDEA—with RSA encryption, using the recipient's public key. The session key acts as the single key that was described previously; the exact same session key is passed with the encrypted file and is used by the file's recipient for decryption. The private key on the recipient end is required to decrypt the IDEA session key only, which then decrypts the file using the single key method.

The use of the RSA public key encryption method to encrypt and decrypt only the session key makes this scheme extremely fast. Encrypting the entire exchange using RSA requires a lot of unnecessary overhead and does not really offer any more security.

How to Get PGP

The main distribution site for PGP in the U.S. is at the Massachusetts Institute of Technology (MIT), at the following address:

```
http://web.mit.edu/network/pgp.html
```

There was a time when you could use FTP and telnet to obtain PGP, but that capability has been removed. The Web page listed previously is now the only legal route to getting PGP in the U.S., short of purchasing a commercial license.

Note

Older books on PGP might detail how to use the FTP and telnet methods of obtaining PGP source code and binaries. These instructions became obsolete in the summer of 1997.

This Web page offers quite a bit of information, including links to public keyservers (where people upload their public keys for others to use), online information regarding PGP usage, pointers to books that cover PGP, and links to other sites that cover PGP issues.

This site only distributes PGP to citizens of the U.S. and Canada, however. A questionnaire that is available through a link to this Web page needs to be filled out before PGP can be obtained. The current version of PGP is version 5.0, and is available on multiple platforms, Linux included.

PGP is free for noncommercial use in the U.S. and Canada. Commercial users must purchase a commercial license from Network Associates (`http://www.nai.com`). This is more an issue with the license for RSAREF (the RSA toolkit, provided by RSA Data Security, Inc.). The commercial versions of PGP are only for Windows95/98/NT and Mac users. There are no known commercial versions of PGP for Linux, regardless of the version number or country of distribution.

Caution

Please note that because encryption software is considered by International Traffic in Arms Regulations (ITAR) to be munitions, exportation of PGP outside of the U.S. and Canada is a serious offense that is punishable by a rather large fine and ten years in prison for each copy you export. Think twice before trying to do this.

The best way to describe the main Web page for PGP at MIT is *cluttered*. It is mostly text, and the link to get to the predownload questionnaire is not obvious. It actually sits about one third of the way down and reads as follows:

```
To obtain the current version of PGP from MIT via the World-Wide Web, click here.
```

The `here` portion is the link that goes to the U.S. questionnaire. There is another questionnaire for Canadian citizens that is available at the top of the Web page (the latter closely resembles the former, with `Canada` in place of `United States` in the questions). You are asked about your citizenship, whether you agree to not export PGP or RSAREF, if you agree to the terms of the RSAREF license (it is linked to the questionnaire so you can read it before answering), and if you plan to use PGP for solely noncommercial purposes. If everything is answered correctly, a page full of links to different versions (source code and precompiled binaries) of PGP is presented.

Download the PGP archives (binary or source code) that you want. Just be sure to download the source code for the UNIX version of PGP at some point during this session.

It is worth noting here that PGP 5.0 is only officially available in the U.S. in precompiled binary form (an international version is available in source code form, but it is questionable as to whether this distribution is legal in the U.S.). The latest U.S. version that is officially available in source code form from MIT is version 2.6.2. Because this is the only version that is available in source code form, it is what is covered in this chapter.

Compiling and Installing PGP

Log in as root and copy the PGP source code file to a directory into which you can extract PGP. You probably need to create a directory under /usr/src that caters only to PGP and RSAREF. For this example, the directory is called /usr/src/PGP-RSA:

```
mkdir /usr/src/PGP-RSA
```

Copy the PGP source code file to this new directory, and then extract it:

```
cp pgp262s.tar.gz /usr/src/PGP-RSA
cd /usr/src/PGP-RSA
tar zxvf pgp262s.tar.gz
```

Table 41.1 shows the other files that are in the directory (besides the source code archive).

TABLE 41.1 FILES CONTAINED WITHIN THE PGP SOURCE CODE ARCHIVE

File	Description
pgp262si.tar.asc	A digital PGP signature for the PGP .tar archive
pgp262si.tar	The .tar archive with PGP source code
rsaref.tar.asc	A digital PGP signature for the RSAREF .tar archive
rsaref.tar	The .tar archive with PGP optimized RSAREF source code
setup.doc	Directions on compiling and installing for various platforms

The .asc files seem a bit odd when you consider that there is currently no PGP installation with which to verify the source code. The idea is that you will verify the .tar files after compiling PGP. Is this the chicken or the egg argument? Perhaps.... But there is no other way to verify the authenticity of the files.

With the main archive extracted, it is time to extract the other two archives. First, extract the PGP source code. This does not create a subdirectory with all the sources; rather, it extracts files directly into the PGP-RSA directory that the archive is sitting in. Because, at this point, the source code files are not compressed, the `tar` command-line parameter for decompression is not required:

```
tar xvf pgp262si.tar
```

This creates four subdirectories—contrib, doc, src, and vmsbuild—and extracts approximately eight files into the PGP-RSA subdirectory.

With that done, extract the RSAREF source code as follows:

```
tar xvf rsaref.tar
```

This one goes in a bit neater than the PGP source code. It creates a subdirectory, called rsaref, for itself off of PGP-RSA and extracts all the source code there.

You now have all the source code that you need decompressed and in its proper place. It is time to start the compilation process.

First, RSAREF must be compiled (PGP needs it, so it comes first). Change to the rsaref/install/unix subdirectory off the PGP-RSA directory and invoke the `make` command. Provided that you have at least a recommended/standard installation of OpenLinux, that is all you need to do to compile RSAREF successfully.

When RSAREF finishes compiling (after a minute or so), change to the /usr/src/PGP_RSA/src directory. There is a long standing bug in PGP 2.6.2 source code that prevents it from compiling under Linux/ELF (which describes literally 100 percent of all Linux distributions today) with the source code in its default state. A little editing of source code is required to get this to work.

In the makefile, look for the following `linux` section:

```
linux:
        $(MAKE) all CC=gcc LD=gcc OBJS_EXT="_80386.o _zmatch.o" \
        CFLAGS="$(RSAINCDIR) -O6 -g3 -DUNIX -DIDEA32 -DASM"
```

You need to add `ASMDEF=-DSYSV` to the `CFLAG` line. The following is the end result:

```
linux:
        $(MAKE) all CC=gcc LD=gcc OBJS_EXT="_80386.o _zmatch.o" \
        CFLAGS="$(RSAINCDIR) -O6 -g3 -DUNIX -DIDEA32 -DASM" ASMDEF=-DSYSV
```

Put the `ASMDEF=-DSYSV` outside the quotes in the `CFLAGS` line; otherwise it does not work.

After doing that and saving the makefile, compile PGP as follows:

```
make linux
```

When the compilation is done, there is a small series of tests that are requested by the included setup.doc file (this file is part of the PGP 2.6.2 source code distribution, and is authored by Perry Metzger, Colin Plumb, Derek Atkins, Jeffrey I. Schiller, and others). These tests are duplicated here:

1. First, create a subdirectory off root's home directory called .pgp (but do not `cd` there).
2. Create a test public/private key pair (use "test" as the ID and the password for the pair) using the following command:

   ```
   pgp -kg
   ```

   See Listing 41.1 for a sample key pair generation session.
3. Add the keys from the keys.asc file in the previous directory to the public key ring:

   ```
   pgp -ka ../keys.asc
   ```

   A number of new keys are added. You are asked if you want to sign the new keys; sign at least one to see how the process looks.
4. Use the following command to heck the key ring:

   ```
   pgp -kc
   ```

   You see the keys you signed with the test ID, and you sec `ultimate` listed in the trust column (you are, after all, the owner of the key ring, so you get ultimate trust privileges).
5. Change to the doc subdirectory off the PGP-RSA directory and encrypt the pgpdoc1.txt file:

   ```
   cd /usr/src/PGP-RSA/doc
   ../src/pgp -e pgpdoc1.txt test -o testfile.pgp
   ```

The resulting testfile.pgp file is compressed and encrypted.

6. Decrypt the testfile.pgp file:

   ```
   ../src/pgp testfile.pgp
   ```

   You are asked for test's password (that is, the ID that is used to encrypt the document). After this information is given, the file decompresses and decrypts. The .pgp extension drops, leaving a file called testfile that is identical to pgpdoc1.txt.

If everything went well, install PGP. A good location for the pgp binary is /usr/bin:

```
cp /usr/src/PGP-RSA/src/pgp /usr/bin
```

Install the documentation for PGP in a new directory called /usr/local/lib/pgp:

```
mkdir /usr/local/lib/pgp
cp /usr/src/PGP-RSA/doc/* /usr/local/lib/pgp
```

Install the man page in /usr/man/man1:

```
cp /usr/src/PGP-RSA/doc/pgp.1 /usr/man/man1
```

Now it is time to decide who gets access to PGP. If you are installing PGP for yourself (if you do not want anybody else on the system to access it), copy the following files to your .pgp subdirectory off your home directory (these are all in /usr/src/PGP-RSA):

```
language.txt
es.hlp
fr.hlp
pgp.hlp
config.txt
```

If you are installing PGP to be used systemwide by all users, place all the files in the /usr/local/lib/pgp directory instead. Some of the settings in the config.txt file need to be perused. For the most part, however, Linux systems are fine with the file the way it is. There is ample explanation for each option in the file, so the options are not discussed here. Just remember that the defaults are generally okay for Linux.

SETTING UP PGP FOR USE

With that done, your first task is to create a legitimate public/private key pair for yourself. Do this while you are logged in as the user that you plan to be logged in as the most, or while you are logged in as the user who you plan to be whenever you encrypt things with PGP. Make sure that there is a .pgp subdirectory created off your home directory (if none exists, create one using `mkdir`).

Following is the command that is used to generate key pairs:

```
pgp -kg
```

Listing 41.1 is a sample key generation session for the fake user Sherman T. Potter, whose machine is rumble.fish.net.

LISTING 41.1 GENERATING A KEY PAIR

```
[stp@rumble user]$ pgp -kg
Pretty Good Privacy(tm) 2.6.2 - Public-key encryption for the masses.
(c) 1990-1994 Philip Zimmermann, Phil's Pretty Good Software. 11 Oct 94
Uses the RSAREF(tm) Toolkit, which is copyright RSA Data Security, Inc.
Distributed by the Massachusetts Institute of Technology.
Export of this software may be restricted by the U.S. government.
Current time: 1998/12/30 08:27 GMT
Pick your RSA key size:
    1)   512 bits- Low commercial grade, fast but less secure
    2)   768 bits- High commercial grade, medium speed, good security
    3)  1024 bits- "Military" grade, slow, highest security
Choose 1, 2, or 3, or enter desired number of bits: 2
Generating an RSA key with a 768-bit modulus.

You need a user ID for your public key.  The desired form for this
user ID is your name, followed by your Email address enclosed in
<angle brackets>, if you have an Email address.
For example:  John Q. Smith <12345.6789@compuserve.com>
Enter a user ID for your public key:
Sherman T. Potter <stp@fish.net>

You need a pass phrase to protect your RSA secret key.
Your pass phrase can be any sentence or phrase and can have many
words, spaces, punctuation, or any other printable characters.

Enter pass phrase: [pass phrase]
Enter same pass phrase again: [same pass phrase]
Note that key generation is a lengthy process.

We need to generate 632 random bits.  This is done by measuring the
time intervals between your keystrokes.  Please enter some random text
on your keyboard until you hear the beep:
### [scrolling numbers]
0 * -Enough, thank you.
.............................**** ............****
Key generation completed.
[stp@rumble user]$
```

At this point, the private/public key pair is ready to use. Both of the files—pubring.pgp, the public key ring, and secring.pgp, the secret key ring—are stored in binary form in your $HOME/.pgp directory. In addition to that, there is a seed file—randseed.bin—that contains the random input that is used to create your keys. Leave all these files intact and in the $HOME/.pgp directory.

MANIPULATING PUBLIC/PRIVATE KEY RINGS

None of this does anyone much good if no one is encrypting anything for you. To allow this to happen, you must share your public key.

There are some public key servers on the Internet to which you need to consider sending your public key if you end up using PGP a lot; that way, people can send you encrypted files without pestering you for your public key. Otherwise, you can simply have a copy of your public key handy in case someone asks for it.

There are two forms that can be taken by the public key: binary and plain text. By default, your pubring.pgp file is binary, so all the keys within are binary as well. The default extraction process extracts a binary version of your public key. The following command does it:

```
pgp -kx youruserID
```

The `youruserID` portion can be fudged a bit to contain enough characters to identify the key that you want to extract. For example, if Sherman T. Potter decides that he wants to extract his public key to give to someone else, he might use the following command to extract his key in binary form:

```
pgp -kx sherman
```

Listing 41.2 shows how the key extraction looks.

Listing 41.2 Extracting a Key from pubring.pgp

```
[stp@rumble ~/.pgp]$ pgp -kx sherman
Pretty Good Privacy(tm) 2.6.2 - Public-key encryption for the masses.
(c) 1990-1994 Philip Zimmermann, Phil's Pretty Good Software. 11 Oct 94
Uses the RSAREF(tm) Toolkit, which is copyright RSA Data Security, Inc.
Distributed by the Massachusetts Institute of Technology.
Export of this software may be restricted by the U.S. government.
Current time: 1998/12/30 23:07 GMT

Extracting from key ring: '/home/stp/.pgp/pubring.pgp', userid "stp".

Key for user ID: Sherman T. Potter <stp@fish.net>
768-bit key, Key ID 78FFC285, created 1998/12/30

Extract the preceding key into which file? shermpub

Key extracted to file 'shermpub.pgp'.
[stp@rumble ~/.pgp]$
```


This creates a file called shermpub.pgp" in $HOME/.pgp that contains a binary version of Sherman T. Potter's public key (the .pgp extension is added automatically). The string `sherman` can be anything within his pubring.pgp file that matches the ID line that is associated with his key.

To see the ID for a key, he can optionally run a key verification and get a listing of the keys in pubring.pgp using the following command:

```
pgp -kv
```

Listing 41.3 shows how the verification looks.

LISTING 41.3 VERIFYING KEYS IN PUBRING.PGP

```
[stp@rumble ~/.pgp]$ pgp -kv
Pretty Good Privacy(tm) 2.6.2 - Public-key encryption for the masses.
(c) 1990-1994 Philip Zimmermann, Phil's Pretty Good Software. 11 Oct 94
Uses the RSAREF(tm) Toolkit, which is copyright RSA Data Security, Inc.
Distributed by the Massachusetts Institute of Technology.
Export of this software may be restricted by the U.S. government.
Current time: 1998/12/30 23:03 GMT

Key ring: '/home/stp/.pgp/pubring.pgp'
Type bits/keyID     Date       User ID
pub   768/78FFC285 1998/12/30 Sherman T. Potter <stp@fish.net>
1 matching key found.
[stp@rumble ~/.pgp]$
```

The italicized line is the line that shows the ID for Sherman's key. This is the same as the ID line that he typed in when he set up his key pair earlier.

But what if Sherman wants to email his key to someone as plain text or publish his public key on his Web page? It happens quite often. Publishing public keys on Web pages and sending them in email messages are very common key distribution methods (short of posting the key on a public key server).

The syntax for doing this is similar to the syntax for extracting a binary public key, but one letter is added to the command line:

```
pgp -kxa sherman
```

The output of this command is basically the same as with the binary key extraction, but this time a file is created in $HOME/.pgp with a .asc extension (the contents of the file are 100 percent ASCII text, hence the extension). When a plain text public key is extracted, the binary version of the key is put through a process known as *ASCII armoring*. Basically, the binary data is translated into ASCII, much like binary data becomes ASCII when it is run through a `uuencode` utility. This enables binary data to be passed back and forth in text-based forums such as email and Web pages.

Tip

Another popular method for passing out PGP public keys is through the `finger` system. Simply put the ASCII version of the public key in your $HOME/.plan file, and whenever anyone runs `finger` against your email address (assuming that your system administrator has not disabled `finger`), they can get your public key. `finger` is going out of style, however, so this might not be the best alternative for passing out public keys.

What needs to be done about other peoples' keys? Does anything need to be done before using them?

The answer is that you must add the keys to your public key ring first. In the exercises that were suggested earlier before finalizing the PGP installation were some public keys that were added to a sample key ring using the following command:

```
pgp -ka ../keys.asc
```

Simply replace `../keys.asc` with the filename (path included, unless it is in the current directory) for the public key that is being added. The same questions that were asked in the earlier exercise are asked every time you add a key, so if you trust the key that you are adding feel free to certify it (there are methods for establishing that a message or file passed to you is authentic and not tampered with. The process is known as *signing* files and is covered in the "Signing Files" section later in this chapter).

Note that if someone sends you a public key, you can also simply run `pgp` against the file that contains the public key to add it to your key ring. PGP can see that the file contains a public key and ask what you want to do with it.

USING PGP

With that all out of the way, it is time to start putting PGP to work. In the following section, you learn how to set up files so that their integrity can be checked and, if necessary, so that you can be warned when they are not received by their intended audiences. This section also discusses how to use public keys to encrypt files that are to be sent to others.

SIGNING FILES

Encrypting files is only one way of maintaining file authenticity and integrity. Another method is signing files. This method takes into account characteristics of the file, and then creates a unique signature using your—or a specified ID's—secret key. If the file is not changed between the time it is signed and the time it reaches its destination, when the file is decrypted or checked with PGP on the recipient's end a message similar to the following appears:

```
File has signature.  Public key is required to check signature. .
Good signature from user "Sherman T. Potter <stp@fish.net>".
Signature made 1998/12/31 00:27 GMT
```

If the file was changed, however, the message looks more like the following:

```
File has signature.  Public key is required to check signature. .
WARNING: Bad signature, doesn't match file contents!

Bad signature from user "Sherman T. Potter <stp@fish.net>".
Signature made 1998/12/31 00:27 GMT
```


The file can still be decrypted, but continuing from this point constitutes an informal agreement that the file's contents are acceptable even if the integrity has been compromised.

There are different ways to sign files. For example, if Sherman just wants to sign the encryptme file and send it to John, he can use the following command:

```
pgp -s encryptme -u sherman
```

This says to sign the encryptme file with Sherman's secret key (the `-u` specifies the ID that is doing the signing) and make the resulting file binary (the default). Of course, the file is not readable in this state because it is not ASCII. To make it a signed ASCII armored file instead, the following command is used:

```
pgp -sa encryptme -u sherman
```

The resulting file looks similar to Listing 41.4.

LISTING 41.4 PGP SIGNED FILE WITH ASCII ARMORING (ENCODED)

```
-----BEGIN PGP MESSAGE-----
Version: 2.6.2

owHrZChlZmUw6zr+eJJb/fWK/4daGRm105j+O7YsP/wviDOT41a52s8/e9KE0t9n
Hrgmo5DJw57SH1gZvo7rXe2td71PC/yb7pc/OUitef/kNe0bzWI+NZYE57AdTNrn
X1P/gKmg7sp23cUZYg5ZLy9fcPyd8r56vYRZzSWB02/WNCVxpuYlF1UWlOSmMgCB
V35Gng4XV3B+bmpJRmZeukJaZnFGpUJmsUJ6Poibn6eQkPqUqqenx+WcmKdQmV+q
kAxUq5BfllqkkJiXopCckZqcrZBZopBfWmLPaRWSkZiXXQxSzhUM1JgL1IMKuLgA
=VoSb
-----END PGP MESSAGE-----
```

This is not exactly readable, however. Sometimes you might want to simply sign—not encode—the file that is being sent so that it is still readable even to users without PGP. To do this, add one letter—t—to the PGP command line:

```
pgp -sta encryptme -u sherman
```

This adds a signature at the end of the ASCII armored file but leaves the rest of the file in its existing state. The `t` parameter makes the text from the encrypted file more palatable to other systems by setting the text style to local character sets. It is recommended that you use this whenever you are sending a file to a machine that is not using the same operating system as you are.

The file that results from the preceding command looks similar to Listing 41.5.

LISTING 41.5 PGP SIGNED FILE WITH ASCII ARMORING (NOT ENCODED)

```
-----BEGIN PGP SIGNED MESSAGE-----

John,

Something fishy is going on here...
Can you come over and check it out?

Thanks...

Sherman


-----BEGIN PGP SIGNATURE-----
Version: 2.6.2
```

```
iQB1AwUBNorId5JGftd4/8KFAQFOvAMAhqJmoszp8NlQWZoSnBKjKwU54RU93NK7
luu/tU6BwQE6lAywETkXEIZfATpPmbLq7dY1hl7u0lur01M4dY7Flm186X7Dbgvo
2DxmCI0a6getdfnuK2y8icGMJi8lY0Jf
=iGBo
-----END PGP SIGNATURE-----
```


This is much more readable—and much more palatable—to those who do not have PGP and therefore cannot decrypt the file. Users who do have PGP can run pgp against this file to see if the signature is good.

At this point, the file is viewable, decodable, and basically readable by anyone who has PGP (or, in the last example, even to non-PGP users). To make a file specific to one single recipient, the file has to be encrypted using the recipient's public key.

ENCRYPTING FILES

Okay, so you have a public key from someone else and you want to encrypt something for that person. The key has been added to the public key ring, a file is ready to be encrypted, and all that is needed is a command to encrypt it.

The following command does the trick:

```
pgp -e filename recipient
```

The `recipient` parameter needs to be enough of an identifier to allow PGP to locate the ID in its public key ring. For instance, use Sherman's encryptme file as an example again:

```
John,

Something fishy is going on here...
Can you come over and check it out?

Thanks...

Sherman
```

The following command can be executed by Sherman to encrypt the encryptme file in such a way that only John can to read it:

```
pgp -e encryptme john
```

This produces the output that is shown in Listing 41.6.

PART VI CH 41

LISTING 41.6 ENCRYPTING A FILE FOR A SPECIFIC USER

```
[stp@rumble ~]$ pgp -e encryptme john
Pretty Good Privacy(tm) 2.6.2 - Public-key encryption for the masses.
(c) 1990-1994 Philip Zimmermann, Phil's Pretty Good Software. 11 Oct 94
Uses the RSAREF(tm) Toolkit, which is copyright RSA Data Security, Inc.
Distributed by the Massachusetts Institute of Technology.
Export of this software may be restricted by the U.S. government.
Current time: 1998/12/30 23:55 GMT
```

continues

LISTING 41.6 CONTINUED

```
Recipients' public key(s) will be used to encrypt.
Key for user ID: John McIntyre <jm@fish.net>
768-bit key, Key ID FABF80ED, created 1998/12/30
.
Ciphertext file: encryptme.pgp
[stp@rumble ~]$
```

As you can see, a file called encryptme.pgp has been created and is ready to be sent to John. This is a binary file because Sherman did not specify that he wanted ASCII armoring. If the command is changed to

```
pgp -ea encryptme john
```

the resulting file is encryptme.asc; it looks similar to Listing 41.7.

LISTING 41.7 ENCRYPTED FILE WITH ASCII ARMORING


```
-----BEGIN PGP MESSAGE-----
Version: 2.6.2

hGwDG3eIG/q/gO0BAwCm14KARgL55ZOYZU7rD0d+3sYd0ItW5a6ZpxCpbSrZI4YG
w9kut765bLui71fZbzxeDvyYnhu5RPiTCiaWEZK8iZcLw8YdsYMlQ1N+nyhZCa8w
qxfHyedwdud/kxZPf02mAAAAeBEuoLDncqoYNH7UZGbwULFAuupLTPnVlXxI/H3e
O77FEggPqkRIIt3zgSVT48dLdVybQEYEvOpNqZQyO67u48KiIhtDOAbl2OnIetnm
VaVeWWM4C2G81KDR3KXHJBerwwA/y3Y49MO3cYRI1P+gAYU9g/clJzOMgQ==
=sQmB
-----END PGP MESSAGE-----
```


This is a much more suitable method if Sherman plans to send John the encrypted file via email.

When John receives this file, he somehow needs to decrypt it before he reads it. The file was encrypted with his public key, and he has the associated secret key, so all he needs to do is run pgp against the encrypted file—it knows what to do from there.

After giving a password for his secret key, the file is decrypted (see Listing 41.8).

LISTING 41.8 DECRYPTING AN ENCRYPTED FILE

```
[jm@tuna ~]$ pgp encryptme.asc
Pretty Good Privacy(tm) 2.6.2 - Public-key encryption for the masses.
(c) 1990-1994 Philip Zimmermann, Phil's Pretty Good Software. 11 Oct 94
Uses the RSAREF(tm) Toolkit, which is copyright RSA Data Security, Inc.
Distributed by the Massachusetts Institute of Technology.
Export of this software may be restricted by the U.S. government.
Current time: 1998/12/31 00:02 GMT
Stripped transport armor from 'encryptme.asc', producing 'encryptme.pgp'.
File is encrypted.  Secret key is required to read it.
Key for user ID: John McIntyre <jm@fish.net>
768-bit key, Key ID FABF80ED, created 1998/12/30
```

```
You need a pass phrase to unlock your RSA secret key.
Enter pass phrase: [password to secret key] Pass phrase is good.\
Just a moment......
Plaintext filename: encryptme
[jm@tuna ~]$
```

Because the file was ASCII armored, it was first decoded back into binary form and then decrypted. If the file that is being decrypted is already binary, this step can be eliminated, but the rest of the decryption process is identical.

If the file is meant for John's eyes only and Sherman is worried about it being tampered with before John gets it, he can sign the file when he encrypts it. This gives an extra layer of insurance that is not there with plain encryption. If the file is tampered with, the signature does not match and a warning is presented (as discussed in the preceding section).

The command to perform these actions resembles a combination of the encryption commands and the signing and ASCII armoring commands:

```
pgp -stae encryptme john -u sherman
```

The resulting file looks similar to a typical ASCII armored encrypted file, but when the file is decrypted, the extra steps that were taken to sign it pay off. It is highly recommended that that you sign all files that are encrypted.

SECURE SHELL (SSH)

SSH is meant to be a secure, encrypted replacement to the Remote Shell (RSH) package. It contains similarly named utilities—`slogin` and `scp` instead of `rlogin` and `rcp`—which have functions that are similar in purpose to those in the RSH package; but SSH provides encryption to its connections, making it much more secure. In addition to its ability to mimic RSH utilities, SSH offers tunneling capabilities that allow other protocols to pipe through it, making almost any routable protocol on your system encryptable.

The same scheme of keys that is used with PGP is used with SSH. Both systems incorporate public and private keys to encrypt their data, and both offer the capability of limiting the audience for the data that is being passed back and forth. The main difference is that PGP protects files, whereas SSH protects network connections.

HOW TO GET SSH

The main home page for SSH is `http://www.ssh.fi`, but it is available all over the Internet. Your best bet is to go to the home page and follow the SSH Products, SSH Protocols, and Downloads links to get to the Web site's download section; from there, download the source tar.gz file. It needs to contain both the client and the server source code.

It is worth noting that there are currently two similar (but nonetheless different) versions of SSH available for downloading: version 1.2.x and version 2.0.x. The latter contains a few enhancements, such as a secure FTP server and matching secure FTP client, but it is yet to be widely used. The former version is much more common, so that is the version that is covered in this chapter.

Caution

One of the encryption items that is offered in SSH—normal RSA routines—violates a U.S. patent that is held by RSA Data Security. If you live in the U.S., use the RSAREF library (which is owned and distributed by RSA Data Security and is legal to use within the U.S.) to replace the normal RSA code that is included in the source code.

If you live outside of the U.S., there is no conflict with the patent because the patent only exists within the U.S.

To get a copy of RSAREF in the U.S. or Canada for use within SSH, follow these steps:

1. Start an FTP session with ftp.rsa.com. Change to the rsaref subdirectory and down load and read the info.reply file and the README file.
2. If you are in the U.S., acknowledge your citizenship, acknowledge the guidelines listed in README, and agree to the licensing terms listed in the info.reply file. From there you need to change to the time-dependent directory listed in README to download the RSAREF source code. Note that if it takes more than a minute or so to read README, you have to download README again to get the latest time-dependent directory name. Also note that this time-dependent directory does not appear in directory listings; you must change straight to the directory, sight unseen, based on the instructions in the README file.

   Within the directory there are two forms of the RSAREF source code (one in tar/compress format, another in zip format). Download the tar/compress source code archive; the zip archive is more of a DOS archive, which you do not want.
3. If you are in Canada, there is a paragraph in the info.reply file that must be emailed to the address that is specified in info.reply; after this, RSAREF—in uuencoded form—is mailed to you. Save the uuencoded message and run `uudecode` on it to create the source code archive in binary form.

Compiling and Installing SSH

Copy the source tar.gz file over to /usr/src, run `tar zxvf` on the file, change to the directory that was created from the archive extraction, and then run the following commands:

```
./configure
make
make install
make install-configs
```

Note

If you are using OpenLinux 2.2 or higher, there are two extra steps for compiling this package (perform these steps right after running `configure`):

1. Edit the Makefile, changing the "DEFS" line to read like this:

   ```
   DEFS = -DHAVE_CONFIG_H -D_GNU_Source $ (COMMERCIAL)
   ```
2. Delete line 437 from the login.c file. This is what it looks like:

   ```
   ux.ut_syslen = strlen (ux.ut_host);
   ```

   Note that there are two lines like this in the same general section of login.c; you want to delete the first one, not the second one.

With those two steps completed, you can execute the three `make` commands.

For most users, that is all that needs to be done. Note that in the first step you could have run

```
./configure --help
```

and gotten a screen full or two (or three) of configuration options that can be set before compiling SSH; but the defaults typically work fine. Look at the listing of configuration options if you want to know how to set/disable certain options.

Note

As was indicated earlier, the RSA code that is included with SSH by default violates some U.S. patents that are held by RSA Data Security. The RSAREF library is to be used to replace this code if you live in the U.S.

To incorporate this library into SSH, create a subdirectory called rsaref2 within the SSH source code directory, copy the RSAREF source code archive into it, and then decompress the source code:

```
mkdir /usr/src/ssh-1.2.26/rsaref2
cd /usr/src/ssh-1.2.26/rsaref2
cp ~/rsaref20.tar.Z .
tar zxvf rsaref20.tar.Z
```

That gets you to a point where you are ready to compile SSH with RSAREF.

You do not need to actually compile RSAREF in advance; the necessary RSAREF files are compiled during the SSH compilation process.

With all that done, change back to the directory to which the SSH source code extracted. Run the configure script, passing a parameter to tell `make` to use the RSAREF library:

```
./configure --with-rsaref
```

This scans for a number of configuration items in addition to the one that you forced on the `configure` command line. A configuration header file (config.h) and a makefile are created, based on what the configuration procedure finds.

When the configuration is done, build the SSH binaries using `make` and `make install` (as mentioned earlier).

The programs that are compiled and installed are listed in Table 41.2.

Table 41.2 Programs and Files Included or Installed with SSH

File	Description
/usr/local/bin/ssh	An RSH replacement that incorporates encryption
/usr/local/bin/slogin	Symbolic link to SSH
/usr/local/sbin/sshd	The SSH server daemon
/usr/local/bin/ssh-keygen	Generates RSA identity key pairs
/usr/local/bin/ssh-agent	Tool that passes authentication information from private keys
/usr/local/bin/ssh-add	Adds private keys to SSH-agent
/usr/local/bin/scp	Secure copy command
/etc/ssh_config	SSH configuration file
/etc/sshd_config	sshd configuration file

There are one or two other utilities that are compiled if X Window system support is configured during the configure process. Because this is not necessary and is not often used, X Window system support is not discussed in this chapter.

Last, a host key that is to be used to identify your system to remote connections is generated and stored in /etc/ssh_host_key, the secret key, and /etc/ssh_host_key.pub, the public key.

SETTING UP THE SSH SERVER

As was mentioned earlier, the SSH server is contained in a daemon called sshd. This server is noninteractive and typically is loaded when the system is booted (usually from /etc/rc.d/rc.local). There are various configuration items offered on the sshd command line, but only the essentials are covered here.

When loading the sshd daemon, you can specify a number of options that control host key generation. At regular intervals, the host key is automatically regenerated by sshd for security reasons. As was indicated earlier, this host key is stored in /etc/ssh_host_key. You can specify not only the time interval between host key regenerations, but also the size of the key that is to be generated.

The port that sshd runs with can be specified. This can be anywhere from 100 to 65535, as long as the port is not being used by any other application.

Table 41.3 lists the command-line parameters that control these settings.

TABLE 41.3 COMMAND-LINE PARAMETERS FOR SSHD

Parameter	Description
`-b` *`bits`*	This is where the number of bits that are used to generate the host key is specified.
`-k` *`interval`*	This specifies how much time is to pass before the host key is regenerated, in seconds. The default is 3600 seconds (one hour).
`-p` *`port`*	Specifies what port sshd is to listen to for incoming connections. The remote slogin client must specify this port (using the -p parameter).

There is a systemwide configuration file that is used by sshd called /etc/sshd_config. Some of the possible configuration items for sshd are not included in this file by default, but those that are not can easily be added with a text editor. Check the man page for sshd to see all the possible configuration options. This chapter covers the ones that are contained within /etc/sshd_config because they are the ones that are most commonly used.

The default configuration file looks similar to Listing 41.9.

LISTING 41.9 DEFAULT /ETC/SSHD_CONFIG FILE

```
# This is ssh server systemwide configuration file.

Port 22
ListenAddress 0.0.0.0
```

```
HostKey etc/ssh_host_key
RandomSeed etc/ssh_random_seed
ServerKeyBits 768
LoginGraceTime 600
KeyRegenerationInterval 3600
PermitRootLogin yes
IgnoreRhosts no
StrictModes yes
QuietMode no
X11Forwarding yes
X11DisplayOffset 10
FascistLogging no
PrintMotd yes
KeepAlive yes
SyslogFacility DAEMON
RhostsAuthentication no
RhostsRSAAuthentication yes
RSAAuthentication yes
PasswordAuthentication yes
PermitEmptyPasswords yes
UseLogin no
# CheckMail no
# PidFile /u/zappa/.ssh/pid
# AllowHosts *.our.com friend.other.com
# DenyHosts lowsecurity.theirs.com *.evil.org evil.org
# Umask 022
# SilentDeny yes
```

Items that are preceded with a # are comments and are ignored by the server.

Table 41.4 lists, in order, the explanations of the different options in this configuration file.

Table 41.4 Configuration Items in the Default /etc/sshd_config File

Configuration Item	Description
`ListenAddress` *`IP_address`*	This specifies the IP address that the server listens on.
`HostKey` *`host_key_location`*	Gives the location of the host key that is to be used with all connections to the server. The default value for this is `/etc/ssh_host_key`.
`RandomSeed` *`random_seed_file`*	Gives the location of the random seed file that is to be used with all connections to the server. The default value for this is `/etc/ssh_random_seed`.
`ServerKeyBits` *`bit_count`*	Tells the number of bits in the host key. The default value for this is `768`.
`LoginGraceTime` *`seconds`*	This specifies a timeout value for people logging in. If they are not logged in by the time this limit is triggered, the connection is dropped. The default value is 600 seconds (ten minutes).

continues

TABLE 41.4 CONTINUED

Configuration Item	Description
`KeyRegenerationInterval` *`seconds`*	True to its name, this option specifies the host key regeneration interval. The default value is 3600 seconds (one hour).
`PermitRootLogin` *`yes/nopwd/no`*	Determines if the root user is allowed to use SSH to log in. The default value is `yes`. The `no` value disables any access to the system for root via SSH. The `nopwd` option states that password-free authenticated connections are allowed. RSH-style authentication needs to be offered via $HOME/.rhosts for this to work. From a security standpoint, it might be a good idea to set this to `no`.
`IgnoreRhosts` *`yes/no`*	Tells sshd whether the RSH authentication files ($HOME/.rhosts and /etc/hosts.equiv) are ignored for all types of SSH authentication. The default setting for this is `no`.
`StrictModes` *`yes/no`*	Tells sshd whether to check the permissions on users' home directories before authenticating them, and if the permissions are too open, to disconnect. The default value is `yes`.
`QuietMode` *`yes/no`*	Tells whether the SSH server is to send its output to system logs. If this is set to `yes`, no logging is done. The default setting is `no`.
`X11Forwarding` *`yes/no`*	Sets whether forwarding of X11 displays is permitted through the SSH server. By default, this is set to `yes`, allowing forwarding to occur. Because there is nothing stopping users from using other forwarding software, this might as well stay set to `yes`.
`X11DisplayOffset` *`display_#`*	To avoid interference between the X11 displays that are being used by SSH and the X11 displays that are being used by users on the server machine, a first available display number can be set using this option. There is no default. XFree86 typically comes up in display 0, so setting this number to somewhere above 0 is helpful. The configuration file specifies display 10 as the first; that is a good first display to offer.
`FascistLogging` *`yes/no`*	`FascistLogging` is equivalent to verbose logging. This option logs quite a bit of information and is considered by some to be an invasion of privacy for users who are connecting to the server. The default value for this is `no`, and needs to probably stay that way unless there is a real security issue that requires verbose logging of SSH connections.

`PrintMotd` *`yes/no`*	On Linux systems, the /etc/motd (Message of the Day) file contains a short blurb of news or brief getting-started instructions that typically show up immediately after login. If this is set to `yes` (which is the default), this same motd file is displayed after users log in via SSH.
`KeepAlive` *`yes/no`*	This option tells whether to send keepalive packets to keep connections going. With this set to `yes`, the only things that can terminate a session are user-forced termination, network failure, or rebooting the system on the remote end. Without this, there is no way for the server to know if there has been a problem on the remote end of the connection; because of this the server can keep the dead connection going indefinitely. The default setting for this option is `yes` and probably needs to stay that way.
`SyslogFacility` *`code`*	This option tells which facility code is used for sshd log entries. The default code is DAEMON. The optional codes are DAEMON, USER, AUTH, LOCAL0, LOCAL1, LOCAL2, LOCAL3, LOCAL4, LOCAL5, LOCAL6, and LOCAL7. DAEMON is sufficient here.
`RhostsAuthentication` *`yes/no`*	This specifies whether password-less authentication á la RSH is offered. This is considered to be more insecure than the other authentication methods, so it is not recommended. If you do incorporate this, remote SSH users need to create an .rhosts file in their home directory on the SSH server machine containing their local machine name and their username, as follows:
localdomain.net localusername	The file has to be mode 600 before you try to authenticate with it: `chmod 600 ~/.rhosts`
`RhostsRSAAuthentication` *`yes/no`*	This incorporates two authentication schemes: the RSH password-less style authentication and RSA host authentication (described in detail later). This is a bit more secure than plain RSH authentication.
`RSAAuthentication` *`yes/no`*	RSA authentication involves using your private and public keys (generated by `ssh-keygen`) to do the authentication for you. The method for setting this up is described later in this chapter. This is considered to be a very good method for providing authentication.
`PasswordAuthentication` *`yes/no`*	Specifies whether password authentication is to be used. If you want to force RSA authentication for `slogin` users on your system, this needs to be set to `no`, and `RSAAuthentication` needs to be set to `yes`.

continues

TABLE 41.4 CONTINUED

Configuration Item	Description
`PermitEmptyPasswords` *yes/no*	If this is set to `yes`, accounts with empty password strings are authenticated (if password authentication is allowed). Blank passwords are common tools for hackers, though, so it is recommended that this be set to `no`. The default setting is `yes`.
`UseLogin` *yes/no*	Tells whether to use the login program to log users in. The default is `no`.
`CheckMail` *yes/no*	If this is set to `yes`, sshd tells the remote user if there is any waiting mail. The default setting is `yes`.
`PidFile` *PID_filename*	This tells the name and location of the file that contains the process ID of sshd. By default, this is set to /var/run/sshd.pid.
`AllowHosts` *host_list*	This contains a list of all the hosts (wildcards `*` and `?` are acceptable in the hostnames) that are allowed to connect to the sshd server. More than one specification can be given, as long as there is a space between host listings. By default, all hosts everywhere are allowed to try to connect.
`DenyHosts` *host_list*	This is the same as `AllowHosts` but in the opposite direction. This option allows the specification of wildcarded hostnames that are not allowed to try to connect to the sshd server.
`Umask` *mask*	This sets the umask (the default file creation mode) for sshd. The system umask setting is typically 022. The default setting for this option is to not set the umask (allow the system running under sshd to do that). Unless there is a real need to change this, leave it out.
`SilentDeny` *yes/no*	If this is set to yes, denied connections are not logged. The default value is no.

It is okay to experiment a bit, but keep in mind that the majority of the defaults are good the way they are. Further options (not many, but some) are available in the man page for sshd.

SETTING UP THE SSH CLIENT

As was mentioned earlier, there is a configuration file for the SSH client that is installed using the `make install-configs` command after compiling SSH.

This file is called /etc/ssh_config, and it contains global configuration information on how the SSH client operates. The settings in this file are considered default settings unless they are overridden by either command-line parameters or by settings in a user's $HOME/.ssh/config file.

The order of configuration precedence is as follows:

- Command-line parameters for SSH
- User-specific configuration options in $HOME/.ssh/config
- Global configuration options in /etc/ssh_config
- Configuration options compiled into the SSH package

The default configuration file for the SSH client contains the code that is shown in Listing 41.10.

LISTING 41.10 DEFAULT /ETC/SSH_CONFIG FILE

```
# This is ssh client systemwide configuration file.  This file provides
# defaults for users, and the values can be changed in per-user configuration
# files or on the command line.

# Configuration data is parsed as follows:
#  1. command line options
#  2. user-specific file
#  3. system-wide file
# Any configuration value is only changed the first time it is set.
# Thus, host-specific definitions should be at the beginning of the
# configuration file, and defaults at the end.

# Site-wide defaults for various options

# Host *
#   ForwardAgent yes
#   ForwardX11 yes
#   RhostsAuthentication yes
#   RhostsRSAAuthentication yes
#   RSAAuthentication yes
#   TISAuthentication no
#   PasswordAuthentication yes
#   FallBackToRsh yes
#   UseRsh no
#   BatchMode no
#   StrictHostKeyChecking no
#   IdentityFile ~/.ssh/identity
#   Port 22
#   Cipher idea
#   EscapeChar ~
```


As you can see, by default there are no options set within this file. In fact, this file does not even contain all the configuration options that are available (nor does it worry about going into them; if you want to know what can go in this file, check the man page for SSH or `slogin`). The settings that you see commented out in this file are the most common settings that SSH users might incorporate. The explanations in Table 41.5 cover these settings.

TABLE 41.5 CONFIGURATION ITEMS IN THE DEFAULT /ETC/SSH_CONFIG FILE

Configuration Item	Description
`ForwardAgent yes/no`	This tells whether you want to offer the services of your authentication agent (covered later in this chapter) to your remote connection.
`ForwardX11 yes/no`	This determines if X Window connections are allowed to pass through the SSH-encrypted connection from the remote host.
`RhostsAuthentication yes/no`	This specifies whether password-less authentication á la RSH is offered. See the description for `RhostsAuthentication` in the "Setting up the SSH Server" section of this chapter for details.
`RhostsRSAAuthentication yes/no`	This incorporates two authentication schemes: the RSH password-less style authentication and RSA host authentication (described in detail later). This is a bit more secure than plain RSH authentication.
`RSAAuthentication yes/no`	RSA authentication involves using your private and public keys (generated by `ssh-keygen`) to do the authentication for you. The method for setting this up is described later in this chapter. This is considered to be a very good method for providing authentication.
`TISAuthentication yes/no`	This authentication is necessary only to connect to TIS (Trusted Information Systems) servers.
`PasswordAuthentication yes/no`	Specifies whether password authentication is to be used. If you want to force RSA authentication for `slogin` users on your system, this needs to be set to `no`, and `RSAAuthentication` needs to be set to `yes`.
`FallBackToRsh yes/no`	If this is set to `yes`, and an encrypted connection was not established, an RSH connection is given (nonencrypted). To prevent nonencrypted connections via `slogin`, set this to `no`.
`UseRsh yes/no`	States whether RSH is to be used to connect to the remote host. It is questionable why anyone might want to enable this. Setting this to `no` is wise.
`BatchMode yes/no`	Sets password querying to on or off (yes or no, respectively). This is meant for scripted functions using SSH where the system is being used noninteractively.
`StrictHostKeyChecking yes/no`	With this option set to `yes`, automatic additions to $HOME/.ssh/known_hosts are disabled, requiring users to manually add remote host keys to the file. This increases security, but it is rather inconvenient. Unless there are serious security concerns regarding SSH connectivity, this probably needs to be set to `no`.

`IdentityFile secret_key_path`	By default, the identity file (which contains your secret key, generated from the `ssh-keygen` program) is stored in $HOME/.ssh/identity. If there is another identity file that is to be used, specify it along with its full path here.
`Port remote_port_number`	This specifies the port on the remote machine to connect to. The default is 22.
`Cipher encryption_algorithm`	This specifies the default or preferred encryption algorithm to be used to encrypt SSH connections. The default, as mentioned earlier, is IDEA. See Table 41.6 (later in this chapter) for optional algorithms.
`EscapeChar` *`escape_char`*	This allows the specification of an escape character. The default is ~. You can set a different character, a Ctrl character combination, or none for no escape character at all. The default is fine unless some application requires that you set it to something different.

Any or all these configuration options can be set in $HOME/.ssh/config for each individual user. Also, there are other configuration options specified in the `slogin` man page that can be set. It is rare that anything beyond the preceding authentication options are changed, though.

Using SSH

A few readers might be put off by SSH after reading about all the available configuration options. There really is no need to panic, though. There is typically nothing wrong with accepting the default SSH configuration as it stands when it is installed. Furthermore, as you can see, the syntax that is used with SSH utilities for most purposes is not complex.

Establishing Encrypted Login Sessions with `slogin`

The most popular utility of the SSH suite is `ssh`, which is symbolically linked as `slogin`. The general syntax for most connections resembles that of `telnet`:

```
slogin remote-host
```

The first time you connect to a remote host, you get a message similar to the following:

```
Host key not found from the list of known hosts.
Are you sure you want to continue connecting (yes/no)? yes
Host 'fish.net' added to the list of known hosts.
Creating random seed file ~/.ssh/random_seed.  This might take a while.
stp@fish.net's password: [password]
```

When you say you want to continue connecting, the remote host is added to the $HOME/.ssh/known_hosts file, you are prompted for your password, and then the connection is established and you are logged in. This only needs to happen once for each remote host (the addition to the known_hosts file, that is) because the host key on the remote system is stored in known_hosts for future connections.

If you are connecting from an account that is different from the one that you want to log in to, you can specify the account on the `slogin` command line using the `-l` parameter:

```
slogin -l username remote-host
```

You are then authenticated as the user that is specified after the `-l`.

The entire time you are connected, the connection looks no different from a typical `telnet` session. When the session is terminated with an `exit` command or Ctrl+D, the SSH encryption ends.

Although there is rarely any reason to do so, you can optionally specify the encryption algorithm that is used to encrypt your connection on the `slogin` command line. By default, IDEA encryption is used. If the remote machine does not support IDEA, however, 3DES is used. If neither of those are supported by the remote machine, or if you simply want to force a specific algorithm, use the `-c` parameter to specify the appropriate algorithm. Choose from the encryption algorithms that are shown in Table 41.6.

TABLE 41.6 ENCRYPTION ALGORITHMS AVAILABLE AT THE `slogin` COMMAND LINE

Algorithm/Parameter	Comment
`Idea`	The default algorithm
`Des`	Data Encryption Standard; considered to be one of the least secure of the offered algorithms
`3des`	Triple-DES; believed to be a bit more secure than DES, but not much more
`Blowfish`	A good 128-bit algorithm
`Arcfour`	Algorithm similar to the RC4 algorithm trademarked by RSA
`None`	Just what it says

For example, to log in as user jm on tuna.fish.net, forcing the `arcfour` algorithm, the `slogin` command looks similar to the following:

```
slogin -l jm -c arcfour tuna.fish.net
```

It is rare that the algorithm needs to be specified, though, so do not think of this option as required. It is good to know about it just in case, though.

One of the more important options offered by `slogin` is the capability to connect to a specific port on the remote machine. Quite often, system administrators run the sshd server on a nonstandard port. The `slogin` program offers the capability to specify the port with the `-p` parameter:

```
slogin -p 8000 tuna.fish.net
```

This tries to connect to port 8000 on tuna.fish.net. Assuming that the server on that machine is running on port 8000, this is the only way to connect to it.

One last option that is worthy of the login discussion is the capability to compress data that is being passed through the SSH connection. On slow connections, such as those that are made through modems, this option can speed things up quite a bit. On fast connections, such as those that are made over a LAN, however, this options seriously slows things down. Therefore, it is only recommended for slow network connections.

The `-C` parameter (note, it is uppercase `C`) enables this compression:

```
slogin -C tuna.fish.net
```

RSA AUTHENTICATION Regular password authentication is not the preferred authentication method; a much more secure method involves using RSA public keys. The keys that you use with a remote host are generated with the `ssh-keygen` program. This authentication method corresponds to the `RSAAuthentication yes` configuration option that was discussed previously.

While you are logged in as the user that you plan to be when you are doing remote logins, create a key pair (public and private) using `ssh-keygen`. This creates two files in your $HOME/.ssh subdirectory: identity (the secret key) and identity.pub (the public key).

Caution

> If you compiled SSH with RSAREF, be aware that there are limitations to the size of the keys that can be generated. RSAREF has problems dealing with large keys, so when you are using `ssh-keygen` to make a key pair, be sure to stay at or below 1024 bits. Do this at the `ssh-keygen` command line as follows:
>
> ssh-keygen -b 896

You need to upload the identity.pub file to your $HOME/.ssh directory on the remote host and rename it authorized_keys (if there is an existing authorized_keys file, add the contents of identity.pub to it).

Be careful when uploading your identity.pub file to the $HOME/.ssh directory on the remote host; if one already exists, it can be overwritten. To avoid this, rename the file before uploading it, or rename it on the `send` command line while you are in your FTP client.

The following step is vitally important: Make sure that your home directory—both on your local machine and on the remote machine—is not group writable. If it is, RSA authentication does not work. Change it with the `chmod` command if necessary:

```
chmod g-w /home/yourusername
```

Of course, if the remote machine has home directories in a location other than /home, revise the preceding path to reflect the accurate location.

After completing these steps, you can use `slogin` to log in to your remote location and not have to pass any password over the network connection. The local identity file is used to authenticate via RSA with the remote authorized_keys file, and the only password that you need to give is for the private key that sits locally on your hard drive.

SSH AUTHENTICATION AGENT There is one other method of authentication that offers password-free connections (that is, you do not even have to give your private key password for RSA encryption). This method incorporates the use of `ssh-agent`, which handles all private key/password authentications after you load your private keys into it. You only give the password for your private key when you load it into the agent; after that, the agent remembers the password and administers it automatically.

Following is an explanation of how it works. First, the `ssh-agent` utility is run with some kind of terminal passed to it on the command line, as follows:

```
[stp@rumble ~]$ ssh-agent xterm
```

`ssh-agent` starts the shell as a child process to itself. When the shell is executed, `ssh-agent` sets a few environment variables that point to itself so that applications can find what port the agent is running on:

```
SSH_AGENT_PID=###
SSH_AUTH_SOCK=/tmp/ssh-username/agent-socket-###
```

The first variable points to the process ID that is assigned to the agent, and the second points to a temporary directory that `ssh-agent` uses for communication with applications (the ssh-username directory changes to reflect the username of the user who started the agent. The `###` in the `agent-socket-###` variable is typically one number lower than the SSH_AGENT_PID).

The method that is used to determine how these variables are set is given at the `ssh-agent` command line. If the agent is started with `-s`, a /bin/sh or /bin/bash type syntax is used. The following is what `ssh-agent` sends out to the terminal program upon execution if `-s` is specified:

```
SSH_AUTH_SOCK=/tmp/ssh-username/agent-socket-###; export SSH_AUTH_SOCK;
SSH_AGENT_PID=###; export SSH_AGENT_PID;
```

Conversely, if `-c` is specified on the command line, /bin/csh (C shell) syntax is given:

```
setenv SSH_AUTH_SOCK /tmp/ssh-username/agent-socket-###;
setenv SSH_AGENT_PID ###;
```

Either method works, depending on the shell that is being started by `ssh-agent`. The default is to use /bin/sh syntax, so users who are accustomed to running C shells ought to consider specifying C shell syntax on the `ssh-agent` command line; otherwise the variables are not set.

After that, the terminal's command prompt is presented. The `ssh-add` program is then run to load your private keys into the agent. Unless a specific key is given on the `ssh-add` command line, $HOME/.ssh/identity (the default private key) is loaded. A password is requested before the key gets loaded. After it is loaded, though, you are ready to go with password-less RSA authentication for all connections that are initiated within the terminal that `ssh-agent` started.

More than one private key can be loaded into ssh-agent using ssh-add. Simply execute ssh-add once for each private key file that is to be loaded. Running ssh-add with -l lists all the currently loaded keys (see Listing 41.11).

LISTING 41.11 ADDING KEYS TO ssh-agent

```
[stp@rumble ~]$ ssh-add
Need passphrase for /home/stp/.ssh/identity (stp@rumble.fish.net).
Enter passphrase: [stp's password]
Identity added: /home/stp/.ssh/identity (stp@rumble.fish.net)
[stp@rumble ~]$ ssh-add -l
1024 37 1448205717319762888850531584488385302360196897060636008262350058З
5974730086732606010969631923044177959123262964453948461941403516170З4640
939983681406018192994060470370905566184699048400957595704194834402298937
93710731049999274292925843384094246235435311424661995341886888772032З742
5703831971963570110
788368799 stp@rumble.fish.net
[stp@rumble ~]$
```

Using slogin or scp (the secure copy command) through a terminal started by ssh-agent looks exactly the same as a regular RSA authenticated connection, but you are not prompted for a password. No other special steps are necessary, and the agent remains active with your private keys until the terminal is exited.

COPYING FILES TO OR FROM REMOTE HOSTS USING SCP

The scp utility is used to copy files from one host to another using SSH. All the same authentication methods that are allowed for slogin are allowed for scp; the only difference is in the command-line parameters and how options are passed (the /etc/ssh_config file is not used with scp).

The basic syntax for scp is rather straightforward:

```
scp file remote_host:path_to_file
```

For example, say Sherman on rumble.fish.net had a 40k file called wharf-bar that he wanted to copy over to his home directory on tuna.fish.net (which is running sshd, by the way). Listing 41.12 covers what that transaction looks like.

LISTING 41.12 COPYING A FILE USING scp

```
[stp@rumble ~]$ scp wharf-bar tuna.fish.net:/home/stp
Enter passphrase for RSA key 'stp@rumble.fish.net': [stp's password]
wharf-bar                 |          40 KB |  40.5 kB/s | ETA: 00:00:00 |
100%

[stp@rumble ~]$
```

Things get a bit trickier when different accounts on the remote system need to be used. For instance, say Sherman has an account on go.fish.net that has a username of sherm. If he wants to copy a file from that system to his local system, he has to specify his username on go.fish.net on the `scp` command line in the same place as on the remote machine:

```
scp sherm@go:/home/sherm/bailey-account .
```

If the SSH connection to the remote machine needs to be authenticated as a user account that is different from the local one, the remote username is specified before the remote machine name, separated with an `@` symbol. A password is requested unless the `scp` session takes place within an `ssh-agent` executed terminal and the $HOME/.ssh/identity file from Sherman's account on go.fish.net is loaded into the agent.

Regarding setting configuration options, `scp` does not use the configuration file that is used by `slogin`. This does not mean that there are no similar configuration options for `scp`, however. Instead of using a configuration file such as /etc/ssh_config, you can specify SSH configuration options on the `scp` command line using `-o`:

```
scp -o "Compression yes' -o 'CompressionLevel 9' sherm@go:/home/sherm/foo
```

Multiple configuration items can be specified as each is preceded by `-o`. Because many SSH configuration parameters consist of two words, single-quotes must surround them to include the space between the words.

Other options are available to `scp` for debugging purposes. See the man page for `scp` if you want to get more details on these debugging features.

TUNNELING PROTOCOLS USING SSH

One of the handy features of SSH is its ability to act as a secure tunnel for other protocols to pass through. In other words, an encrypted tunnel can be established between two machines using SSH, and a specific protocol other than SSH can be told to route itself through the tunnel. This makes it possible to pass network packets back and forth for a particular protocol and have the entire exchange be encrypted even if the protocol itself does not do encryption. You can encrypt just about any protocol by passing it through an SSH tunnel.

Doing so is not very difficult; you simply choose a local port and redirect it to the port that is designated to handle the tunneled protocol on the remote machine. You accomplish the specifications on the command line using ssh's `-L` parameter as follows:

```
ssh -L 4500:ftpserver.fish.net:21 ftpserver
```

This command line redirects local port 4500 (which can be any non-occupied port on the local machine) to port 21 on ftpserver.fish.net. Note that each of the elements of the `-L` parameter are separated with a colon.

This command also logs the user in on ftpserver.fish.net, so an account for the user must already exist on that machine. Remember, `ssh` and `slogin` are symbolically linked, so running `ssh` is the same as running `slogin`.

After establishing the connection to ftpserver.fish.net, the user who created the encrypted SSH tunnel can start another terminal and use the local FTP client to connect to ftpserver, making sure to specify the secured port on the local machine on the command line:

```
ftp localmachine 4500
```

Why FTP to the local machine instead of the FTP server? Because port 4500 on the local machine is the opening to the encrypted pipe between local port 4500 and remote port 21 (the standard FTP port) on the FTP server. Using the FTP client to go straight to the FTP server bypasses this secured tunnel, which defeats the purpose of setting it up in the first place.

The same logic is used to protect other services. Probably the service that is most commonly protected in this manner is POP mail. A similar `ssh` command line is used to set up the secure tunnel:

```
ssh -L 4501:pop.fish.net:110 pop
```

This sets up local port 4501 (assuming 4500 was used already for the FTP tunnel) to be redirected to the POP3 server on pop.fish.net. POP3 is assigned port 110 as a standard port through which to operate, so that is the port to which this tunnel will be directed on the POP server.

From here, POP clients must be set up to access local port 4501 just like the preceding FTP client had to be directed to local port 4500 to get to the encrypted tunnel. Going straight to the POP3 server with the POP mail client bypasses the tunnel.

For example, to use Eric Raymond's `fetchmail` program to download POP3 mail on pop.fish.net (barring any other settings one might have in `fetchmail`'s configuration file, $HOME/.fetchmailrc), the command line looks similar to the following:

```
fetchmail -P 4501 localmachine
```

Note that for this to work, the user who is setting up the tunnel must have an account on the remote system, and the remote system must be running a compatible version of the SSH server.

SUMMARY

This chapter provided an overview of PGP and SSH compilation and usage. There are many different things that you can do with such programs—enough for each to warrant a book of its own. What was covered here will take care of 90 percent of the PGP and SSH usage that is likely to occur, though.

The examples regarding how to use PGP and SSH might all seem like a lot of work, but it is necessary for the sake of security. After using these utilities for a while, it does not seem like a lot of work at all.

For example, on UNIX variants such as Linux it is quite simple to send PGP encrypted messages from a command line. A simple mail command can shoot an encrypted message such as the following off as soon as it is completed:

```
[stp@rumble ~]$ mail jm@fish.net -s "Encrypted File" < encryptme.asc
```

Also, a number of email packages—`exmh`, `Emacs`, and `mutt`, to name a few prominent ones—offer support for PGP encryption if they are compiled or configured to do so.

As for SSH, the syntax for the included utilities is barely more complex than UNIX's `telnet` and `cp` commands. A few more options are offered to ensure secure transactions, but the syntax for most of their usage is very close to the nonsecure alternatives.

It is unfortunate that the ITAR regulations in the U.S. are as strict as they are; otherwise, it might be possible to include these utilities with OpenLinux. As it stands, downloading source code and compiling it is the only known 100 percent legal way to obtain these packages in the U.S. The instructions that are discussed in this chapter are sufficient to allow even a novice to accomplish this.

Although there are really no other chapters in this book that relate directly to the topics that are discussed here, the following chapters might be of interest to you when you are setting up services to use these packages with (or through):

- Chapter 21, "Understanding TCP/IP Fundamentals," covers setting up networking on your OpenLinux system.
- Chapter 30, "IP Firewalling," and Chapter 31, "TCP Wrappers," cover a few other topics that are related to network security.
- Appendix D, "How to Find Other Linux Information," contains pointers to other sources of information on the topics that are discussed in this chapter.

CHAPTER 42

MULTIMEDIA

In this chapter

Linux was once a rather serious infant when it came to multimedia. Now, however, many of the same multimedia features that are found with other operating systems are available to Linux as well. The ones that have garnered the most enthusiasm have been the applications that operate over networks such as the Internet. Streaming audio and video and multimedia documentation distribution have almost become standard in today's Internet.

This chapter discusses a few of the more important packages that offer this functionality; specifically, the commercial Linux sound driver, streaming audio and video, and documentation distribution are covered.

Note that this is not an all-encompassing missive on what is currently available for Linux in the multimedia realm. New plug-ins appear all the time, and there are even plug-ins that make plug-ins out of standalone applications (such as the `Plugger` package). This chapter is also not meant to give full documentation on how to use any of these packages. As with many items that are available for Linux, it is sometimes difficult to find information about where to find programs and—even more importantly—real-life information about how to install them. It is this kind of information that is discussed here.

Open Sound System for Linux

There are two versions of the sound driver system that is used by Linux kernels. One is free (included with the kernel source code) and must be compiled manually and linked into the Linux kernel itself. The other is a commercial product (authored by the same people) that offers more functionality, sound card autodetection (including PnP sound cards), and a much simpler configuration, all at a slight cost.

For many people with common sound cards, the free sound driver package that is included in kernel source code works fine. Even people with PnP sound cards have been known to get them working, although a second utility package—`isapnptools`, which is included with most modern Linux distributions—had to be employed to correctly set up the hardware on the sound card. This is just fine for those who are adventurous, but many people simply do not want to bother with all the work that is involved in getting such a small (but important) thing going on their systems. Then there are those who have sound cards that are simply not supported with the free drivers; there are not many that fall into this category, but they do exist.

As luck would have it, the developers of the free version of the sound driver package offer a commercial version as well: Open Sound System for Linux. Actually, the Open Sound System by 4Front Technologies is offered for a number of different flavors of the UNIX operating system—Linux is just one of them. With Open Sound System, 4Front Technologies is trying to establish a unified sound driver interface for UNIX developers. They are also bringing the kind of sound support that is known on Windows systems to UNIX (previously, only the most basic sound support was offered on any flavor of UNIX; now, with Open Sound System, MIDI and other flashy sound features that were previously limited to other operating systems are available).

This is not, however, why so many Linux users decide to spend the money on a copy of this sound driver package. The main reason they buy it is because they can literally put the files on their system, run an installation script, and within minutes (and sometimes within seconds) they have sound support. Compare this to the hours of tinkering that some people have to go through to get their kernels compiled with correct settings, and you will start to see why the meager cost of the driver package is acceptable.

GETTING AND INSTALLING OPEN SOUND SYSTEM FOR LINUX

The best way to start is to download the demo version and try it yourself. You can download the demo of Open Sound System for Linux (referred to as OSS/Linux) from the main distribution site:

```
http://w4ww.opensound.com
```

Go to the Web page for Linux-x86, and then click the Download button on the left. You are asked for some information about who you are and what kind of system you are running; then you are allowed to download the demo. This demo times out after seven days, but it is sufficient for testing whether the commercial sound driver works with your hardware. Unless your hardware is on the esoteric side, it will work just fine. The demo version is the same as the licensed version, but with a timeout. Applying a license file to the OSS/Linux installation (which is covered later) removes the seven day demo timeout. At the time of this writing, licenses for individual systems are quite inexpensive (starting at $20). They also come with free technical support for one year and free upgrades until 2002 (or until the next major OSS revision is released, such as a version 3.x to 4.x upgrade).

> **Note**
>
> **Be sure to download the version of OSS that matches the version of your Linux kernel! If you are in doubt, execute `uname -v` at a command prompt to see which Linux kernel version you are running.**

RUNNING THE INSTALLATION

The installation of OSS/Linux is really simple. What you download from the site that was mentioned previously is a .tar.gz file that contains the driver package. Create a directory to which to extract the files (for example, oss in your home directory), copy the tar.gz file you downloaded into the directory, and then run the following command to extract the contents:

```
tar zxvf oss??????.tar.gz
```

The results resemble the file list that is shown in Table 42.1.

TABLE 42.1 FILES CONTAINED WITHIN THE OSS/LINUX DEMO

File	Description
INSTALL	Installation instructions
LICENSE	Demo license
`Oss-install`	Installation script
Oss.pkg	An archive containing the binaries that make up the OSS/Linux package

Be sure that there is no sound driver support compiled into your Linux kernel or inserted as modules. Default kernels that ship with OpenLinux do not have the sound driver built in, nor is it inserted as a set of modules; therefore, default installations should be ready for OSS/Linux. If the kernel was recompiled at any point after installation, though, or if sound modules are loaded, all sound driver support must be removed before you try this package.

When you are sure that there is no sound support currently loaded, run the `install` script:

```
./oss-install
```

You are greeted with a screen that contains the license for the package (see Figure 42.1).

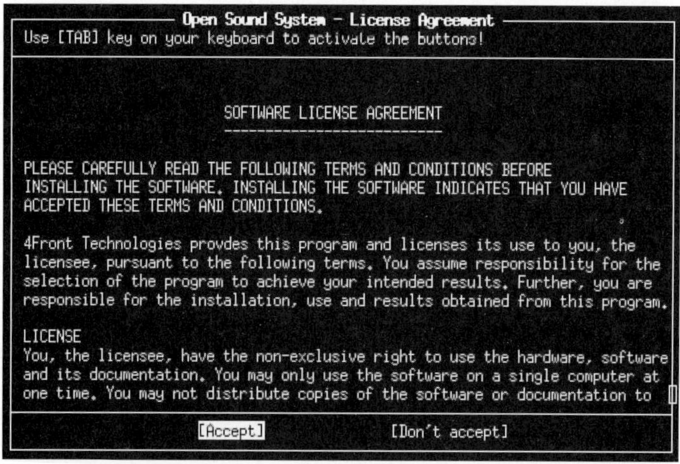

Figure 42.1
Opening OSS/Linux installation screen.

Use the Tab key to move to the Accept option, and press Enter; the release notes appear. Read through these to see if there are any caveats that you need to keep in mind, and then click the OK option at the bottom of the screen.

You are presented with a location to which to install OSS (see Figure 42.2).

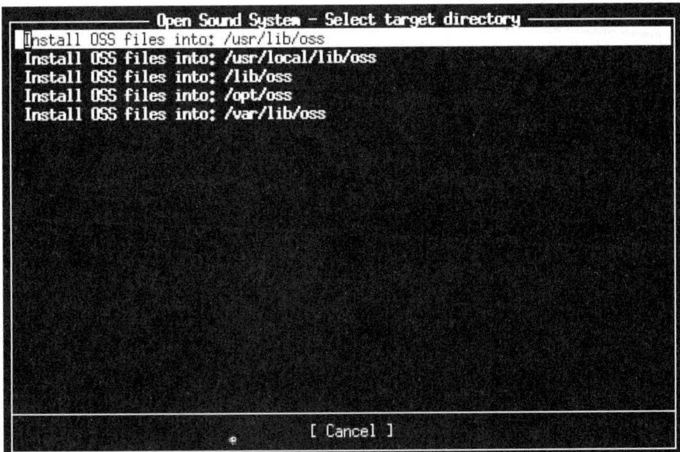

Figure 42.2
Select destination directory.

The default (/usr/lib/oss) is fine; if it is highlighted, press Enter to select it. After you select the destination, the installation program verifies that the version of OSS/Linux matches the version of your Linux kernel. If it matches, the files are installed to the destination directory that you specified.

You are then asked if you want to have OSS probe for the sound card. This is one of the main selling features of this software. Auto-probing for PnP cards does not work in the free version of OSS, but it works beautifully in the commercial version. In most cases, OSS/Linux can find your sound card and set it up for you automatically in a matter of seconds. It is highly recommended that you allow OSS to probe for your sound card.

When a card is found, you are shown the name of the card and prompted to save the configuration. Other options on the menu might be worth exploring, though, to verify that the card was indeed found and that the hardware settings were detected correctly. Verify the configuration first using the Verify configuration menu option; if everything looks okay, save your changes and exit (see Figure 42.3). From there, the sound driver is configured and ready to go.

Before the sound driver can be used, though, it needs to be loaded. There is a program called `soundon`, which ships with OSS/Linux, that does this for you. Manually execute this command to see that it works; if everything goes well and you have sound support, add the `soundon` command to /etc/rc.d/rc.local, somewhere near the end of the file. That way it is started every time the computer starts.

If there is ever a reason for you to unload the driver while the system is running, there is a companion program to `soundon` called `soundoff` that takes care of this for you. Note that this does not need to be run before you shut your system down.

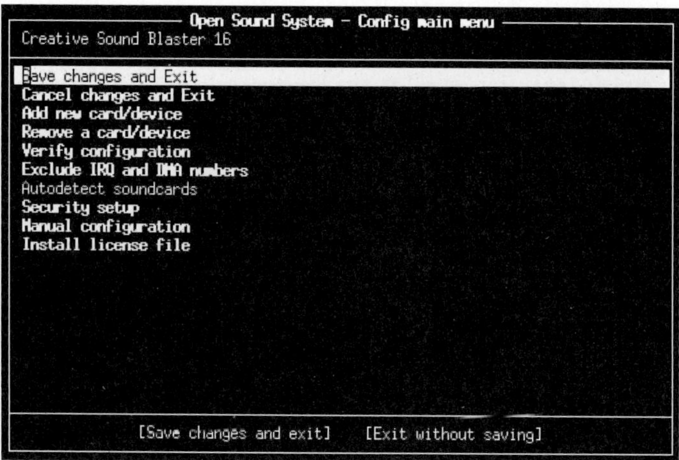

Figure 42.3
Configuration main menu.

CHANGING THE DEFAULT SOUND SETTINGS

One thing that is still bothersome about sound support on Linux is that it tends to default to rather loud settings. One method that people have employed to remedy this is to save settings in the `aumix` program and restore them when the sound driver is loaded. You must first establish that you have the `aumix` program installed, though. Running

```
rpm -q aumix
```

tells you whether you have it. If it is not installed, install it.

After `aumix` is in (and you are logged in as root), start it and set the controls as you want them to be every time you start your system. Then exit `aumix` and execute the following command:

```
aumix -S
```

This writes a file called .aumixrc in root's home directory (/root). Copy this file to /etc/aumixrc. There must not be a period at the beginning of this file when it is copied to /etc. Then, in one of the startup files—probably /etc/rc.d/rc.local, on a line after the line that runs `soundon`—execute the following command:

```
aumix -L
```

This loads the settings in /etc/aumixrc noninteractively, causing your sound system to initialize with settings that are much more reasonable than the defaults.

SUPPORTED SOUND CARDS

The following cards are known to be detectable by the commercial sound driver package (OSS/Linux). Not all of them are completely supported, however. In fact, some are not supported at all yet. Cards that are not supported are labeled as such.

Because this version of the Linux sound driver is not part of the standard kernel sources, the list does not fit in the hardware compatibility appendix (Appendix B). Therefore, it is printed here in Table 42.2.

Table 42.2 Sound Cards Supported by OSS/Linux

Manufacturer	Model
4Front Tech	Virtual Mixer (includes SoftOSS)
	Virtual Synth (SoftOSS) for 486/40
	Virtual Synth (SoftOSS) for 486/66+
	Virtual Synth (SoftOSS) for Alphas
	Virtual Synth (SoftOSS) for MMX/P6/PII
	Virtual Synth (SoftOSS) for P100+
	Virtual Synth (SoftOSS) for PowerPCs
	WaveLoop loopback audio device (Pre BETA)
A-Plus	Sound of Music (OPL3-SA)
A-Trend	Harmony 3DS724 PCI (NOT SUPPORTED YET)
	Harmony 3Ds751 (PCI)
AMD	Interwave reference card
ARC	Probook
AW32 Pro (R2.2-W2)	
AW35 (CS4237)	
AW37 Pro (CS4235)	
AcerMagic	S23
Actech	PCI 388-A3D (NOT SUPPORTED YET)
AdLib	FM synthesizer card
	MSC 16 PnP (CS4235)
Adaptec	AME-1570 (UNSUPPORTED)
Aureal	Vortex PCI (NOT SUPPORTED YET)
Aztech	AZT1008 Sound Device *BETA*
	AZT2320 (NOT FULLY SUPPORTED)
	AZT2320 Sound Device
	AZT3000 Sound Device *BETA*

continues

TABLE 42.2 CONTINUED

Manufacturer	Model
	Sound Galaxy NX Pro
	Sound Galaxy NX Pro 16
	Sound Galaxy WaveRider 32+
	Washington
BTC	Mozart Sound System
	1831 Sound card (ES 1688)
Bravo	Sound Card (OPTi 82C930)
Bull	PowerPC built-in audio
CDR4235-6	
CDR4235-8	
CS32-3DI	
Cardinal	DSP 16 (UNSUPPORTED)
Compaq	Deskpro XL integrated Business Audio
Contributed lowlevel drivers (UNSUPPORTED)	
Creative	EMU8000 add-on (PnP)
	EMU8000 add-on (PnP)
	EMU8000 add-on (PnP)
	Phone Blaster 28.8/33.6
	Sound Blaster 1.0 or 1.5
	Sound Blaster 16
	Sound Blaster 16 ASP
	Sound Blaster 16 PnP (type-1)
	Sound Blaster 16 PnP (type-10)
	Sound Blaster 16 PnP (type-2)
	Sound Blaster 16 PnP (type-3)
	Sound Blaster 16 PnP (type-4)
	Sound Blaster 16 PnP (type-5)
	Sound Blaster 16 PnP (type-6)
	Sound Blaster 16 PnP (type-7)
	Sound Blaster 16 PnP (type-8)
	Sound Blaster 16 PnP (type-9)

Manufacturer	Model
	Sound Blaster 16 Vibra
	Sound Blaster 2.x
	Sound Blaster 32/AWE
	Sound Blaster 32/AWE PnP (type-1)
	Sound Blaster 32/AWE PnP (type-10)
	Sound Blaster 32/AWE PnP (type-2)
	Sound Blaster 32/AWE PnP (type-3)
	Sound Blaster 32/AWE PnP (type-4)
	Sound Blaster 32/AWE PnP (type-5)
	Sound Blaster 32/AWE PnP (type-6)
	Sound Blaster 32/AWE PnP (type-7)
	Sound Blaster 32/AWE PnP (type-8)
	Sound Blaster 32/AWE PnP (type-9)
	Sound Blaster AWE64 (type-1)
	Sound Blaster AWE64 (type-2)
	Sound Blaster AWE64 (type-3)
	Sound Blaster AWE64 (type-4)
	Sound Blaster AWE64 (type-5)
	Sound Blaster AWE64 (type-6)
	Sound Blaster AWE64 (type-7)
	Sound Blaster AWE64 Gold (type-1)
	Sound Blaster AWE64 Gold (type-2)
	Sound Blaster Live (NOT SUPPORTED YET)
	Sound Blaster PCI128
	Sound Blaster PCI64
	Sound Blaster Pro
	ViBRA16C PnP
	ViBRA16CL PnP
	ViBRA16S PnP (type-1)
	ViBRA16S PnP (type-2)
	ViBRA16X PnP (HALF DUPLEX ONLY)
CrystaLake	Crystal Clear Series 100
Crystal Audio	(CS4235)

continues

TABLE 42.2 CONTINUED

Manufacturer	Model
	CRD4236B-1E
	CRD4237B-5
	CRD4237B-8
	CS4614 PCI (NOT SUPPORTED)
	CSC0B35 (CS4236B)
	CX4237B-SIDE
	Onboard PnP Audio (CS4235)
Cyrix	MediaGX built-in audio (NOT SUPPORTED YET)
Dell	Latidude built-in audio
Diamond	Crystal MM PC/104
	Monster Sound MX300 (NOT SUPPORTED YET)
	Sonic Impact (NOT SUPPORTED YET)
Digital	AXP built-in audio
Dream	94PnP Home Studio (NOT SUPPORTED YET)
EON	Bach SP901 (A3D) (NOT SUPPORTED YET)
ESS	PCI (NOT SUPPORTED YET)
	ES1868 Plug and Play AudioDrive
	ES1869 Plug and Play AudioDrive (type-1)
	ES1869 Plug and Play AudioDrive (type-2)
	ES1878 Plug and Play AudioDrive
	ES1879 Plug and Play AudioDrive
	ES1968 Plug and Play AudioDrive
	Maestro-1 PCI (NOT SUPPORTED YET)
	Maestro-2 PCI (NOT SUPPORTED YET)
	Solo-1 PCI (NOT SUPPORTED YET)
Echo	Personal Sound System (UNSUPPORTED)
Ensoniq	AudioPCI (ES1371)
	AudioPCI / Sound Blaster PCI (ES1370)
	Soundscape Elite
	Soundscape PnP model 1
	Soundscape PnP model 2
	Soundscape S-2000

Manufacturer	Model
	Soundscape VIVO
	Soundscape VIVO90
Epson	ActionNote 880 C/CX
Generic	AD1815 based sound card (PnP)
	AD1816 based sound card (PnP)
	AD1816 based sound card (PnP)
	ALS007 based sound card (NOT SUPPORTED)
	ALS100 based sound card (NOT SUPPORTED)
	CMI8330 based sound card (PnP)
	Crystal CS4232 based sound card or motherboard (non PnP)
	Crystal CS4232 by Acer (PnP mode)
	Crystal CS4232 type-1 (PnP mode)
	Crystal CS4232 type-2 (PnP mode)
	Crystal CS4232 type-3 (PnP mode)
	Crystal CS4235 type-1
	Crystal CS4236 (type-1)
	Crystal CS4236 (type-2)
	Crystal CS4236 (type-3)
	Crystal CS4236 based sound card or motherboard (non PnP)
	Crystal CS4236A (type-1)
	Crystal CS4236A (type-2)
	Crystal CS4236B
	Crystal CS4236B
	Crystal CS4237 based sound card
	Crystal CS4237 based sound card or motherboard (non PnP)
	Crystal CS4237B (type-1)
	Crystal CS4237B (type-2)
	Crystal CS4238 based sound card or motherboard (non PnP)
	ESS ES1688 based sound card or motherboard
	ESS ES1788 based sound card or motherboard
	ESS ES1887 based sound card or motherboard
	ESS ES1888 based sound card or motherboard
	ESS ES688 based sound card or motherboard

continues

TABLE 42.2 CONTINUED

Manufacturer	Model
	Jazz16 based sound card
	MAD16 (OPTi 82C928) sound card
	MAD16 Pro (OPTi 82C929) sound card
	MAD16 Pro (OPTi 82C929) sound card (duplex)
	MPU-401 compatible MIDI port
	MPU401 MIDI port (UART mode)
	Mozart sound card (OAK OTI-601 chip)
	OPTi 82C924 based sound card (PnP)
	OPTi 82C924 sound card (non PnP mode)
	OPTi 82C925 based sound card (PnP)
	OPTi 82C930 sound card
	OPTi 82C931
	PSS (ESC614/ADSP2115/AD1848) sound card (NOT SUPPORTED)
	PowerPC built-in audio
	Soundscape based sound card
	Windows Sound System compatible
	Yamaha OPL3-SA (YMF701) based sound card
	Yamaha OPL3-SA2 based sound card (type-1)
	Yamaha OPL3-SA2 based sound card (type-3)
	Yamaha OPL3-SA2 based sound card (type-4)
	Yamaha OPL3-SA3 based sound card
	Yamaha OPL3-SA3 based sound card (type-2)
	Yamaha OPL3-SAx (YMF715/YMF719) non-PnP
Gravis	Ultrasound
	Ultrasound ACE
	Ultrasound Extreme
	Ultrasound MAX
	Ultrasound PnP (with RAM)
	Ultrasound PnP Pro
	Ultrasound with 16-bit daughtercard
HP	OmniBook 2100 (CS4236)

Manufacturer	Model
Home Studio 64 (analog audio only)	
IBM	Studio Feature (CS423X)
	Personal System 8xx (PowerPC) built-in audio
	Personal System 8xx (PowerPC) built-in audio
	RS6000/40P built-in audio
	RS6000/43P built-in audio
Intel	Atlantis built-in audio codec (CS4232)
	Endeavour built-in audio (SB16 Vibra)
Logitech	Soundman 16
	Soundman Games
	Soundman Wave
MED3201 audio card	
Maxi	Sound 32 PnP (analog audio only)
	Sound 64 Dynamic 3D (analog audio only)
Media	Sound SW/32 (non PnP mode)
	Vision Pro Audio Spectrum 16 (PAS16)
	Vision Pro Audio Studio 16
	Vision Thunderboard
MediaTrix	AudioTrix Pro
	Audiotrix 3D XG
MediaVision	ProSonic 16
Microsoft	Windows Sound System board
Motorola	56301 DSP.
	PowerStack II built-in audio
	PowerStack Series E built-in audio
	PowerStack built-in audio
	RiscPC built-in audio - CS4231A
MultiWave	AudioWave Green 16
Music Quest	MIDI connector card (MCC)
	MQX-16 MIDI adapter
	MQX-16S MIDI adapter

continues

TABLE 42.2 CONTINUED

Manufacturer	Model
	MQX-32 MIDI adapter
	MQX-32M MIDI adapter
	PC MIDI card
NEC	Harmony
Orchid	NuSound 3D (NOT SUPPORTED YET)
	SoundDrive 16EZ
	SoundWave 32 (NOT SUPPORTED)
Paradise	DSP-16 (NOT SUPPORTED)
Pine	PT201
Primax	SoundStorm FM 16
	SoundStorm Wave
Quicknet	Internet LineJACK (NOT SUPPORTED YET)
RME	Digi32
	Digi32 Pro
	Digi32/8
Reveal	SC300
	WaveExtreme Pro (with RAM)
Rockwell	WaveArtist chipset (BETA)
Roland	MPU IPC-T MIDI adapter
S3	SonicVibes
Shark	Mako
Sharp	PC8800
Shuttle	Sound System 48
Sonorus	STUDI/O *BETA*
Spacewalker	HOT-255 PCI 3D (PCI)
TerraTec	Maestro 32/96
	EWS64S (NOT SUPPORTED YET)
	EWS64XL (audio only)
	Sound System Base 1 (AD1816)
	Sound System Base 64 (AD1816)
	XLerate (A3D) (NOT SUPPORTED YET)
Tomato	Sound System (OPTi 82C930)

Manufacturer	Model
Trust	Sound Expert De Luxe Wave 32
Turtle Beach	Fiji (NOT SUPPORTED)
	Malibu (NOT FULLY SUPPORTED)
	Maui
	Monte Carlo 928
	Monte Carlo 929
	Montego (NOT SUPPORTED YET)
	Pinnacle (NOT SUPPORTED)
	TBS-2000 (NOT SUPPORTED)
	Tahiti (PRERELEASE, playback only)
	Tropez
	Tropez Plus (audio only)
	Daytona (audio only)
Typhoon	Sound System (non PnP mode)
Videologic	SonicStorm (NOT SUPPORTED YET)
Wearnes	Beethoven ADSP-16 (NOT SUPPORTED)
	Classic 16
Western Digital	Paradise DSP-16 (NOT SUPPORTED)
Yamaha	Sound Edge SW20-PC
	YMF724 PCI (NOT SUPPORTED YET)
Zefiro	Acoustics ZA2 (NOT RECOMMENDED)
Zenith	Z-Player

RealNetworks Products (RealPlayer, Basic Server, RealEncoder)

When it comes to streaming audio and video over networks such as the Internet, one company—RealNetworks—seems to have established the standard to which all others are compared. This is especially true on the Linux platform, where RealNetworks is currently the main show in town. Everything you need for streaming networked audio and video—from client software to servers and encoders—is offered for Linux.

The main attraction here has to be the RealPlayer client software. Using this, anyone with a Linux system that is connected to a network such as the Internet can receive and play audio and video emanating from a RealNetworks server. News, entertainment, radio broadcasts, education, and many other services can be obtained through the use of this software package. Best of all, it is currently available free of charge from RealNetworks.

Note

To get a feel for what this technology can offer, browse some of the audio/video Web sites that are linked to the RealNetworks home Web page (`http://www.real.com`), or check the Live Concerts Web site (`http://www.liveconcerts.com`). There is bound to be something at one of these sites that interests you.

The Basic Server is one in a line of five or more servers that are offered by RealNetworks. This is considered to be a good startup server for Internet streaming, and therefore is the point at which most organizations start when they want to serve audio and video to a few clients over the Internet. Do not be put off by the word *basic*, though; this server can probably do everything that you want it to do as far as serving RealNetworks customers goes.

Before anything can be streamed over a network, however, it must be encoded in a form that the client software on the other end can process. The RealEncoder software encodes .au and .wav files into the RealNetworks format to either be played through a RealNetworks client or passed over the Internet with a server like the one that was just discussed. It also has the capability of capturing audio output through the OSS/Linux sound driver, which allows full streaming input/output action to occur.

The combination of these items can provide not only a great deal of entertainment, but can also provide an important means of communication for companies and organizations that depend on audio and video to convey messages over the Internet. The following sections discuss how to obtain and install this software, and give some general usage instructions where necessary.

GETTING AND INSTALLING REALPLAYER

You can get RealPlayer at the following location:

```
http://www.real.com
```

At the time of this writing, only the regular RealPlayer 5.0 package (consisting of a Netscape plug-in and a standalone application) are available for Linux. There is also currently no commercial (that is, one that costs money) version of RealPlayer for Linux.

When you first arrive at the RealNetworks Web page, you are presented with a small window that enables you to go straight to the download section of the site. If this window does not appear, there is typically a button that takes you there. When you get to the download section of the Web site, you need to fill out a questionnaire. There is an option to Download free RealPlayer after the questionnaire is completed. Select this link. There are various sites within the West and Northwest regions of the U.S., as well as a few sites in Europe and Asia; choose the download site that is closest to you.

After the RealPlayer archive is downloaded, explode it into your home directory (this example uses version 5.0 of RealPlayer for Linux):

```
cp rv50_linux20.tar.gz $HOME
tar zxvf rv50_linux20.tar.gz
```

Table 42.3 lists the files that are extracted into a $HOME/rvplayer5.0 directory.

TABLE 42.3 FILES CONTAINED WITHIN THE REALPLAYER DISTRIBUTION FOR LINUX

File	Description
License.txt	The license for RealPlayer
Mailcap	A mailcap entry for setting up helper applications within other applications (such as mail readers)
Mime.types	MIME types for RealPlayer files to be used with Web browsers
RAObserver.class	
RAPlayer.class	Class files used with Java
README	Instructions on how to pull up documentation on RealPlayer
doc/	Directory containing all the HTML documentation for RealPlayer
index.htm	The main launching point for RealPlayer's documentation; open this file in a Web browser
libdecdnet.so	Shared libraries for various codes that are used by RealPlayer
libra14_4.so	
libra28_8.so	
libradnet.so	
librarv10.so	
librasipr.so	
librv10dec.so	
librvcore.so	Netscape plug-in library
librvplayer.so	Actual Netscape plug-in
rvplayer	Actual executable RealPlayer program
rvplayer.ad	RealPlayer application defaults file (can be edited and the defaults updated by running `xrdb -merge rvplayer.ad`)
welcome.rm ware is working	Sample RealPlayer file used to test whether the player soft-

Note

The following instructions work with new versions of Netscape only.

First, there is a .netscape directory in your home directory. This directory was made automatically when you first started your Netscape browser. Within this directory should be a plugins directory. If there is not one already (there probably is not), create it using `mkdir`:

```
mkdir $HOME/.netscape/plugins
```

Copy the two Java class files that were listed earlier into this plugins directory:

```
cp $HOME/rvplayer5.0/RAObserver.class $HOME/.netscape/plugins
cp $HOME/rvplayer5.0/RAPlayer.class $HOME/.netscape/plugins
```

Next, create a symbolic link from $HOME/rvplayer5.0/librvplayer.so to the plugins directory:

```
ln -s $HOME/rvplayer5.0/librvplayer.so $HOME/.netscape/plugins
```

Next, set two environment variables that point to the $HOME/rvplayer5.0 directory; one that allows the shared libraries within the directory to be found by RealPlayer (both the plug-in and the standalone executable versions), and another that adds the RealPlayer directory to the execution path. This is usually done in the $HOME/.profile file if you are using /bin/bash as your shell (this is the default shell). Create two lines in this file that look similar to the following:

```
export LD_LIBRARY_PATH=$HOME/rvplayer5.0
export PATH=$PATH:/$HOME/rvplayer5.0
```

If you are using /bin/csh, in your $HOME/.cshrc file use the following lines instead:

```
setenv LD_LIBRARY_PATH $HOME/rvplayer5.0
setenv PATH $PATH:$HOME/rvplayer5.0
```

Note

If these environment variables are not set, none of the RealPlayer options (plug-in or standalone applications) work. It is important to keep this in mind. You can not simply add these to $HOME/.profile or $HOME/.cshrc and expect the variables to be set. The terminal that you are in must be exited and another one must be started for either of these files to be executed; or, if you are using /bin/bash, you can `source` .profile into the current terminal, reading in the contents as if you had exited and reentered. The one certain way to make sure that the variables are set is to completely exit the login session that you are currently in and enter it again. All subsequent logins will load the variables successfully, so this does not have to happen each time you want to run RealPlayer.

Next, add the contents of Mime.types and Mailcap to their respective locations (be sure to type these lines in *exactly* or else vital information might be overwritten):

```
cat $HOME/rvplayer5.0/Mime.types >> $HOME/.mime.types
cat $HOME/rvplayer5.0/Mailcap >> $HOME/.mailcap
```

When all files are in their proper places (or are linked to their proper locations) and the environment variables are set and readable by Netscape, start the browser; under the Help menu, select About Plug-ins. You see the RealPlayer plug-in listed.

Next, go into the Edit, Preferences window; select Navigator, Applications, and then select the RealPlayer MIME type from the window. Click the Edit button, and see if the RealPlayer plug-in is selected to be used with that MIME type. If not, select it. Exit the Edit, Preferences window after that. All changes are automatically saved.

That is all there is to installing the plug-in. The standalone application works as well because the path to it is included in the overall execution path for the user. Now change to the $HOME/rvplayer5.0 directory and run the following command to establish that the player application works:

```
rvplayer welcome.rm
```

If the audio and video are operating correctly, you are all set to play streaming RealNetworks audio and video.

Note

If you are using version 5.0 of RealPlayer for Linux and you are running your system with a version 2.2.x Linux kernel (like OpenLinux does), you might have to patch the RealPlayer program before it can play sound. To do this, execute the following commands from within the directory in which RealPlayer resides:

```
dd if=/dev/zero of=rvplayer bs=1 count=1 seek=657586 conv=notrunc
dd if=/dev/zero of=rvplayer bs=1 count=1 seek=665986 conv=notrunc
```

USING REALPLAYER

Regardless of which you are using (Netscape plug-in or standalone application), the RealPlayer opening screen looks the same (see Figure 42.4).

Figure 42.4
Main RealPlayer window—audio and video.

If an audio-only stream is being played, the window is similar, but doesn't have the video portion (see Figure 42.5).

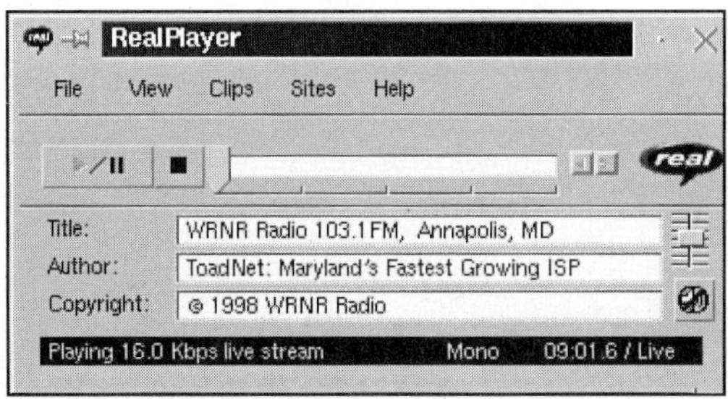

Figure 42.5
Main RealPlayer window–audio only.

As was mentioned earlier, this is RealPlayer 5.0, so it does not have the same channel support that Windows customers might be used to. It is still RealPlayer, though, and the bulk of the controls on the screen will be quite familiar to RealPlayer veterans.

THE FILE MENU

The File menu in RealPlayer offers options that are similar to those on the file menus of Web browsers. Because most people start RealPlayer from a Web browser, this menu does not get very much traffic. But sometimes it is easier to open a RealPlayer URL manually than it is to browse to it. This is especially true when there is a RealPlayer audio/video file that you want to play sitting on your hard drive (such as the welcome.rm file that comes with the software). For these situations, a File menu is available in the player software.

The following sections detail the options that are offered on this menu.

OPEN LOCATION When you open an audio/video stream over a network, what is being opened is a *location*, not a file—even though the address to which you are pointing leads to a file on a remote site. You open an address that is similar to that of a Web page, and it is assumed that at the other end a RealPlayer stream is waiting to be transferred to your player. For this reason, remote audio streams must be opened with the Open Location option from the File menu.

If you choose this option, a window that is similar to Figure 42.6 appears.

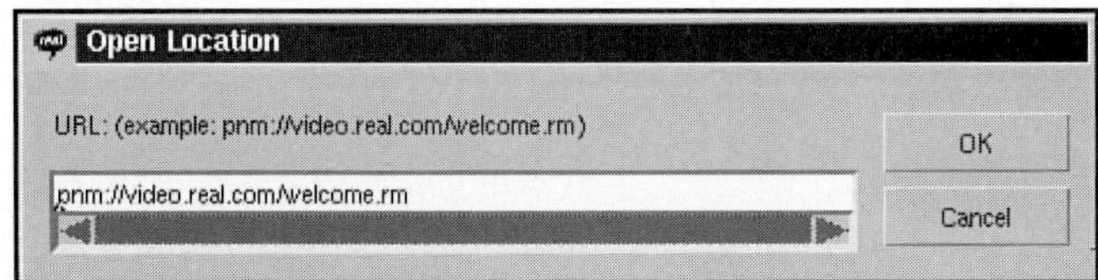

Figure 42.6
The Open Location window.

Only RealPlayer URLs are to be entered in this page (these are typically preceded with `pnm` instead of `http`). Web browsers are not required for opening RealPlayer URLs.

OPEN FILE Contrary to what was described for the Open Location menu option, if you have a RealPlayer audio/video file that is actually sitting on your local machine and that you want to play, you open the file using the Open File option from the File menu. You do this because you are not accessing an audio/video stream residing on a remote site; the location is assumed to be your own personal machine, so only the file name needs to be specified.

The window that is used to open individual RealPlayer audio/video files looks very similar to a typical directory browser (see Figure 42.7).

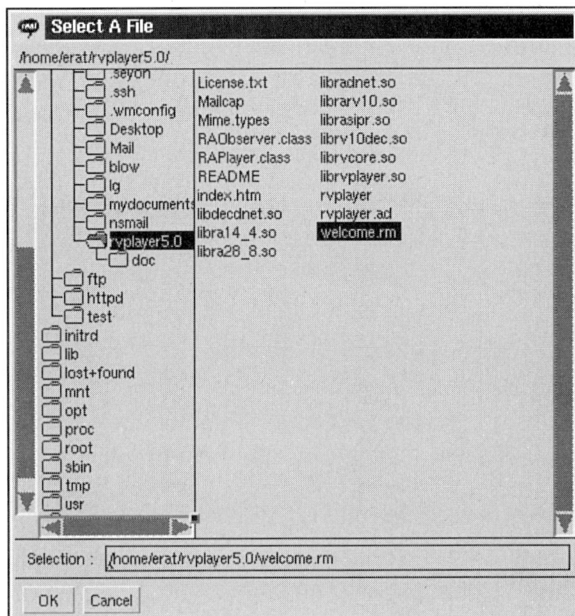

Figure 42.7
The Open File window.

Navigation through the local directory structure is done in the left window, whereas file selection occurs in the right window.

EXIT This option terminates the RealPlayer session and exits.

THE VIEW MENU

The default window for viewing RealPlayer video streams is somewhat small. On a screen that is operating with a low resolution (for example, 640×480 or 800×600), the default window might be a manageable size. But today's monitors can handle much higher resolutions, and at these high resolutions the window can become almost too small to be useful. Changing the size of the view window is the primary function of RealPlayer's View menu.

The following sections describe the options that are offered on this menu.

NORMAL AND ZOOM The first few options on this menu control the viewport size. RealPlayer starts with Normal by default (see Figure 42.4). If you select Zoom from this menu, however, the viewport increases proportionally almost to the width of the window. Note that the Zoom option only increases the viewport size; it does not actually zoom in on portions of the existing viewport.

PREFERENCES In addition to viewport controls, the View menu was chosen to house the menu item that takes you to the preference settings for the software. If you select Preferences on this menu (you cannot be playing any audio or video streams when you do this), the window that is shown in Figure 42.8 appears.

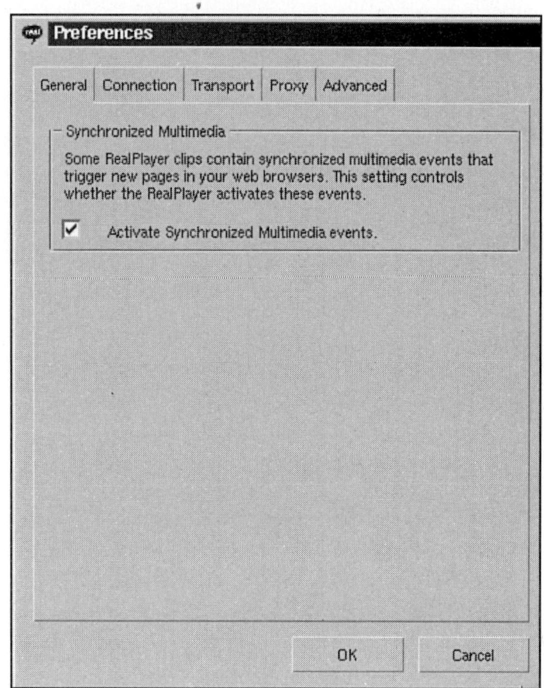

Figure 42.8
The main Preferences window.

The tabs at the top of the screen—General, Connection, Transport, Proxy, and Advanced—take you to different areas of the configuration. On the main preference screen—the General screen—you see that there is only one option: Synchronized multimedia. This enables compatibility with Web pages that are programmed to sync up with RealPlayer streams. It is suggested that this setting remain activated. The next tab takes you to the Connection screen (see Figure 42.9).

Three sections are offered: Bandwidth, Statistics, and Network Timeout.

For Bandwidth, make your selection based on throughput, not on the type of network that is listed afterward. For instance, DSL connections to the Internet probably want to select 112K Dual ISDN in lieu of a missing DSL selection because the throughput is closer to what is actually offered.

The Statistics check box tells your RealPlayer client to send statistical information back to the person who maintains the audio/video servers to which your client connects. Some people might not like the idea that information about their system is being sent to remote sites without their being asked, so this box can be checked off if to disable this feature.

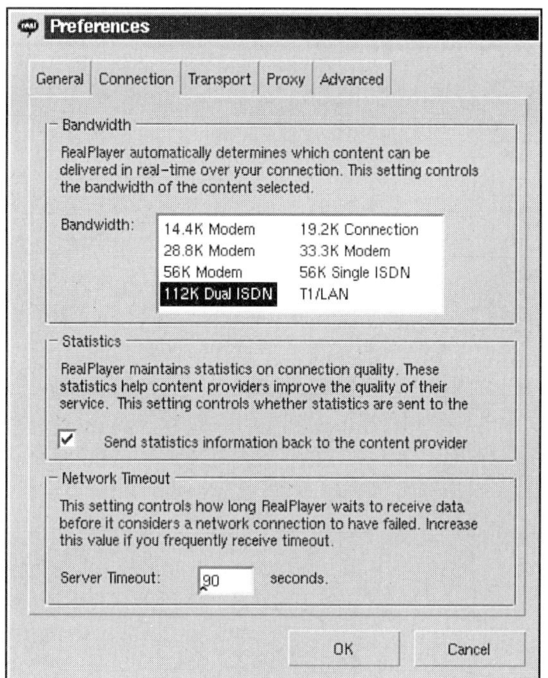

Figure 42.9
Connection preferences.

The last item—Network Timeout—merely gives a timeout, in seconds, to wait for a server to accept a connection from your client.

The Transport tab offers configuration options that control how the routing and protocols that are involved with the network connection are to be handled (see Figure 42.10).

Most people are fine with the default setting, which automatically selects the most efficient transport for you. If the system administrator on your network has configured the Internet gateway system with a specific UDP port for RealPlayer usage, the UDP port can be specified at the bottom of the window.

People who are operating on networks that use certain proxy servers (such as Squid) need to heed the following warning in regard to the transport that is used: Some proxy servers allow RealPlayer streams through, but *only* if they use HTTP as the transport. If you are sitting in front of a system that sits behind one of these proxy servers and you are having problems receiving audio/video streams, this is probably the cause. The Specify transports button in the middle of this window takes you to another window that allows more specific transport configuration (see Figure 42.11).

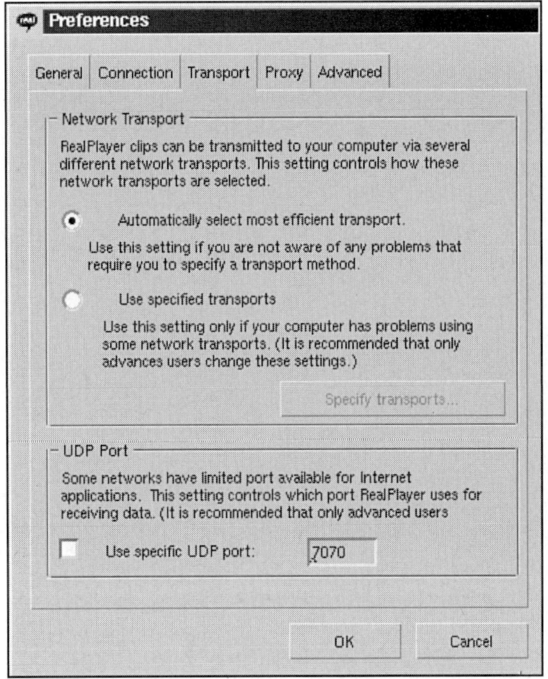

Figure 42.10
Transport preferences.

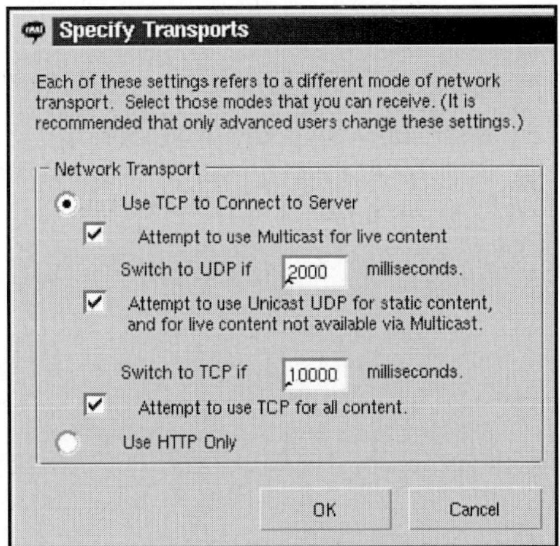

Figure 42.11
Specific transport preferences.

The Use HTTP Only option at the bottom of this window needs to be checked if that is the only transport that is allowed through your proxy server. If this is not required, the defaults for the rest of the settings are fine.

Speaking of proxy servers, the Proxy window is where they are configured (see Figure 42.12).

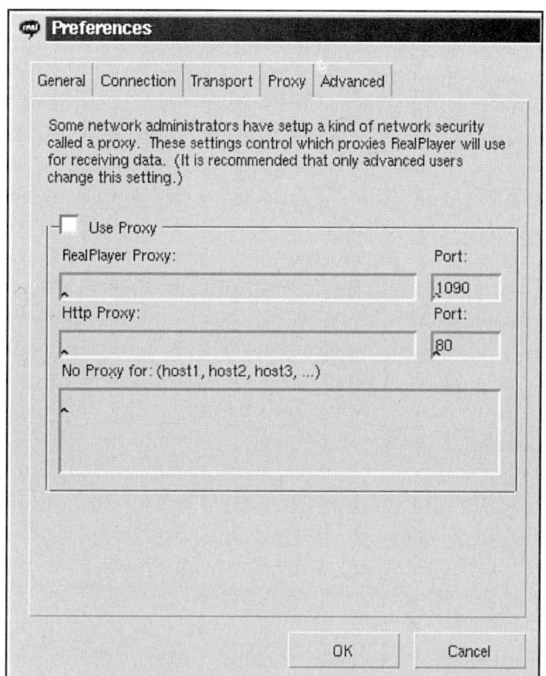

Figure 42.12
Proxy server preferences.

Select the Use Proxy button, and then enter the configuration information to point to your proxy server. The information that needs to be entered is fairly clear; if not, get the proxy server address and port number from the system administrator.

The last of the Preference tabs takes you to the Advanced window (see Figure 42.13).

The only option here is for disabling 16-bit sound. Unless you have an 8-bit sound card (for example, some old Sound Blaster cards) or are having problems playing audio over your 16-bit (or higher) sound card, do not set this option.

STATISTICS The last item on the View menu is a Statistics window (see Figure 42.14).

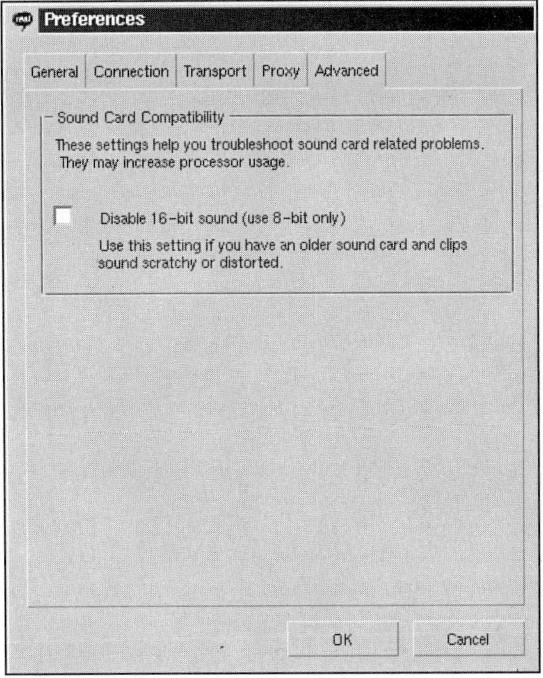

Figure 42.13
Advanced preferences.

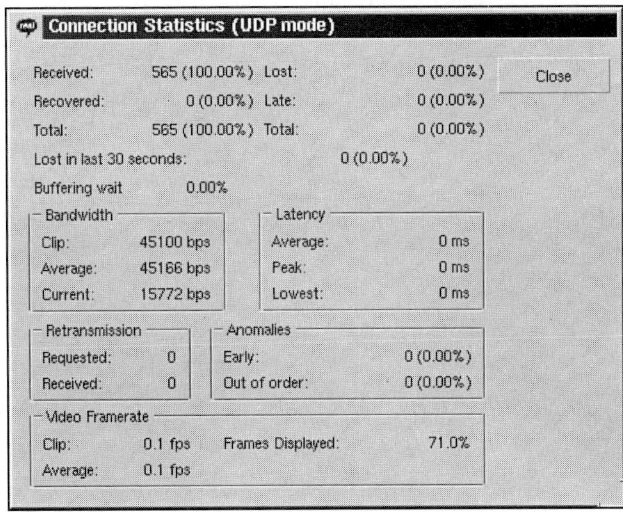

Figure 42.14
Statistics window.

This simply gives you a method of monitoring your connection to remote sites. If any errors occur or network latencies prevent 100 percent of what is sent to be displayed or played, the problems will definitely show themselves in this window. Unless you like to watch numbers tick by, though, this is not a very interesting screen to look at.

The Clips Menu

The Clips menu merely enables you to flip back and forth between recently played audio/video streams.

The Sites Menu

The Sites menu offers some of the more common RealPlayer-capable audio/video Web sites. The items on this menu are not editable in this version of RealPlayer.

The Help Menu

The Help menu offers the typical array of help items, all of which are displayed through an already-running copy of a Netscape browser. But there is one extra feature here: upgrade availability checking. Select About, and the window shown in Figure 42.15 appears.

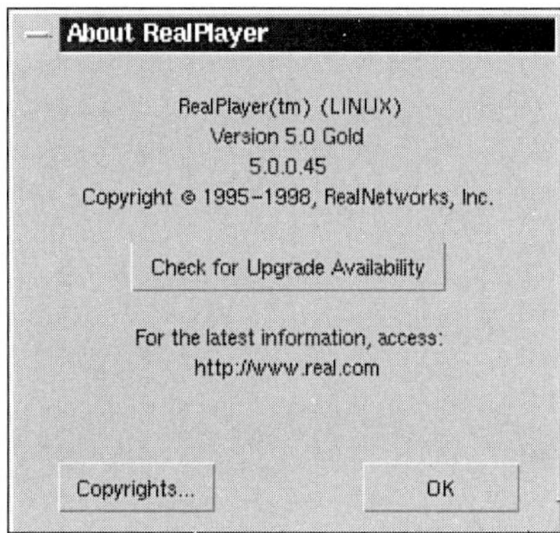

Figure 42.15
About/Upgrade window.

Selecting the Check for Upgrade Availability button starts a check of the distribution site for RealPlayer to see if a more recent version of the software is available. Periodic checking with this feature is wise because there are occasional bug fixes and updates that appear on the distribution site.

Getting and Installing Basic Server

You can download the Linux version of Basic Server from the same Web site that offers RealPlayer. There are two questionnaires that must be completed first: one for personal information, and another to establish how you plan to use the software. After the questions are answered, you can select a site from which to download the software (the same lists for the client software are offered).

One of the items in the first questionnaire asks for your email address. The license file will be mailed to this address, attached to a mail message. Save the license file in a safe place that is accessible during the installation. Be sure to save the file with the name with which it was sent; otherwise it might be rejected during the server installation.

For your purposes, use the g2p1-linux-2_0_30.bin self-extracting archive, which at the time of this writing was the latest version for Linux.

Log in as root, copy the archive into its own directory, and then run the following:

```
chmod +x g2p1-linux-2_0_30.bin
```

Then execute it:

```
./g2p1-linux-2_0_30.bin
```

Some files extract, and then a screen automatically appears:

```
Welcome to the RealServer Setup for UNIX
Setup helps you get RealServer running on your computer.

Setup will step you through the installation process by displaying
informational screens.  Please follow the navigational controls
below:

     Key          Behavior
     ===          ========
     N            Next
     P            Previous
     X            Exit
     F            Finish (Express Installation)

Each input requires the execution of the key above
followed by the [ENTER] key.  Enter [N]ext to continue:
```

Press Enter. The next screen appears, with the following information:

```
If a RealServer license key file has been sent to you,
please enter its directory path below. If you have not
received a RealServer license key file, then this server
will default to a Basic RealServer.
```

Enter the full path and filename of the server license file that was mailed to you. After it is entered, the following appears:

```
Installation and use of RealServer requires
acceptance of the following terms and conditions:
Press [Enter] to display the license text...
```

Pressing Enter displays some of the text within the license file. *You must read this file*! There are *very specific* criteria for using this server, and they are all listed in this license, so you must read this license carefully.

With that finished, you are prompted to accept or reject the license:

```
Choose "Accept" to accept the terms of this
license agreement and continue with RealServer setup.
If you do not accept these terms, enter "No"
and installation of RealServer will be cancelled.
(Default: Accept):
```

Press Enter to accept. Next, indicate where you want to install the software:

```
Enter the complete path to the directory where you want
```

```
to be installed.  You must specify the full
pathname of the directory and have write privileges to
the chosen directory:
```

A good place is /opt/realnetworks/g2serv. If this directory does not exist, a message similar to the following appears:

```
The directory you specified either cannot be created or is
not writable.  Press [Enter] to return to the directory
prompt and choose another directory.
```

If necessary, start another console, log in as root, and create the directory to which you want to install. Then, go back to the console in which the installation is running and enter the path to the location you created.

Next, you are prompted for the username and password settings for server administration:

```
Please enter a username and password that you will use
to access the Web-based RealSystem Administrator, the
RealSystem monitors, and RealSystem live encoders:
Username: [username]

Password: [password]
```

With that finished, you are prompted for some server configuration items (unless there is a specific reason to do otherwise, accepting the defaults is fine):

```
Please enter a port on which RealServer will listen for
PNA connections.  These connections have URLs that begin
with "pnm://": (Default: 7070)

Please enter a port on which RealServer will listen for
RTSP connections.  These connections have URLs that begin
with "rtsp://": (Default: 554)

Please enter a port on which RealServer will listen for
HTTP connections.  These connections have URLs that begin
with "http://": (Default: 8080)

RealServer will listen for RealSystem Administrator
requests on the port shown.  This port has been
initialized to a random value for security.  Please
verify now that this pre-assigned port will not interfere
with ports already in use on your system; you can
change it if necessary. (Default: 2927)
```

After that is done, a report on the settings you selected is presented:

```
You have selected the following RealServer configuration:

Admin Username:         user
Admin Password:         password
Monitor Password:       password
Encoder Username:       user
Encoder Password:       password
PNA Port:               7070
RTSP Port:              554
HTTP Port:              8080
```

```
Admin Port:            2927

Enter [F]inish to begin copying files, or [P]revious
to go back to the previous prompts:
```

Press F+Enter to start installation. After a minute of file shuffling, the following message appears:

```
RealServer installation is complete.
The RealSystem Administrator allows you to configure
and maintain RealServer through an intuitive
Web-based interface. Please note that RealServer
must be running in order to use the Administrator.
Would you like to start RealServer now and launch
the RealSystem Administrator? (Default: Yes)
```

Press Enter, and the following message appears:

```
If at any time you should require technical
assistance, please visit our on-line support area
at http://service.real.com/, or contact our RealServer
technical support team at (206) 674-2681.

Starting RealServer G2...
Please Wait...

Sending RealSystem Administrator URL to browser...

If you do not have a browser installed on this machine,
or your browser failed to display the RealSystem
Administrator, simply type the following URL into the
location field of a browser that can connect to this
machine.
http://rumble.fish.net:2875/admin/index.html


Cleaning up RealServer G2 installation files...
Please Wait...
```

Start the server. If you get some kind of error (a nonfatal error, such as a `cannot find DISPLAY` error) and the server does not start, you can always start the server—after fixing the error—by changing to the installation directory (in this case, /opt/realnetworks/g2serv) and executing the following:

```
./Bin/rmserver rmserver.cfg &
```

You might have to use `killall rmserver` before executing the preceding command. Otherwise, it might not be possible for the server to allocate the ports it needs to use.

The administration Web page prompts you for the username and password of the administrator that you set up during installation. After that, you are in the Web-based administration system for the server.

Note

If you do not have a Web server running on the system to which you just installed Basic Server, the administration Web page might not be accessible. If this happens, simply start your Web server and open the URL that was listed previously.

Using the Basic Server

There really is not much involved in using something such as a server. However, this particular server (as you saw earlier, at the end of the server installation process) has some nice monitoring functions. The Web-based administration interface is somewhat self-explanatory. Those items that are not self-explanatory are beyond the scope of this chapter; look into them by reading the server's documentation. One item that is worth mentioning is that the demonstration items that are offered on the server are mostly made for newer versions of RealPlayer and do not work with the Linux version. Therefore, if testing is being done after the server is installed, it is wise to use a platform that offers a slightly newer version of RealPlayer than the one that is currently offered for Linux.

Getting and Installing RealEncoder

At the time of this writing, RealNetworks is in the process of writing UNIX versions of their recent encoder offerings. Currently, for Linux there is only the RealEncoder 3.1, which is available at the following location:

```
http://proforma.real.com/mario/tools/encoder31.html?wp=798tools
```

As with the other RealNetworks offerings, some questions must be answered prior to downloading the software. After they are answered, you are all set to download the software. Be sure to download the Linux/ELF version because that is the one that is made for systems such as OpenLinux.

Extract the downloaded archive in your home directory. A directory called rmenc is created, and all files are extracted to it. Add the path to the encoder to your execution path. For /bin/bash users, add the following to your $HOME/.profile file:

```
export PATH=$PATH:$HOME/rmenc
```

For /bin/csh users, add the following:

```
setenv PATH $PATH:$HOME/rmenc
```

Of course, the path can be added to the `PATH` statements from either of the other packages you installed earlier, if there are any.

With the correct path set, run the following command to see if everything works:

```
rmenc -H
```

You get a help screen if everything is installed correctly.

USING REALENCODER

The instructions that are contained within the encoder package are fairly complete. There should be no problem getting up to speed quickly. Sample command lines are offered for encoding, along with troubleshooting tips and pointers to Web sites that offer hints on creating high-quality audio with the encoder. The whole thing is command line driven.

ADOBE ACROBAT READER

The Adobe Acrobat Reader is a navigator for platform-independent Portable Document Format (PDF) files. PDF files are PostScript files that are compiled in such a way that they are navigable almost like Web pages. Audio and video can be embedded within PDF files, making them multimedia as well. There are numerous programs that can output PDF files from their documents (programs from Adobe in particular, such as FrameMaker and PageMaker), but the main source of these multimedia documents is Adobe Acrobat itself.

The main Adobe Acrobat software is not free, nor is it currently available for Linux. The reader software, however, is available for Linux free of charge from Adobe's Web site:

`http://www.adobe.com/prodindex/acrobat/readstep.html`

On this page is a short questionnaire in which you give Adobe registration information. After entering this information and specifying the platform for the client that you want to download (operating system, type of Acrobat Reader—the Linux version does not offer search capabilities—and language), a page containing links to the Acrobat Reader archives and installation instructions is presented. Choose the download location that is closest to you.

When you have downloaded the archive, extract the contents using `tar` (version 3.02 is used for this example):

```
tar zxvf ar302lin.tar.Z
```

All the contents are extracted into an ILINXR.install directory. Table 42.4 lists the contents of that directory.

TABLE 42.4 FILES CONTAINED WITHIN THE ACROBAT READER ARCHIVE

File	Description
ILINXR.TAR	The main installation archive (binaries, libraries) for Acrobat Reader for Linux
INSTALL	Installation script
INSTGUID.TXT	Installation instructions
LICREAD.TXT	License for Acrobat Reader
READ.TAR	Fonts and documentation for Acrobat Reader

Change to that directory, log in as root, and run the installation script:

```
cd ILINXR.install
./INSTALL
```

A license agreement is presented, which you must read and agree to (by responding Accept when you are asked) before installation can begin.

The default location for the installation is /usr/local/Acrobat3. This will be fine, unless you want to install it elsewhere. After the installation directory is specified—and, if necessary, created—the software is installed.

To install Acrobat Reader as a Netscape plug-in, a few simple steps need to be taken. First, the /usr/local/Acrobat3/Browsers/intellinux/nppdf.so file needs to be copied into $HOME/.netscape/plugins. Next, the full path to the Acrobat Reader executable binary must be added to the execution path.

For /bin/bash shell users, put this in $HOME/.profile:

```
export PATH=$PATH:/usr/local/Acrobat3/bin
```

For /bin/csh shell users, put this in $HOME/.cshrc:

```
setenv PATH $PATH:/usr/local/Acrobat3/bin
```

Alternatively, simply add `:/usr/local/Acrobat3/bin` to the existing `PATH` statement that was added when RealPlayer was installed, if it was installed as well. As with the installation of the RealPlayer plug-in and application, simply adding the path to the executable files in an environment variable is not enough; the variable must be loaded before the path is recognized, and the best way to ensure that this has happened is to completely exit your login session and log back in.

USING ACROBAT READER

With the path set correctly and the plug-in in its proper place, Netscape is ready to use the Acrobat Reader plug-in. Pulling up a PDF file from a remote site looks similar to Figure 42.16.

Netscape completely swallows the plug-in, running Acrobat within itself. All the controls that are available within the regular standalone application minus the drop-down menus are available within the Netscape plug-in. It is the plug-in version that is most commonly used when viewing PDF files.

The file /usr/local/Acrobat3/Reader/help/reader.pdf contains the online documentation. This file can be accessed from the Help menu on the standalone version of Acrobat Reader, or it can be opened as a file in Netscape.

The documentation for Acrobat Reader is a bit much to read just to get hints on the functions of the toolbar buttons, so Table 42.5 gives a brief overview of them. Note that some of these buttons only exist in the plug-in version of Acrobat Reader on the Linux platform.

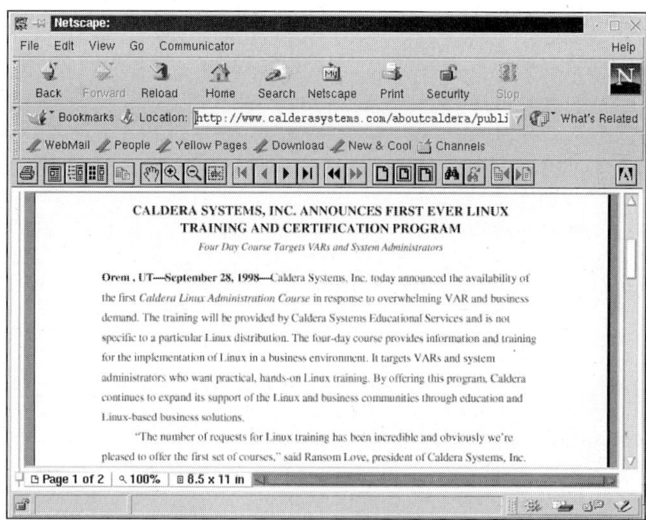

Figure 42.16
Acrobat running as a Netscape plug-in.

TABLE 42.5 BUTTONS AVAILABLE IN THE ACROBAT READER PLUG-IN FOR NETSCAPE

Buttons	Descriptions
	Prints the current document.
	Controls for the viewport. The first button gives only a page view, the second gives a page view with bookmarks, and the third gives a page view with thumbnail images of the pages.
	Copies a selection from the document into the temporary clipboard.
	Controls for movement, zoom, and text selection. The first button selects the hand tool (used to drag the document around the viewport); the next two zoom in and out, respectively; and the fourth allows text selection (text can be selected and pasted into other documents as plain text. This differs from the other Copy button, which copies a selected block from the image without translating it into plain text).
	Page navigation. The first button jumps to page one, the second and third move forward and backward by individual pages, and the last button jumps to the last page.
	Moves to the previous view or goes to the next view, respectively.
	Controls how the page is fit into the window. The first button fits the image, including space around the image, into the viewport; the second fits the page to the upper and lower edges of the viewport; and the third expands the page to 100 percent of the width of the viewport.

Buttons	Descriptions
	Searches a document and repeats the last search, respectively.
	Search previous and search next, respectively.

The last button all the way on the right takes you to the main Acrobat Web page on Adobe's Web site. There, more information can be obtained on upgrades, help topics, and additional software that can help in the creation of PDF files.

SUMMARY

As was mentioned in the beginning of this chapter, this is not meant to be an end-all source of information on multimedia applications for Linux; far from it, actually. Three packages were detailed here that can help get you started with multimedia on Linux. Therefore, think of this chapter as a starting point, not a final reference.

Every month new multimedia applications appear for Linux. The Open Sound System Web site contains numerous links to software that can help with sound processing, recording, and editing. Macromedia, the creators of multimedia plug-ins for Web browsers (among other things), now has a Macromedia Flash plug-in for Netscape on Linux. There are also game development packages, programs for creating 2D and 3D graphics, voice recognition, synchronized presentations, and a slew of other functions that can provide most—if not all—of the same multimedia functionality of other operating systems. The key here is to never stop looking.

Keep the following chapters in mind when you are working with multimedia on Linux:

- Appendix D, "How to Find Other Linux Information," has pointers to many Web sites that can lead to multimedia applications and browser plug-ins that are usable on Linux.
- Chapter 7, "KDE Applications," covers some of KDE's multimedia capabilities.
- Chapter 15, "Software Package Management," contains essential information for installing (and, if necessary, compiling) applications on your OpenLinux system.

PART VII

APPENDIXES

APPENDIX 

Commonly Used Commands

The majority of Linux commands perform functions in exactly the same way as their UNIX equivalents. Many commands are quite cryptic, so the typical challenge with Linux commands is matching the appropriate command with the desired function. The list of commands included in this appendix is not meant to be an all-inclusive list; rather, it is intended to provide a quick reference to commonly used commands and a brief explanation of what each command does. The commands listed here are located in one of four binary directories: /bin, /sbin, /usr/bin, and /usr/sbin.

Each command, with the exception of the self-explanatory `cd` command, has an associated online manual page. These manual pages can be referenced at any time by entering the following at a shell prompt:

```
# man <command>
```

For example, if you wanted to see the manual page for the make directory command (`mkdir`), enter the following at the shell prompt:

```
# man mkdir

MKDIR(1)                                        MKDIR(1)

NAME
    mkdir - make directories

SYNOPSIS
    mkdir  [-p]  [-m  model] [--parents] [--mode=model] [--help]
➥[--version] dir...

DESCRIPTION
   This documentation is no longer being maintained and may be
    inaccurate or incomplete.  The Texinfo documentation is now
   the authoritative source.

   This manual page documents the GNU version of mkdir.  mkdir
   creates a directory with each given name.  By default, the mode
   of created directories is 0777 minus the bits set in the umask.

OPTIONS
```

Whereas the man pages continue to be a good source of information, you will notice in the description of the preceding man page that the man pages are no longer being maintained. The Texinfo documents are now the authoritative source.

The Texinfo documentation can be accessed by typing the `info` command at the shell prompt. A user-friendly version is the X Window–based `tkinfo`. For more detailed information on any of these commands, see the Texinfo documentation or the man pages.

The commands are categorized into one of the following four areas:

- Working with directories
- Working with files
- Networking Utilities
- System Utilities

WORKING WITH DIRECTORIES

Command	Syntax (Example)	Description
`cd`	`cd [`*`path`*`]`	Change directory to the specified path.
	`cd ..`	Change to the parent directory of the current directory.
	`cd -`	Change to the previous working directory, prior to the last `cd` command.
	`cd`	Change to the home directory of the current login ID.
`dir`		See the `ls` command
`ls`	`ls [`*`path`*`]`	List the contents of a directory.
	`ls -l (ll)`	List the files in long format, displaying all file attributes.
	`ls -a`	List all files (including hidden files, sometimes referred to as dot files).
`mkdir`	`mkdir` *`<directory>`*	Make a new directory
`pwd`		Display present working directory.
`mdir`	`rmdir` *`<directory>`*	Remove a directory.

WORKING WITH FILES

Command	Syntax (Example)	Description
`cat`	`cat` *`<file>`*	Most commonly used to display the contents of a file. Derived from the word concatenate, which it also does.
`copy`		See the `cp` command.
`cp`	`cp` *`<source> <dest>`*	Copy a file.
`dd`	`dd if=input of=output`	Most commonly used to convert a file. Can be used to copy image files from one device to another device or file.
`file`	`file` *`<file>`*	Determines the type of a given file.
`grep`	`grep` *`<pattern> <file>`*	Searches a file or files for a specified pattern.
`gzip`	`gzip` *`<name>`*	Compresses a file using Lempel-Ziv coding. Files compressed with this utility have a .gz suffix.
`gunzip`	`gunzip` *`<name>`*	Decompresses a gzipped file.

continues

Command	Syntax (Example)	Description
less	less <*file*>	
	cat <*file*> ¦ less	Similar to the more command but it facilitates backward and forward movement through the file that is being examined. The name is derived from the saying, "Less is more."
ln	ln <*source*> <*dest*>	Used to create links between files or directories.
more	more <*file*>	
	cat <*file*> ¦ more	Used to display the contents of a file, one page at a time.
move		See the mv command.
mv	mv <*source*> <*dest*>	Used to rename a file.
rename		See the mv command.
rm	rm <*file*>	Remove specified file or files.
unzip	unzip [*options*] file	Compression utility that is compatible with similar DOS compression utilities that work with ZIP archives.
vi	vi <*file*>	Full screen editor.
zip	zip [*options*] <*zipfile*>	Creates a ZIP archive.

NETWORKING UTILITIES

Command	Syntax (Example)	Description
dig	dig <*domain*>	Domain information groper. Used to gather information from Domain Name Servers.
dnsdomainname	dnsdomainname	Displays the domain name for the given server.
host	host <*host*>	Look up host or host IP address using Domain Name Server.
hostname	hostname	Displays the fully qualified domain name (FQDN) for the given server.
ifconfig	ifconfig	Displays currently configured network interfaces.
	ifconfig [*interface*]	Configures a network interface.
netstat	netstat	Displays the status of network connections, routing tables and interface statistics.
ping	ping <*host*>	Sends an ECHO_REQUEST packet to the specified host. A response packet is returned by reachable hosts. Commonly used to debug network connections.

Command	Syntax (Example)	Description
nslookup	nslookup	A Name Server lookup utility. Used to query Domain Name Servers.
route	route	Displays the current configuration of the routing table.
	route [*options*]	Configure the IP routing table.
traceroute	traceroute <*host*>	Displays the route of IP packets. Useful for debugging network problems.

SYSTEM UTILITIES

Command	Syntax (Example)	Description
chgrp	chgrp <*group*> <*file*>	Change the group to which a file belongs.
chmod	chmod <*mode*> <*file*>	Change the access permissions of the specified file or files.
chown	chown <*owner*> <*file*>	Change the owner of a given file or files.
date	date	Display the system date setting.
	date <*mmddhhmmyy*>	Set the date.
		mm = month dd = day hh = hour (Military) mm = minute yy = year
df	df	Displays a summary of free disk space for a given file system.
dmesg	dmesg	Displays the startup messages from the last system boot.
du	du	Displays disk usage for the current directory and all subdirectories.
echo	echo	Displays a line of text.
	echo <*$variable*>	
	echo *$PATH*	Commonly used to display the value of a given environment variable.
e2fsck	e2fsck <*file system*>	File system check routine for ext2 file systems.
fdisk	fdisk <*hard drive*> (hard drive = device)	Used to create and/or manipulate a partition table for a given hard drive.

continues

Command	Syntax (Example)	Description
free	free	Displays the total amount of free and used memory. Also shows swap space usage.
fsck	fsck *<file system>*	Front-end program that calls file system check routines for a specific file system type. Defaults to ext2.
fsck.ext2		See e2fsck.
ftpshut	ftpshut	Shuts down ftp services at a specified time.
insmod	insmod *<module>*	Inserts a loadable module.
kill	kill *<PID>*	Kills the specified process.
killall	kill *<name>*	Kill all processes that are executing the specified command.
lilo	lilo	Reinstalls the boot loader.
lsmod	lsmod	Lists all currently loaded modules.
mke2fs	mke2fs *<partition>*	Creates a ext2 type file system on the specified hard drive partition.
mkfs	mkfs *<partition>*	Front-end program that calls make file system routines for a specific file system type. Defaults to ext2.
mkfs.ext2		See mke2fs.
mknod	mknod *<device>* maj min	Makes device files.
modprobe		Used to load a module or a set of dependent modules
mount	mount *<device>* *<dir>*	Mount a file system (device) to a specified directory (mount point).
ps	ps ps aux	Display the process table. Process IDs (PID) for currently running jobs can be identified with this command.
pwconv	pwconv	Used to convert a traditional /etc/passwd file to use shadow passwords.
pwunconv	pwunconv	Converts an existing shadow password system back to the traditional system which uses the /etc/passwd file only.
rdev	rdev [*options*]	Displays or sets values for image root device, swap device, RAM disk size, or video mode.
reboot	reboot	Reboots the system.
showmount	showmount [*options*]	Displays mount information for a given NFS server.
shutdown	shutdown *<time>*	Shuts down the system at a specific time or after a specified delay.

Command	Syntax (Example)	Description
sync	sync	Flushes buffered data to the hard drive.
sysinfo	sysinfo	Displays system information, including kernel specifics, hardware details, and partition information.
tar	tar *<archive>* *<files>*	An archive utility. Used to archive or unarchive a set of files.
	tar -cvf a.tar /etc	Create an archive called a.tar that includes all the files and directories in the /etc directory.
	tar -xvf a.tar	Extract all the files in the a.tar archive.
umount	umount *<device>* umount *<mount point>*	Unmount a previously mounted file system.
zcat		See gzip & gunzip

APPENDIX

HARDWARE COMPATIBILITY LISTS

The title for this appendix is a bit misleading; the tables that are printed here list hardware that has associated drivers included in the source code for the 2.2.1 Linux kernel. Do not consider this to be the final word on hardware support, though; the respective driver authors continuously improve and update their drivers to include support for new hardware, to support existing hardware better, and to clean up bugs in prior versions of their drivers. Also, as is common with Linux kernels, by the time this book is published the version of the Linux kernel will probably be something other than 2.2.1. The driver support that is listed here probably will not waver too much from minor kernel revision to minor kernel revision, though.

Occasionally, new hardware drivers are created that are not immediately included in the kernel source code. So if it looks like something you have is not supported, based on information in these tables, look around a bit before giving up hope. There is a good chance that someone (maybe even the hardware manufacturer) is already working on a Linux driver for your hardware.

The hardware that is covered here is considered essential to operating a networked computer with Linux. Items such as sound cards, cameras, scanners, and other items that are not considered essential for either installation or regular operation cannot be found here. Also, only hardware that runs on ISA, EISA, or PCI PC buses is covered.

Following are a few hints to consider before getting started:

- If you are having problems finding your hardware in this appendix, check hardware that might be compatible with what you have. For instance, many Matsushita CD-ROM drives are shipped as Panasonic drives; likewise for IBM CD-ROM drives, some of which (at least the old ones) are actually made by Mitsumi.
- Do not be afraid to look at a number that is printed on a chip on your motherboard or network card; many of the drivers that are listed here are for chipsets, and are not necessarily brands of cards; so even if something seems to be missing from this, you might still be in luck.
- Where more than one driver is listed for a piece of hardware in any of the tables that follow, the indication is that more than one driver is available for that piece of hardware (not that each driver must be loaded). Note that such devices might behave differently, depending on which of the available drivers is used.

SCSI ADAPTERS

The following SCSI interface cards and chipsets are known to work with the 2.2.1 Linux kernel. Note that if you are going to use modular support for these drivers, you must first load the scsi_mod.o module using `insmod`, and then the driver module for the SCSI interface, and then the device-specific modules that you need from the following list:

Module	Support offered
sd_mod.o	Disk drive support
sr_mod.o	CD-ROM drive support
st.o	Tape drive support
sg.o	Generic SCSI device support (that is, scanners and CD-R drives)

Table B.1 lists the individual SCSI interface drivers.

Table B.1 SCSI Interface Drivers

Vendor	Brand/Model	Driver	Module
AMD	AM53C974	AM53C974.c	AM53C974.o
	AM79C974	AM53C974.c	AM53C974.o
Acard	AEC-671X	atp870u.c	atp870u.o
Adaptec	1502 (cannot be probed for)	aha152x.c	aha152x.o
	1520	aha152x.c	aha152x.o
	1522	aha152x.c	aha152x.o
	1535 (cannot be probed for)	aha1542.c	aha1542.o
	1542 (A,CP,CF)	aha1542.c	aha1542.o
	1740	aha1740.c	aha1740.o
	274x	aic7xxx.c	aic7xxx.o
	284x	aic7xxx.c	aic7xxx.o
	2910B	aic7xxx.c	aic7xxx.o
	2920 (PCI)	fdomain.c	fdomain.o
	2920C	aic7xxx.c	aic7xxx.o
	294x	aic7xxx.c	aic7xxx.o
	2940A	aic7xxx.c	aic7xxx.o
	2944	aic7xxx.c	aic7xxx.o
	2950x	aic7xxx.c	aic7xxx.o
	394x	aic7xxx.c	aic7xxx.o
	3950x	aic7xxx.c	aic7xxx.o
	398x	aic7xxx.c	aic7xxx.o
	aic777x (motherboard)	aic7xxx.c	aic7xxx.o

continues

TABLE B.1 CONTINUED

Vendor	Brand/Model	Driver	Module
	aic785x (motherboard)	aic7xxx.c	aic7xxx.o
	aic786x (7850 ultra)	aic7xxx.c	aic7xxx.o
	aic787x (motherboard)	aic7xxx.c	aic7xxx.o
	aic788x (motherboard)	aic7xxx.c	aic7xxx.o
	aic789x (motherboard)	aic7xxx.c	aic7xxx.o
	aic3860 (motherboard)	aic7xxx.c	aic7xxx.o
AdvanSys	ABP-510	advansys.c	advansys.o
	ABP-542	advansys.c	advansys.o
	ABP-742	advansys.c	advansys.o
	ABP-752	advansys.c	advansys.o
	ABP-842	advansys.c	advansys.o
	ABP-852	advansys.c	advansys.o
	ABP-920	advansys.c	advansys.o
	ABP-930	advansys.c	advansys.o
	ARP-930U	advansys.c	advansys.o
	ABP-930UA	advansys.c	advansys.o
	ABP-940	advansys.c	advansys.o
	ABP-940U	advansys.c	advansys.o
	ABP-940UW	advansys.c	advansys.o
	ABP-950	advansys.c	advansys.o
	ABP-960	advansys.c	advansys.o
	ABP-960U	advansys.c	advansys.o
	ABP-970	advansys.c	advansys.o
	ABP-970U	advansys.c	advansys.o
	ABP-980	advansys.c	advansys.o
	ABP-980U	advansys.c	advansys.o

Vendor	Brand/Model	Driver	Module
	ABP-5140	advansys.c	advansys.o
	ABF-5142	advansys.c	advansys.o
	ABP-5150	advansys.c	advansys.o
Always	IN2000 (ISA)	in2000.c	in2000.o
AMI	MegaRAID	megaraid.c	megaraid.o
	FastDisk adapters (only true BusLogic clones)	BusLogic.c	BusLogic.o
BusLogic	BT-445C	BusLogic.c	BusLogic.o
	BT-445S	BusLogic.c	BusLogic.o
	BT-540CF	BusLogic.c	BusLogic.o
	BT-542B	BusLogic.c	BusLogic.o
	BT-542D	BusLogic.c	BusLogic.o
	BT-545C	BusLogic.c	BusLogic.o
	BT-545S	BusLogic.c	BusLogic.o
	BT-742A	BusLogic.c	BusLogic.o
	BT-747C	BusLogic.c	BusLogic.o
	BT-747D	BusLogic.c	BusLogic.o
	BT-747S	BusLogic.c	BusLogic.o
	BT-757C	BusLogic.c	BusLogic.o
	BT-757CD	BusLogic.c	BusLogic.o
	BT-757D	BusLogic.c	BusLogic.o
	BT-757S	BusLogic.c	BusLogic.o
	BT-946C	BusLogic.c	BusLogic.o
	BT-948	BusLogic.c	BusLogic.o
	BT-956C	BusLogic.c	BusLogic.o
	BT-956CD	BusLogic.c	BusLogic.o
	BT-958	BusLogic.c	BusLogic.o
	BT-958D	BusLogic.c	BusLogic.o
	FlashPoint LT (BT-930) Ultra SCSI-3	BusLogic.c	BusLogic.o
	FlashPoint LT (BT-930R) Ultra SCSI-3 w/ RAIDPlus	BusLogic.c	BusLogic.o

continues

Table B.1 Continued

Vendor	Brand/Model	Driver	Module
	FlashPoint LT (BT-920) Ultra SCSI-3 (BT-930 without BIOS)	BusLogic.c	BusLogic.o
	FlashPoint DL (BT-932) Dual Channel Ultra SCSI-3	BusLogic.c	BusLogic.o
	FlashPoint DL (BT-932R) Ultra SCSI-3 w/ RAIDPlus	BusLogic.c	BusLogic.o
	FlashPoint LW (BT-950) Wide Ultra SCSI-3	BusLogic.c	BusLogic.o
	FlashPoint LW (BT-950R) Wide Ultra SCSI-3 w/ RAIDPlus	BusLogic.c	BusLogic.o
	FlashPoint DW (BT-952) Dual Channel Wide Ultra SCSI-3	BusLogic.c	BusLogic.o
	FlashPoint DW (BT-952R) Dual Channel Wide Ultra SCSI-3 w/ RAIDPlus	BusLogic.c	BusLogic.o
Control Concepts	SCSI/IDE/SIO/ PIO/FDC cards	qlogicfas.c	qlogicfas.o
Dawicontrol	2974	tmscsim.c	tmscsim.o
DPT	EATA_PIO/DASD devices	eata_pio.c	eata_pio.o
	PM2011	eata_dma.c	eata_dma.o
		eata.c	eata.o
	PM2011B/9X	eata.c	eata.o
	PM2012A	eata.c	eata.o
	PM2012B	eata.c	eata.o
		eata_dma.c	eata_dma.o
	PM2021	eata_dma.c	eata_dma.o

Vendor	Brand/Model	Driver	Module
	PM2021A/9X	eata.c	eata.o
	PM2022	eata_dma.c	eata_dma.o
	PM2022A/9X	eata.c	eata.o
	PM2024	eata_dma.c	eata_dma.o
	PM2041	eata_dma.c	eata_drna.o
	PM2042	eata_dma.c	eata_dma.o
	PM2044	eata_dma.c	eata_dma.o
	PM2122	eata_dma.c	eata_dma.o
	PM2122A/9X	eata.c	eata.o
	PM2124	eata_dma.c	eata_dma.o
	PM2144	eata_dma.c	eata_dma.o
	PM2322	eata_dma.c	eata_dma.o
	PM2322A/9X	eata.c	eata.o
	PM3021	eata.c	eata.o
		eata_dma.c	eata_dma.o
	PM3122	eata_dma.c	eata_dma.o
	PM3222	eata.o	eata.o
		eata_dma.c	eata_dma.o
	PM3224	eata.c	eata.o
		eata_dma.c	eata_dma.o
	PM3222W	eata.c	eata.o
	PM3224W	eata.c	eata.o
	PM3332	eata_dma.c	eata_dma.o
	PM3334	eata_dma.c	eata_dma.o
DTC	3180	dtc.c	dtc.o
	3280	dtc.c	dtc.o
Future Domain	TMC-885	seagate.c	seagate.o
	TMC-950	seagate.c	seagate.o
	TMC-1610M	fdomain.c	fdomain.o
	TMC-1610MER	fdomain.c	fdomain.o
	TMC-1610MEX	fdomain.c	fdomain.o
	TMC-1650	fdomain.c	fdomain.o

continues

Table B.1 Continued

Vendor	Brand/Model	Driver	Module
	TMC-1660	fdomain.c	fdomain.o
	TMC-1670	fdomain.c	fdomain.o
	TMC-1680	fdomain.c	fdomain.o
	TMC-1800 based	fdomain.c	fdomain.o
	TMC-18C50 based	fdomain.c	fdomain.o
	TMC-18C30 based	fdomain.c	fdomain.o
	TMC-36C70 based	fdomain.c	fdomain.o
	TMC-3260 (PCI)	fdomain.c	fdomain.o
GVP	Series II SCSI	gvp11.c	gvp11.o
HP	4020i CD-R card	advansys.c	advansys.o
IBM	TMC-1680 based	fdomain.c	fdomain.o
ICP vortex Computer-systeme GmbH	GDT3000/3020	gdth.c	gdth.o
	GDT3000A/3020A/3050A	gdth.c	gdth.o
	GDT3000B/3010A	gdth.c	gdth.o
	GDT2000/2020	gdth.c	gdth.o
	GDT6000/6020/6050	gdth.c	gdth.o
	GDT6000B/6010	gdth.c	gdth.o
	GDT6110/6510	gdth.c	gdth.o
	GDT6120/6520	gdth.c	gdth.o
	GDT6530	gdth.c	gdth.o
	GDT6550	gdth.c	gdth.o
	GDT6117/6517	gdth.c	gdth.o
	GDT6127/6527	gdth.c	gdth.o
	GDT6537	gdth.c	gdth.o
	GDT6557/6557-ECC	gdth.c	gdth.o
	GDT6115/6515	gdth.c	gdth.o
	GDT6125/6525	gdth.c	gdth.o
	GDT6535	gdth.c	gdth.o
	GDT6555/6555-ECC	gdth.c	gdth.o

Vendor	Brand/Model	Driver	Module
	GDT6117RP/6517RP	gdth.c	gdth.o
	GDT6127RP/6527RP	gdth.c	gdth.o
	GDT6537RP	gdth.c	gdth.o
	GDT6557RP	gdth.c	gdth.o
	GDT6111RP/6511RP	gdth.c	gdth.o
	GDT6121RP/6521RP	gdth.c	gdth.o
	GDT6117RD/6517RD	gdth.c	gdth.o
	GDT6127RD/6527RD	gdth.c	gdth.o
	GDT6537RD	gdth.c	gdth.o
	GDT6557RD	gdth.c	gdth.o
	GDT6111RD/6511RD	gdth.c	gdth.o
	GDT6121RD/6521RD	gdth.c	gdth.o
	GDT6118RD/6518RD	gdth.c	gdth.o
	GDT6618RD	gdth.c	gdth.o
	GDT6538RD/6638RD	gdth.c	gdth.o
	GDT6558RD/6658RD	gdth.c	gdth.o
	GDT7118RN/7518RN	gdth.c	gdth.o
	GDT7618RN	gdth.c	gdth.o
	GDT7128RN/7528RN	gdth.c	gdth.o
	GDT7628RN	gdth.c	gdth.o
	GDT7538RN/7638RN	gdth.c	gdth.o
	GDT7558RN/7658RN	gdth.c	gdth.o
	GDT6519RD/6619RD	gdth.c	gdth.o
	GDT6529RD/6629RD	gdth.c	gdth.o
	GDT7519RN/7619RN	gdth.c	gdth.o
	GDT7529RN/7629RN	gdth.c	gdth.o
Initio	INI-910	i91uscsi.c	i91uscsi.o
	INI-9x00/UW	ini9100u.c	Ini9100u.o
Iomega	Jazz Jet PCI (late)	advansys.c	Advansys.o
	Jaz Jet PCI (early)	aic7xxx.c	Aic7xxx.c

continues

TABLE B.1 CONTINUED

Vendor	Brand/Model	Driver	Module
	MatchMaker (par. port)	imm.c	Imm.o
	PPA3 (par.port ZIP)	ppa.c	Ppa.o
	Zip Zoom	aha152x.c	Aha152x.o
Media Vision	Pro Audio Spectrum 16 w/SCSI	pas16.c	pas16.o
	Pro Audio Studio 16	pas16.c	pas16.o
NCR, Symbios Logic, TolerANT	5380	g_NCR5380.c	G_NCR5380.o
	53c400 (no DMA)	g_NCR5380.c	g_NCR5380.o
	53c406a	NCR53c406a.c	NCR53c406a.o
	53c700(chipset)	53c7,8xx.c	53c7,8xx.o
	53c700-66 (chipset)	53c7,8xx.c	53c7,8xx.o
	53c720(chipset)	53c7,8xx.c	53c7,8xx.o
	53c810(chipset)	ncr53c8xx.c	ncr53c8xx.o
		53c7,8xx.c	53c7,8xx.o
	53c810A(chipset)	ncr53c8xx.c	ncr53c8xx.o
	53c815 (chipset)	ncr53c8xx.c	ncr53c8xx.o
	53c820 (chipset)	ncr53c8xx.c	ncr53c8xx.o
		53c7,8xx.c	53c7,8xx.o
	53c825 (chipset)	ncr53c8xx.c	ncr53c8xx.o
	53c825A(chipset)	ncr53c8xx.c	ncr53c8xx.o
	53c860 (chipset)	ncr53c8xx.c	ncr53c8xx.o
	53c875 (chipset)	ncr53c8xx.c	ncr53c8xx.o
	53c876 (chipset)	ncr53c8xx.c	ncr53c8xx.o
	53c895 (chipset)	ncr53c8xx.c	ncr53c8xx.o
Perceptive Solutions	PCI-2000	pci2000.c	pci2000.o
	PCI-2220I	pci2220i.c	pci2220i.o
	PSI-240I	psi240i.c	psi240i.o

Vendor	Brand/Model	Driver	Module
Pro Audio	Spectrum 16	pas16.c	pas16.o
	Studio 16	pas16.c	pas16.o
Qlogic	FastSCSI! (ISA, VLB)	qlogicfas.c	qlogicfas.o
	IQ-PCI (no disconnect)	qlogicisp.c	qlogicisp.o
	IQ-PCI-10	qlogicisp.c	qlogicisp.o
	IQ-PCI-D	qlogicisp.c	qlogicisp.o
	PCI-Basic	tmscsim.c	tmscsim.o
Quantum	ISA-200S	fdomain.c	fdomain.o
	ISA-250MG	fdomain.c	fdomain.o
Seagate	ST01	seagate.c	seagate.o
	ST02	seagate.c	seagate.o
SIIG	i540 SpeedMaster	advansys.c	advansys.o
	i542 SpeedMaster	advansys.c	advansys.o
	Fast SCSI Pro PCI	advansys.c	advansys.o
Tekram	DC390	tmscsim.c	tmscsim.o
	DC390T	tmscsim.c	tmscsim.o
Trantor	T128	t128.c	t128.o
	T128F	t128.c	t128.o
	T130B	g_NCR5380.c	g_NCR5380.o
	T228	t128.c	t128.o
UltraStor	14F (Note: 14F BIOS 2.0 or later is required)	u14-34f.c u1trastor.c	u14-34f.o u1trastor.o
	24F	ultrastor.c	ultrastor.o
	34F	u14-34f.c	u14-34f.o
		u1trastor.c	u1trastor.o
Western Digital	WD7000-FASST2	wd7000.c	wd7000.o
	WD7000-ASC	wd7000.c	wd7000.o
	WD7000-AX(ALPHA)	wd7000.c	wd7000.o
	WD7000-MX(ALPHA)	wd7000.c	wd7000.o
	WD7000-EX(ALPHA)	wd7000.c	wd7000.o

IDE DRIVES

Simply put, if the hard drive in question is an IDE drive, it is supported under Linux. This includes the newer UDMA drives that ship with most modern PCs.

Table B.2 shows a breakdown of the main IDE drivers that are included in the 2.2.1 Linux kernel.

TABLE B.2 IDE DRIVERS

Hardware Type	Driver	Module
Hard Drives	ide.c	ide.o
CD-ROM Drives	ide-cd.c	ide-cd.o
Tape Drives	ide-tape.c	ide-tape.o

Special support is required for removable IDE devices, which are otherwise referred to as IDE *floppy* devices. Table B.3 shows the two main contenders in this category.

TABLE B.3 REMOVABLE IDE DEVICES

Vendor	Brand/Model	Driver	Module
Generic	LS-120	ide-floppy.c	ide-floppy.o
Iomega	ZIP Drive(IDE)	ide-floppy.c	ide-floppy.o

XT HARD DRIVE CONTROLLERS

Table B.4 lists XT hard drives/interfaces that are known to work with the 2.2.1 Linux kernel. In general, any controller that adheres to the standard XT-type hard disk interface works.

TABLE B.4 XT HARD DRIVES AND INTERFACES THAT WORK WITH THE 2.2.1 LINUX KERNEL

Vendor	Brand/Model	Driver	Module
DTC	5150X	xd.c	xd.o
	5150CX	xd.c	xd.o
OMTI	5520	xd.c	xd.o
Seagate	ST11M/R	xd.c	xd.o
	ST11R	xd.c	xd.o
Western Digital	WD1002-27X	xd.c	xd.o
	WD1002AWX1	xd.c	xd.o

Vendor	Brand/Model	Driver	Module
	WD1004A27X	xd.c	xd.o
	WDXT-GEN2	xd.c	xd.o
XEBEC		xd.c	xd.o

CD-ROM Drives

Most SCSI CD-ROM drives with a block size of 512 or 2048 will work. You need to have a supported SCSI adapter to use one of these drives (see the SCSI adapter and device tables earlier in this appendix). Note that some CD-ROM drives are shipped with non-standard SCSI adapters, which might not be supported.

Most CD-ROM drives that are connected via IDE/ATAPI interfaces will work. A few of the vendors who currently ship compatible drives include Aztech, Mitsumi, NEC, Sony, Creative Labs, and Vertos. Some multi-CD changers, such as the NEC CDR-251 and Sanyo's non-standard 3-CD changer, are supported as ATAPI drives and, therefore, do not have a special driver on the list that follows (they are supported by the IDE drivers that were listed earlier). On the other hand, some CyCDROM CD-ROM drives that connect to IDE interfaces are not really IDE drives at all; they use the proprietary drivers that are listed in Table B.5 (in the case of the CyCDROM 940ie and 520ie drives, the Aztech driver is used).

Proprietary CD-ROM Drives

Not all CD-ROM drives can be connected to IDE/ATAPI or SCSI controllers. Most modern CD-ROM drives can, but many older drives use special interfaces that are quite often matched to the drive itself. These are known as *proprietary* drives because of the special needs (drivers, interface cards) that are required to run them.

Table B.5 lists the proprietary CD-ROM drives that are supported by the 2.2.1 Linux kernel.

Table B.5 Proprietary CD-ROM Drives Supported by 2.2.1 Linux Kernel

Vendor	Brand/Model	Driver	Module
Aztech	CDA268-01A	aztcd.c	aztcd.o
Conrad	TXC	aztcd.c	aztcd.o
Creative Labs	CD-200F (CD-200 not fully supported)	sbpcd.c	sbpcd.o
CyCDROM	CR520	aztcd.c	aztcd.o
	CR520ie	aztcd.c	aztcd.o

continues

TABLE B.5 CONTINUED

Vendor	Brand/Model	Driver	Module
	CR540	aztcd.c	aztcd.o
	CR940ie	aztcd.c	aztcd.o
ECS-AT	Vertos 100	sbpcd.c	sbpcd.o
Funai	E2550UA	sbpcd.c	sbpcd.o
	MK4015	sbpcd.c	sbpcd.o
	2800F	sbpcd.c	sbpcd.o
Goldstar/Reveal	R420	gscd.c	gscd.o
IBM	External ISA drive	sbpcd.c	sbpcd.o
Kotobuki	(see Panasonic)		
Lasermate	CR328A	optcd.c	optcd.o
Longshine	LCS-7260	sbpcd.c	sbpcd.o
Matsushita	(see Panasonic)		
Mitsumi	CRMC LU005S	mcd.c	mcd.o
	Fx001S (single speed)	mcd.c	mcd.o
	Fx001S (multisession)	mcdx.c	mcdx.o
	FX001D (double speed)	mcd.c	mcd.o
	Fx001D (multisession)	mcdx.c	mcdx.o
Okano/Wearnes	CDD110	aztec.c	aztec.o
Optics Storage	DOLPHIN 8000 AT	optcd.c	optcd.o
Orchid	CDS-3110	aztcd.c	aztcd.o
Panasonic	CR-521	sbpcd.c	sbpcd.o
	CR-522	sbpcd.c	sbpcd.o
	CR-523	sbpcd.c	sbpcd.o
	CR-562	sbpcd.c	sbpcd.o
	CR-563	sbpcd.c	sbpcd.o
Philips/ LMS	cm206 /w cm260 card	cm206.c	cm206.o

Vendor	Brand/Model	Driver	Module
Sanyo	CDR-H94A	sjcd.c	sjcd.o
Sony	CDU-31A (not probed)	cdu31a.c	cdu31a.o
	CDU-33A (not probed)	cdu31a.c	cdu31a.o
	CDU-510	sonycd535.c	sonycd535.o
	CDU-515	sonycd535.c	sonycd535.o
	CDU-531	sonycd535.c	sonycd535.o
	CDU-535	sonycd535.c	sonycd535.o
Teac	CD-55A	sbpcd.c	sbpcd.o

CD-ROM Drive Interface Cards

Some multimedia kits ship with special interface cards that are used specifically for the included CD-ROM drive. The bulk of them (the ones that are not listed in the previous table) are ISP16 compatible cards. Table B.6 lists the types of ISP16 cards that are known to work with the 2.2.1 Linux kernel. Note that the driver for the interface card must be loaded *before* the driver for the CD-ROM drive.

Table B.6 ISP16 Cards that Work with 2.2.1 Linux Kernel

Vendor	Driver	Module
ISP16	isp16.c	isp16.o
MAD16	isp16.c	isp16.o
Mozart	isp16.c	isp16.o

Parallel Port Drives (PARIDE Drivers)

The following section lists the parallel port devices (CD-ROM drives, hard drives, and tape drives) that are known to work with the 2.2.1 Linux kernel, as well as the procedures that are used to load their associated drivers.

Loading paride drivers as modules requires a few steps:

1. Load the paride.o module using `insmod`.
2. Load the vendor-specific drivers from Table B.7 using `insmod`.
3. Load the paride module that gives the specific support you need. (Select from the modules listed in Table B.7.)

TABLE B.7 PARIDE MODULES

Module	Support offered
pd.o	IDE hard drives
pcd.o	ATAPI CD-ROM drives
pf.o	ATAPI hard drives
pt.o	ATAPI tape drives
pg.o	ATAPI generic drives (CD-R drives specifically)

The Freecom Power CD unit that is listed in Table B.8 consists of a Mitsumi ATAPI drive and a custom chip that implements Freecom's IDE-over-parallel protocol. It seems that this custom chip is based on a truth table that must be loaded by the driver during the initialization of the device. The DOS driver POWER_CD.SYS, which comes with the drive, does this. Because it violates copyrights to include the initialization sequence as part of this driver, the user must arrange for the drive to be initialized from DOS prior to booting Linux (use `LOADLIN` to boot Linux after DOS has initialized the CD-ROM hardware).

Table B.8 lists the vendor-specific parallel port IDE drivers that are included in the 2.2.1 Linux kernel (one or more of these is required to complete step 2 of the preceding process).

TABLE B.8 VENDOR-SPECIFIC PARALLEL PORT IDE DRIVERS

Vendor	Brand/Model	Driver	Module
Arista	Miscellaneous	comm.c	comm.o
ATEN	EH-100	aten.c	aten.o
Avatar	Shark	epat.c	epat.o
DataStor	Commuter adapter	comm.c	comm.o
	EP2000	dstr.c	dstr.o
Fidelity International Technology	TransDisk 2000	fit2.c	fit2.o
	TransDisk 3000	fit3.c	fit3.o
Freecom	Power CD	frpw.c	frpw.o
	IQ Cable	friq.c	friq.o
Hewlett Packard	Tape drives (5GB & 8GB)	epat.c	epat.o
	7100 CD-RW	epat.c	epat.o
	7200 CD-RW	epat.c	epat.o
Imation	SuperDisk LS-120	epat.c	epat.o

Vendor	Brand/Model	Driver	Module
KingByte Information Systems	KBIC-951A	kbic.c	kbic.o
	KBIC-917A	kbic.c	kbic.o
KT Technology	PHd adapter	ktti.c	ktti.o
Maxell	SuperDisk LS-120	epat.c	epat.o
MicroSolutions	backpack CD-ROM	bpck.c	bpck.o
	backpack PD/CD	bpck.c	bpck.o
	backpack Hard Drives	bpck.c	bpck.o
	backpack 8000t Tape Drives	bpck.c	bpck.o
OnSpec Electronics	90c20	on20.c	on20.o
	90c26	on26.c	on26.o
Shuttle Technologies	EPAT	epat.c	epat.o
	EPIA	epia.c	epia.o
SyQuest	EZ-135	epat.c	epat.o
	EZ-230	epat.c	epat.o
	SparQ	epat.c	epat.o

Floppy-Tape Drives

Most QIC-40, QIC-80, QIC-3010, QIC-3020, and QIC-117 floppy tape drives are supported by the ftape driver. Table B.9 lists the drives that are mentioned by name in the 2.2.1 Linux kernel source code. There are no individual, per-device drivers as there are with SCSI or Ethernet cards; all of these are covered under the same ftape.o driver:

Table B.9 Drives Mentioned in 2.2.1 Linux Kernel Source Code

Vendor	Brand/Model	Driver	Module
AIWA	CT-803	ftape	ftape.o
	TD-S1600	ftape	ftape.o
Archive	31250Q (Escom)	ftape	ftape.o
	5580I	ftape	ftape.o

continues

TABLE B.9 CONTINUED

Vendor	Brand/Model	Driver	Module
	S. Hornet (Ident. /Escom)	ftape	ftape.o
	XL9250I (Conner/Escom)	ftape	ftape.o
Colorado	700	ftape	ftape.o
	1400	ftape	ftape.o
	DJ-l0	ftape	ftape.o
	DJ-20	ftape	ftape.o
	FC-10	ftape	ftape.o
	FC-20	ftape	ftape.o
	Tl000 (HP)	ftape	ftape.o
	T3000 (HP)	ftape	ftape.o
ComByte	DoublePlay	ftape	ftape.o
Conner	C250MQ	ftape	ftape.o
	C250MQT	ftape	ftape.o
	TSM420R	ftape	ftape.o
	TSM850R	ftape	ftape.o
	TSMl700R	ftape	ftape.o
	TST800R	ftape	ftape.o
	TST3200R	ftape	ftape.o
COREtape	QIC80	ftape	ftape.o
Exabyte	Eagle-96	ftape	ftape.o
	Eagle-TR3	ftape	ftape.o
Insight	80MB	ftape	ftape.o
Iomega	250	ftape	ftape.o
	700	ftape	ftape.o
	3200	ftape	ftape.o
	Ditto 800	ftape	ftape.o
	Ditto 2GB	ftape	ftape.o
Irwin	80SX	ftape	ftape.o
Mountain	FS8000	ftape	ftape.o
Pertec	MyTape 800	ftape	ftape.o
	MyTape 3200	ftape	ftape.o

Vendor	Brand/Model	Driver	Module
Reveal	TBl400	ftape	ftape.o
Summit	SE 150	ftape	ftape.o
	SE 250	ftape	ftape.o
Teac	700	ftape	ftape.o
	800	ftape	ftape.o
	FT3010TR	ftape	ftape.o
Wangtek	3040F	ftape	ftape.o
	3080F	ftape	ftape.o
	3200	ftape	ftape.o

ETHERNET CARDS

Table B.10 lists the Ethernet cards that are known to work with the 2.2.1 Linux kernel. Note that most generic ISA and PCI Ethernet cards are NE2000 clones. Note also that the 8390.o module needs to be loaded before you load an Ethernet card driver if your card contains an 8390 chip (as do most NE2000 clones).

TABLE B.10 ETHERNET CARDS THAT WORK WITH 2.2.1 LINUX KERNEL

Vendor	Brand/Model	Driver	Module
3Com	Etherlink	3c501.c	3c501.o
	Etherlink II	3c503.c	3c503.o
	Etherlink Plus	3c505.c	3c505.o
	Etherlink 16	3c507.c	3c507.o
	Etherlink III (3c509)	3c509.c	3c509.o
	Etherlink III (3c579)	3c509.c	3c509.o
	Etherlink III (3c590)	3c59x.c	3c59x.o
	Fast Etherlink	3c59x.c	3c59x.o
	Etherlink XL (3c900)	3c59x.c	3c59x.o
	Etherlink XL (3c905)	3c59x.c	3c59x.o
	EtherLink XL (ISA)	3c515.c	3c515.o
	Tigon based (3c985)	acenic.c	acenic.o
Accton	EtherDuo PCI	tulip.c	tulip.o
	EN1207 (all three types)	tulip.c	tulip.o

continues

Table B.10 Continued

Vendor	Brand/Model	Driver	Module
Adaptec	ANA6901/C	tulip.c	tulip.o
	ANA6911/TX	tulip.c	tulip.o
Allied Telesis	AT1500	lance.c	lance.o
	AT1700	at1700.c	at1700.o
	LA100PCI-T	tulip.c	tulip.o
Alteon	AceNIC Gigabit	acenic.c	acenic.o
AMD Lance	PCnet-ISA	lance.c	lance.o
	PCnet-ISA+	lance.c	lance.o
	Pcnet-PCI	lance32.c	lance32.o
		pcnet32.c	pcnet32.o
	PCnet-PCI II	lance.c	lance.o
	PCnet-32	lance32.c	lance32.o
	PCnet-Fast	pcnet32.c	pcnet32.o
Ansel Com.	AC3200 EISA	ac3200.c	ac3200.o
AT-Lan-Tec/ Realtek	RTL8002 (chip)	atp.c	atp.o
	RTL8012 (chip)	atp.c	atp.o
Bay Networks	Netgear FX310 TX 10/100	tulip.c	tulip.o
	Netgear GA620	acenic.c	acenic.o
BOCA	AMD 79C960 based cards	lance.c	lance.o
Cabletron	E2100	e2100.c	e2100.o
CardBus		epic100.c	epic100.o
C-NET	CNE-935	tulip.c	tulip.o
Cogent	EM100	tulip.c	tulip.o
	EM110	tulip.c	tulip.o
	EM400	tulip.c	tulip.o
	EM960	tulip.c	tulip.o
	EM964 Quartet	tulip.c	tulip.o
Compaq	Netelligent 10 T (PCI)	tlan.c	tlan.o
	Netelligent 10 T2(PCI)	tlan.c	tlan.o
	Netelligent 10/100 TX (PCI)	tlan.c	tlan.o

Vendor	Brand/Model	Driver	Module
	Netelligent 10/100 TX UDP (PCI)	tlan.c	tlan.o
	Netelligent 10/100 TX w/ embedded UTP (PCI)	tlan.c	tlan.o
	Integrated Netelligent 10/100 TX (PCI)	tlan.c	tlan.o
	Integrated NetFlex-3/P (PCI)	tlan.c	tlan.o
	NetFlex-3/P (PCI)	tlan.c	tlan.o
	Dual Port Netelligent 10/100 TX (PCI)	tlan.c	tlan.o
Compex	Readylink ENET100-VG4 (EISA/PCI)	hp100.c	hp100.o
	Readylink 2000	ne.c	ne.o
	FreedomLine 100/VG (ISA, EISA, PCI)	hp100.c	hp100.o
Comtrol	Hostess SV-11	hostess_ sv11.c	hostess_ sv11.o
COSA	ISA adapter	cosa.c	cosa.o
Crystal Lan	CS8900	cs89x0.c	cs89x0.o
	CS8920	cs89x0.c	cs89x0.o
Danpex	EN-9400P3	tulip.c	tulip.o
D-Link	DE-530CT	tulip.c	tulip.o
	DE-600	de600 C	de600.o
	DE-620	de620 C	de620.o
	DFE-500-Tx	tulip.c	tulip.o
	DFE-530TX	via-rhine.c	via-rhine.o
DEC	DEPCA	depca.c	depca.o
	DE-100	depca.c	depca.o
	DE-101	depca.c	depca.o
	DE-200 Turbo	depca.c	depca.o
	DE-201 Turbo	depca.c	depca.o
	DE-202 Turbo (TP BNC)	depca.c	depca.o
	DE-203 Turbo (BNC)	ewrk3.c	ewrk3.o
	DE-204 Turbo (TP)	ewrk3.c	ewrk3.o

continues

TABLE B.10 CONTINUED

Vendor	Brand/Model	Driver	Module
	DE-205 Turbo (TP BNC)	ewrk3.c	ewrk3.o
	DE-210	depca.c	depca.o
	DE-422 (EISA)	depca.c	depca.o
	DE-425 (TP BNC EISA)	de4x5.c	de4x5.o
	DE-434 (TP PCI)	de4x5.c	de4x5.o
	DE-435 (TP BNC AUI PCI)	de4x5.c	de4x5.o
	DE-450 (TP BNC AUI PCI)	de4x5.c	de4x5.o
	DE-500 10/100 (PCI)	de4x5.c	de4x5.o
	EtherWORKS	depca.c	depca.o
	EtherWORKS III	ewrk3.c	ewrk3.o
	EtherWORKS 10 (PCI)	tulip.c	tulip.o
	EtherWORKS 10/100 (PCI)	tulip.c	tulip.o
	QSILVER	tulip.c	tulip.o
	DEC chips 21040/21041/ 21140/21142/21143	tulip.c	tulip.o
	DEC chips 21040 (no SROM)/21041A/21140A/ 21142/21143	de4x5.c	de4x5.o
Digi	RightSwitch SE/x	dgrs.c	dgrs.o
Essential	RoadRunner HIPPI	rrunner.c	rrunner.o
Fujitsu	FMV-181	fmv18x.c	fmv18x.o
	FMV-181A	at1700.c	at1700.o
	FMV-182	fmv18x.c	fmv18x.o
	FMV-182A	at1700.c	at1700.o
	FMV-183	fmv18x.c	fmv18x.o
	FMV-183A	at1700.c	at1700.o
	FMV-184	fmv18x.c	fmv18x.o
	FMV-184A	at1700.c	at1700.o
Hewlett Packard	100VG-AnyLan	hp100.c	hp100.o
	27248B (Cascade)	hp100.c	hp100.o
	AMD 79C960 based cards	lance.c	lance.o

Vendor	Brand/Model	Driver	Module
	HP300	hplance.c	hplance.o
	J2405A	lance.c	lance.o
	J2577 (Cascade)	hp100.c	hp100.o
	J2577 (Rev. A Cascade)	hp100.c	hp100.o
	J2573 (Cascade)	hp100.c	hp100.o
	J2573 (Rev. A Cascade)	hp100.c	hp100.o
	J2585 [AB]	hp100.c	hp100.o
	J2970	hp100.c	hp100.o
	J2973	hp100.c	hp100.o
	PC-Lan	hp.c	hp.o
	PC-Lan Plus	hp-plus.c	hp-plus.o
IBM	ThinkPad (built-in network interface)	znet.c	znet.o
ICL	EtherTeam 16I	eth16i.c	eth16i.o
	EtherTeam 32 (EISA)	eth16i.c	eth16i.o
Intel	EtherExpress 16	eexpress.c	eexpress.o
	EtherExpress Pro/10	eepro.c	eepro.o
	EtherExpress Pro/10+	eepro.c	eepro.o
	EtherExpress Pro 100B	eepro100.c	eepro100.o
	Other Intel i82557 based cards	eepro100.c	eepro100.o
Kingston	DEC 21x4x based cards	de4x5.c	de4x5.o
	AMD 79C960 based cards	lance.c	lance.o
	EtherX KNE100TX	tulip.c	tulip.o
	EtherX KNT40T	tulip.c	tulip.o
KTI	ET32P2	ne.c	ne.o
Linksys	AMD 79C960 based cards	lance.c	lance.o
	DEC 21x4x based cards	de4x5.c	de4x5.o
	EtherPCI	tulip.c	tulip.o
Mylex	LNE390	lne390.c	lne390.o
NE1000		ne.c	ne.o
NE2000 (ISA)		ne.c	ne.o
NE2000 (PCI)		ne2k-pci.c	ne2k-pci.o

continues

TABLE B.10 CONTINUED

Vendor	Brand/Model	Driver	Module
NE2100		lance.c	lance.o
		ni65.c	ni65.o
NE2500		lance.c	lance.o
NE3210		ne3210.c	ne3210.o
NetVin	NV5000	ne.c	ne.o
NI5210		ni52.c	ni52.o
NI6510		ni65.c	ni65.o
Olicom	OC-2325	tlan.c	tlan.o
	OC-2183	tlan.c	tlan.o
	OC-2326	tlan.c	tlan.o
Packet Engine	"Yellowfin" G-NIC	yellowfin.c	yellowfin.o
Pure Data	PDI8023-8	wd.c	wd.o
	PDUC8023	wd.c	wd.o
	PDI8023-16	wd.c	wd.o
Racal-Interlan	ES3210 (EISA)	es3210.c	es3210.o
	NI5010	ni5010.c	ni5010.o
Realtek	8029	ne.c	ne.o
	RTL8129/8139 Fast Ethernet	rtl8139.c	rtl8139.o
RedCreek Commun-ications	PCI cards	rcpci45.c	rcpc145.o
Schneider & Koch	G16	sk_g16.c	sk_g16.o
SEEQ	8005 based cards	seeq8005.c	seeq8005.o
SMC	83c790 chips	smc-ultra32.c	smc-ultra32.o
	8432	de4x5.c	de4x5.o
	8432BT	tulip.c	tulip.o
	9000 series	smc9194.c	smc9194.o
	9332 (w/ new SROM)	de4x5.c	de4x5.o
	9332dst	tulip.c	tulip.o
	Ultra	smc-ultra.c	smc-ultra.o

Vendor	Brand/Model	Driver	Module
	EtherEZ (ISA)	smc-ultra.c	smc-ultra.o
	EtherPower 10 (PCI)	tulip.c	tulip.o
	EtherPower 10/100 (PCI)	tulip.c	tulip.o
	Ultra32 EISA	smc-ultra32.c	smc-ultra32.o
	EtherPower II	epic100.c	epic100.o
Surecom	EP-320X	tulip.c	tulip.o
	NE34	ne.c	ne.o
SysKonnect	TR4/16(+) ISA (SK-4190)	sktr.c	sktr.o
	TR4/16(+) PCI (SK-4590)	sktr.c	sktr.o
	TR4/16 PCI (SK-4591)	sktr.c	sktr.o
Thomas Conrad	TC 5048	tulip.c	tulip.o
VIA	86c100A Rhine-II (PCI)	via-rhine.c	via-rhine.o
	82C926 Amazon	ne.c	ne.o
Western Dig.	WD8003	wd.c	wd.o
	WD8013	wd.c	wd.o
Winbond	89C940	ne.c	ne.o
Zenith	Z-Note	znet.c	znet.o
Zynx	ZX312 EtherAction	tulip.c	tulip.o
	ZX314	tulip.c	tulip.o
		de4x5.c	de4x5.o
	ZX315 EtherArray	tulip.c	tulip.o
		de4x5.c	de4x5.o
	ZX342/344/345/346/348/351	tulip.c	tulip.o
	ZX346 10/100 4 port	de4x5.c	de4x5.o

ARCNET CARDS

Table B.11 lists ARCnet interface cards that are known to work with the 2.2.1 Linux kernel. Note that if the modular versions of these drivers are being used, you must first load the arcnet.o module using `insmod`, and then load the card-specific module.

TABLE B.11 ARCNET INTERFACE CARDS

Vendor	Brand/Model	Driver	Module
ARCnet	ARCnet RIM I	arc-rimi.c	arc-rimi.o
	ARCnet card w/ memory mapped COM90xx chipset	com90xx.c	com90xx.o
	ARCnet card w/ COM20020 chipset	com20020.c	com20020.o
	ARCnet card w/ IO mapped COM90xx chipset	com90io.c	com90io.o

FRAME RELAY CARDS

Table B.12 lists frame relay interface cards that are known to work with the 2.2.1 Linux kernel.

There are two utilities that are required to configure these devices: `dlcicfg` and `fradcfg`. Both are available for downloading from the following URL:

`ftp://ftp.invlogic.com/pub/linux`

TABLE B.12 FRAME RELAY INTERFACE CARDS THAT WORK WITH 2.2.1 LINUX KERNEL

Vendor	Brand/Model	Driver	Module
Sangoma	S502A	sdla.c	sdla.o
	S502E	sdla.c	sdla.o
	S508	sdla.c	sdla.o

RADIO MODEM/NETWORK INTERFACES

Table B.13 lists the radio modem cards that are known to work with the 2.2.1 Linux kernel.

TABLE B.13 RADIO MODEM CARDS THAT WORK WITH 2.2.1 LINUX KERNEL

Vendor	Brand/Model	Driver	Module
AT&T	GIS WaveLAN	wavelan.c	wavelan.o
Baycom	EPP modem	baycom_epp.c	baycom_epp.o
	par96	baycom_par.c	baycom_par.o
	par97	baycom_par.c	baycom_par.o
	picpar	baycom_par.c	baycom_par.o
	ser12 (half duplex)	baycom_ser_hdx.c	baycom_ser_hdx.o

Vendor	Brand/Model	Driver	Module
	ser12	baycom_ser_fdx.c	baycom_ser_fdx.o
Creative Labs	SoundBlaster SoundModem	sm.c	sm.o
	SoundBlaster (HF FSK)	hfmodem	hfmodem.o
Gracilis	PackeTwin	pt.c	pt.o
		dmascc.c	dmascc.o
Ottawa Amateur Radio Club	PI	pi2.c dmascc.c	pi2.o dmascc.o
	PI2	pi2.c	pi2.o
		dmascc.c	dmascc.o
WSS	WSS (half duplex only)	sm.c	sm.o
	WSS (HF FSK)	hfmodem	hfmodem.o
z8530 SCC		scc.c	scc.o

TOKEN RING CARDS

The following table lists the Token Ring cards that are known to work with the 2.2.1 Linux kernel.

Vendor	Brand/Model	Driver	Module
IBM	Any non-DMA cards	ibmtr.c	ibmtr.o

FDDI CONTROLLERS

Following are the Fiber Distributed Data Interface (FDDI) interface cards that are known to work with the 2.2.1 Linux kernel:

Vendor	Brand/Model	Driver	Module
DEC	FDDIcontroller (EISA/PCI)	defxx.c	defxx.o

FLOPPY/DISK DRIVES

General floppy disk and disk drive support in the 2.2.1 Linux kernel is quite extensive. To list all the supported drives here is prohibitive. Instead, Table B.14 lists the drives that often require that specific parameters be passed when the floppy driver is loaded. Refer to Appendix C, "Loadable Module Parameters," for more information.

TABLE B.14 FLOPPY/DISK DRIVES

Vendor	Brand/Model	Driver	Module
HP	Omnibook	floppy.c	floppy.o
IBM	L40SX ThinkPad	floppy.c	floppy.o

MICE

Serial mice are supported by the generic serial port support in the 2.2.1 Linux kernel. If the port itself is recognized, so is the mouse that is connected to it. Nonserial mice, however, are a different story. Each requires its own driver based on the type of mouse it is.

Table B.15 lists the nonserial mice that are known to work with the 2.2.1 Linux kernel. Note that bus mice are assumed to be running at IRQ 5, and PS/2 mice are assumed to be running at IRQ 12. Any variations might require some adjustment in the kernel source code and a subsequent kernel recompilation (or in the case of the bus mice, passing a module parameter) to get the mice recognized and working correctly.

TABLE B.15 NONSERIAL MICE THAT WORK WITH 2.2.1 LINUX KERNEL

Vendor	Brand/Model	Driver	Module
ATI	XL	atix1mouse.c	atix1mouse.o
Logitech	Busmouse	busmouse.c	busmouse.o
		msbusmouse.c	msbusmouse.o
Microsoft	Busmouse	msbusmouse.c	msbusmouse.o
PC110	TouchPad	pc110pad.c	pc110pad.o
PS/2	compatibles	pc_keyb.c	pc_keyb.o
"QuickPort"	C&T 82C710 mouse interfaces	qpmouse.c	qpmouse.o

INFRARED (IRDA) HARDWARE

Table B.16 lists the iRDA hardware that is known to work with the 2.2.1 Linux kernel.

TABLE B.16 IRDA HARDWARE

Vendor	Brand/Model	Driver	Module
ACTiSYS	IR-220L (dongle)	actisys.c	actisys.o
	IR-220L+ (dongle)	actisys.c	actisys.o

Vendor	Brand/Model	Driver	Module
Extended Systems	JetEye PC	esi.c	esi.o
Tekram	IrMate IR-210B (dongle)	tekram.c	tekram.o
Sharp	Universal Infrared Communications Controller (UIRCC)	uircc.c	uircc.o
Winbond	W83977AF Super IO chip	w83977af.c	w83977af.o
National Semiconductor	PC87108 chip	pc87108.c	pc87108.o

SERIAL BOARDS

The serial boards that are listed in Table B.17 are known to work with the 2.2.1 Linux kernel.

Note that serial boards such as the STB 4-Com (which simply consist of many standard hardware serial ports on a single card) are supported by the standard serial port driver, which does support IRQ sharing for cards that require it.

Note also that the Cyclades Z boards require a firmware upgrade before the cyclades.o driver works with them. The firmware upgrade can be found at the following URL:

`ftp://ftp.cyclades.com/pub/cyclades/cyclades-z/linux`

TABLE B.17 SERIAL BOARDS THAT WORK WITH 2.2.1 LINUX KERNEL

Vendor	Brand/Model	Driver	Module
Accent	Async	esp.c	esp.o
AST	FourPort	esp.c	esp.o
Comtrol	RocketPort	rocket.c	rocket.o
Cyclades	Cyclom-Y boards	cyclades.c	cyclades.o
	Cyclades-Z boards	cyclades.c	cyclades.o
DigiBoard	EISA/Xem	epca.c	epca.o
	PC/Xe	pcxx.c	pcxx.o
		epca.c	epca.o
	PC/Xem	epca.c	epca.o

continues

TABLE B.17 CONTINUED

Vendor	Brand/Model	Driver	Module
	PC/Xeve	pcxx.c	pcxx.o
		epca.c	epca.o
	PC/Xi	pcxx.c	pcxx.o
		epca.c	epca.o
	PC/Xr	epca.c	epca.o
	PCI/Xem	epca.c	epca.o
	PCI/Xr	epca.c	epca.o
Hayes	ESP	esp.c	esp.o
Multi-Tech	ISI Series	isicom.c	isicom.o
SDL Comm.	RISCom/8	riscom8.c	riscom8.o
Stallion	Brumby	istallion.c	istallion.o
	EasyIO	stallion.c	stallion.o
	EasyConnection 8/32	stallion.c	stallion.o
	EasyConnection 8/64	istallion.c	istallion.o
	ONboard	istallion.c	istallion.o
Specialix	IO8+ multiport	specialix.c	specialix.o

VIDEO CARDS

Table B.18 lists the video cards that are supported by the X Window system that ships with OpenLinux (Xfree86 version 3.3.3). The actual filenames for the servers consist of XF86_ and what is listed in the "Server" column (for instance, the SVGA server filename is XF86_SVGA).

TABLE B.18 VIDEO CARDS

Company	Card	Server
2 the Max	MAXColor S3 Trio64V+	S3
3DLabs	Oxygen GMX	3DLabs
928Movie		S3
AGX (Generic)		AGX
ALG-5434(E)		SVGA

Company	Card	Server
ASUS	3Dexplorer	SVGA
	PCI-AV264CT	Mach64
	PCI-V264CT	Mach64
	VideoMagic PCI V864	S3
	VideoMagic PCI VT64	S3
AT25		SVGA
AT3D		SVGA
ATI	3D Pro Turbo	Mach64
	3D Pro Turbo PC2TV	Mach64
	3D Xpression	Mach64
	3D Xpression+	Mach64
	3D Xpression+ PC2TV	Mach64
	8514 Ultra (no VGA)	Mach8
	All-in-Wonder	Mach64
	All-in-Wonder Pro	Mach64
	Graphics Pro Turbo	Mach64
	Graphics Pro Turbo with AT&T 20C408 RAMDAC	Mach64
	Graphics Pro Turbo with 68860 RAMDAC	Mach64
	Graphics Pro Turbo with 68860B RAMDAC	Mach64
	Graphics Pro Turbo with 68860C RAMDAC	Mach64
	Graphics Pro Turbo with 68875 RAMDAC	Mach64
	Graphics Pro Turbo with CH8398 RAMDAC	Mach64
	Graphics Pro Turbo with STG1702 RAMDAC	Mach64
	Graphics Pro Turbo with STG1703 RAMDAC	Mach64
	Graphics Pro Turbo with TLC34075 RAMDAC	Mach64
	Graphics Pro Turbo 1600	Mach64

continues

TABLE B.18 CONTINUED

Company	Card	Server
	Graphics Ultra	Mach8
	Graphics Ultra Pro	Mach32
	Graphics Xpression w/ 68860 RAMDAC	Mach64
	Graphics Xpression w/ 68860B RAMDAC	Mach64
	Graphics Xpression w/ 68860C RAMDAC	Mach64
	Graphics Xpression w/ 68875 RAMDAC	Mach64
	Graphics Xpression w/ AT&T 20C408 RAMDAC	Mach64
	Graphics Xpression w/ CH8398 RAMDAC	Mach64
	Graphics Xpression w/ Mach64 CT (264CT)	Mach64
	Graphics Xpression w/ STG1702 RAMDAC	Mach64
	Graphics Xpression w/ STG1703 RAMDAC	Mach64
	Graphics Xpression w/ TLC34075 RAMDAC	Mach64
	Intel Maui MU440EX motherboard	Mach64
	Mach32	Mach32
	Mach64	Mach64
	Mach64 w/ 68860 RAMDAC	Mach64
	Mach64 w/ 68860B RAMDAC	Mach64
	Mach64 w/ 68860C RAMDAC	Mach64
	Mach64 w/ 68875 RAMDAC	Mach64
	Mach64 w/ Internal RAMDAC	Mach64
	Mach64 w/ STG1702 RAMDAC	Mach64
	Mach64 w/ STG1703 RAMDAC	Mach64
	Mach64 w/ TLC34075 RAMDAC	Mach64
	Mach64 3D RAGE II	Mach64
	Mach64 3D RAGE II+ DVD	Mach64
	Mach64 3D RAGE IIC	Mach64
	Mach64 3D RAGE Pro	Mach64
	Mach64 CT (264 CT), Internal RAMDAC	Mach64

Company	Card	Server
	Mach64 GT (264 GT), a.k.a. 3D RAGE, Internal RAMDAC	Mach64
	Mach64 VT (264 VT), Internal RAMDAC	Mach64
	Mach64 w/ AT&T 20C408 RAMDAC	Mach64
	Mach64 w/ CH8398 RAMDAC	Mach64
	Mach64 w/ IBM RGB514 RAMDAC	Mach64
	Pro Turbo+PC2TV, 3D RAGE II_DVD	Mach64
	Ultra Plus	Mach32
	Video Xpression	Mach64
	Video Xpression+	Mach64
	WinBoost	Mach64
	WinBoost w/ 68860 RAMDAC	Mach64
	WinBoost w/ 68860B RAMDAC	Mach64
	WinBoost w/ 68860C RAMDAC	Mach64
	WinBoost w/ 68875 RAMDAC	Mach64
	WinBoost w/ AT&T 20C408 RAMDAC	Mach64
	WinBoost w/ CH8398 RAMDAC	Mach64
	WinBoost w/ Mach64 CT (264CT)	Mach64
	WinBoost w/ STG1702 RAMDAC	Mach64
	WinBoost w/ STG1703 RAMDAC	Mach64
	WinBoost w/ TLC34075 RAMDAC	Mach64
	WinCharger	Mach64
	WinCharger w/ AT&T 20C408 RAMDAC	Mach64
	WinCharger w/ 68860 RAMDAC	Mach64
	WinCharger w/ 68860B RAMDAC	Mach64
	WinCharger w/ 68860C RAMDAC	Mach64
	WinCharger w/ 68875 RAMDAC	Mach64
	WinCharger w/ CH8398 RAMDAC	Mach64
	WinCharger w/ Mach64 CT (264CT)	Mach64
	WinCharger w/ STG1702 RAMDAC	Mach64
	WinCharger w/ STG1703 RAMDAC	Mach64
	WinCharger w/ TLC34075 RAMDAC	Mach64

continues

TABLE B.18 CONTINUED

Company	Card	Server
	Win Turbo	Mach64
	WinTurbo w/ AT&T 20C408 RAMDAC	Mach64
	WinTurbo w/ 68860 RAMDAC	Mach64
	WinTurbo w/ 68860B RAMDAC	Mach64
	WinTurbo w/ 68860C RAMDAC	Mach64
	WinTurbo w/ 68875 RAMDAC	Mach64
	WinTurbo w/ CH8398 RAMDAC	Mach64
	WinTurbo w/ Mach64 CT (264CT)	Mach64
	WinTurbo w/ STG1702 RAMDAC	Mach64
	WinTurbo w/ STG1703 RAMDAC	Mach64
	WinTurbo w/ TLC34075 RAMDAC	Mach64
	Wonder SVGA	SVGA
	Xpert 98	Mach64
	Xpert XL	Mach64
	Xpert@Play 98	Mach64
	Xpert@Play PCI and AGP, 3D RAGE Pro	Mach64
	Xpert@Work, 3D RAGE Pro	Mach64
ATrend	ATC-2165A	SVGA
AccelStar	Permedia II AGP	3DLabs
Actix	GE32+ 2MB	S3
	GE32I	S3
	GE64	S3
	ProStar	SVGA
	ProStar 64	SVGA
	Ultra	S3
Acumos	AVGA3	SVGA
Alliance	ProMotion 6422	SVGA
Ark Logic	ARK1000PV (Generic)	SVGA
	ARK1000VL (Generic)	SVGA
	ARK2000MT (Generic)	SVGA
	ARK2000PV (Generic)	SVGA
Avance Logic	2101	SVGA
	2228	SVGA

Company	Card	Server
	2301	SVGA
	2302	SVGA
	2308	SVGA
	2401	SVGA
Binar Graphics	AnyView	SVGA
Boca	Vortex (Sierra RAMDAC)	AGX
California Graphics	SunTracer 6000	SVGA
Canopus Co.	PowerWindow 3DV	SVGA
	Total-3D	SVGA
Cardex	Challenger (Pro)	SVGA
	Cobra	SVGA
	Trio64	S3
	Trio64Pro	S3
Chips & Technologies	CT64200	SVGA
	CT64300	SVGA
	CT65520	SVGA
	CT65525	SVGA
	CT65530	SVGA
	CT65535	SVGA
	CT65540	SVGA
	CT65545	SVGA
	CT65546	SVGA
	CT65548	SVGA
	CT65550	SVGA
	CT65554	SVGA
	CT65555	SVGA
	CT68554	SVGA
	CT69000	SVGA
Cirrus Logic	GD542x	SVGA
	GD543x	SVGA
	GD544x	SVGA

continues

TABLE B.18 CONTINUED

Company	Card	Server
	GD5462	SVGA
	GD5464	SVGA
	GD5465	SVGA
	GD5480	SVGA
	GD62xx (Laptop)	SVGA
	GD64xx (Laptop)	SVGA
	GD754x (Laptop)	SVGA
Colorgraphic	Dual Lightning	SVGA
Compaq	Armada 7380DMT	S3
	Armada 7730MT	S3
Creative Labs	3D Blaster PCI (Verite 1000)	SVGA
	Blaster Exxtreme	3DLabs
	Graphics Blaster 3D	SVGA
	Graphics Blaster Eclipse (OEM model CT6510)	SVGA
	Graphics Blaster MA201	SVGA
	Graphics Blaster MA202	SVGA
	Graphics Blaster MA302	SVGA
	Graphics Blaster MA334	SVGA
DFI-WG1000		SVGA
DFI-WG5000		SVGA
DFI-WG6000		SVGA
DSV3325		SVGA
DSV3326		S3
DataExpert	DSV3325	SVGA
	DSV3365	S3
Dell	S3 805	S3
	onboard ET4000	SVGA
Diamond	Edge 3D	SVGA
	Fire GL 1000	3DLabs
	Fire GL 1000 PRO	3DLabs
	Fire GL 3000	3DLabs
	Speedstar (Plus)	SVGA

Company	Card	Server
	Speedstar 24	SVGA
	Speedstar 24X (not fully supported)	SVGA
	Speedstar 64	SVGA
	Speedstar A50	SVGA
	Speedstar HiColor	SVGA
	Speedstar Pro (not SE)	SVGA
	Speedstar Pro 1100	SVGA
	Speedstar Pro SE (CLGD5430/5434)	SVGA
	Speedstar 64 Graphics 2000/2200	SVGA
	Stealth 24	S3
	Stealth 3D 2000	SVGA
	Stealth 3D 2000 Pro	SVGA
	Stealth 3D 3000	SVGA
	Stealth 3D 4000	SVGA
	Stealth 32	SVGA
	Stealth 64 DRAM SE	S3
	Stealth 64 DRAM w/ S3 SDAC	S3
	Stealth 64 DRAM w/ S3 Trio64	S3
	Stealth 64 VRAM	S3
	Stealth 64 Video VRAM (TI RAMDAC)	S3
	Stealth II S220	SVGA
	Stealth Pro	S3
	Stealth VRAM	S3
	Stealth Video 2500	SVGA
	Stealth Video DRAM	S3
	Stealth 64 Graphics 2001 Series	SVGA
	Stealth 64 Graphics 2xx0 series (864 + SDAC)	S3
	Stealth 64 Graphics 2xx0 series (Trio64)	S3
	Stealth 64 Video 2001 series (2121/2201)	S3
	Stealth 64 Video 2120/2200	S3

continues

TABLE B.18 CONTINUED

Company	Card	Server
	Stealth 64 3200	S3
	Stealth 64 Video 3240/3400 (IBM RAMDAC)	S3
	Stealth 64 Video 3240/3400 (TI RAMDAC)	S3
	Viper 330	SVGA
	Viper 550	SVGA
	Viper PCI 2MB	P9000
	Viper Pro Video	SVGA
	Viper VLB 2MB	P9000
EIZO (VRAM)		AGX
ELSA	ERAZOR II	
	GLoria-4	S3
	GLoria-8	S3
	GLoria Synergy	3DLabs
	GLoria-L	3DLabs
	GLoria-L/MX	3DLabs
	GLoria-S	3DLabs
	GLoria-XL	3DLabs
	Victory ERAZOR	SVGA
	Victory 3D	SVGA
	Victory 3DX	SVGA
	Winner 1000/T2D	S3
	Winner 1000 R3D	SVGA
	Winner 1000AVI (AT&T 20C409 version)	S3
	Winner 1000AVI (SDAC version)	S3
	Winner 1000ISA	S3
	Winner 1000Pro w/ S3 SDAC	S3
	Winner 1000Pro w/ STG1700 or AT&T RAMDAC	S3
	Winner 1000Pro/X	S3
	Winner 1000TRIO	S3

Company	Card	Server
	Winner 1000TRIO/V	S3
	Winner 1000TwinBus	S3
	Winner 1000VL	S3
	Winner 2000	S3
	Winner 2000 Office	3DLabs
	Winner 2000AVI	S3
	Winner 2000AVI/3D	SVGA
	Winner 2000PRO-2	S3
	Winner 2000PRO-4	S3
	Winner 2000PRO/X-2	S3
	Winner 2000PRO/X-4	S3
	Winner 2000PRO/X-8	S3
	Winner 3000	SVGA
	Winner 3000-L-42	SVGA
	Winner 3000-M-22	SVGA
	Winner 3000-S	SVGA
Epson	CardPC (onboard)	SVGA
ET3000 (Generic)		SVGA
ET4000 (Generic)		SVGA
ET4000/W32i, W32p (Generic)		SVGA
ET4000/W32 (Generic)		SVGA
ET6000 (Generic)		SVGA
ET6100 (Generic)		SVGA
ExpertColor	DSV3325	SVGA
	DSV3365	S3
Generic VGA Compatible		VGA16
Genoa	5400	SVGA
	8500VL (-28)	SVGA

continues

TABLE B.18 CONTINUED

Company	Card	Server
	8900 Phantom 32i	SVGA
	Phantom 64i w/ S3 SDAC	S3
	VideoBlitz III AV	S3
Hercules	Dynamite	SVGA
	Dynamite 128/Video	SVGA
	Dynamite Power	SVGA
	Dynamite Pro	SVGA
	Graphite HG210	AGX
	Graphite Power	AGX
	Graphite Pro	AGX
	Graphite Terminator 64	S3
	Graphite Terminator 64/DRAM	S3
	Graphite Terminator Pro 64	S3
	Stingray	SVGA
	Stingray 64/V w/ ICS5342	SVGA
	Stingray 64/V w/ ZoomDAC	SVGA
	Stingray 128 3D	SVGA
	Stingray Pro	SVGA
	Stingray Pro/V	SVGA
	Terminator 3D/DX	SVGA
	Terminator 64/3D	SVGA
	Terminator 64/Video	S3
	Thriller3D	SVGA
Integral	Flashpoint	SVGA
Intel	5430	SVGA
Interay	PMC Viper	SVGA
JAX	8241	S3
Jaton	Video 58P	SVGA
	Video 70P	SVGA
Jazz Multimedia	G-Force 128	SVGA
LeadTek	WinFast 3D S600	SVGA

Company	Card	Server
	WinFast 3D S680	SVGA
	WinFast S200	SVGA
	WinFast S430	S3
	WinFast S510	S3
	WinFast 2300	3DLabs
MELCO	WGP-VG4S	SVGA
	WGP-VX8	SVGA
MSI	MS-4417	SVGA
Matrox	Comet	SVGA
	Marvel II	SVGA
	Millennium 2/4/8MB	SVGA
	Millennium (MGA)	SVGA
	Millennium II 4/8/16 MB	SVGA
	Millennium II AGP	SVGA
	Millennium G200 4/8/16MB	SVGA
	Millennium G200 SD 4/8/16MB	SVGA
	Mystique	SVGA
	Mystique G200 4/8/16MB	SVGA
	Productiva G100 4/8MB	SVGA
MediaGX		SVGA
MediaVision	Proaxcel 128	SVGA
Mirage	Z-128	SVGA
Miro	Crystal 10SD w/ GenDAC	S3
	Crystal 12SD	S3
	Crystal 16S	S3
	Crystal 20SD PCI w/ S3 SDAC	S3
	Crystal 20SD VLB w/ S3 SDAC (BIOS 3.xx)	S3
	Crystal 20SD w/ ICD2061A (BIOS 2.xx)	S3
	Crystal 20SD w/ ICS2494 (BIOS 1.xx)	S3
	Crystal 20SV	S3
	Crystal 22SD	S3

continues

Table B.18 Continued

Company	Card	Server
	Crystal 40SV	S3
	Crystal 80SV	S3
	Crystal 8S	S3
	Crystal DVD	SVGA
	Crystal VRX	SVGA
	MiroVideo 20TD	SVGA
	Video 20SV	S3
	MiroMedia 3D	SVGA
NeoMagic	Laptop/Notebook	SVGA
Number Nine	FX Motion 331	S3
	FX Motion 332	SVGA
	FX Motion 531	S3
	FX Motion 771	S3
	FX Vision 330	S3
	GXE Level 10/11/12	S3
	GXE Level 14/16	S3
	GXE64	S3
	GXE64 Pro	S3
	GXE64 w/ S3 Trio64	S3
	Imagine I-128 (2-8 MB)	I128
	Imagine I-128 Series 2 (2-4 MB)	I128
	Imagine-128-T2R	I128
	Revolution 3D AGP (4-8MB SGRAM)	I128
	Visual 9FX Reality 332	SVGA
Oak	87 ISA (generic)	SVGA
	87 VLB (generic)	SVGA
	ISA card (generic)	SVGA
Ocean/Octek	AVGA-20	SVGA
	Combo-26	SVGA
	Combo-28	SVGA
	VL-VGA-26	SVGA
	VL-VGA-28	SVGA
	VL-VGA-1000	SVGA

Company	Card	Server
Orchid	Celsius (AT&T RAMDAC)	AGX
	Celsius (Sierra RAMDAC)	AGX
	Fahrenheit 1280	S3
	Fahrenheit VA	S3
	Fahrenheit 1280+	S3
	Fahrenheit Video 3D	SVGA
	Kelvin 64	SVGA
	Kelvin 64 VLB Rev. A	SVGA
	Kelvin 64 VLB Rev. B	SVGA
	P9000 VLB	P9000
Paradise	Accelerator Value	SVGA
Paradise/WD	90CXX	SVGA
PC-Chips	M567 Mainboard	SVGA
Pixelview	Combo TV 3D AGP (Prolink)	SVGA
	Combo TV Pro (Prolink)	SVGA
Rendition	Verite 1000	SVGA
	Verite 2x00	SVGA
Revolution	3D (T2R)	I128
RIVA	TNT	SVGA
	128	SVGA
S3	801/805 (Generic)	S3
	801/805 w/ AT&T 20C490 RAMDAC	S3
	801/805 w/ AT&T 20C490 RAMDAC and ICD2061A	S3
	801/805 w/ Chrontel 8391	S3
	801/805 w/ S3 GenDAC	S3
	801/805 w/ SC1148{2,3,4} RAMDAC	S3
	801/805 w/ SC1148{5,7,9} RAMDAC	S3
	864 (Generic)	S3
	864 w/ AT&T 20C498 or 21C498	S3
	864 w/ SDAC (86C716)	S3
	864 w/ STG1703	S3
	868 (Generic)	S3

continues

TABLE B.18 CONTINUED

Company	Card	Server
	868 w/ AT&T 20C409	S3
	868 w/ AT&T 20C498 or 21C498	S3
	868 w/ SDAC (86C716)	S3
	86C260 (Generic)	SVGA
	86C280 (Generic)	SVGA
	86C325 (Generic)	SVGA
	86C357 (Generic)	SVGA
	86C365 (Trio3D) (not fully supported)	VGA16
	86C375 (Generic)	SVGA
	86C385 (Generic)	SVGA
	86C391 (Savage3D) (not fully supported)	VGA16
	86C764 (Generic)	S3
	86C765 (Generic)	S3
	86C775 (Generic)	S3
	86C785 (Generic)	S3
	86C801 (Generic)	S3
	86C805 (Generic)	S3
	86C864 (Generic)	S3
	86C868 (Generic)	S3
	86C911 (Generic)	S3
	86C924 (Generic)	S3
	86C928 (Generic)	S3
	86C964 (Generic)	S3
	86C968 (Generic)	S3
	86C988 (Generic)	SVGA
	86CM65	S3
	911/924 (Generic)	S3
	924 w/ SC1148 DAC	S3
	928 (Generic)	S3
	964 (Generic)	S3
	968 (Generic)	S3

Company	Card	Server
	Aurora64V+ (Generic)	S3
	Savage3D (not fully supported)	VGA16
	Trio3D (not fully supported)	VGA16
	Trio32 (Generic)	S3
	Trio64 (Generic)	S3
	Trio64+ (Generic)	S3
	Trio64V2 (Generic)	S3
	Trio64V2/DX (Generic)	S3
	Trio64V2/GX (Generic)	S3
	ViRGE	SVGA
	ViRGE (Generic)	SVGA
	ViRGE/DX (Generic)	SVGA
	ViRGE/GX (Generic)	SVGA
	ViRGE/GX2 (Generic)	SVGA
	ViRGE/MX (Generic)	SVGA
	ViRGE/MX+ (Generic)	SVGA
	ViRGE/VX (Generic)	SVGA
	Vision864 (Generic)	S3
	Vision868 (Generic)	S3
	Vision964 (Generic)	S3
	Vision968 (Generic)	S3
SHARP	9080	S3
	9090	S3
SNI	PC5H W32	SVGA
	Scenic W32	SVGA
SPEA	Mercury 64	S3
	Mirage	S3
SPEA/V7	Mercury	S3
	Mirage P64	S3
	Mirage P64 w/ S3 Trio64	S3
	Mirage VEGA Plus	SVGA
	ShowTime Plus	SVGA

continues

Table B.18 Continued

Company	Card	Server
STB	Horizon	SVGA
	Horizon Video	SVGA
	LightSpeed	SVGA
	LightSpeed 128	SVGA
	MVP-2	SVGA
	MVP-2 PCI	SVGA
	MVP-2X	SVGA
	MVP-4 PCI	SVGA
	MVP-4X	SVGA
	Nitro (64)	SVGA
	Nitro 3D	SVGA
	Nitro 64 Video	SVGA
	nvidia 128	SVGA
	Pegasus	S3
	Powergraph 64	S3
	Powergraph 64 Video	S3
	Powergraph X-24	S3
	Powergraph 3D	SVGA
	Velocity 3D	SVGA
	Velocity 64 Video	S3
	Velocity 128	SVGA
SiS	3D PRO AGP	SVGA
	5597	SVGA
	5598	SVGA
	6326	SVGA
	SG86C201	SVGA
	SG86C205	SVGA
	SG86C215	SVGA
	SG86C225	SVGA
Sierra	Screaming 3D	SVGA
Sigma	Concorde	SVGA
	Legend	SVGA

Company	Card	Server
Spider	Black Widow	AGX
	Black Widow Plus	AGX
	Tarantula 64	S3
	VLB Plus	SVGA
TechWorks	Thunderbolt	SVGA
	Ultimate 3D	SVGA
Toshiba	Tecra 540CDT	SVGA
	Tecra 550CDT	SVGA
	Tecra 750CDT	SVGA
	Tecra 750DVD	SVGA
Trident	3DImage975 (Generic)	SVGA
	3DImage975 AGP (Generic)	SVGA
	3DImage985 (Generic)	SVGA
	8900/9000 (Generic)	SVGA
	8900D (Generic)	SVGA
	Cyber9382 (Generic)	SVGA
	Cyber9385 (Generic)	SVGA
	Cyber9388 (Generic)	SVGA
	Cyber9397 (Generic)	SVGA
	TGUI9400CXi (Generic)	SVGA
	TGUI9420DGi (Generic)	SVGA
	TGUI9430DGi (Generic)	SVGA
	TGUI9440 (Generic)	SVGA
	TGUI9660 (Generic)	SVGA
	TGUI9680 (Generic)	SVGA
	TGUI9682 (Generic)	SVGA
	TGUI9685 (Generic)	SVGA
	TVGA8800BR (not fully supported)	VGA16
	TVGA8800CS (not fully supported)	VGA16
	TVGA9200CXr (Generic)	SVGA
Unsupported VGA Compatible		VGA16

continues

Table B.18 Continued

Company	Card	Server
VI720		SVGA
VL-41		S3
VidTech	FastMax P20	S3
VideoLogic	GrafixStar 300	S3
	GrafixStar 400	S3
	GrafixStar 500	S3
	GrafixStar 550	SVGA
	GrafixStar 560 (PCI/AGP)	SVGA
	GrafixStar 600	SVGA
	GrafixStar 700	S3
ViewTop PCI		SVGA
WD	90C24 (Laptop)	SVGA
	90C24A or 90C24A2 (Laptop)	SVGA
Weitek	P9100 (Generic)	SVGA
WinFast	3D S600	SVGA
	S200	SVGA
	S430	S3
	S510	S3
XGA-1 (ISA bus)		AGX
XGA-2 (ISA bus)		AGX

APPENDIX 

Loadable Module Parameters

This appendix contains lists of hardware parameters that are supported by the drivers included in the 2.2.1 Linux kernel.

A few guidelines must be specified up front to help with interpretation of the information:

- If the table heading says "Parameter," you specify exactly what is listed (in addition to any extra items in the "Possible Values" column; this generally applies when the parameter in question has an "=" and a value).
- If the table heading says "Option," replace the quoted text with the desired value (using the guidelines that are listed in the "Possible Values" column).

Following is an example. For the floppy driver, there is a parameter for users of IBM ThinkPad computers that indicates what kind of system is being used. If you are using a boot parameter to load the floppy driver, the text entered at the `boot:` prompt looks somewhat similar to the following:

```
linux floppy=thinkpad
```

Note

Boot parameters are always entered at the LILO `boot:` prompt that appears when you start your system. Note that LILO must be installed on your system for this to work. Also, you must always specify the name of the Linux boot option that was set up to boot Linux before you specify boot parameters. If you are in doubt regarding the name of the Linux boot option, press the Tab key at the `boot:` prompt; all boot option names are displayed.

With Ethernet drivers, there are options that can be specified. The position in the boot parameter line almost always affects how the option is interpreted by the driver.

For example, all Ethernet cards have similarly formatted boot parameter lines, each of which starts with an option called `IRQ` in the tables that follow. Specify the actual hardware interrupt for the card in this position of the boot parameter, not the string `IRQ` itself. The format for a basic Ethernet boot parameter line is as follows:

```
ether="IRQ","IO Port","Interface"
```

If the I/O port of an Ethernet card is 320 (specified as 0x320 to indicate to the driver that it is a hexadecimal value—all I/O port values are hexadecimal) and the IRQ is 10, the following can be entered at the Linux `boot:` prompt to boot with the appropriate network card I/O port:

```
boot: linux ether=10,0x320,eth0
```

This says to boot Linux and pass IRQ `10` and I/O port `0x320` to the card that is associated with the first Ethernet interface (eth0)

In cases in which there are both parameters and options for a specific driver, there will be sufficient indication to avoid confusion.

Caution

> Many of the following modules have default values that are probed for when the modules are loaded. Despite the capability to probe for these values, it is extremely dangerous to allow modules to probe for them. Quite often, some of the values for which the module probes are already assigned to other pieces of hardware, which causes the driver probe to either not initialize its hardware (best case scenario) or to lock up the computer (worst case scenario). Therefore, it is highly recommended that you specify parameters when you are loading modules if parameters are available to the driver.

In the following sections, many of the options allow `any valid xxx` to be specified. This says that any of the possible values that work specifically with the hardware can be entered. The settings for a parallel port provide an example of this: Because I/O port addresses on ports are typically either 0x278 or 0x378, it can be said that `any valid IO Port` for a parallel port implies those two addresses. Other I/O port addresses, such as 0x100 or 0x2000, are not included because they do not make sense for that particular type of hardware.

SCSI Interface Drivers

53c7,8xx.o

Boot Parameters

Format:

```
ncr53c700="Memory","IO Port","IRQ","DMA"
ncr53c700-66="Memory","IO Port","IRQ","DMA"
ncr53c710="Memory","IO Port","IRQ","DMA"
ncr53c720="Memory","IO Port","IRQ","DMA"

ncr53c810="Memory","IO Port","IRQ"
ncr53c820="Memory","IO Port","IRQ"
ncr53c825="Memory","IO Port","IRQ"
```

Option	Possible Values	Default Value
`Memory`	Any valid Memory start point	probed
`IO Port`	Any valid I/O Port	probed
`IRQ`	Any valid IRQ	probed
`DMA`	Any valid DMA channel	probed

Module Parameters

No module parameters are provided for this driver.

AM53C974.O

Boot parameter lines for this driver can be stacked at a `boot:` prompt—one for each target SCSI ID—if desired. For example, if there are two devices on an AM53C974 card that require parameters, more than one AM53C974 parameter can be specified at a LILO boot prompt:

```
boot: linux AM53C974=0,1,10,0 AM53C974=0,4,10,0
```

Boot Parameters

Format:

```
AM53C974="Host SCSI ID","Target SCSI ID","Max. Rate","Max. Offset"
```

Option	**Possible Values**	**Default Value**
`Host SCSI ID`	`0–7`	`7`
`Target SCSI ID`	`0–7`	none
`Max. Rate`	`3–10`	`5`
`Max. Offset`	`1–15` bytes, or `0` for `asynchronous`	`0`

Module Parameters

No module parameters are provided for this driver.

ADVANSYS.O

Boot Parameters

This boot parameter is for ISA card detection only. EISA and PCI controllers are always probed by the driver and initialized automatically, regardless of whether a boot parameter is used.

The AdvanSys driver can probe for up to four ISA cards at specific I/O Ports using this parameter. An optional fifth I/O Port is offered to enable debugging output (it is not a real I/O Port, obviously). Note that for this fifth I/O Port to be used, four other I/O Ports must first be specified. If only one AdvanSys controller is in the system, specify the first I/O Port using the standard hex format (`0x###`); use zeros for the next three; and then specify the debug I/O Port, using the syntax described in the following table.

Format:

```
advansys="IO Port"[,"IO Port","IO Port","IO Port"[,0xdeb#]]
```

Option	Possible Values	Default Value
IO Port	Any valid ISA I/O Port, or 0 for no I/O Port (see preceding note) (0x0 disables port scanning, as does specifying advansys= by itself with no parameters)	0x110, 0x210, 0x230, and 0x330 (first through fourth controllers, in order)

0xdeb#	Replace # with:
	0 = errors only
	1 = high-level tracing
	2–f = verbose tracing
		not set

Module Parameters

Format:

```
insmod advansys asc_iopflag=# asc_ioport=0x###[,0x###,0x###,0x###] asc_dbglvl=#
```

Parameter	Possible Values	Default Value

asc_iopflag=#	Replace # with:
	1 = enable I/O Port scanning
	0 = disable I/O Port scanning
		1

asc_ioport=0x###	Replace 0x### with any valid ISA I/O Port	0x110, 0x210, 0x230, and 0x330 (first through fourth controllers, in order)

asc_dbglvl=#	Replace # with:
	0 = errors only
	1 = high-level tracing
	2–f = verbose tracing
		not set

Note that there is no fifth I/O Port setting for debug output as there is with boot parameters; the asc_dbglvl parameter takes care of this.

AHA152X.O

Boot and module parameter lines for this driver can be stacked—one for each card—if desired. Increment the actual parameter name each time another card is added, though (that is, aha152x, aha152x1, aha152x2, aha152x3, and so on).

BOOT PARAMETERS

Format:

```
aha152x="IO Port","IRQ","Host SCSI ID","Reconnect","Parity","Synchronous",
"Reset Delay","Extended Translation"
aha152x1="IO Port","IRQ"",
aha152x2="IO Port","IRQ"", etc.
```

Option	Possible Values	Default Value
IO Port	0x140, 0x340	0x340
IRQ	9–12	11
Host SCSI ID	0–7	7
Reconnect	1 = enabled 0 = disabled	1
Parity	1 = enabled 0 = disabled	1
Synchronous	1 = enabled 0 = disabled	0
Reset Delay	Any integer value	100
Extended Translation	1 = enabled 0 = disabled	0

MODULE PARAMETERS

Format:

```
insmod aha152x aha152x="IO Port","IRQ","Host SCSI ID",
```

The actual module parameters match the preceding boot parameters.

AHA1542.O

BOOT PARAMETERS

Format:

```
aha1542="IO Port","Bus On","Bus Off","DMA Speed"
```

Option	Possible Values	Default Value
`IO Port`	`0x130`, `0x134`, `0x230`, `0x330`, `0x334` (probed at `0x330` and `0x334`) `0x234`, `0x330`, `0x334`	`0x330`, `0x334`
`Bus On`	`2–15` (microseconds)	`11`
`Bus Off`	`1–64`	`4`
`DMA Speed`	`5`, `6`, `7`, `8`, `10` (MB/sec.)	`5`

Module Parameters

No module parameters are provided for this driver.

AHA1740.O

This driver probes for all hardware settings. Therefore, no boot or module parameters are offered for this driver.

AIC7XXX.O

Two parameters—`override_term:0x###` and `stpwlev:0x###`—are not discussed here due to excessive complexity versus utility issues (in other words, trying to explain the difficult syntax of these parameters is not worth the time because very few people ever bother to use them). If you want to look in to these parameters for whatever reason, the /usr/src/linux/drivers/scsi/README.aic7xxx file contains the necessary information.

Boot Parameters

Format:

```
aic7xxx=no_reset,reverse_scan,extended,irq_trigger:#,verbose,no_probe,\
panic_on_abort,dump_card,dump_sequencer,pci_parity:#,tag_info:{...}
```

Parameter	Descriptions/ Possible Values	Default Value
`no_reset`	Disables the SCSI reset delay at system startup	not set
`reverse_scan`	Reverses the order in which multiple SCSI cards are initialized	not set
`extended`	Enables extended translation	not set

continues

continued

Parameter	Descriptions/ Possible Values	Default Value
`irq_trigger:#`	Replace # with: `1` = level triggered interrupts `0` = edge triggered interrupts	probed
`verbose`	Enables verbose messages	not set
`no_probe`	Disables VLB based 2842 and EISA controller probing	not set
`panic_on_abort`	Causes the kernel to panic when the first abort or reset is encountered (for debugging purposes only)	not set
`dump_card`	Tells the driver to display the entirety of all configuration information when the driver initializes	not set
`dump_sequencer`	Same as `dump_card`, but the sequencer RAM is what is dumped	not set
`pci_parity:#`	Replace # with: no number = even parity checking is enabled `1–255` = odd parity checking is enabled `0` = do not check parity	`0`
`tag_info:{...}`	See description that follows	not set

Note

There are extended bitmask options for the `verbose` parameter that was listed previously. These bitmask options can be found in the /usr/src/linux/drivers/scsi/aic7xxx.c source code file. If you want to explore these options, open that file in a pager, such as less, and search for the `#define VERBOSE_XXXXXX` lines.

Description of `tag_info:{...} parameter`

By default, tag queuing is enabled with this driver for all devices. However, individual aic7xxx controllers (whether they are cards or chipsets on a motherboard) and individual devices connected to those controllers can have different settings.

The top-level syntax for this parameter looks similar to the following:

```
tag_info:{{First Controller},{Second Controller},{Third Controller},...}
```


Everything following `tag_info:` must be enclosed in an all-encompassing set of braces. Within each subordinate set of braces are settings for devices on the individual controllers, starting with the first, followed by the second, and so on. Within each set of braces for each interface, a comma-delimited list of tag queue depths can be specified, starting with the device on ID `0` and incrementing through the remaining device IDs on that controller.

Possible settings for each ID on each controller break down as follows:

Value	Description
`0`	Use default tag queue depth (this is the default even if no `0` is specified)
`1–254`	Set tag queue depth to the specified value (it is recommended that nothing higher than `32` be selected here)
`255`	Disable tag queuing entirely for the associated ID

For example, say that there are two aic7xxx controllers in your system, and you want the first ID (ID0) to use a tag queue depth of `12`, and the fourth ID (ID3) to use a tag queue depth of `8`. In addition to that, the third ID (ID2) on the second controller needs a tag queue depth of `32`. The following syntax works for these settings:

```
aic7xxx=tag_info:{{12,,,8},{,,32}}
```

Note that there are some comma-delimited positions that contain no values. The IDs that are associated with these positions simply use the default settings for the controller. Also, you probably noted that not all IDs were given comma-delimited positions in the braces; whatever IDs are not specified also use the controller's default settings. Regardless of what the ID is and regardless of which controller it is on, you must always contain information for individual controllers within their own braces, and you must always start within those braces at that controller's ID0.

MODULE PARAMETERS

Format:

```
insmod aic7xxx aic7xxx=' no_reset.reverse_scan.extended.irq_trigger:#.verbose.\
7895_irq_hack:#.pci_parity:#.tag_info:{...}'
```

As you can see, the format is the same for module parameters as it is for boot parameters with this driver, except that the entire parameter line after `aic7xxx=` must be enclosed in quotes, and all commas must be replaced with periods.

ATP870U.O

No boot or module parameters are provided for this driver.

BUSLOGIC.O

BOOT PARAMETERS

Format:

```
BusLogic=IO:0x###,NoProbe,NoProbeISA,NoProbePCI,NoSortPCI,MultiMasterFirst,\
FlashPointFirst,QueueDepth:#,TaggedQueuing:????,ErrorRecovery:????,\
BusSettleTime:#,InhibitTargetInquiry,TraceProbe,
TraceHardwareReset,TraceConfiguration,TraceErrors,Debug
```

Parameters for multiple BusLogic cards can be stacked either on the boot parameter command line one after the other (that is, `BusLogic=...`, `Buslogic=...`, and so on) or all in one `BusLogic=` *boot parameter*, with each card's settings separated by semicolons.

Parameter	Possible Values	Default Value
`IO:0x###`	Replace `0x###` with an ISA I/O port for which to probe (only used for ISA controllers)	If there is no `IO:0x###` or `NoProbeISA` parameter specified, the following ISA ports are probed: 0x330, 0x334, 0x230, 0x234, 0x130, and 0x134
`NoProbe`	Disables all probing (causing the driver to not initialize any BusLogic controllers)	not set

Parameter	Possible Values	Default Value
`NoProbeISA`	Disables all ISA probing, causing only PCI controllers to be probed	not set
`NoProbePCI`	Disables all PCI probing, causing only ISA controllers to be seen (and PCI MultiMaster controllers with ISA mode set to primary or alternate)	not set
`NoSortPCI`	Allows the PCI BIOS to determine the order in which PCI controllers are initialized	not set
`MultiMasterFirst`	Causes MultiMaster controllers to be initialized before FlashPoint controllers	not set
`FlashPointFirst`	Causes FlashPoint controllers to be initialized before MultiMaster controllers	not set
`QueueDepth:#` (or `QD:#`)	Replace # with the depth at which all tagged queuing-capable devices on the controller are to operate. Optionally, individual devices can have their depth set with a comma-delimited list of depths enclosed in braces: `QueueDepth:[8,,,12]`	Use controller default

continues

continued

Parameter	Possible Values	Default Value
	Omitted values tell the driver to use defaults for the associated device (in the preceding example, the first device has a depth of `8`, the second and third use defaults, and the fourth uses `12`).	
`TaggedQueuing:????` (or `TQ:????`)	Replace `????` with: `Default` = defaults are used, determined by the firmware `Enable` = enables tagged queuing for all devices, regardless of firmware limitations `Disable` = disables all tagged queuing for all devices `<target spec>` = enable queuing on specified devices in a list of the following characters: `Y` = enable `N` = disable `X` = accept firmware defaults	not set
`ErrorRecovery:????` (or `ER:????`)	Replace `????` with: `Default` = driver chooses between the next two options based on the recommendation of the SCSI subsystem	

Parameter	Possible Values	Default Value
	`HardReset` = initiate a SCSI adapter `BusDeviceReset` = attempts to send a reset signal to the target spec (see the following); if the SCSI Bus does not reset, a hard reset signal is sent to the adapter `None` = disables error recovery entirely *`<target spec>`* = enable error recovery on specified devices in a list of the following characters: `D` = use `Default` as described previously `H` = use `HardReset` as described previously `B` = use `BusDeviceReset` as described previously `N` = use `None` as described previously The first character is for ID0, the second is for ID1, the third is for ID2, and so on. No spaces are allowed between letters (for example, `DBNNH`); if the list stops before all IDs are specified, `Default` (or `D`) is used for those that remain.	

continues

continued

Parameter	Possible Values	Default Value
`BusSettleTime:#` (or `BST:#`)	Replace `#` with the number of seconds to wait between SCSI hard resets and sending new SCSI commands.	2
`InhibitTarget Inquiry`	Inhibits `Inquire Target Devices` and `Inquire Installed Devices` inquiries on MultiMaster controllers.	not set
`TraceProbe`	Enables tracing of controller probing	not set
`TraceHardwareReset`	Enables tracing of controller hardware reset	not set
`TraceConfiguration`	Enables tracing of controller configuration	not set
`TraceErrors`	Enables tracing of errors resulting from SCSI commands	not set
`Debug`	Enables all debugging options (all the way back to TraceProbe)	not set

MODULE PARAMETERS

Format:

```
insmod BusLogic
'BusLogic_Options="option1,option2,...;option1,option2,...;option1,\
option2,...""'
```

If multiple BusLogic controllers are in use, each separate controller can have its own set of options on the same line, with semicolons separating each controller's set of options from the next. The options are exactly the same as the boot parameters that were listed in the preceding table. Note that the entire module parameter line must be enclosed in single quotes, and everything following `BusLogic_Option=` must be enclosed in double quotes.

DTC.O

BOOT PARAMETERS

Format:

```
dtc="Memory Base","IRQ"
```

Option	Possible Values	Default Value
`Memory Base`	Any valid Memory Base (probed at 0xcc000, 0xc8000, 0xdc000, and 0xd8000)	probed
`IRQ`	Any valid IRQ (probed at 10, 11, 12, and 15)	probed

MODULE PARAMETERS

No module parameters are offered for this driver.

EATA.O

BOOT PARAMETERS

Format:

```
eata="IO Port"[,"IO Port"],lc:?,tc:?,mq:##,tm:#,ls:?,rs:?,et:?eh:?
```

or

```
eata=0
```

Parameter	Possible Values	Default Value
`IO Port`	Any valid I/O Port. More than one can be specified, in order, if more than one controller exists (probed at 0x1f0 (ISA) first; then, PCI SCSI controllers; then 0x1c88 through 0xfc88 in 0x1000 steps (EISA); then 0x170, 0x230, and 0x330—ISA again)	probed
`lc:?`	Replace `?` with: `y` = enable linked commands	`n`

continues

continued

Parameter	Possible Values	Default Value
	n = disable linked commands	
tc:?	Replace ? with: y = enable tagged commands n = disable tagged commands	n
mq:##	Replace # with the tagged queue depth (between 2 and 32, inclusive)	16

tm:#	Replace # with:
	0 = use head/ordered/simple queue tag sequences
	1 = use only simple queue tags
	2 = use only head queue tags
	3 = use only ordered queue tags
		0

ls:?	Replace ? with: y = enable linked statistics n = disable linked statistics	n
rs:?	Replace ? with: y = enable reverse scanning of PCI boards n = disable reverse scanning	n
et:?	Replace ? with: y = enable extended translation n = disable extended translation	n

`eh:?`	Replace `?` with: `y` = use new SCSI code (2.2.x Linux kernels only!) `n` = use old SCSI code	`n`

The optional boot parameter `eata=0` completely disables the driver.

Module Parameters

Format:

```
insmod eata io_port=0x### linked_comm=# tagged_comm=# max_queue_depth=## \
tag_mode=# link_statistics=# rev_scan=# ext_tran=# use_new_eh_code=#
```

Parameter	**Possible Values**	**Default Value**
`io_port=0x###`	Replace `0x###` with a comma-delimited list of I/O Port addresses to use (see `IO Port` boot parameter for listings of probed ports)	probed
`linked_comm=#`	Replace `#` with: `1` = enable `0` = disable	`0`
`tagged_comm=#`	Replace `#` with: `1` = enable `0` = disable	`0`
`max_queue_depth=##`	Replace `#` with the tagged queue depth (between 2 and 32, inclusive)	`16`
`tag_mode=#`	Replace `#` with: `1` = enable `0` = disable	`0`
`link_statistics=#`	Replace `#` with: `1` = enable `0` = disable	`0`
`rev_scan=#`	Replace `#` with: `1` = enable `0` = disable	`0`

Part VII App C

continues

continued

Parameter	Possible Values	Default Value

`ext_tran=#`	Replace # with:
	1 = enable
	0 = disable
		0

`use_new_eh_code=#`	Replace # with:
	1 = enable (only for 2.2.x Linux kernels!)
	0 = disable
		0

EATA_DMA.O

No boot or module parameters are provided for this driver.

EATA_PIO.O

No boot or module parameters are provided for this driver.

FDOMAIN.O

Boot Parameters

Format:

`fdomain="IO Port","IRQ","Adapter ID"`

Option	Possible Values	Default Value
`IO Port`	Any valid I/O Port (probed at 0x140, 0x150, 0x160, and 0x170)	probed
`IRQ`	Any valid IRQ (probed at 3, 5, 10, 11, 12, 14, and 15)	probed
`Adapter ID`	0–7	7

Module Parameters

`insmod fdomain fdomain="IO Port","IRQ","Adapter ID"`

The module parameter descriptions exactly match those of the similarly named boot parameters.

g_NCR5380.o

Boot Parameters

Format:

```
ncr5380.o="IO Port","IRQ"
```

or

```
ncr53c400="IO Port","IRQ"
```

Option	Possible Values	Default Value
`IO Port`	Any valid I/O Port	None (except for the Trantor 130B, which defaults to 0x350)
`IRQ`	Any valid IRQ, or: `-1` = no IRQ or DMA interrupt `-2` = probe for an IRQ	None (except for the Trantor 130B, which defaults to `5`)

Module Parameters

Format:

```
insmod g_NCR5380 ncr_irq=# ncr_addr=0x### ncr_dma=## ncr_5380=# ncr_53c400=#
```

Parameter	Possible Values	Default Value
`ncr_irq=#`	Replace # with a valid IRQ, or: `254` = probe for an IRQ `255` = no IRQ or DMA interrupt	none
`ncr_addr=0x###`	Replace `0x###` with a valid I/O Port (for port mapped cards such as NCR5380) or a valid Memory Base (for memory mapped cards such as NCR53C400)	none
`ncr_dma=##`	Replace `##` with the DMA channel	none
`ncr_5300=#`	Replace # with: `0` = specifies an NCR5380 adapter `1` = specifies a non-NCR5380 adapter	none

continues

continued

Parameter	Possible Values	Default Value
`ncr_53c400=#`	Replace # with: `0` = specifies an NCR53C400 adapter `1` = specifies a non-NCR53C400 adapter	none

GDTH.O

BOOT PARAMETERS

Format:

```
gdth="IRQ"[,"IRQ2","IRQ3",...],disable=?,reserve_mode:#,reserve_list:C,T,B,L\
[,C,T,B,L,...],reverse_scan:?,max_ids:#,rescan:?
```

or

```
gdth=0
```

Option	Possible Values	Default Value
`IRQ[2,3,4,...]`	Any valid EISA IRQ (for multiple cards, list the IRQs in order)	probed
`disable:?`	Replace `?` with: `Y` = disable the driver `N` = do not disable the driver	`N`
`reserve_mode:#`	Replace # with: `0` = reserve no drives for the “raw” service `1` = reserve only removable drives that did not initialize `2` = reserve all drives that did not initialize	none
`reserve_list: C,B,T,L[,C,T, B,L,...]`	Replace letters with the following: `C` = controller number `B` = channel number	none

Option	Possible Values	Default Value
	T = target number L = LUN number (repeat the sequence for multiple drive reservations)	
reverse_scan:?	Replace ? with: Y = reverse the PCI controller scan order N = do not reverse the PCI controller scan order	N
max_ids:#	Replace # with the maximum target ID count per channel	127
rescan:?	Replace ? with: Y = rescan all channels and IDs N = use all devices found until now	N

The optional boot parameter gdth=0 disables the driver entirely.

Module Parameters

Format:

```
insmod gdth disable=# reserve_mode=# reserve_list=C,B,T,L[,C,B,T,L,...] reverse_\
scan=# max_ids=# rescan=#
```

The descriptions of the various module parameters for this driver exactly match the similarly named boot parameters. The valid options are the same as well, except all instances of Y (yes) are now represented as 1 and all instances of N (no) are now represented as 0.

GVP11.O

Boot Parameters

Format:

```
gvp11=0xFFFFFFFE
```

Option	Possible Values	Default Value
0xFFFFFFFE	Force DMA to use 32-bit address space	DMA uses 24-bit address space

Module Parameters

No module parameters are provided for this driver.

I91USCSI.O

No boot or module parameters are provided for this driver.

IN2000.O

BOOT PARAMETERS

Format:

```
in2000=ioport:0x###,noreset,period:##,disconnect:#,debug:#,proc:#
```

Parameter	Possible Values	Default Value
`ioport=0x###`	Replace `0x###` with any valid I/O Port (probed at 0x100, 0x110, 0x200, and 0x220)	probed
`noreset`	Prevents the SCSI bus from resetting upon startup	not set
`nosync:#`	Replace # with a bitmask value representing the SCSI devices on which you want to prevent sync negotiation (the first seven bits represent the first seven possible devices; `1` means *enable*, `0` means *disable*)	not set
`period:##`	Replace ## with the minimum number of nanoseconds in a SCSI transfer period (options: 250–1000)	`500`
`disconnect:#`	Replace # with: `0` = never allow disconnects `1` = use adaptive disconnects `2` = always allow disconnects	`1`

Parameter	Possible Values	Default Value
`debug:#`	Replace # with the option that matches the desired debug output: `0` = test messages `1` = FIFO messages `2` = queue command messages `3` = execute messages `4` = interrupt messages `5` = transfer messages	none
`proc:#`	Replace # with the option that matches the desired `/proc` output: `0` = version `1` = information `2` = totals `3` = connected `4` = input queue `5` = disc queue `6` = test `7` = stop	none

PART VII

APP C

MODULE PARAMETERS

Format:

```
insmod in2000 setup_strings= ioport:0x###,noreset,period:##,disconnect:#,\
debug:#,proc:#
```

The module parameters exactly match the boot parameters (see the preceding table for details), except the string that precedes the parameters changes from `in2000=` to `setup_strings=` for module parameters.

INI9100.O

No boot or module parameters are provided for this driver.

IMM.O

No boot or module parameters are provided for this driver.

MEGARAID.O

No boot or module parameters are provided for this driver.

NCR53C406A.O

BOOT PARAMETERS

Format:

```
ncr53c406a="IO Port","IRQ","Fast PIO"
```

Option	Possible Values	Default Value
`IO Port`	Any valid I/O Port (probed at 0x230, 0x280, 0x290, 0x300, 0x310, 0x330, 0x340, 0x348, and 0x350)	probed
`IRQ`	Any valid IRQ (probed at 10, 11, 12, and 15; `0` disables the use of IRQs)	probed
`Fast PIO`	`1` = enable fast PIO `0` = enable slow mode	`1`

MODULE PARAMETERS

No module parameters are provided for this driver.

NCR53C8XX.O

BOOT PARAMETERS

Format:

```
ncr53c8xx=mpar:?,spar:?,disc:?,specf:?,ultra:?,fsn:?,tags:#/t#[t#t#...]q#\
[/t#[t#t#...]q#...],sync:##,verb:#,debug:#,burst:##,led:#,wide:#,settle:##,diff:#,
\
irqm:#,revprob:?,pcifix:#,nvram:?,buschk:#
```

or

```
ncr53c8xx=safe:y
```

Parameter	Possible Values	Default Value
`mpar:?`	Replace `?` with: `y` = enable master parity checking `n` = disable master parity checking	`y`

Parameter	Possible Values	Default Value
`spar:?`	Replace `?` with: `y` = enable SCSI parity checking `n` = disable SCSI parity checking	`y`
`disc:?`	Replace `?` with: `y` = allow SCSI disconnects `n` = forbid SCSI disconnects	`y`
`specf:?`	Replace `?` with: `y` or `1` = enable special features `n` or `0` = disable special features `3` = enable special features except for Memory Write And Invalidate (only valid for 810A, 825A, 860 and 875 controllers)	`3`
`ultra:?` (Only applies to 53c860/875/895 controllers)	Replace `?` with: `1` = enable ultra SCSI support `2` = enable Ultra 2 `n` = disable ultra SCSI support (only valid for 860 and 875 controllers)	`1`
`fsn:?`	Replace `?` with: `y` = force synchronous negotiation `n` = do not force synchronous negotiation	`n`
`tags:#/t#[t#t#...]q#[/t#[t#t#...]q#...]`	Replace the first `#` with: `0` or `1` = disable tagged command queuing	`0`

continues

continued

Parameter	Possible Values	Default Value
	2 or higher = enable tagged command queuing, setting the depth to the specified number. Tagged queue depths can be specified after the first #. Each controller's settings is enclosed within two / delimiters, with any number of devices specified within. Different queue depths within each /.../ set are separated with a hyphen. An example is in order: To set a queue depth of 16 on targets 1 and 5 on the first controller, a depth of 24 on target 6 on the same controller, a depth of 16 for target 3 on the second controller, and a depth of 10 on all other targets on all other controllers, the `tags:` parameter looks similar to this: `tags:10/t1t5q16-t6q24/t3q16`	

`sync:##`	Replace # with:
	255 = disable synchronous (forcing asynchronous) transfer mode
		50

Parameter	Possible Values	Default Value
	10 = Ultra-2 SCSI 40 MB/sec. 11 = Ultra-2 SCSI 33 MB/sec. Less than 25 = Ultra SCSI 20 MB/sec. Less than 50 = Fast SCSI-2	

verb:#	Replace # with:
	0 = minimal verbosity level
	1 = normal verbosity level
	2 = extreme verbosity level
		1

debug:#	Replace # with:
	0 = clear debug flags
	or an integer obtained by combining the values of the following options:
	DEBUG_ALLOC 0x1
	DEBUG_PHASE 0x2
	DEBUG_POLL 0x4
	DEBUG_QUEUE 0x8
	DEBUG_RESULT 0x10
	DEBUG_SCATTER 0x20
	DEBUG_SCRIPT 0x40
	DEBUG_TINY 0x80
	DEBUG_TIMING 0x100
	DEBUG_NEGO 0x200
	DEBUG_TAGS 0x400
	DEBUG_FREEZE 0x800
	DEBUG_RESTART 0x1000
		0

burst:##	Replace # with:
	0 = disable burst
	255 = get burst length
		7

continues

continued

Parameter	Possible Values	Default Value
	from initial I/O settings or an integer that is log base 2 of the maximum burst transfer (0 = 1, 1 = 2, 2 = 4, 3 = 8, 4 = 16, 5 = 32, and so on)	
`led:#`	Replace # with: `1` = enable LED support `0` = disable LED support (LED support cannot be enabled unless your motherboard uses an SDMS BIOS)	`0`
`wide:#`	Replace # with: `1` = enable wide SCSI `0` = disable wide SCSI	`1`
`settle:##`	Replace ## with settle time in seconds	`2`
`diff:#`	Replace # with: `0` = never set up differential mode `1` = set up differential mode if BIOS has set it `2` = always set up differential mode `3` = set differential mode if GPIO3 is not set	`0`
`irqm:#`	Replace # with: `0` = "always open drain" IRQ mode `1` = "same as initial settings" IRQ mode `2` = "always totem pole" IRQ mode	`0`

Parameter	Possible Values	Default Value
`revprob:?`	Replace `?` with: `n` = probe chip IDs in this order: 810, 815, 820, 860, 875, 885, 895, 896 `y` = reverse the order of the probe	`n`
`pcifix:#`	Replace `#` with: `0` = do not attempt to fix PCI configuration `1` = set PCI cache-line size register `2` = set write and invalidate bits `3` = increase PCI latency timer according to burst max. `7` = allow the driver to fix up all PCI features	none
`nvram:?`	Replace `?` with: `y` = test controllers for on-board NVRAM `n` = do not test controllers for on-board NVRAM	none
`buschk:#`	Replace `#` with: `0` = no bus check `1` = check the bus and do not attach the controller on error `2` = check the bus and warn on error	none

The optional boot parameter `ncr53c8xx=safe:y` sets the following default values, which are believed to be failsafe:

```
mpar:n,spar:y,disc:n,specf:n,ultra:n,fsn:n,revprob:n,pcifix:0,nvram:y,verb:2,\
tags:0,sync:255,
debug:0,burst:255,led:0,wide:0,settle:10,diff:1,irqm:1,buschk:1
```

Module Parameters

Format:

```
insmod ncr53c8xx ncr53c8xx="mpar:? spar:? disc:? specf:? ultra:? fsn:? tags:# \
sync:## verb:# debug:# burst:## led:# wide:# settle:## diff:# irqm:# revprob:?\
pcifix:# nvram:? buschk:#"
```

or

```
insmod ncr53c8xx ncr53c8xx=safe:y
```

The module parameters for this driver are exactly the same as its boot parameters, but in the parameter line all commas have been replaced with spaces. A `0` or a `1` can replace an `n` or a `y`, respectively, in yes/no parameters.

PAS16.O

Boot Parameters

Format:

```
pas16="IO Port","IRQ"
```

Option	Possible Values	Default Value
`IO Port`	Any valid I/O Port (probed at 0x288, 0x384, 0x388, and 0x38c)	`0x388`
`IRQ`	Any valid IRQ (probed at 10, 12, 14, and 15) or `255` = no IRQ	`10`

Module Parameters

No module parameters are provided for this driver.

PCI2000.O

No boot or module parameters are provided for this driver.

PCI2220I.O

No boot or module parameters are provided for this driver.

PPA.O

Boot Parameters

Format:

```
ppa="IO Port","Mode","Scatter/Gather Buffer Size"
```

Option	Possible Values	Default Value
`IO Port`	Any valid I/O Port (probed at `0x388`)	`0x388`
`Mode`	`0` = autodetect `1` = SPP mode (standard, 4-bit) `2` = PS/2 byte mode `3` = 8-bit EPP mode `4` = 16-bit EPP mode `5` = 32-bit EPP mode	`0`
`Scatter/Gather Buffer Size`	Size of Scatter/Gather buffer	none

Module Parameters

No module parameters are provided for this driver.

PSI240I.O

No boot or module parameters are provided for this driver.

QLOGICFAS.O

No boot or module parameters are provided for this driver. There are, however, I/O Port values that are probed for when the driver is loaded. The following table lists these values, and is provided for information purposes only.

Setting	Probed Values
I/O Port	`0x230` and `0x330`

QLOGICISP.O

No boot or module parameters are provided for this driver. All hardware settings are probed from the PCI BIOS when the driver is initialized.

SEAGATE.O

Boot Parameters

Format:

```
st0x="Memory Base","IRQ"
```

or

```
tmc8xx="Memory Base","IRQ"
```

The first optional parameter in the first line is for Seagate controllers; in the second line, it is for TMC-8xx or TMC-950 controllers. The settings in the following table apply to either.

Option	Possible Values	Default Value
Memory Base	Any valid Memory Base address (probed at 0xc8000, 0xca000, 0xcc000, 0xce000, 0xdc000, and 0xde000)	none
IRQ	Any valid IRQ (probed at 5)	5

Module Parameters

No module parameters are provided for this driver.

T128.O

Boot Parameters

Format:

```
t128="Memory Base","IRQ"
```

Option	Possible Values	Default Value
Memory Base	Any valid Memory Base address (probed at 0xcc000, 0xc8000, 0xdc000, and 0xd8000)	0xcc000
IRQ	Any valid IRQ (probed at 5)	5

Module Parameters

No module parameters are provided for this driver.

TMSCSIM.O

BOOT PARAMETERS

No boot parameters are provided for this driver.

MODULE PARAMETERS

You can only use module parameters for this driver if you are *not* using a DC390 card.

Format:

```
insmod tmscsim tmscsim="Adapter ID","Max. Speed","Device Features","Adapter \
Features","Max. Tagged Commands"
```

Option	Possible Values	Default Value
`Adapter ID`	SCSI adapter ID number (0–7)	7
`Max. Speed`	Maximum speed of the adapter's BIOS, specified with: 0 = 10 MHz 1 = 8.0 MHz 2 = 6.7 MHz 3 = 5.7 MHz 4 = 5.0 MHz 5 = 4.0 MHz 6 = 3.1 MHz 7 = 2 MHz	1
`Device Features`	Per-device features (applies to all supported cards), specified as the sum of the desired values from the following list: 1 = parity check 2 = synchronous negotiation 4 = disconnection 8 is not used (but can be factored into the sum anyway) 16 = tagged queuing	31

continues

continued

Option	Possible Values	Default Value
`Adapter Features`	Adapter features, specified as the sum of the desired values from the following list: 1 is not used (but can be factored into the sum anyway) 2 = use DOS compatible mapping for >1GB drives 4 = reset SCSI bus on startup 8 = active negation 16 is not used (but can be factored into the sum anyway) 32 = check for LUNs >=1	47
`Max. Tagged Commands`	The maximum number of tagged commands. Valid values are as follows: 0 = 2 commands 1 = 4 commands 2 = 8 commands 3 = 16 commands 4 = 32 commands	4

U14-34F.O

BOOT PARAMETERS

Format:

```
u14-34f="IO Port"[,"IO Port","IO Port",...],eh:?,et:?,lc:?,of:?,mq:##
```

or

```
u14-34f=0
```

Option/ Parameter	Possible Values	Default Value
`IO Port`	Any valid I/O Port (probed at 0x330, 0x340, 0x230, 0x240, 0x210, 0x130, and 0x140, in that order) More than one card's I/O Port can be specified, in order, separated by commas.	probed
`eh:?`	Replace `?` with:	`n`
	`y` = use new SCSI code (for 2.2.x Linux kernel only!)	
	`n` = use old SCSI code	`n`
`et:?`	Replace `?` with: `y` = enable extended translation `n` = disable extended translation	
`lc:?`	Replace `?` with: `y` = enable linked commands `n` = disable linked commands	`n`
`of:?`	Replace `?` with: `y` = enable old firmware support `n` = disable old firmware support	`n`
`mq:##`	Replace `##` with the maximum queue depth, anywhere from 2 to 8, inclusive.	`8`

The optional boot parameter `u14-34f=0` disables the driver entirely.

Module Parameters

Format:

```
insmod u14-34f io_port=0x###[,0x###,...] use_new_eh_code=# ext_tran=#
linked_comm=# have_old_firmware=# max_queue_depth=##
```

Parameter	Possible Values	Default Value
io_port=0x###	Replace 0x### with any valid I/O Port (probed at 0x330, 0x340, 0x230, 0x240, 0x210, 0x130, and 0x140, in that order) More than one card's I/O Port can be specified, in order, separated by commas.	probed

use_new_eh_code=#	Replace # with:
	1 = use new SCSI code
	0 = use old SCSI code
		0

ext_tran=#	Replace # with:
	1 = enable extended translation
	0 = disable extended translation
		0

linked_comm=#	Replace # with:
	1 = enable linked commands
	0 = disable linked commands
		0

have_old_firmware=#	Replace # with:
	1 = enable old firmware support
	0 = disable old firmware support
		0

max_queue_depth=##	Replace ## with the maximum queue depth, anywhere from 2 to 8, inclusive.	8

ULTRASTOR.O

No boot or module parameters are provided for this driver. There are, however, IRQ, I/O Port, DMA, and Memory Base values that are probed for when the driver is loaded. The following table lists these values, and is provided for information purposes only.

Setting	Probed Values
IO Port	0x330, 0x340, 0x230, 0x240, 0x210, 0x130, and 0x140
IRQ	15, 14, 11, and 10
DMA Channel	5, 6, and 7
Memory Base	0xC4000, 0xC8000, 0xCC000, 0xD0000, 0xD4000, 0xD8000, and 0xDC000,

WD7000.O

BOOT PARAMETERS

Format:

```
wd7000="IRQ","DMA Channel","IO Port","Bus On","Bus Off"
```

Option	Possible Values	Default Value
IRQ	Any valid IRQ (probed at 3, 4, 5, 7, 9, 10, 11, 12, 14, and 15)	15 for first controller; 11 for second controller
DMA Channel	Any valid DMA Channel (probed at 5, 6, and 7)	6 for first controller; 5 for second controller
IO Port	Any valid I/O Port (probed at 0x0300, 0x0308, 0x0310, 0x0318, 0x0320, 0x0328, 0x0330, 0x0338, 0x0340, 0x0348, 0x0350, 0x0358, 0x0360, 0x0368, 0x0370, 0x0378, 0x0380, 0x0388, 0x0390, 0x0398, 0x03a0, 0x03a8, 0x03b0, 0x03b8, 0x03c0, 0x03c8, 0x03d0, 0x03d8, 0x03e0, 0x03e8, 0x03f0, and 0x03f8)	0x350 for first controller; 0x320 for second controller;
Bus On	Time in nanoseconds for bus on	8000
Bus Off	Time in nanoseconds for bus off	1875

MODULE PARAMETERS

No module parameters are provided for this driver.

IDE DRIVERS

IDE.O

BOOT PARAMETERS

Format (possible parameter lines for controllers only):

```
ideX="IO Port"[,"IO Port"],"IRQ"
ideX=noprobe
ideX="IO Port","CTL"[,"IRQ"]
ideX=autotune
ideX=noautotune
ideX=serialize
ideX=reset
ideX=dma
```

where X is replaced with the IDE controller number starting with 0 (use 1 for the second controller, 2 for the third, and 3 for the fourth).

Options/ Parameters	Possible Values	Default Value
IO Port	Valid I/O Port range starting points for IDE controllers (probed starting at 0x1f0 for ide0, 0x170 for ide1, 0x1e8 for ide2, and 0x168 for ide3). More than one I/O Port can be specified for scanning on the boot parameter line (separated by a comma). The first I/O Port is a range, and the second is an individual port.	0x1f0 (range) and 0x3f6 (specific port) for ide0; 0x170 (range) and 0x376 (specific port) for ide1; 0x1e8 (range) and 0x3ee (specific port) for ide2; 0x168 (range) and 0x36e (specific port) for ide3
IRQ	Valid IRQs for IDE controllers (probes at 14 for ide0, 15 for ide1, 11 for ide2, and 10 for ide3)	14 for ide0; 15 for ide1; 11 for ide2; 10 for ide3

`CTL`	Assumed to be I/O Port plus 0x206	I/O Port plus `0x206`
`noprobe`	Disables the use of this interface	not set
`autotune`	Attempts to tune the interface to optimum speed. Might cause problems with some buggy controllers	not set
`noautotune`	Disables tuning/optimizing the interface	not set
`serialize`	Disables overlap of operations between IDE controllers	not set
`reset`	Reset the interface when the probe is through	not set
`dma`	Automatically configure the DMA channel	not set

A few parameters are reserved for the first IDE controller only (ide0).

Format (for ide0 parameters listed as follows):

`ideX=`*`<parameter from table>`*

Parameters	**Possible Values**	**Default Value**
`dtc2278`	Support for the DTC2278 controller	not set
`ht6560b`	Support for the HT6560B controller	not set
`cmd640_vlb`	Support for VLB controllers that use the CMD640 chipset	not set
`qd6580`	Support for the qd6580 controller	not set
`ali14xx`	Support for ali14xx chipsets (ALI M1439/M1445)	not set
`umc8672`	Support for umc8672 chipsets	not set

Another boot parameter, `idebus=##`, can be used to specify the speed of the IDE bus (replace the `##` with the bus speed between 20 and 66, inclusive). The default value is `40` for PCI systems, `50` for the rest.

Format (possible parameter lines for individual drives only):

```
hdX="Cylinders","Heads","Sectors"
hdX=cdrom
hdX=noprobe
hdX=none
hdX=nowerr
hdX=autotune
hdX=slow
hdX=swapdata
hdX=ide-scsi
```

where `X` is replaced with the letter representation of the IDE drive itself (a being the first IDE drive, as in hda; `b` being the second IDE drive, as in hdb; and so on).

Options/ Parameters	Possible Values	Default Value
`Cylinders, Heads, Sectors`	In general, match these values to those of the drive in question. In odd cases where geometry needs to be spoofed (not common with new controllers), specify the spoofed geometry here.	probed
`cdrom`	Says the drive in question is a CD-ROM drive	not set (but CD-ROM drives are typically detected automatically anyway)
`noprobe`	Do not probe for the drive in question, even if it is present	not set
`none`	Says the drive in question is not present; ignore any CMOS settings and do not probe for it.	not set

`nowerr`	Ignore the WRERR_STAT bit on this drive	not set
`autotune`	Attempt to automatically tune the drive to the fastest PIO mode	not set
`slow`	Insert a pause after each access to the controller	not set
`swapdata`	Byte swap all data	not set
`ide-scsi`	Says to use the ide-scsi driver for the drive in question	not set

Module Parameters

Format:

```
insmod ide options="Parameter1, Parameter2, Parameter3,..."
```

You can specify the same options and parameters that were listed previously in the Boot Parameters section within the `options="..."` quotes.

IDE-CD.O, IDE-FLOPPY.O, IDE-TAPE.O

No boot or module parameters are provided for these drivers. They all depend on the ide.o driver for settings.

XT Controller Driver

XD.O

Boot Parameters

Format:

```
xd="Type","IRQ","IO Port","DMA"
```

Options	Possible Values	Default Value
`Type, IRQ, IO Port, DMA`	These match the settings in your XT controller; check the settings and enter them here	none

Module Parameters

Format:

```
insmod xd nodma xd_geo="Cylinders","Heads","Sectors[,"Cylinders",\
"Heads","Sectors"]
```

Parameters	Possible Values	Default Value
nodma	Do not use DMA	not set
xd_geo=...	Enter the cylinders, heads, and sectors for the drive here, in order. The geometry for more than one drive can be specified; the second drive's geometry starts with the fourth position in the xd_geo= line.	none

Proprietary CD-ROM Drivers

AZTCD.O

Boot Parameter

Format:

```
aztcd="IO Port"[,0x79]
```

Options/ Parameters	Possible Values	Default Value
IO Port	Any valid I/O Port	0x320
0x79	If set, specifies that you want the driver to try harder to find the drive at the I/O Port	not set

Module Parameters

Format:

```
insmod aztcd aztcd=0x###
```

or

```
insmod aztcd aztcd=-1
```

Parameters	Possible Values	Default Value
aztcd=0x###	Replace 0x### with any valid I/O port	0x320

The optional aztcd=-1 parameter tells the driver to probe for the I/O port.

CDU31A.O

There is no autoprobing done by this driver; you must specify parameters to get the hardware recognized.

BOOT PARAMETERS

Format:

```
cdu31a="IO Port","IRQ"[,PAS]
```

Options/ Parameters	Possible Values	Default Value
IO Port	Any valid I/O Port	none
IRQ	Any valid IRQ (0 = do not use an IRQ)	none
PAS	If set, this indicates that the drive is connected to a Pro Audio Spectrum interface card	not set

MODULE PARAMETERS

Format:

```
insmod cdu31a cdu31a_port=0x### cdu31a_irq=#
```

Parameters	Possible Values	Default Value
cdu31a_port=0x###	Replace 0x### with any valid I/O Port	none
cdu31a_irq=#	Replace # with any valid IRQ. If this parameter is left out, IRQs are not used.	none

CM206.O

BOOT PARAMETERS

Format:

```
cm206="IO Port","IRQ"
```

or

```
cm206=auto
```

Options	Possible Values	Default Value
IO Port	Any valid I/O Port (probes from 0x300 to 0x370)	none
IRQ	Any valid IRQ (probes from 3 to 11)	none

The optional `cm206=auto` parameter tells the driver to probe for the settings that were listed previously.

MODULE PARAMETERS

Format:

```
insmod cm206 cm206="IO Port","IRQ" auto_probe=0
```

The format for the module parameters exactly matches that of the boot parameters, except for `auto_probe=0`, which disables all hardware probing.

GSCD.O

BOOT PARAMETERS

```
gscd="IO Port"
```

Options	Possible Values	Default Value
IO Port	Any valid I/O Port (probes at 0x300, 0x310, 0x320, 0x330, 0x340, 0x350, 0x360, 0x370, 0x380, 0x390, 0x3A0, 0x3B0, 0x3C0, 0x3D0, 0x3E0, and 0x3F0)	0x340

MODULE PARAMETERS

Format:

```
insmod gscd gscd="IO Port"
```

The format for the module parameters exactly matches that of the boot parameters.

MCD.O

BOOT PARAMETERS

Format:

```
mcd="IO Port","IRQ"
```

Options	Possible Values	Default Value
`IO Port`	Any valid I/O Port	`0x300`
`IRQ`	Any valid IRQ	`11`

MODULE PARAMETERS

Format:

```
insmod mcd mcd_port=0x### mcd_irq=#
```

Parameters	Possible Values	Default Value
`mcd_port=0x###`	Replace `0x###` with any valid I/O port	`0x300`
`mcd_irq=#` (This parameter *must* follow `mcd_port` on the `insmod` command line)	Replace `#` with any valid IRQ	`11`

MCDX.O

BOOT PARAMETERS

Format:

```
mcdx="IO Port","IRQ"[,"IO Port","IRQ"]
```

Options	Possible Values	Default Value
`IO Port`	Any valid I/O Port	`0x300`
`IRQ`	Any valid IRQ	`11`

More than one drive can be initialized by this driver; specify I/O Port/IRQ pairs on the boot parameter line for each drive, in order.

MODULE PARAMETERS

Format:

```
insmod mcdx.o mcdx_drive_map="IO Port","IRQ"[,"IO Port","IRQ",...]
```

The format for the module parameters (within the `mcdx_drive_map` quotes) exactly matches that of the boot parameters.

OPTCD.O

BOOT PARAMETERS

Format:

```
optcd="IO Port"
```

Options	Possible Values	Default Value
IO Port	Any valid I/O Port (0 disables the driver completely)	0x340

MODULE PARAMETERS

Format:

```
insmod optcd optcd="IO Port"
```

The format for the module parameter exactly matches that of the boot parameter.

SBPCD.O

> **Note**
> This driver is not meant to be used for any IDE/ATAPI CD-ROM drives.

BOOT PARAMETERS

Format:

```
sbpcd="IO Port","Type"
```

Options	Possible Values	Default Value
IO Port	Any valid I/O Port (see listing that follows for probed values)	See the table that follows
Type	0 = LaserMate 1 = SoundBlaster 2 = SoundScape 3 = Teac16bit (Either the numeric or alpha value can be specified.)	See the table that follows

MODULE PARAMETERS

Format:

```
insmod sbpcd sbpcd="IO Port","Type"
```

The format for the module parameter exactly matches that of the boot parameter, except that (because strings are not allowed here) the alpha version of the `Type` parameter is not allowed (only `0`–`3` can be specified).

LISTING OF PROBED VALUES

I/O Port	Type	Description
0x230	1	Soundblaster Pro and 16 (default)
0x300	0	CI-101P (default), WDH-7001C (default), Galaxy (default), Reveal (one default)
0x250	1	OmniCD default, Soundblaster Pro and 16
0x2C0	3	Teac 16-bit cards
0x260	1	OmniCD
0x320	0	Lasermate, CI-101P, WDH-7001C, Galaxy, Reveal (other default), Longshine LCS-6853 (default)
0x338	0	Reveal Sound Wave 32 card model #SC600
0x340	0	Mozart sound card (default), Lasermate, CI-101P
0x360	0	Lasermate, CI-101P
0x270	1	Soundblaster 16
0x670	0	"sound card #9"
0x690	0	"sound card #9"
0x338	2	SPEA Media FX, Ensonic SoundScape (default)
0x328	2	SPEA Media FX
0x348	2	SPEA Media FX
0x634	0	some newer sound cards
0x638	0	some newer sound cards
0x230	1	some newer sound cards
0x630	0	"sound card #9" (default)
0x650	0	"sound card #9"
0x330	0	Lasermate, CI-101P, WDH-7001C
0x350	0	Lasermate, CI-101P
0x358	2	SPEA Media FX
0x370	0	Lasermate, CI-101P
0x290	1	Soundblaster 16
0x310	0	Lasermate, CI-101P, WDH-7001C

SJCD.O

This driver does not use IRQ or DMA channel settings.

BOOT PARAMETERS

Format:

```
sjcd="IO Port"
```

Options	Possible Values	Default Value
`IO Port`	Any valid I/O Port	`0x340`

MODULE PARAMETERS

Format:

```
insmod sjcd sjcd_base=0x###
```

Parameter	Possible Values	Default Value
`sjcd_base=0x###`	Replace `0x###` with any valid I/O Port	`0x340`

SONYCD535.O

BOOT PARAMETERS

Format:

```
sonycd535="IO Port"
```

Options	Possible Values	Default Value
`IO Port`	Any valid I/O Port	none

MODULE PARAMETERS

Format:

```
insmod sonycd535 sonycd535="IO Port"
```

The format for the module parameter exactly matches that of the boot parameter.

CD-ROM INTERFACE CARD DRIVERS

There is currently only one driver: isp16.o

ISP16.O

BOOT PARAMETERS

Format:

```
isp16="IO Port","IRQ","DMA","Drive Type"
```

Options	Possible Values	Default Value
`IO Port`	Any valid I/O Port (probed at 0x340, 0x320, 0x330, and 0x360)	`0x340`
`IRQ`	Any valid IRQ (probed at 3, 5, 7, 9, 10, and 11) `0` indicates that IRQs are not used.	`0`
`DMA`	Any valid DMA channel (probed at 3, 5, 6, and 7) `0` indicates that DMA is not used.	`0`
`Drive Type`	Choose from the following: `noisp16` (skip the initialization of this card altogether), `Sanyo`, `Panasonic`, `Sony`, or `Mitsumi`	`Sanyo`

MODULE PARAMETERS

Format:

```
insmod isp16.o isp16_cdrom_base=0x### isp16_cdrom_irq=# isp16_cdrom_dma=# \
isp16_cdrom_type=????
```

Parameters	Possible Values	Default Value
`isp16_cdrom_base=0x###`	Replace `0x###` with any valid I/O Port (probed at 0x340, 0x320, 0x330, and 0x360)	`0x340`
`isp16_cdrom_irq=#`	Replace # with any valid IRQ (probed at 3, 5, 7, 9, 10, and 11) `0` indicates that IRQs are not used.	`0`

continues

continued

Parameters	Possible Values	Default Value
`isp16_cdrom_dma=#`	Replace `#` with any valid DMA channel (probed at 3, 5, 6, and 7) `0` indicates that DMA is not used.	`0`
`isp16_cdrom_type=????`	Replace `????` with one of the following: `noisp16` (skip the initialization of this card altogether), `Sanyo`, `Panasonic`, `Sony`, or `Mitsumi`	`Sanyo`

PARALLEL PORT DEVICE DRIVERS (PARIDE)

Loading support for these drives is somewhat complex when it is done from a boot parameter. It is much easier to load modules for these items; therefore, for this set of drivers, start with module loading and then move on to loading options through boot parameters.

USING MODULES WITH PARIDE DRIVERS

There are three types of modules that you need to load:

- The main module called paride.o
- Some (or all) of the protocol modules (listed as follows)
- Device type modules (also listed as follows)

After the paride.o module is loaded, any (or all) of the following protocol modules can be loaded:

Protocol Module	Description
aten.o	ATEN EH-100
bpck.o	Microsolutions backpack drives
comm.o	DataStor (old-type) "commuter" adapter
dstr.o	DataStor EP-2000
epat.o	Shuttle EPAT
epia.o	Shuttle EPIA

fit2.o	FIT TD-2000
fit3.o	FIT TD-3000
friq.o	Freecom IQ Cable
frpw.o	Freecom Power
kbic.o	KingByte KBIC-951A and KBIC-971A
ktti.o	KT Technology PHd adapter
on20.o	OnSpec 90c20
on26.o	OnSpec 90c26

Each time you load one of the protocol drivers using `insmod`, a message appears on the screen telling you which devices were found that match the protocol, and what protocol number is assigned to each device. For example, after loading the epat.o and kbic.o modules, the following might appear (this example was borrowed from the paride.txt file that is included with the 2.2.1 Linux kernel source code):


```
# insmod epat
paride: epat registered as protocol 0
# insmod kbic
paride: k951 registered as protocol 1
paride: k971 registered as protocol 2
```

Each time you load protocol drivers, new protocol numbers are assigned, starting with 0. Note that the epat.o module does not necessarily assign protocol 0 to the same device if the module is loaded second instead of first. If the order of the preceding modules were switched, the epat.o module would probably assign the associated device protocol 2, whereas protocols 0 and 1 go with the kbic.o module's devices. It is important to remember the module numbers for these devices for the next step, so write them down if necessary.

After loading the protocols and getting protocol number assignments for the paride devices, you can now load the necessary device type modules. They are described as follows:

Device Module	**Description**
pd.o	IDE disk drive
pcd.o	ATAPI CD-ROM drive
pf.o	ATAPI disk drive
pt.o	ATAPI tape drive
pg.o	ATAPI generic device (currently only used for CD-R drives)

You must first determine what kinds of drives you want to initialize and pass the proper settings on the `insmod` command line using the following format:

```
insmod device-module drive0="IO Port","Protocol" drive1="IO Port","Protocol" \
drive2="IO Port","Protocol" drive3="IO Port","Protocol"
```

By default, each device type module probes one drive using the existing loaded protocols and stops probing after it finds one; but up to four drives can be specified in the `insmod` command line using the preceding syntax. The options can be broken down as follows:

Options	Possible Values	Default Value
`IO Port`	Any valid I/O Port	probed (first drive only; forced in subsequent drives on the `insmod` command line)
`Protocol`	Any valid Protocol number reported by the previously loaded protocol drivers	probed (first drive only; forced in subsequent drives on the `insmod` command line)

Controlling Built-in Paride Drivers

With some understanding of the process of modular paride support and how the different levels of drivers inform each other, it is easier to follow how to use boot parameters to load support for paride devices.

The same information is required to control driver initialization from a boot parameter, but the format of the parameters themselves changes slightly:

```
<device>.drive0="IO Port","Protocol" <device>.drive1="IO Port","Protocol" \
<device>.drive2="IO Port","Protocol" <device>.drive3="IO Port","Protocol"
```

Option	Possible Values	Default Values
`<device>.drive[0-3]`	Replace `<device>` with the appropriate device type from the following list: `pd` = IDE disk `pcd` = ATAPI CD-ROM `pf` = ATAPI disk `pt` = ATAPI tape `pg` = ATAPI generic	none
`IO Port`	Any valid I/O Port	none
`Protocol`	Any valid protocol number reported by the protocol drivers when they loaded (see /var/log/messages or the output of `dmesg` to see what was reported, if you did not catch it when the system booted)	none

If no boot parameters are specified, each driver probes each parallel port using each protocol until one drive is found; then probing stops. Just as with modular support, up to four drives can be specified manually using parameters if you have more than one parallel port drive.

"FLOPPY" TAPE DRIVERS

There is only one driver—ftape.o—that handles these tape drives. The following parameters apply exclusively to that driver.

FTAPE.O

BOOT PARAMETERS

Format:

Each individual boot parameter must be given in the following form:

```
ftape=parameter
```

Unlike the boot parameters for other drivers, the ftape.o driver can not accept boot parameters in one long comma-delimited line. Therefore, it is not uncommon to see multiple `ftape=` lines entered as boot parameters. For example

```
ftape=4,tracing ftape=10,irq ftape=0x310,ioport
```

Options	Possible Values	Default Value
`<IO Port>,ioport`	Replace `<IO Port>` with the I/O port address of your floppy disk controller	probed
`<IRQ>,irq`	Replace `<IRQ>` with the IRQ of the floppy disk controller	probed
`<DMA>,dma`	Replace `<DMA>` with the DMA of the floppy disk controller	probed
`<#>,fc10`	Replace <#> with: `1` = using a Colorado FC-10/20 controller `0` = not using a	`0`

continues

continued

Options	Possible Values	Default Value
	Colorado FC-10/20 controller	
`<#>,mach2`	Replace <#> with: 1 = using a Mountain Mach-2 controller 0 = not using a Mountain Mach-2 controller	0
`<#>,threshold`	Replace <#> with the threshold of the floppy disk controller FIFO	none
`<#>,datarate`	Replace <#> with the maximum data rate for the floppy disk controller	none

Module Parameters

Format:

```
insmod ftape ft_fdc_base=0x### ft_fdc_irq=# ft_fdc_dma=# ft_probe_fc10=# \
ft_mach2=# ft_fdc_threshold=# ft_fdc_rate_limit=#
```

Parameters	Possible Values	Default Value
`fdc_fdc_base=0x###`	Replace 0x### with the I/O port address of your floppy disk controller	probed
`ft_fdc_irq=#`	Replace # with the IRQ of the floppy disk controller	probed
`ft_fdc_dma=#`	Replace # with the DMA of the floppy disk controller	probed

`ft_probe_fc10=#`	Replace # with:
	1 = using a Colorado FC-10/20 controller
	0 = not using a Colorado FC-10/20 controller
		0

`ft_mach2=#`	Replace # with:
	1 = using a Mountain Mach-2 controller
	0 = not using a Mountain Mach-2 controller
		0

`ft_fdc_threshold=#`	Replace # with the threshold of the floppy disk controller FIFO	none
`ft_fdc_rate_limit=#`	Replace # with the maximum data rate for the floppy disk controller	none

Network Card Drivers

The general format of the Ethernet boot parameters follows:

```
ether="IRQ","IO Port","Memory Start","Memory End","Interface"
```

In almost every case, specifying a value of `0` in any position except for the `Interface` position tells the driver to probe for the value that is associated with that option's position. For example, the following line probes for the `IO port`, `Memory Start`, and `Memory End` values on an Ethernet card that uses hardware interrupt 10:

```
ether=10,0,0,0,eth0
```

This looks odd, but it is a perfectly valid boot parameter line.

In the case of PCI cards, the IRQ and I/O Port values are probed from the system's BIOS. There is probably no need to specify these using either boot or module parameters. However, it is highly recommended that you specify these values using module parameters whenever possible (module autoprobing is still an evolving science with Linux).

In all cases, the first nonnumeric parameter is considered to be the Ethernet interface name. Furthermore, in practically all cases, if more than one card is being initialized, boot and module parameters can be stacked on the command line. For example, say you have two NE2000 cards in your system. The following two sample driver parameter lines show how to initialize them both on one command line:

Boot parameters

```
ether=10,0x310,0,0,eth0 ether=11,0x340,0,0,eth1 etc...
```

or module parameters

```
insmod ne io=0x310,0x340 irq=10,11
```

Both lines initialize the same hardware; the only difference is that the first line is for an NE2000 driver that is built into the Linux kernel, whereas the second is for a modular NE2000 driver.

Note

When you are using the OpenLinux module autoloading scheme, be sure to put each module parameter (`io=...`, `irq=...`) on its own line in the /etc/modules/options file that corresponds to the driver (in the case of NE2000 cards, it is /etc/modules/options/ne). The all-on-one-line scheme is only used for insertion of kernel modules from a command prompt or from a script. See Chapter 18, "Kernel Modules," for more details.

3c501.o

Boot Parameters

Format:

```
ether="IRQ","IO Port","Memory Start","Memory End","Interface"
```

Option	Possible Values	Default Value
`IRQ`	Any valid IRQ	5
`IO Port`	Any valid I/O Port (probed at 0x280 and 0x300)	none
`Memory Start`	Any valid Memory Start point	probed
`Memory End`	Any valid Memory End point	probed
`Interface`	eth0, eth1, eth2, eth3	none

Module Parameters

Format:

```
insmod 3c501 irq=# io=0x###
```

Parameter	Possible Values	Default Value
`irq=#`	Replace # with any valid IRQ	5
`io=0x###`	Replace `0x###` with any valid I/O Port (probed at 0x280 and 0x300)	`0x280`

3c503.o

Boot Parameters

Format:

```
ether="IRQ","IO Port","Memory Start","Transceiver","Interface"
```

Option	Possible Values	Default Value
`IRQ`	Any valid IRQ (probed at 3, 4, 5, and 9)	9
`IO Port`	Any valid I/O Port (probed at 0x250, 0x280, 0x2a0, 0x2e0, 0x300, 0x310, 0x330, and 0x350)	none
`Memory Start`	Any valid Memory Start point	probed
`Transceiver`	`0` = internal `1` = external (AUI)	probed
`Interface`	eth0, eth1, eth2, eth3	none

Module Parameters

Format:

```
insmod 3c503 irq=# io=0x### xcvr=#
```

Parameter	Possible Values	Default Value
`irq=#`	Replace # with any valid IRQ (probed at 3, 4, 5, and 9)	9
`io=0x###`	Replace `0x###` with any valid I/O Port (probed at 0x250, 0x280, 0x2a0, 0x2e0, 0x300, 0x310, 0x330, and 0x350)	none

continues

continued

Parameter	Possible Values	Default Value
`xcvr=#`	Replace # with: `0` = internal transceiver `1` = external transceiver (AUI)	none

3c505.o

Boot Parameters

Format:

```
ether="IRQ","IO Port","Memory Start","Memory End","Interface"
```

Option	Possible Values	Default Value
`IRQ`	Any valid IRQ	probed
`IO Port`	Any valid I/O Port (probed at 0x280, 0x300, and 0x310)	probed
`Memory Start`	Any valid Memory Start point	probed
`Memory End`	Any valid Memory End point	probed
`Interface`	eth0, eth1, eth2, eth3	none

Module Parameters

Format:

```
insmod 3c505 irq=# io=0x### dma=#
```

Parameter	Possible Values	Default Value
`irq=#`	Replace # with any valid IRQ	probed
`io=0x###`	Replace `0x###` with any valid I/O Port (probed at 0x280, 0x300, and 0x310)	`0x300`
`dma=#`	Replace # with the card's DMA channel	`6`

3C507.O

BOOT PARAMETERS

Format:

```
ether="IRQ","IO Port","Memory Start","Memory End","Interface"
```

Option	Possible Values	Default Value
`IRQ`	Any valid IRQ	probed
`IO Port`	Any valid I/O Port (probed at 0x280, 0x300, 0x320, and 0x340)	probed
`Memory Start`	Any valid Memory Start point	probed
`Memory End`	Any valid Memory End point	probed
`Interface`	eth0, eth1, eth2, eth3	none

MODULE PARAMETERS

Format:

```
insmod 3c507 irq=# io=0x###
```

Parameter	Possible Values	Default Value
`irq=#`	Replace `#` with any valid IRQ	none
`io=0x###`	Replace `0x###` with any valid I/O Port (probed at 0x280, 0x300, 0x320, and 0x340)	`0x300`

3C509.O

BOOT PARAMETERS

Format:

```
ether="IRQ","IO Port","Memory Start","Memory End","Interface"
```

Option	Possible Values	Default Value
`IRQ`	Any valid IRQ	probed
`IO Port`	Any valid I/O Port (probed at 0xl000, 0x2000, 0x3000,	probed

continues

continued

Option	Possible Values	Default Value
	0x4000, 0x5000, 0x6000, 0x7000, 0x8000, and 0x9000 for EISA; 0xl00, 0xll0, 0x120, 0x130, 0x140, 0x150, 0x160, 0x170, 0x190, and 0x200 for ISA)	
`Memory Start`	Any valid Memory Start point	probed
`Memory End`	Any valid Memory End point	probed
`Interface`	eth0, eth1, eth2, eth3	none

MODULE PARAMETERS

Format:

```
insmod 3c509 irq=# debug=# xcvr=#
```

Parameter	Possible Values	Default Value
`irq=#`	Replace # with any valid IRQ	probed
`debug=#`	Replace # with the desired level of debug output	none

`xcvr=#`	Replace # with:
	0 = internal
	1 = external (AUI)
		none

3C515.O

BOOT PARAMETERS

Format:

```
ether="IRQ","IO Port","Memory Start","Memory End","Interface"
```

Option	Possible Values	Default Value
`IRQ`	Any valid IRQ	probed
`IO Port`	Any valid I/O Port (probed at 0xl00, 0x120, 0x140, 0x160, 0x180, 0x200, 0x220,	probed

	0x240, 0x260, 0x280, 0x300, 0x320, 0x340, 0x360, 0x380, and 0x400)	
`Memory Start`	Any valid Memory Start point	probed
`Memory End`	Any valid Memory End point	probed
`Interface`	eth0, eth1, eth2, eth3	none

Module Parameters

Format:

```
insmod 3c515 debug=# options=?? full_duplex=# rx_copybreak=# \
max_interrupt_work=#
```

Parameter	Possible Values	Default Value
`debug=#`	Replace `#` with the desired verbosity level of the driver's debug messages (`0` = no messages, `1` = minimal messages)	`1`
`options=??`	Replace `??` with media type/duplex settings: `0` = 10Base-T `1` = 10 Mb/sec. AUI `3` = 10Base-2 `4` = 100Base-TX `5` = 100Base-FX `6` = MII `8` = 10Base-T full duplex `12` = 100Base-TX full duplex	none
`full_duplex=#`	Replace `#` with: `1` = enable full duplex `0` = disable full duplex	none

continues

continued

Parameter	Possible Values	Default Value
rx_copybreak=#	Replace # with the copy breakpoint for the copy-only-tiny-frames scheme (setting this to greater than 1518 disables this feature)	200
max_interrupt _work=#	Replace # with the maximum number of events to be handled at each interrupt	20

3C59X.O

BOOT PARAMETERS

No boot parameters are provided for this driver.

MODULE PARAMETERS

Format:

```
insmod 3c59x debug=# rx_copybreak=# max_interrupt_work=# compaq_ioaddr=0x### \
compaq_irq=# compaq_device_id=0x### full_duplex=#
```

Parameter	Possible Values	Default Value
debug=#	Replace # with an integer representation of desired debug output. Values go from 0 (silent) to 6 (highly verbose).	1
rx_copybreak=#	Replace # with the copy breakpoint for the copy-only-tiny-frames scheme (setting this to greater than 1518 disables this feature)	200
max_interrupt _work=#	Replace # with the maximum number of events to handle at each interrupt	20

Parameter	Possible Values	Default Value
compaq_ioaddr=0x###	Replace 0x### with the I/O port of the card (only used if the card is installed on a Compaq with a PCI BIOS)	none
compaq_irq=#	Replace # with the IRQ of the card (only used if the card is installed on a Compaq with a PCI BIOS)	
compaq_device_id=0x###	Replace 0 with the device ID of the card (only used if the card is installed on a Compaq with a PCI BIOS)	0x5900

full_duplex=#	Replace # with:
	1 = enable full duplex
	0 = disable full duplex
		0

AC3200.O

BOOT PARAMETERS

No boot parameters are offered for this driver.

MODULE PARAMETERS

Format:

```
insmod ac3200 irq=# io=0x####
```

Parameter	Possible Values	Default Value
irq=#	Replace # with any valid IRQ	probed
io=0x####	Replace 0x#### with any valid I/O Port (probed at	probed

continues

continued

Parameter	Possible Values	Default Value
	0xl000, 0x2000, 0x3000, 0x4000, 0x5000, 0x6000, 0x7000, 0x8000, and 0x9000 for EISA)	

ACENIC.O

BOOT PARAMETERS

No boot parameters are provided for this driver.

MODULE PARAMETERS

Format:

```
insmod acenic trace=# link=0x#### tx_coal_tick=# rx_coal_tick=# max_tx_desc=# \
max_rx_desc=#
```

Parameter	Possible Values	Default Value
`trace=#`	Replace # with the firmware trace level (used for debugging purposes only)	none
`link=0x####`	Replace `0x####` with: `0x0001` = half duplex `0x0002` = do not negotiate line speed `0x0010` = 10Mb/sec. Link `0x0020` = 100Mb/sec. Link `0x0040` = 1000Mb/sec. Link `0x0100` = do not negotiate flow control `0x0200` = enable RX flow control Y `0x0400` = enable TX flow control Y `0x0270` = negotiate line and flow control	`0x0270`

tx_coal_tick=#	Replace # with the number of coalescing clock ticks to wait for more packets to arrive before interrupting the host, starting from the time the first packet arrives.	none
rx_coal_tick=#	Replace # with the number of coalescing clock ticks to wait for more packets to arrive before interrupting the host, starting after the first packet is transmitted.	none
max_tx_desc=#	Replace # with the maximum number of packets transmitted before interrupting the host.	none
max_rx_desc=#	Replace # with the maximum number of packets received before interrupting the host.	none

APRICOT.O

BOOT PARAMETERS

Format:

```
ether="IRQ","IO Port","Memory Start","Memory End","Interface"
```

Option	Possible Values	Default Value
IRQ	Any valid IRQ	10
IO Port	Any valid I/O Port (only probed at 0x300)	0x300
Memory Start	Any valid Memory Start point	probed

continues

continued

Option	Possible Values	Default Value
`Memory End`	Any valid Memory End point	probed
`Interface`	eth0, eth1, eth2, eth3	none

Module Parameters

Format:

```
insmod apricot irq=# io=0x###
```

Parameter	Possible Values	Default Value
`irq=#`	Replace # with any valid IRQ	`10`
`io=0x###`	Replace `0x###` with any valid I/O Port (only probed at 0x300)	`0x300`

AT1700.O

Boot Parameters

Format:

```
ether="IRQ","IO Port","Memory Start","Memory End","Interface"
```

Option	Possible Values	Default Value
`IRQ`	Any valid IRQ (probed at 3, 4, 5, 9, 10, 11, 14, and 15)	probed
`IO Port`	Any valid I/O Port (probed at 0x220, 0x240, 0x260, 0x280, 0x2a0, 0x2c0, 0x300, and 0x340 for FMV-18x cards; 0x240, 0x260, 0x280, 0x2a0, 0x300, 0x320, 0x340, and 0x380 for AT1700 cards)	probed
`Memory Start`	Any valid Memory Start point	probed
`Memory End`	Any valid Memory End point	probed
`Interface`	eth0, eth1, eth2, eth3	none

MODULE PARAMETERS

Format:

```
insmod at1700 irq=# io=0x### net_debug=#
```

Parameter	Possible Values	Default Value
irq=#	Replace # with any valid IRQ (probed at 3, 4, 5, 9, 10, 11, 14, and 15)	probed
io=0x###	Replace 0x### with any valid I/O Port (probed at 0x220, 0x240, 0x260, 0x280, 0x2a0, 0x2c0, 0x300, and 0x340 for FMV-18x cards; 0x240, 0x260, 0x280, 0x2a0, 0x300, 0x320, 0x340, and 0x380 for AT1700 cards)	0x260

net_debug=#	Replace # with:
	1 = enable messages
	0 = disable messages
		none

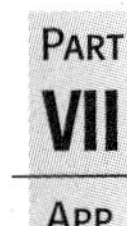

ATP.O

BOOT PARAMETERS

Format:

```
ether="IRQ","IO Port","Transfer Mode","Memory End","Interface"
```

Option	Possible Values	Default Value
IRQ	5 or 7	probed
IO Port	0x278, 0x378, or 0x3bc	probed
Transfer Mode	7 or 4	4
Memory End	Any valid Memory End point	probed
Interface	atp0	atp0

MODULE PARAMETERS

There is no modular support for this driver.

COSA.O

Boot Parameters

No boot parameters are provided for this driver.

Module Parameters

Format:

```
insmod cosa io=0x### irq=# dma=#
```

Parameter	Possible Values	Default Value
io=0x###	Replace 0x### with any valid I/O Port (probed at 0x210, 0x218, 0x220, and 0x228)	probed
irq=#	Replace # with any valid IRQ. Valid values are from 2 to 7 or 10 to 15 (-1 = autoprobe)	-1
dma=#	Replace # with the DMA value of the card. Valid values are 1, 0, or anything between 3 and 7.	none

CS89X0.O

Boot Parameters

No boot parameters are provided for this driver.

Module Parameters

Format:

```
insmod cs89x0 io=0x### irq=# mmode=0x### dma=# media=?? duplex=?? debug=#
```

Parameter	Possible Values	Default Value
io=0x###	Replace 0x### with the I/O Port of the card. Valid values are between 0x200 and 0x360.	0x300
irq=#	Replace # with the IRQ for the card. Valid values are 5, 10, 11, and 12 for CS8900 and 9–15 for CS8920.	10

mmode=0x###	Replace 0x### with any valid memory base address.	0xd0000
dma=#	Replace # with any valid DMA channel	none
media=??	Replace ?? with: rj45 = 10Base-T 2 or aui = AUI auto = autodetect	auto
duplex=??	Replace ?? with: f = full duplex h = half duplex auto = autodetect	f
debug=#	Replace # with the desired level of verbosity of the driver's debug messages (>4 = verbose)	1

DE4X5.O

Boot Parameters

No boot parameters are provided for this driver.

Module Parameters

Format:

```
insmod de4x5 dec_only=# args='eth0:arg1 arg2 arg3 ... eth1:arg1 arg2 arg3...'
```

or

```
insmod de4x5 io=0xABB (For individual boards)
```

Parameter	Possible Values	Default Value
dec_only=#	Replace # with 1 if you want to limit initialization to DEC cards only	not set
args='eth0: arg1... eth1: arg1... eth2: arg1...'	For each interface (eth0, eth1, and so on) select from the following arguments:	not set

continues

continued

Parameter	Possible Values	Default Value
	fdx = full duplex autosense = set media and speed The autosense argument has the following possible sub-arguments: TP, TP_NW, BNC, AUI, BNC_AUI, 100Mb, 10Mb, and AUTO (for example, eth0:autosense=TP)	

The optional io=0xABB parameter is used for setting up individual boards only. Replace 0xABB with a board specification, where A is the bus number and BB is the device number.

DE600.O

BOOT PARAMETERS

Format:

```
ether="IRQ","IO Port","Memory Start","Memory End","Interface"
```

Option	Possible Values	Default Value
IRQ	7	7
IO Port	0x378	0x378
Memory Start	Any valid Memory Start point	probed
Memory End	Any valid Memory End point	probed
Interface	eth0, eth1, eth2, eth3	none

MODULE PARAMETERS

There are no parameters for the modular version of this driver.

DE620.O

BOOT PARAMETERS

Format:

```
ether="IRQ","IO Port","Memory Start","Memory End","Interface"
```

Option	Possible Values	Default Value
IRQ	7	7
IO Port	0x378	0x378
Memory Start	Any valid Memory Start point	probed
Memory End	Any valid Memory End point	probed
Interface	eth0, eth1, eth2, eth3	none

MODULE PARAMETERS

Format:

```
insmod de620 irq=# io=0x### clone=# bnc=# utp=#
```

Parameter	Possible Values	Default Value
irq=#	Replace # with any valid IRQ (probed at 7)	7
io=0x###	Replace 0x### with any valid I/O Port (probed at 0x378)	0x378

clone=#	Replace # with:
	0 = do not skip Ethernet range check
	1 = skip Ethernet range check
		none

bnc=#	Replace # with:
	0 = disable BNC (coax) connector
	1 = enable BNC connector
		none

utp=#	Replace # with:
	0 = disable UTP (twisted pair) connector,
	1 = enable UTP connector
		none

DEPCA.O

BOOT PARAMETERS

No boot parameters are provided for this driver.

MODULE PARAMETERS

Format:

```
insmod depca irq=# io=0x### adapter_name=????? mem=0x#####
```

Parameter	Possible Values	Default Value
irq=#	Replace # with any valid IRQ (probed at 2, 3, 4, 5, and 7 (Depca & Del0x); 5, 9, 10, 11, and 15 (De20x))	7
io=0x###	Replace 0x### with any valid I/O Port (probed at 0x200 and 0x300 for ISA)	0x200
adapter _name=????	Replace ???? with: DEPCA, DE100, DEl01, DE200, DE20l, DE202, DE2l0, or DE422	none
mem=0x#####	Replace 0x##### with: 0xc0000, 0xd0000, 0xe0000	0xd0000

DGRS.O

Boot Parameters

Format:

`ether="IRQ","IO Port","Memory Start","Memory End","Interface"`

Option	Possible Values	Default Value
IRQ	Any valid IRQ (probed at 3, 5, 7, 10, 11, 12, and 15 for EISA)	probed
IO Port	Any valid I/O Port (probed at 0x1000, 0x2000, 0x3000, 0x4000, 0x5000, 0x6000, 0x7000, 0x8000, and 0x9000 for EISA)	probed
Memory Start	Any valid Memory Start point	probed
Memory End	Any valid Memory End point	probed
Interface	eth0, eth1, eth2, eth3	none

Module Parameters

Format:

```
insmod dgrs debug=# dma=# spantree=# hashexpire=# ipaddr=# iptrap=# ipxnet=# \
nicmode=#
```

Parameter	Possible Values	Default Value
debug=#	Replace # with debug printing level	none

dma=#	Replace # with:
	0 = disable
	1 = enable
		none

spantree=#	Replace # with:
	0 = disable
	1 = enable
		none

hashexpire=#	Replace # with address aging time in seconds	300
ipaddr=#	Replace # with SNMP agent's IP address (comma—not period—delimited. For example, 192,168,1,1)	none
iptrap=#	Replace # with SNMP agent's trap address (same format as ipaddr parameter)	none
ipxnet=#	Replace # with SMNP agent's IPX number	none

nicmode=#	Replace # with:
	0 = multiple NIC mode off
	1 = multiple NIC mode on
		none

E2100.O

Boot Parameters

No boot parameters are provided for this driver.

Module Parameters

Format:

```
insmod e2100 irq=# io=0x### mem=0x### xcvr=#
```

Parameter	Possible Values	Default Value
irq=#	Replace # with any valid IRQ (probed at 3, 4, 5, 9, 10, 11, 12, and 15)	probed
io=0x###	Replace 0x### with any valid I/O Port (probed at 0x220, 0x280, 0x300, and 0x380)	probed
mem=0x###	Replace 0x### with the memory start point	probed

xcvr=#	Replace # with:
	0 = internal
	1 = external (AUI)
		probed

EEPRO.O

BOOT PARAMETERS

Format:

```
ether="IRQ","IO Port","Debug","RX Buffer","Interface"
```

Option	Possible Values	Default Value
IRQ	Any valid IRQ (probed at 3, 4, 5, 9, 10, and 11)	probed
IO Port	Any valid I/O Port (probed at 0x200, 0x240, 0x280, 0x2c0, 0x300, 0x320, 0x340, and 0x360)	probed
Debug	Set to 1 or higher for increasing levels of debugging information	none
RX Buffer	Buffer size between 3KB and 24KB (the size must be specified in numbers of kilobytes)	24
Interface	eth0, eth1, eth2, eth3	none

MODULE PARAMETERS

Format:

```
insmod eepro irq=# io=0x### mem=##
```

Parameter	Possible Values	Default Value
irq=#	Replace ## with any valid IRQ (probed at 3, 4, 5, 9, 10, and 11)	probed

io=0x###	Replace 0x### with any valid I/O Port (probed at 0x200, 0x240, 0x280, 0x2c0, 0x300, 0x320, 0x340, and 0x360)	0x200
mem=##	Replace ## with buffer size between 3KB and 24KB (the size must be specified in numbers of kilobytes)	24

EEPRO100.O

Boot Parameters

No boot parameters are provided for this driver.

Module Parameters

Format:

```
insmod eepro100 debug=# options=?? full_duplex=# congenb=# txfifo=# rxfifo=# \
txdmacount=# rxdmacount=# rx_copybreak=# max_interrupt_work=# \
multicast_filter_limit=#
```

Parameter	Possible Values	Default Value
debug=#	Replace # with the desired verbosity level of the driver's debug messages (-1 = disable debug messages)	-1
options=??	Replace ?? with a transceiver override setting or full duplex flag: 16 = full duplex 32 = 100 Mb/sec. only	none

full_duplex=#	Replace # with:
	1 = enable full duplex
	0 = disable full duplex
		1

congenb=#	Replace # with:
	1 = enable congestion control
	0 = disable congestion control
		0

txfifo=#	Replace # with the transceiver FIFO	8

continues

continued

Parameter	Possible Values	Default Value
	threshold. Valid values are 0–15 in 4-byte units (for example, for 32 bytes, choose `8`).	
`rxfifo=#`	Replace # with the receiver FIFO threshold. Valid values are 0–15 in 4-byte units (for example, for 32 bytes, choose `8`).	
`txdmacount=#`	Replace # with: `1–127` = DMA burst length `0` = no preemption `128` = disabled	`128`
`rxdmacount=#`	Replace # with: `1–127` = DMA burst length `0` = no preemption `128` = disabled	`0`
`rx_copybreak=#`	Replace # with the copy breakpoint for the copy-only-tiny-frames scheme (setting this to more than 1518 disables this feature)	`200`
`max_interrupt_work=#`	Replace # with the maximum number of events to handle at each interrupt	20
`multicast_filter_limit=#`	Replace # with the maximum number of multicasts to filter	`64`

EEXPRESS.O

BOOT PARAMETERS

Format:

```
ether="IRQ","IO Port","Memory Start","Memory End","Interface"
```

Option	Possible Values	Default Value
`IRQ`	Any valid IRQ (probed at 3, 4, 5, 9, 10, and 11)	probed
`IO Port`	Any valid I/O Port (probed at 0x270, 0x300, 0x310, 0x320, and 0x340)	probed
`Memory Start`	Any valid Memory Start point	probed
`Memory End`	Any valid Memory End point	probed
`Interface`	eth0, eth1, eth2, eth3	none

MODULE PARAMETERS

Format:

```
insmod eexpress irq=# io=0x###
```

Parameter	Possible Values	Default Value
`irq=#`	Replace `#` with any valid IRQ (probed at 3, 4, 5, 9, 10, and 11)	probed
`io=0x###`	Replace `0x###` with any valid I/O Port (probed at 0x270, 0x300, 0c310, 0x320, and 0x340)	probed

EPIC100.O

BOOT PARAMETERS

No boot parameters are provided for this driver.

MODULE PARAMETERS

Format:

```
insmod epic100 debug=# full_duplex=# rx_copybreak=# max_interrupt_work=#
```

Parameter	Possible Values	Default Value
`debug=#`	Replace # with the desired verbosity level of the driver's debug messages (>4 = verbose)	1

continues

continues

Parameter	Possible Values	Default Value

`full_duplex=#`	Replace # with:
	1 = enable full duplex
	0 = disable full duplex
		1

`rx_copybreak=#`	Replace # with the copy breakpoint for the copy-only-tiny-frames scheme (setting this to more than 1518 disables this feature)	200
`max_interrupt_work=#`	Replace # with the maximum number of events to handle at each interrupt	10

ES3210.O

Boot Parameters

Format:

```
ether="IRQ","IO Port","Memory Start","Memory End","Interface"
```

Option	Possible Values	Default Value
`IRQ`	Any valid IRQ (probed at 3, 4, 5, 6, 7, 8, 9, 10, 11, 12, 14, and 15)	probed
`IO Port`	Any valid I/O Port (probed at 0x1000 to 0x9000 in 0x1000 increments)	probed
`Memory Start`	Any valid Memory Start point	probed
`Memory End`	Any valid Memory End point	probed
`Interface`	eth0, eth1, eth2, eth3	none

Module Parameters

Format:

```
insmod es3210 io=0x### irq=# mem=0x###
```

Parameter	Possible Values	Default Value
`io=0x###`	Replace `0x###` with any valid I/O port (probed at 0x1000 to 0x9000 in 0x1000 increments)	probed
`irq=#`	Replace # with any valid IRQ (probed at 3, 4, 5, 6, 7, 8, 9, 10, 11, 12, 14, and 15)	probed
`mem=0x###`	Replace `0x###` with any valid memory start point	probed

ETH16I.O

Boot Parameters

Format:

```
ether="IRQ","IO Port","Memory Start","Memory End","Interface"
```

Option	Possible Values	Default Value
`IRQ`	Any valid IRQ (probed at 5, 9, 10, and 15 [16i only]; 3, 5, 7, 9, 10, 11, 12, and 15 [32 EISA only])	probed
`IO Port`	Any valid I/O Port (probed at 0x240, 0x260, 0x280, 0x2a0, 0x300, 0x320,0x340, and 0x380 [16i only]; 0x1000, 0x2000, 0x3000, 0x4000, 0x5000, 0x6000, 0x7000, 0x8000, 0x9000, 0xa000, 0xb000, 0xc000, 0xd000, 0xe000, and 0xf000 [32 EISA only])	probed
`Memory Start`	Any valid Memory Start point	probed
`Memory End`	Any valid Memory End point	probed
`Interface`	eth0, eth1, eth2, eth3	none

Module Parameters

Format:

```
insmod eth16i io=0x#### mediatype=??
```

Parameter	Possible Values	Default Value
`ioaddr=0x####`	Replace `0x####` with any valid I/O Port (probed at 0x240, 0x260, 0x280, 0x2a0, 0x300, 0x320,0x340, and 0x380 [16i only]; 0x1000, 0x2000, 0x3000, 0x4000, 0x5000, 0x6000, 0x7000, 0x8000, 0x9000, 0xa000, 0xb000, 0xc000, 0xd000, 0xe000, and 0xf000 [32 EISA only])	`0x2a0`
`mediatype=??`	Replace `??` with one of the following: `bnc`, `tp`, `dix`, `auto`, or `eprom`	none

EWRK3.O

BOOT PARAMETERS

Format:

```
ether="IRQ","IO Port","Memory Start","Memory End","Interface"
```

Option	Possible Values	Default Value
`IRQ`	Any valid IRQ (probed at 3, 5, 9, 10, 11, 12, and 15)	`5`
`IO Port`	Any valid I/O Port (probed at 0xl00, 0x120, 0x140, 0x160, 0x180, 0xlA0, 0xlC0, 0x200, 0x220, 0x240, 0x260, 0x280, 0x2a0, 0x2c0, 0x2e0, 0x300, 0x320, 0x340, 0x360, 0x380, 0x3a0, 0x3c0, 0x3d0, and 0x3e0 [ISA only]; 0x0c00 [EISA only] 0x0c00 [EISA])	`0x300` (ISA)
`Memory Start`	Any valid Memory Start point	probed
`Memory End`	Any valid Memory End point	probed
`Interface`	eth0, eth1, eth2, eth3	none

MODULE PARAMETERS

Format:

```
insmod ewrk3 irq=# io=0x###
```

Parameter	Possible Values	Default Value
`irq=#`	Replace # with any valid IRQ (probed at 3, 5, 9, 10, 11, 12, and 15)	5
`io=0x###`	Replace `0x###` with any valid I/O Port (probed at 0xl00, 0x120, 0x140, 0x160, 0x180, 0xlA0, 0xlC0, 0x200, 0x220, 0x240, 0x260, 0x280, 0x2a0, 0x2c0, 0x2e0, 0x300, 0x320, 0x340, 0x360, 0x380, 0x3a0, 0x3c0, 0x3d0, and 0x3e0 [ISA only]; 0x0c00 [EISA only] 0x0c00 [EISA])	`0x300` (ISA)

FMV18X.O

BOOT PARAMETERS

Format:

```
ether="IRQ","IO Port","Memory Start","Memory End","Interface"
```

Option	Possible Values	Default Value
`IRQ`	Any valid IRQ (probed at 3, 4, 5, 7, 9, 10, 11, and 15)	probed
`IO Port`	Any valid I/O Port (probed at 0x220, 0x240, 0x260, 0x280, 0x2a0, 0x2c0, 0x300, and 0x340)	`0x220`
`Memory Start`	Any valid Memory Start point	probed
`Memory End`	Any valid Memory End point	probed
`Interface`	eth0, eth1, eth2, eth3	none

MODULE PARAMETERS

Format:

```
insmod fmv18x irq=# io=0x### net_debug=#
```

Parameter	Possible Values	Default Value
irq=#	Replace # with any valid IRQ (probed at 3, 4, 5, 7, 9, 10, 11, and 15)	probed
io=0x###	Replace 0x### with any valid I/O Port (probed at 0x220, 0x240, 0x260, 0x280, 0x2a0, 0x2c0, 0x300, and 0x340)	0x220
net_debug=#	Replace # with the desired level of debug messages (>4 = verbose)	1

HOSTESS_SV11.O

Boot Parameters

No boot parameters are offered for this driver.

Module Parameters

Format:

```
insmod hostess_sv11 io=0x### dma=# irq=#
```

Parameter	Possible Values	Default Value
io=0x###	Replace 0x### with any valid I/O Port	0x200
dma=#	Replace # with 1 to enable DMA1/DMA3 for TX/RX	not set
irq=#	Replace # with any valid IRQ	9

HP.O

Boot Parameters

Format:

```
ether="IRQ","IO Port","Memory Start","Memory End","Interface"
```

Option	Possible Values	Default Value
IRQ	Any valid IRQ (probed at 3, 4, 5, 7, 9, 10, and 11 [16-bit only]; 3, 4, 5, 7, and 9 [8-bit only])	5

`IO Port`	Any valid I/O Port (probed at 0x200, 0x240, 0x2c0, 0x280, 0x300, 0x320, and 0x340)	probed
`Memory Start`	Any valid Memory Start point	probed
`Memory End`	Any valid Memory End point	probed
`Interface`	eth0, eth1, eth2, eth3	none

Module Parameters

Format:

```
insmod hp irq=# io=0x###
```

Parameter	Possible Values	Default Value
`irq=#`	Replace `#` with any valid IRQ (probed at 3, 4, 5, 7, 9, 10, and 11 [16 bit-only]; 3, 4, 5, 7, and 9 [8 bit-only])	probed
`io=0x###`	Replace `0x###` with any valid I/O Port (probed at 0x200, 0x240, 0x2c0, 0x280, 0x300, 0x320, and 0x340)	probed

HP100.O

Boot Parameters

Format:

```
hp100_mode=#
```

Parameter	Possible Values	Default Value
`hp100_mode=#`	Replace `#` with: `1` = use busmaster mode `2` = enable shared memory mode `3` = force I/O mapped mode `4` = same as `1`, but reset the enable bit on the card	`1`

Module Parameters

Format:

```
insmod hp100 hp100_rx_ratio=## hp100_priority_tx=# hp100_port=0x#### \
hp100_mode=#
```

Parameter	Possible Values	Default Value
hp100_rx_ratio=##	Replace ## with: 1–99 = percent of onboard memory to be used for receiving packets	none
hp100_priority_tx=#	Replace # with: 0 = outgoing packets are not transmitted as outgoing priority 1 = packets are transmitted as priority	0
hp100_port=0x####	Replace 0x#### with any valid I/O Port (probed at 0xl00, 0x120, 0x140, 0x160, 0x180, 0xlA0, 0xlC0, 0x200, 0x220, 0x240, 0x260, 0x280, 0x2a0, 0x2c0, 0x2e0, 0x300, 0x320, 0x340, 0x360, 0x380, 0x3a0, 0x3c0, 0x3d0, and 0x3e0 [ISA only]; from 0x1c38 to 0x10000 in 0x400 increments [EISA only])	probed
hp100_mode=#	Replace # with: 1 = use busmaster mode 2 = enable shared memory mode 3 = force I/O mapped mode 4 = same as 1, but reset the enable bit on the card	1

HPLANCE.O

No boot or module parameters are offered for this driver.

HP-PLUS.O

BOOT PARAMETERS

Format:

```
ether="IRQ","IO Port","Memory Start","Memory End","Interface"
```

Option	Possible Values	Default Value
`IRQ`	Any valid IRQ	probed
`IO Port`	Any valid I/O Port (probed at 0x200, 0x240, 0x280, 0x200, 0x300, 0x320, and 0x340)	probed
`Memory Start`	Any valid Memory Start point	probed
`Memory End`	Any valid Memory End point	probed
`Interface`	eth0, eth1, eth2, eth3	none

MODULE PARAMETERS

Format:

```
insmod hp-plus irq=# io=0x###
```

Parameter	Possible Values	Default Value
`irq=#`	Replace # with any valid IRQ	probed
`io=0x###`	Replace `0x###` with any valid I/O Port(probed at 0x200, 0x240, 0x280, 0x200, 0x300, 0x320, and 0x340)	probed

LANCE.O

BOOT PARAMETERS

Format:

```
ether="IRQ","IO Port","DMA Channel","Memory End","Interface"
```

Option	Possible Values	Default Value
`IRQ`	Any valid IRQ (probed at 3, 4, 5, 9 [built-in only]; 3, 4, 5, 9, 10, 11, 12, and 15 [hpJ2405A only])	probed
`IO Port`	Any valid I/O Port (probed at 0x300, 0x320, 0x340, and 0x360)	probed
`DMA Channel`	Any valid DMA channel (probed at 3, 5, 6, and 0 [built-in only]; 3, 5, 6, and 7 [hpJ2405A only]; 5, 6, 7, and 3 [all others])	probed
`Memory End`	Any valid Memory End point	probed
`Interface`	eth0, eth1, eth2, eth3	none

MODULE PARAMETERS

Format:

```
insmod lance io=0x### dma=# irq=#
```

Parameter	Possible Values	Default Value
io=0x###	Replace 0x### with any valid I/O port (probed at 0x300, 0x320, 0x340, and 0x360)	probed
dma=#	Replace # with any valid DMA channel (probed at 3, 5, 6, and 0 [built-in only]; 3, 5, 6, and 7 [hpJ2405A only]; 5, 6, 7, and 3 [all others])	probed
irq=#	Replace # with any valid IRQ [probed at 3, 4, 5, 9 (built-in only]; 3, 4, 5, 9, 10, 11, 12, and 15 [hpJ2405A only])	probed

LNE390.O

BOOT PARAMETERS

No boot parameters are provided for this driver.

MODULE PARAMETERS

Format:

```
insmod lne390 io=0x### irq=# mem=0x###
```

Parameter	Possible Values	Default Value
io=0x###	Replace 0x### with any valid I/O Port (probed at 0x1000 to 0x9000 in 0x1000 increments)	probed
irq=#	Replace # with any valid IRQ (probed at 3, 5, 7, 9, 10, 11, 12, and 15)	probed
mem=0x###	Replace 0x### with any valid memory start address	probed

NE.O

BOOT PARAMETERS

Format:

```
ether="IRQ","IO Port","Memory Start","Memory End","Interface"
```

Option	Possible Values	Default Value
IRQ	Any valid IRQ	probed
IO Port	Any valid I/O Port (probed at 0x280, 0x300, 0x320, 0x340, 0x360, and 0x380)	probed
Memory Start	Any valid Memory Start point	probed
Memory End	Any valid Memory End point	probed
Interface	eth0, eth1, eth2, eth3	none

MODULE PARAMETERS

Format:

```
insmod ne irq=# io=0x### bad=0xbad
```

Parameter	Possible Values	Default Value
irq=#	Replace # with any valid IRQ	probed
io=0x### (This parameter *must* be used!)	Replace 0x### with any valid I/O Port (probed at 0x280, 0x300, 0x320, 0x340, and 0x360)	probed
bad=0xbad	Use this parameter if the card has a bad signature or no reset ACK	not set

NE2K_PCI.O

No boot or module parameters are provided for this driver.

NE3210.O

BOOT PARAMETERS

No boot parameters are provided for this driver.

MODULE PARAMETERS

Format:

```
insmod ne3210 io=0x### irq=# mem=0x###
```

Parameter	Possible Values	Default Value
`io=0x###`	Replace `0x###` with any valid I/O Port (probed at 0x1000 to 0x9000 in 0x1000 increments)	probed
`irq=#`	Replace # with any valid IRQ (probed at 3, 5, 7, 9, 10, 11, 12, and 15)	probed
`mem=0x###`	Replace `0x###` with any valid memory start address	probed

NI5010.O

Boot Parameters

No boot parameters are provided for this driver.

Module Parameters

Format:

```
insmod ni5010 io=0x### irq=#
```

Parameter	Possible Values	Default Value
`io=0x###`	Replace `0x###` with any valid I/O Port (probed at 0x300, 0x320, 0x340, 0x360, 0x380, and 0x390)	probed
`irq=#`	Replace # with any valid IRQ	probed

NI52.O

Boot Parameters

Format:

```
ether="IRQ","IO Port","Memory Start","Memory End","Interface"
```

Option	Possible Values	Default Value
`IRQ`	Any valid IRQ	probed
`IO Port`	Any valid I/O Port (probed at 0x280, 0x300, 0x320, 0x340, and 0x360)	probed
`Memory Start`	Any valid Memory Start point (probed 0xd0000, 0xd2000, 0xc8000, 0xca000,	probed

Option	Possible Values	Default Value
	0xd4000, 0xd6000, 0xd8000, 0xcc000, 0xce000, 0xda000, and 0xdc000)	
`Memory End`	Any valid Memory End point	probed
`Interface`	eth0, eth1, eth2, eth3	none

Module Parameters

Format:

```
insmod ni52 irq=# io=0x### memstart=0x##### memend=0x#####
```

Parameter	Possible Values	Default Value
`irq=#`	Replace # with any valid IRQ	probed
`io=0x###`	Replace `0x###` with any valid I/O Port (probed at 0x280, 0x300, 0x320, 0x340, and 0x360)	probed
`memstart=0x#####`	Replace `0x#####` with any valid Memory Start point (probed 0xd0000, 0xd2000, 0xc8000, 0xca000, 0xd4000, 0xd6000, 0xd8000, 0xcc000, 0xce000, 0xda000, and 0xdc000)	probed
`memend=0x#####`	Replace `0x#####` with any valid Memory End point	none

NI65.0

Boot Parameters

Format:

```
ether="IRQ","IO Port","Memory Start","Memory End","Interface"
```

Option	Possible Values	Default Value
`IRQ`	Any valid IRQ (probed at 5, 9, 12, and 15)	probed
`IO Port`	Any valid I/O Port (probed at 0x300, 0x320, 0x340, and 0x360)	probed

continues

continued

Option	Possible Values	Default Value
`Memory Start`	Any valid Memory Start point	probed
`Memory End`	Any valid Memory End point	probed
`Interface`	eth0, eth1, eth2, eth3	none

Module Parameters

Format:

```
insmod ni65 irq=# io=0x## dma=#
```

Parameter	Possible Values	Default Value
`irq=#`	Replace # with any valid IRQ	`9`
`io=0x###`	Replace `0x###` with any valid I/O Port (probed at 0x300, 0x320, 0x340, and 0x360)	`0x360`
`dma=#`	Replace # with DMA channel 3, 5, 6, or 7	none

PCNET32.O

Boot Parameters

No boot parameters are provided for this driver.

Module Parameters

Format:

```
insmod pcnet32 debug=# max_interrupt_work=# rx_copybreak=#
```

Parameter	Possible Values	Default Value
`debug=#`	Replace # with the desired verbosity level of the driver's debug messages (>5 = verbose)	`1`
`max_interrupt_work=#`	Replace # with the maximum number of events to handle at each interrupt	`20`
`rx_copybreak=#`	Replace # with the copy breakpoint for the copy-only-tiny-	`200`

Parameter	Possible Values	Default Value
	frames scheme (setting this to more than 1518 disables this feature)	

RCPCI45.O

No boot or module parameters are provided for this driver.

RRUNNER.O

No boot or module parameters are provided for this driver.

RTL8139.O

Boot Parameters

No boot parameters are provided for this driver.

Module Parameters

Format:

```
insmod rtl8139 full_duplex=# multicast_filter_limit=# \
max_interrupt_work=# debug=#
```

Parameter	Possible Values	Default Value

full_duplex=#	Replace # with:
	1 = enable full duplex
	0 = disable full duplex
		1

multicast_filter _limit=#	Replace # with the maximum number of multicasts to filter	32
max_interrupt _work=#	Replace # with the maximum number of events to handle at each interrupt	20
debug=#	Replace # with the desired verbosity level of the driver's debug messages (4 = verbose)	1

SEEQ8005.O

No boot or module parameters are provided for this driver. There are, however, I/O Port values that are probed for when the driver is loaded. The following table lists these values, and is provided for information purposes only.

Setting	Probed Values
`IO Port`	`0x300`, `0x320`, `0x340`, and `0x360`

SK_G16.O

Boot Parameters

Format:

```
ether="IRQ","IO Port","Memory Start","Memory End","Interface"
```

Option	Possible Values	Default Value
`IRQ`	Any valid IRQ (probed at 3, 5, 9, and 11)	probed
`IO Port`	Any valid I/O Port (probed at 0x100, 0x180, 0x208, 0x220, 0x288, 0x320, 0x328, and 0x390)	probed
`Memory Start`	Any valid Memory Start point	probed
`Memory End`	Any valid memory End point	probed
`Interface`	eth0, eth1, eth2, eth3	none

Module Parameters

There is no modular support for this driver.

SMC9194.O

Boot Parameters

No boot parameters are provided for this driver.

Module Parameters

Format:

```
insmod smc9194 irq=# io=0x### ifport=#
```

Parameter	Possible Values	Default Value
`irq=#`	Replace # with any valid IRQ	none
`io=0x###`	Replace `0x###` with any valid I/O Port (probed at 0x200, 0x220, 0x240, 0x260, 0x280, 0x2A0, 0x2C0, 0x2E0, 0x300, 0x320, 0x340, 0x360, 0x380, 0x3A0, 0x3C0, and 0x3E0)	probed

`ifport=#`	Replace # with: `0` = autodetect, `1` = twisted pair, `2` = AUI or BNC	none

SMC-ULTRA.O

Boot Parameters

Format:

```
ether="IRQ","IO Port","Memory Start","Memory End","Interface"
```

Option	Possible Values	Default Value
`IRQ`	Any valid IRQ (probed at 3, 5, 7, 9, 10, 11, and 15)	probed
`IO Port`	Any valid I/O Port (probed at 0x200, 0x220, 0x240, 0x280, 0x300, 0x340, and 0x380)	probed
`Memory Start`	Any valid Memory Start point	probed
`Memory End`	Any valid Memory End point	probed
`Interface`	eth0, eth1, eth2, eth3	none

Module Parameters

Format:

```
insmod smc-ultra irq=# io=0x###
```

Parameter	Possible Values	Default Value
`irq=#`	Replace # with any valid IRQ (probed at 3, 5, 7, 9, 10, 11, and 15)	probed
`io=0x###`	Replace `0x###` with any valid I/O Port (probed at 0x200, 0x220, 0x240, 0x280, 0x300, 0x340, and 0x380)	probed

SMC-ULTRA32.O

No boot or module parameters are provided for this driver.

TLAN.O

BOOT PARAMETERS

Format:

```
ether=0,0,"AUI","Debug","Interface"
```

Option	Possible Values	Default Value
`0,0`	The first two values in the `ether=` line are not used	none
`AUI`	Choose from the following: `0x1` = aui `0x2` = use `SA_INTERRUPT` flag when reserving the IRQ `0x4` = use half duplex `0x8` = use full duplex `0x10` = use 10Base-T `0x20` = use 100Base-Tx	none
`Debug`	Add the bitmasks that give you the output you want from the following options: `0x1` = Turn on general debugging messages `0x2` = Turn on receive debugging messages `0x4` = Turn on transmit debugging messages `0x8` = Turn on list debugging messages	none

MODULE PARAMETERS

Format:

```
insmod tlan debug=# aui=# duplex=# speed=##
```

Parameter	Possible Values	Default Value
`debug=#`	Replace # with the sum of the bitmasks that give you the output you want. Choose from the following options: `0x1` = Turn on general debugging messages	none

	0x2 = Turn on receive debugging messages 0x4 = Turn on transmit debugging messages 0x8 = Turn on list debugging messages	
aui=#	Replace # with 1 if you want to use the AUI or BNC interface (instead of 10Base-T)	not set

duplex=#	Replace # with:
	1 = half duplex
	2 = full duplex
		none

speed=##	Replace ## with: 10 = 10MBS 100 = 100MBS	none

TULIP.O

Boot Parameters

No boot parameters are provided for this driver.

Module Parameters

Format:

```
insmod tulip debug=# options=# max_interrupt_work=# reverse_probe=# \
rx_copybreak=# full_duplex=#
```

Parameter	Possible Values	Default Value

debug=#	Replace # with:
	1 = normal output,
	2–6 = increase verbosity (6 is the maximum)
		none

options=#	Replace # with:
	0 = Auto-select,
	1 = 10Base-2,
	2 = AUI,
	3 = 100Base-Tx,
	4 = 10Base-T-FD,
	5 = 100Base-Tx-FD,
	6 = 100Base-T4,
		10Base-T

continues

continued

Parameter	Possible Values	Default Value
	7 = 100Base-Fx, 8 = 100Base-Fx-FD, 9 = MII 10Base-T, 10 = MII 10Base-T-FD, 11 = MII (autoselect), 12 = 10Base-T (no autoselect), v0.69 and later only, 13 = MII 100Base-Tx, 14 = MII 100Base-Tx-FD, 15 = MII 100Base-T4	
`max_interrupt _work=#`	Replace # with the maximum number of events to handle at each interrupt	25
`reverse_probe=#`	Replace # with: 1 = enable reverse PCI BIOS probe of multiport chips 0 = disable reverse probe	0
`rx_copybreak=#`	Replace # with the copy breakpoint for the copy-only-tiny-buffer RX structure (values greater than 1518 disable this feature)	100
`full_duplex=#`	Replace # with: 1 = enable full duplex 0 = disable full duplex	0

VIA-RHINE.O

Boot Parameters

No boot parameters are provided for this driver.

Module Parameters

Format:

```
insmod via-rhine max_interrupt_work=# min_pci_latency=# debug=# \
rx_copybreak=# full_duplex=#
```

Parameter	Possible Values	Default Value
max_interrupt_work=#	Replace # with the maximum number of events to handle at each interrupt	20
min_pci_latency=#	Replace # with the setting for the PCI latency timer	64
debug=#	Replace # with the desired verbosity level of the driver's debug messages (0 = quiet, 1 = normal, 7 = verbose)	1
rx_copybreak=#	Replace # with the copy breakpoint for the copy-only-tiny-frames scheme (setting this to greater than 1518 disables this feature)	0

full_duplex=#	Replace # with:
	1 = enable full duplex
	0 = disable full duplex
		1

WD.O

Boot Parameters

Format:

```
ether="IRQ","IO Port","Memory Start","Memory End","Interface"
```

Option	Possible Values	Default Value
IRQ	Any valid IRQ (probed at 3, 4, 5, 7, 9, 10, 11, and 15)	probed
IO Port	Any valid I/O Port (probed at 0x240, 0x280, 0x300, and 0x380)	probed
Memory Start	Any valid Memory Start point	probed
Memory End	Any valid Memory End point	probed
Interface	eth0, eth1, eth2, eth3	none

MODULE PARAMETERS

Format:

```
insmod wd irq=# io=0x### mem=0x### mem_end=0x###
```

Parameter	Possible Values	Default Value
`irq=#`	Replace # with any valid IRQ (probed at 3, 5, 7, 9, 10, 11, and 15)	probed
`io=0x###`	Replace `0x###` with any valid I/O Port (probed at 0x240, 0x280, 0x300, and 0x380)	probed
`mem=0x###`	Replace `0x###` with any valid memory start point	probed
`mem_end=0x###`	Replace `0x###` with any valid memory end point	probed

YELLOWFIN.O

BOOT PARAMETERS

No boot parameters are provided for this driver.

MODULE PARAMETERS

Format:

```
insmod yellowfin max_interrupt_work=# min_pci_latency=# mtu=# debug=#
rx_copybreak=# full_duplex=#
```

Parameter	Possible Values	Default Value
`max_interrupt_work=#`	Replace # with the maximum number of events to handle at each interrupt	`20`
`min_pci_latency=#`	Replace # with the setting for the PCI latency timer	`64`
`mtu=#`	Replace # with the size of the maximum transmission unit	`0`
`debug=#`	Replace # with the desired verbosity level of the driver's	`1`

Parameter	Possible Values	Default Value
	debug messages (5 = verbose)	
rx_copybreak=#	Replace # with the copy breakpoint for the copy-only-tiny-frames scheme (setting this to greater than 1518 disables this feature)	0

full_duplex=#	Replace # with:
	1 = enable full duplex
	0 = disable full duplex
		1

ZNET.O

No boot or module parameters are provided for this driver.

FRAME RELAY CARD DRIVERS

There is currently only one driver: slda.o

No boot or module parameters are provided for this driver. There are, however, IRQ and I/O Port settings that are probed for when the driver is loaded. The following table is being supplied for informational purposes only.

Setting	Probed Values
IRQ	3, 4, 5, 7, 10, 11, 12, and 15
IO Port	0x250, 0x270, 0x280, 0x300, 0x350, 0x360, 0x380, and 0x390

ARCNET CARD DRIVERS

All modular ARCnet support is loaded in two stages: First, the top-level arcnet.o module must be loaded, and then the individual card's module is loaded.

ARCNET.O

No boot or module parameters are provided for this driver.

ARC-RIMI.O

BOOT PARAMETERS

Format:

```
arcrimi="Shared Memory","IRQ","Node ID","Name"
```

Option	Possible Values	Default Value
`Shared Memory`	The address at which Shared Memory begins	none
`IRQ`	Any valid IRQ	none
`Node ID`	The Node ID for the card	none
`Name`	The interface name being used for the card (for instance, if you are not using arc0, put the name of the card that is being used here)	`arc0`

Module Parameters

Format:

```
insmod arc-rimi shmem=0x### irq=# device=?? node=#
```

Parameter	Possible Values	Default Value
`shmem=0x###`	Replace `0x###` with the address at which shared memory starts	none
`irq=#`	Replace `#` with any valid IRQ	none
`device=??`	Replace `??` with the name of the interface being used (for instance, if you are not using arc0, put the name of the interface that is being used here)	`arc0`
`node=#`	Replace `#` with the node ID of the card	none

COM20020.O

Boot Parameters

Format:

```
com20020="IO Port","IRQ","Node ID","Name"
```

Option	Possible Values	Default Value
`IO Port`	Any valid I/O Port	none
`IRQ`	Any valid IRQ	none
`Node ID`	The Node ID for the card	none

Option	Possible Values	Default Value
`Name`	The interface name being used for the card (for instance, if you are not using arc0, put the name of the interface that is being used here)	`arc0`

MODULE PARAMETERS

Format:

```
insmod com20020 io=0x### irq=# node=# device=??
```

Parameter	Possible Values	Default Value
`io=0x###`	Replace `0x###` with any valid I/O port	none
`irq=#`	Replace `#` with any valid IRQ	none
`node=#`	Replace `#` with the node ID of the card	none
`device=??`	Replace `??` with the name of the interface being used (for instance if you are not using arc0, put the name of the interface that is being used here)	`arc0`

COM90IO.O

BOOT PARAMETERS

Format:

```
com90io="IO Port","IRQ","Name"
```

Option	Possible Values	Default Value
`IO Port`	Any valid I/O Port	none
`IRQ`	Any valid IRQ	none
`Name`	The interface name being used for the card (for instance, if you are not using arc0, put the name of the interface that is being used here)	`arc0`

MODULE PARAMETERS

Format:

```
insmod com90io io=0x### irq=# device=??
```

Parameter	Possible Values	Default Value
`io=0x###`	Replace `0x###` with any valid I/O port	none
`irq=#`	Replace `#` with the IRQ of the card	none
`device=??`	Replace `??` with the name of the interface being used (for instance, if you are not using arc0, put the name of the interface that is being used here)	`arc0`

com90xx.o

Boot Parameters

Format:

```
com90xx="IO Port","IRQ","Shared Memory","Name"
```

or

```
com90xx="Name"
```

or

```
com90xx=
```

Option	Possible Values	Default Value
`IO Port`	Any valid I/O Port (probed at 0x200 to 0x3f0 in 0x010 increments [that is, 0x210, 0x220, 0x230, and so on])	none
`IRQ`	Any valid IRQ	none
`Shared Memory`	Any valid Shared Memory start point (probed at 0xa0000 to 0xff800 in increments of 2048)	none
`Name`	The interface name being used for the card (for instance, if you are not using arc0, put the name of the interface that is being used here)	`arc0`

The optional `com90xx=` boot parameter (with nothing after the `=`) is used to disable the driver.

MODULE PARAMETERS

Format:

```
insmod com90xx io=0x### irq=# shmem=0x### device=??
```

Parameter	Possible Values	Default Value
`io=0x###`	Replace `0x###` with any valid I/O port (probed at 0x200 to 0x3f0 in 0x010 increments [that is, 0x210, 0x220, 0x230, and so on])	none
`irq=#`	Replace `#` with any valid IRQ	none
`shmem=0x###`	Replace `0x###` with the address where shared memory starts	none
`device=??`	Replace `??` with the name of the interface being used (for instance if you are not using arc0, put the name of the interface that is being used here)	`arc0`

RADIO MODEM/NETWORK INTERFACE DRIVERS

BAYCOM_EPP.O

BOOT PARAMETERS

Format:

```
baycom="IO Port","Mode"
```

Option	Possible Values	Default Value
`IO Port`	Valid I/O port for the EPP parallel interface	`0x378`
`Mode`	Currently the only valid option is `epp`	`epp`

MODULE PARAMETERS

Format:

```
insmod baycom_epp iobase=0x### mode=??
```

Parameter	Possible Values	Default Value
iobase=0x###	Replace 0x### with the I/O port for the EPP parallel interface	0x378
mode=??	Replace ?? with epp	epp

BAYCOM_PAR.O

BOOT PARAMETERS

No boot parameters are provided for this driver.

MODULE PARAMETERS

Format:

```
insmod baycom_par iobase=0x### mode=??
```

Parameter	Possible Values	Default Value
iobase=0x###	Replace 0x### with the I/O port for the interface (0x378, 0x278, or 0x3bc)	0x378
mode=??	Replace ?? with the operating mode (either par96 for par96/97 cards, or picpar for picpar cards)	picpar

BAYCOM_SER_FDX.O

BOOT PARAMETERS

No boot parameters are provided for this driver.

MODULE PARAMETERS

Format:

```
insmod baycom_ser iobase=0x### mode=?? baud=#### irq=#
```

Parameter	Possible Values	Default Value
iobase=0x###	Replace 0x### with the I/O port for the interface (0x3f8, 0x2d8, 0x3e8, or 0x2e8)	0x3f8
mode=??	Replace ?? with the operating mode. Currently,	ser12*

Parameter	Possible Values	Default Value
	the only valid option is ser12. Add a "*" to the end to enable software DCD (for example, ser12*)	
baud=####	Replace #### with the baud rate. Valid options are from 300 to 4800, inclusive.	1200
irq=#	Replace # with the IRQ. Common values are 3 and 4.	4

BAYCOM_SER_HDX.O

Boot Parameters

No boot parameters are provided for this driver.

Module Parameters

Format:

```
insmod baycom_ser iobase=0x### mode=?? irq=#
```

Parameter	Possible Values	Default Value
iobase=0x###	Replace 0x### with the I/O port for the interface (0x3f8, 0x2d8, 0x3e8, or 0x2e8)	0x3f8
mode=??	Replace ?? with the operating mode. Currently, the only valid option is ser12. Add a * to the end to enable software DCD (for example, ser12*)	ser12*
irq=#	Replace # with the IRQ. Common values are 3 and 4.	4

DMASCC.O

No boot or module parameters are provided for this driver.

HFMODEM.O

Boot Parameters

No boot parameters are provided for this driver.

MODULE PARAMETERS

Format:

```
insmod hfmodem hw=# iobase=0x### irq=# dma=# serio=# pario=# midiio=#
```

Parameter	Possible Values	Default Value

`hw=#`	Replace # with:
	`0 = sbc`
	`1 = wss`
		`0`

`iobase=0x###`	Replace `0x###` with any valid I/O Port	`0x220`
`irq=#`	Replace # with any valid IRQ	7
`dma=#`	Replace # with any valid DMA channel (>=4 for SB16 /32/64, <=3 for all others)	1
`serio=0x###`	Replace `0x###` with an optional serial I/O port to send PTT output	none
`pario=0x###`	Replace `0x###` with an optional parallel I/O port to send PTT output	none
`midiio=0x###`	Replace `0x###` with an optional MIDI I/O port to send PTT output	none

PI2.O

No boot or module parameters are provided for this driver. There are, however, I/O Port settings that are probed for when the driver is loaded. The following table is being supplied for informational purposes only.

Setting	Probed Values
`IO Port`	`0x300`, `0x320`, `0x340`, `0x360`, `0x380`, and `0x3a0`

PT.O

No boot or module parameters are provided for this driver. There are, however, I/O Port settings that are probed for when the driver is loaded. The following table is being supplied for informational purposes only:

Setting	Probed Values
`IO Port`	`0x230`, `0x240`, `0x250`, `0x260`, `0x270`, `0x280`, `0x290`, `0x2a0`, `0x2b0`, `0x300`, `0x330`, and `0x3f0`

SCC.O

No boot or module parameters are provided for this driver. Use of this driver requires downloading the complete z8530drv package from the following FTP site:

`ftp://ftp.uscd.edu/hamradio/packet/tcpip/linux`

SM.O

This driver does not initialize the sound card when it loads (which is very important). For this reason, it is good to load the standard Linux sound driver or the commercial OSS/Linux driver (see Chapter 42, "Multimedia," for more details on OSS/Linux), and then unload it. The last step is important; you cannot run this driver with a Linux sound driver loaded.

Boot Parameters

Format:

```
sm="IO Port","IRQ","DMA"[,"DMA2"[,"Serial IO"[,"Parallel IO"]]],"Mode"
```

Option	Possible Values	Default Value
`IO Port`	Any valid I/O Port	`0x220` for `sbc`, `0x530` for `wss`
`IRQ`	Any valid IRQ	`5` or `7` for `sbc`, `11` for `wss`
`DMA`	Any valid first (low) DMA channel	`1`
`DMA2`	Optional second (high) DMA channel for full duplex	none
`Serial IO`	Optional I/O port for sending output to a serial port	none
`Parallel IO`	Optional I/O port for sending output to a parallel port	none
`Mode`	A combination of two specifications, listed in the form *`hardware:modem`*. Possible values for *`hardware`* include: `sbc` = SoundBlaster `wss` = Windows Sound System	probed

continues

continued

Option	Possible Values	Default Value
	wssfdx = Windows Sound System, full duplex Possible values for *modem* include: afsk1200 = AFSK 1200 baud modem fsk9600 = FSK 9600 baud modem	

MODULE PARAMETERS

Format:

```
insmod sm iobase=0x### irq=# dma=# dma2=# serio=0x### pario=0x### \
midiio=0x### mode=??
```

Parameter	Possible Values	Default Value
iobase=0x###	Replace 0x### with any valid I/O Port	0x220 for sbc, 0x530 for wss
irq=#	Replace # with any valid IRQ	5 or 7 for sbc, 11 for wss
dma=#	Replace # with any valid first (low) DMA channel	1
dma2=#	Replace # with an optional second (high) DMA channel for full duplex	none
serio=0x###	Replace 0x### with an optional serial I/O port to send PTT output	none
pario=0x###	Replace 0x### with an optional parallel I/O port to send PTT output	none
midiio=0x###	Replace 0x### with an optional MIDI I/O port to send PTT output	none
mode=??	Replace ?? with a *hardware*:*modem*	none

Parameter	Possible Values	Default Value
	specification that follows the same guidelines as the `Mode` boot parameter in the preceding table.	

WAVELAN.O

Caution

Changing the default IRQ or I/O Port settings for this driver either with a boot parameter or module parameter is *highly discouraged*. The hardware is meant to be run with certain settings only; straying from these established default settings might cause unreliable hardware operation or total driver failure.

Boot Parameters

Format:

```
ether="IRQ","IO Port","Memory Start","Memory End","Interface"
```

Option	Possible Values	Default Value
`IRQ`	Any valid IRQ	probed
`IO Port`	0x300, 0x390, 0x3E0, 0x3C0, and 0x390 (only probed at 0x390)	`0x390`
`Memory Start`	Any valid Memory Start point	probed
`Memory End`	Any valid Memory End point	probed
`Interface`	eth0, eth1, eth2, eth3	none

Module Parameters

Format:

```
insmod wavelan irq=# io=0x###
```

Parameter	Possible Values	Default Value
`irq=#`	Replace `#` with any valid IRQ	probed
`io=0x###`	Replace `0x###` with any valid I/O Port. Possible values are 0x300, 0x390, 0x3E0, 0x3C0, and 0x390 (only probed at 0x390)	`0x390`

Token Ring Card Drivers

IBMTR.O

Boot Parameters

No boot parameters are provided for this driver.

Module Parameters

Format:

```
insmod ibmtr irq=# io=0x#### mem=0x###
```

Parameter	Possible Values	Default Value
`irq=#`	The only valid option at this time is `0`	none
`io=0x###`	Replace `0x###` with the I/O port of the card. Valid values are either `0xa20` or `0xa24`	`0xa20`
`mem=0x###`	Replace `0x###` with any valid memory start point	none

SKTR.O

Boot Parameters

No boot parameters are provided for this driver.

Module Parameters

Format:

```
insmod sktr io=0x#### irq=# mem=0x###
```

Parameter	Possible Values	Default Value
`io=0x###`	Replace `0x###` with the I/O port of the card. Valid values are `0x0900`, `0x0980`, `0x0a20`, `0x0b20`, `0x1900`, `0x1980`, `0x1a20`, `0x1b20`	none
`irq=#`	Replace `#` with the IRQ of the card. Valid values are `3`, `5`, `9`, `10`, `11`, `12`, and `15`	none
`mem=0x###`	Replace `0x###` with any valid memory start address.	none

FDDI Controller Drivers

The defxx.o driver is the only known driver for FDDI controllers for the 2.2.1 Linux kernel.

No boot or module parameters are provided for this driver.

Floppy Controller Drivers

floppy.o

This is the only driver used for floppy disk drive controllers in the 2.2.1 Linux kernel. The floppy module does not normally require any configuration unless you have an IBM L40SX or ThinkPad, or an HP OmniBook.

Boot Parameters

Format:

```
floppy=parameter1,parameter2,parameter3,...
```

Parameter	Description	Default Value
`asus_pci`	Sets the bitmask to allow only units `0` and `1` (obsolete; always enabled)	enabled
`daring` or `0,daring`	Tells the floppy driver that you have a well-behaved floppy controller. Might speed up the drive, but increases instability. `0,daring` says to use the floppy drive with caution.	disabled
`one_fdc`	Only one floppy controller is present.	enabled
`two_fdc` or *<address>*, `two_fdc`	Two floppy controllers are present. The second controller is to be found at *<address>*, which is in hexadecimal (that is, `0x###`).	`0x370` if `two_fdc` is specified; disabled otherwise
`thinkpad`	Indicates you are using an IBM ThinkPad.	disabled
`0,thinkpad`	Forces the fact that you do *not* have a ThinkPad.	disabled

continues

continued

Parameter	Description	Default Value
`omnibook`	Indicates you are using an OmniBook.	disabled
`nodma`	Disables DMA transfers. Required if you are using an OmniBook or if you get `Unable to allocate DMA memory` errors frequently.	disabled
`yesdma`	Enables DMA transfers.	enabled
`nofifo`	Disables the use of the FIFO. Useful if you get `Bus master arbitration error` messages from your network card while accessing the floppy drive.	disabled
`fifo`	Enables the FIFO.	enabled
`<threshold>`, `fifo_depth`	Sets the FIFO threshold. Higher values cause the driver to handle more interrupt latency, but tend to slow down the system.	no default
`<drive>`, *`<type>`*`,cmos`	Forces certain settings for the drive in relation to the physical CMOS in your system. `drive` = valid drive number `type` = one of the following: `0` = Use CMOS value `1` = 5 1/4" DD `2` = 5 1/4" HD `3` = 3 1/2" DD `4` = 3 1/2" HD `5` = 3 1/2" ED `6` = 3 1/2" ED `16` = none	no default
`unexpected_interrupts`	Says to print a warning whenever an unexpected interrupt is received.	enabled

`no_unexpected_interrupts`	Says to *not* print warnings when unexpected interrupts are received. Required on IBM L40SX laptop systems.	disabled
`L40SX`	Says you have an IBM L40SX laptop	disabled
`broken_dcl`	Says to not use the disk change line (DCL). Some older drives and laptops do not have a DCL; this parameter must be set for those situations.	disabled
`debug`	Print debugging messages.	disabled
`silent_dcl_clear`	Use a quiet DCL clear method.	disabled
`<IRQ>,irq`	Sets the IRQ to `<IRQ>`	6
`<DMA>,dma`	Sets the DMA to `<DMA>`	2
`slow`	Use PS/2 stepping rate	disabled

MODULE PARAMETERS

Format:

```
insmod floppy floppy=parameter1,parameter2,parameter3,...
```

The format for the module parameters following `insmod floppy` is the same format as the boot parameters for this driver.

MOUSE DRIVERS

ATIXLMOUSE.O

No boot or module parameters are provided for this driver. There are, however, IRQ and I/O port values that are probed for when the driver is loaded. The following table lists those values, and is provided for information purposes only.

Setting	**Probed Values**
`IRQ`	`5`
`IO Port`	`0x23d`

BUSMOUSE.O

The default I/O port for this driver is 0x23c. This cannot be changed without editing the actual driver source code and recompiling the driver.

Boot Parameters

No boot parameters are provided for this driver.

Module Parameters

Format:

```
insmod busmouse mouse_irq=#
```

Parameter	Description	Default Value
`mouse_irq=#`	Replace # with the IRQ of the mouse interface	5

MSBUSMOUSE.O

The default I/O port for this driver is `0x23d`. This cannot be changed without editing the actual driver source code and recompiling the driver.

Boot Parameters

No boot parameters are provided for this driver.

Module Parameters

Format:

```
insmod msbusmouse mouse_irq=#
```

Parameter	Description	Default Value
`mouse_irq=#`	Replace # with the IRQ of the mouse interface	5

PC110PAD.O

Boot Parameters

No boot parameters are provided for this driver.

Module Parameters

Format:

```
insmod pc110pad pc110pad_mode=# bounce_interval=# tap_interval=# io=0x### irq=#
```

Parameter	Description	Default Value

`pc110pad_mode=#`	Replace # with:
	1 = raw (byte-by-byte processing)
	2 = rare (debounced up/down and absolute X,Y)
		4

	3 = debug (up/down, debounced, transitions X,Y) 4 = PS/2 compatible	
bounce_interval=#	Replace # with any valid bounce interval	50ms
tap_interval=#	Replace # with any valid tap interval	200ms
io=0x###	Replace 0x### with any valid I/O port.	0x15e0
irq=#	Replace # with any valid IRQ	10

PART VII

APP C

PC_KEYB.O

No boot or module parameters are provided for this driver. There is, however, an IRQ value that is probed for when the driver is loaded. The following table lists that value, and is provided for information purposes only.

Setting	Probed Values
IRQ	12 (can be probed at 9)

QPMOUSE.O

No boot or module parameters are provided for this driver. There are, however, IRQ and I/O port values that are probed for when the driver is loaded. The following table lists those values, and is provided for information purposes only.

Setting	Probed Values
IRQ	12
IO Port	0x310

IRDA (INFRARED DEVICE) DRIVERS

ACTISYS.O

No boot or module parameters are provided for this driver.

ESI.O

No boot or module parameters are provided for this driver.

TEKRAM.O

No boot or module parameters are provided for this driver.

uircc.o

No boot or module parameters are provided for this driver.

w83977af.o

No boot or module parameters are provided for this driver.

pc87108.o

No boot or module parameters are provided for this driver.

Serial Board Drivers

cyclades.o

Boot Parameters

Format:

```
cyclades="IO Port"[,"IO Port2","IO Port3",...]
```

Option	Possible Values	Default Value
`IO Port[2,3,...]`	Any valid I/O Port (probed at `0xd0000`, `0xd2000`, `0xd4000`, `0xd6000`, `0xd8000`, `0xda000`, `0xdc000`, `0xde000`)	probed

Module Parameters

No module parameters are provided for this driver.

epca.o

Only PCI cards are probed by this driver. `digiConfig` values are overridden by boot parameters. Do not use paramcters when you are using this driver with PCI cards.

Boot Parameters

Format:

```
digiepca="Use Card","Type","Alt. Pins","Ports","IO Port","Memory Base"
```

Option	Possible Values	Default Value
`Use Card`	`E` or `1` = enable `d` or `0` = disable	`E` or `1`

`Type`	`PC/Xe` or `0` = PC/Xe (AccelPort) `PC/Xeve` or `1` = PC/Xeve `PC/Xem` or `2` = PC/Xem `PC/Xr` or `2` = PC/Xr (2 applies to both PC/Xr and PC/Xem) `EISA/Xem` or `3` = EISA/Xem `PC/64Xe` or `4` = PC/64Xe `PC/Xi` or `5` = PC/Xi	`PC/Xe` or `0`
`Alt. Pins`	`E` or `1` = enable `D` or `0` = disable	not set
`Ports`	The number of ports on the card	`0`
`IO Port`	Any valid I/O Port	not set
`Memory Base`	Any valid Memory Base	not set

Module Parameters

No module parameters are provided for this driver.

ESP.O

Boot Parameters

No boot parameters are provided for this driver.

Module Parameters

For the `irq=` and `divisor=` parameters, there are eight positions that *must* be filled, even if the number filling the positions is `0`. Each position is mapped to a static I/O port address; each Hayes card that exists at the corresponding I/O port address must have a specified setting (the type of setting is dictated by whether it is an IRQ or a divisor).

The mapping of the eight positions looks similar to the following, in order:

```
0x100,0x140,0x180,0x200,0x240,0x280,0x300,0x380
```

To help illustrate how the positioning of these values works, if you have a Hayes card at I/O port address 0x280 and you want to tell the driver the IRQ is 10, give the following IRQ parameter:

```
insmod esp irq=0,0,0,0,0,10,0,0
```

This tells the driver to assign IRQ 10 to the Hayes card at I/O port address 0x280 and to essentially ignore the rest of the I/O port addresses. The same positioning applies to the `divisor=` parameter (which is explained later).

Format:

```
insmod esp irq=#,#,#,#,#,#,#,# divisor=#,#,#,#,#,#,#,# dma=# rx_trigger=# \
tx_trigger=# flow_off=# flow_on=# rx_timeout=# pio_threshold=#
```

Parameter	Description	Default Value
`irq=#,#,#,#,#,#,#,#`	Replace # with the IRQ that matches the underlying I/O port, if a card exists at that I/O port address (see the preceding explanation). A `0` in any position means that there is no IRQ setting for the position's associated I/O port address.	`0,0,0,0,0,0,0,0`
`divisor=#,#,#,#,#,#,#,#`	Replace # with a divisor value in hex that you want to assign to the underlying I/O port address (see the preceding explanation). These hex values are given from left to right, primary interface to secondary, and so on. For example, if you have a card at I/O port address 0x300, and on the primary port you want to assign a divisor of 4 and on the secondary port you want to assign a divisor of 8, from right to left (in hex formation) the parameter line looks like this: `divisor=0,0,0,0,0,0,0x84,0`	`0,0,0,0,0,0,0,0`
`dma=#`	Replace # with either `1` or `3` to set the DMA channel. Any other value forces the driver to use PIO mode.	none

Parameter	Description	Default Value
`rx_trigger=#`	Replace # with the RX FIFO trigger level. This specifies when the Hayes card is to send an interrupt. Larger values increase the interrupts, but at the expense of possible data loss. This value needs to be lower than the flow-off value. Valid values are between 1 and 1023.	768
`tx_trigger=#`	Replace # with the TX FIFO trigger level. This specifies when the Hayes card is to send an interrupt. Larger values increase the interrupts, but at the expense of possible data loss. Valid values are between 1 and 1023.	768
`flow_off=#`	Replace # with the hardware flow-off level. This must be higher than the flow-on level and higher than the RX trigger. Valid values are between 1 and 1023.	1016
`flow_on=#`	Replace # with the hardware flow-on level. This must be lower than the flow-on level. Valid values are between 1 and 1023.	944

continues

continued

Parameter	Description	Default Value
`rx_timeout=#`	Replace # with the RX timeout value. This indicates how long after receiving the last character the Hayes card is to wait before signaling an interrupt. Higher values increase latency, and excessively low values can cause unnecessary interrupts. Valid values are `0–255`.	`128`
`pio_threshold=#`	Replace # with the threshold (in numbers of characters) for using `PIO` mode instead of `DMA` mode (`PIO` mode can be forced using the `dma=` parameter).	none

ISICOM.O

BOOT PARAMETERS

No boot parameters are provided for this driver.

MODULE PARAMETERS

Format:

```
insmod isicom io=0x### irq=#
```

Parameter	Description	Default Value
`io=0x###`	Replace `0x###` with any valid I/O port	none
`irq=#`	Replace # with any valid IRQ (probed at 2, 3, 4, 5, 7, 10, 11, 12, and 15)	none

ISTALLION.O

When using this driver for any applicable Stallion card (except for the EasyConnection 8/64 PCI card), an additional package of driver utilities has to be downloaded and installed.

The following URL points to a directory on Caldera Systems' FTP site that contains the most recent version of this package:

```
ftp://ftp.calderasystems.com/pub/mirrors/tsx-11/packages/stallion
```

No boot or module parameters are provided this driver. There is, however, one I/O Port value that is probed for when the driver is loaded (for EasyConnection 8/64 boards). The following table lists the I/O Port values that are used for different boards, and is provided for information purposes only.

Setting	Probed Values
IO Port	For EasyConnection 8/64 boards: `0x2a0` For ONboard, Brumby, and Stallion boards: whatever the board itself is set to use For PCI boards: whatever is assigned by the PCI BIOS

PCXX.O

Contrary to convention, boot parameter lines are preceded with the string `digi=`, not `pcxx=`. Multiple `digi=` boot parameter lines can be stacked one after the other for a multiple card setup. They need to be set in order of initialization, of course.

Boot Parameters

Format:

```
digi="Enable","Type","Alternate Pins","Ports","IO Port","Memory Base"
```

Option	Possible Values	Default Value
Enable	`E` or `1` = enable card, `D` or `0` = disable card	`D` or `0`
Type	`PC/Xi` or `0` = PC/Xi, `PC/Xe` or `1` = PC/Xe, `PC/Xeve` or `2` = PC/Xeve	`PC/Xi` or `0`
Alternate Pins	`E` or `1` = enable alternate pin arrangement, `D` or `0` = disable alternate pin arrangement	`E` or `1`
Ports	Number of ports on the card	`16`
IO Port	Any valid I/O Port	`0x200`
Memory Base	Any valid Memory Base	`0xd00000`

MODULE PARAMETERS

Most of the parameters that are offered for the modular driver allow comma-delimited lists that can cover settings for all the cards. These lists are filled in order from the first card to the last. If any particular position in any of the comma-delimited lists is omitted, the card associated with that position uses the default setting for that parameter.

For example, if you want to set the I/O port address for the second card to 0x230, the following parameter line accepts the default I/O port for the first card and assign 0x230 as the I/O port for the second card:

```
insmod pcxx io=,0x230
```

Format:

```
insmod pcxx io=0x###[,0x###,0x###,...] membase=0x###[,0x###,0x###,...] \
memsize=#[,#,#,...] numports=#[,#,#,...] altpin=#[,#,#,...] verbose=# debug=#
```

Parameter	Description	Default Value
`io=0x###[,0x###,...]`	Replace `0x###` with any valid I/O port	`0x200`
`membase=0x###` `[,0x###,...]`	Replace `0x###` with any valid memory base address	`0xd0000`
`memsize=#[,#,...]`	Replace # with any valid memory size (in kilobytes) for the card	not set
`numports=#[,#,...]`	Replace # with the number of ports on the card(s)	`16`
`altpin=#[,#,...]`	Replace # with: `1` = enable alternate pins `0` = disable alternate pins	`0`
`verbose=#`	Replace # with: `1` = enable verbose operation `0` = disable verbose operation	`0`
`debug=#`	Replace # with: `1` = enable debugging output `0` = disable debugging output	`0`

RISCOM8.O

Boot Parameters

Format:

```
riscom8="IO Port 1"[,"IO Port 2","IO Port 3","IO Port 4"]
```

Option	Possible Values	Default Value
`IO Port [1-4]`	Any valid I/O Port (they are listed in order on the boot parameter line, from the first card to the fourth)	`0x220`, `0x240`, `0x250`, `0x260` (in order, from the first card to the fourth)

Module Parameters

Format:

```
insmod riscom8 iobase=0x### [iobase1=0x### iobase2=0x### iobase3=0x###]
```

Parameter	Possible Values	Default Value
`iobase=0x###`	Replace `0x###` with any valid I/O Port (first card)	`0x220`
`iobase[1-3]=0x###`	Replace `0x###` with any valid I/O Port (second through fourth cards)	`0x240`, `0x250`, `0x260` (in order, from the second card to the fourth)

ROCKET.O

Boot Parameters

No boot parameters are provided for this driver.

Module Parameters

Format:

```
insmod rocket board1=0x### board2=0x### board3=0x### board4=0x### \
controller=0x### support_low_speed=#
```

Parameter	Possible Values	Default Value
`board[1-4]=0x###`	Replace `0x###` with any valid I/O port (ISA board)	none

continues

continued

Parameter	Possible Values	Default Value
`controller=0x###`	Replace `0x###` with any valid I/O port (ISA controller)	none
`support_low_speed=#`	Replace # with: `0` = 50 baud `1` = 460400 bps	none

SPECIALIX.O

BOOT PARAMETERS

Format:

`specialix="IO Port","IRQ"[,"IO Port2","IRQ2",...]`

Option	Possible Values	Default Value
`IO Port[2,3,...]]`	Any valid I/O Port (probed at 0x100, 0x180, 0x250, and 0x260 for ISA cards)	In order: `0x100`, `0x180`, `0x250`, and `0x260` for the first four ISA cards
`IRQ[2,3,...]`	Any valid IRQ	none

MODULE PARAMETERS

Format:

`insmod specialix iobase=0x###[,0x###,...] irq=#[,#,...]`

The values for `iobase=` match exactly the `IO Port[2,3,...]` boot parameter values. Likewise, the `irq=` values match exactly the `IRQ[2,3,...]` boot parameter values.

STALLION.O

No boot or module parameters are provided this driver. There is, however, one I/O Port value that is probed for when the driver is loaded (for EasyIO boards). The following table lists the I/O Port values that are used for different boards, and is provided for information purposes only.

Setting	Probed Values
`IO Port`	For EasyIO boards: `0x2a0`

For PCI boards: whatever is assigned by the PCI BIOS

APPENDIX 

How to Find Other Linux Information

With the ever-increasing popularity and notoriety of Linux, the number of Web sites with specific Linux information and documentation is growing at a geometric rate. This list of URLs is by no means all-inclusive. However, it should give you a good idea of what kind of information and software is available for Linux.

OpenLinux Specific

The Caldera Systems Web site contains a great deal of OpenLinux-specific information. A user forum is offered in several areas, including NetWare and Wabi. If you're looking for answers to technical questions in regard to OpenLinux, the Caldera Users email list is known to be a good resource. Many Linux experts are regular contributors to the Caldera Users email list. See the following URL for details:

```
http://www.calderasystems.com/support/forums.html
```

Recently, a new support knowledge base has been added as part of the technical support services. See the following URL for details:

```
http://www.calderasystems.com/support/index.html
```

Much of the OpenLinux documentation is available via the Web as well, at the following URL:

```
http://www.calderasystems.com/doc/
```

The Caldera Systems FTP site also mirrors many Linux related sites, including the complete *Linux Documentation Project* (*LDP*). See the following URLs for details:

```
http://www.calderasystems.com/LDP/
ftp://ftp.caldera.com/pub/mirrors/
```

Linux General

The sites in the following list include information or news about Linux in general. Again, there are many more sites than are listed here, but these are some of the well-known sites.

Linux Standard Base

```
http://www.linuxbase.org/
```

"The goal of the *Linux Standard Base* (*LSB*) is to develop and promote a set of standards that will increase compatibility among Linux distributions and enable software applications to run on any compliant Linux system. In addition, the LSB will help coordinate efforts to recruit software vendors to port and write products for Linux."

LINUX INTERNATIONAL

http://www.li.org

Linux International is a non-profit association of groups, corporations, and others that work toward the promotion of and help direct the growth of the Linux operating system and the Linux community.

XFREE86

http://www.xfree86.org

The XFree86 Project, Inc. is a non-profit organization that produces XFree86. XFree86 is a freely redistributable implementation of the X Window System that runs on UNIX and UNIX-like operating systems (and OS/2).

THE K DESKTOP ENVIRONMENT

http://www.kde.org

KDE is a powerful graphical desktop environment for UNIX workstations. It combines ease of use, contemporary functionality, and outstanding graphical design with the technological superiority of the UNIX operating system.

OPEN SOURCE ORGANIZATION

http://www.opensource.org

Open source software is an idea whose time has finally come. For twenty years it has been building momentum in the technical cultures that built the Internet and the World Wide Web. Now it's breaking out into the commercial world, and that's changing all the rules.

METALAB (FORMERLY SUNSITE)

http://metalab.unc.edu/

TSX-11

ftp://tsx-11.mit.edu/pub/linux/

THE LINUX KERNEL ARCHIVES

http://www.kernel.org

Welcome to the Linux Kernel Archives. This is the primary site for the Linux kernel source, but it has much more than just kernels—it has 20GB of disk space set aside for mirroring the largest Linux-related software archives.

LINUX JOURNAL

`http://www.linuxjournal.com/`

LINUX WEEKLY NEWS

`http://www.lwn.net/`

LINUX WORLD

`http://www.linuxworld.com/`

FRESHMEAT

`http://news.freshmeat.net`

SLASHDOT

`http://www.slashdot.org/`

SPECIFIC COMPONENTS SUPPORT

The following list of sites is more specific in nature, but a wide sampling is included. These sites are just that, a sampling. There are many, many more sites with specific Linux information—and the number of new sites is increasing.

THE LINUX-KERNEL ARCHIVE

`http://www.uwsg.indiana.edu/hypermail/linux/kernel/`

The Linux-kernel list is a majordomo mailing list hosted at `vger.rutgers.edu`. It exists for the discussion of kernel development issues, including new features, bug reports, and announcements of new kernel releases. This list is not for the faint of heart. It is designed for people who have some experience with the kernel and are interested in participating in the development of the kernel.

THE LINUX KERNEL

`http://amelia.db.erau.edu/ldp/LDP/tlk/tlk.html`

This book is for Linux enthusiasts who want to know how the Linux kernel works. It is not an internals manual. Rather, it describes the principles and mechanisms that Linux uses—how and why the Linux kernel works the way that it does. Linux is a moving target; this book is based upon the current, stable, 2.0.33 sources because those are what most individuals and companies are now using.

LINUX SMP

`http://www.linux.org.uk/SMP/title.html`

LINUX LINKS

`http://www.ai.uga.edu/~jae/linux.html`

LINUX FAT32 SUPPORT

`http://bmrc.berkeley.edu/people/chaffee/fat32.html`

LINUX/MICROCONTROLLER HOME PAGE

`http://ryeham.ee.ryerson.ca/uClinux/`

LINUX AT CESDIS

`http://cesdis1.gsfc.nasa.gov/linux-web/`

LINUX IN BUSINESS SETTINGS

`http://www.m-tech.ab.ca/linux-biz/`

MULTICAST AND MBONE ON LINUX—OVERVIEW

`http://www.teksouth.com/linux/multicast/`

The *MBONE* (*Multicast Backbone*) and multicast technology are an exciting branch of Internet technology that might have a major impact on how the Internet is used in the future. Where traditional IP traffic is one sender to one receiver, multicasting has the capability of allowing one sender to many receivers. Propagation can also be set to control how far traffic can go. Traffic can be restricted to a single host, site, or region—or to the whole world.

THE LINUX PROGRAMMER'S BOUNCEPOINT

`http://www.ee.mu.oz.au/linux/programming/`

SSH—PRODUCTS

`http://www.ssh.fi/products/`

This Web site contains security technology from SSH. Communications Security Ltd. forms the security backbone of several well-known products on the worldwide market. The security products are built on tested, public cryptographic algorithms and standardized protocols. This technology provides easy access to security and the best performance available—without compromises in security.

`mgetty + sendfax` DOCUMENTATION CENTRE

`http://www.leo.org/~doering/mgetty/`

Consistent Backspace and Delete Configuration

`http://www.ibbnet.nl/~anne/keyboard.html`

Information on how to configure the behavior of the Backspace key and Delete key can be found at this site.

ISDN for Linux

`ftp://ftp.franken.de/pub/isdn4linux/FAQ/eng-i4l-faq.html`

`Ghostscript`, `Ghostview`, and `Gsview`

`http://www.cs.wisc.edu/~ghost/`

`PStill`—A PS to PDF converter by Frank Siegert

`http://www.this.net/~frank/pstill.html`

`PStill` is a PostScript to Portable Document Format (PDF) converter.

Sound Drivers for Linux (commercial)

`http://www.opensound.com/`

Sound Blaster AWE 32/64 HOWTO

`http://homepage.ruhr-uni-bochum.de/Marcus.Brinkmann/Soundblaster-AWE-HOWTO.html`

This document describes how to install and configure a Sound Blaster 32 (SB AWE 32, SB AWE 64) card from Creative Labs in a Linux System using the AWE Sound Driver Extension written by Takashi Iwai. It also covers some special tools and players for the SB AWE series. Reference system is a Debian GNU/Linux System, but every other Linux Distribution also works.

Linux Parallel Port Home Page

`http://www.torque.net/linux-pp.html`

NSBD: Not-So-Bad Distribution

`http://www.bell-labs.com/project/nsbd/`

Linux PCMCIA Information

`http://hyper.stanford.edu/HyperNews/get/pcmcia/home.html`

BIND, DHCP, INN home page (ISConsortium)

`http://www.isc.org/`

The ISC is a nonprofit corporation dedicated to production-quality software engineering for key Internet standards. Reference implementations of Internet standards often have the weight of *de facto standards* and the ISC wants to make sure that those reference implementations are properly supported. The ISC is also committed to keeping these reference implementations freely available to the Internet community.

The Diald Home Page

http://www.loonie.net/~eschenk/diald.html

Diald provides on demand Internet connectivity for Linux, giving you complete automated control over your SLIP or PPP links. When you need a connection it's there. When you don't, it's not. You'll never need to run a ppp-on or ppp-off script again.

Linux Network Drivers

http://cesdis.gsfc.nasa.gov/linux/drivers/

Linux IP Masquerade Resource

http://ipmasq.cjb.net/

DNS tools

http://www.dns.net/dnsrd/tools.html

Netatalk—Essential for Apple connectivity

http://www.umich.edu/~rsug/netatalk/

Anders: Netatalk: Linux Netatalk-HOWTO

http://thehamptons.com/anders/netatalk/

Netatalk is a package that allows a UNIX machine to supply AppleTalk print and file services on a LAN. The package supports AppleShare IP and classic AppleTalk protocols. With Netatalk, Macintosh computers can mount UNIX volumes and print to UNIX print spools as if they were standard AppleTalk network devices.

Linux Plug-ins for Netscape

http://www.canopy.com/linuxplugins.html

XFree86 Servers by SuSE

http://www.suse.de/XSuSE/XSuSE_E.html

In cooperation with The XFree86 Project, Inc., SuSE GmbH is proud to present a small series of X servers. These servers are based on source code from XFree86-servers, but they are enhanced and extended.

Third-Party Quickcam Software Page

http://www.cs.virginia.edu/~patrick/quickcam/

The Mesa 3D Graphics Library

http://www.ssec.wisc.edu/~brianp/Mesa.html

WhirlGIF 2.01

http://www.msg.net/utility/whirlgif/

BTTV page Frame Grabber for Linux

http://www.thp.Uni-Koeln.DE/~rjkm/linux/bttv.html

XVidCap—X Video Capture for Linux

http://www.komm.hdk-berlin.de/~rasca/xvidcap/

kwintv

http://www.mathematik.uni-kl.de/~wenk/xwintv.html

`kwintv` is a KDE application based on the bttv-driver by Ralph Metzler. `kwintv` enables you to watch TV in a window on your PC screen. It has more or less the same abilities as `xtvscreen`, which is included in the bttv-driver package, but it is based on `Qt`, a C++ GUI application framework by Troll Tech, and integrated in the K Desktop Environment Directory of /pub/Linux/docs/linux-doc-project/module-programming-guide.

INDEX

Symbols

B

E

F

G

H

I

J

K

M

N

O

P

Q

R

S

T

U

V

X

Y

Z

Other Related Titles

UNIX Hints and Hacks
Kirk Waingrow
0-7897-1927-4
$19.99 US/$28.95 CAN

Platinum Edition Using HTML 4, XML, and Java 1.2
Eric Ladd
0-7897-1759-x
$59.99 US/$85.95 CAN

Using Mac OS 8.5
Brad Miser
0-7897-1614-3
$29.99 US/$42.95 CAN

Using UNIX, 2nd Ed.
Steve Moritsugu
0-7897-1632-1
$29.99 US/$42.95 CAN

The Complete Idiot's Guide to UNIX
Bill Wagner
0-7897-1805-7
$16.99 US/$24.95 CAN

Hacking Java: The Java Professional's Resource Kit
Mark Wutka
0-7897-0935-x
$59.99 US/$84.95 CAN

Windows 2000 Hints and Hacks
Bob Chronister
0-7897-1918-5
$19.99 US/$28.95 CAN

The Complete Idiots Guide to C++
Paul Snaith
0-7897-1816-2
$19.99 US/$28.95 CAN

Using C++
Rob McGregor
0-7897-1667-4
$29.99 US/$42.95 CAN

Using Visual InterDev 6
Mike Amundsen
0-7897-1640-2
$29.99 US/$42.95 CAN

www.quecorp.com

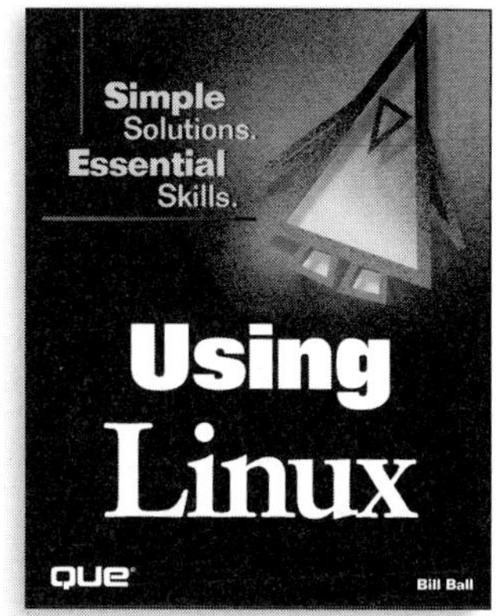

Using Linux
Bill Ball
0-7897-1623-2
$29.99 US/
$42.95 CAN

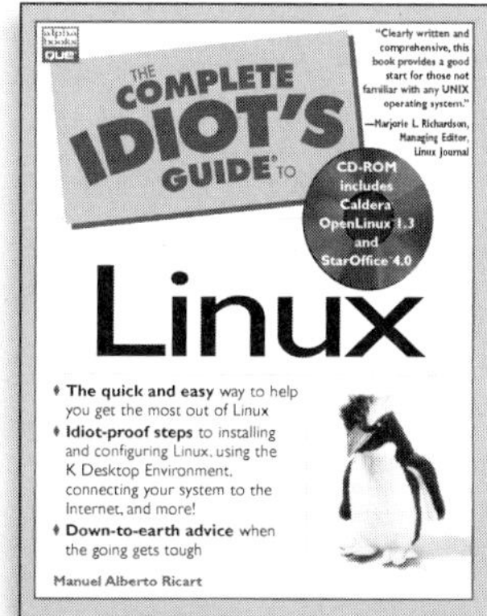

The Complete Idiot's Guide to Linux
Manuel Ricart
0-7897-1826-x
$19.99/US
$28.95 CAN

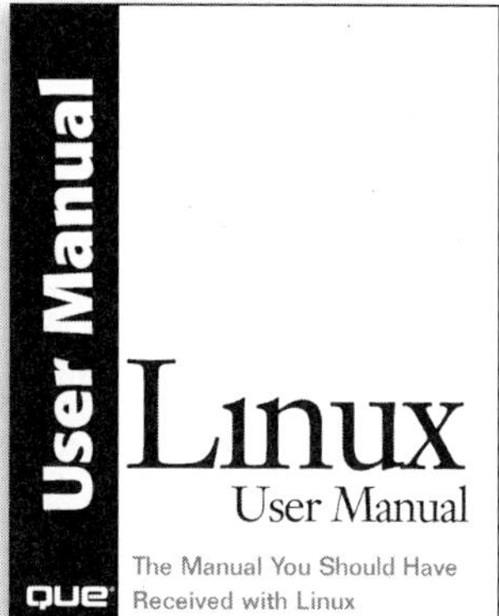

Linux User Manual
Que
0-7897-1877-4
$19.99 US/
$28.95 CAN

All prices are subject to change.

GNU GENERAL PUBLIC LICENSE

Version 2, June 1991

Preamble

The licenses for most software are designed to take away your freedom to share and change it. By contrast, the GNU General Public License is intended to guarantee your freedom to share and change free software--to make sure the software is free for all its users. This General Public License applies to most of the Free Software Foundation's software and to any other program whose authors commit to using it. (Some other Free Software Foundation software is covered by the GNU Library General Public License instead.) You can apply it to your programs, too.

When we speak of free software, we are referring to freedom, not price. Our General Public Licenses are designed to make sure that you have the freedom to distribute copies of free software (and charge for this service if you wish), that you receive source code or can get it if you want it, that you can change the software or use pieces of it in new free programs; and that you know you can do these things.

To protect your rights, we need to make restrictions that forbid anyone to deny you these rights or to ask you to surrender the rights. These restrictions translate to certain responsibilities for you if you distribute copies of the software, or if you modify it.

For example, if you distribute copies of such a program, whether gratis or for a fee, you must give the recipients all the rights that you have. You must make sure that they, too, receive or can get the source code. And you must show them these terms so they know their rights.

We protect your rights with two steps: (1) copyright the software, and (2) offer you this license which gives you legal permission to copy, distribute and/or modify the software.

Also, for each author's protection and ours, we want to make certain that everyone understands that there is no warranty for this free software. If the software is modified by someone else and passed on, we want its recipients to know that what they have is not the original, so that any problems introduced by others will not reflect on the original authors' reputations.

Finally, any free program is threatened constantly by software patents. We wish to avoid the danger that redistributors of a free program will individually obtain patent licenses, in effect making the program proprietary. To prevent this, we have made it clear that any patent must be licensed for everyone's free use or not licensed at all.

The precise terms and conditions for copying, distribution and modification follow.

GNU GENERAL PUBLIC LICENSE

TERMS AND CONDITIONS FOR COPYING, DISTRIBUTION AND MODIFICATION

1. This License applies to any program or other work which contains a notice placed by the copyright holder saying it may be distributed under the terms of this General Public License. The "Program", below, refers to any such program or work, and a "work based on the Program" means either the Program or any derivative work under copyright law: that is to say, a work containing the Program or a portion of it, either verbatim or with modifications and/or translated into another language. (Hereinafter, translation is included without limitation in the term "modification".) Each licensee is addressed as "you".

   Activities other than copying, distribution and modification are not covered by this License; they are outside its scope. The act of running the Program is not restricted, and the output from the Program is covered only if its contents constitute a work based on the Program (independent of having been made by running the Program). Whether that is true depends on what the Program does.

2. You may copy and distribute verbatim copies of the Program's source code as you receive it, in any medium, provided that you conspicuously and appropriately publish on each copy an appropriate copyright notice and disclaimer of warranty; keep intact all the notices that refer to this License and to the absence of any warranty; and give any other recipients of the Program a copy of this License along with the Program.

   You may charge a fee for the physical act of transferring a copy, and you may at your option offer warranty protection in exchange for a fee.

3. You may modify your copy or copies of the Program or any portion of it, thus forming a work based on the Program, and copy and distribute such modifications or work under the terms of Section 1 above, provided that you also meet all of these conditions:

   a) You must cause the modified files to carry prominent notices stating that you changed the files and the date of any change.

   b) You must cause any work that you distribute or publish, that in whole or in part contains or is derived from the Program or any part thereof, to be licensed as a whole at no charge to all third parties under the terms of this License.

   c) If the modified program normally reads commands interactively when run, you must cause it, when started running for such interactive use in the most ordinary way, to print or display an announcement including an appropriate copyright notice and a notice that there is no warranty (or else, saying that you provide a warranty) and that users may redistribute the program under these conditions, and telling the user how to view a copy of this License. (Exception: if the Program itself is interactive but does not normally print such an announcement, your work based on the Program is not required to print an announcement.)

These requirements apply to the modified work as a whole. If identifiable sections of that work are not derived from the Program, and can be reasonably considered independent and separate works in themselves, then this License, and its terms, do not apply to those sections when you distribute them as separate works. But when you distribute the same sections as part of a whole which is a work based on the Program, the distribution of the whole must be on the terms of this License, whose permissions for other licensees extend to the entire whole, and thus to each and every part regardless of who wrote it.

Thus, it is not the intent of this section to claim rights or contest your rights to work written entirely by you; rather, the intent is to exercise the right to control the distribution of derivative or collective works based on the Program.

In addition, mere aggregation of another work not based on the Program with the Program (or with a work based on the Program) on a volume of a storage or distribution medium does not bring the other work under the scope of this License.

4. You may copy and distribute the Program (or a work based on it, under Section 2) in object code or executable form under the terms of Sections 1 and 2 above provided that you also do one of the following:

   a) Accompany it with the complete corresponding machine-readable source code, which must be distributed under the terms of Sections 1 and 2 above on a medium customarily used for software interchange; or,

   b) Accompany it with a written offer, valid for at least three years, to give any third party, for a charge no more than your cost of physically performing source distribution, a complete machine-readable copy of the corresponding source code, to be distributed under the terms of Sections 1 and 2 above on a medium customarily used for software interchange; or,

   c) Accompany it with the information you received as to the offer to distribute corresponding source code. (This alternative is allowed only for noncommercial distribution and only if you received the program in object code or executable form with such an offer, in accord with Subsection b above.)

The source code for a work means the preferred form of the work for making modifications to it. For an executable work, complete source code means all the source code for all modules it contains, plus any associated interface definition files, plus the scripts used to control compilation and installation of the executable. However, as a special exception, the source code distributed need not include anything that is normally distributed (in either source or binary form) with the major components (compiler, kernel, and so on) of the operating system on which the executable runs, unless that component itself accompanies the executable.

If distribution of executable or object code is made by offering access to copy from a designated place, then offering equivalent access to copy the source code from the same place counts as distribution of the source code, even though third parties are not compelled to copy the source along with the object code.

5. You may not copy, modify, sublicense, or distribute the Program except as expressly provided under this License. Any attempt otherwise to copy, modify, sublicense or distribute the Program is void, and will automatically terminate your rights under this License. However, parties who have received copies, or rights, from you under this License will not have their licenses terminated so long as such parties remain in full compliance.

6. You are not required to accept this License, since you have not signed it. However, nothing else grants you permission to modify or distribute the Program or its derivative works. These actions are prohibited by law if you do not accept this License. Therefore, by modifying or distributing the Program (or any work based on the Program), you indicate your acceptance of this License to do so, and all its terms and conditions for copying, distributing or modifying the Program or works based on it.

7. Each time you redistribute the Program (or any work based on the Program), the recipient automatically receives a license from the original licensor to copy, distribute or modify the Program subject to these terms and conditions. You may not impose any further restrictions on the recipients' exercise of the rights granted herein. You are not responsible for enforcing compliance by third parties to this License.

8. If, as a consequence of a court judgment or allegation of patent infringement or for any other reason (not limited to patent issues), conditions are imposed on you (whether by court order, agreement or otherwise) that contradict the conditions of this License, they do not excuse you from the conditions of this License. If you cannot distribute so as to satisfy simultaneously your obligations under this License and any other pertinent obligations, then as a consequence you may not distribute the Program at all. For example, if a patent license would not permit royalty-free redistribution of the Program by all those who receive copies directly or indirectly through you, then the only way you could satisfy both it and this License would be to refrain entirely from distribution of the Program.

   If any portion of this section is held invalid or unenforceable under any particular circumstance, the balance of the section is intended to apply and the section as a whole is intended to apply in other circumstances.

   It is not the purpose of this section to induce you to infringe any patents or other property right claims or to contest validity of any such claims; this section has the sole purpose of protecting the integrity of the free software distribution system, which is implemented by public license practices. Many people have made generous contributions to the wide range of software distributed through that system in reliance on consistent application of that system; it is up to the author/donor to decide if he or she is willing to distribute software through any other system and a licensee cannot impose that choice.

   This section is intended to make thoroughly clear what is believed to be a consequence of the rest of this License.

9. If the distribution and/or use of the Program is restricted in certain countries either by patents or by copyrighted interfaces, the original copyright holder who places the Program under this License may add an explicit geographical distribution limitation excluding those countries, so that distribution is permitted only in or among countries

not thus excluded. In such case, this License incorporates the limitation as if written in the body of this License.

10. The Free Software Foundation may publish revised and/or new versions of the General Public License from time to time. Such new versions will be similar in spirit to the present version, but may differ in detail to address new problems or concerns.

    Each version is given a distinguishing version number. If the Program specifies a version number of this License which applies to it and "any later version", you have the option of following the terms and conditions either of that version or of any later version published by the Free Software Foundation. If the Program does not specify a version number of this License, you may choose any version ever published by the Free Software Foundation.

11. If you wish to incorporate parts of the Program into other free programs whose distribution conditions are different, write to the author to ask for permission. For software which is copyrighted by the Free Software Foundation, write to the Free Software Foundation; we sometimes make exceptions for this. Our decision will be guided by the two goals of preserving the free status of all derivatives of our free software and of promoting the sharing and reuse of software generally.

    NO WARRANTY

12. BECAUSE THE PROGRAM IS LICENSED FREE OF CHARGE, THERE IS NO WARRANTY FOR THE PROGRAM, TO THE EXTENT PERMITTED BY APPLICABLE LAW. EXCEPT WHEN OTHERWISE STATED IN WRITING THE COPYRIGHT HOLDERS AND/OR OTHER PARTIES PROVIDE THE PROGRAM "AS IS" WITHOUT WARRANTY OF ANY KIND, EITHER EXPRESSED OR IMPLIED, INCLUDING, BUT NOT LIMITED TO, THE IMPLIED WARRANTIES OF MERCHANTABILITY AND FITNESS FOR A PARTICULAR PURPOSE. THE ENTIRE RISK AS TO THE QUALITY AND PERFORMANCE OF THE PROGRAM IS WITH YOU. SHOULD THE PROGRAM PROVE DEFECTIVE, YOU ASSUME THE COST OF ALL NECESSARY SERVICING, REPAIR OR CORRECTION.

13. IN NO EVENT UNLESS REQUIRED BY APPLICABLE LAW OR AGREED TO IN WRITING WILL ANY COPYRIGHT HOLDER, OR ANY OTHER PARTY WHO MAY MODIFY AND/OR REDISTRIBUTE THE PROGRAM AS PERMITTED ABOVE, BE LIABLE TO YOU FOR DAMAGES, INCLUDING ANY GENERAL, SPECIAL, INCIDENTAL OR CONSEQUENTIAL DAMAGES ARISING OUT OF THE USE OR INABILITY TO USE THE PROGRAM (INCLUDING BUT NOT LIMITED TO LOSS OF DATA OR DATA BEING RENDERED INACCURATE OR LOSSES SUSTAINED BY YOU OR THIRD PARTIES OR A FAILURE OF THE PROGRAM TO OPERATE WITH ANY OTHER PROGRAMS), EVEN IF SUCH HOLDER OR OTHER PARTY HAS BEEN ADVISED OF THE POSSIBILITY OF SUCH DAMAGES.

END OF TERMS AND CONDITIONS

What's on the Disc

The companion CD-ROM contains Caldera's OpenLinux 2.2.

Installation Instructions

If your computer supports booting directly from a CD-ROM, follow the instructions below for a CD-ROM boot install. Otherwise, you should follow the instructions for a floppy boot install.

CD-ROM Boot Install

1. Insert the Caldera OpenLinux 2.2 CD-ROM in your CD drive.
2. If you want to use Caldera's Windows setup software, launch the setup program by double-clicking on the CD drive, WINSETUP, and SETUP.EXE. Select Install Products and follow the setup instructions. Otherwise, you may proceed to step 2.
2. Restart your computer.
3. You may need to change your BIOS settings to boot from the CD-ROM. Typically, you enter your BIOS setup program with the F2 or DEL key.
4. Make your changes (if any) and exit the BIOS setup utility.
5. When your computer restarts, you will boot into the Caldera OpenLinux setup program.
6. Follow the onscreen prompts to complete the installation.

Floppy Boot Install

If you are using Windows 95 and Windows 98

1. Insert the Caldera OpenLinux 2.2 CD-ROM in your CD drive.
2. If you want to use Caldera's Windows setup software, launch the setup program by double-clicking on the CD drive, WINSETUP, and SETUP.EXE. Select Install Products, and select Create Floppy Install Disks.
3. When you are finished with the boot disk preparation, restart your computer with the boot disk inserted in your floppy drive.
4. You may need to change your BIOS settings to boot from the floppy drive. Typically, you enter your BIOS setup program with the F2 or DEL key.
5. Make your changes (if any) and exit the BIOS setup utility.
6. When your computer restarts, you will boot into the Caldera OpenLinux setup program.
7. Follow the onscreen prompts to complete the installation.

If you are using DOS

1. Navigate to your CD drive and go to the directory \COL\LAUNCH\DOS.
2. Prepare two 1.44 MB floppies by formatting them.
3. Type INSTALL and press <ENTER>. This will prepare your boot floppy and a modules disk, if needed.
4. When you are finished with the boot disk preparation, restart your computer with the boot disk inserted in your floppy drive.
5. You may need to change your BIOS settings to boot from the floppy drive. Typically, you enter your BIOS setup program with the F2 or DEL key.
6. Make your changes (if any) and exit the BIOS setup utility.
7. When your computer restarts, you will boot into the Caldera OpenLinux setup program.
8. Follow the onscreen prompts to complete the installation.

What's on the CD-ROM?

The included CD-ROM contains Caldera's OpenLinux 2.2 which is freely available from Caldera's FTP site. This software includes the following:

- KDE 1.1
- WordPerfect 8
- Netscape Communicator 4.51
- LIZARD, the grapical installation wizard

The following are commercial upgrades which are also available on the included CD-ROM:

- PartitionMagic, Caldera Edition
- BootMagic, Caldera Edition

The following are available in Caldera's commercial package of OpenLinux 2.2:

- StarOffice 5.0
- BRU